CASES AND MATERIALS

ENERGY, ECONOMICS AND THE ENVIRONMENT

by

FRED BOSSELMAN
Professor of Law
Chicago–Kent College of Law

JIM ROSSI
Patricia A. Dore Associate Professor of Law
Florida State University College of Law

JACQUELINE LANG WEAVER
A.A. White Professor of Law
University of Houston Law Center

NEW YORK, NEW YORK
FOUNDATION PRESS

2000

COPYRIGHT © 2000 By FOUNDATION PRESS

       11 Penn Plaza, Tenth Floor
       New York, NY 10001
       Phone Toll Free 1–877–888–1330
       Fax (212) 760–8705
       fdpress.com

All rights reserved
Printed in the United States of America

ISBN 1–56662–900–4

 TEXT IS PRINTED ON 10% POST CONSUMER RECYCLED PAPER

INTRODUCTION

Preface

In both law and business schools, Energy courses were common after the oil price shocks of the 1970s. A number of fine casebooks were written in the early 1980s, responding to the sense of "energy crisis" and "environmental crisis" pervading that period.

As the 1980s progressed, however, declining energy prices, improving economic and environmental conditions, and diminishing Cold War tensions alleviated the sense of crisis. Gradually, schools began to lose interest.

The 1990s, on the other hand, brought about increasing attention to energy issues. The collapse of communism created worldwide interest in the privatization and deregulation of monopolies. Information technology facilitated international business combinations, and increased worldwide awareness about energy alternatives. Meanwhile, confidence about environmental progress faded in the face of worries about the ozone layer, climate change, an asthma epidemic, biogenetics, and our inability to get a handle on air and water pollution from small sources.

During the 1990s, law schools created an increasing number of courses on "regulated industries"—an ironic title given the diminishing role of economic regulation. The law and economics movement continued to expand its influence. Environmental law programs spawned a growing number of sub-specialties, and interest in international law boomed. Natural resources law continued to be dominated by intense political and ideological controversy over the use of public lands, by concern about the long-term supply of resources, and by worries about our reliance on overseas suppliers. In response, there have been excellent new treatises, such as *Energy Law and Policy for the 21st Century* (Rocky Mountain Mineral Law Foundation, 2000) and *Environmental Law: From Resources to Recovery* (West Group, 1993), and a valuable "Nutshell" (*Energy and Natural Resources Law*, West Group, 1992), but no new casebooks.

All of these factors contributed to the authors' belief that the beginning of the new century was an appropriate time for a new casebook on energy, economics and the environment.

Overview of the Casebook

This book is organized roughly on a chronological basis according to the periods in history within which the issues arose. Thus solar and wind power are followed by water power and coal, then oil and gas, electricity, nuclear power and motor vehicles. Throughout the chapters, economic and environmental issues are integrated with energy resource issues. We believe that the material can be taught in many different variations, and we continue to teach it in a somewhat different order every time it is offered.

Chapter One provides an overview of some of the major energy issues facing us in the new century, a review of the regulatory context in which the energy sector operates, and points out some key energy policy failures of the past.

Chapter Two looks at energy in nature. Renewable energy resources are the focus of attention throughout the world, and the chapter looks at some of the property and regulatory issues involved in solar, geothermal and wind power. Because an understanding of energy issues requires an awareness of the scientific underpinnings of energy, some basic physical and biological science principles are woven into the chapter.

Chapter Three introduces the concept of the public utility, central to common law and statutory approaches to energy regulation. Public utility principles are grounded in the history and economics of regulation. The chapter introduces basic aspects of public utility regulation and its limitations, laying the groundwork for the discussions of regulation in later chapters.

Chapter Four traces the history of water power from the early water mill to modern hydroelectric power. Many of the basic property issues underlying energy law today arose in the context of the early water mills. The chapter introduces the role of the Federal Energy Regulatory Commission, and brings out one of the key environmental issues of energy law—the relationship of energy resources to wildlife.

Chapter Five covers the earliest of the fossil fuels to become widely used, coal. Coal has been the focus of many of the leading constitutional cases involving takings, and this chapter emphasizes those issues, which will reappear in many other chapters. It also provides an opportunity to explore the Commerce Clause as a limitation both on federal power and on state power. And a number of the key environmental laws are introduced in the context of their impact on the coal industry.

Chapter Six explores oil, the energy source most familiar to a population of gas-guzzling consumers. It describes how the rule of capture led to wasteful production processes and ultimately to conservation regulation by state commissions. One aspect of this state regulation was market-demand prorationing, a technique used to constrain oil supplies and induce higher prices, imitated by OPEC in the 1970s with massive, worldwide repercussions. The chapter then explores the statutory framework for drilling on the two areas holding the most promise for successful oil and gas development in the United States: the federal offshore Outer Continental Shelf and Alaska. This section explores the issues which arise under the National Environmental Policy Act (NEPA), Alaskan native rights to subsistence hunting and fishing, and state and federal withdrawals of large land areas from oil and gas leasing. The final two sections of the chapter discuss the application of the clean air and water acts to oil and gas operations and the remedial legislation used to address oil spills following the Exxon Valdez catastrophe.

Chapter Seven introduces the reader to the natural gas industry before the 1985 regulatory revolution which sought to undo decades of price controls, shortages, and barriers to pipeline access. It first surveys the many sources of natural gas available for development, including the legal rights to ownership of coalbed methane. The pre-1985 federal framework of control and regulation is then juxtaposed with the parallel development of take-or-pay contracts between private producers and pipeline purchasers. Such contracts later became a major stumbling block in efforts to deregulate the industry, similar to the stranded cost issue in electricity deregulation. The chapter then looks at the conflict between state conservation regulation and federal regulation of the gas industry through the lens of a Supreme Court case on preemption. The chapter concludes with a case detailing the efforts of a state public utility commission to separate the regulated assets from the unregulated assets of a utility company and its entrepreneurial subsidiary which had entered the oil and gas business to mitigate the energy shortages of the 1970s.

Chapter Eight covers the basic principles of rate regulation, with an eye towards the issues introduced by competition, and rate deregulation, in later chapters. The chapter introduces traditional ratemaking principles, such as rate base, operating expenses, and rate of return, and also discusses legal constraints on rate regulation.

Chapter Nine takes up the natural gas industry's transition to competitive markets, as a precursor to the same transition in the electricity industry. The materials illustrate the major problems encountered on the rocky road to restructuring the natural gas industry: industrial bypass; resolving the $20 billion of take-or-pay liabilities owed by pipeline purchasers to producers; and protecting the small consumer. The material excerpts portions of the D.C. Circuit's review of Order 636 and shows the interplay between this court and FERC in the transition process. Potential problems of relying on new, unbundled spot markets for gas supplies are discussed, followed by diverse views of whether restructuring has been a success. Finally, the chapter concludes with another problem of federalism and preemption of state law in an era of free markets in the restructured gas industry.

Chapter Ten introduces electricity. The structure of the existing industry is discussed, along with some explanation of the historical debates that led to the current structure. The chapter discusses the ways in which government laws and policies have tried to promote conservation of electricity. It reviews some of the problems associated with electricity transmission, and it explores the growing interest in small scale, on-site electricity generation. This chapter serves as background for the next four chapters which explore changes taking place in the electricity business.

Chapter Eleven discusses wholesale competition in the electric power industry in the U.S., a major change to the traditional natural monopoly structure of the industry. Given the jurisdictional split between federal and state regulators under federal electric power statutes, most wholesale regulation decisions occur at the federal level. The chapter discusses the major regulatory decisions to date that will define the nature of power competition. In addition, the chapter introduces federal approaches to regulating power transmission and emerging new power generators and brokers in a competitive power industry.

Chapter Twelve reviews the stranded cost issue, a major "transition" issue presented by natural gas and electric power competition. The chapter discusses legal requirements of stranded cost recovery, under the Takings Clause of the U.S. Constitution and under private contract law. Also, policy arguments for and against stranded cost recovery are introduced.

Chapter Thirteen discusses retail competition in the U.S. electric power industry, and also addresses the environmental issues posed more generally by electric power competition. After exploring the structure of retail competition plans, issues such as consumer protection are emphasized. The chapter surveys new approaches to environmental regulation, such as green pricing, and also discusses limitations on state regulation, such as those presented by the Commerce Clause.

Chapter Fourteen explores the use of nuclear power to generate electricity. It reviews the development of new nuclear facilities overseas and discusses the laws that affect the outlook for any resumption of nuclear construction in this country. It reviews some of the problems faced by the nuclear industry in the past, and explores the issues associated with the disposal of radioactive waste, which present the most serious obstacle to the growth of nuclear power.

Chapter Fifteen looks at energy in transportation. After a review of the history of energy in transportation, the chapter focuses on the modern motor vehicle and the ongoing efforts to control its energy consumption and pollution output. It also reviews legal methods being used by state and local governments to promote land use and transportation patterns that will reduce traffic congestion.

Chapter Sixteen launches the reader into the geopolitics of international oil and the legal, environmental and cultural problems of exploring for oil and gas abroad. The chapter first traces the nationalistic birth of OPEC, the rise and fall of oil prices during the 1970s and 1980s, and a statistical overview of the international oil industry. It then compares the early concession agreements used by the major oil companies to exploit oil reserves abroad with the modern forms of agreements used today. An arbitral award arising from Libya's expropriation of oil company assets introduces some of the norms, sources, and procedures of international law used to resolve disputes. Because international petroleum reserves are owned by nation-states, private companies face daunting barriers to suing the state actors from whom they have negotiated petroleum agreements. The chapter presents the major obstacles to litigation, such as sovereign immunity and the act of state doctrine. It then examines the difficult problems of protecting the rights of indigenous people and the fragile ecosystems in which they live by looking at the actual activities of multinational oil companies engaged in developing oil and gas in the rainforests of Ecuador and Peru, and asks whether sustainable development can be achieved in this environment. It also asks whether American courts are the appropriate forum for foreign nationals to bring suits alleging environmental and human rights abuses against U.S. companies operating abroad. The chapter concludes with a review problem which mirrors today's newspaper headlines and shareholder resolutions on the controversy surrounding multinational oil companies in their joint ventures with repressive and corrupt regimes.

Chapter Seventeen examines briefly one of the most complex and contentious scientific issues that presents a major problem for the energy sector – the concern about climate change. After reviewing the scientific basis for the continuing increase in global average temperatures, the chapter summarizes some of the potential impacts and looks at the preliminary efforts of international bodies to achieve some workable consensus on ways to deal with the issue.

Chapter Eighteen discusses the future of economic regulation, including many issues that supplement, but do not neatly fit into, chapters on natural gas and electric power competition. After a review of government efforts to keep energy prices low, such as price caps, the chapter focuses on antitrust merger policy, an issue of paramount importance to the newly reconstituted, and constantly changing, energy industry. The chapter concludes with a discussion of the jurisdictional limits on federal energy regulation, emphasizing the need for cooperative regulatory solutions between federal and state regulators.

A Note on Editing

In common with traditional casebook practice, excerpts from cases, books and other sources have usually been edited to eliminate material not directly relevant to the topic of discussion. Ellipses are routinely used to designate omitted material, but footnotes and citations have often been excised without so indicating. Asterisks are also used to indicate the deletion of substantial amounts of material. Where footnotes have been included, the footnote number from the original precedes our footnote number. Where multiple citations are found in the original, only the West citation or U.S. citation has been included. Concurring and dissenting opinions may have been deleted without notation. A reader who plans to rely on any of the excerpted material as a research source is advised to consult the original.

*

ACKNOWLEDGEMENTS

Fred Bosselman wishes to thank Mark Kaminski, Julie Lucas, Michelle Mishoe, Kristyna Ryan, and the research librarians at Chicago-Kent Law School for their research assistance. A grant from the Marshall T. Ewell fund facilitated work on the book. Dan Tarlock taught from an early draft of the material and provided many helpful comments.

Jim Rossi wishes to thank Kimmy Sharkey, Mike Sjuggerud, and Allison Turnbull for their research assistance, and Erica Bubsey for her diligent support services in draft preparation. Florida State University College of Law provided the educational and research environment, including Summer research support, to support continued experimentation with and updates to these chapter drafts.

Jacqueline Weaver thanks the University of Houston Law Foundation which provided summer research grants to work on this book. She also thanks Dr. Margaret Davis, a first-year student in her Property class with a Ph.D. in Economics and extensive experience in the energy industry, for her superb research assistance. Stewart Schmella, a research assistant in the Faculty Services Department of the library also did a masterful job of finding items. Finally, thanks go to the first class of students to whom she taught this course for their many thoughtful comments on how to improve the casebook: John R. Brown, Buddy Broussard (who continues to update her on industry events from his job as an energy trader), Mary Grace Anderson, Alexandra Colessides, Elizabeth Garrett, Kimberly Klug, Philip Lamsens, Jamie Lavergne, Rebecca Rentz, John Soliz, J. Frank Taylor, and David Walker. Finally, thanks go to Professor Ernest Smith at the University of Texas and Al Boulos, international consultant and negotiator, for their helpful suggestions and review of the chapter on international energy; and to Associate Dean for Academic Affairs Mary Anne Bobinski for her support.

All three authors would like to thank Hilari Hunter for her work in securing copyright permissions for the material excerpted in the casebook.

*

SUMMARY OF CONTENTS

TABLE OF CONTENTS

TABLE OF CASES

Principal cases are in bold type. Non-principal cases are in roman type. References are to Pages.

*

CASES AND MATERIALS

ENERGY, ECONOMICS AND THE ENVIRONMENT

*

CHAPTER 1

ENERGY POLICY

A. THE IMPORTANCE OF ENERGY

The energy sector of the economy is undergoing major changes. Old systems of regulation are being supplanted by policies that emphasize competition. Scientific and technological advances, and wildly fluctuating markets, make companies' long-range plans obsolete quickly. Older firms merge and consolidate across traditional sector boundaries in order to meet the competition of entrepreneurial new entrants. The environmental sciences raise new and increasingly complex issues, such as climate change and the meaning of sustainable development, that impact the energy industries significantly. Privatization of state-owned energy companies reaches to all corners of the globe. It is an exciting time to be working in energy.

1. EMERGING ISSUES: A TOP 10 LIST

We recognize that in approaching a subject such as energy law, students may know more about Jewel's last song than what a joule is.

1

Without pandering to popular culture or to the false comfort that knowledge about the quickly evolving area of energy law and policy can be conveyed in soundbites or consensus predictions, we nonetheless believe that lawyers practicing in this area do confront common themes, and that it is possible to speculate about the major issues they are likely to face in the coming decade.

As co-authors, we have developed our own consensus about some emerging themes. Everyone seems to love "top ten lists." So, in the spirit of the movie "High Fidelity," a romantic pop comedy based on the novel by Nick Hornby, we offer our own "top ten" list of issues in energy law for the coming decade: First, a quick formulation in the polemical style in which they often appear in debate; then, a more nuanced explanation:

1. Are we "locking up" too many of our energy resources—making them unavailable for what may be dubious environmental reasons?

2. Are we blindly following a path toward fossil fuel exhaustion and global overheating while giving only token support to the development of renewable resources?

3. Has our fear of too much federal government power created gridlock in which each state or local government, Indian tribe or neighborhood association can block economically efficient energy policies?

4. Can we attract capital to develop energy resources if constant changes in laws and regulatory policy create an atmosphere of insecurity?

5. Have we failed to create enough incentives for the private sector to build the transmission networks that get energy to where it is needed?

6. Can we meaningfully address the problem of global warming without radically altering our lifestyles and destroying our economic competitiveness?

7. With deregulated energy markets causing increasingly volatile price swings, will elected officials be able to resist the public backlash, especially if rolling brownouts and blackouts accompany the transition?

8. Does our existing regulatory system impose needless roadblocks that hamper the introduction of more efficient energy technologies, such as fuel cells and gas microturbines?

9. Are mega-mergers and cartels in the energy sector producing greedy behemoths that are beyond effective government control?

10. At the local level, will urban sprawl, dying species, traffic congestion and choking air pollution arouse a public desire for a less frantic pace of life and greener communities?

1) *Land availability.* Since so many energy resources are tied to land use, one issue that will undeniably be at the fore is whether land is

available for resource exploitation. In the U.S., the predominant issue is public land availability. Will the U.S. decide to open up the Arctic National Wildlife Refuge or other areas of Alaska to oil and gas leasing? Similarly, will offshore areas (other than the Gulf of Mexico) be open to federal leasing, and will this be with or without the support of the coastal states? The flip side: Will additional areas of public lands be preserved for wilderness or national parks as recreation and preservation uses triumph over development uses? Outside of the U.S., land availability will also be of great significance. Will leasing and development proceed abroad in areas of fragile and unique ecosystems, such as rainforests, coral reefs, and tundra? Or will international pressures from environmental and human rights groups, debt-for-nature swaps, and lack of World Bank or IMF financing result in certain areas being considered "lands unsuitable" for exploitation? A related question: Will the principle of sustainable development become an international norm for oil and gas development? If so, can it work in practice in the oil and gas industry?

2) *Renewable energy.* Will green energy and renewables be able to compete in the marketplace for energy without government subsidies? Should they be subsidized, or are subsidies just boondoggles for special interest groups? What other methods exist, aside from PURPA's avoided cost rates, for encouraging renewable power? Will consumers be willing to pay extra for a "green energy" provider when retail competition in energy comes to their door?

3) *Federalism.* Will the rights or desires of the local population (states, provinces, tribes, and cities) ultimately trump federal development (or nondevelopment) policies? How will the tension be resolved between federal and state jurisdiction over energy resources and over the emerging players in industry? In the electricity context, these players include brokers, marketers, power exchanges, and regional transmission organizations (RTOs). How does the dormant Commerce Clause limit the scope of state regulation–and how does international law limit the scope of national regulation–in a competitive environment?

4) *Regulatory transitions.* Will stable contract and property norms exist to attract energy project financing, especially in light of regulatory transitions in the industry? In recent years, as competition has evolved in the electric power and natural gas industries, restructuring has had to confront the "stranded cost" issue. However, the issue of stability also arises in more traditional applications of contract law and takings jurisprudence in other energy industry sectors, such as coal and oil.

5) *Network regulation.* How will network access for electricity transmission and natural gas pipelines be priced in a competitive environment? Will there be adequate incentives for transmission capacity expansion? Will economic regulation encourage new transmission facilities, such as pipelines to bring the natural gas in Alaska to market in

the lower forty-eight states, and how will new construction hurdle political and environmental opposition?

6) *International climate change.* Will the science of climate change have developed enough so that we will know the full extent to which human use of energy is responsible for global warming? Even if the science is not fully developed, will the precautionary principle result in real reductions in greenhouse gas emissions? Can this be accomplished without significant reductions in energy use? How will the burden of reducing greenhouse gas emissions be allocated between developed and developing nations?

7) *Market volatility.* With increased reliance on markets to deliver energy products and services, will there be greater price and service quality volatility? In the electricity sector, regulators need to address transmission expansion and reliability in electric power because neither federal nor state regulators have the authority to order more transmission. What impact, if any, will this have on reliability? Will there be adequate supplies of natural gas at current prices to meet all of the demands projected for it? Will OPEC continue to have market power over oil prices?

8) *New technologies and the mix of energy uses.* Will small-scale, gas-fired electric generating plants, known as distributed generation, make increasing inroads in the market, and how will this affect the electric power industry? Will the technology for the use of fuel cells in automotive engines continue to improve, and what fuel and fuel distribution system will prove to be the most effective? Does the government have a role to play in encouraging the development of new technologies? Will the growing cost of gas and increasing environmental regulation of coal stimulate interest in a new generation of nuclear power plants? What will be the pace of technological change in clean coal combustion processes, and will coal have a future in the U.S. under the Clean Air Act and the Surface Mining Control and Reclamation Act?

9) *Merger policy and antitrust,* What are the legal and economic issues associated with unbundling the formerly integrated functions of energy companies? Will competitive restructuring ultimately result in antitrust problems due to affiliate transactions, spinoffs, and mergers? How will affiliate transactions be regulated? Do monopoly bottlenecks simply move to gas gathering pipelines at the state level once open access to interstate pipelines succeeds at the federal level? Will the power of private codes of conduct for multinational companies and organizations result in an effective system of corporate and country monitoring of environmental, health and human rights effects of energy development? What antitrust issues will be raised by voluntary regulation? Can antitrust law effectively guard the marketplace against international cartels and mega-mergers?

10) *Emerging environmental issues.* Will concern about salmon and other species at risk force the shutdown of significant amounts of

hydroelectric energy? Will growing traffic congestion due to urban sprawl increase the demand for less energy-intensive patterns of land development? Will the public tolerate transportation of nuclear wastes across America and through local communities to Yucca Mountain for storage? In general, will we, the people, adopt conservation and more sustainable development as a life style in our own backyards? Are higher energy prices a necessary predicate to inducing conservation?

2. SCOPE OF THE BOOK

This book is intended to provide an overview of the legal issues raised in regulation of the energy sector. "Energy law" has been defined as "the allocation of rights and duties concerning the exploitation of all energy resources between individuals, between individuals and governments, between governments and between states." Adrian J. Bradbrook, Energy Law as an Academic Discipline, 14 J. Energy & Nat. Res. L. 193, 194 (1996). At the beginning of the twenty-first century, energy law sits at the intersection of environmental law, natural resources law, and regulated industries.

It also sits at the epicenter of a clash of public values. In fact, the title of this casebook should perhaps be rearranged to Economics, Energy, and the Environment, to place energy in the center of a tug-of-war between the two other forces. We want clean energy, but we don't want high energy prices. We want pristine coasts and coral reefs, untouched tundra and rainforests, and clean air and water, but also, comfortable cars, heat and light at our fingertips, and cold beer. Will technological changes in the energy industry bridge the near-schizophrenic gap between the two sets of values? Will the clash between environmental regulation and competition in the global marketplace lead us to "greener" energy or to less energy, to production at home or imports from foreign lands, to the rebirth of nuclear energy or to planting trees as carbon sinks? What are the lessons of history here?

This casebook provides a framework for readers to use in assessing and analyzing the many forces directed at the energy industry today. It is an interdisciplinary blend of history and future projection, of science and technology, of policies made by many levels of political bodies—local, regional, national, and international—and of legal doctrines as ancient as the common law of custom and as new as the internet-posted administrative rulings of state and federal energy commissioners on energy restructuring. All private actors within this framework—energy producers, distributors, traders, endusers, shareholders, and consumers—will be jostled in this tug-of-war for the "public interest," the balance between clean energy and cheap energy. Some will emerge as winners; others as losers. None will escape the pull of these forces.

Much of the environmental law movement of the last three decades was sparked by energy-related events: the Santa Barbara oil spill, the Exxon Valdez, Chernobyl and Three Mile Island. Much of our legal framework for regulated industries and antitrust law derives from our now century-old experiences with problems of monopoly in the energy industry.

Much of our current energy policy is directed at adjusting our policy framework from an era of energy crisis (the 1970s and early 1980s) to an era of (supposed?) energy availability. Energy law and policy plays on a large stage. It deserves its own casebook.

a.   ENVIRONMENTAL LAW

In most U.S. law schools, the traditional environmental law course surveys the major federal statutes, such as the National Environmental Policy Act, the Clean Air Act, the Federal Water Pollution Control Act, and the various hazardous and solid waste disposal statutes. Many law schools supplement this offering with natural resource courses, which cover water issues. wetlands preservation, wildlife management, biodiversity, and the protection of national parks and other resources, such as timber. These courses focus on the statutory-and common-law bases for regulation across a variety of activities and uses threatening to the environment,

This casebook is designed to bridge the gap between the environmental, natural resources, and regulated industries curriculums. The materials comprise the core readings for an introductory survey to the legal and policy issues concerning energy resources, conservation, and use. Such a course should be of interest to students of both environmental law and economic regulation. Like traditional courses in environmental and natural resources law, this book addresses problems of conservation, externalities, and pollution control. The surveyed topics include: ownership of and access to energy resources; siting of energy facilities, such as pipelines and power plants; and the mechanisms for regulating pollution emission by existing energy sources. In addition, the book introduces long-term planning mechanisms, such as integrated resource planning, and conservation-minded mechanisms, such as demand-side management.

But the scope of this book also departs significantly from the traditional environmental law curriculum offering. First, by providing an in-depth, context-specific study of the environmental issues affecting energy resources, this book provides a focused lens through which to examine the issues raised by environmental regulation. Students are more likely to grasp with depth the basics of environmental regulation if they see the issues recur in similar contexts, as opposed to an unrelated variety of waste-emitting contexts. One commentator has observed that the relationship between energy and environmental law is interesting because "energy issues sometimes divide the environmental movement" and energy law "concentrates on the causes, rather than the effects, of environmental problems." *Id*. at 215–16.

Second, this book promotes a greater awareness of the economic issues affecting the environment than the traditional environmental course, both because of its context-specific approach and because of the history of our regulatory scheme. Many of the topics covered in this book have traditionally been studied as public utility law because most energy sources were believed to possess natural monopoly characteristics and were regulated as public utilities. Natural monopoly conditions exist where a single firm can provide a good or service at a lower average cost than two or more firms. To capture these economies of scale, a single firm is often awarded a monopoly franchise to provide service, but then regulators must prevent the franchised monopoly from earning excess profits at the expense of the consumer. In fact, one way to approach this book is to use it as an example of applied public utility or regulatory law.

Although some may question whether the study of economic regulation has a place in the environmental curriculum, we obviously think it does. An economic approach to resource allocation gives students an understanding of resource use and cost, an approach often slighted or missing from the traditional environmental curriculum. Many environmental law teachers complain that students lack a context for understanding the opportunity costs of environmental regulation. We find that those persons with environmental protection sympathies, sympathies with which we intuitively agree, tend instinctively to favor government regulation—often outright prohibition—of activities that produce any perceived harmful effect on the environment. However, regulation has costs. The material presented here provides a more pragmatic context for the study of environmental issues than often found in the traditional curriculum.

b. NATURAL RESOURCES

The energy industries increasingly employ highly entrepreneurial and creative people. But they do not "create" energy. The laws of thermodynamics tell us that we cannot create energy; we can only *transform* it. We must start with the resources found in nature and convert them to forms suitable to meet our needs. Thus this book begins with an extended review of energy's place in the natural world.

Energy law can effectively be studied in coordination with courses in natural resources law or oil and gas law that focus on the private and public law relating to the extraction of energy resources. While this book does not include a detailed analysis of the leases, concession agreements, and conservation laws applicable to energy extraction, it does provide a solid overview of the different systems used to grant and regulate rights to produce minerals, particularly petroleum, both in the United States and abroad. Energy is only one of the natural resources valued by citizens today. We also value, and indeed put price tags on, otters and sea turtles, whales and wetlands, wilderness and ocean views. Indeed, we swap "debt for nature" internationally to preserve other nations' rainforests. Of all industries in the world, issues of sustainable development most pervade the extractive industries which exploit nonrenewable resources like oil, gas and coal. The classic resource paradigm of the Tragedy of the Commons often appears as an energy policy issue.

c. REGULATED INDUSTRIES

Regulated industries courses in most law schools address many of the problems associated with markets in vital industries such as health care, transportation, food and drugs, telecommunications, and banking. Two very different bodies of economic laws—one general, the other more specific—govern most of these industries. At the general level, each industry is subject to some degree of regulation under state and federal antitrust statutes which promote competition and guard against monopolistic abuses. In terms of doctrine and principles, antitrust law varies little from industry to industry since each industry is subject to the same statutes and case law. More specifically, public utility law, implemented by courts and administrative agencies also applies to many key industries. Public utility law varies more than antitrust law from industry to industry. Industry-specific statutes and regulations usually guide the application of public law principles.

This book provides a fertile context for discussion of reforms in economic and environmental regulation. In recent years the energy industry has moved away from the natural monopoly model and toward market-based mechanisms. This movement provides an excellent context in which to study the interplay between economic competition and environmental protection. How, for instance, can regulators ensure that a competitive electricity industry—one which uses the lowest priced energy source—does not abuse our air, land, or water, or prematurely deplete our supply of non-renewable resources? What is the relationship between market-based mechanisms for energy resource allocation and the market-based mechanisms reformers have embraced in environmental law, such as tradeable air emissions allowances? Are environment-sensitive mechanisms such as integrated resource planning and demand-side management necessarily at odds with competition? By giving students exposure to environmental regulatory mechanisms in the context of energy resource use, this book will supplement—certainly not displace or undermine—the traditional environmental curriculum.

In turn, the complexity of the real environmental issues facing the energy sector presents a challenge to students who approach regulation from a theoretical economic perspective. The values that people attach to the environment are often hard to quantify, and sometimes even hard to define. Recent history is replete with expert economists' prescriptions for addressing environmental issues that died on the vine because they failed to understand public attitudes. An understanding of the history of environmental law brings increasing humility to teacher and student alike.

Last, but certainly not least, this book aspires to prepare students for the practice of energy law—not in the narrower economic context of a traditional public utility law course, but with a fuller sense of responsibility for the environment. The field of energy law promises to be a growing one for years to come as changing regulatory conditions create new legal problems and opportunities. As a specialty, energy law offers a challenging and productive opportunity for lawyers throughout the country. Some students will want to follow up on the materials covered in this book with more specialized courses in topics such as oil and gas law, mining law, federal land and resources law, international energy transactions, international environmental law, government regulation, and administrative law. The world of energy spans all of these.

3. ENERGY RESOURCES AND POLICY

"Energy can be neither created nor destroyed, only converted from one form to another."

—The First Law of Thermodynamics.

"All physical processes proceed in such a way that the availability of the energy involved decreases."

—The Second Law of Thermodynamics.

Energy is "the power by which anything or anybody acts effectively to move or change other things or persons." Howard Mumford Jones, The Age of Energy 104–05 (1971). This is a physical definition of energy, but one which needs some qualification as we begin to immerse ourselves in the legal problems posed by the energy sector of the economy. We cannot live without physical energy, either alone as individuals or together in our society. Even a Robinson Crusoe, stranded alone on a deserted island, is dependent upon energy. After a day of hard work (the exertion of energy), a Crusoe, feeling low on energy, may eat a meal of bananas to energize his body, and that meal will give energy to a whole set of digestive processes—(thankfully) far beyond the scope of this book.

This book is concerned with the societal—not the individual—implications of physical energy. Although burn-out is a low-energy feeling we each may at times have experienced, we happily leave this problem to the doctors, dieticians, psychologists, or astrologists of the world. We will focus our attention in this book on human beings' discovery, creation, transfer, and distribution of physical energy among themselves to improve their collective social lives.

Can you live your daily life without physical energy, so conceived? Think about your daily routine. You wake up to the noise of an alarm clock—powered perhaps by electricity, perhaps by batteries, but even if it is a wind-up mechanical clock it was made in a factory using a variety of energy sources. You turn on the shower. The fact that water comes out of the faucet is impossible without some use of energy to move the water and create pressure. You like your water hot, heated by natural gas, oil, or electricity. You have not left your home and may not have seen another individual, yet you have used a variety of energy resources.

As your day goes on you will rely even more on energy resources. Perhaps you drive a car fueled by gasoline, or take a train powered by electricity or a bus that runs on natural gas. You will sit in a classroom with lights, powered by electricity generated at a nuclear, hydro, or fossil fuel plant. You will eat a warm lunch, or perhaps a cold salad kept crisp by some form of energy. While writing a paper, you—like us—will rely on electricity to power your computer. You will go home and listen to the radio or a compact disk or the TV, or call a friend, perhaps leaving a message on an answering machine. Virtually every minute of your day requires you to use energy resources. Our daily lives would be dull, inefficient, and downright difficult without energy.

a. ENERGY RESOURCES

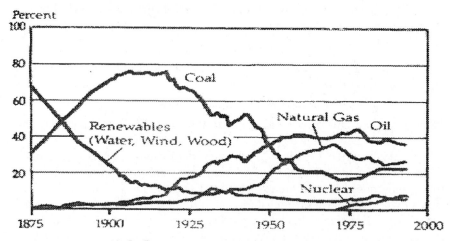

U.S. Primary Energy Use by Source, 1875–1993

Figure 1–1

The predominant energy resources—both in terms of supply and demand—are fossil fuels, such as oil, coal, and natural gas. While fossil fuels as a group are the predominant primary energy resources, renewable energy resources are important as well. Renewable energy resources are of two different types. "Cool" renewable resources do not require burning to convert energy. For example, the Niagara Dam generates electricity by turning turbines with natural water pressure. Similarly, the sun, wind, or underground pressure or heat may generate electricity without the burning of a primary resource. Non-cool renewable resources, such as wood, biomass or waste, must be burned to convert energy.

Electricity is an extremely important energy resource, but it differs fundamentally from the resources mentioned above. Unlike fossil fuel and renewable resources, which can be either primary or secondary resources, electricity is a secondary resource that is dependent on a primary energy resource as an input. Electricity can only be produced by converting any of the primary resources.

Before introducing the legal and policy themes addressed in this book, it is useful to begin by reviewing some facts about the U.S.'s position in the world-wide energy scenario. First, the U.S. has historically had abundant and accessible energy resources, a fact that has no doubt contributed to our economic growth. Almost all of the coal and almost 90 percent of the natural gas consumed in the U.S. is produced from domestic sources. Petroleum imports were a relatively small portion of U.S. demand until the 1970s, when rising demand and falling supply sharply increased oil imports. There is some question as to whether our reliance on domestic resources can continue, but any examination of energy law and policy issues in the

U.S. must recognize that this issue is closely intertwined with our economic and industrial growth.

Second, the U.S. is the largest consumer of energy resources in the world. The U.S. consumes nearly one-fourth of worldwide energy consumption each year. One author notes, "[c]ompared with people elsewhere, Americans are less self-conscious about how unsustainable a high-energy society is and, historically speaking, less aware of the anomaly of high energy use...." David E. Nye, Path Insistence: Comparing European and American Attitudes Toward Energy, 53 J. Intl. Affairs 129, 130 (1999). According to the same author, "Americans have become so 'path dependent' that they only become aware of energy during a blackout or gasoline shortage." *Id.* If this is true, policymakers need to reflect seriously on how the behavior of Americans will change in reaction to legal and economic incentives.

Third, since the energy crises of the 1970s, the U.S. has grown increasingly dependent on fossil fuel imports, particularly petroleum. Overall, the U.S. consumes more energy resources than it produces, and this disparity between demand and supply is particularly large with respect to oil. We consume more oil than any of the other primary energy resources. Over a third of the oil produced in the world is consumed in the United States. As the 1991 Persian Gulf war reminded us, the U.S. is increasingly dependent upon other countries for its oil supply. While oil imports comprised only one-third of U.S. consumption in 1983, by 1990 imports supplied one-half of the oil consumed in the U.S. and the percentage continues to increase steadily. Net gas imports, largely from Canada, are also projected to near one-fifth of U.S. consumption by 2010. So increasingly, any discussion of energy law and policy—even if limited to the U.S.—takes on global ramifications.

Fourth, the fact that we are increasingly so dependent on imported petroleum means that attention is focused on the sector of the economy that uses most of that petroleum, the transportation sector. Automobiles, trucks, airplanes and railroad trains all run on fuels derived from petroleum. The transportation sector in the United States uses a much higher amount of petroleum per person in any other country. This has led to a reexamination of our standards for engines, motor vehicles, and fuels, and even to a reconsideration of the patterns of "urban sprawl" that make us so dependent on the automobile

Fifth, our integrated electricity transmission network ties the United States together and makes possible the dramatic changes in information technology that are fueling the economy. Electricity generation utilizes more than one-third of the primary energy resources consumed in the U.S. The debates about the choice of resources used to produce electricity have been some of the most volatile in American politics, and have produced a complex array of laws that attempt to balance the economic benefits, safety risks, and environmental attributes of the competing fuels: coal, oil, natural gas, uranium, hydro, and various other renewable resources.

Finally, energy resources have had an extensive influence on economic growth and development in the U.S. The estimated value of primary energy sources (inputs) in the U.S. economy is 5 percent of GNP. These primary energy resources have significant uses in the residential, commercial, industrial, and transportation sectors of the economy. With end-use products and services, energy sources comprise as much as 12 percent of GNP. Although the materials in this book may seem specialized at times, their ramifications reverberate far.

b.　U.S. ENERGY POLICY AND LEGISLATION

The vast majority of U.S. energy production, transportation, and distribution resources are privately owned. Why regulate energy resources? Here suffice it to say that this will be a topic we return to time and time again throughout the book. For now, let us limit ourselves to some historical background. For an excellent survey of the history of energy legislation, see David Howard Davis, Energy Politics (4th ed. 1993).

Regulation of energy resources by state and local governments began late in the nineteenth century. The production of oil and gas was regulated by state agencies to avoid physical waste and, not coincidentally, to keep up the price. At the consumption end, local governments typically authorized a private company to sell gas and electricity to the consumer by issuing a franchise that provided that the company's rates and service were subject to local regulation. As these franchises proliferated, state legislatures often preempted the regulation of rates and services by creating a public utility commission.

Until the New Deal era, most energy resources were regulated at the state or local level. This early regulation, primarily by state utility boards, focused on setting the rates for a local monopoly-franchised utility. In 1920, Congress took some nominal steps by passing what is known today as Part I of the Federal Power Act (FPA), which established the Federal Power Commission (FPC) and gave it authority to establish hydroelectric projects on navigable waters. *See* 16 U.S.C. § 791a *et seq.* That year, Congress also passed the Mineral Leasing Act, which brought some consistency to oil and gas leasing on federal lands. *See* 30 U.S.C. § 181.

The New Deal marked the dawn of the era of contemporary federal energy regulation, as well as the growth of economic regulation more generally. In 1935, Congress passed the Public Utility Holding Company Act (PUHCA), to monitor and regulate ownership interests and stock holdings of public utilities. *See* 15 U.S.C. § 79–79z. That same year, Congress added Part II to the FPA, which gave the FPC the authority to regulate wholesale electric utility rates. *See* 16 U.S.C. § 824 *et seq.* In 1938, Congress enacted the Natural Gas Act (NGA), which gave the FPC the authority to regulate the rates of interstate natural gas pipelines. *See* 15 U.S.C. § 717–717z. In 1954, the U.S. Supreme Court extended the FPC's jurisdiction to wellhead prices for interstate natural gas. *See Phillips Petroleum Co. v. Wisconsin*, 347 U.S. 672 (1954). Since then, Congress has continued to address major energy issues in a complex array of environmental and economic statutes that make up the "working capital" of today's energy lawyers.

c. LAW AND POLICY THEMES

As the previous discussion suggests, the regulation of energy resources takes place within a legislative tangle of state and federal statutes, often reviewed by courts using administrative law principles of judicial review. However, many energy issues are also addressed under common-law rules of property and contracts, even in the global arena where private companies contract with government entities for the right to develop state-owned resources. Certain legal and policy themes have a tendency to recur, regardless of the energy source or particular statutory scheme at issue. We will often return to the constitutional themes of federalism under the Commerce Clause and Takings under the Fifth Amendment. Environmental law, antitrust law, and economic regulation appear in every individual resource chapter. International law—both the "hard" law of treaties and international custom and the "softer" law of United Nations resolutions on expropriation, human rights, and the rights of indigenous peoples–already plays an important role in the development of petroleum reserves overseas by multinational companies, many of which have headquarters in the United States. International public law, particularly in the environmental arena, will increasingly affect all of the energy sources, not just petroleum.

B. GOVERNMENT REGULATION

Throughout the history of the United States, the development of new types of energy resources brought questions about whether these resources were appropriate subjects for control as natural monopolies or whether a competitive market could be developed. John D. Rockefeller's success in monopolizing the oil business led to the antitrust laws in the nineteenth century. Samuel Insull's similar success in the electricity business encouraged strict regulation of that industry. But over time, technological advances have made competition among different parts of the energy sector more feasible, and this has revived these age-old questions about the proper system of economic regulation. Meanwhile, however, new layers of environmental and conservation regulation have been added to the regulatory mix.

1. MULTIPLICITY OF REGULATORY AGENCIES

One feature of the energy industries that poses constant problems is the overlapping jurisdiction of a wide variety of regulatory agencies. During the same period as the federal government added regulatory programs specifically addressing energy issues, it also created a wide range of environmental regulatory programs that impacted the energy industries. And in many cases these programs paralleled but did not preempt similar regulatory programs adopted by the state and local governments.

a. FEDERAL AGENCIES

Among the federal agencies, the ones that most directly affect the energy industries are the Department of Energy (DOE), the Department of Interior (DOI), the Federal Energy Regulatory Commission (FERC), the Nuclear Regulatory Commission (NRC) and the Environmental Protection Agency (EPA).

The DOE sponsors energy research and plays a key role in international issues. DOI controls the federal lands, both onshore and offshore, from which much of our coal, oil and gas resources are extracted, and regulates the surface mining of coal. FERC regulates the construction of hydroelectric facilities and oversees the rates of natural gas and electricity to the extent they are transported in interstate commerce.

The NRC regulates the construction and operation of nuclear power plants. EPA administers a variety of environmental programs that affect energy: for example, the Clean Air Act has a major impact on electric power plants and oil refineries and the Oil Pollution Act affects the operation of oil tankers.

By no means is this a complete list of federal regulatory programs that affect the energy industries. For example, the Department of Transportation has played some role in the regulation of oil pipelines and Department of Labor implements safety standards for coal mines. Most of the larger energy companies maintain Washington D.C. offices, or employ legal counsel, to keep track of these regulatory programs.

b. STATE AGENCIES

The state systems of public utility regulation have not been replaced by the new federal regulatory programs. Public utility commissions continue to regulate the rates, facilities and services of the private utilities that supply natural gas and electricity within the state. As we will see, definition of the precise line between state and federal jurisdiction over rates and service has produced a great deal of litigation.

The state governments also have environmental regulatory agencies that administer state programs and cooperate with the EPA in the administration of federal programs. For example, state agencies set water quality standards that have a major impact on the disposal of wastes from the production of energy resources.

c. LOCAL AGENCIES

At the local level, energy companies often must comply with a wide range of land use regulations. Construction of new power lines, for example, is likely to run into local concerns that may be expressed through prohibitory regulations. In some states, many such regulations have been preempted by state law.

Local governments also exercise power over electric and gas companies through control over the local streets, which the companies need to use for delivery of services. In many places, local governments also use regulatory programs as a revenue-raising device through the addition of various fees to consumers' utility bills.

2. FEDERALISM ISSUES

In view of the overlapping nature of the regulatory systems at the federal, state and local levels, it is not surprising that many of the key issues of energy law involve issues of federalism policy. Because the Supreme Court has begun to cast new attention to issues of "states' rights," energy lawyers are beginning to reexamine the constitutionality of some long-accepted balances between state and federal authority.

a. IMPACTS BEYOND JURISDICTIONAL BOUNDARIES

Decisions involving energy resources are subject to the assertion of authority by three sovereigns: the state, the federal government, and the international community. It is useful to ask why the federal government should involve itself in the regulation of energy resources. Don't the states adequately regulate energy resources themselves? As a general matter, local regulation has the advantage of providing a regulatory solution that is most likely to respect and reflect the views of those individuals closest to the energy resources at issue.

However, state regulation may create negative spillover costs—a type of externality—for other states or regions that outweigh the benefits of localized control. In the Northeast, for example, pollution from automobiles may spill over from one state to another, and this may invite some type of federal or regional solution. In addition, economies of scale in production may transcend state borders. For example, although the pollution from automobiles may not drift from one state to another outside of the densely populated Northeast, automobile production does exhibit significant economies of scale: the cost per vehicle of meeting one uniform regulation is much lower than the costs of meeting multiple regulations in multiple states. *See* Margaret A. Walls, U.S. Energy and Environmental Policies: Problems of Federalism and Conflicting Goals, in Making National Energy Policy 95 (Hans H. Landsberg, ed. 1993); *but see* Richard L. Revesz, Rehabilitating Interstate Competition: Rethinking the "Race to the Bottom" Rationale for Federal Environmental Regulation, 67 N.Y.U. L. Rev. 1210 (1992).

b. THE COMMERCE CLAUSE

The U.S. government's authority to regulate energy resources is far reaching under the Commerce Clause. Since 1937, Congress has had the authority to regulate purely intrastate activities that affect interstate commerce, such as electricity and natural gas generation, transmission, distribution.

In many instances, Congress has chosen not to regulate certain energy resource uses. For example, FERC's rate jurisdiction over electricity rates under the FPA extends to only wholesale transactions; Congress has left most matters of retail rate regulation to the states.

This dual regulatory scheme inevitably creates a conflict and has led to much litigation in the energy and environmental areas. As a legal matter, in some instances Congress may explicitly preempt state law, as it is normally allowed to do under the Supremacy Clause. Absent explicit preemption, dual federal and state regulation of energy resources is permissible provided none of the following occurs: state regulation does not frustrate congressional purposes (*Florida Lime & Avocado Growers, Inc. v. Paul*, 373 U.S. 132 (1963)); state law does not regulate conduct in a field Congress intended federal law to occupy exclusively (*California v. ARC America Corp.*, 490 U.S. 93 (1989)); or state law does not conflict directly with federal law. *Transcontinental Gas Pipe Line Corp. v. State Oil and Gas Bd. of Mississippi*, 474 U.S. 409 (1986).

Even in the absence of a federal statute, courts may strike down state statutes that discriminate against out-of-state commerce under the "dormant" Commerce Clause. For example, in *New England Power Co. v. New Hampshire*, 455 U.S. 331 (1982) the Supreme Court held that a state prohibition on the export of locally generated hydropower was unconstitutional for favoring New Hampshire citizens at the expense of out-of-state citizens. The Illinois legislature passed a law that required air quality compliance plans filed by large in-state utilities to consider scrubber installation at their power plants, favoring the usage of Illinois coal in electricity generation facilities. The U.S. Court of Appeals for the Seventh Circuit struck the statute down because it discriminated against out-of-state coal producers in *Alliance for Clean Coal v. Miller*, 44 F.3d 591 (7th Cir.1995). As the states become more concerned about air pollution flowing between the states, dormant Commerce Clause challenges are likely to become more common in the electricity regulation context.

Finally, federal or state regulation of energy resources may conflict with U.S. obligations under international law. Among these obligations are: the General Agreement on Tariffs and Trade and the North American Free Trade Agreement, which constitute an international obligation by the U.S. not to unilaterally impose impediments to trade with most of its energy trading partners; the International Energy Program Agreement, which commits the U.S. to plan for energy emergencies by maintaining oil reserves and supplies, and provide assistance through the International Energy Agency in case of emergency situations; the Nuclear Non–Proliferation Treaty and the programs of the International Atomic Energy Agency, which require the U.S. to restrict certain nuclear and related exports to nonsignatory countries and provide for international inspection systems. The U.S. also has entered into bilateral treaties and agreements with significant obligations concerning energy resources with Canada, Mexico, Venezuela, and Israel. The U.S. has assumed further obligations, particularly concerning global warming and CO_2 emissions, under international environmental treaties.

3.   Competition

One way of understanding the economic and environmental regulation of the energy industry is to view it as governmental reaction to private market failure. Because a market with two or more firms may fail to provide energy resources at a price and quantity which would maximize consumer welfare, the government grants a monopoly franchise to a single firm and regulates its price to guard against monopolist abuses. Similarly, because the market fails to internalize many of the costs of energy resource extraction, conversion, and distribution processes, it is necessary to internalize these costs through environmental controls such as emissions standards, siting proceedings, demand side management, and resource planning procedures.

In addition, in recent years, public choice theory, which applies economic analysis to government institutions and decisionmaking processes, has raised the concern that government regulation itself may be prone to certain failures. If the purpose of government regulation is to correct market failures but regulation as implemented results in solutions that do not approximate the results of a perfectly functioning market, then regulation itself may have imposed unnecessary costs or inhibited self-correcting incentives.

a.   THE LIMITS OF REGULATION

Price and environmental regulation of energy resources are not without their costs, for resource title holders and users as well as society. Regulation often has the unintended effect of falling short of its intended goals for several reasons.

First, the regulatory process may be susceptible to capture by the very interests it is designed to regulate and thus may fall short of its public interest objectives. This has been a recurring problem in the energy regulatory sector. Many of the New Deal modifications to electric utility regulation, which extended federal jurisdiction, were a reaction to this concern. However, as public choice scholars have recently reminded us, promotion of the public interest continues to be thwarted by rent seeking through the regulatory process. *See* George Stigler, The Theory of Economic Regulation, 2 Bell J. Econ. & Management Sci. 137 (1971); Sam Pelzman, Towards a More General Theory of Regulation, 19 J. L. & Econ. 211 (1976).

Second, regulation may cause regulated firms to incur excessive costs or adopt inefficient methods of operation. Economists sometimes refer to this as "X–Inefficiency." *See* John R. Meyer & William B. Tye, Toward Achieving Workable Competition in Industries Undergoing a Transition to Deregulation: A Contractual Equilibrium Approach, 5 Yale J. Reg. 273, 277–79 (1988). For example, to the extent that regulated firms expend their resources to capture the regulatory process, this creates an inefficiency. Richard A. Posner, The Social Costs of Regulation and Monopoly, 83 J. Pol. Econ. 207 (1975). However, even if the "capture" theory of regulation is not entirely descriptive of the actual process, regulation creates artificial—

and sometimes costly—incentives for behavior. Recall that a regulated public utility's rates are calculated on the basis of its revenue requirements, which include both rate base and operating expenses. Some economists have suggested that price regulation has induced many public utilities to artificially inflate their rate base and to overinvest in capital assets—*e.g.*, to build too many power plants for their customer base. Harvey Averch & Leland L. Johnson, Behavior of the Firm Under Regulatory Constraint, 52 Am. Econ. Rev. 1052 (1962). The effect of this has been to create a surplus of power and to inflate the ultimate costs to consumers.

Third, jurisdictional conflicts may create controversies. The most common of these is the conflict between state and federal regulators, creating the unsatisfactory situation "in which two different persons seek to drive one car." *See Louisiana Public Service Commission v. Federal Communications Commission*, 476 U.S. 355 (1986). Such controversies may lead to overregulation, uncertainty, protracted litigation, and an inability to implement a regulatory scheme.

b. COMPETITIVE RESTRUCTURING

Failures in the regulation of energy resources have led regulators to consider market-oriented reforms of the regulatory process. In recent years, this market-oriented approach has driven massive reforms in the natural gas and electric utility contexts. In both contexts, federal regulators have taken a similar approach: unbundling and open access restructuring. In addition, regulators have considered mechanisms such as market-based rates, competitive bidding, and incentive regulation.

Many markets that have been subjected to cost-of-service regulation on the public utility model share a common trait: they are in fact several different markets with varying characteristics. For example, consider the natural gas market. There are thousands of producers and literally millions of consumers of natural gas. Apart from the need to transport gas, the gas sales market is as close to the economist's competitive ideal as any market. Transportation, however, is subject to large economies of scale and is a natural monopoly. Yet historically, sales and transportation have been bundled within a single rate-regulated service. Similarly, electric power generation and electricity transmission have traditionally been bundled into a single rate-regulated service, even though power generation, like natural gas sales, possesses characteristics of a competitive market.

Recognizing the benefits of markets where an industry possesses structurally competitive characteristics, in recent years FERC has implemented unbundling/equal access restructuring in the natural gas industry and has announced its intention to do so in the electric utility industry. This approach has two steps: first, the recognition that, rather than a single market, there are two or more distinctive markets, only one of which is a natural monopoly; second, the implementation of an equal access regulatory scheme that applies only to the natural monopoly market.

Perhaps the simplest example of this two-step approach has already been implemented on a mass scale in the U.S. telecommunications industry. Beginning with the break-up of AT&T in the early 1980s, long-distance and local telephone services were "unbundled", so that regulators and firms were forced to treat them as distinctive markets, rather than a single product provided by a single firm. Long-distance service was deemed to be structurally competitive. However, because AT&T continued to exercise monopoly power over long-distance transmission facilities, AT&T's monopoly was broken up and regulated to ensure open access to new long-distance firms. Today, consumers can choose among a variety of long-distance providers, but are usually captive to local service provision by a single firm.

Similarly, in the natural gas context, FERC completely unbundled pipeline sales and transportation in "Order 636." Order 636 prohibited pipelines from providing a bundled service of sales and transportation. At the same time, however, interstate pipelines were required to provide equal access to storage and transportation services and to file a plan for implementing this new regime. *Pipeline Service Obligations and Revisions to Regulations Governing Self–Implementing Transportation and Regulation of Natural Gas Pipelines After Partial Wellhead Decontrol*, 57 Fed. Reg. 13,267 (1992), *order on reh'g*, 57 Fed. Reg. 36,128 (1992), *order on reh'g*, 57 Fed. Reg. 57,911 (1992), *remanded in part, United Distribution Cos. v. FERC*, 88 F.3d 1105 (D.C.Cir.1996). This has led to an increase in competition for pipeline sales which, many suggest, is likely to accrue to the benefit of consumers. *E.g.*, Robert J. Michaels, The New Age of Natural Gas: How the Regulators Brought Competition, Regulation, Winter 1993, at 68. However, it has also been observed that the costs of implementing Order 636, amounting to about $4.8 billion (General Accounting Office, Costs, Benefits and Concerns Related to FERC's Order 636 16 (1993)), are likely to be disproportionately borne by small consumers. *E.g.*, Joseph Fagan, Note, From Regulation to Deregulation: The Diminishing Role of the Small Consumer Within the Natural Gas Industry, 29 Tulsa L.J. 707 (1994).

FERC has recently made similar steps towards restructuring the electric utility industry. In spring 1996, FERC approved a series of regulations that prohibit utilities from bundling wholesale electricity generation and transmission service. FERC's regulations also require electric utilities to file an equal access transmission plan, which would facilitate competition in power generation markets. *Promoting Wholesale Competition Through Open Access Non-Discriminatory Transmission Services by Public Utilities, Recovery of Stranded Costs by Public Utilities and Transmitting Utilities*, 61 Fed. Reg. 21,539 (1996), *aff'd Transmission Access Policy Study Group v. FERC*, 2000 WL 762706 (D.C.Cir.2000). However, because FERC's electric jurisdiction is less extensive than its natural gas jurisdiction, implementation is primarily taking place at the state level. Some states, such as California, New Hampshire and New York, are well on their way towards implementing a new regulatory regime that would give consumers a choice of their power generator, much as consumers are able to chose their long-distance provider.

In addition, FERC and state utility commissions have embarked upon a series of incremental changes to traditional utility price regulation. More than thirty states have instituted competitive bidding regimes for electric utilities, which require utilities to solicit and consider bids before building new power plants. FERC has approved dozens of market-based rate applications, rates filed in lieu of cost-of-service filings by utilities who meet certain conditions. FERC and many state commissions have also adopted incentive regulation to encourage a variety of non-traditional utilities to enter into power markets. Together, these new regulatory efforts have sparked a considerable growth of new firms in traditional markets as well as the emergence of new pricing markets, such as spot and futures markets.

Regulators have used market-based mechanisms not only to displace price regulation. In the sulfur dioxide context, mandated technologies for coal-fired utility plants have been replaced with tradeable emissions allowances. In implementing a tradeable emissions program, the government gives away limited number of pollution permits but allows the permit holder to trade them, effectively moving them to their highest valued use. However, to date the application of market mechanisms in the traditional pollution context has been limited.

It is unclear how competitive reform of the energy industry will affect environmental regulation mechanisms in the electricity context. Some have criticized the ability of competitive markets to co-exist with centralized decisionmaking mechanisms such as integrated resource planning. *E.g.*, Bernard S. Black and Richard J. Pierce, The Choice Between Markets and Central Planning in Regulating the U.S. Electricity Industry, 93 Colum. L. Rev. 1339 (1993). Others, however, maintain that there is a continued need for such mechanisms to correct market failures (*See* FERC: Electricity Demand Side Bidding: Hearing Before the Subcommittee on Energy and Power of the House Committee on Energy and Commerce, 100th Cong., 2d Sess. 3 (1988) (Statement of Ralph J. Cavanagh)) and to provide critical information for markets to succeed. *See* Carl Pechman, Regulating Power: The Economics of Electricity in the Information Age (1993). Whether price competition and environmental regulation can co-exist in the energy resource context is likely to dominate the agenda of federal and state decisionmakers for decades to come.

C. THE GLOBAL ENVIRONMENT

Energy law is rapidly outgrowing national boundaries. Multinational oil companies have long operated throughout the world, but other parts of the energy industry have expanded internationally as well. American electric companies have expanded by buying electric companies in Europe, and European companies have expanded operations in the United States.

The environmental issues facing the energy sector are also increasingly global in nature. Development of energy resources in the tropical rainforest has implications for global biodiversity. And the most troublesome issue for the energy sector is the widespread and increasingly strong argument that the combustion of fossil fuels threatens to increase global temperatures and cause rising sea levels.

The speed and ubiquity of communication across international boundaries on the internet have brought increasing awareness of international human rights issues. International energy companies working as joint venturers with foreign government entities will have to address the concerns of indigenous people who argue that their own national governments and state-owned oil companies are violating international human rights. The world of energy spans the globe.

D.   Top 5 List of Worst Mistakes

While the top 10 list of emerging issues was forward–looking, their solutions will often draw on the past. Throughout the book, we use the past as a reference point for understanding the future, in the belief that we should be able to learn from our mistakes. In this spirit, we also offer our consensus view of the five worst mistakes in energy law and regulation over the past century.

1) *Using price predictions to make policy.* Irrevocable and long-term policy choices have often been based on price forecasts which failed to account for the power of market forces or technological change. For instance, in the 1970s, the energy industry and government supported programs and investments based on the assumption that oil prices would climb to $70 a barrel in the year 2000. This assumption contributed to decisions to build nuclear plants that later proved uneconomic, relative to alternative energy resources.

2) *Smyth v. Ames,* 169 U.S. 466 (1898). This case endorsed a substantive due process approach to regulation, one that since has been overruled but still lingers in some regulators' decisions, such as recent decisions to compensate stranded costs in the electric power and natural gas industries.

3) *Different environmental standards for incumbents.* The congressional decision to grandfather existing power plants, exempting them from certain requirements of the Clean Air Act, has resulted in thirty years of delay in progress toward cleaner air, as has the failure to regulate diesel fuel at an earlier time.

4) *Reluctance to endorse the common carrier concept in natural gas and electricity transmission.* Until recently, federal regulators failed to recognize that natural gas pipelines and electricity transmission companies are common carriers. Oil pipelines, by contrast, were recognized as common carriers in 1906. As a result, the gas and electricity sectors have required restructuring, often painful to both industry and consumers.

5) *Phillips Petroleum Co. v. Wisconsin,* 347 U.S. 672 (1954). In this case, the Supreme Court regulated the price of natural gas sold by

producers into interstate commerce, transforming a competitive industry into a regulated industry. The approach of federal regulators led to a regulatory morass of gas shortages, enduse allocation, and take-or-pay liabilities. The natural gas precedent has influenced judicial limitations on federal regulation of electricity.

We welcome our readers to amend our lists with ''hits'' of their own as they make their way through the material in this casebook. Time will tell us whether our top issues and mistakes stay on the list as the 21st century counts down.

CHAPTER 2

ENERGY IN NATURE

Outline of Chapter:

A. MEANINGS OF ENERGY

When we speak of energy law and policy we are using the word "energy" in a rather special way. The word "energy" has many meanings in common speech, as the historian Howard Mumford Jones explains:

> It may refer to force or vigor in style, particularly literary style ..., to the exercise of power, to the actual operation, working or activity of man or thing, or to the product or effect of such energy. One may mean by it personal vigor of action or utterance, as when one says that

> Theodore Roosevelt was characterized by energy.... One may mean by it what the physicist tends to mean: the power of doing work possessed at some moment by a body or system of bodies.... Common to all these meanings is the idea of energy as the power by which anything or anybody acts effectively to move or change other things or persons.

Howard Mumford Jones, The Age of Energy 104–05 (Viking, 1971).

Much of modern energy law deals with the fossil fuels, coal, oil and natural gas, and the electricity that these fuels generate. But the source of virtually all of our energy is the sun, which radiates waves of electromagnetic energy and high energy particles into space. Roger G. Barry & Richard J. Chorley, Atmosphere, Weather and Climate 20 (Routledge, 7th ed. 1998). The fossil fuels are the result of natural processes by which the energy the earth receives from the sun was converted into plant material which was eventually buried and compressed into coal or petroleum. And these natural processes continue to play a major role in our evaluation of future policies as we try to determine what fuels will be available for future generations.

1. ENERGY SCIENCE

Understanding the flow of energy through the natural environment is an essential component of all efforts to restore the environment. Duncan T. Patten, Restoration as the Order of the 21st Century: An Ecologist's Perspective, 18 J. Land, Resources, and Envtl. L. 31, 36 (1998). One of the leading ecological scientists has emphasized the importance of energy in understanding the natural world:

> If one were asked to pick out a single common denominator of life on earth, that is, something that is absolutely essential and involved in every action, large or small, the answer would have to be energy....
> The fantastic variety of organisms and functions involved in keeping our life-support systems operating require a great deal of energy....
> All humans should understand the basic principles of energy transformations, because without energy, there can be no life. We should start teaching energetics in the first grade.

Eugene P. Odum, Ecology and Our Endangered Life–Support Systems, (Sinauer, 2d. ed., 1993).

Energy is also one of the key concepts of the physical sciences. The following excerpt is from John Peet, a chemical engineer who has attempted to translate complex scientific principles into terms that people without a background in the physical sciences can understand.

John Peet
Energy and the Ecological Economics of Sustainability
Island Press, 1992.

In the general sense, life on earth (including virtually all activities of human societies) stems, directly or indirectly, from the sun. The sun is the source of effectively all of the energy available to the solar system. The earth is a "consumer" of some of the sun's energy in that energy absorbed from the sun is used to drive atmospheric and life processes before being rejected to the cosmic "heat sink" of outer space. The radiant energy received from the sun supplies heat to the earth's surface and light for the processes of photosynthesis in plants. The complex hierarchy of animal life depends on these flows of energy, from the simplest organisms to the giants of the forest, from bacteria to humans.

Energy from the sun heats the sea and the land, thereby creating convection currents in the atmosphere that result in air movements, evaporation of water from the sea, and rain.

Paths Taken by Incident Solar Radiation In the Atmosphere

Reflected back into space	
From upper atmosphere	30%
From earth's surface	6%
Absorbed by clouds	3%
Absorbed by the atmosphere	14%
Total	53%

At the Earth's Surface

	Ocean Area	Land Area
Evaporation of water	17%	6%
Heating of surface	17%	8%
Total	34%	14%

Of solar radiation that reaches the outer atmosphere, 53 percent never reaches the earth's surface. Of the remaining 48 percent, 34 percent falls on the oceans and 14 percent falls on the land. When energy takes part in activities at the earth's surface, some of it is always degraded into low-temperature heat. This heat is ultimately lost from the earth's system by long-wavelength (infrared) radiation into space. A small part of that energy may be stored for a time, either as plants and animals or as fossil fuels. Eventually, even these will be degraded into low-grade heat. . . .

In a strict scientific sense, *energy* is the ability to do work. This apparently obscure statement means that energy has the ability to cause changes in the physical or chemical nature, structure, or location of matter or things. In this context, "work" has a very specific meaning only vaguely related to the social meaning of the term, with which it should not be confused.

Energy is not a thing that can be seen or touched; it is a concept used to explain changes in the state of matter under certain circumstances. Heating, cooling, chemical change, motion, and so on result from changes in the nature or location of the energetic state of matter. Some such changes alter the structure of matter, as when dough is (chemically) converted into bread by baking (heat energy). Other examples, involving less obvious structural changes, arise when a speeding vehicle (kinetic energy) is slowed by the use of its brakes (heat energy) or when elevated water (high gravitational potential energy) falling to a lower level (low gravitational potential energy) is used to turn turbines (rotating mechanical energy) in a hydroelectric power station to generate electricity (electrical energy).

Energy is thus a generalized attribute of physical transformation and change, not a commodity. Energy may be seen to be *flowing*, as in the case of sunshine, where radiated energy is the basis for the flows of water vapor and air in the atmosphere and for the whole complex system of life on earth. When clouds come between a person and the sun, that person's skin and eyes respond immediately to the change in energy flow.

Energy may be *stored*, in the energy of elevated water in lakes and rivers, in chemical form in plants and animals, or as the highly concentrated stocks of carbon and hydrogen chemically combined in coal, oil, or gas in underground reservoirs. The distinction between stock and flow resources is of vital importance. Only human societies have learned to use large quantities of stock resources to supplement the natural energy flows from the sun. Stock and flow resources are often described, respectively, as *nonrenewable* and *renewable*, since stock resources required millions of years for their formation and cannot be replaced within a time period of relevance to humankind. Flow energy may be stored for relatively short periods in vegetable and animal tissue, and many animals (including, of course, humans) store food for winter use. The flow energy in the water cycle may also be stored for long periods in lakes, glaciers, or aquifers.

All energy has the potential ability to do work. The potential of a form of energy to do work varies according to its nature. Stored energy's potential to do work cannot be exploited, however, until a transformation pathway exists for it to be released. Examples of types of potential energy are as follows:

Gravitational. The height of a lake determines the amount of work that can be done by its water in descending to a lower level.

Mechanical. The energy of motion of a flowing river, the energy stored in a wound-up spring, a rotating flywheel, or a moving object such as a truck can all do work in unwinding or slowing down.

Chemical. Fossil fuels (coal, oil, and gas) contain high concentrations of carbon and hydrogen arranged in structure that bind large quantities of potential energy. The same amounts of carbon and hydrogen bound in carbon dioxide and water (the main products of burning fuels in air) contain much less potential energy.

Nuclear. Uranium and plutonium store energy in their atomic structures. In these atoms, among the largest known, the atomic building blocks (neutrons and protons) are packed tightly into the nucleus of the atom.

When such atoms are "split," fragments are produced, with the release of very large quantities of energy.

Electrical. Lightning is a well-known example of the release of stored electrical energy. The processes inside thunderclouds generate high electrical charges (millions of volts). These build up until the air between the cloud and the earth's surface is able to conduct electricity, whereupon the charge is released and lightning energy "flows."

Thermal. Thermal energy (heat) is available from direct or focused solar radiation, from geothermal sources, and from the burning of fossil fuels, wood, and so on. Its potential depends on the extent to which the temperature achieved is higher than that of its surroundings. Heat may be "stored"; familiar examples are vacuum flasks and hot water bottles. The length of time for which it can be stored depends on the level of insulation; the better the insulation, the slower the rate of cooling. Things do not stay hot indefinitely unless supplied with "new" heat energy.

Flows and transformations of energy into work occur spontaneously only when both the potential and the appropriate pathway exist. If a pathway does not exist, the energy remains at its original potential, either flowing or stored. Water in a lake can turn the turbines of a hydroelectric power station only when it flows (via penstocks) down a gravitational potential to a lower level. Similarly, other forms of stored energy cannot perform work unless they are also released from their stored form and move down an appropriate transformation pathway to a lower potential energy state. The pathway may be a power station or a fire in which coal or wood is burned.

Having done that work, the energy is at a lower level (a lower potential), and experience tells us that *it cannot be used to do the same work again without expenditure of additional energy from outside the system.* In the case of the hydroelectric power station, the only way the water could be used to generate power again at the same station would be for it to be pumped back from the downstream river into the lake above the dam. In practice, this pumping always requires more energy than is obtained by running the water back down through the turbines.

As well as depending on the difference in potential between the stored energy and its surrounding environment, the energy released in a process also depends on the amount of energy in the store. For example, the energy released by a lake depends not only on the difference in height between the lake and the turbine outfall but also on the quantity of water that flows out of the lake through the turbines. The energy available from a tank of gasoline depends on the difference in chemical potentials of the fuel and of the carbon dioxide and water in the exhaust and also on the size of the tank. The "usefulness" of any energy resource depends on its size as well as its potential relative to the baseline energy potential in its local or global environment.

Sunlight performs work in heating the atmosphere and in driving photosynthesis because it comes from a source that is at a temperature of about 6,000 degrees Kelvin (on the Kelvin scale, 0 degrees Kelvin is approximately the temperature of outer space). Since the average temperature of the earth's surface is around 285 degrees Kelvin (about 12 degrees Celsius), solar energy flows "down" a radiation pathway from the sun to outer space, with the earth temporarily intercepting a little of that energy.

Nuclear energy is so highly concentrated that it cannot normally be used directly; it must first be converted in a nuclear reactor into heat, which is then used to raise steam and drive turbines.

Electrical energy is a very useful, high-grade energy source because it is almost entirely capable of conversion into mechanical work through the pathway provided by an electric motor.

Heat is the least useful form of energy in terms of the ability to do work, and low-temperature heat is less useful than high-temperature heat. Water in the oceans of the world is not a useful source of stored energy for ordinary work processes, despite its vast quantity. The difference in temperature (potential) between ocean water and its surroundings is in most cases too small for a useful amount of work to be obtained from it.

Without expenditure of potential energy, there can be no activity in the natural environment. In nature, interaction of sunlight with matter over hundreds of millions of years has enabled the evolution of plants, animals, and ecosystems that provide a multitude of mechanisms for energy transformation and use. These systems exist as the result of prior energy inflows and interactions. Even in ecosystems, development of "natural technologies" depends on the recycling of energy stored from previous inflows....

The basis for all physical activity, on earth as elsewhere in the universe, is the existence of sources of potential energy. This is sometimes more usefully described as *availability*, in that only some forms of energy are, in practice, available for work processes. One form of energy can often be substituted for another; trains can be pulled by locomotives using coal, oil, or electricity, and homes can be heated by many different fuels. Nevertheless, *there is no substitute for energy*. Available energy is an absolutely unsubstitutable input to any physical process. That statement may seem extreme, but it is based on fundamental laws of physics for which no counterevidence has ever been produced.

Thermodynamics—The Science of Energy. Many processes, both in nature and in technology, involve one form of energy being changed into another. Radiation from the sun is changed into heat at the earth's surface; into chemical energy (via photosynthesis) in plants; and into latent heat of vaporization when water evaporates from the sea or from puddles on a road. The science of thermodynamics is a set of bookkeeping principles that enable us to understand and follow energy as it is transformed from one form, or state, to another.

The First Law of Thermodynamics. The first law of thermodynamics, the law of conservation of energy, states: *Energy can be neither created nor destroyed, only converted from one form to another.*

When one energy form is converted into another, the total amount of energy remains constant. When gasoline is burned in an engine, the chemical energy in the fuel is converted into various forms: kinetic energy of motion; potential energy (if the car has been driven up a hill); chemical energy in the carbon dioxide and water of the exhaust gas; heat energy in the exhaust and cooling systems, transmission, brakes, and so on. All of the energy in the fuel can be accounted for, using appropriate measurements.... The accounts always balance; no exception has ever been identified.

The first law of thermodynamics is of only limited use. It does not help us understand why, if energy cannot be destroyed, we cannot reuse the energy in a tank of gasoline. The answer is that although the total energy remains constant, the potential of each subsequent form to do work is not the same as at the start of the process. One cannot pipe exhaust back into the tank and run the car on it. The spent energy is not available for further work to the same extent as was the energy in the original fuel because it has been degraded into lower-temperature and lower-chemical-potential forms. The high temperature of combustion of the gasoline (more than 1,000 degrees Celsius) enables much more of it to be converted into work than do the lower-temperature heat energy (about 100 degrees Celsius) and the minimal quantity of chemical energy in the exhaust gas. We need to formalize this fact, which is where the second law of thermodynamics comes in.

The Second Law of Thermodynamics. The second law of thermodynamics—the entropy law—can be stated as follows: *All physical processes proceed in such a way that the availability of the energy involved decreases.*

What this statement means is that no transformation of energy resources can ever be 100 percent efficient. All processes irrevocably degrade available energy to an unavailable state. In any closed system, whether natural or technological, the total energy available to do work must decrease. Eventually, any system runs out of available energy and comes to a stop.

Many books have been written about this apparently simple law. Equivalent statements (which tell us more about specific topics within thermodynamics) are as follows:

In any transformation of energy, some of it is always degraded.

It is not possible to convert a given quantity of heat (thermal energy) into an equal amount of useful work (mechanical energy).

Heat will not of itself flow from a colder body to a hotter body.

The availability of a quantity of energy can be used only once.

These four statements follow from the previous discussion and also from everyday experience. Nobody has ever built a car that converts all of its gasoline into motion, with no heat release through the radiator or exhaust. A saucepan of water placed on a hot stove does not get colder while the stove gets hotter; nor does it get hotter when removed from the stove altogether. A stone may spontaneously roll down a hill, but it always has to be pushed back up again. The second law of thermodynamics merely formalizes situations that people have known about since the dawn of consciousness.

The second law declares that the material economy *necessarily and unavoidably* degrades the resources that sustain it. Increasing resource scarcity on the one hand and pollution on the other are the results of this unvarying one-way sequence of material consumption and depletion. Even though many natural resources (timber, plants, etc.) can grow again, the rate of natural renewal of resources is, on the world scale, generally smaller than the rate of use. Where stock resources (e.g., fossil fuels and high-quality mineral deposits) are concerned, the renewal process takes place over eons of geological time and is therefore irrelevant compared with the rate at which humans are presently using them.

Entropy. The second law of thermodynamics [can be restated as follows]: *In spontaneous processes, concentrations tend to disperse, structure tends to disappear, and order becomes disorder.* In thermodynamics, there is a concept called *entropy* that is a measure of the amount of energy no longer capable of conversion into work after a transformation process has taken place. It is thus a measure of the unavailability of energy. Entropy can also be shown to be a measure of the level of disorder of a system. Thus, the pile of broken pieces of china on the floor has a greater entropy than would the same plate, unbroken, on the floor, and the plate on the floor has a greater entropy than did the same plate on the table. If the second law is restated in yet another way, still equivalent to the others, in order to bring in the concept of entropy, it becomes this: *All physical processes proceed in such a way that the entropy of the universe increases.*

Primary, Secondary, and Consumer Energy. Some forms of energy exist as such in nature, whereas some must be produced from other forms. Electricity cannot be made available in a controlled form for an economy without its being produced from another form of energy, such as geothermal or nuclear heat, coat, oil, or gas in a power station or elevated water in a hydroelectric station. Those forms of energy that are obtained or extracted without requiring the transformation of significant proportions of other forms of energy are termed *primary energy*; other forms, such as electricity, are *secondary energy*.

All forms of energy are subject to losses in distribution to the consumer. Electricity distribution systems typically "lose" some 10 or 15 percent of the electricity produced by the power stations in transmission along lines to the consumer. Crude oil is subject to refining losses of 5 to 8 percent, representing the oil consumed to drive processes in the refinery. The energy actually delivered to consumers is termed *consumer energy*.

Energy and the Economic Process. The central physical fact about the economic processes of production and consumption is that matter is rearranged. Matter cannot be created or destroyed by an economy, only changed in form. This is the case when ores are processed into motor vehicles and the matter (steel, etc.) in those same vehicles is eventually dissipated as waste by being dumped or recycled as scrap. Some wastes are recyclable, but many have to be assimilated by nature. We know that nature's capacity to absorb waste is limited—often severely—and in such cases, wastes accumulate.

All such processes are associated with the transformation of high-quality available energy into low-quality waste energy. Entropy provides us with a useful index for measuring the accumulation of useless and/or harmful wastes from human economic activity. The entropy concept applies as much to materials (in which energy is a measure of structural order) as to heat flows. (27–43)■

2.   MEASUREMENT OF ENERGY

Energy is measured in a variety of ways in different industries. One of the earliest units of measurement of the power of energy sources was the *horsepower*, which was invented by James Watt as a device to help sell the early steam engines he invented. One horsepower was defined as the ability to pull 33,000 foot-pounds per minute, which was assumed to be the capability of a healthy draft horse.

Vaclav Smil
Energies: An Illustrated Guide to the Biosphere and Civilization

The MIT Press, 1998.

The first problem we encounter in formulating a way to talk about energies is that the common usages of many of the key terms are misleading. As Henk Tennekes has noted, "We have made a terrible mess of simple physical concepts in ordinary life." Few of these muddles are as ubiquitous and annoying as those involving terms such as "energy," "power," and "force."

A knowledge of basic mechanics helps get us started in sorting these terms out. **Force** is defined as the intensity with which we try to displace—push, pull, lift, kick, throw—an object. We can exert a large force even if the huge boulder we are trying to push remains immobile. We accomplish **work**, however, only when the object of our attention moves in the direction of the applied force. In fact, we define the amount of work performed as the product of the force applied and the distance covered. **Energy**, as the common textbook definition puts it, is "the capacity for doing work" and thus will be measured in the same units as work. If we measure force in units of newtons (N, named for Sir Issac Newton) and distance in meters (m), our measure of work will be the awkward-sounding Newton-meter. To simplify, scientists call one Newton-meter a joule (J), named for James Prescott Joule (1818–1889), who published the first accurate calculation of the equivalence of work and heat. The joule is the standard scientific unit for energy and work. **Power** is simply a rate of doing work, that is, an energy flow per unit of time; its measure is thus joules per second. We call one joule per second a watt (W) after James Watt (1736–1819), the inventor of the improved steam engine and the man who set the first standard unit of power, which as it happens was not the watt but horsepower (hp), a unit equal to roughly 750 W.

To go further we need to move from pushing and shoving (which we call mechanical or kinetic energy) to heating (thermal energy). We define a unit called the calorie as the amount of heat needed to raise the temperature of one gram of water from 14.5 to 15.5°C.

Our modern understanding of energy includes a number of profound realizations: that mass and energy are equivalent; that many conversions link various kinds of energies; that no energy is lost during these conversions (this is the first law of thermodynamics); and that this conservation of energy is inexorably accompanied by a loss of utility (the second law of thermodynamics). The first realization—initially called an "amusing and attractive thought" in a letter Einstein wrote to a friend—is summed up in perhaps the best know of all physical equations: $E = mc^2$.

The second realization is demonstrated constantly by myriads of energy conversions throughout the universe. Gravitational energy sets galaxies in motion, keeps the Earth orbiting around the sun, and holds down the atmosphere that makes our planet habitable. Conversion of nuclear energy within the Sun releases an incessant stream of electromagnetic (solar, radiant) energy. A small share of that energy reaches the Earth, which itself also releases geothermal energy. Heat from both these processes sets in motion the atmosphere, the oceans, and the Earth's huge tectonic plates.

Using unadjusted units to quantify this multitude of processes would be inconvenient: actual figures would nearly always be either trailed or preceded by many zeros. Both joules and watts represent very tiny amounts of measured energy and power: about thirty micrograms of coal—or two seconds' worth of a vole's metabolism account for one joule. One watt is the power of a very small burning candle or a hummingbird's rapid flight.

Multiples are inevitable, and we therefore introduce a series of prefixes to abbreviate the most useful multiples; a kilogram of good coal contains nearly thirty million joules, or thirty megajoules (MJ), of energy, and the world now consumes fossil fuels at the rate of roughly ten trillion watts (TW). (xii–xiv)■

B. SOLAR ENERGY

One of the easiest ways to understand the relationship of the sun to energy is to consider the extent to which the sun can be used to heat ordinary homes. The United States Department of Energy, whose mission includes the promotion of economical ways to conserve energy, uses the following pamphlet to explain solar heating in simple terms:

U.S. Dept. of Energy, Solar Energy and You (1993)

Solar energy is heat and light that comes from the sun. Thousands of years ago some people used this energy to heat their homes. Today, solar energy is again helping to heat buildings.

The sun is a giant heat source. If you can collect enough solar heat, you can use it instead of the heat from a furnace. One way to collect heat is to trap solar energy with **solar collectors.** An example of how a solar collector works is a car that has dark seat covers and has all its windows closed tightly. When sunlight passes through the glass windows of the car, it is **absorbed** (taken in) by the dark seat covers and walls and floor. Light that is absorbed changes into heat. If the seat covers are a pale color, such as white or yellow, they would not absorb as much sunlight. So pale colored seats do not become as hot as dark seats.

Now here is an interesting fact about glass: it lets light in, but it does not let all the heat out. Even if it is cold outside, the inside of the car will be warm from the trapped heat. So a solar collector does three things: 1) it allows sunlight inside through glass (or plastic); 2) it absorbs the sunlight and changes it into heat; and 3) it traps most of the heat inside.

Solar collectors become so hot that they can be used as heat sources for a building. There are two kinds of buildings that use solar collectors as heat sources: passive solar buildings and active solar buildings.

In some cases, a whole house itself is a solar collector (just like the car). These houses are called **passive** solar homes because they don't use any special **mechanical equipment** such as pipes, ducts, fans, or pumps. Since the sun shines from the south in North America, passive solar houses are built so that most of the windows face south. They have very few or no windows on the north side.

Some passive homes have greenhouses attached to them to let in light and trap the heat. The greenhouse is also used to grow plants because its many windows provide a lot of sunshine for the plants. Passive houses use walls and floors to absorb solar energy and turn it into heat. Passive homes do not use a mechanical heat distribution system. Instead, a passive home works because hot air is lighter than cold air. Because it is lighter, the hot air will naturally rise to the top of a room, leaving the cold, heavy air near the floor. In a passive home, air that is heated downstairs will naturally flow upstairs. Cold air will flow downstairs and will be heated up again.

To control the amount of heat in a passive solar house, people close doors and windows to keep heated air in and open doors and windows to let heated air out. At night, special heavy curtains or shades are pulled over the windows to keep the daytime heat inside the house. In the summertime, awnings or roof overhangs help to cool the house by shading the windows from the high summer sun.

Some buildings do use special mechanical equipment to collect and distribute solar heat. These buildings have **active** solar heating systems. Active systems use collectors which look like boxes covered with glass. Dark colored metal plates inside the boxes absorb sunlight and change it into heat. Air or water flows through the collectors and is warmed by this heat. The warmed-up air or water is then distributed to the rest of the house just like in an ordinary furnace system. Thermostats are also used to control the delivery of heat in active solar heating systems. Active solar collectors are usually placed high up on roofs where they can collect the greatest amount of sunlight. They are put on the south side of the roof in a place where no trees or tall buildings will shade them.

Solar energy systems must include some ways of storing the heat that was collected during sunny weather.

In active systems, either hot water is moved to large tanks of water, or hot air is moved to bins of rocks beneath the building. When it is needed, the hot water or air is taken back out of storage and sent to the living areas.

In a passive house, heat is absorbed by the thick walls and floors during the day. At night, when it becomes cold outside, warm walls and floors release their heat back into the room. If you have ever leaned up against a sunny brick wall or dark rock on a cold day, you were leaning on warm solar storage.

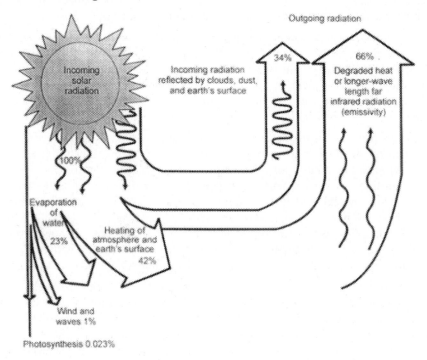

Figure 2-1
Source: Environmental Science: Sustaining the Earth 3ʳᵈ Edition (1991)
G. Tyler Miller, Jr. Wadsworth Publishing Co. (Figure 4.5)

Houses with active or passive solar heating systems also have a furnace, wood burning stove, or some other heat source to provide heat in case there is a long period of cloudy weather. This is called a backup heating system.

Solar energy can be used in many other ways besides heating buildings. Solar **photovoltaic cells** change sunlight directly into electricity; solar energy heats water for homes and businesses; and sunlight can even be used to cook food. As our supplies of precious gas and oil get smaller, we will find new uses for energy from the sun.■

In regions a long way from the equator, reliance on solar energy as a sole source for heating a home would be impractical, but homebuilders are discovering that "passive solar heating" can dramatically reduce heating costs.

Since Betty and Ken Woods went green with their conventional looking 3–bedroom, single-level home, they've slashed their household energy use by 72 percent. The couple's comfortable and durable 2,500–square-foot ranch-style Naperville home, built in 1984 for $103,000, is a super-insulated passive solar design. It has 165 square feet of south-facing, double-glazed windows, with padded interior shutters to prevent heat escape but to allow natural daylight in. It also has floor tile set on three inches of concrete to absorb direct sunlight for space heating. A gas boiler outside the home provides back-up warmth. The air-tight construction uses an air blower to draw in outside air and a filtration system to continually clean and recycle the air. On Saturday, Oct. 17, from 10 a.m. to 4 p.m., the Woods' home, as well as 23 other Illinois entries, including 11 more in the Chicago area, will open to the public as part of the American Solar Energy Society's Third Annual National Tour of Solar Homes.

Ed Meyer's Bolingbrook residence is also on the list. His spacious and sturdy 2,300–square-foot, 2–story, 3–bedroom home, designed by his wife, is well insulated with 6–inch-thick walls, while the second floor's north wall is 1–foot thick and is additionally buffered by a closet that is 2 feet deep. Costing about $110,000 when it was built in 1984, the house also features roof-mounted solar panels for 100 percent hot water heating and a 2–story sun space, a south-facing addition separated from the living room by a sliding glass door that collects direct sun light for space heating. A gas furnace supplies auxiliary heat. "It's fun on a bright sunny day when it's 20 degrees outside and 80 in the sun space. It makes you feel like you're getting something for nothing," chuckles Meyer, an electrical engineer and instructor at BellCore software. His annual heating bills average $120.

Nationwide, solar homes are finding their day in the sun. A million houses are equipped with solar hot water heaters, which average five years of use to recoup their cost. A solar hot water system, which costs

$1,500 to $3,500 would add $5 to $9 a month to a 20–year mortgage while providing monthly energy savings of $15 to $45, according to the Solar Energy Industries Association. Also, more than 10,000 homes are powered entirely by photovoltaics (PV, solar panels that convert sunlight to electricity), another 200,000 use some type of PV technology, and both categories increase 20 percent a year, according to the solar trade group.

Energy efficiency and solar applications are one part of a growing home building trend known loosely as green construction or sustainable development. These efforts have no single definition, but include such topics as orientation and location of a home (including access to transportation), materials, energy efficiency, indoor air quality, and construction waste reduction. The notions have caught the interest of more than maverick builders and idealists. At the International Builders Show in Dallas in January, the National Association of Home Builders Research Center and the Atlanta Home Builders Association will showcase a blueprint and release test results for a 1,200–square–foot "green" home. And, in April, the NAHB will sponsor the National Green Building Conference in Denver. "The very fact that there are six—and many more being considered—local green builder programs (around the U.S.), some of the leading home builder associations are recognizing that there's a demand to be tapped or created for these types of home," says Peter Yost, program manager for resource and environmental analysis at the NAHB Research Center.

Phillip Zonkel, Energy Savers: Homes that slash utility bills are open to the public, Chicago Tribune, Oct. 17, 1998.

Many nations have treated the sunlight that naturally reaches a piece of land as a form of property belonging to the landowner. This is particularly true in countries in the higher latitudes where sunlight seems more precious than it does in more tropical areas. In Japan, for example, construction of an office building requires extensive negotiations with any landowners whose sunlight would be reduced during prime daylight hours. In England, the common law once recognized a doctrine of "ancient lights," which treated the right to receive sunlight as an easement appurtenant to real property. This doctrine has been abandoned in England and in most of the American states. *See Fontainebleau Hotel Corp. v. Forty–Five Twenty–Five, Inc.*, 114 So.2d 357 (Fla.App.1959).

In 1982, the Wisconsin Supreme Court interpreted the common law of that state to provide a potential action in nuisance against a person who built a structure that interfered with the operation of a solar collector. *Prah v. Maretti*, 321 N.W.2d 182 (Wis.1982). Although a number of states have dealt with this issue by statute, relatively few have adopted the Wisconsin rule as a part of the common law. One of those that did is New Hampshire, in the following opinion written by Justice (now United States Supreme Court Justice) Souter:

Tenn v. 889 Associates, Ltd.

500 A.2d 366 (N.H.1985).

■ Souter, J.: The plaintiff, Sylvia Tenn, owns a six-story office building constructed in 1891 at 907–913 Elm Street in Manchester, New Hampshire, known as the Pickering Building. Its south wall is built to the southerly line of its lot. A neighboring building formerly located to the south of the plaintiff's property was built to the same lot line and to a height of nearly four stories, so that up to that height, the south wall of the Pickering Building had no windows. Above the fourth story, a total of twelve windows faced south, as did the glazed south wall of a light shaft, capped with a skylight, which provided light for the offices and halls. Several of the south windows held room air conditioners.

The defendant, 889 Associates, Ltd., now owns the lot south of the Pickering Building. In November, 1983, the defendant's president and treasurer, Michael Ingram, wrote to a representative of the plaintiff, Dr. James Tenn, informing him of the defendant's plans to demolish the existing four-story structure and to replace it with a new one. The letter indicated that the defendant intended to construct the new building, like the old one, to abut the south wall of the Pickering Building, but to a full height of six stories, so that the Pickering Building's room air conditioners would have to be removed. Mr. Ingram offered to meet with Dr. Tenn to describe the plans in more detail.

When they met in December, 1983, Dr. Tenn objected to the plans to block the Pickering Building's south windows and asked Mr. Ingram to redesign the new building with an accommodating set-back of several feet. Mr. Ingram declined to do so and proceeded to seek the requisite zoning variances and building permits.

On April 19, 1984, nearly five months after learning of the defendant's plans, and after demolition of the existing building had already begun, the plaintiff filed the present bill in equity. To the extent that the new building would block the windows and the wall of the light shaft, the plaintiff claimed that it would be a private nuisance.

[T]he substantial issues in this appeal [are] whether the law of private nuisance is broad enough to comprehend a claim of interference with light and air, whether the court correctly applied that law in this case and whether there was a prescriptive right to maintain the air conditioners. In considering the applicability of nuisance law to the interests at stake, it will be helpful to start by canvassing the alternative possibilities that the parties have discussed.

At one extreme there is the English common law doctrine of ancient lights, under which the owner of a window that has enjoyed unobstructed access to sunlight for a sufficient period of time can acquire a prescriptive easement entitling him to prevent an adjoining landowner from obstructing the accustomed light. Comment, Solar Rights: Guaranteeing a Place in the Sun, 57 Or. L. Rev. 94, 108–09 (1977). While in the early days some American courts adopted a similar rule, it fell into disfavor during the nineteenth century. By 1977 "no American common-law jurisdiction affirmatively recognize[d] an ability to acquire an easement of light by prescription," Comment, supra at 112 (footnotes omitted), and "very few, if any, American courts today would uphold a prescriptive right to light," Pfeiffer, Ancient Lights: Legal Protection of Access to Solar Energy, 68 A.B.A.J. 288, 289 (1982).

Historically, there have been three principal reasons for the unpopularity of the doctrine of ancient lights: a desire to foster unimpeded development of real estate, a belief that in an age of artificial illumination light should be classed as an aesthetic rather than a property interest, and a suspicion that the enjoyment of light was so far from a characteristically adverse use that it could not fall within the basic concept of prescriptive use. *See* Comment, *supra* at 110–11; *Prah v. Maretti,* 321 N.W.2d 182, 189 (Wis.1982).

While time has not weakened the third of these historical reasons, the first and second have definitely begun to wane. The desire to encourage unrestricted development has receded as zoning and planning regulations have become more comprehensive, and access to natural light can be expected to justify an increasing degree of protection as the technology of solar energy develops. It does not follow, however, that we should turn to the doctrine of ancient lights to accomplish this purpose. Because the law of zoning is itself one means to recognize an interest in access to light and air, and because, as we will discuss below, the law of nuisance is another, we reject the argument that a prescriptive right to light or air should be recognized at this time. *Cf. Morton v. State,* 181 A.2d 831, 835 (N.H.1962) (assuming possibility of conveyance of rights to light, air, etc.).

At the other extreme among the positions taken in this litigation is the rule customarily identified with *Fontainebleau Hotel Corp. v. Forty–Five Twenty–Five, Inc.,* 114 So.2d 357 (Fla.App.1959), *cert. denied,* 117 So.2d 842 (Fla.1960). In that case the court dissolved a trial court's preliminary injunction against construction of a building that would have cast a shadow over the cabana, pool and sunbathing areas of a neighboring hotel. The court ruled out the possibility of proving a nuisance on the facts before it by affirming Florida's traditional rule, that in the absence of a zoning restriction, a property owner could build up to his property line and as high as he chose. The rule in Fontainebleau thus stands at the furthest remove from the doctrine of ancient lights. Where the latter would limit the neighbor's right to build, the former never would.

The present defendant urges us to adopt the Fontainebleau rule and thereby to refuse any common law recognition to interests in light and air, but we decline to do so. If we were so to limit the ability of the common law to grow, we would in effect be rejecting one of the wise assumptions underlying the traditional law of nuisance: that we cannot anticipate at any one time the variety of predicaments in which protection of property interests or redress for their violation will be justifiable. For it is just this recognition that has led the courts to avoid rigid formulations for determining when an interference with the use of property will be actionable, and to rest instead on the flexible rule that actionable, private nuisance consists of an unreasonable as well as a substantial interference with another person's use and enjoyment of his property. *See Robie v. Lillis*, 299 A.2d 155, 158 (N.H.1972). That is, because we have to anticipate that the uses of property will change over time, we have developed a law of nuisance that protects the use and enjoyment of property when a threatened harm to the plaintiff owner can be said to outweigh the utility of the defendant owner's conduct to himself and to the community. *Id.* at 159.

Viewing the elements and concept of private nuisance as thus formulated in Robie, there is no reason in principle why the law of nuisance should not be applied to claims for the protection of a property owner's interests in light and air, and for reasons already given we believe that considerations of policy support just such an application of nuisance concepts. We therefore hold that the law of private nuisance as expressed in Robie provides the appropriate standard for passing on a property owner's claims of interference with interests in light and air. *See Prah v. Maretti*, 321 N.W.2d 182, 191 (Wis.1982).

Since this is the course that the trial court followed, the third of the substantial issues before us is whether the evidence supported the court's finding that the defendant's building would not be a private nuisance.... The court found, first, that the threatened interference would not be unreasonable. It based this conclusion on findings that nearly all the affected office windows had previously been covered with translucent but not transparent plastic sheets or were blocked by heavy drapes. The southerly openings to the light shaft were covered by translucent but not transparent glass, which admitted substantially less light than the clear skylight above it. It was uncontested that virtually every affected office would continue to receive light from the shaft or from the east or west windows of the building.

The court addressed both the issues of reasonableness and of substantiality when it further found that such interference as there would be would not exceed what was normal under the circumstances. The sites were in the downtown commercial area of Manchester, where buildings commonly buttress and block the sides of adjacent structures. Moreover, the defendant proposed to do no more than the plaintiff's own predecessor had done, by building right to the lot line and to a height of six stories. If, as the plaintiff claimed, this would require expenditures for additional artificial lighting and ventilation systems, she failed to present any evidence that the costs would exceed what was customarily necessary for such buildings.

The court again alluded to the element of substantiality of the threatened interference when it expressly found that little weight should be accorded to the evidence that the Pickering Building would drop in value. This finding was warranted both by the plaintiff's unconvincing evidence on the point, and by this court's holding in Robie that evidence of depreciation in value is to be given little weight in the law of nuisance, since "the law cannot generally protect landowners from fluctuating land values which is a risk necessarily inherent in all land ownership." *Robie v. Lillis,* 299 A.2d at 160.

Thus on the issues of unreasonableness and substantiality the evidence supported the findings. The evidence also supported the court in its more general conclusion under Robie, that the utility to the defendant and to the public of a new office building would outweigh the burden to the plaintiff of installing additional lighting and ventilating equipment. The court therefore was warranted in finding that the building as planned would not be a private nuisance.

We turn now to the final issue of substance. Quite apart from her claims to have protectable interests in light and air, the plaintiff claimed to have an easement to use the defendant's air space for the air conditioners that protruded from the windows. There was no evidence of any express or implied grant of such an easement. Assuming, then, that such an easement could arise by prescription, it was necessary for the plaintiff to "prove by a balance of probabilities twenty years' adverse, continuous, uninterrupted use of [defendant's property] in such a manner as to give notice to the record owner that an adverse claim was being made to it. The nature of the use must [have been] such as to show that the owner knew or ought to have known that the right was being exercised, not in reliance upon his toleration or permission, but without regard to his consent." *Ucietowski v. Novak,* 152 A.2d 614, 618 (N.H.1959) (emphasis added) (citations omitted).

Whether the plaintiff satisfied this standard was an issue of fact to be determined by giving consideration to the peculiar circumstances of an alleged use of small amounts of air space several stories above the ground. *See Ucietowski v. Novak, supra,* 152 A.2d at 618. Thus, acts that might be obtrusive and ostensibly adverse at ground level would not necessarily have the same character high above the street.

Considering these circumstances, the record supports the trial court's finding that the plaintiff did not carry her burden. The evidence indicated that for the required twenty-year period only two or three portable air conditioners had been so placed as to extend several inches into the air space, and that each of these was twelve feet or more above the roof of the building formerly on the defendant's lot. There was no evidence that these air conditioners were or appeared to be permanently installed, that they interfered in any way with the then-current use and enjoyment of the defendant's property or that they physically intruded onto an appreciable portion of defendant's space. In the absence of any such evidence, the trial court was not compelled to conclude that the defendant or his predecessors knew or should have known that the plaintiff was claiming a right to use the defendant's air space for the placement of the air conditioners. Thus, under Ucietowski the trial court reasonably found that no easement had arisen by prescription. *Cf. Matthys v. Swedish Baptist Church of Boston,* 112 N.E. 228 (Mass.1916) (roof of church which extended four feet over property line, from which snow and ice regularly fell onto adjoining land, held sufficiently adverse to create prescriptive easement).

The trial court did not err in dismissing the bill in equity.

Affirmed.■

C. Externalities, The Coase Theorem, and Public Goods

An "externality" is a social cost or benefit that has not been internalized or incurred by the private owner of the resource. Where external costs (also called "spillover costs") are created by an activity, overconsumption may occur because the activity's price is lower than its true costs. 889 Associates' building might be said to create an external cost for Tenn. In fact, the activities of extracting, converting, or distributing energy resources often create costs for others. By burning coal or natural gas, for example, a utility's generation processes may produce pollutants that impose costs on society or other property owners. To the extent these costs are not included in the rates a utility charges customers, this may lead to underpricing, overproduction, and overconsumption of electricity.

Alternatively, where external benefits (also called "spillover benefits") are created by an activity, underconsumption may occur because an activities price is greater than its true costs. Many activities that impose external costs also create external benefits too. For example, 889 Associates' building may create certain benefits as well. Because Tenn will no longer be able to use window air conditioning units, it may utilize more efficient heating and cooling than it would without the new building. In addition, 889 Associates' new building may provide a more aesthetically pleasing facade than the older building, creating benefits for others. Tenn clearly believes that the external costs do not offset any external benefits to her of 889 Associates' new building; otherwise, she would not have sued.

In the article The Problem of Social Cost, a classic in the modern law and economics movement, Ronald Coase argued that the notion of externalities is economically questionable. Coase maintained that voluntary exchange can allocate costs efficiently. So long as parties can bargain freely, they will come to an agreement that minimizes the costs or harms resulting from incompatible property uses. Coase articulated what has come to be known as the Coase Theorem: "It is always possible to modify by transactions in the market the initial delimitation of rights. And, of course, if such market transactions are costless, such a rearrangement of rights will always take place if it would lead to an increase in the value of production." Ronald Coase, The Problem of Social Cost, 3 J. L. & Econ. 1 (1960).

How does the Coase Theorem apply to the *Tenn* fact pattern? According to the Coase theorem, if building the new building is worth more to 889 Associates than the access to air and sunlight is worth to Tenn, the new building will be built so long as 889 Associates have enough resources to bribe Tenn into allowing it. On the other hand, if access to air and sunlight are worth more to Tenn than the new building is worth to 889 Associates, 889 Associates will not build its new building so long as Tenn has sufficient funds to bribe it not to. This is often referred to as the "Invariance

Hypothesis" of the Coase Theorem: as long as the parties face no obstacles to transactions, the allocation of resources will be efficient and that allocation will be the same regardless of how property rights are initially assigned. It simply would not matter what the court does!

The Invariance Hypothesis of the Coase Theorem is seriously flawed, and is not accepted by most economists. The initial assignment of rights may affect the parties' relative wealth. Willingness and ability to pay may be affected by wealth, so the assignment of a right to one party may determine the actual outcome. In addition, transaction costs may be high, especially if information is costly to acquire or if there are multiple parties affected by the decision. For this reason, most economists and legal analysts adopt a more tempered version of the Coase Theorem than the Invariance Thesis. The Coase Theorem is better stated as follows: so long as there are no obstacles to bargaining between the parties involved—i.e., no transaction costs—resources will be allocated efficiently regardless of how initial property rights are assigned. *See* Mark Seidenfeld, Microeconomic Predicates to Law and Economics 91–94 (1996).

Coase's famous article argued, in purely economic terms, that the term "externality" is poorly defined. However, application of Coase's Theorem can also be used to reinforce the basic notion of externalities, a key economic concept in energy and environmental regulation. Part of the explanation for the Coase Theorem is that the potential for voluntary exchange can work to internalize costs that otherwise are external. External costs of an activity may be high where entitlements are not clearly defined.

Contrast privately owned property to what economists call a "public good". Air, sunlight, and wind cannot be owned in the same ways that a ton of coal or a series of power plants and a network of transmission lines can. First, it is difficult or impossible to capture the air, sunlight, or wind. Second, one who claims ownership of the air, sunlight, or wind faces immense difficulties in excluding others for using them. Third, it is difficult to transfer these resources directly.

A public good is a good for which the market itself fails to provide adequate mechanisms to ensure dominion and control, exclusivity, and transferability. The tendency is for the market to undervalue and overconsume such goods where they create negative costs, or to overvalue and underconsume such goods where they produce positive benefits. For example, wind and sunlight are available for free. A user who constructs windmills and solar collectors may make electricity available to consumers at a low cost, since it is not necessary to purchase fuel. However, the windmill or solar collector may obstruct views or use land in ways that generate social costs. Similarly, a utility burning coal to generate electricity may not include damage to the air as a cost in its rate calculation. In this sense, a public good may create externalities. Where a public good is present, private ownership leads to over- or under-consumption.

One solution to such a problem is government regulation. Through the regulation of the siting of wind and solar generation facilities, coupled with regulation of electricity rates, regulators might include the social cost of such activities in the price of electricity. Likewise, through regulation of electricity generation siting and pollution emissions, the full costs of burning coal to generate electricity can be internalized. Much of energy regulation concerns itself with mitigating energy conversion and distribution externalities, and this will be the focus of four core mechanisms studied in this course: siting and permitting regulation, emission regulation, consumption regulation, and long-term resource planning.

With the growth of the Not–In–My–BackYard (NIMBY) syndrome, siting proceedings have become a significant regulatory forum for the discussion of the environmental costs of energy resource use. Before building a natural gas pipeline, an electricity generator, or a transmission line for purposes of selling or distributing energy, a firm must obtain a permit from the state PSC and, normally, the state environmental regulation agency as well. These "siting" proceedings have become an important forum for the discussion of the costs of energy resource use on local concerns, such as property-owners, recreation users, and families. For example, in recent years, siting proceedings have addressed the potential electro-magnetic field risks that high-voltage electricity transmission lines may pose to families and children using adjacent property. In addition to siting proceedings, it is often necessary for energy resource firms to obtain permits which require limitations on use in ways designed to minimize the environmental costs. For example, a firm building an electricity generator is required by the Clean Air Act to apply with the EPA for a permit limiting air pollutant emissions in electricity generation.

Once a firm has complied with siting and use permitting regulation it has permission to go forward with the process of converting its energy resource into an end-use product or service. However, the conversion process itself may also be regulated. Most regulation of energy conversion addresses pollution emission. The traditional mechanisms for regulating pollution emission are technology or design standards—standards that require use of a specific pollution mitigating device, such as scrubbers—or performance standards—standards that specify an emission ceiling but allow the polluter to decide the best technology by which to achieve compliance. The detailed "qualifying facility" criteria for cogenerators promulgated by the Federal Energy Regulatory Commission (FERC) pursuant to the Public Utility Regulatory Policies Act of 1978 (PURPA) are an example of a technology or design standard. These are detailed engineering and operation criteria designed to encourage the use of more efficient electricity generation technologies, including renewable fuels. The Nuclear Regulatory Commission similarly requires technology standards of nuclear facilities designed to generate electricity. New source performance standards under the Clean Air Act are an example of an performance standard. In contrast to technology or design standards, performance standards are articulated in terms of emissions limits, or goals, and the means for achieving these goals are left to the regulated entity. Technology or design standards are easier to enforce than performance standards; on the other hand, performance standards permit flexibility and change.

Increasingly, attempts are being made to link performance standards to market mechanisms so that they will be self-enforcing, or at least reduce the need for the heavy transaction costs associated with detailed government oversight. Examples of this modern approach will be discussed in Chapter Ten.

Daniel A. Farber
Essay: Parody Lost/Pragmatism Regained: The Ironic History of the Coase Theorem

83 Va. L. Rev. 397 (1997).

It is clear from The Problem of Social Cost itself that Coase regarded the assumption of zero transaction costs as unrealistic. Indeed, his previous work made it clear that he regarded transaction costs as not only widespread but essential to understanding the structure of the economy. More recently, he has described his view of the Coase Theorem in broader terms. In discussing what would happen in a world of zero transaction costs, he explains, his aim was not to describe what life would be like in such a world but to provide a simple setting in which to develop the analysis and, what was even more important, to make clear the fundamental role which transaction costs do, and should, play in the fashioning of the institutions which make up the economic system.

He goes on to point out that a world without transaction costs "has very peculiar properties." For example, monopolies would act like competitors, insurance companies would not exist, and there would be no economic basis for the existence of firms. Indeed, he says, since transactions are costless in such a world, it also costs nothing to speed them up, "so that eternity can be experienced in a split second." "It would not seem worthwhile," he concludes, "to spend much time investigating the properties of such a world."

Little wonder that Coase was dismayed to find the world of zero transaction costs described as a Coasean world. Instead, he says, "it is the world of modern economic theory, one which I was hoping to persuade economists to leave." The failure of economists to consider transaction costs is, he believes, the major reason for their inability to account for the operation of the economy in the real world. As a result, their policy proposals are "the stuff that dreams are made of."

Coase's own caustic evaluation of the so-called Coasean world raises the question whether the Coase Theorem should be considered a parody, or at least a caricature, of modern economic theory. The line between the serious and the parodic is not always clear. It is unclear what role the intent of the author or the audience's reaction plays in this distinction—the phrase "unintentional parody" is not an oxymoron, and many an intended parody has been taken seriously by its audience.

Perhaps it is a bit too much to call the Coase Theorem a parody. Besides using it to illustrate the fantastical nature of economic analyses that ignore transaction costs, Coase also intended it as a simple illustration of the reciprocal nature of liability issues. But Coase would probably agree that, to the extent economists take the Coase Theorem as something more than a thought experiment and view it as a serious theory about the economy, they are providing an example of some of the worst flaws of their own paradigm. If not a parody, then, the Coase Theorem has been an invitation to self-parody by its audience.

Given the fact that his intention was to shake economists out of their dominant paradigm and to move them toward a more realistic approach, the enthusiastic reception of the Coase Theorem by armchair theorists was ironic. The Coase Theorem represented the kind of ungrounded theory that Coase hoped to move economists away from. No wonder that Coase laments that "my point of view has not in general commanded assent, nor has my argument, for the most part, been understood." Coase's fame as the discoverer of the Coase Theorem is a most ironic success.

As a further irony, Coase's work may have had the effect of moving some scholars in the direction he desired, not because his arguments were accepted, but because critics were moved to attack the argument they mistakenly thought he was making. When they attacked the Coase Theorem as an economic theory, they were in fact unwitting allies of Coase, who also did not believe it to be a viable economic theory. In mustering their attack on the Coase Theorem, some critics used the very tools that Coase desired—careful consideration of transaction costs and close examination of real institutions. On the theoretical side, consideration of the Coase Theorem helped lead to a refinement of views about strategic bargaining and how it can affect outcomes, leading to a clarification of Coase's concept of transaction costs. On the empirical side, the Donohue and Ellickson studies[1] are just the kind of conscientious empirical investigation that Coase hoped to promote. Thus, his work may have sparked the kind of attention to transaction costs and the type of empirical work he sought. The irony is that the desired reaction came as much from his critics as from his supporters.■

PROBLEM

Rudolph and Bonnie Sher entered into a long term land lease with Stanford University in 1962. The lot they leased was located in one of five model planned subdivisions developed by Stanford for use by faculty and staff. All building and landscaping on subdivision lots was subject to Stanford's prior review and approval. Shortly after the Shers' plans were approved, the Leidermans leased an adjacent lot. They in turn obtained design approval for their home and proceeded with construction.

---

1. [Ed. note] John J. Donohue III, Diverting the Coasean River: Incentive Schemes to Reduce Unemployment Spells, 99 Yale L.J. 549 (1989); Robert C. Ellickson, Of Coase and Cattle: Dispute Resolution Among Neighbors in Shasta County, 38 Stan. L. Rev. 623 (1986).

Both families moved into their new homes in 1963 and have lived there ever since. The Shers' lot fronts on Mayfield Avenue and is situated on the northeast slope of a hill. The Leidermans' lot is southwest of Shers' and occupies the upper slope and the crest of the hill, fronting on Lathrop Drive. The two lots share a common boundary along the Shers' southern— and the Leidermans' northern—property line.

The Shers' home was designed and built to take advantage of the winter sun for heat and light. The home is oriented on the lot so as to present its length towards the south. South-facing windows are relatively larger than others in the house. The south side of the house is also "serrated" to expose the maximum area to the sun. A large south-facing concrete patio operates to radiate sunlight into the home's interior. Skylights add to the light inside the house and an open floor plan in the common areas increases the general circulation of light and air. Roof overhangs are designed at an angle and length to block the hot summer sun while permitting winter sunlight to enter the house. Roof and walls are well insulated. Deciduous trees and shrubs along the southern side of the house aid in shading and cooling in the summer but allow winter sunlight to reach the house. The trial court found that the Sher home is a "passive solar" home. The design features and structures identified above form a system intended to transform solar into thermal energy. The court also found that a concomitant design goal was to create a bright and cheerful living environment. Though the home includes many passive solar features, it does not make use of any "active" solar collectors or panels. Nor does it employ any "thermal mass" for heat storage and distribution. Building materials used throughout were typical and conventional for the time; the house does not contain any special materials primarily selected for effective thermal retention. At the time the Shers and Leidermans designed and built their homes there were no trees on either lot. Over the years both parties, as well as their neighbors, landscaped their properties. As noted above, the Shers' landscaping was designed to enhance and complement their home's effectiveness as a solar system. Between 1963 and approximately 1976 the Liedermans planted a large number of trees, including Monterey pine, eucalyptus, redwood, cedar and acacia. The trial court found that these trees were planted to beautify the appearance of the Leiderman property, to attract birds and other small creatures, and to provide shade and privacy. The court found no intent on the Leidermans' part to deprive the Shers of sunlight.

In 1972, the Shers discovered that certain trees on the Leiderman property cast shadows on the Sher house in the wintertime. The offending trees were topped the following spring and the cost was borne by the Shers. Further tree work was done at the Shers' expense in the winter of 1979. The Leidermans themselves also engaged in certain tree trimming and removal over the years at a cost to them of approximately $4,000. Since 1979, however, the Leidermans have refused either to undertake any further trimming on their own or to cooperate with the Shers in this regard.

At time of trial trees on the Leiderman property completely blocked the sun to much of the Sher home in the winter months. From December

21 to February 10, the central portion of the Sher home was cast in shadow between 10:00 a.m. and 2:00 p.m. The Shers added a skylight over their kitchen area to help alleviate he problem, but now this too is largely shaded during the winter. The shade problem has transformed the formerly cheerful and sunny ambience of the Sher home; the interior is now dark and dismal in the winter months. The shading has also had an adverse impact on the home's thermal performance. The Shers' expert testified that heat loss during the winter months amounted to an equivalent of approximately 60 therms of natural gas. This converts into $30 to $60 per season in heating costs.

Two experts testified that the loss of sunlight to the Shers' house has resulted in a diminution of market value between $15,000 and $45,000. It appears, however, that this loss of value is attributable more to the gloomy atmosphere of the house than to its decreased effectiveness as a solar system. The court also found that the Shers have suffered actual and serious emotional distress as a result of the blockage of sunlight to their home.

In order to restore sunlight to the Shers' home during the winter months it would be necessary to trim certain trees on the Leiderman property, top others and remove those where topping would destroy the character of the tree or possibly kill it. Annual trimming would also be necessary.

The Shers filed a claim for injunctive relief and damages based on a theory of private nuisance. How do you think the cost of this litigation (and earlier negotiations) to the Shers and the Leidermans compares to the economic damage that either party would have suffered from losing the fight? Can you imagine a process to resolve this dispute without incurring significant transaction costs? What values might be endangered by implementing such a procedure?

What noneconomic issues are at stake here? Should a right to use solar energy for home heating be accorded some sort of preference over the right to use solar energy to grow trees? Or is the right to landscape your property deserving of special priority? Why did it prove impossible for the parties to resolve their differences? Are their values incommensurable?

Is the Shers' shade an externality of the Liedermans' tree cultivation? Or is the need to prune the Liedermans' trees an externality of the Shers' demand for the solar energy? Can you see why Professor Coase said that "externality" was hard to define?

If you were assigned to arbitrate this dispute, what result would you propose? How would you rule if you were a judge? *See Sher v. Leiderman*, 226 Cal.Rptr. 698 (Cal. App. 1986).

D. DYNAMIC NATURAL ENERGY

Solar energy is steady but diffuse, but natural energy can also take more violent forms. Humans are awed by the dynamic energy that nature can display. Earthquakes and volcanic eruptions have tremendous destructive power. Tornadoes and tropical storms destroy lives and property every year. Yet the rain produced by storms is necessary if crops are to prosper.

The human race has longed for ways to influence these natural forms of energy. The rain dance is common to many cultures. Today we use more modern sciences such as geomorphology and meteorology to predict, and perhaps influence, the patterns of dynamic natural energy.

The early common law used the term "Acts of God" to describe natural disasters that seemed to be immune from human influence. As science begins to give us increasing mastery over natural forces, the question of separating humans' acts from God's becomes increasingly intricate.

The issue is currently playing out on the international stage in relation to one of the most complex and important issues of our time–climate change, or "global warming" as it is often called. That issue will be dealt with at length in Chapter 17, but it must be understood against the background of the issues discussed in this section.

1.   Subterranean Energy

The earth is basically a giant ball of fire surrounded by a thick layer of cool rock, which is inherently unstable. This instability, coupled with the need for heat to rise, creates geothermal energy that has led to the formation of volcanoes, geysers and hot springs. And the instability sometimes causes massive shifts of subterranean formations that release large amounts of energy in the form of earthquakes. Over the last three million years, the earth has been cooling and a large part of its heat flow has been driving global geotectonics; the movement of the tectonic plates has been accompanied by the release of a geothermal energy in the form of volcanoes and earthquakes. Smil, *supra* at 21.

a.   GEOTHERMAL ENERGY

The volcano is the most violent form in which geothermal energy is released. Many volcanoes are located along the Pacific Ocean in a band dubbed "Ring of Fire." This ring is geologically unstable due to various tectonic plates colliding with each other, causing the ocean floor to sink below the continental crust. These areas are called subduction zones. Magma exists approximately 100 kilometers below the subduction zone. The sinking ocean crust carries with it water under tremendous pressure and temperature, which in turn creates the magma. Magma rises to the surface over a period of several thousand years and either finds or creates the Earth's crust.

Although there are several different types of volcanoes, there is a common structure associated with them all. All volcanoes have an opening at the earth's surface called a vent. The pipe is the route magma takes when rising to the surface during an eruption. The crater is a bowl-shaped depression at the top of the volcano where materials like ash and lava are released. The cone consists of solidified lava, ashes and cinder.

Volcanic eruptions are a natural phenomenon. Magma gathers in a magma chamber, where pressure builds. When the pressure is great enough, the magma is forced through the pipe and out of the vents. The type of eruption that occurs depends on the amount of gases and silica in the magma and whether there are obstacles the magma must pass. Gases and silica affect the viscosity of the magma. Obstacles affect the path of the magma; for example, if there is a blockage in the pipe, there will be a build up of pressure which will cause an explosion. Once magma reaches the surface, it is then called lava. Lava can pour out of the volcano in gentle streams (lava flows) or it can spew into the air. Often rocks are shot into the air as well. These rocks fall back to the earth usually as ash or dust.

Throughout history, volcanic eruptions have been known to cause mass destruction. Perhaps the most famous eruption occurred in 79 A.D. when Mount Vesuvius erupted, burying the cities of Herculaneum, Pompeii, and Stabiae in ash and mud. Because of the layer of ash, Pompeii was discovered partially intact. Another devastating eruption occurred in1883 at Krakatau in the Sunda Strait, located between Java and Sumatra. Thousands of people were killed or injured. Thousands more were forced to abandon their homes and lands. It is believed that Krakatau's eruption led to world climate changes. Over the last 120 years about a dozen volcanic eruptions have been powerful enough to produce dust veils. Barry & Chorley, *supra* at 11. For a detailed history of major volcanic eruptions, *see* Alwyn Scarth, Vulcan's Fury: Man Against the Volcano (Yale University Press, 1999).

Volcanic eruptions create many hazards. One of the most dangerous is the *pyroclastic flow*, which is a mixture of hot gas, ash, and other rocks. This flow travels very quickly down the slopes of the volcano and is certain death to anything caught in the way. *Volcanic ash* often remains as clouds in the air above the volcano and impairs the vision of airplane pilots. *Lahars* are mudflows formed from volcanic materials and water. These cause much economic and environmental damage. The force of a lahar is so great that it typically shears anything caught in its path to ground level. *Lava flows* tend to bury or burn anything they come in contact with and also cause fires which in turn destroy other parts of the environment.

While the thought of a volcano eruption strikes fear in the hearts of many, there are positive qualities associated with volcanoes. Volcanoes play an important role in shaping the earth's surface. The ash layer that forms on the surface near a volcano after an eruption will have long term advantages by adding minerals to the soil, ultimately improving foliage.

Magma is also the key to other forms of geothermal energy, such as geysers and hot springs. Geothermal heat originates from the earth's core, where temperatures reach over 9000 F. Magma that remains beneath the earth's crust heats rock and water. The hot water sometimes travels to the earth's surface as hot springs and geysers, although most stays underground in cracks and porous rocks. Such a formation is known as a geothermal reservoir, and such reservoirs, where available, provide a source of geothermal energy.

In the past, people used geothermal energy from hot springs to bathe and heat buildings. Native Americans used hot springs for cooking and medicine. Today, we drill wells into the geothermal reservoirs to bring the hot water to the surface. Once the water travels to the surface, it is used to generate electricity or for other energy saving measures not related to electricity generation.

Geothermal power plants use steam, heat or hot water from the geothermal reservoirs to spin turbine generators which produce electricity. The water is then returned through an injection well to be reheated and sustain the reservoir. There are three kinds of geothermal power plants. A "dry" steam reservoir produces steam, but very little water. The steam is piped into a "dry" steam power plant that provides the force to spin the turbine generator. A "flash" power plant uses water ranging from 300–700 degrees F. The water is brought to the surface through a production well where some of the water "flashes" into steam, which powers a turbine. A binary power plant uses water that is not hot enough to flash into steam. The water is passed through a heat exchanger, where the heat is transferred to a second liquid that has a lower boiling point than water. The binary liquid flashes to vapor when heated and is used to spin the turbine. The vapor is then condensed and used again.

Geothermal power is a very clean source of energy. The land required for geothermal power plants is generally smaller per megawatt than almost any other type of power plant. There is also much less physical damage to the environment. Rivers do not need to be dammed or forests cut down. Geothermal power is reliable—the plants are located on top of the power source. This eliminates the uncertainties associated with weather and natural disasters, and possible political conflicts that often affect the importation of fossil fuels.

Relatively few places in the world happen to be situated in locations where geothermal energy is available sufficiently close to the surface of the earth that it can be utilized efficiently with current technology. Where it is available, the rights to access this energy have sometimes created disputes not unlike those involving the right to sunlight.

Parks v. Watson

716 F.2d 646 (9th Cir.1983).

■ PER CURIAM:[2]

Gary R. Parks and Max Ansola, Jr., partners in Klamath Valley Company (hereinafter referred to as "Klamath"), appeal from a summary judgment for the City of Klamath Falls, Oregon and its manager Watson (hereinafter collectively referred to as "the City"), in an action under the Civil Rights Act, 42 U.S.C. § 1983 (Supp. V 1981), and the Sherman Act, 15 U.S.C. §§ 1, 2 (1976). In a cross-appeal, the City challenges the district

---

2. The panel consisted of Chief Judge Browning and Circuit Judges Boochever and Wallace. Judge Wallace concurred in part and dissented in part.

court's denial of its motion for an award of attorneys' fees under 42 U.S.C. § 1988 (1976). Klamath's section 1983 and antitrust claims both arose from the City's denial of a request to vacate certain platted City streets unless Klamath dedicated to the City land containing geothermal wells.

In 1978, Klamath acquired two tracts of property located adjacent to Old Fort Road in the city of Klamath Falls. There are four geothermal wells located on the property—two in the northern tract and two in the southern tract. One of the wells in the southern tract is currently operational, providing heat for ten homes located on the tract. Klamath planned to construct 214 apartment units on the northern tract and to heat them with the main geothermal well on the northern tract. Klamath pursued this plan by hiring geothermal heating consultants, developing economic projections and engineering plans, securing a commitment of venture capital, and obtaining a geothermal water permit from the State of Oregon. Klamath also investigated possible uses of the surplus energy produced by the wells which would be available after providing for the existing residences and projected apartment units. Klamath attempted to apply to the City for a utility franchise but was refused an application.

In order to develop its apartment complex, Klamath needed both a zoning change and the vacation of platted City streets on the property. After the City Planning Commission recommended approval of the proposed street vacations and zoning change, the City Council voted to rezone the apartment parcel to allow more dense residential uses.

Things did not go smoothly with Klamath's vacation petition. The City charter provides that when the City vacates a street, the party to whom the property reverts must pay the City just compensation. Negotiations on compensation for the requested vacation occurred between December 1978 and July 1979. Although the parties' description of the preliminary negotiations differ somewhat, the ultimate disagreement between the City and Klamath is quite clear. Klamath was willing to pay $1.00 for each square foot of street that was vacated, and to convey to the City an easement for a 20–foot strip of property near Old Fort Road. However, the City wanted the dedication[3] of that property, because fee ownership of this 20–foot strip of property would give the City rights to the geothermal wells on the northern tract. Klamath did not agree to the dedication. On July 16, 1979, the City Council voted unanimously to deny Klamath's vacation petition. Consequently, Klamath was unable to construct its apartment complex as planned.

Klamath brought suit against the City for conspiracy to restrain competition in and to monopolize the Klamath Falls geothermal heating market. Specifically, Klamath's complaint alleged that by refusing to permit the street vacation for reasonable compensation, the City and others combined to restrain unreasonably the marketing of residential heating by

---

3. [Editors' note] "Dedication" is the term used to describe a conveyance of property in fee to a city to be used for public purposes. "Vacation" is the process by which a city rescinds such a conveyance by "vacating" the property, thereby returning it to the surrounding landowners.

Klamath to potential purchasers in violation of section 1 of the Sherman Act, 15 U.S.C. § 1 (1976). Klamath further alleged that the City denied its vacation request with the intent to create a monopoly in the geothermal heating market in violation of section 2 of the Sherman Act, 15 U.S.C. § 2 (1976), and that the City violated its constitutional rights by denying the vacation petition. . . .

The record suggests that the City was manipulating its vacation authority to exert leverage on Klamath to dedicate the well-site property for little or no compensation. The record further suggests that the City imposed the condition to avoid going through condemnation proceedings to obtain the wells. While governmental entities may negotiate agreements aggressively, . . . they must stop short of imposing unconstitutional conditions. Thus, just as a public employer may not condition an employment contract on the employee forsaking his first amendment rights, *Perry v. Sindermann,* 408 U.S. 593, 598 (1972), the City may not condition street vacation on Klamath waiving its fifth amendment right to just compensation for the geothermal wells. . . . Since the requirement that Klamath Valley Company give its geothermal wells to the City had no rational relationship to any public purpose related to the vacation of the platted streets, the unrelated purpose does not support the requirement that the company surrender its property without just compensation. . . . The condition violates the fifth amendment.

Klamath also claims . . . that requiring it to relinquish the well site violates its equal protection rights. The equal protection clause is offended only if the City's different treatment of Klamath bears no rational relationship to a legitimate governmental purpose. . . . In arguing that the City's vacation decision satisfies this standard, the City [argues that it had] a desire to acquire Klamath's geothermal wells for the City's proposed geothermal heating district. . . . The district court stated that "if the plaintiffs were able to show through discovery that the City was motivated by a desire to acquire the wells, that would still be a rational basis for treating plaintiffs' request differently from other similar requests." Klamath admits that its wells were located within the City's planned geothermal district and that the City's ultimate goal in conditioning the vacation on the dedication of its well-site property was to acquire the wells for the public. We are thus confronted with the question of whether the City's legitimate governmental purpose of acquiring the well sites was rationally related to the vacation of the streets. . . .

There is no justification for distinguishing between vacation petitioners according to whether they possess geothermal wells. To conclude otherwise would permit a city to deny any discretionary benefit, be it a business license, a street vacation, or a parking permit, to a party owning property the city seeks to condemn unless such property is donated to the city. We conclude that the City's interest in acquiring the property is totally unrelated to its statutorily defined interest in determining whether to grant the discretionary benefit, and violates the equal protection clause.

Comment, Unconstitutional Conditions, 73 Harv. L. Rev. 1595, 1600 (1960).

Dismissal of Antitrust Claims. Klamath's complaint alleged that the City's anticompetitive actions prevented it from developing its property as planned, including exploitation of its geothermal wells to heat housing units to be constructed on its property, and from marketing geothermal heat to consumers outside of its own development. . . .

In the present case, the district judge did not find it necessary to decide whether Klamath had stated facts sufficient to support its allegations of an antitrust violation, nor did he pass directly upon the issue of causation. Rather, he concluded that Klamath had not sustained injury to its business or property. In deciding that Klamath failed to establish injury to its business or property, the district judge limited his inquiry to whether Klamath had sustained injury to its business in the market for commercial (off-site) sale of geothermal heat. The district judge excluded consideration of whether Klamath sustained injury to either its residential property development business or its on-site geothermal heating business. He concluded, as a matter of law, that the only injury which could have occurred "by reason of" the alleged antitrust violations was injury to Klamath's off-site geothermal heating business. . . .

Since Klamath was already in the market of providing space heating by geothermal power to ten residences on its southern tract, the district judge should consider whether Klamath had the background and experience necessary to provide space heating to the proposed apartment complex in the northern tract. Klamath had obtained an oral commitment for a ten-year loan of $5,060,107 for the financing of the apartment complex. It had applied for and received zoning changes which would permit the apartment complex to be constructed. Indeed, the City has set forth no facts in its brief which could dispute Klamath's claim that had it not been for the denial of Klamath's vacation petition, it would have successfully expanded its on-site geothermal heating business by supplying heat to the 214 apartment units to be built on its northern tract. Thus, it was error for the district judge to find for the City at this stage of the proceedings on this aspect of the standing issue.

■ WALLACE, J., *concurring in part and dissenting in part:* The City submits as a legitimate governmental purpose its desire to acquire Klamath's geothermal wells for the City's proposed geothermal heating district. Klamath admits that its wells are located within the City's planned geothermal district and that the City's ultimate goal in conditioning the street vacation on the dedication of the well site was to acquire the wells for the public. These concessions preclude our holding that the vacation denial violated the equal protection clause. The acquisition of Klamath's well sites for a city-run geothermal heating district constitutes a legitimate state interest. The only additional inquiry is whether the City's vacation denial was rationally related to the accomplishment of that regulatory purpose. It is clear from the record that the City conditioned the vacation approval and ultimately denied the request in order to acquire Klamath's geothermal drilling rights for the public. Thus, its actions were rationally related to a legitimate state interest. [Judge Wallace therefore dissented on the constitutional issue but concurred that the antitrust issue needed to be retried.]■

NOTES AND COMMENTS

1. Although geothermal energy is found only in a relatively small number of places, the issues presented in this case are common to many other types of energy as well. Some types of energy can be most efficiently utilized by the use of large facilities which provide economies of scale. However, this has often meant monopolization of the resource by a single supplier, which reduces competition and the economies that competition typically creates. This issue will reappear throughout the book.

2. To what extent is it appropriate for public agencies to develop and control energy resources? In many countries, energy development and distribution is controlled by public entities. For example, the Comision Federal de Electricidad of Mexico plans to build one of the largest geothermal energy facilities in the world in Baja California. Mexico Plans Geothermal Generator, Megawatt Daily, Feb. 15, 2000.

Where the federal government grants a patent for title to land to an individual, reserving "all the coal and other minerals in the land so entered and patented, together with the right to prospect for, mine, and remove same . . . ," does the patentee get the right to use geothermal steam under the land or has that right been reserved to the federal government by the quoted language? *See Rosette, Inc. v. United States*, 64 F.Supp.2d 1116 (D.N.M.1999).

The issue of public versus private ownership of energy facilities has recurred from time to time in the United States, and can be seen today in disputes over hydroelectric projects (*See* Chapter Four). As a capitalist country, the United States has opted for private control of most of our energy resources, but at various times in our history we have been persuaded that public ownership of certain resources distributes the costs and benefits more fairly throughout the population. For example, we provide tax advantages for public ownership of facilities and resources by allowing state and local governments to sell bonds free from federal income taxation. As with so many issues, our national policy on public ownership is not necessarily internally consistent.

3. Sometimes attempts by state or local governments to monopolize a particular energy resource may raise a constitutional issue under the interstate commerce clause if it results in discrimination against people from other states. For example, municipal solid waste is an energy resource that can be burned to generate electricity. It is economical to do so, however, only if a large volume of waste can be assembled at a single incinerator. Some local governments have tried to ensure that a large volume of waste would be available by prohibiting their residents from delivering their waste to anyone but the local government, but the Supreme Court held that this discriminated against waste haulers from other

states in violation of the commerce clause. *C & A Carbone, Inc. v. Town of Clarkstown* 511 U.S. 383 (1994)

4. The issue of taking of property without compensation, which arose in *Parks v. Watson*, also arises in connection with almost every other kind of energy resource. The Fifth Amendment of the Constitution provides that the government must provide "just compensation" if it "takes" property. The question of whether a particular government action is or is not a "taking" has proved very difficult for the courts to resolve, as the *Parks* case indicates.

5. The United States Department of Energy has instituted a grant program hoping to boost the use of geothermal energy in the Western states. The announced goal of the program is to supply at least 10% of the energy needs of California, Texas, Utah, Idaho and North Dakota from geothermal sources. In addition, the California Energy Commission has issued research and development grants for the purpose of stimulating the development of geothermal energy.

6. Humans have succeeded in harnessing many forms of natural energy for their own purposes, but there are some times when nature overcomes any feeling of smugness humans may have by delivering energy in a form that both unpredictable and ungovernable. One such form of natural energy is the earthquake.

The Earth is divided into three main layers: the hard outer crust, the soft middle layer, and the center core. The crust is comprised of plates, which move very slowly and have done so for billions of years. These plates shaped the physical features of the Earth. Areas where two or more of the plates meet are called faults. A well-known fault is the San Andreas fault in California. Earthquakes happen when the plates shift suddenly along a fault. The point where an earthquake begins is the focus, and the point on the Earth's surface directly above the focus is the epicenter.

The plate tectonics theory offers a starting point for understanding the forces that cause earthquakes. Plates are thick pieces of rock that make up the outermost 100 km of the Earth. "Tectonics" is used to describe the deformation of the Earth's crust, forces that produce the deformation, and the results of the deformation. Earthquakes occur at the outer portions of the plates, where the rock temperature is relatively low. Convection of rocks is caused by variations of temperature in the Earth's interior. Stress is induced, which results in movement of the overlying plates. The plates normally move at a very slow rate: ranging from two to twelve centimeters per year. Stresses from convection can deform the brittle portions of the overlying plates, creating tremendous energy within the plates. If the stress exceeds the strength of the rocks in the brittle portions, the rocks could suddenly break. This sudden breakage releases the stored energy in the form of earthquakes.

Earthquakes are one of the most destructive forms of energy in nature, insofar as humans are concerned. Despite extensive research, our ability to predict earthquakes is either nonexistent or very limited. And no one has ever come up with a serious proposal to harness the energy of an earth-quake for purposes that humans could utilize.

b. OVERCONSUMPTION OF COMMON PROPERTY

The use of geothermal energy in the United States declined during the 1990s. During 1993, the Energy Information Administration reports that 17.32 trillion Kilowatt-hours of electricity was generated from geothermal sources. By 1997 that number had dropped to 14.57 trillion Kilowatt-hours. Almost all of the geothermal energy utilization is in California, and "several older geothermal fields in California have been depleted beyond their economically useful life and will not resume operation." Energy Information Agency, Renewable Energy Annual 1998.

To a great extent, the rapid depletion of some of these geothermal fields reflects the fact that the geothermal energy is in the form of a "common-pool resource" that becomes the property of anyone who obtains access to it. In the absence of regulation, such common-pool resources may become rapidly depleted because each user will rush to increase his share. This phenomenon has become known as the "Tragedy of the Commons."

In a famous essay, Garrett Hardin argued that when resources exist in a common pool, without individual ownership, they are likely to become victims of "The Tragedy of the Commons." Garrett L. Hardin, The Tragedy of the Commons, 162 Science 1243 (1968). He described this phenomenon by using the example of medieval English farmers who could not prevent overgrazing of common lands because each individual peasant would benefit by grazing one more cow despite that cow's contribution to the overall malnutrition of the herd:

> Picture a pasture open to all. It is to be expected that each herdsman will try to keep as many cattle as possible on the commons.... Explicitly or implicitly, more or less consciously, he asks, "What is the utility to *me* of adding one more animal to my herd?" This utility has one negative and one positive component.

The positive component is one additional animal. The negative component is that all of his animals are a bit weaker. But since "the effects of overgrazing are shared by all the herdsmen," the negative component is overshadowed by the positive benefits of an additional animal.

> Therein is the tragedy. Each man is locked into a system that compels him to increase his herd without limit—in a world that is limited. Ruin is the destination toward which all men rush, each pursuing his own best interest in a society that believes in the freedom of the commons. Freedom in a commons brings ruin to all.

From his parable Hardin drew the conclusion that we must "explicitly exorcize" the "invisible hand" when dealing with problems involving commons. For commons that could not be privatized he favored "coercion." Hardin's metaphor has become widely used to describe a problem that often arises when resources, including energy resources, are commonly owned.

Classical economic theory advocates the privatization of common property to avoid the kind of problems that Hardin describes. *See, e.g.*, Carol Rose, Property and Persuasion 105–108 (Westview, 1994). But as she points out, not all common-pool resources easily lend themselves to that kind of division. For some types of energy resources, in particular, division of the resource into private allotments has proven quite difficult.

In the 1980s, institutions like the World Bank that finance development in third world countries began to express interest in systems to manage common-pool resources. Many of these countries had traditionally relied on common resources as an important element in the local economy. Attempts to intervene in these countries without understanding the existing systems by which common resources were managed sometimes proved to be counterproductive.

In 1985, the National Research Council of the National Academies of Science and Engineering brought together a Panel on Common Property Resource Management to "assess systematically differing institutional arrangements for the effective conservation and utilization of jointly managed resources." National Research Council, Proceedings of the Conference on Common Property Resource Management vii (National Academy Press, 1985). Out of this conference came a research program to study common lands, energy and water resources and "other jointly held resources that constitute the global commons." *Id.*

Current research has found many instances of resource-using communities developing their own informal norms for apportioning common rights effectively. In some cases they found that Hardin's famous "tragedy of the commons" had indeed occurred, but in other instances they found systems of managing common property that appeared to be working well. For example, common grazing lands provided Hardin's example of potential disaster, but a study of common grazing lands in Morocco found that a highly complex body of rules had evolved out of agreements to resolve conflicting claims of nearby villages and tribes. By strictly limiting the seasons of use, the rules allowed the Berber communities to maintain a highly productive and sustainable resource in common ownership. Daniel W. Bromley, ed., Making the Commons Work 229 (San Francisco: ICS Press, 1992).

Many of the common-pool resource studies have looked at third world locations, but other studies found similar examples in highly developed countries. In the Alps of Switzerland, effective rules for the management of common grazing land have been adopted through the processes of Swiss direct democracy. Fikret Berkes, Common Property Resources: Ecology and Community Based Sustainable Development 15 (London: Belhaven Press, 1989). *See generally* Glenn G. Stevenson, Common Property Economics (Cambridge University Press, 1991). Other studies reached similar conclusions in modern American settings. For example, a study of several groundwater systems in semiarid portions of California concluded that locally accepted and managed regulations can sometimes control sharing behavior effectively. Elinor Ostrom, Governing the Commons (Cambridge University Press, 1990).

Because so much of our energy comes from common-pool resources, the study of methods of managing such resources is a potential source of applications that may become useful in the development of energy law. If resources exist as a common pool, to which no one has individual property rights, unique resource management problems are presented. For example, petroleum is usually found underground in reservoirs that have the characteristics of common-pool resources; *i.e.,* the ownership of the resource is divided among a number of separate owners of the land surface but each owner does not have a separately identifiable share of the oil. The resolution of these relationships is a major task of oil and gas law. *See* Chapter Six.

Many other types of resources also exist in common-pool form. When the tanker *Exxon Valdez* cracked open in Alaska's Prince William Sound in 1989 it produced an oil slick that spread for hundreds of miles, devastating the wildlife and natural resources of the Sound. Negligence could easily be established, but who could be a plaintiff? And how could you quantify the damages? The common law had great difficulty in dealing with injuries to common-pool resources because no individual person had a quantifiable share of the right to use such resources. *See Alaska Sport Fishing Ass'n v. Exxon Corp.,* 34 F.3d 769 (9th Cir.1994).

2.   ENERGY IN THE ATMOSPHERE

In contrast to our continuing inability to predict volcanic eruptions or earthquakes, our ability to predict the weather has improved greatly, thanks to an increasing ability to monitor and model the flows of energy through the atmosphere. "The atmosphere acts like a gigantic heat engine in which the constantly maintained difference in temperature existing between the poles and the equator provides the energy supply necessary to drive the planetary atmospheric and ocean circulation." Barry & Chorley, *supra* at 117. These energy flows give rise to the global hydrological cycle, in which water evaporates from the earth's surface to return later in the form of rain or snow.

In the eighteenth century, meteorology was relatively crude, and very little was known of weather patterns and storms. Benjamin Franklin was one of the first to recognize the true nature of electrical storms. By flying a kite during a thunderstorm he was able to confirm that lightning was a form of electricity, which was itself a poorly understood phenomenon at that time. David Freeman Hawke, Franklin 103–105 (Harper & Row, 1976).

By the end of the eighteenth century, weather observers began to share their observations. The invention of the telegraph enabled weather observers to share information almost immediately after it was gathered. In 1870, Congress authorized a government meteorological bureau, which started sending weather reports to some metropolitan newspapers. In 1891, weather observation responsibilities passed to the United States Weather Bureau under the Department of Agriculture. Since that time, there have been great advances in the science and technology of meteorology and climatology. Weather is now tracked by the National Weather Service under the Department of Commerce, using such technology as weather satellites that orbit the Earth and Doppler radar systems. And of course, computers are a key element in processing the enormous amounts of weather information observed on a daily basis.

Our weather is largely controlled by the sun. The sun produces electromagnetic energy, including light, ultraviolet energy and infrared energy. The infrared energy from the Earth's atmosphere and clouds combine with the incoming solar energy to produce the temperature of the air around the Earth. The Earth is surrounded by air masses, several of which control the United States' weather, such as the continental polar air masses which originate over Alaska and Canada.

a.   WIND POWER

Wind also affects weather. About 2% of the solar energy that reaches the earth is ultimately converted to the kinetic energy of wind. Joseph M. Moran et. al., Meteorology: The Atmosphere and the Science of Weather 204 (5th ed., 1997). Wind blows when there is uneven air pressure. Variations in the temperature in the Earth's atmosphere cause differences in air pressure. Movement of air closer to the earth is affected by friction; the wind rubs against trees, hills, buildings, etc., which tend to slow wind down. In the upper atmosphere, the air flow is much smoother. Winds tend to be gustier where terrain is rough and the temperature contrasts between a warm surface and cooler air are common. *See generally* George Bomar, Texas Weather 176–198 (University of Texas Press, 1995).

The use of wind power for the generation of electricity has become a big business. Giant "wind farms" that contain dozens of linked windmills have been erected in many locations. Wind power has its greatest potential where average wind speeds are relatively strong and consistent in direction. In the United States, such "regions include the western High Plains, the Pacific Northwest coast, portions of coastal California, the eastern Great Lakes, the south coast of Texas, and exposed summits and passes in the Rockies and Appalachians." Moran et al., *supra* at 205.

Under PURPA, *supra,* wind power facilities are entitled to favored treatment as a renewable power source if they fit within the statutory definition of a "qualifying facility" (QF). One of the tests for qualification is whether the facility will produce energy from renewable resources. *See, e.g., Southern California Edison Co. v. F.E.R.C.,* 195 F.3d 17 (D.C.Cir.1999) (qualifying status improperly granted where facility needs to supplement renewable energy with natural gas). The Federal Energy Regulatory Commission (FERC) makes the determination of whether a facility qualifies upon application by the builder of the proposed facility.

Wyoming Wind Power, Inc.

34 FERC ¶ 61,152 (1986).

On September 6, 1985, Wyoming Wind Power Inc., (WWP) of Casper, Wyoming, filed an application for certification of a facility as a qualifying small power production facility pursuant to section 292.207 of the Commission's regulations, 18 C.F.R. § 292.207(b). Notice of the application was published in the Federal Register on September 25, 1985, with comments due by October 25, 1985. Timely comments were received from the Office of Endangered Species of the Fish and Wildlife Service of the U.S. Department of the Interior (FWS). No protests or motions to intervene have been filed.

WWP indicates that it will be the sole owner of the facility, which will be located at Simpson's Ridge, in Carbon County, Wyoming. The facility will consist of 200 wind generators rated at 100 kilowatts each, with a total power production capacity of 20 megawatts. Applicant states that it owns no other facility which is located within one mile of the proposed facility and which uses the same energy source. It further states that no electric utility, electric utility holding company, or any combination thereof has any ownership interest in the facility.

FWS raises no issues regarding the proposed facility's status as a qualifying facility (QF). However, FWS suggests that wildlife listed as endangered or threatened species pursuant to the Endangered Species Act (ESA), 16 U.S.C. §§ 1533 et. seq., may inhabit the project area. FWS also states that the Commission is required by section 7 of the ESA to assess the impacts of the project on endangered species that may inhabit the area. FWS recommends that WWP's project be assessed in relation to future wind generation projects proposed for this area and that a cumulative impact analysis be prepared.

With regard to the comments filed by FWS, the Commission concludes that section 7 of the ESA does not apply to Commission orders granting applications for QF status. Section 7(a)(2) states, in relevant part, that "[e]ach federal agency shall, ... insure that any action authorized, funded or carried out by such agency. . . . is not likely to jeopardize the continued existence of any endangered species or result in the destruction or adverse modification of habitat of such species. . . ." A Commission order granting a QF application does not authorize, fund or carry out the construction or operation of any QF. Rather, the Commission simply determines whether or not a project, as described by the applicant, meets the technical and ownership standards for QFs. This is reflected in each order certifying qualifying status, which states that the order does not relieve the facility owner of any State, Federal or local laws regarding construction and operation of the facility, or make any decision with regard to siting. In short, these orders are in the nature of declaratory orders regarding whether the facility meets the technical and ownership standards for QF status. Thus, the provisions of section 7 of the ESA do not apply to this proceeding.

Based on information provided by WWP, WWP's facility, as described in its application, meets the size, fuel use, and ownership requirements established in section 292.203(a) of the Commission's regulations regarding qualification as a small power production facility. The application for certification of qualifying status filed on September 6, 1985, by WWP, pursuant to section 292.207 of the Commission's regulations is hereby granted, provided that the facility operates in the manner described in the application.■

NOTES AND COMMENTS

1.   Environmental organizations support windmills as a renewable source of energy, but in some cases they oppose wind farms that may result in harm to wildlife. The Enron Corporation agreed to relocate a prospective wind farm in California after the National Audubon Society objected that the windmills might pose a threat to the endangered California Condor. Andrew Broman, Environmentalists Pressure Houston–Based Firm to Drop Plans for Wind Farm, Houston Chronicle, Nov. 4, 1999.

2.   The Endangered Species Act, 16 U.S.C. § 1531 *et. seq.*, is one of the most powerful of the federal environmental statutes. When a species (or a subspecies or population of a species) is listed under the Act, all federal agencies must consult with the United States Fish and Wildlife Service before taking any action that might harm the species. Moreover, any person that harms a listed species may be guilty of "taking" the species, which carries criminal penalties under the act. Destruction of the habitat of a listed species can also constitute a taking. For a thorough analysis of the endangered Species Act *see* Michael J. Bean and Melanie J. Rowland, The Evolution of National Wildlife Law, Praeger, 1998.

3.   As the above case indicates, the analysis of the "cumulative impact" of a series of independent actions can present serious difficulties. Each individual action may have only a minor impact, but the aggregate impact could be severe. Is it fair to penalize individual actors on the basis of impacts of which they are only a minor cause? *See* Comment, The Development and Implementation of the Cumulative Impact Analysis Requirement, 8 Public Land Law Rev. 129 (1987). For examples of court decisions requiring cumulative impact analysis, see *Defenders of Wildlife v. Ballard,* 73 F.Supp. 2d 1094 (D.Ariz.1999); *Stewart v. Potts,* 996 F.Supp. 668 (S.D.Tex.1998).

b. STORMS

When winds move large masses of air away from where they are formed, there is often conflict among neighboring air masses. Areas where air masses clash are called fronts. A warm front is where warm air is advancing. A cold front is where cold air is taking over. A stationary front means that neither side is winning. Storms form when gravity pulls colder, heavier air under warmer, lighter air. These contrasts have potential energy. Energy is transformed when air rises and water vapor in it begins condensing into clouds and precipitation. Storms also draw energy from high-speed winds in the upper atmosphere.

Storms can be induced by humans through cloud seeding. Cumulus clouds often contain supercooled water; i.e., water having a temperature below 32 degrees F. but still in liquid form. Airplanes fly through the clouds and spray a substance such as silver iodide that has a crystalline structure similar to ice. When ice particles form in these supercooled clouds, the ice particles grow at the expense of the liquid droplets and become heavy enough to fall in the form of rain.

The use of cloud seeding has been partially successful in some regions. For example, private contractors augment snowfall in California through cloud seeding. The increased snowfall gives power companies, irrigation districts, and municipalities more water when the snow melts. But cloud seeding "may merely redistribute a fixed supply of precipitation." Moran et al., *supra* at 188–89. This may mean that some geographic area gets more while another gets less, which can lead to disputes among neighbors.

Southwest Weather Research, Inc., v. Duncan

319 S.W.2d 940 (Tex.Civ.App.1958).

■ PER CURIAM: This is an appeal from a judgment of the Eighty-third District Court, Jeff Davis County, Texas, said judgment being in the form of an injunction commanding the appellants "to refrain from seeding the clouds by artificial nucleation or otherwise and from in any other manner or way interfering with the clouds and the natural condition of the air, sky, atmosphere and air space of plaintiffs' lands and in the area of plaintiff's lands to in any manner, degree or way affect, control or modify the weather conditions on or about said lands, pending final hearing and determination of this cause; and from further flying over the above-described lands of plaintiffs and discharging any chemicals or other matter or material into the clouds over said lands." Appellees are ranchmen residing in Jeff Davis County, and appellants are owners and operators of certain airplanes and equipment generally used in what they call a "weather modification program", and those who contracted and arranged for their services.

It is not disputed that appellants did operate their airplanes at various times over portions of lands belonging to the appellees, for the purpose of and while engaged in what is commonly called "cloud seeding." Appellants do not deny having done this, and testified through the president of the company that the operation would continue unless restrained. He stated, "We seeded the clouds to attempt to suppress the hail." The controversy is really over appellants' right to seed clouds or otherwise modify weather conditions over appellees' property; the manner of so doing; and the effects resulting therefrom. Appellants stoutly maintain that they can treat clouds in such manner as will prevent the clouds from precipitating hail, and that such operation does not and cannot decrease either the present or ultimate rainfall from any cloud or clouds so treated. Appellants were hired on a hail suppression program by a large number of farmers in and around Fort

Stockton and other areas generally east, or easterly, of Jeff Davis County. It was developed that the farmers' land was frequently ravaged by damaging hail storms, which appellants claim originated in and over the Davis Mountains in the Jeff Davis County area.

The appellees' testimony, on the other hand, which was elicited from some eleven witnesses, was to the effect that this program of cloud seeding destroyed potential rain clouds over their property.

The trial court, in granting the temporary injunction, found as a matter of fact that appellants were engaging in day-to-day flying airplanes over appellees' lands and into the clouds over appellees' lands, and expelling a foreign substance into the clouds above appellees' lands in such a manner that there was a change in the contents of the clouds, causing them to be dissipated and scattered, with the result that the clouds over plaintiffs' lands were prevented from following their natural and usual course of developing rain upon and over and near plaintiffs' lands, thereby resulting in retarded rainfall upon plaintiffs' properties. The court further held that such was injurious to appellees and was in interference of their property rights, and would cause irreparable damage if not restrained.

It has long been decided that in cases of this sort we must affirm the decision of the trial court unless it is clearly shown that he abused his discretion in granting the temporary injunction: Therefore, we must now examine the evidence to see if the trial court's action was proper.

First of all, appellant Kooser, the president of defendant corporation, who was in charge of the operations, when asked if he could prevent or lessen hail, answered as follows: "We feel that we have indicated something along that line in this area." He further admitted that he was trying to and was changing weather conditions, but denied that he depleted any potential or active precipitation, and maintained that, on the contrary, his operation tended to increase precipitation. The experts did not agree in their testimony. Witnesses Quate and Moyer, after qualifying, explained the processes of cloud formation and rain making, and stated positively that seeding clouds, as was done here, with silver iodide or salt brine or both, could not depreciate, deplete or destroy the rain potential of a cloud that was likely to produce rain. They did testify that unimportant clouds with no rain potential could be dissipated. Witness Battle testified that, in his opinion, over-seeding of potential rain clouds could diminish or destroy their rain-making power. All experts agreed that the impregnation of clouds with foreign particles or nuclei would, when carried up to the freezing top of the cloud by a warm updraft, help precipitation to occur by drawing minute droplets of moisture to their surface until they became heavy enough to fall out of the cloud as precipitation. Witness Battle maintained that over-seeding would cause a surplus of nuclei, so that the droplets would never get big enough to fall out. The other two experts denied that this could happen and testified that the type of operation here concerned would increase precipitation and prevent hail. . . .

On behalf of the appellees' position there were eleven witnesses. They testified that on various occasions they had been observing what they considered rain clouds over their property. They testified that these were clouds from which they usually got rain, and which, in their opinion, would probably produce rain. In several instances it had begun to rain or sprinkle. Some of these witnesses testified to a lifetime and others to many years of practical and actual observation of clouds and the formation of those clouds which produced rain. For example, witness Jim Duncan testified he had been in the area since before the turn of the century, and that it was the habit of ranchers to observe and evaluate all clouds with the idea of whether or not rain could be expected therefrom. He testified that his land was ranch land which depended upon the natural elements, such as rain, to grow feed and forage for his livestock. Without detailing the individual testimony of each witness, they all generally agreed that they would be observing a potential rain cloud or thunderhead which they were confident was going to produce rain on their property, when appellants' plane or planes would show up. Now appellants denied ever flying into any clouds, saying that it was dangerous and they wouldn't do it. But witnesses for appellees testified that they had seen the planes going into the clouds. In any event they were generally agreed—all of them—that when the plane or planes showed up and began spraying the foreign substance, that in some ten to twenty minutes the potential rain cloud or thunderhead would be destroyed and dissipated, leaving only a fuzzy or wispy type of mist. As one witness said, it seemed like a "nightmare". Another stated that he would remember it to his "dying day." Now these witnesses all testified flatly that the airplane action destroyed clouds that they felt were going to produce rain on their property, and that such clouds were over their property when the airplane appeared. In several instances the lay witnesses testified that the sprinkle or rain stopped as soon as the airplane began its operation. In another instance it was testified that half of the ranch got a rain and the other half didn't, and the witness blamed this phenomenon on the activity of the airplane and its area of operation.

So, summing up the fact situation or the evidence that was before the trial court, we find that the three appellees and other witnesses testified that they had visually observed the destruction of potential rain clouds over their own property by the equipment of the appellants. They testified that they had seen this happen more than once. The experts differed sharply in the probable effort of a hail suppression program accomplished by the cloud seeding methods used here. The trial court apparently, as reflected by his findings included in the judgment, believed the testimony of the lay witnesses and that part of the expert testimony in harmony with his judgment. This he had a right to do as the trier of facts.

We have carefully considered the voluminous record and exhibits that were admitted in evidence, and have concluded that the trial court had ample evidence on which to base his findings and with which to justify the issuance of the injunction.

Now we must turn to the objections of the appellants, who protest the issuance of the injunction on the grounds, generally, that appellants had every right to do what they were doing in order to protect their crops from hail, and that the facts or credible evidence did not justify the issuance of the injunction. Appellants maintain that appellees have no right to prevent them from flying over appellees' lands; that no one owns the clouds unless it be the State, and that the trial court was without legal right to restrain appellants from pursuing a lawful occupation; also, that the injunction is too broad in its terms.

First of all, it must be noted that here we do not have any governmental agency, State or Federal, and find no legislative regulation. This is exclusively a dispute between private interests. It has been said there is no precedent and no legal justification for the trial court's action. It has long been understood that equity was created for the man who had a right without a remedy, and, as later modified, without an adequate remedy. Appellees urge here that the owner of land also owns in connection therewith certain so-called natural rights, and cites us the following quotation from *Spann v. City of Dallas,* 111 Tex. 350, 235 S.W. 513, 514, in which Chief Justice Nelson Phillips states:

> Property in a thing consists not merely in its ownership and possession, but in the unrestricted right of use, enjoyment and disposal. Anything which destroys any of these elements of property, to that extent destroys the property itself. The substantial value of property lies in its use. If the right of use be denied, the value of the property is annihilated and ownership is rendered a barren right.... The very essence of American constitutions is that the material rights of no man shall be subject to the mere will of another. *Yick Wo v. Hopkins,* 118 U.S. 356....

In California Law Review, December 1957, Volume 45, No. 5, in an article, "Weather Modification", are found the following statements:

> What are the rights of the landowner or public body to natural rainfall? It has been suggested that the right to receive rainfall is one of those "natural rights" which is inherent in the full use of land from the fact of its natural contact with moisture in the air.... Any use of such air or space by others which is injurious to his land, or which constitutes an actual interference with his possession or his beneficial use thereof, would be a trespass for which he would have remedy. *Hinman v. Pacific Air Transport,* 9 Cir., 84 F.2d 755, 758.

Appellees call our attention to various authorities that hold that, although the old ad coelum doctrine has given way to the reality of present-day conditions, an unreasonable and improper use of the air space over the owner's land can constitute a trespass: *Guith v. Consumers Power Co.,* 36 F. Supp. 21; Restatement of the Law of Torts, paragraph 194 etc.; *United States v. Causby,* 328 U.S. 256. Others cases are cited, also, and apparently hold that the land owner, while not owning or controlling the entire air space above his property, is entitled to protection against improper or unreasonable use thereof or entrance thereon.

We believe that under our system of government the landowner is entitled to such precipitation as Nature deigns to bestow. We believe that the landowner is entitled, therefore and thereby, to such rainfall as may come from clouds over his own property that Nature, in her caprice, may provide. It follows, therefore, that this enjoyment of or entitlement to the benefits of Nature should be protected by the courts if interfered with improperly and unlawfully. It must be noted that defendant's planes were based at Fort Stockton, in Pecos County, and had to fly many miles to seed clouds over defendants' lands in Jeff Davis County. We do not mean to say or imply at this time or under the conditions present in this particular case that the landowner has a right to prevent or control weather modification over land not his own. We do not pass upon that point here, and we do not intend any implication to that effect.

There is ample evidence here to sustain the fact findings of the trial court that clouds were destroyed over property of appellees by operations of the appellants. The trial court chose to believe the evidence to that effect, and we hold there was ample evidence to support him in so holding and finding. We further hold that the trial court was justified in restraining appellants from modifying or attempting to modify any clouds or weather over or in the air space over lands of the appellees.■

NOTES AND COMMENTS

1.   In the above opinion, the Court of Civil Appeals granted a preliminary injunction to the respondents to prevent Southwest from seeding clouds until the case could be fully decided on the merits. On appeal, the Texas Supreme Court upheld the preliminary injunction and said it did not need to decide the merits, but remanded the case for trial. *Southwest Weather Research, Inc. v. Jones* , 327 S.W.2d 417 [160 Tex. 104] (Tex. 1959). The case was apparently settled before a decision on the merits was reached.

2.   Section 18.019 of the Texas Water Code now authorizes the Texas Water Commission to contract with private and public agencies for performance of "weather modification or cloud-seeding operations." In 1999, a four year cloud-seeding program was begun in the hope of increasing rainfall over the Edwards aquifer, which supplies drinking water to the City of San Antonio. An article in The Economist suggests that "after five decades of effort, rain-making is starting to gain scientific credibility." Cloudbusting, The Economist, August 26, 1999. But the scientists still disagree about the processes that cause raindrops to form. Barry & Chorley, supra at 86–90.

3.   Some options that governments may choose to take when dealing with atmospheric alterations are discussed in Ray Jay Davis, Law and Urban–Induced Weather Change, 25 U. Tol. L. Rev. 370 (1994). Governments could encourage people to change land use practices, surface material use, and atmospheric emissions. Legal mechanisms are already in place to alter these practices in other contexts and could be useful in controlling atmospheric alterations. These mechanisms include environmental planning, criminal laws, tax laws, and spending laws.

4. Flooding is a predictable consequence of heavy storms in low-lying areas. To alleviate the economic hardship associated with flooding, Congress has passed a national program of flood insurance. Under this program, the federal government shares the risk of flooding with the owners of property at risk.

The rationale behind the passage of the 1968 Flood Insurance Act, 42 U.S.C. § 4001, was to reduce the massive and growing recovery costs born by the Federal government. The "unwise use of the Nation's flood plains" lead to increased annual losses from floods. As a result, the National Flood Insurance Program (NFIP), attempts to connect wise use of the flood plain with affordable and subsidized insurance in order to reduce the cost of subsequent federal disaster and flood protection aid. The NFIP requires local communities to adopt minimum flood management standards to qualify its citizens as insurable. Because of the previous failure of insurance in the private market, NFIP insurance premiums are non-actuarial. Therefore passage of the National Flood Insurance Act recognized that the set premium would take into account the "amount actuarially necessary" and the amount that people were willing to pay. The Federal Emergency Management Agency also offers further reductions in insurance rates to communities who participate in the Community Rating System.

The minimum NFIP guidelines require residential buildings in coastal high hazards areas (areas that would sustain a three foot ocean wave) to be elevated above the 100–year base flood level as they are shown on the Flood Insurance Rate Maps. Landowners must build structures landward of mean high tide, and they cannot alter a floodway if it will increase the level of the base flood discharge. The North Carolina Supreme Court characterized these minimum NFIP requirements as "conditional affirmative duties placed on the landowner's use of his property." The Court reasoned that since they are affirmative duties, they do not "affect in any way the current use" of property. Thus, the owner continues to have a " 'practical' use for his property of 'reasonable value.' " [150][4] This is an important distinction; owners are rarely prohibited from developing land but they must meet regulatory conditions in order to develop the land.

The North Carolina Court used an "ends-means" approach to evaluate the validity of the ordinance as an exercise of state police power. The Court found that the ends sought—the public interest and purpose of the regulation—was valid, and the means used was reasonable. "Enactment of an ordinance which requires that new construction and substantial improvements on property within that flood hazard area be built so as to prevent or minimize this flood damage is 'reasonably necessary' to further the legitimate public goal of preventing or reducing flood damage." The Court next addressed the reason-

4. Responsible Citizens in *Opposition to the Flood Plain Ordinance v. City of Asheville*, 302 S.E.2d 204, 210 (N.C.1983).

ableness of the degree of regulatory interference with the use of the property, and found that the owners were not "deprived of all 'practical' use of the property" and the property retained "'reasonable value.'" Therefore, because the constitutional claims failed, only the common law limits the allowable degree of interference. The Court rejected the arguments that (1) the cost of complying with the regulations was prohibitive, and (2) the ordinance diminished the market value of the property. Mere diminution in value is not enough to sustain a takings challenge, and furthermore, the property owners are not entitled to the best and highest use of their property. The fact that the restrictions are prohibitive of some uses the owner may deem appropriate does not render the ordinance invalid.

Ellen P. Hawes, Coastal Natural Hazards Mitigation: The Erosion Of Regulatory Retreat In South Carolina, 7 S.C. Envt'l L. J. 55, 73–75 (1998). See also *Texas Landowners Rights Ass'n v. Harris,* 453 F.Supp. 1025 (D.D.C.1978), aff'd, 598 F.2d 311 (D.C.Cir.1979), cert. denied, 444 U.S. 927 (1979) (upholding constitutionality of NFIP).

c. *EL NIÑO*

As the above case indicates, it is sometimes difficult to determine whether humans are or are not influencing weather patterns, even on a scale as small as the cloud seeding of Jeff Davis County. When scientists look at worldwide weather patterns, the difficulty of determining whether and to what extent these patterns are affected by human influences is much more difficult, but also much more important. A recent example is the El Niño of 1997–98, which dramatically altered weather patterns around the world, causing at least 2100 deaths and approximately $33 billion in property damage. Curt Suplee, El Niño/La Niña, Nature's Vicious Cycle, National Geographic, March 1999.

The phenomenon of El Niño has captured the public attention only recently. Fishermen originally gave this weather phenomenon its name. A pool of hot water the size of Canada would appear off the west coast of the Americas around Christmastime, so the fishermen gave it the name El Niño for Christ Child. There are records of El Niño's effects on Peru as far back as 1525 and it is possible that the Incas knew of El Niño 13,000 years ago. However, the rest of the world only started paying attention to this climate cycle about twenty-five years ago.

The weather over the Pacific Ocean had been assumed to follow a relatively dependable pattern. The sun warms the uppermost layer of water in the ocean around Australia and Indonesia which causes large quantities of hot, moist air to rise. This creates a low-pressure system at the ocean's surface. The air mass rises and cools, which releases rain, typically in monsoon form. Winds in the upper atmosphere guide the drier air eastward. The air continues to cool and increase in density. When it reaches the coast of the Americas, it is heavy enough to sink, which creates a high-pressure system near the water's surface. The air currents then flow back toward Australia and Indonesia as trade winds. The westward movement of the trade winds pushes the warm top layer of the Pacific Ocean along with them. This causes the warmest water to gather around Indonesia. Along the eastern Pacific, colder subsurface water rises up to replace the warmer layer, which brings nutrients up from the bottom of the ocean. These nutrients help to sustain the food web in the area.[5]

El Niño changes all of that. Periodically, for reasons that have yet to be fully explained, the trade winds disappear. The air pressure pattern reverses itself, which is called the Southern Oscillation. Because there are no trade winds to move the air from the east to the west, the air stays in place and grows warmer. It reaches the point of deep convection, which is the point at which steamy surface air bursts into the upper atmosphere. Water in the upper atmosphere condenses and falls on the west coast of the Americas as torrential rain. Barry & Chorley, *supra* at 276–282. This leads to many other changes. While the Americas experience an increase in rainfall, Australia, Indonesia, and India often experience drought. In North America, the jet streams shift, and the polar jet stream generally stays over Canada, resulting in less cool air over the U.S. Upper level tropical winds also reverse themselves, which takes the tops off cyclones forming in the mid-Atlantic. The number of hurricanes that hit the U.S. tends to be cut in half.

Along with El Niño come abnormal natural disasters. In February 1998, the Piura River in Peru broke its banks due to excessive rainfall caused by El Niño, washing away most of the riverside village of Chato Chico. Luckily, most of the villagers survived. All along the Piura, water pooled, which led to a large mosquito population. The Piura region reported 30,000 cases of malaria in that time period, which is three times the average. Sumatra, Borneo and Malaysia suffered forest fires due to severe droughts. Kenya's rainfall was forty inches above normal. The U.S. experienced mudslides and flash floods from Mississippi to California and tornadoes in Florida.[6]

The use of a name with religious connotations for the Southern Oscillation was undoubtedly a historical accident. But it illustrates the fact that for centuries humans have often believed that weather conditions were either a blessing or a punishment from God. Today, however, modern science suggests that humans themselves often share some responsibility for weather phenomena. Anyone who has experienced a smoggy day in Los

---

5. Research into deep ocean currents may uncover further links between oceanic oscillations and climate. William K. Stevens, Studying Deep Ocean Currents for Clues to Climate, New York Times, Nov. 9, 1999.

6. However, the ability to forecast El Niño has alleviated the distress to a degree. The National Oceanic and Atmospheric Administration ("NOAA") announced the possi-

ble El Niño in April of 1997. Other countries followed soon after with their own predictions. Farmers in northern Peru benefitted from these warnings by planting rice and beans in areas that were normally too dry support them. Fishermen were able to harvest shrimp, which normally thrive in cooler waters.

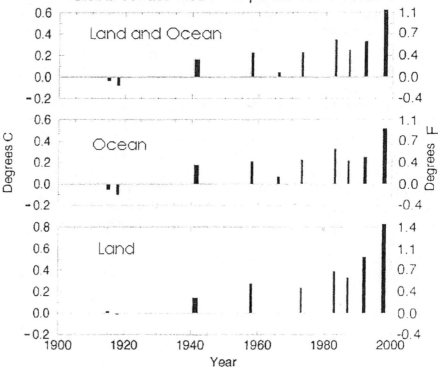

Figure 2–2

Source: www.ncdc.noaa.gov/ol/climate/research/1998/enso/10elnino.html

Angeles, Denver or Phoenix understands that these conditions did not exist before humans occupied the area. Is the recent acceleration of the El Niño phenomenon caused by human actions, or is it simply an "act of God?" We will return to this issue in Chapter Seventeen.

3. THE LEGAL CONCEPT OF "ACTS OF GOD"

Earthquakes, floods, hurricanes, tornadoes, wildfires, and drought have all been responsible for loss of life and destruction of property. While these natural disasters cause much devastation, often something man creates will enhance the effects of nature. Natural disasters have been the source of much litigation. Defendants often use the "act of God" defense, which creates an interesting situation. Where should the line be drawn as to what constitutes an uncompensable act of God and the negligent conduct of a defendant?[7]

The exact origin of the act of God defense is unknown. It was first mentioned in Shelley's Case in the sixteenth century, although no guidance was offered as to how to define an act of God. 76 Eng. Rep. 199 (1579–1581). English courts dealt with the act of God defense for several centuries, but never really formulated clear rules. In *Nugent v. Smith*, the court found that an accident must be due to natural causes, directly and exclusively, and that it "could not have been prevented by any amount of foresight and pains and care reasonably to be expected from him." 1 C.P.D. 423, 444 (1876).

American courts adopted the reasoning of the English courts. In *Polack v. Pioche*, 35 Cal. 416 (1868), the court defined act of God in the following manner: "the [act of God] expression excludes the idea of human agency, and if it appears that a given loss has happened in any way through the intervention of man, it is not an act of God." Today, to support an act of God defense one must show (1) the inability of reasonable human intelligence to foresee an event, and (2) the absence of any human agency causing damage. Basically, if a similar event occurred in the past, could be predicted using modern technology, or foreseeable by some other means, then the act of God defense will not be successful. Even if an act of God occurs, a defendant will not be absolved from negligence if reasonable steps were not taken to minimize the damage. *See*, e.g., *Ismert-Hincke Milling Co. v. Union Pacific R.R. Co.*, 238 F.2d 14 (10th Cir.1956).

Plaintiffs must establish a prima facie case for negligence. Once this is achieved, the burden of proof shifts to the defendant to raise the act of God defense. If this defense fails, liability *is not* automatically established. There is still the matter of whether the risk is foreseeable and if there is a duty to exercise reasonable care.

The act of God defense often comes into play in cases involving joint causation. This occurs when human conduct, along with a natural event combine to cause harm to a third party. Courts often apply the normal rules of joint and several liability. *See e.g., Inland Power & Light Co. v. Grieger*, 91 F.2d 811 (9th Cir.1937) (when an act of God is concurrent with defendant's negligence, defendant is liable as if he had caused the harm). Similarly, if the act of God produces an injury independent of defendant's conduct, the defendant will not be liable. *Krupa v. Farmington River Power Co.*, 157 A.2d 914 (Conn.1959). To summarize, if nature would have produced damage on its own, there is no other liability. But, if defendant's conduct coincides with the natural cause, then there is liability.

---

7. Some attempts to use the act of God defense are quite imaginative. In December 1994, a lawsuit was filed in Springfield, Massachusetts in regard to the intense odor emanating from a regional sewage treatment facility. The city's attorney claimed that the smell was an act of God by stating: "[T]he odors ... are a natural feature of human waste and an act of God for which defendants are not responsible." Sewer-plant Smell called "Act of God," Boston Globe, Dec. 4, 1994, at 42.

How should the act of God defense apply to situations in which humans have modified the environment? Humans have populated areas that were not capable of supporting large numbers of people in their "natural" condition, such as receding shorelines, hillsides and seismic zones that are not geologically stable.[8] To what extent should the public take responsibility for policies that allow people to incur such risks? *See* David R. Godschalk et. al., Natural Hazard Mitigation: Recasting Disaster Policy and Planning, Island Press, 1999.

This issue is currently presented in one of the "hottest" controversies of modern times. To what extent is the apparent warming of the climate a natural occurrence or an event caused by increased burning of fossil fuels to meet our energy needs? The climate change issue is discussed in Chapter Seventeen.

Beneath this controversy lies an even more basic issue. How can we tell what is really "natural" and what isn't? This is one of the dilemmas of the science of ecology.

PROBLEM

The First English Evangelical Lutheran Church of Glendale (First English) brought an action for property damage caused by the flooding of plaintiff's 21–acre private campground, Lutherglen, located at the bottom of a canyon on Angeles Forest Highway, Palmdale, California. Plaintiff purchased Lutherglen in 1957. Twelve acres are flat land, elevated a little above the banks of Mill Creek, a natural watercourse running down the canyon through Lutherglen, and emptying approximately 10 miles below into the Big Tujunga Dam. On this part of the property, First English built a dining hall, two bunkhouses, a caretaker's lodge, an outdoor chapel, and a footbridge across Mill Creek.

The middle fork of Mill Creek (Middle Fork) is the natural drainage channel for the watershed area owned by the National Forest Service (Forest Service) upstream of Lutherglen. The Middle Fork joins Mill Creek about 1–1/2 miles above Lutherglen, just below the point where the Angeles Forest Highway (highway) crosses the Middle Fork at Mileage Marker 16.56 (M.M. 16.56). The highway, built by defendant County of Los Angeles (County) with Forest Service approval, crosses the Middle Fork at about 20 locations in the canyon. At M.M. 16.56, the Middle Fork flows beneath the highway through two metal culverts placed by the County in the highway's solid raised-dirt embankment.

About 3,860 acres of the watershed area were burned in a fire known as the Middle Fire in July 1977. It is undisputed that the Middle Fire

---

8. People sometimes deceive themselves, believing that natural disasters won't cause any harm to them, and ignore warnings of imminent natural disasters. In 1969, 75,000 people fled from Hurricane Camille. However, twenty-five guests of the Richelieu Hotel near Pass Christian, Mississippi ignored the warnings and planned a hurricane party. The hotel collapsed during the storm, killing twenty-three of those people. Ben Funk, Swept Away, N.Y. Times, Sept. 18, 1977, (Magazine), at 38, 39.

created a potential flood hazard. The vegetation of a watershed area normally protects against flooding because the vegetation slows the flow of water, which can then percolate into the soil or be carried away by streams. When the vegetation is burned, however, there is no slowing of the flow, and the crust on the ground formed by the fire's intense heat prevents percolation of water into the soil. Additionally, the ash and debris from the fire increase the bulk of the flow, known as the bulking factor, which increases the erosion damage caused by the runoff.

On February 9 and 10, 1978, a disaster waiting to happen finally arrived. A storm dropped a total of 11 inches of water in the watershed area. A giant wall of water rushed toward the fragile structures people had erected on the banks of the creek. The docile, often dry creek became a raging river and overflowed the banks of the Middle Fork and Mill Creek. The highway's culverts at M.M. 16.56 were inadequate to handle the volume of water. Mill Creek at Lutherglen had a capacity of about 6,000 cubic feet of water per second (cfs). During the storm, the peak runoff just below Lutherglen was 8,800 cfs, 6,100 cfs of which came from Middle Fork and 2,700 cfs of which came from Mill Creek. Normally, had the watershed area not been burned, the flow from Mill Creek would have exceeded the flow from Middle Fork. Approximately 380,000 cubic yards of debris and sediment were carried by the runoff from the watershed area. About 12,000 cubic yards were deposited behind the highway at M.M. 16.56, about 38,000 cubic yards were deposited in Lutherglen, and the rest was deposited at Hansen Dam. The flood drowned 10 people in its path, swept away bridges and buildings, and inflicted millions of dollars in losses. Fortuitously, Lutherglen's planned camp for handicapped children scheduled for that week had been postponed. So no lives were lost on its property when the surging waters engulfed Lutherglen and destroyed its buildings.

Plaintiff filed an inverse condemnation action against the County claiming that the damage to Lutherglen constituted a taking without payment of compensation contrary to article I, section 19 of the California Constitution. The plaintiffs alleged that (1) the defendants are liable because their control of the Middle Fork and the highway at M.M. 16.56 constituted a dangerous condition of public property; and (2) a County ordinance adopted after the flood constituted an unconstitutional taking of property by prohibiting all use of Lutherglen's 21 acres, and (3) the County engaged in cloud seeding during the storm, for which it is liable in tort and inverse condemnation.

Was the forest fire that led to the flood an act of God? What would you need to know about forest management to answer that question?

Was the County negligent in not enlarging the culverts after the fire so that the stream would not flood? What standard would you apply to determine whether the County was unreasonable in failing to enlarge the capacity of the stream?

Once the flood occurred, did the County "take" the church's property by barring a rebuilding of the camp? *See First English Evangelical Luther-*

an Church of Glendale v. County of Los Angeles, 258 Cal.Rptr. 893 (Cal.App.1989).

E.   ENERGY AND ECOLOGY

The science of ecology is the branch of the biological sciences that studies the interrelationships among living things and their environment. Ecologists treat the flow of energy among living things as a key element in the understanding of how nature works.

1.   ENERGY AS THE SOURCE OF LIFE

The importance of the sun as a source of energy is not shown simply by the heat and light that it directly provides. The sun provides the source of energy for all forms of life. The process by which the sun's energy is converted to usable form is through photosynthesis. Plants convert the sun's energy into matter that, directly or indirectly, provides the food that sustains life for all humans and other animals.

a.   THE FOOD WEB

An appreciation of some of the basic premises of ecological science is essential to an understanding of modern energy law. The foundations of modern ecology were laid around the beginning of the twentieth century. Frederic Clements[9] developed a theory that became the prevailing view in ecology through most of the first half of this century. He believed that there was a natural "climax" condition for each part of the earth's landscape, and that if left alone nature would evolve through a series of successions into that climax, which for the Chicago area, for example, might be a forest dominated by oak and beech trees. Once the climax was reached, it would remain in permanent equilibrium unless disturbed by man or some natural disaster, after which it would the return to the climax if left alone.

As ecologists began to study the flow of energy through natural systems, however, they realized that energy needed to be a key component in ecological thinking, and a growing understanding of energy flows began to call into question some of the more simplistic ideas of earlier scientists. More modern theories of ecology began to develop in the 1930s as biologists began to understand the role of energy flows in the natural environment. The English ecologist, Charles Elton, suggested that a guiding principle in the operation of natural communities was the "food chain" in which plants, by using photosynthesis to convert sunlight to food, formed the first link in a chain of nutrition. The next links in the chain were the herbivorous

---

9. Clements' collaborator on an early ecological treatise was Roscoe Pound, who later left the field to study law and eventually became Dean of Harvard Law School and a world renowned authority on jurisprudence.

animals, such as deer or rabbits, which ate the plants; then followed their predators, such as cougars or hawks.

Elton's food chains exist in nature by the thousands, all different but following a common pattern. The plant life that capture the solar energy is always the first link in the chain. And the numbers of individual plants or animals decrease rapidly as one goes up the chain. Grass is common: cougars are rare. Elton called this the "pyramid of numbers." He called the complex of food chains the "food web" and referred to the plants as the "producers" and the animals as either first-or second-order "consumers," depending on whether they ate plants or other animals. As the animals and plants die they are consumed by the "decomposers." The place of each species in the community was referred to as its "niche."

b. ECOSYSTEMS

Another English ecologist, A.G. Tansley, proposed that a new term be created to describe this mass of relationships among living things: the "ecosystem." Donald Worster, in his study of the history of ecological science, points out the importance of this concept:

> Organisms indeed live in closely integrated units, Tansley agreed, but these can best be studied as physical systems, not "organic wholes." Using the ecosystem, all relations among organisms can be described in terms of the purely material exchange of energy and of such chemical substances as water, phosphorus, nitrogen, and other nutrients that are the constituents of "food." These are the real bonds that hold the natural world together; they create a single unit made up of many smaller units—big and little ecosystems. The discovery of the ecosystem ... marked ecology's coming of age as an adjunct of physical science. Henceforth it would gradually cease to be set off as a kind of comprehensive biology, and would instead be increasingly absorbed into the physics of energy systems.[10]

The idea of ecosystems depended on an understanding of the flow of energy through the natural environment. Ecologists applied the second law of thermodynamics to natural systems and mapped energy that flowed from the sun through the earth's ecosystem and then gradually dissipated through entropy in the form of heat being radiated out into space.

The idea of energy coursing through nature was not without its own mystical appeal. One can detect, for example, at least a superficial resemblance between this system and those Eastern philosophies of yogic meditation, transcendental energy, and cosmic kinetics that had so appealed to the Romantic poets. But Tansley's mechanist ecosystem had really nothing in common with the Romantic view of biology—the life-force idea of Goethe and Thoreau. Indeed, it owed nothing to any of its forebears in the history of the science, not even to the crudely

---

10. [Ed. note] For background on the origin of the idea of ecosystems *see* Frank   Benjamin Golley, A History of the Ecosystem Concept in Ecology (1993).

mechanistic biology of the eighteenth century. It was born of entirely different parentage: that is, modern thermodynamic physics, not biology. For the first time, mathematicians could see in ecology the opportunity to quantify. Energy flow could be measured at every point in its progress through the ecosystem; for that matter, so could the cycling of geochemical substances such as nitrogen or carbon.

Donald Worster, Nature's Economy 302–04 (2d. ed. 1994).

The classic empirical study of the operation of an ecosystem was done in 1942 by Raymond Lindeman, who studied Cedar Bog Lake in Minnesota. All resident organisms, he pointed out, may be grouped into a series of "trophic levels". The plant life of the bog, which ranged from cattails to millions of microscopic organisms, were the producers. On these fed the browsers, such as tadpoles, ducks, certain fishes and insects, tiny copepods and other zooplankton. The second-order consumers fed on the browsers; these included other fish, crustaceans, turtles, frogs, and birds. A snapping turtle or an osprey, both carnivorous predators, might represent the third-order consumer. Last came the countless millions of decomposers, bacteria and fungi, which lived in the slimy bottom mud and worked to break down organic substances into recyclable nutrients.

Each of these processes involved a transfer of energy from one trophic level to another. But a large portion of the energy is always lost in the transfer as heat escaping into the atmosphere; what the physicists call "entropy." Lindeman's pioneering research quantified these losses by measuring the "productivity" of each level in the food chain and the "efficiency" of the energy transfers that took place. Productivity refers to the accumulated biomass at any trophic level and the caloric energy required to support that amount of organic matter.

Like a farmer figuring his bushels per acre, the ecologist must harvest the "standing crop" or output at each level, weigh it, and compute the energy it took to grow that crop, whether it be plankton, spruce forest, alfalfa, or grasshoppers. But the ecologist must also estimate how much energy/matter in the crop has been already consumed by herbivores (or birds or budworms), as well as the amount used by the crop itself for its own growth and development. This wider value was the "gross production," the sum total of all energy/matter stored or spent at any trophic level. "Net production" was what was left after the energy/matter utilized in respiration was subtracted. Both figures were given in calories (or gram calories). And "productivity" was expressed in terms of the number of calories used, for one purpose or another, on a single square meter or centimeter during a year.

Once the ecologist had these productivity figures in hand for all the trophic levels, he could discover what happens to the captured solar energy as it moves through the ecosystem. He could calculate, that is, the "ecologic efficiencies" of organisms: how much energy they are able to utilize from lower levels and how much of that they in turn pass on, as well as how much they use up in metabolism. At Cedar Bog Lake, Lindeman discovered that the producers on the first level captured only one-tenth of one percent of the sun's radiation striking the lake's surface . . . The rest of the incident solar radiation was reflected back into space. Of this primary production, over one-fifth was expended in plant respiration, leaving most of the other four-fifths—or the net production—available for the herbivorous consumers. But the herbivores, Lindeman observed, ate only 17 percent of the net production of the plants; the rest went unused or was decomposed. And of what the herbivores did eat, 30 percent was needed for their own metabolism. Then came the carnivores, which consumed only 28.6 percent of their available food energy. To eat more would be to destroy their food base's ability to survive and reproduce effectively; that 28.6 percent was apparently all that they could safely harvest. But the carnivores also used, on the average, 60 percent of their caloric intake in respiration. They had to be more mobile to catch their food, and consequently their metabolism rates were the highest in the food chain.

These efficiency quotients established for Lindeman two main patterns in energy flow. First, organisms become progressively more efficient in their extraction of energy from lower levels as one moves up the food chain. From the 0.10 percent of solar energy captured by the Cedar Bog plants, the efficiency of energy transfer jumped to the 28.6 percent the carnivores harvested from the herbivores' net production (22.3 percent of their gross production). Second, respiration takes an even bigger chunk of the energy as one travels up the chain, rising in Lindeman's sample from 21 percent for plants to 60 percent for carnivores. From these results, it was more than ever clear why Elton's pyramid of numbers had to be so.

Worster, *supra,* at 306–09.

2. STATIC AND DYNAMIC ECOLOGY

Until fairly recently, the dominant school of ecological science continued to follow Clements' theory that every natural area would evolve through a process of succession until it reached "climax"—a state in which all changes in the distribution of plants and animals in that area would cease because the landscape had reached its natural condition of equilibrium. Then each plant and animal species would occupy its niche in perpetual harmony, subject only to temporary disruptions caused by fire, flood or other natural event.

These concepts of climax and equilibrium were adopted by the environmental movement, even though scientists were already beginning to doubt their validity. They fit so neatly into the philosophical idea of a "balance of nature" that they were converted into a simple sound bite: "nature knows best." Simple lessons that the public could understand were needed, and the idea that nature should be left alone fit with the mood of the 1960s. *See* Stephen Bocking, Ecologists and Environmental Policies: A History of Contemporary Ecology 193–202 (Yale University Press, 1997.)

Among modern ecological scientists, however, this static paradigm of equilibrium is being replaced by concepts like "patch dynamics," through which the characteristics of natural areas change as the plants and animals adjust to changing environmental conditions, even where humans impose no direct impact on the area. Dynamic ecological theory recognizes that nature is continually changing and we must evaluate the effects of our activities against this moving target. *See* Kristiina A. Vogt, *et. al.,* Ecosystems: Balancing Science and Management 138–141 (Springer, 1997).

Perceptions of the world as being in a state of constant change are not new. Around 500 B.C., the Greek philosopher Heraclitus of Ephesus based his philosophy on the idea of a world in continual flux. A new sun rises every day, he declared, and you can never step into the same river twice. Philosophers throughout history have debated the relative importance of stability and change.

As ecology has evolved, Clements' idea of a natural condition of equilibrium seems more and more unrealistic. Whether or not equilibrium would occur in the absence of human intervention, an issue about which ecologists continue to disagree, such intervention has now been taking place for many centuries. If ecological science is to provide meaningful answers to real world problems, ecologists increasingly recognize the need to abandon obsolete paradigms and work with the world that actually exists.

A. Dan Tarlock
The Nonequilibrium Paradigm in Ecology and the Partial Unraveling of Environmental Law
27 Loyola of L. A. L. Rev. 1121 (1994).

Many ecologists today believe that it is more useful to think about nature as a set of constantly changing conditions rather than a balanced and perpetual equilibrium. This theory is sometimes characterized as "nonequilibrium ecology."

.... Nonequilibrium ecology rejects the vision of a balance of nature. Further, it rejects the romantic idea that nature should be a place without humans, and returns to the problem posed in Genesis: How should one manage the Garden of Eden after it has been invaded by humans?

In a path-breaking book [Discordant Harmonies: A New Ecology for the Twenty–First Century (1990)], Daniel Botkin has "deconstructed" the equilibrium paradigm as a misguided effort to match science to theological and scientific visions of a perfect universe. His basic argument is that the images of nature that have influenced ecology are static when, in fact, the kinds of problems we face require a dynamic view of nature. This view starts from the premises that human action is one of the principal forces operating on ecosystems and that system disturbances are both predictable and random. Ecosystems are patches or collections of conditions that exist for finite periods of time. Further, the accelerating interaction between humans and the natural environment makes it impossible to return to an ideal state of nature. At best, ecosystems can be managed, but not restored or preserved. Management will be a series of calculated risky experiments: "[N]ature moves and changes and involves risks and uncertainties and . . . our own judgments of our actions must be made against this moving target." Most ecologists now reject any idea of a *balance* of nature, and the nonequilibrium paradigm is now the organizing principle of modern ecology. As one ecologist recently commented, "[t]he idea [of a balance of nature] makes good poetry but bad science.". . . .

The nonequilibrium paradigm does not undermine the case for biodiversity protection because it accepts the principal lesson of ecology: Unregulated, humans harm ecosystems and the magnitude of human intervention is often too great. In many instances, it strengthens the scientific case for ecosystem management, while exacerbating the politics of that management. The scale of management is larger and the emphasis is on the maintenance of processes that produced undisturbed systems. This new paradigm can also serve as the basis for the argument that since nature is in flux, human change is just another "flux" to be tolerated. However, ecologists reject this argument because it undermines the functional, historical, and evolutionary limits of nature.

Adherents to the nonequilibrium paradigm have pioneered a sophisticated new applied science, conservation biology, to protect ecosystems from human insults. To date the science has been stimulated by the need to match protected natural habitats with the survival of listed endangered and threatened species. Conservation biology is a regulatory science that seeks to develop scientific standards that can be applied to regulatory criteria and then to develop the management strategies to meet those standards.

The major institutional change necessitated by the nonequilibrium paradigm is the need to apply adaptive management to biodiversity protection. Students of organizational behavior have always counseled the need for feedback loops to reassess policy as new information accumulates; however, this has never been taken seriously in environmental law and policy. We favor management consistent with the core idea of the rule of law—consistent application of fixed rules to yield a single, final decision. Our environmental laws accept a scientific premise and then require its continued application regardless of subsequent research findings and thinking. For example, the Clean Water Act of 1977 requires that all coastal sewage discharges receive secondary treatment, although there is considerable evidence that this may not always be necessary to achieve environmental objectives. Adaptive management, in contrast, is premised on the assumption that management strategies should change in response to new scientific information. All resource management is an ongoing experiment.

Adaptive management is the end product of a fundamental shift in natural resources management. At the turn of the century, the progressive conservation movement promoted scientific management. For example, until the 1960s, it was assumed that large-scale, multiple-purpose water resources projects were essential to the economic well being of the nation.

Water management meant planning and operating these projects by fixed operating rules to maximize uses—irrigation, hydropower generation, municipal and industrial supply, and flood control. This assumption eroded in the face of the environmental movement. The result is that water resource management rests on some principles that no longer hold true. We rely less on permanent structural solutions and more on adaptive management of existing physical and seminatural systems.

A recent National Research Council–National Academy of Sciences study captures the essence of adaptive management:

> Adaptive planning and management involve a decision making process based on trial, monitoring, and feedback. Rather than developing a fixed goal and an inflexible plan to achieve the goal, adaptive management recognizes the imperfect knowledge of interdependencies existing within and among natural and social systems, which requires plans to be modified as technical knowledge improves. . . .

The idea that all management is an ongoing experiment poses a profound challenge to our legal system because it undermines a core principle of procedural and substantive fairness: finality. We follow Hume and Bentham and seek to confirm settled expectations unless there is a compelling overriding reason, usually one grounded in constitutionally protected norms such as free expression or racial equality. Once a decision is rendered, we expect parties to forever abide by the outcome. Finality takes many forms. Sometimes, it is represented by express doctrines and legislation, such as res judicata, statutes of limitation, and the doctrine of vested rights. On other occasions, finality is implicit. For example, the premise behind an environmental impact statement is that once environmental damage has been fully disclosed, a one-time decision can be made on the merits of the activity, and even if the activity will irrevocably alter the environment, the decision is legitimate and final.

* * *

Though not always reflected in practice, the essential ecological insight of modern wildlife management is that animals, plants, and their physical environment interrelate to form a system. Some wildlife managers have gone beyond a narrow focus on the interaction of wildlife and habitat to a consideration of entire biotic communities and functioning ecosystems.

Conservation biology and its predecessor fields have, however, provided some biologically grounded criteria for reserve design and management. . . . The proper scale for wildlife preserve design and management is that of the regional landscape. The influences of regional processes on local community structures indicate that nature preserves cannot be considered closed, self-supporting systems, but must be viewed as parts interacting within still larger systems. The relatively recent recognition by ecologists that natural systems are dynamic, not static, also suggests that the focus of wildlife conservation should be at the landscape scale. . . .

The foregoing observations have several implications. First, true wildlife conservation will require management of very large areas, such as regional landscapes, for wildlife habitat. While it may be commonsensical that large refuges are better for wildlife, conservation biology also reveals that these areas must be much larger than almost all the existing areas currently devoted to wildlife. Therefore, areas which are not a part of the protected preserve also must be managed to promote wildlife conservation.

Second, where it is not feasible to preserve entire regional landscapes, the connectivity characteristic of natural landscapes should be maintained or restored. Attention to corridors and linkages at various scales can help counter the effects of habitat fragmentation. Even though knowledge of the dispersal patterns of plants and animals is limited, it is widely recognized that watercourses, ridge systems, and other such topographical features, if connected to link habitat fragments, may facilitate the flow of genes, which is important for the long-term fitness of a population, as well as for individuals. The resulting strategy is to optimize the width and variety of natural habitats in landscape linkages. Where wide corridors are no longer available and cannot be restored in the short term, multiple corridors should be used to create "networks" so the full spectrum of native species will be able to move between natural areas. Because of the limitations of current knowledge and potential drawbacks of corridors or networks in some circumstances, their usefulness must be evaluated on a case-by-case basis.

Third, the significant if not pervasive human influence on regional landscapes must be taken into account. In exterminating keystone species and creating habitat islands, man is a formidable biogeographic force. The variety and extent of external threats now facing wildlife refuges underscore this point. Since human beings are members of a species that changes and has been changed by the environment, the new paradigm in ecology suggests human uses should be accommodated in largely natural areas. The management of non-harmful secondary uses within the NWRS demonstrates how humankind can be integrated into wildlife conservation and not separated from the natural environment.

The new paradigm in ecology also should be taken into account in making decisions regarding management of both natural and human-influenced areas. This time may be one of transition from the "old" management of the environment for constancy to a "new" management that takes into account change, risk, and complexity.■

NOTES AND COMMENTS

1.   Some scientists argue that the process of human evolution has given us an innate affection for the natural world around us. *See* Edward O. Wilson, Biophilia (Harvard University Press, 1984). Is there a psychological importance to the idea of the stability of nature that may support retaining it as an objective even in the face of an awareness that nature in fact undergoes constant change? From the perspective of a human lifetime, most of the natural changes in the environment are rather slow–often virtually imperceptible to ordinary observation. For a critique of Professor Tarlock's

analysis, see Eric Freyfogle, A Sand County Almanac at 50: Leopold in the New Century, 30 Envtl L. Rptr. 10058 (2000).

2.   Ecologists have increasingly begun to view natural disasters as part of the normal pattern of ecosystem behavior. "Environmental change is not continuous and gradual, but episodic," and includes not only natural disasters but the recovery period after the disaster. The transition between these states is a natural part of maintaining structure and diversity. Management policies that assume that existing conditions are the natural order of things "lead to systems that lack resilience and may break down from disturbances that were previously absorbed." Crawford S. Holling & Steven Sanderson, Dynamics of (Dis)harmony in Ecological and Social Systems, in Rights to Nature: Ecological, Economic, Cultural, and Political Principles of Institutions for the Environment 57, 58–60 (Susan S. Hanna et. al., eds, Island Press, 1996).

> Conventional resource management is predisposed to block out distur-bance, which may be efficient in a limited sense in the short term. But since disturbance is endogenous to the cyclic processes of ecosystem renewal, conventional resource management tends to increase the potential for larger-scale disturbances and even less predictable and less manageable feedbacks from the environment. These feedbacks, or surprises, can have devastating effects on ecosystems and on societies that depend on the resources that ecosystems generate. As the resili-ence of the buffering capacity of the system gradually declines, flexibili-ty is lost, and the linked social-ecological system becomes more vulner-able to surprise and crisis.

Carl Folke et. al., Ecological practices and social mechanisms for building resilience and sustainability, in Fikret Berkes and Carl Folke, eds., Linking Social and Ecological Systems: Management Practices and Social Mecha-nisms for Building Resilience 441, 415–416 (Cambridge University Press, 1998).

Thus, for example, the management of low-lying land to deter flooding may mean that when a big flood does occur the land will have lost the natural characteristics that enable it to recover from flooding. Similar experiences have been observed when forests are managed to prevent fire, or when agricultural crops are hybridized to promote cold-tolerance. *See* William Stolzenburg, Cold Snap: Warming to the Necessity of Natural Catastrophe, 49 Nature Conservancy #5, p. 14 (September–October 1999) (The science of saving the diversity of life is thinking not about how to dodge the next great disaster but how to roll with the punches.)

3.   Ecological science is now making us realize that attempts to preserve natural areas in a constant state are fraught with difficulty. In managing such areas, increased attention needs to be paid to the importance of the web of interrelationships between those "natural" areas and the areas around them.

> The conservation strategies of the wildlife specialist, however, rely on a particular model of nature—a steady state model in which ecological

characteristics are assumed to oscillate within a relatively narrow range and constantly tend toward a climax condition. This "classical paradigm" in ecology focuses on the end of ecological processes and interactions rather than on the processes, and it considers ecological systems functionally and structurally complete in and of themselves. The wildlife specialist's habitat manipulation and population control conceptually depend upon this paradigm [which] implies that any unit of nature is conservable by itself; that is, systems isolated from direct human influence will maintain themselves in the desired state. These implications have supported a traditional notion of conservation: people are not part of natural systems, so conservation should establish boundaries to exclude them.

Most national laws controlling the use of wildlife are based on the steady-state model. The general approach to managing federal lands in the United States has been described as an "enclave strategy"[11] under which natural parks with definite borders are established in an attempt to isolate nature from most human influences. The wildlife refuges also have definite boundaries even though they admit some human uses. Moreover, the refuges have been managed according to the view that conscious human intervention is necessary to reach the desired state of equilibrium. . . .

Richard J. Fink, National Wildlife Refuges: Theory, Practice, and Prospect, 18 Harv. Envtl. L. Rev. 1 (1994).

Assuming for purposes of argument that the "new paradigm" in ecology is widely accepted, how would you revise the laws relating to the creation and use of the national parks and wildlife refuges to incorporate the principles of the new thinking? For example, assume for purposes of discussion that global warming caused sea levels to rise, and that this caused wetlands that were the key component of a particular wildlife refuge to move landward gradually. Do our systems of property law contain any mechanisms that would allow the natural area to follow the moving ecosystem? *See* Jeffrey W. Niemitz, A Line in the Sand: Global Climate Change and the Future of Coastal Management Policy, 8 Dick. J. Env. L. Pol. 1 (1999). For a discussion of techniques for adaptive management of ecosystems *see* Kristiina A. Vogt et al., Ecosystems: Balancing Science with Management 377–387 (Springer, 1996).

3. THE "LAW OF NATURE"

Many of our environmental statutes assume that the natural condition of an area should be protected. There may be, of course, valid policy reasons unrelated to ecology for retaining certain areas in their natural

---

11. [Ed. note] For a concise summary of the history of United States policies toward the preservation of natural systems, *see* Joseph L. Sax, Nature and Habitat Conservation and Protection in the United States, 20 Ecology L.Q. 47, 49 (1993); Robert B. Keiter, Beyond the Boundary Line: Constructing a Law of Ecosystem Management, 65 U. of Colo. L.Rev. 293, 303–312 (1994).

condition, such as retention of flood waters. But is there a valid basis for protecting natural areas because of their importance in the conversion of the sun's solar energy into products and processes valuable to humans? Should we be concerned about the loss of natural areas that are particularly efficient in energy conservation? How should the law deal with the issues raised by the dynamic theories of ecology? Consider these questions as you read the following two cases:

Florida Power Corp. v. Florida Dept. of Environmental Regulation

638 So.2d 545 (Fla. 1st D.C.A. 1994) review denied, 650 So.2d 989.

■ BARFIELD, J.: Florida Power Corporation (FPC) appeals an order of the Department of Environmental Regulation (DER) denying its application for a wetland resource permit, contending that DER improperly rejected the hearing officer's determination that FPC's project would have no adverse impacts and was not contrary to the public interest....

FPC owns an easement over property in Reedy Creek Swamp, a large mixed wetland forest system in Osceola County, on which it seeks to install an electrical transmission line between Intercession City and Poinciana (the ICP line), which is expected to last at least thirty years....

In December 1989, FPC filed an application with DER for a wetland resource permit to place 353.1 cubic yards of fill to support the transmission poles. The application stated that the fill would impact .0135 acres of jurisdictional wetlands. Prior to obtaining the permit, FPC undertook clearing activities during March–June 1990, cutting all vegetation within the sixty-foot transmission line corridor to the ground or water line. DER conducted a surveillance flight over the project site in June 1990 and visited the site in June and in August. The flight revealed the nearly completed clearing of the forested wetland, and the field appraisals indicated that some dredge and fill had occurred as a result of the land clearing activities. At an on-site meeting in late August 1990, the parties discussed mitigation. FPC eventually offered to preserve one acre of forested wetland, at a site east of the Intercession City substation near State Road 17/92, for each acre of forested wetland impacted.

In September 1990, DER issued a notice of intent to deny the permit request, finding that the proposed installation activities would actually impact approximately 6.01 acres, 5.997 acres of which were "secondary impacts" of the proposed construction (i.e., the clearing activities). It found that the wetland adjacent to State Road 17/92 "will be impacted by minor trimming of branches within the mature forested canopy and by removal of small subcanopy trees beneath the existing corridor," that the main crossing of the swamp "involves secondary impacts to a mature mixed forested wetland" (noting endangered and threatened orchids adjacent to the cleared corridor), and that the wetland south of the main crossing is a cypress community with saw grass as the primary understory. It found that the proposed alignment "has and will continue to result in disturbances to hydric soils and vegetation as a result of the tree cutting, installation and maintenance activities," that the power line "will result in a permanent change in the character of the wetland from a mature mixed forested canopy to a herbaceous wetland," and that this permanent change "is expected to diminish the overall productivity of the system and adversely affect wildlife utilization."

The title to chapter 84–79, Laws of Florida, which created the "Warren S. Henderson Wetlands Protection Act of 1984," Part VIII of chapter 403, Florida Statutes, now entitled "Permitting of Activities in Wetlands," reads ... "... it is the policy of this state to establish reasonable regulatory programs which provide for the preservation and protection of Florida's remaining wetlands to the greatest extent practicable, consistent with private property rights and the balancing of other vital state interests," and "it is the policy of this state to consider the extent to which particular disturbances of wetlands are related to uses or projects which must be located within or in close proximity to the wetland and aquatic environment in order to perform their basic functions, and the extent to which particular disturbances of wetland benefit essential economic development, ..."

Section 403.918, Florida Statutes (1989), which establishes the criteria for granting or denying permits under the Act, provides in part (emphasis supplied):

(2) A permit may not be issued under ss. 403.91–403.929 unless the applicant provides the department with reasonable assurance that the project is not contrary to the public interest. However, for a project which significantly degrades or is within an Outstanding Florida Water, as provided by department rule, the applicant must provide reasonable assurance that the project will be clearly in the public interest.

(a) In determining whether a project is not contrary to the public interest, or is clearly in the public interest, the department shall consider and balance the following criteria:

1. Whether the project will adversely affect the public health, safety, or welfare or the property of others;

2. Whether the project will adversely affect the conservation of fish and wildlife, including endangered or threatened species, or their habitats;

3. Whether the project will adversely affect navigation or the flow of water or cause harmful erosion or shoaling;

4. Whether the project will adversely affect the fishing or recreational values or marine productivity in the vicinity of the project;

5. Whether the project will be of a temporary or permanent nature;

6. Whether the project will adversely affect or will enhance significant historical and archaeological resources under the provisions of s. 267.061; and

7. The current condition and relative value of functions being performed by areas affected by the proposed activity.

(b) If the applicant is unable to otherwise meet the criteria set forth in this subsection, the department, in deciding to grant or deny a permit, shall consider measures proposed by or acceptable to the applicant to mitigate adverse effects which may be caused by the project. . . .

Section 403.919, Florida Statutes (1989), entitled "Equitable distribution," codifies the "cumulative impact doctrine" . . .

[DER] Rule 17–312.300 et seq. establish the criteria for evaluating mitigation proposals. DER must first explore "project modifications that would reduce or eliminate the adverse environmental impacts of the project" and suggest any such modifications, either in addition to or in lieu of mitigation. It may not require mitigation, but it must consider "any mitigation proposed by a permit applicant in accordance with this rule." Rule 17–312.300(7) provides:

The amount, type and location of mitigation, if any, required of electric utilities conducting dredge and fill activities for the purpose of providing energy service shall be determined in conjunction with the criteria in Section 403.918, F.S., in recognition of the fact that such activities generally promote the public interest.

Rule 17–312.340 sets the standards for evaluating mitigation proposals, noting that they must be considered "on a case by case basis" and that offsetting adverse impacts "will usually be best addressed through protection, enhancement or creation of the same type of waters as those being affected by the proposed project."

In March 1991, FPC filed a request for formal administrative hearing . . . The parties stipulated that the proposed project "benefits the public welfare by producing and providing for the reliable transmission of electricity to residents of the State" . . . The five-day hearing centered on the relative condition of the area impacted and the impact of the clearing on the conservation of vegetation, fish and wildlife. FPC admitted that the canopy has been removed in a sixty-foot swath through the swamp and that maintenance activities will result in a change in the corridor from forested wetlands to herbaceous/shrubby wetlands, but it asserted that there has been "no adversity" resulting from the change in the character of the wetlands. DER argued that this was in effect "after-the-fact permitting," that six acres of forested wetland has been removed and will not be replaced, and that what is left is a disturbed herbaceous marsh that will, along with past, present, and future projects, have a cumulative negative effect on Reedy Creek Swamp as a whole. . . .

[Company experts testified] that FPC had evaluated an alternate route which would have followed an existing roadway, but that this route would have been 2.5 miles longer and would have cost $700,000 more. . . . Vegetation would be cut to the ground or water level for seventeen feet on either side of the center line of the sixty-foot wide corridor. The remaining outer thirteen feet on each side would be allowed to regenerate, except for fast-growing trees expected to reach thirty feet or more in height, which would be girdled or treated with EPA approved herbicides by specific and selective application, and that all exotic or nuisance target species would be removed from the entire right-of-way. . . .

Dr. William Dennis . . . was presented as an expert in botany, wetland ecology, and wetland permitting. He testified that there are no trees in the corridor, but that some trees are coppicing (sprouting from stumps), that the herbaceous and shrub plants are essentially the same, and that if there were no maintenance, the corridor would return to forest in 30–50 years. He stated that with maintenance, the shrub species will over time become more dominant, and that wetland functions (storage capacity, recharge potential, water quality, biomass, productivity, habitat) are not diminished, noting that some have probably increased.

Dr. Dennis stated that, as a general rule, herbaceous wetlands are more productive (productivity measured by the amount of plant material accumulated per unit area over time) than forested wetlands. He testified that, while the habitat was definitely changed, he was not aware of any study showing any species adversely affected, and that quite a number of species (for example, wading birds) would be benefitted. . . .

[Steve] Godley [a biological expert] found that the mean "cover" was 85% in the corridor, higher than in the forest, and testified that a study showed that the net primary productivity of herbaceous wetlands is three times higher than in the adjacent flood plain forest, and that the decomposition rate is two or three times higher in the marsh. . . .

As to endangered or threatened species, Godley found that the only endangered reptile, the indigo snake, would be positively affected, that none of the fish or mammals were listed as endangered or threatened, and that of the endangered or threatened birds, three were positively affected (wood stork, little blue heron, snowy egret) because they eat fish, and that the bald eagle, which prefers lakes, would be positively affected. . . .

Godley stated that the ICP corridor had caused a change in the system, but that the wildlife utilization in the whole system is balanced across all kinds of animals and does not appear to have been negatively affected. He testified that the majority of the animal species are likely to be positively affected, and that the species which were negatively affected are "almost at the point of a de minimis effect." He testified that the corridor had not adversely affected recreation and had improved hunting. He did not believe there was a solid scientific basis to indicate that the corridor had fragmented wildlife in the swamp. He discussed nest parasitism (some bird species lay their eggs in other birds' nests), and testified that the brownheaded cowbird likes open spaces and parasitizes warblers and vireos at the edge of the forest, within twenty-five meters, but he did not think the brownheaded cowbird, which is a problem in northeastern upland forests, would view the corridor as an upland habitat....

Anthony Arcuri, with Environmental Consulting & Technology, testified as an expert in wetlands ecology and electric transmission line impacts. He compiled a bibliography of sixty-seven references on ecological impacts of transmission lines in forested wetlands. He also visited the corridor in October 1991, finding that it had revegetated except for the trees and that there appeared to be minimal disturbance to the area. He opined that in general, shifting of forested wetland to herbaceous wetland does not reduce function ascribed to wetland areas, and that some functions are unchanged, while primary productivity increases in the corridor. He found no large-scale invasion of nuisance or exotic species. He stated that "edge effect" increases wildlife utilization, species numbers and diversity, and density of wildlife populations. He acknowledged that the project would cause a permanent shift in the wetland structure, but he stated that he did not feel it would cause a long term impact to the overall function or integrity of the wildlife system. He testified that he felt that the sixty-foot clearing "does not adversely affect Reedy Creek Swamp so as to warrant compensatory mitigation."

Dr. Putz [an associate professor of biology and forestry at the University of Florida] testified [on behalf of DER] that forested wetlands in Florida are being lost faster than any other community type (15% between 1979 and 1987 according to one study of Florida and South Carolina wetlands). He stated that Arcuri's bibliography was good on power line rights-of-way, but lacking on effects of clear cutting, and that it contained "virtually nothing on forest canopy opening." He testified that he thought the literature and Godley's quantitative analysis were "directed attempts," but he acknowledged a study by Randy Kautz with the Florida Game and Freshwater Fish Commission which found that there was no loss of lowland forest.

Bradley Hartman, with the Florida Game and Freshwater Fish Commission, testified as an expert in wildlife management. He and Stephen Lau, also with the Commission, wrote a report for DER in which they found that the wildlife population would be affected by the change in habitat (i.e., replacement of wooded wetlands by open marsh). He stated that there would be an increase in the number of individuals and the number of species because of two habitats located next to each other, but that population of forest animals would be lost because of losses of hardwood mast (seeds and nuts), high canopy, cavities and snags. He testified that they were more interested in regional diversity than in local diversity, and that the corridor could actually reduce the number of species in the regional area. He stated that while there was some additional feeding for the little blue heron and the snowy egret (special concern species), these species do not need more feeding area. He explained the LANDSAT habitat planning project which places emphasis on saving large tracts, more valuable because they buffer themselves. In his opinion, we are losing forested wetlands, resulting in a decline in forested species, some of which are the most rare. . . .

DER's Barbara Bass . . . testified that DER would have been happy to consider other proposals, but that none were submitted by FPC, and that rerouting the line along a road is a reasonable alternative. She stated that the 1:1 mitigation proposed by FPC is inadequate, that there should be at least a 10:1 ratio because of the quality of the swamp and its vulnerability to development, and that it would take sixty years to replace the mature system that was lost. She stated that other projects impact forested wetlands in Reedy Creek Swamp (Continental Development berms and roads, Owens commercial development and access road, Osceola County bridge, Wilderness Joint Venture enforcement case, Walt Disney access road, Walt Disney parking, Reedy Creek Improvement District (RCID) reuse pipeline and access road, RCID bridge, Parker Poinciana DRI, Johnson Island DRI, Pleasant Hill Point DRI, Oak Hill Estates DRI, Celebration Project DRI). She testified that she would prefer to see future crossings of the swamp adjacent to corridors, where disturbance has already occurred.

Dr. Herbert Kale, with Florida Audubon Society, was presented as an expert in ornithology. He testified that he has been to Reedy Creek Swamp many times and that he visited the ICP site in November 1991. He stated that the permanent loss of forested wetland affects woodpeckers and interior forest birds (red-eyed vireo, prothonotary warbler, hermit thrush, ovenbird, northern water thrush), that the corridor brings in wading birds, and that there is an "edge effect" 100–200 meters into the forest. He testified that the corridor is large enough to attract brownheaded cowbirds, who are nest parasites, and that the shiny cowbird is also moving in from the Caribbean. On cross-examination, he stated that the sixty-foot swath is not fatal to any of the forest birds, but "every time you make a cut you're creating problems and reducing habitat."

[The hearing officer recommended that the application for the permit be granted without mitigation.] Based on [her] findings of fact, the hearing officer concluded that FPC had met its burden of proof under section 403.918, that "the minimal changes in the subject six acres will not, as proven by the applicant, produce adverse affects," and that since FPC had met the criteria, "mitigation is unnecessary."

DER filed exceptions to the hearing officer's conclusion that the change in wetland would not result in any adverse impact to the public interest factors of section 403.918(2). . . . DER's Secretary Carol Browner[12] issued an order of remand rejecting DER's exceptions to the hearing officer's findings of fact except for the last one regarding edge effect, which the Secretary characterized as mixing findings of fact with conclusions of law and policy, and erroneously implying that there is a de minimis exception to cumulative impact analysis. She ruled that the hearing officer had construed the "similarity" requirement too narrowly and that the

12.   [Ed. Note] Secretary Browner was appointed in 1993 by President Clinton to be the Administrator of the United States Environmental Protection Agency.

magnitude of a project's environmental impact goes to the weight given it in the cumulative impact analysis, not to whether the project is considered. She found that corridors for roads, pipelines, and power lines are sufficiently similar in their environmental impacts, "not the least of which is the loss of forested wetlands." She ruled that the impact of the DRIs should have been considered either in the cumulative impact analysis or in the secondary impact analysis, and that the burden of proof in both analyses is on the applicant rather than on DER (i.e., FPC had the burden of showing that the suggested projects are not within the basin). She remanded for a revised cumulative impact analysis in which the proposed ICP project would be analyzed in light of the projects referenced in the recommended order, and for additional findings of fact concerning the cumulative and secondary impacts, whether the project is contrary to the public interest, and the adequacy of the proposed mitigation.

[The hearing officer considered the eight existing and two pending dredge and fill projects presented by FPC and issued a supplemental recommended order in which she found that because wetlands were not destroyed in the FPC project under review, as a matter of law mitigation was unnecessary.]

On August 13, 1992, Secretary Browner issued a final order denying FPC's permit application. She accepted the findings of fact in both recommended orders with the following exceptions: that "wetlands" were not destroyed; that the loss of six acres of forested wetlands is not permanent and that the "habitats which were affected when the clearing took place will regenerate and will be reestablished"; that the change from forested wetlands to herbaceous wetlands has not and will not adversely affect threatened plant species, fish or wildlife and that the edge effect "is at least neutral, and is generally positive"; and that there is no adverse impact when the project is considered cumulatively.

As to the hearing officer's finding that "wetlands" were not destroyed, the Secretary ruled that the finding was infused by a policy determination "that herbaceous wetlands are somehow environmentally equivalent to forested wetlands" and rejected this policy determination. She explained: "Forested wetlands are not environmentally equivalent to herbaceous wetlands. Each have their (sic) own unique environmental functions which are not interchangeable" and "the six acres of forested wetlands habitat is lost, i.e., destroyed, regardless of whether it is replaced by a different type of wetland system or by an asphalt parking lot." . . .

The Secretary reconsidered the balancing of the public interest criteria in section 403.918(2) in light of the rejected finding of no adverse impact. She determined that while there are no adverse impacts under criteria 1, 3, 4, and 6, the project has resulted in adverse impacts under criteria 2, 5, and 7. Balancing these adverse effects against the benefit provided, she found that the project is contrary to the public interest. She rejected several of the hearing officer's conclusions of law, and concluded that the mitigation proposed by FPC was not sufficient to offset the adverse impacts of the project. She denied the permit, noting:

This project would have been permitted if FPC had offered sufficient mitigation in its application or during the hearing. Of course, this denial does not preclude FPC from reapplying with legally sufficient mitigation or a modified project.

The parties do not dispute that providing energy service promotes the public interest, that the ICP line must cross the Reedy Creek Swamp, and that some dredge and fill is therefore necessary, requiring a permit from DER. The statute makes it clear that before DER may grant this permit, FPC must provide it with reasonable assurance that the ICP project is not contrary to the public interest, and that in determining whether the ICP project is contrary to the public interest, DER must consider and balance the criteria set out in section 403.918, of which only (2), (5), and (7) are at issue in this case.

FPC admits that it cut down all vegetation to the ground in the ICP right-of-way, removing the forest canopy in a sixty-foot swath through the swamp, and that its proposed maintenance activities will result in a change in the corridor from forested wetlands to herbaceous/shrubby wetlands. FPC's expert witnesses testified that if the corridor were left undisturbed, the forested wetland would regenerate in 30–50 years (i.e., it is technically not "permanently" changed into open marsh). However, they also testified, and the hearing officer found, that FPC plans to maintain the herbaceous/shrubby wetland "over the expected 30–year operational life of the transmission line," by periodically cutting to the ground all vegetation in fifty-feet-wide (at the poles) and thirty-four-feet-wide (between the poles) sections at the center of the corridor, and killing off all trees which will grow higher than thirty feet (i.e., most of the indigenous species) within the sixty-foot corridor.

For purposes of considering and balancing the statutory criteria, there is little doubt that the ICP project will be more permanent than temporary (criterion 5). This leaves the other two criteria at issue: "whether the project will adversely affect the conservation of fish and wildlife, including endangered or threatened species, or their habitats" and "the current condition and relative value of functions being performed by areas affected by the proposed activity."

As DER's attorney observed at the hearing, this is to some extent an after-the-fact permitting process. DER was therefore required to compare the condition of the remote, undisturbed forested wetlands as they existed prior to FPC's clearing of the corridor (and the value of the functions being performed by those forested wetlands) to the condition of the herbaceous/shrubby wetlands that have resulted from the clearing (and the value of the functions being performed by those open wetlands), and to consider also the "edge effect" of the open corridor on the adjacent forested wetlands. Almost no data was presented on the specific forested wetlands before the clearing, except for the ten-year water quality data considered by Dr. Smart. We can know about these forested wetlands only from general qualitative assessments from the experts on both sides that Reedy Creek

Swamp is a high quality wetland area (i.e., the undisturbed forested wetlands where the corridor was cut were of high quality).

The parties do not dispute that there are significant differences between the condition of the site before FPC's clearing activities and the present condition of the site, the most notable being that all the large trees are gone, and that this difference will be maintained by FPC for at least the next thirty years if the permit is granted. The parties also do not generally dispute that, in addition to other wetland functions which remain relatively unchanged, the forested wetland which existed within the area at issue provided a habitat for various species of plants and animals which cannot live in the herbaceous/shrubby wetland resulting from FPC's clearing and maintenance activities, and that the clearing of the corridor affected many of the other plants and animals in the corridor and in the adjacent forest in various ways, some considered positive and some considered negative.

The issues to be resolved are first, the extent of the "adverse" effects on the plants and animals in the corridor and in the adjacent forest, and second, whether these adverse effects outweigh the public benefit which will result from the project, the provision of reliable electric power to the area south of the swamp. The first issue requires factual findings, while the second issue requires a balancing of the adverse effects which are found to exist against the public benefit, to determine whether the project is "contrary to the public interest." s. 403.918(2), Fla. Stat. (1989). In making the latter determination, however, DER must consider not only the impact of the ICP project, but also "the impact of projects which are existing or under construction or for which permits or jurisdictional determinations have been sought" and "the impact of projects which are under review, approved, or vested pursuant to s. 380.06, or other projects which may reasonably be expected to be located within the jurisdictional extent of waters, based upon land use restrictions and regulations." s. 403.919, Fla. Stat. (1989).

The hearing officer essentially dismissed the "cumulative impact analysis" in her recommended order, and Secretary Browner ruled that she had construed the "similarity" requirement too narrowly. When the Secretary remanded for a revised cumulative impact analysis, the hearing officer considered the existing and pending dredge and fill projects, but concluded that because wetlands were not destroyed in the ICP project and FPC provided reasonable assurance that its project will not violate state water quality standards or is not contrary to the public interest, "consideration of these additional projects does not change previous undisturbed findings of fact" (i.e., that the ICP project does not exacerbate the impacts from the other projects).

Secretary Browner correctly rejected the finding that wetlands were not destroyed, on the ground that it was based on a policy determination which she also rejected, "that herbaceous wetlands are somehow environmentally equivalent to forested wetlands." She also properly rejected the finding that there is no adverse impact when this project is considered cumulatively, which was based upon the hearing officer's rejected finding that there was no adverse impact from this project alone. We find that Secretary Browner's rulings were within her discretion in implementing the wetlands protection statutes.

The hearing officer did not find that there were no adverse effects from FPC's clearing of the six acres of forested wetlands. Rather, she found that "based on the limited nature of the project's corridor, the six acre disturbance has been correctly characterized as de minimis." The Secretary ruled that she could not accept, even under the facts of this case, that the loss of six acres of forested wetlands in an area of 31,448 acres of contiguous forested wetlands is de minimis, and that the hearing officer's finding is essentially a conclusion of law that there is a de minimis exception, which "would completely undercut the purpose of the cumulative impact analysis required by Section 403.919." The Secretary properly rejected the hearing officer's conclusion that mitigation was unnecessary because there were no adverse affects from the project. These rulings, and her finding that the mitigation proposed by FPC was not sufficient to offset the adverse impacts of the project, were also within her discretion.

If FPC undertook this extensive and expensive litigation for the purpose of establishing a principle of no mitigation for power line clearing activities through forested wetlands, it has failed in its endeavor. It must now decide whether it will reroute the proposed ICP power line through Reedy Creek Swamp or whether it will offer to preserve an appropriate amount of forested wetlands in mitigation of the adverse effects resulting from its clearing of the proposed ICP corridor.

The final order is affirmed.

■ ZEHMER, J., dissenting: The lengthy recitation of the evidence in the majority opinion confirms my view that the findings of fact in the hearing officer's recommended orders are supported by competent, substantial evidence, and Secretary Browner was bound by these findings of fact. s. 120.57(1)(b)10, Fla. Stat. (1991); *Heifetz v. Department of Business Regulation*, 475 So. 2d 1277 (Fla. 1st DCA 1985). It is clear from the final order that the Secretary disagreed with the hearing officer's findings of fact and therefore modified certain facts to support her conclusion that the activity for which Florida Power sought a dredge and fill permit would result in adverse impacts contrary to the public interest. Yet, no authority permits the Secretary to make such changes in the facts when supported by competent, substantial evidence because of the provisions in subsection 120.57(1)(b)10.

Specifically, Secretary Browner's final order concluded that there is a major difference between forested wetlands and herbaceous wetlands, and that Florida Power had destroyed forested wetlands by clear cutting, thereby leaving instead herbaceous wetlands. This result, she opines, amounts to an adverse impact contrary to the public interest, irrespective of whether the hearing officer's recommended order found as a matter of fact, supported by competent, substantial evidence, that the altered conditions of the land did not factually result in adverse impacts. According to the majority opinion, the Secretary "determined that the public interest in the extent of the impact on the environment from this destruction of the forest was a policy matter for its determination and not a question of fact to be resolved by the hearing officer." Agreeing, the majority affirms the final order on this rationale.

I dissent because I do not agree that this determination is purely a matter of public policy reserved for exclusive decision by the Secretary; rather, the determination must be based on matters of fact determined by the hearing officer on the evidence presented in accordance with section 403.918.

The Secretary's final order found adverse impacts under criteria 2, 5, and 7 based on policy reasons, thereby differing from the hearing officer's findings of fact as to each of those criteria. Criterion 2 involves "whether the project will adversely affect the conservation of fish and wildlife, including endangered or threatened species, or their habitats." Criterion 5 involves "whether the project will be of a temporary or permanent nature." Criterion 7 involves "the current condition and relative value of functions being performed by areas affected by the proposed activity." Each of these criteria is governed by matters of fact on which the applicant and the Department generally present evidence in disputed dredge and fill permitting cases, usually in the form of proof of existing conditions, extensive scientific data, and relevant opinions by qualified experts at a formal subsection 120.57(1) hearing. As often as not, the experts are in disagreement, and it is the function of the hearing officer to judge the credibility and weight of all the evidence, including the contradictory expert opinions, and resolve disputed factual matters, usually by choosing to accept certain expert testimony while rejecting other expert testimony. In my view, that is precisely what the hearing officer did in the instant case. Yet, the Secretary has rejected the hearing officer's findings of fact, not because they were unsupported by competent, substantial evidence, as provided in subsection 120.57(1)(b)(10), but because as a matter of policy the Secretary disagreed with the facts found by the hearing officer. Hence, the Secretary changed the facts under the guise of a policy ruling, asserting that the hearing officer essentially dismissed the ".cumulative impact analysis" in her recommended order and failed to adequately consider the impact of this project (involving approximately 6 acres according to the Department) and other unnamed and undescribed projects expected to be located in the future within this large geographical area known as the Reedy Creek Basin (consisting of over 92,000 acres of upland and wetland habitats, of which some 31,448 acres are characterized as forested wetland). Additionally, the Secretary disagreed with certain policy determinations made by the hearing officer in the recommended order. Affirming the Secretary's ruling, the majority opinion notes that, "Secretary Browner correctly rejected the finding that wetlands were not destroyed, on the ground that it was based on a policy determination which she also rejected, 'that herbaceous wetlands are somehow environmentally equivalent to forested wetlands.'" [Emphasis added.] By characterizing this determination as one of policy rather than fact, the hearing officer's findings can be ignored. This is akin to designating the Secretary as the sole determinator of how land shall be used without regard to the statutory limitations in chapter 403.■

NOTES AND COMMENTS

1.   Assume that the forested wetland that pre-existed the power line was less efficient at converting solar energy than the shrubby wetland that was created by cutting down the trees. Is this a factor that should have been taken into consideration by the Department? Is energy conversion efficiency a value in and of itself? Or is there a presumption that the natural condition of the land is the most desirable from an ecological perspective?

2.   The question of cumulative impact addressed by the court is a troublesome one throughout environmental law. When one can foresee that a multiplicity of small projects will adversely impact the environment, but no single project can be shown to be the cause of significant damage, can individual projects be denied on the ground that they will contribute to the damage? The Supreme Court has suggested that consideration of cumulative impact may be constitutionally required, but it has been in dicta. *See Nollan v. California Coastal Commission*, 483 U.S. 825, 835 (1987).

3.   Do you agree with the dissenting judge that Secretary Browner was dissembling by purporting to use "policy" to overrule the hearing examiner's characterization of the factual evidence? Or do you think the hearing examiner was trying to make policy by the way she characterized the facts? Can you think of ways to clarify the distinction between fact and policy in this area?

4.   The above case arose under a state wetlands protection statute. Most construction projects in wetlands also require a federal "dredge and fill" permit under the Clean Water Act, 33 U.S.C. § 1344. Clearing of vegetation, however, may not constitute "fill" and thus may not trigger the permit requirement. Save Our Wetlands, Inc. v. Sands, 711 F.2d 634, 646–647 (5th Cir.1983).

5.   The siting of new energy facilities often requires highly talented energy lawyers who need to have a basic understanding of many technical issues. The expert testimony quoted in this excerpt is only part of the expert testimony that the court analyzed. Obviously, this litigation was expensive and time consuming. Why do you think the company pursued this expensive litigation rather than abiding by Secretary Browner's interpretation of the statute?

If you had been Florida Power Company's attorney, would you have advised the company that it could proceed to clear the trees on this site without applying for a permit under the wetlands statute? Would you have made that decision on your own, or would you have consulted expert biologists? Would you have sought an informal opinion from the staff of the agency? (The opinion in this case does not tell us whether the company sought legal advice before cutting the trees).

6.   Many states have crafted statutes to coordinate the siting of facilities such as natural gas pipelines, power plants and electricity transmission lines. *See, e.g.,* Mont. Rev. Code Ann. §§ 75–20–101–406 (1997) ("Montana Major Facility Siting Act"); N.Y. Public Service Law §§ 120–130 (McKinney 1997); S.D. Comp. Laws Ann. §§ 49–41B–1—B–38 (1997). The goal of such statutes is to streamline the traditionally extensive regulatory process involved in siting pipelines, power plants and transmission lines. State siting statutes serve to facilitate a public decisionmaking process focused on objective factors. Further, siting statutes often reduce what was previously a local veto over projects by preempting local regulation of certain issues, such as the need for the line or plant or local concerns regarding the environment. Also, siting statutes streamline and coordinate the decision-making of multiple agencies that may have jurisdiction over the project, while still requiring consideration of environmental costs and benefits, as well as alternatives to the project.[13]

To help utilities cope with the permitting process for locating transmission lines, Florida, for example, enacted the Transmission Line Siting Act ("TLSA") in 1980. Those involved in the siting of transmission lines in Florida termed the TLSA "a solution to the regulatory maze." *See* Wade L. Hopping and Carolyn Songer Raepple, A Solution to the Regulatory Maze: The Transmission Line Siting Act, 8 Fla. St. U. L. Rev. 442 (1980). Certification according to the TLSA terms is the sole license required from the state or any local or regional governmental agency to construct a transmission line or to establish the location of a transmission line corridor. *See id.* at 443. Florida's streamlined approach to transmission line siting applies only to transmission lines that are designed to operate at 230 or more kilovolts and that cross a county line, and thus was not available to the Florida Power Co. in the preceding case.

Pursuant to the TLSA, the Florida Public Service Commission (PSC) is first responsible for determining whether a proposed transmission line is needed. *See* Fla. Stat. § 403.537(1)(a) (1997). An electric utility may request a hearing to determine the need for a proposed transmission line, or the PSC may decide to hold a hearing on its own motion. In determining the need for the proposed transmission line, the PSC must consider "the need for electric system reliability and integrity, the need for abundant, low-cost electric energy to assure the economic well-being of the citizens of this state, the appropriate starting and ending point of the line, and other matters within its jurisdiction deemed relevant to the determination of need." *See id.* § 403.537(1)(c).

Transmission line site certification in Florida is subject to the Florida Administrative Procedure Act, and the formal siting process begins when an electric utility submits an application to the Department of Environmental Protection (DEP).[14] An administrative law judge then holds the

---

13. Along these lines, siting overlaps with another tool called "integrated resource planning," discussed further in Chapter 10 and 13.

14. The PSC's determination of need is a pre-requisite to the TLSA certification hearing, and the PSC's need determination is

certification hearing to (1) determine the completeness and the sufficiency of the application; (2) receive the DEP's written analysis of the application; (3) conduct the certification hearing; (4) submit to the siting board (comprised of the Governor and the Cabinet) a recommended order based on the record at the hearing; and (5) rule on motions to intervene. *See id.* § 403.5252; § 403.5253; § 403.527.

The Florida TLSA also contains provisions to prevent the streamlined siting process from blocking public input, while not slowing the process with an overwhelming number of intervenors. Certain enumerated persons and agencies, including local and regional agencies, have party status in the certification hearing. Also, most nonprofit corporations or associations that represent environmental and business interests may become parties to the proceeding by filing a notice of intent at least 15 days prior to the hearing; otherwise such interests may file a motion to intervene in the hearing. Other interested persons may present oral or written communications without becoming a party. Local governments may also hold informational public hearings. *See id.* § 403.5272.

Agency participation is not limited under the TLSA, but electric utilities are not required to apply separately to each agency with an interest in transmission line siting. DEP serves as a central clearinghouse for the application, receiving a wide range of comments, and its report aims to strike "a reasonable balance between the need for the facility as a means of providing abundant low-cost electrical energy and the environmental impact resulting from construction of the line and the location and maintenance of the corridor." *See id.* § 403.521.

The Siting Board's ultimate decision must "fully balance the need for transmission lines with the broad interests of the public." *See id.* The Siting Board's written final order must approve the certification in whole, approve "with such conditions as the board deems appropriate," or deny the certification and state the reasons for issuing the denial. *See id.* 403.529(1). Any party who is adversely affected by the board's decision may seek judicial review before an appellate court.

Other state siting and certification statutes are similar to Florida's in most respects; including statutes in Montana, New York and South Dakota. States have differing kilovolt thresholds for determining which transmission lines qualify for the expedited process, and preempt local regulation in differing ways.[15] Regardless of the differences among states, the universal

---

binding on all parties to the certification hearing. Such need determination is included in a written analysis of the proposal which the Florida Department of Environmental Protection ("DEP") submits to the certification administrative law judge.

15. In New York, all residents of municipalities through which the transmission line may pass must be granted party status in the certification proceeding upon their timely filing of an intent to be a party. *See* N.Y. Public Service Law § 124(j) (McKinney 1997). In both New York and South Dakota, local laws and regulations are superseded only if the approving authority expressly finds that such laws and regulations are unreasonably restrictive. *See id.* at 126(1)(f); S.D. Comp. Laws Ann. § 49–41B–28 (1997).

goal is still to simplify and coordinate the siting and certification process for electric utilities.

Paige v. Fairfield

668 A.2d 340 (Conn.1995).

■ KATZ, J.: The sole issue on appeal is whether trees and wildlife, independent of whether they have economic value, fall within the term "natural resources" as it is used in General Statutes § 22a–19 (a) and (b):

> Administrative proceedings. (a) In any administrative, licensing or other proceeding, and in any judicial review thereof made available by law, the attorney general, any political subdivision of the state, any instrumentality or agency of the state or of a political subdivision thereof, any person, partnership, corporation, association, organization or other legal entity may intervene as a party on the filing of a verified pleading asserting that the proceeding or action for judicial review involves conduct which has, or which is reasonably likely to have, the effect of unreasonably polluting, impairing or destroying the public trust in the air, water or other natural resources of the state.
>
> (b) In any administrative, licensing or other proceeding, the agency shall consider the alleged unreasonable pollution, impairment or destruction of the public trust in the air, water or other natural resources of the state and no conduct shall be authorized or approved which does, or is reasonably likely to, have such effect so long as, considering all relevant surrounding circumstances and factors, there is a feasible and prudent alternative consistent with the reasonable requirements of the public health, safety and welfare."

The record discloses the following undisputed facts. In July, 1991, the defendant Fairfield University (university) filed with the defendant Fairfield town plan and zoning commission (commission) an application to resubdivide a 13.41 acre wooded site into forty building lots along with an application for a special permit to excavate and fill the land. The plaintiffs, Anthony J. Paige and Candace D. Paige, who are property owners of lots that adjoin the subject property, filed a notice of intervention on behalf of the environment in accordance with § 22a–19 (a). They asserted a claim that approval of the application would have an adverse impact on the environment and that, therefore, the university was required to file alternative plans for the commission's consideration. Specifically, the plaintiffs alleged that because development of the subdivision would require clear-cutting of the subject acreage, the development would likely cause unreasonable pollution, impairment or destruction of the public trust in the air, water, wildlife and other natural resources of the state.

Further, the permit issued pursuant to the South Dakota act does not supersede permits required by state agencies; rather, a single, comprehensive application is submitted to all the state-level agencies. *See id.* at 49–41B–24.

[The commission approved the applications; the plaintiffs appealed, claiming that] as a result of the university's plan to clear-cut 13.4 acres of wooded area, the natural resources, in specific, the trees and wildlife that inhabit that area, would be destroyed. According to the plaintiffs, the commission acted "illegally, arbitrarily and in abuse of its discretion . . . by approving the . . . application without considering the proposed development's unreasonable destruction of a natural resource and by failing to consider feasible and prudent alternatives."

The plaintiffs argue that the narrow and restrictive definition of natural resources settled on by the Appellate Court[16] is in derogation of the Environmental Protection Act (act); General Statutes § 22a–1 et seq.; and the applicable Regulations of Connecticut State Agencies promulgated to support its enforcement. We agree that in virtually all statutory references to natural resources, the legislature painted with a broad brush. In view of the various legislative declarations, we conclude that natural resources must be viewed "in terms of values beyond the limited economic product value . . . [and that] a definition of natural resources for the purposes of § 22a–19 should not be restricted to a narrow economic product value standard, but should take into account the broader range of values envisioned by the legislative language." *Paige v. Town Plan & Zoning Commission, supra,* 35 Conn. App. at 670 (Schaller, J., dissenting).

The act, entitled "Environmental Protection Department and State Policy," proclaims as the broad policy behind its enactment: "The air, water, land and other natural resources, taken for granted since the settlement of the state, are now recognized as finite and precious. . . . Human activity must be guided by and in harmony with the system of relationships among the elements of nature. . . . The policy of the state of Connecticut is to conserve, improve and protect its natural resources and environment. . . ." General Statutes § 22a–1. Similarly, the broad policy language found in General Statutes § 22a–36, which defines inland wetlands and watercourses as natural resources, cautions that the destruction of such natural resources "will continue to imperil the quality of the environment thus adversely affecting the ecological, scenic, historic and recreational values and benefits of the state for its citizens now and forever more."

In promulgating regulations regarding its responsibilities, the department of environmental protection (department) has elaborated on what constitutes natural resources. Section 22a–1–1 of the Regulations of Connecticut State Agencies provides that "the department operates according to powers conferred in various titles of the General Statutes relating to management, protection and preservation of the air, water, land, wildlife and other natural resources of the state. . . ." This regulatory enumeration is consistent with the legislature's express reference to plants and wild animals as natural resources in General Statutes § 22a–6a (a), which provides that "such person shall also be liable to the state for the reason-

---

16. [Ed. note] The lower court held that trees and wildlife were natural resources only if they had "economic value," and that those in the case at bar had no such value.

able costs and expenses of the state in restoring the air, waters, lands and other natural resources of the state, including plant, wild animal and aquatic life to their former condition. . . .'' Equally consistent is the use of the term natural resources in General Statutes § 22a–342, which provides that the department, in deciding whether to grant a permit, must consider various factors including "the protection and preservation of the natural resources and ecosystems of the state, including but not limited to ground and surface water, animal, plant and aquatic life, nutrient exchange, and energy flow. . . .'' Therefore, where the legislature has chosen to specifically articulate what is meant by natural resources, it has included trees and wildlife and has given no indication that the term as used throughout the act should be afforded different meanings. Moreover, had the legislature intended the illustrative lists in § 22a–6a (a) or § 22a–342 to be limited to those particular statutes, it could have provided a definitional section within the act to control all the other statutes in which the term is used. *See Neptune Park Assn. v. Steinberg*, 138 Conn. 357, 362, 84 A.2d 687 (1951). The narrow reading of the term natural resources ascribed by the majority of the Appellate Court contradicts the specific illustrations of what the legislature has stated a natural resource includes as found in certain provisions of the act as well as the broad policy language found throughout the act.

Finally, in interpreting a statute, "the general terms will be construed to embrace things of the same general kind or character as those specifically enumerated." *State v. Russell*, 218 Conn. 273, 278, 588 A.2d 1376 (1991). As a natural resource, air, for example, has no traditional economic value because in and of itself it can neither be bought nor sold. Applying this rule of construction, otherwise known as ejusdem generis, because the specific terms of § 22a–19 enumerate resources without economic value, the general terms must be interpreted so as to include resources regardless of their lack of economic value.

Our analysis of legislative intent also takes into account circumstances surrounding the enactment of the provisions under scrutiny. Connecticut is not the only state to have enacted legislation to protect the environment and natural resources. Michigan, Massachusetts, Texas, Pennsylvania, Colorado and California had enacted similar legislation that was reviewed by the drafters of the Connecticut legislation before the adoption of the existing act.

Therefore, we conclude that there is no support for the economic value test in the language of the act, in its stated purpose or in its legislative history. Indeed, given the legislative history and policy of environmental law in Connecticut, the economic value test has little place in our environmental protection statutory scheme. To require a party under § 22a–19 (a) to prove that the state resources he or she is purportedly attempting to protect have economic value is inconsistent with and, indeed, detrimental to all expressed state and federal environmental policies.

It is clear that § 22a–19, consistent with the rest of the act, was intended, not as a mere impediment to developers, but rather as a means to protect the environment from unreasonable adverse impact. We acknowledge the defendants' concerns that residential and commercial development may be burdened as a result of our rejection of the economic value test. Furthermore, we recognize that the intent to balance the tensions of environmental interests with the interests of private landowners to use and develop their land was not ill-conceived.

We understand that it was an overriding fear that "consideration of alternatives pursuant to § 22a–19 (b) for every subdivision in the state"; *Paige v. Town Plan & Zoning Commission, supra*, 35 Conn. App. at 652; would be required that caused a majority of the Appellate Court to generate the narrow economic test. We believe, however, that those fears are unfounded. By requiring the commission to apply the reasonableness standard set forth in § 22a–19 (a), we do not anticipate a sudden influx of citizen intervenors in subdivision applications. Nor do we expect that alternative plans will be required in each case any more than if we were to adopt the economic test espoused by the Appellate Court. "By its plain terms, General Statutes § 22a–19 (b) requires the consideration of alternative plans only where the commission first determines that it is reasonably likely that the project would cause unreasonable pollution, impairment or destruction of the public trust in the natural resource at issue. *See Red Hill Coalition, Inc. v. Town Plan & Zoning Commission, supra,* . . . In view of the factors and standards that govern the determination in each case, any fear that a broad definition will cause alternative plans to be required in virtually every case is plainly unwarranted." (Emphasis in original.) *Paige v. Town Plan & Zoning Commission*, 35 Conn. App. at 672–73 (Schaller, J., dissenting).

Finally, the defendants argue that this case is controlled by *Red Hill Coalition, Inc. v. Town Plan & Zoning Commission*, supra, 212 Conn. 727. In that case, we held that prime agricultural land is not a natural resource under § 22a–19. Prime agricultural land is different from what is claimed to be a natural resource in this case. Prime agricultural land is a subcategory of land subject to human alteration that is kept barren of plant and animal life that would otherwise eventually live on it through natural succession. Agricultural land is not naturally occurring. Consequently, the concerns expressed by this court in *Red Hill Coalition, Inc.*, that including prime agricultural land within the reach of the act would lead to irrational results do not apply here.■

NOTES AND COMMENTS

1.   The Court cites with pride the fact that the state of Connecticut was highly rated in a study that compared the degree of environmental protection among the states. Is there an economic value associated with ratings of this sort? (Connecticut is one of the richest states in the country and has attracted many corporate headquarters, although not all parts of the state have shared this prosperity.)

2.   At the hearing on remand, what type of evidence would the applicant present in the proceedings before the Fairfield commission on the issue of whether the proposed development would unreasonably pollute, impair or destroy the public trust in natural resources? Does the court imply that the applicant must propose mitigation measures that would replace the natural resources that will be lost as a result of the subdivision? How should the issue of cumulative impact be addressed by the local commission?

3.   Would the European colonists who originally settled Connecticut have imagined that their descendants might someday attach a more important value to a patch of woods that to prime agricultural land? Does it matter what they would have thought? As the next excerpt shows, there is a good deal of disagreement today about the appropriate role of land in society.

Joseph L. Sax
Property Rights and the Economy of Nature: Understanding Lucas v. South Carolina Coastal Council

45 Stan. L. Rev. 1433, 1442–45 (1993).

[Professor Sax criticizes the Supreme Court's failure to take into consideration modern scientific knowledge about the relationship of land to the environment in which it is situated. The following (with footnotes omitted) is the heart of his argument:]

There are two fundamentally different views of property rights to which I shall refer as land in the "transformative economy" and land in the "economy of nature." The conventional perspective of private property, the transformative economy, builds on the image of property as a discrete entity that can be made one's own by working it and transforming it into a human artifact. A piece of iron becomes an anvil, a tree becomes lumber, and a forest becomes a farm. Traditional property law treats undeveloped land as essentially inert. The land is there, it may have things on or in it (e.g., timber or coal), but it is in a passive state, waiting to be put to use. Insofar as land is "doing" something—for example, harboring wild animals—property law considers such functions expendable. Indeed, getting rid of the natural, or at least domesticating it, was a primary task of the European settlers of North America.

An ecological view of property, the economy of nature, is fundamentally different. Land is not a passive entity waiting to be transformed by its landowner. Nor is the world comprised of distinct tracts of land, separate pieces independent of each other. Rather, an ecological perspective views land as consisting of systems defined by their function, not by man-made boundaries. Land is already at work, performing important services in its unaltered state. For example, forests regulate the global climate, marshes sustain marine fisheries, and prairie grass holds the soil in place. Transformation diminishes the functioning of this economy and, in fact, is at odds with it.

The ecological perspective is founded on an economy of nature, while the transformative economy has a technological perspective of land as the product of human effort. As Philip Fisher states in Making and Effacing Art: "At the center of technology is the human act of taking power over the world, ending the existence of nature; or, rather, bracketing nature as one component of the productive total system. The world is submitted to an inventory that analyzes it into an array of stocks and resources that can be moved from place to place, broken down through fire and force, and assembled through human decisions into a new object-world, the result of work."

For most of the modern era, the technological use of land has operated to end "the existence of nature." Land has been fenced, excluding wildlife so that it could instead support domesticated grazing animals, agriculture, and human settlements. As William Cronon has shown, a natural subsistence economy that supported indigenous people was systematically replaced by the farming and commercial economy of the European settlers. The property system was a central tool in effecting this transformation. The tension between Native Americans and the European settlers was a "struggle . . . over two ways of living . . . and it expressed itself in how two peoples conceived of property, wealth, and boundaries on the landscape." The settlers' property system invested proprietors with the right to sever natural systems to turn land to "productive" use. Thus, the transformative economy was built on the eradication of the economy of nature.

Even when people acknowledged the toll of development on natural resources, giving birth to the conservation movement in the nineteenth century, there was virtually no impact on the precepts of property law. The concerns of conservation were then largely aesthetic, and ecological understanding was limited. Exceptions existed, especially in understanding the adverse impact of timber harvesting on watersheds, but even as to forests, conservation was largely implemented on distant lands where public ownership prevailed. The principal aim of the early conservation movement was to set aside remote enclaves as public parks, forests, and wildlife refuges, where nature could be preserved while elsewhere the transforming business of society went on as usual.

The burst of concern for controlling industrial pollution also failed to propel nature's economy onto the legal agenda. Conventional pollution laws do not challenge the traditional property system. They do not demand that adjacent land be treated as part of a river's riparian zone nor that it be left to perform natural functions supportive of the river as a marine ecosystem. On the contrary, such laws assume that a river and its adjacent tracts of land are separate entities and that the essential purpose of property law is to maintain their separateness. Thus, they assume development of the land and internalization of the development's effects; they are effectively "no dumping" laws, under which the land and the river are discrete entities.

Benefits that adjacent lands and waters confer upon each other can, with rare exceptions, be terminated at the will of the landowner, because the ecological contributions of adjacent properties are generally disregarded in defining legal rights. For example, if riparian uplands are the habitat for river creatures that come on shore to lay their eggs, landowners are perfectly free to destroy that habitat while putting the land to private use— even though doing so harms the river and its marine life. The existence of such connections between property units was not unknown (though certainly much more is currently known about their importance); rather, until recently society assumed that the termination of natural systems in favor of systems created by human effort was a change for the better. In addition, when significant ecological losses did occur, people believed that the losses could be compensated through technological means. Therefore, landowners developed upstream lands that, in their natural state, had absorbed flood waters. The adverse effects of too much waterflow on downstream lands were either tolerated or replaced technologically, as with flood control dams. Finally, when dams were built, states tried to replace instream losses with fish hatcheries.

Although these differences between the attitudes of the two economies are easy to distinguish in theory, no absolutely firm lines of demarcation exist in either historical experience or legal regimes. Certainly some ecological functions have been recognized and protected by the law. For example, lands adjacent to refuges have been closed to hunting in recognition of the habitat that the land provides for migrating birds. Many situations, however, cannot be definitively categorized as premised on the transformational economy or the economy of nature. In addition, a restriction might serve two quite different functions. For example, timber harvesting near a river's edge is sometimes regulated to prevent siltation of the river. Such regulation might be viewed as either a protection of natural transboundary services, with trees holding soil in place, or an anti-dumping law, where the migration of soil is treated as a consequence of the harvesting, tantamount to a forester jettisoning soil into the river. Similarly, a restriction on building in a flood plain might be viewed as a demand of the economy of nature, preserving the habitat of the protected area, or as a restriction designed to promote human safety by keeping workers and residences out of a hazardous area in the event of a storm. In the same manner, the maintenance of open space could be characterized as either a service in the economy of nature or a limitation on transformation, guided by congestion concerns or aesthetic preferences. These restrictions defy easy classification, but ultimately, for purposes of this analysis, no such classification is needed. It is only necessary to acknowledge the existence of two very different views of what land is and what purposes each view serves.

Viewing land through the lens of nature's economy reduces the significance of property lines. Thus a wetland would be an adjunct of a river, in service to the river as a natural resource. Beach dune land would be the frontal region of a coastal ecosystem extending far beyond the beach itself. A forest would be a habitat for birds and wildlife, rather than simply a discrete tract of land containing the commodity timber. Under such a view the landowner cannot justify development by simply internalizing the effect of such development on other properties. Rather, the landowner's desire to do anything at all creates a problem, because any development affects the delicate ecosystem which the untouched land supports. In an economy of nature the landowner's role is perforce custodial at the outset, before the owner ever transforms the land. Moreover, the object of the custody generally extends beyond the owner's legally defined dominion. The notion that land is solely the owner's property, to develop as the owner pleases, is unacceptable.

This emerging ecological view generates not only a different sense of the appropriate level of development, but also a different attitude towards land and the nature of land ownership itself. The differences might be summarized as follows:

TRANSFORMATIVE ECONOMY	ECONOMY OF NATURE
Tracts are separate. Boundary lines are crucial.	Connections dominate. Ecological services determine land units.
Land is inert/waiting; it is a subject of its owner's dominion.	Land is in service; it is part of a community where single ownership of an ecological service unit is rare.
Land use is governed by private will; any tract can be made into anything. All land is equal in use rights (Blackacre is any tract anywhere).	Land use is governed by ecological needs; land has a destiny, a role to play. Use rights are determined by physical nature (wetland, coastal barrier, wildlife habitat).
	The line between public and private is blurred where maintenance of ecological service is viewed as an owner's responsibility.
Landowners have no obligations.	Landowners have a custodial, affirmative protective role for ecological functions.
Land has a single (transformative purpose).	Land has a dual purpose, both transformative and ecological.
The line between public and private is clear.	The line between public and private is blurred where maintenance of ecological service is viewed as an owner's responsibility.

NOTES AND COMMENTS

1. Are the *Florida Power* and *Paige* cases based on laws that proceed from the underlying assumption of a transformative economy or an economy of nature? Does the economy of nature assume (1) that there is a natural condition of the land, and (2) that ecology counsels that changes in that natural condition are presumptively undesirable? Or can the economy of nature encompass the understanding that natural conditions change over

time? Professor Sax is often cited as one of the leaders of a new "green property" movement. For other examples, *see*: Eric T. Freyfogle, Boundless Lands: Envisioning a New Land Ethic, Island Press, 1998; J. Peter Byrne, Green Property, 7 Const. Comm. 239 (1990); Terry W. Frazier, Protecting Ecological Integrity within the Balancing Function of Property Law, 28 Envtl. L. 53 (1998).

2.   In reading the excerpt from the following case, consider whether the agency is interpreting the relevant statute from the perspective of the transformative economy or the economy of nature:

> The Vermont Environmental Board denied the application of Southview Associates for a permit to build a residential development in Stratton, Vermont. The Board based its decision on the finding that the proposed project failed to meet the requirements of Act 250 criterion 8 pertaining to "necessary wildlife habitat." 10 V.S.A. § 6086(a)(8)(A). Southview proposed to build a 33–lot subdivision for vacation homes on 88 acres of land, situated in a "deeryard" comprising some 280–320 acres. The Board found that, although Stratton once contained 600 acres of deeryard, the 280–320 acre area is the only "active deeryard" in a 10.7–square-mile region. It supports approximately 20 deer over the winter. The deeryard contains two significant areas of mature softwood cover, which is critical deer wintering habitat. One of these areas covers approximately half of the Southview property. The Board found that the softwood stand on the Southview property is necessary to the deer population. The development, it found, would destroy ten acres of this critical habitat, with likely secondary effects in a larger area. Southview submitted a Wildlife Management Plan to mitigate the loss of the ten acres by increasing available deer food and encouraging the growth of immature softwood to replace the cover lost to the development. The Board found, however, that increased food supply would only partially mitigate the adverse effect of the development on the deer, as availability of browse is less important to the deer's survival than good softwood cover, which provides shelter from winter elements and reduces heat loss by radiation. Also, it is critical to the deer population's survival during winter that the deer do not exhaust their fat reserves. Increased physical activity due to the presence of humans, pets, and vehicles would consume these reserves more rapidly. The Board concluded: "As a result of the development, it is likely that there will be a loss of deer in this habitat. It is likely that the deer will abandon the remaining cover altogether and those that remain will be less likely to survive due to the high potential of stress created by wintertime noise and activity from people, vehicles, and pets." The Board concluded further "that the environmental and recreational loss to the public from the destruction and imperilment of the habitat is not outweighed by the economic, social, cultural, recreational or other benefit to the public from the project." Nor did Southview, in the Board's opinion, employ "all feasible and reasonable means of preventing or lessening the destruction and imperilment of the deer habitat." Finally, the Board could not

exclude "the possibility of less intensive development in other areas of the site." The Act 250 permit was accordingly denied.

If you were the attorney for Southview Associates, what arguments would you make in response to the decision. As attorney for the state, how would you respond to Southview's arguments? *See In re Southview Associates*, 153 Vt. 171, 569 A.2d 501 (1989) and *Southview Associates v. Bongartz*, 980 F.2d 84 (2d Cir. 1992), *cert. denied* 507 U.S. 987 (1993).

3.   The management of the national forests by the United States Forest Service has been the focus of highly contentious issues including the implications of clear-cutting on ecological balance. One of the key battlegrounds is long-running litigation relating to the management of national forests in Eastern Texas. The following is an excerpt from an opinion of U.S. District Judge Richard A. Schell of the Eastern District of Texas in this litigation, *Sierra Club v. Glickman*, 974 F.Supp. 905 (E.D.Tex.1997).:

> The Sierra Club, Texas Committee on Natural Resources ("TCONR"), and The Wilderness Society (collectively "Plaintiffs") brought this action challenging the United States Forest Service's management of the National Forests in Texas. The Texas Forestry Association and Southern Timber Purchasers Council (collectively "Timber Intervenors") have intervened. The broad issue before the court is whether the Forest Service is complying with the National Forest Management Act ("NFMA"), 16 U.S.C. §§ 1600–14 and related regulations, 36 C.F.R. § 219.1–.29 (hereinafter "NFMA regulations" or "regulations"). The NFMA and regulations generally require: (1) diversity of plant and animal communities as well as tree species, (2) protection of key resources, and (3) inventorying and monitoring for key resources, diversity, and effects of management activities. Considering the evidence adduced at trial, legal argument of counsel, and the parties' respective proposed findings of fact and conclusions of law, the court is of the opinion that the Forest Service has stepped outside its discretion and acted arbitrarily and capriciously with respect to (1) protecting the key resources of soil and watershed and (2) inventorying and monitoring the wildlife resource, forest diversity, and whether the Forest Service is meeting its objectives and adhering to standards and guidelines with respect to wildlife.

> With respect to the soil resource, the evidence shows that the Forest Service's management activities are causing severe soil erosion and loss of essential organic matter. This loss of soil and organic matter substantially and permanently affects the productivity of the land. Without rich forest soil, plant and animal communities suffer as well as the forest land's ability to produce healthy timber stands. With respect to the watershed resource, Forest Service management practices are causing substantial and permanent (1) erosion within waterways, (2) deposit of soil, silt, and sedimentation in waterways, and (3) disruption of water run-off. Additionally, the Forest Services' practice of permitting timber harvesting in streamside management zones exacerbates the erosion and sedimentation problems and causes the

deposit of logging debris in streams. This derogation of the streams (1) destroys plant, animal, and fish habitat and (2) contributes to flooding.

With respect to the Forest Service's inventorying and monitoring obligations, the Forest Service is not collecting population data on wildlife to ensure viable populations. The Forest Service instead is relying on hypothetical models to assess habitat capability and then assuming that viable populations of species are in existence and well-distributed on the forest land. The Forest Service's failure to collect population data forecloses its ability to evaluate forest diversity in terms of wildlife and to adequately determine the effects of its management activities. The Forest Service's failure to adequately inventory and monitor may be causing permanent and substantial damage to the productivity of the land. Sufficient inventorying and monitoring of forest resources is vital to making sound, forest-management decisions and ultimately protecting the forest resources from permanent impairment. In light of the Federal Defendants' noncompliance with the NFMA and regulations, the court will enjoin certain timber harvesting activities until the Forest Service demonstrates compliance "on-the-ground."

For a discussion of this type of litigation, *See* Oliver A. Houck, On the Law of Biodiversity and Ecosystem Management, 81 Minn. L. Rev. 869, 915–920 (1997).

F.   SUSTAINABLE DEVELOPMENT

Implicit in most of our programs to preserve the natural environment is the idea that we want future generations to be able to have an ability to benefit from that environment in the same way that we have. We want to be able to develop our natural resources, but to do so in a way that does not permanently destroy them. The term for this process is "sustainable development."

Currently, the idea that sustainable development should be both a national and world-wide objective seems to have a great deal of support. In general, the concept of sustainable development means that we should utilize our resources, including our energy resources, in a manner that can be continued indefinitely without making future generations worse off than we are today. *See generally* John C. Dernbach, Sustainable Development as a Framework for National Governance, 49 Case W. Res. L. Rev. 1 (1998).

Some commentators have suggested that the reason that the concept of sustainable development is popular because it is capable of being interpreted in so many different ways that almost any interest group can argue that their position is consistent with sustainability. Sanford E. Gaines, Rethinking Environmental Protection, Competitiveness and International Trade, 1997 U. Chi. Legal F. 231, 232 (1997).[17] Even so, however, the concept has

---

17.   For an interesting study of the way the term "sustainability" is being interpreted in practice, *see* Environmental Law Institute, Sustainability in Practice (1999).

focused beneficial attention on both the current and long range distributional effects of resource policies, which has led to the useful reexamination of many traditional programs.

1. INTERGENERATIONAL EQUITY

The "sustainable development" terminology arose out of the desire to harmonize the objectives of the early environmental movement of the 1970s with the aspirations of third world nations that were seeking to improve their economies. These countries often listened suspiciously to the rhetoric of environmental groups and thought they heard the elite of the prosperous countries trying to keep the developing countries from catching up by denying them a role in the industrialization that caused that prosperity.

The huge differences in the standard of living among the various countries gave credence to that argument. The United States symbolizes to many in the developing countries the kind of a rich country that they might someday become. American exhortations about the importance of environmental protection were particularly resented by those who thought that Americans could far more easily forego a measure of economic advancement than could poorer countries. So the inequality of the current distribution of resources has weakened the effectiveness of the environmental argument.

On the other hand, intergenerational distributional arguments apply as effectively to poor nations as to rich nations. If Zambia uses up its resources today, what will its children have tomorrow?

A United Nations commission chaired by former Prime Minister Bruntland of Norway came out with a report that focused on the concept of sustainable development as one that would be acceptable to both the developed and developing nations. It emphasized that development was good, as long as it was done in a way that did not lead to deprivation for future generations. World Commission on Environment and Development, Our Common Future (United Nations 1987). The Commission defined sustainable development as "development that meets the needs of the present without compromising the ability of future generations to meet their own needs." *Id.* at 43. The mainstream environmental organizations lent their support, and sustainable development soon became a widely accepted objective.[18]

Although the term "sustainability" has a modern ring, the idea behind it has been the official government policy in the United States for most of the last century. The early European settlers of America thought the country's resources were so extensive that there was no need to worry about exhausting them, but with the disappearance of the white pine

---

18. Not all environmental theorists would support the concept. Advocates of "deep ecology" think that it is too accommo- dating to development. Some people in the extractive industries, on the other hand, consider it too restrictive.

forests and the bison towards the end of the nineteenth century, it became apparent that even a large country could exhaust its resources.

Theodore Roosevelt was the leader of a "conservation" movement that became official government policy when he took office. Under his leadership, conservation became defined as "foresight and restraint in the exploitation of the physical sources of wealth as necessary for the perpetuity of civilization and the welfare of present and future generations." Sean Dennis Cashman, America in the Age of the Titans 78 (N.Y.U. Press, 1988). He promoted sustained yield management of the national forests and soil conservation by farmers as part of a long-range conservation strategy. Most of his successors continued to honor conservation as a national objective, although they varied in the importance they placed on it.[19]

Although conservation has usually been a well-accepted national objective in the United States, its implementation has produced numerous distributional controversies. When exploitation of resources is postponed, jobs that would otherwise have been created are lost. To people who are trained in lumbering or mining, for example, the economic impact of these losses is immediate and severe. Sympathy for their circumstances has often modified conservation policies that otherwise might have been adopted.

The modern objective of sustainable development echoes Theodore Roosevelt's policy:

> In a sustainable economy, the fish catch does not exceed the sustainable yield of fisheries, the amount of water pumped from underground aquifers does not exceed aquifer recharge, soil erosion does not exceed the natural rate of new soil formation, tree cutting does not exceed tree planting, and carbon emissions do not exceed the capacity of nature to fix atmospheric CO2. A sustainable economy does not destroy plant and animal species faster than new ones evolve.

Lester Brown et. al., State of the World 1999 15–16 (W.W. Norton, 1999). But modern science and technology have expanded the possibilities of sustainability in ways that Roosevelt's generation could not have anticipated. *See generally* J. B. Ruhl, Sustainable Development: A Five–Dimensional Algorithm for Environmental Law, 18 Stan. Env. L. J. 31 (1999).

2.   INDUSTRIAL ECOLOGY

One outgrowth of the new focus on sustainable development has been increasing attention to the efficient use of energy and other resources in modern industrial processes. Can the principles of the science of ecology be applied beyond the workings of the natural world to help analyze processes of human origin?

---

19. The exception was President Reagan, who appointed an Interior Secretary who was a member of a religious sect that believed the end of the world would occur within a generation and that there was no point in worrying about the welfare of people yet unborn. He led the administration to expand the exploitation of mineral and forest resources on public lands to a degree that caused considerable public outcry. *See* Chapter Six for further discussion of the results.

Clinton J. Andrews
Putting Industrial Ecology Into Place: Evolving Roles for Planners

65 APA Journal 364 (1999).

... A good metaphor expresses complex ideas in neat shorthand, and may become a potent political symbol. "Silent Spring," "Spaceship Earth," and "Gaia" are historical examples from environmental planning and policy. In the last decade, the "industrial ecology" metaphor has gained prominence among environmental researchers and practitioners.

In 1989 physicist Robert Frosch, former NASA chief and then head of research at General Motors (GM), and his GM colleague Nicholas Gallopoulos contributed an article on strategies for manufacturing to a special issue of Scientific American on "Managing Planet Earth." In this article they proposed that firms employ a new type of engineer called an industrial ecologist, arguing that "wastes from one industrial process can serve as the raw materials for another, thereby reducing the impact of industry on the environment". They applied the ecosystem metaphor and observed that the industrial "food web" included many diverse organisms and had room for more. Prescriptively, they called for more physical integration of industrial processes to channel waste materials into closed reuse and recycling loops, more flexible enforcement of hazardous waste handling laws to encourage such loop closing, and more reliance on economic incentives to align pollution reduction and profit maximizing goals.

The phrase "industrial ecology" immediately caught the imagination of many in industry and academia. In early 1991, the consulting firm Arthur D. Little published an environmental agenda for industry based on the industrial ecology concept. Later in 1991, scientists at AT&T Bell Labs organized a colloquium on industrial ecology at the U.S. National Academy of Sciences. This multidisciplinary effort explored many possible interpretations of the industrial ecology metaphor, and for the first time added the perspective of economics to the mix.

In 1992, the multi-agency U.S. Global Change Research Program sponsored 50 researchers in a 2–week summer institute on industrial ecology, inspired more by the work of Ayers on industrial metabolism than by the metaphorizing of Frosch and Gallopoulos. This meeting added significant depth to the field, beginning a synthesis of big-picture research on materials and energy flows with the life-cycle design concern of firms and the pollution prevention objectives of governments. Papers presented at this institute formed the basis for one of the field's first books.

The U.S. National Academy of Engineering ran a series of workshops on technology and the environment that focused on industrial ecology from 1992 onwards. The AT&T Foundation began sponsoring industrial ecology faculty fellowships in 1993; these eventually migrated to successor firms and the U.S. National Science Foundation. The Journal of Industrial Ecology produced its first issue in early 1997. In 1998 the first Gordon Research Conference on industrial ecology was held, as were a variety of policy-oriented worships, including one co-hosted by the President's Council on Environmental Quality. In short, industrial ecology began to acquire some of the trappings of legitimacy as a field of scientific inquiry.

Meanwhile, skeptics also emerged. The heavy involvement of industry in promoting the field made some environmentalists suspicious. Were the calls for regulatory flexibility really calls for regulatory relief? Was the focus on the innovative firm warranted, given that most firms were still reactive foot draggers? Did the field ignore the deeper environmental problems of consumerism, advanced industrial capitalism, and dependence on fossil fuels? Was it all an exercise in "greenwashing"?

Yet even the skeptics agree that the young field of industrial ecology has produced a range of valuable insights. Most are associated with particular materials or industrial sectors. Materials accounting studies have shown that the grand nutrient cycles (global flows of elements crucial to life, including carbon, nitrogen, sulfur and phosphorus) are being transformed: Human flows now exceed natural flows in the global nitrogen cycle, for example. Accounts for heavy metals such as lead and cadmium show that uses such as paint or fuel additives, which dissipate materials widely, endanger humans and ecosystems, and that metal concentrations in mining wastes are often higher than in mined ores. Those studying specific industrial sectors have typically followed the environmental impacts of a product through its life cycle and across all environmental media. Such studies inform product design decisions, such as plastic versus paper cups and electric versus gasoline-powered cars. Much less work has been done on management and policy issues at the sectoral and subnational levels.

From the discussion above, we can distill a working definition of industrial ecology. Industrial ecology takes a systems view of the use and environmental impacts of materials and energy in industrial societies. It employs the ecological analogy in several ways, including analysis of materials flows. It takes a cue from nature by espousing material and product life-cycle management through the parallel paths of better design, reuse, remanufacturing, and recycling. It operates under the premise that because industry is perhaps society's most significant environment actor for bad and good, it should be the focus of analysis. Industrial ecology takes a longer-term perspective than most environmental management approaches and seeks to understand the full picture rather than only the snippets defined by political expedience. . . . ■

NOTES AND COMMENTS

1. An example of the economic by-products of industrial ecology occurred when a study of silver poisoning in San Francisco Bay determined that the silver was coming from a solvent used to fix x-ray images in hospitals and dental offices. The study prompted the creation of a recycling facility to recover silver from waste fixer that produces annual revenues of over $200,000. Jocelyn Kaiser, Turning Engineers into Resource Accountants, 285 Science 685, 686 (July 30, 1999).

2.   The Yale School of Forestry and Environmental Studies web page supports and complements the Journal of Industrial Ecology, published by MIT Press, www.yale.edu/jie.

3.   Although interest in industrial ecology is increasing, many industries have ignored this approach. Should the government be taking steps to promote industrial ecology? What approach would be most successful?

3.   RENEWABLE ENERGY RESOURCES

Sustainable development of energy resources is easiest if the resources are "renewable." The extent to which energy resources are renewable depends on the time scale you use. The sun itself will presumably fade gradually over millions of years. Uranium and related minerals usable as fuel for nuclear power might be exhausted in a few millennia. Coal resources will apparently last for a century or more. Oil and natural gas, however, may have a life span measured in decades at current rates of use.

In today's terminology, renewable energy resources have come to be defined as resources that can be utilized without any discernable reduction in their future availability. Since medieval times, inventors have constantly been searching for cheaper and more reliable sources of renewable energy. The "perpetual motion machine" became a standing joke at the patent office. But modern technology has made the prospect of renewable energy more realistic than before, though still far from broad public acceptance.

Renewable energy resources are often classified into two basic categories: (a) cool resources, which can produce energy without being burned; and (2) hot resources, which require combustion.

a.   COOL RENEWABLES

Solar energy, discussed in Section B of this chapter, is the prototype of a cool renewable energy resource. (This may seem odd given the heat of the sun's rays, but that heat means that solar energy does not have to be burned and is thus classified as a cool resource.) Increasing development of small scale solar energy sources has made such energy available for a wide range of uses where relatively small amounts of energy are needed in remote locations, such as camp stoves, communications satellites, highway sign lighting, and pocket calculators.

Windpower has become one of the most economical sources of renewable energy in windy parts of the world. Huge farms of windmills with blades exceeding 100 feet in length are used to generate electricity. Although these facilities are not without their adverse impacts on wildlife and noise levels, the use of windpower for electricity generation has been growing at a rate of about 25% per year.

Geothermal energy is another cool renewable resource. In those limited locations in which underground steam produces hot springs or geysers, this steam can be used for electric generation. It is generally believed, however, that all of the locations in the United States where it would be practical to harness geothermal energy have already been exploited.

Deepwater energy is an experimental form of renewable energy that has interested many people. Two forms have been the subject of various test projects: (a) tidal power plants, if located in areas where there is a big range in the tides, could be built to operate on the energy generated by the tidal movement; and (b) convection plants, which would build up a circulation of cold deep water that could be used to cool buildings. The City of Toronto is building such a plant that will use water from the lower levels of Lake Ontario.

Ocean resources provide renewable energy in other ways as well. Fish meal and guano from sea birds are common sources of energy-producing fertilizer. At one time whale oil was thought to be a renewable resource, but overuse so depleted the population of whales that it was abandoned as a commercial product.

Hydropower is by far the largest source of cool renewable energy currently being used. Water stored behind dams is released to turn turbines that generate electricity. Because of the extensive environmental impacts of these facilities, however, they are often controversial. The topic of hydropower is the subject of Chapter Four.

Hydrogen-powered fuel cells are currently the form of cool renewable technology that is attracting the most attention.

> Fuel cells use an electrochemical process that combines hydrogen and oxygen, producing water and electricity. Avoiding the inherent inefficiency of combustion, today's top fuel cells are roughly twice as efficient as conventional engines, have no moving parts, require little maintenance, are silent, and emit only water vapor. Unlike today's power plants, they are nearly as economical on a small scale as on a large one. Indeed, they could turn the very notion of a power plant into something more closely resembling a home appliance.

Brown *et. al., supra,* at 28–29. Whether this assessment is overly optimistic remains to be seen.

b.   HOT RENEWABLES

Among the so-called hot renewable resources, the term "biomass" is used to include a wide variety of plant materials that can be burned to provide energy. In primitive regions, wood is often still used as a primary source of energy. Is wood a renewable resource? It is if used in moderation and accompanied by effective replanting of trees. In many poor regions, however, the wood is being depleted faster than it is being replaced.

The burning of waste vegetation from agricultural crops is also a potential energy source that is beginning to be utilized commercially. In tropical climates, for example, sugar cane fields convert solar energy to biomass at very high rates. When the sugar is extracted, the remainder of the plant has traditionally been burned. If this combustion can be converted to electricity it would be renewable as long as the soil would continue to produce crops.[20]

Cogeneration is the term most often used to describe processes that take advantage of heat needed for other purposes to produce electric energy. Many lumber and paper mills, for example, burn the wood chips that are a waste product of their own processes to generate electricity to run the mill.

Municipal solid waste is another source that can be burned to produce electricity in cogeneration facilities. As long as society continues to generate waste this source can be assumed to be renewable. Cogeneration is discussed in Chapter Ten.

Most renewable energy resources that we have discovered are both diffuse, that is, thinly scattered; and sporadic, that is, variable over time. The sun doesn't shine reliably everywhere and all the time, nor does the wind always blow. The availability of hydropower is limited to certain locations and varies with the amount of rainfall. Environmentalists recognize, therefore, that most renewable resources need to be backed up by facilities that use fossil fuel resources.

> Running a modular energy system on renewable resources will require adapting the system to their intermittent nature. A temporary measure might be to build backup generators using efficient gas turbines, fuel cells, or pumped water storage; new technologies such as compressed air, plastic batteries, flywheels, and other energy storage devices also have parts to play.

Brown *et. al., supra* at 30. This lack of what the electric industry calls dispatchability (*i.e.,* the ability to count on being able to dispatch the power to meet demand at any given time) is the biggest handicap for renewable resources. The high cost of capital investment to build plants that produce dispatchable power to back up the unreliable renewable sources remains a major disincentive to the use of renewables in the electricity industry. And the siting procedures with which renewable power plants must comply are no simpler than those for other power plants, and renewable plants often face greater scrutiny because of their novelty. Robert D. Kahn, Siting Struggles: The Unique Challenge of Permitting Renewable Energy Power Plants, 13 Electricity Journal #2 (March 2000).

Nevertheless, there has been a dramatic increase in the extent of private sector investment in research and development of renewable power sources. Major oil and auto companies and electric utilities all have put significant capital into a wide variety of renewable technologies. The possibility of a more sustainable energy economy in the future is beginning to seem a little less like an environmentalists' pipe dream. For a cogent analysis of the major laws affecting renewable power, see Suedeen G. Kelly, Alternative Energy Sources, in James E. Hickey, Jr. et. al., Energy Law and Policy for the 21st Century, Ch. 13 (Rocky Mountain Mineral Law Foundation, 2000).

---

20. Of course the agricultural produce itself is a very important source of energy in the form of food. The "calories" by which we measure our diet are simply units of energy.

4.   THE ECONOMICS OF THE FUTURE

Classical economists recognized that sustainability had a value, but not a very high value. In particular, four elements of economic theory weighed heavily against the importance of sustainability. First, any value that would take place in the future was discounted on the assumption that people would prefer goods now rather than later. Second, the exploitation of natural resources was deemed to be pure gain, ignoring the fact that the resource might be being depleted by the exploitation. Third, it was assumed that if any particular kind of goods or services became scarce and therefore expensive, some substitute would enter the market to replace it. Fourth, it was assumed that each consumer in a free market would always make the decision that maximized her particular values.

a.   DISCOUNT RATES

Discount rates are well accepted tools in financial planning. If you won a million dollars on a lottery, and you were given the choice of taking the full amount now or taking a hundred thousand a year for the next ten years, you would obviously want to take the full amount.[21] But what if the alternative was to take a hundred thousand for twelve years, giving you a total of a million, two hundred thousand? How would you determine what was the most prudent choice?

If you had the million in hand, you could invest it in interest bearing securities and draw down a hundred thousand a year while the interest was accumulating on the remainder. If the interest rate was eight percent, and you drew out a hundred thousand at the beginning of each year, your money would accumulate as follows:

Year	year-end balance
1	972,000
2	941,760
3	909,101
4	873,829
5	835,735
6	794,594
7	750,161
8	702,174
9	650,347
10	594,374
11	533,924
12	468,637

Obviously, if you knew that the interest rate would remain at eight percent for the next twelve years you would want to take the million dollars all at once, because you could invest it and draw down a hundred thousand dollars for twelve years and still have almost half your money left.

---

21. Income tax considerations would, of course, also enter into the financial planning   calculations.

Let us assume, however, that the rate of interest over the next twelve years was going to be only three percent. Which option would be better at that rate?

Year	year-end balance
1	927,000
2	851,810
3	774,364
4	694,595
5	612,432
6	527,805
7	440,639
8	350,858
9	258,375
10	163,126
11	65,019

At a three percent interest rate, if you drew out a hundred thousand dollars at the beginning of each year you would not have enough left to draw out that amount in the twelfth year. Therefore, the option of receiving a hundred thousand dollars a year for twelve years would have been preferable to the option of taking a lump sum up front.

This exercise simply illustrates that the value of future financial benefits depends greatly on the assumptions one makes about the rate of income one can generate on investments while waiting for the future to arrive. Since any such prediction is largely guesswork, no one assumes that calculations such as these are anything but rough guides to financial strategy. But even with conservative interest rate assumptions, one thing is clear: if you carry the calculations out for the length of a generation or more the present value of future benefits is reduced to insignificance.[22] Or as the famous British economist Lord Keynes observed, "in the long run we are all dead."

Consequently, if you accept the classical assumption that everyone wants their benefits as soon as possible, the value of sustainability disappears rapidly as the future years pass. This makes sense insofar as financial benefits are concerned, but what about environmental values? We would like to know that the Everglades would be restored to its natural condition, but how important is it to see it happen right away? Do discount rates make sense in this context? Do we "enter a paradoxical world where we are discouraged from spending present money to provide a distant discounted benefit." Jeffrey M. Gaba, Environmental Ethics and Our Moral Relationship to Future Generations, 24 Colum. J. of Envtl. L. 249, 269 (1999).

Could a good argument be made "for a zero discount rate in decisions taken on behalf of society at large since society, unlike the individual, is

22. The formula for determining the present value of any sum of money to be received in the future is as follows: If i is the assumed annual interest rate, expressed as a decimal, the present value of x dollars to be received in n years from now is $x/(1+i)n$. Thus at an assumed interest rate of 5.5%, the present value of a hundred thousand dollars to be received 30 years from now is about $3,160.

quasi-immortal"? Won't the "wants of future generations" be "just as immediate to them as ours are to us"? Robert Costanza & Herman E. Daly, Natural Capital and Sustainable Development, 6 Conservation Biology 37, 45 (1992). These issues are being intensely debated in the academic literature, as Richard Revesz points out:

Perhaps the two most influential perspectives on what obligations to future generations are encompassed by the principle of sustainable development are those of Edith Brown Weiss and Robert Solow, which are rooted in the traditions of international law and of economics, respectively. Weiss equates sustainable development with intergenerational equity, which she defines by reference to three principles. First, the principle of conservation of options requires each generation to preserve the natural and cultural resource bases so that the options available to future generations are not unduly restricted. Second, the principle of conservation of quality requires each generation to prevent a worsening of the planet's environmental quality. Third, the principle of conservation of access requires each generation to provide its members with equitable rights of access to the legacy of past generations, and to conserve this access for the benefit of future generations.

In contrast, according to Solow, sustainability requires that each future generation have the means to be as well off as its predecessors. He gives content to this principle by proposing a modification to the traditional measure of a nation's economic activity. From Net National Product (NNP)—Gross Domestic Product (GDP) minus the depreciation of fixed capital assets—he would subtract the value of expended nonrenewable resources and environmental assets like clean air and water. Solow argues that each generation must use its nonrenewable and environmental resources in a way that does not detract from the ability of future generations to have a similar standard of living. He admits that certain unique and irreplaceable resources, like certain national parks, should be preserved for their own sake, but maintains that the consumption of non-unique natural and environmental resources ought to be permissible as long as they are replaced by other resources such as equipment or technological knowledge.

The two formulations share important characteristics. First, they define the primary obligation to future generations in terms of a constraint that specifies how much must be left to a subsequent generation. Second, Weiss and Solow would both allow some level of destruction of most natural resources, as long as future generations are compensated in an other way, such as by technological development. Third, they both regard certain natural resources as irreplaceable and would require that such resources be protected for subsequent generations.

In essence, then, under both formulations, every generation must provide the subsequent generation with the means to do at least as well as it did. So, for example, sustainable development would be consistent with the current generation seeking to maximize its own utility, as long as this maximization is subject to a constraint resulting from the need to leave sufficient resources to future generations.

There are, of course, daunting challenges ahead in providing further specificity to the principle. For example, additional work needs to be done to determine how to value the increase in knowledge or the negative long-term environmental effects of economic activity. Also, throughout history, there has been a progressive increase in standards of living. Should the constraint defining one generation's obligation to its successors thus provide for a progressive increase in well-being, so that this pattern may continue? On what basis would that increase be determined? What would be the ethical underpinnings for such a requirement?

Moreover, the link between sustainable development and population policy is not well articulated. The population in any generation is a function of decisions of prior generations. For example, one might argue that if the current generation's actions were to lead to an increase in population, it would have an obligation to provide additional resources so as not to imperil the level of well-being of an average person in the next generation.

Richard L. Revesz, Environmental Regulation, Cost–Benefit Analysis, and the Discounting of Human Lives, 99 Colum. L. Rev. 941 (1999), citing Edith Brown Weiss, Intergenerational Equity: A Legal Framework for Global Environmental Change, in Environmental Change and International Law: New Challenges and Dimensions 385 (Edith Brown Weiss, ed., 1991), and Robert Solow, An Almost Practical Step Toward Sustainability, 19 Resources Policy 162 (1993).[23]

b. DEPLETION

Depletion is another concept that gave classical economists difficulty. If a storekeeper has a stock of a thousand widgets and sells five hundred, she must recognize that she now has five hundred fewer widgets left to sell. Economists and accountants have always recognized that the use of manufactured products depleted the existing inventory.

But there was no such recognition in the case of natural resources. In defining gross national product, the traditional measure of an economy's output, classical theory assumed that any natural resources that were produced were pure gain once the cost of production was subtracted. The fact that there were now fewer natural resources left to be produced was ignored. In other words, no allowance was made for depletion. *See* William D. Nordhaus & Edward C. Kokkelenberg, eds., Nature's Numbers: Expanding the National Economic Accounts to Include the Environment (National

---

23. For other points of view on this important issue, *see* Daniel A. Farber & Paul A. Hemmersbaugh, The Shadow of the Future: Discount Rates, Later Generations, and the Environment, 46 Va. L. Rev. 267 (1993); Lisa Heinzerling, Discounting Our Future, 34 Land & Water L. Rev. 39 (1999); John J. Donohue, III, Why We Should Discount the Views of Those Who Discount Discounting, 108 Yale L. J. 1901 (1999).

Academy Press, 1999). *See also* Joy Hecht, Accounting for the Environment: New Directions for the United States, 14 Natural Resources & Environment 179 (2000).

Ignoring depletion made sense for certain types of calculation, but it seems to defy common sense as long range planning. Daniel H. Cole, What Is the Most Compelling Environmental Issue Facing the World on the Brink of the Twenty–First Century: Accounting for Sustainable Development, 8 Fordham Envt'l L.J. 123 (1996). The classic example is the nation of Nauru, which consists of a single island in the Pacific covered with a thick layer of phosphate that is quite valuable for fertilizer. The people of Nauru debated whether they should mine and sell this phosphate for a good price, eventually leaving them with a barren and useless island that would have to be abandoned. They chose to do so, but to put most of the proceeds in a trust to be invested so that when the phosphate was depleted they would still have its equivalent in other investments. This made sense according to classical economic theory,[24] but as the former citizens of Nauru rapidly lose their homeland they are increasingly questioning the "equivalence" of their investments. John W. Gowdy & Carl N. McDaniel, The Physical Destruction of Nauru, 75 Land Economics 333 (1994).

In recent years there has been intense interest in the reform of economic accounts to better reflect depletion of natural resources. Frances Cairncross, who served as the first environmental editor of *The Economist*, points out that such reforms are a prerequisite if these accounts are to be wisely used by policymakers:

> The main argument for trying to keep track of how economic activity affects the government is that, as management consultants like to say, what is not measured does not happen. Governments that learn to measure economic achievement purely in terms of GNP may make awful mistakes. The more dependent their economies are on natural resources, the worse those mistakes may be.

Frances Cairncross, Costing the Earth: The Challenge for Governments, the Opportunities for Business 40–41 (Harvard Business School Press, 1992). In addition to the National Research Council's work cited above, the Organization for Economic Cooperation and Development is developing a framework for environmental indicators. Organization for Economic Cooperation and Development, Toward Sustainable Development: Environmental Indicators (1998).

c. SUBSTITUTION

Substitution is perhaps the most troublesome of classical economic concepts for many people, not just the Nauruans. The concept of substitution is basically a simple one that we have all observed in practice. If a product becomes scarce, causing the price to rise, many people will choose

24. The Hartwick rule of classical economics says that consumption of exhaustible resources may be held constant if the proceeds deriving from the use of the resources are invested in reproducible capital.

to acquire a substitute product instead if it can provide an equivalent satisfaction at a lower price.

For example, when the housing market in Silicon Valley became tight and prices went through the roof, many people bought cheaper homes in Modesto and endured the long commute. As wild salmon became scarce and expensive, people began to buy the cheaper but relatively tasteless farmed product called euphemistically "Atlantic Salmon." If Coca Cola doubled its price, even confirmed Coke drinkers might switch to Pepsi.

No one doubts that substitution takes place. To classical economists, however, it is simply the natural operation of the market with no negative connotations. They simply assume away any problems by adopting the assumption that technological change can offset any limits to growth that might be associated with a finite supply of natural resources. *See, e.g.,* Robert M. Solow, Resources and Growth, 68 Amer. Econ. Rev. 5 (1978). If you hanker for wild salmon or a house in Silicon Valley, your nostalgia is simply a personal "taste" and thus does not deserve to be considered in economic calculations. As Robert Ayres puts it, "economists have preferred not to examine the concept of technological substitution too closely." Robert U. Ayres, Resources, Environment, and Economics 45 (John Wiley & Sons, 1978). *See also* Daniel S. Levy and David Friedman, The Revenge of the Redwoods; Reconsidering Property Rights and the Economic Allocation of Natural Resources, 61 U. of Chi. L. Rev. 493, 499–502 (1994).

Technology has undoubtedly provided us with substitutes for many resources that became scarce in the past. When whale oil declined it was replaced by petroleum derivatives. The niche formerly occupied by bison has been taken over by carefully hybridized cattle. Opportunities to hike in the wilderness are giving way to theme parks with virtual wilderness rides. To the classical economist this was simply progress, but today many people sense that progress may imply losses of ecological stability and resilience that deserve consideration. And people worry about the assumption that technology will always find a substitute for anything.

Not all economists today are blind adherents to classical theories, of course. A wide range of creative scholarship by economists and scientists from a variety of disciplines has addressed the perplexing issues related to declining resources and increasing waste. The relatively new field of ecological economics is devoted to such efforts.

> The environmental resource base upon which all economic activity ultimately depends includes ecological systems that produce a wide variety of services. This resource base is finite. Furthermore, imprudent use of the environmental resource base may irreversibly reduce the capacity for generating material production in the future. All of this implies that there are limits to the carrying capacity of the planet. It is, of course, possible that improvements in the management of resource systems, accompanied by resource-conserving structural changes in the economy, would enable economic and population growth to take place despite the finiteness of the environmental resource base, at least for some period of time. However, for that to be even conceiva-

ble, signals that effectively reflect increasing scarcities of the resource base need to be generated within the economic system.

[One] useful index of environmental sustainability is ecosystem resilience, [which] is a measure of the magnitude of disturbances that can be absorbed before a system centered on one locally stable equilibrium flips to another. Economic activities are sustainable only if the life-support ecosystems on which they depend are resilient.... The loss of ecosystem resilience is potentially important for at least three reasons. First, the discontinuous change in ecosystem functions as the system flips from one equilibrium to another could be associated with a sudden loss of biological productivity, and so to a reduced capacity to support human life. Second, it may imply an irreversible change in the set of options open both to present and future generations (examples include soil erosion, depletion of groundwater reservoirs, desertification, and loss of biodiversity). Third, discontinuous and irreversible changes from familiar to unfamiliar states increase the uncertainties associated with the environmental effects of economic activities.

If human activities are to be sustainable, we need to ensure that the ecological systems on which our economies depend are resilient. The problem involved in devising environmental policies is to ensure that resilience is maintained, even though the limits on the nature and scale of economic activities thus required are necessarily uncertain.

Kenneth Arrow *et. al.*, Economic Growth, Carrying Capacity, and the Environment, 268 Science 520 (April 28, 1995).

d. CONSUMER SOVEREIGNTY

Many ecological economists suggest that one of the basic tenets of classical economics, the principle of consumer sovereignty, will need to be modified if economics is to be able to deal with the real world that ecologists recognize rather than with a world of assumptions. Economists have traditionally tried to avoid making value judgments by adopting the assumption that people always make wise decisions about what is in their self interest, although they recognize that in a world of imperfect information this assumption is unrealistic. A modern school of behavioral economics tries to use scientific biology and psychology as a springboard to better understanding of economic decisions. *See* Cass Sunstein, ed., Behavioral Law and Economics (Cambridge University Press, 2000).

Nevertheless, some classical economists still argue forcefully that democracy is threatened if outside experts superimpose their value judgments on those of individual. On the other hand, the ecologists ask, "what if the collective individuals are like lemmings headed for a cliff?"

If a self-regulating economic system is to be ecologically sustainable, it should serve a set of consumption and production objectives that are themselves sustainable. But this runs up against a principle of consumer sovereignty that privileges the existing preferences and technologies. If existing preferences and technologies are not ecologically sustainable, then consumer sovereignty implies system instability. This leaves these options: regulate activity levels within the existing structure of preferences, or change that structure of preferences, or both. The appropriate instruments—whether price manipulation, education, changes to property rights, etc.—will vary depending on institutional and other characteristics . . .

Mick Common & Charles Ferrings, Towards an ecological economics of sustainability, 6 Ecological Economics 7, 31 (July, 1992).

Michael Pollan uses the issue of urban sprawl[25] as an example of why he began to question the traditional economic theory of consumer sovereignty. "The free-market think tanks spewed forth studies arguing that sprawl doesn't really exist or that, if it does, . . . the free market has given Americans exactly what their spending decisions say they want. And yet many of us—or maybe I should say some part of most of us—are dismayed by the landscape and traffic that our own dollars and desires have wrought. That's why it is possible both to deplore the arrival of a new Home Depot in my area and also to shop there." Classical economists "would have you believe that the real me, the only one that finally matters, is the shopping me—the consumer; the deploring me should be dismissed as a sentimentalist or elitist or hypocrite."

> Until now, that's been the general view on sprawl, one I've bought into myself. But it overlooks a complicated truth about modern life that conservatives would have us forget. It is that although we are consumers, we are not only consumers, but parents and neighbors and citizens too. The sort of world we bring into being with our dollars does not necessarily match the world we would vote for with our hearts, and one of the things politics is good for is to help us bring those worlds into a more pleasing alignment. What a radical idea.

Michael Pollan, The Way We Live Now: Land of the Free Market, New York Times Magazine, July 11, 1999. *See also* Daphna Lewinsohn–Zamir, Consumer Preferences, Citizen Preferences and the Provision of Public Goods, 108 Yale L.J. 377 (1998).

The basic dilemma posed by these issues pervades almost every aspect of energy policy and will reappear throughout this book. To what extent should government make value judgments for people because its experts are smarter than the rest of the people? It is not a question that deserves a simplistic answer.

---

25. Urban sprawl, discussed in Chapter Fifteen, refers to the low-density, automobile- dependent pattern of land development that has become standard in the United States.

CHAPTER 3

THE CONCEPT OF A PUBLIC UTILITY

Outline of Chapter:
A. Historical Origins
    1. The English Common Law
    2. The Classic American Cases
B. Regulatory Objectives
    1. Natural Monopoly
    2. Price Regulation
C. The Role of the Public Service Commission
D. Limitations on Regulation
    1. Constitutional Limitations
    2. Statutory and Other Jurisdictional Limitations

Public utilities are often privately owned. Yet, historically public utilities have been controlled by different economic and legal expectations than other privately owned businesses. Today, statutes and regulations largely determine the definition of, and benefits and burdens that attach to, public utilities, but the concept of the public utility has a rich history in the common law. Even in the modern so-called "age of statutes," these common law principles are of importance in determining whether certain energy businesses meet the definition of a public utility. More important, common law principles are of relevance in determining the extent of benefits and burdens for modern public utilities. This chapter will provide a basic introduction to the history of these principles in American law, their economic rationales, and their modern analogs.

A. HISTORICAL ORIGINS

Regulation of ferries, sewers, mills, bridges and railroads provide the historical origins for modern public utility regulation. Although sometimes these were government owned and operated, in many, if not most, instances they were privately-owned in England and early America. Looking to the historical examples, can you identify aspects of these business services that differ from other private businesses, such as farming, calculator manufacturing, or hotel and restaurant operation?

1. THE ENGLISH COMMON LAW

Humphry W. Woolrych,
A Treatise on the Law of Waters and Sewers 108–09
(London, W. Benning 1830).

In ancient times, before the necessaries and conveniences of life were supplied in such profusion as at present, it became important to the settlers in and inhabitants of different districts, that they should have free access to some mill for the purpose of grinding their corn. This easement was indispensable, because they required, in the first instance sustenance for their families; and in some cases there might have been an obligation to grind the lord's wheat for his use. Lords of manors, therefore, for the purpose of meeting this exigency, erected mills on their respective domains for the public advantage; but they fettered their gift with this condition that the inhabitants and residents within their respective seignories should bring their corn to be ground at the mill so built up; and this custom, which thus had a reasonable commencement, was called doing suit to the mill. Consequently, whether the millers to whom the respective lords conceded these advantages, make their claim by prescription, which supposes a grant from the lords, or by custom, it seems clear, that this old practice arose originally from a sense of general convenience; and in so strong a point of view does this seem to have been considered, that a man might have claimed the suit by prescription, even from the villeins of a stranger.

In process of years, however, when commerce began to spread, and new erections were prospering on every side, many of the tenants and inhabitants, whose ancestors had derived benefit from the ancient mills, began to employ their own particular workmen, and the old millers found themselves deserted by degrees by those whose duty it was to have continued their support. They were, therefore, necessitated to seek redress, and the writ of *secta ad molendinum,* or *secta molendini,* was the ordinary remedy which they employed upon those occasions. The enforcing of this writ, which is now superseded by the modern action on the case, brought back the inhabitants to the suit and service which they owed.

Again, on the other hand, the millers would sometimes stretch their prerogative too far; and not content with the suit of the tenants and neighbours, would endeavour to lay claim to a more extensive limit than they ought, and thus it was that they were now and then defeated upon actions brought on the one side or the other to try the validity of their customs; or they would even trespass on the rights of the inhabitants, and instead of confining themselves to the usual demand of having all the corn ground at their mills which should be afterwards used in the family, they strove to include within their custom all the corn sold or spent in the neighborhood. This, being an unreasonable custom, was rejected by the courts.■

Tripp v. Frank
100 Eng. Rep. 1234 (1792).

This was an action on the case, wherein the plaintiff declared, that he was possessed of South Ferry, over the Humber; and that the defendant wrongfully carried persons and cattle from Kingston upon Hull to Barton, and other parts of the coast, whereby the plaintiff was injured in his right to his ferry, and lost his tolls.... At the trial before Buller, J. at the last assizes for York, it appeared that the defendant, who was the owner of a market-boat at Barrow, had carried over persons. . . . from Kingston upon Hull to Barrow, to which place they were going, and which lies two miles lower down the Humber than Barton, upon the same coast. It was shown that there was a daily ferry between Kingston and Barton, but none to any other part of the Lincolnshire coast. A verdict was taken for the plaintiff of 1 shilling with liberty for the defendant to enter a nonsuit in case the Court should be of opinion that the plaintiff was not entitled to recover under these circumstances.

[Plaintiff's counsel argued] that if the conduct of the defendant could be justified in this instance, it would render a right of ferry perfectly nugatory. Every person then, by going a little to the right or left of the usual track of the ferry, may equally avoid the ferry: but that would annihilate the right itself. Ferries in general must have some considerable extent upon which their right may operate, otherwise the exclusive privilege would be of no avail. . . . The owners of ferries are bound at their peril to supply them for the public use; and are therefore fairly entitled to preserve the exclusive advantage arising from them. But they admitted, on a question being asked by the Court, that the ferryman was not compellable to provide boats to any place on the Lincolnshire coasts besides Barton.

■ LORD KENYON, CH.J.—It seems to me that the evidence does not support this action. If certain persons wishing to go to Barton had applied to the defendant, and he had carried them at a little distance above or below the ferry, it would have been a fraud on the plaintiff's right, and would be the ground of an action. But here these persons were substantially, and not colourably merely, carried over to a different place; and it is absurd to say that no person shall be permitted to go to any other place on the Humber than that to which the plaintiff chooses to carry them. It is now admitted that the ferryman cannot be compelled to carry passengers to any other place than Barton: then his right must be commensurate with his duty.

■ ASHHURST. J.—The plaintiff's claim is so unreasonable, that it cannot be supported. According to his argument, if a passenger wishes to cross over from Kingston to the Lincolnshire coast three miles eastward, he must necessarily be first carried to Barton, where he would be many miles distant from his place of destination; whereas, if it were not for this ferry, he might go over directly. But the admission which the counsel have made is decisive against the plaintiff.

■ BULLER, J.—The question here is, what right the plaintiff has established by evidence; and that extends only from Hull to Barton, and back again. The question of fraud might arise in this way; by saying that, though the defendant really meant to go to Barton, he went in fraud of the plaintiff's claim a little above or below the ferry. But in this case the defendant had no intention of going to Barton: his place of destination was Barrow, at the distance of two miles from Barton; to which place the plaintiff's right does not extend, and to which he says he is not compellable to go.

■ GROSE, J. of the same opinion.

Rule discharged.■

NOTES AND COMMENTS

1. The feudal system in England allowed the monarchy and the aristocracy to grant themselves and their friends a wide range of privileges. These frequently included the privilege of operating some type of business, such as a flour mill or a ferry, on a monopoly basis—no competition allowed. *See* Matthew Hale, Prerogatives of the King (edited for the Selden Society by D.E.C. Yale, 1976). The courts tempered these privileges by requiring the monopolist to serve all potential customers that requested service.

Consider the following account of the duty to serve in American law:

> [T]he common law duty to serve is as ancient as the Anglo–American concept of equality and, indeed, predates the equal protection language of the federal Constitution by more than seven hundred years of conscious judicial effort. The veneration of the equality norm ... can be traced to the writings of Henry de Bracton, legal counselor to Henry III. Here we first discover the judge-created concept that, at a fundamental level of social organization, all persons similarly situated in terms of need have an enforceable claim of equal, adequate, and nondiscriminatory access to essential services; in addition, this doctrine makes such access largely a governmental responsibility....

> The founding of the American Republic coincided with a second great upheaval ...—the Industrial Revolution. The energy harnessed by Watt transformed the law as it remade the industrial world. Turnpike interests may have doomed the steam coaches, or "teakettles," which sought to traverse conventional road surfaces, but this triumph stamped upon them new obligations to the public. The railroads then emerged as the focus of legal and ideological struggles concerning the duty to serve, much as even now their tracks often divide the more from the less desirable parts of town....

> The emergence of legislative action, and even dominance in railway affairs, did not undercut the doctrine of the duty to serve. The courts remained the prophets of the equality norm. In fact, the appearance of state and, with the 1887 Interstate Commerce Act, federal regulatory legislation meant the enhancement—not eclipse—of the common law duty to serve, as the new branch of government drew on common law precedents for its regulatory activities.

Charles M. Haar & Daniel W. Fessler, The Wrong Side of the Tracks 21–23 (Simon & Schuster 1986). This requirement still plays an important role in American law today: the common law "duty to serve" is presumed to apply to any charter or franchise from the government to operate as a monopoly. *See* Jim Rossi, The Common Law "Duty to Serve" and Protection of Consumers in an Age of Competitive Retail Public Utility Restructuring, 51 Vand. L. Rev. 1233 (1998). Today, however, the nature and extent of the duty is often spelled out in statutes and regulations, and the company often charges customers for the cost of extending service to remote areas. *See, e.g., Deerfield Estates, Inc. v. Township of East Brunswick*, 286 A.2d 498 (N.J.1972).

2. Whenever the government grants someone a monopoly to provide a particular service, the definition of the extent of the monopoly becomes an issue. The problem addressed by the court in *Tripp v. Frank* commonly occurs today in the context of increasing urbanization or technological advancements. For example, when a city expands into formerly rural areas, does the company that provided service to the city automatically expand its territory too? Or does the company that provided service to the rural area retain that privilege? *See, e.g., City of Wichita v. State Corporation Commission*, 592 P.2d 880 (Kan.1979).

3. During the seventeenth and eighteenth centuries, the power of the English crown diminished. Following the "glorious revolution" of the seventeenth century, parliament became the supreme power in the English government. *See* Christopher Hill, The Century of Revolution, 1603–1714 (New York, Norton, rev. ed. 1980). The result was the loss of privilege for many of the old monopolists whose powers were granted by the king. The term "monopoly" began to carry connotations of decadence. *See* Vernon A. Mund, Open Markets: An Essential of Free Enterprise (Harper 1948).

2. THE CLASSIC AMERICAN CASES

In America, the basic common law concepts, such as the duty to serve, were endorsed by most state courts. One of the early issues courts were required to address during the early industrial age was whether the grant of a monopoly franchise guaranteed the monopolist protection against later entrants. The U.S. Supreme Court spoke to the issue in the classic *Charles River Bridge* case in 1837. Today, the case and the principles it stands for remain of great importance; we will return to them in several later chapters.

The Proprietors of the Charles River Bridge v. The Proprietors of the Warren Bridge

36 U.S. 420 (1837).

■ TANEY, J.: [In 1785], a petition was presented to the legislature, by Thomas Russell and others, stating the inconvenience of the transportation by ferries, over Charles river, and the public advantages that would result from a bridge; and praying to be incorporated, for the purpose of erecting a bridge in the place where the ferry between Boston and Charlestown was then kept. Pursuant to this petition, the legislature, on the 9th of March 1785, passed an act incorporating a company, by the name of "The Proprietors of the Charles River Bridge," for the purposes mentioned in the petition. Under this charter, the company were empowered to erect a bridge, in "the place where the ferry was then kept;" certain tolls were granted, and the charter was limited to forty years from the first opening of the bridge for passengers; and from the time the toll commenced, until the expiration of this term ... and at the expiration of the forty years, the bridge was to be the property of the commonwealth [of Massachusetts].

The bridge was accordingly built, and was opened for passengers on the 17th of June 1786. In 1792, the charter was extended to seventy years from the opening of the bridge; and at the expiration of that time, it was to belong to the commonwealth.

In 1828, the legislature of Massachusetts incorporated a company by the name of "The Proprietors of the Warren Bridge," for the purpose of erecting another bridge over Charles river. This bridge is only sixteen rods, at its commencement, on the Charlestown side, from the commencement of the bridge of the plaintiffs; and they are about fifty rods apart, at their termination on the Boston side.

The Warren bridge, by the terms of its charter, was to be surrendered to the state, as soon as the expenses of the proprietors in building and supporting it should be reimbursed; but this period was not, in any event, to exceed six years from the time the company commenced receiving toll.

The bill, among other things, charged as a ground for relief, that the act for the erection of the Warren bridge impaired the obligation of the contract between the commonwealth and the proprietors of the Charles River bridge; and was, therefore, repugnant to the constitution of the United States.

In the argument here, it was admitted, that since the filing of the supplemental bill, a sufficient amount of toll had been reserved by the proprietors of the Warren bridge to reimburse all their expenses, and that the bridge is now the property of the state, and has been made a free bridge; and that the value of the franchise granted to the proprietors of the Charles River bridge, has by this means been entirely destroyed.

The plaintiffs in error insist [t]hat the acts of the legislature of Massachusetts, of 1785 and 1792, by their true construction, necessarily implied, that the legislature would not authorize another bridge, and especially, a free one, by the side of this, and placed in the same line of travel, whereby the franchise granted to the "Proprietors of the Charles River Bridge" should be rendered of no value.

The act of the legislature of Massachusetts, of 1785, by which the plaintiffs were incorporated ... is the grant of certain franchises, by the public, to a private corporation, and in a matter where the public interest is concerned. The rule of construction in such cases is well settled, both in England, and by the decisions of our own tribunals. In the case of the *Proprietors of the Stourbridge Canal v. Wheeley and others*, 2 B. & Ad. 793, the court say, "the canal having been made under an act of parliament, the rights of the plaintiffs are derived entirely from that act. This, like many other cases, is a bargain between a company of adventurers and the public, the terms of which are expressed in the statute; and the rule of construction in all such cases, is now fully established to be this—that any ambiguity in the terms of the contract, must operate against the adventurers, and in favor of the public, and the plaintiffs can claim nothing that is not clearly given them by the act."

Borrowing, as we have done, our system of jurisprudence from the English law; and having adopted, in every other case, civil and criminal, its rules for the construction of statutes; is there anything in our local situation, or in the nature of our political institutions, which should lead us to depart from the principle, where corporations are concerned? We think not; and it would present a singular spectacle, if, while the courts in England are restraining, within the strictest limits, the spirit of monopoly, and exclusive privileges in nature of monopolies, and confining corporations to the privileges plainly given to them in their charter, the courts of this country should be found enlarging these privileges by implication and construing a statute more unfavorably to the public, and to the rights of community, than would be done in a like case in an English court of justice.

Adopting the rule of construction above stated as the settled one, we proceed to apply it to the charter of 1785, to the proprietors of the Charles River bridge. This act of incorporation is in the usual form, and the privileges such as are commonly given to corporations of that kind. It confers on them the ordinary faculties of a corporation, for the purpose of building the bridge; and establishes certain rates of toll, which the company are authorized to take: this is the whole grant. There is no exclusive privilege given to them over the waters of Charles river, above or below their bridge; no right to erect another bridge themselves, nor to prevent other persons from erecting one, no engagement from the state, that another shall not be erected; and no undertaking not to sanction competition, nor to make improvements that may diminish the amount of its income. Upon all these subject, the charter is silent; and nothing is said in it about a line of travel, so much insisted on in the argument, in which they are to have exclusive privileges.

Can such an agreement be implied? The rule of construction before stated is an answer to the question: in charters of this description, no rights are taken from the public, or given to the corporation, beyond those which the words of the charter, by their natural and proper construction, purport to convey.

Indeed, the practice and usage of almost every state in the Union, old enough to have commenced the work of internal improvement, is opposed to the doctrine contended for on the part of the plaintiffs in error. Turnpike roads have been made in succession, on the same line of travel; the later ones interfering materially with the profits of the first. These corporations have, in some instances, been utterly ruined by the introduction of newer and better modes of transportation and traveling. In some cases, railroads have rendered the turnpike roads on the same line of travel so entirely useless, that the franchise of the turnpike corporation is not worth preserving. Yet in none of these cases have the corporation supposed that their privileges were invaded, or any contract violated on the part of the state. The absence of any such controversy, when there must have been so many occasions to give rise to it, proves, that neither states, nor individuals, nor corporations, ever imagined that such a contract could be implied from such charters.

And what would be the fruits of this doctrine of implied contracts, on the part of the states, and of property in a line of travel, by a corporation, if it would now be sanctioned by this court? To what results would it lead us? If it is to be found in the charter to this bridge, the same process of reasoning must discover it, in the various acts which have been passed, within the last forty years, for turnpike companies. If this court should establish the principles now contended for, what is to become of the numerous railroads established on the same line of travel with turnpike companies; and which have rendered the franchises of the turnpike corporations of no value? Let it once be understood, that such charters carry with them these implied contracts, and give this unknown and undefined property in a line of traveling; and you will soon find the old turnpike corporations awakening from their sleep, and calling upon this court to put down the improvements which have taken their place. The millions of property which have been invested in railroads and canals, upon lines of travel which had been before occupied by turnpike corporations, will be put in jeopardy. We shall be thrown back to the improvements of the last century, and obliged to stand still, until the claims of the old turnpike corporations shall be satisfied; and they shall consent to permit these states to avail themselves of the lights of modern science, and to partake of the benefit of those improvements which are now adding to the wealth and prosperity, and the convenience and comfort, of every other part of the civilized world.

The judgment of the supreme judicial court of the commonwealth of Massachusetts, dismissing the plaintiffs' bill, must, therefore, be affirmed, with costs.

■ Story, J., dissenting: [W]ith a view to induce the court to withdraw from all the common rules of reasonable and liberal interpretation in favor of grants, we have been told at the argument, that this very charter is a restriction upon the legislative power; that it is in derogation of the rights and interests of the state, and the people; that it tends to promote monopolies and exclusive privileges; and that it will interpose an insuperable barrier to the progress of improvement. Now, upon every one of these propositions, which are assumed, and not proved, I entertain a directly opposite opinion; and if I did not, I am not prepared to admit the conclusion for which they are adduced. If the legislature has made a grant, which involves any or all of these consequences, it is not for courts of justice to overturn the plain sense of the grant, because it has been improvidently or injuriously made.

But I deny the very ground-work of the argument. This charter is not any restriction upon the legislative power; unless it be true, that because the legislature cannot grant again, what it has already granted, the legislative power is restricted. If so, then every grant of the public land is a restriction upon that power; a doctrine, that has never yet been established, nor (so far as I know) ever contended for. Every grant of a franchise is, so far as that grant extends, necessarily exclusive; and cannot be resumed or interfered with.

Then, again, how is it established, that this is a grant in derogation of the rights and interests of the people? No individual citizen has any right to build a bridge over navigable waters; and consequently, he is deprived of no right, when a grant is made to any other persons for that purpose....

The erection of a bridge may be of the highest utility to the people. It may essentially promote the public convenience, and aid the public interests, and protect the public property. And if no persons can be found willing to undertake such a work, unless they receive in return the exclusive privilege of erecting it, and taking toll; surely, it cannot be said, as of course, that such a grant, under such circumstances, is, per se, against the interests of the people.

Again, it is argued, that the present grant is a grant of a monopoly, and of exclusive privileges; and therefore, to be construed by the most narrow mode of interpretation.

There is great virtue in particular phrases; and when it is once suggested, that a grant is of the nature or tendency of a monopoly, the mind almost instantaneously prepares itself to reject every construction which does not pare it down to the narrowest limits. It is an honest prejudice, which grew up, in former times, from the gross abuses of the royal prerogatives; to which, in America, there are no analogous authorities. But what is a monopoly, as understood in law? It is an exclusive right, granted to a few, of something which was before of common right. Thus, a privilege granted by the king for the sole buying, selling, making, working or using a thing, whereby the subject, in general, is restrained from that liberty of manufacturing or trading, which before he had, is a monopoly.

No sound lawyer will, I presume, assert that the grant of a right to erect a bridge over a navigable stream is a grant of a common right. It was neither a monopoly; nor, in a legal sense, had it any tendency to a monopoly. It took from no citizen what he possessed before; and had no tendency to take it from him. It took, indeed, from the legislature the power of granting the same identical privilege or franchise to any other persons. But this made it no more a monopoly, than the grant of the public stock or funds of a state for a valuable consideration.

But it has been argued, and the argument has been pressed in every form which ingenuity could suggest, that if grants of this nature are to be construed liberally, as conferring any exclusive rights on the grantees, it will interpose an effectual barrier against all general improvements of the country. This is a subject upon which different minds may well arrive at different conclusions, both as to policy and principle. For my own part, I can conceive of no surer plan to arrest all public improvements, founded on private capital and enterprise, that to make the outlay of that capital uncertain and questionable, both as to security and as to productiveness. No man will hazard his capital in any enterprise, in which, if there be a loss, it must be borne exclusively by himself; and if there be success, he has not the slightest security of enjoying the rewards of that success, for a single moment. If the government means to invite its citizens to enlarge the public comforts and conveniences, to establish bridges, or turnpikes, or canals, or railroads, there must be some pledge, that the property will be safe; that the enjoyment will be co-extensive with the grant; and that success will not be the signal of a general combination to overthrow its rights and to take away its profits. And yet, we are told, that all such exclusive grants are to the detriment of the public.

But if there were any foundation for the argument itself, in a general view, it would totally fail in its application to the present case. Here, the grant, however exclusive, is but for a short and limited period, more than two-thirds of which have already elapsed; and when it is gone, the whole property and franchise are to revert to the state. The legislature exercised a wholesome foresight on the subject; and within a reasonable period, it will have an unrestricted authority to do whatever it may choose, in the appropriation of the bridge and its tolls. There is not, then, under any fair aspect of the case, the slightest reason to presume that public improvements either can, or will, be injuriously retarded by a liberal construction of the present grant.

In order to entertain a just view of this subject, we must go back to that period of general bankruptcy, and distress and difficulty. The constitution of the United States was not only not then in existence, but it was not then even dreamed of. The union of the states was crumbling into ruins, under the old confederation. Agriculture, manufactures and commerce were at their lowest ebb. There was infinite danger to all the states, from local interests and jealousies, and from the apparent impossibility of a much longer adherence to that shadow of a government, the continental congress.

This is not all. It is well known, historically, that this was the very first bridge ever constructed, in New England, over navigable tide-waters so near the sea. The rigors of our climate, the dangers from sudden thaws and freezing, and the obstructions from ice in a rapid current, were deemed by many persons to be insuperable obstacles to the success of such a project. . . .

Now, I put it to the common sense of every man, whether if, at the moment of granting the charter, the legislature had said to the proprietors; you shall build the bridge; you shall bear the burdens; you shall be bound by the charges; and your sole reimbursement shall be from the tolls of forty years: and yet we will not even guaranty you any certainty of receiving any tolls; on the contrary; we reserve to ourselves the full power and authority to erect other bridges, toll or free bridges, according to our own free will and pleasure, contiguous to yours, and having the same termini with yours; and if you are successful, we may thus supplant you, divide, destroy your profits, and annihilate your tolls, without annihilating your burdens: if, I say, such had been the language of the legislature, is there a man living, of ordinary discretion or prudence, who would have accepted such a charter, upon such terms?

But it is said, if this is the law, what then is to become of turnpikes and canals? Is the legislature precluded from authorizing new turnpikes or new canals, simply because they cross the path of the old ones, and incidentally diminish their receipt of tolls? The answer is plain. Every turnpike has its local limits and local termini; its points of beginning and of end. No one ever imagined, that the legislature might grant a new turnpike, with exactly the same location and termini. That would be to rescind its first grant. And the opinion of Mr. Chancellor Kent, and all the old authorities on the subject of ferries, support me in the doctrine.

But then again, it is said, that all this rests upon implication, and not upon the words of the charter. What objection can there be to implications, if they arise from the very nature and objects of the grant? If it be indispensable to the full enjoyment of the right to take toll, that it should be exclusive within certain limits, is it not just and reasonable, that it should be so construed? ... If the public exigencies and interests require that the franchise of Charles River bridge should be taken away, or impaired, it may be lawfully done, upon making due compensation to the proprietors.

I maintain, that, upon the principles of common reason and legal interpretation, the present grant carries with it a necessary implication, that the legislature shall do no act to destroy or essentially to impair the franchise; that (as one of the learned judges of the state court expressed it) there is an implied agreement that the state will not grant another bridge between Boston and Charlestown, so near as to draw away the custom from the old one; and (as another learned judge expressed it) that there is an implied agreement of the state to grant the undisturbed use of the bridge and its tolls, so far as respects any acts of its own, or of any persons acting under its authority. . . .

Upon the whole, my judgment is, that the act of the legislature of Massachusetts granting the charter of Warren Bridge, is an act impairing the obligation of the prior contract and grant to the proprietors of Charles River bridge; and, by the constitution of the United States, it is, therefore, utterly void. I am for reversing the decree to the state court (dismissing the bill); and for remanding the cause to the state court for further proceedings, as to law and justice shall appertain.■

Stanley I. Kutler,
Privilege and Creative Destruction:
The Charles River Bridge Case

(Lippincott 1971).

On Bunker Hill Day, 1786, residents of Boston and Charlestown gathered to celebrate their new fortune. At last the two areas were linked by a bridge across the Charles River. Technical skills and entrepreneurial resources, encouraged by the state, had mastered formidable barriers to construct the span. While men had envisioned such a bridge for nearly a century, the costs and physical hazards always made it a risky proposition. But in 1785 the Massachusetts legislature granted a charter to a group of Charlestown businessmen who assumed the risks in exchange for a forty-year guarantee of tolls. With the bridge's completion a year later, the proprietors and townspeople alike could well congratulate themselves on their happy circumstance. There was a steady and sizable flow of goods and persons between the two towns. In place of the old and unreliable ferry, and despite the tolls, communications now were faster and cheaper. And with the successful engineering feat, the proprietors knew that their bridge would continue to provide them with lucrative profits.

Six years later the state extended the charter for another thirty years. The proprietors almost immediately realized their anticipated profits, and then some; by 1814, stock in the corporation sold for over $2,000 per share, up more than 600 percent from the original price.

But in December 1828 there was new cause for rejoicing among some of the townspeople and businessmen, but certainly not among the proprietors and their friends. It was then that a second Charlestown bridge was completed. Overriding the proprietors' claims for exclusive privileges, the Massachusetts legislature had chartered the Warren Bridge Corporation in March 1828 to construct a new bridge nearly adjacent to the existing facility, terminating on the Charlestown side less than ninety yards from the Charles River Bridge. The new company could charge the same tolls as the old, but with a six-year time limit, after which its bridge was to revert to the Commonwealth and become a free avenue.

Constitutional rhetoric and considerations of public policy dominated the controversy over a new bridge. The advocates of a free bridge insisted that the state had never bartered away its right to charter competing franchises, and that the state retained the power to provide improvements for public necessities. In response, the proprietors argued that their charter guaranteed them a vested and exclusive right that could be abrogated only upon the payment of proper compensation. Constitutional principles aside, the antagonists pitched their battle lines around competing views of the state's public policy role. The proponents of a free bridge contended that charter rights should be strictly construed so that privilege would not hamper opportunity or the pressing needs of the community. The Charles River Bridge supporters maintained that the state must scrupulously respect existing titles and interpret their rights liberally in order to ensure a favorable investment climate for future private enterprises.

Defeated in the legislature, the proprietors turned to the courts in defense of their rights. First, in 1828, they sought an injunction from the state supreme court to prevent the completion of the bridge. Daniel Webster and Lemuel Shaw, their distinguished counsel, argued that the Charles River Bridge charter granted exclusive privileges to the corporation, and therefore the legislative act of 1828 impaired the obligation of the contract and was repugnant to the federal constitution. They further contended that the chartering of a new bridge destroyed the tolls—in effect, the property—of the old structure and thus constituted the taking of private property for public use without compensation, in violation of the Massachusetts constitution. The court refused to grant the injunction, however, primarily because of the proprietors' ambiguous claims to exclusive rights. The state court subsequently heard the case on its merits, but in January 1830 dismissed the complainants' bill. The proprietors immediately appealed to the United States Supreme Court.

The Charles River Bridge case was first argued in Washington in 1831, with John Marshall presiding. Despite a determined effort by Justice Joseph Story to secure a judgment for the Charles River Bridge proprietors, the Supreme Court divided on the issue. Subsequent absences and vacancies prevented a decision by the Marshall Court before the Chief Justice's death in 1835. After the appointment of his successor; Roger B. Taney, and before a fully constituted bench, the case was reargued in January 1837. The Court's opinion followed the next month. A clear majority of the Court sustained the state's action and denied the appeal of the proprietors. For Justice Story it was a sad occasion, symbolizing in his mind the evil days that had come upon the court and the law he revered. "With a pained heart, and subdued confidence," Story found himself almost alone as "the last of the old race of judges." . . . .

The Charles River Bridge case had much more at stake than a relatively petty local dispute over a new, free bridge. The Warren Bridge was a symbol for the rapid technological developments competing for public acceptance against existing, privileged property forms. The destruction of vested interest in favor of beneficial change reflected a creative process vital to ongoing development and progress. Within its contemporary setting, and for its historical significance, the case assumes greater meaning if railroads and the development of a new and improved transportation infrastructure—or even the benefits the community could derive from all inventions and scientific knowledge—are substituted for bridges. The competing principles of the parties in the bridge case fundamentally involved the state's role and power of encouraging or implementing innovations for the advantage of the community . . . . ■

NOTES AND COMMENTS

1. One distinguished legal historian summarizes the Charles River Bridge case in the following way: "On one side of the case were the old-money Federalists, who owned many monopoly franchises and argued that private construction of public improvements required monopoly protection for the investors. On the other side was a new group of entrepreneurs, poised to enter American markets. They believed that all markets should be competitive." Herbert Hovenkamp, Enterprise and American Law 1836–1937 (Harv. U. Press 1991) at 110. Who won?

2. Stanley Kutler discusses how corruption may have been present in the initial grant to the proprietors of Charles River Bridge over the alternative charter proposal:

> That the legislature chose to grant a charter to the Russell group for purposes of profit, rather than to the Cabot brothers who had proposed a schedule of tolls that merely would recoup their investment and development costs raises obvious questions of economic ideology and legislative behavior. Beginning in 1792, and in recurring years

afterward, critics of the Charles River Bridge company charged that the proprietors had gained their charter under fraudulent conditions, an allegation never proved. But what motivated the legislature to select the group that frankly sought a long-standing profit arrangement? There may have been some vague, but conscious, perception that the pursuit of profit, even at the public's expense, was a desirable good, one that would regularly attract further investments in behalf of the community. But, more practically, the legislature's decision probably stemmed from the intensive lobbying activities of the Charleston community which was involved most directly, and whose need was clearly greater than that of its neighbors who would have benefitted most from the Cabot's proposal.

Stanley I. Kutler, Privilege and Creative Destruction: The Charles River Bridge Case 11 (1971).

3.   In a concurrence to the Supreme Court's opinion, Justice John McLean characterized the relationship between the state of Massachusetts and the proprietors of the Charles River Bridge as a contract:

> Where the Legislature, with a view of advancing the public interest by the construction of a bridge, a turnpike road, or any other work of public utility, grants a charter, no reason is perceived why such a charter should not be construed by the same rule that governs contracts between individuals....

36 U.S. at 557 (McLean, J., concurring). This regulatory contract rationale for regulation contains an appealing logic. The utility agrees to serve customers and, in return, the state provides the utility protection against new entrants and guarantees recovery of its costs through regulated rates. Judge Kenneth Starr, when sitting on U.S. Court of Appeals for the D.C. Circuit, also endorsed this view of regulation:

> The utility business represents a compact of sorts: a monopoly on service in a particular geographic area (coupled with state conferred rights of eminent domain or condemnation) is granted to the utility in exchange for a regime of intensive regulation, including price regulation, quite alien to the free market. Each party to the contract gets something in the bargain.

Jersey Central Power & Light v. FERC, 810 F.2d 1168, 1189 (D.C.Cir.1987) (Starr, J., concurring). Should the same rules regarding construction of contracts between individuals apply where one of the contracting parties is the government? What incentives do these rules create for the private sector? What approach does the Supreme Court appear to take in the Charles River Bridge case?

4.   The Charles River bridge case is of considerable importance to issues in energy regulation today, as natural gas and electric utilities undergo deregulation and a new infusion of competition. These issues are discussed further in Chapters 11–13.

Munn v. Illinois

94 U.S. 113 (1877).

■ WAITE, C.J.: The question to be determined in this case is whether the general assembly of Illinois can, under the limitations upon the legislative power of the States imposed by the Constitution of the United States, fix by law the maximum of charges for the storage of grain in warehouses at Chicago and other places in the State having not less than one hundred thousand inhabitants, 'in which grain is stored in bulk, and in which the grain of different owners is mixed together, or in which grain is stored in such a manner that the identity of different lots or parcels cannot be accurately preserved.'

It is claimed that such a law is repugnant ... to that part of amendment 14 which ordains that no State shall "deprive any person of life, liberty, or property, without due process of law, nor deny to any person within its jurisdiction the equal protection of the laws."

While this provision of the amendment is new in the Constitution of the United States, as a limitation upon the powers of the States, it is old as a principle of civilized government. It is found in Magna Carta, and, in substance if not in form, in nearly or quite all the constitutions that have been from time to time adopted by the several States of the Union. By the Fifth Amendment, it was introduced into the Constitution of the United States as a limitation upon the powers of the national government, and by the Fourteenth, as a guaranty against any encroachment upon an acknowledged right of citizenship by the legislatures of the States.

When one becomes a member of society, he necessarily parts with some rights or privileges which, as an individual not affected by his relations to others, he might retain. 'A body politic,' as aptly defined in the preamble of the Constitution of Massachusetts, 'is a social compact by which the whole people covenants with each citizen, and each citizen with the whole people, that all shall be governed by certain laws for the common good.' This does not confer power upon the whole people to control rights which are purely and exclusively private, *Thorpe v. R. & B. Railroad Co.*, 27 Vt. 143; but it does authorize the establishment of laws requiring each citizen to so conduct himself, and so use his own property, as not unnecessarily to injure another.

This is the very essence of government, and has found expression in the maxim *sic utere tuo ut alienum non laedas*. From this source come the police powers, which, as was said by Mr. Chief Justice Taney in the *License Cases*, 5 How. 583, "are nothing more or less than the powers of government inherent in every sovereignty, ... that is to say, ... the power to govern men and things." Under these powers the government regulates the conduct of its citizens one towards another, and the manner in which each shall use his own property, when such regulation becomes necessary for the public good. In their exercise it has been customary in England from time immemorial, and in this country from its first colonization, to regulate ferries, common carriers, hackmen, bakers, millers, wharfingers, innkeepers, & c., and in so doing to fix a maximum of charge to be made for services rendered, accommodations furnished, and articles sold.

To this day, statutes are to be found in many of the States on some or all these subjects; and we think it has never yet been successfully contended that such legislation came within any of the constitutional prohibitions against interference with private property. With the Fifth Amendment in force, Congress, in 1820, conferred power upon the city of Washington 'to regulate ... the rates of wharfage at private wharves, ... the sweeping of chimneys, and to fix the rates of fees therefor, ... and the weight and quality of bread,' 3 Stat. 587, sect. 7; and, in 1848, 'to make all necessary regulations respecting hackney carriages and the rates of fare of the same, and the rates of hauling by cartmen, wagoners, carmen, and draymen, and the rates of commission of auctioneers,' 9 *id.* 224, sect. 2.

... Looking, then, to the common law, from whence came the right which the Constitution protects, we find that when private property is 'affected with a public interest, it ceases to be juris privati only.' This was said by Lord Chief Justice Hale more than two hundred years ago, in his treatise De Portibus Maris, 1 Harg. Law Tracts, 78, and has been accepted without objection as an essential element in the law of property ever since. Property does become clothed with a public interest when used in a manner to make it of public consequence, and affect the community at large....

Thus, as to ferries, Lord Hale says, in his treatise De Jure Maris, 1 Harg. Law Tracts, 6, the king has "a right of franchise or privilege, that no man may set up a common ferry for all passengers, without a prescription time out of mind, or a charter from the king. He may make a ferry for his own use or the use of his family, but not for the common use of all the king's subjects passing that way; because it doth in consequence tend to a common charge, and is become a thing of public interest and use, and every man for his passage pays a toll, which is a common charge, and every ferry ought to be under a public regulation, viz., that it give attendance at due times, keep a boat in due order, and take but reasonable toll; for if he fail in these he is finable." So if one owns the soil and landing-places on both banks of a stream, he cannot use them for the purposes of a public ferry, except upon such terms and conditions as the body politic may from time to time impose; and this because the common good requires that all public ways shall be under the control of the public authorities. This privilege or prerogative of the king, who in this connection only represents and gives another name to the body politic, is not primarily for his profit, but for the protection of the people and the promotion of the general welfare.

And the same has been held as to warehouses and warehousemen. In *Aldnutt v. Inglis*, 12 East, 527, decided in 1810, it appeared that the London Dock Company had built warehouses in which wines were taken in store at such rates of charge as the company and the owners might agree upon. Afterwards the company obtained authority, under the general warehousing act, to receive wines from importers before the duties upon the importation were paid; and the question was, whether they could charge arbitrary rates for such storage, or must be content with a reasonable compensation. . . .

But we need not go further. Enough has already been said to show that, when private property is devoted to a public use, it is subject to public regulation. It remains only to ascertain whether the warehouses of these plaintiffs in error, and the business which is carried on there, come within the operation of this principle.

From [a brief filed by plaintiffs] it appears that 'the great producing region of the West and North-west sends its grain by water and rail to Chicago, where the greater part of it is shipped by vessel for transportation to the seaboard by the Great Lakes, and some of it is forwarded by railway to the Eastern ports. . . .Vessels, to some extent, are loaded in the Chicago harbor, and sailed through the St. Lawrence directly to Europe. . . .The quantity [of grain] received in Chicago has made it the greatest grain market in the world. This business has created a demand for means by which the immense quantity of grain can be handled or stored, and these have been found in grain warehouses, which are commonly called elevators, because the grain is elevated from the boat or car, by machinery operated by steam, into the bins prepared for its reception, and elevated from the bins, by a like process, into the vessel or car which is to carry it on. . . .In this way the largest traffic between the citizens of the country north and west of Chicago and the citizens of the country lying on the Atlantic coast north of Washington is in grain which passes through the elevators of Chicago. In this way the trade in grain is carried on by the inhabitants of seven or eight of the great States of the West with four or five of the States lying on the sea-shore, and forms the largest part of inter-state commerce in these States. . . . It has been found impossible to preserve each owner's grain separate, and this has given rise to a system of inspection and grading, by which the grain of different owners is mixed, and receipts issued for the number of bushels which are negotiable, and redeemable in like kind, upon demand. This mode of conducting the business was inaugurated more than twenty years ago, and has grown to immense proportions. The railways have found it impracticable to own such elevators, and public policy forbids the transaction of such business by the carrier; the ownership has, therefore, been by private individuals, who have embarked their capital and devoted their industry to such business as a private pursuit.'

In this connection it must also be borne in mind that, although in 1874 there were in Chicago fourteen warehouses adapted to this particular business, and owned by about thirty persons, nine business firms controlled them, and that the prices charged and received for storage were such 'as have been from year to year agreed upon and established by the different elevators or warehouses in the city of Chicago, and which rates have been annually published in one or more newspapers printed in said city, in the month of January in each year, as the established rates for the year then next ensuing such publication.' Thus it is apparent that all the elevating facilities through which these vast productions 'of seven or eight great

States of the West' must pass on the way 'to four or five of the States on the seashore' may be a 'virtual' monopoly.

Under such circumstances it is difficult to see why, if the common carrier, or the miller, or the ferryman, or the innkeeper, or the wharfinger, or the baker, or the cartman, or the hackney-coachman, pursues a public employment and exercises 'a sort of public office,' these plaintiffs in error do not. They stand, to use again the language of their counsel, in the very 'gateway of commerce,' and take toll from all who pass. Their business most certainly 'tends to a common charge, and is become a thing of public interest and use.' Every bushel of grain for its passage 'pays a toll, which is a common charge,' and, therefore, according to Lord Hale, every such warehouseman 'ought to be under public regulation, viz., that he . . . take but reasonable toll.' Certainly, if any business can be clothed 'with a public interest, and cease to be juris privati only,' this has been. It may not be made so by the operation of the Constitution of Illinois or this statute, but it is by the facts.

In matters not in this case that these plaintiffs in error had built their warehouses and established their business before the regulations complained of were adopted. What they did was from the beginning subject to the power of the body politic to require them to conform to such regulations as might be established by the proper authorities for the common good. They entered upon their business and provided themselves with the means to carry it on subject to this condition. If they did not wish to submit themselves to such interference, they should not have clothed the public with an interest in their concerns. The same principle applies to them that does to a proprietor of a hackney-carriage, and as to him it has never been supposed that he was exempt from regulating statutes or ordinances because he had purchased his horses and carriage and established his business before the statute or the ordinance was adopted.

It is insisted, however, that the owner of property is entitled to a reasonable compensation for its use, even though it be clothed with a public interest, and that what is reasonable is a judicial and not a legislative question.

As has already been shown, the practice has been otherwise. In countries where the common law prevails, it has been customary from time immemorial for the legislature to declare what shall be a reasonable compensation under such circumstances, or, perhaps more properly speaking, to fix a maximum beyond which any charge made would be unreasonable. Undoubtedly, in mere private contracts, relating to matters in which the public has no interest, what is reasonable must be ascertained judicially. But this is because the legislature has no control over such a contract. So, too, in matters which do affect the public interest, and as to which legislative control may be exercised, if there are no statutory regulations upon the subject, the courts must determine what is reasonable. The controlling fact is the power to regulate at all. If that exists, the right to establish the maximum of charge, as one of the means of regulation, is implied. In fact, the common-law rule, which requires the charge to be reasonable, is itself a regulation as to price. Without it the owner could make his rates at will, and compel the public to yield to his terms, or forego the use.

We conclude, therefore, that the statute in question is not repugnant to the Constitution of the United States, and that there is no error in the judgment. In passing upon this case we have not been unmindful of the vast importance of the questions involved. This and cases of a kindred character were argued before us more than a year ago by most eminent counsel, and in a manner worthy of their well-earned reputations. We have kept the cases long under advisement, in order that their decision might be the result of our mature deliberations.

Judgment affirmed.

■ FIELD, J., with whom STRONG J., concurs, dissenting: I am compelled to dissent from the decision of the court in this case, and from the reasons upon which that decision is founded. The principle upon which the opinion of the majority proceeds is, in my judgment, subversive of the rights of private property, heretofore believed to be protected by constitutional guaranties against legislative interference, and is in conflict with the authorities cited in its support. . . .

The declaration of the Constitution of 1870, that private buildings used for private purposes shall be deemed public institutions, does not make them so. The receipt and storage of grain in a building erected by private means for that purpose does not constitute the building a public warehouse. There is no magic in the language, though used by a constitutional convention, which can change a private business into a public one, or alter the character of the building in which the business is transacted. A tailor's or a shoemaker's shop would still retain its private character, even though the assembled wisdom of the State should declare, by organic act or legislative ordinance, that such a place was a public workshop, and that the workmen were public tailors or public shoemakers. One might as well attempt to change the nature of colors, by giving them a new designation. The defendants were no more public warehousemen, as justly observed by counsel, than the merchant who sells his merchandise to the public is a public merchant, or the blacksmith who shoes horses for the public is a public blacksmith; and it was a strange notion that by calling them so they would be brought under legislative control.

If [the majority's approach] be sound law, if there be no protection, either in the principles upon which our republican government is founded, or in the prohibitions of the Constitution against such invasion of private rights, all property and all business in the State are held at the mercy of a majority of its legislature. The public has no greater interest in the use of buildings for the storage of grain than it has in the use of buildings for the residences of families, nor, indeed, any thing like so great an interest; and, according to the doctrine announced, the legislature may fix the rent of all tenements used for residences, without reference to the cost of their erection. If the owner does not like the rates prescribed, he may cease renting his houses. He has granted to the public, says the court, an interest in the use of the buildings, and 'he may withdraw his grant by discontinuing the use; but, so long as he maintains the use, he must submit to the control.' . . .

The power of the State over the property of the citizen under the constitutional guaranty is well defined. The State may take his property for public uses, upon just compensation being made therefor. It may take a portion of his property by way of taxation for the support of the government. It may control the use and possession of his property, so far as may be necessary for the protection of the rights of others, and to secure to them the equal use and enjoyment of their property. The doctrine that each one must so use his own as not to injure his neighbor—sic utere tuo ut alienum non laedas—is the rule by which every member or society must possess and enjoy his property; and all legislation essential to secure this common and equal enjoyment is a legitimate exercise of State authority. Except in cases where property may be destroyed to arrest a conflagration or the ravages of pestilence, or be taken under the pressure of an immediate and overwhelming necessity to prevent a public calamity, the power of the State over the property of the citizen does not extend beyond such limits.

It is only where some right or privilege is conferred by the government or municipality upon the owner, which he can use in connection with his property, or by means of which the use of his property is rendered more valuable to him, or he thereby enjoys an advantage over others, that the compensation to be received by him becomes a legitimate matter of regulation. Submission to the regulation of compensation in such cases is an implied condition of the grant, and the State, in exercising its power of prescribing the compensation, only determines the conditions upon which its concession shall be enjoyed. When the privilege ends, the power of regulation ceases.■

* * *

The *Munn* decision arose out of a long and bitter political battle between farmers and food processors in the Midwest. The context of the dispute is analyzed in William Cronon's book, excerpts from which follow:

William Cronon, Nature's Metropolis (W.W. Norton 1991)

The *Chicago Tribune* led the way in arguing for government intervention against corrupt elevator practices. The *Tribune*, for instance, reported that among farmers in the city's hinterland, "the name of a Chicago warehouseman has become a synonym with that of a pirate. . . . It may be safely affirmed that no man voluntarily sends his grain to Chicago who can send it elsewhere." Negative perceptions of this sort could only hurt the city in general, so booster editors who wished to protect Chicago took it upon themselves to ferret out corruption and hold it up for public condemnation. Because such newspapers were widely read throughout the state, they helped shape public thinking about the issue. Much of the most damaging information that farmers knew about Chicago's markets came to them via the Chicago newspapers, which had in turn learned insider stories from grain traders at the Chicago Board of Trade. If, as many farmers believed, Chicago was the font of corruption in the grain trade, the city also pointed the way to its own redemption.

The constitution's proposed article for regulating grain warehouses had in fact been drafted by none other than a committee of the Board of Trade. This led at least one rural delegate to oppose elevator regulation as "a grain gamblers' article, and not a farmers' article." Another rural delegate thereupon leapt to the measure's defense by declaring that although "this report came from the city of Chicago" and "had its manliness and all its garments laid on there," he was still "willing to receive anything good, that may come out of evil." The *Tribune's* reform editor, Joseph Medill, was himself a delegate and delivered what was probably the convention's most grandiloquent indictment of the elevators:

> The fifty million bushels of grain that pass into and out of the city of Chicago per annum, are controlled absolutely by a few warehouse men and the officers of railways. They form the grand ring, that wrings the sweat and blood out of the producers of Illinois. There is no provision in the fundamental law standing between the unrestricted avarice of monopoly and the common rights of the people; but the great, laborious, patient ox, the farmer, is bitten and bled, harassed and tortured, by these rapacious, blood sucking insects.

With the republican body politic so infested with vermin, Medill argued, only the law could "step between these voracious monopolies and the producers." The new constitution should attack the elevator plague, save the farmer, and redeem Chicago at the same time. . . .

Article 13 as it finally appeared in the 1870 constitution remained largely as Board members had written it. It designated all warehouses in Illinois to be "public," thereby asserting the state's power to regulate their activities and confirming a grain owner's right to inspect the goods stored in such places. Despite the statewide definition of public warehouses, convention delegates understood their real target and did not wish to subject rural warehouse owners to needless cost and regulations. The most important requirements of the article therefore applied only to elevators in cities with over 100,000 inhabitants—and there was only one such city in Illinois. Elevators in Chicago were to post weekly notices of how much grain of each grade they had in store. To prevent them from issuing fraudulent receipts, they were to keep a public registry of all outstanding receipts they had issued. And they were forbidden to mix different grades without permission. Furthermore, all railroads in the state were required to deliver grain to any elevator a shipper desired–and, if necessary, permit new track construction to accomplish this.

The Illinois legislature supplemented Article 13 in 1871 with a series of laws assigning the task of grain inspection to a new Railroad and Warehouse Commission that would henceforth regulate all grain movement and storage in the state. . . . Elevator operators initially contested the legality of the new laws by refusing to take out licenses for themselves, thereby denying that Illinois had a right to regulate their activities. When the state prosecuted them, public outcry about the case was so strong that voters changed the composition of the Illinois supreme court to make sure that the Warehouse Act and other new "Granger laws" would be declared constitutional.

Finally, in 1877, the U.S. Supreme Court issued its famous ruling in *Munn v. Illinois*, establishing forever the principle that grain elevators and other such facilities were "clothed with a public interest" and could not escape state regulation. The name of Ira Munn, Chicago's leading elevator operator, would henceforth be associated with the legal ruling which enabled state governments to regulate the boundary between private interest and public good in economic matters. . . .

Wheat and corn came to Chicago from farms that were themselves radical simplifications of the grassland ecosystem. Farm facilities had destroyed the habitats of dozens of native species to make room for the much smaller bundle of plants that filled the Euroamerican breadbasket. As a result, the vast productive powers of the prairie soil came to concentrate upon a handful of exotic grasses, and the resulting deluge of wheat, corn, and other grains flowed via the railroads into Chicago. And there another simplification occurred. In their raw physical forms, wheat and corn were difficult substances: bulky to store, hard to handle, difficult to value properly. Their minute and endless diversity embodied the equal diversity of the prairie landscape and of the families who toiled to turn that landscape into farms. An older grain-marketing system had preserved the fine distinctions among these natural and human diversities by maintaining the legal connection between physical grain and its owner. But as the production of western grain exploded, and as the ability to move it came to depend on capital investments in railroads and elevators, the linkage between a farm's products and its property rights came to seem worse than useless to the grain traders of Chicago. Moving and trading grain in individual lots was slow, labor-intensive, and costly. By severing physical grain from its ownership rights, one could make it abstract, homogeneous, *liquid*. If the chief symbol of the earlier marketing system was the sack, whose enclosure drew boundaries around crop and property alike, then the symbol of Chicago's abandonment of those boundaries was the golden torrent of the elevator chute. . . .

To understand wheat or corn in the vocabulary of bulls, bears, corners, grades, and futures meant seeing grain as a commodity, not as a living organism planted and harvested by farmers as a crop for people to mill into flour, bake into bread, and eat. As one bewildered delegate to the Illinois Constitutional Convention remarked after trying to read a Chicago market report, "this 'buying short' and 'buying long' and the 'last bulge' is perfect Greek to the grain producer of the State."

By imposing their own order and vocabulary on the world of first nature, the city's traders invented a world of second nature in which they could buy and sell grain as commodity almost independently from grain as crop. "In the business centre of Chicago," wrote a bemused visitor in 1880, "you see not even one 'original package' of the great cereals." In Chicago, the market turned inward upon itself to trade within its own categories and boundaries.■

* * *

Summary: The Common Law Rules for Public Utilities:

1. **Service to public.** It operates a business that is thought to provide a service to the public.

2. **Monopoly power.** It has the legal or *de facto* authority to prevent other businesses from competing with it.

3. **Fixed territory.** A geographical boundary is defined, within which the business is required to provide service.

4. **Duty to serve.** The business has a duty to serve all members of the public, but only for the specific service for which it has a monopoly.

5. **Technological limits.** As technology changes, the nature of the businesses' monopoly may be narrowly construed.

6. **Reasonable prices.** Rates charged by public utilities, which the common law had required be reasonable, could be regulated by the legislative branch. We will consider at some length in Chapter 8 what "reasonable" means.

* * *

The Supreme Court's increasing willingness to allow government to regulate a wider range of businesses occurred at the point in history when a wide range of new technologies for the generation and distribution of energy (and other services) were being developed, as pointed out in the following excerpt.

Charles M. Haar & Daniel W. Fessler, The Wrong Side of the Tracks 142–49

(Simon & Schuster 1986).

In 1865 the first natural gas utility was opened in Fredonia, New York; in 1892 a 120–mile pipeline from wells in Indiana to Chicago made the long-distance transmission of natural gas possible for the first time. Americans in 1878 first saw the electric arc for street and home lighting, followed in 1882 by the first central electric station, with 5500 lamps, at Pearl Street Station, New York. Shortly thereafter, central stations were constructed in Boston, Brooklyn, and Chicago. By 1886, there were forty-seven Edison illuminating companies; more than 1,000 central stations were listed in 1890. The proliferation of waterworks was also impressive—from 136 in 1860 (when fewer than 400 cities had populations over 2500) to over 3000 systems by the end of the century (when there were over 1737 such cities). In 1852, 23,000 miles of telegraph lines were in operation. The Western Union Telegraph Company completed the first telegraph line to the Pacific Coast in 1861, and in 1866 it merged with the two other large telegraph companies. After Alexander Graham Bell constructed the initial pair of magneto telephones in 1875, it was but three years until first New Haven, then San Francisco, Albany, Chicago, St. Louis, Detroit, and Philadelphia had local service. By 1880 there were over 34,000 miles of wire for the nation's 50,000 telephones; the American Telephone and Telegraph Company was organized in 1885 to develop long-distance service. The modern, mechanized American city had been born.

The new utility networks possessed many of the characteristics of common carriers: they provided what were more and more commonly perceived as essential services; they were usually natural or legal monopolies, or both; they exercised the power of eminent domain; and they operated under a franchise from the state or municipality.... [But the view that this new type of business] was not a public enterprise that concerned the courts ... remained the prevailing judicial stance until the United States Supreme Court spoke in *Munn v. Illinois* in 1876. The *Munn* decision, written by Chief Justice Waite, upheld the Illinois statutes that regulated and set maximum rates for warehouses, grain elevators, and railroads. The decision became most memorable for its now-famous delineation of property that becomes "clothed with a public interest when used in a manner to make it of public consequence, and affect the community at large." Waite consulted Lord Hale's famous treatise to support his assertions: "Every bushel of grain for its passage 'pays a toll, which is a common charge,' and, therefore, according to Lord Hale, every such warehouseman 'ought to be under public regulation, viz., that he ... take but reasonable toll.' Certainly, if any business can be clothed 'with a public interest, and cease to be *juris privati* only,' this has been."

Yet beneath the constitutional catchwords "affected with a public interest," the *Munn* case was more fundamentally grounded in the Court's awareness of the shifting social, political, and economic patterns of the post-Civil War period.... In blessing the validity of some governmental control (state regulation by commission) the highest federal judges served as priests of a juridical reformation. The orthodoxy of private competition handed down in the Charles River Bridge decision forty years before had been weakened by the public outcry over abuses and panic attributed to the railroad juggernaut and other malefactors of great power.

By the close of the nineteenth century, courts generally recognized that the common law requirement to proffer equal service should apply to the increasing variety of business affected with a public interest—whether they were common carriers or not....

[Courts have used four different rationales in imposing] the obligation to furnish adequate supply or service without discrimination:

(1) The imposition of a common right to access drawn from the doctrine of services as *a public calling, essential to individual survival within the community;*

(2) The duty to serve all equally, inferred from and recognized as an essential part of *natural monopoly power;*

(3) The duty to serve all parties alike, as a consequence of the *grant of the privileged power of eminent domain; and, finally,*

(4) The duty to serve all equally, *flowing from consent, expressed or (more frequently) implied.*

A notion of reciprocity informs each of the judge-made justifications of the duty to serve. In each case, the court is presenting the elements of a multifaceted *quid pro quo:* if one wants the power to take private property against the wishes of the owner, one has to assume the responsibility of making the land (or the services that spring forth from the land) available to all members of the society; if one claims an exclusive franchise, one has to abide by the rules of the game and provide equal access; if one were going to act like a government, then one assumes the obligations of the sovereign to act in the common interest of all its citizens.

Whichever the rationale proffered, the courts in a pinch could always rest their argument upon "consent." Consent, to them, meant accepting the responsibilities along with the rest of the bargain: if a company has freely chosen to engage in providing a service to the public, then it has voluntarily assented to the appropriate requirements of a public service. Deducing a sufficient incentive for this free choice was easy, for a corporation "has, or must be supposed to have, an equivalent for its consent." Hence, the corporation, it was reasoned, had sought out and willingly assumed the very burdens it was now seeking to negate or avoid.■

NOTES AND COMMENTS

1. In deciding whether the Chicago grain warehouses were devoted to a public use, the court relied on the warehouse companies' own brief in which they bragged about how important they were to the entire Western United States because they served as the shipping point for all of the area's grain. In the nineteenth century, Chicagoans had the reputation of being insufferable braggarts about their great city. It was this trait, not the climate, that gave Chicago the nickname "the Windy City." Emmett Dedmon, Fabulous Chicago 221 (2d. ed. 1981).

2. While today the *Munn* decision may appear obvious, historically it is of great significance. After the Civil War, American States that long had promoted and encouraged railroads and utilities began to regulate them. The *Munn* decision grew out of the varied legislative responses states were taking to the "railroad problem"—a problem associated with large railroad companies that could charge different prices to different customers and control access to transportation markets. It was one of seven cases known as the "Granger cases," historical rulings that tested the constitutional authority of state police power, through legislation, to regulate private businesses.

3. The decision in *Munn* shed some light on the recently enacted Fourteenth Amendment. Justice Stephen J. Field, in a dissent joined by William Strong, made an early plea for substantive due process limitations on

regulation. This view would later be endorsed by the court in *Lochner v. New York*, 198 U.S. 45 (1905), a case which made the Supreme Court the overseer of all kinds of regulatory activity until the mid–1930's.

4. With the growth of regulation, states set up commissions to regulate public utilities. The states usually adopted a series of statutes, one for each type of common public service. Thus there would be a gas act, an electric act and a telephone act, which might eventually be consolidated. But the states usually assigned the power to administer all of these acts to a single board or commission called the "Public Utilities Commission," "Public Service Commission," "Railroad Commission," or "Commerce Commission." The terminology still varies from state to state, but such commissions are commonly referred to generically as "public utility commissions."

5. The Supreme Court's definition of "business affected with a public interest" was further expanded in *Nebbia v. New York*, 291 U.S. 502 (1934). After dairy prices in New York collapsed as a result of oversupply, the legislature commanded a milk control board to fix both maximum and minimum retail milk prices. A grocer, who was convicted for selling milk too cheaply, contested the conviction under the due process and equal protection clauses, arguing that neither the milk business nor retail grocery sales were monopolies or traditional regulated industries. In affirming Nebbia's conviction, the Court said that "affected with a public interest" means "no more than that an industry, for adequate reason, is subject to control for the public good." 291 U.S. at 536. The Court said that "price control, like any other form of regulation, is unconstitutional only if arbitrary, discriminatory, or demonstrably irrelevant to the policy the legislature is free to adopt." 291 U.S. at 539. The *Nebbia* case was seen as an indication that the Court would no longer actively question the extent to which particular businesses could be subjected to regulation. *Lochner*'s reasoning, of course, was expressly overruled only a few years later, in *West Coast Hotel v. Parrish*, 300 U.S. 379 (1937).

6. Following *Munn*, most states interpreted the case as granting them broad authority to set up programs to regulate public utilities. The Court had said that states were free to substitute more detailed statutory rules for the common law principles. Originally, many of the states adopted a series of statutes, one for each type of common public service (e.g., a gas act, an electric act and a telephone act). But the states usually assigned the power to administer all of these acts to a single board or commission called the "Public Utilities Commission" or something similar.

Today, in many states the statutory responsibilities of the commission may all be consolidated in a Public Utilities Act. Typically, these commissions had, and still have, the following basic powers:

1. **Assign territory.** To assign territories through "certificates of public convenience and necessity."

2. **Set service standards.** To enforce the duty to serve by establishing standards of service.

3. Regulate rates. To review the utility's rates and reject those that are not "just and reasonable." This includes the power to review the utility's major capital expenditures, including borrowings, against a standard of "prudent investment."

4. Control abandonment. To prevent the utility from abandoning service without its approval.

Note that these powers generally track the common law rules, but over time the statutes and the rules of the commissions usually provide a lot more detail in the way of guidance to the utility than was obtained from the common law rules.

B. REGULATORY OBJECTIVES

As the previous cases suggest, although American jurisdictions often reject public ownership as the norm, they certainly do not eschew active regulation of privately-owned resources. Why should the government regulate the activities of private energy resource property owners? Several economic rationales lie at the heart of traditional public utility regulation.

1. NATURAL MONOPOLY

The extraction, conversion, and distribution of many energy resources, such as natural gas and electricity, have historically been price regulated to protect against abuses by their owners. Since *Munn v. Illinois*, it has been recognized that certain industries are "clothed with the public interest" and subject to an obligation to provide equal service to all. Firms providing natural gas or electricity to end-use customers have traditionally been regulated as "public utilities"—firms granted a monopoly franchise in a geographic area in return for a duty to serve the public.

For example, Florida Power & Light (FP&L), an investor-owned utility, has been granted an exclusive service territory in Florida in exchange for its promise to provide power to any customer within its service territory at a reasonable rate. This protection against competition within a geographic area is often called a "horizontal monopoly." There are two distinct economic reasons that FP&L is granted this type of a monopoly franchise.

First, FP&L possesses many characteristics of what economists call a classic "natural monopoly"—a single firm that is able to provide a good or service to a market at a lower average cost than two or more firms because of economies of scale or other network economies.[1] Economies of scale occur when the average cost of production declines over the entire range of production for the industry. In addition to simple production efficiency, recent developments in economics focus on network efficiencies. Network economies, a type of economy of scale, may occur when a single firm is able to more efficiently operate than multiple firms, because it is better able to coordinate interdependent aspects of an industry's operations or because it is able to process information more efficiently. For example, it may be

---

1. *See* William W. Sharkey, The Economic Theory of Natural Monopoly (1983).

considered more efficient for a single firm to operate a nationwide distribution network for a product. A single firm may be able to coordinate its operations, such as times for delivery, more efficiently than multiple firms. In addition, the single firm may be able to gather and process information about market supply and demand more efficiently than multiple firms.

Second, it may be advantageous to allow a single firm to provide power service because there are efficiencies to be gained by integrating different market services. This is often called "vertical integration," and its rationales are discussed further in Chapter 7. In the computer industry, for example, it may be efficient for a manufacturer to bundle computer hardware with basic operating system software. A classic example in the energy industry is the electric utility: often, a single firm can more efficiently transport and distribute energy if it serves other market functions, such as power generation, as well.[2]

NOTE ON THE ECONOMICS OF NATURAL MONOPOLY

The economic phenomenon of economies of scale can be illustrated by comparing the general cost functions of different types of firms. A firm's costs can be divided into fixed and variable costs. Fixed costs are the costs associated with the firm's plant; assuming the firm remains in business with a constant plant size, they do not vary with the level of production. Variable costs, however, change with the firm's output level. For example, in making a decision to operate a plant 24 hours a day, as opposed to 12 hours a day, a manufacturing firm raises its variable costs significantly. Total costs represent the sum of fixed and variable costs.

Figure 3-1 illustrates the relationship between total costs and a hypothetical firm's output level. Imagine, for example, that the firm in panel A is a power plant with 250 megawatts (MW) capacity. The horizontal axis represents the firm's operation level, in MW. The vertical axis represents the total costs of production, in dollars. Assume that the fixed costs of the plant are $5 million. Since the firm will have to pay these costs even if it chooses not to operate the plant, the vertical axis begins at $5 million. The graph in panel A is drawn to reflect a cost phenomenon observed in most production processes, including power generation. At low levels of operation, such as those below 50 MWs, variable costs rise rapidly, although at a decreasing rate. Initially, it may take a lot of fuel to fire up the power plant's turbines, just as it takes a lot of fuel to quickly accelerate a car from zero to forty miles per hour. Between the 50 and 200 MW level, variable costs rise more slowly with increased operation levels and output. Once the power plant's turbines are running, additional operation levels are more efficient than the initial startup, for reasons similar to an automobile's improved gas mileage in highway driving. Above the 200 MW level, however, the plant may lose some of its earlier efficiencies. Here costs may climb at a greater rate with each additional unit of output. The shape of this curve suggests that the plant operates most efficiently in the 50 to 200 MW range of output.

2. Harold L. Platt, The Electric City 74-82 (University of Chicago Press; 1991); Paul L. Joskow & Richard Schamalensee, Markets for Power: An Analysis of Electric Utility Deregulation (MIT Press 1983).

The graph in panel B illustrates how this cost phenomenon translates into a relationship between marginal and average costs for the hypothetical

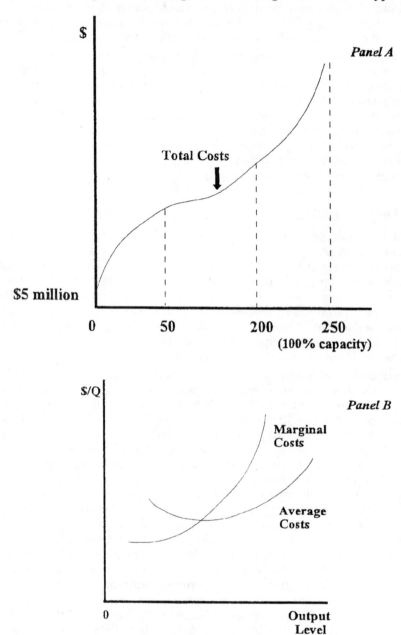

Figure 3-1

The Relationship Between Total Costs, Average Costs, and Marginal Costs

firm. Average costs are calculated by dividing total costs by the output level. The average cost curve in panel B is derived from the curve in panel A; each point in the average cost curve represents total costs divided by the corresponding output level, or the slope of the total cost curve. Marginal (or incremental) costs, by contrast, refer to the costs associated with each additional unit of output. When marginal costs are below average costs average costs fall, and when marginal costs are above average costs average costs rise. Of course, every law student is familiar with this concept: if a law student's average is 75, her GPA will rise if she receives an 80 in torts but will fall if she receives a 70.

Over the long run, nearly all costs are variable. For example, a firm must eventually replace even the plant itself. Cost considerations come into play in determining the optimal size of a firm's plant. These decisions, as well as many regulatory decisions, will depend on the shape of an industry's long run average cost curve. Consider **Figure 3–2**, which represents an entire industry rather than a single firm. A plant of size A has average production costs C1, while a plant of size B has average production costs C2. In the range between A and B, this industry experiences economies of scale: the larger plant produces lower average costs. However, a plant of size C has greater average production costs than size B. Between B and C, the industry experiences diseconomies of scale. The curve connecting these various plant average cost curves corresponds to the industry's long run average cost curve.

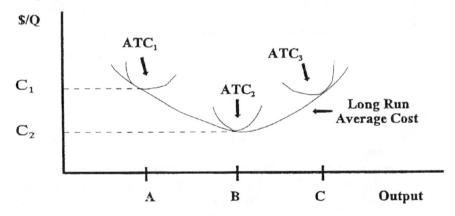

Figure 3-2

Industry-wide Average Costs

What does this long run average cost curve tell us about regulatory policy? A lot depends on the level of demand for an industry's products or services. In an industry with a demand curve similar to that in **Figure 3–3**, firm B would be able to compete more effectively than firm A because firm B's larger size and production scale give it lower average costs. Over time, firm B would drive firm A out of business. In this industry, a single firm is more efficient than two or more firms. If two or more firms operated in this market, prices would be higher and output would be lower, since the quantity demanded would decrease with higher prices. Such a market is called a *natural monopoly*.

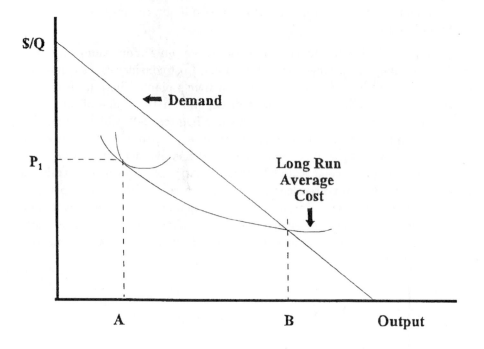

Figure 3-3

Average Cost for a Natural Monopoly Firm

Contrast a natural monopoly market with a competitive market. **Figure 3–4** illustrates a very different relationship between market demand and long run average costs. At price P1, this industry could support five firms. The cost characteristics of various industries are determined primarily by technological issues and transactions costs. Some industries, such as agriculture, have cost curves more like **Figure 3–4** than **Figure 3–3**. These industries will be able to support a larger number of firms. The relationship between long run average costs and demand is the major economic factor in determining the optimal number of firms serving a given market. For further discussion of industry cost characteristics, *see* F.M. Scherer & David Ross, Industrial Market Structure and Economic Performance (Houghton Mifflin Co., 3d ed. 1990); W. Kip Viscusi, John M. Vernon & Joseph E. Harrington, Jr., Economics of Regulation and Antitrust (Heath 1992).

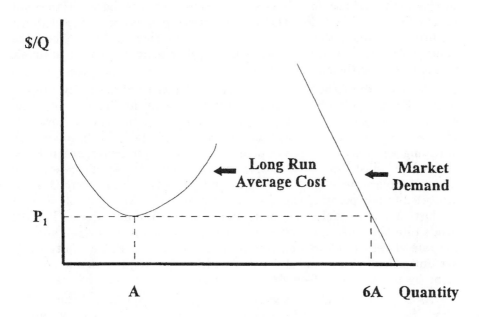

Figure 3-4

Average Cost for a Perfectly Competitive Firm

2.   PRICE REGULATION

The establishment of a monopoly franchise also increases the risk of monopoly pricing, at potential harm to consumers. According to Stephen Breyer, who wrote an important book on the topic of regulation prior to his appointment to the U.S. Supreme Court,

> In a perfectly competitive market, firms expand output to the point where price equals incremental cost—the cost of producing an additional unit of their product. A monopolist, if unregulated, curtails production in order to raise prices. Higher prices mean less demand, but the monopolist willingly forgoes sales—to the extent that he can more than compensate for the lost revenue (from fewer sales) by gaining revenue through increased price on the units that are still sold.

Stephen Breyer, Regulation and Its Reform 15–16 (Harv. U. Press 1982). It is well established that the monopolist faces incentives to charge a price above the competitive level, produce less output than a competitive market, and transfer wealth from consumers to itself.

Price regulation is designed to yield the mix of price, output, and profits approximating that which would be produced by a competitive market. Price regulation began with the local railroad and gas boards of the late nineteenth century. Today, most state public service commissions (PSCs), as well as the Federal Energy Regulatory Commission (FERC), FPC's successor agency, continue to regulate the prices public utilities charge their end-use or wholesale customers on the basis of the cost incurred to provide service. This cost of service regulation is subject to the requirement, under the Takings Clause to the Fifth Amendment of the Constitution, that a utility's investors be allowed to return an adequate rate of return on their investments.[3]

The essence of the traditional formula for calculating utility rates is simple. First, regulators determine a utility's aggregate "revenue requirements"—the amount a utility must earn in a given year to cover its variable and fixed costs,[4] including its cost of capital. The fixed costs of providing service, such as power plants and transmission lines, are included in what is called "rate-base." Revenue requirements (R) are determined through application of the following formula: $R = O + B(r)$, where O is the utility's annual operating expenses (i.e., its costs that vary with its level of production, such a fuel costs, maintenance, and non-union wages), B is the firm's rate base (i.e., its fixed costs, such as its capital resources), and r is the rate of return allowed on the utility's rate base. Next, a utility's rate per unit of energy consumed is calculated by dividing its revenue requirement by the number of energy units consumed by a class of customers.

As a much-simplified example, consider the following: Assume that FP&L incurs $10,000,000 in operating expenses, such as coal or natural gas, and builds its power plant and transmission lines at a cost of $250,-000,000 in order to provide 28,000,000 kwh of service to a single class of residential customers in a given year. Further assume that the average cost of FP&L's various sources of capital—the interest it pays on its debt and the rate of return on its equity—is 10%. FP&L's revenue requirement is $10,000,000 + ($250,000,000 x .10), or $35,000,000. The Florida PSC will set its residential rates at $35,000,000 / 28,000,000, or $1.25 a kwh. Price regulation and its problems are discussed in more detail in Chapter 8, on rate regulation.

NOTE ON THE ECONOMICS OF PRICE REGULATION

Where a monopoly is present, a single firm serves the entire market. Often, in such markets regulators protect monopoly markets, including public utilities, against competitive entrants. The monopolist faces a type of competition in that it cannot charge an infinite price for its products. However, it will be able to charge more than a competitive price without losing so many sales that its price increase is unprofitable.

To illustrate this phenomenon, consider **Figure 3–5**. Assume that the monopolist seeks to maximize its profits and that it charges all consumers the same price. Since the monopolist is the only firm serving the market, the firm's demand curve is the industry demand curve; it is downward

---

3. *Bluefield Waterworks and Improvement Co. v. Public Service Commission*, 262 U.S. 679 (1923); *Federal Power Commission v. Hope Natural Gas Co.*, 320 U.S. 591 (1944).

4. Variable costs change with an increase in a utility's level of production (say, with an extremely hot Summer or cool Winter), while fixed costs do not.

sloping, reflecting that consumers will buy more of a product if the price is lower. The monopolist, like any other firm, must choose the level of output to produce and the price to charge. Like any other firm, it will produce to the point where marginal revenues equal marginal costs. A competitive firm would also produce up to the point where marginal revenue (including a rate of return) equals marginal costs, although a competitive firm would face a very different demand curve; if a market is competitive the demand curve is relatively flat, since the competitive firm will be unable to increase its price significantly without losing all or most of its customers to its competitors. By contrast, the monopolist faces a downward sloping demand curve, indicating its degree of market power over price. It can increase its prices through output restrictions.

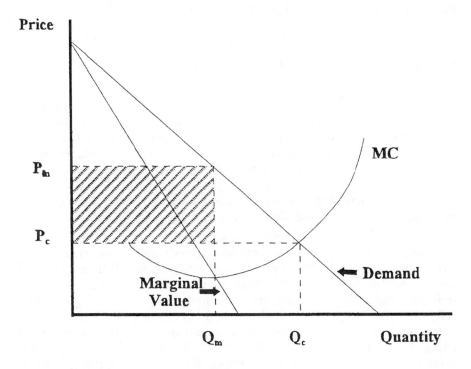

Figure 3-5

Natural Monopoly Pricing

Although the monopolist will follow a basic decisionmaking process very similar to the competitive firm—producing at an output level up to the point additional revenues (including a rate of return) equal additional costs—characteristics of monopolist markets make the outcomes of this process very different. A competitive market would produce QC and charge price PC. The monopolist will produce less and charge a higher price than a competitive market would yield. It will produce QM and charge price PM. In so doing it maximizes its profits.

There are some losses produced by such monopoly pricing that may make government regulation desirable. One such loss is reduced access to products and higher prices, as is reflected in the shaded box of **Figure 3–5**. This shaded box may represent monopoly profits, or money spent by the monopolist to exclude potential rivals. Government might regulate monopoly pricing for a variety of purposes, including protection of consumers against pricing abuses, ensuring monopoly rents are spent on socially valuable items, protecting against the risks of political influence, and limiting size and encourage small business. Operational details of price regulation and its problems are discussed further in Chapter 8, on rate regulation. For further discussion of the basics, *see* Mark Seidenfeld, Microeconomic Predicates to Law and Economics 61–62 (Anderson 1996); Richard A. Posner, Economic Analysis of Law 343–66 (Little Brown, 4th ed. 1992); W. Kip Viscusi, John M. Vernon & Joseph E. Harrington, Jr., Economics of Regulation and Antitrust (Heath 1992).

C. THE ROLE OF THE PUBLIC UTILITY COMMISSION

Public utility regulation is largely controlled by state agencies. Insofar as federal regulation is concerned, in the early part of the twentieth century most public utilities couldn't have been effectively regulated by the federal government because at that time the Supreme Court had a fairly restrictive view of the extent of federal power under the commerce clause. As a result, the more local aspects of public utility operation would have been constitutionally exempt from federal regulation. (This would not necessarily be true today since the companies are more integrated into national networks and the Court takes a more expansive view of federal power under the Commerce Clause.)

Local regulation, on the other hand, was widely seen as ineffective. Originally, it was the cities that tried to regulate public utilities: "Transit, gas and electric companies had extensive, and corrupt, influence in . . . city councils," but business consumers and employee unions were also influential. And the interests of neighboring municipalities and rival utilities "generated intense legal and political controversy." Morton Keller, Regulating a New Economy: Public Policy and Economic Change in America, 1900–1933 58–59 (Harvard Univ. Press, 1990). Many municipal governments offered franchises to private utility operators, subject to a competitive process of franchise review and renewal. Alternatively, the municipal government itself sometime entered into the utility business, which often left regulatory decisions to big city political machines. The result was a decentralized, piecemeal regulatory process, one that provided little uniformity and made many of the private utilities unhappy with the uncertainty of their franchises. State legislatures were sometimes involved in regulatory decisions, but their ability to address serious regulatory problems was seriously limited. So, at the state level the growth of regulation by agency officials can be attributed in large part to the failures of municipal regulation of energy utilities. The creation of state public utility commissions was intended to supersede a pattern of municipal regulation that had proved to be controversial.

"The initiation and development of public service regulation by state commissions owed much to the forces of political reform–under the leadership of men like Charles Evans Hughes of New York and Robert LaFollette of Wisconsin ... [in] response to the excesses of the public service companies and the inadequacies of other methods of control." But many of the companies themselves "encouraged the movement to vest regulatory powers in state commissions–at the expense of municipal authorities [believing that] their operations and investments would be more secure if insulated from politically motivated interference from uninformed (and often corrupt) state and local political factions." William K. Jones, Origins of the Certificate of Public Convenience and Necessity: Developments in the States, 1870–1920, 79 Colum. L. Rev. 426, 432 (1979). Following the leadership of New York and Wisconsin (whose state Public Service Commission legislation was drafted by the University of Wisconsin economist John Commons), many states established state-wide regulatory commissions for public utilities in the early twentieth century. *See* Robert L. Bradley, Jr., The Origins of Political Electricity: Market Failure or Political Optimism, 17 Energy L .J. 59 (1996).

Although initially skeptical, many electric and gas and telephone companies actively began to seek state regulation. They were being bedeviled by all sorts of inconsistent demands by local governments and they saw state regulation as a way to preempt them. Consequently, most public utilities acts preempted local regulation.

Today every state has some sort of commission or agency charged with regulating different types of public utilities in the energy sector. The following excerpt, from the Florida Public Service Commission's (PSC) web site, illustrates the diverse roles modern PSCs and public utility commissions (PUC) play in various states. Some states elect members of PSC or PUCs; others, like Florida, appoint them. Most PSCs and PUCs view their role in a manner similar to Florida's. The role fulfilled by Florida's Office of Public Counsel is met by the state attorney general, other agencies, or private organizations in some other states.

Public Service Commission History

Http://www2.scri.net/psc/general/overview.html

Florida law requires the commission to set rates that provide utilities an opportunity to earn a return on their investment in order to provide adequate and reliable service. However, utility rates must also be reasonable for the customer. The Public Service Commission is the regulatory force that tries to maintain a balance between the utilities and the ratepayers in the state of Florida. It's an important balance to maintain. New technology and changes in federal regulatory policies continually create more and more complex issues that the commission must consider and weigh, fully aware at all times that balance must be kept in the regulatory process. Commissioners' decisions involve hundreds of millions of dollars and affect the lives of millions of people. That's why the PSC wants to help ratepayers better understand the functions of the commission and how the consumer can participate in the ratemaking process.

What Does the PSC Do?

Since the commission's authority requires it to safeguard the interests of both the utilities and citizens of Florida, the PSC regulates the utilities providing electric, gas, telephone, and water and wastewater services. It plays a key role in guaranteeing that you, the consumer, pay fair rates for these services. The PSC's Main Objectives are to:

— Protect consumers from unreasonable rates and terms of service;

— Encourage maximum efficiency in utility company operations and management;

— Ensure public safety and help the public deal with regulated companies; and

— Establish regulatory standards and apply them in a fair and consistent manner.

Who Does the PSC Regulate?

The PSC has rate and service authority over the following utilities:

— 5 investor-owned electric utilities

— 9 investor-owned gas utilities

— 13 local telephone companies

— more than 300 interexchange companies

— more than 700 pay telephone providers

— more than 1,300 water/wastewater systems.

The PSC also has limited jurisdiction over the following utilities:

— 18 rural electric cooperatives

— 33 municipally-owned electric utilities

— 27 municipally-owned gas utilities

How Are Your Rates Set?

Whenever a regulated gas, electric, telephone, or water and wastewater company wants to change its rates, it must come before the PSC for permission. The PSC investigates its request and sets new rate levels if the request is valid. The investigation is extensive, with many PSC staff members helping the commission assess the company's request.

How Are Commissioners Selected?

In the past, three Commissioners were elected in a statewide election, but the 1978 Florida Legislature adopted a bill changing the Commission to a five-member appointed board. The Commissioners are selected for their knowledge and experience in one or more fields substantially related to the duties and functions of the PSC. These fields include such areas as accounting, economics, energy, engineering, finance, natural resource conservation, public affairs, and law.

The governor appoints a Commissioner from nominees selected by the Public Service Commission Nominating Council. The Commissioners are also confirmed by the Florida Senate before serving their four-year terms.

Public Input

The PSC starts an investigation with a hearing within the utility's service area, so the commissioners can hear from customers about the rates and service the utility provides. Customers may comment or ask questions on the proposed rates or make any other statement relating to the utility's operations. The Public Counsel, who represents customers, is also present at these hearings.

Technical Hearings

Later, hearings similar to courtroom proceedings usually are held in Tallahassee [Florida's state capitol], in which evidence from the company and other parties in the case is heard. (Some cases may be conducted in the utility's service area.) Testimony and evidence is presented by expert witnesses in support of each viewpoint represented. Witnesses are cross-examined by the company intervenors, PSC staff, and the Public Counsel's office. This information is important to the commission when it evaluates company requests.

Commission Decisions

After all evidence is presented, the five-member commission reviews the record which has been developed and issues a decision, which concludes the case. The policy decision it makes will determine the level of rates the company will be permitted to collect. However, any party to the case may appeal the commission's decision to the state's appellate court system. Many Floridians—maybe you know the state has a Public Service Commission (PSC), but don't clearly understand what the PSC does. The Florida PSC may well have greater, direct effect on your life than any other state agency.

— How much will the natural gas you use for heating your home cost per month?

— How much will you pay for electricity to run the air conditioner and light your living room?

— How much will it cost for your local telephone service?

The PSC sets the rates utility companies charge for natural gas, electricity and telephone service within the state. In some counties, it even sets the price you pay for the water you drink if your water company is privately owned.■

* * *

The following excerpt discusses some aspects of practice before a PSC:

Charles W. Murphy, Public Service Commission Practice

Florida Bar Journal (January 1995).

Not only are the subject matters of Public Service Commission (PSC) proceedings excruciating, the process involved is somewhat unique in administrative practice. Commission proceedings usually involve the same parties: regulated utilities; potential competitors of those utilities; environmental and user groups; as well as the Office of Public Counsel and Attorney General who represent the interests of the citizens of the state. . . .

Role and Function of PSC

The [Florida] PSC is an agency of the legislative branch, headed by five commissioners, and funded by regulated companies through a regulatory trust fund. The commission regulates certain electric and gas services, telecommunications services, and water and wastewater services.

Traditionally, the commission's role has been to provide rate base regulation of monopoly utility companies as a proxy for competition. In this context, the commission establishes rates and sets service standards. However, because of the advent of cogeneration in the electric industry and competition in the telecommunications industry, the PSC's regulatory responsibilities are evolving.

Because of this evolution, and the diversity of circumstances presented by the companies within each regulated industry, the commission engages in an extensive case-by-case development of regulatory policy prior to undertaking rulemaking. Since most matters before the PSC involve policy considerations, the agency rarely sends cases to DOAH [Florida's centralized panel of administrative law judges]. Rather, the commissioners, or a panel of commissioners, make determinations of substantial interest.

Occasionally the commission reverses upon reconsideration. It seldom loses on appeal. Appeals of commission decisions regarding electric, gas, or telephone rates and services are heard by the Florida Supreme Court. Appeals of other commission actions, including all water and wastewater cases, are heard by the First District Court of Appeal.

How the Commission Decides Cases

Commission dockets are opened to address any number of matters including applications for certification, petitions of various sorts, complaints, rate cases, need determinations, and tariff filings. Soon after a docket is opened, the commission staff establishes a schedule for resolving the case, which is called the "case assignment and scheduling record" (CASR). CASR information is entered into a computerized case management system and is distributed in hard copy to interested parties. All scheduling is subject to approval of the chair.

Extremely controversial matters are sometimes scheduled directly for hearing while other matters are handled with varying degrees of commission review. Very basic administrative matters are processed without the commissioners' direct review. Routine and noncontroversial matters are assigned to the commission's "consent agenda" and voted en masse as Item 2 of the regularly scheduled agenda conference.

Staff prepares detailed recommendations for commission decisions that require more extensive review. Such recommendations are filed 12 days before each commission agenda conference. At the agenda, staff summarizes its recommendation for an item before others are permitted to address the commission. Generally, the commission's action will be based on staff's recommendation with the commissioners either approving, modifying, or denying staff's suggested approach. An order reflecting the commissioners' decision usually is issued within 20 days of the agenda.

Incipient Policy: The Case-by-Case Dilemma

The PSC publishes summaries of commission activity, and recently a private service has begun to track the commission's water and wastewater decisions. However, evolving policy and regulatory trends largely exist as "lore" in the PSC's institutional memory. The existence of lore can make it difficult to anticipate how the commission will respond to a given circumstance or argument. The key to understanding lore is to call the staff attorney assigned to the case and inquire. Within the guidelines of the staff contact rule, you also will want to discuss the matter with the technical/administrative staff member who is assigned to the docket. In turn, these staff members may have to ask their supervisors, but eventually reference to a relevant or related order, or series of orders, will be forthcoming. Although this approach probably goes against your training as an attorney, it is the best strategy to learn what cannot be discovered through standard research methods.

Most matters which come before the commission for an initial determination result in a PAA order. With a PAA order, the commission announces a decision which will become final unless a substantially affected person makes a timely protest. Such a protest triggers a de novo [adjudicative] proceeding on the matter. The commission does not entertain motions for reconsideration of PAA orders; however, such motions may be interpreted as protests and result in a hearing. When a PAA order is protested but the original petition that required commission action is withdrawn prior to hearing, the PAA order is void. On occasion, the commission issues PAA orders which include severable components so that if one aspect of the order is protested, the other aspects remain in force.

Tariffs

Tariffs filed by regulated companies are subject to commission approval. A commission decision regarding a tariff results in a tariff order. The primary distinction between a tariff order and a PAA order is that, unlike a protested PAA order, a tariff order remains in force pending the outcome of the hearing on a timely protest. If a tariff order is protested, any increases in rates are held subject to refund pending the outcome of a hearing. Tariff decisions become controversial when new services, or changes in how services are offered, appear to constitute a change in commission policy. The commission's statutory authority regarding tariff approvals is cast in terms of rate increases. Therefore, it can be argued that approving new services in the guise of a tariff approval exceeds the commission's authority and denies substantially affected parties a meaningful point of entry [intervention] into the process because the service can be offered during the pendency of the [adjudicative] proceeding. Although the commission has taken both views on the issue, it appears that the more specific the policy change, the less likely it is that the commission will approve the change in the context of a tariff approval. In addressing tariff filings, the commission has authority to approve, suspend, or deny the tariff. However, sometimes the commission will decide that if a tariff is modified and refiled within specific parameters, it will be allowed to go into effect without further commission review. The commissioners can also can elect to take no action, in which case the tariff goes into effect (subject to protest) pursuant to a statutory clock.

Show Cause

The commission occasionally finds it necessary to determine whether a penalty should be imposed for violation of its rules, orders, or the applicable statutes. To this end, the commission historically has employed show cause proceedings. However, a show cause order is not significantly different than a PAA order. That is, the show cause order sets a penalty based on an initial determination and, if it is not protested, the penalty is imposed. If the party subject to the show cause order makes a timely response, the penalty becomes just another issue in the subsequent hearing. With this understanding, the commission has begun to use PAA orders to impose penalties.

Practitioner Strategies Regarding Initial Determinations

Bearing in mind that there are rules regarding staff contacts, you should begin to make your case directly with the staff as soon as a docket is opened (or even before). By contacting staff early in the process you can help staff begin to understand your arguments and how your client is affected by the regulatory issues in question.

Hearings can be long as parties explore technical matters in numbing detail. The witnesses are uniformly expert; voir dire is uncommon. True revelations or contradictions are rare. Mercifully, the hearings are somewhat informal. Objections are the exception and, in the past, have tended to be viewed with skepticism from the bench. PSC proceedings are usually not bitterly contested because the utilities have an ongoing regulatory relationship with the commission and refrain from mounting "scorched earth" campaigns in any single proceeding.

Staff's Role in the Hearing Process

While staff is not a party, it can participate "as a party" at hearings in order to develop a complete record. Staff usually does this through cross-examination of witnesses, although occasionally staff will sponsor its own witness(es). Staff also sends truckloads of interrogatories and requests for production of documents. In the telecommunications industry, staff frequently moves discovery responses and deposition transcripts into the hearing record as exhibits. These exhibits are intended to clarify prefiled testimony. However, with this approach, hearing records can become so extensive that the parties may not be able to discern where the case is going. Given the use of deposition transcripts at hearing, you should prepare your witness for the informality of depositions in commission practice.

At hearing, the commissioners listen to the summaries of testimony and cross-examination of witnesses. They have reviewed the prefiled testimony and frequently engage in cross-examination, which can be extensive and sometimes aggressive. While the commissioners tend to approve staff's post-hearing recommendation for most issues, in many instances the commissioners approve some variation of that recommendation, or reject the recommendation entirely for some issues.

[A concern] that is raised periodically involves the role of staff counsel in commission proceedings; namely, that the staff attorney assigned to a case will handle every aspect of that case until it is resolved by the commission. Among other duties, this includes presenting legal arguments to the commission, conducting discovery, and drafting every order issued in the docket.

Generally, staff attorneys view their role as nonadversarial and tend to be generous in helping the parties through a commission proceeding. In representing staff, which is not a party, staff counsel has no motivation to skew a proceeding in any particular direction. Therefore, attempts by outside counsel to use intimidation as a litigation technique against staff attorneys are misguided. There is absolutely nothing to be gained by being abusive to, or attempting to manipulate, a staff attorney. It makes sense to maintain good professional relations with the attorney assigned to your case.■

D.   LIMITATIONS ON REGULATION

1.   CONSTITUTIONAL LIMITATIONS

The constitutional issues raised by regulation are hardly settled, and discussion of them will reappear throughout this book. Even in the post-New Deal era, the Constitution is often invoked to invalidate energy statutes and regulations. Regulation raises the specter of constitutional challenges on the basis of a variety of doctrinal and textual theories.

First, how much judicial deference is appropriate to a Congressional determination that an activity is within its commerce power? In *U.S. v. Lopez*, discussed in Chapter 5, the Supreme Court, in a 5–4 decision in 1995, held invalid a federal statute that criminalized the possession of a gun in a local school zone as beyond Congress' power under the Commerce Clause of the Constitution. The Court reasoned that the statute did not regulate an economic activity that had a "substantial effect" on interstate commerce. After *Lopez*, can the federal government require states to consider certain conservation criteria in approving power plant expansion plans for municipal utilities selling power locally? Regardless of *Lopez's* significance, the Tenth Amendment, which reserves to the states those powers not given to the federal government, remains an important mechanism for challenging energy regulation. *See, e.g., New York v. U.S.*, 505 U.S. 144 (1992); *FERC v. Mississippi*, 456 U.S. 742 (1982).

Second, a state regulatory program may favor one state's economic interests at the expense of the citizens of another state. Such action may violate the "dormant" commerce clause—a judicially created doctrine that has been inferred from the textual language of the commerce clause. *See, e.g., New England Power Co. v. New Hampshire*, 455 U.S. 331 (1982) (state prohibition on the export of locally generated hydropower unconstitutional because it favors New Hampshire citizens at the expense of out-of-state citizens).

Third, a state regulatory program may be preempted by a federal law or program. *See, e.g., Pacific Gas & Electric Co. v. Energy Resources Conservation and Development Comm.*, 461 U.S. 190 (1983). Under the Supremacy Clause of the U.S. Constitution, the federal law takes precedence over state regulation.

Fourth, regulation must comply with the due process clause of the Constitution: due process challenges to regulatory procedures are quite common in the energy context. Such challenges often focus on whether agency decisionmaking processes provided for adequate procedural protections pursuant to the Due Process Clause of the Constitution or the Administrative Procedure Act. *See, e.g., Cajun Electric Power Coop. Inc. v. FERC*, 28 F.3d 173 (D.C.Cir.1994) (per curiam).

Finally, although regulation of a utility is not per se subject to Takings Clause challenges, the Takings Clause does place many constraints on rate regulation. *See, e.g., Duquesne Light Co. v. Barasch*, 488 U.S. 299 (1989). Such limitations may also be invoked in condemnation and siting proceedings.

2.   STATUTORY AND OTHER JURISDICTIONAL LIMITATIONS

The concept that the government may regulate the prices or rates charged by an enterprise if it is "clothed with the public interest" remains the basic rule today—any such business is called a "public utility." However, regulation of public utilities is not exclusively a common law issue. Modern public utilities are legally controlled largely by statutes or regulations. For example, section 205 of the Federal Power Act, 16 U.S.C. § 824d provides for rate regulation of "any public utility" selling electricity to consumers where the transaction is subject to the Federal Energy Regulatory Commission's jurisdiction. Many state statutes provide for similar regulation of electric and natural gas "utilities." Many state statutes also provide for regulation of electric and natural gas "utilities."

Although the common law is useful in interpreting such language, the definition of a public utility remains a contentious issue of statutory interpretation which often makes its way to court. Drawing the line between those businesses that are "clothed" with the public interest and those that are "unclothed" is no less contentious today than it was when *Munn v. Illinois* was decided. For example, should a gas distribution company (a regulated public utility) be allowed to recover from its ratepayers expenses for oil exploration and production (which is unregulated)? *See Committee of Consumer Services v. Public Service Commission*, 595 P.2d 871 (Utah 1979). Or, should a company selling energy conservation and efficiency services have a duty to serve? As competition has grown in the electrical utility industry, many electric utilities now own power marketing or supply companies, which are unregulated. Regulators have been required to police carefully to make sure that ratepayers do not bear the risks of these non-public utility activities.

Before an agency can resolve a matter affecting enterprise, it must have jurisdiction over the enterprise's activities. The initial step for determining an agency's jurisdiction is to look to the common law or the words of the regulatory statute the agency is applying. But the words themselves often will not answer a jurisdictional issue before a court: courts will often be asked to interpret words in light of legislative intent, policy, and the common law. As discussed above, the FERC and most state PSCs have jurisdiction over enterprises deemed to be a "public utility" within the meaning of a regulatory statute. The case that follows raises a more perplexing issue, but a similar exercise in statutory interpretation applies.

California v. Lo–Vaca Gathering Co.

379 U.S. 366 (1965).

■ DOUGLAS, J.: El Paso Natural Gas Co. is an interstate natural gas pipeline company that delivers gas at the Arizona–California border to three California distribution companies. The present controversy concerns gas to be purchased by it in Texas from Lo–Vaca Gathering Co. and Houston Pipe Line Co. Under Lo–Vaca's contract gas produced in Texas is to be delivered to a subsidiary of El Paso's at a Texas point for delivery into its pipeline. The contract contains the following two clauses:

> "All of the gas to be purchased by El Paso from Gatherer [Lo–Vaca] under this agreement shall be used by El Paso solely as fuel in El Paso's compressors, treating plants, boilers, camps and other facilities located outside of the State of Texas. It is understood, however, that said gas will be commingled with other gas being transported in El Paso's pipe line system."

"It is the intent and understanding of the parties hereto that the sale of natural gas hereof is not subject to the jurisdiction of the Federal Power Commission because this sale is not for resale."

This "restricted use" agreement provides for a separate metering of the contract volumes prior to their delivery into El Paso's system. El Paso will meter the gas used for fuel purposes in its New Mexico and Arizona facilities to make certain this amount invariably exceeds the volumes of gas taken from Lo–Vaca under this agreement. . . .

In spite of these "restricted use" covenants it is conceded that the gas sold by Lo–Vaca and Houston to El Paso will flow in a commingled stream with gas from other sources and that at least a portion of the gas will in fact be resold out of Texas.

The Federal Power Commission asserted jurisdiction over these sales as sales in interstate commerce "for resale," as that term is used in § 1 (b) of the Natural Gas Act, 52 Stat. 821, 15 U.S.C. § 717 (1958 ed.) [1][5]

We said in *Connecticut Co. v. Federal Power Comm'n*, 324 U.S. 515, 529, "Federal jurisdiction was to follow the flow of electric energy, an engineering and scientific, rather than a legalistic or governmental, test." And that is the test we have followed under both the Federal Power Act and the Natural Gas Act, except as Congress itself has substituted a so-called legal standard for the technological one. *Id.*, at 530–531. In *Interstate Natural Gas Co. v. Federal Power Comm'n*, 331 U.S. 682, 687, we considered the anatomy of the pipeline system to discover the channel of the constant flow; again in *Federal Power Comm'n v. East Ohio Gas Co.*, 338 U.S. 464, 467; and most recently in *Federal Power Comm'n v. Southern Cal. Edison Co.*, 376 U.S. 205, 209, n. 5. The result of our decisions is to make the sale of gas which crosses a state line at any stage of its movement from wellhead to ultimate consumption "in interstate commerce" within the meaning of the Act.

Attempts have been made by one convention or another to convert a local transaction into one of interstate commerce (*Sprout v. South Bend*, 277 U.S. 163; *Superior Oil Co. v. Mississippi*, 280 U.S. 390) or to make a segment of interstate commerce appear to be only intrastate (*Baltimore & Ohio R. Co. v. Settle*, 260 U.S. 166). But those attempts have failed.

---

5. Section 1 (b) of the Act provides:

"The provisions of this Act shall apply to the transportation of natural gas in interstate commerce, to the sale in interstate commerce of natural gas for resale for ultimate public consumption for domestic, commercial, industrial, or any other use, and to natural-gas companies engaged in such transportation or sale, but shall not apply to any other transportation or sale of natural gas or to the local distribution of natural gas or to the facilities used for such distribution or to the production or gathering of natural gas."

Section 2 (7) of the Act reads as follows:

"When used in this Act, unless the context otherwise requires—

. . .

"(7) 'Interstate commerce' means commerce between any point in a State and any point outside thereof, or between points within the same State but through any place outside thereof, but only insofar as such commerce takes place within the United States."

Similarly, we conclude that when it comes to the question what gas is for "resale" the present contracts should not be able to change the jurisdictional result.

The fact that a substantial part of the gas will be resold, in our view, invokes federal jurisdiction at the outset over the entire transaction. Were suppliers of gas and pipeline companies free to allocate by contract gas from a particular source to a particular use, havoc would be raised with the federal regulatory scheme, as it was construed and applied in *Phillips Petroleum Co. v. Wisconsin*, 347 U.S. 672. A pipeline would then be able to discriminate in favor of its "nonjurisdictional" customers. Moreover, a pipeline company by a contract clause could immunize a particular supplier from the reach of federal regulation as defined by *Phillips Petroleum Co. v. Wisconsin, supra*. There would be created in those and in other ways an "attractive gap" in the federal regulatory scheme (*Federal Power Comm'n v. Transcontinental Gas Pipe Line Corp.*, 365 U.S. 1, 28) which the producing States might have little incentive to close, since the gap would often involve either lower costs to intrastate customers or else merely higher pipeline costs which ultimately would be reflected in rates paid by consumers in other States. Whether cases could be conjured up where in spite of original commingling there might be a separate so-called nonjurisdictional transaction of a precise amount of gas not-for-resale within the meaning of the Act is a question we need not reach....

Reversed.■

* * *

If a statute uses the words "public utility," or instructs regulators to regulated "in the public interest," what does this include? In *National Association For The Advancement of Colored People v. Federal Power Commission*, 425 U.S. 662 (1976), the Court held that the Federal Power Commission, in the performance of its functions under the Federal Power Act and the Natural Gas Act, did not have the authority to prohibit discriminatory employment practices on the part of its regulatees. The Court noted, "The use of the words 'public interest' in the Gas and Power Acts is not a directive to the Commission to seek to eradicate discrimination, but, rather, is a charge to promote the orderly production of plentiful supplies of electric energy and natural gas at just and reasonable rates."

What about the environment? Beginning in the 1960s, many states began to be concerned about air and water pollution. Public utilities were one of the major contributors to air pollution. They hoped that the regulatory role of the public utilities commissions could insulate them from the new environmental agencies that were springing up.

Orange County Air Pollution Control District v. Public Utilities Comm'n

484 P.2d 1361 (1971).

■ PETERS, J.: We are presented in this case with an issue of some importance to urban California: Whether the authority conferred upon the Public

Utilities Commission to grant permission to construct and operate privately owned electric generating units supersedes, in cases of conflict, the authority conferred upon an air pollution control district to condition construction of such units upon compliance with district emission controls.

We conclude that neither the commission nor the district has exclusive or paramount authority. Subject to judicial review provided by law, a utility must comply with the rules and regulations of both the commission and the district. Both the commission and the various districts have jurisdiction over the construction of electric generating units. This jurisdiction is set forth in the statutory schemes governing each agency.

The commission has historically been the agency charged by the Legislature with regulation of privately owned public utilities. Some of the commission's powers are derived by direct grant from the Constitution; others may be conferred by the Legislature, which is given plenary power to confer additional powers upon the commission.

The Legislature has used its authority to confer broad powers upon the commission. The commission 'may supervise and regulate every public utility in the State', may order construction or modification of facilities or equipment, and may fix standards of service to be furnished. No privately owned utility may construct an electric generating unit or plant without first obtaining a certificate of public convenience and necessity from the commission. Finally, public utilities are directed to obey and comply with all commission orders as to any matter affecting its business as a public utility.

Air pollution control districts were created by the Legislature in 1947 to protect the state's 'primary interest in atmospheric purity'. The air pollution control district is the agency charged with enforcing both statewide and district emission controls. The districts may also require that a permit be obtained before any building is constructed or equipment is erected or operated, and may condition the permit upon a showing that the proposed facility will comply with applicable emission controls. The district is empowered to make and enforce emission controls tailored to the peculiar pollution conditions of the district.

The district's enforcement powers are broad. The district air pollution control officer may enter any building or premises to ascertain compliance with emission controls. He may require an applicant for or holder of any permit to provide information disclosing the nature, extent, quantity, or degree of air contaminants which are or may be discharged. A permit may be denied or suspended for refusal to furnish information or failure to comply with applicable emission standards. Failure to obtain a permit, operate a facility in accord with the terms of a permit, or otherwise obey any order, rule, or regulation of an air pollution control district constitutes a misdemeanor. Any violation of statewide or district regulations by any state or local governmental agency or public district may also be enjoined in a civil action.

Southern California Edison Company, real party in interest herein, sought permission to construct and operate two new steam electric generating units (utilizing fossil fuels) at its Huntington Beach generating station. On August 1, 1969, Edison applied to the commission for a certificate of public convenience and necessity covering its proposed construction. On September 30, 1969, Edison similarly applied to the Orange County Air Pollution Control District for a permit covering the proposed new units.

The district took action on Edison's application first. On October 13, 1969, its control officer requested that Edison furnish further information regarding the new units. The information was submitted by letter on November 14. On November 18, 1969, the control officer denied the application, stating that the information submitted was not adequate to show that the units would not violate Health and Safety Code, section 24243.

On December 23, 1969, the district's governing board adopted rule 67, which sets forth specific emission control requirements applicable to all nonmobile fuel burning equipment. The emission requirements of rule 67 are identical to those previously adopted by the Los Angeles district. Petitioners allege in their briefs that identical rules have now been adopted by all other air pollution control districts in the South Coast Air Basin, of which Orange County is a part. This allegation is not denied. On December 29, 1969, the control officer denied Edison's original application on the independent ground that the proposed facility would not comply with rule 67.

The district hearing board continued to hold hearings on Edison's application on December 29 and 30, 1969. On June 17, 1970, the hearing board issued its decision sustaining the control officer's denial of the requested permit "under authority of Rule 20, and, independently and separately thereof . . . under the authority of Rule 67." No judicial review of this decision was requested, although such review is provided for pursuant to sections 24322 and 24323.

The commission held hearings on Edison's application on 19 days between December 17, 1969, and March 9, 1970. The district participated in these hearings, presenting evidence and argument in opposition to the application. The commission was aware that Edison's application had been denied by the district based on rules 20 and 67. Nevertheless, on June 23, 1970, a week after the hearing board's final decision, the commission granted Edison's application and further directed Edison to begin construction immediately.

In its decision the commission did not contradict the district's finding that Edison would not comply with rule 67. The commission recognized, as it must, that sections 24224, 24260, 24263, and 24264, on their face give the district jurisdiction to condition permission to construct a power plant facility upon compliance with district rules and regulations. Without discussion or citation, however, the commission characterized this statutory authority as that of a "local agency."

Having made this assumption, the commission then asserted that its jurisdiction was paramount: "The cases are clear that in matters involving more than strictly local interest the broader regulatory authority, in this case the State through its Public Utilities Commission, should prevail. (*California Water and Telephone Co. v. Los Angeles County*, 253 Cal.App.2d 16 (61 Cal. Rptr. 618); *Los Angeles Railway Corp. v. Los Angeles*, 16 Cal.2d 779, (108 P.2d 430).) As to concurrent jurisdiction, it may well exist as to some matters but ... if ... there is a direct confrontation with the jurisdiction exercised by this Commission ... the jurisdiction of this Commission in the matter is either exclusive or paramount. That was essentially the determination made in the California Water and Telephone Company and the Los Angeles Railway Corp. cases."

The commission correctly stated that local ordinances are controlled by and subject to general state laws and the regulations of statewide agencies regarding matters of statewide concern. Accordingly, the commission has been held to have paramount jurisdiction in cases where it has exercised its authority, and its authority is pitted against that of a local government involving a matter of statewide concern.

Where its jurisdiction conflicts with other than a local agency, commission directives have not been given such controlling effect. The commission, for example, has broad authority to promote the safe operation of utilities. Yet compliance with commission directives does not preclude a jury's finding that the commission's standards did not constitute a minimum standard of reasonable care.

Perhaps an even more relevant issue is jurisdiction to regulate the health and sanitation of common carrier employees. While the commission has been said to have such jurisdiction (37 Ops.Cal.Atty.Gen. (1961) 31, 33), the Industrial Welfare Commission and the Division of Industrial Safety have been held to have concurrent jurisdiction over such matters. The Attorney General's opinion makes it clear that a common carrier must not only obtain an operating permit from the commission and comply with commission orders, but must also comply with pertinent orders of the Industrial Welfare Commission or the Division of Industrial Safety. '(O)wners of common carriers must comply with the orders of each of the agencies so empowered.' (37 Ops.Cal.Atty.Gen. at p. 36; italics added.)

When the Legislature considered the problem of air pollution control in 1947, it was no doubt aware of the jurisdictional limitations of local city and county governments. It is obvious that air is not a matter of purely local concern, and that the effective control of air pollution therefore should be undertaken on a nonlocal basis....

Edison contends that districts have only local powers because they function only with the consent of the county board of supervisors, have boundaries coextensive with that of the county, and have as officers the entire board of supervisors sitting ex officio. What is most significant, however, is the care with which the Legislature separated the legal status of the air pollution control district from that of the county. One prime reason that the board of supervisors must give in its resolution declaring that a district is needed is that 'it is not practical to rely upon the enactment or enforcement of local county and city ordinances to prevent or control ... such pollution.... The board must appropriate separate funds for the operation of the district, deposit such funds in a separate treasury, and record the appropriation as a legal charge against the county. The district is a separate corporate and political body from the county, with powers (inter alia) to sue and be sued, hold or dispose of real property, and contract with the county or city to perform services. Since any contract between a district and a county would be made by two distinct political bodies composed of identical individuals, the Legislature must have intended the district to have a separate existence from that of the county.

The Legislature did not, it is true, intend to occupy the field completely in delegating powers over pollution to air pollution control districts. Aware that some local ordinances of cities and counties might be valid but for the Legislature's intervention, and not wishing to abrogate any power that local governments might have, the Legislature declared that it did not mean to prohibit the 'enactment or enforcement by any county or city of any local ordinance stricter than the provisions of this article and stricter than the rules and regulations adopted (by a district)....' The possible validity of local pollution controls, however, obviously has no effect on the validity of district regulation of nonlocal matters.

It might be contended that the Legislature did not consider the possibility that air pollution control districts might regulate the emissions of public utilities. The possibility of such legislative inadvertence is unlikely. In upholding the Los Angeles County district's rule 67 as reasonable against the attack of a municipally owned utility, the Los Angeles Superior Court noted that 44 percent of the nitrogen oxides discharged from nonvehicular sources in the county came from power plants. (*Department of Water and Power v. Hearing Board of the Air Pollution Control District of the County of Los Angeles*, Los Angeles Superior Court No. 971991, judgment entered July 9, 1970.)

In the instant case it was estimated that 63 percent of the nitrogen oxides from nonvehicular sources in Orange County come from Edison's power plants. It is extremely doubtful that the Legislature, in considering the need for districts with broad powers over private and public 'persons,' did not contemplate district regulation of power plants. There is also no evidence that the Legislature contemplated a patchwork structure in which districts might regulate the emissions of municipally owned utilities but not those of privately owned utilities, and in the absence of such evidence we are unwilling to reach such a result.

We conclude that the Legislature has established one statutory scheme for the general regulation of public utilities, another for the general regulation of air pollution. As in the field of industrial health and sanitation (37 Ops.Cal.Atty.Gen. 31), the commission must share its jurisdiction over utilities regulation where that jurisdiction is made concurrent by another (especially a later) legislative enactment. Here the Legislature has itself enacted specific emission control standards and has erected a comprehensive statutory structure for the adoption of further controls. These controls without doubt apply to public utilities. The Legislature has delegated enforcement of these emission controls to air pollution control districts. Where the district has found that a proposed or existing facility does not comply with applicable regulations, the commission may not order a utility to violate district rulings.

Rather, the Legislature has clearly provided a means by which the utility may challenge a district ruling. 'Any person deeming himself aggrieved ... may maintain a special proceeding in the superior court, to determine the reasonableness and legality of any action of the hearing board.' The superior court, pursuant to Code of Civil Procedure section 1094.5, may then determine the validity of such action. If a court for any reason finds that a discharge in excess of that permitted by district rules and regulations is necessary, it may so order. There is thus little likelihood that the horrific nightmare envisioned by the commission—inadequate electrical service—will become a reality.

The commission has acted in excess of its jurisdiction in purporting to overrule the Orange County Air Pollution Control District's denial of Edison's application. The order of the commission is annulled, without prejudice to Edison's right to seek judicial review of the district's order pursuant to section 24322. ■

NOTES AND COMMENTS

1. As the California example illustrates, environmental and economic regulation of public utilities often overlap significantly. Not only do they overlap, but different regulators may be charged with implementing environmental and economic goals. What is the effect of this on regulatory objectives? On the industry? On consumers? On the environment?

2. In *Grand Council of the Crees (of Quebec) v. Federal Energy Regulatory Commission*, 198 F.3d 950 (D.C.Cir. 2000), a panel for the U.S. Court of Appeals for the D.C. Circuit addressed a similar issue under federal economic regulation. The Federal Power Act charges the Federal Energy Regulatory Commission (FERC) to set rates for electric utilities within its jurisdiction at a "just and reasonable" level. *See* 16 U.S.C. § 824d(a). Groups appealing FERC's rate decisions based their standing on allegations that the agency's decision, by impacting the uses of electricity, will "devastate the lives, environment, culture and economy of the Crees" and "will destroy fish and wildlife upon which Cree fisherman, trappers and hunters depend." 198 F.3d at 954. The D.C. Circuit, however, denied standing to these groups, holding that the environmental concerns they raised are outside of the zone of interests of FERC's statutory mandate to set "just and reasonable" rates. The panel reasoned that "[T]he fixing of 'just and reasonable' rates[] involves a balancing of the investor and consumer interests," but that "[b]oth interests are economic and tied directly to the transaction regulated." *Id.* at 956. The D.C. Circuit also noted that, "The Supreme Court has never indicated that the discretion of an agency setting

'just and reasonable' rates for sale of a simple, fungible product or service should, or even could, encompass considerations of environmental impact (except, of course, as the need to meet environmental requirements may affect the firm's costs)." *Id.* at 957. The court also gave weight to the fact that FERC had affirmatively forsworn environmental considerations in adjudicating rates.

3.   Peter Huber argues that the multiple agencies regulating the utility industry result in "only a cycle of ecstasy and agony" in the electricity industry. According to him, "Utilities may be pleased with regulatory inertia when the issue is emissions from older, coal-fired power plants, but they are dismayed when regulatory paralysis smother a half-built nuclear power station." Environmentalists fare no better: "Those who favor more electricity production are pleased that it is enormously difficult to shut down older powerplants, regardless of how unsafe or dirty those plants may be." Huber concludes "There is something in the system for everyone, but always something negative. Where can any of the contending parties turn for affirmative regulatory leadership?" *See* Peter Huber, Electricity and the Environment: In Search of Regulatory Authority, 100 Harv. L. Rev. 1002, 1054 (1987). Is there a better way to regulate a utility industry? Do other activities that are subject to regulation, such as product safety, suffer the same problem?

CHAPTER 4

WATER POWER

A. WATER AS A SOURCE OF ENERGY

If water is located at any place higher than the level of the area towards which it seeks to flow, it has potential gravitational energy, as discussed in Chapter Two. From the dawn of recorded history, humans have experimented with ways to turn that potential energy into useful kinetic energy.

1. THE WATER MILL

One of the first devices to utilize the force of falling water as a source of energy was the simple water mill. Flowing water in a river turned some sort of paddle wheel attached to a drive shaft that connected it to some type of machinery. The earliest examples were mills to grind grain, as described in the excerpt from Woolrych in Chapter Three. Both windmills and watermills were common in the medieval world, but watermills were far more abundant; in the Domesday Book count of 1086, there were 5624 mills in southern and eastern England, or one for every 350 people.

By the eighteenth century, water mills were widely used in England to run factories that created textiles, tools and other commodities. To the English settlers of North America, the search for water power was the obvious way to control one of the most important sources of energy. After the revolutionary war, Americans wanted to establish their economic independence from England by manufacturing their own goods, such as clothing and tools, which had traditionally been imported from England. To do so, they needed to utilize the water power potential of the rivers flowing into the Atlantic Ocean, which proved to be easiest in the rolling terrain of New England.

This New England regional complex had an interdependence and an inner dynamic that shaped the role of the textile industry in the national economy. Geographically, the industry spread inward along the rivers of New England, eventually studding the great waterpower sites with clusters of large mills and housing for workers. Mill towns were connected by river, canal, turnpike, and eventually railroad to major mercantile centers, which imported the raw cotton, shipped the finished goods, and served as general supply centers and managerial and financial headquarters. D.W. Meinig, II The Shaping of America 377 (1993).

Most of America's first important industrial facilities were located along Northeastern rivers at locations where dams could be built to run mills powered by water wheels. Even after coal-fired steam engines were common in New England in the mid 1850s, steam was still about three times more expensive than water as a prime mover. Vaclav Smil, Energy in World History 108 (1994).

Effective use of water power usually required the construction of a dam that would store large quantities of water. As the needs of industry grew, higher and higher dams were needed to provide the power. The difference in the height of the water above and below the dam is called the "head" of the dam. As the height of the head increased, flooding of lands behind the dam increased, which often created conflict between mill owners and farmers whose land was flooded.

When a mill dam is built and the reservoir filled, the water is then released in a steady flow so that the water mill will run continuously and evenly. Because the construction of a dam affected the landowners both above and below the dam, legal rules were needed for determining the rights of the various landowners. These rules set precedents that influenced the development of energy law as new and more powerful sources of potential energy came into operation later in the century.

The ability to capture a "higher head" of water by building a dam was a rearrangement of the natural flows of energy. Water that naturally would have flowed freely downstream was captured and held by the dam so that its potential energy could be used to turn the mill's machinery. The dam reduced the amount of water (and potential energy) that would otherwise be available to downstream landowners and also caused flooding of the land adjacent to the river upstream from the dam.

American courts wrestled with the legal issues arising out of these energy transfers. As you consider the ways in which the lawmakers attempted to resolve this conflict, think about the similarities and differences between the capture of the potential energy in water and the capture of the potential energy in sunlight, as discussed in Chapter Two.

2.   IMPACT ON PROPERTY RIGHTS

Fiske v. Framingham Manufacturing Co.

29 Mass. (29 Pick) 68 (1831).

Action on the case. The plaintiff alleges that he is owner of a tract of meadow land situate in Natick, on one side of and near a pond, called Wansemog Pond, and that the defendants, by drawing water from the pond, overflowed his land, whereby his hay was injured.

■ SHAW C. J.: The statutes in regard to mills, and the rights and liabilities of mill-owners in relation to flowing the lands of others, are to be regarded as statutes in pari materia and to be construed together as one system of regulations.

By the Statute 1824, c. 153, § 1, it is provided, that when any person shall complain that he sustains damage in his lands, by their being flowed, whether situated above or below any mill dam, the court may order, & c. It is well settled, that in all these cases, where the party is entitled to his damage upon complaint, under the statute, his common law remedy by an action on the case is taken away.

In the case of *Wolcott Woollen Manuf. Co. v. Upham,* 5 Pick. 292, a construction was put upon this statute, and it was there held, as under the former one, that where the statute remedy by complaint applies, the common law remedy by action on the case is taken away. It was further held, in that case, that a dam erected several miles above a mill for the purpose of raising a head of water, and creating a reservoir, for the use of such mill, is a mill dam within the meaning of the act, and a remedy for damage done by the water flowing away from the dam of such reservoir, must be sought under the statute. Were the plaintiff's meadow situated on a natural stream, and the defendants' dam erected above it, on a natural stream, there would be nothing to distinguish this from the case cited, and the question is, whether the statute can apply to an artificial stream created by means of a canal.

The statute of 1824 makes no distinction in terms or by implication, between a natural stream, and a canal or artificial stream. But, as already suggested, this statute is to be construed with the other statutes in pari materia, and regarded not as establishing a new principle, but as enlarging and extending a beneficial remedy, before given in certain cases, to other analogous cases. The statute of 1796 is but a revision of a former law, and the origin of these regulations is to be found in the provincial statute of 1714. They are somewhat at variance with that absolute right of dominion and enjoyment which every proprietor is supposed by law to have in his own soil; and in ascertaining their extent, it will be useful to inquire into the principle upon which they are founded. We think they will be found to rest for their justification, partly upon the interest which the community at large has in the use and employment of mills, and partly upon the nature of the property, which is often so situated, that it could not be beneficially used without the aid of this power. A stream of water often runs through the lands of several proprietors. One may have a sufficient mill-site on his own land, with ample space on his own land for a mill pond or reservoir, but yet, from the operation of the well known physical law, that fluids will seek and find a level, he cannot use his own property without flowing the water back more or less on the lands of some other proprietor. We think the power given by statute was intended to apply to such cases, and that the legislature meant to provide, that as the public interest in such case coincides with that of the mill-owner, and as the mill-owner and the owner of lands to be flowed cannot both enjoy their full rights, without some interference, the latter shall yield to the former, so far that the former may keep up his mill and head of water, notwithstanding the damage done to the latter, upon payment of an equitable compensation for the real damage sustained, to be ascertained in the mode provided by the statute.

From this view of the object and purpose of the statute, we think it quite manifest, that it was designed to provide for the most useful and beneficial occupation and enjoyment of natural streams and water-courses, where the absolute right of each proprietor to use his own land and water privileges, at his own pleasure, cannot be fully enjoyed, and one must of necessity, in some degree, yield to the other. But we think it would be an extension of the principle not warranted by the statute, if it were so construed as to authorize one person to make a canal or artificial stream in such manner as to lead the water into the lands of another; and in such case, therefore, the right of the party whose lands are flowed, to recover damages by an action at common law, is not taken away or impaired.

It appears by the facts reported, that the sluice and gate, through which the water was drawn which flooded the plaintiff's meadow, were not placed upon any natural stream, but upon a canal or artificial cut, by means of which the water flowed through the plaintiff's meadow, where it did not flow before; and therefore the Court are of opinion, for the reasons before given, that the statute does not apply, and that the plaintiff is not barred by it from his remedy at common law.

Nonsuit taken off and the cause to stand for trial.■

Morton J. Horwitz
The Transformation of American Law, 1780–1860 (1977)

The various acts to encourage the construction of mills offer some of the earliest illustrations of American willingness to sacrifice the sanctity of private property in the interest of promoting economic development. The first such statute, enacted by the Massachusetts colonial legislature in 1713, envisioned a procedure for compensating landowners when a "small quantity" of their property was flooded by the raising of waters for mill dams. The statutory procedure was rarely used, however, since the Massachusetts courts refused to construe the act to eliminate the traditional common law remedies for trespass or nuisance. After the act was amended in 1795 and 1798, mill owners began to argue that it provided an exclusive remedy for the flooding of lands. As a result, the mill acts adopted in a large number of states and territories on the model of the Massachusetts law were, more than any other legal measure, crucial in dethroning landed property from the supreme position it had occupied in the eighteenth century world view, and ultimately, in transforming real estate into just another cash-valued commodity. The history of the acts is a major source of information on the relationship of law to economic change. For reasons of convenience the discussion that follows concentrates on the Massachusetts experience which, though particularly rich, is not atypical.

Under the 1795 Massachusetts statute, Act of Feb. 27, 1795, ch. 74, [1794–96] Mass. Acts & Resolves 443, an owner of a mill situated on any nonnavigable stream was permitted to raise a dam and flood the land of his neighbor, so long as he compensated him according to the procedures established by the act. The injured party was limited to yearly damages, instead of a lump sum payment, even if the land was permanently flooded, and the initial estimate of annual damages continued from year to year unless one of the parties came into court and showed that circumstances had changed. The act conferred extensive discretion on the jury, which, in addition to determining damages, could prescribe the height to which a dam could be raised as well as the time of year that lands could be flooded. Unlike the statutes in some states, such as Virginia, *See Wroe v. Harris*, 2 Va. (2 Wash.) 126 (1795), the Massachusetts law authorized the mill owner to flood neighboring lands without seeking prior court permission. Thus, except for the power of the jury to regulate their future actions, there was no procedure for determining in advance the utility of allowing mill owners to overflow particular lands.

The exclusive remedial procedures of the mill acts foreclosed four important alternative avenues to relief:

First, they cut off the traditional action for trespass to land, in which a plaintiff was not required to prove actual injury in order to recover. In a mill act proceeding a defendant could escape all liability by showing that, on balance, flooding actually benefitted the plaintiff.

Second, the statutory damage formula removed the possibility of imposing punitive damages in trespass or nuisance. The common law view had been that unless punitive damages could be imposed, it might pay the wrongdoer to "keep it up forever; and thus one individual will be enabled to take from another his property against his consent, and detain it from him as long as he pleases."

A third form of relief at common law allowed an affected landowner to resort to self-help to abate a nuisance. Indeed, there are a number of reported cases in which mill dams not covered by the protection of the mill acts were torn down by neighbors claiming to enforce their common law rights.

Finally, the acts foreclosed the possibility of permanently enjoining a mill owner for having created a nuisance.

In the early nineteenth century the need to provide a doctrinal rationale for the extraordinary power that the mill acts delegated to a few individuals was acute. Not only had the use of water power vastly expanded in the century since the original Massachusetts act, but there was also a major difference between the eighteenth century grist mill, which was understood to be open to the public, and the more recently established saw, paper, and cotton mills, many of which served only the proprietor.

By 1814, the significance of the growing separation between public and private enterprise was only beginning to penetrate the judicial mind. Some still conceived of mills as a form of public enterprise in which competition was impermissible. Business corporations were only beginning to upset the old corporate model, in which the raison d'être of chartered associations was their service to the public. Nor is there any evidence that the increasingly private nature of mills, which was painfully evident to everyone fifteen years later, had as yet caused judges the slightest conceptual difficulty. At this time in Virginia, for example, where the old corporate model still prevailed, judges were also clear that the state's mill act could be defended on the ground that "the property of another is, as it were, seized on, or subjected to injury, to a certain extent, it being considered in fact for the public use." *Skipwith v. Young,* 19 Va. (5 Munf.) 276, 278 (1816).

The dramatic growth of cotton mills after 1815 provided the greatest incentive for mill owners to flood adjoining land and, in turn, brought to a head a heated controversy over the nature of property rights. The original mill dams were relatively small operations that caused some upstream flooding when proprietors held back water in order to generate power. With the growth of large integrated cotton mills, however, the flooding of more lands became necessary not only because larger dams held back greater quantities of water but also because of the need to generate power by releasing an enormous flow of water downstream. In light of this fact, the Massachusetts legislature amended the mill act in 1825 to allow the flooding of "lands ... situated either above or below any mill dam." Act of Feb. 26, 1825, ch. 153, § 1 [1822–25] Mass. Laws 658.

Extension of the mill act to manufacturing establishments brought forth a storm of bitter opposition. One theme—that manufacturing establishments were private institutions—appeared over and over again.... The nearly unanimous denunciation of the mill acts soon brought forth a degree of change. From 1830, when Lemuel Shaw began his thirty year tenure as chief justice, the Massachusetts court began a marked retreat away from its earlier reluctant, but expansive, interpretation of the act. Conceding that the mill acts "are somewhat at variance with that absolute right of dominion and enjoyment which every proprietor is supposed by law to have in his own soil," *Fiske v. Framingham Mfg. Co.,* 29 Mass. (12 Pick.) 68, 70 (1832), Shaw nevertheless proceeded to offer a dual justification for the acts. The legislation could be defended, he wrote, "partly upon the interest which the community at large has, in the use and employment of mills"—a theory of eminent domain—"and partly upon the nature of the property, which is often so situated, that it could not be beneficially used without the aid of this power." *Id.* at 70–71. However artificial it may have been in the existing context, Shaw argued that the mill act "was designed to provide for the most useful and beneficial occupation and enjoyment of natural streams and water-courses, where the absolute right of each proprietor, to use his own land and water privileges, at his own pleasure, cannot be fully enjoyed, and one must of necessity, in some degree, yield to the other." *Id.* at 71–72.

The main contribution of Shaw's formulation was to force courts to see that a conception of absolute and exclusive dominion over property was incompatible with the needs of industrial development. Whether the rationale for state intervention was eminent domain or a more explicit recognition of the relativity of property rights, under the influence of the mill acts men had come to regard property as an instrumental value in the service of the paramount goal of promoting economic growth.■

NOTES AND COMMENTS

1. When the mill owner's dam flooded the farmer's land, a natural resource (i.e., agricultural land) was lost that could have converted the sun's energy into crops. On the other hand, the stored water in the dam was potential energy that could be converted to kinetic energy that would grind corn or convert cotton into textiles. Was the dam's conversion of energy more efficient (i.e., did it create less entropy) than the farmer's conversion of solar energy into corn or cotton? How would such efficiency be measured? Did the rules of law created in Massachusetts to resolve the conflicts between the mill owner and the farmer take into account any differences in relative efficiency of energy conversion?

2. If the mill owner were required to pay the farmer the value of her land, would the relative market values of the respective parcels of land automatically take into account the relative efficiency of the mill owner's and the farmer's conversion of energy?

3. "The Virginia Mill Act provided significant protection for landowners against incursions by the mills and was interpreted in a way that made it quite difficult to construct a mill.... First, the Act protected landowners directly by requiring millers to obtain permission from a court before flooding nearby land and by ensuring that the millers paid adequate damages. Second, judges added extra protection for landowners by construing the act very strictly, often finding technical reasons to forbid construction of a mill. Thus, the Virginia Mill Act did allow for some industrial development, but without enriching 'men of commerce and industry' at the expense of less powerful groups or running roughshod over other interests." Note: Water Law and Economic Power: A Reinterpretation of Morton Horwitz's Subsidy Thesis 77 Va. L.Rev. 397 (1991). What differences between the conditions in Massachusetts and Virginia might have contributed to the development of different laws governing the balance of power between millowners and farmers?

4. The Mill Acts effectively gave mill owners a power of private eminent domain to flood their neighbors' land as long as they paid damages. In 1991, Peter Dorey, who had purchased an old mill near Foster Pond in

Bridgton Maine, sought a declaratory judgment that he was entitled to increase the height of the dam under the Maine Mill Act, which was similar to the Massachusetts Act. His action would cause flooding for forty-four owners of waterfront property on the pond. How should the court decide the case? *See Dorey v. Estate of Spicer*, 715 A.2d 182 (Me.1998).

B. Hydroelectric Power

Early in the twentieth century, the technology for the use and distribution of electricity became readily available (see Chapter Ten), leading to a search for the most efficient way of generating electricity. One of the earliest technologies to be developed was a relatively simple one; the rotating movement of the traditional water mill was transferred to a turbine, which generated electric current. Such electricity became known as hydroelectric power (also called hydropower or simply hydro).

1. The Era of the Big Dams

The mountains of the western United States were one of the first places in which the promoters of hydroelectric power sought appropriate sites for power plants. Because of the terrain, all of the major western rivers dropped long distances between their source and their mouth, thus providing large amounts of potential gravitational energy. If dams could be built at key locations, this energy could be used to generate a great deal of electricity.

The builders of some of the largest dams were two federal agencies, the Bureau of Reclamation and the U. S. Army Corps of Engineers. Projects such as the Colorado River's Boulder Dam (later renamed Hoover Dam after the President who was one of its strongest backers) and the Columbia River's Grand Coulee Dam were triumphs of engineering that still awe people by their size. These agencies also built hundreds of smaller dams as Congressional delegations sought to bring federal money into their districts.

With the election of President Franklin Roosevelt and the "New Deal" policies he espoused, the role of the federal government in hydroelectric power was intensified. The Congress created the Tennessee Valley Authority as a federal agency with a monopoly on electric generation in the valley of the Tennessee River and its tributaries, and it began the construction of a whole series of dams to produce power. In the northwest, another federal agency, the Bonneville Power Authority, was created to harness the power potential of the Columbia River. The reservoirs created by these dams displaced thousands of people, but the promised economic benefits of the new technology were so great that the minor hardship (Congress provided fairly generous compensation) was widely seen as simply the price of progress.

Meanwhile, private power companies were also seeking sites for dams to provide hydroelectric power. Before 1920, private hydropower projects on Federal lands and waterways were authorized either through revocable licenses granted by the Secretary of War, Interior or Agriculture or by special legislation enacted by Congress. The 1920 Federal Water Power Act struck a balance between promoting development of private hydropower on Federal waterways and lands and the need to condition the use of those public resources to protect the public interest; in particular protection of fishing interests and national parks and other reservations. The original Act set up a three member Federal Power Commission—composed of the Secretaries of War, Agriculture and the Interior—to oversee the development of private hydropower. Congress required private builders of hydro projects to obtain an FPC license for any dam they built.

In 1930, Congress reconstituted the Commission by substituting full-time Commissioners for the Cabinet members. These responsibilities are now codified as part of the Federal Power Act, 16 U.S.C. § 792 *et seq.*, and given to the Federal Energy Regulatory Commission (FERC), the FPC's successor agency. The Act also gave other federal agencies a major role in the process of attaching conditions to project licenses to ensure that federal interests such as fishing and recreation would be protected. Their authorities include:

- mandatory conditions for the adequate protection and utilization of reservations occupied by a project, such as Indian reservations, refuge lands, certain units of the national park system and national forests (Section 4(e));

- mandatory conditions for fish passage (Section 18);

- mandatory conditions to prevent the loss of, or damage to, fish and wildlife resources for projects exempted from licensing (Section 30(c));

- recommendations for the protection, mitigation and enhancement of fish and wildlife resources (including related spawning grounds and habitat) to which FERC must give due weight (Section 100(j)); and

- recommendations for the protection of recreation, cultural resources and irrigation (Section 10(a)).

As of 1998, there were 1,630 FERC-authorized hydropower projects in the United States—involving approximately 2,000 dams—with a combined installed capacity of 53,211 megawatts. Hydropower projects provide relatively cheap electricity, but they also can cause significant damage to aquatic and riparian environments by altering the fundamental physical, chemical and biological processes of river systems. They can block and impede fish migration, dewater streams or otherwise destroy existing natural habitat, cause shoreline and bank erosion, block the downstream flow of nutrients and sediments, destroy sensitive cultural resources such as archeological sites, and affect recreational opportunities.

2. THE ROLE OF THE PUBLIC SECTOR

The extent to which hydroelectric power should be developed by public or private entities was a bitterly fought issue in the early decades of the technology. The electric power industry was being developed largely by private corporations, and they and their backers thought hydro should be developed in the same way. Others argued that the waters of the rivers were public waters, and that the energy generated thereby should not be given to private companies. The final legislation was a compromise, authorizing the licensing of private projects but giving the federal government a preference if it wished to build the project itself.

Udall v. FPC

387 U.S. 428 (1967).

■ DOUGLAS, J.: The Federal Power Commission has awarded Pacific Northwest Power Company (a joint venture of four private power companies) a license to construct a hydroelectric power project at High Mountain Sheep, a site on the Snake River, a mile upstream from its confluence with the Salmon. 31 F.P.C. 247, 1051. The Court of Appeals approved the action, 358 F.2d 840 (D.C.Cir.); and we granted the petitions for certiorari. 385 U.S. 926, 927.

The primary question in the cases involves an interpretation of § 7 (b) of the Federal Water Power Act of 1920, as amended by the Federal Power Act, 49 Stat. 842, 16 U.S.C. § 800 (b), which provides:

> Whenever, in the judgment of the Commission, the development of any water resources for public purposes should be undertaken by the United States itself, the Commission shall not approve any application for any project affecting such development, but shall cause to be made such examinations, surveys, reports, plans, and estimates of the cost of the proposed development as it may find necessary, and shall submit its findings to Congress with such recommendations as it may find appropriate concerning such development.

The question turns on whether § 7 (b) requires a showing that licensing of a private, state, or municipal agency[1] is a satisfactory alterna-

---

1. Section 4 of the Act provides in part:

"The Commission is hereby authorized and empowered—

(a) To make investigations and to collect and record data concerning the utilization of the water resources of any region to be developed, the water-power industry and its relation to other industries and to interstate or foreign commerce, and concerning the location, capacity, development costs, and relation to markets of power sites, and whether the power from Government dams can be advantageously used by the United States for its public purposes, and what is a fair value of such power, to the extent the Commission may deem necessary or useful for the purposes of this Act

. . .

(e) To issue licenses to citizens of the United States, or to any association of such citizens, or to any corporation organized under the laws of the United States or any State thereof, or to any State or municipality for the purpose of constructing, operating, and main-

tive to federal development. We put the question that way because the present record is largely silent on the relative merits of federal and nonfederal development. What transpired is as follows:

Both Pacific Northwest and Washington Public Power Supply System, allegedly a "municipality" under § 4 (e) and under § 7 (a) of the Act,[2] filed applications for licenses on mutually exclusive sites; and they were consolidated for hearing. Before the hearing the Commission solicited the views of the Secretary of the Interior. The Secretary urged postponement of the licensing of either project while means of protecting the salmon and other fisheries were studied. That was on March 15, 1961. But the hearings went forward and on June 28, 1962, after the record before the Examiner was closed, but before he rendered his decision, the Secretary wrote the Commission urging it to recommend to Congress the consideration of federal construction of High Mountain Sheep. The Commission reopened the record to allow the Secretary's letter to be incorporated and invited the parties to file supplemental briefs in response to it. On October 8, 1962, the Examiner rendered his decision, recommending that Pacific Northwest receive the license. He disposed of the issue of federal development on the ground that there "is no evidence in this record that Federal development will provide greater flood control, power benefits, fish passage, navigation or recreation; and there is substantial evidence to the contrary."

The Secretary asked for leave to intervene and to file exceptions to the Examiner's decision[3]. The Commission allowed intervention "limited to

taining dams, water conduits, reservoirs, power houses, transmission lines, or other project works necessary or convenient for the development and improvement of navigation and for the development, transmission, and utilization of power across, along, from, or in any of the streams or other bodies of water over which Congress has jurisdiction under its authority to regulate commerce with foreign nations and among the several States, or upon any part of the public lands and reservations of the United States (including the Territories), or for the purpose of utilizing the surplus water or water power from any Government dam, except as herein provided...." 49 Stat. 839, 840, 16 U.S.C. §§ 797 (a), (e).

2. See n. 1, *supra*, for § 4 (e). Section 7 (a) of the Act provides: "In issuing preliminary permits hereunder or licenses where no preliminary permit has been issued and in issuing licenses to new licensees under section 15 hereof the Commission shall give preference to applications therefor by States and municipalities, provided the plans for the same are deemed by the Commission equally well adapted, or shall within a reasonable time to be fixed by the Commission be made

equally well adapted, to conserve and utilize in the public interest the water resources of the region...." 49 Stat. 842, 16 U.S.C. § 800 (a).

3. The Secretary argued that federal development of High Mountain Sheep is necessary because (1) hydraulic and electrical coordination with other Columbia River Basin projects, particularly the federal dams already or to be constructed on the downstream sites, could be more effectively achieved if High Mountain Sheep is a part of the federal system; (2) federal development will assure maximum use of the federal northwest transmission grid, thus contributing to maximum repayment of the federal investment in transmission, which will, in turn, redound to the benefit of the power consumers; (3) federal development would provide greater flexibility and protection in the management of fish resources; (4) flood control could better be effected by flexible federal operation; (5) storage releases for navigation requirements could be made under federal ownership and supervision with less effect on power supply; (6) federal development can better provide recreational fa-

filing of exceptions to the Presiding Examiner's decision and participation in such oral argument as might subsequently be ordered."

The Secretary filed exceptions and participated in oral argument. The Commission on February 5, 1964, affirmed the Examiner saying that it agreed with him "that the record supports no reason why federal development should be superior," observing that "[while] we have extensive material before us on the position of the Secretary of the Interior, there is no evidence in the record presented by him to support his position." 31 F.P.C., at 275.

It went on to say that it found "nothing in this record to indicate" that the public purposes of the dam (flood control, etc.) would not be served as adequately by Pacific Northwest as they would under federal development. And it added, "We agree that the Secretary (or any single operator) normally would have a superior ability to co-ordinate the operations of HMS with the other affected projects on the river. But there is no evidence upon which we can determine the scope or the seriousness of this matter in the context of a river system which already has a number of different project operators and an existing co-ordination system, i.e., the Northwest Power Pool." *Id.* at 276–277.

The Secretary petitioned for a rehearing, asking that the record be opened to permit him to supply the evidentiary deficiencies. A rehearing, but not a reopening of the record, was granted; and the Commission shortly reaffirmed its original decision with modifications not material here.

The issue of federal development has never been explored in this record. The applicants introduced no evidence addressed to that question; and the Commission denied the Secretary an opportunity to do so though his application was timely. The issue was of course briefed and argued; yet no factual inquiry was undertaken. Section 7 (b) says "Whenever, in the judgment of the Commission, the development of any water resources for public purposes should be undertaken by the United States itself," the Commission shall not approve other applications. Yet the Commission by its rulings on the applications of the Secretary to intervene and to reopen precluded it from having the informed judgment that § 7(b) commands.

We indicate no judgment on the merits. We do know that on the Snake–Columbia waterway between High Mountain Sheep and the ocean, eight hydroelectric dams have been built and another authorized. These are federal projects; and if another dam is to be built, the question whether it should be under federal auspices looms large. Timed releases of stored water at High Mountain Sheep may affect navigability; they may affect hydroelectric production of the downstream dams when the river level is too low for the generators to be operated at maximum capacity; they may affect irrigation; and they may protect salmon runs when the water

cilities for an expanding population. The Secretary noted, however, that immediate construction of the project would produce an excess of power in the Pacific Northwest which would cause large losses to Bonneville Power Administration and severe harm to the region's economy.

downstream is too hot or insufficiently oxygenated. Federal versus private or municipal control may conceivably make a vast difference in the functioning of the vast river complex.

Beyond that is the question whether any dam should be constructed. As to this the Secretary in his letter to the Commission dated November 21, 1960, in pleading for a deferment of consideration of applications stated:

> In carrying out this Department's responsibility for the protection and conservation of the vital Northwest anadromous fishery resource and in light of the fact that the power to be available as a result of ratification of the proposed Columbia River treaty with Canada will provide needed time which can be devoted to further efforts to resolve the fishery problems presently posed by these applications, we believe that it is unnecessary at this time and for some years to come to undertake any project in this area.

> You may be assured that the Fish and Wildlife Service of this Department will continue, with renewed emphasis, the engineering and research studies that must be done before we can be assured that the passage of anadromous fish can be provided for at these proposed projects.

Since the cases must be remanded to the Commission, it is appropriate to refer to that aspect of the cases.

Section 10 (a) of the Act provides that "the project adopted" shall be such "as in the judgment of the Commission will be best adapted to a comprehensive plan for improving or developing a waterway ... and for other beneficial public uses, including recreational purposes."

The objective of protecting "recreational purposes" means more than that the reservoir created by the dam will be the best one possible or practical from a recreational viewpoint. There are already eight lower dams on this Columbia River system and a ninth one authorized; and if the Secretary is right in fearing that this additional dam would destroy the waterway as spawning grounds for anadromous fish (salmon and steelhead) or seriously impair that function, the project is put in an entirely different light. The importance of salmon and steelhead in our outdoor life as well as in commerce is so great that there certainly comes a time when their destruction might necessitate a halt in so-called "improvement" or "development" of waterways. The destruction of anadromous fish in our western waters is so notorious that we cannot believe that Congress through the present Act authorized their ultimate demise.

Mr. Justice Holmes once wrote that "A river is more than an amenity, it is a treasure." *New Jersey v. New York*, 283 U.S. 336, 342. That dictum is relevant here for the Commission under § 10 of the 1920 Act, as amended, must take into consideration not only hydroelectric power, navigation, and flood control, but also the "recreational purposes" served by the river. And, as we have noted, the Secretary of the Interior has a mandate under the 1965 Act to study recommendations concerning water development programs for the purpose of the conservation of anadromous fish. Thus apart from § 7 (b) of the 1920 Act, as amended, the Secretary by reason of § 2 of the 1965 Act comes to the Federal Power Commission with a special mandate from Congress, a mandate that gives him special standing to appear, to intervene, to introduce evidence on the proposed river development program, and to participate fully in the administrative proceedings.

In his letter of November 21, 1960, the Secretary noted that, due to increased power resources, the projects could be safely deferred. "These projects could extend the time still further, as could also be the case in the event nuclear power materialized at Hanford in the 1960–1970 period. This possibility, as you know, has been under intensive study by your staff for the Atomic Energy Commission...."

By 1980 nuclear energy "should represent a significant proportion of world power production." *Id.* at 109. By the end of the century "nuclear energy may account for about one-third of our total energy consumption." Ibid. "By the middle of the next century it seems likely that most of our energy needs will be satisfied by nuclear energy." *Id.* at 110.

Some of these time schedules are within the period of the 50–year licenses granted by the Commission.

Nuclear energy is coming to the Columbia River basin by 1975. For plans are afoot to build a plant on the Trogan site, 14 miles north of St. Helens. This one plant will have a capacity of 1,000,000 kws. This emphasizes the relevancy of the Secretary's reference to production and distribution of nuclear energy at the Hanford Thermal Project which he called "most important of all" and which Congress has authorized. 76 Stat. 604.

The need to destroy the river as a waterway, the desirability of its demise, the choices available to satisfy future demands for energy—these are all relevant to a decision under § 7 and § 10 but they were largely untouched by the Commission.

On our remand there should be an exploration of these neglected phases of the cases, as well as the other points raised by the Secretary.

We express no opinion on the merits. It is not our task to determine whether any dam at all should be built or whether if one is authorized it should be private or public. If the ultimate ruling under § 7 (b) is that the decision concerning the High Mountain Sheep site should be made by the Congress, the factors we have mentioned will be among the many considerations it doubtless will appraise. If the ultimate decision under § 7 (b) is the other way, the Commission will not have discharged its functions under the Act unless it makes an informed judgment on these phases of the cases. We reverse the judgment and remand the case to the Court of Appeals with instructions to remand to the Commission.

Each remand is for further proceedings consistent with this opinion.

[Justice Harlan, with whom Justice Stewart joined, dissented on the ground that the Commission's decision was supported by substantial evidence.]■

NOTES AND COMMENTS

1. The opinion of the Supreme Court in the *Udall* case came at the beginning of a decade of heightened environmental sensitivity that produced much federal environmental legislation. The case is often cited as one of the earliest examples of the "hard look" doctrine, which was used extensively by federal courts in the 1970s to force federal agencies to examine the environmental implications of their decisions. See James Oakes, The Judicial Role in Environmental Law, 52 N.Y.U. L. Rev. 498 (1977).

2. The Court's citation to predictions that nuclear power would replace the need for traditional sources of power generation now seems rather ironic. Not only has such power proven to be more expensive than was then anticipated, but the environmental opposition to it has been even more intense than to hydroelectric projects. Nuclear power is discussed in Chapter Fourteen. This is not the last example you will see of a confidently voiced energy prediction that proves widely off the mark.

3. The history of hydropower development reflects a theme that will be seen again and again in the history of technology, and particularly energy technology. A new and more efficient way of producing energy is discovered and the public is willing to sacrifice other objectives in order to bring it about. Some years later, when the technology is no longer at the forefront, the public often has difficulty remembering why it was willing to make such sacrifices. *See* Richard White, The Organic Machine: The Remaking of the Columbia River, Hill & Wang, 1995. The dilemma of the *Charles River Bridge* case (*see* Chapter Three) is repeated over and over in the history of energy law.

4. The High Mountain Sheep Dam was never built. Eight years after the Udall decision, Congress included the proposed dam site in the Hells Canyon National Recreation Area, thereby prohibiting the construction of dams and preserving the area's free-flowing rivers and salmon habitat. However, the "designation did nothing to restore the spring fish flows that young Idaho salmon needed to survive the eight federal dams that now obstructed their journey from their spawning grounds to the ocean." Michael C. Blumm and F. Lorraine Bodi, in The Northwest Salmon Crisis: A Documentary History, Joseph Cone and Sandy Ridlington, eds., Oregon State University Press, 1996.

5. Snake River politics is just as volatile today as it was in the 1960s. The Snake River is home to many species of fish, including several species listed as "endangered," including steelhead and chinook salmon. It is estimated that millions of salmon returned to the Snake and Columbia Rivers each year to spawn, and now only a few hundred thousand make the journey. Many things have contributed to the decline in fish stock in the Snake River, such as over-harvesting, and effects on the habitat from farming, grazing, mining, logging, etc. But most people agree that dams significantly contributed to the salmons' decline, especially those dams that eliminate access to fresh water for spawning purposes. Scientists believe that the

salmon need more natural river conditions—cold, clean, free-flowing water—to remain a viable species.

There are many dams in the Columbia and Snake River basin, eight of which are operated by the United States Army Corps of Engineers ("USACE"). The USACE implemented several mechanisms in efforts to preserve the existing fish population. Adult fish ladders are used to assist the adult salmon in forging their way upstream to places to spawn. Juvenile fish bypass systems are also in place, to allow juvenile fish to make their way to the ocean. However, these bypass systems involve the fish going through a turbine or over a dam spillway, which can be detrimental to the fish. Another measure being used to aid in the preservation of fish species is the trap and haul method. Fish are caught and transported by truck around the hydropower projects and then released back into the river.

Currently, environmental groups are pushing the USACE to partially remove four lower Snake River dams to promote recovery of salmon. *See* Michael C. Blumm, *et. al.*, Symposium on Water Law: Saving Snake River Water and Salmon Simultaneously, 28 Envtl. L. 997 (1998). The USACE is trying to model the various factors affecting the salmon in order to decide how to proceed. See www.nwd.usace.army.mil. The Oregon Natural Resources Council's cost-benefit analysis estimates that restoration of salmon populations through dam removal would result in a net economic benefit of $87 million. www.onrc.org/wild_oregon/salmonriver98/salmonriver98.html. (The Oregon Natural Resources Council is a conservation organization that promotes environmental protection in Oregon).

Some environmental organizations have their eyes on even larger dams. The Glen Canyon dam in the Colorado River is one of the largest dams in the country. In 1996, the Sierra Club voted to support the decommissioning of the dam in order to protect various endangered species of fish in the Colorado River. Scott K. Miller, Undamming Glen Canyon: Lunacy, Rationality, or Prophecy?, 19 Stan. Envtl. L. J. 121 (2000).

6. Once a particular fish population has been listed as an endangered or threatened species under the Endangered Species Act, 16 U.S.C. § 1531 et. seq., the powerful sanctions of the Act begin to play a dominant role in the management of the river. Federal wildlife agencies need to sign off on federal projects or federal permits that affect the river. 16 U.S.C. § 1536. It becomes unlawful to "take" any such fish, 16 U.S.C. § 1538, including taking through habitat destruction. *Palila v. Hawaii Dept. of Land and Natural Resources*, 639 F.2d 495 (9th Cir.1981). The management of the Columbia and Snake Rivers is now subject to very different legal rules that it was at the time the *Udall* case was decided. "The Columbia Basin is now awash with ESA listings of salmonids. No fewer than twelve Columbia Basin salmonid species are currently under ESA protection. When the decade dawned, there were no salmonid listings at all. Within a seven-year period, the ESA has assumed a dominant role in salmon law and policy in the basin." Michael C. Blumm & Greg D. Corbin, Salmon and the Endangered Species Act: Lessons from the Columbia Basin, 74 Washington L.

Rev. 519, 586 (1999). *See also* John M. Volkman, How Do You Learn From a River? Managing Uncertainty in Species Conservation Policy, 74 Wash. L. Rev. 719 (1999).

But will it really make a difference? Some commentators suggest that the tough language of the Endangered Species Act has been watered down by flexible administration. "The empirical experience with Section 7 consultation can be summed up simply: large numbers, few project stoppages." William H. Rodgers, Jr., Environmental Law 1011 (West Group, 2d. ed. 1994). *See* also Blumm & Corbin, *supra*, at 524, 598–599.

The American legal system has always recognized that public ownership is one acceptable alternative for managing energy resources, even though it has been less common than private ownership. The government itself might take title to a coal mine or to an electric utility's facilities. In certain instances, government ownership may have advantages over private ownership. Due to market failures, private ownership may under- or over-price energy resources, or may fail to make them available to certain classes of customers. Once the government assumes ownership of energy resources, the political process monitors and guards against the failures of private property in the market. The government could pass the cost of resources through to users or consumers by charging higher usage fees or rates. Debate over the advantages and disadvantages of government ownership of hydropower resources has been particularly intense.

Robert L. Bradley, Jr.
The Origins of Political Electricity: Market Failure or Political Opportunism

17 Energy L.J. 59 (1996)

The first federal hydro project was built by the Interior Department's Bureau of Reclamation in 1909 in northeastern Utah. Another twenty irrigation and reclamation power projects would follow by 1932, totaling 138 megawatts. The War Department completed the Wilson Dam in 1925 and used its power for wartime materials. By this time, a federal law (see below) was in place to regulate the Wilson Dam and future hydro projects.

Federal Water Power Act of 1920. After six years of Congressional debate, the Federal Water Power Act of 1920 (FWPA), the first major federal law regulating the power industry, was enacted. The law established the Federal Power Commission (FPC), composed of the secretaries of War, Interior, and Commerce, to:

1. gather information concerning the use of domestic water resources for power development and investigate the relationship of the U.S. water power industry to other industries and interstate and foreign commerce;

2. determine "whether the power from Government dams can be advantageously used by the United States for its public purposes, and what is a fair value of such power;"

3. issue licenses up to fifty years to new investor-owned or municipal power projects on federal waterways and lands "for the purpose of utilizing the surplus water or water power from any Government dam."

4. require licensees to make comprehensive cost determinations, disclose all financial information, and establish a uniform system of accounts in any new or improved federal water project;

5. set "reasonable, nondiscriminatory, and just" (cost based) rates for water power in interstate or foreign commerce in accordance with the Interstate Commerce Act of 1887;

6. set a "reasonable" rate of return for all licensed projects with any "excess" earnings after twenty years either expropriated or applied to reduce net investment;

7. assess annual charges for the use of government property, the administration of this Act, and to collect excess profits except for nonprofits and government projects not using federal dams;

8. require "reasonable" investments to improve navigation, or if not reasonable, use federal money for said improvements;

9. require project construction to begin within two years of when the license is issued and take possession of unfinished projects after a two-year notification;

10. issue a new license or take over all projects after the fifty-year original license expires;

11. regulate unregulated state projects until the state itself does so if a complaint is filed; and

12. exempt minor hydro projects (those under one hundred horsepower) from all provisions of this law except for the fifty-year license.

The FWPA enjoyed industry and business support. Although regulated, private developers finally could gain entry to at least some water sites....

Reorganization of the Federal Power Commission. Under the 1920 act, the FPC was not an independent commission but a hybrid regulatory body run by representatives from three other agencies. Very little regulating was done, and what was done was considered inadequate. This lead to a reorganization in 1930 whereby the FPC became an independent agency. The number of commissioners was raised from three to five, and the commissioners had to originate from outside the industry they regulated, be from different political backgrounds, and be full-time members. The new FPC also was authorized to hire staff and contract for the materials "necessary to execute its functions." These changes positioned the FPC for its increased responsibilities that would come with both electricity and natural gas.

FDR's Public Power Initiatives. As governor of New York in the 1920s, Franklin Roosevelt endorsed municipal provision of electric power to ensure that more Americans gained access to power and to use as a "yardstick" enterprise to compete against investor-owned utilities. Power provision to FDR was "a national problem," and in his first term as president he formulated a National Power Policy not only to bring interstate electricity under federal public utility regulation but also to make electricity "more broadly available at cheaper rates to industry, to domestic and to agricultural consumers." Hydropower as a federal public works program and rural subsidy program was key.

Three major laws ... would follow as part of FDR's public works program to promote economic recovery during the Great Depression.

1. **Tennessee Valley Authority.** On April 10, 1933, FDR proposed a major hydro project to Congress to rectify "the continued idleness of a great national investment in the Tennessee Valley." The next month, Congress approved the Tennessee Valley Act (TVA) "in the interest of national defense and for agricultural and industrial development, and to improve navigation in the Tennessee River and to control the destructive flood waters." The Act established a three-member board with eminent domain powers to "construct dams, reservoirs, power houses, power structures, transmission lines ... and to unite the various power installations into one or more systems by transmission lines." The agency was empowered to "produce, distribute, and sell electric power" with preference to "States, counties, municipalities, and cooperative organizations of citizens and farmers, not organized or doing business for profit, but primarily for the purpose of supplying electricity to its own citizens or members." Contracts could be for up to twenty years, and agreements with for-profit entities could be voided with five years' notice if the power was needed on the non-profit side.... The fateful decision made by Congress was to construct and operate the facilities as a public project. Numerous applications for private development languished before Congress between 1903 and 1933 without approval. Two Tennessee utilities applied for federal permits to invest between $60 and $100 million to develop eleven waterpower sites only to encounter years of inaction. The result of government provision was a competitive antagonism between TVA and neighboring private systems who were discriminated against under the preference system and feared taxpayer-funded raiding that led to litigation and obstructionism that retarded rural electrification. Facilities were also duplicated.

2. **Rural Electrification Act of 1936.** In early 1935, FDR endorsed a program to subsidize rural electrification to which Congress responded with a $100 million appropriation. On May 11, 1935, FDR issued an executive order creating a new agency to transmit electricity "to as many farms as possible in the shortest possible time, and to have it used in quantities sufficient to affect rural life." The Rural Electrification Administration (REA) was empowered to make loans to private

and public parties to finance connections with farms. As a public works program, 90% of involved workers had to originate from the relief rolls unless an exemption was granted by the REA. The next year the program was put on a more permanent basis with the passage of the Rural Electrification Act. The REA was instructed to "make loans in the several States and Territories of the United States for rural electrification and the furnishing of electric energy to persons in rural areas [defined as residing in population centers under 1,500 persons] who are not receiving central station service." The REA was appropriated $50 million for fiscal year 1937 and $40 million for each of the next eight years to finance generation, transmission, and distribution facilities. Loans for such assets could not exceed 85% of the principal amount and had to be fully amortized over a twenty-five-year period (with a maximum five-year extension) at an interest rate paid by the government on long term debt. Financing preference was given to governmental bodies and private cooperatives and nonprofits....

3.   Bonneville Power Administration Act of 1937. Federal monies to develop the water resources of the Pacific Northwest were first allocated by Congress in 1933 as part of the employment program of the Public Works Administration. An additional allocation followed two years later in the Rivers and Harbors Improvement Act. The final push was the Bonneville Power Administration Act of 1937 (BPA), which authorized the Secretary of War to "provide, construct, operate, maintain, and improve at [the dam projects under construction at Bonneville, Oregon and North Bonneville, Washington] such machines, equipment, and facilities for the generation of electric energy ... to develop such electricity as rapidly as markets may be found therefor." To "encourage the widest possible use of all electricity," the Bonneville Power Administrator was authorized to construct transmission facilities to interconnect with other markets. Eminent domain rights were granted to facilitate land requisition associated with the above....

FDR's policy of "direct and indirect competition in reducing electricity prices ... including yardstick federal power projects, birch rod potential competition from municipalities and rural cooperatives, [and] well-publicized annual rate surveys" has been found by one business historian to be "quite sound." This analysis adds the caveats, however, that (1) rates could have fallen further still without FDR's activism, and (2) the "administrative costs, rent-seeking costs, price discrimination practices, government subsidies, and other factors" related to his activism would have to be assessed. While the first point can probably be discounted—more generation and distribution investment would surely increase supply to lower prices compared to its absence—the second point raises a very obvious issue: a large dedication of taxpayer resources amid Depression scarcity was not a free lunch. But the foregone opportunity of FDR's action was not so much his inaction. It was the deregulation of electric utilities and privatized electric provision to let market forces guide the industry where, by definition, no taxpayer or regulatory costs would be incurred.■

3.   PRIVATIZATION

A market economy, such as ours, relies on pervasive private ownership of resources. In its pure theoretical form, private property ownership is characterized by dominion and control (the power to define the use of the property), exclusivity (the power to exclude others from using the property) and transferability (the power to transfer use or title of the property to another owner). The 1990's saw a movement toward privatization throughout the world. The collapse of the Soviet Union brought recognition that many publicly-owned enterprises were both economically inefficient and environmentally disastrous.

This privatization movement has had relatively little impact on the energy industries of the United States insofar as at their domestic operations are concerned. In the U.S., most energy resources, as well as most of the infrastructure for extracting, transporting, and distributing energy to consumers, were already privately owned. Peabody Coal Company owns the ton of coal that it extracts from its mine; likewise, Detroit Edison, a private investor-owned utility, owns the power plants and transmission lines it uses to generate and distribute its electricity, as well as the electrons that it makes available to residential customers.

While public ownership has been the recent norm in several socialist countries, such as China and the former Soviet Union, the U.S. system has opted for a scheme of predominantly private energy resource ownership coupled with regulation. The U.S. system recognizes that public ownership may be subject to manipulation and capture by private interests, and may only succeed at the cost of efficiency. However, there have been two significant historical exceptions to the norm of private ownership of energy resources in the U.S.

First, many electrical generation projects were planned, built, and have been operated by the government. For example. one of the largest power projects in U.S. history—the Tennessee Valley Authority—was conceived and in many respects continues to operate under government ownership. One of the greatest proponents of public ownership of energy resource projects was Franklin D. Roosevelt who, as governor of New York in the late 1920s and early 30s, fought for public ownership of hydroelectric power projects. Roosevelt's populist vision was that the nation's natural resources—such as the Niagara Falls—are owned by the people and public ownership is the most effective way to return these resources—such as the vigor of the Niagara—to the people through low electricity rates.

The concept of public ownership was not the norm then, nor is it today. However, today many municipal governments continue to own and operate electrical generation, transmission, and distribution facilities. In addition, the government continues to own and operate several hydroelectric facilities and to distribute this power via the five federal power marketing agencies: Alaska Power Administration, Bonneville Power Administration, Southeastern Power Administration, Southwestern Power Administration, and Western Area Power Administration. The government gives a preference to municipalities and other public bodies in the sale of this power. It is important to note, though, that most electrical and natural gas "public utilities" are not owned by the government but are privately owned by shareholders.

Second, in many instances the land on which many energy resources are located remains under public ownership. For example, many of the coal reserves in the Western U.S. lie below land owned by the U.S. government. Under the Mining Act of 1872, 30 U.S.C. § 26 *et seq.* individuals were encouraged to prospect, explore, and develop the mineral resources below federal land. Effectively, this statute enshrined a federal policy that encouraged the prompt development of mineral resources without regard to the impact on the land and its surroundings. Once an individual located minerals and established a claim, the locator had "the exclusive right of possession and enjoyment of all of the surface...." *Id.* at § 26. Today, this outright giveaway of mineral resources is questionable.

Although the government no longer gives away the rights to fossil-fuel minerals on its land,[4] it continues to own substantial mineral reserves in coal, oil, and natural gas and allows private individuals and firms to extract these reserves for a fee. The current regulatory approach also favors the restoration of the surface of such lands to their original condition. This introduces a form of ownership that is extremely important to oil and gas law: the leasehold, or the right to use property owned by someone else for a limited term. *See* Chapter 6.

Even absent government regulation, complete private ownership does not imply that a resource holder can use an energy resource in whatever manner she pleases. Private ownership of energy resources is subject to important common-law rules that limit the nature of that ownership such as the law of nuisance, requirements for subjacent lateral support, the public trust doctrine and the federal navigational servitude.

4.   THE RENEWABILITY OF HYDROPOWER

Given modern concerns about whether energy resources are renewable, the question of whether hydropower is truly a renewable resource has assumed increasing importance. As the Udall case suggests, by the 1960s most of the desirable dam sites in the United States were then occupied by hydroelectric projects. The power being generated was relatively cheap and was appreciated by the residents of the particular region, but opposition to further hydroelectric development was building at the national level. This opposition was based on three unrelated issues: (a) as the cost of these projects increased, residents of areas which lacked useful dam sites argued that these hydro projects were prime examples of "pork barrel politics;"[5]

---

4. The Mining Act of 1872 has since been modified by the Mineral Leasing Act of 1920, 30 U.S.C. § 181 *et seq.* and the Federal Coal Leasing Amendments Act of 1975, 30 U.S.C. § 201 *et seq.*

5. The term "pork barrel" is used to describe projects funded by all of the federal taxpayers that primarily benefit the people of a particular state or congressional district.

(b) recreational users of rivers, including the newly popular rafting industry, complained that fewer and fewer rivers could still be utilized for their purposes; and (c) commercial and sport fishing interests were increasingly realizing the extent to which dams were interfering with the ability of fish to reproduce.

Despite these concerns, however, the construction of hydro projects revived sharply in the mid–1980s when overseas crises forced up the price of oil and made Americans conscious of their dependence on imported oil. In response, Congress passed the Public Utility Regulatory Policies Act of 1982 ("PURPA," 16 U.S.C. § 2601 *et seq.*) which included (among many other provisions, some of which will be dealt with in later chapters) a series of incentives to encourage the building by private companies of small hydroelectric projects.

To those concerned with energy policy in 1982, hydropower had the distinct advantage of being renewable. In other words, the fact that the water was used to generate energy would not diminish the amount of water that would be available in the future. Renewable sources of energy were contrasted with nonrenewable sources such as coal, oil and natural gas, which existed in finite amounts and were being depleted by our current use of them. To the extent that more power could be generated from renewable resources, our dependence on depleting resources (and foreign resources) could be reduced. In response to the perception of an "energy crisis," therefore, Congress provided incentives that brought thousands of new hydro license applications to the Federal Energy Regulation Commission. Although the legislation recognized the impact that dams might have on fish populations, and the Act required the FERC to give consideration to the views of state and federal wildlife agencies, the final decision was the FERC's.

Should hydropower be considered a truly renewable resource? Traditionally, hydroelectric power has been considered a renewable energy source. The continuous flow of water in many of our nation's rivers has served as a relatively inexpensive way to produce electricity since water flow is virtually endless. And in view of recent concerns that the combustion of fossil fuels contributes to climate change (*see* Chapter Seventeen), in licensing proceedings the FERC has begun to evaluate the extent to which a hydropower facility displaces fossil fuel-burning plants. *Avista Corporation*, 90 FERC ¶ 61,167 (slip opinion p. 40, February 23, 2000).

However, many now argue that hydropower is *not* renewable because of the environmental impacts. Construction of dams saturated thousands of acres of land. Wildlife habitats have been severely altered or destroyed, chiefly by turning a free-flowing river into a series of pools and dams. Fish stocks near many of the hydro projects are dwindling rapidly. Many of these environmental impacts are irreversible or would take many years to correct. Because of this kind of environmental impacts, several states refuse to treat hydropower as renewable energy when establishing rules requiring local electric utilities to obtain a percentage of electric generation from renewable sources. See Chapter Ten.

C.   THE FEDERAL ENERGY REGULATORY COMMISSION

The Federal Energy Regulatory Commission (FERC) plays a key role in the development of energy law. FERC deals with hundreds of hydroelectric projects, most of them much smaller than the dams at issue in the *Udall* case. As an example, we will look at the way that one particular hydro project was handled by the FERC. This example also illustrates the way in which the licensing process is affected by the National Environmental Policy Act, 42 U.S.C. § 4331 et. seq. As background, the following sections of the statutes and regulations describe briefly the structure of the FERC and the way it makes a decision about whether to license a dam (which, of course, is only one of many decisions over which it has responsibility.) The excerpted sections are only a small part of the body of law that governs FERC's operations.

Volume 42, U.S. Code § 7171. Appointment and administration

(a) Federal Energy Regulatory Commission; establishment. There is hereby established within the Department an independent regulatory commission to be known as the Federal Energy Regulatory Commission.

(b) Composition; term of office; conflict of interest.

(1) The Commission shall be composed of five members appointed by the President, by and with the advice and consent of the Senate. One of the members shall be designated by the President as Chairman. Members shall hold office for a term of 5 years and may be removed by the President only for inefficiency, neglect of duty, or malfeasance in office. Not more than three members of the Commission shall be members of the same political party. Any Commissioner appointed to fill a vacancy occurring prior to the expiration of the term for which his predecessor was appointed shall be appointed only for the remainder of such term. A Commissioner may continue to serve after the expiration of his term until his successor is appointed and has been confirmed and taken the oath of Office, except that such Commissioner shall not serve beyond the end of the session of the Congress in which such term expires. Members of the Commission shall not engage in any other business, vocation or employment while serving on the Commission.

(2) Notwithstanding the third sentence of paragraph (1), the terms of members first taking office after the date of enactment of the Federal Energy Regulatory Commission Member Term Act of 1990 [enacted April 11, 1990] shall expire as follows:

(A) In the case of members appointed to succeed members whose terms expire in 1991, one such member's term shall expire on June 30, 1994, and one such member's term shall expire on June 30, 1995, as designated by the President at the time of appointment.

(B) In the case of members appointed to succeed members whose terms expire in 1992, one such member's term shall expire on June 30, 1996, and one such member's term shall expire on June 30, 1997, as designated by the President at the time of appointment.

(C) In the case of the member appointed to succeed the member whose term expires in 1993, such member's term shall expire on June 30, 1998.

(c) Duties and responsibilities of Chairman. The Chairman shall be responsible on behalf of the Commission for the executive and administrative operation of the Commission, including functions of the Commission with respect to (1) the appointment and employment of hearing examiners in accordance with the provisions of title 5, United States Code [5 U.S.C. §§ 1 *et seq.*], (2) the selection, appointment, and fixing of the compensation of such personnel as he deems necessary, including an executive director, (3) the supervision of personnel employed by or assigned to the Commission, except that each member of the Commission may select and supervise personnel for his personal staff, (4) the distribution of business among personnel and among administrative units of the Commission, and (5) the procurement of services of experts and consultants in accordance with section 3109 of title 5, United States Code. The Secretary shall provide to the Commission such support and facilities as the Commission determines it needs to carry out its functions.

(d) Supervision and direction of members, employees, or other personnel of Commission. In the performance of their functions, the members, employees, or other personnel of the Commission shall not be responsible to or subject to the supervision or direction of any officer, employee, or agent of any other part of the Department.

Volume 18, Code of Federal Regulations

§ 375.101   The Commission.

(a) Establishment. The Federal Energy Regulatory Commission is an independent regulatory commission within the Department of Energy established by section 401 of the DOE Act.

(b) Offices. The principal office of the Commission is at 825 North Capitol Street, NE., Washington, D.C. 20426. Regional offices are maintained at Atlanta, Ga., Chicago, Ill., Fort Worth, Texas, New York, N.Y., and San Francisco, Calif.

(c) Hours. Unless the Chairman otherwise directs, the offices of the Commission are open each day, except Saturdays, Sundays, and Holidays, from 8:30 a.m. to 5:00 p.m.

(d) Sessions. The Commission may meet and exercise its powers at any place in the United States. The time and place of meetings of the Commission are announced in advance as provided in § 375.204.

(e) Quorum. A quorum for the transaction of business consists of at least three members present.

(f) Action by Commissioners or representatives. The Commission may, by one or more of its members or by such agents as it may designate, conduct any hearing, or other inquiry necessary or appropriate to its functions, except that nothing in this paragraph supercedes the provisions of section 556, of Title 5, United States Code relating to Administrative Law Judges.

§ 375.105 Filings.

(a) Filings in pending proceedings. All filings in proceedings referred to in § 375.104 shall be made with the Secretary.

(b) Filings in connection with functions transferred to the Commission. All persons required to file periodic or other reports with any agency or commission whose functions are transferred under such Act to the Commission shall file such reports which relate to those transferred functions with the Secretary. The Commission hereby continues in effect all previously-approved forms for making periodic or other reports.

(c) Where to make filings. All filings of documents with the Commission shall be made with the Secretary. The address for filings to be made with the Secretary is: Secretary, Federal Energy Regulatory Commission, 825 N. Capitol St., NE., Washington, DC 20426. Where a document to be filed with the Secretary is hand-delivered, it shall be submitted to Room 3110, 825 North Capitol Street, NE., Washington, DC 20426. Documents received after regular business hours are deemed to have been filed on the next regular business day.

§ 375.301 Purpose and subdelegations.

(a) The purpose of this subpart is to set forth the authorities that the Commission has delegated to staff officials. Any action by a staff official under the authority of this subpart may be appealed to the Commission in accordance with § 385.1902 of this chapter.

(b) Where the Commission, in delegating functions to specified Commission officials, permits an official to further delegate those functions to a designee of such official, designee shall mean the deputy of such official, the head of a division, or a comparable official as designated by the official to whom the direct delegation is made.

(c) For purposes of Subpart C, uncontested and in uncontested cases mean that no motion to intervene, or notice of intervention, in opposition to the pending matter made under § 385.214 (intervention) has been received by the Commission.

§ 375.308 Delegations to the Director of the Office of Energy Projects.

The Commission authorizes the Director or the Director's designee to:

(a) Take appropriate action on uncontested applications and on applications for which the only motion or notice of intervention is filed by a competing preliminary permit or exemption applicant that does not propose and substantiate materially different plans to develop, conserve, and utilize the water resources of the region for the following:

(1) Licenses (including original, new, and transmission line licenses) under part I of the Federal Power Act;

(2) Exemptions from all or part of the licensing requirements of part I of the Federal Power Act; and

(3) Preliminary permits for proposed projects.

(b) Take appropriate action on uncontested applications for:

(1) Amendments (including changes in the use or disposal of water power project lands or waters or in the boundaries of water power projects) to licenses (including original, new, and transmission line licenses) under part I of the Federal Power Act, exemptions from all or part of the requirements of part I of the Federal Power Act, and preliminary permits; and

(2) Surrenders of licenses (including original and new), exemptions, and preliminary permits.

1.   JURISDICTION

A hydroelectric project does not need the approval of the FERC unless it is located on a river over which the Commission has jurisdiction. A publicly-owned water authority in Fairfax County, Virginia, had built two dams on the Occoquan River to store water for public water supply. It included hydroelectric power generating facilities to supplement its own need for electricity to run its water pumping operations. The Authority did not think it needed to get a license from the FERC, but the FERC's Director of Hydropower Licensing disagreed. The Authority appealed his decision to the full Commission:

Fairfax County Water Authority

43 F.E.R.C. ¶ 61,062 (1988).

By orders issued January 21, 1987 and March 16, 1987, the Director, Office of Hydropower Licensing (Director), determined that the Fairfax County Water Authority's (Authority) Upper and Lower Occoquan Projects, located on the Occoquan River in Fairfax County, Virginia, are required to be licensed pursuant to Section 23(b)(1) of the Federal Power Act, 16 U.S.C. § 817(1) (1982) (FPA). The Director concluded that the projects are located on a stretch of the Occoquan River that is navigable within the meaning of Section 3(8) of the FPA, 16 U.S.C. § 796(8). Accordingly, the orders required the Authority to file license applications for the Occoquan projects.

The Authority filed timely appeals of the January 21 and March 16 orders, arguing that the Director erred in concluding that the stretch of the Occoquan River where the projects are located is navigable. The Authority also claims that the projects do not affect the interests of interstate or foreign commerce....

Section 23(b)(1) of the FPA would require licensing of the Occoquan projects if: (1) they are located on a navigable water of the United States; (2) they occupy lands of the United States; (3) they utilize surplus water or water power from a government dam; or (4) they are located on a body of water over which Congress has Commerce Clause jurisdiction, project construction occurred on or after August 26, 1935, and the projects affect the interests of interstate commerce. Since the Authority's projects do not occupy lands of the United States or utilize surplus water or water power from a government dam, whether the projects are required to be licensed depends on whether they are located on a navigable water or come within the scope of (4) above.

Navigability. Under Section 3(8) of the FPA[6], navigable waters are generally those streams which in their natural or improved condition are used or suitable for use for the transportation of persons or property in interstate or foreign commerce, including any interrupting falls, shallows, or rapids compelling land carriage. *See United States v. Appalachian Electric Power Co.,* 311 U.S. 377 (1940).

The Occoquan River rises in Loudoun, Fairfax, and Fauquier Counties and drains the upper part of Prince William County. It is formed by the junction, about a mile south of Brentsville, Virginia, of Broad Run and Cedar Run, and thence flows northeast to where it is joined by Bull Run and continues in a generally southeast direction for approximately 14 miles to the Potomac River. The Occoquan River crosses the fall-line[7] just before it reaches the town of Occoquan, which is the head of tidewater, and up to which there is a navigable depth of five feet at low tide and seven feet at high tide. A fall, now partially inundated by the dams of the Occoquan projects, begins approximately three miles above the head of tidewater and continues down to tide, falling about 80 feet in that distance. At its mouth, the Occoquan River is five miles wide. At the head of tide, approximately six to seven miles above, it narrows to 75 yards.

The Director relied on a 1938 Federal Power Commission Report on the Potomac River Basin to conclude that the Occoquan projects are located on a stretch of the Occoquan River that is navigable. The 1938 Report indicates, and the Authority agrees, that for six miles above its mouth the

6. Section 3(8) provides: "navigable waters" means those parts of streams or other bodies of water over which Congress has jurisdiction under its authority to regulate commerce with foreign nations and among the several States, and which either in their natural or improved condition notwithstanding interruptions between the navigable parts of such streams or waters by falls, shallows, or rapids compelling land carriage, are used or suitable for use for the transportation of persons or property in interstate or foreign commerce, including therein all such interrupting falls, shallows, or rapids, together with such other parts of streams as shall have been authorized by Congress for improvement by the United States or shall have been recommended to Congress for such improvement after investigation under its authority.

7. The fall-line is an imaginary boundary line separating the middle and western water-shed divisions from the eastern division, which extends from the coast to the head of tidewater and navigation. It marks the last considerable fall on the rivers. *See* United States Department of the Interior, Report on the Water Power of the United States, Middle–Atlantic Water–Shed 520 (1885).

river is navigable. However, the Authority claims that the projects are located above the navigable tidal reach, which extends to the town of Occoquan just below the falls.

Staff inspection reveals that the upper project is located where the falls once existed, approximately one and one-half miles above the head of tidewater. Nevertheless, the falls are navigable waters if the river above the falls is navigable. *See Rochester Gas Elec. Corp. v. FPC*, 344 F.2d 594, 595 (2d Cir.1965). However, the 1938 Report does not indicate any use of the river above the town of Occoquan for transportation of commerce, and additional research regarding this stretch has uncovered no substantial evidence to support a finding that the river, in the vicinity of the upper project, is navigable.

Effect on Interstate Commerce. The Occoquan River is a body of water that Congress has authority to regulate under the Commerce Clause,[8] and project construction at the site occurred after 1935. Accordingly, a license is required to operate the Occoquan projects if they affect the interests of interstate or foreign commerce.

The Authority states that all of the energy from the Occoquan projects is used to serve its own power needs and that therefore the projects do not affect the interests of interstate commerce. The Authority claims in the alternative that, while it admittedly purchases less power from its supplier, Virginia Electric and Power Company (VEPCO), because of the projects' generation, any resultant effect on interstate commerce is too minimal to meet the "real and substantial" standard used in *City of Centralia v. FERC,* 661 F.2d 787 (9th Cir.1981).

In *FPC v. Union Electric Co. (Taum Sauk),* 381 U.S. 90, 96 (1965), the Supreme Court interpreted Section 23(b)'s reference to "affecting the interests of interstate commerce," finding that Congress had invoked "its full authority over commerce, without qualification, to define what projects on non-navigable streams are required to be licensed." The Court held that the central purpose of the FPA to provide comprehensive control over uses of the nation's water resources would be more fully served if the Commission "considers the impact of the project on the full spectrum of commerce interests." *Id.* at 98, 101. Since Part I of the FPA thus embodies the full reach of the Commerce Clause, whether projects generate to transmit energy across state lines or feed into an interstate power system for distribution is not dispositive of the effect on interstate commerce issue. Rather, the relevant point of inquiry is the relationship between the activity to be regulated and interstate commerce. Thus, if a project on a Commerce Clause water with post–1935 construction affects any of the broad range of commerce clause interests, it is required to be licensed under Section 23(b)(1) of the FPA. Moreover, as noted by the Centralia court, *supra,* 661 F.2d at 789, even if the project itself does not substantial-

---

8. The Occoquan River is a tributary of the Potomac, a navigable river, and thus comes within the scope of the Commerce Clause. See *FPC v. Union Electric Co.,* 381 U.S. 90, 97 (1965).

ly affect the interests of commerce, it can nevertheless be reached if it belongs to a class of projects whose activities affect interstate commerce, [and] a substantial effect can be measured by the cumulative effect of a class of activities. *See Wickard v. Filburn*, 317 U.S. 111 (1942).

The Authority operates the Occoquan projects to provide power generation for its water supply pumping station located in the town of Occoquan. The upper project contains two 500–kW synchronous generating units, and the lower project contains a single 350–kW synchronous generating unit. The generators' 4.16–kV terminals are continuously paralleled with the 4.16–kV incoming utility circuit from VEPCO's 34.5/4.16–kV, 16.2–MVA Aqua Substation. Direction of power flow over this utility circuit is always toward the project, since the project load always exceeds its generating capability. The magnitude of this flow varies, depending upon the relative levels of project generation and load. The respective estimated average annual output of the upper and lower projects is 4,320,000 kwh and 1,296,000 kwh. The projects supply an estimated 24.29 percent of the Authority's needs on an annual basis. The remainder of the Authority's energy needs is met with purchases from VEPCO. VEPCO's system serves load in Virginia, North Carolina, and West Virginia, and is directly connected with Allegheny Power, Appalachian Power Company, Carolina Power and Light Company, and Potomac Electric Power Company.

The units within this interstate system are interlocked electromagnetically, and thus the actions of one unit within the system affect every other generating unit in the system. *See FPC v. Florida Power & Light Co.*, 404 U.S. 453 (1972); *Indiana & Michigan Electric Co. v. FPC*, 365 F.2d 180 (7th Cir.1966).... To the extent the projects do or do not generate, they affect the functioning of the interstate energy and thus interstate commerce, because they increase or decrease the amount of power that other resources must produce to keep the system balanced.

An interconnected project that generates to supply its own power needs, thereby displacing power that would otherwise be purchased from the interstate system, affects the operation of the system as does the project that generates to directly sell energy, because both affect the supply of and the demand for energy.

The foregoing demonstrates the effect of the Occoquan projects on electricity as a basic element of interstate commerce.

Since the projects are located on Commerce Clause waters, involve post–1935 construction, and affect the interests of interstate or foreign commerce, they are required to be licensed pursuant to Section 23(b)(1) of the FPA.

The Commission orders:(A)The appeals filed by the Fairfax County Water Authority on February 9, 1987, in Docket No. UL87–3–001, and on April 10, 1987, in Docket No. UL87–9–001, are denied.(B) Fairfax County Water Authority must file with the Secretary of the Commission, within 45 days of the date of this order, an expeditious schedule for submitting a license....■

NOTES AND COMMENTS

1. The definition of navigable water in the Federal Power Act is specific to that act only. The various statutory and judge-made definitions of navigability have created a long history of legal puzzles. *See generally* A. Dan Tarlock, Law of Water Rights and Resources § 9.03 (1995).

Federal jurisdiction over navigable waterways has evolved since the formation of our country. The distinction between navigable and non-navigable waterways first arose in a commerce clause context. The Commerce Clause "comprehends navigation, within the limits of every state in the Union; so far as that navigation may be, in any manner, connected with 'commerce with foreign nations, or among the several states, or with the Indian Tribes.'" *Gibbons v. Ogden,* 22 U.S. (9 Wheat) 1, 197 (1824). For some time after this decision, federal policies dealt only with protection and enhancement of navigation, a power that was exercised often, usually to improve the navigable capacity of water bodies. The Report of the President's Water Resources Policy Commission, Vol. 3 Water Resources Law 87–91 (1950).

The first challenge to the definition of navigable waterways came with the effects that tidal movements had on navigability. Until 1851, inland lake and river systems were not considered navigable waterways. In 1851, the Supreme Court adopted "suitability for commercial navigation" as the test for federal jurisdiction. *The Propeller Genesee Chief v. Fitzhugh,* 53 U.S. (12 How.) 443 (1851). This test worked well for the larger bodies of water, but did not include smaller rivers and lakes. Several years later, the test changed to include rivers which are "navigable in fact. And they are in their ordinary condition as highways of commerce, over which trade and travel are or may be conducted in the customary modes of trade and travel over water." *The Daniel Ball,* 77 U.S. (10 Wall.) 557, 563 (1871).

The "navigation in fact" test is still used today, however it has been expanded by the Supreme Court. Federal jurisdiction was first extended to obstructions and diversions on non-navigable portions of navigable rivers. *U.S. v. Rio Grande Dam & Irrigation Co.,* 174 U.S. 690 (1899). Federal jurisdiction then extended to rivers that could be made navigable by "reasonable improvement." *U.S. v. Appalachian Elec. Power Co.,* 311 U.S. 377 (1940). Currently, courts must consider whether a river (1) is presently in use or suitable for use, or (2) was used or suitable for use in the past, or (3) could be made usable by reasonable improvements. *Rochester Gas and Elec. Corp. v. FPC,* 344 F.2d 594, 596 (2d Cir.), *cert. denied,* 382 U.S. 832 (1965). This is the controlling test for FERC jurisdiction.

The environmental movement of the 1960's created confusion in the definition of navigable waters. Environmentalists exerted pressure on the federal government to regulate the protection of shallow water bodies and wetlands. During this period, courts were split as to whether small streams were navigable or not. Those that denied federal jurisdiction did so if the parties could not produce substantial evidence of past commercial navigation or that navigation is possible by reasonable improvements. *U.S. v.*

Crow, Pope & Land Enters., Inc., 340 F.Supp. 25 (N.D.Ga.1972). Other courts allowed federal jurisdiction if the river served commercial recreational purposes. *U.S. v. Underwood*, 344 F.Supp. 486 (M.D.Fla.1972). Commerce Clause opinions were cited by courts for support that federal jurisdiction did not hinge upon a water body being navigable in fact. *Id.*

The definition of navigable water in the Clean Water Act codified the most recent of the courts' definitions. Navigable waters, as defined in the Clean Water Act, are "the Waters of the United States, including the territorial seas." Federal jurisdiction has been extended to small tributaries and associated groundwater, lagoons separated from the ocean, to landlocked lakes and associated wetlands. *See Quivira Mining Co. v. U.S. EPA,* 765 F.2d 126 (10th Cir.1985); *Boone v. U.S.,* 944 F.2d 1489 (9th Cir.1991); *U.S. v. Byrd,* 609 F.2d 1204 (7th Cir.1979); *Slagle v. U.S.,* 809 F.Supp. 704 (D.Minn.1992).

2. In *Federal Power Commission v. Florida Power & Light Co.*, cited by the Commission in the above opinion, the Supreme Court held that any electric system that is connected to a network of power lines that crosses state lines is subject to federal regulation pursuant to the interstate commerce clause. The power flow within state lines is subject to federal regulation if a utility is connected to an interstate grid, even if the utility does not transmit energy beyond the state's borders, because the power has the potential to be in interstate commerce. *Id.* This ruling was reaffirmed in *New England Power Co. v. New Hampshire*, 455 U.S. 331 (1982), where the court held that FERC has regulatory jurisdiction over transmission service performed by a utility connected to the interstate network. Virtually all electric systems are so connected, other than those in Hawaii, Alaska and arguably Texas. Congress, however, has never chosen to exercise fully the federal regulatory power, so by far the largest share of the regulation of the electric industry remains with the state governments. See Chapter Ten.

2. ROLE OF THE STATES

After FERC determined that it had jurisdiction, the Fairfax County Water Authority applied for a license for its Occoquan Projects from FERC's office of hydropower licensing. The license was issued almost three years later in the following decision:

Fairfax County Water Authority

54 F.E.R.C. ¶ 62,142 (1991).

Office Director Order Issuing License (Minor Project), March 5, 1991.

Fred E. Springer, Director, Office of Hydropower Licensing: Fairfax County Water Authority filed a license application under Part I of the Federal Power Act (Act) to operate and maintain the Occoquan River Hydro Project located on the Occoquan River, in Fairfax and Prince William Counties, Virginia. The project would affect the interests of interstate or foreign commerce.

Notice of the application has been published. No protests or motions to intervene were filed in this proceeding, and no agency objected to issuance of this license. Comments received from interested agencies and individuals have been fully considered in determining whether to issue this license.

License Term and Back Annual Charges. This project should have been licensed in 1973, the date when the hydroelectric project began generation. As is proposed here, for projects involving no new construction, the Commission's practice is to issue licenses that expire 30 years from issuance. Because this project should have been previously licensed and for purposes of assessing annual charges, the effective date of this license will be backdated 18 years and the license will expire 30 years from issuance. Annual charges will be assessed from the effective date.

Comprehensive Development. Sections 4(e) and 10(a)(1) of the Act, 16 U.S.C. §§ 797(e) and 803(a)(1), respectively, require the Commission to give equal consideration to all uses of the waterway on which a project is located. When the Commission reviews a proposed project, the recreational, fish and wildlife, and other non-developmental values of the involved waterway are considered along with power and other developmental values. In determining whether, and under what conditions, a hydropower license should be issued, the Commission must weigh the various economic and environmental tradeoffs involved in the decision.

The project would generate approximately 4,672 megawatt hours of electrical energy per year. The project also provides for long-term energy conservation and displacement of fossil-fueled electric power plant generation for the betterment of air quality and the conservation of fossil fuels.

We evaluated the effects of project operation on the environmental resources of the project area and the environmental assessment (EA) provides a discussion of the measures to protect and enhance these environmental resources. We conclude that present project operation and measures proposed by Fairfax County and the staff are adequate to protect the environmental resources in the project's impact area. These measures include ... designing, constructing, and operating sluices at each of the project's dams in order to safely move fish downstream of the project dams. We did not ... adopt the recommendations by the Virginia Department of Game and Inland Fisheries (VDGIF) and U.S. Fish and Wildlife Service (FWS) to install and operate a trap and haul fish passage facility. The trap and haul facility would, on an annual levelized basis, cost more than the value of the project energy.

Alternatives to issuing a license for the Occoquan River Project were also considered. These alternatives included the proposed project with our recommended mitigative measures, denial of the license application, and a no-action alternative. We have concluded that issuing the license for the project with our mitigative and enhancement measures, is the preferred option for two reasons: (1) the environmental effects of continued operation of the project would be minor with the implementation of the proposed enhancement measures; and (2) the electricity generated from a renewable resource would be used by Fairfax County, thus reducing the use of existing fossil-fueled, steam-electric generating plants and, in turn, reducing atmospheric pollution and possible global warming. We also concluded that denial of the license would deprive the applicant of the energy produced by the project without providing any dam safety oversight or environmental benefits.

The Director Orders:

(A) This license is issued to the Fairfax County Water Authority (licensee), effective January 1, 1973, and expiring February 28, 2021, to operate and maintain the Occoquan River Hydro Project. This license is subject to the terms and conditions of the Act, which is incorporated by reference as part of this license, and subject to the regulations the Commission issues under the provisions of the Act.

[The director's order described the applicant's project and set forth various conditions attached to the license. Appended to the order was an Environmental Assessment (EA) that supported the decision of the FERC staff not to require installation of a fish trap and haul facility at the project. The EA discussed the impact of the dam on fish:]

Since 1935, 65 fish species have been collected from the Occoquan River Basin. The upper Occoquan Reservoir has a resident assemblage of warm water species including: northern pike, tiger muskellunge, largemouth bass, walleye pike, striped bass, channel catfish, bluegill, black crappie, white perch, gizzard shad, and hybrid of a cross between striped bass and white bass, known locally as wipers.

In addition, anadromous alosids (American shad, blueback herring, and alewife) also occur in the Occoquan River Basin and have been collected in the upper Occoquan Reservoir. We assume that both the resident and anadromous fish species may also occur in the lower Occoquan Reservoir.

Similar for many migratory fishes in the Chesapeake Bay, anadromous alosids have also declined in abundance over the last 30 years. Commercial landings of river herring (i.e., blueback herring and alewife), for example, have decreased by over 90 percent since the early 1960's (Chesapeake Bay Foundation, 1989). The uses of river herring for commercial purposes include human consumption, bait, and industrial products (i.e., fertilizer). The decrease in commercial landings have been attributed to the cumulative effects associated with over fishing, pollution, siltation, and obstructed access to historical spawning areas. Anadromous alosids are ecologically important as a food resource. Juvenile alosids serve as a food resource for smallmouth bass and other freshwater piscivores, and marine fish, such as striped bass, utilize small alosids, in particular alewife and blueback herring, as forage.

Fairfax County investigated available spawning habitat for the following anadromous fish species in the upper reaches of the Occoquan River Basin: American shad; blueback herring; and alewife. Completed during April 1989, the study consisted of an aerial reconnaissance and a ground survey. The results of the study, as summarized by Fairfax County, are as follows:

Of the 63 miles of free flowing stream in the drainage above the upper project dam:

(1) no suitable spawning habitat was identified for American shad; (2) about one-third or 21 miles of stream were identified as marginally suitable for blueback herring spawning (run and riffle habitat); and(3)about two-thirds or 42 miles of stream were identified as suitable for alewife spawning (pool habitat).

American shad spawn in run (moderately fast flowing) habitat. American shad spawning habitat is characterized as having a depth greater than 1.5 feet and a water velocity between 1 foot per second (ft/s) and 3 ft/s. The substrate must be free of silt and DO concentrations should exceed 4 mg/l. The Fairfax County investigation showed that spawning habitat in tributary streams upstream of the upper dam does not meet these depth and velocity criteria for American shad and, thus, these stream areas are considered unsuitable for American shad spawning.

Blueback herring spawning habitat is characterized as having a depth greater than 1.0 foot and a water velocity of 1 ft/s to 3 ft/s. Blueback herring prefer a hard substrate and a DO concentration greater than 4 mg/l. Spawning habitat identified by Fairfax County for blueback herring in tributary streams upstream of the upper dam marginally meet the depth and velocity criteria for blueback herring.

Alewife spawn in habitat characterized by slow-moving water with a depth of 0.5 feet and water velocity of less than 0.5 ft/s. The substrate may be soft and DO concentrations should exceed 4 mg/l. As shown by Fairfax County's study, alewife spawning habitat was identified in the tributary streams of the upper Occoquan Reservoir that meets the depth and velocity criteria for this fish species.

Alewife presently occur in the upper Occoquan Reservoir, however, the population has declined since 1984. The accidental introduction of gizzard shad in the upper Occoquan Reservoir at some time in the early 1980's coincides with the sharp decline in the alewife population. Currently, the alewife population remains small in comparison to the gizzard shad population. . . .

Upstream fish passage: Anadromous alosid fish species have been identified as important fish resources in the project area by the fish and wildlife agencies. Consequently, the VDGIF, the U.S. Fish and Wildlife Service (FWS), and the National Marine Fisheries Service (NFS) recommended that Fairfax County construct, operate, and maintain a trap and haul facility immediately downstream of the lower dam to provide upstream fish passage for river herrings (i.e., blueback herring and alewife) into the upper Occoquan Reservoir. In addition, these agencies recommended that Fairfax County undertake a three-year long study to determine whether spawning habitat in the Occoquan River Basin is sufficient to support these species upon initiation of the trap and haul operations. If the study determines that the trap and haul facility improves upstream fish populations for these species, the facility should be retained; if not, the facilities should be turned over to a state or federal entity for use elsewhere (Virginia Council on the Environment, letter dated April 13, 1990).

As part of the consultation process, the applicant investigated available spawning habitat for American shad, blueback herring, and alewife, in the tributary streams of the upper Occoquan Reservoir. While alewife are established in the upper Occoquan Reservoir, the population has declined since 1984. Fairfax County suggests that interspecific competition with gizzard shad coupled with the stocking of hybrid striped bass by the VDGIF, as well as other environmental factors, are responsible for the decline in the alewife populations. The VDGIF hypothesizes that the outmigration of adult and juvenile alewife was responsible for the observed population decline since 1984. Fairfax County counters that if outmigration was responsible for the decline in the alewife population, the declines would have also been observed immediately after the introductions of alewife by the VDGIF in the upper Occoquan Reservoir in the past, and would have been observed over several years after these introductions.

There is no documentation of the historical presence of alosids upstream of the project dams in the Occoquan River Basin. Neither the VDGIF nor the U.S. National Museum of Natural History have records confirming the occurrence of alosids upstream of the project dams prior to their construction. Hydraulic analyses performed by Fairfax County indicated that alosids may have been unable to negotiate in the steep stream gradient found between the lower dam and the service pump station located 1,600 feet downstream of the lower dam. Fairfax County concludes that there is little benefit to be derived from providing upstream fish passage at the project.

While the VDGIF seemed initially to agree with Fairfax County's conclusions, VDGIF now maintains that a trap and haul facility at the project dams is necessary for the future management of alosids in the Occoquan River Basin (letters dated July 10, 1989, September 29, 1989, and April 26, 1990). The VDGIF has stated that the amount of suitable spawning habitat in the tributary streams of the upper Occoquan Reservoir is adequate to warrant installation of a trap and haul facility at the Occoquan River Project.

We requested that the VDGIF, FWS, and NFS provide additional information to us in order to support the need for the recommended trap and haul operation (letter dated February 26, 1990). Among other items, we asked each of the agencies to provide information on how the fishery planning and management goals of their agency were considered in their recommendations for the trap and haul program at the Occoquan River Project. The FWS and NFS did not respond to our request for the information. The VDGIF responded by stating the following:

(1) "while the numbers of alosids migrating to the project area cannot be estimated, it is considered to be significant";

(2) "the 62.9 miles of alewife and blueback herring spawning habitat deemed marginally suitable by Fairfax County is, nevertheless, significant"; and

(3) "the tributary streams of the upper Occoquan Reservoir provide 42.2 stream miles of satisfactory alewife spawning habitat".

The VDGIF further indicated that their participation in an interagency restoration plan for the Chesapeake Bay requires the restoration of all the Bay's anadromous fish stocks to their historical spawning areas. Ongoing efforts are in progress throughout the Chesapeake Bay region to restore anadromous fishes to their historical spawning areas upstream from man-made blockages. Most such habitats, according to the VDGIF, have been blocked to fish passage 80 to 100 years and downstream populations are, in many cases, depleted.

Interspecific competition between alewife and gizzard shad may be the reason for the decline in the alewife population, as postulated by Fairfax County. Juvenile alewife have been observed as being a size-selective predator on zooplankton. Juvenile gizzard shad, of the same size, have been shown to be extremely efficient pump filter feeders and are not known to be size selective. The competitive exclusion of one species by another, based on the efficiency of food resource utilization, has occurred between other planktivorous fish. For example, the brook silverside (Labidesthes sicculs) was rapidly replaced by the introduction of the inland silverside (Menidia beryllina) in the Texoma Reservoir located in Oklahoma. Complete replacement occurred in less than two years. Therefore, we believe it can be argued that the introduction of gizzard shad in the upper Occoquan Reservoir could account for the decrease in the alewife population by competitive interaction between the species.

Since it appears that gizzard shad was unintentionally introduced into the upper Occoquan Reservoir, it is interpreted that gizzard shad is an undesirable species. If this is the case, then it follows that the introduction of gizzard shad into areas where it is not presently established would be undesirable.[9] Furthermore, the same mechanisms which resulted in the decrease in the alewife population in the Occoquan Reservoir could continue to operate in areas within the upper Occoquan Reservoir where future introductions of alewife would occur as a result of a trap and haul operation. These mechanisms could similarly decrease any future benefits envisioned with the agencies' recommendation for Fairfax County to implement a trap and haul program at the project.

The upper reaches of the Occoquan River Basin drain western Prince William County and eastern Fauquier County. Both of these counties have experienced explosive growth in residential housing construction that have

---

9. [Ed. Note] Perhaps the unfortunate choice of name given the poor gizzard shad has made it difficult to obtain sympathy for it. In one case in which the FERC did require an applicant to provide compensation for the destruction of gizzard shad, the decision was reversed by the D.C. Circuit, which found it difficult to attach any value to the species. *City of New Martinsville v. Federal Energy Regulatory Commission,* 102 F.3d 567 (D.C.Cir.1996).

contributed to the heavy sediment load found entering the upper Occoquan Reservoir. These areas are likely to continue to experience such growth in the foreseeable future. Sediment loads higher than 100 mg/l have been shown to be deleterious to the development of alosids (Mullen et al., 1986). Thus, it is likely that alosid species will not be able to spawn successfully due to the heavy sediment loads (e.g. 100 to 500 mg/l) carried downstream during storm events into any available spawning habitat areas.

We conclude that little or no benefit to alosid populations is expected to be derived from providing upstream fish passage at the Occoquan River Project at this time because:

(1) gizzard shad in the reservoir may be out competing alewife;

(2) gizzard shad would continue to invade areas where it is not presently established, and would continue to compete with alewife to the detriment of any future alosid introductions associated with implementation of a trap and haul program; and

(3) sediment loads entering the upper Occoquan Reservoir adversely affect available alosid spawning habitat, and, as a result, satisfactory alosid spawning habitat is marginal in the tributaries upstream of the upper dam.

Because of these reasons, we conclude that the existing operation of the Occoquan River Project has not contributed to significant cumulative impacts to anadromous fish populations in the Chesapeake Bay region.

While we believe that providing fish passage at the Occoquan River Project is not warranted at this time, it may, however, be appropriate in the future. Fish passage at the project may be beneficial when it is demonstrated that the number of fish to be passed will significantly contribute to alosid populations in the Chesapeake Bay. Future events that we believe must first occur to consider implementation of upstream fish passage at the Occoquan River Project include the following: available alosid spawning habitat in other areas of the Chesapeake Bay Basin should first reach carrying capacity; a reduction of suspended sediments in the upper Occoquan Reservoir should occur; the cause(s) of the existing alewife population decrease in the upper Occoquan Reservoir should be determined by federal and state fishery agencies; a substantial decrease in the gizzard shad population in the Occoquan Reservoir needs to occur; and a comprehensive fish passage program for the Occoquan River Basin should be developed by the federal and state fishery agencies. Therefore, we do not agree with the agencies' recommendations to implement a trap and haul program at the Occoquan River Project at this time.

In addition, we have also found that the installation and operation of a trap and haul program at the Occoquan River Project would make the project economically inviable. . . .

We asked Fairfax County to provide additional information on the agencies' recommended trap and haul program to include a description of the facilities, the criteria that would be used for monitoring the effectiveness of any implemented trap and haul program, and the costs of constructing, operating, monitoring, and maintaining the facilities. Fairfax County filed the information with the Commission on June 11, 1990.

The facilities would consist of a Denile-type fish ladder (approximately 26 feet-long) that would be installed at the upstream side of the Low Service Pump Station tailrace (1,600 feet downstream from the lower dam) which would allow fish passage up to the trapping tank; bucket hoist and lift; sorting and return tank; holding tanks; loading pad; and, service building and fish transport trucks. Fish would be transported to a release site at Fountainhead Park (along the north side of the upper Occoquan Reservoir or, possibly, at the Bull Run Marina, located near the mouth of Bull Run in the Bull Run arm of the upper Occoquan Reservoir. The facilities would be operated for approximately 6 weeks each year (during a 10 week period) between March 15 and May 31.

The monitoring program to determine the effectiveness of the trap and haul program would include: monitoring the number of fish passed, identification of spawning locations, estimates of numbers of juveniles moving into the reservoir and passing over the dams; estimates of trap efficiency; and estimates of fish mortality during transport and during passage over the existing spillway.

Fairfax County estimated the initial materials and construction costs of the trap and haul facilities to be $971,500 and the initial costs of the monitoring program to be $90,350. Fairfax County also estimated the annual operating costs of the trap and haul facilities to be $89,400 and subsequent annual costs of the monitoring program at $159,900. Table 1 provides the component costs of the construction, operation, and maintenance of the trap and haul facilities.

We have analyzed the economic feasibility of the agencies' recommended trap and haul fish program at the Occoquan River Project. The economics of the project were based on the following assumptions:

(1) the project generates an average of 4,672 MWh of energy annually;

(2) the value of the project's power is 56 mills/kwh in 1991, escalating 5 percent annually;

(3) the 1991 hydroelectric operation and maintenance cost of 15 mills/kwh, escalating 5 percent annually;

(4) the first 10 years of operation and maintenance for the trap and haul facility would cost $249,000 annually, escalating 5 percent annually thereafter; and

(5) construction costs for the trap and haul facility, approximately $1,061,900, could be financed with 9-percent tax exempt bonds; or, alternatively, construction costs that could not be financed through tax-exempt bonds and 11-percent taxable bonds would have to be issued.

Table 2 shows the results of our analysis based on the assumption that 9-percent tax-exempt bonds could be issued. Table 3 shows the results if 11-percent taxable bonds would have to be issued.

The cost of the trap and haul facility would be greater than the value of the power generated by the project for a period greater than 50 years. Consequently, installation and operation of a trap and haul facility as recommended by the fish and wildlife agencies would make the project economically inviable. It is reasonable to expect, therefore, that Fairfax County would surrender a license requiring the trap and haul facility, rather than pass on the higher costs to its water supply customers.∎

NOTES AND COMMENTS

1. In 1986, Congress amended the Federal Power Act to require FERC to "give equal consideration" not only to "power and development purposes" but "energy conservation, ... fish and wildlife ... recreational opportunities, and the preservation of other aspects of environmental quality." 16 U.S.C. § 797(e). It also required that licensed projects "be best adapted to a comprehensive plan ... for the adequate protection, mitigation, and enhancement of fish and wildlife (including related spawning grounds and habitat ..." 16 U.S.C. § 803(a).

At the time, conservation groups thought they had achieved a great victory. But both FERC and the courts have interpreted this language as merely requiring that environmental issues be given consideration in licensing proceedings, not that they be accorded any particular weight. *See, e.g.,* U.S. Dept. of the Interior v. FERC, 952 F.2d 538 (D.C.Cir.1992).

2. The National Environmental Policy Act of 1969 ("NEPA"), which was discussed in the *Fairfax Water Authority* opinion, is largely a procedural statute, which sets it apart from other important pieces of environmental legislation. The enactment of NEPA established environmental policies for the United States, and created the President's Council on Environmental Quality ("CEQ"). The CEQ oversees the implementation of NEPA. NEPA requires federal agencies to prepare an environmental impact statement ("EIS") when making the decision to take "major federal action significantly affecting the quality of the human environment." § 102(2)(C), 42 U.S.C. § 4332 (2)(C) (1999). The idea behind NEPA is that the quality of final federal decisions will be greater if information is provided to the decision-maker and to the public.

An environmental assessment ("EA") is performed prior to the preparation of an EIS to determine if the federal action will affect the human environment. The EA describes the proposed action and a brief discussion of alternatives to the action in order to help the agency determine if an EIS in necessary. If the agency determines that an EIS is unnecessary, a "Finding of No Significant Impact" ("FONSI") is prepared giving reasons for this conclusion. At this point, no further action is taken under NEPA. The great majority of agency decisions on NEPA compliance conclude that an EIS is not necessary.[10]

---

10. If an EIS is necessary, the agency will publish a "notice of intent" to prepare   and EIS. The agency will also note the scope of the EIS and the important issues that will

Only federal actions are subject to NEPA requirements. Federal actions naturally include actions by the federal government, such as issuance of regulations or construction of federal facilities. Federal actions include actions of private parties having a significant degree of federal involvement, especially if the activity requires a federal permit. Federal actions also include specific projects that receive major funding from the federal government. If the federal money is provided for general use, this makes the line for "federal" action fuzzy.

It is sometimes difficult to know if an agency's intentions amount to "action" or "proposed action." Agencies constantly plan things, and courts are often asked to determine if those plans have reached the "proposed action" stage. NEPA compliance is only required if there is an actual proposal for action put forth by the agency, not merely the formulation of proposals. *Kleppe v. Sierra Club,* 427 U.S. 390 (1976). Federal *inaction* generally does not generally require compliance with NEPA.

Whether a federal action is "major" or "significantly affects the human environment" is usually determined on a case-by-case basis. Generally, the direct and indirect environmental impacts are analyzed, along with the cumulative effects of related actions. An action that appears minor at first glance may require NEPA compliance if it is part of a pattern of actions. CEQ regulations also allow the agency to prepare a programmatic EIS, which considers the cumulative impacts of the smaller actions and identifies alternatives to the whole project. Later site specific EAs would consider the local effects and address alternatives related to that specific component rather than reconsidering general issues.

The "human environment" has been interpreted to mean the physical environment, and so does not cover activities having only social and economic effects. For example, the psychological and sociological effects of constructing jail facilities in a residential area is not covered by NEPA, but the possible increase in crime is covered by NEPA. *Hanly v. Kleindienst (II),* 471 F.2d 823 (2d Cir. 1972).

be addressed. A draft EIS is then prepared, giving complete analysis of the project, alternatives, actions to mitigate adverse effects, and possible environmental consequences. Upon completion, a draft EIS must be made available for public comment. Public comments must be included in the record of the final agency decision. The agency must respond to public comments and modify the draft if necessary, and the final EIS is then prepared. Final agency actions are subject to judicial review, usually to review the decision not to prepare an EIS or whether the procedural requirements of NEPA have been met. An EIS must contain several key components. Alternatives to the proposed action must be considered. § 102(2)(C)(iii), 42 U.S.C. § 4332(2)(C)(iii); § 102(2)(E), 42 U.S.C. § 4332(2)(E). Only reasonable alternatives need be identified. These must include a discussion of the "no action" alternative, reasonable alternatives that would eliminate or lessen the need for the proposed action, and alternatives that would mitigate the environmental impacts of the proposed action. Sometimes, there is inadequate scientific information about the environmental effects of a proposed action. At the very least, the agency must disclose what information is lacking. An agency may choose to prepare a "worst case analysis" as a way of dealing with the unknown. An agency may also be required to prepare a supplemental EIS in the event that new information becomes available or the design of the proposal changes.

If the agency's action or proposed action requires an EIS, another set of issues is raised. One issue is when the agency action is actually a series of related actions. Often, the agency will divide a project into smaller segments, hence the term "segmentation". If the agency only addresses each segment individually, the cumulative effects of the action may not be addressed, therefore the full impact of the action is not considered. The courts and the CEQ offer criteria to consider when determining if an EIS is only needed for a segment of a federal action: whether the series of actions are related, if the first action has an "independent utility", and if there are cumulative impacts of the series of actions, those should be addressed in the EIS.

Some critics of NEPA believe that federal agencies do not seriously take into account the environmental impacts of proposed actions. They charge that agencies do not consider alternatives to the proposed action that would interfere with the agency's goals. NEPA has also been criticized for the generation of mountains of paperwork and litigation. Supporters of NEPA believe that NEPA has a positive effect on agency action. Many of the most harmful environmental impacts are avoided due to the information generated by environmental analyses. Additionally, the "arbitrary and capricious" review standard forces agencies to consider relevant information carefully since they have to give an explanation for decisions made.

3. In the *Fairfax Water Authority* case, the Water Authority hired a consultant to prepare a draft EA which was submitted to the FERC in the hope that the FERC would adopt it and make a Finding of No Significant Impact (FONSI). The great majority of NEPA compliance actions are handled in this way. *See* Rodgers, *supra*, at 893–896. The key issue becomes the nature and extent of the conditions that the agency will impose on the project in order to make the finding that the impact is not significant.

When these conditions are designed to reduce the impact of the project, or to create environmental benefits that would offset the harmful impact of the projects, the process is known as mitigation. Here the FERC was trying to determine whether the environmental impacts of Fairfax County's project were sufficiently significant to require mitigation, and if so, the nature of that mitigation. Environmental lawyers spend much of their time trying to resolve such issues.

4. Is it possible for an agency to quantify and weigh the competing values of wild fish and electric power? Can environmental values be stated in dollars? Consider the following quote from the noted ecologist, Eugene P. Odum: "Money is related to energy, since it takes energy to make money. Money is a counterflow to energy in that money flows out of cities and farms to pay for the energy and materials that flow in. The trouble is that money tracks human-made goods and services but not the equally important natural goods and services. At the ecosystem level, money enters the picture only when a natural resource is converted into marketable goods and services, leaving unpriced (and therefore not appreciated) all the work of the natural system that sustains this resource." Eugene P. Odum, Ecology and Our Endangered Life Support Systems 105 (2d ed. 1993).

As the quote from Odum indicates, our present systems of accounting assume that when we use a natural resource we are creating an asset, even though we are depleting the long term supply of the resource. Many economists and accountants are debating ways in which our systems of cost accounting could be changed to take into account depletion of natural resources. *See* Chapter Two.

D. STATE WATER QUALITY STANDARDS

In addition to the role state wildlife agencies play in FERC hydropower proceedings, the states may choose to play another and more powerful role in these proceedings through their water quality agencies. In *Public Utility Dist. #1 of Jefferson County v. Washington Department of Ecology,* 511 U.S. 700 (1994), the United States Supreme Court held that where the State of Washington adopted a requirement that a river maintain a minimum rate of flow to protect fish, such a requirement was a "water quality standard" and FERC could not approve a hydroelectric project unless the state certified that it would be consistent with that standard.

The Clean Water Act ("CWA") is designed to improve or maintain the water quality of the nation's water bodies. 33 U.S.C. § 1251(a). State and Federal governments each have important roles in the implementation of the CWA. The EPA is required to set technology-based standards for individual discharges in the nation's navigable waterways. States are required to set water quality goals that are designed to protect human health for all intrastate waters. 33 U.S.C. §§ 1251(a)(2), 1311 (b)(1)(C), 1313. States must enforce these water quality standards and also approve water quality certification before a federal license or permit may be issued. 33 U.S.C. § 1341.

Petitioners in *PUD No. 1* proposed to build a hydroelectric project on federally owned land. Because of this, the petitioners were required to obtain a license from FERC for the facility and certification from the state for water quality. The Washington Department of Ecology issued a certification requiring that the petitioners maintain a minimum stream flow in order to protect fisheries in the areas to be affected by the dam. Petitioners argued that under the CWA the state only had the authority to regulate discharges, not stream flow. The Court disagreed with this position, quoting 401(d) of the CWA, which provides "any certification shall set forth 'any effluent limitations and other limitations ... necessary to assure that any applicant' will comply with various provisions of the Act and appropriate state law requirements." The Court found that this section of the CWA applies to the applicant, not to the particular discharge, which allows the state to impose other limitations as needed. *PUD No. 1 v. Washington Department of Ecology,* 511 U.S. 700, 711 (1994).

The Court also found that water quality standards adopted pursuant to the CWA are included in the "other limitations" of the 401(d) certification process. Certification may be conditioned on these limitations if necessary to gain compliance with state water quality standards. States may also require that an application for certification comply with the designated uses of a water body. *Id.* at 1910.

Petitioners also argued that the CWA regulates water quality, not water quantity. The Court found this distinction to be "artificial":

> "In many cases, water quantity is closely related to water quality; a sufficient lowering of the water quantity in a body of water could destroy all of its designated uses, be it for drinking water, recreation, navigation or, as here, as a fishery. In any event, there is recognition in the Clean Water Act itself that reduced stream flow, *i.e.*, diminishment of water quantity, can constitute water pollution. First, the Act's definition of pollution as 'the man-made or man induced alteration of the chemical, physical, biological, and radiological integrity of the water' encompasses the effects of reduced water quantity. 33 U.S.C. § 1362(19). This broad conception of pollution—one which expressly evinces Congress' concern with the physical and biological integrity of water—refutes petitioners' assertion that the Act draws a sharp distinction between the regulation of water 'quantity' and water 'quality.' Moreover, § 304 of the Act expressly recognizes that water 'pollution' may result from 'changes in the movement, flow, or circulation of any navigable waters ..., including changes caused by the construction of dams.' 33 U.S.C. § 1314(f). This concern with the flowage effects of dams and other diversions is also embodied in EPA regulations, which expressly require existing dams to be operated to attain designated uses. 40 C.F.R. § 131.10(g)(4) (1992)."

The Court concluded that minimum stream flow requirements were acceptable state water quality standards. The result was to substantially increase the power of the states in hydropower licensing.

Following that decision, the Second Circuit Court of Appeals had occasion to consider some limits imposed by the State of Vermont on certain hydropower projects in that state that were on FERC's licensing agenda.

American Rivers, Inc. v. Federal Energy Regulatory Comm'n

129 F.3d 99 (2d Cir.1997).

■ WALKER, J.: Petitioners, the State of Vermont and American Rivers, Inc., seek review of several orders issued by the Federal Energy Regulatory Commission ("FERC" or "Commission") licensing six hydropower projects located on rivers within the State of Vermont. The dispute surrounds (1) the authority of the State under § 401 of the Clean Water Act ("CWA"), 33 U.S.C. § 1341, to certify—prior to the issuance of a federal license—that such projects will comply with federal and state water quality standards and (2) the appropriate route for review of a state's certification decisions. The Commission argues that, when it determines that a state has exceeded the scope of its authority under § 401 in imposing certain pre-license conditions, it may refuse to include the ultra vires conditions in its license as it did in each of the proceedings at issue.

Petitioners contend that the Commission is bound by the language of § 401 to incorporate all state-imposed certification conditions into hydropower licenses and that the legality of such conditions can only be challenged by the licensee in a court of appropriate jurisdiction. We agree with petitioners and, thus, grant the petition for review, vacate the Commission's orders, and remand.

The principal order under review in this proceeding arises from the efforts of the Tunbridge Mill Corporation ("Tunbridge") to obtain a license from FERC for the operation of a small hydroelectric facility on the First Branch of the White River in Orange County, Vermont, restoring an historic mill site in Tunbridge Village. Pursuant to § 401(a)(1) of the CWA, 33 U.S.C. § 1341(a)(1), an applicant for a federal license for any activity that may result in a discharge into the navigable waters of the United States must apply for a certification from the state in which the discharge originates (or will originate) that the licensed activity will comply with state and federal water quality standards. *See P.U.D. No. 1 of Jefferson County v. Washington Dep't of Ecology*, 511 U.S. 700 (1994). Such certifications, in accordance with § 401(d), 33 U.S.C. § 1341(d), shall

> set forth any effluent limitations and other limitations, and monitoring requirements necessary to assure that any applicant for a Federal license or permit will comply with any applicable effluent limitations and other limitations, under section 1311 or 1312 of this title, standard of performance under section 1316 of this title, or prohibition, effluent standard, or pretreatment standard under section 1317 of this title, and with any other appropriate requirement of State law set forth in such certification. . . .

The CWA further provides that the state certification "shall become a condition on any Federal license or permit subject to the provisions of this section." *Id.*

The [Vermont natural resources agency] issued a draft certification on September 18, 1991, for public notice and comment in compliance with § 401(a)(1), 33 U.S.C. § 1341(a)(1), and Vermont law. A week later, on September 25, 1991, the certification was issued. No one challenged the ruling through the state's process of administrative and judicial review, and thus the certification became final fifteen days later. *See* 10 Vt. Stat. Ann. § 1024(a).

As issued, the certification contained eighteen conditions (designated by letters "A" through "R"), three of which, P, J, and L, are relevant for our purposes. Condition P reserves the right in Vermont to amend (or "reopen") the certification when appropriate. Condition J requires Tunbridge to submit to the state for review and approval any plans for significant changes to the project. Finally, condition L requires Tunbridge to seek clearance from the state before commencing construction so that the state may ensure that plans are in place to control erosion and manage water flows.

Certificate in hand, Tunbridge sought a license from FERC, which is vested with authority under 4(e) of the Federal Power Act ("FPA"), 16 U.S.C. § 797(e), to issue licenses for "the development, transmission, and utilization of power across, along, from, or in any of the streams or other bodies of water over which Congress has jurisdiction...." FERC may issue such licenses "whenever the contemplated improvement is, in the judgment of the Commission, desirable and justified in the public interest," *id.*, and "best adapted to a comprehensive plan ... for the improvement and utilization of water-power development, for the adequate protection, mitigation, and enhancement of fish and wildlife ... , and for other beneficial public uses," 16 U.S.C. § 803 (a)(1).

On July 15, 1994, FERC ... granted Tunbridge a 40–year license "to construct, operate, and maintain the Tunbridge Mill Project." However, ... FERC found that conditions P, J, and L were beyond the scope of Vermont's authority under the CWA. Accordingly, FERC refused to incorporate them into the Tunbridge license. Vermont and American Rivers now seek review in this court of the Commission's determination.

Prior to Tunbridge Mill, FERC had held that it was required by § 401 to include in its licenses all conditions imposed by a state in its certifications notwithstanding the Commission's view that the conditions were beyond a state's authority under § 401.

In Tunbridge Mill, however, the Commission reversed field, finding that "to the extent that states include conditions that are unrelated to water quality, these conditions are beyond the scope of Section 401 and are thus unlawful." "We conclude that we have the authority to determine that such conditions do not become terms and conditions of the licenses we issue." *Id.* The Commission reasoned, in part: "We believe that, in light of Congress' determination that the Commission should have the paramount role in hydropower licensing process, whether certain state conditions are outside the scope of Section 401(d) is a federal question to be answered by the Commission."

The principal dispute between petitioners and the Commission in this case surrounds the relative scope of authority of the states and the Commission under the CWA and the FPA. Petitioners' contention is straightforward, resting on statutory language. In their view, the plain language of § 401(d) indicates that FERC has no authority to review and reject the substance of a state certification or the conditions contained therein and must incorporate into its licenses the conditions as they appear in state certifications. FERC disagrees, arguing that the language of § 401(d) is not as clear as petitioners would have it. Rather, FERC contends, it is bound to accede only to those conditions that are within a state's authority under § 401, that is, conditions that are reasonably related to water quality and that otherwise conform to the dictates of § 401. The Commission also argues that without the authority to reject state-imposed § 401 conditions its Congressionally mandated role under the FPA of ensuring comprehensive planning and development of hydro-power would be undermined.

The Clean Water Act. Before considering the Commission's contentions regarding the CWA, we note that FERC's interpretation of § 401, or any other provision of the CWA, receives no judicial deference under the doctrine of Chevron USA, Inc. v. Natural Resources Defense Council, 467 U.S. 837 (1984), because the Commission is not Congressionally authorized to administer the CWA. *See* 33 U.S.C. § 1251(d) ("Except as otherwise expressly provided in this chapter, the Administrator of the Environmental Protection Agency ... shall administer this chapter."); *see also* West v. Bowen, 879 F.2d 1122, 1137 (3d Cir.1989) (holding that "no deference is owed an agency's interpretation of another agency's statute"). Thus, we review de novo the Commission's construction of the CWA.

We begin, as we must, with the statute itself. In this case, the statutory language is clear. Section 401(a), which is directed both to prospective licensees and to the federal licensing agency (in this case, the Commission), provides, in relevant part:

> Any applicant for a Federal license or permit to conduct any activity ... which may result in any discharge into the navigable waters, shall provide the licensing or permitting agency a certification from the State in which the discharge originates or will originate.... No license or permit shall be granted until the certification required by this section has been obtained or has been waived.... No license or permit shall be granted if certification has been denied by the State....

33 U.S.C. § 1341(a). More important, § 401(d), reads, in pertinent part:

> Any certification provided under this section ... shall become a condition on any Federal license or permit subject to the provisions of this section.

33 U.S.C. § 1341(d).

This language is unequivocal, leaving little room for FERC to argue that it has authority to reject state conditions it finds to be ultra vires. Rather, in this case, to the extent that the Commission contends that Congress intended to vest it with authority to reject "unlawful" state conditions, the Commission faces a difficult task since it is generally assumed—absent a clearly expressed legislative intention to the contrary—"that Congress expresses its purposes through the ordinary meaning of the words it uses...." *Escondido Mut. Water Co. v. La Jolla Band of Mission Indians*, 466 U.S. 765, 772 (1984).

The Commission argues that, notwithstanding the mandatory language of the provision, § 401(d) itself restricts the substantive authority of states to impose conditions: "Section 401 authorizes states to impose only conditions that relate to water quality." This is plainly true. Section 401(d), reasonably read in light of its purpose, restricts conditions that states can impose to those affecting water quality in one manner or another. *See* P.U.D. No. 1 of Jefferson County, 114 S. Ct. at 1909 (holding that a state's authority to impose conditions under § 401(d) "is not unbounded"). However, this is not tantamount to a delegation to FERC of the authority to decide which conditions are within the confines of § 401(d) and which are not. And this is the crux of the dispute in this case.

In *Escondido Mut. Water Co. v. La Jolla Band of Mission Indians*, 466 U.S. 765 (1984)—a case which the Commission goes to great lengths to distinguish—the Supreme Court was called upon to consider a strikingly analogous factual and legal scenario. At issue was a pre-license certification scheme within the FPA itself, permitting (in this instance) the Secretary of the Interior to impose requirements on licenses issued "within" any Native American "reservation." In particular, this certification scheme, § 4(e) of the FPA, 16 U.S.C. § 797(e), provides that licenses issued under this provision "shall be subject to and contain such conditions as the Secretary of the department under whose supervision such reservation falls shall deem necessary for the adequate protection and utilization of such reserva- tion." 16 U.S.C. § 797(e). FERC, however, refused to accept the Secretary's conditions, and an aggrieved party sought review. In construing § 4(e), the Supreme Court focused closely on the provision's plain language, remark- ing that "the mandatory nature of the language chosen by Congress appears to require that the Commission include the Secretary's conditions in the license even if it disagrees with them." *Escondido*, 466 U.S. at 772. Consistent with this view, the Court gave effect to the plain language of 4(e), 16 U.S.C. § 797(e), finding no "clear expressions of legislative intent to the contrary." *Id.*

Although Escondido arose in a different context, it is instructive in this case for several reasons. In both contexts, FERC is required in clear statutory language to incorporate conditions imposed by an independent governmental agency with special expertise, in Escondido, the Department of the Interior, 16 U.S.C. § 797(e), and in this instance, the states, *see* 33 U.S.C. § 1251(b) ("It is the policy of the Congress to recognize, preserve, and protect the primary responsibilities and rights of States to prevent, reduce, and eliminate pollution. . . ."); *see also United States v. Puerto Rico*, 721 F.2d 832, 838 (1st Cir.1983) ("states are the prime bulwark in the effort to abate water pollution"). In both cases, the Commission attempted to ignore this command and substitute its own judgment for that of the certifying agency. In both cases, the real issue in dispute is not whether there are limits on the certifying agency's authority to impose conditions on federal licenses, but "whether the Commission is empowered to decide when the . . . conditions exceed the permissible limits." *Escondido*, 466 U.S. at 777. In neither case do the underlying statutes or their schemes for administrative and judicial review suggest that Congress wanted the Com- mission to second-guess the imposition of conditions.

Finally, and most persuasively, in both cases the Commission argued that without the authority to review conditions imposed by the certifying agency its ability to carry out its statutory mission would be compromised. In *Escondido*, notwithstanding this contention, the Supreme Court found that absent a challenge by the applicant-licensee, the Interior Secretary's conditions must either be incorporated in full into any license that it issues or the Commission must deny the license altogether. 466 U.S. at 778 n.20. In reaching this conclusion, the Court expressly addressed difficulties inherent in such a statutory scheme, difficulties the Commission decries in this case:

> We note that in the unlikely event that none of the parties to the licensing proceeding seeks review, the conditions will go into effect notwithstanding the Commission's objection to them since the Commission is not authorized to seek review of its own decisions. The possibility that this might occur does not, however, dissuade us from interpreting the statute in accordance with its plain meaning. Congress apparently decided that if no party was interested in the differences between the Commission and the Secretary, the dispute would best be resolved in a nonjudicial forum.

Id.

The Commission's efforts to distinguish Escondido are unavailing.

The Federal Power Act. Independent of FERC's concerns that Vermont's 401 conditions violate the terms of the CWA, the Commission contends that the 401 conditions run afoul of the FPA. The Commission primarily fears that "to accept the conditions proposed would give the state the kind of governance and enforcement authority that is critical and exclusive to the Commission's responsibility to administer a license under the Federal Power Act, a power the Courts have repeatedly concluded belongs exclusively to the Commission." Brief of the Fed. Energy Regulatory Comm'n at 16. In particular, FERC argues (1) that the conditions that impose deadlines on construction conflict with § 13 of the FPA, 16 U.S.C. § 806, which places construction deadlines largely within the discretion of the Commission and generally contemplates that construction will be commenced within two years of the date of the license, *see First Iowa Hydro–Elec. Coop. v. Federal Power Comm'n,* 328 U.S. 152, 168 n. 13 (1946); (2) that the reopener conditions and pre-approval conditions violate § 6 of the FPA, 16 U.S.C. § 799, which provides that a license, once issued, "may be revoked only for the reasons and in the manner prescribed under the provisions of this chapter, and may be altered or surrendered only upon mutual agreement between the licensee and the Commission," as well as other provisions of the FPA, see 16 U.S.C. § 803(b), 820, 823b; and, (3) more generally, that the conditions "eviscerate[] the carefully balanced approach" to environmental concerns expressed in the Electric Consumers Protection Act ("ECPA"), Pub.L. No. 99–495, 100 Stat. 1243 (1986), amending the FPA, *see, e.g.,* 16 U.S.C. §§ 797(e), 803(a), 803(j).

We have no quarrel with the Commission's assertion that the FPA represents a congressional intention to establish "a broad federal role in the development and licensing of hydroelectric power." *California v. Federal Energy Regulatory Comm'n,* 495 U.S. 490, 496 (1990). Nor do we dispute that the FPA has a wide preemptive reach. *Id.* The CWA, however, has diminished this preemptive reach by expressly requiring the Commission to incorporate into its licenses state-imposed water-quality conditions. *See* 33 U.S.C. § 1341(a)(1). Although we are sympathetic to the Commission's suggestion that without the authority to reject states' conditions that are beyond the scope of § 401, the preemptive reach of the FPA may be narrowed at the will of the states, *see, e.g.,* Brief of Amici Curiae Edison Elec. Inst. at 14, the Commission's concerns are overblown.

The Commission fails to acknowledge appropriately its ability to protect its mandate from incursion by exercising the authority to refuse to issue a hydropower license altogether if the Commission concludes that a license, as conditioned, sufficiently impairs its authority under the FPA. *See, e.g., Escondido,* 466 U.S. at 778 n.20. If the Commission is concerned that the conditions imposed by a state "intrude[] upon the Commission's exclusive authority under the FPA," Brief of the Fed. Energy Regulatory Comm'n at 44, nothing in the CWA prevents it from protecting its field of authority by simply refusing to issue the license as so conditioned.

The Commission, however, has chosen to forgo this route, arguing that refusing to issue a license is not a "practical option" in relicensing cases. *Id.* at 20 n.10. Although we understand that refusing to relicense a hydroelectric project would result in the disassembly of the project, presenting "serious practical and economic problems" and affecting all manner of local interests, id., the Commission's dissatisfaction with the remedy of license denial is not reason enough to turn a blind eye to FERC's assumption of authority to review and reject a state's 401 conditions. Rather, the Commission must establish that the authority it proposes is rooted in a Congressional mandate. And this they have failed to do.

Finally, with respect to the ECPA amendments to the FPA, the Commission is mistaken. Under these provisions, the Commission must "give equal consideration to ... the protection, mitigation of damage to, and enhancement of, fish and wildlife ... and the preservation of other aspects of environmental quality," 16 U.S.C. § 797(e), and must impose conditions, based on recommendations of relevant federal agencies and affected states, to "protect, mitigate damages to, and enhance, fish and wildlife ... affected by the development, operation, and management of the project ...," 16 U.S.C. § 803(j)(1). *See United States Dep't of Interior v. Federal Energy Regulatory Comm'n,* 952 F.2d 538, 543 (D.C.Cir.1992) (describing environmental aspects of the ECPA amendments). The Commission argues that absent the authority to reject state-imposed conditions beyond the scope of § 401 of the CWA, the carefully balanced approach of the ECPA amendments, in general, and § 10(j), 16 U.S.C. 803(j), in particular, would be "eviscerated ... through the simple expedient of [states'] labeling ... recommendations 'conditions' to the Section 401 certification." Brief of the Fed. Energy Regulatory Comm'n at 39. In short, the Commission is concerned that it would be "held hostage" to every state imposed condition, compromising its role under the ECPA amendments of reconciling competing interests. *Id.* Such a result, the Commission contends, is impermissible under § 511(a) of the CWA, 33 U.S.C. § 1371(a), which provides, in part, that the Act "shall not be construed as ... limiting the authority or functions of any officer or agency of the United States under any other law or regulation not inconsistent with this chapter...."

The Commission's claim that the CWA—as we construe it—and the ECPA amendments are incompatible must be rejected. The Commission's concern that states will hold the Commission hostage through the § 401 process is misplaced because states' authority under § 401 is circumscribed in notable respects. First, applicants for state certification may challenge in courts of appropriate jurisdiction any state-imposed condition that exceeds a state's authority under § 401. In so doing, licensees will surely protect themselves against state-imposed ultra vires conditions. Second, even assuming that certification applicants will not always challenge ultra vires state conditions, the Commission may protect its mandate by refusing to issue a license which, as conditioned, conflicts with the FPA. In so doing, the Commission will not only protect its mandate but also signal to states and licensees the limits of its tolerance. Third, and most important, to the extent that the existence of states' authority to impose 401 conditions may otherwise conflict with the ECPA amendments, the ECPA is inconsistent with the terms of the CWA, thus, making inapplicable § 511(a) of the CWA. *See* 33 U.S.C. § 1371(a) (the Act "shall not be construed as ... limiting the authority or functions of any officer or agency of the United States under any other law or regulation not inconsistent with this chapter ...").

We have considered the Commission's remaining arguments and find them to be without merit. For the foregoing reasons, we grant the petition for review, vacate the orders of the Commission, and remand for proceedings consistent with this opinion.■

NOTES AND COMMENTS

1.   Upon remand, the FERC issued the license subject to the state's conditions. *Tunbridge Mill Corporation*, 82 FERC ¶ 61,265 (1998). For a discussion of the impact of the *American Rivers* case, *see* Comment: Who's in Charge Here? The Shrinking Role of the Federal Energy Regulatory Commission in Hydropower Licensing, 70 U. Of Colo. L. Rev. 603 (1999).

2.   American Indian Tribes share with the States the power to set conditions on water usage within reservations. Tribes have been active participants in the negotiations on many of the contested hydropower licensing proceedings. *See* Jane Marz, *et. al.*, Tribal Jurisdiction over Reservation Water Quality and Quantity, 43 S. D. L. Rev. 315 (1998).

3.   In another case brought by the same plaintiff, *American Rivers v. FERC*, 201 F.3d 1186 (9th Cir., 2000), the court held that FERC lacks authority to question the validity of a condition proposed by the U.S. Department of the Interior requiring the applicant to build a "fishway." Subsequently, in *Public Utility Dist. No. 1 of Okanogan County*, 90 FERC ¶ 61,169 (2000), the Commission rescinded an earlier order and denied a license application for the Enloe Dam project rather than approve the project with a fish ladder demanded by the National Marine Fisheries Service (NMFS). Most of the reservoir would have been in British Columbia, and the Canadian authorities objected to the introduction of steelhead trout and other anadromous fish into Canadian waters. NMFS, on the

other hand, argued that it was obligated to insist on a fish ladder because the dam otherwise would "take" steelhead trout protected under the ESA.

E. Hydropower Project Relicensing

Hydropower projects receive licenses for a fixed term of years. Hundreds of the early project licenses have now expired, and applications are pending before FERC to reissue many of these licenses. "Between 1993 and 2010, the licenses for 419 projects have expired or will expire. Many of the largest projects will expire between 2005 and 2010.... Some re-licenses have been granted and some projects are operating on annual permits pending decision." Marla E. Mansfield, Hydroelectric Power, in James E. Hickey, Jr., Energy Law and Policy for the 21st Century 11–19 (Rocky Mountain Mineral Law Foundation, 2000). In many cases, these applications have produced political controversy and have raised difficult legal issues.

The Federal Power Act gives general administrative authority to FERC for hydropower licensing. 16 U.S.C. § 825(h). FERC has the authority to issue original licenses for hydropower projects that have not yet been built and "new" licenses for existing projects whose licenses have expired. 16 U.S.C. §§ 797(e), 808. Before issuing a license, FERC must satisfy two requirements. *Id* at § 797(e). Section 4(e) of the FPA provides that "licenses shall be issued within any reservation[11] only after a finding by the Commission that the license will not interfere or be inconsistent with the purpose for which such reservation was created or acquired." *Id*. Under this provision, FERC must evaluate a project's compatibility with the reservation's original purpose. *Id*. Next, section 4(e) of the FPA states that licenses "shall be subject to and contain such conditions as the Secretary of the department under whose supervision such reservation falls shall deem necessary for adequate protection and utilization of such reservations." *Id*. Because of this, FERC must include in the project license any conditions recommended by the appropriate land-administering agency. *Id*. The D.C. Circuit held in *Southern California Edison Co. v. FERC*, 116 F.3d 507 (D.C.Cir.1997), that the mandatory conditions in 4(e) apply to reissued licenses as well as original licenses. *See generally* Mansfield, *supra*.

The Federal Power Act requires that the relicensing of hydropower projects be done in accordance with the laws and regulations in effect at the time of the relicensing. The nature of the mitigation and enhancement measures required and recommended by the Department of the Interior and the other non-FERC federal agencies vary depending upon the impacts of a particular hydropower project. Typical conditions address both how a

---

11. Reservation is defined as "national forests, tribal lands embraced within Indian reservations, military reservations, and other lands and interests in lands owned by the United States, and withdrawn, reserved, or withheld from private appropriation under the public land laws" as well as "lands and interests in lands acquired and held for any public purposes." 16 U.S.C. § 796(2).

project is physically operated and non-operational mitigation, such as habitat enhancement or replacement, fish stocking and shoreline protection. In 1997, FERC revised its regulations by offering an alternative "collaborative" process that integrates the existing pre-filing consultation process required of license applicants with environmental review of the project. *See* 62 Fed. Reg. 59802 (November 5, 1997). The process for relicensing hydro projects, with particular emphasis on potential settlement procedures, is discussed in Note: A Case Study for Stakeholders: An Alternative to Traditional Hydroelectric Licensing, 18 Energy L.J. 405 (1997).

The collaborative process resulted in the issuance of a license to the Avista Corporation for the Noxon Rapids and Cabinet Gorge projects in Idaho and Montana. *Avista Corporation*, 90 FERC ¶ 61,167 (2000). The new license was in substance a relicense of two projects originally licensed in the 1950s. The new license was conditioned on compliance with a settlement agreement entered into by the applicant and 25 other parties, including Indian Tribes, state and federal wildlife agencies, and private conservation groups. The effect of the settlement agreement was to make the license what the FERC staff calls a "living license," in which the wildlife and other environmental issues will be dealt with by adaptive management, rather than pursuant to conditions locked into the original issuance of the license. In issuing the license, the Commission said: "We congratulate the parties for their extensive and ultimately successful efforts to reach consensus on so many significant aspects of operation of the Clark Fork Project over the term of a new license. We also commend our staff for their assistance to the parties in developing a sound framework for a continuing collaborative approach to the management of the project in the public interest." (Slip opinion at 16–17).

One of the more contentious issues in relicensing proceedings is whether FERC can and should order a licensee to remove a dam when the license expires. FERC announced in a policy statement issued in February, 1995, that it had the authority to order dam decommissioning at relicensing. Project Decommissioning at Relicensing: Policy Statement, 60 Fed Reg. 30 (1995) (18 C.F.R. pt. 2.24 (1997)). FERC says it has the power to deny a license if it cannot be "fashioned" in accordance with statutory standards.[12]

---

12. FERC takes the position that it may issue a license even if it is considered uneconomic; that is, the hydro project may be allowed to operate and not make a profit. An example of this is with the Cushman Hydroelectric Project No. 460 located on the Skokomish River. FERC issued a relicensing order on July 30, 1998 stating that the public interest would be best served by the continuation of power production and that the licensee must use more measures to protect and enhance environmental resources affected by the project. City of Tacoma, 84 FERC ¶ 61,107. FERC stated the conditions placed on the renewed license strike an appropriate balance between developmental and environmental values for the new license term. *Id.* Furthermore, the Federal Water Power Act of 1920 does not guarantee that a licensee will make a profit. If a license must be renewed, it should be done under current conditions, not under the conditions that the original license was issued. *Id.* See Beth C. Bryant, FERC's Dam Decommissioning Authority under the Federal Power Act, 74 Wash. L. Rev. 95 (1999).

FERC issued the first denial of a license and order of dam removal to Edwards Manufacturing Company. 81 FERC ¶ 61,255 (1997). FERC decided that the continued operation of Edwards Dam on the Kennebec River was against the public interest and that the negative impacts of the dam could not be mitigated by current technology. An EIS was issued pursuant to NEPA in 1997. FERC concluded, among other things, that the removal of the Edwards Dam would provide access to more of the Kennebec river for several fish species. Estimates showed removal of the dam would be significantly less expensive than installing the necessary environmental protections, including appropriate fish passages. The nature and extent of FERC's authority to require dam removal upon decommissioning has yet to be decided by the courts. The Edwards Dam case settled before a court had a chance to rule on the issue. Dam ownership transferred to the state of Maine on January 1, 1999. Funding for dam removal and fishery restoration came entirely from private sources in exchange for environmental mitigation credit. On July 1, 1999, the Edwards Dam was effectively removed. *See* John McPhee, Farewell to the Nineteenth Century: The Breaching of Edwards Dam, 75 The New Yorker #28, p.44, Sept. 27, 1999.

Some dam operators have suggested that dam decommissioning may amount to a regulatory taking for which the licensees should be compensated. Under the Fifth Amendment to the United States Constitution. Compensation may be required even if there is no physical taking of private property, if there is a severe interference with property rights through regulation. *Kaiser Aetna v. U.S.,* 444 U.S. 164 (1979). *Lucas v. South Carolina Coastal Council,* 505 U.S. 1003 (1992), held that if a regulation deprives a landowner of 100% of the land's economic value, then just compensation is required, regardless of whether the regulation serves a legitimate public interest. (The regulation in the case prohibited the construction of permanent structures on beachfront property in order to preserve South Carolina's beaches from erosion.) But, said the Court, if the regulation "encompasses property interests that were not a part of the owner's title to begin with" there can be no taking.

There is speculation as to how this exception applies to dam decommissioning. Licensees assert they have an interest in the hydro project lands, the physical structures, water use rights, and even the FERC license and should therefore be compensated if ordered to decommission a dam. However, it is difficult to say that there is property interest in an expired license. A FERC license may be considered a "regulatory contract" between the licensee and the federal government. Existing FERC licenses may be regarded as property rights. But, once the license expires, the contract ends and the property right no longer exists. *See U.S. v. Fuller,* 409 U.S. 488 (1973) (taking of grazing land required no compensation for any value added to the lands by the permits.) One court has held that the *Fuller* case is the relevant precedent if the federal government condemns a licensed hydroelectric project, so that the project is to be appraised as if its license will not be renewed. *U.S. v. 42.13 Acres of Land,* 73 F.3d 953 (9th Cir.1996).

Hydropower project owners also do not have a property interest in the value of water power or the value of the land as a hydropower site. *See U.S. v. Chandler–Dunbar Water Power Co.,* 229 U.S. 53 (1913) (compensation not required for lost water use for power production when federal government condemned land in order to take navigable river flow for interstate commerce and revoked a hydropower license); *see also U.S. v. Grand River Dam Authority,* 363 U.S. 229 (1960) (the U.S. has a superior navigation easement which precludes private ownership of the water or its flow). But compensation for the condemnation of private riparian land was required in *U.S. v. Kelly,* 243 U.S. 316 (1917). *See* Katharine Costenbader, Damning Dams: Bearing the Cost of Restoring America's Rivers, 6 Geo. Mason L. Rev. 635 (1998); Comment, FERC's Dam Decommissioning Authority under the Federal Power Act, 74 Wash. L. Rev. 95 (1999); Richard Stavros, Hydro Relicensing Redux: Will Dams Be Saved?, Public Utilities Fortnightly, April 1, 2000, p. 26.

CHAPTER 5

COAL

Outline of Chapter:

A. THE EVOLUTION OF THE MODERN COAL INDUSTRY

The coal industry has evolved from a highly labor intensive industry plagued by health and safety problems to a highly mechanized industry heavily dependent on huge strip mining operations that are plagued by environmental problems. Many of its traditional markets have disappeared, yet it still supplies the majority of the fuel that produces electricity in the United States.

The coal industry is one of the most heavily regulated industries in the United States. Various constitutional challenges to federal and state regulations of the coal industry have produced some of the most important decisions in American constitutional history. These decisions involve two of the issues that recur throughout energy law: (1) At what point does regulation force a business to assume an unfair economic burden; and (2)

231

what is the line that separates permissible federal regulatory power and state regulatory power.

Before addressing these issues, it is important to understand the important role that coal has played in the development of the United States, and the changing nature of the coal industry in today's environment.

1.   FROM WOOD TO COAL

Ever since prehistoric humans discovered how to make fire they have been cutting down trees to obtain wood as a fuel. Wood, along with muscles, water and wind, continued to be the dominant source of energy until the mid-nineteenth century. In the United States today, wood is still used as a fuel in fireplaces and wood stoves, but it accounts for only a minute fraction of our energy usage.

In some less developed societies, however, wood remains an important fuel. In some parts of the world the forests have been largely destroyed to provide wood for fuel. Many parts of the Mideast that are semi-deserts today were described as heavily forested in biblical times. Even today, very poor countries such as Albania and Haiti are suffering serious soil erosion problems because the people need wood as a source of energy.

Peat is another fuel that has a long history. Peat is the remains of wetland vegetation that has formed a coherent mass. For centuries it has been dug and used as fireplace fuel in many parts of the world. But peat's heating efficiency is very low, and it produces lots of smoke.

When geological changes cause peat to be buried under layers of rock, the peat becomes compressed and turns into coal. This compression packs a lot of potential energy into a small space, with the result that coal is a much more efficient fuel than peat.

Coal varies greatly in heat content and in sulfur content. The relative efficiency of different types and grades of coal can vary significantly depending on differences in original vegetation and, more importantly, in the magnitude and duration of transforming temperatures and pressures.

Anthracites and the best bituminous coals—ancient fuels derived primarily from the wood of large, scaly-barked trees laid down in immense coastal swamps more than two hundred million years ago— break up to reveal hard, jet-black facets of virtually pure carbon. These fuels contain hardly any water and very little ash, and their heat values are near 30 MJ/kg. In contrast, the youngest lignites are soft, often crumbly, clayish, fairly wet chunks of brownish hues. They contain large shares of ash and water, often a great deal of sulfur, and their energy density is as low as 10 MJ/kg, inferior to air-dried wood.

Not surprisingly, all large lignite-producing nations call them brown coals. As with their drawbacks, the redeeming qualities of brown coals spring from their relative immaturity: their deposits are often very thick, quite level and close to the surface, conditions making a large-scale extraction in huge open-cast mines very economical.

Vaclav Smil, Energies: An Illustrated Guide to the Biosphere and Civilization 136–137, The MIT Press, 1999.

But a switch to coal is not just a simple matter of replacing one energy base with another. Coal is more difficult to extract and process than wood or peat because it takes a great deal more energy to transform it into a usable state. Jeremy Rifkin suggests that this may reflect a universal principle: the second law of thermodynamics. "The available energy in the world is constantly being dissipated. The more available sources of energy are always the first to be used. Each succeeding environment relies on a less available form of energy than the one preceding it. It is more difficult to mine coal and process it than it is to cut down trees. It's still more difficult to drill and process oil, and even harder to split atoms for nuclear energy" Jeremy Rifkin with Ted Howard, Entropy: A New World View 85 (1985).

2. The Industrial Revolution

Coal not only provided a more efficient source of heat than wood, it was a sufficiently concentrated form of energy that it became practical to convert it to motion through the use of the steam engine. The development of the steam engine was the foundation of the dramatic change in living conditions that became known as the Industrial Revolution.

James Trefil, A Scientist in the City (Doubleday, 1994)

One way of looking at the Industrial Revolution is to say that in the late 1700s, people learned how to tap the solar energy stored in fossil fuels—first coal, then oil and natural gas—instead of the solar energy stored in plant and animal tissues.

The story of fossil fuels isn't so very different from the story of glucose: Energy from the sun drives photosynthesis and is stored in plant fibers. When the plant dies, it and its cargo of energy are buried, perhaps in a swamp or bog, and over millions of years are converted into a fossil fuel. We human beings have mechanisms built into our cells to tap the solar energy stored in plant and animal tissues, but we need to build some sort of machine to get at the energy stored in fossil fuels. The Industrial Revolution had to wait until the first of these machines—the steam engine—came along.

That the steam engine was invented by James Watt is one of those things that everyone knows to be true but is nonetheless false. The first steam engine in the modern age was built in England in 1712 by a man named Thomas Newcomen. It was a pretty simple system. Coal was used to boil water to make steam, which was injected into a cylinder with a piston in it. The expansion of the steam drove the piston up, and when the piston got to the top, cold water was squirted into the cylinder to condense the steam. This created a vacuum in the cylinder, and the pressure of the outside air pushed the piston back down so that the whole cycle could start again.

The Newcomen engine was a cumbersome, inefficient affair. It sometimes required several minutes for the piston to go up and down, and the cylinder had to be heated and cooled on each stroke. Nevertheless, it was an immediate commercial success in coal mines, where there was a constant need to pump water from the tunnels and where the engine began replacing the horses that had been used up to that time. (Our habit of rating engines in horsepower traces its ancestry back to this particular episode of technology replacement.)

Watt's contribution to the steam engine came in a whole series of improvements to the original design—a separate chamber to condense the steam, a gear system that converted the up-and-down motion of the piston into the rotary motion of a shaft, and so on. His steam engine was the basis upon which the modern city was built, although, to be honest, the engine's potential wasn't universally recognized at first. In fact, the first spinning machine installed in Watt's native Scotland after his invention came on the market was powered by two Newfoundland dogs on a treadmill!

By modern standards, Watt's machine, even with all the improvements, was still incredibly inefficient. An engine capable of generating as much power as a modern lawn mower, for example, filled a two-story building. But for engineers in the eighteenth century, such a comparison was meaningless. For the first time, they didn't have to search for space near running water or keep a stable full of horses to run their machines. Instead, they could pick the site where they wanted power, shovel in some coal, and let 'er rip.

Over the years, the steam engine developed into many forms. It drove the railroads that carried goods and people into the growing cities; it carried ships across oceans regardless of the wind; and most important, it powered the factories that filled those ships with goods and those cities with workers. For all its success, however, the steam engine has proved to have a fundamental drawback. Once you pare away the fancy additions, all the bells and whistles, all steam engines share one central property—they deliver energy mechanically, by making a shaft move or a wheel spin. This is a serious limitation on the steam engine's usefulness, because it means that the power must be developed close to the place where it will be used. Whatever is to be moved by the engine has to be connected to it. The great puffs of smoke issuing from a steam locomotive are a reminder of the fact that you have to carry both the coal and the engine along with you if you expect the wheels to turn. You can see the same thing in photos and etchings of turn-of-the-century factories, where long lines of lathes or other machines are run by belts connected to rotating overhead shafts near the factory ceiling. This meant that when the great manufacturing cities of the nineteenth century were built, every factory with power-driven machinery had to have its own steam engine (or engines) and supply of coal.■

3. COAL RESERVES IN THE UNITED STATES

Coal remains one of the major sources of energy in the United States and throughout much of the world today. The conversion of coal to energy

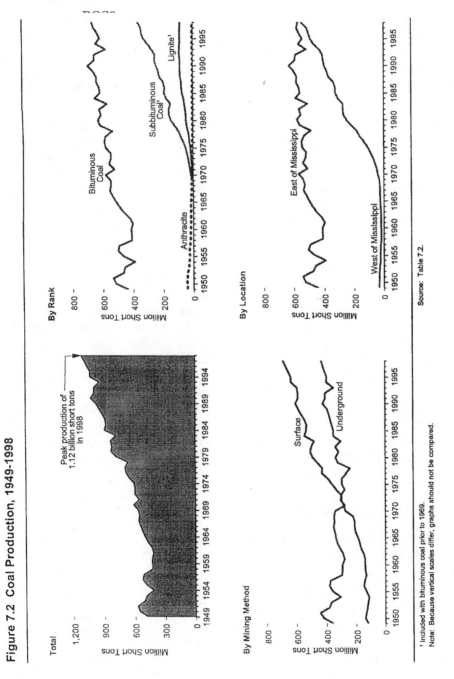

Figure 7.2 Coal Production, 1949–1998

Source: Table 7.2.

[1] Included with bituminous coal prior to 1969.
Note: Because vertical scales differ, graphs should not be compared.

Figure 5–1

requires four steps: mining, processing, transportation, and combustion. The big coal companies typically operate large mines that often ship their entire output to a few major users such as power plants or large factories, but some coal is mined by smaller companies that sell to wholesalers.

In the United States, coal was initially found primarily in the Appalachian Mountains, particularly in Pennsylvania and West Virginia. As the nation expanded westward, coal mines were opened first in the Midwestern states and, more recently, in the Rocky Mountain area. Today, nearly one-fourth of the nation's coal reserves are in Montana, with another 14% in neighboring Wyoming.

It is difficult to estimate the exact amount of coal buried underground, but there is no question that the United States has enormous coal reserves, probably in the neighborhood of five hundred billion tons of readily extractable coal. Almost half of this coal is in the Rocky Mountain area, but significant coal reserves remain in Illinois, West Virginia, Kentucky, Pennsylvania and Ohio. However, the increasing abandonment of small mines in these states has contributed to a significant loss of potential coal reserves[1].

The predominant type of coal in the eastern United States has a high heat content but usually has a high sulfur content as well, which means that it will create high volumes of sulfur dioxide when burned. Typical western coal, on the other hand, has less sulfur but also has a lower heat content, which means that more tons of coal must be mined and shipped to produce the same energy. Historically, these regional differences have had a major impact on the politics of coal in the United States. Congressional representatives from the Eastern states have tended to support requirements for the installation of power plant scrubbers, which would remove sulfur compounds from the emitted stack gas and thus allow the plants to continue to burn high-sulfur coal. Representatives from the Rocky Mountain states have tended to promote laws that would promote shipment of low-sulfur Western coal to power plants in the East and Midwest. *See* Bruce A. Ackerman and William T. Hassler, Clean Coal/Dirty Air, Yale University Press, 1981.

4. CHANGING MARKETS FOR COAL

Iron and steel used to be big consumers of coal in the form of coke. Now, much of our steel is imported, and what is made here doesn't use

---

1. Small blocks of coal are not amenable to the larger-scale, higher-technology mining that can boost average productivity rates. The closing of these small mines has left significant coal reserves permanently unmineable. Some operators choose to extract only the quickest-or easiest-to-mine parts of a coal deposit or only the highest-grade coal that will fetch a premium price, leaving the rest, which will probably be spoiled by caving and weathering. With prices low and competition keen, coal deposits once regarded as reserves at producing properties were found to be no longer marketable. If reserve blocks contain coal of moderate to high sulfur content, for which markets are shrinking, the changes of permanent closure are high. *See* Bonskowksi, *supra* at 8–9.

much coke any more. Today less than 5% of American coal goes to the steel industry.

It is the electric utilities that now consume about nine-tenths of the coal mined in the United States. About 10% of coal is used for industrial

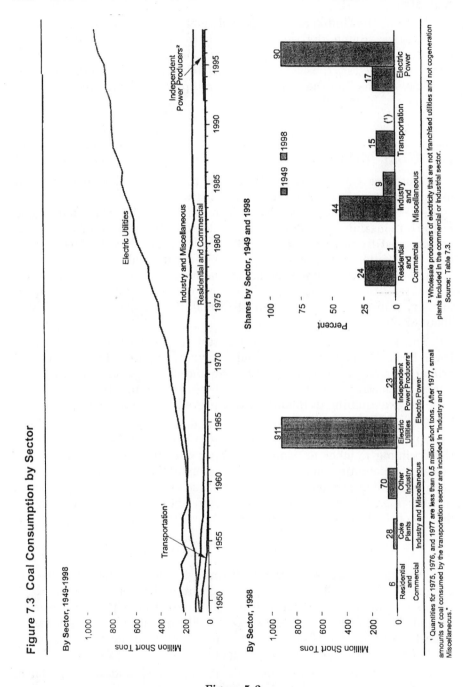

Figure 7.3 Coal Consumption by Sector

Figure 5–2

purposes, such as cement plants and foundries. The heaviest use of coal tends to be in the eastern-central part of the country, from Pennsylvania to Missouri. Less coal is used on the East and West Coasts. But the state that burns the most coal is Texas, mostly lignite that is used for power generation.

In 1997, the United States exported more than 83.5 million tons of coal to countries around the world. *See* Richard Bonskowski, The U.S. Coal Industry in the 1990s 19, Energy Information Administration, September, 1999. Nevertheless, the widespread availability of coal resources in other countries means that the export market will probably be limited to particular grades of high-quality coal.

B.   COAL MINING

Mines are thriving in the West, but they are closing in many coal-mining areas east of the Mississippi. Although coal production in the United States increased from 890 million tons in 1986 to 1090 million tons in 1997, thousands of small mines have closed as the total number of mines has declined from almost 4500 in 1986 to less than 2000 by 1998. Small-mine production between 1991 and 1997 declined about half causing a sharp decline in the number of jobs in the industry. This gradual switch to larger-scale, higher-technology mining has cut the number of jobs in the industry almost by half between 1986 and 1997, from about 155,000 to about 82,000.

The jobs have also been moving west, particularly into the Powder River Basin of Wyoming, where huge new surface mines have become the primary source of fuel for electric generation. In eastern underground mines, productivity per miner has also increased through the use of larger-scale longwall mining techniques and improved cutting technology.

The decline in underground mining and the growth of surface mining has aggravated the legal problems of the industry in two key respects: (1) the declining number of companies engaged in underground mining has depleted a potential source of financial support for remedying the health and environmental problems created by these mines, and (2) the increasing number of surface mines has aroused significant opposition to the transformation of the landscape that they create.

1.   HEALTH AND SAFETY IN UNDERGROUND MINING

Originally, most coal was mined through underground methods—the digging of shafts and tunnels spreading out underground from a single minehead. Although this creates highly intensive activity on the surface around the minehead, it does not necessarily appear to have a substantial impact on the surface of most of the land under which the coal lies because most of the work takes place underground.

Underground coal mines pose significant health and safety problems for the mine workers: (1) Methane gas, which is commonly found in association with coal, is potentially explosive and can also cause asphyxiation, so underground mines must be carefully ventilated. (2) As the coal is removed from an underground seam there is always a danger that the mine shaft will collapse, crushing anyone who happens to be in it; engineering plans to prevent mine collapse are not always successful. (3) Coal miners inhale large amounts of coal dust which, over a period of years, can cause black lung disease, a progressive loss of lung capacity that can be fatal unless the miner retires promptly after the initial diagnosis. Alan Derickson, Black Lung: Anatomy of a Public Health Disaster (Cornell University Press, 1998).

Public attention focused on the hazards of coal mining in the 1960s. Congress passed the Federal Coal Mine Health and Safety Act of 1969, 30 U.S.C. § 801 *et seq.*, and the Black Lung Benefits Act of 1972, 30 U.S.C. § 900 *et seq.* The latter statute required coal companies to pay benefits to miners who had contracted the disease, including some who had left the companies' employ long ago. *Usery v. Turner Elkhorn Mining Co.*, 428 U.S. 1 (1976) (upholding retroactive application of Act).

Because the onset of black lung disease and other work-related illnesses may arise long after the miner quits working, the attribution of the injury to a particular employer has proven to be a problem, especially because many mining companies have gone out of business in the interim. The Coal Industry Retiree Health Benefit Act of 1992, 26 U.S.C. § 9701 *et seq.*, increased the responsibility of mining companies to pay lifetime medical benefits to miners. It adopted the policy that coal mining companies were retroactively liable for these health benefits if they had been in the coal business after the point in time when there was a "general understanding" between the industry and the United Mine Workers that lifetime health benefits would be paid. The retroactive elements of the Act were challenged by Eastern Enterprises, a company that had gotten out of the coal business many years ago[2], but now found itself responsible for the medical costs of some retired miners.

When Eastern Enterprises decided to challenge the application of the 1992 statute to it, there were a number of possible constitutional clauses available:

(1) The Constitution provides that "No ... ex post facto Law shall be passed" (Art. I, § 9(3)).

(2) The Fifth Amendment to the Constitution provides that "No person ... shall be deprived of life, liberty, or property, without due process of law."

(3) The same Fifth Amendment says "nor shall private property be taken for public use, without just compensation."

---

2. Eastern Enterprises is the parent corporation of Boston Gas Company, the largest distributor of natural gas in New England, and of Midland Enterprises, Inc., the leading barge carrier of coal. See Note, Non-traditional Takings and the Coal Act, 20 Energy L. J. 117, 123 (1999).

The ex post facto clause might appear to be the most closely suited to an attack on retroactive regulation. But early in constitutional history the Supreme Court held that this clause prohibits retroactivity in criminal cases but not in civil cases. *See* Harold J. Krent, The Puzzling Boundary Between Criminal and Civil Retroactive Lawmaking, 84 Geo. L. J. 2143 (1996).

The due process clause is another option. The Supreme Court has held that some government regulations may violate that clause if the regulations are so harsh that they infringe on "substantive due process." In the late nineteenth and early twentieth century the Supreme Court frequently used the theory of substantive due process to strike down legislation that affected business. This period in the Court's history is usually characterized as the "Lochner era" in reference to *Lochner v. New York*, 198 U.S. 45 (1905), in which the Court held that a law forbidding employers to make bakers work more than 10 hours a day violated the employers' rights to substantive due process. Then, in the mid 1930s, the Court effectively overruled *Lochner* and many of its other substantive due process cases and began to apply the due process clause only to discrimination against minorities rather than to regulation of business. See Howard Gillman, The Constitution Besieged 175–193 (Duke University Press, 1993).

The third option is the taking clause. During the Lochner era, the Court rarely used the taking clause to test the validity of regulations. More recently, however, the Court has begun to expand the use of the taking clause to strike down economic regulations of business. The Court in *Agins v. Tiburon*, 447 U.S. 255 (1980) said in dicta that a regulation could be a taking if it failed to advance legitimate governmental interests. This led many commentators to wonder whether the Court intended to use the taking clause much like the Lochner-era Court used substantive due process.

Meanwhile, the law of substantive due process has also been evolving. The current Supreme Court is badly split on the meaning of, and even the very existence of, substantive due process—a split that mirrors the strong differences within the Court on the issue of abortion. The famous case of *Roe v. Wade*, 410 U.S. 113 (1973), held that a woman's right to an abortion was protected by the doctrine of substantive due process. Since that time, the Justices who are most strongly opposed to abortion have grown increasingly vehement in their opposition to the doctrine of substantive due process, to the point where Justices Scalia and Thomas have taken the firm position that the very idea of substantive due process should be abolished. *See, e.g., United States v. Carlton*, 512 U.S. 26 (1994); *Albright v. Oliver*, 510 U.S. 266 (1994). On the other hand, some federal circuits have continued to use substantive due process in economic regulation decisions. Michael J. Phillips, The Slow Return of Economic Substantive Due Process, 49 Syracuse L. Rev. 917 (1999).

Given this turbulent stage in constitutional history, Eastern Enterprises logically decided to include counts challenging the Coal Industry Retiree

Health Benefit Act under both the substantive due process and taking clauses.

Eastern Enterprises alleged that it had been in the coal business only until 1966, at which time it spun off its coal business to a subsidiary that it later sold. The Act assigned Eastern the responsibility for paying the medical benefits of certain miners if the miners had worked for Eastern prior to 1966 and had not worked for any other currently existing mine operator since that time. In 1998, the Supreme Court held the Act unconstitutional as applied to Eastern in one of the most confusing opinions in recent Court history. Although the Court held the application of the Act to Eastern to be unconstitutional, there was no majority agreement on which clause of the Constitution had been violated. Four justices found that the Act constituted a taking of property without just compensation, but refused to consider the issue of substantive due process. One justice, Justice Kennedy, found that there was no taking, but held that the Act violated substantive due process as applied to Eastern Enterprises. Four dissenters would have upheld the Act. They agreed with Justice Kennedy that there was no taking, and they agreed that the Act should be tested on grounds of substantive due process, but they said that the statute did *not* violate substantive due process. *Eastern Enterprises v. Apfel,* 524 U.S. 498 (1998).

In the course of his opinion, Justice Kennedy interpreted the taking clause in a new way; he said that a liability to make a monetary payment, such as a tax or a fee, could never be the subject of a taking because it did not involve an "identified property interest" that was protected by the taking clause. The four dissenting justices all announced their agreement with Justice Kennedy on this issue. As a result, a majority of the Court now supports an interpretation of the taking clause that would appear to make it completely inapplicable to statutes such as the Coal Industry Retiree Health Benefit Act.

Therefore the Eastern Enterprises case produced the highly unusual result of a part of a statute being found invalid but with no majority agreeing on the reason for the invalidity. The lack of any consistent rationale for the Court's result has posed difficult problems for the lower courts, as the following case illustrates. The case arose because the *Eastern Enterprises* decision struck down the Act as applied to a coal company that had left the business in 1966, but it left open the issue of the Act's validity to other companies who had continued in business after that time. The companies in the following case stayed in the coal business through the 1970s, but they argued that the precedent of *Eastern Enterprises* should protect them as well.

Unity Real Estate Co. v. Hudson
178 F.3d 649 (3d Cir.) cert. denied 120 S.Ct. 396 (1999).

■ BECKER, C.J.: In *Eastern Enterprises v. Apfel,* 524 U.S. 498, (1998), the Supreme Court held unconstitutional the portion of the 1992 Coal Industry Retiree Health Benefit Act (Coal Act), 26 U.S.C. §§ 9701–9722 (1994 &

Supp. II), that required former coal mine operators to pay for health benefits for retired miners and their dependents, as applied to a former operator who last signed a coal industry benefit agreement [an "NBCWA"] in 1964. In this case, we are asked to apply *Eastern* to former coal mine operators who were signatories to coal industry agreements in 1978 and thereafter. *Eastern* was decided by a sharply divided Court, and the parties disagree as to what, if any, principles commanded a majority.

The plaintiffs, Unity Real Estate ("Unity") and Barnes & Tucker Co. ("B & T"), challenge the Coal Act as applied to them as both a violation of substantive due process and an unconstitutional uncompensated taking. Although it is an exceedingly close question, and we are highly sympathetic to plaintiffs' unfortunate situation, in which retroactively imposed liability operates to bind them to commitments they had thought satisfied when they left the coal industry, we conclude that the Act is constitutional as applied to these plaintiffs. Accordingly, their recourse must be to Congress rather than to the courts.

First, we conclude, albeit with substantial hesitation, that the Coal Act does not violate due process. Our due process inquiry proceeds in two parts. We acknowledge at the outset that there is a gap between what the contracts between the union and the mining companies required and what the Coal Act now mandates from those former mining companies. Because this is a substantive due process challenge, we accord deference to Congress's judgments, based on the report and recommendations of the Coal Commission. While reasonable minds could differ on the point, we are satisfied that the agreements signed by the plaintiffs in 1978 and thereafter promised that miners and their dependents would receive lifetime benefits from the benefit funds, and that, at all events, these agreements informed reasonable expectations that the benefits would continue for life. Similarly, we conclude that it was reasonable for Congress to conclude that the plaintiffs' withdrawal from the funds contributed to the funds' financial instability, though the agreements themselves permitted withdrawal. The history of coal mining in this country also supports Congress's decision to step in when the funds that provided health benefits to retired miners began to falter.

The question we must then answer is whether those congressional judgments provide enough of a rationale for closing the gap between the contracts and the needs of the benefit funds through the mechanism of the Coal Act. Consistent with our due process jurisprudence, we ask whether the Coal Act was a rational response to the problems Congress identified, taking into account the Act's retroactivity, which is highly disfavored in our legal culture. In light of Congress's findings and in the context of extensive government regulation of the coal industry, we hold that it was not fundamentally unfair or unjust for Congress to conclude that the former coal companies should be responsible for paying for such benefits, even if they were no longer contractually obligated to pay into the benefit funds. The retroactive scope of this enactment, especially as applied to plaintiff

Unity (eleven years), approaches the edge of permissible legislative action, but we cannot say that the law is beyond the legislative power.

We also decline to find a compensable taking on the ground that the Coal Act will put the plaintiffs out of business, because it is contrary to the reasoning of a majority of the Supreme Court in *Eastern*. Moreover, granting relief whenever a plaintiff could credibly argue that it would be driven out of business by a regulation would create major difficulties in evaluating the constitutionality of much modern legislation. We therefore decline to construe this regulatory burden as a "categorical taking" analogous to the total destruction of the value of a specific piece of real property.

[The court then analyzed the Supreme Court's *Eastern Enterprises* opinion:] Eastern Enterprises was involved in coal mining until 1965, and signed every NBCWA from 1947 until 1964. It was assigned liability for over 1000 miners, based on Eastern's status as the pre–1978 signatory for whom the miners had worked for the longest period of time; its total liability was estimated to be between $50 and $100 million. Eastern sued, claiming that the Coal Act was unconstitutional.

Four Justices concluded that the Act was a compensable taking as to Eastern. The plurality looked to three factors of particular significance in determining whether a taking had occurred: the economic impact of the regulation, its interference with reasonable investment-backed expectations, and the retroactive character of the government action. The plurality examined several previous cases to set the stage for its analysis [and] summarized this line of cases as follows:

> Our opinions make clear that Congress has considerable leeway to fashion economic legislation, including the power to affect contractual commitments between private parties. Congress also may impose retroactive liability to some degree, particularly where it is "confined to short and limited periods required by the practicalities of producing national legislation." Our decisions, however, have left open the possibility that legislation might be unconstitutional if it imposes severe retroactive liability on a limited class of parties that could not have anticipated the liability, and the extent of that liability is substantially disproportionate to the parties' experience.

Eastern, 118 S. Ct. at 2149 (plurality). The plurality held that the Coal Act, as applied to Eastern, presented such an extreme case. On the economic impact factor of the takings test, the plurality found "no doubt that the Coal Act has forced a considerable financial burden upon Eastern," between $50 and $100 million. *Id.* (plurality). The plurality referred to previous cases requiring that liability be proportional to a party's experience with the object of the challenged legislation. In the pension plan cases, the parties had voluntarily negotiated and maintained pension plans, at least for a while, and consequently their statutorily imposed liability was linked to their own conduct. *See id.* at 2149–50 (plurality). Eastern did not participate in the negotiations for the 1974 or subsequent NBCWAs, nor did it agree to make contributions thereunder. "[The 1974, 1978, and subsequent agreements] first suggest an industry commitment to the funding of lifetime health benefits for both retirees and their family members." *Id.* at 2150 (plurality).

The plurality then concluded that the Coal Act substantially interfered with Eastern's reasonable investment-backed expectations. *See id.* at 2151 (plurality). It reasoned that retroactivity is generally disfavored in the law, and that the length of the period of retroactivity and the extent of Eastern's liability raised substantial questions of fairness. *See id.* at 2152 (plurality). Finally, the plurality found the nature of the government action to be quite unusual, because the liability imposed was substantial, based on conduct thirty to fifty years in the past, and unrelated to any commitment Eastern made or injury it caused. *See id.* at 2153 (plurality).

The plurality declined to reach Eastern's substantive due process argument, although it noted that takings and due process analyses are often correlated. *See id.* (plurality). The plurality reiterated the Court's past concerns about using the "vague contours" of the due process clause to nullify laws. *Eastern,* 118 S. Ct. at 2153 (plurality) (citation omitted). Justice Thomas agreed with the plurality's Takings Clause analysis but wrote separately to reaffirm his belief that the Ex Post Facto Clause would also apply to Eastern's predicament. *See id.* at 2154 (Thomas, J., concurring).

Justice Kennedy concurred in the judgment, providing the critical fifth vote to strike the law down as applied to Eastern. He found takings analysis inapplicable: "The Coal Act imposes a staggering financial burden on the petitioner ... but it regulates the former mine owner without regard to property. It does not operate upon or alter an identified property interest, and it is not applicable to or measured by a property interest." *Id.* at 2154 (Kennedy, J., concurring). Instead, he emphasized the law's distaste for retroactivity and found that the Coal Act's extreme retroactivity violated due process as applied to Eastern. *See id.* at 2158–59 (Kennedy, J., concurring). When the Court upheld retroactive legislation in the past, he noted, the statutes at issue were "remedial, designed to impose an actual, measurable cost of [the employer's] business which the employer had been able to avoid in the past." *Id.* at 2159 (Kennedy, J., concurring) (citation and internal quotation marks omitted) (alteration in original). Justice Kennedy concluded that "statutes may be invalidated on due process grounds only under the most egregious of circumstances. This case represents one of the rare instances in which even such a permissive standard has been violated." *Id.* (Kennedy, J., concurring).

Four Justices dissented, finding neither a taking nor a due process violation.

[The Court of Appeals then concluded that the key issue in the case then pending before it was whether companies that had stayed in the coal business through 1981, like the present plaintiffs, were distinguishable from Eastern because the bargaining agreements entered into during the time period between 1978 and 1981 implicitly promised the miners that they would receive lifetime health benefits.]

Unlike Eastern, Unity and B & T, as members of the Bituminous Coal Operators' Association (BCOA), participated in the negotiations that created the post–1978 funding structure. They benefitted from the NBCWAs by obtaining labor peace. Although the contract allowed the companies to unload their obligations to the retirees onto the Trustees, they should reasonably have anticipated that such a strategy would threaten the Funds and might well prompt a congressional response. . . . The question is what reasonable expectations the coal companies' actions created. While an expectation cannot be reasonable without some foundation in the real world, an explicit representation that the companies would provide lifetime benefits is not required, since reasonable expectations may arise from a consistent course of conduct as well.

Plaintiffs and amici argue that the coal companies never made any promises, implicit or explicit, or raised any expectations of lifetime benefits. They first point to the text of the NBCWAs, which did not themselves require the coal companies to provide lifetime benefits under all circumstances. . . . It is true that the funding contribution requirements were limited to the life of the agreement, "ending when this Agreement is terminated," in 1978 and subsequent NBCWAs. Yet all of these arguments have the same fundamental weakness, which is that they go to the contract and not to the reasonable expectations that might have been created by the contract. The United Mine Workers Association (UMWA) negotiator's testimony is a particularly strong example of this: the parties could have agreed to eliminate benefits in any given negotiation, but there was no realistic chance that they would. . . .

Ultimately, although the issue is close, we conclude that the Coal Act is targeted to address the problem of insufficient resources in the benefit funds and that it puts the burden on those who, in Congress's reasonable judgment, should bear it. The law's retroactivity is troubling, yet given the nature of the commitments at issue and the relationship of Coal Act liabilities to past acts in the industry, we cannot say that the Act violates due process.

■ ALDISERT, J., concurring: As a native of Carnegie, Pennsylvania—a coal mining and steel mill town near Pittsburgh—who is old enough to remember the organizational efforts of John L. Lewis in the coal fields in the 1930s and the 1947 Krug–Lewis Agreement, I no doubt have a unique perspective. I know first-hand the mantra of every coal miner through decades of strikes and picketing: "No Contract, No Work."

To the miner, the actual contract controlled, not the expectation of future agreements. Without the contract in hand, the miners would not pick up their lamps at the lamp house and descend into the shafts. They worked under the precise language in a given contract and under no other representations. The sordid history of the coal company towns that surrounded Carnegie, and the inhumane treatment of the miners and their families prior to effective unionization in the mines, impelled the miners to require thereafter that every representation of working conditions and benefits be set forth in clear language in a hard-fought written collective bargaining agreement.

The foregoing discussion is but my gratuitous interpretation of some of the history and contents of the Wage Agreements, and admittedly, it may be contrary to that expressed in most other judicial opinions. My views and those of judges with contrary interpretations are important in one respect only: My views and those of other judges are totally irrelevant. What is relevant is only that on the basis of evidence before it, Congress concluded that a promise of lifetime benefits had been made. This furnished the rational basis for enacting the controversial provisions of the Coal Act.

This, too, must be said. I am conscious that in light of the view that we take here, the handwriting is on the wall that a kind of hydraulic pressure will generate economic disasters in companies whose financial circumstances are similar to Unity and Barnes and Tucker. Without additional and more realistic Congressional intervention, we may see a phenomenon of the "last man standing," as companies disappear from the economic scene and responsibility for paying benefits shifts to surviving companies. If this case is any example and a forerunner of things to come, the operation of the present statutory solution to the vexing health benefit problem of retirees and their dependents may serve as a full employment program for bankruptcy lawyers of companies unable to make prescribed payments. Sadly, I do not believe that this statement is an argumentum ad terrorem.

I join in the judgment of the court.■

NOTES AND COMMENTS

1. Professor Jan Laitos of the University of Denver Law School has been suggesting for some years that retroactivity is one of the Court's half-hidden concerns in all property rights cases, not just takings cases. See Jan G. Laitos, Legislative Retroactivity, 52 Wash. U. J. Urb. & Contemp. L. 81 (1997). In his 1999 treatise on property rights, he cites the *Eastern Enterprises* opinion as a vindication of his position. For his extended discussion of the history of the Supreme Court's retroactivity decisions and their modern relevance, see Jan Laitos, The Law of Property Rights Protection, Chs. 13–16 (1999).

2. On the other hand, the Supreme Court in *Eastern Enterprises* is certainly not saying that all retroactive legislation is invalid on its face.[3] Both the plurality opinion by Justice O'Connor[4] and Justice Kennedy's

---

3. It should be noted, however, that a brief concurrence by Justice Thomas suggests that he may be willing to go that far (524 U.S. at 538, Thomas J., concurring).

4. "[L]egislation might be unconstitutional if it imposes severe retroactive liability on a limited class of parties that could not have anticipated the liability, and the extent of that liability is substantially disproportion-

ate to the parties' experience." 524 U.S. at 528–29. Legislation that "singles out certain employers to bear a burden that is substantial in amount, based on the employers' conduct far in the past, and unrelated to any commitment that the employers made or to any injury they caused, the governmental action implicates fundamental principles of

concurrence carefully limit their discussion to the specific facts of that particular company's situation. Professor Mark Tushnet refers to such narrowly limited opinions as "judicial minimalism," and calls *Eastern Enterprises* the best recent example because "it used so many standards and made each important to the conclusion." Mark Tushnet, The New Constitutional Order and the Chastening of Constitutional Aspiration, 113 Harv. L. Rev. 29, 92–93 (1999). Is the most that we can discern from the *Eastern Enterprises* opinions that the Court may be telling us that it will employ some higher level of scrutiny in reviewing laws that have "severe retroactive" effect? Will the Court ever be able to come up with a bright line rule that alerts us to the degree of retroactivity that would be permitted?

3. Justice Kennedy's interpretation of the taking clause as being limited to the protection of identified property interests, concurred in by the four dissenters, appears to substantially limit the extent to which regulatory takings claims can be made outside the traditional context of property regulation. He interprets the taking clause to apply only to the taking of specific property interests, and says that a demand for payment of a fee does not "operate upon or alter an identified property interest" (*Eastern*, 524 U.S. at 540, opinion of Kennedy J.). The fact that the coal companies were being asked to make cash contributions takes the case out of the realm of the taking clause; an exaction in cash can be invalidated only if it violates substantive due process.[5] The reason for this limitation on the taking clause is the need to provide "some necessary predictability" for state and local governments. The extreme difficulty "in determining whether there is a taking or a regulation" means that "extending regulatory takings analysis to the amorphous class of cases" involving fees and taxes "would throw one of the most difficult and litigated areas of the law into confusion, subjecting States and municipalities to the potential of new and unforeseen claims in vast amounts." (*Id.* at 542). Identification of the specific property right allegedly taken is important "lest all governmental action be subjected to examination under the constitutional prohibition against taking without compensation, with the attendant potential for money damages." (*Id.* at 543). The four dissenting justices agreed with this part of Justice Kennedy's opinion.

To what extent does this new interpretation of the taking clause limit the ability of energy businesses to challenge other forms of government regulation as a taking? See *Commonwealth Edison Company v. United*

---

fairness underlying the Taking Clause." 524 U.S. at 537.

5. "The coal act does not appropriate, transfer or encumber an estate in land (*e.g.*, a lien on a particular piece of property), a valuable interest in an intangible (*e.g.*, intellectual property), or even a bank account or accrued interest. The law simply imposes an obligation to perform an act, the payment of benefits. The statute is indifferent as to how

the regulated entity elects to comply or the property it uses to do so. To the extent it affects property interests, it does so in a manner similar to many laws; but until today, none were thought to constitute takings. To call this sort of governmental action a taking as a matter of constitutional interpretation is both imprecise and, with all due respect, unwise." 524 U.S. at 540 (opinion of Kennedy, J.).

States, 46 Fed.Cl. 29, reconsideration denied, 46 Fed.Cl. 158 (2000)(government fee assessed on power companies for environmental cleanup of uranium enrichment sites cannot be a taking). Can Congress now evade effective judicial scrutiny by enforcing regulations solely through financial penalties that do not "operate upon or alter an identified property interest?" Is the same limitation applicable to state and local governments? Remember that the taking clause applies to state and local regulation as well as federal regulation. What effect does this interpretation of the taking clause have on the arguments of electric utilities who claim that the introduction of competition to the electricity business would constitute a taking of their "stranded costs?" (See Chapter 12).

4.   The Coal Act does not involve the acquisition of any property or money by the government, but requires the coal companies to pay money directly to a fund for the coal miners. Does the fact that the government is transferring wealth from one group to another, rather than acquiring a property interest itself, suggest the need for an analysis under the due process clause rather than the taking clause? *See* John V. Orth, Taking from A and Giving to B: Substantive Due Process and the Case of the Shifting Paradigm, 14 Constitutional Commentary 337 (1997).

5.   Today, surface mining (called strip mining by its critics) is the most efficient way of mining coal if the coal is relatively near the surface. About three-fifths of the coal mined in the United States is currently mined by surface mining using huge shovels the size of a multistory building. Surface mining does not create the same health and safety issues for the mine workers as underground mining. Moreover, surface mining is much less labor-intensive, so the productivity of each employee is far higher than in underground mines. On the other hand, the impact of surface mining on the use of the surface of the land is more extensive than the impact of underground mining (see § 2b of this chapter).

2.   EXTERNALITIES OF COAL MINING

In addition to the health and safety problems of mining workers, coal mining often has serious adverse impacts on other people who are not associated with the coal industry. These impacts have led to extensive legislation designed to regulate these impacts.

a.   UNDERGROUND MINING EXTERNALITIES

Underground mining was the only method of coal mining used in the 19th century and it still accounts for at least a third of the coal produced in the United States. A mine shaft is drilled down to the coal seam. Then tunnels are excavated through the seam. Two specific problems associated with underground mining have posed major regulatory issues: (1) Mines cause subsidence of the surface; either intentional, in the case of longwall mining[6], or accidental after the mine is abandoned and the support system

---

6.   Longwall mining is a modern system of underground mining that uses highly auto-   mated coal cutting machines that excavate the entire coal seam and allow the earth

collapses; and (2) Mines tap into seams of minerals and heavy metals that then leak out of the mines into streams or aquifers where they become water pollutants.

i. Subsidence

Coal mine subsidence is the lowering of strata overlying a coal mine, including the land surface, caused by the extraction of underground coal. This lowering of the strata can have devastating effects. It often causes substantial damage to foundations, walls, other structural members, and the integrity of houses and buildings. Subsidence frequently causes sink-holes or troughs in land which make the land difficult or impossible to develop. Its effect on farming has been well documented: many subsided areas cannot be plowed or properly prepared. Subsidence can also cause the loss of groundwater and surface ponds. *Keystone Bituminous Coal Assn. v. DeBenedictis,* 480 U.S. 470 (1987).

In the famous case of *Pennsylvania Coal Co. v. Mahon,* 260 U.S. 393 (1922), the Supreme Court held that the Kohler Act, a Pennsylvania statute that prevented coal companies from mining coal in a way that caused subsidence to the owner of a surface estate, was invalid as a taking of property without just compensation. Justice Holmes, writing for the majority, opined that

> This is the case of a single private house. No doubt there is a public interest even in this, as there is in every purchase and sale and in all that happens within the commonwealth. Some existing rights may be modified even in such a case. *Rideout v. Knox, 148 Mass. 368.* But usually in ordinary private affairs the public interest does not warrant much of this kind of interference. A source of damage to such a house is not a public nuisance even if similar damage is inflicted on others in different places. The damage is not common or public. *Wesson v. Washburn Iron Co., 13 Allen, 95, 103.* The extent of the public interest is shown by the statute to be limited, since the statute ordinarily does not apply to land when the surface is owned by the owner of the coal. Furthermore, it is not justified as a protection of personal safety. That could be provided for by notice. Indeed the very foundation of this bill is that the defendant gave timely notice of its intent to mine under the house. On the other hand the extent of the taking is great. It purports to abolish what is recognized in Pennsylvania as an estate in land—a very valuable estate[7]—and what is declared by the Court below to be a contract hitherto binding the plaintiffs.

---

above the seam to subside after excavation is complete. J. Thomas Lane II, Fire in the Hole to Longwall Shears: Old Law Applied to New Technology and other Longwall Mining Issues, 96 W.Va. L. Rev. 577 (1994).

7. [Ed. Note] Under Pennsylvania law, the right to mine coal in a way that destroyed the support for the surface is called the "support estate" and is treated as a separate property interest.

What makes the right to mine coal valuable is that it can be exercised with profit. To make it commercially impracticable to mine certain coal has very nearly the same effect for constitutional purposes as appropriating or destroying it. This we think that we are warranted in assuming that the statute does.

The *Pennsylvania Coal* decision represented the first time that the Supreme Court had held that a regulation could be "tantamount to a taking." In recent years, the Court has devoted increased attention to the issue of regulatory takings.

Sixty-five years after the initial *Pennsylvania Coal* decision, The Court returned to the issue of coal mine subsidence. In *Keystone Bituminous Coal Ass'n v. DeBenedictis,* 480 U.S. 470 (1987), the Court upheld another Pennsylvania statute preventing coal companies from mining coal in a way that caused subsidence to roads, schools and other public facilities. The Court distinguished the earlier case on the ground that it was designed only to rearrange the rights among private parties, while the later statute was designed to protect public safety.

In the advisory portion of the Court's opinion, Justice Holmes rested on two propositions, both critical to the Court's decision. First, because it served only private interests, not health or safety, the Kohler Act could not be "sustained as an exercise of the police power." *Id.* at 414. Second, the statute made it "commercially impracticable" to mine "certain coal" in the areas affected by the Kohler Act.

This assumption was not unreasonable in view of the fact that the Kohler Act may be read to prohibit mining that causes any subsidence—not just subsidence that results in damage to surface structures. The record in this case indicates that subsidence will almost always occur eventually.

The holdings and assumptions of the Court in *Pennsylvania Coal* provide obvious and necessary reasons for distinguishing *Pennsylvania Coal* from the case before us today.... First, unlike the Kohler Act, the character of the governmental action involved here leans heavily against finding a taking; the Commonwealth of Pennsylvania has acted to arrest what it perceives to be a significant threat to the common welfare. Second, there is no record in this case to support a finding, similar to the one the Court made in *Pennsylvania Coal*, that the Subsidence Act makes it impossible for petitioners to profitably engage in their business, or that there has been undue interference with their investment-backed expectations.

Unlike the Kohler Act, which was passed upon in *Pennsylvania Coal*, the Subsidence Act does not merely involve a balancing of the private economic interests of coal companies against the private interests of the surface owners. The Pennsylvania Legislature specifically found that important public interests are served by enforcing a policy that is designed to minimize subsidence in certain areas.

None of the indicia of a statute enacted solely for the benefit of private parties identified in Justice Holmes' opinion are present here. First, Justice Holmes explained that the Kohler Act was a "private benefit" statute since it "ordinarily does not apply to land when the surface is owned by the owner of the coal." 260 U.S., at 414. The Subsidence Act, by contrast, has no such exception. The current surface owner may only waive the protection of the Act if the DER [Pennsylvania Department of Environmental Regulation] consents. *See* 25 Pa. Code § 89.145(b) (1983). Moreover, the Court was forced to reject the Commonwealth's safety justification for the Kohler Act because it found that the Commonwealth's interest in safety could as easily have been accomplished through a notice requirement to landowners. The Subsidence Act, by contrast, is designed to accomplish a number of widely varying interests, with reference to which petitioners have not suggested alternative methods through which the Commonwealth could proceed.

After Keystone, the courts have had difficulty deciding whether to award damages to coal companies that have been denied permits. Where the federal government refused to issue a permit to mine coal to a company on the ground of a risk of public injury because of large cracks in the ground, collapsing structures, and breaks in gas, water and electrical lines, the federal circuit found that the mining company was not deprived of all beneficial use because "the nature of the owner's estate shows that the prescribed use interests were not part of the title to begin with." *M. & J. Coal Company v. United States*, 47 F.3d 1148 (Fed.Cir.1995). But see *Machipongo Land and Coal Company, Inc. v. Commonwealth of Pennsylvania*, 719 A.2d 19 (Pa.Commw.1998) (discussing various theories for measuring the extent to which the regulation diminishes the company's interest) and *Eastern Minerals International, Inc. v. U.S.*, 36 Fed. Cl. 541 (1996)(holding that an inexcusable delay in issuing a mining permit may constitute a taking).

Congress entered the dispute in 1992 by adding a new § 720 to the Mining Act, see Energy Policy Act of 1992, Pub. L. No. 102–486, sec. 2504(a)(1), § 720, 106 Stat. 2776, 3104 (1992), which provides:

(a) Requirements. Underground coal mining operations conducted after October 24, 1992, shall comply with each of the following requirements:

(1) Promptly repair, or compensate for, material damage resulting from subsidence caused to any occupied residential dwelling and structures related thereto, or non-commercial building due to underground coal mining operations. Repair of damage shall include rehabilitation, restoration, or replacement of the damaged occupied residential dwelling and structures related thereto, or non-commercial building. Compensation shall be provided to the owner of the damaged occupied residential dwelling and structures related thereto or non-commercial building and shall be in the full amount of the diminution in value resulting from the subsidence. Compensation may be accomplished by

the purchase, prior to mining, of a noncancellable premium-prepaid insurance policy.

(2) Promptly replace any drinking, domestic, or residential water supply from a well or spring in existence prior to the application for a surface coal mining and reclamation permit, which has been affected by contamination, diminution, or interruption resulting from underground coal mining operations. Nothing in this section shall be construed to prohibit or interrupt underground coal mining operations.

The D.C. Circuit Court of Appeals upheld regulations promulgated under the Energy Policy Act requiring coal companies to repair or fully compensate homeowners for property damage caused by subsidence, even if a waiver agreement was in place. *National Mining Ass'n v. Babbitt*, 172 F.3d 906 (D.C.Cir., 1999). The National Mining Association (NMA) had challenged the regulation as unreasonable "to the extent it purports to nullify prior agreements between owners of eligible structures and underground mine operators." The NMA argued that if the statute authorizes the annulment of waiver agreements, landowners would receive a windfall, and coal mining companies could suffer an unconstitutional taking of contract rights through a "double recovery" scheme, in which the mining company first pays a landowner for subsidence damage by buying waiver rights and then has to pay again for post-mining damage through the Energy Policy Act.

The government argued in response that there would be no "double recovery" because the cost of the waiver would be subtracted from the post-mining damage amount. The court agreed with the government's position.

NMA also argued that interference with contract rights is a per se taking. The court disagreed, citing the rule from *Connolly v. Pension Benefit Guaranty Corp.*, 475 U.S. 211, 224 (1986): "legislation [that] disregards or destroys existing contractual rights does not always transform the regulation into an illegal taking." NMA should have been prepared to demonstrate why "(1) the economic impact of the regulation on the claimant; (2) the extent to which the regulation has interfered with investment-backed expectations; and (3) the character of the governmental action" show that an unconstitutional taking would result.(quoting *Penn Cent. Transp. Co. v. City of New York*, 438 U.S. 104, 124 (1978)).

At the present time, therefore, coal mining companies are responsible for most significant damages caused by subsidence. Although Justice Holmes' famous opinion in *Pennsylvania Coal* is still widely cited, the factual context on which it was based now appears to be obsolete.

ii.   *Acid Mine Drainage*

Acid mine drainage can be associated with either surface mining or underground mining, and often results in water polluted with not only with high acidity but with toxic substances. The purpose of the Clean Water Act ("CWA") "is to restore and maintain the chemical, physical, and biological integrity of the nation's waters." 33 U.S.C. § 1251. The idea is to use technology-based effluent limitations and water quality-based ambient standards to achieve swimmable and fishable water throughout the United States. These standards are implemented through the national pollutant discharge elimination system ("NPDES") permit. The NPDES permit applies to discharges from point sources. 33 U.S.C. § 1342. Individual states are responsible for administering the CWA. The EPA may administer a program only if the state's program is found to be inappropriate.

The CWA makes the discharge of any pollutant into navigable waters by any person unlawful, except when in compliance with designated sections of the statute. 33 U.S.C. 1§ 362. A pollutant is basically anything other than sewage from vessels or fluids used to facilitate the production from an oil or gas well.[8] Discharge of a pollutant is the addition of any pollutant to navigable waters from a point source. Navigable waters are the waters of the United States including the territorial seas. 40 C.F.R. § 122.2 (1998). "Point source" is broadly defined, and includes pipes, tunnels and animal feed lots. 33 U.S.C. § 1362(14).

Drainage from a mine is treated as a point source that requires an NPDES permit under the Clean Water Act (*Trustees for Alaska v. EPA,* 749 F.2d 549 (9th Cir.1984)) unless the drainage is merely stormwater runoff. 33 U.S.C. § 1342 (*l*) (2).

Under the Clean Water Act, the EPA and state environmental agencies seek to prevent the development and release of acid mine drainage by requiring either active or passive treatment systems. An active system may be manual or mechanical and requires the periodic addition of reagents, ongoing support, and maintenance; for example, adding lime to a treatment pool to raise the pH of an acidic discharge. Passive systems are designed to be self-sustaining and use chemical or biological processes that rely on no external support. For example, constructed wetlands are sometimes used to treat mine drainage because many of the plant species that comprise wetlands thrive on acidic material.

U.S. v. Law

979 F.2d 977 (4th Cir.) cert. denied 507 U.S. 1030 (1993).

■ Per curiam: Lewis R. Law and Mine Management, Inc. appeal their felony convictions for violating the Clean Water Act, 33 U.S.C. § 1319(c)(2) ("CWA") by knowingly discharging polluted water into Wolf and Arbuckle Creeks in Fayette County, West Virginia without a National Pollution Discharge Elimination System ("NPDES") permit. Finding no reversible error, we affirm.

In 1977 Lewis R. Law formed Mine Management, Inc. ("MMI"), a West Virginia corporation, to engage in various coal-related business activities. From MMI's inception, Law was its sole officer and stockholder. In

---

8. Pollution from oil and gas wells is dealt with under other statutes. See Chapter Six.

1980, MMI purchased 241 acres from the New River Company ("New River"). The conveyance included an aged coal preparation plant, masses of coal refuse ("gob piles"), and a water treatment system. New River installed this system in the late 1970s to collect, divert, treat, and discharge runoff and leachate from a gob pile that covered a large portion of the subject property.

The water treatment system was designed to reduce the acidity and metal content of drainage from the gob pile. The system comprised a collection pond near Wolf Creek, a pump, and piping that channeled the collected water over a ridge and through a hopper, which dispensed soda ash briquettes to raise the pH of the water. Iron and manganese then precipitated out as the water flowed through two settling ponds before its discharge into Arbuckle Creek.

The water treatment system was subject to an NPDES permit when MMI purchased the site. Despite repeated notice, however, neither MMI nor Law ever applied for, or was granted, an NPDES permit authorizing discharges into Wolf or Arbuckle Creeks. Due to MMI's failure to operate the water treatment system effectively, acid mine drainage discharged from the collection pond into Wolf Creek, or from the second settling pond into Arbuckle Creek, on at least 16 occasions between March, 1987 and November 15, 1991. Law and MMI were indicted for violating the CWA, 33 U.S.C.§ 1319(c)(2), tried to a jury, and found guilty. Law was sentenced to two years in prison and Law and MMI were fined $80,000.00 each.

Law and MMI challenge their convictions on two grounds. They argue, first, that the trial court instructed the jury erroneously on the law governing their case and, second, that the court abused its discretion in barring evidence regarding New River's alleged policy of concealing preexisting environmental problems from prospective purchasers of its property. We reject both grounds of appeal.

Under the CWA, it is a felony to (a) knowingly (b) discharge (c) a pollutant (d) from a point source (e) into a navigable water of the United States (f) without, or in violation of, an NPDES permit. See 33 U.S.C. §§ 1311(a), 1319(c)(2), 1342(a); *Arkansas v. Oklahoma*, 112 S. Ct. 1046, 1054 (1992); see also 33 U.S.C. § 1362(12) (defining "discharge" as "any addition of any pollutant to navigable waters from any point source") (emphases added). Appellants do not contest that they added untreated acid mine drainage to Wolf and Arbuckle Creeks from the collection pond and the settling pond, respectively, knowing that they lacked the requisite NPDES permit.

In challenging the trial court's jury instructions, however, appellants contend that the CWA imposes liability only upon the generators of pollutants discharged into navigable waters of the United States, and not upon persons over whose property preexisting pollutants are passed along to flow finally into navigable waters. They contend that the trial court erred by refusing to instruct the jury that no responsibility lies for discharging pollutants that originate beyond one's own property, and by instructing the jury instead that

... it is not a defense to the charge that the water discharged from the point source came from some other place or places before its discharge from the point source. It is not a defense to this action that some, or all, of the pollutants discharged from a point source originated at places not on the defendants' property. This is because the offense consists of the knowing discharge of a pollutant from a point source into a water of the United States [without, or in violation of, an NPDES permit]. J App 489–90

Appellants rely for this contention upon decisions in *National Wildlife Federation v. Consumers Power Co.,* 862 F.2d 580 (6th Cir.1988), *National Wildlife Federation v. Gorsuch,* 224 U.S. App. D.C. 41, 693 F.2d 156 (D.C.Cir.1982), and *Appalachian Power Co. v. Train,* 545 F.2d 1351 (4th Cir.1976). In these cases, operators of power plants and dams diverted, then released, navigable waters of the United States. The appellate courts held that where "pollutants" existed in the waters of the United States before contact with these facilities, the mere diversion in the flow of the waters did not constitute"additions" of pollutants to the waters. *Consumers Power,* 862 F.2d at 585–86; *Gorsuch,* 693 F.2d at 174–75; *Train,* 545 F.2d at 1377–78. Appellants sought to square their case with these decisions by showing that the headwaters of Wolf and Arbuckle Creeks originated, and were polluted, before entering their water treatment system, so that, like the power plant and dam operators, they had no duty to remove preexisting pollutants.

With respect to pollutants preexisting in the waters of the United States, where the flow of the waters is merely diverted, the trial court's jury instructions did not state the law with strict accuracy ("it is not a defense ... that some, or all, of the pollutants ... originated at places not on the defendants' property"). The error was harmless, however, because, as a matter of law, appellants' water treatment system was not part of the waters of the United States; to the contrary, the system constituted a point source.

Unlike the river and lake waters diverted in *Consumers Power, Gorsuch,* and *Train,* appellants' water treatment system collected runoff and leachate subject to an NPDES permit under the CWA, and therefore was not part of the "waters of the United States." *See* 40 C.F.R. § 122.2(g) ("Waste treatment systems, including treatment ponds and lagoons designed to meet the requirements of CWA ... are not waters of the United States."). The origin of pollutants in the treatment and collection ponds is therefore irrelevant. The proper focus is upon the discharge from the ponds into Wolf and Arbuckle Creeks.

Appellants' treatment system is also unlike the power plants and dams at issue in *Consumers Power, Gorsuch,* and *Train* because it clearly satisfies the statutory definition of "point source." *See* 40 C.F.R. § 122.2 (a "point source" is "any discernible, confined and discrete conveyance, including but not limited to any pipe, ditch, channel, ... conduit, ... discrete fissure, ... [or] landfill leachate collection system ... from which pollutants are or may be discharged" (emphasis added); "discharge" includes "surface runoff which is collected or channeled by man"); see also *Sierra Club v. Abston Constr. Co.*, 620 F.2d 41, 47 (5th Cir.1980) (collection and channeling of runoff constitutes a point source). Because appellants' treatment system was, as a matter of law, not part of the waters of the United States but instead a point source, the trial court's instructions to the jury were without prejudicial error.

Appellants also claim that the trial court abused its discretion in excluding evidence concerning New River's alleged policy of concealing existing environmental problems from prospective purchasers. Under the foregoing analysis of the CWA, the relevant *mens rea* issue was Law's knowledge as of March, 1987, that the ponds were discharging pollutants into the creeks without, or in violation of, an NPDES permit. Appellants' attempts to cross-examine former New River employees Louis Briguglio and Don Reedy regarding the alleged policy were therefore properly excluded as irrelevant. Law's testimony regarding his conversations with Briguglio were properly excluded as hearsay.

For the foregoing reasons, we affirm the convictions of Lewis R. Law and Mine Management, Inc. on all counts.■

NOTES AND COMMENTS

1. There are two main categories of criteria with which compliance is required under the Clean Water Act. (A) Technology-based effluent limits establish discharge requirements from coal mining point sources based on control technology. The regulations require compliance with numerical limits based on the capacities of technologies examined, but do not prescribe the use of a particular technology. Technology-based limits are used to ensure the uniform adoption of advanced effluent standards across entire industry groups without considering the discharge locations or water quality in the receiving water body. 40 C.F.R.§ 434. (B) Water quality standards are based on the physical qualities of the water body and are designed to protect the designated uses of that water body. Individual states set their own water quality standards, subject to EPA approval. These standards must "protect the public health or welfare, enhance the quality of the water, and serve the purposes of the CWA." 33 U.S.C. § 1313(c)(20(A). NPDES permit limitations are then established regardless of the availability or effectiveness of treatment technologies. If the existing water quality is above what is necessary to support designated activities, the water quality standards cannot be set lower than what currently exists. Waters that have been designated "special national resources" may not be degraded at all. 40 C.F.R. §§ 131.10, 131.12.

The EPA has addressed coal mining point sources in the CWA regulations. 40 C.F.R. § 434. The regulations pertaining to acid mine drainage ("AMD") involve drainage from active mines as well as areas on or beneath land disturbed by coal mining activities. The NPDES permit program would require a permit for a mine even after the close of operations if a discharge occurs, but there is little incentive to comply with a permit once mining is finished. Often coal companies become insolvent or the responsible owner no longer exists. Caroline Henrich, Acid Mine Drainage: Common Law, SMCRA, and the Clean Water Act, 10 J. Nat. Resources & Envtl. L. 235 (1994–95). For these reasons, CWA compliance is usually applied only to active mining sites. Mary J. Hackett, Remining and the Water Quality Act of 1987: Operators Beware!, 13 Colum. J. Envtl. L. 79, 115–17 (1987).

Drainage from abandoned underground coal mines is often a major water pollution problem in those areas where coal has been mined for many years, and many such mines have been placed on the National Priority List under the Comprehensive Environmental Response, Compensation, and Liability Act (CERCLA), 42 U.S.C. § 9601 *et seq.* This problem is often aggravated in the East because of the high sulfur content of the coal. *See* William H. Rodgers, Jr., Environmental Law 724 (West Publishing, 2d ed. 1994).

2.   Does *U.S. v. Law* mean that if anyone owns a point source that is discharging pollutants into water of the United States without a permit, that person is in violation of the CWA, regardless of where the pollutants originated? A review of the joint appendix in the record of the case shows the complexity of the situation faced by Law and MMI.[9]

Law formed Mine Management Company in 1977 to engage in various business activities related to the coal industry. MMI leased the right to recover coal from the property owned by New River Company. Prior to this, New River Company operated the Lochgelly mine on the site. Coal mining activities also took place on the property adjacent to the site. Refuse from New River's coal processing was dumped at the site, resulting in a gob pile that covered approximately 100 acres of the surface, and approximately 100 feet deep. The head waters of the Wolf and Arbuckle Creeks are located near the foot of this gob pile. New River installed a series of collection ponds on the Wolf and Arbuckle Creeks to treat acid mine drainage in 1979. New River acquired an NPDES permit, which was in place when MMI purchased the property.

MMI purchased 241 acres of the surface of the property owned by New River, including the various treatment ponds, in 1980. Between 1980 and 1991, Law was informed on numerous occasions that an NPDES permit was required for the treatment ponds on his property. Law failed to comply.

Conflicting evidence was presented at trial as to how acid mine drainage entered the Wolf Creek collection pond. Prosecution experts testified that acid drainage (AMD) leached from the surface of the gob pile as a result of rain and the migration of water through the pile. Defense experts testified that the AMD came from underground springs contaminated as a result of mining activities on other properties adjacent to MMI's

---

9.   *See generally* Phillip B. Scott, S. Benjamin Bryant, Criminal Enforcement of the Clean Water Act in the Coal Fields: United States v. Law and Beyond, 95 W.Va. L. Rev. 663 (Spring, 1993).

site. Law argued that he had no duty to treat the AMD because he was the surface owner and could not be required to treat pollutants generated below the surface. However, Law's argument was unpersuasive because the statute does not require that the defendant create the pollutants. The CWA does not regulate the generation of pollutants, but the addition of pollutants to navigable waters. See *Natural Resources Defense Council v. U.S. EPA*, 859 F.2d 156, 170 (D.C.Cir.1988) (CWA jurisdiction limited to regulation of discharge of pollutants).

If Law's argument were accepted, could a mining company discharge pollutants as long as the pollutants were generated by someone else? In the coal fields, could the CWA be circumvented by severing (1) the AMD producing estate, (2) the subsurface from the AMD discharging estate, and (3) the surface? Should there be special treatment of environmental criminal defendants, sometimes called "green collar" criminals, in regard to the criminal intent requirement? *See* Lawrence Friedman & H. Hamilton Hackney III, Questions of Intent: Environmental Crimes and "Public Welfare" Offenses, 10 Villanova Envtl L. J. 1 (1999).

3. Another one of Law's challenges was that the Wolf and Arbuckle Creeks were polluted before entering the collection ponds. He claimed that the ponds added no additional pollutants and therefore were not regulated by the CWA. This argument was based on evidence that the original headwaters of the stream extended to the area now covered by the gob pile and that the ponds lay in the original stream beds. This argument rested on an analogy to the reservoirs created by power plants and dams. Law relied on a long line of cases holding that power plants and dams, which merely divert or accumulate waters of the United States and then release those waters, do not require an NPDES permits if they do not physically add pollutants from the outside world into those waters, and they are not required to remove pollutants from the waters that were already there. The *Law* court rejected this analogy. The court held that the treatment ponds were a part of Law's water treatment system and the waters in them were not waters of the United States, unlike the reservoir behind the dam in a river. Thus when water was discharged from the treatment pond into a river, it was a discharge into the waters of the United States and therefore subject to the CWA. *See Rayle Coal Co. v. Chief, Division of Water Resources*, 401 S.E.2d 682 (W.Va. 1990).

4. Is criminal prosecution the appropriate way to deter environmental crimes? Federal environmental laws typically provide that any responsible officer of a corporation can be held criminally responsible for violations if they knew or should have known that the corporation was violating environmental regulations. *United States v. Johnson & Towers*, 741 F.2d 662, 663 (3d Cir.1984), cert. denied 469 U.S. 1208 (1985). The field of environmental law has had schizoid problems trying to decide whether it is trying to punish "bad guys" or simply setting aspirational objectives to control inevitable and pervasive pollution. Richard Lazarus, Meeting the Demands of Integration in the Evolution of Environmental Law: Reforming Environmental Criminal Law, 83 Geo. L.J. 2407 (1995).

b. SURFACE MINING EXTERNALITIES

Although surface mining lacks the pervasive health and safety problems of underground mining, it has a massive impact on the landscape. As the mining equipment has grown in size and efficiency, its ability to reach deep into the earth and permanently transform its surface has greatly exceeded the expectations of people familiar only with early forms of strip mining.

Since 1977, the Federal Surface Mining Control and Reclamation Act ("SMCRA", 30 U.S.C. § 1201 *et seq.*) has imposed regulations on strip mining to mitigate the adverse effects on the use of the surface of the land. In general, where the land is capable of being farmed, mining companies must restore the original surface; in other cases, they must leave it in a way that retards erosion. Land that is classified as prime farmland is not supposed to be mined at all. Agricultural interests were among the strong proponents of tough legislation designed to protect farmland.

Mining companies must get approval of reclamation plans before proceeding to mine. Under these plans the company must: (1) restore the land to a condition capable of supporting uses as good as existed before; (2) restore the approximate original contour of the land; (3) stabilize the soil; (4) spread the topsoil back over the area; and (5) revegetate the site.

i. *Federalism Issues*

From the beginning, questions were raised about whether a *national* program was the appropriate way to deal with surface mining. First, surface mining for coal was concentrated in a relatively small number of states, and was not on the radar screen of many people outside these areas. Second, the issues associated with surface mining differ greatly depending on the terrain and climate of the particular region; the Appalachian ridges, the Illinois prairies, and the high plains of Montana vary so greatly in terms of geomorphology and climate that the ability to generalize on national standards was in question.

Despite these doubts, Congress passed SMCRA to "establish a nationwide program to protect society and the environment from the adverse effects of surface coal mining operations" while assuring that there is an adequate supply of coal to meet the nation's energy needs. 30 U.S.C. § 1202(a), (f). Like the CAA and CWA, SMCRA is a cooperative effort between the federal and state governments to control surface mining. The federal role is administered by the Office of Surface mining (OSM) in the Department of the Interior.

Congress did provide for a great deal of state participation in the program. States may get federal approval to administer the Act themselves. Under SMCRA, a state may obtain jurisdiction for regulating surface mining on non-federal lands within the state by submitting a program proposal to the Secretary of the Interior. 30 U.S.C. § 1253. Once a state achieves "primacy," the federal Office of Surface Mining acts only as an overseer and its authority is limited.

States may submit any proposed changes in the surface mining program to the Director of the Office of Surface Mining. 30 C.F.R. § 732.17. The director may approve the changes upon a finding that the amendment is consistent with SMCRA, 30 U.S.C. § 1253(a)(7), and consistent with the implementation of SMCRA 30 C.F.R § 730.5. These amendments must also comply with other federal environmental laws, such as the Clean Water Act. 30 U.S.C. § 1292 (a)(3). *Fincastle Mining, Inc. v. Babbitt*, 842 F.Supp. 204 (W.D.Va.1993).

The adoption of SMCRA was challenged by a number of states that thought the federal government was infringing on states' traditional responsibilities. SMCRA was one of a number of federal environmental statutes passed in the 1970s pursuant to the authority of Congress under the interstate commerce power. Little doubt was expressed about the basic constitutional authority of the federal government to regulate most of the problems addressed by this environmental legislation. It was obvious that air and water moved across state lines, so legislation designed to control the pollution of these media was clearly within the scope of the federal government's power under the interstate commerce clause of the Constitution. SMCRA, on the other hand, posed a more complex constitutional issue. The primary externality of surface mining might be characterized as "land pollution," and land is more localized than air or water.

The coal industry initially challenged SMCRA as an overreaching of federal power under the commerce clause, and district judges in Indiana and Virginia initially held the statute invalid. A district judge in Indiana, in *Indiana v. Andrus*, 501 F.Supp. 452 (S.D.Ind.1980), held (1) that the sections of SMCRA designed to protect prime farmland are directed at facets of surface coal mining which have no substantial and adverse effects on interstate commerce; (2) that the prime farmland provisions are not related to the removal of air and water pollution and are, therefore, not reasonably and plainly adapted to the legitimate end of removing any substantial adverse effect on interstate commerce; and (3) that all of these sections are not within powers delegated to Congress and are unlawful as being contrary to the Tenth Amendment to the Constitution. He also held unconstitutional the "approximate original contour provisions, the topsoiling requirements, the areas unsuitable for surface mining provisions, [and those provisions] which combine to require a commitment by an operator to a certain postmining land use" because they "are not directed at the alleviation of water or air pollution, to the extent there are such effects, and are not means reasonably and plainly adapted to removing any substantial and adverse effect on interstate commerce. These sections are outside the enumerated powers of Congress and are, therefore, unconstitutional and unlawful."

The district judge went on to hold that these provisions of the statute also violated the Tenth Amendment, which reserves to the states those powers not delegated to the federal government:

> Land use control and planning is a traditional or integral governmental function or area of State sovereignty. This is required because of the

very diverse geography, climate, natural resources, population density and economic structures within the various States, and this was expressly recognized by Congress in 30 U.S.C. § 1201(f) of the Act. Land use control and regulation has historically always been exercised by State governments. It is one of the most severe and restrictive governmental powers, considering its effect on individuals' property and on local governments as cities, counties and States. Land use planning and control most directly affect the people, industry and governmental entities directly connected with the land involved.

The judge also ruled that SMCRA constituted "displacement, regulation and altering of the management structure and operation of the traditional area of State sovereignty or integral governmental function of land use planning and control" in violation of the Tenth Amendment.

The federal government appealed to the United States Supreme Court from both the Indiana and Virginia decisions. The Court reversed and upheld the validity of the statute in two separate opinions, *Hodel v. Virginia Surface Mining & Reclamation Assn., Inc.*, 452 U.S. 264 (1981) and *Hodel v. Indiana*, 452 U.S. 314 (1981). In the latter case the Court said "In our view, Congress was entitled to find that the protection of prime farmland is a federal interest that may be addressed through Commerce Clause legislation. ...The court incorrectly assumed that the Act's goals are limited to preventing air and water pollution.... Congress was also concerned about preserving the productive capacity of mined lands and protecting the public from health and safety hazards that may result from surface coal mining. All the provisions invalidated by the court below are reasonably calculated to further these legitimate goals."

The Supreme Court also rejected summarily the district court's Tenth Amendment analysis:

The District Court ruled that the real purpose and effect of the Act is land-use regulation, which, in the court's view, is a traditional state governmental function. ... We hold that the District Court erred in concluding that the challenged provisions of the Act contravene the Tenth Amendment. The sections of the Act under attack in this case regulate only the activities of surface mine operators who are private individuals and businesses, and the District Court's conclusion that the Act directly regulates the States as States is untenable.

The Court also reversed the district court on the issues of the takings and due process clauses.

The Court's analysis of the interstate commerce clause in the two *Hodel* opinions was almost routine. Between 1937 and 1995, the Court never held a federal statute invalid for exceeding federal power under the commerce clause. That string was broken by the Court's decision in *United States v. Lopez*, 514 U.S. 549 (1995) in which the Court struck down a federal statute making it a crime to carry a gun within a certain distance of a school. The crucial votes in the 5–4 decision were provided by Justice Kennedy and Justice O'Connor, who joined in a concurring opinion written by Justice Kennedy, which noted that earlier decisions upholding "the exercise of federal power where commercial transactions were the subject of regulation [is] within the fair ambit of the Court's practical conception of commercial regulation and are not called in question by our decision today...."

[U]nlike the earlier cases to come before the Court here neither the actors nor their conduct have a commercial character, and neither the purposes nor the design of the statute have an evident commercial nexus. The statute makes the simple possession of a gun within 1,000 feet of the grounds of the school a criminal offense. In a sense any conduct in this interdependent world of ours has an ultimate commercial origin or consequence, but we have not yet said the commerce power may reach so far. If Congress attempts that extension, then at the least we must inquire whether the exercise of national power seeks to intrude upon an area of traditional state concern.

An interference of these dimensions occurs here, for it is well established that education is a traditional concern of the States.... The proximity to schools, including of course schools owned and operated by the States or their subdivisions, is the very premise for making the conduct criminal. In these circumstances, we have a particular duty to insure that the federal-state balance is not destroyed.

Does the standard set forth in Justice Kennedy's opinion threaten SMCRA's continuing validity?[10] Can you think of any federal laws regulating energy that might not have "an evident commercial nexus?"

ii. Enforcement Issues

The regulations adopted by the Secretary of Interior under SMCRA were also subjected to numerous challenges in the courts. Final rules setting out the responsibilities of the Office of Surface Mining ("OSM") were adopted near the end of President Carter's term. These were challenged by the coal industry, but in 1981 a new Secretary of the Interior took office in the Reagan administration, with the result that the regulations were significantly relaxed, which in turn led to litigation by environmental groups.

On paper, SMCRA is one of the toughest environmental statutes on the books. In practice, there is often little support for enforcing the act to the letter. The cost of restoring the site to permit agricultural use is often much greater than the cost of simply keeping it safe and forested.

---

10. Prior to 1937, when the Supreme Court reversed its earlier narrow readings of the commerce clause, it was well accepted that "mining" was a local activity that was not within federal control under the commerce power. Federal authority began only when the mined products moved into the stream of commerce. In *Lopez*, Justices Kennedy and O'Connor make it clear that they would not reopen the Court's 1937 reversal of those decisions. In a separate concurrence, Justice Thomas suggested a willingness to do so.

The permitting requirements of SMCRA say that a permit is necessary before any person may engage in surface mining operations. 30 U.S.C. § 1256(a). The permit application requires the mine operators to plan the mining operation in detail, identify adverse effects on the environment, and devise a reclamation plan. The permit application must be denied if the owner has unabated violations of SMCRA or other environmental laws.

The permit must contain details regarding timing of the operation, and engineering and design provisions that will ensure field performance. The permit must be revoked or suspended if the operation is in non-compliance.

Reclamation requirements are often the most controversial issues in a SMCRA permit. SMCRA is designed to assure "complete reclamation of mine sites." *Cat Run Coal Co. v. Babbitt,* 932 F.Supp. 772, 774–5 (S.D.W.Va.1996). Every operator of a mining operation must post a bond which is calculated to ensure that the commitments set forth in the permit are carried out. 30 U.S.C. § 1259(a). The bond requirement ensures that funds are available to reclaim mined lands if an operator defaults and to give incentive to comply with the reclamation requirements. See Barlow Burke, Reclaiming the Law of Suretyship, 21 So. Ill. U. L. J. 449 (1997).

To be released from liability under SMCRA, an operator must apply to the appropriate agency and demonstrate performance of the reclamation work required under SMCRA and the bond. 30 U.S.C. § 1269(c). The appropriate agency inspects the reclamation work. First, the operator must complete backfilling, grading, and drainage control in accordance with the reclamation plan. Then the operator must revegetate the regraded mine lands. Finally, if the agency finds that all reclamation requirements have been met, it will release the reclamation bond.

National Wildlife Federation v. Lujan

950 F.2d 765 (D.C.Cir.1991).

■ RANDOLPH, J.: Surface coal mining is a temporary use of the land. When mining ends the land must be restored. After revegetation is complete, and sufficient time has passed to ensure its success—5 years in the east, 10 years in the arid west—a mine operator who has fulfilled all legal requirements is entitled to have his performance bond released. The principal question in this case is whether under the Surface Mining Control and Reclamation Act of 1977, 30 U.S.C. §§ 1201–1328 (1988), regulatory jurisdiction may then be terminated. The Secretary of the Interior issued regulations so providing. *See* 52 Fed. Reg. 24,092 (1987) (Notice of Proposed Rulemaking); 53 Fed. Reg. 44,356 (1988) (Final Rule). The district court, at the behest of the National Wildlife Federation and others ("NWF"), struck them down. *National Wildlife Federation v. Interior Dep't,* 31 Env't Rep. Cas. (BNA) 2034, 2040–41 (D.D.C.1990). Because we find the Act silent on the issue presented and the Secretary's interpretation permissible, we reverse.

As night follows day, litigation follows rulemaking under this statute. Since the Act's passage in 1977, in cases challenging regulations, our opinions have described in considerable detail the Act's structure and operation. We shall assume familiarity with those opinions. In brief, the Act is intended to protect the environment from the adverse effects of surface coal mining while ensuring an adequate supply of coal to meet the nation's energy requirements. 30 U.S.C. § 1202(a), (f). Section 501(b) directs the Secretary to promulgate regulations establishing regulatory procedures and performance standards "conforming to the provisions of" the Act (30 U.S.C. § 1251(b)). Section 515 contains detailed "environmental protection performance standards" applicable to "all surface coal mining and reclamation operations." 30 U.S.C. § 1265. Through the Office of Surface Mining Reclamation and Enforcement ("OSMRE"), the Secretary is to take steps "necessary to insure compliance with" the Act. 30 U.S.C. § 1211(a), (c)(1). The states too have a significant role to play. After an interim period of federal regulation, states had the option of proposing plans for implementing the Act consistent with federal standards on non-federal lands. When the Secretary approved the programs submitted by the states, those states became primarily responsible for regulating surface coal mining and reclamation in the non-federal areas within their borders. 30 U.S.C. § 1253. In states not having an approved program, the Secretary implemented a federal program. 30 U.S.C. § 1254(a), (b). The "permanent program" regulations issued under section 501(b) set standards for federally-approved state programs and for the federal program that takes effect when a State fails to "implement, enforce, or maintain" its program. 30 U.S.C. § 1254(a). Enforcement is carried out by the "regulatory authority," that is, the state agency administering the federally-approved program, the Secretary administering a federal program, or OSMRE conducting oversight of state programs. *See* 30 C.F.R. § 700.5.

The primary means of ensuring compliance is the permit system established in sections 506 through 514 and section 515(a). 30 U.S.C. §§ 1256–1264, 1265(a). A permit is required for "any surface coal mining operations." 30 U.S.C. § 1256. Summaries of applications for permits must be published, and objections may be submitted by local agencies or by "any person having an interest which ... may be adversely affected" by a proposed operation. 30 U.S.C. § 1263. Each application must include a reclamation plan. Section 507(d), 30 U.S.C. § 1257(d). A reclamation plan describes the present use of the land, proposed and possible post-mining uses of the land, and what steps the operator will take to ensure the viability of the latter. Among other things, the plan must show how the operator will achieve soil reconstruction and revegetation of the mined area. Section 508, 30 U.S.C. § 1258. A permit application can only be approved if it demonstrates that "all requirements" of the Act have been satisfied and that "reclamation as required by [the Act] ... can be accomplished." 30 U.S.C. § 1260.

Section 509 requires the operator to post a performance bond in an amount sufficient to secure completion of reclamation. The operator and the surety remain liable under the bond for the duration of the surface mining and reclamation operation and until the end of the "revegetation period" (5 or 10 years) prescribed by section 515(20). 30 U.S.C. § 1259(b). At that time, the operator may petition the regulatory authority for release of the bond. The petition must be published, and is subject to the same opportunities for comment and hearing as the permit application. 30 C.F.R. § 800.40(a)(2), (b)(2). Further, "no bond shall be fully released ... until reclamation requirements of the Act and the permit are fully met." *Id.* § 800.40(c)(3).

Prior to this rulemaking, the relationship between bond release and continuing regulatory jurisdiction was unclear. 53 Fed. Reg. 44,356 (1988). State authorities would decline to act on violations reported after bond release, even when the allegation was that the bond had been released improperly. In some such cases, OSMRE would re-assert jurisdiction directly. *Id.* This led to confusion about whether a site was or was not subject to the Act. In order to end this confusion, the Secretary promulgated the rules at issue, which specify when regulatory jurisdiction over a site terminates. *Id.* Thus, 30 C.F.R. § 700.11(d)(1) provides that "a regulatory authority may terminate its jurisdiction ... over [a] reclaimed site" when (and only when) the authority determines (either independently or pursuant to a bond release) that "all requirements imposed" have been completed. *Id.* By tying termination of jurisdiction to bond release, the Secretary sought to resolve doubts about the former, while imposing minimum standards for the latter on the state authorities.

In the district court NWF claimed that it was "premature" to terminate regulatory jurisdiction at the time of bond release. Complaint of National Wildlife Federation at 14, Civ. No. 88–3345 (D.D.C. filed Nov. 17, 1988). The district court interpreted NWF's complaint not simply as an objection to timing, but as an attack on "the concept of terminating jurisdiction." *National Wildlife Federation v. Interior Dept.*, 31 Env't Rep. Cas. (BNA) at 2039. Seizing on language found in section 521 of the Act, 30 U.S.C. § 1271, the court noted that the Secretary was under "an ongoing duty ... to correct violations ... without limitation." 31 Env't Rep. Cas. (BNA) at 2040. The court also believed that allowing termination of jurisdiction would "hinder" the Act's goal of "protecting the environment." *Id.* at 2041. In view of these considerations, the court believed it proper to interpret Congress' silence on the precise question of termination of jurisdiction as a call for perpetual regulation. *Id.*

The district court's opinion and NWF's claim of prematurity suffer from the same flaw. Section 521 cannot be read to express or assume that regulatory jurisdiction over a surface coal mining and reclamation operation must continue forever. It is true that section 521 requires the regulatory authority to "take ... action" "whenever" a violation occurs, 30 U.S.C. § 1271(a)(1) (emphasis added). But by "action," section 521 means primarily the issuance of an order requiring "cessation of surface coal mining and reclamation operations." 30 U.S.C. § 1271(a)(2). Section 521(a)(2) also empowers the Secretary to impose other "affirmative obligations" on the operator; these, however, are to be exacted "in addition to the cessation order," 30 U.S.C. § 1271(a)(2). It thus appears that Congress contemplated enforcement actions only during mining and reclamation operations. If the site were no longer the scene of a "surface coal mining and reclamation operation," and it could not be by the time the bond is released, it would be difficult to see how section 521 could nevertheless continue to apply. The regulation, then, cannot be upheld or struck down solely by reference to Congress' intent, at least not as that intent was expressed in section 521....

NWF apparently believes that because, under the regulations, it is possible for some operators to avoid liability for violations of the Act that are undiscovered or undiscoverable at the time of bond release, the regulations improperly fail to promote the Act's purpose: protection of the environment. The Act, however, was a compromise, designed both to protect the environment and to ensure an adequate supply of coal to meet the nation's energy requirements. *See* 30 U.S.C. § 1202(a), (f). The Secretary struck a reasonable balance between these competing interests in his interpretation of the Act (and, as noted above, responded to NWF's concerns about unabated environmental harm by adding 30 C.F.R. § 700.11(d)(2)).

The regulation also strikes a reasonable balance between the gradual increase, due to improving technology, in what legitimately may be demanded of an operator, and an operator's need for certainty regarding closed sites. "It would not be appropriate . . . to require operators who had . . . met the standards of their permits and the applicable regulatory program to . . . reclaim [closed sites] in accordance with new technology." 53 Fed. Reg. 44,361 (1988).

In short, we find the regulation consistent with the goals of the Act and a reasonable interpretation of it. Furthermore, the factors supporting "the concept of terminating jurisdiction," 31 Env't Rep. Cas. (BNA) at 2039, buttress the Secretary's decision to use bond release as the point at which termination occurs. Until bond release the operator is still liable, and an attempt to terminate jurisdiction sooner would violate the terms of the Act. Nothing in the statute speaks in fixed temporal terms of regulation after bond release. Under the regulation that is the point at which the regulatory authority must "sign off" on the reclamation project. Bond release also has the advantage of being an independently identifiable point in time. For these reasons the Secretary's choice was not arbitrary or capricious. Accordingly, we reverse the district court's judgment insofar as it invalidated 30 C.F.R. § 700.11(d).■

NOTES AND COMMENTS

1.   The coal industry estimates that more than two million acres of mined lands have been reclaimed in the past twenty years. This represents an area larger than the state of Delaware. Reclamation involves the following steps: leveling off fill soil by bulldozers, placing topsoil or approved substitute over graded area, reseeding with native vegetation, crops and/or trees,

and monitoring the area for many years to ensure success of reclamation. National Coal Mining Association, Fast Facts About Coal, www.nma.org.

Coal mining lands have been restored to a variety of uses. Farming is one of the most common post-mining land uses. Housing development is often used for mined lands located near urban centers. Often, special uses arise out of reclamation projects. For example, the OSM coordinates the use of trees grown on reclaimed coal mine lands in Maryland for the National Christmas Pageant of Peace tree-lighting ceremony in Washington, D.C. A former coal mine in West Virginia now includes a little league baseball field. Post mining land uses, www.osmre.gove.

2.   Depending on the nature of the soils and terrain and on the desired end use, the time that it takes to determine with some confidence whether reclamation has been successfully accomplished can range from a few years to many decades. In most instances, the mining companies are not enthusiastic about retaining responsibility for sites that are no longer producing income, but once the company's deep pocket disappears, conditions on the site may deteriorate. Can you think of other solutions for the long-term maintenance of reclaimed mining sites?

3.   Definition of the relative powers of the federal and state agencies under SMCRA remains a source of controversy. *See* Robert E. Beck, The Federal Role Under the Surface Mining Control and Reclamation Act of 1977 (SMCRA) on Nonfederal Lands After State Primacy, 31 Tulsa L. J. 677 (1996). The D.C. Circuit upheld the regulations of the federal Office of Surface Mining under which it retains backup authority to issue a notice of violation even though it has delegated to a state agency primary enforcement authority. *National Mining Ass'n v. U.S. Dept. of the Interior,* 70 F.3d 1345 (D.C.Cir.1995).

c.   MOUNTAIN–TOP MINING

The most controversial form of surface mining has been the so-called "mountain-top mining" that has become prevalent in southern Appalachia, particularly West Virginia. In the southern part of the state, the terrain consists primarily of ridges and valleys. The mine operators use surface mining equipment to take off the tops of the ridges to expose coal seams. The overburden is dumped into the adjacent valleys.

State interpretations of Federal regulations in the late 1990's allowed increases in the numbers and sizes of steep slope surface mining operations, including extensive mountain-top removal mines in West Virginia. The EIA reports that these mines "can out-compete their more moderately scaled competitors because they tend to achieve higher recovery rates from greater numbers of multiple coalbeds than conventional contour mines. However, they produce large amounts of disturbed rock and unrecovered coal." Bonskowski, *supra* at p. 23.

In West Virginia, mine operators have been allowed to dispose of the overburden from the mountaintop mines in "valley fills" that turn natural stream valleys into relatively level reclaimed plateaus. *See* Comment,

Regulatory Violations in the Mining Industry: Mountaintop Removal Mine Valley Fills Violate the Federal Clean Water Act, 100 W. Va. L. Rev. 691 (1998). A controversial statute was passed in early 1998 that liberalized state policies on valley fills and intensified opposition to the practices. The prospects for continuing this form of mining hinge on the outcome of a suit filed in 1998 by citizens and environmentalists in West Virginia, claiming inadequate protection of surface stream waters in valley fills. In *Bragg v. Robertson*, 72 F.Supp.2d 642 (S.D.W.Va.1999), the district court held that such valley fills violated regulations under SMCRA that prohibited permits for valley fills that would adversely affect the normal flow or gradient of a stream, affect fish migration or materially damage water quality or quantity. The court found that "When valley fills are permitted in intermittent and perennial streams, they destroy those stream segments. The normal flow and gradient of the stream is now buried under millions of cubic yards of excess spoil waste material, an extremely adverse effect. If there are fish, they cannot migrate. If there is any life form that cannot acclimate to life deep in a rubble pile, it is eliminated. No effect on related environmental values is more adverse than obliteration. Under a valley fill, the water quantity of the stream becomes zero. Because there is no stream, there is no water quality." 72 F.Supp.2d at 661–662. The judge stayed his ruling pending an appeal to the Fourth Circuit Court of Appeals in response to an outcry from the industry and the Governor. Court Ruling Puts W. Va. Mining at Risk, The Washington Post, October 24, 1999.

Meanwhile, the federal agencies are in the process of preparing a programmatic environmental impact statement on the mountain top mining activities in the Appalachian region. Information on the EIS can be found at *www.epa.gov/region3/mtntop*. The editor of Coal Age noted that the controversy over mountaintop mining meant that in the Eastern states in 1999, underground mining produced more coal than surface mining, reversing earlier trends. Steve Fiscor, Big Ten in the East, Coal Age, March, 2000.

3.   MINERAL RIGHTS

The English common law, which was incorporated into American law, gave the owner of the surface of the land the right to all minerals underneath it, but it allowed the "mineral rights" to land to be separated from the right to use the surface of the land because lawyers needed to develop a vehicle for allowing a mining company to control the mining without having to assume all of the responsibility for the uses on the surface.

The terms defining the mineral rights vary with the needs of the parties. For example, the rights might be to all minerals, just coal, coal in a particular seam, or coal of a particular grade. The landowner and the mining company may define the rights conveyed in any manner they choose. Once the mineral rights are divided as a separate interest, they can be transferred independently from the surface. Often, the mineral rights are leased rather than purchased from the surface owner.

The modern mineral rights deed or lease will spell out the obligations of each party in regard to, among other things, (1) the extent to which a mineral owner has a right to use the surface for mine openings, roads, etc.; (2) the extent to which the mine operator is liable for subsidence of the land; and (3) whether the mineral rights owner has an obligation to explore and develop the minerals within a particular time.

Where underground mining is contemplated, coal mining companies typically purchase only the mineral rights from the landowner rather than purchasing a fee simple interest in the land on which the coal was located. Because the surface owner could continue to farm or develop the land for a profit while the mining was taking place underneath it, she would normally ask a lower price for the mineral rights than for the property as a whole.

Surface mining has become prevalent only since the 1950s. If a coal company purchased the mineral rights from a landowner at a time when the only known method of mining was underground mining, does the coal company now have the right to remove the coal by surface mining, thus effectively destroying the value of the surface owner's interest? This contentious issue has been a source of both legal and political battles in the coal mining states.

Ward v. Harding

860 S.W.2d 280 (Ky.1993), cert. denied, 510 U.S. 1177 (1994).

■ LAMBERT, J.: With ratification of Section 19(2) of the Constitution of Kentucky,[1][11] the people swept away decades of litigation and numerous court decisions addressing the proper construction of so-called "broad form" deeds. By the amendment, the people have declared that henceforth in instruments of conveyance of the type at issue here, it shall be held, in the absence of clear and convincing evidence to the contrary, that coal extraction be only by the known methods in the area at the time the instruments were executed.

11. Amendment proposed by Acts 1988, Ch. 117, § 1, ratified November, 1988. The full text of Section 19(2) of the Constitution of Kentucky is as follows:

In any instrument heretofore or hereafter executed purporting to sever the surface and mineral estates or to grant a mineral estate or to grant a right to extract minerals, which fails to state or describe in express and specific terms the method of coal extraction to be employed, or where said instrument contains language subordinating the surface estate to the mineral estate, it shall be held, in the absence of clear and convinc-ing evidence to the contrary, that the intention of the parties to the instrument was that the coal be extracted only by the method or methods of commercial coal extraction commonly known to be in use in Kentucky in the area affected at the time the instrument was executed, and that the mineral estate be dominant to the surface estate for the purposes of coal extraction by only the method or methods of commercial coal extraction commonly known to be in use in Kentucky in the area affected at the time the instrument was executed.

The issue joined between appellants and appellees is whether a broad form deed mineral owner may, by virtue of that instrument alone, engage in surface mining. The trial court ruled in favor of appellants, the surface owners, holding, *inter alia*, that:

> The parties to the original conveyance contemplated mining by the underground method [in a manner] which would not destroy the surface. . . .

The genesis of this controversy was early in the twentieth century. John C.C. Mayo and others traveled throughout Eastern Kentucky and obtained instruments of conveyance whereby large numbers of landowners conveyed the minerals underlying their real property. Typically Mayo deeds and others of their genre conveyed all minerals which underlay the surface, granted rights to use the surface to such an extent as was necessary or convenient to gain access to the minerals, contained an express waiver of liability for damages to the surface, and reserved to the surface owner only such rights as were consistent with the other provisions of the instrument. . . . For the most part, this Court's decisions rendered during the first half of the twentieth century demonstrated an inclination toward enforcement of the literal language of the instrument and resolution of ambiguity against the grantor.

It should be emphasized, however, that the early decisions, with the exception of dictum in *Rudd v. Hayden*, 265 Ky. 495, 97 S.W.2d 35 (1936), were exclusively in the context of deep mining methods of coal extraction. See *Martin v. Kentucky Oak Mining Co.*, 429 S.W.2d 395 (Ky.1968), Hill, J., dissenting at 401.

With the advent of equipment capable of moving massive amounts of earth, the controversy took on a new dimension. As technology progressed, mineral owners and their successors in interest acquired the capability of removing previously inaccessible or economically unfeasible coal by means of strip mining or other mining methods which caused profound disturbance of the surface. The issue which then emerged was whether or to what extent, and with or without compensation for damages, the mineral owner was entitled to destroy the surface to extract the coal. This Court's decision in *Buchanan v. Watson*, 290 S.W.2d 40 (Ky.1956) . . . stripped the landowner of any right to restrict the mining method and rendered him a virtual tenant on his land.

In the years which have followed Buchanan, there have been various efforts toward modification of its holding, but not until *Akers v. Baldwin*, 736 S.W.2d 294 (Ky.1987), was there any appreciable change, and even then its central holding remained wholly intact. In Akers, this Court's plurality opinion invalidated a portion of KRS § 381.940 which is virtually identical to the Constitutional Amendment here under review. In so doing, the Court relied upon the separation of powers provisions of the Constitution of Kentucky, § 27, 28 and 109, and held that

> [C]ourts are the proper forums to determine the issues presented in the interpretation of past transactions, as in this case. . . . "The

General Assembly has, by enacting this statute, reached across the years and has arbitrarily determined the rights of the parties and their successors to deeds and other documents."

Akers at 309.

[In another decision,] the Court invalidated an Act which required the signature of the surface owner before strip mining would be permitted. *Dept. for Natural Resources v. No. 8 Ltd.*, 528 S.W.2d 684 (Ky.1975). In so holding, it was determined that the purpose of the Act was to modify the economic bargaining power of private parties under their contracts rather than serve any public purpose. Essential to the holding was the conclusion that the original contract granted the mineral owner the right to engage in surface mining.

We begin our discussion of the constitutionality of the 1988 Amendment with a further review of the law as it existed immediately prior thereto. Our most recent decision in this arena was *Akers v. Baldwin*, *supra*, a decision in which three Justices concurred in the plurality opinion and one Justice concurred by separate opinion. In dissent, three Justices rendered two separate opinions. Despite their differences as to the result, an examination of these four opinions reveals a remarkable agreement as to the fundamental question of the intention of the parties at the time the instruments were created. The plurality opinion by Chief Justice Stephens acknowledged that

> It is highly unlikely that any parties to a deed or lease would enter into an agreement which creates two separate estates in land knowing or contemplating that one of those estates—the surface—could and would be totally destroyed, and leaving that estate owner without anything, without damages to the injured party being allowed. The obliteration of the surface would never have been anticipated by the grantor of the mineral estate. *Id.* at 306–307. The evidence in this case and the evidence generally is that strip mining, as it is practiced today, was non-existent in the early 1900's, when most, if not all, of the broad form deeds were executed. This Court takes judicial notice of that fact. *Id.* at 308–309.

[T]he Court was unanimous in its conclusion that the parties to such instruments did not contemplate strip mining as the means by which the coal would be removed from the earth and that the original conveyance anticipated no such mining right. Nevertheless, and despite this view, four members of the Court concluded that the doctrine of stare decisis and the desirability of stability in the law were sufficient to sustain the rule in *Buchanan v. Watson* despite the implicit recognition that it was erroneous.

As it was neither fair nor just to deny damages for surface destruction, it is neither fair nor just to permit surface mining contrary to the wishes of the surface owner and beyond the contemplation of the original parties to those instruments. As we now hold the firm conviction that the conveyance of minerals by means of a broad form deed did not include the right to strip mine, we hereby overrule that portion of *Buchanan v. Watson* and its progeny which survived our decision in *Akers v. Baldwin*. As this Court's decision in *Buchanan v. Watson* presumed a right to surface mine merely by virtue of the ownership of mineral rights, by this decision we hold that no such presumption shall hereafter exist.

Properly framed, the question here is not what the parties actually intended, but what they would have intended if significant surface destruction had been contemplated. In circumstances where there is no actual intent, a court should presume a reasonable intent.... To achieve the proper construction of a broad form deed, the Court must examine not only the language of the instrument, but determine the intentions of the parties in the manner described hereinabove.

Despite our view that the right to strip mine was not a right properly flowing from the original conveyance, we must nevertheless consider appellees' claim that Section 19(2) of the Constitution of Kentucky violates Article I, Section 10 of the Constitution of the United States, the "Contract Clause." As we have said hereinabove, at the time of the original mineral conveyance, the parties could not have intended any substantial disturbance of the surface. The original contract did not create a right to surface mine; this right, such as it was, arose by court decision half a century after the conveyance. While appellees acquired their mineral ownership after our decision in Buchanan and with an expectation of the right to strip mine, they acquired no greater right than their vendors possessed. *York v. Perkins*, Ky., 269 S.W.2d 242 (1954); *Vanhoose v. Fairchild*, 145 Ky. 700, 141 S.W. 75 (1911). Akers went astray when it elevated the rights of those who acquired their interest subsequent to Buchanan to immunity from modification. Those who acquired such interests knew or should have known that Buchanan was not indisputable nor irrefutable and that in time its holding could be reconsidered and amended or overruled. To grant immunity from change is to concede that one may acquire a vested interest in the decision of a court, a proposition universally rejected. The applicable rule is well stated as follows:

> There is no vested right in the decisions of a court, and a change of decisions of a state court does not constitute the passing of a law, although the effect of such change is to impair the validity of a contract made in reliance on prior decisions.

16A Am.Jur.2d, Constitutional Law, § 703 (1979).

The Contract Clause protects only those rights which are embraced in the contract at the time it is entered into.... This Court's improvidently rendered decision in Buchanan amounted to an unforeseen windfall for mineral owners in complete derogation of the rights of surface owners. Surely, the Contract Clause does not prevent restoration of the original contract.

Appellees likewise claim that Section 19(2) of the Constitution of Kentucky constitutes a "taking" of private property for public use without just compensation in violation of the Fifth and Fourteenth Amendments to the Constitution of the United States. In substance, they contend that passage of the Constitutional Amendment deprives them of a property right by rendering it economically unfeasible to recover their minerals.

At the outset, we have difficulty bringing this case within the ambit of "takings" jurisprudence. The Constitutional Amendment here does not amount to a new regulation or land use restriction. It is simply the codification of a rule of contract construction designed to give effect to the original intention of the parties, a construction we believe to be entirely correct. While the Act of the General Assembly which proposed the Amendment recited limited public purposes as a justification, the overwhelming purpose was to correct what the General Assembly and the people believed to have been erroneous contract interpretations by this Court.

That an owner's right of use may be limited to the interests originally acquired was recognized in the Supreme Court's most recent pronouncement on the issue at hand, *Lucas v. South Carolina Coastal Council,* 112 S. Ct. 2886 (1992). There, a newly enacted state regulation prohibited erection of any permanent habitable structure and was found to have rendered the land valueless. The Court framed the issue as whether the Act's dramatic effect on the economic value of the land accomplished a taking which required just compensation. Discussing the effect of such a new regulation, a fact not present here, the Court nevertheless recognized that compensation was not required if

> "the owner's estate shows that the proscribed use interests were not part of his title to begin with. This accords, we think, with our 'takings' jurisprudence, which has traditionally been guided by the understandings of our citizens regarding the content of, and the State's power over, the 'bundle of rights' that they acquire when they obtain title to property." 112 S. Ct. at 2899.

The Court recognized that regulatory action may diminish or eliminate economically productive uses of land providing it does not destroy all permissible uses under relevant property law principles. When the principles in Lucas are applied here, it would appear that appellees have a common law right to remove their coal in accordance with the instrument of severance and in the manner contemplated therein, but are without any protected right to retain benefits claimed by virtue of our previous decisions. Manifestly, the determination of property rights acquired by virtue of written instruments is a matter of State law. *Texaco, Inc. v. Short,* 454 U.S. 516 (1982). As appellee's entitlement to remove their minerals in accordance with the instrument of acquisition has not been affected by Section 19(2) of the Constitution of Kentucky, there has been no violation of the Fifth and Fourteenth Amendments to the Constitution of the United States.

In final analysis, it is appropriate to review the matters decided herein and express our view as to the legal significance of Section 19(2) of the Constitution of Kentucky. For more than twenty years now, there has been growing disfavor among the Justices of this Court with the Buchanan construction of broad form deeds. In that time, the Legislature has twice sought to modify our interpretation, and in each instance, we have held its

Act unconstitutional. This Court has evolved from one in which we unanimously declared the right to strip mine to one in which each of seven Justices have acknowledged that the original parties did not anticipate any substantial disturbance of the surface estate. The culmination of the judicial and public debate was a Constitutional Amendment approved by more than 82% of the voters in the November, 1988, General Election. The effect of the Amendment, apart from the obvious effect of overruling numerous decisions of this Court, was to codify a rule of construction which we now hold to have been at all times the proper rule, our decisions to the contrary notwithstanding. In discerning no violation of the Constitution of the United States in Section 19(2) of the Constitution of Kentucky, we have also determined that it is in accord with the common law of this jurisdiction, and embrace it as reflective of the views of this Court.

For the foregoing reasons, the opinion of the Court of Appeals is reversed and the judgment of the trial court reinstated.

■ LEIBSON, J., with whom STEPHENS, C.J., and REYNOLDS, J., concur, dissenting: Respectfully, I dissent. Considering my oath to support our Kentucky Constitution (and, of course, its Amendments), to dissent in present circumstances is an onerous task. I do so only from a strong sense of conviction that there are compelling reasons; reasons that must be stated.

The Majority Opinion has lost sight of the judicial function. The first paragraph of the Majority Opinion trumpets that through the enactment of the Broad Form Deed Amendment "the people have declared that henceforth" Broad Form Deeds do not convey the right to strip mine without the surface owner's consent, and have "swept away" "numerous court decisions" to the contrary. The Majority Opinion fails to appreciate that, while majoritarian rule applies to state legislative enactments and state constitutional amendments, court cases are different. They must be decided according to law, not by the will of the majority. The majority cannot dictate contract rights previously transferred by a deed because the U.S. Constitution, Art. 1, Sec. 10, guarantees the individual citizen's vested contract rights: "No state shall … pass any … Law impairing the Obligation of Contracts."

The Majority Opinion treats two separate issues as one. The first issue is the rights conveyed by a Broad Form Deed, which by its terms conveyed the mineral estate and authorized the grantee to use the surface in any manner which may be deemed necessary or convenient for the exercise and enjoyment of the property rights conveyed. Do such deeds convey to the grantee the right to engage in surface mining without first obtaining permission from the persons presently holding title to the surface estate regardless of the mining methods extant at the time of the deed? We have so held in a long and unbroken line of cases, both old and recent.

The second and separate issue only arises if we continue to recognize that a Broad Form Deed conveys such right. If we recognize the rights conveyed by a Broad Form Deed include the right to engage in surface mining to remove the minerals without first obtaining further consent from the surface owner, does the recently enacted amendment to the Kentucky

Constitution, now codified as Sec. 19(2) of the Constitution, by denying mineral owners such right, violate the Federal Constitution?

Of course, a majority of this Court has the raw power to overrule precedent, both recent and long-standing, construing the rights conveyed by the forms used in ancient documents. But should we do so when the parties have not raised the issue and presented compelling reasons to believe our previous decisions erred in construing the documents? Should we do so because of popular clamor for a different result? No, not even when public opinion is expressed through a constitutional amendment. Of course the constitutional amendment overrides judicial precedent to the contrary, but that does not mean it was wrong. It is one thing to say the constitutional amendment is now the law, and an entirely different thing to say passing the constitutional amendment proves previous judicial decisions were erroneous. Contrary to the lead paragraph in the Majority Opinion, the "people" have not "swept away ... numerous court decisions addressing the proper construction of the so-called 'broad form' deeds." It is our Court which now "sweep[s] away" an unbroken line of precedents, and public opinion can provide neither reason nor excuse.... If the new state constitutional amendment conflicts with the Federal "Contract Clause" it is as much a Federal constitution violation as the previous 1984 statutory enactment....

There is a corollary to this problem that I address briefly before concluding this dissent. The Fifth Amendment to the U.S. Constitution, which is applicable to the states through the Fourteenth Amendment, provides "nor shall private property be taken for public use, without just compensation."

In the present case, taking from the mineral owners the right to mine the surface where it is otherwise "commercially impracticable" to remove the coal, cannot be justified under federal "Taking Clause" jurisprudence even were we to assume that such taking could be justified to promote the general welfare. This is because the coal company has not been compensated for the "taking" of its property (its mining rights). *See Pennsylvania Coal Co. v. Mahon*, 260 U.S. 393 (1922). The only way to circumvent the obvious dilemma is to declare, as the Majority has done, that Broad Form Deeds give no surface mining rights to the mineral owners in the first place. To do so it is necessary to overrule precedent, both long-standing and recent, in a case where we have been presented no new or compelling reasons aside from public clamor against our previous decisions. Our Court bowed to the will of the majority at the sacrifice of individual rights protected in the United States Constitution which we are obligated to defend.

For the reasons stated I would hold the state constitutional amendment is in conflict with the Federal Constitution.■

NOTES AND COMMENTS

1. Is the majority being realistic in saying that mineral owners should have known that a long line of cases might be overruled? Would a

practicing lawyer have given an opinion to that effect prior to this decision? *See* Note: Ward v. Harding, Kentucky Strips Miners of Dominate Rights, Burying a Century of Litigation, 21 N. Ky. L. Rev. 649 (1994). The United States Supreme Court passed up the opportunity to decide some interesting questions when it denied certiorari in this case.

2.   Is this constitutional amendment just a wealth distribution measure that requires mining companies to go back and pay more to the surface owners? Or will it have the effect of reducing the amount of strip mining because owners will refuse to negotiate? Does the surface owner have an absolute property right to prevent the mineral owner from extracting the coal by surface mining, or just a liability right to receive compensation?

3.   The longwall method of underground mining is another mining technique that was unknown at the time many mineral rights were granted. This method often produces a great deal of surface subsidence. With the longwall method, entries into the coal seam are made and supported by pillars. The mining equipment is moved to the furthest point on the panel and begins cutting toward the front. As the machine moves forward, the supports collapse, along with the overburden. Extraction is around 90%, but subsidence is usually immediate. S. Peng & H. Chaing, Longwall Mining (1984).

In *Smerdell v. Consolidation Coal Co.*, 806 F.Supp. 1278 (N.D.W.Va. 1992) the owners of the surface had waived all claims for damages from subsidence in 1905. The current owners of the surface claimed that their predecessors' waiver was no longer valid because the coal company had switched to the longwall mining method. The district court held that the effect of changed circumstances, such as the development of new mining techniques, on an unambiguous written instrument was not subject to judicial interpretation, and that the right to subjacent support was waived no matter what method of coal extraction is used. *See also* Lane, *supra* at 611–615.

4.   Today, it is most common for the surface owner to lease the mineral rights to the mining company for a modest cash rental plus a significant percentage of the minerals that are found—this is known as a royalty interest. For example, the surface owner might retain a 1/8 royalty interest in all coal discovered and produced from under the land. The mining company will want the lease to set out its right to erect structures and build roads on the land, if underground mining is contemplated.

Whether underground or surface mining is contemplated, the lease should expressly set out the methods of mining that are anticipated. The owner will also want to know what type of land reclamation the mining company contemplates when the mining operation has been completed.

The Mayo deeds at issue in *Ward*, and the court's construction of them prior to that decision, reflected the attitude prevalent in the nineteenth century—that because coal was dramatically increasing peoples' ability to produce goods and raise their standard of living, the law ought to construe instruments in a way that encouraged the production of this valuable commodity. *See generally* Morton J. Horwitz, The Transformation of American Law, 1780–1860 (Harvard University Press, 1977). Only much later did people fully realize some of the adverse impacts of coal mining.

5. A large part of the remaining coal reserves underlie federal lands in the western states, so companies seeking to mine this coal must comply with the complex laws relating to federal public lands. Coal on federal lands is under the jurisdiction of the Department of the Interior, where different aspects of coal production are handled by different agencies, including the Bureau of Land Management and the Minerals Management Service. For an analysis of these federal regulations, *see* Marla E. Mansfield, Coal, in James E. Hickey et. al., Energy Law & Policy in the 21st Century, Ch. 9 (Rocky Mountain Mineral Law Foundation, 2000).

6. Texas has extensive deposits of brown coal known as lignite, much of which can be mined by surface mining methods. Under Texas law, a landowner's conveyance of the rights to "oil, gas and other minerals" has been construed not to convey the rights to any lignite that is near the surface. *Reed v. Wylie*, 597 S.W.2d 743 (Tex.1980).

PROBLEM

The Rith Energy Company was denied a mining permit under SMCRA and brought suit in the United States Court of Federal Claims. The government sought to dismiss the complaint, arguing as follows:

Plaintiff's just compensation claim fails because plaintiff does not possess the compensable expectancy it presumes. First, one of plaintiff's two leases, the Eagle/Boylan lease, allows the mining of coal only by underground methods. As to that lease, plaintiff's "bundle of rights" never included the expectancy to surface mine at all. *Lucas v. South Carolina Coastal Council*, 505 U.S. 1003, 1027 (1992).

Second, plaintiff's claim in essence presumes it possesses a constitutionally protected right to mine in a particular manner. However, the property interests under which plaintiff has mined, and seeks to mine further, were created after the enactment of SMCRA. Accordingly, when plaintiff received those interests, its expectancies were already affected by the restrictions of the Act. Thus, it could have acquired no right to mine in a manner which was in violation of the Act. *M & J Coal Co. v. United States*, 30 Fed. Cl. 360, 369 (1994), *aff'd*, 47 F.3d 1148 (Fed.Cir.1995), *cert. denied*, 516 U.S. 808 (1995). In other words, before plaintiff's interests were created, SMCRA required that a permit be denied if the operator would not be able to reclaim the site or if mining operations would cause offsite hydrologic impacts. Plaintiff could have acquired no right to mine in a manner which was already prohibited by the Act. For that reason alone, Rith's just compensation claim must fail. . . .

Finally, the governmental action challenged here is itself reactive to plaintiff's seeking to engage in a mining method with nuisance-like impacts. Measured against a variety of factors, including longstanding federal regulation under SMCRA and the risk that the mining practices in which plaintiff sought to engage would have nuisance-like consequences under state law, plaintiff could have acquired no "historically rooted" expectancy—no "property" for purposes of Fifth Amendment compensation—to mine in a manner which would cause nuisance-like impacts. The "background principles" analysis articulated in *Lucas v. South Carolina Coastal Council* confirms that, when acquired, Rith's right to mine could not have included an expectation of being allowed to mine if to do so would cause a nuisance.

Are the government's arguments persuasive? How would you respond on behalf of the plaintiff? What additional facts would you like to know? *See Rith Energy, Inc. v. United States*, 44 Fed. Cl. 108 (1999). An appeal of the court's decision is quite likely.

C. COAL TRANSPORTATION

As a relatively heavy fuel, coal has always cost a lot to ship to markets. Seventy-five percent of all coal shipments are handled by railroads and barge lines. Trucks and conveyor systems are also used to move coal, but primarily over short distances. The price of coal to the consumer is thus heavily affected by the distance from its markets and the relative efficiency of the transportation routes between the mine and the market. Eastern coal tends to be more expensive at the mine, but for power plants in the East its transportation costs are lower due to shorter hauls. Eastern coal is often shipped by barge, which makes transportation costs even lower. Western coal is less expensive at the mine. However, it is usually shipped great distances by rail, making transportation expense higher. Energy Information Administration, Challenges of Electric Power Industry Restructuring for Fuel Suppliers, Sept. 1998, at 21.

As deregulated railroads consolidated in the late 1980's and the 1990's, they increasingly used large unit trains with lighter-weight, high-capacity cars, and added new sections of track, to help move coal from Wyoming's Powder River Basin to the Midwest. They also offered lower ton-per-mile rates and coordinated efforts with barge line operators to improve rail-barge transloading facilities, incorporating coal-blending capabilities. This served the need of new customers of Western coal whose boilers often required some ratio of bituminous coal to be blended with the new low-sulfur subbituminous coal for proper combustion.

The relationship between the coal industry and the railroads has had its ups and downs. They have joined forces on many lobbying projects. Coal shipping is beneficial to the railroads, which receive almost one-fourth of their gross revenue from coal shipments. Coal transportation costs have decreased even though the average distance coal must travel has increased. This has contributed to the competitiveness between the western coal sources in the eastern markets. But the competitiveness of the different markets is sensitive to rail rates and small differences can make one regional market much more favorable than another.

Recently there is an increasing tension between the two industries because the major railroads are merging, often over the objections of the coal companies. *See, e.g., Western Coal Traffic League v. Surface Transportation Board*, 169 F.3d 775 (D.C.Cir.1999). In 1970, there were 71 Class I railroad companies. By 1996, there were only nine Class I railroad companies. Mergers over the past sixteen years have resulted in only two major railroads in the west, the Burlington Northern and the Union Pacific. A recent proposal will leave only two major railroad lines in the eastern part of the country as well.[12]

The reduction in competition has made it possible for the railroads to raise rates over segments of track on which coal needs to be moved. The coal shippers are concerned that the railroads will charge discriminatory rates, favoring coal producers and power plants that create the most profitable traffic. Shippers argue that they will have fewer choices for coal deliveries. "Captive shippers," those that only have one transportation option, are particularly concerned. *See* Salvatore Massa, Injecting Competition in the Railroad Industry Through Access, 26 Transp. L.J. 283 (1999).

The railroads insist that competition will be adequate and longer operations will result in lower costs to the coal shippers. They argue that in order for coal shippers to compete with each other, they should "take advantage of economies of scale through mergers and acquisitions." Rail companies also believe that the larger geographic scope of operations will broaden markets for coal producers and offer more coal supply choices for electricity generators. *See* Energy Information Agency, Challenge of Electric Power Industry Restructuring for Fuel Suppliers (Sept. 1998).

MidAmerican Energy Co. v. Surface Transportation Board

169 F.3d 1099 (8th Cir.1999).

■ WOLLMAN, J.: Petition for Review of an Order of the Surface Transportation Board. This is a consolidated action involving MidAmerican Energy Company (MidAmerican), Central Power & Light Company (CP & L), and Pennsylvania Power & Light Company (PP & L) (collectively the utilities). They petition for review of two orders of the Surface Transportation Board (the Board) dismissing their complaints against rail carriers. The carriers cross-appeal from the portion of the Board's decisions regarding reasonableness review of contractual shipping rates, arguing that the issue was

12. The coal companies, it should be noted, have also been engaged in consolidation. The top 10 coal companies control 61% of the nation's coal output, up from 35% a decade earlier. William R. Long, Coal's Hot Competition Forges a Breed of Giants, N.Y. Times, February 21, 1998. The major oil companies, which had invested heavily in coal during the 1970's, have sold virtually all their coal assets throughout the world. Large German and South African coal companies have been expanding their activities. Gerard McCloskey, Coal Rush Goes Into Reverse, Financial Times, Sept. 23, 1999.

not ripe for adjudication. We affirm the dismissal of the utilities' complaints. We dismiss the cross-appeal for lack of jurisdiction.

I.

MidAmerican ships coal approximately 750 miles from the Powder River Basin in Wyoming to its generating facility near Sergeant Bluff, Iowa. At the time it filed its complaint, MidAmerican was shipping the coal from origin to destination under contract with the Union Pacific Railroad (UP). This contract was scheduled to expire at the end of 1997. Anticipating the contract's expiration, MidAmerican began to compare UP's rates with those of other carriers to obtain the most favorable shipping rates. The only other carrier offering rail service originating in the Powder River Basin is the Burlington Northern Railroad (BN).

BN does not service the final 90 miles of the route, a stretch from Council Bluffs, Iowa, to the generating station. Such a rail segment is commonly termed a "bottleneck," because it is serviced by only one carrier. Thus, MidAmerican could not directly compare the rates of BN and UP, as UP is the only carrier capable of shipping all the way to the generating station. To obtain a competitive rate for the 660–mile stretch from Wyoming to Council Bluffs, MidAmerican requested that UP provide a rate for its service over the bottleneck.

UP refused to provide the rate. Instead, it provided a rate for the entire route from the Powder River Basin to the generating station. This precluded MidAmerican from using BN as a carrier from Wyoming to Council Bluffs, essentially extending the bottleneck over the entire 750–mile route. Consequently, MidAmerican brought an action before the Board requesting a rate prescription over the 90–mile bottleneck segment. Although MidAmerican could not challenge a local "unit-train" rate for the bottleneck service, it asked the Board to prescribe a reasonable rate for the bottleneck if it found the published "class" rate for the 90–mile stretch unreasonable.[2][13]

CP & L transports coal from the Powder River Basin in Wyoming to its Coleto Creek generating station in Texas. Although both BN and UP offer rail service originating at the coal mines, the Southern Pacific Railroad

13. A local unit-train rate is a published rate applicable to transport of a trainload of a specific good between two points on a carrier's line. A local class rate, on the other hand, is a published rate applicable to transport of a certain type of good in smaller quantities between two points on a carrier's line. Railroads must maintain class rates because of their common carrier obligation to transport goods to any point on their lines upon request by a shipper. *See Thompson v. United States*, 343 U.S. 549, 558, 96 L. Ed. 1134, 72 S. Ct. 978 (1952); *Westinghouse Elec. Corp. v. United States*, 388 F. Supp. 1309, 1311 (W.D.Pa.1975) (*citing New York v. United States*, 331 U.S. 284, 289–90, 91 L. Ed. 1492, 67 S. Ct. 1207 (1947)). Because it is more costly for carriers to offer service for unspecified quantities of goods, however, class rates are seldom used and are generally significantly higher over the same stretch of rail. See Routing Restrictions over *Seatrain Lines, Inc.*, 296 I.C.C. 767, 773 (1955); *Burlington Northern, Inc. v. United States*, 555 F.2d 637, 639 (8th Cir.1977) (noting that a class rate for coal shipment was more than double the unit-train rate).

(SP) is the only carrier from an interchange point in Victoria, Texas, to Coleto Creek. UP's lines run from Wyoming to Victoria; BN's lines run from Wyoming to Fort Worth, Texas, where SP's service to Victoria and Coleto Creek begins. Therefore, UP and BN directly compete on the portion of the route from Wyoming to Fort Worth. SP and UP directly compete on the portion from Fort Worth to Victoria. After both BN and UP indicated a willingness to offer competitive rates for their service, CP & L requested that SP provide it a local unit-train rate for the segment from Fort Worth to Coleto Creek, which represented SP's longest haul, or for the bottleneck from Victoria to Coleto Creek.

SP refused to provide either rate, offering instead to provide a joint rate with UP. CP & L chose to obtain a unit-train rate from UP for service from Wyoming to Victoria, and to ship from Victoria to Coleto Creek under SP's class rate. It could thus take advantage of neither the competition between UP and BN from Wyoming to Fort Worth, nor the competition between SP and UP from Fort Worth to Victoria. Subsequently, CP & L brought a complaint before the Board challenging the class rate as unreasonable and requesting a rate prescription for the bottleneck segment.

SP's class rate for the coal shipment from Victoria to Coleto Creek was $19.95 per ton. At the Board's hearing, CP & L offered the testimony of eight expert witnesses that the highest reasonable rate for this stretch was $0.63 per ton, less than one-thirtieth of the actual class rate charged. [The court also described the facts of two similar cases that had been consolidated]

In considering the utilities' requests, the Board grappled with the tension between two competing policies expressed in the Interstate Commerce Act (the Act). Under 49 U.S.C. § 10701a(a) (1995) (now 10701(c)), rail carriers possess broad discretion in setting rates and routes. This reflects Congress's goal of deregulating the railroad industry and allowing railroads to achieve revenue adequacy by competing on a free-market basis. Under sections 10101a(6) and 10701a(b) (now 10101(6) and 10701(d)), however, some rate regulation is required when carriers possess monopoly power over a section of rail. These provisions codify railroads' common carrier obligations, which require them to provide service at reasonable rates to all shippers upon request.

The Board resolved this tension in favor of the "rate freedom" of bottleneck carriers. Specifically, it held that bottleneck carriers satisfy their common carrier duties and thus comply with the Act by providing origin-to-destination service that includes the bottleneck, as in MidAmerican's case, or by providing joint or proportional service with other carriers that includes transportation over the bottleneck. In addition, the Board held that shippers may not challenge class rates as an "indirect basis for obtaining prescription of a local unit-train rate" for bottleneck segments. Subsequently, the utilities moved for clarification and reconsideration of the decision. The Board responded by issuing a second decision, granting in part the motion for clarification and denying the motion for reconsideration. *See Central Power & Light Co. v. Southern Pac. Transp. Co.,* No.

41242, at (Surface Transp. Bd. Apr. 28, 1997) (Bottleneck II). The utilities appeal from both rulings.

II.

Before we address the specific issues raised in these cases, we briefly review the relevant history of railroad regulation. From its passage in 1887 until the mid–1970s, the Interstate Commerce Act provided for a strict regulatory framework to govern the federal railroad industry. This legislative approach resulted in an industry chronically plagued by capital short-falls and service inefficiencies. *See* H.R. Rep. No. 96–1035, at 33 (1980), *reprinted in* 1980 U.S.C.C.A.N. 3978, 3978; *Coal Exporters Ass'n of United States v. United States,* 240 U.S. App. D.C. 256, 745 F.2d 76, 81 (D.C.Cir. 1984).

To assure railroads greater freedom in establishing routes and rates, Congress modified the Act with the Railroad Revitalization and Regulatory Reform Act (4R Act), Pub. L. No. 94–210, 90 Stat. 31 (1976), and the Staggers Rail Act (Staggers Act), Pub. L. No. 96–448, 94 Stat. 1895 (1980). *See* H.R. Conf. Rep. No. 96–1430, at 79 (1980), *reprinted* in 1980 U.S.C.C.A.N. 3978, 4110. These acts were intended to end "decades of ICC control over maximum rates and to permit carriers not having market dominance to set rates in response to their perception of market conditions." *Midtec Paper Corp. v. United States,* 857 F.2d 1487, 1506 (D.C.Cir. 1988).

Underlying these reform efforts was the notion that market forces would operate in the rail industry as they do in other spheres. Congress believed that free competition for rail services would ensure that consumer demand dictated the optimal rate level, while facilitating enough long-term capital investment to maintain adequate service. Congress was also mindful, however, that the free market would protect consumers only if there was "effective" competition. Therefore, the new enactments included provisions allowing regulatory intervention where competition would not control prices. *See* 4R Act § 101(b), 90 Stat. 31, 33; Staggers Act § 101(a), 49 U.S.C. § 10101a(6) (now 10101(6)); *Coal Exporters,* 745 F.2d at 81 n.6.

Indeed, in bottleneck situations the Staggers Act actually "increased the ICC's regulatory power—by authorizing the agency to require railroads to enter into agreements to 'switch' other railroads' cars to and from shippers located along each other's lines...." *Baltimore Gas & Elec. Co. v. United States,* 260 U.S. App. D.C. 1, 817 F.2d 108, 113 (D.C.Cir.1987);*see* 49 U.S.C. § 11103 (now 11102). After the 4R and Staggers Acts, the agency (previously the ICC, now the Surface Transportation Board) is still required to use rate prescription and other remedies such as reciprocal switching arrangements to ensure reasonable shipping rates on bottlenecks. It is also responsible for ensuring that free competition is preserved to the greatest extent possible on non-bottleneck segments.

Congress's decision to deregulate the railroad industry has been largely successful. Experts for both sides in these cases have acknowledged that competition has led to more efficient routes, increased profits, better service, and an enhanced ability to attract capital investment. *See, e.g.,* Verified Statement of William J. Baumol & Robert D. Willig at 6–7, J.A. at 1111–12; Verified Statement of Alfred E. Kahn at 15–16, J.A. at 2931–32. However, the experts dispute the role of bottleneck rail segments in increasing profits and facilitating the overall revenue adequacy of the railroad industry.

III.

We have jurisdiction under 28 U.S.C. §§ 2321 and 2341 (Supp. 1998), which provide for review of the Board's decisions. Because Congress has entrusted the Board with interpreting and administering the Act, in reviewing its decisions we ask only whether they are " 'based on a permissible construction of the statute.' "

As the utilities and shipper organizations assert, carriers are bound both at common law and under the Act to "provide ... transportation or service on reasonable request" to any shipper. *GS Roofing,* 143 F.3d at 391. This duty not only requires carriers to provide service on their lines, but also requires rates for such service to be reasonable. *See Thompson,* 343 U.S. at 554; 49 U.S.C. § 10701a(b) (now 10701(d)).

As the Board and the railroads assert, however, there are significant limitations to the common carrier duties. It is usually at the discretion of the carrier how it wishes to satisfy its duty to provide rates and service. *See* 49 U.S.C. § 10701a(a) (now 10701(c)). Further, a carrier generally may provide common carrier service in a manner that protects its "long hauls." *See* 49 U.S.C. § 10705(a) (now 10705(a)). The Board may order a carrier to provide service over a shorter haul than it wishes only if the Board first makes specific findings under the Act. *See Id.* § 10705(a)(2). Thus, a carrier such as UP may normally choose to provide service to a shipper such as MidAmerican over a route longer than the 90 miles from Council Bluffs to Sergeant Bluff, unless the longer route would be "unreasonably long" or inefficient.

Therefore, the Act protects both shippers and carriers. It guarantees that shippers will receive rail service at reasonable rates, and it allows carriers to provide such service in a manner that achieves revenue adequacy.

The Board has recognized that an important part of achieving revenue adequacy is differential pricing. *See Consolidated Rail Corp. v. United States,* 812 F.2d 1444, 1453–54 (3d Cir.1987) (*citing* Coal Rate Guidelines, Nationwide, 1 I.C.C. 2d 520 (1985)). This is a practice by which carriers charge a higher mark-up on rail segments where demand elasticity is low, such as bottlenecks, to compensate for low mark-ups on competitive segments. *See Coal Rate Guidelines,* 1 I.C.C. 2d at 526–27. Therefore, "services may be priced above their attributable costs according to observable market demand, but only to the extent necessary to cover total costs, including return on investment of an efficient carrier." *Id.* at 533–34. Accordingly, in reviewing the reasonableness of bottleneck rates, the Board allows bottleneck carriers to charge up to stand-alone cost (SAC), a level that is significantly higher than marginal cost.[10][14]

In the present case, the Board determined that exploiting bottlenecks by refusing to provide separately challengeable bottleneck rates also assists carriers in achieving revenue adequacy. Specifically, in the MidAmerican case, allowing UP to provide only an origin-to-destination rate enables it to charge up to SAC over the entire 750–mile route, rather than just over the 90–mile section from Council Bluffs to Sergeant Bluff. Were UP required to provide a separate bottleneck rate, it would be forced to charge lower competitive rates from the mine to Council Bluffs. Based on these economic factors and extensive expert testimony, the Board concluded that the Act did not require carriers to provide separate bottleneck rates.

Regardless of how we would resolve the tension in the Act if we were to independently rule on the utilities' claims, we cannot say that the Board's interpretation was incorrect. The Board's considerable expertise in the economic underpinnings of the railroad industry is entitled to a great degree of deference, and its decision to allow carriers to determine how they wish to fulfill their duties under the Act is consistent with the current national railroad policy of maximizing carrier discretion in setting routes and rates. Because the utilities have not demonstrated that the Board's rulings were incorrect, we affirm the Board's dismissal of the utilities' complaints.■

NOTES AND COMMENTS

1. What policy reasons justify a system in which the railroads can charge monopolistic prices to captive customers in order to be able to reduce rates to other customers? Are the railroads engaged in a business in which they cannot be expected to make a profit in the free market? Compare the *Market Street Railway* case, discussed in Chapter 8, *infra*. Is the Staggers Act simply a well-hidden redistributional subsidy by which some of the costs of operating a railroad system are shifted to the consumers of electric power?

2. In many instances, the electric utilities entered into contracts to purchase the output of a coal mine and transport it by a particular railroad at a time when the electric utility was subject to traditional rate regulation, which allowed the utility to pass its costs on to the consumers. Today, many of these utilities are facing increasing competition (see Chapter Eleven, *infra*) and are much more concerned about their costs.

3. The Surface Transportation Board has modified its regulations to reduce the evidentiary requirements for shipper seeking to prove that a

---

14. Stand-alone cost represents the minimum amount that a hypothetical carrier, or the shipper itself, would have to spend to build a new rail line to compete over the bottleneck segment. *See Coal Rate Guidelines*, 1 I.C.C. 2d at 528–29. This measure better allows railroads to achieve true revenue adequacy, because it takes into account profits and the cost of long-term capital investment, while marginal cost does not. *See id.* at 526.

railroad has "market dominance" over a particular route. Shippers now need to show only that the railroad dominated the transportation market; they no longer need to present evidence on the broader issues of product and geographic competition. Surface Transportation Board, Market Dominance Determinations, Ex Parte No. 627 (Dec. 21, 1998).

4. The District of Columbia Court of Appeals, in a case that it held in abeyance until the Eighth Circuit decided the *MidAmerican* case, upheld the STB's bottleneck policy against an argument by the railroads that the policy was too favorable to shippers. "We think the Board adequately reconciled the particular statutory tensions raised by the Bottleneck cases; confronting the unenviable task of balancing the rail carriers' rate and route prerogatives and the shippers' contract rights, the Board produced what is, on balance, a reasonable policy." *Union Pacific Railroad Co. v. STB*, 202 F.3d 337, 344–45 (D.C.Cir.2000).

D. COAL COMBUSTION

The only economically productive function of coal is to be burned. Consequently, if a coal mining company is to operate profitably it must find a customer that wants to burn coal. In modern times, that has increasingly meant an electric utility.

1. COAL CONTRACTS

In the modern coal market, in which entire mines are constructed for the purpose of supplying one or more power plants, the contract between the coal mining company and the power company will inevitably cover a long period of time. Both parties will need to estimate demand and supply over a long period, and the contract will need to provide for the possibility that these estimates may be wrong.

Business and Professional People for the Public Interest v. Illinois Commerce Commission

585 N.E.2d 1032 (Ill.1991).

■ CLARK, J.: [In an appeal from a rate decision of the Illinois Commerce Commission, Commonwealth Edison ("Edison")] argues that the Commission improperly excluded $383.3 million of western coal reserves from its rate base. Edison had included this amount in its budget as property held for future use. The Commission found that none of the reserves qualified as property held for future use, although some of the reserves may be included in Edison's rate base as part of its fossil fuel inventory.

The coal reserves at issue here are an outgrowth of coal purchase contracts Edison entered into in the 1970s. At that time Edison agreed to purchase certain quantities of coal over an extended period of time. Because the demand for electricity did not grow as fast as Edison had expected, in the 1980s the company did not need as much coal as it had previously agreed to purchase. In 1982 and 1983, the company negotiated with its suppliers to reduce the amount of coal to be delivered currently. These negotiations resulted in "agreements to defer actual mining of some coal in exchange for the company's agreement to make certain prepayments and receive what is called an 'interest' in the coal in the ground; i.e., the coal reserves at issue here." In essence, the company prepaid its suppliers for the coal under the terms of the base contract, less the cost of mining and delivering the coal. In return, the company obtained the right to defer delivery of the coal until some future date. When the coal is actually needed, Edison will pay only the cost of mining and delivery. Thus, under the base coal contracts and related deferral agreements, Edison has hedged against future increases in the price of the coal. Edison now wants to include the value of these coal reserves as property held for future use.

" 'Property held for future use' refers to a utility's investment in property which is not currently being used to provide service to its customers but which will be used in the future to provide such service." *City of Chicago v. Illinois Commerce Comm'n* 133 Ill. App. 3d 435, 440 (1985). Generally a "utility is entitled to earn a return on its investment in property held for future use if the property was acquired in good faith with a definite plan for its use and it is reasonably acquired and retained to serve the utility's customers." (*Id.* at 441) Edison argues that because the Commission previously found that the base coal contracts and the deferral contracts were prudent, the company may include the amount of coal expected to be used during the next 10 years in its rate base as property held for future use.

The Commission previously considered the ratemaking treatment of these coal reserves in Docket No. 83—0537 [and] held that the " 'reserve coal' is not property which is used and useful in providing utility service, or which is highly likely to be so used and useful in the future under a plan for its use." (61 Pub. Util. Rep. 4th at 10.) Therefore, the Commission excluded the coal reserves from Edison's rate base and ignored the coal reserve contracts for ratemaking purposes. Instead, the Commission directed Edison "to account for the cost of the reserve coal when it is used, for ratemaking purposes, as if the coal was being bought currently on the open market; Edison should not use the then-current base coal contract price." 61 Pub. Util. Rep. 4th at 10.

In the Remand Order, the Commission "reaffirm[ed] its decision in Docket 83—0537 as to the treatment of these coal reserves," and also found that the coal reserves "are essentially coal inventory." By treating the coal reserves as inventory, the Commission permitted Edison to include in its rate base only that amount of the reserves which was deemed proper as fossil fuel inventory. Therefore, under the Remand Order none of the reserves was included as property held for future use.

In the Rate Order the Commission again "reaffirme[ed] its decision in Docket 83—0537 as to the treatment of these coal reserves." Although the Rate Order did not specifically adopt the Commission's findings contained in the Remand Order, the Rate Order "noted that the Commission also rejected this same proposal in [the Remand Order]." We believe this statement from the Rate Order was intended to reaffirm the Commission's finding that the coal reserves are coal inventory. We conclude that the Commission's classification of the coal reserves as inventory is within the sound discretion of the Commission and is supported by the evidence.

Edison states that the Commission's prior orders relating to the treatment of the coal reserves are irrelevant to the present rate case because the prior orders were based on the amount of reserve coal which Edison expected to use under conditions prevailing at the time of the orders. Because the amount of coal Edison expects to use has changed, Edison argues the Commission must evaluate this issue de novo to determine the amount of coal reserves to be included in Edison's rate base. We agree with Edison that changing conditions will affect the amount of coal reserves to be included in rate base. However, we believe the Commission properly considered these changed conditions when it decided the issue of fossil fuel inventory. We note that Edison does not challenge the Commission's findings on that issue.■

NOTES AND COMMENTS

1.   The consulting firm, Resource Data International, published a study in 1999 which purported to analyze the relative success of various power companies in contracting for coal at competitive prices. Its report concluded that by the year 2003 a quarter of the country's power plant capacity will be paying higher fuel costs for coal than could be achieved with new natural gas-fired power plants. The report cites three utilities, American Electric Power, Southern Company, and Commonwealth Edison, as burdened with coal contracts that "resulted in each company paying $300 million over and above market prices for coal delivered to their power plants in 1998." Competition Threatens Coal–Fired Units, 13 Electricity Daily #86 (Nov. 3, 1999).

2.   Consumer groups have sometimes argued that electric utilities are deliberately paying high prices for coal today in exchange for agreements to get cheaper coal in a few years time. They allege that the companies' objective is to prepare to be more competitive when electricity deregulation becomes a reality. The North Carolina Utilities Commission recently rejected such an argument, but the Carolina Utility Consumers Association plans to appeal. *Re Carolina Power & Light Company*, 1999 WL 827712 (North Carolina Utilities Commission, 1999)

3.   Many long-term coal contracts provide for the arbitration of disputes, but it is not unusual for the disputes to end up in court anyway. *See ANR Coal Co., Inc. v. Cogentrix of North Carolina, Inc.*, 173 F.3d 493 (4th Cir.1999).

2.   EXTERNALITIES OF COAL COMBUSTION

In the early days of the Industrial Revolution, smoke from the burning of coal was seen as a good thing. Throughout the 1800s "Americans had come to associate smoke with all those positive changes attributed to coal: production, prosperity, and progress." David Stradling, Smokestacks and Progressives: Environmentalists, Engineers, and Air Quality in America, 1881—1951 14, Johns Hopkins University Press, 1999. As industrialization became more prevalent, however, coal smoke became an annoyance. Then as medical science became more aware of the relationship between air pollution and respiratory disease, coal smoke began to be viewed not just as a nuisance but as a serious health hazard.

a.   EARLY AIR POLLUTION REGULATIONS

The Clean Air Act ("CAA") was first enacted in 1955 under the name "Air Pollution Control Act," which provided only for "research and technical assistance relating to air pollution control." Pub.L. No. 91–604, 60 Stat. 322. (1955). In 1970, Congress gave the CAA teeth by establishing its current form and placing deadlines for compliance with environmental standards regarding air pollution. Clean Air Act,§ 110(a)(1), 42 U.S.C. § 7410 (1998). Each state has primacy for assuring that the air quality within its borders meets a minimum standard. The states are responsible for submitting a state implementation plan ("SIP") to the EPA. A SIP must specify how the state will achieve and maintain national ambient air quality standards ("NAAQS"). NAAQS were established for six criteria pollutants. Regions that do not meet the NAAQS for one or more criteria pollutants are considered "non-attainment" areas.

One of the six criteria pollutants is sulfur dioxide, which is produced by the combustion of coal, particularly the so-called high-sulfur coal. In the compromise that produced the Clean Air Act of 1970, existing coal-burning plants were not required to conform to New Source Performance Standards (NSPS) that were imposed on new plants. Instead, if an old plant was causing the sulfur dioxide to exceed EPA standards in their local area, the plant operator typically built a taller stack, which had the effect of dissipating the sulfur compounds over longer distances.

b.   THE ACID RAIN PROGRAM

As the power plants raised their stacks, residents of states downwind of the power plants soon begin to notice that this dispersed sulfur dioxide and other sulfur compounds were entering their states and being caught by clouds and dissolved in rain. The sulfur acidified the rainwater and produced what became known as "acid rain."

More than two-thirds of the acid produced is the result of the use of coal in power plants and smelter processes. Although for many years the power companies argued that the harm caused by acid rain was minor, it was generally blamed with causing reduced growth of some trees and crops and with making some lakes and streams less hospitable for fish.

In the late 1970s, Congress and the EPA thought that the problem of acid rain should be solved by requiring power plants to install "scrubbers" which would remove the sulfur compounds from the emission stream. (See the Burtraw & Swift article, *infra.*) But the industry objected vigorously to the high cost of this equipment.

The CAA was amended in 1990 to target acid rain more specifically. 42 U.S.C. §§ 7401–7642 (1998). The utility companies are encouraged to buy pollution control technologies, such as scrubbers, or to switch to low sulfur coal. If these reductions result in a greater reduction in pollution than the standards require, the companies receive credits for each ton of pollutants reduced below the established limits. These credits may be sold to other utilities. The idea is that there would be an overall reduction in air pollutants, even though some facilities would be allowed to emit more pollutants than the average, as long as the total aggregate pollution was within the legal limit.

The effect of the acid rain program was to facilitate increased reliance on coal-burning power plants and increase overall coal consumption, but with a switch toward greater use of low sulfur coal from the Western states.

The following article was written by representatives of two organizations that played a prominent role in designing and promoting the acid rain program that was adopted in 1990.

Dallas Burtraw and Byron Swift, A New Standard of Performance: An Analysis of the Clean Air Act's Acid Rain Program

26 Environmental Law Reporter 10411 (1996).

The Acid Rain Program enacted in Title IV of the 1990 Clean Air Act Amendments contains two innovative features that represent dramatic departures from conventional environmental regulation. First, the program sets an overall cap on SO_2 emissions at approximately one-half of historic levels. The usual approach has been to calculate allowable emission rates based on engineering assessments of technological feasibility and modeling of ambient environmental quality.

The program's second innovative feature is that it allows operators of affected facilities—primarily electric utilities—to trade emission allowances between their own facilities or with other utilities in order to save costs in achieving the overall national emissions cap. Hence, an individual facility may implement abatement measures that depart from an engineering prescription of the cleanest possible technology for that facility. But in order to do so, it must find alternative ways of reducing emissions or it must compensate another utility to reduce emissions accordingly.

This Article explores the program's successes, as well as its potential shortcomings and improvements. The Article shows that it is the adoption of an emissions cap approach that has led to the most significant cost reductions and ensured the achievement of the program's environmental goals. The program's allowance trading provisions have assisted in reducing compliance costs, but they have not led to extensive trading between firms, though they have been used within firms. . . .

An emission cap differs in important ways from traditional environmental regulation, which prescribes particular emission rates for each point source and has tended to force adoption of an associated specific technology. Instead, individual affected facilities are allocated a quantity of emission allowances each year at no cost. To reduce its emissions to equal its allowance allocation, an individual facility can choose among competing technologies with varying emission rates, including scrubbing, fuel blending, fuel switching, and clean coal technology. The facility can also seek to reduce demand by its customers.

Newly built facilities are given no allowances, and must obtain them from existing plants. Absent the ability to transfer allowances between facilities, the emission cap would create a performance standard for individual facilities that gives operators the flexibility to choose the facility's cheapest compliance option, but would deny the flexibility to minimize costs over several facilities. The NSPS in effect since 1979 did not afford such flexibility for two reasons. First, it limited technology choices to end-of-pipe treatment, precluding abatement through process changes or volume or demand reduction, neither of which changed effluent rates.

Second, while the NSPS, being based on emission rates, was ostensibly a performance standard, it limited technology choices to flue gas desulfurization, or scrubbing, by setting a specific percentage reduction in emissions that provided no room for deviation from the benchmark technology. Often emission rates, monitoring, and enforcement are geared to currently available technology. Pursuing innovative approaches under these circumstances poses a substantial risk of being found in noncompliance with little chance of reward. In addition, there is no incentive to pursue additional reductions, even if they can be achieved at relatively low cost. In general, while nominally performance standards, many if not most effluent rate limits become technology standards when the rate itself specifies a percentage reduction in effluent, or the permitting agencies in practice require certain technologies as the only permissible way of achieving the standards. Certainly in the case of the SO_2 NSPS, scrubbing was the only way to meet the standard.

The second significant innovation in the Acid Rain Program was the provision for trading allowances. Title IV's emission cap applies to the industry rather than to individual facilities, and allowances are transferable between facilities and bankable over time. If a utility reduces its emissions below its endowed emission level, it can switch those allowances to another of its units, bank them for future use, or sell them. This provision of the program allows even greater programmatic cost savings by creating incentives for plants with the lowest costs of SO_2 reduction to reduce emissions, and switch or sell their allowances to plants or other utilities with higher costs, profiting both firms and minimizing overall compliance costs.

Through the market for transferable allowances, this incentive-based approach allows utilities to determine how and where to achieve emission reductions. Utilities may use different technologies at different facilities, achieve compliance at only some of their facilities or units, or transfer allowances to other utilities. These changes have led to significant cost savings in achieving an environmentally stringent standard, and have resulted in a dramatic shift to process change instead of end-of-the-pipe treatment....

[B]y far the most significant reason for lower costs has been the flexibility afforded utilities under the program to switch to low-sulfur coal as a means of compliance. This has driven competition and technology improvements in the coal and rail haul industry, which in turn have led to a dramatic reduction in the delivered cost of low-sulfur coal. A review of changes in the receipts for coal distinguished by sulfur content reveals that between 1990 and 1994 use of low-sulfur coal (defined as less than 0.6 pounds (lbs.) sulfur per million British thermal units (mmBtu)) increased by 28 percent while its price fell by 9 percent. Meanwhile, sales of high-sulfur coal (defined as greater than 1.67 lb. sulfur per mmBtu) fell by 18 percent, though prices fell by only 6 percent....

The consequence of reduced low-sulfur coal prices, combined with the ability to exploit low-sulfur coal resulting from the flexibility of Title IV, is that in Phase I many plants that are not relying on scrubbers are arguably complying with the Acid Rain Program at virtually no cost or at a savings. A study by Resources Data International estimates that the savings to such firms may be as much as $158 million annually during Phase I.

The decline in coal prices driven by the availability of cheap, low-sulfur western coal has led some to speculate that some of the emission reductions that are occurring under Title IV would have happened anyway. Indeed, early emissions reductions are observable in 1993 and 1994, before Phase I took full effect. The trend toward early reductions suggests the possibility that the Acid Rain Program did little more than accelerate a trend that was otherwise occurring. Econometric analysis by A. Denny Ellerman and Juan–Pablo Montero has verified that, to some extent, this is the case. They conclude that Title IV should get some, but not all, of the credit for the decrease in emissions that has resulted from the increased use of western coal....

One important reason trading has been lighter than many analysts originally expected is the role played by low-sulfur coal in meeting compliance requirements. The decline in rail transport costs, coupled with ample supplies of low-sulfur coal, makes it a commonly available option with comparably low marginal costs at many different facilities. Nonetheless, the GAO has identified 80 utilities in Phase I with emission reduction costs higher, and sometimes significantly higher, than current allowance prices. In principle, within a system of transferable emission allowances, a firm with relatively high marginal costs of emission reduction would have an incentive to take advantage of another firm's relatively low marginal costs. [The authors go on to identify various tax and regulatory rules that have provided a disincentive to trading of allowances by utilities.]■

NOTES AND COMMENTS

1. The price of an allowance for emission of one ton of SO_2, originally estimated to be $750 by some analysts, has at times dropped to below $100. The EPA auction for allowances in March 1996, which may underestimate the current value of an allowance due to its institutional features, yielded an average price of $68.14 per ton for an allowance usable in the current period, and a price of $65.36 per ton for an allowance useable in the year 2002.

As of mid–1999 allowances were selling in the $200 range, but those prices were still far below the prices anticipated at the time the legislation was adopted. Towards the end of 1999, the EPA initiated litigation against a number of utilities who allegedly evaded New Source Performance Standards improperly. Matthew L. Wald, EPA is Ordering 392 Plants to Cut Pollution in Half, New York Times, Dec. 18, 1999. Thereafter the price of an allowance dropped below $150 per ton. SO2 Market is Getting Clobbered as Regulatory Uncertainties Persist, Utility Environment Report, January 14, 2000.

2. A study by the Environmental Law Institute demonstrates that state laws constrain trading of allowances, which can preclude the innovation, and reduce the cost savings, normally associated with this regulatory method. Many state public utility commissions lack rules governing allowance transactions, which creates uncertainty and presents a significant barrier to risk-averse utilities. In addition, in most states the standard rules governing the allowed rate of return, the depreciation rate, and the risk that expenses, such as allowance purchases, may not be recoverable in electricity rates are all less favorable to allowance transactions. Furthermore, prohibitions against shareholder earnings on capital gains (but not capital losses) impose one-sided risks on utilities that purchase allowances. Douglas R. Bohi, Utilities and State Regulators Are Failing to Take Advantage of Emission Allowance Trading, Elec.J., Mar. 1994, at 20. An additional problem has been explicit attempts by legislatures to prohibit trades that might undermine local economic activity, such as the production of coal. All of these factors have discouraged utilities' willingness to purchase allowances. Byron Swift, Barriers to Environmental Technology Innovation and Use, 28 ELR 10202, 10209 (1998). For a critique of the legislative process that led to the acid rain program , see Lisa Heinzerling, Selling Pollution, Forcing Democracy, 14 Stan. Envtl. L. J. 300 (1995).

3. Unfortunately, the reduction in sulfur dioxide emissions resulting from the acid rain program does not yet appear to have stemmed the acidification of the waters of the Northeast. A study by the General Accounting Office "raises sharp questions about the effectiveness of the Clean Air Act amendments of 1990, which set tough restrictions on smokestack emissions of sulfur and nitrogen, the two components of acid rain. The report shows that while sulfur levels have declined substantially in a vast majority of the Adirondacks waterways, nitrogen levels have continued to rise in nearly half of them. In water, nitrogen turns to nitric acid, which can damage fish larvae and create conditions that poison adult fish." James Dao, Acid Rain

Law Found to Fail in Adirondacks New York Times p.A1, March 27, 2000. Utility representatives argue that the reductions in nitrogen oxide that took effect in 1996 and 2000 will alleviate the problem, but have not yet been reflected in the GAO's data. *Id.*

4.   The United States Government is basing its support for a system of trading emission allowances for greenhouse gases on the success of the trading of allowances in the acid rain program. The greenhouse gas issue is discussed in Chapter Seventeen. One irony of the interrelationship between the acid rain program and the climate change issue is that the principal result of the acid rain program has been to keep existing coal-fired power plants in operation by allowing the use of low sulfur coal. This has contributed significantly to the increased emission of carbon dioxide, the most prevalent greenhouse gas, that the United States has experienced since 1990.

c.   STATE ATTEMPTS TO FAVOR LOCAL COAL

The big losers in the compromise that produced the 1990 Clean Air Act Amendments were the states in which high-sulfur coal was mined. A number of these states sought to adopt laws or regulations that would discourage their local electric companies from switching from local high-sulfur coal to low-sulfur coal from out of state. But it proved difficult to enact such rules without violating the dormant Commerce Clause of the Constitution.

The term "dormant" commerce clause refers to the fact that the Supreme Court has used the interstate commerce clause of the Constitution as a limitation on the power of the states to regulate businesses that are involved in interstate commerce. When used in this manner, the clause is often referred to as the "dormant" commerce clause, a reference to the fact that although the Constitution does not specifically say that the states may not regulate interstate commerce, the Court has held that such a limitation is implicit (i.e., dormant) in the grant of power to Congress to regulate interstate commerce. In the last fifty years, cases arising under the dormant commerce clause that contest the validity of state regulation have been far more frequent than cases challenging federal power under the direct application of the commerce clause. *See* Dan T. Coenen, Business Subsidies and the Dormant Commerce Clause, 107 Yale L. J. 965 (1998).

Alliance for Clean Coal v. Miller

44 F.3d 591 (7th Cir.1995).

■ CUMMINGS, J.: Plaintiff Alliance for Clean Coal ("Alliance") is a Virginia trade association whose members include Colorado and Oregon coal companies and three railroads that transport coal. The defendants are the chairman and six commissioners of the Illinois Commerce Commission in charge of the administration and enforcement of the Illinois Public Utilities Act.

Coal has long been and continues to be the most important source of fuel for the generation of electric power in this country, accounting for 56 percent of all electricity generated in 1992. Electric utilities, the primary consumers of domestic coal, burned 78 percent of the 998 million tons of coal produced in the United States in 1992. Coal is produced in over half the states and is sold in a highly competitive national market. *See* Alliance Ex. 10.

Coal's sulfur content varies greatly depending on its geographical origin. Western coal, mined west of the Rocky Mountains, generally has the lowest sulfur content of any coal produced in the country. Coal mined in the "Illinois Basin," which includes most of Illinois and parts of Indiana and western Kentucky, is relatively high in sulfur. Burning coal emits sulfur dioxide in an amount proportional to the coal's sulfur content. *See generally* Bruce A. Ackerman & William T. Hassler, Clean Coal/ Dirty Air (1981).

In the 1970 Amendment to the Clean Air Act, Congress authorized the Environmental Protection Agency ("EPA") to set new standards to regulate various emissions, including sulfur dioxide. See 42 U.S.C. § 7411 (1970) (amended 1977). The EPA provided for two methods to control sulfur dioxide emissions: (1) the use of low sulfur coal; and (2) the use of pollution control devices ("scrubbers").

In 1977 Congress again amended the Clean Air Act, requiring new electric plants to build scrubbers. By requiring scrubbers regardless of the sulfur content of the coal burned, Congress essentially eliminated for new facilities the low-sulfur coal compliance option that had been available under the 1970 Amendment.

In 1990 Congress once again amended the Act, this time requiring a drastic two-stage reduction in industrial sulfur dioxide emissions in an attempt to combat acid rain. The 1990 Act implements a market-driven approach to emissions regulation, allowing for the free transfer of emission "allowances." The Act is aimed at reducing sulfur dioxide emissions in the most efficient manner and, like the 1970 Act, allows electric generating plants to meet the emission standards in the cheapest way possible. The principal methods of compliance now include installing new scrubbers, using low-sulfur coal, switching to another fuel source, or buying additional emission allowances.

The 1990 amendments meant the end of the salad days for high-sulfur coal-producing states such as Illinois. Low-sulfur western coal once again offered a viable alternative to the continued burning of high-sulfur coal combined with the installation of expensive new scrubbers. Faced with potentially damaging competition for the local coal industry, in 1991 the Illinois General Assembly passed the Coal Act, an addition to the Utilities Act, concerning implementation and compliance with the 1990 Clean Air Act amendments. *See* 220 ILCS 5/8–402.1. Under the Coal Act, utilities must formulate Clean Air Act compliance plans which must be approved by the Illinois Commerce Commission. In preparing and approving these compliance plans, the utilities and the Commerce Commission are required to:

> Take into account the need for utilities to comply in a manner which minimizes to the extent consistent with the other goals and objectives of this Section the impact of compliance on rates for service, the need to use coal mined in Illinois in an environmentally responsible manner in the production of electricity and the need to maintain and preserve as a valuable State resource the mining of coal in Illinois. 220 ILCS 5/8–402.1(a).

The Act encourages the installation of scrubbers to allow the continued burning of Illinois coal, stating that the combination can be an environmentally responsible and cost effective means of compliance when the impact on personal income in this State of changing the fuel used at such generating plants so as to displace coal mined in Illinois is taken into account. *Id.*

The four largest generating plants in Illinois currently burning Illinois coal are required to include the installation of scrubbers in their compliance plans so that they will be able to continue their use of Illinois coal. The cost of these scrubbers will be deemed "used and useful" when placed in operation and the utilities are guaranteed that they will be able to include the costs in their rate base. The Act further provides that the Commerce Commission must approve any 10 percent or greater decrease in the use of Illinois coal by a utility.

Plaintiff asked the district court to declare the Illinois Coal Act repugnant to the Commerce Clause of the federal Constitution and to enjoin its enforcement. In December 1993, District Judge Conlon handed down a memorandum opinion and order granting such relief. *Alliance for Clean Coal v. Craig,* 840 F. Supp. 554 (N.D.Ill.1993). The court enjoined the Illinois Commerce Commission from enforcing the Illinois Coal Act and voided federal Clean Air Act compliance plans approved in reliance on the Illinois Coal Act.

On appeal, the defendant commissioners request that we dismiss the case for want of jurisdiction or, if we reach the merits, reverse the judgment below....

Alliance attacks the constitutionality of the Illinois Coal Act under the Commerce Clause of the Constitution. That clause provides that "the Congress shall have power ... to regulate commerce ... among the several states." Article I, Section 8, Clause 3. It has long been interpreted to have a "negative" aspect that denies the states the power to discriminate against or burden the interstate flow of articles of commerce.... "If a statute discriminates against interstate commerce either on its face or in its practical effect, it is subject to the strictest scrutiny ... 'Where simple economic protectionism is effected by state legislation, a virtual per se rule of invalidity has been erected.'" *DeHart v. Town of Austin,* 39 F.3d 718, 723 (7th Cir.1994), *quoting Philadelphia v. New Jersey,* 437 U.S. 617, 624.

Two recent Supreme Court cases interpreting the negative Commerce Clause are controlling here. In *Oregon Waste Systems v. Department of Environmental Quality,* 128 L. Ed. 2d 13, 114 S. Ct. 1345, the Court held that the negative Commerce Clause prohibited a state surcharge on the disposal of solid waste generated out of state. *In West Lynn Creamery, Inc. v. Healy,* 129 L. Ed. 2d 157, 114 S. Ct. 2205, the Court struck down a Massachusetts milk-pricing order which employed a tax on all milk sold to fund a subsidy to in-state producers. Because the Illinois Coal Act, like the milk-pricing order in West Lynn, has the same effect as a "tariff or customs duty—neutralizing the advantage possessed by lower cost out of state producers," it too is repugnant to the Commerce Clause and the principle of a unitary national economy which that clause was intended to establish. *West Lynn,* 114 S. Ct. at 2212.

The Illinois Coal Act is a none-too-subtle attempt to prevent Illinois electric utilities from switching to low-sulfur western coal as a Clean Air Act compliance option. Indeed, the statute itself states that the Illinois General Assembly determined that there was "the need to use coal mined in Illinois" and "the need to maintain and preserve as a valuable State resource the mining of coal in Illinois." 220 ILCS 5/8–402.1(a). The Act implements this protectionist policy in four ways. First, it tilts the overall playing field by requiring that commissioners take account of the effect on the local coal industry when considering compliance plans. *Id.* Second, the Act requires that certain large generating units install scrubbers "to enable them to continue to burn Illinois coal." 220 ILCS 5/8–402.1(e). Third, the Act guarantees that the cost of these scrubbers can be included in the utility's rate base and passed through to consumers, even where the use of low-sulfur western coal would be a cheaper compliance option. 220 ILCS 5/8–402.1(e) and 220 ILCS 5/9–212. Finally, the Act requires Commerce Commission approval before a utility can make a change in fuel that would result in a 10 percent or greater decrease in the utility's use of Illinois coal. In determining whether to grant approval, the Commerce Commission "shall consider the impact on employment related to the production of coal in Illinois." 220 ILCS 5/8–508. The intended effect of these provisions is to foreclose the use of low-sulfur western coal by Illinois utilities as a means of complying with the Clean Air Act. This of course amounts to discriminatory state action forbidden by the Commerce Clause.

Illinois seeks to save the Act by claiming that it merely "encourages" the local coal industry and does not in fact discriminate. This argument rings hollow. The Illinois Coal Act cannot continue to exist merely because it does not facially compel the use of Illinois coal or forbid the use of out-of-state coal. As recognized in *West Lynn Creamery,* even ingenious discrimination is forbidden by the Commerce Clause. 114 S. Ct. at 2215. By "encouraging" the use of Illinois coal, the Act discriminates against western coal by making it a less viable compliance option for Illinois generating plants. Moreover, the requirement that certain generators be equipped with scrubbers essentially mandates that these generators burn Illinois coal: that is the purpose of the scrubber requirement, and the Commerce Commission would likely not allow the pass-through of the then-unnecessary additional cost of low-sulfur western coal. Such a mandate runs directly afoul of *Wyoming v. Oklahoma*, 502 U.S. 437 (requirement that Oklahoma generating plants burn 10 percent Oklahoma coal held to violate the Commerce Clause). Similarly, the guaranteed pass-through of the scrubber cost to rate-payers is equivalent to the minimum price fixing for the benefit of local producers held unconstitutional in *Baldwin v. G.A.F. Seelig, Inc.*, 294 U.S. 511.

Illinois argues that it has merely "agreed to 'subsidize' the cost of generating electricity through the use of Illinois coal by requiring its own citizens to bear the cost of pollution control devices." First, the fact that Illinois rate-payers are footing the bill does not cure the discriminatory impact on western coal producers. As the Supreme Court noted in rejecting an identical argument in West Lynn, "the cost of a tariff is also borne primarily by local consumers yet a tariff is the paradigmatic Commerce Clause violation." *West Lynn*, 114 S. Ct. at 2216–2217. Second, Illinois' characterization of the Act as an "agreement to subsidize" does not suffice to fit this case into the "market participant" exception to the negative Commerce Clause created in *Hughes v. Alexandria Scrap Corp.*, 426 U.S. 794. Illinois is not acting as a purchaser of either coal or electricity but as a regulator of utilities. The fact that its regulatory action "has the purpose and effect of subsidizing a particular industry . . . does not transform it into a form of state participation in the free market." *New Energy Co. of Indiana v. Limbach*, 486 U.S. 269, 277 (state tax credit for the use of Ohio-produced ethanol violated the Commerce Clause).

Finally, defendants champion the Illinois Coal Act as a means of protecting Illinois and its citizens from economic harm that would result from a decline in the local coal industry. Such concerns do not justify discrimination against out-of-state producers. "Preservation of local industry by protecting it from the rigors of interstate competition is the hallmark of economic protection that the Commerce Clause prohibit." *West Lynn*, 114 S. Ct. at 2217.

The purpose of the Illinois Coal Act was "to maintain and preserve . . . the mining of coal in Illinois" and to continue "to use Illinois coal as a fuel source." 220 ILCS 5/8–402.1(a). The Illinois Commerce Commission was required to take into account "the need to use coal mined in Illinois." *Id.* The obvious intent was to eliminate western coal use by Illinois generating plants, thus effectively discriminating against western coal. The Commerce Clause compels us to invalidate this statute, and consequently the compliance plans thereunder.

Judgment affirmed.

■ CUDAHY, J., concurring: Although the framework provided by the majority opinion is supportable, I believe that it is incomplete and, at the same time, may overstate the case. When all the conflicting considerations are weighed, there is some basis for concluding that Illinois has crossed the constitutional line, but its actions are probably only the first in a series of efforts to accommodate conflicting but important and legitimate public policies. . . .

The State's most effective argument is that we are dealing with a local (retail) ratemaking and electric operations problem over which the states have plenary authority. Appellants Br. at 33; see *Arkansas Elec. Coop. v. Arkansas Public Serv. Comm'n*, 461 U.S. 375, 395 (1983) (replacing the bright line distinction between state regulation of retail versus wholesale electricity sales with the balancing test of modern Commerce Clause jurisprudence, but reaffirming the general premise of "leaving regulation of retail utility rates largely to the States.") The basic principle under the Coal Act (as elsewhere) for the conduct of electric operations is to arrive at the "least cost" solution. The State argues, in accordance with unimpeachable economic theory, that "cost" means "social cost" and should include the cost of providing compensation for the sectors of society suffering injury from the lost Illinois coal business (such as the cost of unemployment compensation and loss of tax revenue). This is an "externality" not incorporated in ordinary commercial calculations but is a real cost to society nonetheless.

The answer to this argument seems to be that this is an externality that the states may not recognize since the Commerce Clause effectively precludes consideration of local economic damage as a legitimate reason to handicap interstate commerce. *Wyoming*, 112 S. Ct. at 800 ("When the state statute amounts to simple economic protectionism, a virtually per se rule of invalidity has applied."). Another way of handling this problem would be to offset the externality of damage to the Illinois coal industry with the additional externality of the long-term benefit accruing to Illinois from the free trade bias of the Constitution. In any event, the external cost of damage to the Illinois coal industry is something that presumably may not be recognized in computation of "least cost" for present purposes.

Nonetheless, the assurance of rate base treatment for scrubbers (which provide a capability for using Illinois coal) seems a tenuous basis for finding a violation of the Commerce Clause. I believe no Supreme Court case goes so far as clearly to support the conclusion that this is a violation although the trend of the Court's decisions may point this far. (*See* discussion above of *Wyoming*, 502 U.S. 437; *New Energy*, 486 U.S. 269; *Bacchus Imports*, 468 U.S. 263.) It is difficult to perceive the realities here since, as discussed above, we do not know the price and cost relationships involved and, in addition, it is hard to know how far this statute takes us beyond the already existing commercial and regulatory biases.

In this connection, I assume that both the utilities and the Illinois Commerce Commission may have reason to favor Illinois coal even without this legislation. The utilities are pervasively state regulated and simply as a matter of political prudence one would expect them to be more sensitive to major Illinois political and economic interests—like the coal industry and the labor it employs—than to the needs of the same interests in Wyoming or Montana. Similarly, the members of the Illinois Commerce Commission are appointed by a Governor dependent for votes on Illinois' coal-producing areas. One would not expect them to be hard at work furthering the aims of out-of-state mines or railroads. The mandates of the Coal Act may bring a local bias into more focus, but I doubt that they bring about a fundamental shift in preference.

I am also inclined to consider this legislation as possibly vulnerable under the Supremacy Clause. In contrast to the 1978 law, when Congress ordered scrubbers for all new coal plants, in 1990 ... there seems to have been a disposition to leave the matter to the markets. It might be argued that Congress intended to "occupy the field" with a market-based approach, eschewing any mandatory measures. If this were the case, any "putting of thumbs on the scale" by the states might be preempted by the prescribed market-oriented methodology. The relevant Court cases, however, seem to make much easier the striking down of state legislation on Commerce Clause grounds, where relatively little burden or interstate commerce need be shown, than on grounds of preemption, where the requirements seem quite exacting. *See English v. General Electric Co.,* 496 U.S. 72 (1990); *Pacific Gas and Electric,* 461 U.S. 190.

These somewhat inconsistent considerations seem to create a conundrum in the case before us, whatever the standard for striking down state "encouragement" to local industry. In the end, I join, but with significant reservations, in the result reached by the majority opinion.■

NOTES AND COMMENTS

1. The 1990 Clean Air Act Amendments (CAAA90) subjected several hundred existing coal-fired electric generating units to stricter regulation, but gave all power producers greater discretion to create least costly overall strategies to achieve national pollution control targets. The most likely compliance option for the 435, mostly older, electric power units affected by Phase I of the CAAA90 was to switch to low-sulfur coal, and Powder River Basin (PRB) coal was potentially a less expensive source for many of them. During the 2 to 3 years following CAAA90, legislatures and other authorities in Oklahoma, Illinois, Indiana, and Kentucky passed legislation or took other steps to protect in-State coal mining jobs through legal requirements or economic incentives designed to persuade in-State utilities to burn local high-sulfur coals and to install flue gas scrubbers. By 1995 these challenges had been overcome as a result of decisions such as the preceding case finding that the laws violated the interstate commerce clause *See also Alliance for Clean Coal v. Bayh,* 72 F.3d 556 (7th Cir.1995).

2. Western coal already controlled a major part of U.S. coal production by 1990—more than 32 percent—but these rulings encouraged Western coal producers and, especially, Western railroads to invest in equipment and infrastructure improvements. That in turn reassured electricity generators concerned that new fuel switching might overburden the capacity of the systems to deliver, which had begun to happen in 1993 and 1994. Bonskowski, supra at p. 20. In 1999, for the first time, more coal was produced from West of the Mississippi than from East of the Mississippi, and that trend is projected to continue.

d.   CONTINUING AIR POLLUTION CONTROVERSIES

Changes in power plant operation in response to the EPA's acid rain reduction program have brought about substantial reductions in emissions of sulfates. But as the saying goes, no good deed goes unpunished. In 1997, EPA announced the adoption of stricter ambient air quality standards for ozone and a new standard for fine particulate matter. The agency suggested that further reductions in power plant emissions would be needed in order to achieve compliance with these new criteria.[15] The standards were challenged by the affected industries, and on May 14, 1999, a panel of the D.C. Circuit held them invalid because they were based on an erroneous interpretation of EPA's authority under the statute. American Trucking Ass'n v. U.S. E.P.A., 175 F.3d 1027 (D.C.Cir.1999) cert. granted, 68 U.S.L.W. 3724, 68 U.S.L.W. 3739 (2000). *See* Case Note, 113 Harv. L. Rev. 1051 (2000). The court's opinion appears to revive a "non-delegation doctrine" that has been dormant since the 1930s. Cass R. Sunstein, Is the Clean Air Act Unconstitutional?, 98 Mich. L. Rev. 303 (1999).

In addition, however, the EPA has moved forward with other regulations. Its New Source Performance Standards for nitrogen oxide emissions from power plants have been upheld by the D.C. Circuit. *Lignite Energy Council v. U.S. E.P.A.*, 198 F.3d 930 (D.C.Cir.1999). And that court also upheld an EPA rule issued in 1998 that requires 22 states and the District of Columbia to revise their state implementation plans to mitigate the interstate transfer of ozone; this rule is assumed to be aimed at older coal-fired power plants in the South Central states. *State of Michigan v. U.S. E.P.A.*, ___ F.3d ___, 2000 WL 180650 (D.C.Cir.2000). Moreover, as noted above, the EPA and the State of New York have brought litigation charging that many operators of coal-fired power plants have illegally rebuilt old plants that had received exemptions from that standards for new plants on the theory that they would be closed when they reached the end of their useful life.

E.   THE FUTURE OF COAL

Coal has major advantages and disadvantages as an energy source. Its biggest advantage is the sheer volume of it that is available; we will not need to worry about worldwide coal shortages for many generations. Second, the reserves of coal within the United States are sufficiently great that we need not be concerned about interruptions caused by international conflict, which gives coal a major advantage over oil.

Coal has the disadvantage of being a relatively dirty fuel, which means that much more money must be spent on pollution control equipment if one burns burn coal rather than oil or especially natural gas. Second, the

---

15. Electric industry representatives have expressed doubt that power plants are a key source of fine particulate matter, pointing to a lack of monitoring data and modeling procedures for tracking these pollutants. 28 BNA Environment Reporter #9 (June 27, 1997) at 401.

externalities caused by the mining of coal, as described above, are quite significant. Third, and perhaps most important, coal has the big disadvantage of being relatively inflexible in the way it can be used. While it can be conveniently burned under boilers, the cost of transforming it into a liquid or gas that can be more easily transported remains prohibitive, and in our increasingly mobile society this limitation is increasingly serious.

Coal mining has changed much in the last half of the twentieth century. There are several emerging trends: Air pollution problems have led to a heavy emphasis on the quality of coal, particularly in regard to sulfur content. Western mines are accounting for an increased share in total production. Electric utilities have come to dominate the market for coal, typically buying in large quantities. There are fewer total active mines, but the active mines are larger in size. The overall production is increasing in surface mines, as well as underground production from longwall mining.

The market for electric generation, on which coal is heavily dependent, is undergoing major structural changes (see Chapters 11–13, *infra*). For new electric generating plants, natural gas is a powerful competitor to coal:

> Natural gas during the 1990's has captured a significant portion of new electric generating capacity—a section that went primarily to coal-fired units in the previous decade. Real-dollar prices of natural gas, though volatile, have been declining in recent years as supply systems, delivery systems, and market mechanisms have adjusted to natural gas deregulation and new operating routines. Technological advances in combustion—the highly efficient natural gas turbine-based combined-cycle (NGCC) system—along with structural changes in electricity distribution systems have made natural gas the fuel of choice for 88 percent of new utility-owned generating units scheduled to go online between 1998 and 2007. In addition, nonutility generating capacity is currently only 9 to 10 percent as large as utility, but 60 percent of nonutility planned additions, between 1998 and 2001, will be gas-fired. Though environmentally preferable and quicker and less costly to install, most new NGCC units will supplement rather than supplant baseload generating capacity. The NGCC units will add only 6 percent to utility net generation capacity.

> Competition from natural gas has temporarily slowed the growth of new coal-fired generation capacity but consumption of coal still increased by 28 percent from 1986 through 1997, 90 percent of which, by 1997, was used to generate electricity. Coal-fired units account for only 5 percent of planned new units between 1998 and 2007 but coal-fired net generation capacity is projected to grow because of anticipated increased utilization and, after 2007, additions to new capacity. EIA projections between 1997 and 2010, considering scheduled generating capacity additions and baseload mix, anticipate nearly a 14–percent increase in annual coal consumption at electricity generators. These projections, and others like them, provide reasonable assurance of long-term coal markets and motivate large companies, especially with tradi-

tional ties to coal, to hold investment positions in coal for the long term.

Bonskowski, *supra* at p. 18. Whether these EIA projections will hold up may depend to a great extent on what happens to natural gas prices and environmental laws over the next decade.

Perhaps the biggest unknown in coal's future is how the United States and the world will ultimately respond to the problem of the greenhouse effect and its potential warming of the atmosphere. Coal combustion is one of the leading causes of carbon dioxide emissions, and a switch to virtually any other fuel would cause significant reduction in greenhouse gas impact. The issue is discussed in Chapter Seventeen.

CHAPTER 6

OIL

A.   SOME BASICS

1.   THE LONG TERM PRICE OF OIL

Fluctuations in the price of oil have driven much of the legislation enacted by both state and federal governments in the United States. Here is a long-term view of this key determinant of our energy policies:

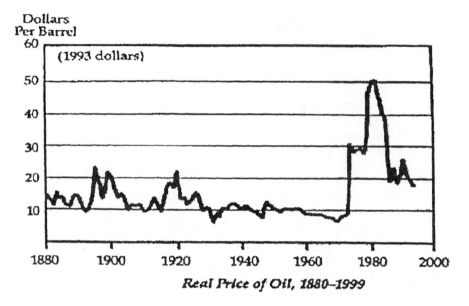

Figure 6–1

Source: Authors' extrapolation from EIA data.

2.   TERMINOLOGY

"Petroleum" is found in certain geological formations under the surface of the earth. In place, it typically consists of a mixture of liquid hydrocarbons called "crude oil," and various gaseous hydrocarbons, primarily methane, known as "natural gas."[1] Like coal, petroleum is considered a fossil fuel because it is the byproduct of millennia of decay and compression of organic material.

For many purposes, the law treats petroleum as a single commodity regardless of whether it consists of crude oil, natural gas or a mixture thereof. For example, standard leases between landowners and oil compa-

---

1. The line between liquid and gas will vary depending on pressure and temperature. For example, condensate is a liquid recovered at the surface from hydrocarbons that were initially in a gaseous phase in the reservoir and in the well bore. The gas condenses into a liquid at the lower temperatures and pressures of the surface.

nies apply to both oil and gas. For other purposes, however, oil and gas[2] have separate legal characteristics; *e.g.*, the system of federal regulation of oil pipelines has been quite different from that of gas pipelines.

Petroleum is found underground in locations where impervious rock forms some sort of dome or trap that prevents the petroleum, which is located in the pore spaces of rock such as sandstone or limestone, from migrating to the surface. If the quantities of discovered petroleum are large enough to be produced profitably, the location is given a specific name, such as "the Seminole field." Such fields are often referred to as pools or reservoirs, but these "pools" are not huge holes or caves in the ground. The pools are sedimentary rocks, which look and feel like concrete. If you spill gasoline or motor oil onto a concrete pavement, much of the liquid will seep into the tiny pore spaces of the concrete rather than remain in a puddle on the surface. Similarly, in reservoirs, oil and gas are stored in the tiny pore spaces of sedimentary rocks, but they are under pressure caused by the weight of hundreds of feet of overlying silt and rock.

Some fields produce only gas (often with accompanying condensate liquids dripped out at the surface), and some produce mainly oil, inevitably accompanied by gas called "casinghead gas." This gas was originally dissolved in the oil underground, but when the pressure is lowered, the gas comes out of solution, much like bubbles of carbon dioxide in a soda drink are released when you pop the top off a soda can.

The oil in some fields is so fully saturated with natural gas that the gas forms a separate layer of lighter hydrocarbons sitting on top of the oil called a "gas cap." Often, the oil and gas layers sit on top of a layer of salt water which is also trapped in the porous rock as pictured in Figure 6–2 below.

The largest oil field in the United States is the Prudhoe Bay field in Alaska. It is a gas cap field containing billions of barrels of oil and trillions of cubic feet of natural gas. To date, only the oil is being produced because it can be shipped 770 miles south through the Trans–Alaskan pipeline to tankers and markets in the lower 48. The increasingly large quantity of gas which comes up with the oil is reinjected back into the reservoir, awaiting a gas pipeline or technological change that can convert the gas to a liquid at competitive market prices. Technology currently exists to convert gas to a liquid called LNG (for liquefied natural gas). Some energy-poor countries like Japan import LNG from energy-rich nations which have no domestic markets for their gas, but this is expensive gas.

---

2. The term "gas" is commonly used as a shorthand term for "gasoline," a liquid derivative of crude oil. In this book, the term "gas" refers to natural gas unless the context makes it obvious that gasoline is intended.

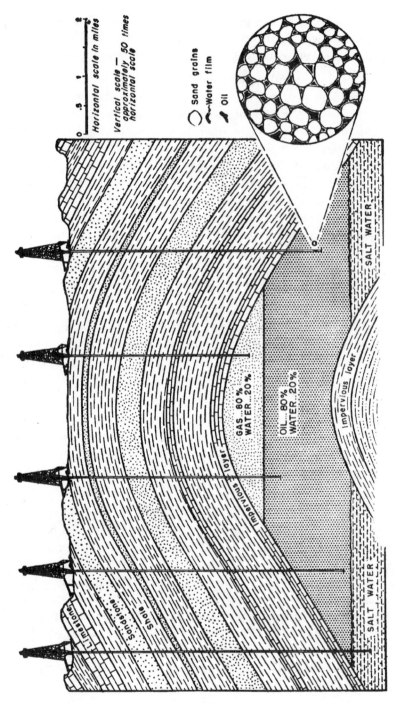

Figure 6–2

[Distribution of fluids within a reservoir. At right is a magnified view of sand grains, with film of water around each grain and oil in remainder of pore space. Source: Richard C. Maxwell, Stephen F. Williams, Patrick H. Martin, Bruce M. Kramer, Oil and Gas: Cases and Materials 9 (6th ed. 1992, Foundation Press).]

3. THE OIL AND GAS LEASE

The United States is unique in that private landowners can own oil and gas and other minerals in the ground as real property. In virtually all the other countries of the world, the state owns the mineral resources. In these countries, oil and gas are typically developed by national oil companies, such as Pemex in Mexico or the Chinese National Petroleum Company, often in joint ventures with multinational corporations such as Exxon and British Petroleum (BP) or Royal Dutch Shell. The relationship between the host country and the corporation is discussed in Chapter 16 on International Petroleum.

In the United States, private ownership of oil and gas has created a body of oil and gas law governed by the common law of property, contract, and tort. This common law operates within a complex framework of state conservation legislation and federal statutes. In addition to this system of private ownership, our federal government owns substantial mineral resources on public lands through its ownership of about 30 percent of the total land area in the United States, located mostly in the western states and Alaska. *E.g.*, 83 percent of Nevada and 68 percent of Alaska are federal land. The federal government also owns the outer continental shelf which produces much oil and gas from offshore wells drilled in the Gulf of Mexico and other coastal areas. The coastal states usually own the first three miles of offshore lands, at which point federal jurisdiction begins. (See Section 6(E) of this Chapter).

Despite this diverse system of private, state, and federal ownership of minerals in the U.S., the exploration and production of oil and gas are typically done pursuant to an "oil and gas lease" between the landowner as lessor (whether private or public) and an oil company (the "operator") as lessee. This core contract is designed to meet the unique needs of an industry exploring for and producing a substance hidden thousands of feet underground. The lessee wants the right, but not the duty, to develop a leasehold for a certain time. If promising deposits are found, the lessee wants the right to hold the lease for as long as profitable production continues.

The typical lessor does not have the capital or technical expertise to develop the oil and gas himself and does not want to bear the costs and risks of drilling and producing wells. Therefore, the lessor transfers the exclusive right to develop the minerals to the lessee in return for a cost-free share of production, called a royalty. In addition, the lessor will bargain with the lessee for a bonus—a one-time cash payment to the lessor for signing the lease. In "hot" territory where discoveries have been found on nearby acreage, the bonus may amount to thousands of dollars an acre. In "wildcat" territory where no operators have yet drilled, the bonus may be a few dollars an acre. If a lessee never drills, or drills only dry holes, the lessor's royalty payments are zero because there is no production, but the lessor has at least received the upfront bonus payment. When the lessor is the state or federal government, leases are usually awarded through competitive auctions to the company that submits the highest bonus bid for a particular tract.

The complex relationship between the lessor and lessee is the mainstay of courses in oil and gas law, but it is premised on these straightforward economic goals of the two parties to the lease. Briefly, a typical oil and gas lease includes three basic clauses:

1.   A granting clause that transfers the mineral estate under the described land to the lessee from the lessor.

2.   The habendum clause which reads "this lease shall be for a primary term of ___ (blank to be filled in) years and as long thereafter as oil or gas is produced from said land."

3.   The royalty clause which grants the lessor a 1/8 royalty on all the oil and gas produced from the lease.

NOTES AND COMMENTS

1.   Test your knowledge of the lessor/lessee relationship:

(a) If you are the lessee, will you bargain for a three year or a ten year primary term in the blank in the habendum clause? If you are the lessor, which will you prefer?

(b) The lessee usually hands the lessor a printed lease form with a 1/8 royalty printed in the royalty clause and hopes that the lessor will not bargain for a higher royalty. However, when oil and gas prices are high and leases are valuable, lessors may be able to secure a 1/6 or greater royalty share. The larger the cost-free royalty, the less money remains for the lessee to pay for all the costs of producing the oil and gas. Conversely, when oil prices dip to record lows, why might a lessor grant temporary royalty relief to a lessee and lower royalties until prices rise to an agreed level? (*See, e.g.*, the Deepwater Royalty Relief Act, which provides incentives to develop domestic deepwater resources by providing royalty holidays for initial production increments).

(c)   If a lessee signs a lease on January 1, 1995 containing a three-year primary term, and has no production on January 1, 1998, what happens to the lease? What if the lessee has no production but is drilling a well on that day? What if the lessee has drilled a number of good wells, but is not yet producing the oil or gas because no pipeline connection exists?

(d) The giant East Texas oil field was discovered on October 9, 1930. Many leases in this field were signed in the 1930s "for 10 years and as long thereafter as oil and gas are produced." The wells on the western part of this field have now "watered out" as the oil has migrated from west to east due to the natural reservoir drive in the field. Are the leases still alive on the western acreage? On the eastern acreage? Is it "fair" to allow the lessees and lessors of eastern wells to produce the oil which originated from someone else's land to the west?

(e) You are the employee for Bigg Oil Company responsible for submitting bids on tracts offered for lease on the outer continental shelf by the Minerals Management Service (the federal agency within the Department of Interior). Would your supervisors or shareholders be happy with you if you won the bid for Tract 91 by offering $1.1 billion when the second highest bidder offered $500,000? What does this difference tell you about the risks of exploration?

2.   The lessee under a typical lease never promises to drill even a single well. If the lessee never drills and never secures production, the lease will terminate automatically at the end of the primary term because of the wording of the habendum clause. Lessors often seek to encourage drilling by contracting for the lessee's payment of annual delay rentals in exchange for the privilege of delaying the commencement of a well. Thus, if a lease has a primary term of 10 years and the lessee does not drill by the end of the first year, the lessee will have to pay delay rentals if it wants to extend the lease for another year. Nonetheless, it is still the lessee's option to either drill or pay delay rentals; there is no contractual obligation to drill.

4.   THE OIL BUSINESS

Between the wellhead and an end–user's gasoline tank, stove top, boiler or blast furnace, oil and gas are transported and processed from lower-valued hydrocarbons, often produced in remote areas of the country, to higher-valued products used in populated centers of industrial activity. The largest companies in the industry are often vertically integrated and operate in all five stages of the value chain: 1. exploration; 2. production; 3. refining; 4. distribution; and 5. marketing. However, a significant number of small, medium, and large size companies also operate as "independent" producers, refiners, transporters and marketers, active in just one or two of the stages. Natural gas is treated like oil for purposes of exploration and production, but it is distributed and marketed through different networks than those used for oil. Crude oil usually flows to a refinery for processing into gasoline, jet fuel, diesel and other products, while gas is often processed in the field to recover hydrocarbon liquids and to eliminate undesirable elements like sulfur and water. The gas then needs no further refining.

a.   EXPLORATION

The exploration staff is led by petroleum geologists who use tools such as seismographs, magnetic surveys from NASA satellites, gravimeters and infrared remote sensors to unlock the earth's buried secrets. Geologists look for underground formations of porous, permeable rock which have trapped oil and gas as illustrated in Figure 6–2.

Despite technological improvements, any exploratory "wildcat" well remains a gamble. In 1975, only 3 out of 100 exploratory wells drilled were commercially successful.[3] Technological progress in supercomputers in the 1990s has allowed the processing of enormous amounts of data from geological surveys. Computers can now produce brightly colored 3–D seismic images which virtually shout "drill here." Three–D seismic can greatly increase the probability of successful drilling. Still, even promising loca-

---

3. Science Service, Petroleum (Nelson Doubleday Inc., 1975) at 27; American Petroleum Institute, Facts about Oil, (no date) at 8: From the Houston Chronicle, July 3, 1999, at 2C: "Conoco will take a $19 million charge in the second quarter to write off an unsuccessful deepwater wildcat well near New Zealand,... [I]t drilled the well 90 miles northwest of Auckland in 4,800 feet of water and found no commercial reserves."

tions can result in "dusters" or dry holes rather than the "gushers" depicted in movies like "Giant."[4]

Today, most of the easy places to find petroleum in the United States have been explored. The most promising areas for discoveries are in deep offshore waters and in the remote Arctic where the challenges and costs of drilling are great. Many of the major oil companies have reallocated their exploration budgets to overseas ventures in places like Russia, China, and Nigeria, where large political risks are added to geological risk and the financial risk of highly fluctuating oil prices.

b. PRODUCTION

The efficient recovery of crude oil from the tiny pore spaces of the reservoir rock is technically rather complicated. When a well bore penetrates the formation, resulting in an area of low pressure, the pressure differential causes oil to flow into the well. Yet crude oil cannot expel itself from the rock. It is the compressed gas or water trapped in the reservoir with the oil that expands in response to the lower pressure at the well bore. The expanding gas or water forces the oil up and out of the well in a displacement process and provides the continuing pressure essential for producing oil without the use of pumps. If the original field pressure is low, or has decreased over time as oil is withdrawn, wells will need to be put "on the pump."

Three types of oil displacement mechanisms exist either alone or in combination. They are the dissolved gas drive, the gas-cap drive, and the water drive.

In the ***dissolved gas drive***, oil in the reservoir contains gas in solution. This dissolved gas expands as a result of the pressure gradient around the well bore and comes out of solution. This free gas fills the void spaces once occupied by the oil flowing out of the well. As oil production proceeds, pressure is reduced throughout the reservoir and more and more gas is freed from solution everywhere. Eventually, the free gas begins to flow into the well along with the oil. The gas-oil ratio of the well increases and reservoir pressure declines continuously until all of the gas originally contained in the reservoir has been withdrawn. At this point there is no more pressure to expel the oil and oil production ceases. Unfortunately, only 10 to 30 percent of the oil in the reservoir can be recovered in a dissolved gas drive.

In the ***gas-cap drive***, the upper part of the reservoir is filled with gas, and oil with dissolved gas lies beneath the gas cap. When a well is drilled into the lower oil zone, the pressure differential causes the compressed gas in the gas cap to expand. The gas cannot expand upward through the impervious rock that traps the hydrocarbons, so it expands into the lower

---

4. No driller today would want to dance in a fountain of black crude erupting from a discovery well like James Dean (playing Jett Rink) does in the movie "Giant." Blowout preventers and proper drilling techniques are used today to prevent such spectacular, but environmentally disastrous, scenes.

oil zone, driving the oil toward the low-pressure area at the well bore. This oil migration continues as the gas cap expands to fill the space voided by withdrawn oil, until the gas invades the lower part of the formation and enters the well. Then, the gas-oil ratio rises sharply, reservoir pressure declines rapidly, and when the gas completely fills the original oil zone, oil production ceases. However, a properly controlled gas-cap drive can result in recovery rates of 25 to 50 percent of the oil. If gas production is prohibited from the gas cap, and oil wells are located to produce only from the lower parts of the reservoir, the gas in the gas cap can be retained in the formation for a longer period of time. This maintains pressure in the reservoir and allows more oil to be flushed out. The same effects can be had if any gas produced from the gas cap is returned continuously to the formation.

In a *water drive* field, the oil lies atop a layer of compressed water which expands upward slightly when the pressure reduction from the well bore spreads outward. Water is a more effective pushing agent than gas and can "scrub" the reservoir rock more thoroughly as it migrates through the pore spaces. The water drives the oil in front of it toward the well bore. Eventually, as the water invades the oil zone, more water and less oil are produced from the wells. Oil production ceases when the cost of operating the uppermost wells exceeds the value of the oil withdrawn from them. It is not loss of pressure that causes abandonment of the reservoir but the fact that the oil content of the rock has been depleted. Recovery rates of 75 to 85 percent are possible if the reservoir is operated to preserve the flushing action of the water. This requires that the oil be produced largely from wells located in the upper part of the reservoir having low water-oil ratios . Wells bottomed in the lower zone will produce large amounts of water with the oil and will dissipate the reservoir's source of pressure unless the withdrawn water is continually reinjected into the formation

Thus, two factors must be controlled to produce a reservoir efficiently: (1) the rate of production; and (2) the location of wells. A controlled rate of production maintains reservoir pressure by preventing the rapid release of dissolved gas from solution. It also assures that the boundary between the migrating oil and the advancing gas or water front is fairly uniform so that the entire reservoir is effectively flushed without bypassing areas of oil-saturated rock.

The proper location of wells also increases recovery rates. No wells should be allowed to produce gas from the gas cap until all of the oil is flushed out; and oil wells in a water-drive field should be located high on the structure where they will not prematurely produce large amounts of water and dissipate the water drive.

Thus, for each reservoir there is generally a dominant displacement mechanism, an optimal pattern of well locations, and a maximum efficient rate of production (called the MER) which, if exceeded, will lead to an avoidable loss of ultimate oil recovery. The MER of a field is determined technically through engineering studies. The use of the MER to control production rates is probably the single most important conservation measure for assuring efficient oil recovery.

Further improvements in production efficiency can result from artificial pressure maintenance activities such as injecting water or gas into the reservoir. The injected gas or water may be recycled from the reservoir or brought in from extraneous sources. Many of the older fields in West Texas are being repressured with carbon dioxide delivered through a 400–mile pipeline from natural deposits of this gas in Colorado.

The recovery of natural gas is much less complicated than recovery of crude oil because gas is highly expansible. It can be recovered from porous rock simply by allowing it to migrate by expansion into the low-pressure area around the well bore. This process commonly can recover 90 percent or more of the original gas in place. Recovery rates less than this occur only when the permeability of the reservoir rock is so low that gas cannot flow freely into the well bore. This is called a "tight sand" formation. Operators will often use hydraulic fracturing to create cracks in the formation so that the gas can flow freely. Fluids are forced under high pressure down the well bore to crack the tight formation. In "Project Gas Buggy," one of the more spectacular efforts to promote the peaceful use of atomic energy after World War II, the federal government exploded a nuclear bomb underground in New Mexico to fracture the formation and stimulate the flow of gas. Although a technical success, the gas was too radioactive to market.

c.   REFINING

Crude oil in its natural state is of little practical value. It is a complex chemical compound consisting of a mixture of hundreds of hydrocarbon compounds, each having its own boiling point. Refining separates these compounds into desired products such as gasoline, jet fuel, kerosene, diesel fuel, heating oil, and asphalt. Petroleum hydrocarbons are also the source of many feedstocks for chemical plants producing everything from nylons to insecticides.

Refining first separates the hydrocarbons in crude oil by heating them and distilling the different vapor streams which result at different temperatures. Heated crude oil is sent to a fractionation tower which may be a hundred feet high.

The hydrocarbons with the lowest boiling points, such as gasoline, will vaporize first. As other hydrocarbons rise and then cool, they condense at different heights in the tower and are withdrawn as separate products, as shown in Figure 6–3.

Distillation of crude oil into its fractions does not produce the correct proportion of products demanded by the marketplace. For example, it produces relatively small amounts of gasoline. Therefore, refineries use thermal cracking and catalytic cracking to break larger hydrocarbon molecules into smaller ones that will rise to the top of the fractionation tower.

FRACTIONATION

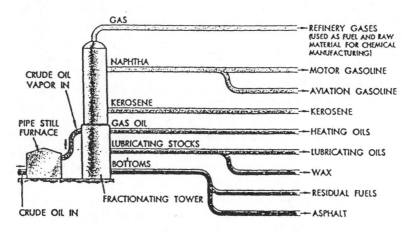

Figure 6–3. Science Service, Petroleum at 35 (undated).

Oil refineries pose major problems of air and water pollution. Many refineries are located in sensitive coastal areas because they are designed to receive and ship products by tanker. In addition, refineries process tremendous quantities of liquids and vapors at high temperatures and high pressures. Explosions and blasts, while rare, can kill and injure workers and seriously affect the health and property of people living in surrounding neighborhoods.

As noted earlier, natural gas is not refined in the way that crude oil is. The gas that comes out of the well may require some treatment, such as removal of sulfur, but this is a much simpler operation than the refining of petroleum.

d. TRANSPORTATION AND DISTRIBUTION

In general, the method of distributing petroleum compounds varies with their relative weight. Heavy compounds, like asphalt, usually go by truck, rail or barge. Liquids can vary from heavy crude, which is like molasses, to gasoline, which evaporates readily. Heavy crude usually goes by tanker or barge, although it may go by pipeline if it is not too heavy to flow. Refined products are typically distributed by pipeline to a terminal and then by truck or train to the ultimate user. Natural gas can be liquefied and shipped by LNG tankers, but it is far more commonly transported by pipeline.

The retail marketing of gasoline is discussed in Chapter 15. Crude oil is a "niche" fuel. Its refined products are used primarily in the transportation sector of the U.S. economy. In 1997, this sector used 78 percent of the oil consumed in the United States.

A "spaghetti bowl" of pipes underlies cities like Houston located near producing fields and refinery complexes. A large network of interstate pipelines moves oil and gas from the producing states to consuming centers. Pipelines are specialized for natural gas and different types of petroleum products. In 1906, oil pipelines were regulated as common carriers by federal law. *See* the Hepburn Act Amendment of 1906, Pub. L. No. 357, 34 Stat. 584 (1906). At that time, the major pipeline companies attempted to circumvent this Act by transporting only oil produced from their own leases or purchased at the wellhead, thereby refusing to hold themselves out as public pipelines for hire. In *The Pipeline Cases*, 234 U.S. 548 (1914), the U.S. Supreme Court held that the 1906 law applied to interstate pipelines, even if the pipeline owned the oil being transported. Justices Holmes wrote: "Availing itself of its monopoly of the means of transportation the Standard Oil Company refused through its subordinates to carry any oil unless the same was sold to it or to them and through them to it on terms more or less dictated by itself. In this way it made itself master of the fields without the necessity of owning them and carried ... a great subject of international commerce coming from many owners but, by the duress of which the Standard Oil Company was master, carrying it all as its own." *Id.* at 559. *See* George S. Wolbert, Jr., The Pipe Line Story, 4 Okla. L. Rev. 305–36 (1951); Edwin I. Malet, Oil Pipelines as Common Carriers: Issues of Form and Substance, 20 Hous. L. Rev. 801 (1983).

The technology for gas pipelines did not exist in 1906. Gas pipelines were regulated in 1938 when the Natural Gas Act was passed in recognition of the monopoly power of interstate gas pipelines.

B. THE EARLY HISTORY OF PETROLEUM

1. OIL BEFORE PETROLEUM

a. OF WHALES AND WAX

In the newly formed United States, the primary source of power for mills and other growing industries was water power. Water could turn wheels, but it could not produce light. For illumination, most people still relied on candles and fireplaces. Wealthier people were able to light their homes with oil lamps, which produced a brighter and more reliable flame, but the animal and vegetable fats used to fuel such lamps were expensive. The premium fuel, whale oil, became increasingly expensive as the whalers wiped out the whale populations of the Atlantic and had to travel to the Antarctic to obtain supplies.

Until the end of the eighteenth century, artificial indoor light came only in units of one candle. Bright illumination was possible only through massive multiplication of these tiny sources. Candles convert only about 0.01 percent of their chemical energy into light. The bright spot in a candle flame has an average irradiance (rate of energy falling on a unit area) just 20 percent higher than clear sky. The first eighteenth-century lighting innovations doubled and tripled this low performance. In 1794, Aime Argand introduced lamps that could be regulated for maximum luminosity by using wick holders with a central air supply and chimneys to draw in the air. Soon afterward came the first lighting gas made from coal. This was "town gas" which was piped into street lamps and the homes of middle- and upper-class families in urban areas. Town gas was too expensive for many households, however. For more than half of the nineteenth century, tens of millions of rural households around the world continued to fill their lamps with an exotic biomass fuel—the oil rendered from the blubber of sperm whales.

Whaling, a poorly paid and dangerous way of life—portrayed so unforgettably in 1851 in Melville's "Moby Dick"—reached its peak just before 1850. The American whaling fleet, by far the largest in the world, had a record total of more than 7900 vessels in 1846. As the number of sperm whales dwindled and competition from coal gas and kerosene increased, whaling rapidly declined. This was the first Tragedy of the Commons to affect America's energy supplies.

b. KEROSENE

In the 1850s a Canadian inventor discovered a way to extract a liquid from natural deposits of tar and asphalt. He called this liquid, which could be burned in existing oil lamps, kerosene. Although expensive, it produced higher quality illumination than vegetable or animal oils, and a number of firms began to produce it. The kerosene lamp then became a common fixture in the homes and offices of the wealthy.

The growing market for kerosene increased the interest in learning more about the still mysterious properties of oil. This interest "arose from pure necessity," writes Daniel Yergin, because "[b]urgeoning populations and the spreading economic development of the industrial revolution had increased the demand for artificial illumination beyond the simple wick dipped into some animal grease or vegetable fat, which was the best that most could afford over the ages, if they could afford anything at all."[5]

c. THE FIRST OIL WELL

As storm clouds were gathering for the Civil War, the discovery of oil in Pennsylvania foretold a breakthrough in energy utilization that would rank with the great technological advances of all time. The tar-like substances that provided the source material for kerosene were scarce and difficult to process, so kerosene remained an expensive luxury. Until 1859, petroleum was gathered from natural seeps and springs or skimmed off ponds. Then, in 1859, the Pennsylvania Rock Oil Company hired Edwin Drake to drill a well near an old oil spring, using a rig made from an old steam engine and an iron bit attached by a rope to a wooden windlass. The drill bit hit oil at 69 feet below the surface. "Drake's Folly" had proved the practicality of a new technique for tapping liquid petroleum from the earth.

---

5. Daniel Yergin, The Prize: The Epic Quest for Oil, Money and Power 22–23 (1991). Yergin's book is the classic history of the oil industry. A documentary, based on the book, is periodically aired by public television stations and is also available in videocassette form.

The discovery that oil could be found by drilling sparked a "gold rush" into the northwestern Pennsylvania region. Wild speculation in land followed as prospectors rushed into the area to try their luck. No one knew why oil could be found in one place but not another, so whenever someone struck oil everyone else scurried to buy up the rights to nearby land. "Close-ology" was the geology of the day. In 1861, the first refinery went into operation in this region, producing mostly kerosene. To supply more distant refineries, railroads built spurs into the region, and in 1865 a railroad tank car was developed especially for carrying crude in two large wooden tanks. As large quantities of Pennsylvania oil reached the market, the price of kerosene dropped dramatically and the kerosene lamp became the basic source of lighting for homes and businesses all over the eastern United States.

2. THE RULE OF CAPTURE: THE TRAGEDY OF THE COMMONS I

The discovery of oil, and then natural gas, from wells tapping underground reservoirs, posed a novel legal question. Who owned the oil and gas? The courts' resolution of this issue had a major impact on the way that the oil business was conducted.

Barnard v. Monongahela Natural Gas Co.

216 Pa. 362, 65 A. 801 (1907).

[Daniel and Elizabeth Barnard brought a bill in equity against the Monangahela Natural Gas Company for an injunction and an accounting. The plaintiffs owned a 66–acre farm adjoining the 156–acre farm owned by James Barnard. The gas company held leases on both farms. James' farm joined the other Barnards' farm in such a way that one corner of his farm formed an angle of about 12 degrees less than a right angle. A circle large enough to include ten acres with its center at this corner would enclose 2½ acres of James' land and 7½ acres of Daniel and Elizabeth's land. The gas company drilled a well on James' farm near the corner of this angle, only 35 feet from the line dividing the two farms.

On appeal, the supreme court, *per curiam*, dismissed the bill in equity, quoting the opinion of the court below as follows:]

The first question stated broadly is this: "Can a landowner in gas territory drill a well on his farm close to the line of his adjoining landowner and draw from the land of the latter three-fourths of the gas that his well may produce without so invading the property rights of the adjoining landowner as to be legally accountable therefore?" There is no doubt that the oil and gas confined in the oil and gas-bearing sands of a farm belong to the one who holds title to the farm, but it is also recognized, both as a question of fact and law, that oil and gas are fugitive in their nature, and will by reason of inherent pressure seek any opening from the earth's surface that may reach the sand where they are confined. . . .

The right of every landowner to drill a well on his own land at whatever spot he may see fit certainly must be conceded. If, then, the landowner drills on his own land at such a spot as best subserves his purposes, what is the standing of the adjoining landowner whose oil or gas may be drained by this well? He certainly ought not to be allowed to stop his neighbor from developing his own farm. There is no certain way of ascertaining how much of the oil and gas that comes out of the well was when in situ under this farm and how much under that. What then has been held to be the law? It is this, as we understand it, every landowner or his lessee may locate his wells wherever he pleases, regardless of the interests of others. He may distribute them over the whole farm or locate them only on one part of it. He may crowd the adjoining farms so as to enable him to draw the oil and gas from them. What then can the neighbor do? Nothing; only go and do likewise. He must protect his own oil and gas. He knows it is wild and will run away if it finds an opening and it is his business to keep it at home. This may not be the best rule; but neither the Legislature nor our highest court has given us any better. No doubt many thousands of dollars have been expended 'in protecting lines' in oil and gas territory that would not have been expended if some rule had existed by which it could have been avoided. Injunction certainly is not the remedy. If so, just how far must the landowner be from the line of his neighbor to avoid the blow of 'this strong arm of the law'?■

NOTES AND COMMENTS

1. The rule of capture adopted for oil and gas was based, perhaps surprisingly, on the principle expressed in the famous case of *Pierson v. Post*, 3 Cai. R. 175 (N.Y.Sup.1805) involving ownership of a wild fox. In *Westmoreland & Cambria Natural Gas Co. v. De Witt*, 130 Pa. 235, 18 A. 724 (1889), the court wrote:

> Water and oil, and still more strongly gas, may be classed by themselves, if the analogy be not too fanciful, as minerals ferae naturae. In common with animals, and unlike other minerals, they have the power and the tendency to escape without the volition of the owner. Their "fugitive and wandering existence within the limits of a particular tract was uncertain." . . . They belong to the owner of the land, and are part of it, so long as they are on or in it, and are subject to his control; but when they escape, and go into other land . . . the title of the former owner is gone. Possession of the land, therefore is not necessarily possession of the gas.

2. The rule of capture has been adopted in all oil and gas producing states. On January 10, 1901, the greatest gusher the world had ever seen erupted in Spindletop, Texas, spewing over 75,000 barrels of oil a day over the coastal plain. Does it surprise you that Spindletop's Boiler Avenue looked like this in 1903?

Figure 6–4

Boiler Avenue at Spindletop. Photo courtesy of American Petroleum Institute. This photo and many others, just as picturesque, appear in Walter Rundell, Jr., Early Texas Oil: A Photographic History 1866–1936 (Texas A & M Press 1977).

Land that had once been pig pastures sold for as much as $900,000 an acre. A glut of oil dropped the price to as little as three cents a barrel, while a cup of water cost five cents. The boom, however, was short-lived. Rapid and uncontrolled production depleted the field's pressure so quickly that by 1903 the field had begun to decline and within ten years, Spindletop was a virtual ghost town. Less than five percent of the field's oil was produced.

3. Many natural gas reservoirs have produced all of the native gas originally in the pore spaces of the reservoir formation. These depleted reservoirs are valuable "pieces of rock," especially when they are located

near cities or industry, because they can be used to store gas which has been produced and transported from other distant fields. The gas is pumped into the pore spaces of the depleted reservoir and then can be quickly extracted when, for instance, a cold snap hits and homeowners all turn up the thermostats on their gas furnaces. Underground storage is usually the only feasible and safe method of storing large quantities of natural gas.

In *Lone Star Gas Co. v. Murchison*, 353 S.W.2d 870 (Tex.Civ.App. 1962), the plaintiff, Lone Star, was a public utility engaged in the business of distributing natural gas to a large number of customers. Because the demand for gas, especially for residential use, fluctuates widely, Lone Star stored gas during periods of low demand and withdrew it to meet periods of peak demand. Lone Star had acquired the rights to all of the underground formation except for a small amount of acreage underlying the Jackson land. The Jacksons leased this land to Murchison and he drilled a well into the gas formation and started extracting large quantities of gas. Lone Star sought an injunction to prevent the Murchison well from producing gas, and also sued for damages for conversion of its gas.

Should the rule of capture apply to stored gas? The Texas courts said no, holding that stored gas is the personal property of the storer.

Could Murchison then claim that Lone Star was trespassing on his property? Lone Star's gas molecules were invading his mineral estate without his permission. The court ducked this question, writing that "[t]he status of this record is such ... that we must, as Ulysses 'lash ourselves to the mast and resist Siren's songs' of trespass." *Id.* at 875. How would you be tempted to rule on the trespass issue? If you find a trespass, would you grant Murchison an injunction against the gas storer? What if it is impossible for Lone Star to "fence off" its part of the reservoir? Unlike wild animals, Lone Star cannot corral its molecules into a holding pen to prevent them from escaping on to Murchison's tract. Yet an injunction will destroy the value of the reservoir as a storage device. Lone Star could offer to lease Murchison's subsurface estate. If other landowners had leased for a dollar an acre, do you think Murchison will accept this amount? Or will he demand, say, $1,000 an acre, to buy out his trespass cause of action? Is this "extortion" to allow Murchison to extract monopoly rents from Lonestar?

If you were a Texas legislator, would you vote for a statute which authorized public utility companies to exercise the right of eminent domain over depleted gas reservoirs which can be used for storage? Why would such a law operate in the public interest?

3.   An early Kentucky case held that the rule of capture applied to stored gas. *See Hammonds v. Central Kentucky Natural Gas Co.*, 75 S.W.2d 204 (1934). In 1987, the Kentucky Supreme Court was asked to render a declaratory judgment by joint petition of a bank and a gas storer. The bank wanted to loan the gas company $24 million to finance the purchase of gas to be stored in a Kentucky field. The question arose: Should the bank secure its loan with a lien against the gas as personal property under Article 9 of the Uniform Commercial Code, or with a real estate mortgage?

In *Texas American Energy Corp. v. Citizens Fidelity Bank & Trust Co.*, 736 S.W.2d 25 (Ky.1987), the court distinguished the earlier *Hammonds* case as follows:

> In *Hammonds* there was a known "leak" in the gas storage reservoir inasmuch as Mrs. Hammonds' land was, in fact, a part of the natural reservoir, though not controlled by the storage company. In the case at hand, however, it has been stipulated that the gas reservoir has total integrity, and the gas cannot escape nor can it be extracted by anyone other than [Texas American Energy]. Using the *ferae naturae* analogy, [Texas American] has captured the wild fox, hence reducing it to personal property. The fox has not been released in another forest, permitting it to revert to the common property of mankind; but rather, the fox has only been released in a private confinement zoo. The fox is no less under the control of [Texas American] than if it were on a leash.

Id. at 28.

4. Are there any other limits to the rule of capture under the common law in addition to the exception for stored gas? Suppose the driller next door to you negligently blows out a well, creating an enormous low pressure area to which your gas rapidly flows and erupts in a fiery inferno that can be seen for miles around. Is the driller shielded from liability for draining all of your gas because of the rule of capture?

Elliff v. Texon Drilling Co.

210 S.W.2d 558 (Tex. 1948).

[Plaintiff owned land overlying a gas field. Defendant was engaged in drilling a well on the neighboring tract only 466 feet east of plaintiff's property line. The well struck gas under high pressure, and exploded and burned, resulting in the waste of a large part of the petroleum in the reservoir. Plaintiff sought to recover damages for the hydrocarbons lost from underneath plaintiff's land. The jury found that the drilling company had been negligent in blowing out the well.]

■ FOLLEY, J.: ... In our state the landowner is regarded as having absolute title in severalty to the oil and gas in place beneath his land [citations]. The only qualification of that rule of ownership is that it must be considered in connection with the law of capture and is subject to police regulations. The oil and gas beneath the soil are considered a part of the realty. Each owner of land owns separately, distinctly and exclusively all the oil and gas under his land and is accorded the usual remedies against trespassers who appropriate the minerals or destroy their market value.

The conflict in the decisions of the various states with reference to the character of ownership is traceable to some extent to the divergent views entertained by the courts, particularly in the earlier cases, as to the nature and migratory character of oil and gas in the soil. 31A Tex. Jur. 24, Sec. 5. In the absence of common law precedent, and owing to the lack of scientific information as to the movement of these minerals, some of the courts have sought by analogy to compare oil and gas to other types of property such as wild animals, birds, subterranean waters, and other migratory things, with reference to which the common law had established rules denying any character of ownership prior to capture. However, as was said by Professor A. W. Walker, Jr., of the School of Law of the University of Texas: "There is no oil or gas producing state today which follows the wild-animal analogy to its logical conclusion that the landowner has no property interest in the oil and gas in place." 16 T.L.R. 370, 371. In the light of modern scientific knowledge these early analogies have been disproved, and courts generally have come to recognize that oil and gas, as commonly found in underground reservoirs, are securely entrapped in a static condition in the original pool, and, ordinarily, so remain until disturbed by penetrations from the surface. It is further established, nevertheless, that these minerals will migrate across property lines towards any low pressure area created by production from the common pool. This migratory character of oil and gas has given rise to the so-called rule or law of capture. That rule simply is that the owner of a tract of land acquires title to the oil or gas which he produces from wells on his land, though part of the oil or gas may have migrated from adjoining lands. He may thus appropriate the oil and gas that have flowed from adjacent lands without the consent of the owner of those lands, and without incurring liability to him for drainage. The nonliability is based upon the theory that after the drainage the title or property interest of the former owned is gone. This rule, at first blush, would seem to conflict with the view of absolute ownership of the minerals in place, but it was otherwise decided in the early case of *Stephens County v. Mid–Kansas Oil & Gas Co.*, 254 S.W. 290, 292 (1923). Mr. Justice Greenwood there stated:

"The objection lacks substantial foundation that gas or oil in a certain tract of land cannot be owned in place, because subject to appropriation, without the consent of the owner of the tract, through drainage from wells on adjacent lands. If the owners of adjacent lands have the right to appropriate, without liability, the gas and oil underlying their neighbor's land, then their neighbor has the correlative right to appropriate, through like methods of drainage, the gas and oil underlying the tracts adjacent to his own."

Thus it is seen that, notwithstanding the fact that oil and gas beneath the surface are subject both to capture and administrative regulation, the fundamental rule of absolute ownership of the minerals in place is not affected in our state. In recognition of such ownership, our courts, in decisions involving well-spacing regulations of our Railroad Commission, have frequently announced the sound view that each landowner should be afforded the opportunity to produce his fair share of the recoverable oil and gas beneath his land, which is but another way of recognizing the existence of correlative rights between the various landowners over a common reservoir of oil or gas.

It must be conceded that under the law of capture there is no liability for reasonable and legitimate drainage from the common pool. The land-owner is privileged to sink as many wells as he desires upon his tract of land and extract therefrom and appropriate all the oil and gas that he may produce, so long as he operates within the spirit and purpose of conservation statutes and orders of the Railroad Commission. These laws and regulations are designed to afford each owner a reasonable opportunity to produce his proportionate part of the oil and gas from the entire pool and to prevent operating practices injurious to the common reservoir. In this manner, if all operators exercise the same degree of skill and diligence, each owner will recover in most instances his fair share of the oil and gas. This reasonable opportunity to produce his fair share of the oil and gas is the landowner's common law right under our theory of absolute ownership of the minerals in place. But from the very nature of this theory the right of each land holder is qualified, and is limited to legitimate operations. Each owner whose land overlies the basin has a like interest, and each must of necessity exercise his right with some regard to the rights of others. No owner should be permitted to carry on his operations in reckless or lawless irresponsibility, but must submit to such limitations as are necessary to enable each to get his own.

While we are cognizant of the fact that there is a certain amount of reasonable and necessary waste incident to the production of oil and gas to which the non-liability rule must also apply, we do not think this immunity should be extended so as to include the negligent waste or destruction of the oil and gas.

In Summers, Oil and Gas, Permanent Edition, Volume 1, page 142, correlative rights of owners of land in a common source of supply of oil and gas are discussed and described in the following language:

"These existing property relations, called the correlative rights of the owners of land in the common source of supply, were not created by the statute, but held to exist because of the peculiar physical facts of oil and gas. The term 'correlative rights' is merely a convenient method of indicating that each owner of land in a common source of supply of oil and gas has legal privileges as against other owners of land therein to take oil or gas therefrom by lawful operations conducted on his own land; that each such owner has duties to the other owners not to exercise his privilege of taking so as to injure the common source of supply; and that each such owner has rights that other owners not exercise their privileges of taking so as to injure the common source of supply."

. . .

In like manner, the negligent waste and destruction of petitioners' gas and distillate was neither a legitimate drainage of the minerals from beneath their lands nor a lawful or reasonable appropriation of them. Consequently, the petitioners did not lose their right, title and interest in them under the law of capture. At the time of their removal they belonged to petitioner, and their wrongful dissipation deprived these owners of the right and opportunity to produce them. That right is forever lost, the same cannot be restored, and petitioners are without an adequate legal remedy unless we allow a recovery under the same common law which governs other actions for damages and under which the property rights in oil and gas are vested. This remedy should not be denied.

... The fact that the major portion of the gas and distillate[6] escaped from the well on respondents' premises is immaterial. Irrespective of the opening from which the minerals escaped, they belonged to the petitioners and the loss was the same. They would not have been dissipated at any opening except for the wrongful conduct of the respondents. Being responsible for the loss they are in no position to deny liability because the gas and distillate did not escape through the surface of petitioners' lands.■

C.   STATE CONSERVATION REGULATION

1.   PREVENTING PHYSICAL WASTE

Ohio Oil Co. v. Indiana

177 U.S. 190 (1900).

[The state of Indiana adopted a statute in 1893, requiring the operator of any oil or gas well to confine the flow of oil or gas into a pipeline or other safe receptacle within two days of discovery. The state attorney general sued the Ohio Oil Company to enjoin it from allowing gas to escape. Ohio Oil had drilled five wells producing both oil and gas. The oil stratum was connected with a large gas reservoir which supplied fuel to cities in the area. The complaint stated that maintenance of "back pressure" was necessary to prevent salt water encroachment, and the continued flow of gas from defendant's well destroyed this pressure.[7] Ohio Oil contended that it was impossible to produce the oil without producing the gas; that the gas had no value to the defendant; and that enforcing the statute deprived it of the right to produce oil.]

■ WHITE, J.: The assignments of error all in substance are resolvable into one proposition; which is, that the enforcement of the provisions of the Indiana statute as against the plaintiff in error, constituted a taking of private property without adequate compensation, and therefore amounted to a denial of due process of law in violation of the Fourteenth Amendment.

When this proposition is analyzed by the light of the facts which are admitted on the record, it becomes apparent that the foundation upon which it must rest involves two contentions which are in conflict one with

---

6. Editors' note: Distillate is condensate, *i.e.*, the liquids dripped out of "wet" gas.

7. From the court's description, the field appeared to have a gas-cap drive and a water drive. Ohio Oil had drilled oil wells which were producing large amounts of casinghead gas. Until the late 1950s, casinghead gas was often an undesirable byproduct of oil production. Operators burned it at the well head, which is called "flaring."

the other; in other words, the argument by which alone it is possible to sustain the claim becomes, when truly comprehended, self-destructive. Thus, it is apparent, from the admitted facts, that the oil and gas are commingled and contained in a natural reservoir which lies beneath an extensive area of country, and that as thus situated the gas and oil are capable of flowing from place to place, and are hence susceptible of being drawn off by wells from any point, provided they penetrate into the reservoir.... From this it must necessarily come to pass that the entire volume of gas and oil is in some measure liable to be decreased by the act of any one who, within the superficial area, bores wells from the surface and strikes the reservoir containing the oil and gas. And hence, of course, it is certain, if there can be no authority exerted by law to prevent the waste of the entire supply of gas and oil, or either, that the power which exists in every one who has the right to bore from the surface and tap the reservoir involves, in its ultimate conception, the unrestrained license to waste the entire contents of the reservoir by allowing the gas to be drawn off and to be dispersed in the atmospheric air, and by permitting the oil to flow without use or benefit to any one. These things being lawful, as they must be if the acts stated cannot be controlled by law, it follows that no particular individual having a right to make borings can complain, and thus the entire product of oil and gas can be destroyed by any one of the surface owners. The proposition, then, which denies the power in the State to regulate by law the manner in which the gas and oil may be appropriated, and thus prevent their destruction, of necessity involves the assertion that there can be no right of ownership in and to the oil and gas before the same have been actually appropriated by being brought into the possession of some particular person. But it cannot be that property as to a specified thing vests in one who has no right to prevent any other person from taking or destroying the object which is asserted to be the subject of the right of property. The whole contention, therefore, comes to this: that property has been taken without due process of law, in violation of the Fourteenth Amendment, because of the fact that the thing taken was not property, and could not, therefore, be brought within the guarantees ordained for the protection of property....

Hence it is that the legislative power, from the peculiar nature of the right and the objects upon which it is to be exerted, can be manifested for the purpose of protecting all the collective owners ... by preventing waste. This necessarily implied legislative authority is borne out by the analogy suggested by things *ferae naturae* which it is unquestioned the legislature has the authority to forbid all from taking, in order to protect them from undue destruction, so that the right of the common owners, the public, to reduce to possession, may be ultimately efficaciously enjoyed. Viewed, then, as a statute to protect or to prevent the waste of the common property ... [the law here attached] is a statute protecting private property and preventing it from being taken by one of the common owners without regard to the enjoyment of the others....

[W]e cannot say that the statute amounts to a taking of private property, when it is but a regulation by the State of Indiana of a subject which especially comes within its lawful authority.█

NOTES AND COMMENTS

1. *Ohio Oil Co. v. Indiana* was one of the earliest cases to recognize the doctrine of correlative rights, which appeared in the *Elliff v. Texon Drilling Co.* case *supra* involving negligent drainage. The doctrine holds that each owner of a common source of supply has both legal rights and legal duties toward the other owners. The strongest right continues to be the rule of capture if exercised properly under common law tort principles and in compliance with a broad range of state conservation laws which were enacted after 1900. Does the doctrine of correlative rights guarantee that each owner of a common reservoir receive a fair share of the oil and gas in the reservoir, even if that owner never drills a well? Or does it guarantee only the opportunity to produce a fair share, which if unexercised, allows one owner to drain another without liability?

2.   Does this Indiana statute ensure that this reservoir will be produced at its Maximum Efficient Rate of Recovery (MER)? Should any wells be producing gas from the gas cap? Should Ohio Oil be allowed to market its gas rather than reinject it into the gas cap?

2.   DEMAND AND SUPPLY: PREVENTING ECONOMIC WASTE WITH MARKET DEMAND PRORATIONING

With the discovery of oil at Spindletop in 1901, the mad rush was on to explore for oil in Texas and the neighboring states of Oklahoma and Louisiana. Many large oil and gas fields were discovered in the next few decades, leading to a sharp increase in oil production in the familiar "boom and bust" pattern caused by the rule of capture. Fortuitously, the invention of the gasoline-powered engine sparked an enormous increase in the demand for gasoline. In the 19th century, the primary use for petroleum had been for kerosene. In the 20th century, the primary use soon became gasoline for the "horseless carriage." Kerosene sales shrank to negligible levels after Thomas Edison's invention of the incandescent light bulb.

The excessive well drilling and wasteful production engendered by the rule of capture were difficult to ignore. States began to enact conservation legislation like that in *Ohio Oil,* and created regulatory agencies to implement the new laws. Many states enacted well spacing rules which provided that no well could be drilled on less than a certain number of acres or closer than so many feet from an existing well. However, these regulations were often not enforced in situations where small lots already existed. Moreover, well spacing alone did not address the most important factor affecting the ultimate percentage of oil recovered from a field: the field's production rate.

In addition, producers were battered by the widely fluctuating swings in the price of oil. Flush production from the Seminole field in Oklahoma and the great East Texas field caused the price to drop from three dollars a barrel in 1920 to as low as ten cents a barrel in the early 1930s. Some operators imposed voluntary controls on themselves, such as a moratorium on new drilling until pipeline capacity and storage facilities were enlarged to handle the increased flow. However, most voluntary efforts to conserve were doomed to failure under the inexorable logic of the Tragedy of the Commons. Many operators pressed their state legislators to enact pro-rationing statutes which would authorize a state agency to restrict production in a field by establishing a maximum "allowable" that each well could produce. Inevitably, such a statute was challenged in court.

Champlin Refining Co. v. Corporation Commission of Oklahoma

286 U.S. 210 (1932).

■ BUTLER, J.: The refining company by this suit seeks to enjoin the commission, attorney general and other state officers from enforcing certain provisions of c. 25 of the laws of Oklahoma enacted February 11, 1915,[1][8] and certain orders of the commission on the ground that they are

8. C.O.S. 1921, §§ 7954–7963.

§ 1. That the production of crude oil or petroleum in the State of Oklahoma, in such a manner and under such conditions as to constitute waste, is hereby prohibited. [§ 7954.]

§ 2. That the taking of crude oil or petroleum from any oil-bearing sand or sands in the State of Oklahoma at a time when there is not a market demand therefor at the well at a price equivalent to the actual value of such crude oil or petroleum is hereby prohibited, and the actual value of such crude oil or petroleum at any time shall be the average value as near as may be ascertained in the United States at retail of the by-products of such crude oil or petroleum when refined less the cost and a reasonable profit in the business of transporting, refining and marketing the same, and the Corporation Commission of this State is hereby invested with the authority and power to investigate and determine from time to time the actual value of such crude oil or petroleum by the standard herein provided, and when so determined said Commission shall promulgate its findings by its orders duly made and recorded, and publish the same in some newspaper of general circulation in the State. [§ 7955.]

§ 3. That the term "waste" as used herein, in addition to its ordinary meaning, shall include economic waste, underground waste, surface waste, and waste incident to the production of crude oil or petroleum in excess of transportation or marketing facilities or reasonable market demands. The Corporation Commission shall have authority to make rules and regulations for the prevention of such wastes, and for the protection of all fresh water strata, and oil and gas bearing strata, encountered in any well drilled for oil. [§ 7956.]

§ 4. That whenever the full production from any common source of supply of crude oil or petroleum in this State can only be obtained under conditions constituting waste as herein defined, then any person, firm or corporation, having the right to drill into and produce oil from any such common source of supply, may take therefrom only such proportion of all crude oil and petroleum that may be produced therefrom, without waste, as the production of the well or wells of any such person, firm or corporation, bears to the total production of such common source of supply. The Corporation Commission is authorized to so regulate the taking of crude oil or petroleum from any or all such common sources of supply, within the State of Oklahoma, as to

repugnant to the due process and equal protection clauses of the Fourteenth Amendment and the commerce clause.

The Act prohibits the production of petroleum in such a manner or under such conditions as constitute waste. Section 3 defines waste to include—in addition to its ordinary meaning—economic, underground and surface waste, and waste incident to production in excess of transportation or marketing facilities or reasonable market demands, and empowers the commission to make rules and regulations for the prevention of such wastes. Whenever full production from any common source can only be obtained under conditions constituting waste, one having the right to produce oil from such source may take only such proportion of all that may be produced therefrom without waste as the production of his wells bears to the total. The commission is authorized to regulate the taking of oil from common sources so as to prevent unreasonable discrimination in favor of one source as against others.

The [plaintiff has nine wells in the] Greater Seminole [field which] covers a territory fifteen to twenty by eight to ten miles and has eight or more distinct pools in formations which do not overlie each other. The first pool was discovered in 1925 and by June 15, 1931, there were 2141 producing wells having potential production of 564,908 barrels per day. The wells are separately owned and operated by 80 lessees. About three-fourths of them, owning wells with 40 per cent. of the total potential capacity of the field, have no pipelines or refineries and are entirely dependent for an outlet for their crude upon others who purchase and transport oil. Five companies, owning wells with about 13 per cent. of the potential production, have pipelines or refinery connections affording a partial outlet for their production. Nineteen other companies own or control pipelines extending into this area having a daily capacity of 468,200 barrels, and most of them from time to time purchase oil from other producers in the field.

Crude oil and natural gas occur together or in close proximity to each other, and the gas in a pool moves the contents toward the point of least resistance. When wells are drilled into a pool the oil and gas move from place to place. If some of the wells are permitted to produce a greater proportion of their capacity than others, drainage occurs from the less active to the more active.... Where proportional taking from the wells in flush pools is not enforced, operators who do not have physical or market outlets are forced to produce to capacity in order to prevent drainage to others having adequate outlets. In Oklahoma prior to the passage of the Act, large quantities of oil produced in excess of transportation facilities or demand therefor were stored in surface tanks, and by reason of seepage, rain, fire and evaporation enormous waste occurred. Uncontrolled flow of flush or semi-flush wells for any considerable period exhausts an excessive

prevent the inequitable or unfair taking, from a common source of supply, of such crude oil or petroleum, by any person, firm, or corporation, and to prevent unreasonable discrimination in favor of any one such common source of supply as against another. [§ 7957.]

amount of pressure, wastefully uses the gas and greatly lessens ultimate recovery....

The first of the present series of proration orders took effect August 1, 1927, and applied to the then flush and semi-flush pools in the Seminole.... In order No. 5189, June 30, 1930, [the Corporation Commission] found that the potential production in the United States was approximately 4,730,000 barrels per day and that imports amounted to about 300,000 barrels, creating a supply of over 5,000,000 barrels as against an estimated domestic and export demand of 2,800,000 barrels.... The orders ... operated to restrict plaintiff to much less than the potential production of its nine wells in the Seminole pools.

The court found that at all times covered by orders involved there was a serious potential overproduction throughout the United States and particularly in the flush and semi-flush pools in the Seminole and Oklahoma City fields; that, if no curtailment were applied, crude oil for lack of market demand and adequate storage tanks would inevitably go into earthen storage and be wasted; that the full potential production exceeded all transportation and marketing facilities and market demands; that accordingly it was necessary, in order to prevent waste, that production of flush and semi-flush pools should be restricted as directed by the proration orders, and that to enforce such curtailment, with equity and justice to the several producers in each pool, it was necessary to enforce proportional taking from each well and lease therein and that, upon the testimony of operators and others, a comprehensive plan of curtailment and proration conforming to the rules prescribed in the Act was adopted by the commission and was set forth in its orders.

[The district court also found that none] of the commission's orders has been made for the purpose of fixing the price of crude oil or has had that effect. When the first order was made the price was more than two dollars per barrel, but it declined until at the time of the trial it was only thirty-five cents. In each case the commission has allowed to be produced the full amount of the market demand for each pool. It has never entered any order under § 2 of the Act.

It was not shown that the commission intended to limit the amount of oil entering interstate commerce for the purpose of controlling the price of crude oil or its products or of eliminating plaintiff or any producer or refiner from competition, or that there was any combination among plaintiff's competitors for the purpose of restricting interstate commerce in crude oil or its products, or that any operators' committee made up of plaintiff's competitors formulated the proration orders.

The evidence before the trial court undoubtedly sustains the findings above referred to, and they are adopted here.

1.   Plaintiff here insists that the Act is repugnant to the due process and equal protection clauses of the Fourteenth Amendment.

Plaintiff insists that it has a vested right to drill wells upon the lands covered by its leases and to take all the natural flow of oil and gas therefrom so long as it does so without physical waste and devotes the production to commercial uses. But if plaintiff should take all the flow of its wells, there would inevitably result great physical waste, even if its entire production should be devoted to useful purposes. The improvident use of natural gas pressure inevitably attending such operations would cause great diminution in the quantity of crude oil ultimately to be recovered from the pool. Other lessees and owners of land above the pool would be compelled, for self-protection against plaintiff's taking, also to draw from the common source and so to add to the wasteful use of lifting pressure. And because of the lack, especially on the part of the non-integrated operators, of means of transportation or appropriate storage and of market demand, the contest would, as is made plain by the evidence and findings, result in surface waste of large quantities of crude oil. . . .

It is not shown that the rule for proration prescribed in § 4 or any other provision here involved amounts to or authorizes arbitrary interference with private business or plaintiff's property rights or that such statutory rule is not reasonably calculated to prevent the wastes specified in § 3.

We put aside plaintiff's contentions resting upon the claim that § 2 or § 3 authorizes or contemplates directly or indirectly regulation of prices of crude oil. The commission has never made an order under § 2. The court found that none of the proration orders here involved were made for the purpose of fixing prices. The fact that the commission never limited production below market demand, and the great and long continued downward trend of prices contemporaneously with the enforcement of proration, strongly support the finding that the orders assailed have not had that effect. . . .

2. Plaintiff contends that the Act and proration orders operate to burden interstate commerce in crude oil and its products in violation of the commerce clause. It is clear that the regulations prescribed and authorized by the Act and the proration established by the commission apply only to production and not to sales or transportation of crude oil or its products. Such production is essentially a mining operation and therefore is not a part of interstate commerce even though the product obtained is intended to be and in fact is immediately shipped in such commerce. . . .[9] No violation of the commerce clause is shown.

3. Plaintiff assails the proration orders as unauthorized, lacking basis in fact and arbitrary. But it failed to show that the orders were not based upon just and reasonable determinations of the governing facts: namely, that proportion of all crude oil, which may be produced from a common source without waste, that the production of plaintiff's wells bears to the total production from such source. . . .

---

9. Editors' note: As noted in Chapter 5 *supra*, the cases on which the Court was relying were overturned in 1937.

As plaintiff has failed to prove that any order in force at the time of the trial was not in accordance with the rule prescribed by § 4 or otherwise invalid, the part of the decree from which it appealed will be affirmed....■

NOTES AND COMMENTS

1.   Champlin was a vertically integrated oil company engaged in producing and refining crude oil and transporting and marketing it and its products in interstate commerce. Its refinery had a daily capacity of 15,000 barrels of crude. It owned 735 tank cars, operated 470 miles of pipeline and had 256 wholesale and 263 retail gasoline stations supplied from its refinery. At the refinery it had gas-tight steel storage tanks which could hold 645,000 barrels of petroleum and its products. It did not use earthen storage, nor did it allow its crude "to run at large, or waste any oil produced at its wells. All that it can produce will be utilized for commercial purposes." *Id.* at 226–27. How, then, was Champlin wasting oil? Did the court uphold the prorationing statute because it prevented waste by restricting the field's output to its MER? Or because it protected correlative rights by assuring fair shares of production to all operators? Or, because it raised the price of oil (coincidently providing tax revenues to the state treasury) by restricting output far below the field's MER?

2.   What is the relationship between restricting a field's production to its MER to prevent physical waste, and restricting production to meet market demand and prevent economic waste? Suppose the MER of a field would allow 500,000 barrels per day of production, but the market "demands" only 30 percent of this amount. Wells in this field will be allowed to produce a total of 150,000 barrels per day. Return to Figure 6–1. Does market-demand prorationing account for the remarkable stability in the price of crude oil from about 1930 until 1973?

Here is a chart of the market demand factor (MDF) applied to Texas fields from 1950 through 1975:

Year	% MDF	Year	% MDF	Year	% MDF
1950	63	1960	28	1970	72
1951	76	1961	28	1971	73
1952	71	1962	27	1972	94
1953	65	1963	28	1973	100
1954	53	1964	28	1974	100
1955	53	1965	29	1975	100
1956	52	1966	34		
1957	47	1967	41		
1958	33	1968	45		
1959	34	1969	52		

The data show that wells were prorated to 28 percent of their capacity in 1960, *i.e.*, a well that could produce 100 barrels a day was restricted to 28 barrels. If the nation demanded more crude oil to satisfy its hunger for gasoline in the post-war years, the Texas Railroad Commission could simply raise the MDF to 41 percent. Producers would turn the valves on their wells, and more oil would flow.

Over these same years, the domestic cost of drilling rose because new fields were generally smaller and deeper than the large discoveries of old. As costs rose, fewer producers drilled new wells. The United States imported increasing quantities of crude oil from supergiant fields developed abroad, especially in Saudi Arabia.[10] In what year was the U.S. first vulnerable to an Arab embargo of imports to our shores?

3. If Texas severely prorated its wells to market demand, but other producing states like Oklahoma or Louisiana did not, Texas producers would lose market share to their competitors in other states, a clearly unacceptable result. So how was market demand prorationing to be coordinated among all the major producing states? In 1934, Secretary of the Interior Harold Ickes was pushing for federal control of the petroleum industry to prevent the rampant waste of oil and gas. His plan used a public utility model to regulate the industry. To forestall federal intervention, the governors of Oklahoma, Texas, and other producing states met to devise an interstate oil compact as an alternative. The governor of Oklahoma pressed for a compact which would allocate the federal Bureau of Mines' monthly estimates of national market demand to the states as binding quotas, resulting in a clear and direct mechanism for price-fixing. Texas resisted this degree of interference in its affairs. In the end, Texas prevailed. In 1935, the Interstate Compact to Conserve Oil and Gas was created and approved by the President and Congress. The compact now has 30 member states and 6 associate members. It relies on voluntary agreements to accomplish its objectives. *See* Erich W. Zimmermann, Conservation in the Production of Petroleum 201–236 (1957). Given this history, what do you think was Oklahoma's objective in restricting production so severely in the *Champlin* case?

4. Support for proration was not universal in the industry. Some smaller companies viewed prorationing as a conspiracy by the major oil companies to bankrupt the independent producer by depriving him of the cash flow from flush production. Some believed that by appealing to state agencies for production controls, the oil industry was drifting toward governmental control. Chief Justice Fletcher Riley of the Supreme Court of Oklahoma, in a dissenting opinion, expressed this viewpoint: "In my opinion, proration of oil was born of monopoly, sired by arbitrary power, and its progeny (such as these orders) is the deformed child whose playmates are graft, theft, bribery and corruption." *H.F. Wilcox Oil & Gas Co. v. State*, 162 Okla. 89 (1933).

In the East Texas field, producers regularly ignored Railroad Commission prorationing orders. In July 1931, 1,300 wells were producing 1.4 million barrels of oil per day. The price dropped below ten cents a barrel. Finally, in August, the Texas Governor declared martial law and sent the National Guard into the field to shut down every well. Troops patrolled the field. Military officers ran a prorationing office and re-opened the wells

---

10. In 1996, the average production per well in the U.S. was 11.2 barrels of oil per day. Wells in Saudi Arabia averaged 6000 barrels per day. 2 Energy Law and Transactions (David J. Muchow and William A. Mogel, eds.) Appendix 10, at 51–82 (1999).

with a maximum allowable of 225 barrels of oil per day per well. *See* James H. Keahy, Jr., The Texas Mineral Interest Pooling Act: End of an Era, 4 Natural Resources Lawyer 359, at 360–61. The shutdown was effective in raising the price of oil, and this considerably tamed the opposition to market-demand prorationing.

5.   How is the state conservation agency to determine each producer's "fair share" of the total field allowable? Should every well be allowed to produce the same amount, regardless of how much acreage it drains? (This is the "per well" allowable system which the National Guard used). Is it fair that the owner of one well on a town lot no bigger than 1/10 of an acre be allowed to produce the same amount of oil as the owner of a well on a ten acre tract? Should the owner of the ten acre tract be granted additional wells as exceptions to the field's well spacing rule requiring at least ten acres for a well permit? If so, won't this encourage unnecessary well drilling, just like occurred under the rule of capture?

6.   As the science of petroleum engineering progressed, state conservation agencies adopted larger and larger spacing units. As a rule of thumb, one well can drain oil from about 40 acres. A gas well can drain from about 640 acres. Assume you own a one acre tract in the Excalibur oil field. The 40–acre spacing rule prohibits you from getting a well permit to drill. Your neighbor owns a 40–acre tract and drills a well close to your boundary in a field that is determined to be 4,000 acres large. The conservation commission sets the total field allowable equal to a market demand of 4,000 barrels a day for the field. The commission allocates this total using a prorationing formula based on acreage. Under this formula your neighbor can produce 40 of these barrels because she owns 40/4,000 (or one percent) of the acreage in the field. While your neighbor is selling the 40 barrels for $3 per barrel, (or $120 a day in revenues), you are producing nothing. Are your correlative rights protected in this scenario?

Suppose the commission grants you an exception to the spacing rule so that your oil will not be confiscated through drainage to your neighbor's well. If you drill and produce your own well, you will be granted an allowable of 1/4000, or one barrel of oil per day. If oil is selling for $3 dollars a barrel, you will have revenues of $3 a day. This amount does not cover the costs of drilling and producing the well on your one acre. You will lose money. Are your correlative rights protected in this scenario?

Suppose the commission grants every well in the field the same allowable of 40 barrels of oil per day. Now your well on your one acre is profitable to drill and produce. Does this prorationing formula protect the correlative rights of your neighbor?

Can you think of a better way to run an oil field? Many states enacted compulsory pooling laws. These statutes allow the conservation commission to pool small tracts into acreage large enough to secure a well permit under the spacing rules. All the owners with interests in the pooled acreage share in the production from the one well, usually on a surface acreage basis. Thus, four owners, owning 1, 5, 10, and 24 acres respectively, could be pooled into a 40–acre unit on which one well would be drilled. The owner would receive 1/40, 5/40, 10/40 and 24/40, respectively, of the productions. Does pooling protect correlative rights and prevent the waste of unnecessary well drilling?

3. SECONDARY RECOVERY: THE TRAGEDY OF THE COMMONS PART II

Because many U.S. fields were produced so inefficiently under the rule of capture, much oil remained in the reservoirs after the reservoir drive was depleted. Secondary recovery can sweep this oil up. In 1979, secondary recovery accounted for about 60 percent of Texas's total oil production and about 38 percent of Oklahoma's. In a typical secondary recovery operation, injected gas or water is used to drive oil away from the high-pressured injection wells toward producing wells. A waterflood operation commonly uses a five-spot pattern which places injection wells at the corners of a square and a producing well at the center. The injected water pushes a bank of oil toward the producing well. In recent years, advanced forms of secondary recovery–called enhanced oil recovery—have been devised. For example, carbon dioxide is piped from a large natural reservoir of CO_2 in Colorado some 400 miles to large oil fields in West Texas. There it is injected and miscibly displaces oil from the pore spaces of the rock. Sometimes chemical surfactants and polymers are added to waterflooding to better "scrub" the rock clean of the clinging oil.

Do conservation laws and the common law maximize the efficiency of these "second chance" operations? This question arose in the following case:

Railroad Commission of Texas v. Manziel

361 S.W.2d 560 (Tex.1962).

■ SMITH, J.: This direct appeal is the result of a suit filed by the appellees, Dorothy N. Manziel et al. in the 126th District Court of Travis County, Texas, to set aside and cancel an order of the Railroad Commission of December 12, 1960, permitting the appellants, the Whelan Brothers, to drill and inject water in their Eldridge #11 well located at an irregular spacing on the Whelan Brothers-Vickie Lynn unit 206 feet south of the boundary of the Manziel Estate–Mathis lease in the Vickie Lynn Field, Marion County, Texas. The Railroad Commission was the original defendant in this action; the Whelan Brothers intervened and aligned themselves in defense of the Railroad Commission's order. For convenience the parties will hereinafter be referred to as the Whelans, the Manziels and the Commission.

In addition to alleging irregularities in connection with the Whelans' application for the permit, the Manziels attacked the Commission's order on the grounds that it would cause waste, that it would result in the confiscation of the Manziels' property, that the permit was not necessary to protect the correlative rights of the Whelans', and that the order was in violation of the Commission's own rules.

After trial, the District Court entered a judgment canceling the order allowing the Whelans to inject water at the irregular location, enjoining its enforcement and enjoining the Whelans from injecting water in their Eldridge #11 well under said order. The judgment of the District Court has been brought to this court for review. . . .

The Vickie Lynn Field was discovered in February, 1956, and field rules were established by the Commission, effective August 20, 1956. The rules provide for 80–acre production units with the wells to be located on that unit 660 feet from lease lines. A well located 660 feet and more from lease lines is referred to as being at a regular location while a well located at a less distance is said to be at an irregular location. All the wells in the field were drilled according to this plan except the Manziel–Mathis lease and the well located thereon is spaced 330 feet north of the adjoining Whelan unit.

At the time of the trial, the Vickie Lynn Field was divided into three separate and distinct areas. The Whelans' property is referred to as the Whelan Brothers–Vickie Lynn Unit, and includes about 900 productive acres on which 11 producing wells have been drilled. The Manziels are the only other operators in the field and they control two units, the largest of which is referred to as the Manziel Estate–Whelan lease; it comprises about 1,135 producing acres and has 10 wells. The other unit is made up of three leases sometimes collectively referred to as the Hollandsworth leases (separately known as the Mathis, the Combs, and the Coleman leases), which were not acquired by the Manziels until 1960. The Mathis lease contains 40.36 acres, with one well; and the Combs and Coleman leases each include 80 acres, with one well on each lease. For a better understanding of the relative size and location of each of the units involved, a plat drawn from Exhibit 'A' is attached.

The field has not been unitized as a whole, but the Whelans have unitized all of the properties of which they are lessees; however, no unitization agreement has been made between the Whelans and the Manziels. The Manziels have not unitized all of the properties under their control, and the situation in the Vickie Lynn Field is further complicated by the fact that the Manziels have a waterflood program on their Whelan lease, and have no such program on their Hollandsworth leases.

The Vickie Lynn Field is in a solution gas drive reservoir, and it is estimated that between 816 barrels to 824 barrels of oil per acre foot were originally in place beneath the field. As production was carried out, the resultant displacement and the failure to maintain adequate pressure has caused the original pressure to drop from 2650 pounds per square inch to the point where it is now of an average of 371 pounds per square inch. The present low pressure in the reservoir means that the remaining oil is "dead," and from the record it appears that the best means of recovery thereof is by the secondary method of waterflooding.

The Hollandsworth leases of the Manziels are located in the northwestern part of the field, and the result of the production from these leases and the effect of the existing water injection programs on the Manziel Estate–

Whelan lease and on the Whelan Brothers–Vickie Lynn Unit is to push the oil in a northwesterly direction to the Hollandsworth leases. The purpose of the Whelans Eldridge #11 well is to increase reservoir pressure and to minimize the amount of oil which is pushed from their unit, across lease

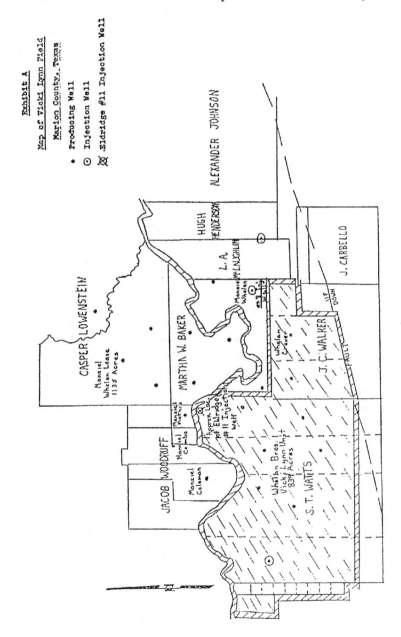

Exhibit A

lines, to the Hollandsworth leases, and particularly the Manziel Estate–Mathis lease. Of the Hollandsworth leases, the Manziel Estate–Mathis lease is in the closest proximity to the operations of the Eldridge #11 well of the Whelans, and if the operations can be held valid in relation to the Mathis lease they are valid as to the rest. It is the Whelans' contention that in a situation such as exists in this field their waterflood program must have the dual purpose of efficient recovery of oil from producing wells on their property and the prevention, so far as is possible, of the loss of oil from beneath their lease due to the pushing or drainage of oil to other properties.

If all the oil here in question were located under one tract, it is established that the most recovery from the *entire field* would be through a plan of peripheral flooding around the edges to the field, thus sweeping the oil from the south and southwest down-structure to the north and northwest. In regard to the Whelan Brothers–Vickie Lynn Unit it was shown that the flooding pattern was planned so recovery of an estimated 930,000 barrels of oil from under that lease could be made. The plan was not set up out of a consideration of what pattern would result in the most recovery from the entire field; but rather a plan was used that would result in the most recovery from that *one lease*. (Emphasis in original.)

Water injected into an oil reservoir generally spreads out radially from the injection well bore, and it is impossible to restrict the advance of the water to lease lines. For example, water injected into the Manziel Estate #8 well has already crossed the boundary of the Whelans' unit and as more water is injected further encroachment will take place until finally the Whelans' Craver well is drowned out. It is just such an encroachment upon the Mathis lease by water injected in the Whelans' unit that the Manziels seek to prevent.

Regardless of whether the Eldridge #11 well is located at a regular or irregular location any water injection program on the Whelans' unit will cause oil to be pushed from their unit to the Hollandsworth leases. However, it is estimated that four times as much of the oil presently beneath the Whelans' lease will be pushed to the Hollandsworth leases if the injection well is located 660 feet from the lease line as opposed to a 206–foot location. On the other hand, the Manziels–Mathis well would have an estimated life of 32 months if the Eldridge #11 well is placed at a regular location 660 feet from lease lines while if the irregular spacing is used the life of the well would be reduced to 3½ to 8 months depending on the rate of production and injection of the respective wells.

During the primary stage of the field, the Mathis lease enjoyed a great drainage advantage as is shown by the following production figures:

PRIMARY RECOVERY

	Acres	Production	% of Oil in Place Before Production	% of Total Field Recovery	Wells
Mathis	40.36	44,034 bbls.	1.8%–2.4%	5.8%	1
Remainder of field	2,195.00	709,006 bbls.	97.6%–98.8%	94.2%	23

Now, however, the field is in a secondary recovery stage, and with the location of the Eldridge #11 well at a 206–foot location these additional figures are relevant:

SECONDARY RECOVERY

	Acres	Estimated Production	Estimated % of Total Secondary Recovery	# of Injection Wells
Mathis	40.36	9,202	.83%	0
Remainder of Field	2,195.00	1,090,798	99.17%	4

The Commission takes the position that it must have the authority to grant the location of water injection wells to prevent drainage and to protect correlative rights in order to encourage operators to initiate secondary recovery programs. The Commission contends that there would be no incentive to engage in this method of increasing the recovery of oil unless the operator is allowed to use effective methods to prevent oil from being pushed from beneath his property.

The Manziels concede that the Whelans have the right to protect their leases from drainage, and that the Commission has the power to issue reasonable orders to aid such a purpose if it is found to be necessary to drill the well at an irregular location in order to prevent waste or to prevent confiscation of the Whelans' property. However, after conceding this right and power, the Manziels assert that the Commission may not authorize, or the Whelans carry out, a trespass by injected water that will result in the premature destruction of their producing Mathis well. It is asserted that such authorization is violative of Art. 6029(4) Vernon's Annotated Civil Statutes which provides that the Commission is to require wells to be drilled and operated in such a manner as to prevent injury to adjoining property. They further assert that the order permitting the water injection into the irregularly located Eldridge #11 well of the Whelans deprives them of their property without due process of law. . . .

The Commission has adopted no fieldwide spacing rule for water injection wells, but has made special orders as to each operator desiring to waterflood. On August 15, 1960, over a year after the Manziels had instituted similar operations on their Whelan lease, the Whelans were authorized to conduct secondary recovery operations on their Vickie Lynn Unit. The special order provided: '. . . that as the pressure maintenance operation progresses, said operators may expand the injection facilities and may use for injection purposes additional wells . . .; and provided, further, that no injection well location will be approved at or nearer to a lease boundary line than a regular location (660 feet) for producing wells projected to this reservoir unless and until the operators furnish waivers from any such offsetting operators or until evidence that such offsetting operator has been notified and that no protest is made to the Commission concerning such location within ten days after such request for approval of the injection well location is received by the Commission's Engineering Department.' From the wording of this order we interpret it to be the intention of the Commission to authorize the Whelans to inject water in irregularly located wells if the Manziels waived objection; but if the Manziels did not waive, then the Commission, as was done, would conduct a hearing to see whether, under the facts shown, the proposed exception should be granted.

The parties agree that the Commission has the power to grant exception to the order if the evidence establishes that it is necessary to drill a well at an irregular location in order to prevent waste or to prevent confiscation of property. If the right to the exception is supported by substantial evidence, the exact location of the well is in the Commission's sound discretion. Thus, a principal issue presented for determination by this court is whether there is substantial evidence in the record which establishes that it is necessary for the injection well to be placed at an irregular location to prevent either the confiscation of the Whelans' property or waste in the field. However, before discussing this issue, we deem it appropriate to dispose of other issues raised on this appeal.

Trespass

The Manziels pleaded that the injection of salt water by the Whelans in the Eldridge #11 well will cause damage to their producing wells, and will result in loss and injury to their oil and gas interests due to premature flooding. They assert, and we agree, that under our liberal rules of pleading, this wording is sufficient to give rise to the issue of trespass in considering the status of encroaching secondary recovery waters.

The subsurface invasion of adjoining mineral estates by injected salt water of a secondary recovery project is to be expected, and in the case at bar we are not confronted with the tort aspects of such practices. Neither is the question raised as to whether the Commission's authorization of such operations throws a protective cloak around the injecting operator who might otherwise be subjected to the risks of liability for actual damages to the adjoining property; rather we are faced with an issue of whether a trespass is committed when secondary recovery waters from an authorized secondary recovery project cross lease lines.

In seeking to answer this question, we have examined cases covering almost every aspect of the oil and gas industry in this state where the plaintiff has gone into court against an operator on adjoining property who has caused some type of damage to or encroachment in the plaintiff's subsurface estate. In only one situation have we found an injunction granted on the applied theory of trespass.[11] With one exception, all others

---

11. Editors' note: The one exception involved "slant well" drilling when a lessee of Tract A started drilling on the surface of Tract A but bottomed the well under Tract B.

have involved questions of liability for negligence] with which we are not here concerned.

To constitute trespass there must be some physical entry upon the land by some "thing," *Gregg v. Delhi–Taylor Oil Corp.*, Tex., 344 S.W.2d 411 (1961); but is injected water that crosses lease lines from an authorized secondary project the type of "thing" that may be said to render the adjoining operator guilty of trespass? . . .

In considering the legal consequences of the injection of secondary recovery forces into the subsurface structures, one authority, Williams and Meyers, supra, has stated:

"What may be called a 'negative rule of capture' appears to be developing. Just as under the rule of capture a land owner may capture such oil or gas as will migrate from adjoining premises to a well bottomed on his own land, so also may he inject into a formation substances which may migrate through the structure to the land of others, even if it thus results in the displacement under such land of more valuable with less valuable substances (e.g., the displacement of wet gas by dry gas)."

Secondary recovery operations are carried on to increase the ultimate recovery of oil and gas, and it is established that pressure maintenance projects will result in more recovery than was obtained by primary methods. It cannot be disputed that such operations should be encouraged, for as the pressure behind the primary production dissipates, the greater is the public necessity for applying secondary recovery forces. It is obvious that secondary recovery programs could not and would not be conducted if any adjoining operator could stop the project on the ground of subsurface trespass. As is pointed out by amicus curiae, if the Manziels' theory of subsurface trespass be accepted, the injection of salt water in the East Texas field has caused subsurface trespasses of the greatest magnitude.

The orthodox rules and principles applied by the courts as regards surface invasions of land may not be appropriately applied to subsurface invasions as arise out of the secondary recovery of natural resources. If the intrusions of salt water are to be regarded as trespassory in character, then under common notions of surface invasions, the justifying public policy considerations behind secondary recovery operations could not be reached in considering the validity and reasonableness of such operations. *See* Keeton and Jones: "Tort Liability and the Oil and Gas Industry II," 39 Tex. Law Rev. 253 at p. 268. Certainly, it is relevant to consider and weigh the interests of society and the oil and gas industry as a whole against the interests of the individual operator who is damaged; and if the authorized activities in an adjoining secondary recovery unit are found to be based on some substantial, justifying occasion, then this court should sustain their validity.

We conclude that if, in the valid exercise of its authority to prevent waste, protect correlative rights, or in the exercise of other powers within its jurisdiction, the Commission authorizes secondary recovery projects, a trespass does not occur when the injected, secondary recovery forces move across lease lines, and the operations are not subject to an injunction on that basis. The technical rules of trespass have no place in the consideration of the validity of the orders of the Commission.

The Statutes

The Manziels further assert that the Commission, in authorizing the irregular spacing of the Eldridge #11 well, has violated the legislative command of Article 6029(4) that wells shall be operated in such manner as to prevent injury to adjoining property. However, they would not make the same objection if the well in question was in a regular location. Under the statute, secondary recovery operations need not be field wide, but may be conducted in one or more but less than all of the units of the reservoir. Such operations are primarily concerned with increasing the ultimate recovery of oil and gas and the prevention of waste. In any case in which secondary recovery procedures are used on one tract of a nonunitized field, it can be expected that eventually there will be a subsurface invasion of adjacent properties. If such operations are to have optimum success there is no way to prevent the eventual flooding of every well in the field. Unquestionably, the legislature was fully cognizant of this fact when it enacted Article 6008b, Vernon's Annotated Civil Statutes,[8][12] and regardless of what may be said to the contrary, the legislature has made it the policy of this state to encourage the secondary recovery of oil. It is matter of common knowledge that secondary recovery methods sometimes result in more recovery than the total procured through primary production. Indeed, only 15% of the oil in place can be recovered by primary methods in the case at bar. It is thus concluded that Article 6029(4) has no application to authorized, secondary recovery projects, and that the provisions of Article 6008b control in such instances.

Validity of Order

This being a case of first impression in this state, resort has been made to analogous cases from other jurisdictions. In the cases examined, the issue of trespass was not asserted, and regardless of the fact that there was migration across lease lines, the orders of the Conservation Commissions were upheld if they were supported by substantial evidence, and in the

---

12. Article 6008b, § 1: "Subject to approval of the Railroad Commission of Texas . . . persons owning or controlling production, leases, royalties, or other interests in separate properties in the same oil field, gas field, or oil and gas field, may voluntarily enter into and perform agreements for the following purposes:" (A) To establish pooled units necessary to effect secondary recovery operations for oil or gas, including those known as cycling, recycling, repressuring, water flooding, and pressure maintenance and to establish and operate cooperative facilities necessary for said secondary operations; "(B) . . . 'Such agreements shall not become lawful nor effective until the Commission finds, after application, notice and hearing:' " 1. . . . that the rights of the owners of all the interests in the field, whether signers of the unit agreement or not, would be protected under its operation. "All agreements executed hereunder shall be subject to any valid order, rule, or regulation of the Commission relating to location, spacing, proration, conservation, or other matters within the authority of the Commission. . . ."

public interest and were necessary to protect correlative rights or to prevent waste in the field.

In *Syverson et al. v. North Dakota State Industrial Commission,,* 111 N.W.2d 128 (N.D.Sup.Ct.1961), all the operators in the field decided to unitize in order to carry out a program of pressure maintenance, by the injection of water. A voluntary agreement was drafted and approved by the Commission, and Amerada Petroleum Corporation was designated as the unit operator. The operators succeeded in obtaining 98% of the mineral and royalty owners to agree thereto. Syverson refused to join on the grounds that he would not be paid enough if he were in the unit. The operators filed an application to authorize the beginning of injections and Syverson contested the granting of the application. The application was granted. The Commission pointed out that Syverson's interest was not within the area covered by the agreement, and that there was no showing that they would suffer actual damages.

The question presented on appeal was whether Amerada had the right to repressure the entire field by water injection into wells covered by the agreement. The court sustained the order of the Commission in finding that there was competent evidence to support the position of the Commission, that the program was in the public interest and was necessary to prevent waste and to protect correlative rights. In holding that regardless of the Syverson's non-joinder, the Commission had the power to order, and Amerada, the right to carry out, field-wide repressuring the court stated:

"By refusing to join such agreement, however, appellants may not, at the same time prevent other interests in the field developing adjoining tracts. . . . Whatever the result would be if the appellants could show actual damages, they are certainly not entitled to complain in the absence of such a showing."

Reed v. Texas Co., (1959), 159 N.E.2d 641, is more closely in point. There, three owners of a portion of the reservoir who had not entered into the pressure maintenance project sought an injunction against the Texas Company to require the discontinuance of a field-wide waterflooding program. Reed contended that the operation was forcing oil, to which they had "title," from under their property. The program involved the placing of injection wells around the periphery and others in the interior area of the pool. The latter were spotted as close to boundaries of leaseholds as was practical, so as to diffuse the pressure and minimize the migration of oil from one leasehold to another. The Chancellor heard testimony concerning the physical condition of the pool and the production history of each well in the field. The prayer for injunction was denied and an appeal followed.

In holding that the denial of the injunction should be sustained the court commented:

"If a minority of one or more persons affected by the operations could prevent it by refusing to join in the agreement, they could then force the others to choose between leaving a large part of the oil underground, or consent to granting the dissidents an unreasonably large percentage of the oil. *In other words, the power to block a repressure program by refusing to sign the unitization agreement, would be the power to insist upon unjust enrichment. Surely a court of equity should not support such a rule."* (Emphasis added.)

"As to whether the plan in this case was reasonable and fair to all parties, there was a dispute, but the Chancellor heard the testimony, therefore, *this court looks only to the question of whether there is substantial evidence to support the result."* (Emphasis added.)

These authorities, in principle, support our view that it was the purpose of the Legislature in adopting our conservation laws that in any oil or gas field the Commission should have power, even the duty, to prevent undue drainage of oil across lease lines. The Commission has two primary duties in the administration and control of our oil and gas industry. It must look to each field as a whole to determine what is necessary to prevent waste while at the same time countering this consideration with a view toward allowing each operator to recover his fair share of the oil in place beneath his land. In carrying out these duties, there has devolved upon the Commission the power to promulgate rules, orders and regulations that control the industry, and such are issued pursuant to the police power of the state, and that power may invade the right of the owner of the land to the oil in place under his land as long as it is based on some justifying occasion, and is not exercised in an unreasonable or arbitrary manner. *See Brown v. Humble Oil and Refining Co.*, 126 Tex. 296, 87 S.W.2d 1069, 99 A.L.R. 1107, 101 A.L.R. 1393, (1935).

The rules of ownership are of prime importance, but in this consideration the rights of one do not exceed the rights of another. As to oil and gas, the surface proprietors within the field have the coequal right to take from the common source of supply. It follows from the nature of oil and gas that the use by one of his power to seek to convert a part of the common reservoir to actual possession may result in an undue portion being attributed to one of the possessors of the right to the detriment of the other. Hence, it is within the Commission's power to protect the vested rights of all the collective owners, by securing a just distribution, and to reach the like end by preventing waste.

There is no dispute as to the necessity of injecting larger amounts of water into the reservoir to prevent waste in the field, and from the evidence it appears that regardless of whether the Eldridge #11 well is located at a regular or irregular spacing there will be no appreciable difference in the amount of oil recoverable from the reservoir as a whole. The only dispute is as to where the necessary injection well should be located to serve the dual purpose of facilitating efficient recovery of oil and the protection of the correlative rights of the Whelans. If we are to sustain the validity of the order involved here, it must be on the ground that there is substantial evidence that the exception is necessary to protect correlative rights and prevent undue drainage.

The evidence shows that the Manziel–Mathis lease comprises 40.36 acres with an estimated 184 productive acre feet underlying. It is further estimated that approximately 816 to 824 barrels of oil per acre foot were originally in place in the field. The Whelan Brothers' expert testified that an estimated 118,296 barrels of oil was the total amount of oil in place under the Mathis tract. It is estimated that only between 17,744 barrels to 22,700 barrels of this total amount was recoverable by primary means. However, the production figures show that as of Sept. 1, 1961, the Mathis well has actually produced 45,720 barrels[9][13] of oil.

It is established that the effect of the existing pattern of flooding is to cause the remaining oil in the field to be pushed toward the Mathis lease, and due to the high rate of production from the Mathis well, the process is being aided by a great disparity in pressures.[10][14] According to the testimony of the Whelans' expert, a large amount of the estimated 118,296 bbls. of oil originally in place under the Mathis lease lies to the north of the Mathis well and will not be produced from under that lease due to pressure differentials. It appears that the pressure is greater in the south, east and west than in the north and northwest. It stands to reason that under these conditions, the drainage from the Whelan Brothers–Vickie Lynn Unit will continue.

The Manziels' expert witness testified that without the Whelans' Eldridge #11 well being used for injection purposes, that the primary life of the Mathis well would be from 3 to 5 years with only a 'small' benefit from past water injections, and that from Sept. 1, 1961, to the end of production from the Mathis well, an additional 61,000 bbls. of oil will be recovered. However, it appears that without instituting repressure operations of their own on the Mathis lease, the Manziels will reap the benefit of the repressure operations of adjoining tracts and recover approximately 106,-720 bbls. of oil while there was only, at the most, 22,700 bbls. of oil originally in place recoverable by primary methods. Thus, while the remainder of the field is only able to recover approximately 15% of the total amount of oil in place beneath their tracts without resorting to secondary operations; the Manziels may recover an amount equal to 90% of the total recoverable reserves in place under the Mathis lease without resorting to such operations. In other words, unless the Eldridge #11 well is used for injection purposes, the Mathis well will recover over 5 times the amount of oil it would have been able to recover if primary production had been adjusted according to the proportion of productive acre feet beneath the Mathis lease. Admittedly, this disparity would be caused by drainage from other leases.

From these figures it is established that without resorting to secondary operations on its Hollandsworth leases, and continuing to rely on primary methods of production, the Manziel Estate–Mathis lease has, and will

---

13. Thus, while owning only an estimated 1.8 to 2.4% of the total productive feet in the field, the Manziel–Mathis well has had 5.8% of the field's total primary recovery.

14. It is shown that the pressure at the Mathis well is only 87 pounds per square inch, while the pressure at the Eldridge #11 well is 551 pounds per square inch; the remaining wells in the field report pressures varying from 254 to 328 pounds per square inch.

continue to, produce far in excess of its fair share of the oil in place originally recoverable through the use of such methods. It further appears that unless the order granting the exception is held to be valid, the production will even further exceed the fair share of the primary recovery. Clearly, the Mathis lease has produced, will produce, and will retain thereunder an amount of oil that is its fair share of both the primary and secondary stages of recovery.

We are of the opinion that the order of the Railroad Commission of Texas should be upheld on the ground that there is substantial evidence that the exception here in question is necessary to protect the correlative rights of the Whelan Brothers–Vickie Lynn Unit and to prevent drainage from such unit across lease lines to the Manziel Estate's Hollandsworth leases, and particularly the Mathis lease. Therefore, the judgment of the trial court is reversed and judgment is here rendered that the permanent injunctions granted by the trial court against the Railroad Commission of Texas and the Whelans be dissolved, and that the Manziels take nothing.■

NOTES AND COMMENTS

1.   How does *Manziel* illustrate the same Tragedy of the Commons problem that arose under the rule of capture?

2.   Why didn't the Manziels simply agree to cooperate with the Whelans and pay for their fair share of the waterflooding operation, reaping their fair share of the profits? With cooperation, the total size of the "pie" to be split between M and W would be larger because the two operators would save the costs of drilling unnecessary injection wells along lease lines as barriers to the flow of oil. Is the problem determining the formula to measure each operator's "fair share" (the same contentious issue that arose under prorationing)?

In *Gilmore v. Oil & Gas Conservation Comm'n*, 642 P.2d 773 (Wyo. 1982), the operators met for three years, trying to develop a formula that would reach the minimum 75 percent level of approval required by statute before the commission could force the remaining 25 percent of the acreage into the unit. The 81 different lessees considered 71 formulas without success. They then used computers to analyze voting patterns and "split the baby" using eleven different factors in the formula for dividing proceeds from the operation. This formula achieved 75.89 percent approval. One unhappy operator appealed the commission order to unitize the field on the basis that its correlative rights were not adequately protected. The Wyoming Supreme Court wrote: "Appellant seems to expect perfection. Justice was accomplished here, as much as could be under the circumstances. This litigation should end." *Id.* at 781.

3.   Footnote 12 of the *Manziel* case cites to the Texas voluntary unitization statute. Unitization is the joint, coordinated operation of all, or a substantial part, of a reservoir as a single unit by all the different operators holding leases in the field. This term should be distinguished from "pooling" which is the process of combining small tracts of land into acreage

large enough to secure a drilling permit to meet the spacing rules of the conservation commission. Pooling prevents the drilling of unnecessary wells and protects the correlative rights of all the owners being drained by the one well on the spacing unit and usually occurs during primary production. Unitization combines many spacing units into a fieldwide unit, usually to conduct secondary recovery operations.

Why would states require that voluntary units secure commission approval? Why would major operators desire the state's blessing for their private contract to produce cooperatively?

4. Most states have compulsory unitization statutes like that in *Gilmore* (note 2 above), which allow the conservation agency to force holdouts, like the Manziels, into a unit that is expected to increase the total recovery from the field. However, such a statute was castigated by the Texas independent producers for years as "substitution of force for persuasion . . . another fetter on the step of Freedom, another move down the road towards confiscation, tyranny, and unmorality" whose advocates were "socialists, bureaucrats, self-seeking politicians [and] fuzzy thinkers of the left." L.P. Thomas, Prospects for Compulsory Unitization in Texas, 44 Texas L. Rev. 510 at 524 (1966). By 1998, the lack of such a statute was retarding secondary recovery in West Texas fields to such an extent that the Texas Independent Producers and Royalty Association drafted and supported a compulsory unitization bill. However, it never reached the floor of the legislature. Many of the largest fields in Texas have been unitized because the Railroad Commission armtwisted the operators to unitize "voluntarily" by shutting in the fields or prorating them severely under the agency's broad authority to prevent waste. *See* Jacqueline L. Weaver, Unitization of Oil and Gas Fields in Texas: A Study of Legislative, Administrative and Judicial Policies 137–166 (1986).

5. The court in *Manziel* says that "in the case at bar we are not confronted with the tort aspects" of secondary recovery operations, yet it then proceeds to analyze the issue of trespass in great detail. Is the trespass part of the opinion dictum then? If the Manziels cannot obtain an injunction against this approved waterflooding operation, can they secure damages if they can show that their mineral estate was prematurely destroyed by the saltwater injections?

The "negative rule of capture" which appeared to be developing in 1962 has not come to pass. Operators who have been injured by a rival's secondary recovery have been able to secure damages, if proved. At the same time, the courts have worked strenuously to prevent the holdout from being unjustly enriched by the repressuring operation of other hard-working producers on adjoining acreage. *See* Patrick H. Martin and Bruce M. Kramer, 6 Williams and Meyers Oil and Gas Law, § 204.5 (1998), which now concludes:

> It is extremely hazardous, therefore, to engage in a secondary recovery program in the absence of unitization (voluntary or compulsory) of all premises which may be adversely affected by injection of fluids.

6.   Because minerals in the United States can be privately owned, mineral estates are often subdivided by deeds or by wills or intestacy laws as the property is transferred from one generation to another. The mineral estates often become subdivided into smaller and smaller physical tracts over time, or ownership becomes subdivided into increasingly small and more numerous fractional interests owned in cotenancy or some other form of concurrent ownership. Often both events occur. Such subdivision and fractionalization of privately owned interests cause serious problems for lessees. For example, as early as 1928, a cotenant who owned an undivided 1/768 interest in a tract of land in West Virginia prevented its development; the 131–acre tract would have to be partitioned into separately owned tracts before a lessee could drill. Law v. Heck, 106 W.Va. 296, 145 S.E. 601 (1928). Even though the common law in most states today would allow one cotenant to lease or drill without the consent of all the others, the developing cotenant must still account to the nondeveloping cotenants for their share of profits from any producing operations. Over time, dozens of relatives may come to own fractional interests. Many owners end up being paid a percentage interest that begins in the sixth decimal place. This owner will receive less than $10 a month from a well's oil production worth $1 million a month. Few wells produce that much revenue in one month, so thousands of royalty owners are due only a few pennies. The administrative costs to lessees of accounting to so many owners for their rightful shares of a well's revenues are very high. *See* Owen L. Anderson & Ernest E. Smith, The Use of Law to Promote Domestic Exploration and Production, 50 Inst. of Oil & Gas L. & Tax'n 2–1 (1999)

This is one reason that lessees have sought to explore in areas where large tracts of land are available owned by a single lessor–the government. Such lands are available offshore the United States on the outer continental shelf, on federal or state-owned land in the western United States and Alaska, and throughout the rest of the world where private ownership of minerals is not recognized. Here, the government owns all the oil and gas. The next two sections look at these areas of the world.

D.   THE GEOPOLITICS OF OIL

American oil exports fueled the victorious Allied forces in both World Wars I and II. However, after the second World War, U.S dominance in crude oil production quickly faded as the enormous oil fields of the Mideast came on stream. The United States moved from oil exporter to importer. While the world was soon awash with crude oil for the two decades following the end of the war, excess reserves in the United States dwindled as fewer new fields were discovered at home and consumer demand for oil and its products zoomed. This nation was becoming ever more dependent on imports of crude oil from foreign countries that were increasingly nationalistic and anti-American. The stage was set for the massive oil shocks of the 1970s, precipitated by the Arab countries' embargo of oil to the West and Japan in late 1973.

A more detailed account of the rise of OPEC, the Organization of Petroleum Exporting Countries, and its Arab counterpart (OAPEC) appears at the start of Chapter 16 on International Petroleum. This account is also useful reading as background to the current chapter, because it explains the roller coaster rise and fall of the price of oil in Figure 6–1 from 1973 to 1985. In brief, the dramatic price increases of the 1970s ultimately led to massive conservation efforts by importing countries and to the rapid development of diversified sources of new crude supplies in many new parts of the world. The price of oil plummeted in the early 1980s. Market forces seemed triumphant.

Today, crude oil is traded as a commodity, much like grain and pork bellies. However, the market for crude is by no means free of the geopolitical forces which have dominated its production since the early 1900s when Great Britain (through British Petroleum), the Netherlands (through Royal Dutch Shell) and the United States (through Standard Oil) battled for spheres of influence over global oil supplies. Today, many more players compete on the international scene—state-run oil companies, majors, independents, organizations of producer and consumer nations, and the nations themselves. Still, something other than free market forces appears to underlie the more recent gyroscopic fall and rise of crude oil prices, from about nine dollars a barrel in December 1999 to over $30 a barrel in March 2000. International oil diplomacy remains an important part of the foreign policy of the United States, as witnessed by Project Desert Storm in 1990–91 when U.S. troops were sent to the Persian Gulf to defend Kuwait against Iraqi invasion. However colorful the history of the domestic oil industry in the U.S., it pales in comparison to the international scene.

The relationship between private, multinational companies and host governments, often acting through their own national oil companies is far more complicated that the leasing transaction between a government lessor in the United States and private operators. Chapter 16 explores this relationship and other issues unique to international operations. Multinational companies abroad face political risks which are magnitudes greater than those in the United States. Here are some examples:

Columbia

"In the sacred tradition of Colombia's U'Wa Indians, oil flows through the veins of a living Mother Earth and drilling destroys nature's lifeblood. So says Berito Kuwaru'wa, explaining why the tribe's 5,000 members have threatened to jump off a cliff to their deaths if Occidental Petroleum Corp. drills for oil on its ancestral territory–an area of oil-rich northeastern Columbia in the shadow of the Andes mountain range. For the third year, the U'wa tribal elder has traveled from his remote home in the Colombian cloud forest to Los Angeles to protest at Occidental's annual shareholder meeting. 'Mother Earth is cut, is trampled, her vein is cut and blood is sucked out,' said Kuwaru'wa. Occidental has not drilled on the U'wa ancestral land but operates the block for the Colombian government to explore for oil on lots that include traditional U'wa territory. In a letter to shareholders, Occidental said it already had relinquished part of land that lay within the reservation, but did not rule out exploration in other areas within the U'wa's land." Houston Chronicle, April 30, 1999, Business Section at 1.

Nigeria

"Activists in southern Nigeria claimed Thursday to have captured and shut down 61 oil wells and a pipeline flow station operated by Houston-based Shell Co. in an effort to pressure the government for development funds. . . . The capture of oil platforms, wells and pipeline stations by activists and militant youths is common through out Nigeria's Niger Delta, where most of the country's oil is drilled. . . . Nigeria is the world's sixth largest exporter of oil, which brings in billions of dollars each year in profits. The Delta was sorely neglected by a succession of corrupt military leaders who robbed most of the country's oil wealth." Houston Chronicle, July 9, 1999, at 24A.

Russia

"The board of Russia's largest shipping company elected a ranking official [Mr. Lugovets] of the Russian Government as the company's chairman today, bowing to pressure from a powerful regional governor who has expressed anger over the influence of foreign investors in post-communist Russia. . . . Last month, Mr. Nazdratenko [governor of the region of Primorsky] is suspected of having threatened to jail a British member of the [Far Eastern Shipping Company's] board, Andrew Fox, if several demands were not met, among them election of Mr. Lugovets to the chairmanship. Mr. Nazdratenko also demanded that 7 percent of the shares owned by foreign investors, who hold 42 percent of the company, be sold to the Government of Primorsky, which already owns some shares, Mr. Fox said.

Acquiring those shares would give Mr. Nazdratenko effective control of the company. Formerly state-run, it is a major employer, with 11,400 workers and 112 ships. . . .

Far Eastern Shipping does most of its business in dollars and other hard currency, with annual revenue of $370 million, which has raised speculation that [the governor] may want access to that money to help finance his coming re-election campaign. Many foreign investors and their Russian allies had opposed Mr. Lugovets for the position. But he won in a 6–5 vote after an American board member, Richard Thomas, who had worked at Mr. Fox's firm until recently, broke ranks with the other foreigners and cast an affirmative vote. The reasons behind Mr. Thomas's decision were not clear, and he could not be reached today." Russell Working, Foreign Investors Lose a Round at Russian Ship Concern, New York Times, July 7, 1999, at C4.

Under circumstances like these, what expected rate of return would be required to attract foreign investors to develop petroleum resources abroad? Perhaps drilling "at home" on the outer continental shelf is more attractive. This is the most promising area of development in the U.S. today.

E.   Offshore Oil and Gas

1.   Introduction

About 18 percent of U.S. oil production and 27 percent of gas production comes from wells on the federal offshore outer continental shelf (OCS). It is estimated that over half of our nation's undiscovered oil and gas reserves lie on the OCS, particularly in the Gulf of Mexico. The late 1990s have seen a resurgence of drilling offshore in the Gulf of Mexico due to a number of factors: (1) new knowledge of how sands were deposited far from shore (as far as 130 miles) in the Gulf of Mexico millions of years ago in flood-related currents from the Mississippi River; (2) 3–D seismic technology; (3) the 1995 Deep Water Royalty Relief Act which exempts up to 87.5 million barrels of oil from royalty payments from each newly discovered field; and (4) advances in the evolution of offshore oil platforms from towers that rest on the sea bottom to floating or guyed structures, some of which are taller than the Sears Tower in Chicago. Peter Wilson, Science and Technology in the Offshore Oil Industry, Natural Resources & Environment, Spring 1990, at 552.

Little political opposition exists to drilling in the Gulf of Mexico. However, other coastal states, notably California, Massachusetts, and Florida have not been so welcoming. And Alaska presents its own unique set of environmental and political challenges as the following material will demonstrate.

2.   The Statutory Framework

One event, above all, was the catalyst for the wave of environmental legislation enacted from 1969 onwards: the Santa Barbara oil spill of January 28, 1969. In 1966 the first federal leases on the Pacific offshore were issued in the Santa Barbara Channel. As Union Oil drilled the fifth well on its Platform A in the channel, the well blew out. Eleven days passed before the well was plugged and some 24,000 to 71,000 barrels of oil spilled into the channel and onto nearby beaches. Figure 6–5 depicts the ensuing tsunami of environmental legislation:

When Figure 6–5 is superimposed on Figure 6–1, the wave of environmental protection closely coincides with the rocketing price of crude oil following the 1973 embargo and its ensuing decade of energy shocks and crisis. Energy competed with the environment for national attention. Could a balance be struck? Nowhere was this question more sharply framed than on the outer continental shelf and Alaska, the two areas of highest potential to provide a staggering nation with the domestic crude oil so essential to the transportation sector.

After the Santa Barbara spill, in rapid succession, Congress enacted the National Environmental Policy Act of 1969 (NEPA), the Marine Protec-

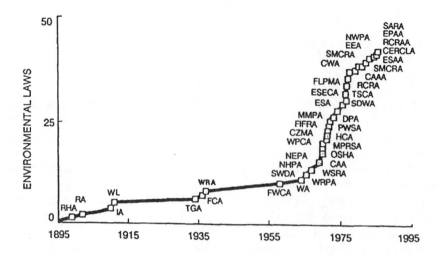

1899 - River and Harbors Act (RHA)
1902 - Reclamation Act (RA)
1910 - Insecticide Act (IA)
1911 - Weeks Law (WL)
1934 - Taylor Grazing Act (TGA)
1937 - Flood Control Act (FCA)
1937 - Wildlife Restoration Act (WRA)
1958 - Fish and Wildlife Coordination Act (FWCA)
1964 - Wilderness Act (WA)
1965 - Solid Waste Disposal Act (SWDA)
1965 - Water Resources Planning Act (WRPA)
1966 - National Historic Preservation Act (NHPA)
1968 - Wild and Scenic Rivers Act (WSRA)
1969 - National Environmental Policy Act (NEPA)
1970 - Clean Air Act (CAA)
1970 - Occupational Safety and Health Act (OSHA)
1972 - Water Pollution Control Act (WPCA)
1972 - Marine Protection, Research and
        Sanctuaries Act (MPRSA)
1972 - Coastal Zone Management Act (CZMA)
1972 - Home Control Act (HCA)
1972 - Federal Insecticide, Fungicide and
        Rodenticide Act (FIFRA)
1972 - Parks and Waterways Safety Act (PWSA)
1972 - Marine Mammal Protection Act (MMPA)

1973 - Endangered Species Act (ESA)
1974 - Deepwater Port Act (DPA)
1974 - Safe Drinking Water Act (SDWA)
1974 - Energy Supply and Environmental
        Coordination Act (ESECA)
1976 - Toxic Substances Control Act (TSCA)
1976 - Federal Land Policy and Management Act (FLPMA)
1976 - Resource Conservation and Recovery Act (RCRA)
1977 - Clean Air Act Amendments (CAAA)
1977 - Clean Water Act (CWA)
1977 - Surface Mining Control and Reclamation Act
        (SMCRA)
1977 - Soil and Water Resources Conservation Act
        (SWRCA)
1978 - Endangered Species Act Amendments (ESAA)
1978 - Environmental Education Act (EEA)
1980 - Comprehensive Environmental Response
        Compensation and Liability Act (CERCLA)
1982 - Nuclear Waste Policy Act (NWPA)
1984 - Resource Conservation and Recovery Act
        Amendments (RCRAA)
1984 - Environmental Programs and Assistance Act (EPAA)
1986 - Safe Drinking Water Act Amendments (SDWAA)
1986 - Superfund Amendments and Reorganization Act
        (SARA)

Figure 6–5

Source: National Academy of Engineering, Energy: Production, Consumption and Consequences 185 (National Academy Press 1990).

tion, Research and Sanctuaries Act of 1972, the Coastal Zone Management Act of 1972, the Marine Mammal Protection Act of 1972, and the Endangered Species Act of 1973, followed by the massive Clean Water and Clean Air Acts of 1977. In 1978, Congress significantly revised the Outer Continental Shelf Lands Act (OCSLA) of 1953, reflecting widespread dissatisfaction with the Department of Interior's administration of the earlier law. The 1978 amendments expanded the role of state and local government officials in the federal OCS leasing process in the hopes that this action would quell the unrelenting litigation between many coastal states and the Department of the Interior, so that OCS oil could be expeditiously developed in the wake of the first and second price shocks. However, opposition to OCS leasing continued unabated in states like California, except that the states now had additional legal mechanisms to fight the federal government in its attempts to develop domestic oil and gas. The "cooperative federalism" scheme championed in the CZMA was failing miserably.

In 1977, the Interior Department prepared another lease sale off the Santa Barbara coast. In the following case, the U.S. Supreme Court was called upon to interpret the CZMA of 1972 and the amendments (OCSLA) of 1978 in the context of this leasing decision. While the Court's interpretation of "directly affecting" in this case has been subsequently overturned by a 1990 amendment to the CZMA, the case still provides a good history of the 1972 and 1978 acts and a nice description of the potential adverse impacts of offshore leasing on coastal states. Better yet, the strong dissenting opinion of four justices sharply illuminates the policy choice which Congress confronted when it amended the CZMA in 1990.

Secretary of Interior v. California

464 U.S. 312 (1984).

■ O'CONNOR, J.: This case arises out of the Department of Interior's sale of oil and gas leases on the outer continental shelf off the coast of California. We must determine whether the sale is an activity "directly affecting" the coastal zone under § 307(c)(1) of the Coastal Zone Management Act (CZMA). That section provides in its entirety:

> "Each Federal agency conducting or supporting activities directly affecting the coastal zone shall conduct or support those activities in a manner which is, to the maximum extent practicable, consistent with approved state management programs." 16 U.S.C. § 1456(c)(1).

We conclude that the Secretary of the Interior's sale of outer continental shelf oil and gas leases is not an activity "directly affecting" the coastal zone within the meaning of the statute.

I

CZMA defines the "coastal zone" to include state but not federal land near the shorelines of the several coastal states, as well as coastal waters extending "seaward to the outer limit of the United States territorial sea." 16 U.S.C. § 1453(1). The territorial sea for states bordering on the Pacific or Atlantic Oceans extends three geographical miles seaward from the coastline. *See* 43 U.S.C. § 1301; United States v. California, 381 U.S. 139, (1965). Submerged lands subject to the jurisdiction of the *United States* that lie beyond the territorial sea constitute the "outer continental shelf" (OCS). *See* 43 U.S.C. § 1331(a). By virtue of the Submerged Lands Act, passed in 1953, the coastal zone belongs to the states, while the OCS belongs to the federal government.[15] 43 U.S.C. §§ 1302, 1311.

---

15. Editors' note: In 1950, the Supreme Court ruled that the entire continental shelf was under federal control (*United States v. Texas*, 339 U.S. 707 (1950) and cases cited

CZMA was enacted in 1972 to encourage the prudent management and conservation of natural resources in the coastal zone. Congress found that the "increasing and competing demands upon the lands and waters of our coastal zone" had "resulted in the loss of living marine resources, wildlife, nutrient-rich areas, permanent and adverse changes to ecological systems, decreasing open space for public use, and shoreline erosion." 16 U.S.C. § 1451(c). Accordingly, Congress declared a national policy to protect the coastal zone, to encourage the states to develop coastal zone management programs, to promote cooperation between federal and state agencies engaged in programs affecting the coastal zone, and to encourage broad participation in the development of coastal zone management programs. 16 U.S.C. § 1452.

Through a system of grants and other incentives, CZMA encourages each coastal state to develop a coastal management plan. Further grants and other benefits are made available to a coastal state after its management plan receives federal approval from the Secretary of Commerce. To obtain such approval a state plan must adequately consider the "national interest" and "the views of the Federal agencies principally affected by such program." 16 U.S.C. §§ 1455(c)(8), 1456(b).

Once a state plan has been approved, CZMA § 307(c)(1) requires federal activities "conducting or supporting activities directly affecting the coastal zone" to be "consistent" with the state plan "to the maximum extent practicable." 16 U.S.C. § 1456(c)(1). The Commerce Department has promulgated regulations implementing that provision. Those regulations require federal agencies to prepare a "consistency determination" document in support of any activity that will "directly affect" the coastal zone of a state with an approved management plan. The document must identify the "direct effects" of the activity and inform state agencies how the activity has been tailored to achieve consistency with the state program. 15 C.F.R. § 930.34, 930.39 (1983).

II

OCS lease sales are conducted by the Department of the Interior (Interior). Oil and gas companies submit bids and the high bidders receive priority in the eventual exploration and development of oil and gas resources situated in the submerged lands on the OCS. A lessee does not, however, acquire an immediate or absolute right to explore for, develop, or produce oil or gas on the OCS; those activities require separate, subsequent federal authorization.

therein), but in 1953 Congress passed the Submerged Lands Act which gave the states the rights to certain offshore waters, typically three miles seaward of the shore. However, Texas and Florida prevailed in their historical claims to extend their territorial sea jurisdiction to three marine leagues, or about ten miles seaward. This jurisdictional "wrinkle" has enriched Texas state coffers by millions of dollars. *See* Francis J. Gaynor, Beyond All Boundaries–a Study of Marine Jurisdiction of the State of Texas–Past History and Current Issues, 17 Hous. J. Int'l L. 253 (1994).

In 1977, the Department of Commerce approved the California Coastal Management Plan. The same year, Interior began preparing Lease Sale No. 53—a sale of OCS leases off the California coast near Santa Barbara. Interior first asked several state and federal agencies to report on potential oil and gas resources in this area. The Agency then requested bidders, federal and state agencies, environmental organizations, and the public, to identify which of 2036 tracts in the area should be offered for lease. In October 1978, Interior announced the tentative selection of 243 tracts, including 115 tracts situated in the Santa Maria Basin located off western Santa Barbara. Various meetings were then held with state agencies. Consultations with other federal agencies were also initiated. Interior issued a Draft Environmental Impact Statement in April, 1980.

On July 8, 1980 the California Coastal Commission informed Interior that it had determined Lease Sale No. 53 to be an activity "directly affecting" the California coastal zone. The state commission therefore demanded a consistency determination—a showing by Interior that the lease sale would be "consistent" to the "maximum extent practicable" with the state coastal zone management program. Interior responded that the Lease Sale would not "directly affect" the California coastal zone. Nevertheless, Interior decided to remove 128 tracts, located in four northern basins, from the proposed lease sale, leaving only the 115 tracts in the Santa Maria Basin. In September 1980, Interior issued a final Environmental Impact Statement. On October 27, 1980, it published a proposed notice of sale, limiting bidding to the remaining 115 blocks in the Santa Maria Basin. 45 Fed. Reg. 71140 (1980).

On December 16, 1980, the state commission reiterated its view that the sale of the remaining tracts in the Santa Maria Basin "directly affected" the California coastal zone. The commission expressed its concern that oil spills on the OCS could threaten the southern sea otter, whose range was within 12 miles of the 31 challenged tracts. The commission explained that it "has been consistent in objecting to proposed offshore oil development within specific buffer zones around special sensitive marine mammal and seabird breeding areas...." *App.* 77. The commission concluded that 31 more tracts should be removed from the sale because "leasing within 12 miles of the Sea Otter Range in Santa Maria Basin would not be consistent" with the California Coastal Management Program.

Interior rejected the State's demands. In the Secretary's view, no consistency review was required because the lease sale did not engage CZMA § 307(c)(1), and the Governor's request was not binding because it failed to strike a reasonable balance between the national and local interests. On April 10, 1981, Interior announced that the lease sale of the 115 tracts would go forward, and on April 27 issued a final notice of sale. 46 Fed. Reg. 23674 (1981).

Respondents filed two substantially similar suits in federal district court to enjoin the sale of 29 tracts situated within 12 miles of the Sea Otter range. Both complaints alleged, inter alia, Interior's violation of

§ 307(c)(1) of CZMA. They argued that leasing sets in motion a chain of events that culminates in oil and gas development, and that leasing therefore "directly affects" the coastal zone within the meaning of § 307(c)(1).

The district court entered a summary judgment for respondents on the CZMA claim. The Court of Appeals for the Ninth Circuit affirmed that portion of the district court judgment that required a consistency determination before the sale. We granted certiorari, and we now reverse.

III

Whether the sale of leases on the OCS is an activity "directly affecting" the coastal zone is not self-evident. As already noted, OCS leases involve submerged lands outside the coastal zone, and as we shall discuss, an OCS lease authorizes the holder to engage only in preliminary exploration; further administrative approval is required before full exploration or development may begin. Both sides concede that the preliminary exploration itself has no significant effect on the coastal zone. Both also agree that a lease sale is one ... in a series of decisions that may culminate in activities directly affecting that zone.

A

We are urged to focus first on the plain language of § 307(c)(1). Interior contends that "directly affecting" means "[h]av[ing] a [d]irect, [i]dentifiable [i]mpact on [t]he [c]oastal [z]one." Brief for Federal Petitioners 20. Respondents insist that the phrase means "[i]nitiat[ing] a [s]eries of [e]vents of [c]oastal [m]anagement [c]onsequence." Brief for Respondents State of California, et al. 10. But CZMA nowhere defines or explains which federal activities should be viewed as "directly affecting" the coastal zone, and the alternative verbal formulations proposed by the parties, both of which are superficially plausible, find no support in the Act itself.

B

OCSLA was enacted in 1953 to authorize federal leasing of the OCS for oil and gas development. The Act was amended in 1978 to provide for the "expeditious and orderly development, subject to environmental safeguards," of resources on the OCS. 43 U.S.C. 1332(3) (1976 ed., Supp. III). As amended, OCSLA confirms that at least since 1978 the sale of a lease has been a distinct stage of the OCS administrative process, carefully separated from the issuance of a federal license or permit to explore, develop, or produce gas or oil on the OCS.

The leases in dispute here, however, were sold in 1981. By then it was quite clear that a lease sale by Interior did not involve the submission or approval of "any plan for the exploration or development of, or production from" the leased tract. Under the amended OCSLA, the purchase of a lease entitles the purchaser only to priority over other interested parties in submitting for federal approval a plan for exploration, production, or development. Actual submission and approval or disapproval of such plans occurs separately and later.

Since 1978 there have been four distinct statutory stages to developing an offshore oil well: (1) formulation of a five year leasing plan by the Department of the Interior; (2) lease sales; (3) exploration by the lessees; (4) development and production. Each stage involves separate regulatory review that may, but need not, conclude in the transfer to lease purchasers of rights to conduct additional activities on the OCS. And each stage includes specific requirements for consultation with Congress, between federal agencies, or with the States. Formal review of consistency with state coastal management plans is expressly reserved for the last two stages.

(1) Preparation of a leasing program. The first stage of OCS planning is the creation of a leasing program. Interior is required to prepare a 5–year schedule of proposed OCS lease sales. 43 U.S.C. § 1344 (1976 ed., Supp. III). During the preparation of that program Interior must solicit comments from interested federal agencies and the governors of affected states, and must respond in writing to all comments or requests received from the state governors. 43 U.S.C. § 1344 (1976 ed., Supp. III). The proposed leasing program is then submitted to the President and Congress, together with comments received by the Secretary from the governor of the affected state. 43 U.S.C. § 1344(d)(2) (1976 ed., Supp. III).

Plainly, prospective lease purchasers acquire no rights to explore, produce, or develop at this first stage of OCSLA planning, and consistency review provisions of CZMA § 307(c)(3)(B) are therefore not engaged. There is also no suggestion that CZMA § 307(c)(1) consistency requirements operate here, though we note that preparation and submission to Congress of the leasing program could readily be characterized as "initiat[ing] a [s]eries of [e]vents of [c]oastal [m]anagement [c]onsequence." Brief for Respondents State of California, et al. 10.

(2) Lease sales. The second stage of OCS planning—the stage in dispute here—involves the solicitation of bids and the issuance of offshore leases. 43 U.S.C. § 1337(a) (1976 ed., Supp. III). Requirements of the National Environmental Protection Act and the Endangered Species Act must be met first. The governor of any affected state is given a formal opportunity to submit recommendations regarding the "size, timing, or location" of a proposed lease sale. 43 U.S.C. § 1345(a) (1976 ed., Supp. III). Interior is required to accept these recommendations if it determines they strike a reasonable balance between the national interest and the well-being of the citizens of the affected state. 43 U.S.C. § 1345(c) (1976 ed., Supp. III). Local governments are also permitted to submit recommendations, and the Secretary "may" accept these. 43 U.S.C. § 1345(a), (c) (1976 ed., Supp. III). The Secretary may then proceed with the actual lease sale. Lease purchasers acquire the right to conduct only limited "preliminary" activities on the OCS—geophysical and other surveys that do not involve seabed penetrations greater than 300 feet and that do not result in any significant environmental impacts. 30 C.F.R § 250.34–1 (1982).

Again, there is no suggestion that these activities in themselves "directly affect" the coastal zone. But by purchasing a lease, lessees acquire no right to do anything more. Under the plain language of OCSLA, the purchase of a lease entails no right to proceed with full exploration, development, or production that might trigger CZMA § 307(c)(3)(B); the lessee acquires only a priority in submitting plans to conduct those activities. If these plans, when ultimately submitted, are disapproved, no further exploration or development is permitted.

(3) Exploration. The third stage of OCS planning involves review of more extensive exploration plans submitted to Interior by lessees. 43 U.S.C. § 1340 (1976 ed., Supp. III). Exploration may not proceed until an exploration plan has been approved. A lessee's plan must include a certification that the proposed activities comply with any applicable state management program developed under CZMA. OCSLA expressly provides for federal disapproval of a plan that is not consistent with an applicable state management plan unless the Secretary of Commerce finds that the plan is consistent with CZMA goals or in the interest of national security. 43 U.S.C. § 1340(c)(2) (1976 ed., Supp. III). The plan must also be disapproved if it would "probably cause serious harm or damage . . . to the marine, coastal, or human environment. . . ." 43 U.S.C. §§ 1334(a)(2)(A)(I), 1340(c)(1) (1976 ed., Supp. III). If a plan is disapproved for the latter reason, the Secretary may "cancel such lease and the lessee shall be entitled to compensation. . . ." 43 U.S.C. § 1340(c)(1) (1976 ed., Supp. III).

There is, of course, no question that CZMA consistency review requirements operate here. CZMA § 307(c)(3)(B) expressly applies, and as noted, OCSLA itself refers to the applicable CZMA provision.

(4) Development and production. The fourth and final stage is development and production. 43 U.S.C. § 1351 (1976 ed., Supp. III). The lessee must submit another plan to Interior. The Secretary must forward the plan to the governor of any affected state and, on request, to the local governments of affected states, for comment and review. 43 U.S.C. §§ 1345(a), 1351(a)(3) (1976 ed., Supp. III). Again, the governor's recommendations must be accepted, and the local governments' may be accepted, if they strike a reasonable balance between local and national interests. Reasons for accepting or rejecting a governor's recommendations must be communicated in writing to the governor. 43 U.S.C. § 1345(c) (1976 ed., Supp. III). In addition, the development and production plan must be consistent with the applicable state coastal management program. The State can veto the plan as "inconsistent," and the veto can be overridden only by the Secretary of Commerce. 43 U.S.C. § 1351(d) (1976 ed., Supp. III). A plan may also be disapproved if it would "probably cause serious harm or damage . . . to the marine, coastal or human environments." 43 U.S.C. § 1351(h)(1)(D)(I) (1976 ed., Supp. III). If a plan is disapproved for the latter reason, the lease may again be canceled and the lessee is entitled to compensation. 43 U.S.C. § 1351(h)(2)(C) (1976 ed., Supp. III).

Once again, the applicability of CZMA to this fourth stage of OCS planning is not in doubt. CZMA § 307(c)(3)(B) applies by its own terms, and is also expressly invoked by OCSLA.

Congress has thus taken pains to separate the various federal decisions involved in formulating a leasing program, conducting lease sales, authorizing exploration, and allowing development and production. Since 1978, the purchase of an OCS lease, standing alone, entails no right to explore, develop, or produce oil and gas resources on the OCS. The first two stages are not subject to consistency review; instead input from State governors and local governments is solicited by the Secretary of Interior. The last two stages invite further input for governors or local governments, but also require formal consistency review. States with approved CZMA plans retain considerable authority to veto inconsistent exploration or development and production plans put forward in those latter stages. The stated reason for this four part division was to forestall premature litigation regarding adverse environmental effects that all agree will flow, if at all, only from the latter stages of OCS exploration and production. . . .

It is argued, nonetheless, that a lease sale is a crucial step. Large sums of money change hands, and the sale may therefore generate momentum that makes eventual exploration, development, and production inevitable. On the other side, it is argued that consistency review at the lease sale stage is at best inefficient, and at worst impossible: Leases are sold before it is certain if, where, or how exploration will actually occur.

The choice between these two policy arguments is not ours to make; it has already been made by Congress. In the 1978 OCSLA amendments Congress decided that the better course is to postpone consistency review until the two later stages of OCS planning, and to rely on less formal input from State governors and local governments in the two earlier ones. It is not for us to negate the lengthy, detailed, and coordinated provisions of CZMA § 307(c)(3)(B), and OCSLA §§ 1344–1346 and 1351, by a superficially plausible but ultimately unsupportable construction of two words in CZMA § 307(c)(1).

V

Collaboration among state and federal agencies is certainly preferable to confrontation in or out of the courts. In view of the substantial consistency requirements imposed at the exploration, development, and production stages of OCS planning, the Department of the Interior, as well as private bidders on OCS leases, might be well advised to ensure in advance that anticipated OCS operations can be conducted harmoniously with state coastal management programs. But our review of the history of CZMA § 307(c)(1), and the coordinated structures of the amended CZMA and OCSLA, persuades us that Congress did not intend § 307(c)(1) to mandate consistency review at the lease sale stage.

Accordingly, the decision of the Court of Appeals for the Ninth Circuit is reversed insofar as it requires petitioners to conduct consistency review pursuant to CZMA § 307(c)(1) before proceeding with Lease Sale No. 53.

It is so ordered.

■ JUSTICE STEVENS, with whom JUSTICE BRENNAN, JUSTICE MARSHALL, and JUSTICE BLACKMUN join, dissenting: In this case, the State of California is attempting to enforce a federal statutory right. Its coastal zone management program was approved by the Federal Government pursuant to a statute enacted in 1972. In § 307(c)(1) of that statute, the Coastal Zone Management Act (CZMA), the Federal Government made a promise to California:

> "Each Federal agency conducting or supporting activities directly affecting the coastal zone shall conduct or support those activities in a manner which is, to the maximum extent practicable, consistent with approved state management programs." 86 Stat. 1285, 16 U.S.C. § 1456(c)(1) (1982).

The question in this case is whether the Secretary of the Interior was conducting an activity directly affecting the California Coastal Zone when he sold oil and gas leases in the Pacific ocean area immediately adjacent to that zone. One would think that this question could be easily answered simply by reference to a question of fact—does this sale of leases directly affect the coastal zone? The District Court made a finding that it did, which the Court of Appeals affirmed, and which is not disturbed by the Court. Based on a straightforward reading of the statute, one would think that that would be the end of the case. . . .

[The dissent then conducted its own review of the plain language and legislative history of the CZMA:]

The majority's construction of § 307(c)(1) is squarely at odds with [the purpose of the CZMA]. Orderly, long-range, cooperative planning dictates that the consistency requirement must apply to OCS leasing decisions. The sale of OCS leases involves the expenditure of millions of dollars.[15][16] If exploration and development of the leased tracts cannot be squared with the requirements of the CZMA, it would be in everyone's interest to determine that as early as possible. On the other hand, if exploration and development of the tracts would be consistent with the state management plan, a pre-leasing consistency determination would provide assurances to prospective purchasers and hence enhance the value of the tracts to the Federal Government and, concomitantly, the public. Advance planning can only minimize the risk of either loss or inconsistency that may ultimately confront all interested parties. It is directly contrary to the legislative scheme not to make a consistency determination at the earliest possible point. Such a construction must be rejected.

There is no dispute about the fact that the Secretary's selection of lease tracts and lease terms constituted decisions of major importance to

---

16. In the lease sale at issue in this case, $220 million was bid on the disputed tracts.

the coastal zone. The District Court described some of the effects of those decisions:

* * *

"The Secretarial Issue Document ('SID'), prepared in October 1980 by the Department of Interior to aid the Secretary in his decision, contains voluminous information indicative of the direct effects of this project on the coastal zone. For instance, the SID contains a table showing the overall probability of an oil spill impacting a point within the sea otter range during the life of the project in the northern portion of the Santa Maria Basin to be 52%. Both the SID and the EIS [Environmental Impact Statement] contain statistics showing the likelihood of oil spills during the life of the leases; based on the unrevised USGS estimates, 1.65 spills are expected during the project conducted in the Santa Maria subarea. According to the SID, the probability of an oil spill is even higher when the revised USGS figures are utilized.

"... Both documents refer to impacts upon air and water quality, marine and coastal ecosystems, commercial fisheries, recreation and sportfishing, navigation, cultural resources, and socio-economic factors. For instance, the EIS states that '[n]ormal offshore operations would have unavoidable effects ... on the quality of the surrounding water.' Pipelaying, drilling, and construction, chronic spills from platforms, and the discharge of treated sewage contribute to the degradation of water quality in the area. As to commercial fisheries, drilling muds and cuttings 'could significantly affect fish and invertebrate populations'; the spot prawn fishery in the Santa Maria Basin is particularly vulnerable to this physical disruption. In reference to recreation and sportfishing, the EIS indicates the possibility of adverse impacts as a result of the competition for land between recreation and OCS/related onshore facilities as a result of the temporary disruption of recreation areas caused by pipeline burial. There are the additional risks of 'the degradation of the aesthetic environment conducive to recreation and the damage to recreational sites as a result of an oil spill.' Another impact on the coastal zone will occur as a result of the migration of labor into the area during the early years of the oil and gas operations. Impacts on the level of employment and the size of the population in the coastal region are also predicted.

"The SID notes that there are artifacts of history interest as well as aboriginal archaeological sites reported in the area of the Santa Maria tracts. The FWS and NMFS biological opinions, appended to the SID, indicate the likelihood that development and production activities may jeopardize the existence of the southern sea otter and the gray whale.

"These effects constitute only a partial list. Further enumeration is unnecessary. The threshold test under § 307(c)(1) would in fact be satisfied by a finding of a single direct effect upon the coastal zone.

Although the evidence of direct effects is substantial, such a showing is not required by the CZMA.''

520 F.Supp. 1359, 1380–1382 (C.D.Cal.1981). . . .

I therefore respectfully dissent.■

NOTES AND COMMENTS

1.   In an omitted footnote in this case, the majority opinion noted that the California Coastal Commission had warned: "Any attempt to explore or develop these tracts will face the strong possibility of an objection to a consistency certification of the Plan of Exploration or Development." What projected rate of return would warrant the political risks of leasing in the Santa Barbara Channel? What property right have lessees bought in exchange for the $221 million spent in bids? Do you agree that "[t]he price of confirming federal supremacy was destruction of the protectible property aspects of the offshore leasehold?" *See* George C. Coggins and Doris K. Nagel, "Nothing Beside Remains": The Legal Legacy of James G. Watt's Tenure as Secretary of the Interior on Federal Land Law and Policy, 17 Environmental Affairs 474 at 527 (1990). Keep these questions in mind as you read the material on OCS leasing moratoria in part 4 of this section below.

In mid–1999, Chevron sold its interests in offshore California fields, ending 41 years of production along the state's coast. Instead, it will focus on exploration projects in Kazakhstan, West Africa and the Gulf of Mexico. Houston Chronicle, Business Briefs, July 3, 1999, at 2C.

2.   Section 307(c)(1)(A) of the CZMA currently reads: "Each Federal agency activity within or outside the coastal zone that affects any land or water use or natural resource of the coastal zone shall be carried out in a manner which is consistent to the maximum extent practicable with the enforceable policies of approved State management programs." 16 USCA § 1456(c)(1)(A) (1999 Supp.). How does this amendment affect the balance between federal and state power over control of vital OCS resources? Does it give states a veto power over OCS leasing?

Section 307(c)(1)(B) allows the President, under certain conditions, to exempt a specific federal agency activity from compliance with the new consistency requirements if the President determines such a waiver is "in the paramount interest of the United States."

3.   Walter Mead, a professor of economics at the University of California at Santa Barbara, testified on March 11, 1969 before the Senate Subcommittee on Antitrust and Monopoly which was investigating government intervention in petroleum markets. After analyzing the combined effects of the Mandatory Oil Import Program, the tariff on imported crude oil, market demand prorationing by the states, and the percentage depletion allowance–all of which resulted in subsidizing the domestic oil industry and shielding it from international price competition–he stated: "The oil spillage case in the Santa Barbara Channel is directly related to the subsidy

system. Leases were purchased and drilling occurred in the California offshore area because operations were made profitable by the subsidy legislation. Under free market conditions, oil prices would be substantially lower, tax costs substantially higher, and the profit inducement to buy leases in the Channel would probably be lacking.... In addition, ... we have the external cost (aptly called 'spillover costs' even before this oil spillage case) of environmental pollution." Walter Mead, The System of Government Subsidies in the Oil Industry, 10 Nat. Res. J. 113 at 123–24 (1970).

Professor Mead recommended that the subsidies be phased out so that "the massive burden of resource misallocation in this industry be removed as a drag on this nation's strength." In light of subsequent events, do you agree with Professor Mead's advice?

4.   The staged structure of offshore oil development explicated in *Secretary of Interior v. California* has ramifications for the Environmental Impact Statement process required for any major federal activity significantly affecting the human environment under NEPA.

In *Village of False Pass v. Clark,* 733 F.2d 605 (9th Cir.1984), the court explained the interaction among OCSLA, NEPA, and the Endangered Species Act (ESA), in a case involving "an important marine environment, rare whales, large sums of money, [and] a search for increasingly scarce energy resources." *Id.* at 607.

In this case, the Secretary of Interior had approved federal leasing in the St. George Basin, located off the west coast of Alaska in the Bering Sea, "the gateway to virtually every marine mammal, fish, and bird species moving between the North Pacific and the Bering Sea." The Basin potentially held oil reserves of 1.12 billion barrels for which oil companies were willing to spend almost half a billion dollars for the right to investigate the chance (rated at 28 to 37 percent) of discovering such commercial quantities.

The Village of False Pass and other interveners argued that the Secretary had abused his discretion under NEPA by failing to perform a worst case analysis in the EIS of an oil spill of 100,000 barrels or larger occurring while whales migrated nearby. In response, the court wrote:

> The village would have a better argument for the importance of a worst case analysis at the lease sale stage of a 100,000 barrel oil spill if that were the only time the Secretary could review the potential environmental impacts of those leases.... As our earlier discussion of OCSLA's three stage process made clear, however, NEPA may require an environmental impact statement at each stage: leasing, exploration, and production and development. Furthermore, each stage remains separate. The completion of one stage does not entitle a lessee to begin the next [citing *Secretary of Interior v. California*].

A strong dissent in *False Pass* argued that the *California* case should not affect the interpretation of NEPA's requirements. The earlier case held that the OCSLA lease sale stage did not "directly affect" the coastal zone so as to require a consistency review under the CZMA. But the purposes of NEPA are different, explained the dissent:

> Prior to sale, the Secretary has absolute discretion to decline to lease an OCS tract. *See* 43 U.S.C. § 1344(a). He can therefore decline to lease on the ground that exploration or development will run a small but real risk of immense environmental harm. Once the Secretary leases a tract, however, he loses that freedom, and consequently commits himself to incur such a risk. The reasons why the Secretary loses his freedom upon sale of the leases are both legal and practical.

> As a legal matter, the Secretary is allowed to cancel an existing lease for environmental reasons only if he determines that:

>> (I) continued activity ... *would probably cause* serious harm or damage to ... [the] environment; (ii) the threat of harm or damage will not disappear or decrease to an acceptable extent within a reasonable period of time; and (iii) the advantages of cancellation outweigh the advantages of continuing such lease or permit in force.

> 43 U.S.C. § 1334(a)(2)(A)(emphasis added); 43 U.S.C. § 1351(h)(1)(D). The requirement of a determination that continued activity "would *probably* cause serious harm to the environment" is a forceful restriction on the Secretary's authority. At least under ordinary circumstances, it prohibits cancellation because of the possibility of a major oil spill; ... a major oil spill is not a *probable* occurrence, but rather is "an event of low probability but catastrophic effects." The effect of the statute, therefore is that sale of the leases ends the Secretary's right to call a total halt to exploration and development out of concern over remote environmental catastrophes....

> It is true that the Secretary's power to *suspend* operations remains broad, but we have held that the power to suspend is exceeded when the suspension is so open-ended as to amount to a cancellation of a lease. *Union Oil Co. of California v. Morton,* 512 F.2d 743, 750–51 (9th Cir.1975). Suspension is therefore a temporary remedy, and being temporary, cannot eliminate the possibility of a major oil spill. Only cancellation can do that."

Id. at 617–18.

5.   The *Village of False Pass* case also involved the Endangered Species Act (ESA) and whales. Section 7(a)(2) of the Act requires that every federal agency "insure that any action authorized, funded, or carried out by such agency ... is not likely to jeopardize the continued existence of any endangered species or threatened species" or adversely modify its critical habitat. 16 U.S.C.A 1536(a)(2) (1985). The majority opinion states that "ESA appears to apply equally to each stage [of offshore activity] of its own force and effect." *Id.* at 609. The court found no violation of the ESA because the Secretary had placed special disclaimers in the Notice of Lease Sale, stating that the Secretary retained authority to regulate seismic testing and to suspend drilling whenever migrating whales came close enough to be subject to the risk of spilled oil. The opinion continues:

The Village characterizes these [disclaimers] as "only a plan for later action." We conclude that, given the Fisheries Service's general recommendations about oil spills and exploration stage seismic testing, the Secretary could properly limit his action at the lease sale stage to a plan for later implementation. The ESA applies to every federal action.... The lease sale decision itself could not directly place gray or right whales in jeopardy, and the plan insures that the many agency actions that may follow indirectly from the sale will not either.

By choosing this plan, however, the Secretary recognizes his obligation under ESA to implement it. *See generally Conservation Law Foundation of New England, Inc. v. Andrus*, 623 F. 2d at 715. With each exploration plan, development and production plan, or permit to drill, the Secretary must: implicitly conclude that any approval does not affect an endangered species, *see* 50 C.F.R. § 402.04(a)(2) (1982); take appropriate steps to insure, on the basis of his previous consultation with the Fisheries Service, the absence of jeopardy to an endangered species; or reinitiate formal consultation, *see*, e.g., *Village of False Pass v. Watt*, 565 F. Supp. at 1161 & n.28 (strong suggestion that formal consultation about oil spill risks on whales will be required at the exploration stage); 50 C.F.R. § 402.04(h) (1982).

The monitoring agreement with the Fisheries Service will help the Secretary take these steps and diligently pursue ESA compliance after the lease sale, *see Village of False Pass v. Watt*, 565 F. Supp. at 1161. The Secretary's own regulations require an environmental report from each lessee for each exploration plan, ... and development and production plan.... Approval of these plans may even require a full environmental impact statement. *See* 30 C.F.R. § 250.34–4(a) (1982); *see also* 43 U.S.C. § 1351(e) (OCSLA); 42 U.S.C. § 4332(2)(C) (NEPA). Even if not a full environmental impact statement, these reports and plans must include information about marine mammal use of the area. *See* 30 C.F.R. § 250.34–3(a)(1)(I)(G)(4) (1982).... This means that the Secretary will have precise, site-specific information in each case to insure the best compliance with ESA.

These regulations, promulgated in part under OCSLA, help make the Secretary's plan a real safeguard. Neither the regulations, nor OCSLA itself, dilute the full application of ESA to actions by the Secretary....

Could the Secretary of Interior cancel a lease permanently because she found that exploration on the tract would jeopardize an endangered species and no temporary suspension could "unjeopardize" it? Would the lessee be entitled to compensation for lease cancellation?

Continue to keep these questions in mind as you approach the material on OCS leasing moratoria.

7. Can the best-made plans either predict or adjust to the disequilibrium of Mother Nature's own cycles? Consider the following:

Killer whales that normally hunt seals and sea lions are now feeding on sea otters and creating an ecological crisis along the entire Aleutian island chain of western Alaska.

Researchers say that the sudden loss of thousands of sea otters is allowing a boom in the population of sea urchins and these animals in turn, are stripping the undersea kelp forest, laying bare vast areas that once were lush with the marine plant.

The whole coastal ecosystem in western Alaska is now affected, says James Estes, a marine ecologist with the U.S. Geological Survey. Estes said the research demonstrates how disrupting just one link in a food chain can threaten an entire ecological system.... "The otters are down about 90 percent in the areas that we studied while the sea urchins have increased by about tenfold," said Estes....

Normally there is a delicate balance of life in the western Alaska waters, with sea lions and seals feeding on fish and the killer whales preying on the sea lions and seals. Sea urchins graze on the kelp beds while sea otters feed on the urchins. This keeps the urchin population in check and allows the kelp beds to thrive providing a home to hundreds of species.

But Estes said that starting in the late 1980s, the sea lion and seal population crashed and is now about a 10th of normal. Deprived of their normal food, killer whales turned to the sea otter.

The otter is much smaller than the sea lions and seals so the killer whales must eat more to get the same nourishment.

Estes said he and his colleagues estimate that a single killer whale will have to eat 1,825 otters a year to get its required nourishment. At that rate, it would take just four killer whales feeding only on sea otters to cause a crash of the sea otter population throughout most of the Aleutian Island chain.

Houston Chronicle, "Killer whales' search for new food source blamed for ecological crisis," Oct. 16, 1998, at 9A.

This study can be found in 282 Science 390–91 and 473–76 (Oct. 16, 1998). As one ecologist said, "It's just mindblowing that as few as four whales could cause an ecosystem effect over such a huge part of the Earth." *Id.* at 390. The researchers suspect that the seal and sea lion populations have declined because of intensified trawler fishing in the Bering Sea, although warmer ocean temperatures or the local extinction of baleen whales may also be the cause. The extinction of the baleen whale has allowed one fish, the pollock, which is low in fat, to flourish.

7.   In a study of oil and gas leasing on federal onshore lands, the National Research Council was informed by the federal agencies that, as a rule of thumb, about 10 percent of all oil and gas leases issued are ever drilled on, and about 10 percent of those drilled on ever produce oil and gas. Does this rule of thumb bolster the views of the majority? Should NEPA generate paperwork evaluating speculative possibilities that are a long shot? *See*

Park County Resource Council, Inc. v. U.S. Dep't of Agriculture, 817 F.2d 609 (10th Cir.1987) (lease issuance not a major federal action significantly affecting the human environment in a national forest because, among other factors, future drilling was "nebulous").

Until 1987, federal onshore leasing was conducted under the Mineral Leasing Act of 1920. In 1987, Congress enacted FOOGLRA, the Federal Onshore Oil and Gas Leasing Reform Act to amend serious deficiencies in the 1920 Act. Onshore production of oil and gas from federal lands is small compared to OCS production. For a full discussion of onshore leasing, *see* George C. Coggins and Robert L. Glicksman, 3 Public Natural Resources Law, Ch. 23 (1997).

3.   Alaska

a.   ABORIGINAL RIGHTS TO SUBSISTENCE HUNTING AND FISHING

Prudhoe Bay on Alaska's North Slope is the largest oil field in North America, one-and-a-half times larger than the East Texas field. It was discovered in late 1967 on land which the state of Alaska had selected (with some foresight) under the Alaskan Statehood Act of 1958. This Act gave Alaska the right to select over 100 million acres from the vacant and unreserved lands which had once been federal territory. Natives objected to many of the state's selections and by 1968 had filed land claims over 80 percent of Alaska. Congress stepped in to resolve the competing state, federal, and Native ownership claims. In the Alaskan Native Claims Settlement Act (ANCSA) of 1971, Congress allowed Native Alaskans to select 44 million acres of land, but in return, the Native Alaskans were required to relinquish all aboriginal rights to the exclusive use of the lands and waters in Alaska. These aboriginal rights were based on the immemorial custom and practice of the natives and their ancestors dating from long before the United States asserted sovereignty over Alaska. The rights of Indians to hunt and fish for subsistence had long been recognized as "not much less necessary to [their] existence ... than the atmosphere they breathed." *United States v. Winans,* 198 U.S. 371, 381 (1905). The Settlement Act vested land titles in native Villages and Regional Corporations, but did not specifically address Native subsistence. Much of Alaska remained in federal hands as national parks, forests, wilderness and wildlife refuges.

The Settlement Act's inadequate protection of Native subsistence rights resulted in the passage of the Alaska National Interest Lands Conservation Act (ANILCA) nine years later. At that time, much of Alaska's rural population lived a subsistence life style based on harvesting wild resources such as salmon, seals, caribou, bear, and berries. Subsistence living is more than a matter of providing food and shelter to households hundreds of miles from markets. It is a cultural way of life involving special skills, communal attitudes, and spiritual ceremony passed down from generation to generation. Title VIII of ANILCA established a priority for nonwasteful subsistence fishing and hunting on federal lands.

Inevitably, perhaps, OCS leasing came into conflict with the subsistence rights of some Native Alaskan Eskimo tribes living in small villages along the coasts, and the court was called upon to resolve this dispute between an endangered life style and OCS leasing.

Amoco Production Co. v. Village of Gambell

480 U.S. 531 (1987).

■ WHITE, J.: Petitioner Secretary of the Interior granted oil and gas leases to petitioner oil companies in the Norton Sound (Lease Sale 57) and Navarin Basin (Lease Sale 83) areas of the Bering Sea under the Outer Continental Shelf Lands Act (OCSLA), 67 Stat. 462, as amended, 43 U.S.C. § 1331 *et seq.* (1982 ed. and Supp. III). The Court of Appeals for the Ninth Circuit directed the entry of a preliminary injunction against all activity in connection with the leases because it concluded that it was likely that the Secretary had failed to comply with § 810 of the Alaska National Interest Lands Conservation Act (ANILCA), 94 Stat. 2371, 16 U.S.C. § 3120, prior to issuing the leases. We granted certiorari, 476 U.S. 1157, 106 S.Ct. 2274, 90 L.Ed.2d 717, and we now reverse.

I

When the Secretary of the Interior proposed Outer Continental Shelf (OCS) Lease Sale 57, the Alaska Native villages of Gambell and Stebbins sought to enjoin him from proceeding with the sale, claiming that it would adversely affect their aboriginal rights to hunt and fish on the OCS and that the Secretary had failed to comply with ANILCA § 810(a), 16 U.S.C. § 3120(a), which provides protection for natural resources used for subsistence in Alaska.[2][17] The District Court denied their motion for a preliminary injunction and thereafter granted summary judgment in favor of the Secretary and oil company intervenors, holding that the villagers had no

17. Section 810(a), 16 U.S.C. § 3120(a), provides: "In determining whether to withdraw, reserve, lease, or otherwise permit the use, occupancy, or disposition of public lands under any provision of law authorizing such actions, the head of the Federal agency having primary jurisdiction over such lands or his designee shall evaluate the effect of such use, occupancy, or disposition on subsistence uses and needs, the availability of other lands for the purposes sought to be achieved, and other alternatives which would reduce or eliminate the use, occupancy, or disposition of public lands needed for subsistence purposes. No such withdrawal, reservation, lease, permit, or other use, occupancy or disposition of such lands which would significantly restrict subsistence uses shall be effected until the head of such Federal agency—

"(1) gives notice to the appropriate State agency and the appropriate local committees and regional councils established pursuant to section 3115 of this title;

"(2) gives notice of, and holds, a hearing in the vicinity of the area involved; and

"(3) determines that (A) such a significant restriction of subsistence uses is necessary, consistent with sound management principles for the utilization of the public lands, (B) the proposed activity will involve the minimal amount of public lands necessary to accomplish the purposes of such use, occupancy or other disposition, and (C) reasonable steps will be taken to minimize adverse impacts upon subsistence uses and resources resulting from such actions."

aboriginal rights on the OCS and that ANILCA did not apply to the OCS.[3][18]

The Court of Appeals for the Ninth Circuit affirmed the District Court's ruling on aboriginal rights, although on different grounds, and reversed the ruling on the scope of ANILCA § 810. *People of Gambell v. Clark*, 746 F.2d 572 (1984) (Gambell I). With respect to the claim of aboriginal rights, the court assumed without deciding that the villagers once had aboriginal rights to hunt and fish in the Norton Sound, but concluded that these rights had been extinguished by § 4(b) of the Alaska Native Claims Settlement Act (ANCSA), 85 Stat. 690, 43 U.S.C. § 1603(b). That section provides:

"All aboriginal titles, if any, and claims of aboriginal title in Alaska based on use and occupancy, including submerged land underneath all water areas, both inland and offshore, and including any aboriginal hunting or fishing rights that may exist, are hereby extinguished."

The Court of Appeals construed the phrase "in Alaska" to mean "the geographic region, including the contiguous continental shelf and the waters above it, and not merely the area within the strict legal boundaries of the State of Alaska." 746 F.2d, at 575. Finding the phrase ambiguous, the court examined the legislative history and concluded that Congress wrote the extinguishment provision broadly "to accomplish a complete and final settlement of aboriginal claims and avoid further litigation of such claims." Ibid. The court then concluded that ANILCA § 810 had the same geographical scope as ANCSA § 4(b):

"[The villages] make a compelling argument that the provisions of Title VIII of [ANILCA] protecting subsistence uses were intended to have the same territorial scope as provisions of the earlier Claims Settlement Act extinguishing Native hunting and fishing rights. The two statutory provisions are clearly related. When Congress adopted the Claims Settlement Act it was aware that extinguishing Native rights might threaten subsistence hunting and fishing by Alaska Natives.... It is a reasonable assumption that Congress intended the preference and procedural protections for subsistence uses mandated by Title VIII of [ANILCA] to be co-extensive with the extinguishment of aboriginal rights that made those measures necessary." 746 F.2d, at 579–580.

The court found support for this view in ANILCA's legislative history. But, according to the Court of Appeals, "[t]he most compelling reason for resolving the ambiguous language of Title VIII in favor of coverage of outer continental shelf lands and waters is that Title VIII was adopted to benefit the Natives." Id. at 581. The court acknowledged the familiar rule of

---

18. The villages appealed and moved to enjoin the issuance of the leases pending appeal. The Ninth Circuit denied the motion and on May 10, 1983, 59 tracts were leased for bonus payments totaling over $300 million. While the appeal was pending, the Secretary approved exploration plans submitted by the lessees under 43 U.S.C. § 1340 (1982 ed. and Supp. III) and they proceeded with exploration during the summer of 1984. The Secretary also proceeded with Lease Sale 83 on April 17, 1984, which resulted in the leasing of 163 tracts for total bonus payments of over $500 million.

statutory construction that doubtful expressions must be resolved in favor of Indians. See *Alaska Pacific Fisheries v. United States*, 248 U.S. 78, 89 (1918). It then remanded to the District Court the questions whether the Secretary had substantially complied with ANILCA § 810 in the course of complying with other environmental statutes,[5][19] and if not, whether the leases should be voided.

In compliance with the Court of Appeals' decision, the Secretary prepared a postsale evaluation of possible impacts on subsistence uses from Lease Sale 57.[6][20] The Secretary found that the execution of the leases, which permitted lessees to conduct only limited preliminary activities on the OCS, had not and would not significantly restrict subsistence uses. He further found that the exploration stage activities, including seismic activities and exploratory drilling, that had occurred in Norton Sound had not significantly restricted subsistence uses and were not likely to do so in the future. Finally, he found that, if development and production activities were ever conducted, which was not likely, they might, in the event of a major oil spill, significantly restrict subsistence uses for limited periods in limited areas.

In April 1985, the villages sought a preliminary injunction in the District Court against exploratory activities in Norton Sound. At the same time, the village of Gambell, joined by Nunam Kitlutsisti, an organization

---

19. The Coastal Zone Management Act, 16 U.S.C. § 1451 *et seq.* (1982 ed. and Supp. III), Marine Protection, Research, and Sanctuaries Act, 16 U.S.C. § 1431 *et seq.* (1982 ed. and Supp. III), Marine Mammal Protection Act, 16 U.S.C. § 1361 *et seq.* (1982 ed. and Supp. III), Fishery Conservation and Management Act, 16 U.S.C. § 1801 *et seq.* (1982 ed. and Supp. III), Endangered Species Act, 16 U.S.C. § 1531 *et seq.* (1982 ed. and Supp. III), and National Environmental Policy Act, 42 U.S.C. § 4331 *et seq.* (1982 ed. and Supp. III), all apply to activities on the OCS. Pursuant to the National Environmental Policy Act (NEPA), the Department of the Interior drafted in 1982 a 332–page Final Environmental Impact Statement (EIS) on proposed Lease Sale 57. Interior analyzed in the EIS the effects that the lease sale, and subsequent exploration, development, and production, could conceivably have on "subsistence uses," as defined by ANILCA § 803, 16 U.S.C. § 3113. The EIS documented the fish and shellfish, sea mammal, bird, and land animal resources utilized by the villages in the region, including Gambell and Stebbins, and analyzed the sensitivity of these resources to oil spills, other exploration and development impacts, and harvest pressure. EIS 47–53, 136–148. The EIS also considered

the sociocultural impact of changes in the availability of subsistence resources. Interior concluded as follows:

"While some changes in local subsistence use and take may occur with this proposal, the probability of significant disturbance, in the form of long-term reduction of subsistence take, large-scale disruption of subsistence harvesting activities, or significant reductions in primary resources utilized for subsistence is unlikely for the region as a whole. For Savoonga, and to a lesser extent other 'big sea mammal hunting' villages (Diomede, Gambell, King Island, Wales) due to a relatively greater vulnerability to oil spill events, the short-term disturbance is more likely, particularly during the peak development period." EIS 142 ...

20. ... The Secretary examined the effects on subsistence uses of Lease Sale 57 itself, present and future exploratory activities, and development and production activities, which the Secretary estimated had a 13% probability of being undertaken.... The Secretary stressed that a definite evaluation with respect to the latter stage could only be made if and when plans for development and production were submitted and that a separate § 810 evaluation would be prepared at that time.

of Yukon Delta Natives, filed a complaint seeking to void Lease Sale 83 and to enjoin imminent exploratory drilling in the Navarin Basin. The District Court consolidated the motions for preliminary injunctions and denied them.... [W]ith respect to the postsale evaluation for Lease Sale 57, the District Court concluded that because development and production activities, if they ever occurred, could significantly restrict subsistence uses in certain areas, the Secretary was required to conduct the hearing and make the findings required by §§ 810(a)(1)-(3) prior to conducting the lease sale. Nevertheless, the court concluded that injunctive relief was not appropriate based on the following findings:

"(1) That delay in the exploration of the OCS may cause irreparable harm to this nation's quest for new oil resources and energy independence. Expedited exploration as a policy is stated in OCSLA. See 43 U.S.C. § 1332(3);

"(2) That exploration will not significantly restrict subsistence resources; and

"(3) That the Secretary continues to possess power to control and shape the off-shore leasing process. Therefore, if the ANILCA subsistence studies require alteration of the leasing conditions or configuration the Secretary will be able to remedy any harm caused by the violation." *Id.*, at 62a–63a.

Accordingly, applying the traditional test for a preliminary injunction, the court concluded that the balance of irreparable harm did not favor the movants; in addition, the public interest favored continued oil exploration and such exploration in this case would not cause the type of harm that ANILCA was designed to prevent.

Respondents appealed from the District Court's denial of a preliminary injunction. The Ninth Circuit reversed. People of Gambell v. Hodel, 774 F.2d 1414 (1985) (Gambell II). The court, agreeing that the villages had established a strong likelihood of success on the merits, concluded that the District Court had not properly balanced irreparable harm and had not properly evaluated the public interest. Relying on its earlier decision in Save Our Ecosystems v. Clark, 747 F.2d 1240, 1250 (1984), the court stated: " 'Irreparable damage is presumed when an agency fails to evaluate thoroughly the environmental impact of a proposed action.' " 774 F.2d, at 1423. It ruled that "injunctive relief is the appropriate remedy for a violation of an environmental statute absent rare or unusual circumstances." Ibid. "Unusual circumstances" are those in which an injunction would interfere with a long-term contractual relationship, Forelaws on Board v. Johnson, 743 F.2d 677 (9th Cir.1984), or would result in irreparable harm to the environment, American Motorcyclist Assn. v. Watt, 714 F.2d 962, 966 (9th Cir.1983). 774 F.2d, at 1423–1425. The court found no such circumstances in the instant case. The Ninth Circuit also concluded that the policy declared in OCSLA to expedite exploration of the OCS had been superseded by ANILCA's policy to preserve the subsistence culture of Alaska Natives....

II

[In this part of the opinion, the Court held that the Ninth Circuit had erred in issuing a preliminary injunction. Because the District Court had found that exploration would not significantly affect subsistence uses and the Secretary continued to possess the power to control later stages of the offshore leasing process, there was little probability of irreparable injury to the Native Alaskans. The Court continued. "[O]n the other side of the balance of harms was the fact that the oil company petitioners had committed approximately $70 million to exploration to be conducted during the summer of 1985 which they would have lost without chance of recovery had exploration been enjoined."]

III

Petitioners also contend that the Court of Appeals erred in holding that ANILCA § 810 applies to the OCS. We agree. By its plain language, that provision imposes obligations on federal agencies with respect to decisions affecting use of federal lands *within the boundaries of the State of Alaska.* Section 810 applies to "public lands." Section 102 of ANILCA, 16 U.S.C. § 3102, defines "public lands," and included terms, for purposes of the Act as follows:

"(1) The term 'land' means lands, waters, and interests therein.

"(2) The term 'Federal land' means lands the title to which is in the United States after December 2, 1980.

"(3) The term 'public lands' means land situated *in Alaska* which, after December 2, 1980, are Federal lands, except [land selected by the State of Alaska or granted to the State under the Alaska Statehood Act, 72 Stat. 339, or any other provision of federal law, land selected by a Native Corporation under ANCSA, and lands referred to in ANCSA § 19(b), 43 U.S.C. § 1618(b)]." (Emphasis added.)

The phrase "in Alaska" has a precise geographic/political meaning. The boundaries of the State of Alaska can be delineated with exactitude. The State of Alaska was "admitted into the Union on an equal footing with the other States," and its boundaries were defined as "all the territory, together with the territorial waters appurtenant thereto, now included in the Territory of Alaska." Alaska Statehood Act (Statehood Act) §§ 1, 2, 72 Stat. 339. Under § 4 of the Submerged Lands Act, 43 U.S.C. § 1312, the seaward boundary of a coastal State extends to a line three miles from its coastline. At that line, the OCS commences. OCSLA § 2(a), 43 U.S.C. § 1331(a). By definition, the OCS is not situated in the State of Alaska. Nevertheless, the Ninth Circuit concluded that "in Alaska" should be construed in a general, "nontechnical" sense to mean the geographic region of Alaska, including the Outer Continental Shelf. 746 F.2d at 579. We reject the notion that Congress was merely waving its hand in the general direction of northwest North America when it defined the scope of ANILCA as "Federal lands" "situated in Alaska." Although language seldom attains the precision of a mathematical symbol, where an expression is capable of precise definition, we will give effect to that meaning absent strong evidence that Congress actually intended another meaning. . . .

■ JUSTICE STEVENS, with whom JUSTICE SCALIA joins, concurring in part and concurring in the judgment: Given the Court's holding that § 810 of the Alaska National Interest Lands Conservation Act (ANILCA), 94 Stat. 2371, 16 U.S.C. § 3120, does not apply to the Outer Continental Shelf, it is unnecessary to decide whether the Court of Appeals applied the proper standard in determining the availability of injunctive relief. Accordingly, I join only Parts I and III of the Court's opinion.■

NOTES AND COMMENTS

1. Is there stronger protection for endangered species or for endangered people in the network of laws governing OCS leasing?

A similar conflict between endangered species and endangered people has arisen over the Inuit right to hunt the bowhead whale. Inuits are Eskimo natives of the Arctic, often referred to as "the People of the Whale" because their culture and values are rooted in whale hunting and sharing of the harvest. Whale hunting provides them with food, clothing, light, and heat, and is the central ritual of their community life. Archeological evidence suggests that their ancestors have hunted the bowhead whale for 2,500 years. Yet commercial overhunting of the bowhead has led the international community, through the International Whaling Commission, to establish a moratorium on bowhead hunting. The moratorium spells death for the Inuit culture. Rupa Gupta Note: Indigenous Peoples and the International Environmental Community, 74 N.Y.U.L.Rev. 1741 (1999). Gupta argues that Inuits should have a formal role on the Whaling Commission so that their views and their extensive traditional knowledge of the bowhead whales life cycle can be heard in the regulatory forum. Any international regime based on principles of sustainable development should integrate indigenous knowledge and practices into a regime of co-management of resources rather than relying only on scientific experts from the Western communities.

"Only with a heightened sensitivity to the interdependence of Inuit cultural and physical survival will the international community solve the problems posed by the global commons. Historically, indigenous populations have been marginalized and viewed by the international community through a narrow lens of assimilation. A member of one indigenous community expresses the danger inherent in such a perspective:

> The surest way to kill us is to separate us from our part of the Earth. Once separated, we will either perish in body or our minds and spirits will be altered so that we end up mimicking foreign ways, adopt foreign languages, accept foreign thoughts and build a foreign prison around our indigenous spirits which suffocates [us]. . . . Over time, we lose our identity and eventually die or are cripples as we suffer under the name of 'assimilation' into another society." *Id.* at 1784–85.

Chapter 16 on International Petroleum considers in more detail the rights of indigenous peoples, this time in the context of drilling for oil and gas in tropical rainforests.

2. Why did the majority of the Supreme Court decide the injunction issue? If preliminary injunctions against federal lease sales are automatically granted, it is easier for opponents to block federal programs that are found to be in "probable" conflict with environmental laws. Faced with the real prospect of delays due to preliminary injunctions issued under a vague "public interest" standard, oil companies may withdraw from participating in bids for leases.

In *Sierra Club v. Georgia Power Co.*, 180 F.3d 1309 (11th Cir.1999), the court of appeals upheld the district court's finding that a preliminary injunction requested by the Sierra Club would be adverse to the public interest. The Sierra Club sought the injunction to require Georgia Power to meet the temperature discharge limits in its Clean Water Act permit. Hot water discharges from the plant had resulted in fish kills. The Sierra Club contended that the company could meet its permitted discharge temperatures by reducing the amount of power generated in the plant. The company contended that it could not do so without seriously impacting the power generated throughout its entire electrical grid. Noting that the fish kills were "temporary, not significant and limited to a small percentage of the lake," the court found that the potential harm of reduced electrical power during summer heatwaves outweighed the potential injury to the lake.

3. A moratorium is essentially an "injunction" issued by either the Executive or Congressional branch prohibiting leasing. Frustrated with the results of litigation, the coastal states used their political clout, quite successfully, to press for moratoria on OCS leasing off the Pacific and Atlantic coasts, as discussed in the next section.

4.   MORATORIA AND WITHDRAWALS OF LAND FROM LEASING

a.   OFFSHORE

The moratorium movement gained momentum when James Watt became Secretary of the Interior under Ronald Reagan in 1981 and proposed to lease virtually the entire federal offshore area. Almost one billion acres were to be offered for lease during the five-year period from 1982–1987. This amounted to 25 times as much land as was offered during the entire period from 1954 to 1980. In 1982, Congress responded by writing into the DOI's 1982 appropriations bill a prohibition against offering certain areas for lease in California. By 1989, succeeding appropriation bills had extended the moratoria to more than 181 million acres off the coasts of California, the North Atlantic, and the Eastern Gulf of Mexico (near Florida). This "off limits" acreage equaled more than twice the acreage that had been leased in the entire history of the OCS program. The reasons for the Congressional moratoria have been summarized as follows:

They were partly a political response to the intractable approach of former Secretary Watt toward placing one billion acres of OCS for lease sale. The rapid pace and magnitude of leasing proposed under this program undermined the ability of state and local governments to adequately assess the environmental impact of leasing and to plan for OCS development. The Reagan administration's continued support for the areawide leasing concept and its refusal to delete areas of environmental sensitivity and economic importance from lease sales was perceived by coastal states and environmental groups as a resource program weighted heavily toward energy production, irrespective of legitimate state concerns for balanced OCS development. The administration's opposition to continued funding for state coastal management programs, OCS revenue sharing, and consistency requirements lead [sic] states and local citizens to conclude that they were taking all the risks of OCS activity but receiving none of the benefits in return.

G. Kevin Jones, Understanding the Debate over Congressionally Imposed Moratoria on Outer Continental Shelf Leasing, 9 Temp. Envtl L. & Tech. J. 117 at 144 (1990).

The domestic oil industry characterized the moratoria thusly: "If a foreign power had managed to do to us what we have done to ourselves, to shape our energy policy so disastrously, we would call it an act of war." *Id.* at 147. In the first two years of the Watt program, eight of the 15 scheduled lease sales were challenged in court, resulting in major delays and uncertainties in the program rather than Watt's hoped-for acceleration. ARCO forfeited a $30 million investment by abandoning a high potential area off California because of the litigation. *Id.* at 163.

The leasing fiasco, and Secretary Watt's other controversial efforts to privatize and develop America's public lands ultimately led to his resignation in 1983 (sparked by his refusal to allow the Beach Boys to perform at a free outdoor concert on the Washington D.C. mall), and to the following ditty:

"Buy the shores of Gitche Gumee
Buy the shining offshore leases
Buy the shining mining leases
Giving me the credit due me,
And you'll be as rich as Croesus

* * *

Thus spake Watt in his ascendence,
Pillar of Conservatism,
Glowing with a great resplendence
Til he brewed a mess of pottage
That created massive schism.

* * *

Even in the Great White Cottage

* * *

> Thereupon Watt drew dismissal,
> Drew dismissal unexpected
> When the Wise Men blew the whistle:
> Reagan must be re-elected."

Felicia Lamport, The Song of High Watt (1983), N.Y. Times, Oct. 28 1983, Sec. 4 at 19 (copyright Felicia Lamport, as reprinted in George C. Coggins and Doris K. Nagel, "Nothing Beside Remains": The Legal Legacy of James G. Watt's Tenure as Secretary of the Interior on Federal Land Law and Policy, 17 Environmental Affairs 473 (1990).

President Reagan's subsequent five-year leasing programs were also amply litigated. *See* Edward A. Fitzgerald, Natural Resources Defense Council v. Hodel: The Evolution of Interior's Five Year Outer Continental Shelf Oil and Gas Leasing, 12 Temp. Envtl. L. & Tech. J. 1 (1993). Subsequent presidents have taken the ditty to heart (undoubtedly also influenced by the sharp drop in oil prices in 1981 that crimped demand for federal leases). In 1990, President Bush canceled all lease sales pending off California, Washington, Oregon, Florida, and the Georges Bank area off New England (one of the richest fishing areas in the world). *Id.* at 44–45. Further, he issued a moratorium on leasing in these areas until the year 2002. President Clinton's latest OCS leasing plan for 1997 to 2002 leaves the Atlantic and Pacific coasts untouched. Annual sales are scheduled in the Gulf of Mexico, with one sale being considered in the Eastern Gulf in deep water more than 100 miles off Florida. Five sales are contemplated in Alaska. *See* The Proposed Final Outer Continental Shelf Oil and Gas Leasing Program for 1997–2002 (August 1996) available at the Minerals Management Services website at www.mms.gov. The program emphasizes a new approach to decisionmaking:

> This program is unique in its development from the bottom up and its grounding in the principle of working in partnership with affected parties to develop a reliable schedule of lease offerings so that the new program can serve as a framework for collaboration among parties. The Secretary has decided, for this program, to give greater weight to the following two OCS Lands Act section 18 criteria: (1) laws, goals, and policies of affected States and (2) location of regions with respect to other uses of the sea and seabed. He has concluded that any lesser weighting of these latter two criteria at this time would be counterproductive to long-term development of the OCS. *Id.* at 2.

In 1998, President Clinton extended through the year 2012 the Bush moratoria against drilling off most of the U.S. coastline, except in the Gulf Coast and parts of Alaska. The American Petroleum Institute responded: "The extension is unfortunate because it ignores the near-perfect performance of the American petroleum industry in operating offshore in a safe and environmentally sensitive manner. U.S. government statistics show that natural seeps from the ocean floor introduce 100 times more crude oil into U.S. marine waters than do the petroleum industry's offshore activities." In turn, the Natural Gas Supply Association said cleaner air and increased use of affordable, clean-burning natural gas depended on access to the large gas fields off the nation's coasts. The moratoria made projections of a 35 percent growth in U.S. gas consumption by 2010 or 2015 "virtually untenable." Oil & Gas J., June 22, 1998 at 32.

The moratoria do not extend to 40 existing undeveloped oil and gas leases off the coast of California near Santa Barbara. Oil companies had paid $1.2 billion for the leases between 1968 and 1984. Development of these leases was halted in 1993 when the oil companies agreed to work with federal and county authorities to conduct a study on the impact of development on local communities. The ban was to expire in June 1999 after the research study was completed. As of July 1999, the MMS was still finalizing the study (called COOGER, the California Offshore Oil and Gas Energy Report) and Governor Davis was vowing to block any effort by the DOI to extend the leases without further study. A spokesman for Conoco, one of the companies involved, said the delay "has been going on for so many years, [that] it's not anything that has affected our work a great deal. We don't know anything different." Jennifer Walsh, Drilling Ban Extended Off Calif. Coast, Houston Chronicle, June 26, 1999 at C1.

Can recalcitrant coastal states be lured into accepting oil and gas development through a revenue sharing mechanism that gives them more of the OCS bounty? States currently receive 50 percent of federal onshore oil and gas revenues, but such largesse does not extend to the OCS. Six states with OCS production directly bordering their submerged lands began to receive 27 percent of certain federal offshore revenues in 1986. Legislation has been proposed which designates 50 percent of OCS revenues (about $2.5 billion a year) for grants to coastal states and to fund nationwide conservation and wildlife programs. Under one such bill, Senate Bill 25 (proposing the Conservation and Reinvestment Act of 1999), all 34 states bordering the oceans or the Great Lakes would share the revenues, although OCS production borders only six states. Senator Mary Landrieu of Louisiana, a chief sponsor, included all 34 states in the bill in order to deliver 60 votes, the number needed to override a potential Senate filibuster. The proposed Conservation and Reinvestment Act is discussed in Edward A. Fitzgerald, The Conservation and Reinvestment Act of 1999: Outer Continental Shelf Revenue Sharing, 30 ELR 10165 (Mar. 2000).

In testimony before the Senate Energy and Natural Resources Committee on S.B. 25 on January 27, 1999, Mark Van Putten, President of the World Wildlife Fund, endorsed the concept that federal revenues should go to mitigate the environmental impacts of offshore drilling, but objected to the use of funds to encourage more OCS development. In his view, the legislation should be amended to exclude new leasing revenues or revenues received from production in areas that are currently subject to leasing moratoria.

Some OCS lease revenues are already earmarked for the Land and Water Conservation Fund (LWCF), created in 1965, to finance new recreational areas and improve existing national parks, refuges, and forests. LWCF grants to states have added two million acres to state and local government recreational lands. However, actual spending from this fund has been far below the amounts authorized. *See generally* Robert E. Glicksman & George C. Coggins, Federal Recreation Land Policy: The Rise and Decline of the Land and Water Conservation Fund, 9 Colum. J. Envt'l L. 125 (1984).

NOTES AND QUESTIONS

If states cannot be "bought off" to accept OCS leasing activities off their coastlines, will oil companies that have paid millions of dollars in bonus money for leases that cannot be developed be entitled to compensation? In *Marathon Oil Co. v. United States,* 158 F.3d 1253, *reversed sub. nom., Mobil Oil Exploration & Producing Southeast, Inc.,* 2000 WL 807187 (June 26, 2000), the Circuit Court of Appeals refused to order restitution of $156 million in bonuses paid by Marathon and Mobil for leases 45 miles off the coast of North Carolina. This court held that these two oil companies were sophisticated lessees who bargained "with their legal eyes wide open" for nothing more than a lottery ticket, giving them the right to explore if they could secure a state consistency certificate or a federal override of a state's refusal to find consistency. 158 F.3d at 1258. This court cited *Secretary of Interior v. California,* 464 U.S. 312 (1984), excerpted in the text *supra,* for its view of the nature of a lessee's property rights in an OCS lease, and a provision of OCSLA which reads: "Lessee shall not be entitled to compensation" for lease cancellation if its activities "do not receive concurrence by such State with respect to the consistency certification" and the Secretary of Commerce refuses to override the state disapproval.

The U.S. Supreme Court, with a lone dissent by Justice Stevens, reversed and ordered the restitution of the $156 million in the following opinion:

Mobil Oil Exploration & Producing Southeast, Inc. v. United States

2000 WL 807187, ___ U.S. ___.
(June 26, 2000).

■ BREYER, J. Two oil companies, petitioners here, seek restitution of $156 million they paid the Government in return for lease contracts giving them rights to explore for and develop oil off the North Carolina coast. The rights were not absolute, but were conditioned on the companies' obtaining a set of further governmental permissions. The companies claim that the Government repudiated the contracts when it denied them certain elements of the permission-seeking opportunities that the contracts had promised. We agree that the Government broke its promise; it repudiated the contracts; and it must give the companies their money back.

I A

A description at the outset of the few basic contract law principles applicable to this case will help the reader understand the significance of the complex factual circumstances that follow. "When the United States enters into contract relations, its rights and duties therein are governed generally by the law applicable to contracts between private individuals." United States v. Winstar Corp., 518 U.S. 839, 895, 116 S.Ct. 2432, 135 L.Ed.2d 964 (1996) (plurality opinion) (internal quotation marks omitted). The Restatement of Contracts reflects many of the principles of contract law that are applicable to this case. As set forth in the Restatement of Contracts, the relevant principles specify that, when one party to a contract repudiates that contract, the other party "is entitled to restitution for any benefit that he has conferred on" the repudiating party "by way of part performance or reliance." Restatement (Second) of Contracts § 373 (1979) (hereinafter Restatement). The Restatement explains that "repudiation" is a "statement by the obligor to the obligee indicating that the obligor will commit a breach that would of itself give the obligee a claim for damages for total breach." *Id.*, § 250. And "total breach" is a breach that "so substantially impairs the value of the contract to the injured party at the time of the breach that it is just in the circumstances to allow him to recover damages based on all his remaining rights to performance." *Id.*, § 243.

As applied to this case, these principles amount to the following: If the Government said it would break, or did break, an important contractual promise, thereby "substantially impair[ing] the value of the contract[s]" to the companies, *ibid.*, then (unless the companies waived their rights to restitution) the Government must give the companies their money back. And it must do so whether the contracts would, or would not, ultimately have proved financially beneficial to the companies. The Restatement illustrates this point as follows:

> "A contracts to sell a tract of land to B for $100,000. After B has made a part payment of $20,000, A wrongfully refuses to transfer title. B can recover the $20,000 in restitution. The result is the same even if the market price of the land is only $70,000, so that performance would have been disadvantageous to B." Id., § 373, Comment a, Illustration 1.

B

In 1981, in return for up-front "bonus" payments to the United States of about $158 million (plus annual rental payments), the companies received 10–year renewable lease contracts with the United States. In these contracts, the United States promised the companies, among other things, that they could explore for oil off the North Carolina coast and develop any oil that they found (subject to further royalty payments) provided that the companies received exploration and development permissions in accordance with various statutes and regulations to which the lease contracts were made "subject."

The statutes and regulations, the terms of which in effect were incorporated into the contracts, made clear that obtaining the necessary permissions might not be an easy matter. In particular, the Outer Continental Shelf Lands Act (OCSLA), 67 Stat. 462, as amended, 43 U.S.C. § 1331 *et seq.* (1994 ed. and Supp. III), and the Coastal Zone Management Act of 1972 (CZMA), 16 U.S.C. § 1451 *et seq.*, specify that leaseholding companies wishing to explore and drill must successfully complete the following four procedures.

First, a company must prepare and obtain Department of the Interior approval for a Plan of Exploration. 43 U.S.C. § 1340(c). Interior must approve a submitted Exploration Plan unless it finds, after "consider[ing] available relevant environmental information," § 1346(d), that the proposed exploration

> "would probably cause serious harm or damage to life (including fish and other aquatic life), to property, to any mineral . . ., to the national security or defense, or to the marine, coastal, or human environment." § 1334(a)(2)(A)(i).

Where approval is warranted, Interior must act quickly—within "thirty days" of the company's submission of a proposed Plan. § 1340(c)(1).

Second, the company must obtain an exploratory well drilling permit. To do so, it must certify (under CZMA) that its Exploration Plan is consistent with the coastal zone management program of each affected State. 16 U.S.C. § 1456(c)(3). If a State objects, the certification fails, unless the Secretary of Commerce overrides the State's objection. If Commerce rules against the State, then Interior may grant the permit. § 1456(c)(3)(A).

Third, where waste discharge into ocean waters is at issue, the company must obtain a National Pollutant Discharge Elimination System permit from the Environmental Protection Agency. 33 U.S.C. §§ 1311(a), 1342(a). It can obtain this permit only if affected States agree that its Exploration Plan is consistent with the state coastal zone management programs or (as just explained) the Secretary of Commerce overrides the state objections. 16 U.S.C. § 1456.

Fourth, if exploration is successful, the company must prepare, and obtain Interior approval for a Development and Production Plan—a Plan that describes the proposed drilling and related environmental safeguards. 43 U.S.C. § 1351. Again, Interior's approval is conditioned upon certification that the Plan is consistent with state coastal zone management plans—a certification to which States can object, subject to Commerce Department override. § 1351(a)(3).

C

The events at issue here concern the first two steps of the process just described—Interior's consideration of a submitted Exploration Plan and the companies' submission of the CZMA "consistency certification" necessary to obtain an exploratory well drilling permit. The relevant circumstances are the following:

1. In 1981, the companies and the Government entered into the lease contracts. The companies paid the Government $158 million in up-front cash "bonus" payments.

2. In 1989, the companies, Interior, and North Carolina entered into a memorandum of understanding. In that memorandum, the companies promised that they would submit an initial draft Exploration Plan to North Carolina before they submitted their final Exploration Plan to Interior. Interior promised that it would prepare an environmental report on the initial draft. It also agreed to suspend the companies' annual lease payments (about $250,000 per year) while the companies prepared the initial draft and while any state objections to the companies' CZMA consistency certifications were being worked out, with the life of each lease being extended accordingly.

3. In September 1989, the companies submitted their initial draft Exploration Plan to North Carolina. Ten months later, Interior issued the promised ("informal" pre-submission) environmental report, after a review which all parties concede was "extensive and intensive." App. 179 (deposition of David Courtland O'Neal, former Assistant Secretary of the Interior) (agreeing that the review was "the most extensive and intensive" ever "afforded an exploration well in the outer continental shelf (OCS) program"). Interior concluded that the proposed exploration would not "significantly affec[t]" the marine environment or "the quality of the human environment."

4. On August 20, 1990, the companies submitted both their final Exploration Plan and their CZMA "consistency certification" to Interior.

5. Just two days earlier, on August 18, 1990, a new law, the Outer Banks Protection Act (OBPA), § 6003, 104 Stat. 555, had come into effect. That law prohibited the Secretary of the Interior from approving any Exploration Plan or Development and Production Plan or to award any drilling permit until (a) a new OBPA-created Environmental Sciences Review Panel had reported to the Secretary, (b) the Secretary had certified to Congress that he had sufficient information to make these OCSLA-required approval decisions, and (c) Congress had been in session an additional 45 days, but (d) in no event could he issue an approval or permit for the next 13 months (until October 1991). § 6003(c)(3). OBPA also required the Secretary, in his certification, to explain and justify in detail any differences between his own certified conclusions and the new Panel's recommendations. § 6003(c)(3)(A)(ii)(II).

6. About five weeks later, and in light of the new statute, Interior wrote a letter to the Governor of North Carolina with a copy to petitioner Mobil. It said that the final submitted Exploration Plan "is deemed to be approvable in all respects." It added:

"[W]e are required to approve an Exploration Plan unless it is inconsistent with applicable law or because it would result in serious harm to the environment. Because we have found that Mobil's Plan fully complies with the law and will have only negligible effect on the environment, we are not authorized to disapprove the Plan or require its modification." App. to Pet. for Cert. in No. 99–253, at 194a (letter from Regional Director Bruce Weetman to the Honorable James G. Martin, Governor of North Carolina, dated Sept. 28, 1996).

But, it noted, the new law, the "Outer Banks Protection Act (OBPA) of 1990 . . . prohibits the approval of any Exploration Plan at this time." It concluded, "because we are currently prohibited from approving it, the Plan will remain on file until the requirements of the OBPA are met." In the meantime a "suspension has been granted to all leases offshore the State of North Carolina."

About 18 months later, the Secretary of the Interior, after receiving the new Panel's report, certified to Congress that he had enough information to consider the companies' Exploration Plan. He added, however, that he would not consider the Plan until he received certain further studies that the new Panel had recommended.

7.   In November 1990, North Carolina objected to the companies' CZMA consistency certification on the ground that Mobil had not provided sufficient information about possible environmental impact. A month later, the companies asked the Secretary of Commerce to override North Carolina's objection.

8.   In 1994, the Secretary of Commerce rejected the companies' override request, relying in large part on the fact that the new Panel had found a lack of adequate information in respect to certain environmental issues.

9.   In 1996, Congress repealed OBPA. § 109, 110 Stat. 1321–177.

D

In October 1992, after all but the two last-mentioned events had taken place, petitioners joined a breach-of-contract lawsuit brought in the Court of Federal Claims. On motions for summary judgment, the court found that the United States had broken its contractual promise to follow OCSLA's provisions, in particular the provision requiring Interior to approve an Exploration Plan that satisfied OCSLA's requirements within 30 days of its submission to Interior. The United States thereby repudiated the contracts. And that repudiation entitled the companies to restitution of the up-front cash "bonus" payments it had made. Conoco Inc. v. United States, 35 Fed. Cl. 309 (1996).

A panel of the Court of Appeals for the Federal Circuit reversed, one judge dissenting. The panel held that the Government's refusal to consider the companies' final Exploration Plan was not the "operative cause" of any failure to carry out the contracts' terms because the State's objection to the companies' CZMA "consistency statement" would have prevented the companies from exploring regardless. 177 F.3d 1331 (C.A.Fed.1999).

We granted certiorari to review the Federal Circuit's decision.

II

The record makes clear (1) that OCSLA required Interior to approve "within thirty days" a submitted Exploration Plan that satisfies OCSLA's requirements, (2) that Interior told Mobil the companies' submitted Plan met those requirements, (3) that Interior told Mobil it would not approve the companies' submitted Plan for at least 13 months, and likely longer, and (4) that Interior did not approve (or disapprove) the Plan, ever. The Government does not deny that the contracts, made "pursuant to" and "subject to" OCSLA, incorporated OCSLA provisions as promises. The Government further concedes, as it must, that relevant contract law entitles a contracting party to restitution if the other party "substantially" breached a contract or communicated its intent to do so. See Restatement § 373(1); 11 W. Jaeger, Williston on Contracts § 1312, p. 109 (3d ed.1968) (hereinafter Williston); 5 A. Corbin, Contracts § 1104, p. 560 (1964); see also Ankeny v. Clark, 148 U.S. 345, 353, 13 S.Ct. 617, 37 L.Ed. 475 (1893). Yet the Government denies that it must refund the companies' money.

This is because, in the Government's view, it did not breach the contracts or communicate its intent to do so; any breach was not "substantial"; and the companies waived their rights to restitution regardless. We shall consider each of these arguments in turn.

A

The Government's "no breach" arguments depend upon the contract provisions that "subject" the contracts to various statutes and regulations. Those provisions state that the contracts are "subject to" (1) OCSLA, (2) "Sections 302 and 303 of the Department of Energy Organization Act," (3) "all regulations issued pursuant to such statutes and in existence upon the effective date of" the contracts, (4) "all regulations issued pursuant to such statutes in the future which provide for the prevention of waste and the conservation" of Outer Continental Shelf resources, and (5) "all other applicable statutes and regulations." The Government says that these provisions incorporate into the contracts, not only the OCSLA provisions we have mentioned, but also certain other statutory provisions and regulations that, in the Government's view, granted Interior the legal authority to refuse to approve the submitted Exploration Plan, while suspending the leases instead.

. . .

... [T]he Government refers to 30 CFR § 250.110(b)(4) (1999), formerly codified at 30 CFR § 250.10(b)(4) (1997), a regulation stating that "[t]he Regional Supervisor may ... direct ... a suspension of any operation or activity ... [when the] suspension is necessary for the implementation of the requirements of the National Environmental Policy Act or to conduct an environmental analysis." The Government says that this regulation permitted the Secretary of the Interior to suspend the companies' leases because that suspension was "necessary ... to conduct an environmental analysis," namely, the analysis demanded by the new statute, OBPA.

The "environmental analysis" referred to, however, is an analysis the need for which was created by OBPA, a later enacted statute. The lease contracts say that they are subject to then-existing regulations and to certain future regulations, those issued pursuant to OCSLA and §§ 302 and 303 of the Department of Energy Organization Act. This explicit reference to future regulations makes it clear that the catchall provision that references "all other applicable . . . regulations," must include only statutes and regulations already existing at the time of the contract, a conclusion not questioned here by the Government. Hence, these provisions mean that the contracts are not subject to future regulations promulgated under other statutes, such as new statutes like OBPA. Without some such contractual provision limiting the Government's power to impose new and different requirements, the companies would have spent $158 million to buy next to nothing. In any event, the Court of Claims so interpreted the lease; the Federal Circuit did not disagree with that interpretation; nor does the Government here dispute it.

Instead, the Government points out that the regulation in question—the regulation authorizing a governmental suspension in order to conduct "an environmental analysis"—was not itself a future regulation. Rather, a similar regulation existed at the time the parties signed the contracts, 30 CFR § 250.12(a)(iv) (1981), and, in any event, it was promulgated under OCSLA, a statute exempted from the contracts' temporal restriction. But that fact, while true, is not sufficient to produce the incorporation of future statutory requirements, which is what the Government needs to prevail. If the pre-existing regulation's words, "an environmental analysis," were to apply to analyses mandated by future statutes, then they would make the companies subject to the same unknown future requirements that the contracts' specific temporal restrictions were intended to avoid. Consequently, whatever the regulation's words might mean in other contexts, we believe the contracts before us must be interpreted as excluding the words "environmental analysis" insofar as those words would incorporate the requirements of future statutes and future regulations excluded by the contracts' provisions. Hence, they would not incorporate into the contracts requirements imposed by a new statute such as OBPA.

Third, the Government refers to OCSLA, 43 U.S.C. § 1334(a)(1), which, after granting Interior rulemaking authority, says that Interior's

> "regulations . . . shall include . . . provisions . . . for the suspension . . . of any operation . . . pursuant to any lease . . . if there is a threat of serious, irreparable, or immediate harm or damage to life . . ., to property, to any mineral deposits . . ., or to the marine, coastal, or human environment." (Emphasis added.)

The Government points to the OBPA Conference Report, which says that any OBPA-caused delay is "related to . . . environmental protection" and to the need "for the collection and analysis of crucial oceanographic, ecological, and socioeconomic data," to "prevent a public harm." H.R. Conf.

Rep. No. 101–653, p. 163 (1990). At oral argument, the Government noted that the OBPA mentions "tourism" in North Carolina as a "major industry . . . which is subject to potentially significant disruption by offshore oil or gas development." § 6003(b)(3). From this, the Government infers that the pre-existing OCSLA provision authorized the suspension in light of a "threat of . . . serious harm" to a "human environment."

The fatal flaw in this argument, however, arises out of the Interior Department's own statement—a statement made when citing OBPA to explain its approval delay. Interior then said that the Exploration Plan "fully complies" with current legal requirements. And the OCSLA statutory provision quoted above was the most pertinent of those current requirements. The Government did not deny the accuracy of Interior's statement, either in its brief filed here or its brief filed in the Court of Appeals. Insofar as the Government means to suggest that the new statute, OBPA, changed the relevant OCSLA standard (or that OBPA language and history somehow constitute findings Interior must incorporate by reference), it must mean that OBPA in effect created a new requirement. For the reasons set out however, any such new requirement would not be incorporated into the contracts.

Finally, we note that Interior itself, when imposing the lengthy approval delay, did not rely upon any of the regulations to which the Government now refers. Rather, it relied upon, and cited, a different regulation, 30 CFR § 250.110(b)(7) (1999), which gives Interior the power to suspend leases when "necessary to comply with judicial decrees prohibiting production or any other operation or activity." The Government concedes that no judicial decree was involved in this case and does not rely upon this regulation here.

We conclude, for these reasons, that the Government violated the contracts. Indeed, as Interior pointed out in its letter to North Carolina, the new statute, OBPA, required Interior to impose the contract-violating delay. ("The [OBPA] contains provisions that specifically prohibit the Minerals Management Service from approving any Exploration Plan, approving any Application for Permit to Drill, or permitting any drilling offshore the State of North Carolina until at least October 1, 1991"). It therefore made clear to Interior and to the companies that the United States had to violate the contracts' terms and would continue to do so.

. . .

We do not say that the changes made by the statute were unjustified. We say only that they were changes of a kind that the contracts did not foresee. They were changes in those approval procedures and standards that the contracts had incorporated through cross-reference. The Government has not convinced us that Interior's actions were authorized by any other contractually cross-referenced provision. Hence, in communicating to the companies its intent to follow OBPA, the United States was communicating its intent to violate the contracts.

B

The Government next argues that any violation of the contracts' terms was not significant; hence there was no "substantial" or "material" breach that could have amounted to a "repudiation." In particular, it says that OCSLA's 30–day approval period "does not function as the 'essence' of these agreements." The Court of Claims concluded, however, that timely and fair consideration of a submitted Exploration Plan was a "necessary reciprocal obligation," indeed, that any "contrary interpretation would render the bargain illusory." 35 Fed. Cl., at 327. We agree.

We recognize that the lease contracts gave the companies more than rights to obtain approvals. They also gave the companies rights to explore for, and to develop, oil. But the need to obtain Government approvals so qualified the likely future enjoyment of the exploration and development rights that the contract, in practice, amounted primarily to an opportunity to try to obtain exploration and development rights in accordance with the procedures and under the standards specified in the cross-referenced statutes and regulations. Under these circumstances, if the companies did not at least buy a promise that the Government would not deviate significantly from those procedures and standards, then what did they buy?

The Government's modification of the contract-incorporated processes was not technical or insubstantial. It did not announce an (OBPA-required) approval delay of a few days or weeks, but of 13 months minimum, and likely much longer. The delay turned out to be at least four years. And lengthy delays matter, particularly where several successive agency approvals are at stake. Whether an applicant approaches Commerce with an Interior Department approval already in hand can make a difference (as can failure to have obtained that earlier approval). Moreover, as we have pointed out, OBPA changed the contract-referenced procedures in several other ways as well. . . .

D

Finally, the Government argues that repudiation could not have hurt the companies. Since the companies could not have met the CZMA consistency requirements, they could not have explored (or ultimately drilled) for oil in any event. Hence, OBPA caused them no damage. As the Government puts it, the companies have already received "such damages as were actually caused by the [Exploration Plan approval] delay," namely, none. This argument, however, misses the basic legal point. The oil companies do not seek damages for breach of contract. They seek restitution of their initial payments. Because the Government repudiated the lease contracts, the law entitles the companies to that restitution whether the contracts would, or would not, ultimately have produced a financial gain or led them to obtain a definite right to explore. If a lottery operator fails to deliver a purchased ticket, the purchaser can get his money back—whether or not he eventually would have won the lottery. And if one party to a contract, whether oil company or ordinary citizen, advances the other party money, principles of restitution normally require the latter, upon repudiation, to refund that money. Restatement § 373.

III

Contract law expresses no view about the wisdom of OBPA. We have examined only that statute's consistency with the promises that the earlier contracts contained. We find that the oil companies gave the United States $158 million in return for a contractual promise to follow the terms of pre-existing statutes and regulations. The new statute prevented the Government from keeping that promise. The breach "substantially impair[ed] the value of the contract [s]." *Id.*, § 243. And therefore the Government must give the companies their money back.

■ JUSTICE STEVENS, dissenting.

Since the 1953 passage of the Outer Continental Shelf Lands Act (OCSLA), 43 U.S.C. § 1331 *et seq.*, the United States Government has conducted more than a hundred lease sales of the type at stake today, and bidders have paid the United States more than $55 billion for the opportunity to develop the mineral resources made available under those leases. The United States, as lessor, and petitioners, as lessees, clearly had a mutual interest in the successful exploration, development, and production of oil in the Manteo Unit pursuant to the leases executed in 1981. If production were achieved, the United States would benefit both from the substantial royalties it would receive and from the significant addition to the Nation's energy supply. Self-interest, as well as its duties under the leases, thus led the Government to expend substantial resources over the course of 19 years in the hope of seeing this project realized.

From the outset, however, it was apparent that the Outer Banks project might not succeed for a variety of reasons. Among those was the risk that the State of North Carolina would exercise its right to object to the completion of the project. That was a risk that the parties knowingly assumed. They did not, however, assume the risk that Congress would enact additional legislation that would delay the completion of what would obviously be a lengthy project in any event. I therefore agree with the Court that the Government did breach its contract with petitioners in failing to approve, within 30 days of its receipt, the plan of exploration petitioners submitted. As the Court describes,the leases incorporate the provisions of the OCSLA into their terms, and the OCSLA, correspondingly, sets down this 30-day requirement in plain language. 43 U.S.C. § 1340(c).

I do not, however, believe that the appropriate remedy for the Government's breach is for petitioners to recover their full initial investment. When the entire relationship between the parties is considered, with particular reference to the impact of North Carolina's foreseeable exercise of its right to object to the project, it is clear that the remedy ordered by the Court is excessive. I would hold that petitioners are entitled at best to damages resulting from the delay caused by the Government's failure to approve the plan within the requisite time.

I

To understand the nature of the breach, and the appropriate remedy for it, it is necessary to supplement the Court's chronological account. From the time petitioners began discussing their interest in drilling an exploratory well 45 miles off the coast from Cape Hatteras in the fall of 1988, until (and even after) the enactment of the Outer Banks Protection Act (OBPA), § 6003, on August 18, 1990, their exploration proposal was fraught with problems. It was clear to petitioners as early as October 6, 1988 (and almost certainly before), that the State of North Carolina, whose approval petitioners knew they had to have under their lease terms in order to obtain the requisite permits from the Department of the Interior (DOI), was not going to go along readily. . . .

That is why petitioners pursued multiparty negotiations with the Federal Government and the State to help facilitate the eventual approval of their proposal. As part of these negotiations, petitioners entered into a memorandum of understanding with North Carolina and the Federal Government, and, according to the terms of that agreement, submitted a draft plan of exploration (POE) to DOI and to the State. The Government also agreed to prepare draft and final environmental impact reports on petitioners' draft POE and to participate in public meetings and hearings regarding the draft POE and the Government's findings about its environmental impact. Among other things, this agreement resulted in the Government's preparation in 1990 of a three-volume, 2,000–page special environmental report on the proposed project, released on June 1 of that year.

Although the State thereafter continued to express its dissatisfaction . . . petitioners nonetheless submitted a final POE to DOI on August 20, 1990, pursuant to the lease contract terms. . . .

Following petitioners' submission of the final POE, DOI then had a duty, under the terms of the OCSLA as incorporated into the lease contract, to approve that plan "within thirty days of its submission." 43 U.S.C. § 1340(c)(1). In other words, DOI had until September 19, 1990, to consider the submitted plan and, provided that the plan was complete and otherwise satisfied the OCSLA criteria, to issue its statement of approval. (Issuing its "approval," of course, is different from granting petitioners any "license or permit for any activity described in detail in an exploration plan and affecting any land use or water use" in a State's coastal zone, § 1340(c)(2); actual permission to proceed had to wait for the State's CZMA certification.) Despite this hard deadline, September 19 came and went without DOI's issuance of approval.

DOI's explanation came two days later, on September 21, 1990, in a letter to Mobil Oil from the MMS's Acting Regional Supervisor for Field Operations, Lawrence Ake. Without commenting on DOI's substantive assessment of the POE, the Ake letter stated that the OBPA "specifically prohibit[s]" the MMS from approving any POE "until at least October 1, 1991." "Consequently," Mr. Ake explained, the MMS was suspending operation on the Manteo Unit leases "in accordance with 30 CFR § 250.10(b)(7)," a regulation issued pursuant to the OCSLA and, of course, incorporated thereby into the parties' lease agreement. One week after that, on September 28, 1990, the MMS's Regional Director, Bruce Weetman, sent a letter to Governor Martin of North Carolina, elaborating on MMS's actions upon receipt of the August 20 POE. According to Weetman, the POE "was deemed complete on August 30, and transmitted to other Federal Agencies and the State of North Carolina on that date. Timely comments were received from the State of North Carolina and the U.S. Coast Guard. An analysis of the potential environmental effects associated with the Plan was conducted, an Environmental Assessment (EA) was prepared, and a Finding of No Significant Impact (FONSI) was made." Based on these steps taken by the MMS, it concluded that the POE was "approvable" but that the MMS was "currently prohibited from approving it." Thus, the letter concluded, the POE would "remain on file" pending the resolution of the OBPA requirements, and the lease suspensions would continue in force in the interim.

II

In my judgment, the Government's failure to meet the required 30–day deadline on September 19, 1990, despite the fact that the POE was in a form that merited approval, was a breach of its contractual obligation to the contrary. After this, its statement in the September 21 Ake letter that the OBPA prohibited approval until at least October 1991 must also be seen as a signal of its intent to remain in breach of the 30–day deadline requirement for the coming year. The question with which the Court is faced, however, is not whether the United States was in breach, but whether, in light of the Government's actions, petitioners are entitled to restitution rather than damages, the usual remedy for a breach of contract.

... [An] injured party may obtain restitution only if the action "so substantially impairs the value of the contract to the injured party ... that it is just in the circumstances to allow him to recover damages based on all his remaining rights to performance." In short, there is only repudiation if there is an action that would amount to a total breach, and there is only such a breach if the suspect action destroys the essential object of the contract. It is thus necessary to assess the significance or "materiality" of the Government's breach.

Beyond this, it is important to underscore as well that restitution is appropriate only when it is "just in the circumstances." Restatement (Second) § 243. This requires us to look not only to the circumstances of the breach itself, but to the equities of the situation as a whole....

III

Given these requirements, I am not persuaded that the actions by the Government amounted either to a repudiation of the contracts altogether, or to a total breach by way of its neglect of an "essential" contractual provision.

I would, at the outset, reject the suggestion that there was a repudiation here, anticipatory or otherwise, for two reasons. First, and most basic, the Government continued to perform under the contractual terms as best it could even after the OBPA's passage. Second, the breach-by-delay forecast in the Ake letter was not "of sufficient gravity that, if the breach actually occurred, it would of itself give the obligee a claim for damages for total breach."

While acknowledging the OBPA's temporary moratorium on plan approvals, the Ake letter to petitioner Mobil states that the Government is imposing a lease suspension—rather than a cancellation or recision [sic]— and even references an existing, OCSLA regulatory obligation pursuant to which it is attempting to act. The Weetman letter explains in detail the actions the MMS took in carefully considering petitioners' POE submission; it evaluated the plan for its compliance with the OCSLA's provisions, transmitted it to other agencies and the State for their consideration, took the comments of those entities into account, conducted the requisite analyses, and prepared the requisite findings—all subsequent to the OBPA's enactment. It cannot be doubted that the Government intended to continue performing the contract to the extent it thought legally permissible post-OBPA.

Indeed, petitioners' own conduct is inconsistent with the contention that the Government had, as of August 18, 1990, or indeed as of September 19, 1990, fully repudiated its obligations under the parties' contracts.... [I]t was after the enactment of the OBPA that petitioners submitted their final plan to the DOI—just as if they understood there still to be an existing set of contractual conditions to be fulfilled and expected to fulfill them. Petitioners, moreover, accepted the Government's proffered lease suspensions, and indeed, themselves subsequently requested that the suspensions remain in effect "from June 8, 1992 forward" under 30 CFR § 250.10(b)(6) (1990), an OCSLA regulation providing for continued lease suspension at the lessee's request "to allow for inordinate delays encountered by the lessee in obtaining required permits or consents, including administrative or judicial challenges or appeals."

After the State of North Carolina filed its formal CZMA objections on November 19, 1990 (indicating that the State believed a contract still existed), petitioners promptly sought in December 1990—again under statutory terms incorporated into the contracts—to have the Secretary of Commerce override the objections, 43 U.S.C. § 1340(c)(1), to make it possible for the exploration permits to issue. In a response explainable solely on the basis that the Government still believed itself to be performing contractually obligatory terms, the Secretary of Commerce undertook to evaluate petitioners' request that the Secretary override the State's CZMA objections. This administrative review process has, I do not doubt, required a substantial expenditure of the time and resources of the Departments of Commerce and Interior, along with the 12 other administrative agencies whose comments the Secretary of Commerce solicited in evaluating the request to override and in issuing, on September 2, 1994, a lengthy "Decision and Findings" in which he declined to do so.

And petitioners were not finished with the leases yet. After petitioners received this adverse judgment from Commerce, they sought the additional lease suspensions described, insisting that "the time period to seek judicial review of the Secretary's decisions had not expired when the MMS terminated the [pre-existing] suspensions," and that "[s]ince the Secretary's decision is being challenged, it is not a final decision and will not be until it is upheld by a final nonappealable judgment issued from a court with competent jurisdiction," id., at 2a. Indeed, petitioners have pending in the United States District Court for the District of Columbia at this very moment their appeal from the Secretary of Commerce's denial of petitioners' override request of North Carolina's CZMA objections. Mobil Oil Exploration & Producing Southeast, Inc. v. Daley, No. 95–93 SSH (filed Mar. 8, 2000).

Absent, then, any repudiation, we are left with the possibility that the nature of the Government's breach was so "essential" or "total" in the scope of the parties' contractual relationship as to justify the remedy of restitution.... The OBPA was not passed as an amendment to statutes that the leases by their terms incorporated, nor did the OBPA state that its terms were to be considered incorporated into then existing leases; it was, rather, an action external to the contract, capable of affecting the parties' actions but not of itself changing the contract terms. The OBPA did, of course, impose a legal duty upon the Secretary of the Interior to take actions (and to refrain from taking actions) inconsistent with the Government's existing legal obligations to the lessees. Had the Secretary chosen, despite the OBPA, to issue the required approval, he presumably could have been haled into court and compelled to rescind the approval in compliance with the OBPA requirement. But that this possibility remained after the passage of the OBPA reinforces the conclusion that it was not until the Secretary actually took action inconsistent with his contractual obligations that the Government came into breach.

. . .

Whether the breach was sufficiently "substantial" or material to justify restitution depends on what impact, if any, the breach had at the time the breach occurred on the successful completion of the project. See E. Farnsworth, Contracts § 8.16 (3d ed. 1999) ("The time for determining materiality is the time of the breach and not the time that the contract was made.... Most significant is the extent to which the breach will deprive the injured party of the benefit that it justifiably expected"). In this action the answer must be close to none. Sixty days after the Government entered into breach—from September 19, 1990, to November 19, 1990—the State of North Carolina filed its formal objection to CZMA certification with the United States. As the OCSLA makes clear, "The Secretary shall not grant any license or permit for any activity described in detail in an exploration plan and affecting any land use or water use in the coastal zone of a State with a coastal zone management program ... unless the State concurs or is conclusively presumed to concur with the consistency certification accompanying such plan ..., or the Secretary of Commerce makes the finding [overriding the State's objection]." 43 U.S.C. § 1340(c)(2) (emphasis added); see also § 1351(d). While this objection remained in effect, the project could not go forward unless the objection was set aside by the Secretary of Commerce. Thus, the Government's breach effectively delayed matters during the period between September 19, 1990, and November 19, 1990. Thereafter, implementation was contractually precluded by North Carolina.

. . .

In the end, the Court's central reason for finding the breach "not technical or insubstantial" is that "lengthy delays matter." I certainly agree with that statement as a general principle. But in this action, that principle does not justify petitioners' request for restitution.... As with any venture of this magnitude, this undertaking was rife with possibilities for "lengthy delays," ... The OBPA was not, to be sure, a cause for delay that petitioners may have anticipated in signing onto the lease. But the State's CZMA and NPDES objections, and the subsequent "inordinate delays" for appeals, certainly were.... Any long-term venture of this complexity and significance is bound to be a gamble. The fact that North Carolina was holding all the aces should not give petitioners the right now to play with an entirely new deck of cards.

IV

The risk that North Carolina would frustrate performance of the leases executed in 1981 was foreseeable from the date the leases were signed. It seems clear to me that the State's objections, rather than the enactment of OBPA, is the primary explanation for petitioners' decision to take steps to avoid suffering the consequences of the bargain they made. As a result of the Court's action today, petitioners will enjoy a windfall reprieve that Congress foolishly provided them in its decision to pass legislation that, while validly responding to a political constituency that opposed the development of the Outer Banks, caused the Government to breach its own contract. Viewed in the context of the entire transaction, petitioners may well be entitled to a modest damages recovery for the two months of delay attributable to the Government's breach. But restitution is not a default remedy; it is available only when a court deems it, in all of the circumstances, just. A breach that itself caused at most a delay of two months in a protracted enterprise of this magnitude does not justify the $156 million draconian remedy that the Court delivers.

Accordingly, I respectfully dissent.

NOTES AND QUESTIONS

1. Does it surprise you that the Supreme Court granted writ on a case which revolves around basic principles of private contract law? Do the major differences between the majority and the dissent involve interpretations of law or of the underlying facts in the case?

2.   Should the Secretary of Interior, despite the OBPA, have issued approval to the POE? If so, and the state of North Carolina had secured a judicial decree enjoining the Secretary's actions, would the Secretary then have been authorized to suspend the leases? One of the OCSLA regulations reads as follows:

> The Regional Supervisor may also direct ... suspension of any operation or activity, including production, because ... (7)[t]he suspension is necessary to comply with judicial decrees prohibiting production or any other operation or activity, or the permitting of those activities. 30 CFR § 250.10(b)(7) (1990).

Would this sequence of events have affected the majority's opinion?

b. ONSHORE

Withdrawals of federal onshore land from oil and gas and other resource development have also occurred throughout our nation's history. For example, the Congressional branch has often acted to create National Parks and Wilderness Areas in which development is forbidden. When Congress has refused to act quickly to protect areas against commercial activity, presidents have acted unilaterally under the Antiquities Act of 1906. This Act authorizes the President "in his discretion to declare by public proclamation historic landmarks, historic and prehistoric structures and other objects of historic or scientific interest that are situated upon the lands owned or controlled by the Government of the United States to be national monuments." 16 U.S.C.A. § 431. President Roosevelt withdrew 270,000 acres of the Grand Canyon from mining claims under this Act in 1920.

More recently, President Clinton used the 1906 Act to set aside 1.8 million acres in southeast Utah's canyonlands as the Grand Staircase Escalante National Monument. The President's move blocked plans by a Dutch company, Andalex Resources, to develop a coal reserve twice the size of Manhattan located in the middle of the set-aside area. The state of Utah owns about 180,000 acres of scattered tracts in the monument areas. Income from these state lands supports public education in Utah. Senator Frank Murkowski (R–Alaska), chair of the Senate Energy and Natural Resources Committee, issued a statement claiming that the president's decision would cost the Utah education system as much as $1 billion in lost revenues from coal and other mineral development. He also claimed that the monument might be locking up as much as 62 billion tons of clean, low-sulfur coal, which would force utilities to burn dirtier coal and exacerbate air pollution. BNA Daily Report for Executives, Sept. 19, 1996 at A–31.

The new National Monument also contains 59 federal oil and gas leases owned by Conoco covering 108,000 acres. In September 1997, the Interior Department's Bureau of Land Management approved exploratory drilling of a single well by Conoco on an existing lease to test for the existence of millions of barrels of oil suspected to lie underneath the red rocks. Secretary Bruce Babbitt viewed a fight over this permit as unwarranted because the odds of striking oil were so slight and President Clinton's proclamation creating the monument recognized valid existing rights. Other federal agencies and environmentalists warned that the precedent could lead to "widespread development, marking the area for decades to come with tall rigs, networks of roads and pipelines, bright lights blotting out the stars above ballfield-size drilling pads, and impoundments of toxic drilling mud despoiling pristine habitats." John H. Cushman, Jr., "U.S. Approves Test Oil Drilling On National Parkland in Utah," New York Times, Sept. 9, 1997, at A1.

The Utah withdrawal was wrathfully denounced by the entire Utah delegation to Congress. Such withdrawals create many of the same state/federal conflicts over the use of the public lands as the OCS has engendered, except that the roles are usually reversed. The Western states have generally taken a pro-development stance against the use of executive or congressional powers to withdraw land from resource use. A full accounting of the many laws and policies for resource use and management on federal lands demands its own course. An excellent case book, Federal Public Land and Resources Law by George Coggins, Charles Wilkinson and John Leshy awaits the eager student.

c.   THE ARCTIC NATIONAL WILDLIFE REFUGE (ANWR)

Prudhoe Bay understandably focused oil industry attention on the north coast of Alaska. In 1983, Mukluk, the world's most expensive dry hole costing $2 billion, was drilled 14 miles off the north coast, 65 miles northwest of Prudhoe Bay. Despite this setback, the oil industry continues to eye the area just to the east of Prudhoe Bay, known as the Alaskan National Wildlife Refuge or "ANWR". When Alaska was granted statehood, Congress reserved many tracts of land under various categories of federal land management. ANWR is a 19 million acre tract managed by the U.S. Fish and Wildlife Service to protect wildlife, particularly large migrating herds of caribou. Under federal law, oil leasing is prohibited.

The climate on the North Slope is hostile, with long winters and brief summers. Caribou are the predominant mammal and mosquitoes the predominant insect during the brief summer. Some 165,000 caribou make up the Porcupine herd that occupies ANWR. Every June they trek to the coast of ANWR to give birth to their young. They stay there during July and August and then migrate to the Brooks range for the winter. About 5,000 Eskimo of the Inupiat tribe live on the North Slope as traditional hunters whose life style is intimately tied to the caribou herd.

Because ANWR and its offshore area are thought to hold the brightest prospects for finding large oil fields in the United States, the oil industry has sought to open up ANWR to leasing. The industry argues that development of ANWR is an important way to reduce our reliance on imported oil. While both the Reagan and Bush administrations supported legislation that would allow such development, environmental groups opposed any such proposal and defeated its inclusion in what eventually became the Energy Policy Act of 1992. *See* Lisa J. Booth, Comment, Arctic National Wildlife Refuge: A Crown Jewel in Jeopardy, 9 Pub. Land Rev. 105 (1988).

The strength of the opposing views has not waned, as can be seen from the following excerpts from editorials: "ANWR is one of only two areas in the U.S. that holds out hope for additions to reserves in the billions of barrels and to production in the millions of barrels per day. It is one of only two areas with which the U.S. can compete internationally for significant amounts of exploration and development capital. The other area is off-shore." Editorial, Oil & Gas Journal, Aug. 22, 1994.

An example of the opposing view is found in a July 14, 1994, editorial of the New York Times advocating "full wilderness protection to the magnificent Arctic refuge Coastal Plain, often called America's Serengeti. The only North Slope area not open to oil extraction, it continues to lie in the gunsights of the insatiable oil industry. The plain will not be assured its proper place as a legacy to future generations without wilderness protection now."

d. SUBMERGED LANDS OFF ANWR

While the debates over the future of ANWR were proceeding, the state government was seeking to lease submerged lands off ANWR for oil exploration. The United States claimed that certain submerged lands located within three miles of the Arctic coast were retained by the federal government, even though under the Equal Footing doctrine, these lands typically would have been conveyed to Alaska at the time of statehood.

In *United States v. State of Alaska*, 521 U.S. 1 (1997), the Supreme Court overturned the recommendations of a special master and held that the federal government did not transfer title to these submerged lands to Alaska at statehood in 1959. The Court held that it was the intent of Congress to retain federal jurisdiction over offshore submerged lands within the boundaries of the Arctic National Wildlife Refuge and also within the boundaries of the National Petroleum Reserve. The decision was hailed by environmentalists because it blocked Alaska's claim of sole authority to open up ANWR's submerged lands to oil and gas development. Discovery of oil in the submerged lands inevitably would pressure Congress to open up ANWR. The Alaskan Governor predictably vowed to continue to fight "for the rights of Alaskans to develop Alaska resources." BNA, Daily Report for Executives, June 23, 1997, at A–7.

With attempts to open up ANWR thwarted, attention turned to the National Petroleum Reserve, which occupies over 23 million acres of land and offshore waters to the west of Prudhoe Bay, as shown on the map in Fig. 6–6 below.

In August 1998, the Department of the Interior issued a proposal that would allow leasing and drilling in the northeast quadrant of the reserve. Hailed as a "new chapter in conservation management," the proposal followed an 18–month planning process by DOI, the state of Alaska, and the North Slope Bureau. The quadrant contains an area the size of New Jersey. Its northern section of shallow lakes and tundra is heavily used by geese during the molting season and by Teshekpuk caribou for calving.

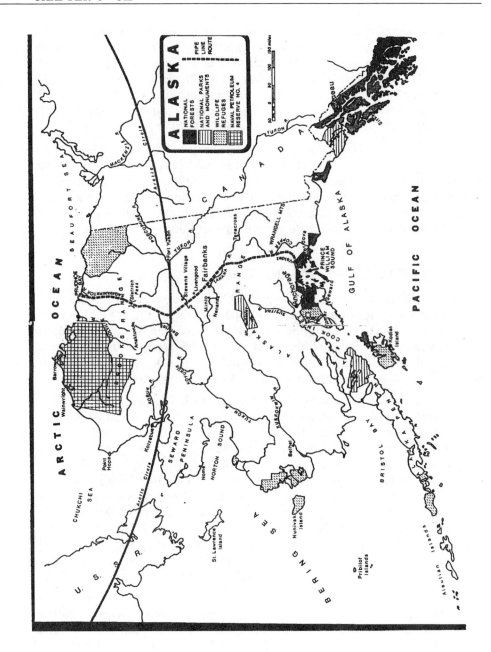

Figure 6–6

Under the proposal, almost all the shallow lakes are off limits to leasing, and permanent oil and gas surface occupancy is prohibited on most locations important for fish and subsistence use. The leasing process was triggered by a request from the Alaskan Governor to President Clinton. BNA Daily Report for Executives, Aug. 7, 1998, A–31. The draft plan and environmental impact statement are published at 62 Fed. Reg. 65,440 (1997). Exploratory activities are also underway on adjacent state lands.

The Department of Energy and the domestic oil industry have recently undertaken an intensive campaign to publicize how advanced oil and gas technologies have resulted in considerable environmental progress compared to past practices. Figure 6–7 below is one of the "before" and "after" exhibits of the "footprints" left in the tundra by drilling sites in 1995 versus 1970.

BOS18

The Evolution of a Drill Site: 1970 to Present

1st Generation
(1970)

2nd Generation
(1980)

3rd Generation
(1985)

4th Generation
(1995)

scale
1' = 500'

65 acres   24 acres   18 acres   8.7 acres

Source: www.anwr.org

According to the   t with today's technology, its footprint would be 64 percent smaller than its current size. Drilling pads would be 74 percent smaller and roads would cover 58 percent less surface. Department of Energy, Environmental Benefits of Advanced Oil and Gas Exploration and Production Technology 59 (1999). This report is available on the web at www.fe.doe.gov/oil_gas/environ_rpt/index.html. It includes an impressive set of photos and graphics. Oil companies now build ice-based roads, bridges, airstrips, and drilling pads for exploration activities. They are cheaper than gravel and leave virtually no footprint, because the ice structures simply thaw and melt in the spring. BP Exploration (Alaska) has gone one step further; it has built insulated ice pads for drilling rigs, thus extending the drilling season. *Id.* at 58. Almost all drilling operations on the Alaskan North Slope are done in the bitter cold of winter. ARCO and BP also developed a process that takes the drill cuttings (the bits of reservoir rock that the drill bit pierces) and converts them to road construction materials, since the cuttings' composition is essentially identical to that of native gravel. *Id.* at Section on "Sensitive Environments" pp. 36–37.

An industry-oriented website promoting the opening up of ANWR is at http://www.anwr.org/ and has a stunning "photo gallery" on its homepage index, which will show ice roads, bears and caribou at play around oil pipelines, and the tundra.

In February 2000, BP Exploration Alaska was sentenced to the $500,-000 maximum criminal penalty for failing to report a hazardous substance release under CERCLA (the Superfund law). The company admitted to illegally discharging waste oil and hazardous substances by injecting them down the outer rims of their oil wells on the North Slope from 1993 until 1995 when a whistleblower revealed the practice. BP will also implement a $15 million environmental management system as a condition of probation, averting further charges under the Resource Conservation and Recovery Act (RCRA). BNA Daily Report for Executives, Feb. 16, 2000, A–11.

F. THE ENVIRONMENTAL IMPACT OF OIL

1. SUMMARY OVERVIEW OF IMPACTS

The production, transport, refining, and consumption of oil and petroleum products have a significant environmental impact. Margaret Carswell of the Economic Research Service prepared the following summary of some of the major areas of concern.

Margriet F. Carswell, Balancing Energy and the Environment 179, 182–85 in The Environment of Oil (Richard J. Gilbert, ed., 1993).

Air Quality. Energy development and use can affect air quality in many ways. Both onshore and offshore production pollute the air with emissions from drilling equipment, escaping hydrocarbons, flaring of natural gas, and emissions form support vehicles. Pipelines contribute very little to air pollution during normal operations although there may be some emissions produced during transfer from wells or to refineries or tankers. Tankers and barge tugs emit hydrocarbons when under power and may have fugitive vapors escape during cargo transfer. However, the consumption of oil and gas contributes most greatly to air quality degradation. The incomplete combustion of petroleum products yields carbon monoxide, hydrocarbons, oxidation products, and particulates. The principal stationary-source contributors are inorganic and organic chemical plants, iron and steel mills, petroleum refiners, pulp and paper mills, electric-power plants, and nonferrous-metal smelters. By weight alone, motor vehicles contribute nearly half of the total pollutants attributable to the fact that carbon monoxide constitutes such a large proportion of emissions.

Water Quality. Degradation of water quality can occur in the marine environment or in surface or ground freshwater supplies. Both onshore and offshore production require the proper disposal of produced water.[2][21] Produced water is the largest source of contaminants from offshore oil and gas development, where up to 1 barrel of produced water is obtained for each barrel of crude oil that is recovered. Improper disposal can contaminate the marine environment or freshwater supplies. The disposal of drilling muds can also present problems, especially during offshore production.[3][22]

Oil spills from offshore production and discharges from tankers and barges have added many polluting constituents to water environments, and these events are discussed at greater length below. From all sources, about 6 million tons of oil pollutants get to the ocean each year. Consumption of petroleum products contributes to some water pollution indirectly through the deposition of airborne contaminants. In addition, individuals disposing of engine oil have unknowingly jeopardized their own water sources, since one quart of crankcase oil that reaches a source of clean water will cause 250,000 gallons to be unusable for a drinking water supply. Leaking gasoline storage tanks also can constitute a severe problem for fresh groundwater supplies, and many service stations have been required to replace tanks and remove contaminated soil.

Biological Resources. Both plants and animals can be affected directly by petroleum development activities or indirectly through the air and water quality changes discussed above. The integrity of an ecosystem can be destroyed if only one link in the food chain is eliminated. Therefore, environmentalists tend to focus on an indicator species such as the caribou in Alaska when protesting energy development projects. Such a focus can be misleading if the species chosen is not the most predictive indicator of ecosystem health. The species is often chosen because it is easily identified and tracked. Public opinion is often swayed by the careful choice of an indicator species—popularly known as a "charismatic megafauna." Land-based production and transport can affect large territories during construction and by blocking migratory patterns with pipelines. Environmentalists also claim that oil production will open wilderness areas up for further development, thus endangering scarce biological resources.

Unfortunately, scientific knowledge of the complex interactions and dynamic nature of ecosystems is not adequate to accurately determine the effects of petroleum development on biological resources. Therefore, many environmentalists recommend erring on the side of caution (precluding development) until more is known. The relative benefits and costs of gaining more knowledge are seldom considered, however. Oil spills from onshore wells and pipelines have been relatively small and confined to a limited area. The greatest damage from such spills occurs when petroleum

21. Produced water is the aqueous waste that has existed in the interstitial spaces of fossil fuel-bearing formations for thousands of years. Produced water may contain elevated concentrations of metals, hydrocarbons, and other organic substances.

22. Drilling muds are used to remove cuttings from under the drill bit, to control well pressure, to cool and lubricate the drill string, and to seal the well. They can contain clay minerals, barite, trace metals, sodium hydroxide, biocides, diesel fuel, and other minor constituents.

residues reach either surface or groundwater supplies. Offshore production spills and discharges from tankers and barges are potentially more damaging because they can contaminate large areas of the marine environment and directly threaten biological resources. In addition, little is known about the chronic exposure of marine resources to drilling muds and produced water that are the byproducts of offshore production. Neither refining nor consumption affect biological resources directly, although there is a possible secondary impact from degraded water and air.

Social and Economic Impacts. Environmental degradation has social and economic impacts with both monetary and nonmonetary components. Tourism and recreation industries and commercial fisheries will decline after an oil spill. Air pollution caused by the consumption of petroleum may deteriorate buildings. Health can be threatened by polluted air and water supplies and aesthetic values will be lessened when ecosystems are damaged. In addition, if the assimilative capacity of the environment to absorb wastes is decreased by oil development activities, other sectors of the economy may have to pay more to dispose of wastes.■

2.   OFFSHORE WASTES AND THE CLEAN WATER ACT

All too frequently, regulations designed to improve one environmental condition create an environmental problem elsewhere. Pollutants removed from the air end up in the water, and vice versa. This phenomenon is nowhere more evident than in the problem of disposing of wastes from offshore oil platforms. Such a platform is a world in microcosm. As waste products are generated, they can typically be deposited in the ocean, burned at the platform, or shipped back to shore for burial.

The EPA, after long study and debate, issued regulations governing offshore disposal. The regulations were challenged by both industry and environmentalists (the Natural Resources Defense Council). In a voluminous decision, the Sixth Circuit addressed the complaints of both sides. For those students who have not had a course in Environmental Law, the Clean Water Act presents a maze of almost impenetrable acronyms, largely defining the severity of technological controls required by industry. Yet the legal issues can be clearly grasped in the excerpted version of this case, which illustrates both the workings of the Clean Water Act and the working of judges tackling complex technical issues.

BP Exploration & Oil, Inc. v. EPA

66 F.3d 784 (6th Cir.1995).

■ BATCHELDER, J.: In these consolidated cases, petitioners BP Exploration & Oil, Inc., American Petroleum Institute, Conoco Inc., Marathon Oil Co., Natural Resources Defense Council, Inc., and Svedala Industries, Inc., challenge the effluent limitations promulgated for the offshore oil and gas industry by the United States Environmental Protection Agency under the Clean Water Act. For the reasons that follow, we affirm the effluent limitations promulgated by the Environmental Protection Agency (EPA) for the offshore oil and gas industry.

I.

The disputed effluent limitations guidelines are the final regulations and standards of performance for the "Offshore Subcategory of the Oil and Gas Extraction Point Source Category," published pursuant to sections 301, 304, and 306 of the Clean Water Act (CWA or "Act"). 33 U.S.C.A. §§ 1311, 1314, 1316 (West 1986).... These regulations (the "Final Rule") were also formulated in response to a Consent Decree entered on April 5, 1990, in *NRDC v. Reilly*, C.A. No. 79–3442 (D.D.C.) (subsequently modified on May 28, 1992). The Final Rule became effective on April 5, 1993, ending a process that began in 1975 with EPA's publication of interim guidelines for the offshore oil and gas industry.

Petitioners BP Exploration & Oil, Inc., American Petroleum Institute, Conoco Inc., Marathon Oil Co., and Svedala, Inc. (hereinafter referred to as "Industry petitioners"), contend that the effluent standards are too stringent. Generally, Industry petitioners allege that the Environmental Protection Agency (EPA) violated the CWA by (1) setting an unreasonable standard for the discharge of oil and grease in effluent discharges, (2) prohibiting the discharge of certain drilling wastes within three miles of shore, and (3) banning the discharge of contaminated sand. At the other end of the spectrum, petitioner Natural Resources Defense Council, Inc. (NRDC), representing environmental interests, contends that EPA violated the CWA by promulgating effluent standards that are generally too lenient. In short, NRDC alleges that EPA (1) illegally rejected zero discharge of drilling wastes, (2) violated the Act by failing to regulate radioactive pollutants in discharged water, and (3) should have required reinjection of polluted water.

A. The Clean Water Act

The objective of the CWA "is to restore and maintain the chemical, physical, and biological integrity of the Nation's waters." § 1251. Congress' original goal was for the discharge of all pollutants into navigable waters to be eliminated by the year 1985. § 1251(a)(1). Consequently, the discharge of any pollutant is illegal unless made in compliance with the provisions of the CWA. Because numerous other courts have fully described the CWA, *see E.I. du Pont de Nemours & Co. v. Train*, 430 U.S. 112 (1977), it is unnecessary here to include more than an outline of the statutory structure for promulgating effluent limitations.

The CWA directs EPA to formulate national effluent limitation guidelines for those entities that discharge pollutants into the navigable waters of the United States. In formulating these guidelines, the CWA directs EPA to institute progressively more stringent effluent discharge guidelines in stages. Congress intended EPA to consider numerous factors in addition to pollution reduction: "The Committee believes that there must be a reasonable relationship between costs and benefits if there is to be an effective and workable program." Clean Water Act of 1972, Pub. L. No. 92–500, 1972 U.S.C.C.A.N. (86 Stat.) 3713.

At the first stage of pollutant reduction, EPA is to determine the level of effluent reduction achievable within an industry with the implementation of the "best practicable control technology currently available" (BPT). § 314(b)(1)(A). In general, BPT is the average of the best existing performances by industrial plants of various sizes, ages, and unit processes within the point source category or subcategory. In arriving at BPT for an industry, EPA is to consider several factors, including the total cost of the application of the technology in relation to the effluent reduction benefits to be achieved from such application.[4][23] For the offshore oil and gas subcategory, BPT was to be achieved by July 1, 1977. § 1311(b)(1)(A).

At the second stage, EPA is to set generally more stringent standards for toxic and conventional pollutants. For toxic pollutants, EPA is to set the standard for the "best available technology economically achievable" (BAT). BAT represents, at a minimum, the best economically achievable performance in the industrial category or subcategory. *NRDC, Inc. v. EPA,* 863 F.2d 1420, 1426 (9th Cir.1988) (*citing EPA v. National Crushed Stone Ass'n*, 449 U.S. 64, 74 (1980)). Compared to BPT, BAT calls for more stringent control technology that is both technically available and economically achievable. Among the factors that EPA must consider and take into account when setting BAT are the cost of achieving such effluent reduction and the non-water quality environmental impact including the energy requirements of the technology. § 1314(b)(2)(B). For the offshore oil and gas subcategory, BAT was to be achieved by July 1, 1987. § 1311(b)(2)(A).

Conventional pollutants[8][24] are treated differently from toxics under the CWA. Pursuant to 1977 amendments to the Act, a new standard was conceived for conventional pollutants entitled "best conventional pollutant control technology" (BCT). This standard is designed to control conventional pollutants about which much is known but for which stringent BAT standards might require unnecessary treatment. Congress intended for BCT to prevent the implementation of technology for technology's sake. BCT is not an additional level of control, but replaces BAT for conventional pollutants.

Consequently, the technology chosen as BCT must pass a two-part "cost reasonableness" test. *American Paper Institute v. EPA*, 660 F.2d 954 (4th Cir.1981). According to the Act, the Administrator shall include in the determination of BCT

---

23. Other factors EPA must consider are the age of equipment and facilities involved, the process employed, the engineering aspects of the application of various types of control techniques, process changes, non-water quality environmental impacts, and such other factors as the Administrator deems appropriate. § 1314(b)(1)(B); *see also Environmental Protection Agency v. National* *Crushed Stone Ass'n*, 449 U.S. 64, 71 n. 10 (1980).

24. Conventional pollutants include biochemical oxygen demand (BOD), total suspended solids (TSS) (nonfilterable), pH, fecal coliform, oil and grease. 40 C.F.R.§ 401.16 (1994).

[a] consideration of the reasonableness of the relationship between the costs of attaining a reduction in effluents and the effluent reduction benefits derived, and the comparison of the cost and level of reduction of such pollutants from the discharge from publicly owned treatment works [POTWs] to the cost and level of reduction of such pollutants from a class or category of industrial sources....

§ 1314(b)(4)(B). The first part of the BCT cost test is referred to as the "industry cost-effectiveness test"; the second part is known as the "POTW test."

Finally, the CWA directs EPA to establish a separate standard for new sources of pollutants. These "new source performance standards" (NSPS) require application of the technology chosen as BAT to remove all types of pollutants from new sources within each category. § 1316. Factors to be considered in formulating NSPS include the cost of achieving such effluent reduction and any non-water quality environmental impact and energy requirements. § 1316 (b)(1)(B).

* * *

C. The Industry

EPA identified a total of 2,550 offshore structures that will be affected by the Final Rule. Of these structures, 2,517 are located in the Gulf of Mexico, 32 are located off the coast of California, and one is located off the coast of Alaska. Petitioners challenge those portions of EPA's Final Rule relating to (1) produced water, (2) drilling fluids and drill cuttings, and (3) produced sand. Although wastewater originates both from the exploration and development process and from the production phase of the oil and gas industry's offshore operations, drilling fluids make up the majority of the effluent produced from exploration and development, and produced water represents a majority of the effluent from production. Produced sand is a minimal component of the effluent from production.

D. The Standard of Review

When a court reviews an agency's construction of a statute, it is confronted with two inquiries. First and foremost is whether Congress has directly spoken to the matter at issue. *Chevron, U.S.A., Inc. v. NRDC, Inc.*, 467 U.S. 837, 842 (1984). "If the intent of Congress is clear, that is the end of the matter; for the court, as well as the agency, must give effect to the unambiguously expressed intent of Congress." *Id.* at 842–43.... If the court decides that Congress has not directly addressed the precise issue at hand, however, the court may not simply dictate its own construction of the statute. *Id.* at 843. "Rather, if the statute is silent or ambiguous with respect to the specific issue, the question for the court is whether the agency's answer is based on a permissible construction of the statute." Id.

. . .

The language of the Act clearly manifests Congress' intention that EPA formulate BPT, BAT, BCT, and NSPS within certain time deadlines and having considered various factors. § 1311(b). Congress set forth the goal of the Act and left its implementation and details to the EPA. In construing regulations promulgated by EPA, we heed the wide latitude given the Secretary by the CWA. *Cf. Babbitt v. Sweet Home Chapter*, 115 S.Ct. 2407, 2416 (1995) (interpreting the Endangered Species Act). It has long been recognized that a great deal of deference should be given to an agency's construction of a statutory scheme that it is entrusted to administer. *Chevron*, 467 U.S. at 844. Along with the regulatory expertise required to enforce the CWA, "we owe some degree of deference to the Secretary's reasonable interpretation." *Babbitt*, 115 S. Ct. at 2416 (citation omitted).

EPA promulgated the 1993 effluent guidelines through informal rulemaking. The scope of review over the informal rulemaking process is generally governed by section 10(e)(2) of the Administrative Procedure Act (APA), 5 U.S.C.A. § 706(2) (West 1977); *Weyerhaeuser Co. v. Costle*, 590 F.2d 1011, 1024 (D.C.Cir.1978). According to this section, a court must "hold unlawful and set aside agency action, findings, and conclusions found to be ... arbitrary, capricious, an abuse of discretion, or otherwise not in accordance with law...." 5 U.S.C. § 706(2)(A). *See generally Citizens to Preserve Overton Park, Inc. v. Volpe*, 401 U.S. 402, 415–17 (1971). The D.C. Circuit has described the court's administrative review function as divisible into three categories: statutory, procedural, and substantive. *Weyerhaeuser*, 590 F.2d at 1024.

In the present case, neither EPA's statutory authority nor the procedural steps taken has been challenged. Only substantive aspects of the Final Rule are being challenged. Consequently, this Court must determine "whether the agency 'abuse[d its] discretion' (or was 'arbitrary' or 'capricious') in exercising the quasi-legislative authority delegated to it by Congress, or, on the other hand, whether its 'decision was based on a consideration of the relevant factors and [was not the product of] a clear error of judgment.' " *Weyerhaeuser*, 590 F.2d at 1025 (*quoting Citizens to Preserve Overton Park*, 401 U.S. at 416).

Finally, this Court will defer in large part to EPA's scientific findings. "In assessing difficult issues of scientific method and laboratory procedure, we must defer to a great extent to the expertise of the EPA." *NRDC, Inc. v. EPA*, 863 F.2d 1420, 1430 (9th Cir.1988) (*citing Baltimore Gas & Elec. Co. v. NRDC, Inc.*, 462 U.S. 87, 103 (1983)). In *Baltimore Gas & Elec. Co.*, "the Supreme Court recognized that a reviewing court should be at its most deferential in reviewing an agency's scientific determinations in an area within the agency's expertise." *NRDC v. EPA*, 863 F.2d at 1430.

II.

A. Produced Water

The bulk of produced water is water trapped in underground reservoirs along with oil and gas that eventually rises to the surface with the produced oil and gas. Most of the oil and gas in the produced water is separated as part of the oil and gas extraction process. The remaining produced water, still containing some oil and grease, is then discharged overboard or otherwise disposed of. Produced water also includes the injection water used for secondary oil recovery and various well treatment chemicals added during production and oil and gas extraction. Produced water is the highest volume waste source in the offshore oil and gas industry.

Under the Final Rule, EPA determined that BAT and NSPS would be set to limit the discharge of oil and grease[9][25] in produced water to a daily maximum of 42 mg/l and a monthly average of 29 mg/l, based on the improved operating performance of gas flotation technology (otherwise referred to as improved gas flotation). BCT for produced water was set by the Final Rule to equal current BPT limitations (72 mg/l daily maximum, 48 mg/l 30–day average).

Gas flotation is a technology that forces small gas bubbles into the wastewater to be treated. As the bubbles rise through the produced water, they attach themselves to any oil droplets in their paths. As the gas and oil are separated from the wastewater, they rise to the surface, where they are skimmed away. EPA characterizes "improved performance" gas flotation as the gas flotation technology enhanced through improved operation and maintenance, more operator attention to treatment systems operations, chemical pretreatment to enhance system effectiveness, and possible resizing of certain treatment system components for increased treatment efficiency....

In setting the limits, EPA used the "median" platform from the 83 Platform Composite Study. In other words, 50 percent of the platforms in the study discharged higher levels of pollutant, and 50 percent of the platforms discharged lower levels of pollutant. The daily maximum limitation was set so that there would be a 99 percent likelihood that a physical composite sample taken from the median platform would have a total oil and grease measurement less than or equal to that limitation. The monthly average was set so that there would be a 95 percent probability that a monthly average taken from the median platform would also be less than or equal to that limitation. EPA estimates that 60 percent of the platforms in the composite of 83 platforms already meet the new BAT limitations. For those platforms that do not already meet the new BAT standard, chemical coagulants can be used to improve the removal of dissolved or soluble oil.

In light of the deference due the EPA, especially concerning scientific and technical data, Industry petitioners have not proven their claim that improved gas flotation does not remove "dissolved" oil or that EPA violated either the CWA or the APA by using Method 413.1 to measure oil and grease in produced water.

2.   Radioactive Pollutants in Produced Water

Also in relation to produced water, petitioner NRDC argues that EPA illegally refused to regulate radioactive pollutants in produced water, despite NRDC's contention that ample record evidence proves the presence and negative impacts of radionuclides. In contrast, EPA maintains that the

---

25. Although oil and grease are conventional pollutants rather than toxics, oil and grease are limited under BAT and NSPS as an "indicator" pollutant to measure discharge of toxic and nonconventional pollutants.

agency was justified in its decision not to regulate radionuclides in produced water because inadequate information existed to issue rules regarding the radionuclides, Radium 226 and Radium 228 (referred to as NORM). According to the EPA, the CWA does not require the promulgation or implementation of regulations if there is not sufficient evidence on which to base those regulations. As EPA argues, the agency is continuing to gather information on radionuclides and could issue regulations in the future if the compiled information shows a need for such regulation. See § 1314(e). In fact, EPA has stated its intent to require radium monitoring as part of the permitting process for offshore oil and gas producers. . . .

The present case is unlike NRDC v. EPA, in which the Ninth Circuit concluded that EPA should not delay requiring such technologically feasible limitations as BAT in order to wait for precise cost figures. NRDC v. EPA, 863 F.2d at 1426. In this case, EPA has legitimately declined to regulate radionuclides in produced water due to the lack of data on radionuclides in produced water-particularly information on the environmental and health harms presented by NORM. In light of EPA's discretion to promulgate this Final Rule, we agree that EPA reasonably decided that insufficient evidence existed to regulate this pollutant in produced water at this time.

3.   Reinjection of Produced Water

The NRDC also contends that EPA illegally refused to require zero discharge of produced waters through reinjection because record evidence shows that reinjection is technologically and economically feasible. . . .

EPA admits that reinjection may be technologically feasible.[14][26] The only evidence that reinjection may not be feasible is the possibility that geographic formations in some areas may preclude reinjection. However, EPA's rejection of reinjection as a BAT, while based in part on concerns regarding feasibility, was, more importantly, based on several relevant factors, such as unacceptably high economic and nonwater quality environmental impacts.

EPA estimates the cost of implementing reinjection as BAT and NSPS would exceed several billion dollars. The extraordinary cost was one basis for rejecting reinjection, although NRDC is correct that EPA did not conclusively determine that reinjection was not economically attainable. In addition to the high expense of reinjection, the negative impact reinjection would have on air emissions and the loss of production resulting from reinjection combined to cause EPA to reject reinjection for BAT and NSPS.

EPA estimates that the implementation of reinjection at existing platforms in the Gulf and Alaska alone would increase the emission of air

---

26. A majority of the platforms in California already reinject their produced water to enable recover of the heavy crude oil that is typically produced in that part of the country. The only offshore rig in Alaska also reinjects its produced water in order to comply with state regulation. Reinjection of produced water is much less common in the Gulf of Mexico, although some studies have shown it to be feasible there as well. It is important to remember, however, that of 2,500 offshore platforms, only 33 platforms are located off the coast of California and Alaska.

pollutants by 1,041 tons/year for BAT and 849 tons/year for NSPS. The existing air quality of Southern California is so bad that reinjection was not considered an option at all. Reinjection was also rejected based on the increased energy required to run the reinjection pumps. According to EPA, reinjection would result in additional energy requirements of 977,000 barrels of oil equivalent (BOE)/year for BAT and 785,000 BOE/year for NSPS. Finally, EPA projected that reinjection would result in a one percent loss in production. (It is worth noting that one percent of oil and gas production from the Gulf of Mexico amounts to several million BOE/year.) The accumulation of these factors led EPA to reject reinjection as BAT and NSPS for produced water.

We think that EPA acted within its statutory authority in rejecting zero discharge based on reinjection. As EPA correctly points out, NRDC's contention that economic, energy, and nonwater quality environmental impacts are less important than achieving zero discharge merely reflects NRDC's disagreement on a policy level. This Court may not substitute NRDC's judgment, any more than our own, for that of the EPA.

B. Drilling Fluids and Drill Cuttings

Drilling fluid (also called drilling mud) is any fluid sent down the drillhole to aid the drilling process. This includes fluid used to maintain hydrostatic pressure in the well, lubricate and cool the drill bit, remove drill cuttings from the well, and stabilize the walls of the well during drilling or work over operations. The fluid is pumped down the drill pipe and through the drill bit. At the bottom of the hole, it sweeps crushed rock drill cuttings from beneath the bit, carries them back to the surface, is separated from drill cuttings and is discharged or is returned to the mud tank for recirculation.

Under the Final Rule, EPA prohibits all discharge of drilling fluids and drill cuttings from wells located within three nautical miles from shore for the Gulf and California regions. The BAT, NSPS, and BCT all require any dischargers within the three-mile limit to transport drilling fluids and drill cuttings to shore by barge and to dispose of the discharge in landfills. Beyond the three-mile limit, drilling fluids and drill cuttings may be discharged under BCT after meeting the limitation for no discharge of free oil measured by the static sheen test.[17][27] BAT and NSPS for dischargers beyond the three-mile limit are more stringent, requiring compliance with four basic requirements.[18][28]

Industry petitioners challenge the EPA's decision to impose the zero discharge limitation on drilling fluids and drill cuttings discharged within

---

27. Fluids fail the static sheen test if a "sheen, iridescence, gloss, or increased reflectance" appears on the surface of test seawater after drilling fluid samples are introduced into ambient seawater in a container having an air-to-liquid interface area of 1,000 cm. 50 Fed. Reg. 34,592, 34,627 (1985).

28. These requirements are: (1) a toxicity limitation set at 30,000 ppm in the suspended particulate phase; (2) a prohibition on the discharge of diesel oil; (3) no discharge of free oil based on the static sheen test; and (4) a limitation on cadmium and mercury in barite of 3 mg/kg and 1 mg/kg, respectively.

three miles of shore in the Gulf and California regions. The BAT, NSPS, and BCT chosen for these dischargers is to barge the drilling fluids and cuttings to shore to be disposed of in landfills. Industry petitioners assert that EPA acted arbitrarily and violated the CWA by (1) improperly calculating the BCT cost test, (2) regulating drill cuttings as Total Suspended Solids (TSS), and (3) failing adequately to consider the cost factor in its BAT and NSPS determination.

1. BCT Cost Test

The BCT cost test is made up of two parts, the POTW test and the industry cost-effectiveness test. The portion of the BCT cost test at issue here, the industry cost-effectiveness test, has been translated into the following mathematical formula:

$$\frac{\text{BCT cost/lb.} - \text{BPT cost/lb.}}{\text{BPT cost/lb.} - \text{preBPT cost/lb.}} < 1.29$$

Based on this formula, EPA's first step was to calculate the existing cost of BPT under which some drilling muds were hauled to shore when they did not meet the "no free oil" test. EPA then calculated the BCT cost of hauling all drilling muds and cuttings within the Final Rule's three-mile limit.

Industry petitioners allege that EPA made two mistakes in calculating the cost of BPT. First, Industry petitioners contend that EPA mistakenly classified the costs of substituting mineral oil for diesel oil as a BPT cost. EPA candidly admits that it did commit this error. EPA contends, however, that this mistake was harmless error because, even with a substitution cost of zero (which EPA does not concede), the BCT level chosen still passes the BCT cost test once Industry petitioners' second contention is rejected.

Industry petitioners' second contention is that EPA exaggerated BPT onshore disposal costs for oil-based muds. According to Industry petitioners, no cost should be attributed to the onshore disposal of oil-based muds because dischargers actually sell the muds to mud companies who recondition the mud for reuse as drilling fluids. Industry petitioners assert that a correct calculation of the BPT cost should include only the transportation of oil-based muds to shore. As Industry petitioners view it, a recalculation of the industry cost-effectiveness test, omitting the cost attributed to product substitution and the cost attributed to the disposal of oil-based muds, causes EPA's zero discharge BCT level to fail the BCT cost test. EPA counters that Industry petitioners are not permitted to raise their claim relating to the disposal cost of oil-based muds, because the issue was not raised during the rulemaking process. The requirement that a party raise its concerns to an agency prior to the publication of the final rule promotes agency autonomy and judicial efficiency. *Ohio v. EPA*, 997 F.2d 1520, 1528–29 (D.C.Cir.1993). Industry petitioners counter that they could not have raised this issue earlier because EPA's calculations were not available until the Rule was published. Industry petitioners' claim is not persuasive, however, because although the exact calculations may have been unavailable, we find ample record evidence that Industry petitioners had sufficient notice that disposal costs of oil-based muds were being considered by EPA as part of the BCT cost test.

Even if Industry petitioners had the right to raise this issue, EPA persuasively argues that some cost must be associated with disposal of oil-based muds. For example, EPA suggests that there will be some solids in the process that still require disposal because they will not pass the no free oil test; that reconditioning all of the drilling fluid may not be feasible; and that for those fluids that are reused, there is probably some limit to the number of times such reuse can occur. Logically, there must be some cost associated with the reconditioning operation itself. EPA claims that all of these factors make the Industry petitioners' argument for zero disposal cost an unreasonable one. We are persuaded by EPA that its revised BPT calculation passes the BCT cost test. When EPA drops the mistaken amount included for product substitution, and leaves the rest of the numbers the same, the result of the equation is 1.239. This figure is still lower than the permissible threshold of 1.29.

2. Regulating Drill Cuttings as TSS

Industry petitioners also argue that EPA improperly classified, and then regulated, drill cuttings as Total Suspended Solids (TSS). According to Industry petitioners, it is arbitrary to ban an entire waste stream (such as all drill cuttings) as TSS when only a small portion of the waste is actually suspended. In Industry petitioners' opinion, a large percentage of the drill cuttings are heavy bits of rock that sink immediately to the ocean floor and should therefore not be classified as TSS.

EPA counters that drill cuttings are classified as TSS because they fit within the definition of TSS. According to EPA, TSS is defined as "nonfilterable residue." This definition requires only that the substance will not pass through a glass filter. Consequently, EPA uses Method 160.2[20][29] to measure the amount of solid retained by a fiber filter. Because the drill cuttings discharged by oil and gas producers will not pass through such a filter, drill cuttings are, by EPA's definition, TSS. Industry petitioners maintain that it is illogical to include drill cuttings in a test method that is intended to filter much smaller particles. According to Method 160.2, the practical range of material to be measured is 4 mg/l to 20,000 mg/l. However, as Industry petitioners point out, a representative drill cutting sample is over 1.1 million mg/l. We are persuaded by Industry's argument that EPA has arbitrarily classified drill cuttings as TSS. It is error for EPA to classify drill cuttings, typically on the magnitude of 1.1 million mg/l, by measuring TSS using a test designed to include only particles smaller than 20,000 mg/l. Despite the deference due to EPA in its choice of analytical methodology and testing procedures, it is apparent to this Court that most drill cuttings may not qualify as TSS because they are not "suspended." Our view is further bolstered by another of EPA's own tests, Method 160.5, which measures residue classified as "settleable." 40 C.F.R. § 136.3, Table

29. EPA's Method 160.2 entails filtering a sample of the industrial waste through a glass fiber filter and then weighing the retained residue after it has dried.

1B (1994). The drill cuttings discharged from the oil and gas development and production phases should not be measured by Method 160.2 unless they fit within that test's practical guidelines.

Despite our belief that EPA may have erred in classifying drill cuttings as TSS, it appears senseless here to remand this portion of the Final Rule. Because BAT and NSPS for drill cuttings require the same technological control on drill cuttings as BCT, that is, zero discharge within three nautical miles of shore and no discharge of free oil beyond three miles, altering BCT in this case would not change the result. Furthermore, even if EPA improperly classified drill cuttings as TSS, the agency is not precluded from regulating drill cuttings as an indicator for oil and grease. It is well documented that once drill cuttings are separated from the reusable drilling mud, they continue to carry drilling fluid residues of conventional and toxic pollutants. It is apparent in this specific situation that altering BCT would not in any way change the treatment of drill cuttings in the Gulf of Mexico, California, or Alaska. In this case, therefore, we will not disturb the EPA's treatment of drill cuttings as TSS in the Final Rule although we find some merit in Industry petitioners' allegation.

3.   BAT and NSPS Cost Calculation

Finally, Industry petitioners challenge the BAT and NSPS levels set by EPA for drilling fluids and cuttings. The BAT and NSPS for dischargers within three miles of shore (excluding Alaska) require zero discharge of the pollutant by barging the mud and cuttings to shore for onshore disposal. Industry petitioners contend that EPA failed to consider adequately the relevant factors required, specifically the cost of barging. Phrased another way, Industry petitioners claim that the BAT and NSPS levels were improperly promulgated because the environmental benefits of the limitations are negligible.

EPA counters that it has discretion whether or not to use cost considerations under BAT and NSPS, and that EPA need only find that the technology is technically and economically achievable and that the cost of the technology is "reasonable." *NRDC v. EPA*, 863 F.2d at 1426; *see also CPC Int'l Inc. v. Train*, 540 F.2d 1329, 1341–42 (8th Cir.1976) (setting NSPS does not require cost-benefit analysis, "what is required ... is a thorough study of initial and annual costs and an affirmative conclusion that these costs can be reasonably borne by the industry"), cert. denied, 430 U.S. 966 (1977). The CWA does not require a precise calculation of BAT and NSPS costs. *NRDC v. EPA*, 863 F.2d at 1426. Congress intended that EPA have discretion "to decide how to account for the consideration factors, and how much weight to give each factor." *Weyerhaeuser*, 590 F.2d at 1045.

Industry petitioners maintain that when environmental benefits are de minimis, the regulation is not valid. However, EPA points to several environmental benefits of the zero discharge rule, primarily, the decrease in pollutants ingested by fish and shellfish and passed along the food chain. Among the non-monetary benefits of zero discharge is the reduction in recreation degradation. Industry petitioners maintain that zero discharge is not necessary because simply meeting the four basic requirements under BAT for dischargers outside the three mile limit reduces virtually any pollution harm. However, Industry petitioners have not carried their burden of showing that zero discharge does not achieve any additional environmental benefit.

We are persuaded that EPA acted within its discretion in setting BAT and NSPS for drilling muds and drill cuttings.

4.   Nonwater Quality Environmental Impacts

In promulgating the permissible discharge of drilling fluids and cuttings in this part of the Final Rule, EPA determined that zero discharge for all offshore platforms in the Gulf, California and Alaska was technologically available (through barging to shore) and economically achievable ($12.3 million for drilling fluids, $6.6 million for drill cuttings). However, unacceptably high nonwater quality environmental impacts led EPA to establish the three-mile zero discharge limit for the Gulf and California. In the Gulf of Mexico, EPA rejected zero discharge beyond three miles from shore because of a lack of landfill capacity in the region. In California, zero discharge beyond three miles was rejected because of its serious impact on air pollution. NRDC challenges each of these decisions.

a.   Volume of Waste and Landfill Capacity in Gulf

NRDC contends (1) that EPA overestimated the volume of waste that would be generated by platforms outside the three-mile limit, and (2) underestimated land disposal capacity. According to NRDC, correcting these errors clears the way for a zero discharge requirement for drilling fluids and drill cuttings from all oil and gas rigs in the Gulf of Mexico.

EPA estimated the landfill capacity in the Gulf region over the next 15 years and determined that 8.5 million barrels of waste could be disposed each year. Because the landfills in that area are already receiving 3 million barrels of waste each year from other sources, EPA calculated that only an additional 5.5 million barrels of waste from offshore sources could be accommodated. EPA then examined the amount of waste that would be generated offshore if a zero discharge limitation were in place for all platforms. It was estimated that offshore platforms would generate 6.6 million barrels/year. In addition to the 1.1 million barrels/year already being produced by coastal drilling operations, the total amount of drilling wastes generated totals 7.7 million barrels of waste per year. Because EPA estimated landfill capacity at only 5.5 million barrels each year, EPA devised its three-mile mark, beyond which platforms are not required to comply with zero discharge.

NRDC first contends that EPA overestimated the amount of waste that would require disposal by use of the zero discharge limit. NRDC claims that EPA used poor solids control technology in its calculations. Solids control technology removes drill cuttings from the drilling fluid system and reduces the total amount of drilling wastes that cannot be reused. As EPA points out, however, improved solids control technology only increases the volume of drill cuttings separated from reusable drilling fluid. Consequently, EPA found that the additional waste reduction that might be achieved is minimal. NRDC also raised the oil-based muds issue, contending that such muds are reused and that EPA did not take this into consideration. EPA maintains that reconditioning oil-based muds cannot eliminate all drilling fluids from the waste stream and that, therefore, any reuse does not drastically change its calculations.

NRDC also contends that EPA underestimated the landfill capacity of the Gulf region. NRDC believes that EPA ruled out acceptable landfills for insufficient reasons. For example, in its estimation of landfill capacity, EPA did not include landfills that are not now in operation. NRDC contends that those landfills currently are not operating because of a lack of demand. If it were more economically productive for those landfills to operate, NRDC presumes that more space would open up for drilling wastes. Nor did EPA consider landfills whose licenses are currently suspended. NRDC asserts that those sites might regain their licenses. Despite NRDC's contentions, however, this Court would have to engage in pure speculation to determine whether landfill operators would reopen or regain their licenses. Furthermore, the confusion cited by NRDC over the names of several of the landfills in the EPA estimate is adequately explained by the fact that several landfills are known by more than one name.

Finally, NRDC criticizes EPA for failing to include in its estimate of landfill capacity any sites equipped to accept hazardous wastes. However, EPA purposely omitted hazardous landfill sites due to the high demand for such hazardous sites. According to EPA, the decision to exclude hazardous sites from its estimation of total landfill capacity is consistent with its 1988 decision not to regulate oil and gas under the hazardous waste portion of the Resource Conservation and Recovery Act (RCRA), 42 U.S.C. §§ 6901–6987. It is EPA's position that hazardous waste sites must be reserved for disposing of those substances that are more hazardous and dangerous than drilling fluids and drill cuttings.

This Court believes that EPA has both the discretion and the expertise to make the decisions and value judgments behind its rejection of the zero discharge option beyond three miles off the shore of the Gulf of Mexico. Furthermore, EPA continuously reevaluated data and collected comments on the estimated volume of drilling fluids and cuttings, revising its information as recently as 1993. It is clear from the record that EPA made the decisions NRDC challenges after considering all of the options raised by the NRDC and after weighing the benefits and drawbacks of those options. We find that EPA's decisions are not arbitrary or capricious, nor are they the result of an abuse of the agency's discretion.

b.   Air Quality Impact in California

NRDC also alleges that EPA illegally rejected zero discharge of drilling wastes in California beyond the three-mile limit. Having found zero discharge to be achievable in the California region, EPA nevertheless rejected zero discharge beyond the three-mile limit, based on the severity of the air pollution in Southern California. In EPA's opinion, the increased air emissions that would result from barging all drilling wastes from offshore platforms to the coast of California vastly outweighed the benefit of a zero discharge limitation beyond three miles from shore.

NRDC generally charges that EPA cannot reject zero discharge on the basis of possible increased air emissions. According to NRDC, EPA cannot reject a limit based on nonwater quality environmental impacts unless the impacts are "wholly disproportionate" to the possible pollution reduction. NRDC also argues that the estimated addition of 54 tons/year of air pollution off the coast of California is small compared to the present degree of air pollution in California, and that offshore platforms that increase air emissions would be able to purchase pollution offsets to compensate for the increased air pollution. We find each of NRDC's arguments unpersuasive.

The overriding principle in our review of the Final Rule is that the agency has broad discretion to weigh all relevant factors during rulemaking. The CWA does not state what weight should be accorded to the relevant factors; rather, the Act gives EPA the discretion to make those determinations. *NRDC v. EPA*, 863 F.2d at 1426. Compared to the benefit of a zero discharge requirement for all California offshore platforms, EPA views this increase in air pollution to be unjustified.

Furthermore, Southern California is a severe nonattainment area under the measurements of the Clean Air Act (CAA).[21][30] There is some doubt that emissions offsets are available at any cost. Even if offsets could be purchased by offshore oil producers, they would cost approximately $15,000 per ton of nitrogen dioxide and $5,000 per ton of hydrocarbons.

If any entity has the ability to weigh the relative impact of two different environmental harms, it is the EPA. Here, EPA has weighed all the factors and has decided to compromise by requiring zero discharge within a three-mile limit. In the absence of a showing of clear error or abuse of discretion, this Court will not overturn EPA's determination....

For the foregoing reasons, we AFFIRM the Final Rule for the offshore oil and gas subcategory promulgated by EPA pursuant to the CWA.■

NOTES AND COMMENTS

1. Do you feel confident in either the EPA's or the judge's ability to understand the technical or economic aspects of an industrial activity? Is there a better way to formulate control standards than through formal rulemaking procedures under the Administrative Procedure Act? Regulatory negotiations, or "reg-negs" are a form of alternative dispute resolution designed to bring together potential litigants to resolve differences before a proposed rule is published. In 1985, Santa Barbara County sued Exxon to force better air pollution controls on its offshore platforms. The MMS held three years of reg-negs with five different caucuses (the oil industry,

---

30. It is convenient in this case for NRDC to make its argument for zero discharge beyond EPA's three-mile limit at the expense of compliance with the Clean Air Act. We reject the temptation to speculate about NRDC's seeming willingness to sacrifice clean air for a more stringent discharge regulation.

environmentalists, federal, state, and local governments), but to no avail. The reg-neg process failed because of disputes about factual issues, the complexity of technical issues, and whipsawing national politics. *See* William Fulton, "Reg–Neg: How California's First Regulatory Negotiations Fell Victim to the Politics of Offshore Drilling, 9 Calif. Lawyer 65 (Nov. 1989). Exxon did agree, however, to fully electrify its Santa Ynez project (in lieu of diesel fuel) at a cost of millions of dollars. *Id.* at 136. Does this victory for Santa Barbara simply move pollution around, perhaps to the coal-fired power plants near the Grand Canyon?

2. Most high-volume wastes from oil and gas drilling are exempt from the mandates of the Resource Conservation and Recovery Act (RCRA) of 1976. This act creates a cradle-to-grave program for managing solid hazardous wastes in landfills. Produced water, drilling fluids, and other wastes uniquely associated with oil and gas drilling and production were exempted from the act because Congress feared the economic impact on the energy industry of subjecting these huge quantities of wastes to the strict requirements of Subtitle C of RCRA. An EPA report, required under RCRA, determined that this impact would cost the industry from $1 billion to $6.5 billion and result in oil production declines that would raise the price of oil by as much as 76 cents per barrel, costing consumers $4.5 billion per year. The EPA decided that removal of the exemption was not justified based on a further finding that current disposal methods for such wastes were not causing significant damage to human health or the environment. This exemption is controversial and is periodically attacked by environmental groups. *See generally,* Daniel L. McKay, RCRA's Oil Field Wastes Exemption and CERCLA's Petroleum Exclusion: Are They Justified?, 15 J. Energy, Nat. Resources, & Envtl. L. 41 (1995).

G. OIL TRANSPORTATION

1. OIL SPILLS

Tanker accidents have created some of the most telegenic of environmental disasters. We have all seen the television pictures of oil-soaked birds and dead otters which demonstrate the destructiveness of major oil spills.

The safety of oil tanker shipments requires a system in which the people who operate the system remain in a continual state of sharp awareness and preparedness. Think about this human element as you read about the famous 1989 Alaskan oil spill and Congress's reaction to it.

Art Davidson, In the Wake of the Exxon Valdez: The Story of America's Most Devastating Oil Spill, 10–18
Sierra Club Books, 1990

By 9:00 p.m., [on March 23, 1989] the Exxon Valdez was ready to depart. Earlier, Third Mate Gregory Cousins had tested the vessel's navigation equipment: radar, gyro compass, automatic pilot, course indicator, rudder control, and other sophisticated instrumentation. At 9:12 p.m., the tanker's last mooring line was detached from the pier and two tugs nudged the Exxon Valdez from its berth. On the bridge were harbor pilot Ed Murphy and Captain Hazelwood. Coast Guard regulations require that harbor pilots—who are trained to know about navigational hazards in local waters—be contracted to guide tankers from port to open water. Earlier, when they were boarding, Murphy had smelled alcohol on Hazelwood's breath but had said nothing about it.

At 9:21 p.m., Murphy, directing the vessel's speed and course settings, began to steer the Exxon Valdez out of the harbor toward Valdez Narrows, 7 miles from port. The Narrows, a channel that forms the entrance to Valdez Bay, is 1,700 yards wide. Middle Rock, a rock in the channel sometimes called "the can opener," reduces the minimum usable width to 900 yards. In computer simulations before the route was sanctioned, pilots repeatedly wrecked their imaginary tankers on Middle Rock. However, with the help of escort tugs and harbor pilots, tankers three football fields long had successfully negotiated the Narrows for eleven years. "We all know what the stakes are," said one longtime Valdez harbor pilot. "You've always got to be on your toes. I see these ships as eggs that are a quarter of a mile long. You can't make mistakes with them. A mistake ends your career."

The Exxon Valdez steamed through the Narrows in relatively calm weather: a 10–mph breeze from the north, with 4–mile visibility through low clouds and some snow and fog. With Murphy at the helm of the vessel, Hazelwood left the bridge, which was highly unusual and against company policy. But the two men had known each other for years and had eaten together that afternoon. Murphy mentioned nothing; he knew Hazelwood well and respected his seamanship. On a previous passage through the Narrows, when Murphy was piloting the ship, Hazelwood had helped avert disaster. "It was a winter night with very limited visibility. I was making a course change on Potato Point, and we were accelerating," Murphy recalled later. "The quartermaster applied the helm the wrong way.... The loaded vessel was rapidly swinging toward the beach. Captain Hazelwood picked up that mistake even before I did."

On this March 23 evening, the Exxon Valdez passed through the Narrows without mishap. Fourteen miles out of port, the tanker reached Rocky Point, where harbor pilots normally transfer command of a ship back to the captain. Murphy had to order Hazelwood called back to the bridge. When Hazelwood returned to the control room, Murphy again noticed the smell of alcohol on the captain's breath. However, a Valdez harbor pilot had never challenged a captain's command of his vessel. A pilot's continued employment by a given vessel can depend on the captain's good will. Murphy decided that Hazelwood looked fit and focused enough to assume command. At 11:20 p.m., Captain Joseph Hazelwood took control of the Exxon Valdez.

In the dimly lit radar room atop the three-story Coast Guard station in Valdez, civilian radar man Gordon Taylor watched a bright orange ring on the radar scope. The ring represented the Exxon Valdez as it moved from the terminal out through the Narrows. At Rocky Point, radar coverage became fainter and Taylor found it difficult to read. "You can pick up vessels off Bligh Island if there are no squalls, no heavy seas, no wind, and the radar is tuned up and working well," Taylor explained later. He added that it's easy to lose track of a tanker. "The vessel is there one sweep; the next, no vessel."

In 1981, James Woodle, then the Valdez Coast Guard commander, had recommended that the Coast Guard radar system be improved. He had wanted to ensure sharp vessel coverage between Bligh Island and the leading edge of the Columbia Glacier. The U.S. Geological Survey had predicted even more extensive glacial ice floes over the next ten to thirty years, and Woodle had argued that "placement of a radar site on either Glacier Island or Bligh Island could prove to be an invaluable tool.... Expanded radar coverage in this area is strongly recommended."

The Coast Guard had not acted on Woodle's recommendation, because it deemed the additional radar sites, at $100,000 a year, "cost prohibitive." In fact, budget cuts and the transfer of personnel to President Reagan's war on drugs had continually drained money from the Valdez Coast Guard budget and had whittled its staff from thirty-seven to twenty-four since the pipeline's completion in 1977.

Far from pushing for the recommended additions, Commander Steve McCall, who took over as the Coast Guard's ranking officer in Valdez in 1986, favored a downgraded system. "It's been twelve years since the tankers began operating, and nothing major has gone wrong," McCall had commented regarding the recommended radar upgrade. "So a lot of things have changed from what people thought was necessary in 1977.... We started downgrading in 1984.... We changed the radars in '82, and made manpower cuts.... How much do you really need to watch a ship that is going in and out, all by itself, with nobody around it?"

As the Exxon Valdez approached the edge of radar coverage, Hazelwood radioed the Coast Guard that he was "heading outbound and increasing speed."

At 11:24 p.m., harbor pilot Ed Murphy, who had already turned over command to Hazelwood, left the tanker and boarded a pilot boat that would speed him back to the port of Valdez. Hazelwood radioed Traffic Valdez, the Coast Guard's radio monitoring station:

Hazelwood: We've departed a pilot. At this time hooking up to sea speed. And ETA [estimated time of arrival] to make it out [past Naked Island] on 0 100 [1:00 a.m.]. Over.

Traffic Valdez: Roger, Request an updated ice report when you go down through there. Over.

Hazelwood: Okay. Was just about to tell you that judging by our radar I will probably divert from TSS [Traffic Separation Scheme] and end up in an inbound lane. Over.

Traffic Valdez: No reported traffic. I got the Chevron California one hour out and the ARCO Alaska is right behind him. But they are an hour out from Hinchinbrook.

Hazelwood: That'd be fine, yeah. We may end up over in the inbound lane, outbound track. We'll notify you when we ... cross over the separation zone. Over.

Shortly after Hazelwood notified the Coast Guard that he was going to divert from the Traffic Separation Scheme (designated one-way inbound and outbound tanker lanes), he radioed that he was going to angle left and reduce speed in order to work through some floating ice: "At the present time I am going to alter my course to 200 [degrees] and reduce speed about 12 knots to wind my way through the ice. And Naked Island ETA may be a little out of whack. But once we're clear of the ice, out of Columbia Bay, we'll give you another shout. Over." However, despite Hazelwood's assurance to the Coast Guard, the ship's speed was not reduced.

At 11:40 p.m., the night shift took over at the Coast Guard station back in Valdez. Radar man Taylor had seen the Exxon Valdez "blinking on and off the screen" but had lost the vessel by this time. Before heading home, Taylor told his replacement, Bruce Blanford, that the Exxon Valdez was crossing into the separation zone—possibly into the northbound lane to avoid the ice.

However, Hazelwood did not notify the Coast Guard when he left the traffic separation zone. And instead of ending up in the inbound lane, he went on through the inbound lane, taking the tanker farther off course. In one transmission, he mistakenly identified his vessel as the Exxon Baton Rouge, and his speech was slurred.

At the Coast Guard station, it was now Blanford's responsibility to track tankers and warn of impending danger. Instead of trying to locate the Exxon Valdez on radar or trying to monitor its movements by radio, Blanford began to rearrange the tanker traffic data sheets. To track the progress of the tankers traveling in and out of Valdez, he moved stacks of paper, each representing a different vessel, around the room.

"As soon as [Taylor] left and I got everything sorted out in my mind, I checked all of the vessel data sheets," Blanford would report. "We each have our little way of keeping things straight in our heads and keeping our watches flowing smoothly. I'm left-handed. The rest of them are right-handed, so they all set their sheets up [one] way and I set mine up this way. And so I go through and get them where I can understand them. And I generally lay [the sheets for each tanker] from left to right.... When their sheets end up all the way on the right-hand side, a tanker would be in Valdez."

By the time Blanford had arranged his stacks of paper to represent vessels going to and from the port, the Exxon Valdez was nearing the ice. "After I got things squared away, so to speak, I went down and got a cup of coffee," Blanford said. "I may have been gone a couple of minutes. I really couldn't say how long."

Meanwhile, on the Exxon Valdez, Third Mate Gregory Cousins had joined Hazelwood on the bridge to make a navigational fix on the vessel's position in the sound. The night was too dark for the seaman on watch to see any bergs, but ice was silhouetted on the radar screen. It was an extensive floe—thousands of chunks of ice had broken from the Columbia Glacier and were being massed together by the current. Cousins and Hazelwood discussed skirting the ice. Some of the ice, broken into pieces the size of a car and smaller, were of little consequence to a tanker. But the massive bergs—those the size of a house and larger, the ones they called growlers—caused concern. However, Cousins couldn't tell from the radar screen whether there were any growlers out there in the night.

The northern edge of the floe appeared to be two miles dead ahead. At their current course setting, they would run into it. The ice was backed up to Columbia Glacier, so they couldn't pass it to the right. To the left of the ice was a gap of nine-tenths of a mile between the edge of the ice and Bligh Reef. They could wait until the ice moved, or reduce speed and work their way through the ice. Captain Hazelwood chose another option: turn and enter the gap between the ice and the reef. The ship was still accelerating.

Hazelwood ordered the helmsman to alter their course "180 degrees to port"—to turn left across the 2,000–yard-wide zone separating inbound and outbound traffic and continue across the 1,500–yard-wide inbound lane. A well-timed right turn would be necessary to avoid Bligh Reef, which lay six miles ahead in the darkness. There would be little room for error. The vessel needed at least six-tenths of a mile to make the turn, and the gap between the ice and Bligh Reef was only nine-tenths of a mile wide. The tanker itself was nearly two-tenths of a mile long. The tanker would have to start its turn well before the gap between the ice and the reef if it was to make it through.

At 11:46 p.m., Maureen Jones left her cabin to go on duty. Captain Hazelwood relayed an order to her to stand on the bridge wing instead of standing her watch from the bow. Although 800 feet farther from the front of the boat, she would have the advantage of watching for hazards and buoy lights from a high position. She went to the bridge as requested.

As Jones came on duty, Helmsman Harry Claar's shift was coming to an end. Claar's job as helmsman was to physically move the steering wheel at the direction of the captain or qualified mates. Hazelwood gave him two last orders: to accelerate to sea speed and to put the ship on automatic pilot. Both commands were highly unusual. Speed was normally reduced when ice was encountered, both to minimize impact with bergs and to allow the crew more time to plot vessel position, make course adjustments, and react to an emergency. The automatic pilot—almost never used in the sound—would have to be released if any course changes had to be made.

Though puzzled by Hazelwood's orders, Claar increased speed and locked the controls on automatic pilot. He was then replaced at the helm by Robert Kagan.

On the bridge, Hazelwood told Cousins he was going below and asked if he felt comfortable navigating alone. Cousins had made only a few voyages with Hazelwood, and he had never maneuvered the Exxon Valdez in tight quarters. Nevertheless, he replied, "Yes, I feel I can manage the situation."

Standard Coast Guard procedure dictates that in the presence of danger, two officers must be on the bridge. The junior of the two is responsible for fixing the location of the vessel. The senior officer is responsible for directing the vessel's course based on this navigational information. Before leaving Cousins alone on the bridge, Hazelwood told him to make a right turn when the ship was across from the Busby Island light and to skirt the edge of the ice—but he neither gave Cousins an exact course to follow nor plotted a line on the chart. If he had, Hazelwood might have noticed that it was virtually impossible to turn abeam the Busby light and also miss the ice.

Hazelwood left the bridge at 11:53 p.m. "to send a few messages from [my] cabin." Cousins was now the only officer on the bridge. The chief mate and second mate were off duty, resting. Moments after the captain left, Cousins, who had not heard Hazelwood's orders to Claar, discovered that the vessel was on automatic pilot, and he shifted it back into manual mode. The ship was still headed on a 180–degree course toward Bligh Reef, and Cousins faced a critical maneuver: he had to avoid the ice but couldn't wait too long before turning. The vessel was increasing speed.

At 11:55 p.m., Cousins called Hazelwood to say, "I think there's a chance that we may get into the edge of this ice."

Hazelwood said, "Okay," and asked if the second mate had made it to the bridge yet. Cousins replied that the second mate hadn't arrived. They talked for less than a minute and neither mentioned slowing the vessel down.

Once more, Cousins assured the captain that he could handle things and then told the helmsman to make a 10–degree right turn. Cousins turned again to the radar, trying to locate the leading edge of ice. As he concentrated on the ice, Cousins may have lost track of time for a few minutes. He was peering at the radar screen when the tanker slipped past the Busby Island light without beginning to turn.

It was nearly midnight, the beginning of Good Friday, March 24, when Maureen Jones, now on watch, noticed that the red light on the Bligh Reef buoy was to the ship's right. Red navigational lights are placed to the right of ships returning to port, and almost every seaman knows the adage "red, right, returning." Since the Exxon Valdez was leaving port, the light should have been on the left side, to port. Jones alerted Cousins that "a red light was flashing every four seconds to starboard."

At virtually the same moment, though the ship was turning slowly, Cousins concluded that the tanker had not responded to his 10–degree right-turn command. He immediately ordered a 20–degree right turn, and this time he noticed the vessel responding.

Jones called Cousins a second time. She had a more accurate count on the red light; it was flashing every five seconds. It was still on the wrong side of the ship.

Cousins ordered a hard right and called Hazelwood, saying, "I think we are in serious trouble."

At 12:04 a.m., the Exxon Valdez shuddered. Hazelwood raced to the bridge. After first impact, the tanker advanced 600 feet before it ground to a halt on Bligh Reef.

Hazelwood didn't try to back off the reef. With the engines running full speed forward, he ordered a hard right, then a hard left. In the engine room, the chief engineer did not know they had grounded; he couldn't figure out why the system was overloading.

Chief Mate James Kunkel had been sleeping in his quarters, but awoke at first impact. "The vessel began to shudder and I heard a clang, clang, clang. I feared for my life. I thought I would never see my wife again. I knew my world would never be the same," Kunkel recalled.■

2.   REMEDIAL LEGISLATION: OPA 90

The Exxon Valdez spill was to the Oil Pollution Act of 1990 (often called OPA 90) as the Santa Barbara spill was to NEPA and the Coastal Zone Management Act. OPA 90 passed the Senate without a single dissenting vote, even though attempts to strengthen oil spill laws had foundered for years until then. Perhaps the following figure, showing the extent of the Exxon Valdez spill juxtaposed against the west and east coasts, explains the unanimity:

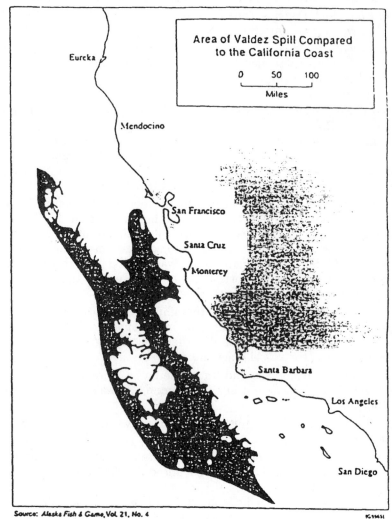

Source: *Alaska Fish & Game, Vol. 21, No. 4*

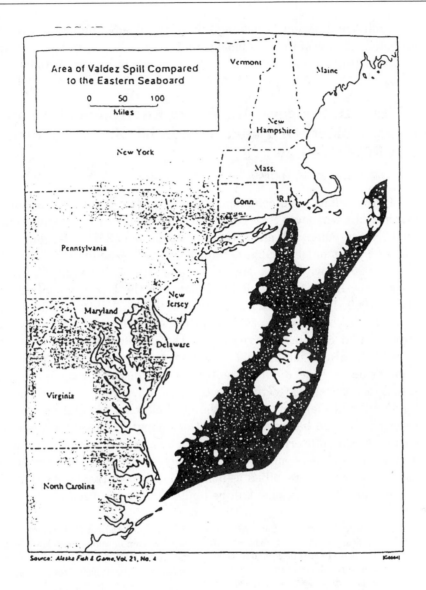

Figure 6–8

Reprinted from William H. Rodgers, Jr., 2 Environmental Law: Air & Water 192–93 (Supp. 1999).

Professor Rodgers, a leading authority on environmental law and an avid student of evolutionary biology and its interface with law, has written an interesting commentary on the likely success of certain sections of OPA:

William H. Rodgers, Jr., Where Environmental Law and Biology Meet: Of Panda's Thumbs, Statutory Sleepers, and Effective Law

65 U. Colo. L. Rev. 25, 66–74 (1993).

One is tempted to condemn without further inquiry false behavioral assumptions whenever they appear in law. Delusions of compliance are an unlikely ingredient of an effective rule of law.[257][31] To gain further enlightenment on this subject, though, we will examine the Oil Pollution Act of 1990, which became law on August 18th of that year. The 1990 Act marked the initial Congressional response to the Exxon Valdez oil spill of March 1989. In an approximate way, the Exxon Valdez accident was the product of a combination of failures that included erratic navigation by an incapacitated captain in a vulnerable vessel under poorly planned conditions.[259][32] In a long (ninety-one pages), comprehensive (amendments were made to nine different statutes), and detailed response, Congress spread solutions across this spectrum of navigation, operations, vessel condition, and planning. Behind the Oil Pollution Act of 1990 are a wide variety of human behavioral assumptions about bad-weather observations, upstart second-officers, clever programmers, casual use of the auto-pilot, aggressive engineers, and careful planners. But it is the specter of the drunken captain, personified as Joseph Hazelwood, that drove this legislative engine. Our discussion will be limited to the legalized mutiny and the

---

31. Margaret Gruter, Law And The Mind: Biological Origins Of Human Behavior 21 (1991). "The effectiveness of law will be proportional to the degree to which the function of a particular law complements the function of the behavior that the law intends to regulate." *Id.*

32. ...

The findings of the Alaska Oil Spill Commission make clear that whatever the captain's shortcomings, the Exxon Valdez oil spill was an accident that was bound to happen: the combination of regulatory and corporate complacency, crew fatigue, insufficient personnel, insufficient radar, and insufficiently rigorous loading practices, as well as insufficient response preparations, created the preconditions for predictable spill disasters in the oil transport system. Alaska Oil Spill Comm'n, Spill: The Wreck Of The Exxon Valdez, Implications For Safe Transportation Of Oil iv (1990).

planning provisions. The central question is whether these measures represent effective law.

a.   Legalized Mutiny and the Myth of Compliance

Section 4104 of the 1990 Act tackles the problem of the drunken captain by obliging the second-in-command to take over the vessel temporarily "when the [two] next most senior licensed officers on a vessel reasonably believe that the master or individual in charge of the vessel is under the influence of alcohol or a dangerous drug and is incapable of commanding the vessel." Assuming for the moment that this law is meant to serve a functional and not merely an aesthetic purpose, namely, the elimination of the risk of accident due to captain drunkenness, can we say anything useful about the effectiveness of this law as adjudged from a behavioral perspective? Borrowing from ethology, we will attempt to construct for this law a compliancegram, which can be defined as a description of the range and probability of behaviors that must coincide in order to achieve the professed objective of the law. So viewed, this legalized mutiny can be expected to happen if one of the junior officers knows of the law (K), recognizes the risk (R), overcomes (O) his hesitation to initiate a takeover, persuades (P) his colleague to join in the endeavor, and defeats (D) other practical barriers to the takeover.

What are the probabilities that all conditions (K, R, O, P, D) will be satisfied to bring the vessel under safe command? Knowledge (K) of the law is usually assumed for legal purposes, and for good reason since the assumption is unlikely to be established as an empirical matter. One is left to speculation as to whether and how junior officers will be advised of their mutiny rights. The option to take over the vessel may well be spelled out in various directives, commands, manuals, and rules known best by the novitiates and least by the veterans. The possibility may be mentioned (featured?) in a mandatory (optional?) meeting on compliance with the oil spill rules. Each officer might be given the full text (all 91 pages?) of the Oil Pollution Act of 1990, which makes it a theoretical possibility that Section 4104 could be read and understood by at least a tiny fraction of the licensed merchant mariners. One suspects that years of education would be necessary to elevate the mutiny-option rule to the status of plausible hypothesis among working junior officers. There is no ship's lawyer, and if there were, he would be working for the captain. There is no report either of any captain posting a notice on a bulkhead spelling out the "Mutiny Option." A conservative estimate of the probability of the (K) requirement being satisfied is 1:5.

Risk recognition (R) is not a serious barrier to compliance, but a knowledge of human behavior could help in the analysis. Surely the mate can recognize a drunken captain when he sees one (and avoid the risk of confusing inebriation with, say, a stroke) although the use of "drugs" other than alcohol might give rise to odd behavior creating some ambiguities in interpretation. The big problem with risk recognition (R) is in appreciating that the drunken captain is "incapable" of commanding the vessel. The situation is bound to be ambiguous (the captain might be only slightly drunk, or indisposed to interfere, or soon to be so drunk that he can't interfere, or waters could be calm, or the automatic-pilot dependable, etc.), and ambiguity can be resolved as non-threatening in the mind of a junior officer. There is evidence also that self-deception may be at work to convince both the captain and the junior officers that the risks are non-emergent.[265][33] We will assign a probability of 1:2 that a junior officer will recognize (R) the captain-drunkenness risk when it appears on the scene.

Having recognized the risk, will the mate overcome (O) hesitation to put in motion the machinery of this legalized mutiny? Even with personal safety at stake, the behavioral constraints against this sort of challenge to authority are formidable. Within primate bands the very idea of a "temporary" takeover of leadership is implausible because of small rewards and high risks of subsequent retaliation. Sociological studies of modern bureaucracies underscore the difficulties of encouraging communication contrary to established norms,[266][34] much less direct challenges to the authority of the leadership. In the maritime world, of course, centuries of tradition have accorded the captain a role of unquestioned authority, and those in the business are entirely familiar with the career-threatening consequences of challenging these traditions. Junior officers who will rock this boat will be made of stern and unusual stuff. We will fix the probabilities of O being satisfied as 1:12.

Having convinced himself, will junior officer A be able to persuade (P) junior officer B to go along with the takeover? There are a number of variables here we can not account for: is this a case of a subordinate attempting to persuade a superior, or a superior a subordinate? Are the junior officers friends or rivals? Or long-term acquaintances or relative strangers? Was the decision to take over the vessel jointly arrived at, or did one overcome hesitation and make a commitment to action before seeking to persuade the other? The severity of the emergency obviously will influence the resolution of K and P by both actors. With this said, the second officer, like the first, will be contemplating a course of action under highly ambiguous and stressful conditions that will be of some considerable risk to her career. Even with the support of a colleague, the probability of the P barrier being overcome is not high—1:10 is the choice.

Even with the juniors committed to overthrowing the captain's authority, we must add a factor (D) to account for other miscellaneous obstacles that might stand in the way of a successful shift of power. What if the captain resists, and resists with force? Will the crew cooperate? Systems of formal approval (e.g., radio communication) might be superimposed on the

33. *See* Robert Trivers & Huey P. Newton, The Crash of Flight 90: Doomed By Self–Deception? Sci. Dig., Nov. 1982, at 66.

34. *See* Presidential Comm'n On The Space Shuttle Challenger Accident, Report To The President chs. 4–5, 95–96, 99, 101, 107 (1986) (the contractors (Morton Thiokol) recommended against the launch because of concerns regarding O-ring temperatures, ran into opposition from middle-level NASA managers and Morton Thiokol's superiors (one key person was told to "take off his engineering hat and put on his management hat,") took another "perspective" under this pressure, identified an "ambiguity" in the data, and caved in by withdrawing the no-launch recommendation; NASA upper-level management responsible for the launch were never informed about the safety concerns or the engineers' opposition).

process to constrain the choices otherwise open to the junior officers. Or what if the ship's doctor announces an interpretation of "under the influence" that deviates from the conclusion of the juniors? Or the turmoil of the moment may lend itself to a "nobody in charge" solution where the junior officers can take some steps to combat the pollution risk while protecting themselves from the career risks that might attend a complete takeover. These D obstacles will be assigned a probability of 1:2 of preventing the shift in command envisaged by the law.

Our compliancegram for the legalized mutiny rule tells us, then, that a limited knowledge of the law compounded with difficulties of recognizing the risk and of conforming to the legal mandates will lead to a low rate of compliance. The combined probabilities of K (1:5), R (1:2), O (1:12), P (1:10), and D (1:2) amount to 1:2400. Put another way, this law can be expected to repair one of every 2,400 drunken-captain, oil-spill-risk enhancements. This is not an effective law. A legislator might vote for the measure on symbolic grounds or because it does not hurt but not because it materially reduces the risks of oil spills from the navigation of tankers.

b.   Planning and the Attrition of Time

Oil spill contingency plans have been a primary exhibit in the law of water pollution since the 1960s, and the concept received a thorough empirical test in the wake of the Exxon Valdez disaster:

> The fishermen of Prince William Sound watched in the hours after the wreck on Bligh Reef as eleven million gallons poured out into their waters. On Friday morning, some of them hired a small airplane to fly out from Cordova to survey the wreck. "It was eerie," said Riki Ott. "On the radio, the whole world was talking about the disaster. People in the lower forty-eight were busily planning volunteer cleanup and animal rescue units to support the official response forces, but here in Prince William Sound lay the Exxon Valdez completely quiet, surrounded by a pool of oil a mile across, with blue fog vapors rising from it, just a few people standing on the deck, shaking their heads, looking at this catastrophe, and no one out there doing anything on the water." That morning, nine hours after the spill, the fishermen could fly around the oil slick in only eight minutes. And they waited, watching, expecting the official governmental and corporate mechanisms to jump into action, as so often promised in contingency plans, political representations, and courtroom proceedings. For almost forty hours the weather of Prince William Sound was uncharacteristically generous. The normal winds of March were nowhere to be seen; the seas were calm and the oil stayed in a compact floating mass near the Exxon Valdez. But no one showed up with the necessary skimming barges, the containment booms, the storage materials and clean-up equipment so confidently promised earlier. And then at the end of the second day, the winds came back with a vengeance. One fisherman looked up from Valdez Sunday afternoon and saw a ribbon of snow blowing off the shoulder of one of the mountain peaks. "Uh-oh," he

said, "there it goes," and within 24 hours the oil had blown forty miles southeastward, out of control forevermore, as the official players still continued to try to figure out what to do.[270][35]

The reasons for this contingency nonresponse are not much in doubt: confusion of authority (all looked to Alyeska), lack of preparedness (Exxon took over command of the response operation within twenty-four hours but was untrained for the job), staff limitations (supervision of all operations at the Valdez terminal was assigned to one-half the time of one full-time Alaska Department of Environmental Conservation field person), shortages of equipment (skimming barges, containment booms), lack of expertise (not enough people to operate the equipment, interpret the tides, etc.). It is another question, of course, and not a trivial one, to ask whether any response would have sufficed to contain the 10.8 million gallons of crude oil that found its way into the waters of Prince William Sound on March 22, 1989.

How did Congress respond to this demonstrated failure of contingency planning? By adding to the Act "an extremely elaborate system of contingency planning, consisting of a national response unit ("NRU"), Coast Guard strike teams, Coast Guard district response groups, area committees, area contingency plans, and individual vessel and facility response plans." The facility and vessel response plans, which have their own histories going back to 1973, must be written to combat a "worst case discharge" and are expected to cover topics such as training, equipment testing, unannounced drills, and planned responses. They are supposed to dovetail in unspecified ways with similar legal requirements under the Emergency Planning and Community–Right-to-Know Act.

[Professor Rodgers then develops a compliancegram for OPA's mandated contingency plans, and concludes]:

To complete the calculations, then, our compliancegram for the contingency planning requirements advises us that even if the plans are written, they are unlikely to be adequate, and if adequate they are unlikely to be implemented, and if implemented they are unlikely to be successful. The combined probabilities of [each of these events] are 1:12,000. Rephrased, a Las Vegas gambler would fix the odds of the next million-gallon spill being stopped by a contingency plan as 12,000:1. The contingency plan requirements of the 1990 Act are not an effective tool for stopping major spills. A legislator might vote for the measure on symbolic grounds or because it is packaged with other effective provisions or because a plan might be helpful for dealing with small spills in confined waters.■

NOTES AND COMMENTS

1. How do you prevent people working in areas of safety hazard from growing complacent after years of no trouble? The same problem affects

35. Zygmunt J.B. Plater, Essay, "A Modern Political Tribalism in Natural Re-   source Management," 11 Pub. Land L. Rev. 1, at 1–9 (1990).

any business in which the risk of failure is small but the cost of failure is catastrophic, such as the nuclear power industry. Boredom is apparently another problem. In March 2000, workers at a British company that makes plutonium fuel for nuclear reactors reportedly were bored counting fuel pellets for shipment and instead falsified numbers. New York Times, Mar. 22, 2000.

Does the saga of the Exxon Valdez affect your opinion about whether a "worst case analysis" of a 100,000 barrel oil spill should have been included in the challenged EIS in *Village of False Pass*, discussed in note 4 on p. 361? *See* Edward A. Fitzgerald, The Rise and Fall of Worst Case Analysis, 18 Dayton L. Rev. 1 (1992). OPA now requires a "worst case" response plan, defined as a spill of a vessel's entire cargo in adverse weather, as part of the national contingency plan, area contingency plans, and the facility response plans. Are plans likely to work in the event of a worst case disaster?

From the Houston Chronicle, Feb. 22, 1999, at 7A:

> Public health infrastructures in the United States and Canada, in their current states, would be devastated by a "high-impact" bioterrorism event in which an attacker uses modern germ technology, officials say.
>
> A telltale scenario—role-played by public health experts using smallpox as the biological agent involved and epidemic response plans similar to those in many American cities–left 15,000 people dead over two months and 80 million dead within a year, primarily because of insufficient global vaccine supplies.
>
> "We blew it," said Dr. Michael Ascher, . . . one of a number of experts asked to make decisions as the scenario played out. "It clearly got out of control. Whatever planning we had . . . didn't work. I think this is the harsh reality, what would happen."

Laurie Garrett, "Smallpox Bioterrorism Exercise Proves Disaster in Preparedness."

2.   Are Rodgers' statistics convincing? Or would this methodology seem to make almost anything seem improbable? The Chairman of the Flight Safety Foundation commented as follows on the cause of the cargo fire that led a Valujet to crash in the Everglades in 1998: "Who would ever have thought somebody would one day mislabel the package [of oxygen generators], never put the safety caps on them, throw them into a rough box and put them into a hold full of things that would burn? . . . There are so many minute probabilities there." New York Times, Feb. 6, 2000, at A16.

3.   Are there other ways to deal with the problem of the drunken captain? Of human error? The U.S. Coast Guard reports that since 1990, the number of spills of more than 10,000 gallons in the U.S. decreased by about 50 percent. Perhaps the legislation has had a positive effect, despite Prof. Rodgers' pessimism, or because of other sections of the law. As you read the following summary of other provisions of the act, ask how they might affect the compliancegram for preventing oil spills:

(A) Owners and operators of vessels or facilities are strictly liable for cleanup costs and damages caused by discharges of oil. Sec. 1002, 33 U.S.C. § 2702.

(B) The federal liability limit was raised to $1,200 per gross ton, eight times the liability cap under the Clean Water Act. Sec. 1004.

(C) A new $1 billion Oil Spill Liability Trust fund is available to pay for cleanup costs in excess of the liability limit, funded by a five-cent-per-barrel tax on oil. The entire amount can be used for one spill, with up to $500 million for payments for damage to natural resources. (Exxon incurred expenses of $3.5 billion as a result of the spill, including $2.2 billion in cleanup costs, about $1 billion in payments to state and federal governments; and $300 million in voluntary payments to cover actual damages of those who sought compensatory payments from lost income).

(D) OPA 90 requires more drug and alcohol reporting, testing and retesting of merchant mariners., and limits the number of hours worked to prevent exhaustion.

(E) All newly constructed tankers must have double hulls, and existing tankers must be retrofitted for double hulls under a phased in schedule over 20 years. 33 U.S.C. § 4115.

(F) Civil penalties were dramatically increased, as were criminal sanctions for failure to report discharges.

(G) OPA 90 expressly denies any intent to preempt more stringent state laws regarding oil spills, such as laws imposing unlimited liability. Sec. 1018, 33 U.S.C. § 2718. Many states have enacted such laws. *See, e.g.,* Gary V. Pesko, Comment: Spillover from the *Exxon Valdez*: North Carolina's New Offshore Oil Spill Statute, 68 Envtl L. 1214 (1990). Following the Valdez spill, the state of Washington enacted laws that require tanker operators to comply with the state's "best achievable protection (BAP)" regulations. These regulations consisted of many operating and personnel rules, such as requirements that all deck officers be proficient in English and able to speak a language understood by the crew; that the crew have completed a comprehensive state training program; and that the navigation watch be composed of at least two licensed deck officers, a helmsman, and a lookout. The International Association of Independent Tanker Owners (Intertanko) brought suit, alleging that 16 of the BAP regulations were federally preempted. The lower courts upheld almost all of the 16 rules, relying on OPA's expression of non-preemption.

However, in *U.S. v. Locke,* 120 S.Ct. 1135 (2000), the Supreme Court held that reliance on OPA's savings clause was misplaced. OPA's non-preemption effect was limited to state laws involving oil spill liability, similar to the Florida law which the Court had upheld in *Askew v. American Waterways Operators, Inc.,* 411 U.S. 325 (1973). OPA' s passage did not affect the preemptive powers of another federal statute, the Ports and Waterways Safety Act of 1972 (as amended in 1978). The Supreme Court had ruled in 1978, in *Ray v. Atlantic Richfield Co.,* 435 U.S. 151 (1978), that this Ports Safety Act preempted many of Washington state's earlier attempts to regulate tanker traffic in Puget Sound (much of it carrying crude oil from the Alaskan North Slope) by restricting tanker size, tanker design, and pilotage requirements. OPA's saving clause reads that "Nothing in this Act" shall "affect, or be construed or interpreted as preempting, the authority of any State" to impose "any additional liability or requirements with respect to (A) the discharge of oil. . . ." The Court found that these savings clauses applied only to Title I of OPA, captioned Oil Pollution and Compensation, and not to the whole Act, because the clause was placed in Title I. Title I does not regulate vessel operation, design, or manning, which were the subject of Washington's 16 BAP rules. Legislative history showed that Congress shared the court's view that OPA "does not disturb the Supreme Court's decision in *Ray*." In short, maritime commerce is largely a matter for federal and international regulation, unless "peculiarities of local waters" call for special, local regulations (such as requiring a local tug escort or local pilot in Puget Sound). Many of Washington's requirements applied at all times in all waters and so could not survive the *Ray* preemption test.

The Court concluded "When one contemplates the weight and immense mass of oil ever in transit by tankers, the oil's proximity to coastal life, and its destructive power even if a spill occurs far upon the open sea, international, federal, and state regulation may be insufficient protection. Sufficiency, however, is not the question before us. The issue is not adequate regulation but political responsibility; and it is, in large measure, for Congress and the Coast Guard to confront whether their regulatory scheme, which demands a high degree of uniformity, is adequate." 120 S.Ct. at 1152.

4.   The reach of OPA's strict liability provisions was tested in Rice v. Harken Exploration Co., 89 F.Supp.2d 820 (N.D. Tex.1999), when owners of the Big Creek Ranch in the Panhandle of Texas sued Harken, seeking $38 million in damages and remediation for discharging pollutants from drilling operations onto ranch land and into a small seasonal creek. The creek flowed into the Canadian River, which flows into the Arkansas River, which flows into the Mississippi River, which flows into the Gulf of Mexico, some 500 miles distant. Under OPA, a person operating an onshore facility is liable if the facility has discharged oil, or poses a substantial threat of discharging oil into the nation's navigable waters. 33 U.S.C. secs. 2701(32), 2702(a). Under OPA, the ranchers had to prove two elements: (1) that a discharge of oil occurred, and (2) that it threatened navigable waters. The Clean Water Act and OPA define "navigable waters" very broadly, as "waters of the United States". Courts have interpreted the Clean Water Act expansively to mean any natural surface water in the U.S., including sloughs, wetlands, and prairie potholes that have some connection to interstate commerce. Should OPA be similarly interpreted to apply to discharges of oil on the Big Creek Ranch? Would your answer change if Harken had prepared a Spill Prevention Control Plan under OPA for its Panhandle leases?

5.   How would you create the incentives to ensure that plans for responding to oil spills are understood and implemented? The techniques for cleaning up after an oil spill are themselves controversial. For example,

should dispersants be used to break the oil into smaller particles which will sink to the bottom? The pros and cons of dispersants are discussed in International Maritime Organization, Manual on Oil Pollution, sec. 4, pp. 123–51 (1988). For a description of the program for cleaning up Prince William Sound after the Exxon Valdez wreck, *see* Jeff Wheelwright, Degrees of Disaster (1994).

The tenth anniversary of the spill in March 1999 spawned assessments of the Sound's recovery. Bald eagles and river otters are fully recovered; three bird species, Pacific herring, sea otters, clams, mussels, and pink and sockeye salmon are recovering; killer whales, harbor seals, and four bird species are not recovering. *See* 195 National Geographic (March 1999) at 98.

A volunteer who organized citizens to hand-scrub the oil off hundreds of otters and birds now looks back on this effort: "Exxon spent $80,000 per otter that survived the cleaning, but at least half of those are thought to have died soon after they were released. So it was closer to $160,000 per animal. I think that money would have been better spent restoring and protecting habitat." Sierra, "Sea of Crude, Legacy of Hope," Mar/April 1999 at 81. Nearly $700 million of Exxon's settlement with the state and federal governments has been used to purchase over half a million acres of spectacular Alaskan coastline to preserve as parks and wildlife refuges.

6.   On November 18, 1997, the D.C. Circuit upheld most of the regulations implementing the natural resources damages sections of the Oil Pollution Act of 1990. *General Electric Company v. U.S. Dep't of Commerce*, 128 F.3d 767 (D.C.Cir.1997). The regulations allow, but do not require, the use of contingent value methodology in measuring natural resource damages. *See also Kennecott Utah Copper Corp. v. U.S. Dep't of the Interior*, 88 F.3d 1191 (D.C.Cir.1996).

7.   Litigation arising out of the Exxon Valdez spill lingers on. Exxon is appealing a $5 billion punitive judgment award in the Ninth Circuit. *See also, Exxon Shipping Co. v. Airport Depot Diner, Inc.*, 120 F.3d 166 (9th Cir.1997); and *In re Exxon Valdez; Alaska Native Class v. Exxon Corp.*, 104 F.3d 1196 (9th Cir.1997) (class action based on public nuisance brought by Alaskan Natives for injury to their subsistence way of life dismissed for failure to prove "special injury"; damage suffered by the Natives varied only in magnitude, not in kind, from that suffered by all Alaskans). The conviction of Captain Hazelwood of the criminal charge of negligent discharge of oil was upheld by the Alaska Supreme Court. *State of Alaska v. Hazelwood*, 946 P.2d 875 (1997).

8.   Almost twice as much oil is released into the marine environment from municipal wastes and urban runoff as from major tanker accidents. *See* National Research Council, Oil in the Sea: Inputs, Fates, and Effects 82 (1985). What laws can change the behavior of the weekend "do it yourselfer" who dumps used engine oil down storm sewers?

9.   Outside the jurisdiction of the United States, a complex series of international treaties governs claims for compensation for damage from oil spills. These treaties are administered by the International Maritime Organization based in London, and claims are paid out of the International Oil

Pollution Compensation Fund. In general, the types of damage for which compensation is available are somewhat more limited than in the United States, and the amount of damages is determined through administrative procedures rather than by a jury, which tends to result in smaller awards, but the time for processing awards is usually quite expeditious.

3.   Oil Pipelines

a.   PIPELINE SAFETY

Safety regulations for oil pipelines are enforced by the United States Department of Transportation (DOT) under the Hazardous Liquids Pipeline Safety Act, as amended by the Pipeline Safety Act of 1992 (*see* 49 U.S.C. § 2001). In the 1992 act, Congress increased inspection requirements, especially of underwater pipelines, brought some formerly exempt lines under DOT regulation, and required pipelines to use certain state-of-the-art technologies in their regular inspection programs. In 1994, Alyeska, the operator of the Trans Alaskan Pipeline settled several whistleblower suits charging it with intimidation of employees who pointed out safety and other problems with the operations during a government-ordered audit in 1993. In 1999, Alyeska presented a 225–page report to Congress which found that retaliation against whistleblowers was still a problem and was retarding quality control and the updating of technical work. The new manager of Alyeska vowed to change the company's old culture of resistance to criticism and change. New York Times, Sept. 22, 1999, at B4. Alyeska is largely owned by Exxon, BPAmoco, and Arco.

In January 2000, Koch Industries, one of the largest pipeline operators in the U.S. agreed to pay a $30 million fine, the largest civil environmental penalty ever collected to date. The EPA had found that Koch had failed to inspect its lines for cracks or corrosion, resulting in leaks of 3 million gallons of crude oil, gasoline, and other oil products in 300 separate incidents in the past 9 years. Instead of doing inspections, it apparently was cheaper for Koch to find pipeline flaws by waiting for them to break. New York Times, Jan. 14, 2000, at A21. In the same month, an 8–ton anchor dropped accidently from a drilling rig being towed in the Gulf of Mexico, rupturing an offshore pipeline and causing an oil slick two miles wide and two miles long. New York Times, Jan. 23, 2000, at A20.

Can best technology and eternal vigilance prevent the following kind of disaster, which occurred in October 1994 near Houston, Texas after several days of rainstorms? The pipeline ruptures had enough impact on the availability of oil on the East coast to raise the market price of oil substantially.

Gaynell Terrell, Emergency Alert Issued on Pipelines, Houston Post, Oct. 26, 1994, at A1

Federal officials issued an emergency bulletin nationwide Tuesday to operators of oil and gas pipelines in flood plains in an effort to deter another disaster like the explosions and fires in the San Jacinto River. At the same time, comprehensive inspections began on all Houston-area pipelines to determine on a case-by-case basis which pipelines can return to service.

About 30 pipelines under the flood-swollen San Jacinto were shut off after a 40–inch main pipeline carrying gasoline and owned by Colonial Pipeline Co. ruptured last Thursday, fueling a fire that sent 120 people to the hospital, most with throat or lung irritation. Three more pipelines ruptured, adding diesel, heating oil and crude to the mix. More than 20 nearby homes and other buildings caught fire and the spill sent streaks of black oil 20 miles downstream toward Galveston Bay.

So far, 6,000 barrels of oil and water have been collected, with more absorbed by sponge-like booms placed in the water. The Coast Guard estimated 1.5 million barrels of oil leaked into the flooded river, but much of it burned or evaporated. Also Tuesday, Texas Land Commissioner Garry Mauro announced his agency has already begun efforts to seed patches of the slick with oil-eating microbes.

D.K. Sharma, the U.S. Department of Transportation's top pipeline safety official, said the agency is sending 10 of its 35 pipeline inspectors and field engineers to the Houston area. All 30 pipelines here are thought to have been affected in some way by record flooding. Sharma said new rules already under consideration would require specifically placed valves and leak detectors on hazardous material pipelines. The rules will be accelerated by about a year, he said.

A thorough study of the nation's pipeline system—and its ability to withstand disaster—will also be conducted. "Over the long term, we must also determine what changes may be necessary to assure that pipelines have the best chance possible of withstanding inevitable, but often unpredictable, natural disasters," he said.

Mauro said the pipeline ruptures and fire have been devastating to the area both environmentally and economically. "I think a lot of us were surprised at the distance between the shut-off valves (on some of the pipelines)," he said. Colonial officials said last week it was 10 miles between valves on its No. 1 line, but workers couldn't reach the closest valves because of the floodwaters. At one point product from about 30 miles of pipeline was feeding the inferno.■

NOTE AND COMMENT

In August, 1999, the Office of Pipeline Safety reported that the average amount of oil spilled per pipeline incident fell by 31 percent since 1993, due to a federal program requiring all pipeline operators to review their emergency response plans, as required by the Oil Pollution Act of 1990. The Office credited the decline to faster and more effective responses to spills resulting from company exercises in organizing Spill Management Teams. BNA Daily Report for Executives, Sept. 1, 1999, at A15.

b. COMMON CARRIERS

Oil pipeline companies are often owned by the major oil companies, but at both the interstate and intrastate level they are regulated as common carriers. This means that they must offer to transmit oil for anyone at the same rate.

Unlike electricity and natural gas, oil is not a homogeneous commodity. Everything from fairly heavy oil to lighter products like gasoline can be carried in pipelines. The same pipeline often carries different commodities; a solid ball is put into the line between shipments of different commodities, and the ball is forced through the line by the pressure of the liquids behind it.

Intrastate rates for shipment of oil by pipeline are typically regulated by whatever state agency regulates oil and gas. Interstate rates are regulated by FERC, which took over that role from the Interstate Commerce Commission.

c. COMPETITION

Is it safer to ship oil by tanker than by pipeline? At present, the state of Florida gets all of its oil, even oil produced in Texas and Louisiana, by tanker. For years, the oil companies have sought authority to build an oil pipeline from those states into Florida. Their efforts have consistently been frustrated by opposition from local Florida "environmental" groups, some of which have been funded by shipping interests.

Campion Walsh, Shipping Companies Lead Florida Effort to Block Oil Pipeline,

Oil Daily, Aug. 26, 1994 at 165

Southeast Florida maritime interests, concerned about new competition for transportation of petroleum products, are subsidizing efforts to block construction of the first interstate oil products pipeline into Florida, industry sources say. The Florida Alliance, an association of shipping companies that operate at Port Everglades in southeast Florida, has been funding Friends of Lloyd, the environmental group leading protests against Colonial Pipeline Co.'s proposed spur extension into northern Florida just west of Tallahassee, industry sources tell The Oil Daily.

The alliance has helped pay for lawsuits against the project filed by Friends of Lloyd President Robert Rackleff. Rackleff has argued in the suits that pipelines require more federal and state regulation because they spill twice as much oil as tankers and barges on an average annual basis. Nearly all of the 259 million bbl of oil and oil products arriving annually in Florida are transported in barges and tankers. And Port Everglades is currently the largest delivery site for vehicle fuels entering Florida.■

As this example indicates, the business of transporting energy is a highly competitive one in which it is often difficult to make a reasoned evaluation of the various alternatives.

NATURAL GAS REGULATION BEFORE 1985

A. SOME BASICS

1. INDUSTRY STRUCTURE

a. THE PHYSICAL FLOW THROUGH FOUR ENTITIES

Natural gas flows through a continuous chain of links between four major types of business entities:

Producers. These are the operators of the oil and gas fields that produce natural gas. For the most part, they are the same companies that produce oil because the two hydrocarbons are so often found together and are leased together in the same oil and gas lease discussed in the Oil Chapter. Gas is gathered in small-diameter pipelines from all the wells in a field; run through processing facilities in the field to remove water and impurities; compressed to boost its pressure so that it will flow into a large transmission pipeline; and transported to storage or marketing centers as depicted in Figure 7–1:

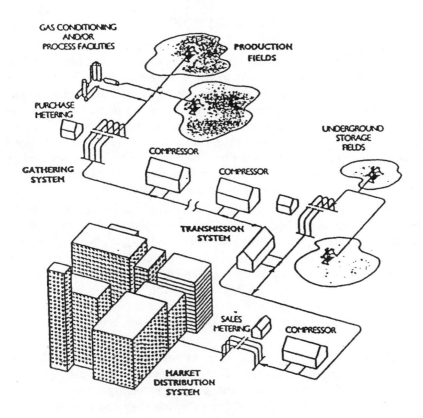

Typical
Natural Gas
Pipeline System

GAS CONDITIONING
AND/OR
PROCESS FACILITIES

PRODUCTION
FIELDS

PURCHASE
METERING

UNDERGROUND
STORAGE
FIELDS

GATHERING
SYSTEM

COMPRESSOR

COMPRESSOR

TRANSMISSION
SYSTEM

SALES
METERING

COMPRESSOR

MARKET
DISTRIBUTION
SYSTEM

Figure 7–1

Source: 2 Energy Law and Transactions, p. 50–108 (David J. Muchow & William A. Mogel eds., 1999) (Matthew Bender).

Pipelines. Interstate pipeline companies have, for antitrust reasons, been independent from the producers. They are separate companies that have been set up to move the gas from the states where it is produced to other regions where it is desired as a fuel. Interstate pipelines are regulated by the Federal Energy Regulatory Commission (FERC). In large producing and consuming states like Texas, many intrastate pipelines also exist. These are regulated by a state agency, often the public utility commission.

Distributors or LDCs. In each urban area there is usually a "gas company" that distributes gas through gas mains under the streets to homes for heating and cooking, and to commercial and industrial businesses. These local distribution companies are known as LDCs or distributors. They are usually investor-owned utilities regulated by the state public utility commission, but in some cases municipalities operate the gas distribution business.

Industrial Users. Gas is used as fuel in a wide variety of industrial processes from boilers to blast furnaces. Industrial users often use very large volumes of gas and are quite sensitive to its price.

b. THE BASICS OF PIPELINE OPERATIONS

The market for natural gas has wide seasonal variations. In the northern states, the most common use for natural gas is for space heating. This means that usage is very high in the winter and much lower in the summer. The laws of physics tell us there are limits on how much gas can be pushed through a pipe, depending on the size of the pipe and the degree of pressure. Natural gas is under considerable pressure in a transmission line, but there are limits on the extent to which it can be compressed without risking a rupture, which can be disastrous. Thus a pipeline system must be designed to have enough capacity to meet the demands of customers on the coldest day. The coldest day is known as the "peak."

This means that on many summer days, there is plenty of room in the pipe, but when cold snaps hit, pipeline capacity often reaches its limit. To address this imbalance, two different methods have typically been employed. First, depleted reservoirs nearer to consuming areas are converted to gas storage areas by piping in new gas in the summer, injecting it into the reservoir, and drawing it out in the following winter. (Gas storage is discussed in Chapter 6). Especially in the last decade, gas storage facilities have greatly expanded and this alleviates, but does not eliminate, the peaking problem.

Second, many industrial users, such as petrochemical plants or steel mills, can use very large quantities of gas on a year round basis, *i.e.*, they have a "high load factor." They are also large enough that they can maintain alternative coal or oil facilities to which they can switch if gas is not available or if gas becomes relatively expensive compared to substitute fuels. These customers are very desirable for a pipeline company, which is always seeking to maximize the use of its facilities on a year-round basis.

To attract these customers, pipeline companies designed "interruptible" rates, which allow industrial customers to buy gas at low rates on condition that they can be cut off on cold days if the capacity is needed for heating customers. The pipelines developed certain basic rate design principles that were generally accepted by the regulatory commissions:

The "interruptible" customer pays a rate based primarily on the amount of gas it actually uses, called the "usage" or "commodity" charge.

The "firm" customer (like the residential consumer with a low load factor) pays a two-part rate. The first part is based on the actual amount of gas used, *i.e.*, the usage or commodity rate. In addition, the firm customer pays for the right to demand service even on the coldest day. This second part of the rate is called a "reservation" or "demand" charge.

If it gets so cold that even a cutoff of the industrial customers is inadequate to free up enough gas to serve the firm customers, LDCs typically establish priority lists to allocate gas among the firm customers.

Usually the customers that will suffer the least damage from a shutdown
are the first to be cut off, but any such action is an emergency situation to
be avoided if at all possible.

c. CHANGING INDUSTRY LANDSCAPES

The business relationships among these four sectors were well established until the energy shocks of the 1970s forced a radical restructuring of
the industry. Historically, the pipelines bought gas from producers, transported it to markets, and sold it to distributors and industrial users.
Because financing to construct a pipeline was not available unless the
company could show that it had an assured source of supply and demand
for twenty years or so, pipeline companies entered into long-term contracts
to buy gas from producers, usually at relatively fixed prices. Similarly,
distributors entered into long-term agreements to buy gas from the pipelines at rates approved by the state public utility commission.

The physical flow of gas and the straightforward buy/sell arrangements
in the gas chain from the "upstream" wells to the "downstream" consumer
before the restructuring are depicted in Figure 7–2 below. The pipeline
basically acted as a merchant, buying gas from the producer at one end and
then selling it to the LDC at the other.

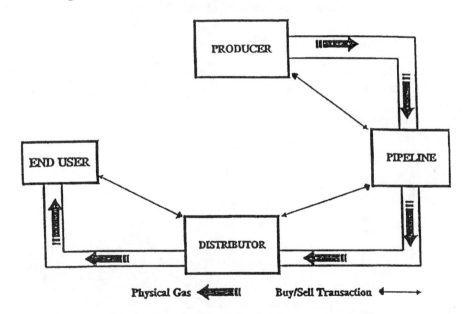

Figure 7–2. Historical Marketplace for Gas.

Today, the physical flow of gas follows the same pattern from the
wellhead through pipelines to the users, but the buy/sell financial transactions involve new players and new risk management tools created in
response to fast-moving market forces. The new landscape is depicted in
Figure 7–3 below. This chapter describes the pre–1985 evolution of the gas
industry. Chapter 9 describes the post–1985 revolution, after an excursion
into ratemaking regulation in Chapter 8.

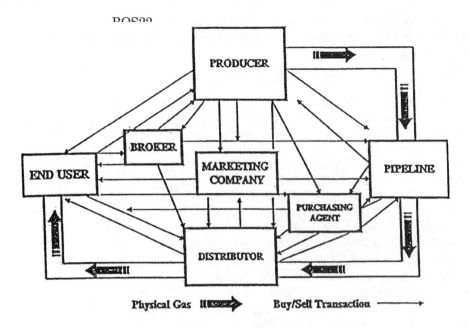

Figure 7–3. Today's Marketplace for Gas.

2.   GAS PRICES

As with oil, the long-term price of natural gas explains much about natural gas law and policy. Here is the price of gas from 1949–1998:

Wellhead, 1949-1998

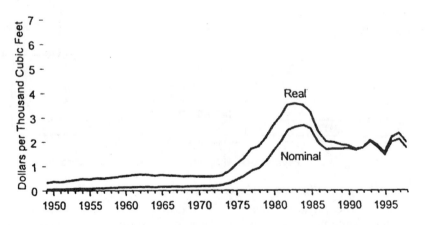

Figure 7–4. Natural Gas Wellhead Prices 1949–1998. * Real prices in 1992 dollars.

Source: Energy Information Administration.

A comparison of gas prices with the prices of the other two fossil fuels—crude oil and coal—during the key decades of 1960–1990 shows the following pattern:

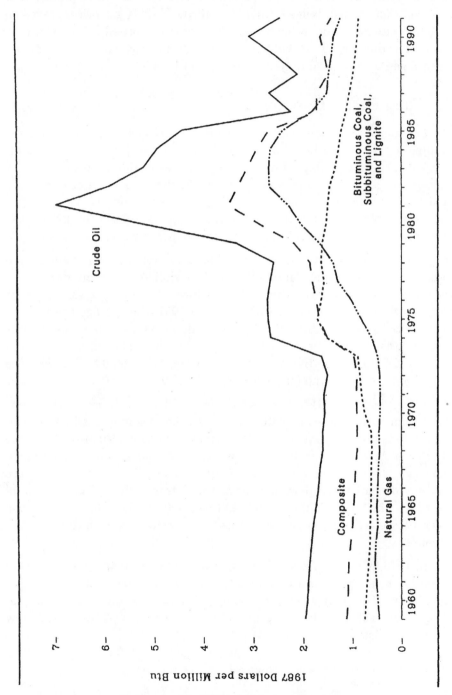

Figure 7–5. Fossil Fuel Prices 1959–1991.

Source: Energy Information Administration.

Two trends are evident. First, natural gas prices turned sharply upwards in 1973 with the first Oil Shock, but did not reach such a lofty peak as crude oil; and second, gas prices resisted the 1981 plunge that crude oil experienced. Indeed, from 1981 through 1985, gas prices stayed on a high plateau, while other fossil fuel prices dropped. This aberrant behavior is due largely to the perverse legal framework created to regulate natural gas, as discussed in Section B of this Chapter.

3.   FROM EXCESS GAS TO SHORTAGE

For many years, gas was an unwanted byproduct of the hunt for oil. Finding a gas field rather than an oil field was a serious disappointment. For years, operators simply flared casinghead gas at the wellhead. (Casinghead gas is gas which inevitably accompanies the production of oil). Many Houstonians can still remember driving at night from Houston to the Galveston beach, 30 miles away, through oil fields so brightly illuminated by the gas flares that they could read a newspaper in the car.

In the 1920s and 1930s, huge gas fields covering millions of acres were discovered in the Texas Panhandle and in Oklahoma, but the gas was in the wrong place—far from the populated East coast. The excess supply of gas was reflected in its price. From 1935 to 1951, the average price of gas on a BTU basis was about 6 cents per million BTUs, while the price of crude oil rose from 18 cents to 43 cents on the same BTU basis.[1] Thus, gas sold for 1/3 to 1/7 of the equivalent heating value of oil. Gas was the "Cinderella" of fuels, the forgotten stepchild of oil.

After World War II, during which crude oil was in very short supply, natural gas began to come into its own as the cleanest of all fuels. The interstate gas transmission system expanded and provided new and more distant markets for this fuel. Gas is about 30 times more expensive to transport than oil (on an energy equivalent basis), so its markets are crucially dependent on development of this infrastructure. The passage of the Clean Air Act in 1970 elevated gas to a premium fuel. But by this time, federal price controls on gas had already begun to create shortages in gas supplies.

In 1978, when interstate pipelines were forced to curtail and ration gas to endusers along the East coast, and Congress was debating the passage of the Natural Gas Policy Act as a solution to the shortages, the National Geographic featured this fuel in an article asking "Natural Gas–How Much, How Soon?":

---

1. Erich W. Zimmermann, Conservation in the Production of Petroleum 237–51 (1957).

Bryan Hodgson, "Natural Gas: the Search Goes On,"

154 Nat'l Geographic 632–51 (Nov. 1978).

"Natural gas? We could have it running out our ears", says Dr. Paul Jones. "But first we've got to accept some new ideas about petroleum geology.

He stabs a finger at a map of the Texas–Louisiana coastal region, which is barely recognizable beneath a crazy-quilt pattern of subsurface contour lines.

"Those lines could lead us to more gas than we've ever dreamed of, enough for centuries," says Paul. "They mark the geopressure systems— 150,000 square miles of porous shale and sandstone saturated with hot brine at abnormally high pressures. There's good scientific evidence that. this brine could contain as much as 50,000 trillion cubic feet of gas. That's equal to 2,500 times our present yearly production."

As a hydrologist, Paul has spent thirty years—most of them with the U.S. Geological Survey—studying the critical role of underground water in the earth's geological history. Some of his ideas are still sheer heresy to many petroleum experts. But he is one of a growing band of scientists, engineers, and hard-nosed production men who reject the dire predictions that United States gas resources will soon be exhausted.

Instead, they want to rewrite the petroleum-geology textbooks to include six "unconventional" gas sources long dismissed as too difficult or too costly to exploit:

Geopressure zones. Interest is focused on the Gulf Coast region, but researchers have identified several other U.S. regions that also may contain significant resources.

Deep basins. Today drillers are finding unheralded quantities of gas at depths between 15,000 and 30,000 feet.

Western "tight sands." In the Rockies drillers have learned how to extract gas from concrete-hard sandstones estimated to contain some 800 trillion cubic feet (TCF).

Coal seams. An estimated 850 TCF of gas exists in the nation's coal seams at depths as great as 6,000 feet.

Devonian shales. More than 1,000 TCF is believed trapped in dense rock underlying 90,000 square miles of Appalachia.

Methane hydrates. At certain pressures and temperatures, methane and water form an icelike substance beneath permafrost and in deep-ocean bottoms. Undetected in nature until the mid–1960's, hydrates may have captured enormous quantities of gas thought to have dissipated millennia ago.

"If we recover only a small percentage of all this gas, we'd more than quadruple our present estimates of potential resources," says one government researcher. "But this is scarcely mentioned as a possibility in our energy plans."

He's right. In April 1977 federal policy-makers wrote a virtual obituary for natural gas. A 14 percent production drop by 1985 would compound already critical shortages. Industry and government reserve estimates were almost identical: about 208 TCF, barely a ten-year supply at today's consumption rate of some 19 TCF annually.

That spelled trouble. Today [in 1978] natural gas supplies 41 percent of our nontransportation energy, serving 41 million homes and providing 40 percent of industrial needs. It is our cleanest fossil fuel, and also the cheapest, with interstate prices rigidly controlled since 1954. In early 1978, residential consumers paid an average of $2.34 per thousand cubic feet, compared to $11 for an equivalent amount of electricity.

But with gas price deregulation on the horizon, higher fuel bills are a certainty.

The planners are turning to massive engineering projects for new gas supplies. Liquefied natural gas (LNG), chilled to minus 260°F and imported by tanker from Algeria or Indonesia, may cost five dollars per thousand cubic feet delivered to U.S. pipelines by 1985—more than double the controlled price of new domestic gas. The 4,800–mile Alaska gas pipeline also will require a five-dollar price, as would synthetic gas produced from coal in a series of proposed 1.6–billion-dollar plants backed by the government. "But we could drill a thousand exploration wells for the cost of one coal-gas plant," says my government friend. "If we're wrong about unconventional resources, we'd soon find out. If we're right, we'd find huge new energy supplies in our own backyard—with a very good chance that they'd be cheaper than the alternatives, and reduce our dependency on imported fuels."

Methane Pervasive in Nature

Nature's gas isn't hard to find. Cows belch it. Swamps bubble with it. You can make your own by mixing organic waste with water in an airtight tank. Anaerobic bacteria digest the waste and produce methane, the principal ingredient of natural gas. They've been doing it for four billion years, helping make methane the world's most pervasive hydrocarbon.

Finding petroleum hydrocarbons—gas and oil—is more complex. It's a gambler's game, and nature has stacked the deck. . . .

For decades oilmen treated gas as a necessary evil. It provided most of the pressure that caused oil to flow to the surface. But it caused deadly blowouts. There was no market for it. Since 1859, night skies have glared hellishly over the world's oil fields as trillions of cubic feet of natural gas flared uselessly away. Not until the 1930's was the first major U.S. pipeline built to carry gas as a lowly by-product of oil.

Things have changed. In the U.S., laws severely restrict flaring. Today gas travels through a million-mile, 50–billion-dollar pipeline network. Eighty percent of our supply comes from the gas-only reservoirs disdained by the oil pioneers.

The legacy of that disdain lives on. For years gas price controls were based on its byproduct status. Researchers concentrated relatively little effort outside the areas where oil, vastly more profitable, might be found. Unconventional gas resources were largely ignored and poorly understood.

Now that, too, is changing. A new breed of pioneers, armed with new technology and new ideas, has entered the gambler's game.

Hot liquid spurts furiously from the high-pressure valve. Dr. Denton Wieland fills a beaker and holds it to the light with a connoisseur's eye. "Good, clean stuff," he says, and offers it to me.

I take it reverently. It's a very special vintage—hot, salty water, aged for millions of years and foaming with natural gas like warm champagne. It is an actual sample of geopressurized methane, the most exciting unconventional gas source of all.

Government Probes Geopressure Zone

We're sweltering on a barge moored in Tigre Lagoon, deep in the humid coastal marsh of southern Louisiana. Dr. Wieland, a veteran petroleum engineer, is working on the U.S. Department of Energy's first geopressure test well, Edna Delcambre #1. It is producing as much as 10,000 barrels of water a day from a sandstone aquifer 12,600 feet below, where pressure is almost 11,000 pounds per square inch and the temperature is 240°F. The gas is collected by an elaborate manifold system, and the water is forced by its own pressure down another well bore for disposal 2,500 feet underground. . . .

And the results are dramatic. Gas production is 150 percent higher than originally predicted.

"We expected 20 cubic feet per 42–gallon barrel of water," Dr. Wieland says. "But we're getting 50 cubic feet."

The new data delights Dr. Paul Jones, reinforcing theories he's held for years.

"We know that enormous quantities of gas are dissolved in geopressure waters. The reasons are complicated], but basically here's what happens:

"The amount varies with temperature pressure, and salinity. Recent research indicates that water may dissolve as much as 1,000 cubic feet of gas per barrel at 30,000 feet. Near the 20,000–foot level, with lower pressures, its saturation capacity is about 100 cubic feet. Now, over geologic time, these waters have been forced upward. As they encounter lower pressures, gas comes out of solution in tiny bubbles. As more water passes through the pressure-drop zone, the number of bubbles increases. They move upward with the water. When they collect beneath geologic traps, free-gas reservoirs are formed. Today, many such reservoirs in the Gulf Coast geopressure zones are producing trillions of cubic feet a year.

"But the aquifers are vastly more extensive than the free-gas pockets. Virtually all the water is gas saturated. That is the gas we must learn to recover."

Paul published his theories in 1975, not long after ending his career with the U.S. Geological Survey. His research was a key factor in a USGS study estimating that sandstone and shale in Gulf geopressure areas contain some 60,000 TCF of dissolved gas. . . .

Coal Hides Cleaner Fuel

"Digging isn't the only way to get energy from coal," says Harvey Price. "By drilling into seams for methane, we think production could reach a trillion cubic feet a year by 1985, the equivalent of 40 million tons of coal—with no environmental problems."

Price is an executive with a Houston petroleum-engineering firm that has made a specialty of unconventional gas. Already he has ten coal-seam drilling projects across the U.S. Recent core samples from Pennsylvania coal beds indicate gas resources of seven to nine billion cubic feet per square mile, half of which Price thinks is recoverable.

"This isn't potential gas—it's here today," says Price.

Resource estimates are huge—850 trillion cubic feet, according to a 1977 Federal Power Commission study. "We think it's closer to 1,000 trillion," Price says. "They left out several basins."

Coal-seam methane is nothing new. Miners have feared and fought it for years, and thousands have died in methane-triggered explosions. In 1964 the U.S. Bureau of Mines began a research program designed to remove the deadly hazard and cut ventilation costs by drilling into coal seams before they were mined.

"We've produced more than two billion cubic feet since 1972 in just one West Virginia seam," says Maurice Deul, who started the project. "And just last year a small horizontal borehole produced between 60 and 70 million cubic feet from a Utah seam. We're planning a full-scale program there."

Degassing can permit a 10 to 20 percent coal-production increase, but horizontal drilling is not the most economical way to tap the huge gas resource.

"The gas flows slowly, with very little pressure," says Ed Talone, who worked on the Bureau of Mines program before joining Price in 1976. "So we fracture the seams with liquids. That can increase the flow eight-to twentyfold."

Coal companies fiercely resist this idea, claiming that fracturing can create cracks in overlying rock, endangering mining operations. But Bureau of Mines studies of three fractured seams that were later mined showed no such damage, and one major company has already drilled and fractured more than a dozen sites on its coal leases.

"That's not the main issue," says Talone. "Coal companies own the coal, but in the East few of them have clear title to the gas. Until that's resolved, it will be a bigger roadblock than the technology. Meanwhile, we're starting another program. We think there's a lot of gas in Devonian shale."

Eye in Space Aids Shale Probe

"But it's hard to get," says Dick McClish, an energy specialist for Ohio's Department of Energy. "We're looking for help from out in space."

He unrolls a large map overlay covered with lines like scattered dry spaghetti.

"This is Ohio's share of the Devonian sediments. The lines are surface faults, plotted from satellite pictures. We think they'll lead us to underground fault systems where shale-gas production is best."

Devonian shale contains an estimated 1,000 trillion cubic feet of gas beneath 90,000 square miles of seven Appalachian states. Ten percent of the gas can be recovered by modern methods, according to the U.S. Department of Energy's Technology Center in Morgantown, West Virginia.

Shale gave birth to the U.S. gas industry in 1821, when the first well was sunk at Fredonia, New York. It produced only a few thousand cubic feet a day for 35 years. Low productivity and long life are typical of Appalachia's 10,000 shale wells. But the Big Sandy field of eastern Kentucky has produced three trillion cubic feet since 1914.

"We'd like to find some more fields like that," says Dick McClish. "The space survey has given us some promising sites. The state is putting up 1.3 million dollars for drilling in Ohio this year, and private investors another 1.7 million. They'll get the gas—and we'll get the most sophisticated Ohio Devonian core sampling ever. A real challenge—and every 5,600 cubic feet of gas means one less barrel of oil imported. . . ."

"We don't really know what we've got in Appalachia," says J. Pasini III, a senior engineer at the Morgantown Energy Technology Center. "The big companies pulled out years ago, and there's been almost no real exploration for fifty years. They're starting to come back now—and not just for fun."

Soviets Predict 300–Century Supply

For sheer optimism about the future of natural gas, Soviet scientists win hands down. They estimate that a 30,000–year world supply lies trapped in layers that most petroleum geologists hadn't dreamed of.

These layers, called methane hydrates, are made of water and gas, which solidify naturally underground at certain temperatures and pressures. Extensive hydrate deposits were discovered beneath Siberian permafrost in 1969. Drilling through them, the Russians discovered that huge volumes of free gas were trapped underneath. The implications are staggering.

For years geologists believed that most of the world's natural gas escaped millions of years ago from areas that lacked traps of impermeable rock.

But hydrates are also impermeable. And the proper temperature–pressure conditions occur not only in permafrost regions, but in gas-rich deep ocean sediments as well. If hydrate layers exist there, the Russians said, they may contain 1.7 million trillion cubic feet of gas.

Evidence is growing. A U.S. Geological Survey team headed by Dr. Arthur Grantz has found seismic evidence that thousands of square miles of hydrate layers may exist beneath the Beaufort Sea north of Alaska. Others have found hydrate indications off the Atlantic coast of North and South America. And they believe hydrates may explain the large quantities of methane found in hundreds of locations by the National Science Foundation's Deep Sea Drilling Project since 1968.

McIver [an Exxon scientist who studied hydrate samples at Prudhoe Bay] believes the first commercial hydrate production will come from the shallow and accessible permafrost regions onshore—but not until conventional Arctic gas has been fully developed. Deep-sea hydrates must await much research and major new offshore drilling technology.

Is Barnyard Gas Next?

Technology. Economics. Statistics. At first it seemed to me that natural gas was nothing else. Now I've traveled the land to meet men who are cheerfully testing ideas against the earth's endless mystery.

I must confess their optimism has rubbed off. And if they're wrong, I know some other optimists, with some quite different ideas.

Jim Samis, for instance. In Oklahoma he shows me around his three-million-dollar plant, which makes more than a million cubic feet of methane each day from cow manure and recycles the residue into high-quality cattle feed and fertilizer. "This isn't a pilot plant," he says. We're in business."

Or Dr. Joseph Katz. In a basement workshop at Argonne National Laboratory in Illinois, he has bred thousands of generations of algae, and has learned to simulate aspects of photosynthesis—the means by which green plants convert sunlight into energy.

"That energy, electron by electron, drives the chemistry on which all organic life is based," he says. "Someday we will learn to use this principle to make fuel and food as nature does—quietly, and without any fuss." ■

NOTES AND COMMENTS

1. As you read the rest of this chapter and Chapter 9, ask yourself if the optimism of these energy pioneers in 1978 about the future of natural gas supplies was well-based, with the advantage of 20 years of hindsight. In addition to price, what will be some of the major barriers to development of some of these unconventional gas sources? *E.g.*, what problems are likely to arise with the development of methane hydrates from the Arctic?

In May 1999, the House Science Subcommittee on Energy and Environment approved a bill to authorize a $45 million research program on the energy potential of methane hydrate. A methane hydrate is a cage-like lattice of ice in which molecules of methane are trapped. Geologists now estimate that the amount of methane trapped inside hydrates is about twice the amount of carbon held in all fossil fuels on the planet. Hydrates produce minimal amounts of $CO2$ and particulates and no sulfur when burned; however, releases of methane to the atmosphere could result in a massive injection of greenhouse gases. BNA Daily Executive Report, May 13, 1999 at A–29.

The November 1978 issue of the National Geographic has photos and maps illustrating much of the excerpted text and is highly recommended reading, if you can dig the issue out of your family's attic.

2. Hydraulic fracturing of tight sands to increase the flow of gas is a well-known technology. Suppose one operator does a successful "frac" job and creates cracks in the reservoir which extend underneath the adjoining landowner's tract. Is this a trespass? What if the frac job increases the well's productivity by 1800 percent? Should the rule of capture apply to the increased production which is being drained from the tract next door? Does *Railroad Commission v. Manziel*, discussed in Chapter 6, shed light on these issues? *See* Ernest E. Smith and Jacqueline Lang Weaver, Texas Law of Oil and Gas pp. 7–19 to 7–21 (1998).

3. The environmental impacts of gas exploration and production are very similar to those discussed in the Oil Chapter, except that gas does not spill. When a gas well blows out, the gas vents into the air or else burns. The Safe Drinking Water Act (SDWA) of 1974 is of special note, however, because it regulates underground injection wells to assure that they do not pollute groundwater reservoirs which serve as sources of drinking water. Wells used in oil and gas operations are classified as Class II wells under the federal Underground Injection Control (UIC) program of the SDWA. Thousands of disposal wells reinject saltwater from oil and gas production underground. (On average, 8.5 barrels of water are brought up with every barrel of crude oil produced in the U.S.) Other wells are used to direct oil and gas into underground storage. All of these types of wells are regulated by the Environmental Protection Agency (EPA), usually through delegations to state environmental agencies. For years, fracturing wells to stimulate gas production was not considered to be subject to the permitting requirements of the SDWA. The EPA regulated only underground injection wells whose principal function was injection of fluids. However, in *Leaf Environmental Assistance Foundation (LEAF) v. EPA*, 118 F.3d 1467 (11th Cir.1997), the court found that hydraulic fracturing constituted "underground injection" under Part C of the SDWA. The *LEAF* case involved hydraulic fracturing of coal beds to produce natural gas, a technique discussed in the upcoming *Southern Ute* case *infra*. In response to *LEAF*, the state of Alabama incorporated hydraulic fracturing of coal beds into its EPA–approved UIC program. *See* 40 C.F.R. sec. 147.52 (2000). Two issues arise: First, will other states be forced to follow the hydraulic fracturing of gas wells in non-coal related gas reservoirs; and second, will this precedent affect hydraulic fracturing of gas wells in non-coal related gas reservoirs?

Sometimes, oil and gas wells encounter hydrogen sulfide, the gas with the "rotten egg" odor known to all high school chemistry students. This gas is colorless, corrosive, and highly toxic. In 1975, nine persons died from exposure to hydrogen sulfide when a well experienced equipment failure. This widely publicized tragedy prompted much tighter regulations, including contingency plans for evacuation and alerting the public, special worker training, and protective breathing equipment. (Methane, the natural gas used in homes, is odorless in its natural state. Gas utilities add an odor to it so that householders will be able to detect leaks more easily).

4. Coalbed methane production has soared in the United States. So much so, that it is no longer unconventional to produce it. Its ownership has been much litigated, however, as the following case illustrates.

Amoco Production Co. v. Southern Ute Indian Tribe

526 U.S. 865 (1999).

■ KENNEDY, J.: Land patents issued pursuant to the Coal Lands Acts of 1909 and 1910 conveyed to the patentee the land and everything in it, except the "coal," which was reserved to the United States. Coal Lands Act of 1909 (1909 Act), 35 Stat. 844, 30 U.S.C. § 81; Coal Lands Act of 1910 (1910 Act), ch. 318, 36 Stat. 583, 30 U.S.C. §§ 83–85. The United States Court of Appeals for the Tenth Circuit determined that the reservation of "coal" includes gas found within the coal formation, commonly referred to as coalbed methane gas (CBM gas). *See* 151 F.3d 1251, 1256 (1998) (en banc). We granted certiorari, 525 U.S. ___, 119 S. Ct. 921 (1999), and now reverse.

I

During the second half of the nineteenth century, Congress sought to encourage the settlement of the West by providing land in fee simple absolute to homesteaders who entered and cultivated tracts of a designated size for a period of years. *See, e.g.,* 1862 Homestead Act, 12 Stat. 392; 1877 Desert Land Act, ch. 107, 19 Stat. 377, as amended, 43 U.S.C. §§ 321–323. Public lands classified as valuable for coal were exempted from entry under the general land-grant statutes and instead were made available for purchase under the 1864 Coal Lands Act, ch. 205, § 1, 13 Stat. 343, and the 1873 Coal Lands Act, ch. 279, § 1, 17 Stat. 607, which set a maximum limit of 160 acres on individual entry and minimum prices of $10 to $20 an acre. Lands purchased under these early Coal Lands Acts—like lands patented under the Homestead Acts—were conveyed to the entryman in fee simple absolute, with no reservation of any part of the coal or mineral estate to the United States. The coal mined from the lands purchased under the Coal Lands Acts and from other reserves fueled the Industrial Revolution.

At the turn of the twentieth century, however, a coal famine struck the West. *See* Hearings on Coal Lands and Coal–Land Laws of the United States before the House Committee on Public Lands, 59th Cong., 2d Sess., 11–13 (1906) (testimony of Edgar E. Clark, Interstate Commerce Commissioner). At the same time, evidence of widespread fraud in the administration of federal coal lands came to light. Lacking the resources to make an independent assessment of the coal content of each individual land tract, the Department of the Interior in classifying public lands had relied for the most part on the affidavits of entrymen. *Watt v. Western Nuclear, Inc.*, 462 U.S. 36, 48, and n. 9 (1983). Railroads and other coal interests had exploited the system to avoid paying for coal lands and to evade acreage restrictions by convincing individuals to falsify affidavits, acquire lands for homesteading, and then turn the land over to them. C. Mayer & G. Riley, Public Domain, Private Dominion 117–118 (1985).

In 1906, President Theodore Roosevelt responded to the perceived crisis by withdrawing 64 million acres of public land thought to contain coal from disposition under the public land laws. *Western Nuclear*, 462 U.S., at 48–49. As a result, even homesteaders who had entered and worked the land in good faith lost the opportunity to make it their own unless they could prove to the land office that the land was not valuable for coal.

President Roosevelt's order outraged homesteaders and western interests, and Congress struggled for the next three years to construct a compromise that would reconcile the competing interests of protecting settlers and managing federal coal lands for the public good. President Roosevelt and others urged Congress to begin issuing limited patents that would sever the surface and mineral estates and allow for separate disposal of each. *See id.*, at 49 (quoting Special Message to Congress, Jan. 22, 1909, 15 Messages and Papers of the Presidents 7266). Although various bills were introduced in Congress that would have severed the estates—some of which would have reserved "natural gas" as well as "coal" to the United States—none was enacted. *See* 41 Cong. Rec. 630 (1907) (bill by Rep. Volstead "reserving coal, lignite, petroleum, and natural-gas deposits from disposal . . . under existing land laws"); *id.*, at 1483–1484 (bill by Sen. La Follette providing for the sale of surface lands, but "reserving from entry and sale the mineral rights to coal and other materials mined for fuel, oil, gas, or asphalt"); *id.*, at 1788 (bill by Sen. Nelson "to provide for the reservation of the coal, lignite, oil, and natural gas in the public lands").

Finally, Congress passed the Coal Lands Act of 1909, which authorized the Federal Government, for the first time, to issue limited land patents. In contrast to the broad reservations of mineral rights proposed in the failed bills, however, the 1909 Act provided for only a narrow reservation. The Act authorized issuance of patents to individuals who had already made good-faith agricultural entries onto tracts later identified as coal lands, but the issuance was to be subject to "a reservation to the United States of all coal in said lands, and the right to prospect for, mine, and remove the same." 30 U.S.C. § 81. The Act also permitted the patentee to "mine coal for use on the land for domestic purposes prior to the disposal by the United States of the coal deposit." *Ibid.* A similar Act in 1910 opened the remaining coal lands to new entry under the homestead laws, subject to the same reservation of coal to the United States. 30 U.S.C. §§ 83–85.

Among the lands patented to settlers under the 1909 and 1910 Acts were former reservation lands of the Southern Ute Indian Tribe, which the

Tribe had ceded to the United States in 1880 in return for certain allotted lands provided for their settlement. Act of June 15, 1880, ch. 223, 21 Stat. 199. In 1938, the United States restored to the Tribe, in trust, title to the ceded reservation lands still owned by the United States, including the reserved coal in lands patented under the 1909 and 1910 Acts. As a result, the Tribe now has equitable title to the coal in lands within its reservation settled by homesteaders under the 1909 and 1910 Acts.

We are advised that over 20 million acres of land were patented under the 1909 and 1910 Acts and that the lands—including those lands in which the Tribe owns the coal—contain large quantities of CBM gas. Brief for Montana et al. as Amici Curiae 2. At the time the Acts were passed, CBM gas had long been considered a dangerous waste product of coal mining. By the 1970's, however, it was apparent that CBM gas could be a significant energy resource, *see* Duel & Kimm, Coalbed Gas: A Source of Natural Gas, Oil & Gas J., June 16, 1975, p. 47, and, in the shadow of the Arab oil embargo, the Federal Government began to encourage the immediate production of CBM gas through grants, *see* 42 U.S.C. §§ 5901–5915 (1994 ed. and Supp. III), and substantial tax credits, *see* 26 U.S.C. § 29 (1994 ed. and Supp. III).

Commercial development of CBM gas was hampered, however, by uncertainty over its ownership. "In order to expedite the development of this energy source," the Solicitor of the Department of the Interior issued a 1981 opinion concluding that the reservation of coal to the United States in the 1909 and 1910 Acts did not encompass CBM gas. *See* Ownership of and Right to Extract Coalbed Gas in Federal Coal Deposits, 88 Interior Dec. 538, 539. In reliance on the Solicitor's 1981 opinion, oil and gas companies entered into leases to produce CBM gas with individual landowners holding title under 1909 and 1910 Act patents to some 200,000 acres in which the Tribe owns the coal.

In 1991, the Tribe brought suit in Federal District Court against petitioners, the royalty owners and producers under the oil and gas leases covering that land, and the federal agencies and officials responsible for the administration of lands held in trust for the Tribe. The Tribe sought, inter alia, a declaration that Congress' reservation of coal in the 1909 and 1910 Acts extended to CBM gas, so that the Tribe—not the successors in interest of the land patentees—owned the CBM gas.

The District Court granted summary judgment for the defendants, holding that the plain meaning of "coal" is the "solid rock substance" used as fuel, which does not include CBM gas. 874 F.Supp. 1142, 1154 (D.Colo. 1995). On appeal, a panel of the Court of Appeals reversed. 119 F.3d 816, 819 (C.A.10 1997). The court then granted rehearing en banc on the question whether the term "coal" in the 1909 and 1910 Acts "unambiguously excludes or includes CBM." 151 F.3d, at 1256. Over a dissenting opinion by Judge Tacha, joined by two other judges, the en banc court agreed with the panel. *Ibid.* The court held that the term "coal" was ambiguous. *Ibid.* It invoked the interpretive canon that ambiguities in land grants should be resolved in favor of the sovereign and concluded that the coal reservation encompassed CBM gas. *Ibid.*

The United States did not petition for, or participate in, the rehearing en banc. Instead, it filed a supplemental brief explaining that the Solicitor of the Interior was reconsidering the 1981 Solicitor's opinion in light of the panel's decision. Brief for Federal Respondents 14, n. 8. On the day the Government's response to petitioners' certiorari petition was due, *see id.*, at 47, n. 37, the Solicitor of the Interior withdrew the 1981 opinion in a one-line order, *see* Addendum to Brief for Federal Respondents in Opposition 1a. The United States now supports the Tribe's position that CBM gas is coal reserved by the 1909 and 1910 Acts.

II

We begin our discussion as the parties did, with a brief overview of the chemistry and composition of coal. Coal is a heterogeneous, noncrystalline sedimentary rock composed primarily of carbonaceous materials. *See, e.g.,* Gorbaty & Larsen, Coal Structure and Reactivity, in 3 Encyclopedia of Physical Science and Technology 437 (R. Meyers ed., 2d ed.1992). It is formed over millions of years from decaying plant material that settles on the bottom of swamps and is converted by microbiological processes into peat. Van Krevelen, Coal 90 (3d ed.1993). Over time, the resulting peat beds are buried by sedimentary deposits. *Id.*, at 91. As the beds sink deeper and deeper into the earth's crust, the peat is transformed by chemical reactions which increase the carbon content of the fossilized plant material. *Ibid.* The process in which peat transforms into coal is referred to as coalification. *Ibid.*

The coalification process generates methane and other gases. R. Rogers, Coalbed Methane: Principles and Practice 148 (1994). Because coal is porous, some of that gas is retained in the coal. CBM gas exists in the coal in three basic states: as free gas; as gas dissolved in the water in coal; and as gas "adsorped" on the solid surface of the coal, that is, held to the surface by weak forces called van der Waals forces. *Id.*, at 16–17, 117. These are the same three states or conditions in which gas is stored in other rock formations. Because of the large surface area of coal pores, however, a much higher proportion of the gas is adsorped on the surface of coal than is adsorped in other rock. *Id.*, at 16–17. When pressure on the coalbed is decreased, the gas in the coal formation escapes. As a result, CBM gas is released from coal as the coal is mined and brought to the surface.

III

While the modern science of coal provides a useful backdrop for our discussion and is consistent with our ultimate disposition, it does not answer the question presented to us. The question is not whether, given what scientists know today, it makes sense to regard CBM gas as a constituent of coal but whether Congress so regarded it in 1909 and 1910. In interpreting statutory mineral reservations like the one at issue here, we have emphasized that Congress "was dealing with a practical subject in a practical way" and that it intended the terms of the reservation to be understood in "their ordinary and popular sense." *Burke v. Southern Pacific R. Co.*, 234 U.S. 669 (1914) (rejecting "scientific test" for determining whether a reservation of "mineral lands" included "petroleum lands"); *see also Perrin v. United States* 444 U.S. 37, 42 (1979) ("[U]nless otherwise defined, words will be interpreted as taking their ordinary, contemporary, common meaning" at the time Congress enacted the statute). We are persuaded that the common conception of coal at the time Congress passed the 1909 and 1910 Acts was the solid rock substance that was the country's primary energy resource.

A

At the time the Acts were passed, most dictionaries defined coal as the solid fuel resource. For example, one contemporary dictionary defined coal as a "solid and more or less distinctly stratified mineral, varying in color from dark-brown to black, brittle, combustible, and used as fuel, not fusible without decomposition and very insoluble." 2 Century Dictionary and Cyclopedia 1067(1906). *See also* American Dictionary of the English Language 244 (N. Webster 1889) (defining "coal" as a "black, or brownish black, solid, combustible substance, consisting, like charcoal, mainly of carbon, but more compact"); 2 New English Dictionary on Historical Principles 549 (J. Murray ed. 1893) (defining coal as a "mineral, solid, hard, opaque, black, or blackish, found in seams or strata in the earth, and largely used as fuel"); Webster's New International Dictionary of the English Language 424 (W. Harris & F. Allen eds.1916) (defining coal as a "black, or brownish black, solid, combustible mineral substance").

In contrast, dictionaries of the day defined CBM gas—then called "marsh gas," "methane," or "fire-damp"—as a distinct substance, a gas "contained in" or "given off by" coal, but not as coal itself. *See, e.g.,* 3 Century Dictionary and Cyclopedia 2229 (1906) (defining "fire-damp" as "[t]he gas contained in coal, often given off by it in large quantities, and exploding, on ignition, when mixed with atmospheric air"; noting that "[f]ire-damp is a source of great danger to life in coal-mines") As these dictionary definitions suggest, the common understanding of coal in 1909 and 1910 would not have encompassed CBM gas, both because it is a gas rather than a solid mineral and because it was understood as a distinct substance that escaped from coal as the coal was mined, rather than as a part of the coal itself.

B

As a practical matter, moreover, it is clear that, by reserving coal in the 1909 and 1910 Act patents, Congress intended to reserve only the solid rock fuel that was mined, shipped throughout the country, and then burned to power the Nation's railroads, ships, and factories. *Cf. Leo Sheep Co. v. United States*, 440 U.S. 668, 682 (1979) (public land statutes should be interpreted in light of "the condition of the country when the acts were passed" (internal quotation marks omitted)). In contrast to natural gas, which was not yet an important source of fuel at the turn of the century, coal was the primary energy for the Industrial Revolution. *See, e.g.,* D. Yergin, The Prize 543 (1991). *See* also Brief for Federal Respondents 30 (recognizing that the three primary sources of energy in the United States at the turn of the century were coal, oil, and wood, and that natural gas—even from conventional reservoirs—was not yet an important energy resource).

As the history recounted in Part I, supra, establishes, Congress passed the 1909 and 1910 Acts to address concerns over the short supply, mismanagement, and fraudulent acquisition of this solid rock fuel resource. Rejecting broader proposals, Congress chose a narrow reservation of the resource that would address the exigencies of the crisis at hand without unduly burdening the rights of homesteaders or impeding the settlement of the West.

It is evident that Congress viewed CBM gas not as part of the solid fuel resource it was attempting to conserve and manage but as a dangerous waste product, which escaped from coal as the coal was mined. Congress was well aware by 1909 that the natural gas found in coal formations was released during coal mining and posed a serious threat to mine safety. Explosions in coal mines sparked by CBM gas occurred with distressing frequency in the late nineteenth and early twentieth centuries. Brief for National Mining Association as Amicus Curiae 7. Congress was also well aware that the CBM gas needed to be vented to the greatest extent possible. Almost 20 years prior to the passage of the 1909 and 1910 Acts, Congress had enacted the first federal coal-mine-safety law which, among other provisions, prescribed specific ventilation standards for coal mines of a certain depth "so as to dilute and render harmless ... the noxious or poisonous gases." 1891 Territorial Mine Inspection Act, § 6, 26 Stat. 1105. *See also* 3 Century Dictionary and Cyclopedia, supra, at 2229 (explaining the dangers associated with fire-damp).

That CBM gas was considered a dangerous waste product which escaped from coal, rather than part of the valuable coal fuel itself, is also confirmed by the fact that coal companies venting the gas to prevent its accumulation in the mines made no attempt to capture or preserve it. The more gas that escaped from the coal once it was brought to the surface, the better it was for the mining companies because it decreased the risk of a dangerous gas buildup during transport and storage. *Cf.* E. Moore, Coal: Its Properties, Analysis, Classification, Geology, Extraction, Uses and Distribution 308 (1922) (noting that the presence of gases such as methane in the coal increases the risk of spontaneous combustion of the coal during storage).

(The fact that CBM gas was known to escape naturally from coal distinguishes it from the "producer gas" that was generated from coal in the 1800's. Brief for Federal Respondents 30. Producer gas was produced by "destructive distillation, that is, by heating the coal to a temperature where it decomposed chemically." App. at 531 (reproducing Perry, The Gasification of Coal, Scientific American 230, (Mar.1974)). The natural escape of CBM gas from the coal also distinguishes CBM gas from other "volatile matter," expelled when coal is heated, or liquid "coal extracts," which "can be extracted though the use of appropriate solvents." Brief for Federal Respondents 26–27. The United States' expressed concern that if the coal reservation does not encompass CBM gas it does not encompass these "components" of coal, *see ibid.*, is unfounded.)

There is some evidence of limited and sporadic exploitation of CBM gas as a fuel prior to the passage of the 1909 and 1910 Acts. *See, e.g.,* E. Craig & M. Myers, Ownership of Methane Gas in Coalbeds, 24 Rocky Mt. Min. L. Inst. 767, 768 (1978) ("As early as 1746, methane was being drained from an English coal mine through pipes and used for heating"); *see also United States Steel Corp. v. Hoge,* 503 Pa. 140, 146, 468 A.2d 1380, 1383 (1983) (noting that as early as 1900, "certain wells were drilled [into coalbeds in Pennsylvania, which] produced coalbed gas"). It seems unlikely, though, that Congress considered this limited drilling for CBM gas. To the extent Congress had an awareness of it, there is every reason to think it viewed the extraction of CBM gas as drilling for natural gas, not mining coal.

That distinction is significant because the question before us is not whether Congress would have thought that CBM gas had some fuel value, but whether Congress considered it part of the coal fuel. When it enacted the 1909 and 1910 Acts, Congress did not reserve all minerals or energy resources in the lands. It reserved only coal, and then only in lands that were specifically identified as valuable for coal. It chose not to reserve oil, natural gas, or any other known or potential energy resources.

The limited nature of the 1909 and 1910 Act reservations is confirmed by subsequent congressional enactments. When Congress wanted to reserve gas rights that might yield valuable fuel, it did so in explicit terms. In 1912, for example, Congress enacted a statute that reserved "oil and gas" in Utah lands. Act of Aug. 24, 1912, 37 Stat. 496. In addition, both the 1912 Act and a later Act passed in 1914 continued the tradition begun in the 1909 and 1910 Acts of reserving only those minerals enumerated in the statute. *See ibid.*; Act of July 17, 1914, 38 Stat. 509, as amended, 30 U.S.C. §§ 121–123 (providing that "lands withdrawn or classified as phosphate, nitrate, potash, oil, gas or asphaltic minerals, or which are valuable for those deposits" could be patented, subject to a reservation to the United States of "the deposits on account of which the lands so patented were withdrawn or classified or reported as valuable"). It was not until 1916 that Congress passed a public lands act containing a general reservation of valuable minerals in the lands. *See* Stock–Raising Homestead Act, ch. 9, 39 Stat. 862, as amended, 43 U.S.C. § 299 (reserving "all the coal and other minerals in the lands" in all lands patented under the Act). *See also Western Nuclear,* 462 U.S., at 49 ("Unlike the preceding statutes containing mineral reservations, the [1916 Stock–Raising Homestead Act] was not limited to lands classified as mineral in character, and it did not reserve only specifically identified minerals").

C

Respondents contend that Congress did not reserve the solid coal but convey the CBM gas because the resulting split estate would be impractical and would make mining the coal difficult because the miners would have to capture and preserve the CBM gas that escaped during mining. *See, e.g.,* Brief for Respondent Southern Ute Indian Tribe 46; *see also id.,* at 25–26 (emphasizing that the reservation includes the right to "mine" the coal, "indicating that Congress reserved all rights needed to develop the underlying coal" including the right to vent CBM gas during mining). We doubt Congress would have given much consideration to these problems, however, because—as noted above—it does not appear to have given consideration to the possibility that CBM gas would one day be a profitable energy source developed on a large scale.

It may be true, nonetheless, that the right to mine the coal implies the right to release gas incident to coal mining where it is necessary and reasonable to do so. The right to dissipate the CBM gas where reasonable and necessary to mine the coal does not, however, imply the ownership of the gas in the first instance. Rather, it simply reflects the established common-law right of the owner of one mineral estate to use, and even damage, a neighboring estate as necessary and reasonable to the extraction of his own minerals. *See, e.g., Williams v. Gibson,* 84 Ala. 228, 4 So. 350 (1888); Rocky Mountain Mineral Foundation, 6 American Law of Mining § 200.04 (2d ed.1997). Given that split estates were already common at the time the 1909 and 1910 Acts were passed, *see, e.g., Chartiers Block Coal Co. v. Mellon,* 152 Pa. 286, 25 A. 597 (1893), and that the common law has proved adequate to the task of resolving the resulting conflicts between estates, there is no reason to think that the prospect of a split estate would have deterred Congress from reserving only the coal.

Were a case to arise in which there are two commercially valuable estates and one is to be damaged in the course of extracting the other, a dispute might result, but it could be resolved in the ordinary course of negotiation or adjudication. That is not the issue before us, however. The question is one of ownership, not of damage or injury.

In all events, even were we to construe the coal reservation to encompass CBM gas, a split estate would result. The United States concedes (and the Tribe does not dispute) that once the gas originating in the coal formation migrates to surrounding rock formations it belongs to the natural gas, rather than the coal, estate. *See* Brief for Federal Respondents 35; Brief for Respondent Southern Ute Indian Tribe 3, n. 4. Natural gas from other sources may also exist in the lands at issue. Including the CBM gas in the coal reservation would, therefore, create a split gas estate that would be at least as difficult to administer as a split coal/CBM gas estate. If CBM gas were reserved with the coal estate, those developing the natural gas resources in the land would have to allocate the gas between the natural gas and coal estates based on some assessment of how much had migrated outside the coal itself. There is no reason to think Congress would have been more concerned about the creation of a split coal/CBM gas estate than the creation of a split gas estate.

Because we conclude that the most natural interpretation of "coal" as used in the 1909 and 1910 Acts does not encompass CBM gas, we need not consider the applicability of the canon that ambiguities in land grants are construed in favor of the sovereign or the competing canons relied on by petitioners.

The judgment of the Court of Appeals is reversed.

It is so ordered.

■ JUSTICE BREYER took no part in the consideration or decision of this case.

■ GINSBURG, J.: I would affirm the judgment below substantially for the reasons stated by the Court of Appeals and the federal respondents. *See* 151 F.3d 1251, 1256–1267 (C.A.10 1998) (en banc); Brief for Federal Respondents 14–16. As the Court recognizes, in 1909 and 1910 coalbed methane gas (CBM) was a liability. *See* ante, at 1723, 1725–1726. Congress did not contemplate that the surface owner would be responsible for it. More likely, Congress would have assumed that the coal owner had dominion over, and attendant responsibility for, CBM. I do not find it clear that Congress understood dominion would shift if and when the liability became an asset. I would therefore apply the canon that ambiguities in land grants are construed in favor of the sovereign. *See Watt v. Western Nuclear, Inc.*, 462 U.S. 36, 59 (1983) (noting "established rule that land grants are construed favorably to the Government, that nothing passes except what is conveyed in clear language, and that if there are doubts they are resolved for the Government, not against it" (internal quotation marks omitted)).■

NOTES AND COMMENTS

1. An estimated $200 million of CBM was located underneath the Ute land. The holding of this case will apply to another 16 million acres of land with similar split ownership.

2. CBM received a significant tax credit, known as the IRS Section 29 tax credit. 26 U.S.C. § 29 (2000). CBM is less environmentally friendly than conventional coal to produce. Coals seams contain much water as well as methane. It often takes many months to pump off the water from the seams before the gas can be produced. The safe disposal of this water is a major expense.

In *Perlman v. Pioneer Limited Partnership*, 918 F.2d 1244 (5th Cir. 1990), William Perlman had leased land in Wyoming and Montana on which he sought to develop coal seam gas using his patented "Perlman Process." One well was drilled using this process and resulted in so much water production that the state conservation commission ordered the lessee to do hydrological studies to determine the effect of his process on Wyoming's water resources. Perlman then concluded that the Wyoming regulators had hindered his performance under the lease and invoked the force majeure clause to cancel the lease which required him to spend $1.5 million in developing the acreage. The court held that Perlman's performance was not excused because state officials had never refused to permit Perlman's operations; they merely required advance studies, a standard and foreseeable event. Moreover, Perlman had a duty under his lease to make a reasonable effort to remove any force majeure condition rather than give up and walk away.

3. CBM is very similar to the natural gas found in oil deposits and is a valuable energy source. However, its potential has been slow to be realized because of uncertainty surrounding property rights in CBM. CBM can exist as free gas in the macropores (fractures) of the coal seam, but most CBM adheres to the micropores within the internal structure of the coal itself. The pressure exerted on the CBM trapped in the coal is greater than atmospheric pressure. Mining of the coal therefore releases CBM in a two step process: CBM is released from the coal micropores and into the surrounding macropores; the CBM then proceeds from the macropores to the mine surface following the decrease in pressure. Deeper coal beds are subject to higher pressure and temperature, and will therefore have a higher CBM content.

Production Techniques.

There are several techniques for CBM extraction and production. One method simply employs traditional natural gas technology to extract CBM from the coal bed through vertical wells independent from any mining of the coal itself. Other methods for CBM production have been developed to extract the gas in conjunction with the coal mining operation. Where the gas yield is insufficient, hydrofracturing is used. This process involves injection of pressurized fluid into the coalbed to enhance the fracture system, which in turn allows the release of more CBM into the borehole.

Another method is used with the longwall mining of coal. CBM can be extracted from vertical holes called "gob wells," which drain CBM from the "gob zone" (the area of fractured rock created when the overburden caves into the unsupported, mined-out area). Large quantities of CBM are often released from the collapse and fracture of the overburden into the resulting rubble creating the gob zone. To ventilate these gob areas, vertical boreholes are drilled in advance of mining. Production of gob gases therefore begins shortly after the overburden collapses and forms the gob zone. Gob gases often contain methane released from several different sources: (1) CBM released from residual coal in the primary seam, from thin and unminable coal seams in the roof and floor, or from separate mine workings nearby; (2) strata gases that escaped from the coal seams and became trapped in non-coal strata; and (3) natural gas that originated in non-coal strata.

Property Rights in Coal Bed Methane on private lands.

While *Amoco v. Southern Ute Indian Tribe, supra* decided the ownership of CBM under certain land patents, the courts have often been asked to decide the same issue under common law rules governing private contracts. The common law offers a number choices, as summarized below.

As you consider potential rules regarding ownership of CBM, recall *Ward v. Harding* in the Coal Chapter. The court there held that "broad form deeds" convey only those rights capable of contemplation at the time of the deed, and therefore could not have granted a right to stripmine coal. Should this test be used when analyzing gas and coal leases? Here are the leading common law possibilities:

i.   CBM is Gas.

Under this rule, CBM is viewed definitionally as a gas and therefore falls within the ordinary meaning of the terms "gas" or "natural gas" as used in standard mineral conveyances. A federal bankruptcy court has held that under Alabama law, CBM in the form of gob gas is the property of the owner of gas rights, not the owner of coal rights. *In re Hillsborough Holdings Corp.*, 207 Bankr. 299 (1997). There is, however, an important practical objection to this approach; coal owners must vent the CBM for safety reasons when mining, and they fear suits by gas owners will prevent them from venting the CBM.

ii.   CBM is Coal.

Coal owners claim ownership of CBM on the basis that it is physically intermixed with the coal itself, and should therefore be included within any grant or reservation of coal rights. This position is also supported by a number of commentators. In *United States Steel Corp. v. Hoge*, 503 Pa. 140, 468 A.2d 1380 (1983), the court held that the owner of the coal bed is the owner of the CBM contained in the coal but will lose ownership once the CBM migrates out of the coal bed to the adjoining strata. There is also a practical problem with the "CBM is coal" rule. Much of the CBM released during coal mining does not come from the actual coal seam being mined, but instead comes from the overburden or other strata that fracture and collapse as a result of the mining operation. Ownership of CBM based on ownership of the coal would not extend to any CBM that migrated from other non-coal strata, so gob gas would have to be apportioned between the coal bed owner and the owner of the surrounding strata.

iii.   Priority at Severance

Some commentators suggest that competing claims between coal and gas owners should be resolved under a "first in time" theory, whereby rights accrue in the order in which the competing deeds or leases were created. Others suggest that priority of severance leads to an arbitrary result.

iv.   Case-by-Case Analysis

A case-by-case analysis rejects strict rules such as "CBM is gas" or "CBM is coal," and looks to other factors beyond priority at severance. Additional factors include the specific language of the lease, the state of knowledge or opinion regarding CBM at the time of drafting, and any other evidence that demonstrates intent at the time of drafting. Each case would be decided on its own facts, without reference to presumptions such as "CBM is gas" or "CBM is coal." A court would look only to the instant transaction between the parties, an approach which is quite labor-intensive for both lawyers and judges.

v. Successive Ownership

Under the rule of successive ownership, coal owners would have title to the CBM absorbed within the coal, but would not retain title to any CBM that escapes into other strata or that enters the gob zone as a result of longwall mining (since it would no longer be intermixed with the coal). In *Hoge, supra*, the Pennsylvania Supreme Court may have given at least implicit approval to this rule. The successive ownership rule may lead to an unhappy result for coal owners. Under the rule, it is unlikely that a coal owner could claim a right to gob gas, which constitutes a major portion of the CBM released during longwall mining. If the coal owner has rights only to the coal seam, and not the surrounding strata, any CBM released into the gob zone would no longer be intermixed with the coal, causing the coal owner to lose the right of ownership.

vi. Mutual Simultaneous Rights

Under this rule, gas owners would have title to CBM but coal owners would have the right to capture the CBM in the process of removing it from their mines, as an exercise of the coal owner's "incidental mining rights" (mineral rights transfers impliedly include any incidental rights that are reasonably necessary to facilitate extraction of the mineral). The basis for the coal owner's right of capture would be a responsibility to ventilate the mines for safety purposes.

4. An extensive survey of coalbed methane issues, especially those arising in the Appalachian area, is contained in Elizabeth A. McClanahan, Coalbed Methane: Myths, Facts, and the Legends of its History and the Legislative and Regulatory Climate Into the 21st Century, 48 Okla. L. Rev. 471 (1995). A western focus on CBM issues appears in Kurt M. Petersen, Coalbed Gas Development in the Western United States: Legal Issues and Operational Concerns, 7th Ann. Rocky Mtn Min. L. Inst., ch. 13 (1991).

5. As noted earlier, uncertainty regarding property rights has curtailed CBM production, most notably in Virginia and West Virginia, but legislation at both the federal and state level has been enacted to address a part of the problem. These statutes create a temporary bypass of the ownership disputes, allowing CBM production via "forced pooling" pending final resolution of the property claims in court, without addressing the underlying property law issue. See 42 U.S.C. § 13368; Va. Code Ann. §§ 45.1–361.ff; W.Va. Code §§ 22–21–ff. See Jeff L. Lewin, Coalbed Methane: Recent Court Decisions Leave Ownership "Up in the Air," But New Federal and State Legislation Should Facilitate Production, 96 W. Va. L. Rev. 577 (1994).

B. Federal Framework of Natural Gas Regulation

1. Overview

The Natural Gas Act of 1938 still operates today, largely unchanged, as the primary federal statute regulating interstate transportation of gas. It is now clothed in six decades of case law interpreting its framework, including the famous, or rather infamous, case of *Phillips v. Wisconsin* that has been blamed for creating the serious gas shortages of the 1960s and 1970s. A second statute, the Natural Gas Policy Act (NGPA) of 1978, was enacted to overrule the *Phillips* case and undo the gas shortages. This Act died a well-deserved death (in the opinion of most observers) when Congress passed the Wellhead Decontrol Act of 1989, decreeing the end of federal price controls on all gas as of 1993.

The foremost scholar of natural gas regulation has summarized these two acts and previewed the revolution to come in the following article, which provides a whirlwind tour of the past and present structure of the industry as it moved from Figure 7–2 to Figure 7–3.

Richard J. Pierce, Jr., "The Evolution of Natural Gas Regulatory Policy,"

Natural Resources and Environment 53–85 (Summer 1995).

Deregulation of the market for natural gas surely ranks as one of the most significant accomplishments in natural resources law over the past decade. During the period 1985 to 1995, the Federal Energy Regulatory Commission (FERC) accomplished this massive task by, in effect, reversing through regulatory decisionmaking a pair of unfortunate public policy errors made by Congress in 1938 and by the U.S. Supreme Court in 1954. The results of FERC's carefully constructed deregulatory program are impressive. They include at least a $5 billion annual improvement in aggregate social welfare and significant air quality improvements attributable to use of natural gas to displace dirtier fuels.

The history of regulation and deregulation of the natural gas industry is worth recounting because it provides insights that can be useful in identifying potential ways of attaining socially beneficial results in many analogous contexts. The ongoing effort to create a competitive electricity market is an obvious case in point. *See* Richard Pierce, The State of the Transition to Competitive Markets in Natural Gas and Electricity, 15 Energy L.J. 323 (1994); Richard J. Pierce, Using the Gas Industry as a Guide to Reconstituting the Electricity Industry, 13 J. Res. in L. & Econ. 7 (1991).

The story begins in the 1920s. The development of high-tensile steel and electric welding permitted the construction of high-pressure steel pipelines that allowed gas to be transported long distances at relatively low costs. State public utility commissions (PUCs) attempted to regulate the then newly emerging business of transporting natural gas across state lines for resale in states other than the state in which the gas was produced. It made sense to regulate interstate pipelines because interstate transportation of gas, like distribution of gas by local distribution companies (LDCs), was a natural monopoly function, characterized by large economies of scale and high barriers to entry. State regulation of interstate transportation of gas created intolerable problems, however. The firms that engaged in this new activity were subjected both to conflicting regulatory orders from different states and to regulatory policies that were designed to help the residents of one state at the expense of residents of other states.

The Supreme Court responded to these problems with a trilogy of opinions in which it held that the dormant Commerce Clause prohibited any state from regulating interstate transportation or wholesales of gas. *PUC v. Attleboro Steam & Electricity Co.*, 273 U.S. 83 (1927); *Missouri v. Kansas Gas Co.*, 265 U.S. 298 (1924); *Pennsylvania v. West Virginia*, 262 U.S. 553 (1923).

The Supreme Court performed a constructive function by redefining the geographic scope of the problem and by prohibiting an attempted solution that could only exacerbate the problem. The basic problem remained, however: interstate transportation of gas was a natural monopoly function that required regulation by someone. In response to numerous complaints from consumers and producers about alleged abuses of monopoly power by interstate pipelines, Congress assigned the Federal Trade Commission (FTC) the duty to study the gas industry to determine whether there was a need for federal regulation of the industry. In 1935, the FTC submitted a comprehensive, high quality report in which it concluded that interstate transportation of gas was a natural monopoly that should be regulated by a federal agency. The FTC found that pipelines were exercising their monopoly power by extracting high prices from LDCs.

Up to this point, there is no basis to criticize the performance of any of the institutions that played roles in the policymaking process. Each institution performed its role in an exemplary manner. In 1938, however, Congress made a decision that ultimately produced a series of unfortunate results. The FTC found a justification to regulate only interstate transportation of gas. This could have been accomplished easily by subjecting interstate gas pipelines to federal regulation as common carriers; the method of regulation Congress had imposed on interstate oil pipelines decades earlier. Gas pipelines objected to this treatment, however. They sought to preserve their monopoly relationship with LDCs and their monopsony relationship with producers. Common carrier status would strip them of their monopoly and monopsony power by forcing them to transport gas owned by third parties.

Pipelines successfully urged Congress to impose a different form of regulation. In the Natural Gas Act of 1938 (NGA), Congress instructed the Federal Power Commission (FPC) to regulate interstate pipelines as if they were utilities. Congress prohibited the FPC from requiring any pipeline to transport gas for a third party. This policy decision enabled interstate pipelines to use their monopoly power over gas transportation to create and to maintain monopsony power in the market for the purchase of gas at the wellhead and monopoly power in the market for the sale of gas to LDCs. The available evidence suggests that FPC regulation of pipelines as utilities was not effective. *See* Breyer & MacAvoy, Energy Regulation By The Federal Commission (1974). The FPC was able to perform the difficult task assigned it with no serious adverse effects, however, for sixteen years.

In 1954, a five-Justice majority of the Supreme Court made the second major public policy error. In *Phillips Petroleum Co. v. Wisconsin*, 347 U.S. 672 (1954), the Court held that NGA required the FPC to regulate the price of natural gas sold by independent gas producers in interstate commerce. The five-Justice majority focused exclusively on the words Congress used to describe the scope of the FPC's regulatory jurisdiction. The majority ignored both the long-standing contrary interpretation of the statute by the agency responsible for its implementation and the effects of the alternative interpretations of the statute that were consistent with the ambiguous language of the statute....

Unlike transportation of gas, production of gas is not a natural monopoly. It is an activity characterized by low economies of scale and low barriers to entry. Thousands of firms compete to produce gas and to make wellhead sales. The FTC had not detected any problem of monopoly power in producing gas and selling it at the wellhead in the comprehensive investigation of the gas industry it conducted during the 1930s, and the FPC saw no justification to regulate producer prices. Indeed, producers were among the victims of interstate pipelines—pipelines used their monopsony power in the producing fields to depress the wellhead price of gas, just as they used their monopoly power to sell gas to LDCs at excessive prices.

The Supreme Court assigned the FPC an impossible task in *Phillips*. No agency can impose price controls on a structurally competitive market without creating a shortage of the regulated product or service. Between 1954 and 1960 the FPC attempted to implement the Court's mandate in *Phillips* in a manner that had little effect. The FPC attempted to set a maximum rate applicable to sales made by each producer by determining the costs incurred by each of the thousands of producers. By 1960, it had completed ten rate cases and had developed a backlog of 2,900 pending cases. At this point, the Supreme Court issued an opinion in which it chastised the FPC for the slow rate at which it was implementing the mandate of *Phillips* and held that the FPC could not authorize any new sales to the interstate market unless and until it established price ceilings applicable to the gas that the producer proposed to sell. *Atlantic Refining Co. v. Public Service Commission of New York,* 360 U.S. 378 (1959). In 1961, the FPC responded to the Court's decision in *Atlantic Refining* by switching to a new method of implementing the *Phillips* decision. The FPC established rates applicable to all gas produced in each producing area based on the agency's estimate of the average historical cost of finding and producing a unit of gas in each area.

The new method was effective; its effect was to create a gas shortage. The gas shortage began to manifest itself initially in forms that were invisible to the public. Price controls reduced the rate of exploration for new supplies of gas. That in turn, reduced the inventory of gas supplies available to the interstate market. Eventually, the available inventory declined to the point at which deliverability could not be sustained at levels sufficient to meet demand. In 1969, fifteen years after the *Phillips* decision, the effects of that decision emerged in a publicly visible form. Interstate pipelines began to reduce their deliveries to LDCs. The deliverability shortage grew rapidly during the early 1970s. By the unusually cold winter of 1976–1977, the shortage had reached the point at which gas service was no longer available to most prospective new customers; thousands of manufacturing plants and schools were closed by service curtailments; and, over 1 million workers were laid off because of their employer's inability to obtain gas.

Congress had debated the wisdom of the Court's decision in *Phillips* nearly continuously between 1954 and 1977. It came close to reversing that decision legislatively in 1955 and again in 1976, but ignorance with respect to basic principles of microeconomics induced many legislators to believe that price controls benefitted consumers. The severe shortages of 1976–1977 finally forced Congress to act. Congress enacted the Natural Gas Policy Act of 1978 (NGPA), in which it instructed the FPC, then recently renamed the Federal Energy Regulatory Commission (FERC), to implement a new regulatory regime applicable to the gas industry. The NGPA regulatory regime was extraordinarily complicated: it divided gas supplies into over a score of different categories, each subject to different rules and statutory price ceilings-*See* Richard J. Pierce, Reconsidering the Roles of Regulation and Competition in the Natural Gas Industry, 97 Harv. L. Rev. 345 (1983).

In one sense, NGPA was a major breakthrough. It was designed ultimately to deregulate the wellhead gas market, and it did create the conditions in which FERC ultimately was able to accomplish that task. In another sense however, NGPA was a catastrophe. Congress drafted NGPA based on the assumption that market forces are relatively weak and require many years to yield beneficial results. Congress assumed that the quantity of gas demanded and supplied would change slowly in response to changes in the price of gas. Thus, for instance, Congress scheduled deregulation to take place gradually over a period of many years, with most gas subject to constantly increasing statutory price ceilings for a decade or more. Congress expected the statutory ceiling prices to remain below the market price of gas for the entire period in which the NGPA authorized gradual replacement of ceiling prices with prices determined by market forces. Congress also expected the shortage to persist for many years. Instead, as the price of gas increased, the quantity of gas demanded fell rapidly, the quantity of gas supplied rose rapidly, and the market price of gas plummeted to well below the statutory ceiling prices.

In the meantime, however, pipelines had entered into thousands of long-term contracts to purchase large volumes of gas at the ceiling prices established by NGPA. Because the NGA insulated pipelines from competition for the sale of gas, they were not particularly concerned about the risk that they would lose sales to competitors if they committed to buy gas at prices well above the price at which gas would sell in a competitive market. Within a few years after enactment of NGPA, the flawed assumptions on which the statute was based became apparent to all market participants and observers. The NGA and the NGPA combined to create market conditions attainable only through regulation—a large surplus of gas that coexisted with consumer prices far in excess of the price that would exist in an unregulated market.

By the mid–1980s, FERC confronted a daunting task. It had to change the regulatory rules applicable to the gas market in ways that would eliminate the severe adverse effects of decades of misguided policy decisions made with respect to that market. FERC proved to be up to that challenge, however, Between 1985 and 1992, FERC took a series of regulatory actions that had the effect of reversing the many disastrous policy decisions that were made between 1938 and 1978. The details of FERC's successful strategy are too intricate to recount in this summary, but two regulatory actions formed the core of that strategy. The first took place in 1985 when FERC issued Order 436. That order used regulatory sticks and carrots to coerce interstate pipelines into agreeing to become "equal access" carriers; pipelines obligated themselves to transport gas owned by third parties on terms equivalent to the terms on which the pipelines transported their own gas. A year later, in Order 451, FERC changed the rules with respect to ceiling prices in ways that allowed producers and pipelines to adjust their prices to be compatible with the new relationship between gas supply and demand. The Order 436 equal access policy and the Order 451 flexible pricing policy went a long way toward eliminating pipelines' monopoly power in the wholesale gas market and toward forcing producers and pipelines to sell gas at market-based prices. With pipelines operating under equal access tariffs, LDCs and industrial consumers were free to buy gas directly from thousands of producers and independent marketers. That access to competing suppliers forced pipelines and producers to lower their prices significantly. Consumer prices plummeted; the quantity of gas consumed increased; and, the gas surplus began to dissipate.

FERC encountered one major impediment to implementation of its critical initial step toward reforming the gas market. By allowing third-party sellers to compete with pipelines in the wholesale gas market, FERC's new policies had the effect of forcing pipelines to lower the prices they charged LDCs to a level consistent with market forces. That, in turn. exposed pipelines to the risk of losing approximately $20 billion attributable to the long-term contracts in which they had committed to buy large quantities of gas at above-market prices. Pipelines were understandably reluctant to absorb such enormous losses. Pipelines pursued a multifaceted litigation strategy that was designed to stall the process of implementing the new market-based regulatory strategy and to reallocate to other market participants the bulk of the cost of their problem contracts. Eventually, the costs of the problem contracts were allocated among pipelines, producers, LDCs, and consumers. The legal disputes over the appropriate allocation of those costs delayed the transition process, however, and made the process painful for all market participants. That complicated litigation took place over the period 1985 to 1995 at FERC, at state PUCs, and in hundreds of state and federal courts. . . .

By 1989, Congress was sufficiently impressed with the results of FERC's regulatory restructuring that it enacted the Natural Gas Wellhead Decontrol Act. That statute ratified FERC's de facto deregulation of the gas sales market, formally eliminated all wellhead price ceilings effective on January 1, 1993, and encouraged FERC to take such further actions as it deemed appropriate to create a fully competitive gas sales market. FERC responded to the admonition in the 1989 Wellhead Decontrol Act with its second major policy initiative. In 1992 FERC issued Order 636. That order completed the process of deregulating the gas sales market. It required interstate pipelines to provide fully unbundled services; henceforth, pipelines were required to sell separately transportation services, storage services, and natural gas. After Order 636, LDCs and industrial consumers were free to purchase gas, storage services, and even transportation services from scores of potential suppliers.

The participants in the gas market have responded to the spur of competition by implementing numerous efficiency-enhancing commercial and technological innovations. Gas is being found, produced, stored, and transported at much lower cost than was the case a decade ago. Gas is traded constantly at dozens of market hubs at constantly changing spot prices. Hundreds of new pipeline interconnections have transformed the previously fragmented transportation system into a closely integrated network that links all North American supplies with all markets in the United States and Canada. Electronic bulletin boards allow market participants to engage in continuous trade with respect to transportation capacity so that all gas can move from supply areas to market areas over the least expensive route. Market participants have changed their methods of using storage in a variety of ways that have simultaneously reduced costs and increased service reliability

The deregulated gas market performed extremely well during the unusually cold 1993–1994 winter. That performance was in sharp contrast both to the miserable performance of the then-regulated gas industry during the severe 1976–1977 winter and to the disappointing performance of the still-regulated electricity industry during the 1993–1994 winter. The gas industry continued to provide reliable service even in extreme conditions, while all industrial, commercial. and governmental activities in the middle Atlantic states had to be halted for a day in January 1994 to avoid a complete electricity blackout of that region.

Some work remains to be done to ensure that all consumers reap the full benefits of FERC's deregulatory restructuring of the gas industry. State PUCs are in the process of discovering that their traditional methods of regulating LDCs are incompatible with the dynamic, robustly competitive wholesale gas market FERC has created. PUCs will have no choice but to adopt more flexible, market-driven methods of regulating LDCs. Those new regulatory techniques will benefit all gas consumers. *See* Richard J. Pierce, Regulation and Competition in Natural Gas Distribution (1990).

FERC's extraordinary success in subjecting the gas industry to the unmatched discipline of a competitive market should be a source of many lessons that can be valuable in efforts to restructure other industries whose performance has been disappointing. The closely analogous electricity industry provides the most obvious candidate for similar restructuring. By restructuring that industry, we can improve the industry's performance dramatically and reduce the nation's electricity bill by approximately $24 billion a year. *See* Black and Pierce, The Choice Between Markets and Central Planning in Regulating the U.S. Electricity Industry, 93 Colum. L. Rev. 1339 (1993)....■

2.   THE NATURAL GAS ACT OF 1938

The NGA of 1938 adopted cost-of-service ratemaking to control the monopoly power of pipelines, rather than the common carrier model of open access. Yet, until the Supreme Court's opinion in *Phillips Petroleum Co. v. Wisconsin*, 347 U.S. 672 (1954), Professor Pierce, in the above-cited work, says that this policy choice was relatively harmless. Then, the Court interpreted the FPC's jurisdiction to include regulating the prices at which independent producers could sell their gas to pipelines. The FPC's jurisdiction is set out in section 1(b) of the Act (15 U.S.C. sec. 717b):

> [T]his chapter shall apply to the transportation of natural gas in interstate commerce, to the sale in interstate commerce of natural gas for resale for ultimate public consumption for domestic, commercial, industrial, or any other use, and to natural-gas companies engaged in such transportation or sale, but shall not apply to any other transportation or sale of natural gas or to the local distribution of natural gas or to the facilities used for such distribution or to the production or gathering of natural gas.

Phillips Petroleum was a gas producer engaged in the production, gathering, processing and sale of gas. It did not engage in the interstate transmission of gas, and it was not affiliated with any interstate pipeline company. Phillips simply sold its gas to five different interstate pipeline companies, which then transported and resold it to consumers and LDCs in 14 different states.

What prompted the state of Wisconsin to bring suit in the 1950s seeking FPC regulation of producers' prices at the wellhead? For more than two decades, many end users had been buying gas under 20–year contracts at prices fixed in the 1930s when gas had been hugely in excess. Prices in many of these contracts were set at about one cent per thousand cubic foot (MCF). After World War II, new pipelines opened up the large Eastern markets. The demand for gas increased briskly, and the amount available to market slowed as producers reinjected gas back into reservoirs in order to increase oil recovery. Gas prices responded to the forces of supply and demand and started to advance. By the mid–1950s, many old gas contracts came up for renewal, and prices were jumping as much as ten-fold to about 15 cents per MCF. Lawyers in the cold state of Wisconsin argued that the FPC was required to regulate the wellhead price of gas under the language of section 1(b) quoted above.

The FPC issued an order denying jurisdiction over independent producers like Phillips, based on the express exemption of "production and gathering" in the statute. The FPC therefore refused to investigate the reasonableness of Phillips's gas prices. This set the stage for the Supreme Court's majority opinion interpreting section 1(b):

> In general, petitioners [Phillips, and the state of Texas] contend that Congress intended to regulate only the interstate pipeline companies since certain alleged excesses of those companies were the evil which brought about the legislation. If such were the case, we have difficulty in perceiving why the Commission's jurisdiction over the transportation *or* sale for resale in interstate commerce of natural gas is granted in the disjunctive. It would have sufficed to give the Commission jurisdiction over only those natural-gas companies that engage in "transportation" or "transportation and sale for resale" in interstate commerce, if only interstate pipeline companies were intended to be covered. [citations omitted].

> Rather we believe that the legislative history indicates a congressional intent to give the Commission jurisdiction over the rates of all wholesales of natural gas in interstate commerce, whether by a pipeline company or not and whether occurring before, during or after transmission by an interstate pipeline company. There can be no dispute that the overriding congressional purpose was to plug the "gap" in regulation of natural-gas companies resulting from judicial decisions prohibiting on federal constitutional grounds, state regulation of many of the interstate commerce aspects of the natural-gas business. *Id.* 682–83. . . .

> Regulation of the sales in interstate commerce for resale made by a so-called independent natural-gas producer is not essentially different from regulation of such sales when made by an affiliate of an interstate pipeline company. In both cases, the rates charged may have a direct and substantial effect on the price paid by the ultimate consumers. Protection of consumers against exploitation at the hands of natural-gas companies was the primary aim of the Natural Gas Act. *Id.* at 685.

Justice Douglas dissented:

> The sale by this independent producer is a "sale in interstate commerce . . . for resale." It is also an integral part of "the production or gathering of natural gas." . . . So we must make a choice. . . .

> There are practical considerations which . . . lead me to conclude that we should not reverse the Commission in the present case. If Phillips' sales can be regulated, then the Commission can set a rate base for Phillips. A rate base for Phillips must of necessity include all of Phillips' producing and gathering properties; and supervision over its operating expenses. . . . The fastening of rate regulation on this independent producer brings "the production or gathering of natural gas" under effective federal control, in spite of the fact that Congress has made that phase . . . exempt from regulation. The effect is certain

to be profound.... The sales price determines his profits. And his profits and the profits of all the other gatherers, whose gas moves into the interstate pipelines, have profound effects on the rate of production, the methods of production, the old wells that are continued in production, the new ones explored, etc. Regulating the price at which the independent producer can sell his gas regulates his business in the most vital way any business can be regulated. That regulation largely nullifies the exemption granted by Congress. *Id.* at 690.

Justices Clark and Burton also dissented, citing additional concerns:

By today's decision the Court restricts the phrase "production and gathering" to "the physical activities, facilities, and properties" used in production and gathering. Such a gloss strips the words of their substance. If the Congress so intended, then it left for state regulation only a mass of empty pipe, vacant processing plants and thousands of hollow wells with scarecrow derricks, monuments to this new extension of federal power.... The states have been for over 35 years and are now enforcing regulatory laws covering production and gathering ... proration of gas, ratable taking, unitization of fields, processing of casinghead gas ... well spacing, repressuring, abandonment of wells, marginal area development, and other devices.... There can be no doubt ... that federal regulation of production and gathering will collide and substantially interfere with and hinder the enforcement of these state regulatory measures. We cannot square this result with the House Report on this Act which states that the subsequently enacted bill "is so drawn as to complement and in no manner usurp State regulatory authority." *Id.* at 695–96.

3. THE NATURAL GAS POLICY ACT OF 1978

The *Phillips* decision led to a dual system for selling natural gas: an intrastate and an interstate market. By 1978, producers' sales into the interstate market, with its low federally regulated prices, had dried up. Gas was available to intrastate users in the producing states, but only at a higher price. The 1976 shortages along the East coast led to the popular Texas bumper sticker "Drive 70 and freeze a Yankee in the dark." The new regulatory regime implemented by Congress in 1978 regulated both the intrastate and interstate gas markets and established 27 different pricing categories for natural gas, depending on whether the gas came from existing wells, new wells, stripper wells, high-cost wells, offshore wells and a number of other factors. The different categories had different price escalators, so some gas was allowed to increase more in price than other gas (even though the molecules of gas were essentially identical). Congress also authorized the deregulation of some categories of gas, such as high cost gas, as early as November 1979. Here is a graph showing the major categories of gas and the maximum legal prices allowed for each under the NGPA:

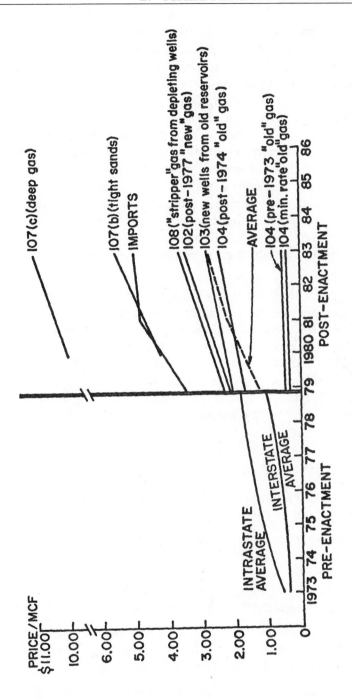

Figure 7-6

Price path of natural gas, before and after enactment of the Natural Gas Policy Act of 1978. After enactment of NGPA, intrastate gas was placed under federal control. The dashed line represents the common (interstate and intrastate) average price. The graph shows only a few of the many categories of gas established by NGPA.

Source: Connie C. Barlow & Arlon R. Tussing, Regulation and Deregulation of Natural Gas, in Free Market Energy, p. 63 (S. Fred Singer ed. 1984). (Universe Books)

To what ends was this hydra-headed pricing system created? Congress attempted to achieve many goals: First, it unified FERC control over all natural gas production, so that a national policy could be exerted over all gas sales. Second, it sought to protect residential and commercial consumers from huge, abrupt price shocks. Third, it sought to prevent producers from collecting monopoly rents or excess profits on "old" gas from already existing wells, while at the same time encouraging producers to drill new wells to alleviate shortages by offering incentive prices on newly discovered gas, especially from high-cost areas. Fourth, the NGPA sought to deregulate most gas prices gradually by January 1, 1985, giving consumers time to adjust to the forecast price increases. (Some high-cost gas was deregulated as early as November 1979, the date that FERC was to implement the "incremental pricing" rate design discussed below.) And fifth, it sought to promote the flow of gas into the interstate market where shortages were most severe.

In the long run, the most important achievement of the NGPA was to free natural gas prices from the utility-type, cost of service ratemaking imposed on it by the *Phillips* reading of the NGA. Congress itself determined what the just and reasonable rates were for different kinds of gas under the NGPA, and ultimately the market would set this price without bureaucratic interference. The path to this end result was rocky, however, because of the $20 billion take-or-pay problem which grew out of the private system of long-term contracts that pipeline merchants had with producers.

4.   TAKE-OR-PAY

Most contracts between selling producers and pipeline purchasers negotiated in the 1970s contained a provision similar to the following:

> "Seller agrees to sell and deliver to Buyer, and Buyer agrees to purchase and take, or pay for if available and not taken, Seller's pro rata part of the following quantities of gas produced from the reserves committed to this contract, to wit, a Quantity of gas equal to 85% of Seller's delivery capacity"[2]

Why would a purchaser sign an agreement to pay for gas that it takes and also pay for gas that it doesn't take? Professor John Lowe explains in this excerpt from Oil and Gas Law 288–90 (3d ed. West 1995):

> Take-or-pay payments are generally associated with long-term gas sales contracts, and from the time that interstate pipelines were constructed in the 1930s until the mid–1980s, long term contracts were

---

2. Delivery capacity was defined as the amount of gas which could be efficiently withdrawn from the wells on the lease under prudent operating practices and in accord with all applicable rules and regulations.

the norm. . . . The clause provides the producer with a guaranteed minimum cash flow in return for dedicating the gas supply to the purchaser; once the gas is dedicated, the producer cannot sell it elsewhere even if the purchaser does not take the gas. . . . Producers have historically viewed take-or-pay clauses as a guarantee of a minimum cash flow and a protection against the risk that purchasers will "bank" contracted gas in the ground. Pipelines saw take-or-pay clauses as a non-price premium for gas commitment; they paid nothing so long as they took the gas they expected to need.

In the energy crisis of the 1970s, however, take-or-pay provisions became a substitute for price competition. Price regulation under the Natural Gas Act of 1938 and the Natural Gas Policy Act of 1978 set maximum lawful prices for gas of different "vintages" and classifications that quickly became the going price. Barred from competing for the gas supplies that they needed to supply their customers, pipeline companies competed by offering attractive non-price terms, particularly take-or-pay provisions. Producers saw the clauses as risk shifting devices that would protect them against demand fluctuations. Take-or-pay percentages increased from as low as 35 percent in the early 1970s to 90 percent at the height of the boom.

5.   TAKE-OR-PAY MEETS THE NGPA AND MARKET FORCES

Now let us hear from two economists how take-or-pay contracts combined with the NGPA and FERC's "rolled in" gas pricing policy to produce the perverse market effect of rising gas prices at a time of excess gas supplies:

James M. Griffin and Henry B. Steele, Energy Economics and Policy pp. 301–303

(Academic Press 1986, 2d Ed.).

The general expectation of the 1978 act seems to have been that new gas prices would rise to their true competitive wellhead values, while old gas would continue to be underpriced for the benefit of the consumer as long as it lasted. These expectations were not to be realized. Gas prices increased more rapidly than had been anticipated, largely because pipelines with large quantities of cheap old gas could bid above-market prices for new gas and pass the higher average cost of supplies along to utility companies. The utilities in turn could cover these charges by averaging in the cost of this new gas with other old gas supplies they might have from other pipeline contracts and presenting a higher gas bill to their consumers. Gas pipelines could do this because their profits depended upon maintaining a high percentage of pipeline capacity utilization, and not upon the margin between purchase cost and resale price, which was closely regulated. Natural gas prices also increased for other reasons. The Federal Energy Regulatory Commission (successor to the FPC in gas price control matters) favored gas price increases for reasons of economic efficiency, and took a number of steps to facilitate price hikes, especially for new gas. The most important categories of new gas were completely decontrolled by FERC action in 1979.... [Deregulated] deep gas had skyrocketed to over $9.00 per mcf by 1980, contrasted with certain vintages of old gas that were selling for $.50 per mcf. Thus ... natural gas prices [increased] quite significantly during the period 1978–84, and it is very interesting to investigate the reasons for these increases.

Much of the blame for the rapid increase in the price of new gas has been directed at gas pipeline companies, particularly those with large supplies of underpriced old gas, but in a broader context these pipelines acted as agents rather than principals. The more fundamental causes of pipeline imprudence are (1) the whole scheme of gas price regulation, which over a period of years systematically underpriced new as well as old gas and hence created continual excess demand for any gas available at regulated prices; (2) inefficient price regulation of utility companies, which should have been required to charge prices based on the marginal cost of gas supplies rather than the weighted average cost; (3) less than optimal regulation of pipeline companies, such that their incentives to operate efficiently were impaired; and (4) a legal tradition of very inflexible long-term contracts for the sale of gas to pipelines....

Since gas was persistently underpriced in the market, whatever could be produced could readily be sold. Regulated companies often lead a rather sheltered life. They focus their skills on the manipulation of the regulators, and not on keeping abreast of the whole market at all times. Why bother to pinpoint total potential gas demand when you can sell all you can produce, or resell all you can buy? Since the early 1960s, many forces had combined to produce an increasing excess demand for gas, including environmental regulations that placed a premium on gas as a fuel because of its freedom from major air pollution problems. Pipelines in particular were convinced as of 1978–80 that the gas shortage would be perpetual, since they felt oil prices would continue to rise over time, and under the new regulations, gas prices would never quite catch up. Thus it followed that they should control as many gas reserves as they could: get the gas reserves under contract, regardless of price or contract terms.

After deregulation of high-cost new gas, supplies increased sharply in response to the very high prices offered by pipelines. A gas pipeline company with large reserves under contract at less than 50 cents per mcf could afford to contract for new reserves at $5.00 or more per mcf and still keep its weighted average of acquisition costs at or below the price that a utility company could pass on to its customers—at least, to its residential customers. [Ed. note: This method of averaging costs is called "rolled–in pricing"].

Not only did the price of new and deep gas increase sharply, but the gas producers insisted upon contract terms, other than price, that were very favorable to them: high deliverability rates, favorable "take-or-pay" provisions, ... "most favored nation" clauses, which guaranteed that higher prices paid to anyone else in a field would automatically trigger an increase to all producers in that field, and similar provisions.[3]

The pipeline companies' strategy was based on the assumption that gas consumption would never fall, since OPEC prices would always rise and gas prices would always lag behind oil prices. But gas consumption eventually fell. By the 1980s, high OPEC prices had induced energy conservation efforts everywhere. Initially oil consumption suffered before gas consumption declined. By late 1981 oil prices were slowly falling and gas prices were still rapidly increasing under the provisions of the 1978 gas act. It is apparent that some time in 1982 oil and gas prices converged and the gas market finally cleared. For the first time in roughly 20 years, excess demand for gas no longer existed....

Within a surprisingly short period of time, gas prices came to be determined by competition and not by regulation. Under these circumstances, guaranteed price escalation under inflation adjustment clauses became a disadvantage, and the "take-or-pay" contracts signed in earlier years by pipeline companies became the casket in which pipelines were to be buried.

Both price and delivery quantities of new gas had been set in concrete [in contracts] with fixed prices and the "take or pay" provision.

What did the pipelines do? Seemingly, the only option was to fight. If pipelines had to pay for gas they could not sell, it was clearly less expensive to them to pay for unpurchased cheap gas than for unpurchased expensive gas. So in the early 1980s, the natural gas market witnessed the paradox of low-cost reserves being shut-in or under-produced, while high-cost new gas was being produced as close to capacity as demand would permit. Such a policy maximizes total supply cost rather than minimizes it! Nevertheless, it was perfectly logical for pipelines to behave this way under existing legal, regulatory, and market constraints.

This was no solution, however, because as old gas was shut-in, the average price of gas to the consumer rose, causing additional reductions in natural gas consumption. As gas consumption fell further, pipelines were finally forced to cut purchases of high-cost new gas, in violation of contract terms, and lawsuits rapidly multiplied. If contracts on new gas were enforced, many pipelines faced bankruptcy. Bills were introduced in Congress to abrogate the terms of gas contracts already in existence, a rather novel proposal in the context of orthodox contract law. As the January 1, 1985 deadline for gas price deregulation approached, demand was falling, prices to consumers were rising, gas producers were suffering from a burden of shut-in production, many pipelines were grasping at the straws

---

3. [Editor's note: A most favored nation clause reads: "If at any time after the execution of this contract, Buyer shall enter into a contract to purchase gas similar in quality at a price higher than the price hereunder, then Buyer shall immediately increase the price of gas received hereunder to equal the price under the other contract." This is a two-party favored nations clause. A third-party favored nations clause provides that the buyer will pay seller a price equal to the highest price paid by any buyer to any seller in the same area.

of legal doctrines such as *force majeure* to save, them from ruin, and the FERC was having difficulties explaining how old gas prices could have risen so rapidly under continued price regulation.

The fundamental cause of all these market dislocations was the tradition of underpricing gas through regulation. As long as gas was underpriced, excess demand existed and it was obviously more important for the gas industry to forecast FERC policy than to forecast gas demand. Once the all-embracing nature of the regulatory context is understood, the self-confessed "imprudence" and "stupidity" of the pipelines becomes more comprehensible. . . .

It is straightforward to prescribe where policy should ultimately take us. It is less obvious how to get there. . . . [I]t should be clear that "rolled in" pricing coupled with differential pricing of new and old gas creates gross market distortions. . . . [P]olicy should aim for a single price of gas, irrespective of when it was found or how difficult it was to find. Does this mean immediate decontrol of all gas vintages still held under controls? In the event of complete decontrol, gas producers individually would be motivated to exploit all the terms in existing contracts to maximize price hikes, particularly those relating to receiving prices equal to the highest price received by any producer in a given field. If high-cost new gas production exists with contract prices well above competitive levels—and such production is rather widespread, . . . then gas producers will simply price themselves out of the market. Not only would utility companies be unlikely to recognize such high prices, when passed on to them by the pipelines, as eligible for inclusion in the rate base, but utility demand itself would dwindle away as final user demand proved inadequate to sustain consumption levels at much higher prices. Industrial users would switch first, leaving residential users with a higher fixed cost allocation (for both pipeline and utility investment) to be covered in their rates. This in turn would provoke revolt by residential users, with the probable passage of laws in some states that would regulate gas utilities more harshly. There would be demands everywhere for fresh legislation to "solve" the new gas price problems.

Thus a worst-case scenario can readily be devised that would result in disaster. On the other hand, gas producers as a group may see reasons to act more temperately. Since the gas pipelines are their only customers, it would not seem optimal to take steps that would destroy them. Voluntary renegotiations, contract by contract, might lead to more efficient resource allocation than the passage of extremely detailed national laws changing the terms of individual gas contracts. A major problem with voluntary renegotiations is that producers may be less willing to negotiate than pipelines. Existing contracts seem to give them an advantage in the event of decontrol; the market realities of excess supply at existing prices mean that they are likely to lose revenues at the present time, to the extent that prices are exposed to short-run competitive forces. Most producers believe that currently depressed prices will disappear in the long run as the present gas surplus is worked through, so they feel that delay will work in their interest. Under such circumstances negotiations may not begin readily or proceed rapidly.■

NOTES AND COMMENTS

1.   Chapter 9 describes how FERC, the pipelines, producers, and the courts solved this mess. Before advancing to this material, be sure that you understand why the natural gas market experienced such price rigidity between 1982 and 1985, when gas shortages no longer existed. Was the effect caused solely by government regulation? After all, the NGPA set maximum legal prices, but producers could always sell their gas for less than the maximum if they wanted. Was the problem embedded in the private contracts between producers and purchasers? What particular clauses caused rigidities in price and quantity? Is there any indication that monopoly power was causing too-high prices?

2.   Surprisingly, an NGPA case came before the Fifth Circuit in 1997, long after the act had ceased to exist. The NGPA classifications for high-cost gas are used by the Internal Revenue Service for assessing eligibility for tax credits. The following case gives the reader some idea of the task Congress gave to FERC and state regulatory agencies in classifying every gas well in the United States in the right NGPA category. It also demonstrates how law often lags behind advances in technology.

WRT Energy Corp. v. Federal Energy Regulatory Comm'n

107 F.3d 314 (5th Cir.1997).

■ BARKSDALE, HIGGENBOTHAM and GARZA, C.Js.: The principal issue at hand is whether natural gas wells, which previously produced from a gas cap and were subsequently fitted with new technology for removing gas from the brine in the aquifer, qualify as producing "high-cost natural gas" pursuant to the Natural Gas Policy Act, 15 U.S.C. § 3301 *et. seq.* (repealed 1989). Reversing determinations by the Louisiana Department of Natural Resources, Office of Conservation, the Federal Energy Regulatory Commission ruled that the gas did not qualify. We AFFIRM.

WRT Energy Corporation has five wells in Louisiana which extract brine from an aquifer and then use recently-developed vortoil hydrocyclones to separate natural gas from the brine. Prior to installation of this new technology, each well had produced natural gas by tapping a "cap" of gas which had broken free from the brine and migrated to the top of the aquifer.

As the gas cap was depleted, however, the pressure in the well decreased. This pressure reduction allowed gas which had been dissolved in the brine to resolve out of it; but, it also allowed the brine which occupied the underlying aquifer to move upward, replacing all or part of the area previously occupied by the gas cap. This resulted in fewer well perforations exposed to free gas, and the well began to produce more and more brine with the gas, until the well "watered out." As a result, the wells were going to be plugged.

WRT's new process reaches more gas by allowing the production of gas which never broke free of the brine, but it is more costly than the usual extraction of natural gas; and, as with any new application of technology, there is an amount of risk involved. Accordingly, WRT applied for special treatment of these five wells under the Natural Gas Policy Act (NGPA).

The purpose of this special treatment is to encourage the production of natural gas sources, such as geopressured brine, which would not otherwise be economical to exploit. 1978 U.S.C.C.A.N. 8800, 9003. WRT sought relief under § 107 of the NGPA, 15 U.S.C. § 3317, which provided an incentive to produce "high-cost natural gas." For qualifying gas, the producer could elect either a pricing benefit under the NGPA, or a tax benefit. 15 U.S.C. § 3317(d); 26 U.S.C. § 29(c). One way to qualify—the route taken by WRT—is if the gas is "produced from geopressured brine." Because the NGPA was repealed effective 1 January 1993, the pricing benefits are no longer of use. But remaining is the potential tax benefit, which is not directly at issue in this proceeding, as discussed infra. 26 U.S.C. § 29(c).

As defined by the FERC, "geopressured brine" is subsurface fluid that has at least 10,000 parts of dissolved solids for every million parts water, and has an initial reservoir geopressure gradient over .465 pounds of pressure per square inch for each vertical foot of depth. 18 C.F.R. § 272.103. By FERC regulation, in order for gas to qualify as being "produced from geopressured brine," the gas must be "dissolved [in the brine] before initial production." 18 C.F.R. § 272.103(c).

Gas exists in brine in two states: (1) in solution—when the gas is dissolved in the brine; and (2) in free but immobile form—when the gas has fallen out of solution (or resolved) but remains trapped in the brine, without migrating to the top to form or join a gas cap. The NGPA and its regulations make no mention of the treatment of gas which is not dissolved in the brine, but exists instead in free immobile form in the brine without rising to form or join a gas cap. On the other hand, the FERC has expressly rejected the possibility that gas cap gas could qualify as gas "produced from geopressured brine"; early on, it required that, in order to qualify, the gas had to be dissolved in the brine. Interim Rules Defining and Deregulating Certain High-cost Natural Gas, FERC Regulations Preambles 1977–81, 44 Fed.Reg. 61,950 (29 October 1979); Final Rules Defining and Deregulating Certain High-cost Natural Gas, FERC Regulations Preambles 1977–81, 45 Fed.Reg. 28,092 (28 April 1980).

WRT faced two hurdles in order for the gas to be classified as being "produced from geopressured brine": (1) the wells had previously success-fully produced gas cap gas, before "watering out"; and (2) the brine now being extracted carried natural gas in two different states: dissolved gas which met the FERC's definition as having come from brine, and free immobile gas. Exacerbating matters is the fact that it is not known with certainty how much of each type of gas is produced and no one seems to be able to measure how much of the free immobile gas resolved as a result of the prior gas cap production.

There is a two-step process for deciding whether natural gas qualifies as "high-cost". 15 U.S.C. § 3317(c). First, the appropriate state or federal agency makes a determination; next, the FERC makes the conclusive determination, reviewing the earlier determination for substantial evidence. The FERC's determination is reviewable in a United States Court of Appeals.

Consistent with this process, after WRT installed a vortoil hydrocyclone at one of its wells as a test subject, it received a determination from the Louisiana Office of Conservation (LOC) that the well qualified as producing high-cost natural gas. The vortoil units were then installed at the other four wells; the LOC also certified them as producing high-cost gas. It found that, although all the wells had previously produced gas cap gas, the gas now produced is not from caps, but is either dissolved, or is in free immobile form, in the brine.

These positive determinations were transmitted to the FERC in April and May 1994.

[In April 1995 FERC issued a final order denying qualification to WRT's wells as high-cost wells. The court found that WRT had standing to appeal as an aggrieved party because FERC's final order would be detrimental to WRT's efforts to obtain a tax credit, even though the IRS is not bound to follow the FERC ruling]. . . .

This much is certain: the NGPA is a complex statute, one that was designed to control natural gas pricing and yet allow sufficient flexibility so that prices would encourage the production of gas that is more difficult to produce. . . .

To this end, the FERC is given quite a bit of discretion. For example, for the first sale of high-cost natural gas, the FERC could set a price above "the otherwise applicable maximum lawful price to the extent that such special price is necessary to provide reasonable incentives for the production of such . . . gas." *Id.* § 3317(b). . . .

Obviously pertinent to whether wells which previously produced gas cap gas can qualify as high-cost is the fact that the NGPA enumerated four methods for producing gas that might qualify as high-cost:

(1) produced from any well the surface drilling of which began on or after February 19, 1977, if such production is from a completion location which is located at a depth of more than 15,000 feet;

(2) produced from geopressured brine;

(3) occluded natural gas produced from coal seams;

(4) produced from Devonian shale. . . .

15 U.S.C. § 3317(c)(1)–(4). Each of these types involves higher cost to produce than usual gas production. Moreover, this section contains a fifth

"catch-all" category; the FERC could determine that a well presented "extraordinary risks or costs." *Id.* § 3317(c)(5)....

The apparent intent of Congress, as discussed by the FERC for its final finding, was to reward producers who incurred, "the high-costs of brine disposal from the start," and to grant the FERC a great deal of authority over the way in which the incentives are implemented. In fact, as discussed infra, the FERC noted in its final finding that the NGPA and its regulations have never been read to intend to reward a producer for a well, all or part of the cost of which had been recouped by producing from a gas cap, and which later produces, as an added bonus, the gas both dissolved and trapped (free immobile) in the brine....

Furthermore, the question at hand was touched on by the FERC in the preamble to its interim regulations:

> Gas not dissolved in brine, such as gas caps, may be economically produced through less expensive conventional production techniques and is not a high-cost gas. Therefore, *if the gas has broken free from the brine before initial production (before any fluids are withdrawn from the reservoir), it will not qualify under this definition.*

44 Fed.Reg. 61,950 (*emphasis added*). In the preamble to the final regulations, the FERC did not alter this position, stating in relevant part that "qualification under this category of gas relates only to whether the gas is dissolved gas produced from geopressured brine"; ...

As noted, portions of the gas in issue are dissolved in the brine, but other portions are free, yet immobile. This finding is not challenged by WRT, and is supported by substantial evidence. Restated, it is undisputed that all of the gas is not dissolved in the brine....

There is no definition for when the gas has "broken free": when it resolves out of the brine and becomes free immobile gas, or when it actually escapes the brine and forms or joins a gas cap. In the light of such questions, we defer to the promulgating agency....

Based on the NGPA, the FERC's arguments here, and its admission that the new technology was not available and therefore not considered during its rule making, there is reason to believe that it had not fully considered the question of free immobile gas. But, in the face of the clear statement in the regulation that, in order to qualify as high-cost, the gas must be "dissolved before initial production", we must apply it as written. Therefore, we rely on this plain language that the gas must be dissolved in the brine in order to qualify as coming "from" the brine.

For the foregoing reasons, the final finding of the Federal Energy Regulatory Commission is AFFIRMED.■

NOTES AND COMMENTS

1. Do you agree with Congress that geopressured methane production should be subsidized by the taxpayer? Coalbed methane production? What

public interest is served? Why would the State of Louisiana be more likely to certify this well for special tax treatment than FERC?

6.   ROLLED–IN PRICING AND INCREMENTAL PRICING: PROTECTING THE RESIDENTIAL CONSUMER

The rolled in pricing discussed in the Griffin and Steele excerpt (which allowed a pipeline to sell gas by averaging the costs of old 50 cents gas and new $5.00 gas) was not without its critics, nor without its legal battles. In *United Gas Pipe Line Co. v.* FERC. 649 F.2d 1110 (5th Cir.1981), *reh'g denied,* 664 F.2d 289 (1981), the court upheld a FERC order that refused to allow rolled in pricing for emergency gas purchases, because such pricing was unduly discriminatory in violation of the NGA. Under the NGA, FERC is charged with assuring that the rates of natural gas companies are just and reasonable. In the mid–1970s, United Gas Pipe Line experienced such severe shortages of natural gas that it had to curtail deliveries. FERC approved a curtailment plan which divided United's customers into three classes according to end use. Residential consumers were Priority I; gas used as feedstock by direct industrial customers was Priority II; and gas for all other industrial users was Priority III.

FERC also allowed United to make emergency purchases of gas, which it did, paying high prices for this gas. When United submitted new tariffs to recover the cost of the emergency gas on a rolled-in basis, Brooklyn Union Gas Company and Elizabeth Town Gas Company intervened and protested. They were LDCs which purchased gas from other pipelines which in turn purchased the gas from United. The intervenors insisted that proportional allocation of the cost of the emergency purchases among all customers was unduly discriminatory in light of United's curtailment plan. The demand of high priority customers (like intervenors) could be satisfied from the gas supply normally available to United under long-term contracts at lower prices. Since the emergency purchases were made solely to meet the demand of low priority customers, they should bear the burden of the premium price of the emergency gas. FERC agreed, and prohibited United from using rolled-in pricing to recover its emergency-gas costs "unless there is a direct benefit to all classes of customers."

FERC explained its reasons for disallowing rolled–in pricing in United's case: (1) it resulted in gross discrimination against high priority customers, and (2) it failed to encourage conservation of natural gas and substitution of more abundant fuels. The Court accepted FERC's explanation, as shown in the following excerpt from this case:

> Section 5(a) of the Natural Gas Act, 15 U.S.C.A. § 717d(a), requires the Commission to ferret out and remedy "unduly discriminatory" practices. Under United's court-ordered curtailment plan "high-priority customers have experienced very little curtailment." Order at 8. Since low priority customers are the primary beneficiaries of emergency gas, the Commission concluded that it is only just that they pay for it. Rolled-in pricing imposed a substantial cost burden on many

customers who received no benefit from emergency purchases, and the Commission concluded that United's pricing system resulted in "overwhelming discrimination" against high priority customers and in favor of low priority customers. Order at 10.

If the finding of discrimination is a corollary of the curtailment plan, the Commission's second consideration that brokered sales of emergency gas will serve to promote the efficient use of gas by United's customers may be said to follow from some of the same conclusions that went into the formulation of he[sic] plan. Those with alternative energy sources and those who could most easily reduce consumption or deal with supply disruptions were given the lowest priority and are the first to be curtailed. *See* Southern Natural Gas Co.

When a curtailment plan groups customers according to their ability and willingness to find substitute fuel, the goal of encouraging efficient utilization of gas will be further served by allocating high cost gas to low priority customers. Although the Commission was not free to uncritically impose high cost gas on low priority customers, *cf. Elizabethtown Gas Co. v. FERC*, 575 F.2d 885 (D.C.Cir.1978); *Fort Pierce Util. Auth. v. FPC*, 526 F.2d 993 (5th Cir.1976); *Mississippi Pub. Serv. Comm'n v. FPC*, 522 F.2d 1345 (5th Cir.1975), *cert. denied*, 429 U.S. 870 (1976) (Commission has jurisdiction to order high priority customers to compensate curtailed low priority customers for their off-line purchases, and must develop its record on the issue), here the Commission specifically found that allocating high cost emergency gas to United's low priority customers will encourage them to find substitute fuels and make more efficient use of the gas they do receive. Order at 8.

The NGPA provided a different mechanism, more regular than emergency purchases, for interstate pipelines facing shortages to purchase gas. In Sections 311 and 312 of the Act, intrastate pipelines were authorized to sell natural gas to interstate pipelines (at NGPA controlled prices) without subjecting themselves to the full panoply of NGA jurisdiction over rates, entry, abandonment, etc. United stopped making emergency purchases and began making high-priced gas purchases under Sections 311 and 312. FERC allowed rolled–in pricing for this gas. Another LDC serving residential customers, LaClede, argued that these types of gas purchases were merely a substitute for the prior purchase of emergency gas and rolled–in pricing should be prohibited, as in the *United Gas Pipe Line* case above.

The *United Gas* case was decided before the enactment of the NGPA. In *Laclede Gas Co. v. FERC*, 722 F.2d 272 (5th Cir.1984), the court upheld FERC's rolled–in pricing, under sections of the NGPA designed to allow gas to flow more freely from intrastate to interstate markets. The court distinguished *United* as follows:

> First of all, the *United* case by its terms referred only to emergency gas transactions. Furthermore, although similarities do exist between the emergency program and Sections 311–312 gas, FERC correctly stated in Opinion No. 159–A that the policies behind the two

programs differ substantially. Emergency gas may be purchased only when the pipeline is in curtailment, when curtailment is imminent, or when the pipeline must meet a sudden unexpected increase in demand. 18 C.F.R. § 157.46(a). By contrast, Sections 311 and 312 gas may be purchased at any time. The House Ad Hoc Committee on Energy stated in reference to the House precursor to NGPA Sections 311–312: "The amendment facilitates development of a national natural gas transportation network without subjecting intrastate pipelines, already regulated by State agencies, to FPC regulation over the entirety of their operations." ... *See* Ringleb, Natural Gas Producer Price Regulation Under the NGPA: Regulatory Failure, Alternatives, and Reform, 20 Houston L.Rev. 709, 722 n. 66 ("The most obvious intent of Congress [in § 311] was to provide a mechanism allowing the surplus gas in the intrastate market to be sold to the interstate market.")....
The fact that the NGPA retained emergency gas provisions in Section 303 along with Sections 311 and 312 is further evidence that the two programs embody distinct policies.

As FERC points out, the statutory time frames of emergency gas and Sections 311–312 gas also differ. Emergency gas transactions are limited to sixty days. 18 C.F.R. § 157.48(b). The initial Section 311 gas purchases may be as long as two years, and additional two year extensions may be authorized. Section 312 does not limit the duration of an assignment under Section 312 of an intrastate pipeline's right to purchase surplus gas.

Other distinctions between emergency gas and Sections 311–312 gas are thoroughly explicated by both the Administrative Law Judge and by FERC. Because Sections 311 and 312 purchases were intended to do more than forestall temporary emergency situations, the Commission concluded that Sections 311–312 gas is an integral part of United's overall supply. Unlike emergency gas, Sections 311–312 gas is not purchased solely for the benefit of one priority group in the curtailment plan. Thus FERC determined it to be just and reasonable for the cost of Sections 311–312 gas to be rolled-in to the costs of all customers. *See United Gas Pipe Line v. Federal Energy Regulatory Commission*, 649 F.2d 1110, 1115 (5th Cir.1981). *See also Battle Creek Gas Co. v. Federal Power Commission*, 281 F.2d 42, 46 (D.C.Cir.1960). Rather than an unexplained departure from past precedent, we find the Commission's decision to be a reasoned explanation of why the differences between emergency gas and Sections 311–312 gas justify rolled-in pricing in the 311–312 case, ...

On top of the 27 pricing categories for natural gas and FERC's policies for rolled–in (sometimes) prices, Title II of the NGPA introduced "incremental pricing," a rate design with the single goal of shifting the increased cost of gas from residential consumers to industrial users, but without driving industrial users to convert to other fuels. The legislative objective was to subsidize the favored class of residential gas users at the expense of the disfavored class, but not to the extent that industrial users would swing off of gas, thereby leaving no industrial buyers to bargain with pipelines to keep prices low as the pipelines bargained with producers for the newly deregulated gas. (Residential consumers or their representatives were not considered good bargaining agents because their demand for gas was inelastic; *i.e.*, they could not threaten to switch to another fuel if prices were raised too high). The intricacy of Congressional tinkering with this system of "ordering the market" defies summary description. If you want to try and make sense of either the economics or the politics of incremental pricing, read Carol Cormie, Incremental Pricing Under the Natural Gas Policy Act of 1978, 57 Denver L. Rev. 1 (1979); and William A. Mogel and William R. Mapes, Jr., Assessment of Incremental Pricing under the Natural Gas Policy Act, 29 Catholic U. L. Rev. 763 (1980).

After reading Chapter 8 on rate making, ask yourself if rolled–in pricing accords with the economist's prescription to price gas or electricity to consumers at its longrun marginal cost. Rolled–in pricing is still an issue when pipelines expand an existing facility to serve new customers. Who should bear the costs of the expansion: all customers or only the new customers?

C. PREEMPTION AND STATE CONSERVATION REGULATION

The inevitable conflict between producer rate regulation and state conservation laws, presaged by the dissenting justices in *Phillips* came to pass under the NGPA of 1978. In the following case, the U.S. Supreme Court had to determine whether Congressional policy had left room for state ratable–take laws to operate in the new federal scheme. The facts in this case typified scenarios in gas fields throughout the United States at that time.

Transcontinental Gas Pipe Line Corp. v. State Oil & Gas Board of Mississippi

474 U.S. 409 (1986).

[The Mississippi Oil and Gas Board's Rule 48 required the purchaser of natural gas from a common pool to buy the gas from each of the owners of such pool in proportion to their share of the ownership. This procedure is known as "ratable take." Transcontinental (Transco) had long–term contracts to purchase gas from some but not all owners of the gas in the Harper Sand Pool. The market price of gas had dropped significantly since the contracts were signed, and Transco refused to purchase gas from those owners with which it had no contracts, except at a much lower price. The state board held that Transco had violated Rule 48. Transco brought suit in the state court, arguing that state ratable–take orders had been held to be preempted by the Natural Gas Act (NGA) in *Northern Natural Gas Co. v. State Corp. Commission of Kansas*, 372 U.S. 84 (1963). The Mississippi Supreme Court held that such preemption had been negated by Congress's enactment of the Natural Gas Policy Act of 1978 (NGPA), 15 U.S.C. § 3301 *et. seq.* The United States Supreme Court reversed.]

■ BLACKMUN, J.: If the Gas Board's action were analyzed under the standard used in Northern Natural, it clearly would be pre-empted. Whether that decision governs this case depends on whether Congress, in enacting the NGPA, altered those characteristics of the federal regulatory scheme which provided the basis in Northern Natural for a finding of preemption....

Northern Natural's finding of preemption [rested] on two considerations. First, Congress had created a comprehensive regulatory scheme, and ratable-take orders fell within the limits of that scheme rather than within the category of regulatory questions reserved for the States. Second, in the absence of ratable-take requirements, purchasers would choose a different, and presumably less costly, purchasing pattern. By requiring pipelines to follow the more costly pattern, Kansas' order conflicted with the federal interest in protecting consumers by ensuring low prices.

Under the NGA, the Federal Power Commission's comprehensive regulatory scheme involved "utility-type ratemaking" control over prices and supplies. *See* Haase, The Federal Role in Implementing the Natural Gas Policy Act of 1978, 16 Houston L.Rev. 1067, 1079 (1979). The FPC set price ceilings for sales from producers to pipelines and regulated the prices pipelines could charge their downstream customers. But "[i]n the early 1970's, it became apparent that the regulatory structure was not working." *Public Service Comm'n of New York v. Mid–Louisiana Gas Co.,* 463 U.S. 319, 330 (1983). The Nation began to experience serious gas shortages. The NGA's "artificial pricing scheme" was said to be a "major cause" of the imbalance between supply and demand.

In response, Congress enacted the NGPA, which "has been justly described as 'a comprehensive statute to govern future natural gas regulation.' " *Mid-Louisiana Gas Co.,* 463 U.S., at 332, *quoting* Note, Legislative History of the Natural Gas Policy Act, 59 Texas L. Rev. 101, 116 (1980). The aim of federal regulation remains to assure adequate supplies of natural gas at fair prices, but the NGPA reflects a congressional belief that a new system of natural gas pricing was needed to balance supply and demand. *See* S.Rep. No. 95–436, at 10. The new federal role is to "overse[e] a national market price regulatory scheme." Haase, 16 Houston L. Rev., at 1079; *see* S.Rep. No. 95–436, at 21 (NGPA implements "a new commodity value pricing approach"). The NGPA therefore does not constitute a federal retreat from a comprehensive gas policy. Indeed, the NGPA in some respects expanded federal control, since it granted FERC jurisdiction over the intrastate market for the first time. *See* the Act's §§ 311 and 312, 15 U.S.C. §§ 3371 and 3372.

Appellees argue, however, that §§ 601(a)(1)(B)(I) and (ii), 15 U.S.C. §§ 3431(a)(1)(B)(I) and (ii), stripped FERC of jurisdiction over the Harper Sand pool gas which was the subject of the Gas Board's Rule 48 order, thereby leaving the State free to regulate Transco's purchases. Section 601(a)(1)(B) states that "the provisions of [the NGA] and the jurisdiction of the Commission under such Act shall not apply solely by reason of any first sale" of high-cost or new natural gas. Moreover, although FERC retains some control over pipelines' downstream pricing practices, § 601(c)(2) requires FERC to permit Transco to pass along to its customers the cost of the gas it purchases "except to the extent the Commission determines that the amount paid was excessive due to fraud, abuse, or similar grounds." According to appellees, FERC's regulation of Transco's involvement with high-cost gas can now concern itself only with Transco's sales to its customers; FERC, it is said, cannot interfere with Transco's purchases of new natural gas from its suppliers. Appellees believe that the Gas Board order concerns only this latter relationship, and therefore is not pre-empted by federal regulation of other aspects of the gas industry.

That FERC can no longer step in to regulate directly the prices at which pipelines purchase high-cost gas, however, has little to do with whether state regulations that affect a pipeline's costs and purchasing patterns impermissibly intrude upon federal concerns. Mississippi's action directly undermines Congress' determination that the supply, the demand, and the price of high-cost gas be determined by market forces. To the extent that Congress denied FERC the power to regulate affirmatively particular aspects of the first sale of gas, it did so because it wanted to leave determination of supply and first-sale price to the market. "[A] federal decision to forgo regulation in a given area may imply an authoritative federal determination that the area is best left *un*regulated, and in that event would have as much preemptive force as a decision *to* regulate" (emphasis in original). *Arkansas Electric Cooperative Corp. v. Arkansas Public Service Comm'n*, 461 U.S., at 384.

The proper question in this case is not whether FERC has affirmative regulatory power over wellhead sales of § 107 gas, but whether Congress, in revising a comprehensive federal regulatory scheme to give market forces a more significant role in determining the supply, the demand, and the price of natural gas, intended to give the States the power it had denied FERC. The answer to the latter question must be in the negative. First, when Congress meant to vest additional regulatory authority in the States it did so explicitly. *See* §§ 503(c) and 602(a), 15 U.S.C. §§ 3413(c) and 3432(a). Second, although FERC may now possess less regulatory jurisdiction over the "intricate relationship between the purchasers' cost structures and eventual costs to wholesale customers who sell to consumers in other States," *Northern Natural*, 372 U.S., at 92, than it did under the old regime, that relationship is still a subject of deep federal concern. FERC still must review Transco's pricing practices, even though its review of Transco's purchasing behavior has been circumscribed. In light of Congress' intent to move toward a less regulated national natural gas market, its decision to remove jurisdiction from FERC cannot be interpreted as an invitation to the States to impose additional regulations.

Mississippi's order also runs afoul of other concerns identified in *Northern Natural*. First, it disturbs the uniformity of the federal scheme, since interstate pipelines will be forced to comply with varied state regulations of their purchasing practices. In light of the NGPA's unification of the interstate and intrastate markets, the contention that Congress meant to permit the States to impose inconsistent regulations is especially unavailing. Second, Mississippi's order would have the effect of increasing the ultimate price to consumers. Take-or-pay provisions are standard industrywide.... Pipelines are already committed to purchase gas in excess of market demand. Mississippi's rule will require Transco to take delivery of noncontract gas; this will lead Transco not to take delivery of contract gas elsewhere, thus triggering take-or-pay provisions. Transco's customers will ultimately bear such increased costs....

The change in regulatory perspective embodied in the NGPA rested in significant part on the belief that direct federal price control exacerbated supply and demand problems by preventing the market from making long-term adjustments.[6][4] Mississippi's actions threaten to distort the market once again by artificially increasing supply and price. Although, in the long run, producers and pipelines may be able to adjust their selling and purchasing patterns to take account of ratable-take orders, requiring such future adjustments in an industry where long-term contracts are the norm will postpone achievement of Congress' aims in enacting the NGPA. We therefore conclude that Mississippi's ratable-take order is pre-empted.

Because we have concluded that the Gas Board's order is pre-empted by the NGA and NGPA, we need not reach the question whether, absent federal occupation of the field, Mississippi's action would nevertheless run afoul of the Commerce Clause.

The judgment of the Supreme Court of Mississippi is therefore reversed.

It is so ordered.

■ REHNQUIST, J., dissenting: I believe that the NGPA's removal of such gas from the NGA takes this case outside the purview of Northern Natural, and that a ratable-take rule such as that imposed by Mississippi is consistent with the NGPA's purpose of decontrolling the wellhead price of high-cost gas.

Congress passed the NGA in 1938 in response to this Court's holding that the Commerce Clause prevented States from directly regulating the wholesale prices of natural gas sold in interstate commerce. *See Missouri v. Kansas Natural Gas Co.*, 265 U.S. 298 (1924). The purpose of the NGA was "to occupy the field of wholesale sales of natural gas in interstate commerce." *Exxon Corp. v. Eagerton*, 462 U.S. 176, 184 (1983). In 1954 this Court [in] *Phillips Petroleum Co. v. Wisconsin*, 347 U.S. 672, interpreted the NGA as creating exclusive federal jurisdiction over the regulation of

---

4. The dissent's complaint that Congress did not intend to decontrol supply and demand, at 714, n. 5, misses the point. Congress clearly intended to eliminate the distortive effects that NGA price control had had on supply and demand. To suggest that Congress was willing to replace this distortion with a distortion on price caused by a State's decision to require pipelines and, ultimately, interstate consumers, to purchase gas they do not want—the purpose of the order in this case—requires taking an artificially formalistic view of what Congress sought to achieve in the NGPA.

natural gas in interstate commerce, extending the NGA's coverage to both downstream and local sales, though not to the production and gathering of natural gas.

Northern Natural Gas Co. v. State Corporation Comm'n of Kansas, was decided against this backdrop. The Court reasoned that the NGA "leaves no room either for direct state regulation of the prices of interstate wholesales of natural gas, . . . or for state regulations which would indirectly" regulate price. Because ratable-take rules apply to purchasers, they indirectly regulate price and therefore "invalidly invade the federal agency's exclusive domain" of sales regulation. Finally, the Court explained that although "States do possess power to allocate and conserve scarce natural resources upon and beneath their lands," they may not use means such as ratable-take rules that "threaten effectuation of the federal regulatory scheme."

The NGPA was passed in 1978 in response to chronic interstate gas shortages caused by price ceilings imposed pursuant to the NGA. Its purpose was to decontrol the wellhead price of natural gas sold to interstate pipelines, allowing prices to rise according to market conditions and causing shortages to vanish. To accomplish this purpose, it divided the supply of gas into three major categories: high-cost gas, new gas, and old gas. . . . It removed the wellhead sales of high-cost and new gas from the coverage of the NGA. 15 U.S.C. § 3431(a)(1)(B). It then established formulas for the gradual decontrol of the wellhead prices of such gas. *See* 15 U.S.C. §§ 3312(b), 3313(b), 3317(a). The wellhead price of high-cost gas was totally decontrolled in November 1979. *See* 15 U.S.C. § 3331(b); Pierce, *supra*, at 87–88. Ceilings continue to apply to the wellhead prices of old gas. *See id.*, at 88–89. Because gas from the Harper Sand Gas Pool qualifies as high-cost gas, the NGA no longer covers its wellhead price. Therefore, *Northern Natural* does not govern this case. Rather, the issue is whether Mississippi's ratable-take rule stands as an obstacle to the full accomplishment of the NGPA's purpose.

The purpose of the NGPA with respect to high-cost gas is to eliminate governmental controls on the wellhead price of such gas. State regulation that interferes with this purpose is pre-empted. *See Arkansas Electric Cooperative Corp. v. Arkansas Public Service Comm'n*, 461 U.S. 375, 384 (1983). State regulation that merely defines property rights or establishes contractual rules, however, does not interfere with this purpose. Markets depend upon such rules to function efficiently.

Ratable-take rules serve the twin interests of conservation and fair dealing by removing the incentive for "drainage." On its face, the ratable-take rule here is completely consistent with the free market determination of the wellhead price of high-cost gas. Like any compulsory unitization rule, it gives joint owners the incentive to price at the same level as a single owner. But it will not affect the spot market price of gas in any other way. It is similarly price neutral in the context of long-term contracting. The rule is merely one of a number of legal rules that regulates the contractual relations of parties in the State of Mississippi as in other States. The Court, however, seems to equate Mississippi's rule requiring equitable dealing on the part of pipeline companies purchasing from common owners of gas pools as akin to a tax or a subsidy, both of which do tend to distort free market prices.

Unlike taxes or subsidies, however, rules regulating the conditions of contracts have only an attenuated effect on the operation of the free market. Their effect is often to promote the efficient operation of the market rather than to inhibit or distort it the way a tax or subsidy might. A ratable-take rule applied to a common pool eliminates the inefficiencies associated with the perverse incentives of common ownership of a gas pool. It is different from a rule that would require any out-of-state pipeline that purchases gas from one in-state pool of gas to purchase equal amounts from every other in-state pool. This latter type of rule might well burden interstate commerce or violate the free market purpose of the NGPA. But a ratable-take rule applied to a common pool promotes, rather than inhibits, the efficiency of a competitive market. Moreover, States have historically included ratable-take rules in developing the body of law applicable to natural gas extraction. *See, e.g., Champlin Refining Co. v. Corporation Comm'n of Oklahoma*, 286 U.S. 210, 233 (1932). One may agree that Congress wished to return to the free market determination of the price of high-cost gas without concluding that Mississippi's ratable-take rule frustrates that wish.

I believe that Mississippi's ratable-take rule as applied to high-cost gas offends neither FERC's jurisdiction [nor] the applicable provisions of the NGPA. I would therefore affirm the judgment of the Supreme Court of Mississippi.■

NOTES AND COMMENTS

1. Do the majority and the dissent disagree about the Congressional intent behind the NGPA's pricing policies? Does the majority interpret the NGPA's goal as keeping gas prices low? Does the dissent disagree? What was the NGPA policy regarding gas prices? If it was to ultimately let the market determine the price, then this price might be high or low, depending on supply and demand. How did the Mississippi ratable–take statute interfere with the forces of supply and demand in the gas market? How did it interfere with private contractual relations? Does the split in the Court reflect different views of federalism, of "state's rights," rather than a difference in interpreting the NGPA's pricing policy?

2. Could Mississippi have accomplished the result it wanted by issuing a market-demand prorationing order rather than a ratable–take order? A prorationing order would restrict the producer from producing more than the market demanded. This type of order does not aim directly at interstate purchasers of gas. Yet the interstate pipeline is certainly affected by such an order. If the producers with whom the pipeline has long-term contracts can no longer supply the quantities demanded by the pipeline because their wells have been cut back by a state prorationing order, then the pipeline

will have to buy gas from other producers. Doesn't this solve the correlative rights problem of drainage? How does this scenario affect the pipeline's take-or-pay liabilities? Can the pipeline be forced to pay for gas that it does not take because the state conservation agency prohibits producers from producing at their deliverability capacity and instead cuts producers to, say, 35 percent of capacity? Reread the take-or-pay clause quoted on page 448 of this chapter. Now do you understand why pipeline companies with large take-or-pay liabilities preferred prorationing rules over ratable–take rules? Are state prorationing rules preempted under the reasoning of *Phillips* and the majority in *Transco?*

3. In 1985, FERC began to issue a series of orders that separated the traditional functions of the participants in the natural gas supply business into new combinations. FERC sought to transform gas pipelines into open–access common carriers (the regulatory model which Congress had failed to enact in 1938) without waiting for Congress to amend the NGA. The story of this revolution is told in Chapter 9.

D. STATE PUBLIC UTILITY REGULATION

While Congress, FERC, and the federal courts were busily engaged in adopting, adapting to, or interpreting the many federal laws enacted to solve the energy crisis, the state public utility commissions with jurisdiction over LDC's, the investor-owned utilities which distribute gas locally in intrastate markets, also faced new problems. One such problem involved the proper treatment of the regulated utilities' non-regulated business ventures. Many utilities integrated backwards into the ownership of energy resources by investing in oil and gas exploration and production businesses or by buying coal fields. Oil production and coal mining are not within the jurisdiction of the state utility commissions. Or are they? The following excerpt from a Michigan Public Service Commission case, *Re Michigan Consolidated Gas Company*, 78 P.U.R.3d 321, 323–24 (1968) aptly describes the problem, and offers one solution:

> Michigan Consolidated has for many years been engaged in an exploration program to discover gas producing fields. This commission has during this period allowed Michigan Consolidated to include gas exploration costs in its "cost of service" as a legitimate part of its expenses properly chargeable to its utility customers.
>
> In its exploration program, Michigan Consolidated did not deliberately set out to discover only oil or only gas fields. It secured leases and drilled wells where geological or geophysical service indicated some promise of either event. Thus, discovery of oil fields was not by design, but rather by accident and incidental to its gas exploration program.
>
> Michigan Consolidated developed oil production in the Big Hand field in 1963 and discovered the Hardy Dam oil field in 1966. As is the case with most so-called oil fields, these reservoirs contain both oil and gas, and both flow or are pumped through the same wellbores to the

surface where the oil and gas are separated. In these fields, the resultant oil is sold to refineries. Some of the gas is used for field purposes and the remainder is vented. Michigan Consolidated's management decided to treat these production facilities as nonjurisdictional and take the profits therefrom 'below the line' to inure to the benefit of its stockholders.

The record shows that the gas utility customers have already paid the exploration expenses leading to the development of these oil production properties through the cost of maintaining an active geological and reservoir engineering staff, obtaining leases, and drilling exploratory wells. Until these exploratory wells are drilled, it is not possible to determine whether the ultimate production from a particular lease will be oil or gas, or both. Moreover, Michigan Consolidated has charged some dry holes related to oil production to its gas operations, while venting gas produced with the oil. We also consider it significant that gas which has been vented from the wells producing oil in the Big Hand field will soon be gathered and ultimately utilized by Michigan Consolidated in serving its gas utility customers.

Consequently, we find that these oil production facilities cannot be considered as a separate non-utility operation, but are incidental to the natural gas exploration program and a part of Michigan Consolidated's gas utility operation. For these reasons, Michigan Consolidated's investment in these oil production facilities, as well as the revenues and expenses associated therewith, should and shall be treated and recorded as utility plant and utility operations for rate-making and accounting purposes.

The Michigan solution seems straightforward and in the public interest: The private investor/shareholders in a utility provide the risk capital and bear the risk of loss or profit in that enterprise. But if facility enterprises are placed in the rate base, then they become subject to state utility ratemaking controls, and if ratepayers have been charged for these facilities and have borne this risk, then ratepayers should also reap the benefits of the enterprise. Gain should follow risk.

In fact, however, the public interest may not be so easy to determine, as shown in the case of *Committee of Consumer Services v. Public Service Commission of Utah*, 595 P.2d 871 (Utah 1979). In this case, the Commission had issued orders allowing a utility, Mountain Fuel Supply to segregate its utility and non-utility assets and then to transfer the non-utility assets, which consisted of oil wells, to a separate affiliate Wexpro. The oil assets were being transferred to Wexpro at a depreciated book value of $33 million, even though Mountain Fuel's expert estimated that the property had a fair market value of $150 million. (The proposed sale was to occur in 1976; review Figure 6–1 to understand why the fair market value was so high relative to book value). If this property was a utility asset, then the Utah commission would have jurisdiction over the sale to Wexpro and could police the sale of this valuable asset. The Commission, after much indecision which seems to have caused considerable havoc in the financial markets, allowed the transfer to proceed because it did not involve utility assets over which it had jurisdiction.

The Utah Supreme Court reversed the Commission's order allowing the transfer and remanded the issue for additional hearings. The high stakes at issue obviously caused high feelings about "ratepayer ripoffs" and "Damocles swords" of regulatory uncertainty. Justice Maughan wrote an opinion in which three justices concurred and one did not participate. Justice Wilkins offered a thoughtful dissent which saw the public interest quite differently.

Before reading this opinion, it is useful to recall that oil and gas are often, but not always, found together in the same reservoir. The Texas regulatory commission uses the following chart to classify gas wells. Some gas wells produce only gas, called non-associated gas. But all oil fields produce some gas, either from a separate gas-cap which sits on top of the oil (associated gas) or from gas which is dissolved in the oil and comes out of solution at the casinghead (the top of the well). When a public utility sets out to find gas, and winds up with oil and its accompanying gas, how are the regulated gas assets to be separated from the unregulated oil assets?

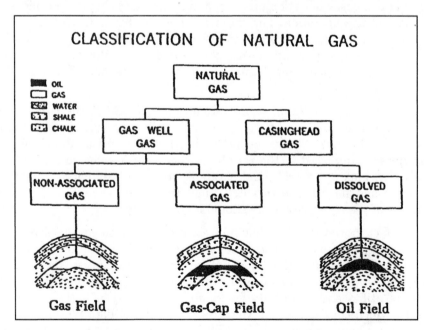

Figure 7–7

Ernest E. Smith & Jacqueline Lang Weaver, 2 Texas Law of Oil and Gas at p. 8–23 (2d ed. 1999).

Committee of Consumer Services v. Public Service Comm'n

595 P.2d 871 (Utah 1979).

■ Maughan, Justice:

Petitioners seek review of an order of the Public Service Commission approving an amended purchase and sale agreement, and an amended joint exploration agreement. Both of these were modified by the Commission. They related to Mountain Fuel Supply and its wholly owned subsidiary, Wexpro. The order is reversed and the matter is remanded for a hearing in accordance with the principles set forth in this opinion. . . .

The order was predicated on the validity of the classification by Mountain Fuel of its utility and non-utility assets, and the conclusion the Commission had no jurisdiction over the non-utility assets and the transfer of those assets to a non-utility corporate entity. These conclusions were premised on the erroneous assumption there was no correlation or connection between the contributions by the ratepayers, through an annual exploration and development expense included in the rate base, and the ensuing benefits from this program.

The key to the nature of misunderstanding of the majority of the Commission is well expressed in the dissent of Commissioner Rigtrup, who stated:

> The Commission's Report and Order represents a fundamental abdication by the Commission of its statutory responsibility to protect the public interest. The result of this abdication, which allows the transfer to an unregulated company of well over $150 million worth of assets discovered and developed with funds provided by the ratepayers of this state, under prior order of this Commission, can only be characterized a regulatory outrage.

In the conclusion to his dissent, Commissioner Rigtrup stated:

> . . . I would conclude that the exploration acreage held by Mountain Fuel over the years was used or useful in its natural gas utility business, and should have always been classified as utility assets. The fact that revenues from 'oil' or other liquid hydrocarbons have become very significant during the last few years does not change the basic character of those assets. However, it appears that the shareholders of Mountain Fuel have come to expect an unregulated return from oil properties, for which the risk capital was largely derived in rates charged its customers as ordered by the Commission. . . .

In evaluating the order of the Commission, it is important to review the two avowed purposes of Mountain Fuel in creating Wexpro: first, to provide and maintain a vigorous exploration program in order that Mountain Fuel might secure natural gas reserves for the future; second, "to remove regulatory uncertainty from the non-utility properties of the company which has hung like Damocles (sic) sword over the properties and assets of Mountain Fuel since 1972."

The latter purpose was the consequence of a finding by the Commission, in a report and order of January 14, 1974, that the oil operations were so incidental to and inseparable from the production and sale of natural gas as to be part of Mountain Fuel's utility operations; and any other treatment would be purely arbitrary, conjectural, and speculative. The Commission had ordered the investments, revenues, and expenses of the oil operations be included in the appropriate utility accounts, for rate-making purposes. Subsequently, the Commission had rescinded the order for the "roll in" of the oil properties, but the findings were not rejected. These findings, in regard to the inseparable nature of the oil and gas operations, were the sword of Damocles Mountain Fuel sought to have beaten into a non-regulated oil derrick.

In the current order, in finding No. 42, the majority of the Commission concluded that the language of the January 14, 1974, Report and Order "with respect to the ratepayer risk, ratepayer rip-off and exploitation of Mountain Fuel customers is erroneous and should not stand as fact or law." The dissent responded it was unnecessary for the majority to overrule the prior order. The dissent stated:

> ... The attempt of Mountain Fuel to obtain a ruling in this case which it could not get in Case No. 6668 is not only an affront to the members of the former Commission, but should offend reasonable sensitivities of this Commission.

There are certain basic principles which should be reviewed prior to the evaluation of the positions of the contesting parties.

First, it is the duty of a public utility corporation to operate in such a manner as to give to the consumers the most favorable rate reasonably possible. This duty stems from the fact the State has conferred on the utility the exclusive right to sell and distribute gas. As a consequence, the utility bears a trust relationship to its customers and must conduct its operations on that basis and not as though it were engaged in a private enterprise with no restrictions as to its income.

Second, under the general concepts of public utility law, risk capital is provided by the investor; it is this group which bears the risk of loss as developer of a public utility. It is only to the extent the facilities developed are used and useful to the consumer that they are included in the rate base.

Third, under the "no-profits-to-affiliates" rule, any amount paid as a profit by a company to any other with which it is directly or indirectly in a control relationship cannot properly be included in the rate base. The basis of the rule is that a profit made by an enterprise dealing with itself does not represent a cost. The rationale underlying this concept proceeds from a simple premise:

> If the relationship between two contracting parties is so close that they lose their individual identity and are, in fact, one, there can be no 'actual legitimate cost' involved in the payment of profits, since it would be tantamount to a company's paying itself a profit for interdepartmental services. (Citations)

... Intracompany transactions cannot be used to create an artificial or inflated price to be charged consumers....

This Court would be remiss in its duty if it did not cite the findings of the Commission, wherein it is said Mountain Fuel has been permitted to pay itself a profit for interdepartmental services. Heretofore, under Mountain Fuel's classification system, when an oil well has been developed and has been placed in the non-utility account, the non-utility account has been credited with the field price of the associated gas rather than the cost of service price. Under the amended purchase and sale agreement, there is a provision for Mountain Fuel to purchase, at market price rather than cost of service, the gas discovered on properties acquired by Wexpro, other than transferred acreage and that which comes to it under the joint exploration agreement. This provision violates the "no-profits-to-affiliates" rule....

Mountain Fuel has maintained a utility account #105 in which has been held the unexplored or wildcat acreage. These assets have been deemed used and useful in the utility business by the Commission and have been included as capital assets in the rate base. As previously noted a utility is usually precluded from including in the rate base any capital asset, until it is developed, and then only to the extent the asset is used and useful in rendering the consumer service.

The determination of the Commission that this undeveloped acreage was used and useful in the utility business was consistent with statutory provisions. Under 54–2–1(30), the definition of a public utility includes a gas corporation, where the gas is sold or furnished to any consumer within this state for domestic, industrial or commercial use. Under 54–2–1(18), the definition of a gas corporation includes every corporation and person owning, controlling, operating or managing any gas plant for public service, within this state, or for the selling or furnishing of natural gas to any consumer or consumers within this state for domestic, commercial or industrial use. The key definition is the statutory one of gas plant. 54–2–1(17) provides:

> The term "gas plant" includes all real estate and fixtures and personal property owned, controlled, operated or managed in connection with or to facilitate the production, generation, transmission, delivery or furnishing of gas (natural or manufactured) for light, heat, or power.

Under this broad definition, the undeveloped acreage may properly be deemed an asset of the gas plant, because it is owned to facilitate the production of gas.

As early as 1957, the Commission found funds for exploration and development were a just and reasonable expense as part of the utility function of Mountain Fuel. As a result the company maintained accounts #795, #796, #797, #798 as utility expense accounts. Covered under these direct exploration expenses were costs for lease maintenance (delayed rentals), non-productive well drilling (dry hole exploration), abandoned leases, and other authorized exploration expenses. Since 1960, $44,981,000 has been authorized by the Commission as a utility exploration expense, which has been reflected in the rates and charges for the sale of natural gas. Between 1966 and 1976, the utility expense account paid for 73.3 percent of dry hole exploration and the non-utility account paid 26.7 percent of this expense. The utility expense account paid 95 percent of the canceled and delayed rentals on leases and the non-utility account paid 5 percent of this expense. Of the total exploration expenses for the ten year period, $37,250,000 was paid from the utility account, and $8,222,000 was paid by the non-utility account. It was not until 1972 that the Commission ordered the non-utility account to pay a portion of the exploration and development expenses; that year this account was ordered to bear $300,000 of the expense. In 1974, the non-utility account was ordered to pay 32.88 percent of this expense, and in 1975 the amount was increased to 50 percent.

Thus, as early as 1957, the traditional principles of utility law were modified by the Commission, e. g., generally the investor supplies the risk capital and sustains the losses in a speculative venture; the ratepayer only pays a return on that portion of the investment which is found used and useful in rendering the utility service. Although the exploration and development costs which were reflected in the rates and charges were characterized as a just and reasonable expense of the utility by the Commission, these charges were, in effect, a capital contribution to a speculative venture for the purpose of developing oil and gas sources. However, these charges can be justified under the broad statutory definition of a gas plant insofar as they are used to develop property owned, controlled, operated or managed by the gas corporation, to facilitate the production of gas.

What are the consequences to Mountain Fuel of the ratepayers being the primary source of the risk capital throughout the years? Mountain Fuel responds that the consumer benefits by being assured of a continuing supply of gas, at cost of service prices.

This response is insufficient, since under the statute the charges for exploration and development can be sustained only if they were utilized on property held as a utility asset, and the property remains classified as a utility asset after it is developed. This is so regardless of the nature of the hydrocarbons recovered. Mountain Fuel sustains a trust relationship to its customers, and it has a duty to conduct its operations in such a manner as to give to the consumers the most favorable rate reasonably possible. When the expenses to develop the utility properties were included in the rate base, the ratepayers were entitled to share in the benefit by having the net profits on the oil, and other hydrocarbon substances, sold by Mountain Fuel to others, applied to reduce the cost of gas.

Mountain Fuel, according to the findings, developed a system of classification based on custom or usage. This classification was never reduced to writing by either the utility or the Commission. If the exploration and development produced a successful well, it was classified as oil or gas based on the "value of production." This system involved measuring the product at the well head, or field separator facility, and then comparing the field price of gas and oil. Whichever substance had greater value determined whether the site was a gas or an oil well. Thus, any disparity between gas and oil prices at the time of classification could play a decisive role in determining whether it was a gas or an oil well. If it were a gas well, the drilling costs were capitalized and the well was held in a utility account, and any incidental gas and oil sales were credited to a utility account. If it were an oil well, the drilling costs were capitalized and held in the non-utility account; any associated gas was credited at field price to the non-utility account. In addition, any acreage logically related to the discovery was transferred and capitalized in the corresponding account.

. . .

The properties in the non-utility account, under this classification system, were the subject matter of the purchase and sale agreement. In its initial determination, the Commission limited the issue as to whether the properties in the non-utility account, which Mountain Fuel proposed to transfer to Wexpro, were properly held in this account under Mountain Fuel's system of classification. The Commission reasoned if they were non-utility properties under Mountain Fuel's classification, the Commission had no jurisdiction. The petitioners urged until there was an evidentiary hearing to determine whether, in fact, these properties were non-utility assets, there was an insufficient factual basis to determine the issue of the Commission's jurisdiction. We agree.

The classification of this property is of utmost importance, since this property is being transferred to Wexpro at a depreciated book value of $33.1 million. The claimed gross revenue from this property for 1976 was approximately $39 million. An expert from Mountain Fuel estimated the fair market value of the property at $150 million. If, in fact, after a hearing the property should be classified as a utility asset, the ratepayers by this transfer, would be deprived of benefits to which they are entitled.

The net effect of the Commission's initial determination was that their jurisdiction was based on Mountain Fuel's classification. This classification, in turn, was based on the value of production; and whether the substance was deemed gas or oil was based upon the end use of the product. There is no statutory or legal basis to sustain such a classification. . . .

. . .

The order approving the amended purchase and sale agreement must be reversed, and there must be an evidentiary hearing. The Commission must reassess the transfer and determine whether the properties were utility assets. The following is the criteria by which the properties should be classified:

(1) Was the property, while undeveloped, held in the utility capital account (Account #105), upon which a rate of return was paid by the ratepayers?

(2) Were any funds from the utility exploration and development expense accounts (Accounts #795, #796, #797, and #798) applied to the development of the acreage?

(3) Has any natural gas or natural gas liquids been produced from the acreage?

If the answer to any of these is in the affirmative, the assets are utility property. Any transfer of a utility asset should be for fair market value so an appropriate benefit therefrom will redound to the credit of the ratepayers. Furthermore, before approving the transfer of a utility asset, the Commission should determine whether the transaction is detrimental to the ratepayer, and whether it is in the public interest.

. . .

[As to Mountain Fuel's claim that a different system of classification of their assets would constitute a confiscation of property, the court held]:

There are elements of fantasy involved in the claim that a utility asset, which has been held and developed as a utility expense, undergoes a transfiguration into a non-utility asset by virtue of the value of the type of hydrocarbons recovered. To claim the "oil" operations constitute a separate business is a straw man to distract the unwary. If the assets involved, under the tests set forth in this opinion, be utility assets, they are subject to regulation.

Where an activity or business is affected with the public interest, the courts have universally held that to subject such activity or business to regulation does not violate either the Fifth Amendment or the Fourteenth Amendment of the Federal Constitution.

■ ELLETT, C. J. and CROCKETT and HALL, JJ., concur.

■ STEWART, J., does not participate herein.

■ WILKINS, J., dissenting: In 1935, five small companies were merged to form Mountain Fuel. One of the companies produced oil, and its assets were categorized as non-utility and carried in accounts separate from the utility accounts which covered the four gas-producing companies. Mountain Fuel subsequently adopted and has consistently used the Uniform System of Accounts for Natural Gas Companies promulgated by the Federal Power Commission in 1940.

As Mountain Fuel's exploration and development program expanded, it discovered gas wells and oil wells and some wells which produced both. Although it discovered much more gas than oil it became necessary for Mountain Fuel to classify the wells which produced both as either gas or oil so it could assign them to the appropriate utility or non-utility account. Essentially gas was categorized as that hydrocarbon product which was capable, after contaminants and liquids were removed, of being placed in a natural gas pipeline for transmission and distribution. Oil was defined as all other hydrocarbon products which before or after treatment were, under industry standards, normally sold and transferred in a container or tank and delivered to a refinery.

Actually this definition applied only [to] . . . a small percentage of the producing wells. For example, in the ten year period from 1966 to 1976, Mountain Fuel drilled 163 successful wells and only 22 contained both gas and oil. Of those, only one had as close a ratio between gas and oil production as 60 percent to 40 percent.... If the value of the natural gas in the well exceeded that of the oil, the well was classified as a gas well. All associated expenses for drilling and completing the gas well were capitalized in the #101 utility account. If the well was classified an oil producer, all associated expenses were capitalized in the #121 non-utility account.

The Commission approved this accounting system, ruling it did not have jurisdiction over the non-utility accounts in June, 1948, November, 1953, February, 1957, July, 1968, and in February, 1972. The classification system was challenged more vigorously in this decade, when the non-utility oil accounts became enormously valuable as a result of the Organization of Petroleum Exporting Countries' ("OPEC") oil management and pricing policies which had material impact in 1973 and following years.

Mountain Fuel's exploration and development program has also been under attack in this case. Through equity and debt financing and retained earnings, Mountain Fuel has raised investment capital to purchase or lease unexplored acreage. This acreage was held for future use in Mountain Fuel's #105 utility account. Acreage in this account was treated as a capital cost, and Mountain Fuel's annual exploration and development expense, included in the rate base, was never used to finance its acquisition. The acreage in this #105 utility account has been included in the rate base, as a capital asset, to the extent that consumers paid a rate of return to shareholders on their investment in that property.

From its formation, Mountain Fuel has maintained an aggressive and extensive exploration program. It produces over 30 percent of its entire system's requirements, one of the highest percentages in the United States. This gas comes to consumers at cost of service, or about $.40 per Mcf (thousand cubic feet), rather than market price, which averaged $1.17 per Mcf in 1977, or pipeline price, which in 1977 was $1.48 per Mcf. Petitioners do not dispute Mountain Fuel's testimony that its Utah customers pay the lowest, or among the lowest, rates of any gas utility customers in the country. To develop this low-cost gas and the reserves, the Commission has allowed Mountain Fuel to reflect as one of its operating costs, an exploration expense in its rate base. Like other costs in the rate base, this exploration and development expense was paid from general corporate resources, not a special, earmarked development fund. This exploration expense paid for such items as delay rentals on exploration acreage, abandoned leases, geophysical work, and non-productive well drilling, or dry holes. It did not pay for the initial lease or purchase acquisition, successful well drilling costs, completion costs, producing costs, costs to connect the well to a pipeline, or costs to construct and maintain pipelines. These latter costs, being capital costs, were borne by Mountain Fuel through equity and debt financing and retained earnings.

Exploration expense money was used to develop acreage held in the #105 utility account. If exploration resulted in a gas discovery, the project costs to that point were ... spread prospectively over the estimated well life after transfer to the utility #101 account by capitalizing those costs and taking deductions for each year's depreciation and depletion. So, the costs of successful wells were never included in the money allotted as annual exploration and development expenses. It is the cost of lease maintenance, geophysical work, and, most importantly, dry holes, included in the rate base, which is disputed here. The Commission heard conflicting testimony on whether or not the non-utility operations paid part of the exploration expenses prior to 1972. Mountain Fuel's exhibits, including certified audit reports, show that between 1960 and 1970 the non-utility operations had paid $430,544 for dry holes, or 3.2 percent of the total exploration expenses of the company. During that same period, the revenues attributable to the non-utility accounts constituted 3.1 percent of the total company revenues....

[The justice then describes the Commission's past orders allocating increasing amounts of monies from the nonutility accounts to the utility accounts in 1972 through 1974 after Mountain Fuels efforts had discovered several oil fields.]

In the 1973 and 1974 hearings, the Commission was urged to consolidate Mountain Fuel's non-utility and utility accounts for rate-making purposes. It finally did so in its January 14, 1974 Order on the basis that the oil and natural gas operations were inseparable from each other. Trading in Mountain Fuel's stock was suspended the following day to prevent what Mountain Fuel characterized as financial disaster. One week later the Commission entered an Order setting aside that part of the January 14 Order merging the non-utility and utility accounts. It did not, at that time, set aside its January 14 findings. The Commission also granted a petition for rehearing, and on July 18, 1974, entered a final Order affirming the January 21, 1974 Order....

Significantly, no petition for certiorari to this Court was taken asserting the inconsistency of the January 14, 1974 findings with the January 21 or July 18, 1974 Order, and in the Final Order in the Wexpro case, the Commission found that

> "the language of the January 14 Report and Order in Case No. 6668 with respect to the ratepayer risk, ratepayer rip-off and exploitation of Mountain Fuel customers is erroneous and should not stand as fact or law. All prior and subsequent Orders of the Commission reached an opposite conclusion based on a correct balancing of the interests of customers and shareholders of the company and this Commission herein affirms that long line of precedent...."

Regulatory jurisdiction over the non-utility operations has continued to be at issue in every Mountain Fuel rate case since 1974. This has resulted in substantial shareholder unrest as well as uncertainty in the capital markets. Early in 1976, some Mountain Fuel shareholders waged a proxy battle for control of the company, the central issue of which was the continued attack on the non-utility properties. The commission in this case heard testimony that Mountain Fuel was unable to market a $20,000,000 common equity issuance of stock because of this uncertainty, and that Wexpro has also been unable to engage in capital financing. As long as Mountain Fuel remains a publicly held, capital intensive corporation, its financial capabilities are of extreme importance to the Commission. The evidence before the Commission disclosed that it is imperative that Mountain Fuel be able to finance its capital expenditures, for when the company falters, rates increase, utility services deteriorate, and the gas customer suffers. In short, the Commission found that a financially distressed utility benefits no one, least of all those who will have to depend on its services in the future.

To alleviate this regulatory uncertainty and to encourage successful re-entry into the capital markets, Mountain Fuel formed Wexpro, and it was for these reasons that the Commission found the [purchase and sale of assets to Wexpro] to be in the public interest.

. . .

[In this second excerpt from the dissenting opinion, Justice Wilkins summarizes how the majority determined that these oil assets were utility property under Utah's statutes (the chain of definitions which moved from the definition of "public utility" to that of "gas corporation" to that of "gas plant" to that of "real estate . . . owned . . . to facilitate the production . . . of gas) and then presents his own views]:

It seems to me that the reasoning of the majority opinion begs the vital question. Because the undeveloped property was initially placed in the #105 utility account, the Court today assumes that we are compelled by Sec. 54–2–1(17) to conclude that that property became " . . . real estate . . . (which was) owned . . . to facilitate the production . . . of gas . . ." and hence was and is utility property. . . .

Why? The record undeniably reveals that Mountain Fuel, with the approval of the Commission, segregated its non-utility oil properties from its utility accounts from the beginning, and these properties were always treated as non-utility in nature and excluded from the utility account, rate base, and rate of return. And the initial inclusion of these properties, along with gas properties when all properties were undeveloped acreage into the #105 utility account should not vitiate this traditional segregation, which has had consistent Commission approval, and thereby transform now the utility and non-utility businesses into one estate. The irony of mandating, in effect, this merger is particularly striking, I believe, when the very policy and precedent which allowed a utility and non-utility classification greatly contributed to producing the lowest, or among the lowest, gas rates to the ratepayers of Mountain Fuel in this country, as well as producing significant natural gas reserves. In short the very format of historical classification that was established, and followed, produced an exploration and development program which eventuated in signal benefits to the ratepayers, Mountain Fuel, and the stockholders.

* * *

[Justice Wilkins then addressed the three basic principles of utility law upon which the majority opinion based its findings and views. This third and final excerpt from his opinion is a good introduction to the methods used by courts to police affiliate transactions, an issue which pervades the study of energy law because many of the players in the industry have a network of affiliates in both related and unrelated enterprises:]

These [three] principles are: first, that public utilities sustain a trust relationship to their ratepayers; second, that risk capital for utility development is provided by investors in the utility and that property is included in the rate base to the extent that it is used and useful; and third, that any amount paid to a company as a profit by a utility which controls that company cannot be included as a charge in the rate base (the "no profits to affiliates" rule). I disagree with these principles or the majority's application of them to this case.

First, I find no statutory authority in this State's Public Utility Code, or any case law in Utah supporting the proposition that the relationship between a public utility and its ratepayers is fiduciary or one of trust. As a regulated monopoly, a public utility may not do business in the same manner as it could were it not regulated. Sec. 54–4–2 imposes on the Public Service Commission the standard of regulating public utilities in a reasonable manner consistent with the public interest. If a public utility conforms its practices to the public interest, neither the Commission nor this Court have cause for misgivings. The term "public interest", however, encompasses more than protection of the class of ratepayers at the expense of all others, contrary to what I believe to be the implication of the majority opinion. It necessitates balancing the interests of the utility's ratepayers, its shareholders and the public itself within the utility's area of service. Until the Legislature amends the statutes to provide for a trust or fiduciary responsibility from the utility to its ratepayers, this Court, I believe, should adhere to those statutory mandates now in force as the Commission below has done.

Second, I have no quarrel with the observation made in the majority opinion that utility shareholders provide risk capital. I address the majority's use of that principle *infra* in this dissent. But here, I comment on references in the majority opinion to facilities (undeveloped acreage) which are used and useful to the consumer as includable assets in the rate base for reasons now noted. Traditionally, this undeveloped acreage in this case was included in the rate base. But the majority opinion weaves that fact into an argument that this inclusion was justified under a broad definition of a gas plant in Sec. 54–2–1(17), . . . and makes the oil properties utility properties.

The argument eludes me. Rather than concluding, as does the majority opinion, that ". . . traditional principles of utility law were modified . . ." by the Commission in permitting this inclusion, but that Sec. 54–2–1(17) justifies this modification, I find another analysis to be legally sounder. It may be, arguendo, that a rate of return should not traditionally have been allowed on this acreage, but the question of placing the undeveloped acreage in the #105 utility account, and the Commission's allowance thereof, was not addressed, argued or appealed to this Court at the times the acreage was placed in that account, nor in the petition for certiorari in this case. So that question is not before us. And that error, if any particularly in view of all of the evidence in this case, does not, in some self-propelling manner convert unregulated oil into a regulated category under the Commission.

Third, I think the "no profits to affiliates" rule has no application to the facts of this case. The cases cited by the majority opinion,[20][5] concerning profits paid to affiliated construction companies formed by their parent utilities and rights to purchase gas at cost of service reserved in a contract which was regulated by the Federal Power Commission, describe the basic tenets of this rule. Arising under federal regulatory law and cited mostly in federal cases, it has been invoked where a "dummy" corporation is formed as an affiliate to perform services for the utility (a) where the affiliate has no assets or capital of its own, or (b) where the profits paid to the affiliate were fictitious, fraudulent or collusive. The affiliate susceptible to this rule may be so dependent upon the utility that it has no legitimate business existence of its own. The rule has not been interpreted in the cases cited by the majority opinion to disallow all profits paid to affiliated companies. It is a rule narrow in scope, and Courts have cautioned against its expansion.

Cities Service Gas is easily distinguishable from the instant case. There the pipeline utility spun-off to an affiliate its utility owned and federally regulated property from which it purchased gas at cost of service. The transferred property was not non-utility, unregulated oil producing property as in the case here. When the affiliate transferred the property to a non-affiliated company, reaping a $21 million profit to the parent, the United States Court of Appeals for the Tenth Circuit, although discussing the "no profits to affiliates" rule, affirmed the Federal Power Commission's ruling to price the purchased gas at cost of service rather than the contract amount on the basis that the cost of service rate had been reserved in the Federal Power Commission's grant of the original certificate to the affiliate, which reservation could not be dissipated by alienation to a non-affiliated third party.

In the *Utah Power & Light* case, Mr. Justice Wolfe concluded for this Court that the utility's wholly owned subsidiary, a "dummy" corporation with no assets or capital of its own, was doing construction work for the parent-utility with the parent's assets, and that in such a relationship there was "no reasonable basis as far as rate making is concerned upon which it could be paid more than actual costs."

Such is not the case here. The evidence in this case discloses that Wexpro is adequately capitalized and, in my judgment, owns substantial assets. Its oil production constitutes a legitimate business objective independent of the utility-parent's, Mountain Fuel's, objectives, and it is not formed for, or involved in, the construction of a capital asset for its parent.

Florida Gas is no authority for the majority's position. Indeed, the Fifth Circuit, on remand to the Federal Power Commission, disallowed

---

5. Florida Gas Transmission Company v. Federal Power Commission, 362 F.2d 331 (5th Cir.1966); Utah Power & Light Co. v. Public Service Commission, 107 Utah 155, 152 P.2d 542 (1944); Cities Service Gas Company v. Federal Power Commission, 424 F.2d 411 (10th Cir.1969), *cert. denied*, 400 U.S. 801 (1970).

application of the "no profits to affiliates" rule. In that case, four engineering and construction firms were formed from the sale of 37.5 percent of the utility's stock, and neither the utility nor the four-company group controlled the other. The Federal Power Commission, relying on federal regulations and opinions not applicable to this case, and Section 10 of the Clayton Act, disallowed, as part of the utility's cost of service, the profits paid to the four company group. The United States Court of Appeals for the Fifth Circuit reversed the Commission because the profits paid were actual, legitimate costs, with no fraud, collusion or fiction involved in their payment, and remanded the case to the Federal Power Commission to determine whether the profits were reasonable without applying the "no profits to affiliates" rule.

In this case, none of the parties had the opportunity to address this rule below or here. Further, petitioners, after a six-month investigation and audit of Wexpro, raised no claims of fictitious, fraudulent or collusively paid profits, and do not raise such a claim here in their petition or in their briefs.

The majority opinion today heralds an unfortunate principle by applying the "no profits to affiliates" rule to this case, I believe. In so doing, it ignores the criteria outlined in the cases it cites as authority, and, further, erroneously assumes (1) that Wexpro is a utility and holds utility property, and (2) that the relationship between Mountain Fuel's utility accounts and Wexpro is so close that acts conducted between them are tantamount to a single intracompany business.

Petitioners attack the Commission's findings and conclusions that the [Wexpro purchase and sale] were in the public interest. They assert error in the Commission's failure to adopt their principle of "gain follows risk," . . . .

Such statements evince a disregard for basic accounting principles, *i.e.*, the distinction between expense and capital expenditures. Mountain Fuel, through money supplied by its investors, not its ratepayers, acquired the property it explores and develops for hydrocarbon production. This property is a capital asset, and Mountain Fuel incurred a capital, investment risk when it acquired it. Money used to explore the property, up to that point where the type of hydrocarbon production from the property is ascertained, was expense money. Part of it was acquired from the ratepayers through monies received by them in payment of their gas bills as was part of the other operating expenses of Mountain Fuel. Money which is spent for expenses is usually deducted, for tax purposes, in the year it is spent, and it is treated entirely differently than money spent to capitalize an asset. Certainly its expenditure constitutes no investment or capital risk. Simply, the ratepayer is not assuming an investment risk. The risk the ratepayer assumes because the Commission permits Mountain Fuel the expense is the risk that exploration will prove more costly than purchases from other producers. The ratepayer's reward for assuming such risk is that the savings Mountain Fuel realizes from finding its own gas must pass through to that ratepayer.

The record in this case shows that Mountain Fuel's oil has always been treated as the source of reward for those who take investment risk, whose money is used for acquisition of both oil prospects and gas prospects, and whose investment may evanesce if Mountain Fuel cannot remain competitive. The record also shows that cost savings attributable to Mountain Fuel's gas exploration program have been substantial and have passed to ratepayers. I cannot see how prospects for that kind of benefit to Mountain Fuel's customers can be enhanced by removing incentives for investors to supply capital for Mountain Fuel's lease acquisitions and oil-oriented drilling.■

NOTES AND COMMENTS

1. Now is it so obvious what is in the public interest in the Utah case? Are the basic principles of utility rate regulation so simple to apply? Should regulated enterprises be allowed to engage in any unregulated enterprises? What are the dangers to the public interest? What are the possible gains? Can stockholders of any public utility ever make a successful claim of a taking when the rules change? Many regulated industries have now formed affiliates to operate in related but deregulated areas. How should this relationship be policed to serve the public interest?

Many utilities have diversified into seemingly unrelated fields such as insurance, banking, and real estate through the formation of holding companies which segregate the nonutility subsidiaries from the utility subsidiary. The federal government, through the Securities Exchange Commission (SEC), has regulated the structure of holding companies since 1935 under the Public Utility Holding Company Act (PUHCA). Before the passage of PUHCA, utility holding companies had often operated subsidiaries in speculative ventures that contributed nothing to the effective, integrated management of the enterprises. By 1986, perhaps reflecting the success of the Act, only 12 holding companies were federally registered under PUHCA, accounting for some 20 percent of the revenues of all electric utilities in the United States. Most holding companies have been structured to be exempt from PUHCA, which shifts the burden of policing these companies from the SEC to state PUCs. For an analysis of the pros and cons of allowing regulated utilities to form unregulated subsidiaries and a proposal for effective state regulation of this structure, *see* Jeffrey Knapp, Effective State Regulation of Energy Utility Diversification, 136 U. Pa. L. Rev. 1667 (1988).

2. Many electric utilities bought or formed coal companies during the late 1960s and 1970s when oil and gas became scarce and expensive as fuels for their generating facilities. The coal company was often a "captive" of the utility in the sense that almost all of the coal company's production went to the parent utility. The coal companies were set up as separate affiliates of the utility. Do you understand why this arrangement might be worrisome to a state public utility commission? Might the parent company be tempted to buy coal from its captive at a higher-than-market price? Profits captured

in this way by the captive coal company would inure to the benefit of stockholders and to the detriment of ratepayers.

For further reading, *see* Mark Sievers, An Economic Analysis of Utility–Coal Company Relationships, 8 J. Energy L. & Policy 27 (1987) which identifies four economic problems in the utility-coal relationship: (1) the cost inflation problem (as identified *supra* in this note); (2) the coal monopoly problem; (3) the utility monopoly problem; and (4) the utility monopsony problem.

An overarching question about the current energy industry restructuring is whether competition and some "light-handed regulation" by FERC and state PUCs will suffice to police the new restructured marketplace, or whether antitrust law will be required as the policing agent that ultimately assures consumers enjoy the benefits of deregulation.

CHAPTER 8

RATE REGULATION

Outline of Chapter:

A. THE REGULATORY PROCESS

1. THEORIES OF REGULATION

The history of enterprise in the U.S. suggests a variety of rationales for regulation. Political, economic, and legal considerations are involved. Skeptics of governmental regulation (as well as many public choice economists) may describe regulation as the result of strong political forces—whether industry, environmental groups, or consumers—mustering the support to protect their interests.[1] By contrast, as is discussed in Chapter Three, many neoclassical economists explain regulation as a response to the market failures introduced by natural monopoly, ensuring that prices and quantities in naturally monopolistic markets approximate those of a competitive market. Still another theory of regulation is based on deliberative democracy—that some enterprises are inextricably linked to the public good and the process of government regulation is most likely to promote the public interest, rather than purely private gain.[2]

---

1. A good summary of this literature is included in George Priest, The Origins of Regulation and the "Theories of Regulation" Debate, 36 J. L. Econ. & Org. 289 (1993). For early works arguing this general thesis *see* Sam Peltzman, Towards a More General Theory of Regulation, 19 J. L. & Econ. 211 (1976); George Stigler, The Theory of Economic Regulation, 2 Bell J. Econ. & Mgmt. Sci. 3 (1971).

2. *See* Paul L. Joskow & Roger Noll, Regulation in Theory and Practice: An Overview, in Studies in Public Utility Regulation (Gary Fromm, ed., MIT Press 1981).

While all of these theories provide a useful and relevant lens through which to view public utility regulation, perhaps the most powerful analytical tool—indeed, the tool most widely accepted by regulators in market economies—comes from the neoclassical economists. We live in a market economy, one in which competition is valued both for its process and its outcomes.

As was discussed in Chapter 3, the neoclassical economic model views regulation as a tool to approximate the behavior of a firm in a perfectly competitive market. A perfectly competitive market assumes certain conditions: a firm faces multiple buyers and sellers in the market, all firms and buyers have equal access to information, the costs of transaction between any seller and buyer are extremely low, and there are no significant impediments to market entry and exit. Given such conditions, the neoclassical economic model shows that perfectly competitive firms will price their products or services at marginal cost—the cost to the firm of producing one additional unit of output. If a firm prices above marginal cost, the lure of economic profits will result in new firms entering the market and, as supply increases, driving price downward towards marginal cost. By contrast, if a firm was to price below marginal cost, the cost of each new unit of production or sales would exceed the revenue from the additional unit; since firms cannot stay in operation for long if their costs exceed their revenues, some firms would be likely to exit such a market and, as supply decreases, drive price upward towards marginal cost.

However, most markets which are price regulated are not perfectly competitive. While a perfectly competitive market marks one extreme of the neoclassical market spectrum (indeed, its ideal), at the other end of the spectrum is natural monopoly: a market that can be served at a lower average cost by a single firm than by two or more firms. As was illustrated in Chapter Three, a market is a natural monopoly if it faces decreasing average costs over its entire range of production; a single firm in such a market could increase its production or sales at a lower average cost than if a new entrant were to also compete in the market.

Consider, for example, electricity distribution. Assume that one firm serves the entire city of Chicago by building a local transmission network to reach all customers and by centralizing its power generation and distribution decisions. Once a firm has built a transmission network to serve a fraction of the customers throughout this densely populated urban area (say the largest customers, such as factories, hotels, and large retail establishments), it will be cheaper for that same firm to increase its customer base incrementally than for a new firm to begin a network from scratch to serve additional customers (such as smaller residential customers). Indeed, we could imagine the unnecessary duplication that would result if multiple utilities were required to build transmission lines to the same neighborhoods to provide electricity to different customers. Electricity distribution is characterized by economies of scale: the cost of transmitting electricity decreases over the entire range of production for the market.

Thus, it is cheaper for a single firm to expand its operations than for additional firms to enter the market.

For this reason, governments grant certain utilities and common carriers a monopoly franchise to provide service to a specified geographic area. A monopoly is able to provide more reliable and economic service in markets that face significant economies of scale.

However, once a utility has been granted a monopoly franchise, this raises a new problem: the specter of monopoly pricing. It is well established that the monopolist faces strong incentives to charge a price higher and produce less of a good or service than a perfectly competitive market would yield. For this reason, monopoly franchises are typically subject to some sort of price regulation.[3]

2. REGULATORY AGENCIES

Although the concept of a public utility has common law roots, today most utility regulation begins with a provision of a statute or state constitution that designates the enterprises to be regulated and the type of regulatory powers that may be exercised over them.

At the national level, public utility regulation is implemented by the Federal Energy Regulatory Commission (FERC), formerly the Federal Power Commission (FPC). FERC derives its regulatory powers from three primary statutes: the Natural Gas Act (NGA), which regulates natural gas sales; the Federal Power Act (FPA), which regulates sales of electricity for resale (i.e., wholesale sales) in interstate commerce; and the Interstate Commerce Act (ICA), which gives FERC jurisdiction over the shipment of oil by pipeline. As outlined in Chapter 4, FERC is composed of five commissioners appointed by the President and confirmed by the Senate. Commissioners are appointed for a term of four years, but no more than three members of FERC can be from the same political party. FERC is an "independent" agency: it performs legislative functions and the President's removal power is limited. In addition to limitations on the number of FERC members from a single political party, the President may only remove FERC commissioners for "inefficiency, neglect of duty, or malfeasance in office," not for simple disagreement with policies. 42 U.S.C. § 7171. In addition to its five commissioners, FERC employs a staff of approximately 1500, which includes lawyers, accountants, engineers, and economists as well as "street-level" bureaucrats.

State regulatory control is exercised by a specialized agency of government called the Public Service Commission, Public Utility Commission, Railroad Commission, or Corporation Commission. (These state agencies, discussed in Chapter 3, will be referred to generically as "PSCs.") The

---

3. Some argue that the presence of a single firm need not necessarily lead to monopolistic pricing. *See* Harold Demsetz, Why Regulate Utilities?, 9 J. L. & Econ. 55 (1968). In addition, more modern work in contesta-ble market theory calls into question monopoly pricing. *See* Elizabeth E. Bailey and William J. Baumol, Deregulation and the Theory of Contestable Markets, 1 Yale J. on Reg. 111 (1984).

practice for selecting PSC members varies from state to state: some are elected, while others are appointed by the state governor or legislature. Similar to the FERC, most PSCs have a staff of lawyers, accountants, engineers, and economists, although the training and experience of the staff members varies widely from state to state.

While both FERC and state PSCs have the power to initiate actions on their own, they are generally reactive regulatory bodies. A regulated utility will come to the agency to increase its rates or change its existing structure. Alternatively, a prospective entrant may seek to provide service in a regulated market, drawing complaints from customers or competitors. Agencies will often be asked to resolve such matters.

Although the process varies from state to state and in different contexts at the federal level, most public utility regulation imposes the following general requirements:

1) **Certificate of Convenience and Necessity:** The business must obtain permission to enter into and operate within the regulated market. This is achieved by securing a "certificate of convenience and necessity."

2) **Monopoly Franchise:** As part of this licensing process, the government often creates a monopoly by establishing an exclusive geographic franchise. Within this service area, the utility has the right to serve the market without competition.

3) **Duty to Serve:** In return for this exclusive service territory, the government often requires the utility to provide a certain level of service to all customers within the service territory. The utility has a duty to serve customers and cannot selectively choose its customer base for its own private gain, nor may it abandon facilities without PSC approval.

4) **Price Regulation:** The regulatory body will allow the utility to charge only "just and reasonable" rates to customers. This is normally done on the basis of the cost of providing service to each class of customers.

For example, consider two separate industries: food packaging and electricity distribution. A new entrant to the food packaging business (Packco) need not seek government permission to build and operate its plant. However, before building a power transmission line, a power generator (Genco) must obtain a certificate of convenience and necessity from the relevant state authority, usually a PSC. Packco will likely compete with numerous other food packaging companies within the same geographic market. By contrast, Genco may seek an exclusive service territory and may ask the PSC to grant a monopoly franchise. If the PSC has approved Genco's franchise, Genco will no longer face competition in this geographic area. If granted a franchise, the PSC will require Genco to serve all customers within its territory and will ensure that it charges these customers just and reasonable rates. Packco, however, will continue to face competition from other food packaging companies, as well as potential new entrants to the food packaging business. Although certain aspects of the food packaging business may be regulated, such as the information that may be presented on certain products and the materials that may be used,

Packco will charge the price that the market yields, not a price set by regulators.

B. Principles of Rate Regulation

1. Regulation of Rates Based on Cost of Service

As is discussed in Chapter Three, rate regulation is one way of limiting losses, in higher price and reduced output, associated with granting a monopoly. At the same time, rate regulation is designed to assure that a regulated firm earns what it needs to remain in business. Regulators achieve these goals by attempting price at a level that would approximate a competitive market. Since no comparable competitive market for natural monopoly services exists, regulators set rates based on the cost of service, including a fair rate of return on investment.

Cost of service regulation begins with calculation of a firm's revenue requirements—i.e., the total amount a utility needs to recover from its customers to cover its costs. Revenue requirements (R) can be stated as the following formula:

$R = B^*r + O$

The variables to this formula include:

> R the utility's revenue requirement—the total amount the firm needs to recover from its customers to cover its costs.
>
> B the utility's rate base, representing its capital investment in plant and other assets.
>
> r the rate of return regulators allow the utility to earn on its rate base.
>
> O the utility's operating expenses, or expenses such as fuel and labor that may vary with its level of production.

This formula may be deceptive, since the calculation of R is rarely simple, but it expresses the basic components and the details are discussed further below. Once R has been calculated, rates can be set for customers. For example, if rates are set on a per unit basis for customers, $P = R/V$ where P is the price per unit the firm is permitted to charge, R is the firm's allowed revenue requirements, and V is the number of units of volume of the product the firm expects to sell.

a. RATE BASE AND RATE OF RETURN

Rate base, B, and rate of return, r, are often treated as distinct issues in rate cases before regulatory commissions. Each of these elements has been the subject of much litigation. What legal protections constrain application of this formula for the protection of consumers? For investors and utilities? The following case, decided by the Supreme Court in an era in which the Court was beginning to recognize stronger constitutional protections of private property under a doctrine known as "substantive due process," illustrates some of the legal limitations on the setting of utility rates.

Smyth v. Ames

169 U.S. 466 (1898).

[Railroads argued that a Nebraska statute establishing maximum rates applicable to rail service within the state violated the constitutional prohibition on taking private property without just compensation. After comparing the revenues each railroad would have earned by charging the prescribed rate with each railroad's operating costs for each of several years, the Court addressed the issue of rate base.]

■ HARLAN, J.: A corporation maintaining a public highway, although it owns the property it employs for accomplishing public objects, must be held to have accepted its rights, privileges and franchises subject to the condition that the government creating it, or the government within whose limits it conducts its business, may by legislation protect the people against unreasonable charges for the services rendered by it. It cannot be assumed that any railroad corporation, accepting franchises, rights and privileges at the hands of the public, ever supposed that it acquired, or that it was intended to grant to it, the power to construct and maintain a public highway simply for its benefit, without regard to the rights of the public. But it is equally true that the corporation performing such public services and the people financially interested in its business and affairs have rights that may not be invaded by legislative enactment in disregard of the fundamental guarantees for the protection of property. The corporation may not be required to use its property for the benefit of the public without receiving just compensation for the services rendered by it. How such compensation may be ascertained, and what are the necessary elements in such an inquiry, will always be an embarrassing question. As said in [*Turnpike Co. v. Sandford,* 164 U.S. 578, 596, 597,]:

> "Each case must depend upon its special facts; and when a court, without assuming itself to prescribe rates, is required to determine whether the rates prescribed by the legislature for a corporation controlling a public highway are, as an entirety, so unjust as to destroy the value of its property for all the purposes for which it was acquired, its duty is to take into consideration the interests both of the public and of the owner of the property, together with all other circumstances that are fairly to be considered in determining whether the legislature has, under the guise of regulating rates, exceeded its constitutional authority, and practically deprived the owner of property without due process of law.... The utmost that any corporation operating a public highway can rightfully demand at the hands of the legislature, when exerting its general powers, is that it receive what, under all the circumstances, is such compensation for the use of its property as will be just both to it and to the public."

We hold, however, that the basis of all calculations as to the reasonableness of rates to be charged by a corporation maintaining a highway under legislative sanction must be the fair value of the property being used by it for the convenience of the public. And in order to ascertain that value, the original cost of construction, the amount expended in permanent improvements, the amount and market value of its bonds and stock, the present as compared with the original cost of construction, the probable earning capacity of the property under particular rates prescribed by statute, and the sum required to meet operating expenses, are all matters for consideration, and are to be given such weight as may be just and right in each case. We do not say that there may not be other matters to be regarded in estimating the value of the property. What the company is entitled to ask is a fair return upon the value of that which it employs for the public convenience. On the other hand, what the public is entitled to demand is that no more be exacted from it for the use of a public highway than the services rendered by it are reasonably worth. But even upon this basis, and determining the probable effect of the act of 1893 by ascertaining what could have been its effect if it had been in operation during the three years immediately preceding its passage, we perceive no ground on the record for reversing the decree of the Circuit Court. On the contrary, we are of opinion that as to most of the companies in question there would have been, under such rates as were established by the act of 1893, an actual loss in each of the years ending June 30, 1891, 1892 and 1893; and that, in the exceptional cases above stated, when two of the companies would have earned something above operating expenses, in particular years, the receipts or gains, above operating expenses, would have been too small to affect the general conclusion that the act, if enforced, would have deprived each of the railroad companies involved in these suits of the just compensation secured to them by the Constitution. Under the evidence there is no ground for saying that the operating expenses of any of the companies were greater than necessary.■

NOTES AND COMMENTS

1. Does this case concern rate base or rate of return? Because *Smyth v. Ames* is generally concerned with the "fair value of the property being used," it is more concerned with a utility's assets, or rate base, than its rate of return, or the cost the utility must pay to attract investors.

2. How helpful is the term "fair value" as a substantive legal requirement? The Court suggests that four criteria are relevant in the determination of "fair value": 1) "original cost of construction"; 2) "the amount and market values of [the utility's] bonds and stocks"; 3) "the present as compared with the original cost of construction"; 4) "the probable earning capacity of the property under particular rates prescribed." Does this give PSCs and subsequent courts a meaningful standard to apply? Is there any difference between 2) and 4)? Are these really concerns in calculating rate base?

3. As is discussed below, later cases repudiate the "fair value" doctrine. The doctrine did, however, reign during the *Lochner* era. *See* Stephen A, Siegel, Understanding the *Lochner* Era: Lessons from the Controversy Over Railroad and Utility Rate Regulation, 70 Va. L. Rev. 187 (1984).

* * *

Smyth v. Ames is now only history, but the following cases both remain good law:

Bluefield Water Works & Improvement Co. v. Public Service Commission

262 U.S. 679 (1923).

■ BUTLER, J.: The company contends that the rate of return is too low and confiscatory. What annual rate will constitute just compensation depends upon many circumstances and must be determined by the exercise of a fair and enlightened judgment, having regard to all relevant facts. A public utility is entitled to such rates as will permit it to earn a return on the value of the property which it employs for the convenience of the public equal to that generally being made at the same time and in the same general part of the country on investments in other business undertakings which are attended by corresponding risks and uncertainties; but it has no constitutional right to profits such as are realized or anticipated in highly profitable enterprises or speculative ventures. The return should be reasonably sufficient to assure confidence in the financial soundness of the utility and should be adequate, under efficient and economical management, to maintain and support its credit and enable it to raise the money necessary for the proper discharge of its public duties. A rate of return may be reasonable at one time and become too high or too low by changes affecting opportunities for investment, the money market and business conditions generally.■

Federal Power Commission v. Hope Natural Gas Co.

320 U.S. 591 (1944).

■ DOUGLAS, J.: The primary issue in these cases concerns the validity under the Natural Gas Act of 1938 (52 Stat. 821, 15 U.S.C. 717) of a rate order issued by the Federal Power Commission reducing the rates chargeable by Hope Natural Gas Co. . . .

The Commission established an interstate rate base of $33,712,526 which, it found, represented the "actual legitimate cost" of the company's interstate property less depletion and depreciation and plus unoperated acreage, working capital and future net capital additions. The Commission, beginning with book cost, made certain adjustments not necessary to relate here and found the "actual legitimate cost" of the plant in interstate service to be $51,957,416, as of December 31, 1940. It deducted accrued depletion and depreciation, which it found to be $22,328,016 on an "economic-service-life" basis. . . .

Hope introduced evidence from which it estimated reproduction cost of the property at $97,000,000. It also presented a so-called trended "original cost" estimate which exceeded $105,000,000. The latter was designed "to indicate what the original cost of the property would have been if 1938 material and labor prices had prevailed throughout the whole period of the piecemeal construction of the company's property since 1898." 44 PUR. (N. S.), pp. 8–9. Hope estimated by the "per cent condition" method accrued depreciation at about 35% of reproduction cost new. On that basis Hope contended for a rate base of $66,000,000. The Commission refused to place any reliance on reproduction cost new, saying that it was "not predicated upon facts" and was "too conjectural and illusory to be given any weight in these proceedings." *Id.*, p. 8. It likewise refused to give any "probative value" to trended "original cost" since it was "not founded in fact" but was "basically erroneous" and produced "irrational results." . . .

The fixing of prices, like other applications of the police power, may reduce the value of the property which is being regulated. But the fact that the value is reduced does not mean that the regulation is invalid. *Block v. Hirsh*, 256 U.S. 135, 155–157; *Nebbia v. New York*, 291 U.S. 502, 523–539 and cases cited. It does, however, indicate that "fair value" is the end product of the process of rate-making not the starting point as the Circuit Court of Appeals held. The heart of the matter is that rates cannot be made to depend upon "fair value" when the value of the going enterprise depends on earnings under whatever rates may be anticipated.

We held in *Federal Power Commission v. Natural Gas Pipeline Co., supra*, that the Commission was not bound to the use of any single formula or combination of formulae in determining rates. Its rate-making function, moreover, involves the making of "pragmatic adjustments." p. 586. And when the Commission's order is challenged in the courts, the question is whether that order "viewed in its entirety" meets the requirements of the Act. *Id.*, p. 586. Under the statutory standard of "just and reasonable" it is the result reached not the method employed which is controlling. *Cf. Los Angeles Gas & Electric Corp. v. Railroad Commission*, 289 U.S. 287, 304–305, 314; *West Ohio Gas Co. v. Public Utilities Commission (No. 1)*, 294 U.S. 63, 70; *West v. Chesapeake & Potomac Tel. Co.*, 295 U.S. 662, 692–693 (dissenting opinion). It is not theory but the impact of the rate order which counts. If the total effect of the rate order cannot be said to be unjust and unreasonable, judicial inquiry under the Act is at an end. The fact that the method employed to reach that result may contain infirmities is not then important. Moreover, the Commission's order does not become suspect by reason of the fact that it is challenged. It is the product of expert judgment which carries a presumption of validity. And he who would upset the rate order under the Act carries the heavy burden of making a convincing showing that it is invalid because it is unjust and unreasonable in its consequences. . . .

The rate-making process under the Act, i.e., the fixing of "just and reasonable" rates, involves a balancing of the investor and the consumer interests. Thus we stated in the *Natural Gas Pipeline Co.* case that "regulation does not insure that the business shall produce net revenues." 315 U.S. p. 590. But such considerations aside, the investor interest has a legitimate concern with the financial integrity of the company whose rates are being regulated. From the investor or company point of view it is important that there be enough revenue not only for operating expenses but also for the capital costs of the business. These include service on the debt and dividends on the stock. *Cf. Chicago & Grand Trunk Ry. Co. v. Wellman*, 143 U.S. 339, 345–346. By that standard the return to the equity owner should be commensurate with returns on investments in other enterprises having corresponding risks. That return, moreover, should be sufficient to assure confidence in the financial integrity of the enterprise, so as to maintain its credit and to attract capital. *See Missouri ex rel. Southwestern Bell Tel. Co. v. Public Service Commission*, 262 U.S. 276, 291 (Mr. Justice Brandeis concurring). The conditions under which more or less might be allowed are not important here. Nor is it important to this case to determine the various permissible ways in which any rate base on which the return is computed might be arrived at. For we are of the view that the end result in this case cannot be condemned under the Act as unjust and unreasonable from the investor or company viewpoint. . . .

As we have noted, the Commission fixed a rate of return which permits Hope to earn $2,191,314 annually. In determining that amount it stressed the importance of maintaining the financial integrity of the company. It considered the financial history of Hope and a vast array of data bearing on the natural gas industry, related businesses, and general economic conditions. . . .

In view of these various considerations we cannot say that an annual return of $2,191,314 is not "just and reasonable" within the meaning of the Act. Rates which enable the company to operate successfully, to maintain its financial integrity, to attract capital, and to compensate its investors for the risks assumed certainly cannot be condemned as invalid, even though they might produce only a meager return on the so-called "fair value" rate base.■

Market St. R.R. Co. v. R.R. Comm. of California

324 U.S. 548 (1945).

■ JACKSON, J.: The Market Street Railway Company at the commencement of these proceedings operated a system of passenger transportation by street car and by bus in San Francisco and its environs. The Railroad Commission of California instituted on its own motion an inquiry into the Company's rates and service. After hearings, an order was promulgated reducing the fare from seven to six cents. The Company obtained review by the Supreme Court of California. It also obtained a stay of the Commission's order, conditioned upon impounding the disputed one cent per passenger to abide settlement of the issues upon which its ownership would depend. The Supreme Court of California affirmed the order and appeal is taken to this Court.

Meanwhile the Company sold its operative properties to the City of San Francisco. The case is saved from being moot only because its decision is necessary to determine whether the Company is entitled to the impounded portion of the fares or whether the money shall be refunded to passengers making claims and unclaimed amounts thereof be paid over to the state, as required by conditions of the stay order.

The appeal raises constitutional issues only. The contention is that the order [is] a taking of its property [since] it would force the Company to operate at a loss because the Commission used a rate base of $7,950,000, the price at which appellant had offered to sell its operative properties to the City, and did not consider reproduction cost, historical cost, prudent investment, or capitalization bases, on any of which under conventional accounting the six-cent fare would produce no return on its property and would force a substantial operating deficit upon the Company.

The appellant ... invokes many decisions of this Court in which statements have been made that seem to support its contentions. But it should be noted at the outset that most of our cases deal with utilities which had earning opportunities, and public regulation curtailed earnings otherwise possible. But if there were no public regulation at all, this appellant would be a particularly ailing unit of a generally sick industry. The problem of reconciling the patrons' needs and the investors' rights in an enterprise that has passed its zenith of opportunity and usefulness, whose investment already is impaired by economic forces, and whose earning possibilities are already invaded by competition from other forms of transportation, is quite a different problem. The Company's practical situation throws important light on the question of whether the rate reduction has taken its property.

Transportation history of San Francisco follows a pattern not unfamiliar. This property has passed through cycles of competition, consolidation and monopoly, and new forms of competition; it has seen days of prosperity, decline, and salvage. In the 1850's an omnibus service began to operate in San Francisco. In the 1860's came the horse car. The 1870's saw the beginning of the cable car, for which the contour of the city was peculiarly adapted. The Market Street Railway Company was incorporated in 1893 and took over 11 of the 17 street car lines then independently operated in the city. In 1902, United Railroads of San Francisco was organized. This consolidated under one operating control properties of the Market Street Company and five other lines, comprising 229 miles of track, much of which was cable-operated. It suffered greatly from the earthquake and fire of 1906, but carried out a considerable program of reconstruction between 1906 and 1910. In 1921 it failed to pay interest on outstanding bonds. Bondholders acquired the properties and revived the Market Street Railway Company, which had been a dormant subsidiary of United, to operate them.

In 1912 the City and County of San Francisco began operation of a municipal street railway line. This line is not and never has been under the Railroad Commission's jurisdiction. It expanded rapidly, its routes in some instances parallel those of appellant, and its competition has been serious. Throughout the period of competition the municipal lines have operated on a five-cent fare. The Market Street Line also operated on a five-cent fare until July 6, 1937. In that year it applied to the Commission for an increase to a seven-cent fare. This was denied, but a two-cent transfer charge and other adjustments were authorized. In March 1938 the Company again petitioned for a seven-cent fare, with reduction for school children. The Commission authorized a seven-cent fare, but required some concession to token buyers. A few months later the Company again asked a straight seven-cent fare and relief from the token rate. The Commission directed the Company to apply to the City for permission to abandon certain lines and to protect it against "jitney competition," stipulating that the seven-cent fare could be made effective if the City failed to respond. The City did not act, and the seven-cent fare became effective January 1, 1939.

But the increase of fare brought no increase of revenue. Both traffic and revenue continued to decline, and in 1941 reached the lowest point in twenty years. Then came war, bringing accelerated activity, increase of population of the city, rubber and gas shortage, restrictions on purchase of new and retirement of many old automobiles. Traffic and revenues showed a sudden increase. The Commission found, however, that the service had constantly deteriorated and was worse under the seven-cent fare than under the former five-cent rate. It recognized that some of the causes were beyond the Company's control. But after allowance for those causes, it also found evidence of long-time neglect, mismanagement, and indifference to urgent public need. It found the Company's service inferior to the service of the municipal lines, although appellant charged a 40 per cent higher fare. Defects in service consisted of failure to operate on schedule, long intervals between cars, followed by several cars operating with little headway, overloading, inadequate inspection, and inadequately maintained rolling stock. The Company had some 70 cars out of operation and in storage because of shortage of manpower. Its street car rolling stock was obsolete, 73 electric cars and 12 cable cars being out of service. None of the cars was modern. . . .

Reviewing the financial results of fare increases, the Commission concluded that the Company would reap no lasting benefit from rates in excess of five cents, due to the tendency of a higher rate to discourage patronage. The war traffic the Commission thought temporary. But it concluded that a six-cent fare would sufficiently stimulate traffic to leave after operating expenses approximately a six per cent return on a rate base of $7,950,000. This was the figure at which the Company had offered to sell its operative properties to the City. Accordingly the Commission found the six cents to be a reasonable rate to the Company and to be all or more than the reasonable value of the services being rendered to patrons. It considered this rate to be experimental and kept the proceeding open for such further orders as might be just and reasonable. The Company applied for rehearing on substantially the grounds it urges here. Its arguments were considered at length in an opinion which denied rehearing. The Supreme Court of California overruled all of the Company's objections and affirmed the Commission's order.

The reduced rate never took effect. The Company obtained delay from the Commission and a stay order from the Court. It then sold its properties to the City, which took over and continued the seven-cent fare. So the anticipations of the Commission as to increased patronage from the rate reduction never have been put to the test of experience. Our review considers only whether the order was valid when and as made.

The order is asserted to be invalid because it is said to be confiscatory and to compel appellant to operate at a loss. The Commission used a rate base of $7,950,000, the price at which the property had been offered to the City, and the six-cent rate is not calculated to permit any return on a greater valuation. Before we consider the validity of this rate base, we may well consider what alternatives the case presents. No study of the present cost of reproduction is shown, no present fair value is suggested. Nor do we think it important. Apart from familiar objections to the reproduction-cost method, no responsible person would think of reproducing the present plant, consisting in substantial part of cable cars and obsolete equipment. There is no basis for assuming that anyone, in the light of conditions which prevail in the street-surface railroad industry generally, would consider reproducing any street railway system. It was no constitutional error to proceed to fix a rate in disregard of theoretical reproduction costs.

The Commission in 1920 made a valuation study of appellant's properties and found an historical reproduction cost of road and equipment to be $29,715,147. This valuation, brought forward by adding additions and betterments and deducting retirements, shows a total amount for road and equipment as of December 31, 1942 of $25,343,543.

Actual investment is not disclosed by the record. It does disclose that the book value of appellant's properties as of December 31, 1942 was $41,768,505.20.

The Company's outstanding securities at the end of 1942, issued with the approval of the Commission, totaled $37,921,323.96 at face value. They consisted of common stock of over $10,000,000; 3 different classes of preferred stock of $21,000,000; first mortgage bonds of $4,217,500; equipment notes of $735,748.28; and additional long-term debt of $1,041,625.68.

Not one of these nor any combination of them affords a practical or possible rate base, nor does the Company suggest that allowance of any rate will earn it a return upon any of these. It has not itself ventured to ask a rate higher than seven cents, although the inadequacy of its yield to take care of the financial requirements of the Company has for some time been apparent. This company obviously is up against a sort of law of diminishing returns; the greater amount it collects per ride, the less amount it collects per car mile. It has long been recognized that this form of transportation could be preserved only by the most complete cooperation between management and public and the most enlightened efforts to make the service attractive to patrons.[8][4] It is obvious that, for whatever cause, the appellant has not succeeded in maintaining its service on a paying basis.

It is idle to discuss holdings of cases or to distinguish quotations in decisions of this or other courts which have dealt with utilities whose economic situation would yield a permanent profit, denied or limited only by public regulation. While the Company does not assert that it would be economically practicable to obtain a return on its investment, it strongly contends that the order is confiscatory by the tests of *Federal Power Commission v. Hope Natural Gas Co.*, 320 U.S. 591, 603, 605, from which it claims to be entitled to a return "sufficient to assure confidence in the financial integrity of the enterprise, so as to maintain its credit and to attract capital" and to "enable the company to operate successfully, to maintain its financial integrity, to attract capital, and to compensate its investors for the risks assumed." Those considerations, advanced in that case (which was reviewed pursuant to statute rather than under the Fourteenth Amendment), concerned a company which had advantage of an economic position which promised to yield what was held to be an excessive return on its investment and on its securities. They obviously are inapplicable to a company whose financial integrity already is hopelessly undermined, which could not attract capital on any possible rate, and where investors recognize as lost a part of what they have put in. It was noted in the *Hope Natural Gas* case that regulation does not assure that the regulated business make a profit. 320 U.S. at 603; *see Federal Power Commission v. Natural Gas Pipeline Co.*, 315 U.S. 575, 590. All that was held was that a company could not complain if the return which was allowed made it possible for the company to operate successfully. There was no suggestion that less might not be allowed when the amount allowed was all that the company could earn. Without analyzing rate cases in detail, it may be safely generalized that the due process clause never has been held by this Court to require a commission to fix rates on the present reproduction value of something no one would presently want to reproduce, or on the historical valuation of a property whose history and current financial statements showed the value no longer to exist, or on an investment after it

---

4. In May of 1919 the Secretary of Commerce and the Secretary of Labor joined in a letter to President Wilson, advising him that 50 or more urban street railway systems representing a considerable percentage of the electric railway mileage was in the hands of receivers, affecting some of the largest cities of the country, and that other systems were on the verge of insolvency and the industry as a whole was virtually bankrupt. They urged the appointment of a commission to study and report upon the problem. President Wilson on June 1, 1919 named a commission which held extensive public hearings. The first witness was ex-President William Howard Taft, speaking for the National War Labor Board, and others, including leading municipal and railway officials and such experienced persons in the problem of regulation as Newton D. Baker, Milo R. Maltbie, Morris L. Cook, Joseph B. Eastman, and many others. Proceedings of the Federal Electric Railways Commission, v. 1. An exhaustive report with many recommendations was made. *See* Analysis of the Electric Railway Problem prepared for the Federal Electric Railways Commission by De Los F. Wilcox, New York City, 1921. Its recommendations were extensive, including certain changes both by the municipalities and by the companies affected. The recommendations were not generally heeded by either.

has vanished, even if once prudently made, or to maintain the credit of a concern whose securities already are impaired. The due process clause has been applied to prevent governmental destruction of existing economic values. It has not and cannot be applied to insure values or to restore values that have been lost by the operation of economic forces.

The owners of a property dedicated to the public service cannot be said to suffer injury if a rate is fixed for an experimental period, which probably will produce a fair return on the present fair value of their property. If it has lost all value except salvage, they suffer no loss if they earn a return on salvage value. If the property has no prospect of salvage except through dismantling and sale for scrap, the scrap value for such of it as is to be scrapped may represent its present worth. In this case the owners were fortunate in having a potential buyer. Negotiations had long been under way. The operative properties were twice offered to the City of San Francisco for $7,950,000 and twice the voters rejected the proposition. Ultimately the properties were sold for $7,500,000. The evidence shows that the president of the Company reported to the directors "that the price mentioned is the amount that has been agreed upon for the purchase by the City and County of San Francisco of the operative properties of the Company after negotiations in respect thereto which covered a considerable period of time and, as previously mentioned, is the best price obtainable therefor." Upon this understanding the Board of Directors ratified the offer and directed the officers to consummate it.

It is now contended that this offer was calculated by a capitalization of earning power and that this Court condemned such a basis of valuation in *Federal Power Commission v. Hope Natural Gas Co.*, 320 U.S. 591, 601, when it said, "The heart of the matter is that rates cannot be made to depend upon 'fair value' when the value of the going enterprise depends on earnings under whatever rates may be anticipated." The pronouncement in the *Hope* case was directed to a situation where the demand for the service permitted such a range of choice in rates as would greatly affect the value of the property. No such choice appears open to the appellant. Apart from a little brief war-time prosperity, it seems doubtful whether any rate would yield appellant's operating expenses.

Under these circumstances we do not find that anything has been taken from the appellant by the impact of public regulation. If the expectations of the Commission as to traffic increase were well founded, it would earn under this rate on the salvage value of its property, which is the only value it is shown to have. If expectations of increased traffic were unfounded, it could probably not earn a return from any rate that could be devised. We are unable to find that the order in this case is in violation of constitutional prohibitions, however unfortunate the plight of the appellant.

We have considered appellant's complaints in considerable detail because the case in so many ways departs from the usual rate case. We find no constitutional infirmity in the result or in the procedure by which it is reached. The judgment of the Supreme Court of California is therefore

Affirmed.■

NOTES

1. This case addresses the liability of government for changes in technological and economic conditions in an industry. During the early twentieth century, the streetcar industry faced enormous pressures from the growth of subway, bus, and other transportation systems (including roads and parking for the ordinary automobile). Many of these other modes of transportation became possible because of technological innovations and changes in economic conditions. What case from earlier in the book does this scenario remind you of?

2. Today, cable cars in San Francisco charge $2.00, are overflowing with customers, and are seen as an asset to the city. Some of this continued viability in the industry may be due to public ownership of the resource. Notice that the company alleging damages in *Market Street Railway* sold their properties to the City of San Francisco, which continues to operate the cable car system. Would the cable car have survived without public ownership?

* * *

Rate of return, like most ratemaking issues, raises complex accounting, economics, and forecasting matters. It is an extremely important issue, since its calculation reflects the time value of the investors' money and utility investments are often financed over long periods of time.

At its most basic level, a rate of return represents the utility's cost of capital–i.e., the opportunity it forgoes by using its capital to provide utility services rather than engage in some other profitable activity. Cost of capital can be broken into two main components: 1) the cost of money that is borrowed on both a long- and short-term basis, also known as "debt"; and 2) money received by the utility in exchange for its stock, or "equity."

The equity capital of a public utility is generally of two types: (1) preferred and (2) common. The former is essentially the same as long-term debt capital as regards specified and agreed rates of return or dividends and times of payment. While the consequences of nonpayment are not as onerous, dividends on or the cost of the preferred stock capital of a public utility nevertheless must be paid before any dividends may be paid on common stock.

The common equity capital of a public utility is that which incurs the highest risk. Unlike most debt capital, its ultimate recovery by those who furnished the funds is not secured by liens against the property of the utility, and, unlike both debt capital and preferred stock investors, those who hold common stock are not entitled to any agreed or assured rate of return on their investment. In short, their earnings consist of the net remaining from revenues after all other creditors of the public utility, including long-term debt and preferred stock investors, have been paid. While the return on this type of capital is actually measured by the amount of net income from gross receipts so remaining, this actual return is not necessarily synonymous with the cost of this category of capital. The cost or rate of return a public utility must pay or be able to pay in order to obtain common equity funds from the private capital markets is set for the company by the market, not by this commission or the company. It is particularly important to stress and recognize that the cost of a public utility's common equity capital is simply another cost of furnishing service, which is not generically different from any of its other costs. Those who furnish common equity capital to a utility, whether by purchasing new stock of the company or by permitting the company to retain and invest their earnings in new plant and equipment, expect and are entitled to a return or earnings for the use of their money by the utility. In an economic sense, this return represents the company's cost of the common equity capital employed, just as rent on an office building leased by the company or wages to those who work for the company constitute costs to it.

Re Public Service Company of New Mexico, 8 P.U.R.4th 113 (N.M.P.S.C. 1975).

Equity is the more difficult cost for regulators to determine. Since there is rarely a fixed commitment to a dividend rate, the actual cost of floating a stock issue is uncertain. "Investors' decisions are largely based on a utility's expected earnings and upon their stability, as well as upon alternative uses of investment funds. Yet, since the allowable amount of earnings is the object of a rate case, a commission's decision, in turn, will affect investors' decisions." Charles F. Phillips, Jr., The Regulation of Public Utilities 394 (3d ed. 1993). Two principle methods are used to estimate the cost of equity capital: the "market-determined" standard, which focuses on investor expectations in terms of the utility's earnings, dividends and market prices; and a "comparable earnings" standard, which focuses on what capital can earn in various alternative investments with comparable risks. *Id.*

A related issue in measuring cost of capital is determining the appropriate capital structure. Since the interest rate on debt is normally lower than the cost of equity capital (why?), the overall cost of capital will be lower when the debt-equity ratio is high. Some argue that regulators should look to the ideal rather than actual capital structure, in order to minimize the possibility that utility capitalization decisions are made based on rate regulation decisions. As the utility industries moves towards competition, as is discussed in Chapters 9, 11, and 13, debt-equity ratios have moved upward.

As the United States Supreme Court acknowledged in *Bluefield Water Works & Improvement Co. v. Public Service Commission*, 262 U.S. 679 (1923), there are constitutional limits on the setting of cost of common equity capital:

A public utility is entitled to such rates as will permit it to earn a return on the value of the property which it employs for the convenience of the public equal to that generally being made at the same time and in the same general part of the country on investments in other business undertakings which are attended by corresponding risks and uncertainties; but it has no constitutional right to profits such as are realized or anticipated in highly profitable enterprises or speculative ventures. The return should be reasonably sufficient to assure confidence in the financial soundness of the utility, and should be adequate under efficient and economical management, to maintain and support its credit and to enable it to raise the money necessary for the proper discharge of its public duty. A rate of return may be reasonable at one time, and become too high or too low by change affecting opportunities for investment, the money market and business conditions generally.

In *Federal Power Commission v. Hope Natural Gas Co.*, 320 U.S. 591 (1944), where the court endorsed an "end result" test, it also specified three conditions of a fair return on the invested capital of a public utility: (1) it should be sufficient to maintain the financial integrity of the utility; (2) it should be sufficient to compensate the utility's investors for the risks assumed; (3) it should be sufficient to enable the utility to attract needed new capital.

NOTES AND COMMENTS

1. Regulated firms use a two-step strategy to maximize their returns to shareholders. First, they attempt to obtain a rate of return, r, that exceeds the actual cost of capital. Second, they may overinvest in capital, producing a product of B and r that is greater than the actual cost of capital used. *See* Harvey Averch & Leland L. Johnson, Behavior of the Firm Under Regulatory Constraint, 52 Am. Econ. Rev. 1052 (1962).

2. What are the capital sources available to a firm? Like any other business enterprise, an energy utility needs to attract investors. Generally a firm has two options in raising capital: debt (bond obligations) and equity (stock). Capital structure refers to a firm's mix of debt and equity. Would an unregulated firm ever intentionally choose a suboptimal mix of capital? No. Because it competes in markets as a buyer of capital, the unregulated firm faces strong economic incentives to choose the debt-equity ratio that minimizes its risk-adjusted cost of capital. Cost of service regulation, by guaranteeing a utility a minimum rate of return, reduces the strength of this incentive. How likely are regulators to determine a firm's correct capital structure—i.e., the mix of debt and equity the regulated firm would face in a competitive market?

3. *Smyth* required regulators to use "fair value" in determining rate base. Generally the choice for determining "fair value" comes down to two alternatives: original cost (or historical cost) and reproduction cost (or present cost). Early on, the Court read *Smyth* to require a regulator to consider both. In several cases decided between 1898 and 1944, the Supreme Court held rate decisions unconstitutionally confiscatory where an

agency gave undue consideration to original cost and insufficient consideration to reproductive cost. *See, e.g., Missouri ex rel. Southwestern Bell Telephone Co. v. Missouri PSC*, 262 U.S. 276 (1923). Holmes and Brandeis, in a concurrence to that case, dissented from the majority's reliance on the indeterminate "fair value" standard of Smyth.

In the 1944 *Hope* case, a majority agreed with Holmes and Brandeis' 1923 concurrence: "If the total effect of the rate order cannot be said to be unjust and unreasonable, judicial inquiry under the Act is at an end.... Rates which enable the company to operate successfully ... cannot be condemned as invalid, even though they might produce only a meager return on the so-called 'fair value' rate base." 320 U.S. at 602–05. *Hope* marks a departure from Smyth's "fair value" standard—a standard first enunciated during the rise of the substantive due process era of the late nineteenth and early twentieth centuries. *See* Basil L. Copeland, Jr. & Walter W. Nixon, III, Procedural Versus Substantive Economic Due Process for Public Utilities, 12 Energy L.J. 81 (1991).

4.   In *Permian Basin Area Rate Cases*, 390 U.S. 747 (1968), the Court reviewed Commission orders setting area-wide rates for gas producers. Writing for the majority, Justice Harlan affirmed *Hope*, stating that a court reviewing rate orders must assure itself both that "each of the order's essential elements is supported by substantial evidence" and that "the order may reasonably be expected to maintain financial integrity, attract necessary capital, and fairly compensate investors for the risks they have assumed, and yet provide appropriate protection to the relevant public interests, both existing and foreseeable." *Id.* at 792. In examining the end result of the rate order, a court cannot affirm simply because each subpart of that order, taken in isolation, was permissible; it must be the case "that they do not together produce arbitrary or unreasonable consequences." The reviewing court, according to Harlan, must determine that "the record before the Commission contained evidence sufficient to establish that these rates, as adjusted, will maintain the industry's credit and continue to attract capital." *Id.* at 812.

5.   The most recent case addressing rate base and rate of return decided by the Supreme Court is *Duquesne Light Co. v. Barasch*, 488 U.S. 299 (1989), which is discussed further below.

b.   RATE–SETTING OBJECTIVES

What interests should a regulator take into account in determining whether rates are just and reasonable? Certainly, as the above excerpt suggests, regulators are concerned with ensuring that the utility and its investors are provided with sufficient revenue to keep the utility operational. However, utility rate filings are often subject to challenge by a myriad of non-utility interest groups with a stake in the outcome: consumers, who seek the lowest possible rates; environmental groups who may seek to increase rates to discourage wasteful consumption, or have regulators force the utility to adopt conservation-enhancing mechanisms; and public advocates, such as state attorneys general or consumer protection offices, who may advocate some version of the public interest. The preferences of these interest groups often clash.

So what objectives should regulators consider when setting rates? First, as the readings have suggested, regulators should attempt to ensure that the utility meets its revenue requirement. This includes not only the payment of operating expenses, but the cost of capital as well. Cost of capital is not pure profit or gain for the utility and its shareholders; maintenance of a minimum cost of capital is in the public interest as well. As the New Mexico PSC suggests, if a utility does not receive a competitive rate of return, existing investors may find alternative investments. While consumers are justifiably concerned with paying high rates to subsidize utility profits, they certainly would not want to see their local utility struggling to stay one-step away from bankruptcy.

A second objective of rate-setting is economic efficiency. Rates should encourage the regulated enterprise to provide service at the lowest social cost and explore ways to further reduce costs through better management and the adoption of newer, more efficient technological processes.

A third objective is environmental. Approved rates should not encourage waste or encourage uses that are threatening to the environment or energy resource base. This is certainly related to the second objective: if all social costs (including environmental costs) are fully internalized in the rate making process, then efficient rates will reflect environmental costs as well as the financial costs necessary for a utility to continue to provide service. However, environmental costs are often not fully internalized for two reasons. As a practical matter, it is difficult to quantify the actual impact of a certain energy conversion or distribution process on the environment. In addition, many environmental costs affect parties or deplete resources outside of a regulatory body's jurisdiction.

A final regulatory objective is social and distributional. Should some customers—say wealthy or middle-class suburban customers—pay higher rates to subsidize other customers—say low income urban customers—or to build a distribution network to serve rural customers? Should a state that has adopted a policy of encouraging manufacturing set rates for industrial customers low?

c.   COMMON RATE CASE ISSUES

There are several classic treatises on rate regulation. *See, e.g.*, James C. Bonbright, Albert L. Danielson & David R. Kamerschien, Principles of Public Utility Rates (2d ed. 1988); Paul J. Garfield & Wallace F. Lovejoy, Public Utility Economics (1964); Charles Phillips, The Regulation of Public Utilities (3d ed. 1993). Some common issues raised in utility rate cases include the following:

The Test Year. The purpose of a rate case is to set utility rates for the future. A utility is seeking approval for the rate it will charge its customers for months or years to come—at least until another rate increase is approved. However, it is impossible to obtain exact financial information for a future year. For this reason, regulators use what is known as a "test year" in setting rates. This is a hypothetical future period into which regulators attempt to forecast a utility's revenue requirements: its operating expenses (O), rate base (B) and rate of return (r). Like any forecast, use of a test year depends upon certain assumptions about consumer demand, input prices, and the state of the economy in general. In actuality, some years may provide for over recovery of costs and other years may provide for under recovery.

Determining Rate Base. Recall the two alternatives presented in *Smyth v. Ames*: reproduction cost or original (historical) cost. In *Union Electric Company v. Illinois Commerce Commission*, the Illinois Supreme Court adopted an original cost approach. 77 Ill.2d 364, 396 N.E.2d 510 (1979). The Court noted: "... [A] cost based rate reflects the amount of capital whereas a value rate base reflects the value of assets which the utility has devoted to serving the public." *Id.* at 516. FERC bases property valuations on original cost, as do the vast majority of state PSCs.

Does the calculation of rate base on reproduction cost give utility shareholders a windfall? Or does it encourage an efficient allocation of resources? During a period of inflation, the rates of regulated utilities may be lower than the rates of non-regulated enterprises with which they compete (which would reflect reproduction cost). This could increase the demand for the services of a regulated utility and lead to an uneconomical expansion of capacity. For discussion of the merits of reproduction cost versus original cost, *see* Charles F. Phillips, Jr., The Regulation of Public Utilities 299–307 (1984).

Appeals. An interested party aggrieved by the procedural consideration or end result of a utility rate case may appeal. The Johnston Act, 28 U.S.C. § 1342, prohibits a U.S. District Court from exercising jurisdiction over a rate appeal from a state PSC where there is an adequate remedy in state court. The proper avenue for appeal of a state PSC rate determination is through the state court system and then to the U.S. Supreme court. Under the FPA and NGA, FERC rate cases are appealed to the U.S. Court of Appeals for the D.C. Circuit or the circuit within which the utility or aggrieved party sits.

On appeal, challenges to rate proceedings may focus not only on the substance of public utility law, but also on the procedures by which agencies make their factual, policy, and legal determinations. Rate cases often involve hearings before the decisionmaking body, during which the utility and intervening parties are given an opportunity to present expert testimony in support of their positions in both oral and written form and are given an opportunity to seek discovery of and cross-exam the testimony of other parties. Hearings can last from a period of days to months. Normally, uncontested factual findings do not require a hearing before an agency. However, a hearing is required where an agency is making a factual determination under contest by a party or where the agency is making a new policy or legal decision. *See Cajun Electric Power Coop. v. FERC*, 28 F.3d 173 (D.C.Cir.1994). Often, an agency will make generic policy and legal decisions through a process called notice and comment rulemaking.

Antitrust law. Rate regulation may implicate legal concerns under sections 1 and 2 of the Sherman Act, which address agreements in restraint of trade and illegal monopolization, respectively. For example, rate cases often raise concerns of price fixing (a section 1 problem) and price squeeze (a section 2 problem). *See, e.g.*, Lawrence J. Spiwak, Is the Price Squeeze Doctrine Still Viable in Fully-Regulated Energy Markets?, 14 Energy L.J. 75 (1993). Under the doctrine of primary jurisdiction—along with a doctrine called the "state action doctrine" (see Chapter Thirteen)—agencies responsible for enforcing state and federal antitrust laws often defer to the price regulation schemes applied by state PSCs and FERC where the agency is engaged in a pervasive scheme of regulation. However, if an agency's approval of activity initiated by a firm is only pro forma or if the agency failed to evaluate fully the effects of the firm's activities on competition, there is some room for antitrust enforcement. *See Hughes Tool Co. v. Trans World Airlines*, 409 U.S. 363 (1973). If the costs of pervasive agency regulation are higher than the costs of competition as enforced through antitrust litigation, what is the most efficient regulatory scheme? See discussion of competition in Chapter Eleven, below.

d.   "USED AND USEFUL" PROPERTY

Recall that *Smyth v. Ames* refers to "the fair value of the property being used" in its definition of rate base. In *Denver Union Stock Yard Co. v. U.S.*, 304 U.S. 470, 475 (1938) the Court held that property not used or useful in providing regulated services does not have to be included in rate base. What has come to be known as the "used and useful" doctrine prohibits the inclusion of rate base of assets used exclusively to provide unregulated goods or services, or assets that are technologically or economically obsolete. How does a regulator determine whether property is used and useful? The clearest example is where a utility has placed the most economical plant into operation to meet a specific customer demand. It is beyond dispute that such a facility is used and useful. Beyond this, regulators have been flexible in applying the used and useful doctrine on an ad hoc basis. As the following two cases address, however, there is some constitutional limitation on regulators' decisions to deem property used and useful.

Jersey Central Power & Light Co. v. Federal Energy Regulatory Commission
810 F.2d 1168 (D.C.Cir.1987).

[The Federal Energy Regulatory Commission allowed Jersey Central Power and Light Co. to amortize a $397 million investment in a canceled nuclear plant over a fifteen-year period. Jersey Central was not allowed, however, to include the unamortized balance in its rate base, because FERC determined the plant was not "used and useful." The effect of this treatment meant that the interest costs of the $397 million were charged to shareholders while the principal costs were charged to ratepayers over a fifteen-year period.]

■ BORK, J.: Jersey Central Power and Light Company petitions for review of Federal Energy Regulatory Commission orders modifying the electric utility's proposed rate schedules and requiring the company to file reduced rates. Jersey Central charges that it alleged facts which, if proven, show that the reduced rates are confiscatory and violate its statutory and constitutional rights as defined by the Supreme Court in *FPC v. Hope Natural Gas Co.*, 320 U.S. 591 (1944). Though it is probable that the facts alleged, if true, would establish an invasion of the company's rights, the Commission refused the company a hearing and reduced its rates summarily.

The decision of the Commission is vacated and the case remanded for a hearing at which Jersey Central may finally have its claim addressed. . . .

The teaching of [*Hope* and *Permian Basin*] is straightforward. In reviewing a rate order courts must determine whether or not the end result of that order constitutes a reasonable balancing, based on factual findings, of the investor interest in maintaining financial integrity and access to capital markets and the consumer interest in being charged non-exploitative rates. Moreover, an order cannot be justified simply by a showing that each of the choices underlying it was reasonable; those choices must still add up to a reasonable result. . . .

The allegations made by Jersey Central and the testimony it offered track the standards of *Hope* and *Permian Basin* exactly. The *Hope* Court stated that the return ought to be "sufficient to ensure confidence in the financial integrity of the enterprise, so as to maintain its credit and to attract capital," and that "it is important that there be enough revenue not only for operating expenses but also for the capital costs of the business. These include service on the debt and dividends on the stock." 320 U.S. at 603. *Permian Basin* reaffirmed that the reviewing court "must determine" whether the Commission's rate order may reasonably be expected to "maintain financial integrity" and "attract necessary capital." 390 U.S. at 792. Jersey Central alleged that it had paid no dividends on its common stock for four years and faced a further prolonged inability to pay such dividends. [It also alleged] that the company was unable to sell senior securities; that its only source of external capital was the Revolving Credit Agreement, which was subject to termination and which placed the outstanding bank loans the company was allowed to maintain below the level necessary for the upcoming year; that the need to pay interest on the company's debt and dividends on its preferred stock meant that common equity investors not only were earning a zero return, but were also forced to pay these interest costs and dividends and that "continued confiscation of earnings from the common equity holder . . . will prolong the Company's inability to restore itself to a recognized level of credit worthiness"; that its "inability to realize fully its operating and capital costs so as to provide a fair rate of return on its invested capital has pushed its financial capability to the limits"; that "adequate and prompt relief is necessary in order to maintain the past high quality of service"; and that the rate increase requested was "the minimum necessary to restore the financial integrity of the Company."

The Commission maintains that because excluding the unamortized portion of a canceled plant investment from the rate base had previously been upheld as permissible, any rate order that rests on such a decision is unimpeachable. But that would turn our focus from the end result to the methodology, and evade the question whether the component decisions together produce just and reasonable consequences. We would be back with the assertion made in *Jersey Central I* that "the end result test is to be applied ... only to those assets which valid Commission rules permit to be included in the rate base." 730 F.2d at 823. That statement was one which neither party endorsed. It was incorrect. The fact that a particular rate-making standard is generally permissible does not per se legitimate the end result of the rate orders it produces. . . .

In addition to prohibiting rates so low as to be confiscatory, the holding of Hope Natural Gas makes clear that exploitative rates are illegal as well. If the inclusion of property not currently used and useful in the rate base automatically constituted exploitation of consumers, as one of the amici maintains, then the commission would be justified in excluding such property summarily even in cases where the utility pleads acute financial distress. A regulated utility has no constitutional right to a profit, *see FPC v. Natural Gas Pipeline Co.*, 315 U.S. at 590, and a company that is unable to survive without charging exploitative rates has no entitlement to such rates. *Market Street Ry. v. Railroad Comm'n of Cal.*, 324 U.S. 548 (1945). But we have already held that including prudent investments in the rate base is not in and of itself exploitative, and no party has denied that the Forked River investment was prudent. Indeed, when the regulated company is permitted to earn a return not on the market value of the property used by the public, *see Smyth v. Ames*, but rather on the original cost of the investment, placing prudent investments in the rate base would seem a more sensible policy than a strict application of "used and useful," for under this approach it is the investment, and not the property used, which is viewed as having been taken by the public. The investor interest described in *Hope*, after all, is an interest in return on investment. *Hope*, 320 U.S. at 603.

The central point, however, is this: it is impossible for us to say at this juncture whether including the unamortized portion of Forked River in the rate base would exploit consumers in this case, or whether its exclusion, on the facts of this case, constitutes confiscation, for no findings of fact have been made concerning the consequences of the rate order. Nor, for the same reason, can we make a judgment about the higher rate of return the utility sought as an alternative to inclusion in the rate base of its unamortized investment. Jersey Central has presented allegations which, if true, suggest that the rate order almost certainly does not meet the requirements of *Hope Natural Gas*, for the company has been shut off from long-term capital, is wholly dependent for short-term capital on a revolving credit arrangement that can be canceled at any time, and has been unable to pay dividends for four years. In addition, Jersey Central points out that the rates proposed in its filing would remain lower than those of neighboring utilities, which at least suggests, though it does not demonstrate, that the proposed rates would not exploit consumers. The Commission treated those allegations as irrelevant and hence has presented us with no basis on which to affirm its rate order. The necessary findings are simply not there for us to review. When the Commission conducts the requisite balancing of consumer and investor interests, based upon factual findings, that balancing will be judicially reviewable and will be affirmed if supported by substantial evidence. That is the point at which deference to agency expertise will be appropriate and necessary. But where, as here, the Commission has reached its determination by flatly refusing to consider a factor to which it is undeniably required to give some weight, its decision cannot stand. *Citizens to Preserve Overton Park, Inc. v. Volpe*, 401 U.S. 402, 416 (1971). The case should therefore be remanded to the Commission for a hearing at which the Commission can determine whether the rate order it issued constituted a reasonable balancing of the interests the Supreme Court has designated as relevant to the setting of a just and reasonable rate.

■ Starr, J., concurring: The Commission's stated justification for summarily dismissing these allegations was the weight of its prior "used and useful" precedent. But as the court's opinion shows, that body of precedent did not constitute as iron-clad a rule as the Commission would have us believe. It is certainly not evident from those precedents that the rule could be summarily applied in the face of the financial demise of the regulated entity.

Indeed, the Commission as a matter of policy has departed over the years from the strictures of the "used and useful" rule. This is illustrated by its treatment of "construction work in progress" (CWIP), part of which, the Commission recently determined, can be included in a utility's rate base. *See Mid–Tex Electric Cooperative v. FERC*, 773 F.2d 327 (D.C.Cir. 1985). In that proceeding, the Commission recognized that its own practice admits of "widely recognized exceptions and departures" from the "used and useful" rule, "particularly when there are countervailing public interest considerations." *See* 48 Fed. Reg. 24,323, 24,335 (June 1, 1983) (CWIP final rule). In that setting, financial difficulties in the electric utility industry played a significant role in the Commission's decision to bend the rule. *See id.* at 24,332; 773 F.2d at 332–34. *See also, e.g., Tennessee Gas Pipeline Co. v. FERC*, 606 F.2d 1094, 1109–10 (D.C.Cir.1979) (departure from "used and useful" to permit rate base treatment of natural gas prepayment is justified as means of encouraging development of additional gas reserves), *cert. denied*, 445 U.S. 920 (1980).

This policy of flexibility, it seems to me, reflects the practical reality of the electric utility industry, namely that investments in plant and equipment are enormously costly. Rigid adherence to "used and useful" doctrines would doubtless imperil the viability of some utilities; thus, while not articulating its results in *Hope* or "takings" terms, the Commission—whether as a matter of policy or perceived constitutional obligation—has in the past taken these realities into account and provided relief for utilities in various forms.

The utility business represents a compact of sorts; a monopoly on service in a particular geographical area (coupled with state-conferred rights of eminent domain or condemnation) is granted to the utility in exchange for a regime of intensive regulation, including price regulation, quite alien to the free market. *Cf. Permian Basin*, 390 U.S. at 756–57 (unlike public utilities, producers of natural gas "enjoy no franchises or guaranteed areas of service" and are "intensely competitive"). Each party to the compact gets something in the bargain. As a general rule, utility investors are provided a level of stability in earnings and value less likely to be attained in the unregulated or moderately regulated sector; in turn, ratepayers are afforded universal, non-discriminatory service and protection from monopolistic profits through political control over an economic enterprise. Whether this regime is wise or not is, needless to say, not before us.

In the setting of rate regulation, when does a taking from the investors occur? It seems to me that it occurs only when a regulated rate is confiscatory, which is a short-hand way of saying that an unreasonable balance has been struck in the regulation process so as unreasonably to favor ratepayer interests at the substantial expense of investor interests. Thus, in my view, a taking does not occur when financial resources are committed to the enterprise. That is especially so since a utility's capital investment is made not simply in satisfaction of legal obligations to provide service to the public but in anticipation of profits on the investment. The utility is not a servant to the state; it is a for-profit enterprise which incurs legal obligations in exchange for state-conferred benefits. A profit-seeking capital investment is scarcely the sort of deprivation of possession, use, enjoyment, and ownership of property which can conceptually be deemed a taking. *See generally* R. Epstein, Takings 63–92 (1985). Indeed, it would seem odd to consider as a taking government's disavowal of any interest in property which remains unregulated and which reflects a profit-seeking investment.

For me, the prudent investment rule is, taken alone, too weighted for constitutional analysis in favor of the utility. It lacks balance. But so too, the "used and useful" rule, taken alone, is skewed heavily in favor of ratepayers. It also lacks balance. In the modern setting, neither regime, mechanically applied with full rigor, will likely achieve justice among the competing interests of investor and ratepayers so as to avoid confiscation of the utility's property or a taking of the property of ratepayers through unjustifiably exorbitant rates. Each approach, however, provides important insights about the ultimate object of the regulatory process, which is to achieve a just result in rate regulation. And that is the mission commanded by the Fifth Amendment. Unlike garden-variety takings, the requirements of the Takings Clause are satisfied in the rate regulatory setting when justice is done, that is to say the striking of a reasonable balance between competing interests.

Thus it is that a taking occurs not when an investment is made (even one under legal obligation), but when the balance between investor and ratepayer interests—the very function of utility regulation—is struck unjustly. Although the agency has broad latitude in striking the balance, the Constitution nonetheless requires that the end result reflect a reasonable balancing of the interests of investors and ratepayers. As we have seen, both investors and ratepayers were the intended beneficiaries of the Forked River investment; both should presumptively have to share in the loss. Filling in the gaps, the making of the specific judgments that constitutes the difficult part of this enterprise, belongs in the first instance to the politically accountable branches, specifically to the experts in the agency, not to generalist judges.

■ MIKVA, J., with whom CHIEF JUDGE WALD, and JUDGES ROBINSON and EDWARDS join, dissenting: The real mischief of today's decision lies not in the majority's belief that the utility has raised an issue of fact necessitating a hearing, but in its determination that Jersey Central has actually made out a case of constitutional confiscation. As Justice Douglas remarked, "he who would upset the rate order under the Act carries the heavy burden of making a convincing showing that it is invalid because it is unjust and unreasonable in its consequences." *Hope*, 320 U.S. at 602. The majority believes that Jersey Central can meet this burden. We simply cannot swallow the majority's assertion that "it is probable that the facts alleged [by Jersey Central], if true, would establish an invasion of the company's rights." In our view, it is beyond cavil that Jersey Central has not presented allegations which, if true, would establish that the Commission's orders result in unjust and unreasonable rates.

Permian Basin teaches that if the Commission reasonably balances consumer and investor interests, then the resulting rate is not confiscatory. The separate opinion ably translates this into a working definition of a confiscatory rate: it exists when "an unreasonable balance has been struck in the regulation process so as unreasonably to favor ratepayer interests at the substantial expense of investor interests." The majority appears to agree with the teaching of *Permian Basin*. The lesson it gleans, however, is incongruous. According to the majority, balancing competing interests is not enough; a rate is confiscatory if it does not satisfy the "legitimate investor interest" outlined by the Court in *Hope*. This interpretation of *Hope* and *Permian Basin* is implausible.

. . . The *Hope* court did not define "unjust or unreasonable"; nor did it articulate when a rate would be confiscatory. It certainly did not hold that the end result could be condemned if the investor criteria defined in the case were not fulfilled. Indeed, it expressly noted that its holding made no suggestion that more or less might not be allowed. 320 U.S. at 603; *see Market Street*, 324 U.S. at 566.

This understanding of *Hope* is the only way to reconcile the Court's recitation of investor interests with its avowal that "regulation does not insure that the business shall produce net revenues." *See Hope*, 320 U.S. at 603 (*quoting Natural Gas Pipeline*, 315 U.S. at 590). Investor interests are only one factor in the assessment of constitutionally reasonable, therefore non-confiscatory, rates. *Permian Basin*, 390 U.S. at 769. In any instance, the rate must also "provide appropriate protection to the relevant public interests, both existing and foreseeable." *Id.* at 792. A just and reasonable rate which results from balancing these conflicting interests might not provide "enough revenue not only for operating expenses but also for the capital costs of the business ... includ[ing] service on the debt and dividends on the stock." *See Hope*, 320 U.S. at 603.

The Court made this abundantly clear in *Market Street*.... Neither the regulatory process nor the fifth amendment shelter a utility from market forces. Thus, contrary to the majority's intimations, rates do not fall outside the zone of reasonableness merely because they do not enable the company to operate at a profit or do not permit investors to recover all their losses....

Application of this principle is readily apparent in the Commission's current treatment of electric utility plants, investments prudent when made but sometimes frustrated in fruition. If the investment is successful, the customer benefits from controlled rates for the service provided. But the ratepayer also shares the costs if the investment fails; he must pay for the expenditure made on an unproductive facility from which he obtains no service. From the investor's viewpoint, price regulation cabins both his upside and downside risk. He cannot collect the windfall benefits if the project is a boon; he does not bear all costs if the project is a bust. Electric utility stockholders do not lose equity in the non-serviceable facility, as they might in the marketplace. They simply do not procure a return on the investment.

The majority quibbles with this risk allocation; it would prefer a world in which the investor is guaranteed a return on his investment, if prudent when made. Its resultant holding today is directly at odds with fundamental principles laid out in *Hope* and its progeny. Adherence to the majority's insistence on the inclusion of prudent investments in the rate base would virtually insulate investors in public utilities from the risks involved in free market business. This would drastically diminish protection of the public interest by thrusting the entire risk of a failed investment onto the ratepayers....■

* * *

Duquesne Light Company v. Barasch

488 U.S. 299 (1989).

■ REHNQUIST, C. J.: Pennsylvania law required that rates for electricity be fixed without consideration of a utility's expenditures for electrical generating facilities which were planned but never built, even though the expenditures were prudent and reasonable when made. The Supreme Court of Pennsylvania held that such a law did not take the utilities' property in violation of the Fifth Amendment to the United States Constitution. We agree with that conclusion, and hold that a state scheme of utility regulation does not "take" property simply because it disallows recovery of capital investments that are not "used and useful in service to the public." 66 Pa. Const. Stat. § 1315 (Supp.1988).

* * *

In response to predictions of increased demand for electricity, Duquesne Light Company (Duquesne) and Pennsylvania Power Company (Penn Power) joined a venture in 1967 to build more generating capacity. The project, known as the Central Area Power Coordination Group (CAPCO), involved three other electric utilities and had as its objective the construction of seven large nuclear generating units. In 1980 the participants canceled plans for construction of four of the plants. Intervening events, including the Arab oil embargo and the accident at Three Mile Island, had radically changed the outlook both for growth in the demand for electricity and for nuclear energy as a desirable way of meeting that demand. At the time of the cancellation, Duquesne's share of the preliminary construction costs associated with the four halted plants was $34,697,-389. Penn Power had invested $9,569,665.

In 1980, and again in 1981, Duquesne sought permission from the Pennsylvania Public Utility Commission (PSC) to recoup its expenditures for the unbuilt plants over a 10–year period. The Commission deferred ruling on the request until it received the report from its investigation of the CAPCO construction. That report was issued in late 1982. The report found that Duquesne and Penn Power could not be faulted for initiating the construction of more nuclear generating capacity at the time they joined the CAPCO project in 1967. The projections at that time indicated a growing demand for electricity and a cost advantage to nuclear capacity. It also found that the intervening events which ultimately confounded the predictions could not have been predicted, and that work on the four nuclear plants was stopped at the proper time. In summing up, the Administrative Law Judge found "that the CAPCO decisions in regard to the [canceled plants] at every stage to their cancellation, were reasonable and prudent." He recommended that Duquesne and Penn Power be allowed to amortize their sunk costs in the project over a 10–year period. The PSC adopted the conclusions of the report.

In 1982, Duquesne again came before the PSC to obtain a rate increase. Again, it sought to amortize its expenditures on the canceled plants over 10 years. In January 1983, the PSC issued a final order which granted Duquesne the authority to increase its revenues $105.8 million to a total yearly revenue in excess of $800 million. The rate increase included $3.5 million in revenue representing the first payment of the 10–year amortization of Duquesne's $35 million loss in the CAPCO plants.

The Pennsylvania Office of the Consumer Advocate (Consumer Advocate) moved the PSC for reconsideration in light of a state law enacted about a month before the close of the 1982 Duquesne rate proceeding. The Act amended the Pennsylvania Utility Code by limiting "the consideration of certain costs in the rate base." It provided that "the cost of construction or expansion of a facility undertaken by a public utility producing ... electricity shall not be made a part of the rate base nor otherwise included in the rates charged by the electric utility until such time as the facility is used and useful in service to the public." On reconsideration, the PSC affirmed its original rate order. It read the new law as excluding the costs of canceled plants (obviously not used and useful) from the rate base, but not as preventing their recovery through amortization.... [The Pennsylvania Supreme Court affirmed, holding that exclusion from rate base was not a taking in violation of the Fifth Amendment of the U.S. Constitution.]

* * *

As public utilities, both Duquesne and Penn Power are under a state statutory duty to serve the public. A Pennsylvania statute provides that "[e]very public utility shall furnish and maintain adequate, efficient, safe, and reasonable service and facilities" and that "[s]uch service also shall be reasonably continuous and without unreasonable interruptions or delay." 66 Pa. Const. Stat. § 1501 (1986). Although their assets are employed in the public interest to provide consumers of the State with electric power, they are owned and operated by private investors. This partly public, partly private status of utility property creates its own set of questions under the Takings Clause of the Fifth Amendment.

The guiding principle has been that the Constitution protects utilities from being limited to a charge for their property serving the public which is so "unjust" as to be confiscatory. If the rate does not afford sufficient compensation, the State has taken the use of utility property without paying just compensation and so violated the Fifth and Fourteenth Amendments. As has been observed, however, "[h]ow such compensation may be ascertained, and what are the necessary elements in such an inquiry, will always be an embarrassing question." *Smyth v. Ames*, 169 U.S. 466, 546, (1898). *See also Permian Basin Area Rate Cases*, 390 U.S. 747, 790, (1968) ("[N]either law nor economics has yet devised generally accepted standards for the evaluation of rate-making orders").

At one time, it was thought that the Constitution required rates to be set according to the actual present value of the assets employed in the public service. This method, known as the "fair value" rule, is exemplified by the decision in *Smyth v. Ames, supra*. Under the fair value approach, a "company is entitled to ask ... a fair return upon the value of that which it employs for the public convenience," while on the other hand, "the public is entitled to demand ... that no more be exacted from it for the use of [utility property] than the services rendered by it are reasonably worth." 169 U.S., at 547. In theory the *Smyth v. Ames* fair value standard mimics the operation of the competitive market. To the extent utilities' investments in plants are good ones (because their benefits exceed their costs) they are rewarded with an opportunity to earn an "above-cost" return, that is, a fair return on the current "market value" of the plant. To the extent utilities' investments turn out to be bad ones (such as plants that are canceled and so never used and useful to the public), the utilities suffer because the investments have no fair value and so justify no return.

Although the fair value rule gives utilities strong incentive to manage their affairs well and to provide efficient service to the public, it suffered from practical difficulties which ultimately led to its abandonment as a constitutional requirement.[5]⁵ In response to these problems, Justice Brandeis had advocated an alternative approach as the constitutional minimum, what has become known as the "prudent investment" or "historical cost" rule. He accepted the *Smyth v. Ames* eminent domain analogy, but concluded that what was "taken" by public utility regulation is not specific physical assets that are to be individually valued, but the capital prudently devoted to the public utility enterprise by the utilities' owners. *Missouri ex rel. Southwestern Bell Telephone Co. v. Public Service Comm'n,* 262 U.S. 276, 291 (1923) (dissenting opinion). Under the prudent investment rule, the utility is compensated for all prudent investments at their actual cost when made (their "historical" cost), irrespective of whether individual investments are deemed necessary or beneficial in hindsight. The utilities incur fewer risks, but are limited to a standard rate of return on the actual amount of money reasonably invested.[6]⁶

Forty-five years ago in the landmark case of *FPC v. Hope Natural Gas Co.,* 320 U.S. 591 (1944), this Court abandoned the rule of *Smyth v. Ames,* and held that the "fair value" rule is not the only constitutionally acceptable method of fixing utility rates. In *Hope* we ruled that historical cost was a valid basis on which to calculate utility compensation. 320 U.S., at 605 ("Rates which enable [a] company to operate successfully, to maintain its financial integrity, to attract capital, and to compensate its investors for the risk assumed certainly cannot be condemned as invalid, even though they might produce only a meager return on the so called "fair value rate base"). We also acknowledged in that case that all of the subsidiary aspects of valuation for ratemaking purposes could not properly be characterized as having a constitutional dimension, despite the fact that they might affect property rights to some degree. Today we reaffirm these teachings of *Hope*

---

5. Perhaps the most serious problem associated with the fair value rule was the "laborious and baffling task of finding the present value of the utility." The exchange value of a utility's assets, such as powerplants, could not be set by a market price because such assets were rarely bought and sold. Nor could the capital assets be valued by the stream of income they produced because setting that stream of income was the very object of the rate proceeding. According to Brandeis, the *Smyth v. Ames* test usually degenerated to proofs about how much it would cost to reconstruct the asset in question, a hopelessly hypothetical, complex, and inexact process.

6. The system avoids the difficult valuation problems encountered under the *Smyth v. Ames* test because it relies on the actual historical cost of investments as the basis for setting the rate. The amount of a utility's actual outlays for assets in the public service is more easily ascertained by a ratemaking body because less judgment is required than in valuing an asset.

Natural Gas: "[I]t is not theory but the impact of the rate order which counts. If the total effect of the rate order cannot be said to be unreasonable, judicial inquiry . . . is at an end. The fact that the method employed to reach that result may contain infirmities is not then important." *Id.*, at 602. This language, of course, does not dispense with all of the constitutional difficulties when a utility raises a claim that the rate which it is permitted to charge is so low as to be confiscatory: whether a particular rate is "unjust" or "unreasonable" will depend to some extent on what is a fair rate of return given the risks under a particular rate-setting system, and on the amount of capital upon which the investors are entitled to earn that return. At the margins, these questions have constitutional overtones.

Pennsylvania determines rates under a slightly modified form of the historical cost/prudent investment system. Neither Duquesne nor Penn Power alleges that the total effect of the rate order arrived at within this system is unjust or unreasonable. In fact the overall effect is well within the bounds of *Hope*, even with total exclusion of the CAPCO costs. Duquesne was authorized to earn a 16.14% return on common equity and an 11.64% overall return on a rate base of nearly $1.8 billion. Its $35 million investment in the canceled plants comprises roughly 1.9% of its total base. The denial of plant amortization will reduce its annual allowance by 0.4%. Similarly, Penn Power was allowed a charge of 15.72% return on common equity and a 12.02% overall return. Its investment in the CAPCO plants comprises only 2.4% of its $401.8 million rate base. The denial of amortized recovery of its $9.6 million investment in CAPCO will reduce its annual revenue allowance by only 0.5%.

Given these numbers, it appears that the PSC would have acted within the constitutional range of reasonableness if it had allowed amortization of the CAPCO costs but set a lower rate of return on equity with the result that Duquesne and Penn Power received the same revenue they will under the instant orders on remand. The overall impact of the rate orders, then, is not constitutionally objectionable. No argument has been made that these slightly reduced rates jeopardize the financial integrity of the companies, either by leaving them insufficient operating capital or by impeding their ability to raise future capital. Nor has it been demonstrated that these rates are inadequate to compensate current equity holders for the risk associated with their investments under a modified prudent investment scheme.

Instead, appellants argue that the Constitution requires that subsidiary aspects of Pennsylvania's ratemaking methodology be examined piecemeal. One aspect which they find objectionable is the constraint Act 335 places on the PSC's decisions. They urge that such legislative direction to the PSC impermissibly interferes with the PSC's duty to balance consumer and investor interest under *Permian Basin*, 390 U.S., at 792. Appellants also note the theoretical inconsistency of Act 335, suddenly and selectively applying the used and useful requirement, normally associated with the fair value approach, in the context of Pennsylvania's system based on historical cost. Neither of the errors appellants perceive in this case is of constitutional magnitude.

It cannot seriously be contended that the Constitution prevents state legislatures from giving specific instructions to their utility commissions. We have never doubted that state legislatures are competent bodies to set utility rates. And the Pennsylvania PSC is essentially an administrative arm of the legislature. This is not to say that any system of ratemaking applied by a utilities commission, including the specific instructions it has received from its legislature, will necessarily be constitutional. But if the system fails to pass muster, it will not be because the legislature has performed part of the work.

Similarly, an otherwise reasonable rate is not subject to constitutional attack by questioning the theoretical consistency of the method that produced it. "It is not theory, but the impact of the rate order which counts." *Hope*, 320 U.S., at 602. The economic judgments required in rate proceedings are often hopelessly complex and do not admit of a single correct result. The Constitution is not designed to arbitrate these economic niceties. Errors to the detriment of one party may well be canceled out by countervailing errors or allowances in another part of the rate proceeding. The Constitution protects the utility from the net effect of the rate order on its property. Inconsistencies in one aspect of the methodology have no constitutional effect on the utility's property if they are compensated by countervailing factors in some other aspect.

Admittedly, the impact of certain rates can only be evaluated in the context of the system under which they are imposed. One of the elements always relevant to setting the rate under Hope is the return investors expect given the risk of the enterprise. *Id.*, at 603 ("[R]eturn to the equity owner should be commensurate with returns on investments in other enterprises having corresponding risks"); *Bluefield Water Works & Improvement Co. v. Public Service Comm'n of West Virginia*, 262 U.S. 679, 692–693 (1923) ("A public utility is entitled to such rates as will permit it to earn a return ... equal to that generally being made at the same time and in the same general part of the country on investments in other business undertakings which are attended by corresponding risks and uncertainties"). The risks a utility faces are in large part defined by the rate methodology because utilities are virtually always public monopolies dealing in an essential service, and so relatively immune to the usual market risks. Consequently, a State's decision to arbitrarily switch back and forth between methodologies in a way which required investors to bear the risk of bad investments at some times while denying them the benefit of good investments at others would raise serious constitutional questions. But the instant case does not present this question. At all relevant times, Pennsylvania's rate system has been predominantly but not entirely based on historical cost and it has not been shown that the rate orders as modified by Act 335 fail to give a reasonable rate of return on equity given the risks under such a regime. We therefore hold that Act 335's limited effect on the rate order at issue does not result in a constitutionally impermissible rate. Finally we address the suggestion of the Pennsylvania Electric Association as amicus that the prudent investment rule should be adopted as the constitutional standard. We think that the adoption of any such rule would signal a retreat from 45 years of decisional law in this area which would be as unwarranted as it would be unsettling. Hope clearly held that "the Commission was not bound to the use of any single formula or combination of formulae in determining rates." 320 U.S., at 602.■

NOTES AND COMMENTS

1. On rehearing in *Jersey Central III*, the Commission sustained the amortization scheme after holding a hearing. *See Jersey Cent. Power & Light*, 49 FERC ¶ 63,004 (1989).

2. Does *Duquesne* resolve the differences between the majority and dissent in *Jersey Central III*? Would the Supreme Court have sided with the majority, the dissent, or Judge Starr's concurrence? The *Duquesne* case raises the relationship between regulatory takings and takings in the ratemaking context. Should utility regulation that is found to satisfy the *Hope* "end results" test be subjected to additional tests to determine whether or not the regulation results in "confiscation" and is a "regulatory taking"? *See* Richard Goldsmith, Utility Rates and 'Takings,' 10 Energy L.J. 241 (1989). Judge Starr, in his concurrence to *Jersey Central III*, suggests that the Hope test operates independent of the takings tests that might apply in other contexts, and the dissent appears to agree.

Duquesne purports to reaffirm *Hope*, but there is considerable disagreement over whether the Court opened the door to second-guessing regulators' choices of measures for rate base. According to some commentators, "a wolf in sheep's clothing, the *Duquesne* opinion has resurrected the language of substantive economic due process, and has the potential for undoing everything for which *Hope* stood." Basil M. Copeland, Jr. & Walter W. Nixon, III, Procedural Versus Substantive Economic Due Process for Public Utilities, 12 Energy L.J. 81, 89 (1991). Does the language of *Duquesne* support Copeland and Nixon's argument? Others disagree with this reading, maintaining that *Hope* and *Duquesne* effectively remove the judiciary from constitutional review of ratemaking. *See* Richard J. Pierce, Jr., Public Utility Regulatory Takings: Should the Judiciary Attempt to Police the Political Institutions?, 77 Geo. L.J. 2031, 2062 (1989). The approach of lower courts in adjudicating recent takings challenges in the ratemaking context seem to lend more support for Pierce's views on the issue. *See* discussion of stranded costs in Chapter Twelve.

3. Even if original cost is chosen as the method for valuing rate base, there is still a significant question as to how original cost should be determined. As an accounting matter, rate base, B, does not remain constant from year-to-year; rather, a utility's investments in capital assets depreciate over their useful lives and are eventually retired, scrapped, or sold. Assets are capitalized over their useful years, not expensed in a single

year. By contrast, variable expenses are expensed during the periods in which they are consumed.

For example, many modern consumers finance automobiles over a 4–5 year period; in doing this, the consumer spreads the cost of the automobile over its most useful years. By contrast, in buying a hamburger, the cost is incurred immediately. If the hamburger is bought on a on credit card, it is charged simultaneous with consumption of the hamburger. Only an unwise or financially irresponsible consumer would pay for hamburger over a 4 or 5 year period. When assets are paid for over time, their original value needs to be adjusted to take into account what has already been paid and used. Depreciation, d, represents the cumulative amount of assets that have been retired for accounting purposes. Rate base, B, is typically adjusted by d, by subtracting d from V, the gross value of the utility's capital investment.

In *Jersey Central III*, briefly excerpted above, Jersey City's investment of $397 million in the canceled Forked River nuclear plant was at issue. FERC allowed Jersey City to amortize its $397 million investment over a fifteen-year period. (Amortization is the functional equivalent of depreciation; it expenses a portion of an intangible asset's value over its useful life.) It did not, however, allow Jersey City to put the unamortized balance in rate base, because the plant was not "used and useful." As a result, interest costs are charged to shareholders while principal costs are charged to ratepayers over the fifteen year period. In other words, the firm loses the time value of its money by only recovering a portion of the $397 million as an operating expense. To the utility, failure to include depreciation in rate base can make a large difference in revenue requirements, as it may deny the utility (and its investors) the ability to earn a rate of return on the entire capital investment.

4. If depreciation is included in rate base, there are basically two approaches available to regulators in applying d to B: depreciated original cost (DOC) and trended original cost (TOC). Both measure the amount of fixed investment for the provision of utility service in actual dollars, as adjusted, not only for depreciation, but also for some complicated accounting concepts—e.g., allowance for funds used during construction and normalized taxes—which are beyond the scope of our discussion.

Under DOC, assets are depreciated on what accountants call a "straight-line" basis—i.e., rate base declines at a steady rate over the useful life of the asset as d increases at a steady rate. Under DOC a front-end asset load is created: investors in early years pay higher rates on the new assets, while investors in later years pay lower rates on the depreciated plant. (As rate base is depreciated, smaller and smaller portions of rate base are left to which apply cost of capital.)

With TOC, rate base is increased by an inflation factor at the same time that the facilities are depreciated over their remaining useful life of the asset. FERC has give the following example to illustrate the TOC method:

Assume a new pipeline with an original equity investment of $1,000. Also assume that a just and reasonable overall rate of return on equity would be 16 percent and that 7 percent of that represents inflation. That leaves 9 percent as a so-called "real" rate of return. In its first year of service, the pipeline would be entitled to earn $90 (9 percent times $1,000) and $70 (7 percent times $1,000) would be capitalized into its equity rate base to be amortized over the life of the property starting with the first year, along with the depreciation on the $1,000. If that life were twenty years, in addition to the return of $90, the pipeline would be entitled to recover, in the first year, $3.50 as amortization ($70 divided by 20), $50 as depreciation ($1,000 divided by 20), its embedded debt cost, and depreciation associated with debt investment. This process would continue over the life of the property until the rate base (assuming no salvage value) hit zero. Unless changed in a rate case, the real rate, which should be relatively stable, would be 9 percent each year. The inflation rate would vary as the chosen inflation index varies.

Williams Pipe Line Company, 31 FERC ¶ 61,377 at 61,834 (1985).

Unlike DOC, application of TOC results in a rate base that increases in the initial year of operation and then turns downward until the facilities are fully depreciated. TOC and DOC are essentially the same except for their treatment of inflation. TOC has been advanced as a mechanism that will more nearly replicate competitive markets, by avoiding the front-loading problem of DOC. For criticism, *see* Henry E. Kilpatrick, Jr. & Dennis H. Melvin, The Trended Vs. Depreciated Original Cost Controversy: How Real Are the Real Returns?, 12 Energy L. J. 323 (1991).

5. Application of the used and useful doctrine is controversial in instances where a utility has invested in plants that are never completed or when a utility builds plants beyond its needs to serve customers. Are power plants under construction "used and useful"? On one hand, the electric generating plant that is not yet producing electricity is not "used and useful" to customers. On the other hand, the construction expense and length of time required to create the new generating facility suggests the utility should get at least some recovery for its expenses from the commission.

As Judge Starr notes in his concurrence to *Jersey Central III*, FERC has departed from the used and useful rule to allow utilities to include a portion of the costs of construction work in progress in rate base. Utilities in every state are allowed to include at least a portion of CWIP in rate base. FERC allows utilities to include in rate base up to 50 percent of CWIP allocable to electric power sales and 100 percent of CWIP associated with pollution control and fuel conversion facilities. 48 Fed. Reg. 24,323; 18 C.F.R. §§ 35.12, 35.13, 35.26, *remanded in Mid–Tex Electric Coop. v. FERC*, 773 F.2d 327 (D.C.Cir.1985); *Mid-Tex Electric Coop. v. FERC*, 864 F.2d 156 (D.C.Cir.1988).

In *Legislative Utility Consumers' Council v. Public Service Company*, 119 N.H. 332, 402 A.2d 626 (1979), the New Hampshire Supreme Court upheld the state PSC's inclusion in rate base of construction work in progress (CWIP) of $111,258,428 to finance construction of the Seabrook nuclear generating plant. The Legislative Utility Consumer's Council, a legislative agency comprised of state legislators statutorily authorized to intervene in rate proceedings on behalf of consumers, contested the commission's inclusion of in the company's rate base as contravening the "used and useful" requirement, which was codified in New Hampshire. The court noted:

> . . . The commission should consider whether the CWIP asked to be included in the rate base represents the cost of money expended for raising capital to finance construction that is undertaken upon sound business judgment and in accordance with a definite plan to meet the needs of future utility consumers. . . .

The factual determination that the commission had to make in its used and useful analysis was whether the company's CWIP represents an expenditure incurred in raising capital to finance a reasonable construction program that will inure to the benefit of energy consumers by assuring a future supply of electricity. . . .

We next consider the LUCC's argument that inclusion of CWIP in the company's rate base violates the basic "just and reasonable" principle of RSA ch. 378. The thrust of the LUCC's position is that including CWIP in the rate base forces present ratepayers to pay costs that should fall on future ratepayers who will actually benefit from the plant under construction when it comes on line. The LUCC argues that the traditional AFUDC treatment of CWIP, whereby it is capitalized and collected from future ratepayers via inclusion in the rate base over the period of the useful life of the plant when it comes on line, is required by the "just and reasonable" principle. The LUCC suggests that "the inclusion of CWIP [in the current rate base] is detrimental to present consumers while providing a windfall to future consumers."

We reject the LUCC's contention that AFUDC treatment of CWIP is mandated by law. The commission's decision to include CWIP in the rate base instead of capitalizing it in an AFUDC account is a factual one to be made on a case-by-case basis. Incorporating the burden of proof standard of RSA 378:8, we hold that "the burden of proving the necessity" of including CWIP in the rate base instead of employing traditional AFUDC treatment is upon the public utility. In the present case, we cannot say that "a clear preponderance of the evidence before [us]," demonstrates that the commission erroneously decided that the company has met its burden. RSA 541:13.

. . . The building of a nuclear powered generating facility requires very substantial lines of bank credit for the early construction stages. Immediate financing must be available. If credit is not forthcoming, the construction program will be jeopardized. *Amyot, supra* at 281. Because it is fundamental that rate making must take into account the need for the utility to maintain the confidence of investors, *Bluefield Water Works & Improvement Co. v. Pub. Serv. Comm'n*, 262 U.S. 679, 693 (1923); *accord, Federal Power Comm'n v. Hope Natural Gas Co.,*

320 U.S. 591, 603 (1944), the commission properly exercised its regulatory function by allowing the company to prove the necessity of including its CWIP in the rate base. . . .

Ratepayers like taxpayers come and go but ratepayers like taxpayers cannot expect to be charged solely on the basis of their individual benefit. Schools and other public buildings are benefitting the taxpayers today but were fully paid for by taxpayers of yesterday. . . .

If CWIP is not allowed in rate base, a firm cannot earn a current rate of return on its investment. However, it is permitted to use an alternative method of recovering the cost of capital invested in CWIP during the period before new plant is placed into service through an account known as Allowance for Funds Used During Construction (AFUDC); the firm accumulates in AFUDC an amount each year that represents the annual cost of capital in its CWIP account. Once a plant is completed and placed in service, all costs of the plant, including the accumulated AFUDC, are transferred to the firm's rate base. This allows the firm to earn a return on its CWIP, but the receipt of that money is deferred until after the plant is in service. In the above case, the New Hampshire Supreme Court rejected this approach:

The commission also evaluated alternative ratemaking approaches to that of including CWIP in the rate base. It considered full normalization of tax benefits of accelerated depreciation and allowing a higher return on equity capital. It found that these methods were "disadvantageous and undesirable in many respects." The commission relied on witness Trawicki's testimony to reject the alternative of allowing a higher return on equity capital. Trawicki stated "that such an alternative would result in an inflated return which is unrealistic when compared to other utilities and it could have the effect of establishing an inappropriate precedent." In rejecting the option of full normalization of tax benefits from accelerated depreciation, the commission found that this method would not generate enough funds to remedy the company's revenue deficiency and also that this procedure is imprecise and not readily controllable. The commission's report elaborated on the reasoning favoring CWIP in the rate base as the most desirable ratemaking approach.

We find that setting a rate of return higher than normal [on equity capital] would impose the same burdens on customers, that is, the rates would be the same while providing none of the advantages of the CWIP method, that is, a future reduction in rates because of a smaller future rate base. In other words, if the interest on the CWIP component is paid for today, it will not be included in the rate tomorrow. If CWIP were not allowed and the needed cash revenue were generated through a rate of return, the Company would continue to accumulate AFUDC along conventional accounting principles and eventually add this total amount to the total capitalization of plant. Thus, there would be no future reduction in rates stemming from discontinuance of AFUDC. . . .

6. Used and useful, as a criteria for including costs in rate base, serves to protect current generations from bearing the burden of paying for the capital necessary to generate energy for future generations. Does this create the right incentives for energy consumption? What are the effects of the doctrine on technological innovation? Does allowing recovery of CWIP serve any useful distributive or economic purpose?

7. The used and useful doctrine has been most controversial in the nuclear context, where many expensive plants took longer to build than was initially planned and were never fully utilized to the benefit of consumers. Consider the following excerpt:

James A. Throgmorton, Planning as Persuasive Storytelling: The Rhetorical Construction of Chicago's Electric Future
University of Chicago Press 70–72, 244–45 (1996).

In 1956, [Commonwealth] Edison obtained the ICC's permission to build Dresden 1, the nation's first full-scale, privately financed nuclear power plant. Almost one decade later, with its forecasts showing the demand for electric power growing at 7 percent per year, and believing that nuclear power would be the best way of providing adequate and reliable power in the future, Edison announced a major expansion of what has become the nation's largest program to construct nuclear power plants. Between 1965 and 1973, the company announced its intention to build twelve or more large nuclear units at its Dresden, Quad Cities, Zion, LaSalle, Byron, and Braidwood stations. More specifically, in 1970, 1972, and 1973, Edison applied to the ICC for "certificates of public convenience and necessity" to authorize and direct construction of six nuclear generating units totaling approximately 6,600 MW at its LaSalle, Byron, and Braidwood stations. According to material submitted with those applications, the units would be completed by 1980 at a cost of $2.5 billion (ICC 1980a; ICC 1985b; BPI and CUB 1989b). They would extend the modernist story of a regulated natural monopoly building larger power plants that increased earnings and reduced consumer rates.

This was an ambitious plan. As time passed, it also proved to be highly controversial and difficult to carry out completely or on time. The plan assumed that the economic stability of the 1960s would continue. It also assumed that nuclear power plants, which heretofore had been designed as 300 MW units, could easily be modified to operate equally efficiently at the 1,000 MW scale. Consequently this plan was shaken by the energy price shocks of the 1970s, by price inflation, by the 1979 nuclear accident at Three Mile Island. Moreover, it was assaulted by the rise of consumer, environmental, and antinuclear movements.

Edison's plants took longer to build, and they cost much more than expected. The last of the six nuclear units was not completed until 1988, and the final construction cost turned out to be approximately $13.7 billion (see table 4.1). Thus Edison's nuclear plan was completed eight years behind schedule and $11.2 billion over budget!

To pay for its increasingly expensive plants, the company had to apply for a series of large rate increases. As the price of electricity increased, the rate of growth in demand for electric power declined. Edison's capacity and load factors decreased, while its reserve margin increased. Faced with steadily increasing electricity prices, consumers looked for alternative ways of obtaining needed power and energy services. . . .

And the commissioners—ah, the commissioners they struggled to "balance the interests" of characters who were beginning to bewilder them by telling very different stories about planning and ratemaking in Illinois, stories that implied fundamental changes in the very notion of balancing interests through regulatory action. . . .

The data said that demand for electric power in Edison's service area had been growing at an average annual rate of 7.8 percent from 1961 through 1973. The data said that peak load—which stood at 10,943 megawatts in 1970—would grow to 17,850 megawatts in 1977 and that the company would need to add almost 7,000 megawatts of additional generating capacity to meet that demand. The data showed that nuclear power would provide the least costly way of generating the additional power. Consequently, the one best solution to the problem (or opportunity) of rapidly increasing demand was for Edison to build six new nuclear power generating units, each with a capacity of 1,100 megawatts, at its LaSalle, Byron, and Braidwood stations. Cost estimates showed that construction of those units would be completed by 1980 at a cost of $2.506 billion. Net present value revenue projections showed that the rates (prices) consumers pay for electric power would decline as the plants began generating useful power.

Confident in its forecasts and plan, Edison began building its six nuclear units in the early 1970s. However, the company soon encountered a series of difficulties (all due, of course, to factors beyond its control) which endangered that plan. Rather than growing at 7.8 percent, peak demand grew at an average annual rate of 2.3 percent from 1974 through 1988. Rather than growing by 6,900 megawatts between 1970 and 1977, peak load grew by 2,990 megawatts. (As of 1990 it still had not reached the load Edison projected for 1977.) Rather than costing approximately $400 per kilowatt, Edison's last six nuclear units turned out to cost almost $2,100. Rather than declining, the average rates that Edison charged its customers (measured in terms of gross operating revenues divided by kilowatt-hour sales) increased from 4.51¢/kWh to 7.35¢/kWh in constant 1982 dollars. Despite these difficulties, the company did finish building its six nuclear units. But it did not finish them until 1988 at a total cost of $13.7 billion, and along the way it had to increase its rates by 63 percent (in constant 1982 dollars), saw its earnings drop from $4.75 per common share in 1987 to $0.08 in 1991, and had to cut its dividends from $3 per common share in 1987 to $1.60 per share in 1991.

Rigidly focused on completing the company's troubled expansion plan, on cutting a clear path through the wilderness below, Edison's managers found that they could no longer simply contemplate and control the future from their central plateau. To their dismay, the plan and its tidal wave of rate increases motivated consumer, environmental, antinuclear, community groups, and sympathetic elected officials to coalesce in opposition. Instead of simply presenting evidence that justified the plan, Edison's planners and managers had to descend from their plateau and then try to persuade specific audiences at specific times in specific contexts, in the face of determined opposition.■

e. OPERATING EXPENSES

The day-to-day operational decisions of a regulated utility remain largely in the hands of its management. Operating and maintenance expenses are often recorded in the utility's actual books and records, so their identification and measurement does not pose the same challenge as other aspects of the ratemaking formula. FERC and state PSCs generally defer to private management regarding the utility's decisions as to what type of fuel to purchase, the need for more service workers, or a salary increase for management.

Depreciation and taxes are operating expenses for most utilities. Although, as is noted above, depreciation is typically deducted from capital investment to determine rate base, depreciation for the relevant period is also included as an operating expense. So, although the utility's rate base may be declining with time, the utility is able to recover the value of the reduction in value from customers.

Although operating expenses generally comprise around 75% of a utility's revenue requirements, in practice operating expenses may be the least controversial of the costs in the ratemaking formula. Deference is the standard with respect to operating expenses, but not every expense item is rubber-stamped for rate inclusion by FERC or state PSCs. In dictum, *Smyth v. Ames* qualified its description of the operating costs, O, a utility must be allowed to recover: "Under the evidence there is no ground for saying that the operating expenses of any companies were greater than necessary." This has come to be known as the "prudent expenditure" and "prudent investment" doctrines. Regulators will disallow operating expenses or investments that do not meet the prudence standards. These two standards are distinct. A decision to build (prudent investment) is evaluated separately from the reasonableness of costs once that decision has been made (prudent expenditure). In evacuating prudence, regulators apply a general presumption of managerial competence. *See Missouri ex rel. Southwestern Bell Tel. Co. v. Public Serv. Comm'n*, 262 U.S. 276 (1923).

While the prudent investment doctrine is primarily a rate base issue, FERC and state PSCs have disallowed many operating expenses under the prudent expenditure standard. For example, state commissions have also disallowed from rate recovery portions of wages they deem to be excessive. *See, e.g., Southwestern Bell Tel. Co. v. Arkansas Pub. Serv. Comm'n*, 715 S.W.2d 451 (1986); *Southern Cal. Edison Co. v. Public Util. Comm'n*, 20

Cal.3d 813 (1978). In addition, the costs of unnecessary advertising[7] and charitable contributions have regularly been disallowed. *See, e.g., Central Maine Power Co.*, 26 P.U.R.4th 407 (Maine PSC 1978) (disallowing advertisements designed to influence pending rate proceedings as "political"); *Cleveland v. PSC*, 406 N.E.2d 1370 (Ohio 1980) (disallowing charitable contributions "not reasonably necessary to produce safe, reliable service to utility customers").

Should the prudence of each of a utility's charitable contributions be evaluated, or is it the overall amount of the contribution that should be subject to a reasonableness standard? In *Business & Professional People v. Illinois Commerce Comm'n*, 585 N.E.2d 1032 (Ill.1991), the Illinois Supreme Court held that is the overall amount of expenses that are important to the assessment of just and reasonable rates. Commonwealth Edison argued that the Commission arbitrarily disallowed $1.269 million of charitable contributions from Edison's operating expenses. The Court reasoned:

> Edison is correct that the Act prohibits the Commission from "disallowing by rule, as an operating expense, any portion of a reasonable donation for public welfare or charitable purposes." (Ill. Rev. Stat. 1987, ch. 111 2/3, par. 9—227.) However, section 9—227 does not provide that every donation Edison makes to a qualified organization is presumed reasonable. Edison still has the burden of showing that a donation is reasonable in amount. When this burden of proof is considered, the Act merely states that the Commission shall not disallow any portion of that amount which Edison has shown to be reasonable in amount. Contrary to Edison's position, we believe that the Commission must determine the reasonableness of the amount of contributions based on the total contributions rather than on an individualized basis. There are numerous charitable organizations worthy of Edison's support. If Edison were to make a reasonable donation to each of these organizations, the aggregate total of the donations could very easily exceed a reasonable amount.

The Court refused to substitute its judgement for the Commission on which requested charitable expenses to exclude from an overall reasonable amount.

Another prevalent operational expense is fuel costs or the costs of purchased power (i.e., wholesale power bought by a utility for resale to its customers). Since its is costly to evaluate rates on a continuing basis, many regulators have provided for automatic adjustments in the price and quantity of fuel used through a Fuel Adjustment Clause (F.A.C.). The Illinois Supreme Court has commented:

> Perhaps the most significant operating expenses utilities incur are fuel costs. In 1973, a four-fold increase in petroleum prices and the escala-

---

7. The U.S. Supreme Court has recognized that utility advertising may raise First Amendment concerns. *Consolidated Edison Co. v. Public Service Commission*, 447 U.S. 530 (1980); *Central Hudson Gas & Electric Corp. v. PSC of New York*, 447 U.S. 557 (1980).

tion of coal and natural gas prices left utilities with far higher rates than those based on test year projections. Thus, utilities faced a revenue shortfall. A response to this development was the fuel adjustment clause. The fuel adjustment clause (FAC) is a statutory or regulatory rule that allows a utility to automatically pass through to rates increased fuel costs, without the need for a formal rate proceeding. From the utility's perspective, this allows a closer matching of actual expenses and the revenues received from consumer rates. Consumers may also benefit if fuel costs decrease between rate filings. However, FACs also reduce incentives for utilities to negotiate low fuel costs.

Business & Professional People v. Illinois Commerce Comm'n, 585 N.E.2d 1032 (Ill.1991).

In *Southern California Edison v. Public Utilities Comm.*, 20 Cal.3d 813, 821–23 (1978), the California Supreme Court noted, however, that usage of a F.A.C. on the basis of entirely forecasted data can lead to over collection of revenues by utilities:

> Not surprisingly, at the hearings below Edison's witness was extremely reluctant to admit that the company in fact treated such overcollections as earnings; rather, he took refuge in the repeated assertion that the funds could not be "isolated" from Edison's overall revenues. It clearly appears from published figures, however, that Edison's overcollections pursuant to the fuel clause were not only large in the absolute sense, they amounted to a very significant proportion of the company's general revenue picture. For example, for the year 1974 Edison reported a total net income from all sources of $218.3 million; yet during the same 12–month period, according to Edison's own figures filed with the commission in compliance with the decision under review, Edison's net fuel clause overcollections were $122.5 million—in other words, they constituted more than 56 percent of the company's system-wide net income for the entire year. Moreover, that net income was itself 47.8 percent higher than in the previous year, even though sales were lower; Edison's reported earnings per share were $4.10 for 1974, as compared with $2.70 for 1973; and the company's board of directors voted to increase the common stock dividend in 1974, the first such raise in three years. (Annual Rep., p. 4.) In announcing all these benefits to the shareholders, Edison acknowledged that the fuel clause adjustments, together with a general rate increase in late 1973, "contributed substantially to higher revenues."

These continuing overcollections by Edison and other electric utility companies did not pass unnoticed. On the contrary, they triggered a sequence of public complaints, investigations, and proposals for reform or abolition of the entire fuel clause procedure. Among the most vocal critics were consumer groups (e.g., The Fuel–Adjustment Caper (Nov. 1974) 39 Consumer Rep. 836) and organs of the Congress (*see* Rep. of Subcom. on Oversight and Investigations of House Com. on

Interstate and Foreign Commerce on Electric Utility Automatic Fuel Adjustment Clauses (Oct. 1975) passim).

While sharing many of the concerns voiced by critics of the clause, the commission determined that the cost adjustment concept should be preserved but the clause should be modified to eliminate the defects revealed by experience. The principal such defect, as we have seen, was the provision authorizing Edison to base its calculations on a prediction of its fossil fuel needs for the 12–month period following each application for a billing adjustment, premised on the assumption that "average" weather conditions would prevail throughout that time. The commission abandoned this procedure, and in lieu thereof adopted a clause which operates on a "recorded data" basis, i.e., on the actual fuel expenses incurred by the utility during the period preceding its application for a billing adjustment. The utility is now required to maintain a monthly "balancing account," into which it will enter the amount by which its actual energy cost for the month was greater or less than the revenue generated by the clause; and on each occasion hereafter that the clause is invoked, the billing factor will be adjusted so as to bring the balance of this account back to zero. By this device the possibility of large over-or undercollections accumulating in the future is eliminated. And because the commission expanded the clause to include all sources of purchased energy—e.g., nuclear and geothermal, in addition to fossil fuels—it renamed the device the "energy cost adjustment clause."

Id. The Court held that adjustment clause did not result in retroactive ratemaking. *Id.*

NOTES AND COMMENTS

1. Operating expenses may also be disallowed if they are underrepresentative (or nonrecurring). Generally non-recurring expenses, such as repair expenses attributable to a hurricane or excess fuel costs incurred during an excessively hot summer, will not be used as a basis for test year recovery of expenses, but will be allowed one-time recovery as extraordinary expenses. In addition, some operating expenses simply may not qualify for agency regulation. *See Sandstone Resources, Inc. v. FERC*, 973 F.2d 956 (D.C.Cir. 1992) (costs incurred in removing liquid brine from natural gas held to be nonrecoverable production costs).

2. How would you oppose or defend the inclusion of the following as legitimate utility operating expenses? Are all of these operating expenses, or should some of them be included in rate base?

    — A contribution to an industry-wide Gas Research Institute. *See PUC of Colorado v. FERC*, 660 F.2d 821 (D.C.Cir.1981).

    — Research programs in solar energy and nuclear reactor technology standards. *See Caldwell v. PUC*, 613 P.2d 328 (Colo.1980).

— A discount on electric charges for company employees. *See Central Maine Power Co. v. PUC*, 405 A.2d 153 (Me.1979).

— A commercial scale plant demonstrating a new coal gasification technique. *See Transwestern Pipeline Co. v. FERC*, 626 F.2d 1266 (5th Cir.1980).

— Expenses incurred when a plant under construction is abandoned. *See Office of Consumers' Council v. Public Utilities Commission*, 67 Ohio St.2d 153, 423 N.E.2d 820 (1981).

— Advertising expenses encouraging the conservation of electricity.

— Flyers included with utility bills responding to allegations that a utility's nuclear facilities are unsafe.

— A utility-sponsored research lab to investigate the effects of electro-magnetic fields from power lines.

— The medical costs for future retired employees.

Should a utility be allowed to recover attorneys fees incurred defending claims of environmental harm during construction of a new gas or power transmission line? The following case illustrates the skepticism with which regulators have treated such claims for recovery. Why was the agency reversed?

Iroquois Gas Transmission System v. Federal Energy Regulatory Commission,

145 F.3d 398 (D.C.Cir.1998).

■ Williams, J.:

Iroquois Gas Transmission System, L.P., ran up substantial legal defense costs as a result of federal investigations into environmental violations committed in its construction of a natural gas pipeline. The Federal Energy Regulatory Commission issued orders excluding these legal costs from the rate base used to calculate Iroquois's permissible charges, explaining that Iroquois had failed to carry the burden of proving that the costs were prudently incurred. Iroquois says the orders were grounded in an impermissible presumption of non-recoverability and asks us to set them aside, relying primarily on our decisions in *Mountain States Telephone and Telegraph Co. v. FCC*, 939 F.2d 1021 (D.C.Cir.1991) ("Mountain States I") and *Mountain States Telephone and Telegraph Co. v. FCC*, 939 F.2d 1035 (D.C.Cir.1991) ("Mountain States II"). Because the Commission has failed to come to grips with the questions that Mountain States II said must be answered when addressing a utility's recovery of legal expenses, we remand the case for a more reasoned decision.

* * *

In November 1990 the Commission granted Iroquois a certificate of public convenience and necessity under Section 7 of the Natural Gas Act (the "Act"), authorizing the company to build and operate a new pipeline stretching from the Canadian border to Long Island. The pipeline went into full service in January 1992. Before long, however, Iroquois found itself in trouble for environmental violations. Around November 1991 the U.S. Attorney's Office for the Northern District of New York, in conjunction with the FBI and the Environmental Protection Agency, began an investigation into whether Iroquois's construction activities violated the Clean Water Act. The record suggests that the investigation focused on points where the pipeline crossed creeks and streams in upstate New York, allegedly discharging silt and sediment in violation of Iroquois's Clean Water Act permit, and on Iroquois's alleged failure to build so-called trench breakers, which control soil erosion and pipeline corrosion. An Army Corps of Engineers inspection report from early 1992 cited a potential overall penalty of more than $115,000,000. Civil investigations, presumably closely related, were also undertaken by the U.S. Attorney's offices for the Northern, Eastern, and Southern Districts of New York. In addition, FERC's own enforcement staff launched a separate investigation to determine whether Iroquois had violated the environment-related conditions of its Section 7 certificate. Ultimately an Iroquois affiliate and four of its employees entered into guilty pleas and a civil settlement costing $22 million in fines and penalties, and Iroquois consented to a settlement with the Commission admitting violations of environmental conditions in its certificate and agreeing not to pass the fines and penalties on to its ratepayers. *Iroquois Gas Transmission System, L.P.*, 75 FERC ¶ 61,205 (1996).

In the course of resolving these disputes Iroquois ran up a legal bill of more than $15,000,000. While the various investigations were still under way, Iroquois filed with the Commission for a general rate increase to recover its pipeline construction costs. The rate proceeding culminated in a settlement between Iroquois and its customers resolving all issues except the rate and accounting treatment of the legal defense costs. Hearings on these reserved issues were held before an administrative law judge, who determined that the legal costs were not unrecoverable per se, and observed that "[t]he participants have presented nothing to rebut Iroquois's position that the legal costs were incurred as an appropriate and normal response to investigatory activities arising from the construction undertaken to provide service to the ratepayers." *Iroquois Gas Transmission System, L.P.*, 72 FERC ¶ 63,004, at 65,027 (1995).

The Commission reversed the ALJ's initial decision and held that Iroquois's legal defense costs could not be included in its rate base. *Iroquois Gas Transmission System, L.P.*, 77 FERC ¶ 61,288 (1996). "Allowing recovery of Iroquois' litigation expenses," the Commission concluded,

> would fail to recognize the interests of Iroquois' ratepayers, shared by the Commission, that emanate from Section 7 of the NGA. These interests are to ensure that the pipeline is built in compliance with all applicable federal environmental and safety laws so as to prevent any future personal injuries or environmental damage.

Id. at 62,280. The Commission based its disallowance of recovery on Iroquois's failure to demonstrate any countervailing economic or noneconomic benefit to ratepayers from the activities that gave rise to the investigations. The Commission denied Iroquois's request for rehearing, *Iroquois Gas Transmission System, L.P.*, 78 FERC ¶ 61,216 (1997), and later rejected similar claims in a second rate case filed by Iroquois. *Iroquois Gas Transmission System, L.P.*, 77 FERC ¶ 61,352, at 62,538 (1996), rehearing denied, 80 FERC ¶ 61,199, at 61,797–98 (1997). Iroquois petitioned for review in this court.

At the outset the Commission concedes two propositions, one general and one specific to this case. First, the Commission admits that although the Act gives the natural gas company the burden of showing that a proposed rate increase is just and reasonable, 15 U.S.C. § 717c(e), as a matter of FERC practice "a natural gas company is ordinarily not required to show that all of its expenditures were prudent unless serious doubts are raised regarding the prudence of those costs." FERC Br. at 24. *See, e.g., Trans World Airlines, Inc. v. CAB*, 385 F.2d 648, 657 (D.C.Cir.1967); *Minnesota Power & Light Co.*, 11 FERC ¶ 61,312, at 61,645 (1980). Second, the Commission does not seriously contest that it effectively raised a presumption against recovery in this case, putting the burden on Iroquois to demonstrate that its expenditures were prudently incurred. *See* 78 FERC at 61,927 ("[S]ince [Iroquois] was seeking to recover the legal defense costs in its rates, it had the burden of proving that the costs were just and reasonable."). Indeed, at times the Commission seemed to erect something close to an irrebuttable presumption against recovery. See id. ("Iroquois placed itself in the untenable position of arguing that its illegal activities, supposedly taken to save time and money during construction, were in the interests of its ratepayers, and, therefore, just and reasonable.") (emphasis added).

The Commission contends, however, that it adequately justified its decision to invert the normal presumption in this case, because Iroquois's legal costs by their very nature raised a serious doubt as to prudence (i.e., because they grew out of civil and criminal violations). *See* FERC Br. at 24. One immediate problem with this approach is that as of the time the hearing was held before the ALJ no violations had been proven or admitted; the investigations were still ongoing and the precise contours of any eventual charges were still uncertain. But even if that problem is put aside, the Commission runs into another barrier: our decisions in the Mountain States cases.

In Mountain States I we held that the Federal Communications Commission had failed to provide a reasoned justification for its presumption that antitrust litigation expenses incurred by AT & T could not be recovered from ratepayers. 939 F.2d at 1029–35. "Illegality of carrier conduct from which an antitrust litigation expense stems," we concluded, "does not inexorably compel or warrant either rejection or stigmatization of the expense as a factor in rate calculations." *Id.* at 1031. We noted that in two tax decisions the Supreme Court had described litigation expenses—even those incurred in a losing cause—as ordinary and legitimate costs of doing business. *Id.* at 1031–32 (*citing Commissioner v. Heininger*, 320 U.S. 467,

64 S.Ct. 249, 88 L.Ed. 171 (1943), and *Commissioner v. Tellier*, 383 U.S. 687, 86 S.Ct. 1118, 16 L.Ed.2d 185 (1966)).

In Mountain States II, issued the same day as Mountain States I, we reviewed a new FCC regulation governing the accounting treatment of litigation expenses generally. The new rule attached a presumption of non-recoverability to all litigation expenses that resulted in an adverse final judgment or post-judgment settlement in any federal statutory case, unless the regulated company could show that ratepayers benefitted from the underlying activity. 939 F.2d at 1039. Holding that "the FCC may disallow any expense incurred as a result of carrier conduct that cannot reasonably be expected to benefit ratepayers," id. at 1043, we found the new rule quite sensible in the context of antitrust violations, since the effect of such violations is typically to injure consumers. But we went on to say that the FCC had inadequately justified its application of the new rule to statutory violations beyond antitrust, where an absence of ratepayer benefit "is neither self-evident, as it is in the antitrust context, nor bolstered by either analytical or empirical support." Id. at 1044. By the same token we rejected the FCC's "terse assertion" that violations of federal statutory law "raise public policy implications" sufficient to justify presumptive disallowance of associated litigation costs. Id. at 1045.

We emphasized in Mountain States II that the FCC had not taken sufficient account of the perverse incentive effects set in motion by a presumption against recovery of litigation expenses. Such a presumption, we observed, was likely to induce excessive caution in carriers, causing them to shun activities that might conceivably be found to violate federal law, even when those activities promise benefits to ratepayers. Id. at 1046. We illustrated the point in a passage whose uncanny relevance to the instant case calls for full quotation:

> Consider the following example: A carrier has to choose between instituting a strict pollution monitoring policy or a lax policy that is arguably sufficient under the law and would cost $50,000 less than the strict policy. The carrier will surely be sued under a federal statute if it adopts the lax policy, and there is a 10% chance that it will lose; if it does, the plaintiff would recover $100,000, making the expected or ex ante cost of the lawsuit ($100,000 x .10 =) $10,000. Thus the carrier reasonably determines that adopting the lax policy will produce a net benefit of $40,000 to the ratepayers, who would otherwise have to pay the cost of the strict monitoring policy. It would be misleading to say that requiring ratepayers to bear the cost of the resulting judgment, if any, causes them to subsidize the carrier's illegal activity. The carrier made the "right" decision, i.e., what the ratepayers would have decided in their own economic self-interest; it just turned out to be the "wrong" decision as a matter of how the law was finally interpreted. Perhaps the agency has a more capacious notion of ratepayer benefit than merely paying lower rates. If it does, however, it has neither said as much nor indicated why ratepayers are generally harmed in some non-economic way by the violation of federal statutes.

Id. at 1044–45.

The Commission quoted this passage in its initial order, *see* 77 FERC at 62,279–80, acknowledging its relevance but claiming to find refuge in its final two sentences. While the FCC in Mountain States II had failed to articulate any noneconomic harm flowing from violations of federal statute law, the Commission said, here Iroquois's ratepayers have a general interest in compliance with federal environmental and safety laws, and thus are harmed whenever those laws are violated. 77 FERC at 62,280. The inclusion of environmental compliance requirements in Iroquois's Section 7 certificate, according to the Commission, represented an "implicit recognition that it would be appropriate for ratepayers to pay costs that may be incurred to build a pipeline in an environmentally responsible manner. It is not reasonable then to elevate the ratepayer interest in saving time and money to such a preeminent position in the interests to be considered when deciding whether costs are recoverable in the rates." *Id.*

We pause here to note that the Commission correctly placed its initial focus on the prospect of ratepayer benefits from the underlying activity rather than from the litigation. Even though it is commonly prudent (in the conventional sense of the term) to incur legal expenses in defending conduct that turns out to have been illegal, there appears no reason why ratepayers should bear the expense of defending conduct that had no ex ante prospect of benefitting them. *See* Mountain States II, 939 F.2d at 1043.

Nonetheless, we find the Commission's treatment of Mountain States II unconvincing. The asserted ratepayer interest in compliance with environmental and safety laws is virtually as generic as the amorphous "public policy implications" we found inadequate to justify the presumption of nonrecoverability in Mountain States II, 939 F.2d at 1045. Because all citizens share an interest in widespread compliance, not just with environmental or safety laws but with laws of any kind, the Commission's approach would result in the presumptive disallowance of all litigation expenses leading to anything short of outright triumph for the regulated entity.

More important, the Commission's approach utterly fails to respond to the problem of incentives posed in Mountain States II. Iroquois's ratepayers, in common with the general population of upstate New York, undoubtedly share an interest in maintaining the purity of the region's creeks and streams. But the same ratepayers have a unique and concentrated interest in timely and efficient pipeline construction. Although our concurring colleague asserts that some ratepayers would willingly pay higher rates in exchange for assurances of environmental compliance, see Concurring Op. at 276–77, laws obligating firms to satisfy environmental standards are necessary precisely because most consumers, if given a choice, appear unwilling to pay the full cost of satisfying higher standards. If consumer demand were actually enough to cause ordinary firms in competitive industries to incur the costs of protecting the environment, there would be little need for environmental regulation.

Indeed, because of the limitation of the utility's rates to recovery of cost under the statute's "just and reasonable" formula, the ratepayers have the same interest in optimizing environmental compliance costs as they would if they built the pipeline themselves through a cooperative or a partnership. As our opinion in Mountain States II made clear, a firm incurring optimal environmental compliance costs will on occasion take measures that are ultimately found illegal. In Mountain States II's example, where a saving of $50,000 runs a 10% risk of triggering $100,000 in additional costs, the ex ante expected benefit for the ratepayers is $40,000. Contrary to our concurring colleague's suggestion, see Concurring Op. at 277, Mountain States II does not establish a ratemaking principle that affirmatively encourages regulated companies to violate environment-related certificate conditions. It does, however, recognize that ratepayers often benefit from activities that tack reasonably close to the wind, and that policies inducing management to pursue absolutely risk-free environmental compliance measures are therefore not, on their face, in the ratepayers' interest.

Yet the Commission's approach seems sure to chill some lawful activity beneficial to ratepayers; indeed, it would seem calculated to encourage regulated firms to avoid any and all litigation risks. "[L]awsuits are a recurring fact of life in operating a business," Mountain States I, 939 F.2d at 1034, and in the area of federal environmental regulation the line between permissible and impermissible conduct is often drawn in (muddy) water. *Compare United States v. Mango*, 997 F.Supp. 264, 285 (N.D.N.Y. 1998) (holding that CWA authorized Army Corps of Engineers to regulate Iroquois's "backfilling of trenches excavated in waterways and wetland areas") with id. at 283–87, 295–98 (holding that CWA does not authorize Corps to impose permit conditions not related to discharge of dredged or fill material, such as those designed to prevent wetland drainage).[8] Thus the Commission must do a better job of explaining why all activities that turn out to violate environmental laws should be presumed unlikely "to benefit ratepayers," as required for presumptive disallowance under Mountain States II, 939 F.2d at 1043.

The Commission's attempted distinction of *Appalachian Electric Power Co. v. FPC*, 218 F.2d 773 (4th Cir.1955), is also insubstantial. There the Fourth Circuit held that legal costs incurred by a regulated utility in an unsuccessful challenge to the Commission's jurisdiction over a proposed power plant were recoverable from ratepayers as expenses necessary to the development of the project. According to the Commission, the costs of the jurisdictional challenge in Appalachian were an example of "normal civil litigation" costs; other examples given by the Commission were the "cost of attorneys hired to secure any state or federal permits, or litigation to perfect eminent domain rights or to establish property values." 77 FERC at 62,281. Iroquois's case is different, the Commission said, because it "is not

---

8. [Editors note:] On appeal, the district court decision cited here was reversed and the Second Circuit held that the condi-

tions attached by the Corps were proper. *U.S. v. Mango*, 199 F.3d 85 (2d Cir.1999).

the type of case where a regulated company, interpreting the law in a manner most favorable to the company, loses a court case." Id. In fact that description seems, at least at first glance, to fit Iroquois's case quite snugly. Beyond offering a few conclusory statements ("there is no punitive aspect associated with the loss of a challenge [to] the agency's regulatory jurisdiction," id.), the Commission never explains why action based on a legal interpretation "most favorable to the company" should have been presumptively beneficial to ratepayers in Appalachian but presumptively harmful here.

In short, the Commission has not made clear which types of legal defense costs are presumed recoverable for ratemaking purposes and which not, or why the costs here belong on the nonrecoverable side of the line. Particularly in light of the explicit discussion of pollution laws in Mountain States II, the Commission's burden here requires more than the making of general allusions to the public interest in compliance with environmental statutes or with Section 7 certificate requirements. Of course, we do not reach the ultimate question whether Iroquois's legal defense costs were in fact prudently or imprudently incurred, and thus whether they may or may not be borne by the ratepayers. We hold only that the Commission has not adequately justified its apparent decision to impose upon Iroquois the burden of proving that its activities benefitted ratepayers.

The case is remanded to the Commission for further proceedings consistent with this opinion.

So ordered.

■ WALD, J., concurring in the judgment:

Although I agree that this case must be remanded for further consideration, I write separately to emphasize the breadth of the analysis FERC should undertake on remand. Although the ultimate issue in this case is who is to bear Iroquois's litigation costs, not whether Iroquois's conduct was legal or illegal, the latter consideration is certainly relevant, in my view. It is worth noting, therefore, that Iroquois admitted violating several environmental-related conditions of its section 7 certificate, and our discussion of whether it is "just and reasonable" for the company to then shift the litigation costs related to those violations to its ratepayers should in no way be read as directing FERC to ignore the harm to the environment that has been suffered as a result of those violations. Rather, I think it important that the calculus of whether a rate is reasonable take into consideration noneconomic benefit as well as economic benefit. It may well be true that a thoroughly informed ratepayer will prefer a cheaper product obtained by way of environmental violations over a more expensive product produced legally. But I'm not sure that this can be presumed to be the case, as the majority opinion appears to assume. In an antitrust case, as Mountain States II recognized, the analysis is easier: A presumption that litigation expenses associated with a violation of the antitrust laws are disallowed is reasonable because we can assume that consumers would prefer to buy products in a competitive market, since competition is presumed to make products both cheaper and better. Thus, it would be difficult to show that anticompetitive conduct would be beneficial to rate-payers in any way. Here, however, the equation is not so simple: We cannot presume that noncompliance with environmental regulations would be a benefit to ratepayers if the economic costs of compliance outweigh the economic costs of noncompliance, since the noneconomic benefit of compli-ance must also enter the calculus. It may well be the case, for example, that a ratepayer would prefer to pay higher rates in exchange for the assurance that the pipeline from which it obtains its gas is in compliance with environmental laws. (I can imagine several reasons for this preference: for the goodwill benefits compliance confers, to aid in thwarting litigation, or even because the ratepayer lives in the geographic area for which noncom-pliance is proposed and will suffer as a citizen.) I agree that under our precedent FERC's simple assertion that ratepayers have an interest in compliance with the law is insufficient to disallow recovery of Iroquois's litigation costs. As Mountain States II holds, FERC must also take into consideration the economic benefits noncompliance may confer, though I must admit I have a good deal of trouble with the proposition that FERC can validly attach an environmental condition on a section 7 permit, but the company is simultaneously encouraged by ratemaking principles to violate it if it can build the pipeline cheaper or faster by doing so. That kind of law makes no sense to me. But I also believe that even the Mountain States II calculus is far more expansive than the majority opinion suggests. By seeming to give priority to economic over noneconomic considerations, I fear that the majority will dissuade FERC from adequately considering the environmental costs of Iroquois's conduct, costs that may well affect the decision about whether forcing ratepayers to bear its litigation costs is indeed "just and reasonable."■

f.   INTERGENERATIONAL ALLOCATION

The most controversial expense issue regulators currently face is the intergenerational allocation of costs in utility rates. The general principle of cost of service ratemaking is that customers should pay for the costs of the services they consume. However, as issues such as CWIP, depreciation, and the FAC illustrate, it is much simpler to state the principle than make it work in practice. Consumers today, through items such as CWIP, may pay for services that benefit future generations. Although commissions general-ly frown upon "retroactive ratemaking," there is no hard and fast rule that commissions or courts use to match costs and benefits across generations. It generally comes down to balancing the various interests before the regulator.

In this balancing of interests, since future generations are not repre-sented it might be expected that often the costs associated with benefits to today's ratepayers are passed on to future generations. Ratepayers today are paying for services that may have unanticipated costs for future generations. As a result, future generations may pay greater rates to benefit today's consumers.

As an example, billions of dollars are at stake in the recovery of nuclear "decommissioning" costs—the costs utilities must incur when nuclear plants producing power today are retired 10, 20, or 30 years into the future to seal off radioactive waste and return nuclear facilities to a low-risk status. Regulators failed to account for these costs in determining the prudence of nuclear construction. Because it would be unfair to impose these costs on future ratepayers, utilities have been required to seek recovery in current rates.

Commonwealth Edison Company: Proposed General Increase in Electric Rates

158 P.U.R. 4th 458 (Ill. Commerce Comm. 1995).

On February 10, 1994, Commonwealth Edison Company ("Edison" or "Company") filed with the Illinois Commerce Commission (the "Commission") certain revised tariff schedules and amendments (collectively "the Filed Tariffs") by which it proposed to increase annual revenues by about 7.9%, or $460.3, which includes a base rate increase of $461.7 million, decreased meter lease revenues of $2.2 million and increased fuel adjustment revenues of $.8 million. . . .

Edison requests approval of $170.3 million annually to be paid directly into its external decommissioning trust funds. This amount, which represents an increase over the currently authorized level of $127.1 million, as allowed in Docket 90–0169, is attributable to: (1) site-specific or generic regional decommissioning cost estimates in 1993 dollars prepared by Edison witness Mingst; (2) Edison's intention to use the immediate dismantlement or "DECON" method; (3) its plan to return the sites of its nuclear plants to "greenfield" status, i.e., to demolish both radioactive and non-radioactive structures rather than leave the nonradioactive structures standing; (4) a 5.3% annual escalation rate derived from the Nuclear Regulatory Commission ("NRC") formula; (5) estimated rates of return on investments in the external decommissioning trust funds; and (6) a 25% contingency factor. Edison contends that these assumptions are consistent with state and federal laws requiring owners of nuclear generating facilities to provide reasonable assurance that adequate funds will be available to decommission those facilities at the end of their operating lives.

Edison claims that it has no incentive to overestimate its decommissioning costs because all funds will be deposited in trusts beyond its control. Thus, overestimating such costs would raise the Company's rates, making it less competitive, without providing any additional funds to the Company itself. Moreover, Edison maintains that since the Company is required by law to pay its decommissioning collections directly into external trust funds outside its control, and ultimately would be required to refund any unneeded funds to ratepayers, it does not benefit at all from these collections. . . .

Edison intends to demolish both radioactive and nonradioactive structures on the sites of its nuclear units and thereby return these sites to greenfield status. As Mr. Mingst stated, "non-radioactive plant structures are demolished for safety and environmental reasons," and "[a]ll responsible organizations plan for the eventual demolition" of such structures. Therefore, "[i]t is a standard industry practice to include the costs of demolishing the nonradioactive structures as a necessary component of total decommissioning costs." Also, the 1978 Battelle/Pacific Northwest Laboratories ("Battelle") site-specific decommissioning cost studies of the reference Trojan and WNP–2 nuclear plants, which have served as the bases for NRC rules, included the costs of nonradioactive demolition as normal decommissioning costs. . . .

Based upon the evidence in the record, the Commission denies any funds to return sites to greenfield status. The burden is on the Company to prove that it will not re-use old structures. The Company has failed to convince the Commission that nonradioactive structures will not be used in the future. The Commission cannot allow ratepayers to pay for returning facilities to greenfield status when, in fact, some facilities may be re-used.

In addition, this Commission does not have a statutory obligation to return sites to greenfield status. Illinois law mandates that decommissioning trusts be established to fund the costs of decommissioning. However, it does not require that sites be returned to greenfield status. It is also clear from the evidence in the record that the NRC does not mandate greenfield status.

From a technical perspective, it is not clear from the evidence in the record that greenfield status is a commonly accepted decommissioning practice. The Commission was persuaded by the evidence that potential changes in regulations may encourage use of nonradioactive portions of facilities. Given the technical changes that will occur, it would be unwise for the Commission to allow funds for greenfield status without being certain that nonradioactive facilities will be returned to greenfield status. . . . ■

g.   RATE DESIGN

The intergenerational cost allocation problem illustrates the issue of rate design. Even once revenue requirements are determined, regulators must decide who, among the various customer classes, should pay the costs of service. Several rate design issues may arise, among them demand and energy charges, marginal cost pricing, or seasonal or peak load pricing.

In terms of the cost of service rate formula, distinct costs of service can be allocated to distinct customer classes. For example, it may be more costly for a utility to build the distribution infrastructure to serve the hundreds of residential customers in a development than to serve one or two very large industrials customers, even though the two classes—residential and industrial—may consume similar total amounts of energy.

In allocating costs to classes of customers, including residential, industrial, and small business customers, regulators use two billing components: demand and energy charges. Demand charges generally refer to the portion of utility costs allocated to a customer group to meet the aggregate demand of that group. In other words, these costs represent the amount of plant and other fixed assets allocated to a customer group through a utility rate base ($B*r$). Energy charges generally refer to the cost of providing a certain number of units of energy to a class of customers. These costs vary with the amount consumed (e.g., fuel) and thus represent the amount of a company's operating expenses allocated to a class of customers (O). On a customer's bill, distinct charges for demand and energy will appear. Depending on how "firm" the customer's service is—i.e., the level of reliability the utility has guaranteed—the appropriate charges will be assessed. Because many industrial customers take service on an "interruptible" basis, their bills have small demand components relative to the portion of their bill attributed to energy charges (given the large number of units that they consume). By contrast, residential customers generally have high demand components (given that they need "firm" power) relative to the energy charges on their bills.

Fuels Research Council, Inc. v. Federal Power Comm.

374 F.2d 842 (7th Cir. 1967).

[Three coal associations and the mineworkers union challenged the FPC's approval of the rate design of two interstate pipelines, Natural Gas Pipeline Company of America and Midwestern Gas Trans mission Company. The Commission upheld a two-part rate structure, in which most of the capital cost of the pipeline facilities was charged to firm customers based on the maximum amount of gas to which they were entitled (the "demand" component) while the rates for industrial customers who bought gas on an interruptible basis were largely based on the volume of gas that they actually used (the "commodity" component). The coal associations appealed the Commission's decision to the Seventh Circuit Court of Appeals.]

■ SWYGERT, J.: The first step in setting the rates to be charged by a regulated pipeline is the determination of the pipeline's "cost of service," that is, the total revenues required to cover the pipeline's cost of operation plus a fair return on its investment. Once the cost of service has been ascertained, rates are "designed" to recover it. For reasons allegedly related to different types of services desired by different customers but more realistically attributable to the basic economic laws of supply and demand as they concern natural gas, the "designing" operation is not reducible to a simple mathematical exercise.

One "demand" for gas, the demand by those consumers who can be made to pay for both the pipeline and the gas flowing through it, is highly seasonal in the midwestern states. The desirability of gas for domestic and commercial space heating purposes in the winter, the "peak" period, is such that the demand for gas during that period by this type of consumer far exceeds the demand by the same consumer at other times of the year. This economic fact creates a "valley" period, a capacity in the pipeline to supply other potential users during the "non-peak" season, including many whose "demand" is constant but so low that they would never become users if they were compelled to pay a proportionate share of the pipeline's cost of service. The valley periods might well go unfilled were it not for the principle, widely accepted by rate-makers, that a more complete utilization of existing facilities spreads the costs of the entire system to whatever extent the additional utilization contributes to the fixed costs of the facilities over and above the payment of variable costs.

The rate-making theory urged upon us blends a concept of "peak cost-responsibility" with a desire to take advantage of the above principle in the following manner. First, the proposition that a pipeline is built to serve the peak period demand is accepted as a fact.[9] Stated another way, the pipeline capacity provided to take care of the demand on peak days of the system is viewed as creating the bulk of the fixed costs of the pipeline company. These costs do not depend upon the amount of gas flowing through the pipeline. The variable or "volumetric" costs of pipeline operation are essentially related to the amount of gas transported and sold; they are incurred in proportion to the gas actually used. It follows that those responsible for the creation of the peak demand would bear the entire cost of pipeline operation were it not for the opportunity provided by "valley filling" or "off peak" sales. Sales during valley periods (sales to those who will take gas if the price is right), since they do not require the construction of additional facilities, may and should be made at variable cost plus (as the Commission puts it) "such amounts in addition thereto as may be determined to be a proper contribution to the fixed charges," so that the fixed costs can be spread over more sales units, thus reducing the per unit costs.

The theory just described and the recognition that a pipeline's cost of service encompasses both fixed costs and variable costs have been reflected by ratemakers in the form of two-part rates. The rates are split into "demand" and "commodity" components. The demand component is a charge intended to reflect the fact that a customer has contracted for the right to take a given quantity of gas during the peak period. The demand charge is imposed whether the gas is actually taken from the system or not. The commodity component is a charge based upon the volume of gas consumed by each customer. The combination of these charges, multiplied by the anticipated units of the demand component to be contracted for plus the anticipated units of gas to be actually sold is expected to generate revenues equal to the cost of service. The significant problem posed by the two-part formula concerns the allocation of the costs of pipeline operation to the demand and commodity components, more specifically, to the deter-

---

9. See generally, Bonbright, Principles of Public Utility Rates (1961). But see the view expressed by Mr. Justice Jackson in *Colorado Interstate Gas Co. v. FPC*, 324 U.S. 581, 615, 65 S. Ct. 829, 845, 89 L. Ed. 1206 (1945) (concurring opinion), that "I do not think it can be accepted as a principle of public regulation that industrial gas may have a free ride because the pipe line and compressor have to operate anyway * * *."

mination of what contribution to the fixed costs of the system is to be recovered by the commodity charge. In the instant case the problem is accentuated, not because the customers of the pipeline, the distribution companies, have different peak demands, but due to the fact that the price of gas to certain customers of the distribution companies during the "valley" periods is based upon the commodity component of the pipelines' rate design.

At the hearing before the examiner, the coal associations argued that two-part rates for Midwestern and Natural were invalid, that the proper rate was a straight one-part rate representing the average cost of each unit of gas sold to the distributors. They introduced expert testimony to indicate the one-part rate which would be necessary to recover Midwestern's cost of service. In their brief on this petition for review, the coal associations do not directly attack the validity of two-part rates, but they do argue inferentially that the only permissible rates are those which reflect average unit costs.

We agree with the Commission that it may approve the formulation of a two-part rate structure. The demand-commodity formula has long been a rate device of regulatory agencies and there can be no objection to the use of it (or any other formula) in designing the recovery of a pipeline's cost of service, absent some indication that the results of its application may be in violation of the Natural Gas Act. Demand-commodity methods producing different rates for different types of services have been justified both because it is thought that the costs necessitated by the various services differ, *Mississippi River Fuel Corp. v. FPC*, 163 F.2d 433, 437–438, (D.C.Cir.1947), and because of the principle that fuller use of closed utility systems involving fixed costs results in lower unit costs. *National Coal Ass'n v. FPC*, 247 F.2d 86, 87 (D.C.Cir.1957)....

At the hearing before the examiner the coal associations offered evidence to show the impact of pipeline rates on the consumption of coal in the Chicago area. The examiner excluded the evidence as improper for consideration in a section 5(a) proceeding. The coal associations do not challenge the examiner's ruling directly but seek to avoid it by other means. Thus they alternately argue competitive injury to coal and assert that they are "persons" within that portion of section 4(b) (1) of the act, *15 U.S.C. § 717c*(b) (1), which states that "no natural-gas company shall * * * make or grant any undue preference or advantage to any person or subject any person to any undue prejudice or disadvantage * * *." The coal associations say that the rate designs approved by the Commission grant an "undue advantage" to the distributors and subject coal producers to "undue prejudice," and that therefore their effect upon the coal industry should be considered in a section 5(a) proceeding to determine whether rates are "unjust, unreasonable, unduly discriminatory, or preferential." The examiner answered this contention by saying that section 4(b) (1) deals with discriminations and preferences between different gas customers and does not apply to the effect of gas rates upon competing fuels. In view of the congressional purpose of the act to protect consumers against exploitation, we think that this is the proper construction. The interpretation urged by the coal associations would produce a result contrary to the authority of *FPC v. Hope Natural Gas Co.,* 320 U.S. 591, 602 (1944) and *Alston Coal Co. v. FPC,* 137 F.2d 740 (10th Cir. 1943), which held that the economic effect of pipeline rates upon competing fuels is not open for consideration in a section 5(a) proceeding. In Hope, the Court stated:

> It is also pointed out that West Virginia has a large interest in coal and oil as well as in gas and that these forms of fuel are competitive. When the price of gas is materially cheapened, consumers turn to that fuel in preference to the others. As a result this lowering of the price of natural gas will have the effect of depreciating the price of West Virginia coal and oil.
>
> . . .
>
> We have considered these contentions at length in view of the earnestness with which they have been urged upon us. We have searched the legislative history of the Natural Gas Act for any indication that Congress entrusted to the Commission the various considerations which West Virginia has advanced here. And our conclusion is that Congress did not. 320 U.S. at 609, 64 S. Ct. at 291.

The Commission takes the position that although a competitor may not intervene in rate proceedings under sections 4 and 5 of the act to argue his own injury, a competitor may participate in such proceedings to insure the protection of the public interest by offering evidence and argument relating to the factors pertinent to the Commission's determination. In this proceeding the coal associations are free to challenge the rates of Natural and Midwestern as "unjust, unreasonable, unduly discriminatory, or preferential," but only as the rates affect the distributors and their customers. Thus, even though the Commission considers competitive fuel prices in approving rate designs, competitors of the distributors may not urge competitive injury in design proceedings. This situation may seem anomalous, but for the reasons expressed in *FPC v. Hope Natural Gas Co., supra,* the matter is not open to question . . . .

The record supports the findings of the Commission and warrants the conclusion that the rate designs of Natural and Midwestern are just and reasonable. The order is affirmed.■

NOTES AND COMMENTS

1. Economists have long argued that all of a firm's capital costs, such as pipelines and compressor stations, should be included entirely in the demand charge of a two-part rate because a company's decision to invest in capital facilities is based on the maximum demand for the firm's product. Therefore, these "capacity" costs should be allocated to those customers who require service in periods of peak demand, in proportion to the maximum number of units of service that they are entitled to demand.

For many years, however, the FPC and its successor, FERC, used a compromise formula in which roughly half the capacity costs were included in the demand charge and the other half in the commodity charge. In 1992, however, the FERC in Order 636, discussed in Chapter Nine, switched to a rate design in which all capacity costs are included in the demand charge and are thus paid only by the firm customers. See Richard J. Pierce, Jr., and Ernest Gellhorn, Regulated Industries in a Nutshell 202–203 (West Group, 3d ed., 1994).

2. Gas and electricity distribution companies often use a three part rate structure. In addition to a demand and commodity component, they include a "customer" component, which is a fixed amount per customer to cover such charges as meter reading and billing, which do not vary either with total amount used or with maximum demand.

* * *

While, as is discussed in Chapter Three, we entertain the myth that natural monopoly prices should approximate marginal costs, the rate formula suggests a different pricing criterion. Because utility rates are set based on the cost of service, regulated utility prices more closely approximate average costs—not marginal costs, as a competitive market would yield. Yet, the disparity between average and marginal costs for some customer classes have led to some problems in the industry. For example, if average costs exceed marginal costs, utilities are more than compensated at a rate adequate to stay in business. In contrast, if marginal costs exceed average costs, utilities may find themselves in a profitability squeeze. Pricing at average cost makes no economic sense. Yet it is extremely difficult for regulators to adopt marginal cost pricing, given the lack of a complete and accurate system for evaluating utility marginal cost information. At the same time, pricing solely on the basis of marginal costs might have a disproportionate impact on some customers, particularly smaller ones.

For a long time, utilities were encouraged to build capacity and sell as much energy as possible to customers. Through the 1960s and early 1970s, technological improvements and growing economies of scale led electric utilities to build new and more efficient power plants. New power plant projects were very large—typically in the 1000 MW range. Once a power plant project was under construction, sales and marketing experts attempted to sell the excess capacity by encouraging large industrial users to abandon their in-house generating facilities, adding new customers to their geographic service areas, and encouraging greater electric usage by existing customers (e.g., the "all electric home" in the 1960s). A rate structure arose that favored the large industrial customer, recognizing that some customers could easily shift to alternative fuel sources or self-generation.[10] However, even advocates of small consumers were unabashed in their goal

---

10. The phenomenon known as "Ramsey Pricing," borrowed from taxation, advises regulators to set price higher for consumers with price-inelastic demand if they wish to maximize revenues. *See* Frank P. Ramsey, A Contribution to the Theory of Taxation, 37 Econ. J. 47 (1927).

of settings rates as low as possible for all customers. During this period of capacity expansion, electric utilities were more concerned with increasing consumer demand and covering capacity costs, not with having insufficient capacity to serve their customers.

About twenty-five years ago, attitudes toward rate design began to change. With the dawn of a grass-roots inspired environmental movement and the establishment of environmental interest groups at the state, local and national levels, conservation—not increased consumption—became an important concern for regulators. The oil crisis of the mid–1970s magnified the importance of conservation as one means of bringing about U.S. energy independence. New environmental legislation required the installation of pollution control equipment and added regulatory delay to the licensing of new power plants, thus making new power plant construction very expensive. Moreover, in the 1970s, utilities incurred construction and fuel cost overruns and, with improvements to the efficiency of power plants as small as 250 MW, an end to economies of scale in power generation; soon it was not only environmental groups and progressive regulators who were concerned with the traditional rate structure, but utilities as well.

In the early 1970s, conservation—which avoided the need to build new power plants—replaced merchandising of kilowatt hours at the lowest possible cost as a regulatory objective. This forced a rethinking of the rates that different customer groups must pay to cover utility expenses and capital costs. Remember that a utility has an obligation to meet consumer demand, whatever that might be. However, electricity poses a unique problem because, unlike natural gas and oil, it cannot be stored. This raises an issue that utilities often face: short-term mismatches between supply and demand. When the temperature reaches 105 degrees, everyone wants their air conditioning to work at full power, without interruption. To help encourage conservation, many regulars approved inclining block rates— rates that increase with additional units of use—or adopted "peak load" pricing—cost of service principles that charge higher rates during those "peak periods when the utility is operating at or near capacity. Like limited supply urban taxi cabs that charge higher rates during rush hours to encourage cab-pooling or alternatives, such as walking or taking a train, many utilities charge higher rates during peak periods to discourage use. During nonpeak periods, their rates may go down again to encourage more customer use.

By the mid–1980s, excess supply was again a concern of many electric utilities. This led to the re-emergence of many utilities offering low rates to maintain industrial customers. Many utilities with excess capacity also stand to benefit from the recent efforts to introduce competition into the electric utility industry, as discussed in Chapter Eleven.

Re Central Maine Power Company
150 P.U.R.4th 229 (Maine PUC 1994).

When we review an electric utility's request for an increase in its base or fuel rates, our perspective is largely historic; we look in fine detail at all the ways the utility has spent its money during a recent actual year, to determine whether its overall revenues in the year ahead could suffice to pay the costs of the service needed. Although inevitably requiring much judgment about the likely levels of future costs and revenues and about the prudence of the utility's management of its operations, such "revenue requirement" cases are rooted in historic accounting data.

When, instead, we review a utility's long-term resource plans, projected cost structures, and rate design proposals, our perspective is largely forward-looking and uncertain. We ask how a utility can best meet its customers' needs over the long-term planning period? What are the most likely costs? How should those costs be assigned to each class of customer? How should the costs be reflected in the pricing details of the specific rate structures offered? To answer these questions, we must look into an uncertain future, choose among competing planning strategies on the basis of educated judgments about future supply and demand conditions, and decide how those choices can best be reflected in the design of rates. Thus, this case leads us neither to specify the annual revenue amount that rates should be designed to allow the utility to collect, nor to say how much revenue should be collected from each rate class, and with what rate structure. Instead, our tasks here are to find the general utility planning strategy that best comports with the public interest, and to develop a set of general guidelines that can be used by CMP in a subsequent case to translate that strategy and its underlying costs into a specific rate design proposal. . . .

Declining Block Rates

. . . [W]e turn first to the single, key question on which much of the argument in the case has centered: Should public policy allow or encourage CMP to promote load growth through a broad adoption of a rate structure known as "declining block" rates? In electric utility parlance, a rate structure in which the average price paid per kilowatt-hour remains the same at different levels of monthly usage is known as a "flat rate." If the average price per kilowatt-hour changes with usage, the rate is either "declining" or "inclining," according to whether it falls or rises with usage; because declining rates were once very common, an inclining rate has at times been known as an "inverted" rate. When the rate is flat within broad ranges or "blocks" of usage, but changes between blocks, it is either an "inclining block" or "declining block" rate. Since 1986, CMP's rate for most of its residential customers, known as Rate A, has had an "inclining block" structure, in which the price per kWh for the first 400 kWh per month is 20 percent lower than the price for usage above 400 kWh per month. Other customers, including high-use residential customers who are on time-of-use rates, and commercial and industrial customers, have a more complicated bill that includes a fixed monthly customer charge. For the higher-use rate classes, the bill includes a demand charge as well. Both of these can cause the overall average rate per kilowatt-hour paid to vary considerably with usage. However, the energy charge component of these rates is currently a flat rate per kWh used.

In this case, CMP has asked us to approve the concept of replacing the inclining block structure of residential Rate A, and the flat rate energy charge of other residential and many commercial customers, with a declining block rate, so that the "tail block" monthly consumption above certain thresholds would be priced at a much lower rate. According to CMP, the purpose of this proposal is to improve economic efficiency, to make the price of electricity more competitive with oil for space or water heating, and, implicitly, to encourage a general increase in usage of electricity. In reviewing the evidence and argument developed in this case over the past year, we find that CMP has not made a convincing case for such a substantial revision to our long-standing rate design policies. The record lacks evidence on the likely extent of customer response to CMP's proposed changes in rate structure; we have no basis to say with any confidence that CMP's overall revenue would be higher than otherwise as a result of such changes. Given the normal expectations about demand elasticity, revenue would probably fall. Consistent with the virtual consensus among the other parties to the case, we are persuaded that the pursuit of economic efficiency through declining block rates, as the AARP put it, "does not ensure any additional revenue contribution and, indeed, gives rise to a substantial risk of revenue erosion, especially in the short run."

We do know, however, that a major rate design change such as a broad move to declining block rates would be likely to cause large increases in the bills paid by many customers, in order to offset the large decreases to high-use customers; simply changing the current inclining block structure of Rate A to a flat rate would cause the bills of the many customers using less than 400 kWh per month to go up by 12 percent, on average. (In January of 1992, the number of these customers was nearly 150,000; in August, more than 200,000.) Thus, the uncertain benefits of increased economic efficiency from the imposition of declining block rates would be bought at the certain expense of large rate changes for many customers. We find CMP's proposal especially unwise at this time of unusually high customer sensitivity to further changes in electric rates and low public confidence in the utility's ability to control its costs and charge reasonable rates.

Even if it could be shown that a change to declining block rates would be likely to yield at least a short-run revenue increase, we are not persuaded that such a move would be in the public interest. CMP argues that its current cost situation, in which marginal costs are well below average costs, will persist indefinitely, as a result of future cost-saving technologies and competitive pressures, and that rates should therefore be designed to encourage load growth. The record provides little support for such untempered optimism. Instead, the evidence shows that current cost relationships result to a significant degree from a temporary excess of "base-loaded" resources and expensive long-term power purchases. A strategy of encouraging marginal usage through broad adoption of declining rates would run a substantial risk of higher costs and rates, as current excesses diminish and new resources are needed. . . .

We find that rates should continue to reflect the long-run marginal costs of service and the differences in costs between seasons and among times of day. As a general matter, making cost-based rate elements (such as variation with time of use) optional is likely to create adverse selection problems for other ratepayers, and thus would be inequitable, as customers with higher-cost usage patterns select the more beneficial rate and ultimately cause class rates to rise. In designing rates, the customer charge, if any, should reflect marginal customer costs; the demand charge, if any, should reflect the marginal capacity costs of generation, transmission, and distribution. For rate classes without a demand charge, we have seen no evidence that demand costs are disproportionately driven by usage in the lower usage blocks. If, for any rate class without a separately stated demand charge, a utility wishes to structure rates in blocks according to total energy used, then the rates for each block should reflect the total long-term cost of capacity associated with that usage.

As a general matter, promotional pricing should be "risk-averse" by requiring that discounted rates be set high enough to have a high probability of exceeding the relevant marginal costs. We will separately review the Conservation Group proposal to allow special promotion of certain electric end uses. CMP also should offer cost-based rates for backup and maintenance service. In calculating long-run avoided costs, transmission and distribution costs should be included.

Methods. To estimate the long-term marginal cost of generation, utilities should use the cost of the least capital-intensive capacity option. Marginal energy costs should be estimated using a forward-looking average of annual marginal energy costs, with the average calculated using estimated costs for a period beginning with the rate-effective period and extending six years.

Legal Context

The Legislature and Congress have provided statutory guidance to the Commission in deciding the questions presented in this proceeding, but as we will explain, this statutory guidance is not determinative of any issue before us in this investigation.

This investigation is concerned with CMP's resource planning, rate structures and long-term avoided and marginal costs. Our regulatory policies in these areas have been shaped first and foremost by the enactment of the Federal Public Utilities Regulatory Policies Act of 1978, Pub. L. No. 95–617, 92 Stat. 3117 (PURPA). The relevant provisions of PURPA are designed to encourage the adoption of certain regulatory practices. The goals as stated by Congress are:

. . . to encourage—

1.   conservation of energy supplied by electric utilities;

2.   the optimization of the efficiency of the use of facilities and resources by electric utilities; and

3.   equitable rates to electric consumers.

Section 101, 92 Stat. 3120, enacting 16 U.S.C.A. § 2611 (1985). To achieve these goals, Congress directed state utility regulatory commissions to consider the adoption and implementation of specific rate design and regulatory standards.

PURPA sets forth six primary rate design standards, which we summarized in an earlier rate design proceeding:

1. Cost of Service—Rates charged to each class of electric consumers should, to the extent practicable, reflect the cost of providing service.

Methods used to determine cost of service should identify differences in cost due to variations in daily or seasonal time of use and due to variations in customer demand in energy components of cost. [16 U.S.C.A. § 1621(d)(1)]

2. Declining Block Rates—The energy component of a rate should not decrease as consumption increases, except to the extent that such a rate reflects decreases in cost to the utility in providing the service. [16 U.S.C.A. § 1621(d)(2)]

3. Time of Day Rates—Rates should be based on the cost of providing service at different times of the day if the long run benefits are likely to exceed the metering and other costs associated with such rates. [16 U.S.C.A. § 1621(d)(3)]

4. Seasonal Rates—Rates should vary by seasons of the year to the extent that costs vary seasonably. [16 U.S.C.A. § 1621(d)(4)]

5. Interruptible Rates—Industrial and commercial consumers should be offered interruptible rates which reflect the cost of providing such service. [16 U.S.C.A. § 1621(d)(5)]

6. Load Management Techniques—Consumers should be offered non-pricing techniques designed to provide useful energy or capacity management advantages to the extent they are practicable, cost effective, and reliable. [16 U.S.C.A. § 1621(d)(6)] *Re: Bangor Hydro–Electric Company*, Docket No. 80–108, slip op. at 2 (Me. PSC, 1985)

In 1979, the Maine Legislature enacted the Electric Rate Reform Act (ERRA), 35–A M.R.S.A. §§ 3151–55. As part of the ERRA, the Legislature required the Commission, to the extent feasible, to consider and adopt the federal rate design standards established by PURPA and, for any standard or standards not adopted, to provide the facts and rationales supporting the rejection of the standard.

The ERRA also provides a policy basis that governs rate design, coinciding in most major respects with PURPA. For instance, the purpose of the ERRA is to "require the Commission to relate electric rates more closely to the costs of providing electric service." 35–A M.R.S.A. § 3152(1)(A) (supp. 1992). There are broad policy statements in both PURPA and ERRA that rate design should promote conservation, efficient use of resources and equity. The ERRA also directs the Commission, when ordering rate design improvements, to "consider rate design stability" and to "assure the revenue requirement of the utility." 35–A M.R.S.A. § 3154(1).

The Commission adopted the six federal standards contained in PURPA in the so-called PURPA investigation for CMP, *Re: Central Maine Power Company* (Cost of Service and Rate Design), Docket No. 80–66 (Me. PSC, Sep. 11, 1985). The Commission did not adopt specific rate designs in the CMP PURPA investigation but did establish several overriding principles relevant to designing rates. Among these was the policy that rates should reflect the marginal costs of service, including daily and seasonal cost differences. While the Commission found that flat rates for residential customers were proper, the Commission also stated that time-of-use and inclining block rates would be implemented if future cost studies supported such results. *Id.*

The Commission established new rate designs for CMP and Bangor Hydro–Electric Company during 1985 and 1986. *Re: Bangor Hydro–Electric Company, Investigation of Cost of Service and Rate Design*, Docket No. 85–209 (Me. PSC, Oct. 1, 1986); *Re: Central Maine Power Company, Investigation Into Cost of Service and Rate Design*, Docket No. 86–002 (Me. PSC, Oct. 3 and Oct. 17, 1986). In the BHE proceeding, the Commission adopted what became known as a "hybrid" approach, wherein customer class revenue responsibility would be based on embedded costs, while the design of rates within classes would reflect marginal costs and time-of-use cost differentials. BHE Docket No. 85–209 at 4, 8. The same approach was adopted for CMP in Docket No. 86–002. In the BHE docket, the Commission expressed the preference, where cost differences were shown, to implement seasonal and time-of-day rates. . . .

Despite the "hybrid" approach, the increased importance of marginal cost information was emphasized in nearly every rate design case throughout the 1980s. For instance, in *Re: Bangor Hydro–Electric Company*, Docket No. 86–242 (Me. PSC, Dec. 22, 1987), we said that as a general policy matter, the Commission is moving toward greater reliance on long-run marginal costs as the basis for setting prices. This policy also means that customer class revenue requirements will be set on a long-run marginal cost basis. *Id.* at 90.

In that docket, the Commission for the first time stated a policy preference for using marginal cost studies for allocating costs to customer class, as well as for rate design within the classes.

Our most recent rate design case for CMP occurred during 1989 and 1990. *Re: Central Maine Power Company*, Docket No. 89–068 (Me. PSC, Mar. 29, 1991). The Commission decided to replace the "hybrid" approach, so that both customer class revenue responsibilities and rate design within classes would be based on marginal cost. Equity would then be best achieved, "because each customer and class will pay on the basis of what it would cost if service to that customer or class were expanded." *Id.* at 26. The Commission found that embedded cost allocation methods sent distorted price signals because such methods allocate costs to rate classes on the basis of historic average total cost calculations, which may have only a coincidental connection to current, forward-looking estimates of marginal cost. Furthermore, because the hybrid approach mixed class revenue allocations based on embedded cost with marginal cost rate design within classes, large anomalies among rate elements occurred in implementing Docket No. 86–002.

In addressing the problem of reconciling the marginal cost approach to the Company's total revenue requirement, we adopted the equiproportional marginal cost (EPMC) method, under which the difference between total revenue requirement and marginal costs incurred to serve each class is allocated in proportion to the marginal costs. We stated that:

> The Commission recognizes that full pursuit of its efficiency goals would suggest the use of an inverse elasticity (Ramsey) rule to reconcile the total cost arrived at under the marginal cost approach to the Company's overall revenue requirement. However, in the absence of reliable customer elasticity information, equity dictates that the EPMC reconciliation method be used at least for the present time. This is because it is fair for each class to be responsible for the embedded revenue requirement in proportion to its share of total marginal cost.

Id. at 26–27.

In the most recent legislative session, sections 3152 and 3153–A were both amended to add the consideration of reduced electric rates, along with reduced electric costs, in the setting of electric rates and in developing conservation programs. P.L. 1993, c. 402 (An Act to Minimize Electric Rates). In fact, the Commission "shall give equivalent consideration to the goals of minimizing cost and minimizing rates of electricity to consumers." The following language was also contained in P.L. 1993, c. 402, although not included in Title 35–A: Sec.

> 3.   Construction. Nothing in this Act is intended or may be construed to discourage energy conservation and demand management programs or to encourage continued or additional use of electric baseboard resistance heating systems. Nothing in this Act may be construed to encourage or discourage the development or implementation of any particular rate design.
>
> As a result of giving equal consideration to the goals of minimizing costs and minimizing rates pursuant to this Act, the Public Utilities Commission may not adopt any rate design that results in increased rates for residential customers with usage or less than 750 kilowatt hours per month. Nothing in the preceding sentence may be construed to prohibit the Public Utilities Commission from increasing rates for residential customers with usage of less than 750 kilowatt hours per month to the extent justified by other legitimate rational principles or legislative mandates.

There is no real disagreement as to the legal principles explained above or their interpretation. The disagreements among the parties, as explained below, are about factual issues or the relevance of various facts in determining the proper costs of service that should be reflected in CMP's rates at this time. Still, these legal principles and the regulatory "common law" developed in implementing them will guide us in resolving the factual and policy disputes. . . .

In planning, building, and operating an electric power system, a utility can choose among various types of generating plant. For some, like nuclear power plants, the fixed (capital) costs are high and the variable (fuel) costs are low. In other words, they are relatively expensive to build and cheap to run. For others, like diesel units or combustion turbines, the opposite conditions hold; with low capital costs per kilowatt of capacity and high fuel costs per kilowatt-hour of energy, they are relatively cheap to build but expensive to run. Because the total power demanded by its customers varies widely, and not always predictably, with the hour, day, and season, a utility needs a balanced mix of generation types if it is to produce power at the lowest overall cost per kilowatt-hour generated.

The "base load" portion of the power demand, comes from uses that are in constant operation, such as refrigerators, hospitals, and three-shifts-per-day factories. The base load has the highest "load factor," or ratio of total energy (kilowatt-hours) used over the course of the year to maximum demand (kilowatts) placed on the system at one time. For this reason, it can be served most economically with "base-load" generation that has relatively low energy costs (and relatively high capital cost). Conversely, the "peak load" portion of the power demand, that occurs in only a few hours of the year, such as in the late afternoon on a very cold winter weekday, can be served most economically with "peaking" generation that has relatively low capital costs (but high energy costs). At intermediate points on the load curve, "cycling" units with an intermediate balance of costs, such as CMP's Wyman 4 oil burner, may be the most economical choice. On the customer's side of the meter, there are DSM measures analogous to base-load generation, such as water heater insulation, and to peaking units, such as interruptible power contracts and water heater control programs.

Given a range of energy resource options, one can find the optimum mix to serve a utility's load pattern at lowest overall cost. In CMP's case, the current resource mix is out of balance. Additions to its own base-load plant, combined during the last decade with large blocks of power purchased from qualifying facilities (QF) under "must-run" contract terms, have produced an uneconomic resource mix under today's cost and load conditions.

Excess must-run/baseload generation has driven CMP's average costs and rates up. It has also driven CMP's marginal costs down; excess baseload, although not the optimal mix, nevertheless means that dispatchable peaking capacity, with its higher energy cost, is needed less. CMP, through its witness Peaco, estimates that its system is about 400 megawatts out of balance; that is, to achieve the optimum resource mix under today's planning assumptions, CMP would need to replace some 400 MW of existing base-load capacity with more readily dispatchable resources. If CMP's system were in balance, Staff witness Huntington found, marginal energy costs would increase by some 38 percent on a weighted average basis, with the increases ranging from 15 percent in the winter on-peak period to as much as 63 percent in the non-winter, off-peak period. CMP's total marginal costs would increase by more than 20 percent relative to current levels, if its generation system were in balance. Much of CMP's

must-run capacity is from QF purchased power contracts that are themselves very expensive, averaging over 9 cents/kWh....

We agree with Staff and OPA that marginal energy costs matter, and
are sensitive to the supply mix, especially when (as now) that mix is out of
balance. This result suggests, as discussed below, that marginal cost
projections will be less reliable when significant swings in the supply mix
are likely....

Clearly, the widespread connection of non-utility generation to the
power grid during the last decade has made the power industry more
competitive, putting a lid on generation costs. During the same period, and
as an intended result of the same public policies that opened the grid to
competition, innovative technologies to capture waste heat through cogeneration and achieve other efficiencies with smaller units and renewable
fuels has added new fuels and diversity to power generation and reduced
the demand for and price of oil. Although these innovations initially cost
almost as much as the projected cost of the utility plants they displaced, the
technologies have resulted in lower costs as they have matured.

Arguably, the electric utility industry may have a "flatter" cost structure today than it had in 1991, when we were last designing CMP's rates.
In the interim, avoided costs have continued to drop. General inflation
rates have declined and interest rates are sharply lower, both of which tend
to reduce the construction costs of new generating capacity. The design of
natural gas-fired electric generation, whether with combustion turbines or
combined-cycle units, has continued to improve, and wind generators may
have become increasingly cost-effective. The potential addition of significant gas pipeline capacity in New England, combined with changes in
federal regulation of gas pipelines, make gas-fired electric units an increasingly viable source of generation in the NEPOOL region, especially considering their suitability as peaking and cycling facilities. With more excess
capacity at CMP and in New England today than we anticipated in 1991,
the cost of serving new load is less today than we expected it to be. All of
these observations tend to support the inference that the long-run average
cost curve for the generation of electricity may have shifted downward
since 1991, and also may have today less of an upward slope than it
appeared to have in 1991....

Rate structure policies

Our investigation in this proceeding of CMP's long-term costs has been
designed to provide the basis for decisions about CMP's general rate
structure policies, such as the relative desirability of inclining block rates,
flat rates, and declining block rates; the desirability of time-of-use rates;
and the desirability of rates designed to encourage increases in the use of
electricity over the long term. In this section, we review the record evidence
on fifteen such rate policy issues raised in this case, working from the
general to the specific.

Should rates in general reflect the long-run marginal cost of service?

Uncertainty is inherent in planning scenarios for the optimal power
supply 25 years or more into the future. Trying to make current rates

reflect true long-run costs, over the period in which the system can be substantially rebuilt and thus "reoptimized," may sound like a fool's errand, but we do not agree that today's prices can completely ignore such costs. CMP, like most utility companies, continues to invest in very long-lived assets. Much of its new T & D plant, for example, will still be in service a decade or more beyond the 25–year horizon that it alleges "it makes no sense" to consider in pricing. When making long-term investment decisions, utilities reduce future costs and returns to a present value using some appropriate discount rate. Long-term avoided costs of competing resource options are similarly discounted. This technique properly places greater weight on the near-term and less on the more distant future.

Logically, the costs underlying rate design should be viewed from a similar perspective. CMP must already use long-term cost projections as the basis for a great many of the utility's planning decisions, many of which we will have to live with for decades. We, therefore, reject both CMP's claim that the proper planning horizon for pricing purposes is five years or less, and the CCUC position that all such projections, short or long, are too uncertain to serve as the basis for rate design. We agree with the general principle that we should not pursue short-run efficiency at the expense of long-run efficiency. . . .

Reliance on CMP's short-run marginal costs for rate design purposes also raises serious questions of fairness. . . . [W]hen the resource mix is seriously out of balance on the side of excess base-load capacity, as it is today, the system will display unusually low marginal energy costs, particularly in off-peak periods. If these low marginal costs were used to allocate revenue among customer classes (the EPMC method) and to design rate components (energy and demand charges), customers with high load factors would receive, in effect, a windfall. Other customers, especially those with low load factors or with usage concentrated in peak and shoulder hours, would pay disproportionately for the cost of the system imbalances. Since no one has suggested any causal link between the usage patterns of the customers so affected and the costs imposed by the suboptimal planning, and we find it hard even to imagine such a linkage, the end result of short-run cost approach is clearly inequitable.

Overall, we see no reason to abandon our long-standing policy of taking a long view of costs when designing rates. . . . Over the past decade, as more diverse and flexible resource options and strategies have become available, CMP's investment horizon has contracted. Therefore, we instruct the parties to develop marginal costs for the six-year period, 1995 through 2000. To the extent that the planning horizon affects the calculation of marginal capacity costs, the same time frame should be used.■

NOTES AND COMMENTS

1.   Marginal cost and peak load pricing are discussed in *In re Rate Design for Electric Corporations*, 15 P.U.R.4th 434 (N.Y.1976); *In re Madison Gas*

& *Electric Co.*, 5 P.U.R.4th 28 (Wis. 1974). For an examination of the background and impact of peak-load pricing by a former Wisconsin PSC commissioner (Richard Cudahy, now a judge on the U.S. Court of Appeals for the Seventh Circuit), *see* Cudahy & Malko, Electric Peak–Load Pricing: Madison Gas & Beyond, 1976 Wis. L. Rev. 47. For a good examination of electric pricing issues, *see* Hunington, The Rapid Emergence of Marginal Cost Pricing and the Regulation of Electric Utility Rate Structures, 55 Boston U. L. Rev. 689 (1975).

2. The same conservation principles apply outside of the energy context as well. For example, in *Brydon v. East Bay Municipal Utility District*, 24 Cal.App.4th 178 (App. 1st Dist. 1994), a California water utility adopted an inclining block rate for water conservation as a part of its comprehensive Drought Management Program. The inclining block structure imposes higher charges per unit of water as the level of customer consumption increases. The court held that the inclining block rates did not violate California Proposition 13 prohibition on "special taxes" absent approval of 2/3 of the voters. "Special taxes" are fees that "exceed the reasonable cost of providing the service or regulatory activity for which the fee is charged and which is not levied for general revenue purposes." *Id.* at 187. The court concluded that the District, by acting prospectively to create incentives for conservation through water rates rather than waiting for apocalyptic drought circumstances to develop, had developed a "well-conceived and eminently reasonable" Drought Management Program. *Id.* at 204.

3. A useful exercise on ratemaking has been written by William Anderson and is available in the Computer–Assisted Legal Instruction (CALI) administrative law library. Now would be a good time to work parts A–E of this exercise, which should be available through your law library.

2. RATE REGULATION BASED ON NON-COST FACTORS

a. "LIFE–LINE" RATES

One of the more controversial issues in rate design involves special rates to benefit low-income groups. An issue that has been the subject of some debate is whether low-income rates are undertaken not on the basis of cost considerations, but distributional fairness. Some have suggested that, with low-income programs, like "lifeline" rates, service for some customers is subsidized at a cost well below marginal or average costs, a subsidy borne by other ratepayers. *Mountain States* examines this argument.

Mountain States Legal Foundation v. Public Utilities Comm'n

590 P.2d 495 (Colo.1979).

■ HODGES, J.: Plaintiffs-appellees, Mountain States Legal Foundation and Colorado Association of Commerce and Industry, commenced separate actions in the trial court challenging Public Utilities Commission (PSC) decisions which established a reduced gas rate for low-income elderly and low-income disabled persons. The trial court entered a judgment which set aside these decisions. It held that the adoption of this special reduced rate exceeded the PSC's authority under Article XXV of the Colorado Constitution and violated section 40–3–106(1), C.R.S. 1973. The appellant PSC and intervener-appellant Mountain Plains Congress of Senior Organizations urge reversal. We affirm the trial court's judgment.

On November 8, 1977, the PSC, in two decisions, ordered gas utilities under its regulatory authority to implement a discount gas rate plan for low-income elderly and low-income disabled persons. The low-income customers who would be eligible for the discounted gas rate are "identified" through a procedure utilized by the Department of Revenue to administer the Colorado property and rent credit program.

In order to qualify for the discounted rate, a customer must have been a full year resident of Colorado; the customer must be 65 years of age or older or be the surviving spouse, 58 years old or older, of a deceased spouse who met the age requirement, or the customer must be receiving full disability benefits from a bona fide public or private insurance plan; and if the discounted gas rate plan were to go into effect during the 1978–1979 heating season, a customer would have to have an income of $7,300 or less if single, and $8,300 or less if married. These income standards are different from those which were in effect during the 1977–1978 heating season because of a legislative change in the standards for the Colorado property tax and rent credit.

The resulting revenue loss for the discounted services would be recovered by higher rates on all other customers.

We give full recognition to the fact that many of our state's elderly live on fixed incomes which are severely strained by today's inflationary economy, as are low-income disabled persons who are often shut out of the employment market. While efforts to provide economic relief to such needy persons are laudatory, the PSC has limited authority to implement a rate structure which is designed to provide financial assistance as a social policy to a narrow group of utility customers, especially where that low rate is financed by its remaining customers.

In *Mountain States Telephone and Telegraph Co. v. Public Utilities Commission*, 576 P.2d 544 (Colo.1978), we held that Article XXV of the Colorado Constitution gives the PSC full legislative authority to regulate public utilities. We noted in that case, however, that the legislative authority in public utility matters delegated by Article XXV to the PSC could be restricted by statute. *Id.* at 547. It is clear in the case before us that the PSC's authority to order preferential utility rates to effect social policy has, in fact, been restricted by the legislature's enactment of section 40–3–106(1), C.R.S. 1973 and section 40–3–102, C.R.S. 1973.

Section 40–3–106(1), C.R.S. 1973, prohibits public utilities from granting preferential rates to any person, and section 40–3–102, C.R.S. 1973, requires the PSC to prevent unjust discriminatory rates. When the PSC ordered the utility companies to provide a lower rate to selected customers unrelated to the cost or type of the service provided, it violated section 40–3–106(1)'s prohibition against preferential rates. In this instance, the discount rate benefits an unquestionably deserving group, the low-income elderly and the low-income disabled. This, unfortunately, does not make the rate less preferential. To find otherwise would empower the PSC, an appointed, non-elected body, to create a special rate for any group it determined to be deserving. The legislature clearly provided against such discretionary power when it prohibited public utilities from granting "any preference." In addition, section 40–3–102, C.R.S. 1973, directs the PSC to prevent unjust discriminatory rates. Establishing a discount gas rate plan which differentiates between economically needy individuals who receive the same service is unjustly discriminatory.... affirm the judgment of the trial court.

■ CARRIGAN, J., dissenting: The majority opinion depends entirely on characterization of the special rate classification here involved as a "preference" forbidden by section 40–3–106(1). Thus the decisive issue is whether the instant rate classification is so clearly of the type that the legislature intended to forbid when it enacted that section that it must be held to be a "preference" as a matter of law. The majority opinion cites no precedent or other authority for its holding and we have found no case law from any state dealing with the issue. Moreover the majority opinion fails to define the term "preference" for guidance of the P.U.C. in future cases. In effect the majority opinion has condemned the rate scheme here involved by saying, "We can't define a "preference' but we know one when we see one." Such an ad hoc determination does not provide needed rational standards as precedent for future cases....

Apparently, the purpose of section 40–3–106(1) was to prevent the public utilities' then-common practice of favoring certain customers with lower utility rates to the competitive disadvantage of others in the same class of customers similarly situated. *Columbia Gas of N.Y., Inc. v. N.Y. State Elec. & Gas Co.*, 28 N.Y.2d 117, 268 N.E.2d 790 (1971); *Hays v. Pennsylvania Co.*, 12 Fed. 309 (N.D. Ohio 1882).

The issue, therefore, becomes whether the statutory language so clearly forbids the P.U.C.'s rate classification plan that this Court, as a matter of law, must outlaw it rather than leaving the decision whether to overrule it to the General Assembly as a matter of state policy.

In the law the word "preference" denotes giving an advantage or priority to one or more claimants in a manner which discriminates unjustly or unreasonably against other claimants in the same class. This connotation of the term clearly was intended by section 40–3–106(1), for in the sentence immediately following the use of the term "preference" in that section, public utilities are forbidden to "establish or maintain any unreasonable difference as to rates...." If only unreasonable rate differentials are forbidden, it is plainly implied that reasonable differences in rates are not forbidden. It follows that a classification for rate purposes should not be considered a "preference" if the classification is reasonable.

This rationale is further buttressed by section 40–3–102, C.R.S. 1973, which empowers the P.U.C. "to prevent unjust discriminations . . . in the rates, charges and tariffs of . . . public utilities. . . ." The clear implication is that just discrimination in rates may be tolerated.

Whether a particular classification among ratepayers is "unreasonable" or "unjust" is a question on which this court has no more expertise than the P.U.C. or the General Assembly. Indeed we probably have less. Such questions are at bottom fact issues, or at best mixed law-fact issues. They involve social policy determinations rather than legal decisionmaking.

The P.U.C. as a specialized, quasi-legislative agency is a particularly appropriate body to effectuate—at least in the first instance—the legislative factfinding and policymaking function incident to setting rates. It possesses unique expertise and the capacity to analyze the complex technical, economic, and social information necessary to set public utility rates intelligently and fairly. The constitution, as well as the statute governing P.U.C. rate regulation, wisely leave to the P.U.C. the initial authority to determine policy. Colo. Const., Art. XXV; Section 40–3–101, C.R.S. 1973. . . . ■

NOTES AND COMMENTS

1. Does the "lifeline" principle make sense? Would it be better to price energy resources at marginal cost to ensure the most efficient allocation of resources? "Lifeline rates," which encourage pricing below marginal cost, seem to run counter to this proposition.

2. As the *Mountain States* case suggests, any rate that creates an unjustified preference for one class of customers seems inconsistent with well-accepted principles of public utility law. Several states, however, have recognized "lifeline" rates. Is this inconsistent with the goals of public utility law, as we have studied them to this point?

3. Is there any sound economic rationale for subsidizing low-income customers? Is this an instance of market failure for which some regulatory solution may be justified? Or is this a pure redistributive program that serves non-cost goals?

Charging and collecting rates are two different actions. Many customers who are charged rates may never pay them, and utilities are often required to undergo costly collection efforts, sometimes at a cost to all customers. One way to conceptualize of low-income rates is as based upon cost. As Roger Colton describes:

> The National Consumer Law Center has developed the energy assurance program (EAP) to address these dual problems [charging as opposed to collecting rates]. The EAP recognizes that some households simply do not have sufficient income to pay for the basic necessities of life, including energy. There is no question but that this inability to pay is a social problem. There is no question, however, that this

inability to pay also represents a business problem for utilities. For these households, regardless of the number of disconnect notices sent, regardless of the number of times service is disconnected, regardless of the type of payment plan that is offered, there will be insufficient household funds available to pay utility bills. A utility can recognize this fact and seek to collect what it can, while minimizing collection expenses, or a utility can deny this fact and devote its time, energy, and attention to what will prove to be fruitless and expensive collection attempts....

The EAP is not simply sound social policy. It is based on sound regulatory principles as well. A utility is required to operate with all reasonable efficiency. This is part and parcel of the obligation to provide least-cost service. Accordingly, utilities should pursue all reasonable means of minimizing the total revenue requirement, including the adoption of innovative credit and collection techniques.

Roger D. Colton, "A Cost-based Response to Low-income Energy Problems," Public Utilities Fortnightly, March 1, 1991. As Colton see it, this type of a program "is not designed to serve as a social program providing rate discounts to low-income households." Instead, it "is intended to be a collection device. It is a means of collection that will maximize the receipt of revenue from customers who cannot afford to pay their bills, while at the same time minimizing all of the expenses associated with delinquent payments." This makes some sense in a rate-regulated system: since fixed costs do not vary with the amount of service consumed, if a customer can cover at least the variable costs attributed to that customer, in the short-run other customers are not made any worse off. Colton states:

The concept behind this statement is simple: It is better to collect 95 percent of a $70 bill than it is to collect 50 percent of a $100 bill....

Removing a nonpaying customer from the utility system does not necessarily result in the least-cost provision of service to all remaining ratepayers. Whenever a customer's service is disconnected, two things happen. The company does avoid the variable cost of delivering that unit of energy to the household. However, the company also foregoes the revenue that would have been collected from the household but for the disconnection of service.

To the extent that the revenue would have exceeded the variable cost of delivering the energy (whether it be gas or electricity), other ratepayers lose a contribution toward the payment of the fixed charges of the company. In this instance, the disconnection of service leaves remaining, paying customers worse off than had the disconnection not occurred.

In general, there is an advantage to all ratepayers from keeping as many households on the system as possible. So long as households pay the variable costs of delivering the energy they consume, other ratepayers are no worse off. To the extent that households pay anything beyond the variable cost of the energy they consume, they are making a contribution toward the fixed costs of the system and all ratepayers are better off than they would have been had those households been disconnected. It is thus cost-effective for the utility, and for all remaining ratepayers, to provide payment-troubled customers with an incentive to make reduced payments (even when full payment cannot be made) by deciding not to disconnect so long as these customers continue to pay more than the variable cost of providing service. In essence, this proposal is no different than the treatment that many states accord their large natural gas and telecommunications customers who have the ability and inclination to engage in bypass. In effect, these residential customers who, because of their inability to pay their utility bill, would be disconnected from the utility system and forced to move to alternative sources of home energy, would be treated as opportunity sales by the utility.

Id. Roger Colton's article was written in response to Howard M. Spinner's article, "Choosing an Efficient Energy Assistance Program," which appeared in the December 20, 1990 issue of the Public Utilities Fortnightly. For further development of the concept, *see* Roger D. Colton, The Duty of a Public Utility to Mitigate 'Damages' from Nonpayment Through the Offer of Conservation Programs, 3 B.U. Pub. Interest L.J. 239 (1993); Roger D. Colton & Mike Sheehan, A New Basis for Conservation Programs for the Poor: Expanding the Concept of Avoided Costs, 21 Clearinghouse Review 135 (1987).

4. Subsidies for low-income energy consumers have received congressional attention. PURPA supported low income rate concepts. 16 U.S.C. § 2624. In addition, federal agencies, such as the formerly-named Department of Housing and Urban Development, provide assistance (approximately one billion dollars annually) to the poor in meeting their energy needs through a number of federal programs. *See* Steven Ferry, In from the Cold: Energy Efficiency and the Reform of HUD's Utility Allowance System, 32 Harv. J. on Legis. 145 (1995); Steven Ferry, Cold Power: Energy and Public Housing, 23 Harv. J. on Legis. 33 (1986).

5. *Mountain States* is out-of-date in its analysis of the issue of low-income rates and possibly inconsistent with the approach of most utility commissions today. Although states today rarely even consider "lifeline" rates, low-income rate discounts are now prevalent, for reasons similar to those articulated by Roger Colton. According to Peter Fox–Penner:

In recent years [] state utility commissions have begun to use discount rates as a more cost-effective alternative than other low-income programs. Utility regulators reason that it is less expensive to provide affordable utility rates to low-income households in the first place, than to provide service at higher rates, incur the costs of providing working capital to cover unpaid arrears, spend money on credit and collection, and still write-off a substantial part of the unbilled revenue to certain customers as uncollectible. By offering such affordable rates, utilities have found that they actually can increase the revenues they collect and decrease the expenses they incur in the process of collection, to the benefit of all involved, including nonparticipating customers.

Peter Fox–Penner, Electric Utility Restructuring: A Guide to the Competitive Era 325 (1997).

6. Do the benefits of administering any low income rate program exceed the potential costs? For example, how will a PSC distinguish between low-income and middle-income and wealthy residential customers? Can it establish an eligibility test? What is the best way to do this?

b. OTHER NON–COST–BASED THEORIES OF REGULATION

In recent years, dissatisfaction with cost-based regulation has been expressed by many observers. Both in this country and abroad, legislatures and regulatory agencies have been exploring completely different approaches to the subject of utility pricing.

One of the most popular non-cost methods of pricing is price ceilings or caps. To counteract the effects of inflation and save the regulatory costs associated with calculate revenue requirements, regulators will limit the charges utilities can pass on to certain customers. For instance, the British government, adopted price ceilings when it privatized its telecommunications industry in 1984, and several federal state regulators in the U.S. have experimented with price level regulation as well. In some instances, utilities may favor price caps since they give utilities the ability to make their own decisions about expenditures without regulatory oversight. And, if a utility can find ways to decrease its costs, it may keep some or all of the additional revenue it generates as profit. Regulators may find price caps attractive too, since they may create incentives for utilities to become productive.

Nevertheless, price level regulation has not been widespread in the U.S. Regulators are unable to accurately set ceiling prices: when utilities make excess profits public pressure leads regulators to return to cost of service regulation, yet if utilities are making little or no profits they will pressure regulators to raise ceiling prices. See Richard J. Pierce, Price Level Regulation Based on Inflation is Not An Attractive Alternative to Profit Level Regulation, 84 N.W. U. L. Rev. 665 (1990) (reviewing Jordan Jay Hillman & Robert Braeutigam, Price Level Regulation for Diversified Public Utilities (1989)). In the electric utility industry, as states have attempted to adopt deregulation plans, some consumer advocates have embraced (and some states have adopted) price caps or mandatory price reductions, as is discussed in Chapters 13 and 18.

Other non-cost methods of pricing include market-based pricing, incentive regulation, and economic development regulation. These theories will be discussed in the context of the regulation of electricity prices in Chapter Eleven.

CHAPTER 9

COMPETITIVE MARKETS IN NATURAL GAS

A. THE TRANSITION TO A COMPETITIVE INDUSTRY

Today the natural gas business would hardly be recognized by the people who knew it in the 1970s. A highly regulated, conservative industry has been transformed into a very competitive business featuring entrepreneurs and marketers who would be equally at home on Wall Street. (Refer back to Figures 7–2 and 7–3 in Chapter 7 to view the changing landscape.)

1. THE GORDIAN KNOT OF PRE–1985 GAS REGULATION: REVIEW

Chapter 7 left the gas industry tied into a Gordian knot. Demand was falling but gas prices were rising. Congress had passed the Natural Gas Policy Act of 1978, partially decontrolling gas prices, but leaving a 27–category system of classifying wells for pricing purposes. Pipelines rolled the price of low-cost old gas into the price of high-cost gas newly freed from price controls. Rigidities in the long-term contracts between producers and pipeline purchasers, caused by take-or-pay clauses and most favored nations clauses, meant prices could not fall, even when a "bubble" of excess gas appeared by 1982.

This bubble was most unexpected. The underlying assumption of the NGPA was that shortages and high prices would be a fact of life for years to come. However, domestic producers had responded vigorously to the increased incentives offered by the new federal pricing policies. Meanwhile, industrial end users had often shifted to coal or heavy fuel oil rather than risk gas curtailments and the vagaries of federal pricing policies like incremental pricing. The excess gas bubble coincided with the Third Oil Shock. Conservation of oil by consumers and newly found oil supplies (developed around the world in response to the skyrocketing oil prices of the First and Second Oil Shocks) resulted in a dramatic drop in oil prices in 1981. The stage was set for the marketplace to reign in energy.

Residential consumers of gas, however, did not experience the benefits of any price decrease. The Local Distributing Companies (LDCs) supplying residential customers had entered into long-term contracts to buy gas from the pipelines which were similar to the long-term contracts between the pipelines and the producers. The distributors typically had "minimum bill" contracts with the pipelines which functioned like take-or-pay contracts, *i.e.*, the distributors were required to pay for certain minimum amounts of gas whether or not they needed this amount to fill their customers' demands. Many industrial users had swung off of gas on to alternate fuel sources, so this customer base had declined. As a result, LDCs, facing an oversupply of gas in a declining industrial market, had to raise rates to the captive consumer market to offset the withdrawal of industrial users from the market. This created the perverse effect of residential consumers' gas bills rising while the market price of gas was falling.

Many regulators found this situation discomforting—but the alternative of pipeline bankruptcy was equally distressing. And the potential of bankruptcy was very real for many pipelines, which would have meant that the pipeline bondholders and stockholders would take a big hit. Local distributing companies and their investors were also suffering, so the pressure for relief was intense. FERC began to issue a series of orders that proposed to separate the traditional functions of the participants to allow flexible markets for gas to develop.

2. INDUSTRIAL BYPASS

FERC's initial attempt to alleviate the problem came by addressing an issue that had long been one of the most contentious in the industry: the complaint of big industrial customers that they were paying rates for natural gas that were set higher than they should be in order to keep down the price of gas for residential users. These industries were eager to negotiate their own purchases of gas directly from producers and to pay the pipelines for the cost of transportation only, thus leaving the local distributing company out of the transaction.

FERC's initial step toward the resolution of the take-or-pay problem was addressed in the following opinion by Judge (now Justice) Scalia, written when he was still on the D.C. Circuit:

Maryland People's Counsel v. FERC

761 F.2d 768 (D.C.Cir.1985).

■ SCALIA, J.: This is a challenge to the Federal Energy Regulatory Commission's approval of what it described as an "experimental increase in [natural gas] pipeline competition." That increase was to be achieved by agreement of a pipeline and its producers to amend the high-priced gas purchase contracts entered into between them in earlier years, so as to permit the producers to sell the committed gas elsewhere (at current market prices), crediting the volume of such sales against the pipeline's high-priced purchase obligations. This challenge is brought, curiously enough, not by the competing pipelines or producers to whose flanks this new spur of competition is being applied, but by representatives of the putative beneficiaries, customers of the pipeline system. Their complaint is that, under the arrangements approved by the Commission, the only customers eligible to purchase the cheaper released gas are industrial users who would, at the higher gas prices agreed to in the original contracts, switch to an alternate fuel. They claim that because of this limitation "captive customers" of the pipeline—those who do not have alternate fuel sources to which they may turn—receive no net benefit, but to the contrary suffer a net loss from the arrangement. The principal issue before us is whether the Commission set forth a reasonable basis for believing that the program it approved will benefit all pipeline ratepayers.

A modest understanding of the complex regulatory background of this dispute is necessary to evaluate the arguments made before us. Pipelines regulated by the Natural Gas Act transport natural gas from producers to distributors and end-users in other states. Ordinarily (though not invariably) they purchase the gas on their own account and resell it to their customers. While they may transport gas purchased directly by distributors or end-users from producers, they have no common-carrier obligation to do so. Their rates to distributors (but not to end-users) are regulated by FERC. However, while that portion of the rate attributable to transportation costs (the fixed and incremental costs of constructing and operating the pipeline) is determined by standard public utility rate-making techniques, the much larger portion attributable to the cost of the transported gas is effectively unregulated at the pipeline stage. FERC permits that cost to be passed through, without assuring that the purchase price was a prudent one. A pipeline's purchase costs for all the gas it acquires are averaged to determine the appropriate gas-cost component of its rates.

Previously, lack of gas price regulation at the pipeline stage would have made little difference, since FERC (or more accurately its predecessor, the Federal Power Commission) regulated gas prices (for interstate gas) at the wellhead, controlling the maximum prices that producers could charge.

Because it fixed those prices well below market, a large discrepancy developed between the price for interstate gas and the price for unregulated intrastate gas, and gas production was withheld from the interstate market. After the interstate gas shortages and curtailments of 1976–77, Congress almost entirely terminated Commission wellhead-price regulation, and provided in the Natural Gas Policy Act of 1978, 15 U.S.C. §§ 3301–3432 (1982) ("NGPA"), statutorily prescribed wellhead price ceilings for various categories of gas, in both inter-state and intra-state markets.

The problem ultimately giving rise to the present litigation is that the 1978 predictions of the 1985 market were much in error. Factors ranging from the increased wellhead prices and impending total decontrol, to greater energy conservation, to the lower prices of competing fuels, have turned the natural gas shortages of the 1970's into a natural gas surplus. Thus, as early as the summer of 1983—a year and a half before the scheduled deregulation of new gas—the formulary statutory maximum price for new gas had already reached or exceeded the market-clearing price in many geographic markets. . . . Pipelines, however, by reason of their practice of entering into long-term contracts with producers, were already locked into purchases, for years to come, of NGPA unregulated gas and new gas in volumes and at prices based upon the 1978 expectations.

If all natural gas customers were as a practical matter compelled to buy gas, the consequence of this miscalculation would merely be that they would be paying more for the gas they purchase than it is now "worth." In fact, however, many existing customers (and many would-be customers whose new business was contemplated in the pipelines' long-term purchases) can shift to alternate fuels that are cheaper than the gas that has been purchased by the pipelines (though not cheaper than the current market price of gas). The departure of these customers imposes two added burdens upon the customers that remain: (1) the "fixed cost" component of their rates will rise, because it must now be divided among a smaller number of ratepayers, and (2) the gas cost component of their rates will rise even further above its already-inflated level, since the pipelines' average gas cost per unit volume will be substantially increased by "take-or-pay" liabilities to producers—that is, liabilities under standard provisions of their long-term contracts requiring payment for a minimum volume of purchase whether or not it is in fact taken. Of course these additional increases make it worthwhile for even more customers to leave the system, so that the situation becomes still worse.

To meet this situation, . . . one pipeline, Columbia Gas Transmission Corporation ("Columbia") . . . concluded . . . an agreement with its largest supplier, Exxon Corporation. The core of the agreement was that Columbia would release its contract rights to certain categories of gas in specified Exxon fields (subject to retraction if Columbia should need the gas to fulfill its customer obligations), and would transport that released gas to direct purchasers from Exxon on Columbia's system; in exchange for which Exxon would credit Columbia's take-or-pay liability with the volume of released gas sold, on Columbia's system or elsewhere. Sales by Exxon to customers off Columbia's system would be subject to a right of first refusal by Columbia's customers.

[FERC approved this so-called special marketing program ("SMP") subject to certain conditions: It required Columbia to permit all its suppliers, not merely Exxon, to participate in the SMP; it expanded somewhat the category of eligible released gas purchasers; and it authorized other pipelines to initiate SMPs similar to Columbia's. Shortly thereafter, Maryland People's Counsel (MPC) filed a timely petition for review.]

The issue presented for our review is a narrow one. We have not been asked to pass on the Commission's general authority to approve SMPs such as Columbia's, but only on its power to permit exclusion, from the category of authorized purchasers of released gas under such an SMP, of the pipeline's captive customers or (as the Commission calls them) "core market"—i.e., those customers who have no readily available alternative source of fuel. Paragraph J of the Commission's order, as finally amended, provided as follows:

> (J) Any gas released and sold under this program to distributors or end users which are served, directly or indirectly, by any pipeline (provided that no tariff provision prevents such sale), shall be limited to new loads not previously served by natural gas or to requirements which are being or would otherwise be served by: (1) alternative fuels; (2) producer direct sales arrangements; (3) gas made available under industrial sales programs, or other similar programs; (4) gas sold by pipelines under special discount rates, or in off-system sales; (5) propane or synthetic natural gas; or (6) interruptible sales service schedules.

[The effect of this limitation of eligible participants is that captive customers of the Columbia system are excluded from purchasing the cheaper released gas.]

The Commission recognized that Paragraph J raised substantial competitive concerns.... Nonetheless, the Commission justified the program as essential to avoid saddling captive customers with an increased share of the fixed costs of gas pipelines as fuel-switchable customers left the system because of high prices. The Commission reasoned that if the SMP increased volumes of gas transported through the pipeline, the fixed costs could be spread over greater volumes, thereby lowering the costs assigned to each share. Thus, even though the SMP was limited to certain eligible customers, ineligible customers would benefit directly from the reduction in the portion of fixed costs they would be forced to bear. *See* Final Columbia SMP Order, *supra*, 26 F.E.R.C. (CCH) at ¶ ¶ 61, 087–88.

MPC, however, raised several arguments not responded to by the Commission. Most important, the Commission's fixed cost saving rationale does not explain why such savings would not similarly accrue to the benefit of captive customers in the absence of the Paragraph J limitation on eligible purchasers. Additional SMP sales would presumably still occur, and fixed costs would still be spread to the benefit of captive customers....

On this appeal, the rationale the Commission advances most strenuously in defense of Paragraph J is that competition between pipelines for one another's "core" or captive market would not necessarily be in the public interest. The Commission's order expressed this point as follows:

> [W]e are not yet prepared to say that competition for the firm markets would achieve a net benefit. The pipelines have made long-term supply commitments, have designed their operations, and have major investments in pipeline capacity and other facilities, e.g., above ground and underground storage and synthetic gas, in order to serve these markets. Under competition, there would be winners and losers and the pipelines that lost firm markets would be forced to attempt to recover their costs from other captive markets that were unable to take advantage of competition. The shifting of these costs could constitute undue discrimination. On the other hand, failure to recover these costs could place the pipeline in financial jeopardy which could affect the reliability of service to those customers and consumers dependent upon the pipeline.

Final Columbia SMP Order, *supra*, 26 F.E.R.C. (CCH) at ¶ 61,087.

This "winners and losers" rationale plainly cannot support the Paragraph J limitation. In the first place, in order to avoid competition between pipelines for "core" markets it was not necessary to exclude those markets entirely from the SMP. The same result could have been achieved by permitting each pipeline to transport only to its own captive customers the gas that is released from its system supply. Reply Brief for MPC at 30. In other words, even if the Commission was justified in preventing pipeline-to-pipeline competition, it offered no justification for limiting producer-to-producer competition within a particular pipeline's service area. Moreover, even if competition between pipelines were allowed, it is quite possible that the downward pressure exerted by competition on gas prices (constituting 85 percent of the captive customers' rates) would outweigh any increased fixed cost burden—enabling even the "loser" pipelines to stay in business by charging their remaining customers higher fixed costs but overall lower rates. The Commission did not even consider this possibility. . . .

It would be an exaggeration to say that this petition for review has required us to evaluate whether the Commission had, if not the better side, at least a reasonable side, of the argument with MPC over the effects of these orders. On a number of obviously significant points that MPC raised, there is simply no argument to evaluate: the Commission proceeded on its course with no comment, or with comment that was patently unresponsive. As far as we can tell from the record before us, the Commission's decision was not "based on a consideration of the relevant factors," *State Farm*, 463 U.S. at 43, and was therefore invalid.

Since the orders at issue in this case have already expired, in lieu of mandate we will issue a certified copy of this opinion. As noted earlier, successor orders have already been challenged in other proceedings before this court. By accompanying orders, we are directing the Commission and intervenors on behalf of the Commission in those cases, *Maryland People's*

Counsel v. FERC, 760 F.2d 318, and *Laclede Gas Co. v. FERC*, 760 F.2d 318, to show cause why the successor orders should not be vacated and remanded for reconsideration in light of this opinion.

Petition granted.■

NOTES AND COMMENTS

1.   In a companion case, the court also remanded to the FERC its new process for obtaining "blanket certificates," by which a pipeline could obtain the right to transport gas for others without obtaining FERC approval of each transaction. As with the special marketing program, the court's objection was not to the process itself but to FERC's restriction of the process to large interruptible customers. *See Maryland People's Counsel v. FERC,* 761 F.2d 780, (D.C.Cir. 1985).

2.   The court uses the term "captive customers" to describe the distributors who were served by Columbia's pipeline system. If the distributor was not near enough to another pipeline to obtain economical service, and if its business consisted solely of supplying customers with natural gas, then it was truly a captive. The end users were also captive customers of the distributor to a degree, but many of them had the choice of switching to alternative fuels. Even residential homeowners sometimes switch between gas and oil based on price differentials, and as both oil and gas prices rose during this period the sales of wood stoves skyrocketed. But the economies of scale typically make it much easier for a large user, such as an industrial plant, to save money by switching fuels, and this technical difference underlies the conflict between residential and industrial users that continues to be a basic theme in the political battles over energy regulation.

3.   FERC's cautious approach, which the court criticized in the *Maryland Peoples' Counsel* opinion, reflected extreme nervousness in the financial markets about a switch to a competitive natural gas industry. The pipeline networks had been very expensive to build and their financing had largely been provided by the purchasers of pipeline bonds. If a pipeline lost out in the competitive market, its bondholders would not receive their interest payments. These bonds were held by financial institutions, trusts, pension funds and individuals all across the country, and they were a big factor in the political equation. Fortunately, by this time most of the pipelines had been in existence for many years and their bonds were being paid off as their terms expired, so concern for the bondholders investments was decreasing with time.

4.   Judge Scalia said that he was not deciding the case on the merits of the FERC decision, but only on the question of whether the decision "was based on a consideration of the relevant factors." In *Udall v. FPC*, discussed in Chapter Four, Justice Douglas said the same thing. Are you convinced? Is there some factor in energy law cases that encourages judicial activism?

3.   RESTRUCTURING BEGINS

After a number of abortive efforts, FERC finally succeeded in encouraging pipelines and producers to negotiate compromises of their take-or-pay contracts. And following the court's lead, FERC began to expand the "bypass" concept to a full-scale restructuring of the industry, as summarized in these excerpts:

> A series of regulatory crises forced deregulation in stages: First, wellhead prices; second, gas contracts; and finally, pipeline transportation. As markets responded, the Federal Energy Regulatory Commission (FERC) and the state regulatory commissions were forced to change. The growing efficiency of markets demanded better access to services. "Bypass," that quaint industry term for access to markets, emerged as a goal for gas users and suppliers. Regulators answered with the now-famous series of "open access" orders permitting shippers to bypass pipelines as sellers of gas and letting pipelines elect to transport gas under contract. By about 1985, enough pipelines had opened up that gas buyers and sellers could deal directly with one another and make arrangements to transport gas with assurance. This development marked the beginning of the modern gas market.

> By 1989, a mature form of competition had come to natural gas. Enough pipelines had opened their systems to form a pipeline network. Markets had evolved far enough to coordinate gas and transmission trading. The gas market had gained the broad participation of buyers and sellers, giving it the depth and liquidity characteristic of a competitive market. The gas pipeline industry is no longer a natural monopoly.

Arthur De Vany and W. David Walls, The Triumph of Markets in Natural Gas, Public Utilities Fortnightly, April 15, 1995, at 21.

4.   PAYING FOR TAKE–OR–PAY

This federal restructuring then presented state public utility commissions with the issue of how the costs incurred by the pipelines to get out of their take-or-pay contracts would be treated for ratemaking purposes. The following case is an example of how these issues were dealt with in one state.

Hamm v. Public Service Comm'n of South Carolina

425 S.E.2d 28 (S.C.1992).

■ FINNEY, J.: This is an appeal from a circuit court order reversing and remanding orders of the South Carolina Public Service Commission, which permitted a levelized surcharge based upon a combination of both the volumetric and deficiency-based systems to recover from retail gas customers take-or-pay charges incurred at the wholesale level. We affirm in part and reverse in part.

To compensate the wholesaler for risks involved in the merchandising of natural gas, the retailer agrees to take, or pay for if not taken, a minimum quantity of gas. These take-or-pay (TOP) provisions operate to compensate wholesalers for exclusive commitments of natural gas reserves to a specific sales contract and serves [sic] to allocate the risks between the parties.

On September 23, 1988, Appellant South Carolina Pipeline Corporation (Pipeline) filed an application with Appellant South Carolina Public Service Commission (Commission) for approval of a charge to be added to its customers' monthly cost of gas to empower Pipeline to recover TOP costs paid to its wholesale natural gas supplier.

Subsequently, Appellants South Carolina Electric & Gas Company and Respondents Piedmont Natural Gas Company, Inc. (Piedmont), South Carolina Energy Users Committee (SCEUC), and Steven W. Hamm, Consumer Advocate for the State of South Carolina (Consumer Advocate), were permitted to intervene. Thereafter, the American Gas Association was allowed to file an Amicus Curiae brief.

On April 3–6, 1988, the Commission conducted an evidentiary hearing during which the two controlling issues of this appeal were raised. First, how much, if any, of TOP costs should Pipeline be permitted to recover from its customers. Second, if permitted, by what method should TOP costs be allocated among Pipeline's customers. On May 31, 1988, the Commission issued Order No. 89–520 in which it approved the implementation of levelized billing on or after June 1, 1989, and imposed a collection methodology. Respondents separately petitioned for rehearing, and on July 12, 1988, by Order No. 89–703, the Commission denied a rehearing and clarified certain determinations in Order No. 89–520.

Respondents petitioned for judicial review, and the cases were consolidated for hearing. Pursuant to SCEUC's motion to stay portions of Orders Nos. 89–520 and 89–703, the circuit court stayed implementation of a deficiency-based collection methodology pending issuance of a final order after a hearing on the merits of the case. After considering briefs and hearing oral arguments, the circuit court reversed the Commission orders and remanded the case based upon its finding that the decision of the Commission was not supported by the evidence and was arbitrary and capricious as a matter of law. This appeal followed. . . .

We address first the issue of whether Pipeline is entitled to recover from its customers the full amount of TOP charges. The circuit court found that TOP costs do not reflect purchased gas costs. Based upon its reasoning that TOP charges arise out of a failure to purchase gas, the court concluded there was no basis in fact or in law which would mandate their recovery through a purchased-gas expense recovery mechanism.

Appellants Commission and Pipeline argue that TOP costs approved by the Federal Energy Regulation Commission (FERC) may be treated as cost of gas under Pipeline's tariff and recovered from Pipeline's customers. We agree.

Mandated FERC rates may be passed on to customers pursuant to the filed-rate doctrine, a federal preemption rule which requires states to accord binding effect to filed rates approved by the FERC. *See General Motors Corp. v. Illinois Commerce Comm'n*, 143 Ill.2d 407, 574 N.E.2d 650 (1991); *Mississippi Power and Light Co. v. Mississippi*, 487 U.S. 354 (1988); *Nantahala Power and Light Co. v. Thornburg*, 476 U.S. 953 (1986).

Local gas companies are permitted to pass on to customers TOP charges if such charges are neither illegal, arbitrary nor unreasonable. Additionally, the Commission must authorize sufficient revenue to afford utilities the opportunity to recover expenses and the capital cost of doing business. *Southern Bell Telephone and Telegraph v. South Carolina Public Service Comm'n*, 270 S.C. 590, 244 S.E.2d 278 (1978). . . .

The Commission found that because the rates and surcharges Pipeline pays for gas are federally approved and imposed as a cost of gas, the Commission was bound to allow Pipeline to recover from its South Carolina customers Pipeline's full gas costs in the absence of a Commission finding of imprudent purchasing practices. Specifically, Pipeline's existing tariff provisions permit Pipeline to pass on to its customers all costs and surcharges imposed on gas purchased from intrastate pipelines. Moreover, the record reflects no challenge by any party as to the prudency of Pipeline's purchasing practices.

We conclude that the record evinces substantial evidence to support the Commission's findings that Pipeline is entitled to recoup TOP costs in full and that, with regard to this issue, the record reflects neither arbitrariness nor capriciousness as a matter of law.

We next consider whether the Commission's method of allocating TOP costs among Pipeline's customers is proper. The circuit court found that the deficiency-based portion of the Commission-authorized allocation constituted retroactive ratemaking. We agree.

The Commission adopted a 50% volumetric and 50% deficiency-based collection methodology, a combination of the collection methods supported by the parties. Under the volumetric system, TOP liability is reasonably apportioned according to the degree to which individual customers have benefitted from the recent restructuring of the natural gas industry. A deficiency-based allocation ascribes TOP liability according to the reasonable measure of an individual customer's responsibility for the incurrence of such costs.

The commission-approved method allowed Pipeline to prepay its lump sum direct bill liability and charge interest on the prepaid amounts pending collection. Ultimately, the volumetric provision would require Pipeline's customers to pay a surcharge on each unit of gas purchased by them in the future. The deficiency aspect would permit the allocation of TOP charges based on the customers' gas purchase "deficiencies" during the period 1982–1986 as compared with their 1981 purchases.

Appellants contend TOP costs are current and that the Commission's decision established a mechanism to recover Pipeline's current costs. Appellants argue further that demand costs have customarily been assessed on the basis of past events and peak demand for the allocation of current costs of service. . . .

S.C.Code Ann. § 58–5–240 (Cum.Supp.1990) requires a public utility to have rates filed and approved by the Commission prior to implementation of such rates; the intent being to insure that customers know prior to purchase what rate is charged.

The Commission asserts that the deficiency method was approved by the FERC. However, in *Associated Gas Distributors* [893 F.2d 349 (D.C.Cir. 1989)] the United States Court of Appeals for the District of Columbia held that the deficiency allocation method approved by the FERC violates the filed-rate doctrine and constitutes retroactive ratemaking.

Appellants seek to distinguish this controversy by arguing that respondents were put on notice through Pipeline's tariffs, which permitted recovery of TOP costs as costs of gas.

Even if notice to the respondents of the potential for TOP liability solved any conflict with the filed-rate doctrine, it cannot be argued that such notice apprized of any rate and method of recovery, or that retroactive recovery would be permitted. Pipeline's customers were entitled to rely on the contractual rates in effect at such time in the past as they chose to purchase or refrain from purchasing gas. This Court finds the deficiency-based collection methodology for recoupment of TOP charges to be arbitrary and capricious as a matter of law.

Accordingly, we reverse the circuit court's holding that, in toto, the findings of the Commission are without evidentiary support and are arbitrary and capricious as a matter of law. We reinstate so much of the Commission's order as holds that Pipeline is entitled to recover from its customers 100% of its FERC-approved TOP costs.

We affirm so much of the circuit court's order as finds that a deficiency-based levelized charge to customers for TOP costs is prohibited in that it constitutes retroactive ratemaking. The issue of methodology for recoupment of FERC approved TOP charges is reversed and remanded to the Commission for reconsideration consistent with the order of the circuit court.■

NOTES AND COMMENTS

1. This opinion discusses some principles of ratemaking that may be difficult to understand at this stage. Despite the court's use of some technical jargon, however, the issues involved in the case are not complex and can be understood without an in-depth knowledge of ratemaking.

2. Both parts two and three of the opinion involve the operation of the "filed-rate doctrine." In its simplest form, this doctrine says that if someone pays for services at a rate that has been filed with and approved by the proper regulatory agency then the legality of that rate should not be subject to being reopened in later proceedings. Conversely, if a company agrees to

provide a service to a particular customer at a rate different than the legally filed rate, then its promise is void. *American Telephone & Telegraph Co. v. Central Office Telephone, Inc.*, 524 U.S. 214 (1998).

3. Parts two and three of the opinion illustrate the difference between two key elements of ratemaking: rate level and rate design. In part two the court is determining the total amount of money that the local company may pass on to its customers (the "rate level"). In part three the court is addressing the question of which classes of customers should pay which share of the total amount ("rate design").

4. The take-or-pay problem also caused a flurry of law suits between the producer and the landowner from whom the producer had leased the tracts to explore for and develop oil or gas. The typical oil and gas lease signed between these two parties granted the landowner, as lessor, a one-eighth royalty on oil or gas produced by the lessee. (Review the lease provisions in Chapter 6 on Oil). The lessee-producer's gas sales contract with the pipeline committed the pipeline to either take the gas (and pay the agreed price for it) or to pay the producer for gas which the pipeline opted not to take (because it had no market for it). When the pipeline exercised the option of paying for the gas without taking it, lessees received large sums of money, even though the gas remained in the ground. Was the lessee-producer required to share one-eighth of these TOP payments with the landowner? Similarly, when the pipeline made cash payments, often in the millions of dollars, to "buy out" (*i.e.*, terminate) or "buy down" (reduce the gas price agreed to) these take-or-pay contracts, was the landowner entitled to a share under the lease?

Producers argued that the TOP payments were made for gas *not* produced. The gas remained in the ground and the landowner would receive royalties on it later when it was produced under a new, renegotiated contract. Landowners argued that their lessee was receiving the TOP payments only because of the existence of the lessors' gas. The typical lease states that royalties are to be paid on oil or gas *"produced from said land"* or on *"production saved, removed or sold from the leased area."* Given this language, who do you expect would win these TOP lawsuits? Not surprisingly, producers generally won. "Production" has been interpreted to mean the physical severance of gas from the underground reservoir. *See, e.g., Diamond Shamrock Exploration Co. v. Hodel*, 853 F.2d 1159 (5th Cir. 1988) *Condra v. Quinoco Petroleum, Inc.*, 954 S.W.2d 68 (Tex.App.1997); *Trans-American Natural Gas Corp. v. Finkelstein*, 933 S.W.2d 591 (Tex.App. 1996).

Would the result differ, however, if the royalty clause required payment of "royalty on gas sold by Lessee of one-eighth of the amount realized at the well from such sales."? What if the court views the oil and gas lease as a "cooperative venture" or "symbiotic endeavor" in which the lessor contributes land and the lessee contributes capital and expertise to develop the oil and gas for the mutual benefit of both parties? In a minority of states, royalty interest owners have won the right to share in some TOP payments based on lease language and construction such as this. *See, e.g.,*

Frey v. Amoco Prod. Co., 603 So.2d 166 (La.1992); and *Klein v. Jones,* 980 F.2d 521 (8th Cir. 1992), *aff'd after remand,* 73 F.3d 779 (8th Cir. 1996), *cert. denied,* 519 U.S. 815 (1996).

B.   ORDER 636 AND ITS IMPLEMENTATION

1.   OVERVIEW; ORDER 636 IN THE COURT

The most important of the FERC restructuring orders is Order 636, issued in April 1992. The basic policy behind FERC's restructuring is that the pipelines are to become primarily transporters of gas owned by others. LDCs and industrial customers will purchase gas directly from producers or on the open market and will then negotiate with a pipeline to transport the gas for them. Thus the pipeline will become analogous to a railroad or trucking company that handles goods owned by others rather than by the rail or truck line. Pipelines will cease to be merchants, buying and selling gas, and will become transporters only. Before reading some major (but drastically shortened) parts of the 150–page opinion of the D.C. Circuit court reviewing Order 636, here is an overview of the key provisions and some of the jargon of Order 636:

a.   Functional unbundling. The widely used term for the separation of one line of business from another is "unbundling." The pipelines were directed to separate their gas merchant sales services from their transportation services. This required changes in the internal organization of the companies, which in the past had primarily transported only gas they bought and sold themselves. Because the pipelines were not required to actually divest themselves of one of these two divisions, Order 636 did not require a true unbundling, although the pipelines had the option to do so. The Order only demanded that an internal "Chinese wall" be created within the company to prevent the exchange of information between the two divisions except on the same terms as available to competitors. For this reason the process became known as "functional" unbundling.

b.   Storage Access. Most pipelines operate storage fields near their major markets, consisting of depleted oil or gas reservoirs into which gas can be pumped in the summer and withdrawn in the winter. Order 636 directed the pipelines to provide equal access to these storage fields to all shippers of gas and on terms comparable to the pipeline's own gas.

c.   Transportation Access. The pipelines were required to file rate schedules ("tariffs") showing that all shippers of gas could buy transportation service from the pipeline at the same rate as the pipeline charged customers who bought gas owned by the pipeline.

d.   Electronic Notification. Pipelines were required to install information technology that would give their customers equal and timely access to the prices and conditions of transportation service. These are referred to as "electronic bulletin boards" or "EBBs".

e. Capacity Release. Pipelines are required to implement a "capacity release" program so that firm shippers, *i.e.*, those who have committed to pay for space in the pipeline, can release unwanted space to companies who need the capacity. Thus contracts for pipeline capacity can be bought and sold on the market.

f. Common Rate Design. All pipelines were required to compute their rates for transportation services on the basis of the same formula.

The process of issuing the restructuring orders for each individual pipeline is now substantially completed, and the pipelines are operating under the new regime. The validity of Order 636 was upheld on appeal, although several minor issues were remanded to FERC for reconsideration. The following excerpts from the case first review some familiar background to Order 636 and its predecessor Order 436. This section of the opinion explains why Order 436 was only partially successful in providing "open access" pipelines, causing FERC to issue Order 636's mandatory unbundling to achieve full success. The excerpts then address three other major parts of the order: First, how would curtailment work, not in the traditional context of a shortage in gas supplies, but in the new context of a shortage in pipeline space due to unexpected events? Second, did FERC have jurisdiction to regulate the newly created market in buying and selling pipeline space? This market is the focus of the "capacity release" program. Third, and yet again, who would bear the burden of the costs of transition, mainly take-or-pay costs? The pipelines? All or some of their customers? Gas producers? Or should all interested groups share the costs somehow?

As you read these excerpts, note how the restructuring of the gas industry was a constant back-and-forth between FERC and the D.C. Circuit.

United Distribution Companies v. Federal Energy Regulatory Comm'n

88 F.3d 1105 (D.C.Cir.1996).

■ PER CURIAM: In Order No. 636, the Federal Energy Regulatory Commission ("Commission" or "FERC") took the latest step in its decade-long restructuring of the natural gas industry, in which the Commission has gradually withdrawn from direct regulation of certain industry sectors in favor of a policy of "light-handed regulation" when market forces make that possible. We review briefly the regulatory background for natural gas. . . .

A. Background: Natural Gas Industry Structure

The natural gas industry is functionally separated into production, transportation, and distribution. Traditionally, before the move to open-access transportation, a producer extracted the gas and sold it at the wellhead to a pipeline company. The pipeline company then transported the gas through high-pressure pipelines and re-sold it to a local distribution company (LDC). The LDC in turn distributed the gas through its local mains to residential and industrial users.

The Natural Gas Act (NGA), ch. 556, 52 Stat. 821 (1938) (codified as amended at 15 U.S.C. §§ 717–717w (1994)), enacted in 1938, gave the Commission jurisdiction over sales for resale in interstate commerce and over the interstate transportation of gas, but left the regulation of local distribution to the states. NGA § 1(b), 15 U.S.C. § 717(b). The NGA was intended to fill the regulatory gap left by a series of Supreme Court decisions that interpreted the dormant Commerce Clause to preclude state regulation of interstate transportation and of wholesale gas sales. *See Arkansas Elec. Coop. Corp. v. Arkansas Pub. Serv. Comm'n*, 461 U.S. 375, 377–80 (1983). The overriding purpose of the NGA is "to protect consumers against exploitation at the hands of natural gas companies." *FPC v. Louisiana Power & Light Co.*, 406 U.S. 621, 631 (1972) (*quoting FPC v. Hope Natural Gas Co.*, 320 U.S. 591, 610 (1944)). Federal regulation of the natural gas industry is thus designed to curb pipelines' potential monopoly power over gas transportation. The enormous economies of scale involved in the construction of natural gas pipelines tend to make the transportation of gas a natural monopoly. Indeed, even with the expansion of the national pipeline grid, or network, in recent decades, many "captive" customers remain served by a single pipeline. Order No. 436, P 30,665, at 31,473.

Even though the market function potentially subject to monopoly power is the transportation of gas, for many years the Commission also regulated the price and terms of sales by producers to interstate pipelines. *See Phillips Petroleum Co. v. Wisconsin*, 347 U.S. 672, 677–84 (1954). Producer price regulation was widely regarded as a failure, introducing severe distortions into what otherwise would have been a well-functioning producer sales market. *See* Stephen G. Breyer & Paul W. MacAvoy, Energy Regulation by The Federal Power Commission 56–88 (1974). When a severe gas shortage developed in the 1970s, Congress enacted the Natural Gas Policy Act of 1978 (NGPA), Pub. L. No. 95–621, 92 Stat. 3351 (codified as amended at 15 U.S.C. §§ 3301–3432 (1994)), which gradually phased out producer price regulation. Under the NGPA's partially regulated producer-price system, many pipelines entered into long-term contractual obligations, in what were known as "take-or-pay" provisions, to purchase minimum quantities of gas from producers at costs that proved to be well above current market prices of gas. *See* Richard J. Pierce, Jr., Reconstituting the Natural Gas Industry from Wellhead to Burnertip, 9 Energy L.J. 1, 11–16 (1988).

The problem of pipelines' take-or-pay settlement costs has plagued the industry and the Commission over the last fifteen years. The Commission's initial response to escalating pipeline take-or-pay liabilities was to authorize pipelines to offer less expensive sales of third-party (non-pipeline-owned) gas to non-captive customers while still offering only higher-priced pipeline gas to captive customers. The court struck down these measures because the Commission "had not adequately attended to the agency's prime constituency," captive customers vulnerable to pipelines' market power. *Maryland People's Counsel v. FERC*, 761 F.2d 780, 781 (D.C.Cir. 1985) (MPC II); *see also Maryland People's Counsel v. FERC*, 761 F.2d 768, 776 (D.C.Cir.1985) (MPC I). In response to the court's decisions in MPC I and MPC II, the Commission embarked on its landmark Order No. 436 rulemaking. *See* Order No. 436, P 30,665, at 31,467.

B.   Order No. 436: Open–Access Transportation

In Order No. 436, the Commission began the transition toward removing pipelines from the gas-sales business and confining them to a more limited role as gas transporters. Under a new Part 284 of its regulations, the Commission conditioned receipt of a blanket certificate for firm transportation of third-party gas on the pipeline's acceptance of non-discrimination requirements guaranteeing equal access for all customers to the new service. Order No. 436, P 30,665, at 31,497–518. In effect, the Commission for the first time imposed the duties of common carriers upon interstate pipelines. *See Associated Gas Distributors v. FERC*, 824 F.2d 981, 997 (D.C.Cir.1987) (AGD I), *cert. denied*, 485 U.S. 1006 (1988). By recognizing that anti-competitive conditions in the industry arose from pipeline control over access to transportation capacity, the equal-access requirements of Order No. 436 regulated the natural-monopoly conditions directly. In addition, every open-access pipeline was required to allow its existing bundled firm-sales customers to convert to firm-transportation service and, at the customer's option, to reduce its firm-transportation entitlement (its "contract demand"). Order No. 436, P 30,665, at 31,518–33. Moreover, the Commission established a flexible rate structure under which transportation charges were limited to the maximum approved rate (based on fully allocated costs) but pipelines could selectively discount down to the minimum approved rate (based on average variable cost). *Id.* at 31,533–49.

The court largely approved Order No. 436, but the principal stumbling-block was the unresolved problem of uneconomical pipeline-producer contracts in the transition to the unbundled environment. The Commission had decided not to provide pipelines with relief from their take-or-pay liabilities, even though the introduction of open-access transportation in Order No. 436 would likely exacerbate the problem by reducing pipeline sales. AGD I, 824 F.2d at 1021–23. After the court remanded the case on the ground that the Commission's inaction on take-or-pay did not exhibit reasoned decision making in light of open access, *id.* at 1030, the Commission adopted various interim measures in Order No. 500. First, it instituted a "crediting mechanism," under which a pipeline could apply any third-party gas that it transported toward the pipeline's minimum-purchase obligation from that particular producer. Order No. 500, P 30,761, at 30,779–84. Second, the Commission adopted two alternative cost-recovery mechanisms. As customary, a pipeline could recover all of its prudently incurred costs in its commodity (sales) charges, although that could prove difficult for pipelines with shrinking sales-customer bases. In the alternative, under the equitable-sharing approach, a pipeline offering open-access transportation could, if it voluntarily absorbed between twenty-five and fifty percent of the costs, recover an equal share of the costs through a "fixed charge" and recover the remaining amount (up to fifty percent) through a volumetric surcharge based on total throughput (and thus borne by both sales and transportation customers alike). *Id.* at 30, 784–92; 18 C.F.R. § 2.104. Third, the Commission authorized pipelines not recovering take-or-pay costs in any other manner to impose a "gas inventory charge" (GIC), a fixed charge for "standing ready" to deliver gas—the sales analogue to a reservation charge. Order No. 500, P 30,761, at 30,792–94; 18 C.F.R. § 2.105.

The Commission's alternative solutions to the problem of take-or-pay settlement costs in Order No. 500 fared poorly on judicial review. First, the court remanded the crediting mechanism for an explanation of whether the Commission had the requisite authority under § 7 of the NGA. *American Gas Ass'n v. FERC*, 888 F.2d 136, 148–49 (D.C.Cir.1989) (AGA I). After the Commission explained its § 7 authority for the crediting mechanism in Order No. 500–H, the court upheld the crediting mechanism. *American Gas Ass'n v. FERC*, 912 F.2d 1496, 1509–13 (D.C.Cir.1990) (AGA II). Second, the court struck down the equitable-sharing cost-recovery mechanism on the ground that the Commission's "purchase deficiency" method for calculating the "fixed charge," which assigned costs to each customer based on how much its purchases had declined over the relevant preceding period, violated the filed-rate doctrine. *Associated Gas Distributors v. FERC*, 893 F.2d 349, 354–57 (D.C.Cir.1989) (AGD II), *reh'g en banc denied*, 898 F.2d 809 (D.C.Cir.), *cert. denied*, 498 U.S. 907 (1990). The Commission responded to the invalidation of the "purchase deficiency" method in AGD II by adopting Order No. 528, which allowed pipelines, in the "fixed charge," to pass through a portion of costs to customers based on any of several measures of current (rather than past) demand or usage, with the intent of avoiding the filed-rate problem. Order No. 528, P 61,163, at 61,597–98. Finally, the court struck down the Commission's approval of a GIC on a particular pipeline because it had given undue weight to the pipeline's customers' having agreed to the GIC and failed adequately to consider the interests of end-users. *Tejas Power Corp. v. FERC*, 908 F.2d 998, 1003–05 (D.C.Cir.1990).

Congress completed the process of deregulating the producer sales market by enacting the Natural Gas Wellhead Decontrol Act of 1989, Pub. L. No. 101–60, 103 Stat. 157 (codified in scattered sections of 15 U.S.C.). As the House Committee on Energy and Commerce emphasized, the Commission's creation of open-access transportation was "essential" to Congress' decision completely to deregulate wellhead sales. H.R. REP. NO. 29, 101st Cong., 1st Sess. 6 (1989). The committee report declared also that "both the FERC and the courts are strongly urged to retain and improve this competitive structure in order to maximize the benefits of decontrol." *Id.* The committee expected that, by ensuring that "all buyers [are] free to reach the lowest-selling producer," *id.*, open-access transportation would allow the more efficient producers to emerge, leading to lower prices for consumers, *id.* at 3, 7.

C.   Order No. 636: Mandatory Unbundling

In Order No. 636, the Commission declared the open-access requirements of Order No. 436 a partial success. The Commission found that pipeline firm sales, which in 1984 had been over 90 percent of deliveries to market, had declined by 1990 to 21 percent. Order No. 636, P 30,939, at 30,399 tbl. 1. On the other hand, only 28 percent of deliveries to market in 1990 were firm transportation, whereas 51 percent of deliveries used interruptible transportation. *Id.* at 30,399 & n.61. The Commission concluded that many customers had not taken advantage of Order No. 436's option to convert from firm-sales to firm-transportation service because the firm-transportation component of bundled firm-sales service was "superior in quality" to stand-alone firm-transportation service. *Id.* at 30, 402. In particular, the Commission found that stand-alone firm-transportation service was often subject to daily scheduling and balancing requirements, as well as to penalties for variances from projected purchases in excess of ten percent. Moreover, pipelines usually did not offer storage capacity on a contractual basis to stand-alone firm-transportation shippers. *Id.* The result was that many of the non-converted customers used the pipelines' firm-sales service during times of peak demand but in non-peak periods bought third-party gas and transported it with interruptible transportation. The Commission found that "it is often cheaper for pipeline sales customers to buy gas on the spot market, and pay the pipeline's demand charge plus the interruptible rate, than to purchase the pipeline's gas." *Id.* at 30,400. Because of the distortions in the sales market, these customers often paid twice for transportation services and still received an inferior form of transportation (interruptible rather than firm). *Id.* Because of the anti-competitive effect on the industry, the Commission found that pipelines' bundled firm-sales service violated §§ 4(b) and 5(a) of the NGA. *Id.* at 30,405.

The Commission's remedy for these anti-competitive conditions, and the principal innovation of Order No. 636, was mandatory unbundling of pipelines' sales and transportation services. By making the separation of the two functions mandatory, the Commission expects that pipelines' monopoly power over transportation will no longer distort the sales market. Order No. 636, P 30,939, at 30,406–13; Order No. 636–A, P 30,950, at 30,527–46; Order No. 636–B, P 61,272, at 61,988–92. To replace the firm-transportation component of bundled firm-sales service, the Commission introduced the concept of "no-notice firm transportation," stand-alone firm transportation without penalties. Those customers who receive bundled firm-sales service have the right, during the restructuring process, to switch to no-notice firm-transportation service. Pipelines that did not offer bundled firm-sales service are not required to offer no-notice transportation; but if they do, they must offer no-notice transportation on a non-discriminatory basis.

In contrast to the continued regulation of the transportation market, the Commission essentially deregulated the pipeline sales market. The Commission issued every Part 284 pipeline a blanket certificate authorizing gas sales. Although acknowledging that "only Congress can 'deregulate,' "the Commission "instituted light-handed regulation, relying upon market forces at the wellhead or in the field to constrain unbundled pipeline sale for resale gas prices within the NGA's "just and reasonable standard." Order No. 636, P 30,939, at 30,440. The Commission reasoned that open-access transportation, combined with its finding that "adequate divertible gas supplies exist in all pipeline markets," would ensure that the free market for gas sales would keep rates within the zone of reasonableness.

The Commission also undertook several measures to ensure that the pipeline grid, or network, functions as a whole in a more competitive fashion. First, open-access pipelines may not inhibit the development of "market centers," which are pipeline intersections that allow customers to take advantage of many more transportation routes and choose between sellers from different natural gas production areas. Similarly, open-access pipelines may not interfere with the development of "pooling areas," which allow the aggregation of gas supplies at a production area. [ ] Finally, as part of the move toward open-access transportation, the Commission required Part 284 pipelines to allow shippers to deliver gas at any delivery point without penalty and to allow customers to receive gas at any receipt point without penalty.

Even though this is the court's first occasion to address Order No. 636, which was enacted in 1992, we do not write on a clean slate. Beginning with MPC I and MPC II, the court has consistently required the Commission to protect consumers against pipelines' monopoly power. No longer reluctantly engaged in the unbundling enterprise, the Commission has responded by initiating sweeping changes with Order No. 636. Accordingly, we review the Commission's exercise of its authority under the NGA in light of the principles that the court has already applied in this area.

* * *

After two comprehensive rehearing orders, Orders No. 636–A and No. 636–B, the Commission denied further rehearing. . . . We consolidated with this case petitions for review of the Commission's decision to prohibit buy/sell agreements, and of the Commission's decision to end capacity-brokering programs. We ordered the petitioners to file briefs in consolidated industry groups: pipelines; local distribution companies (LDCs); small distributors and municipalities; industrial end-users; electric generators; and public utility commissions (PUCs).

The petitioners do not challenge the mandatory unbundling remedy itself. At issue on review are numerous other aspects of Order No. 636 involving changes that the Commission undertook as part of its comprehensive restructuring of the natural gas industry. . . .

* * *

II.C. Curtailment

When supply shortages arose in the natural gas industry during the 1970s, the Commission adopted end-use curtailment plans to protect high-priority customers from an interruption of supply. *See generally Consolidated Edison Co. v. FERC*, 676 F.2d 763, 765–67 (D.C.Cir.1982); *North Carolina v. FERC*, 584 F.2d 1003, 1006–08 (D.C.Cir.1978). In 1973, the Commission found itself "impelled to direct curtailment on the basis of end use rather than on the basis of contract simply because contracts do not necessarily serve the public interest requirement of efficient allocation of this wasting resource." Order No. 467, 49 F.P.C. 85, 86 (*quoting Arkansas Louisiana Gas Co.*, 49 F.P.C. 53, 66 (1973)), *order on reh'g*, 49 F.P.C. 217, *order on reh'g*, 49 F.P.C. 583 (1973), *petitions for review dismissed sub nom. Pacific Gas & Elec. Co. v. FPC*, 506 F.2d 33 (D.C.Cir.1974). The Commission's end-use curtailment schemes were essentially enacted into law by title IV of the Natural Gas Policy Act of 1978 (NGPA), which establishes the following priority system:

Whenever there is an insufficient supply, under the Act first in line to receive gas are schools, small business, residences, hospitals, and all others for whom a curtailment of natural gas could endanger life, health, or the maintenance of physical property. After these "high-priority" users have been satisfied, next in line are those who will put the gas to "essential agricultural uses," followed by those who will use the gas for "essential industrial process or feedstock uses," followed by everyone else. *Process Gas Consumers Group v. United States Dep't of Agriculture*, 657 F.2d 459, 460 (D.C.Cir.1981) (Process Gas I); *see also* 18 C.F.R. §§ 281.201–281.215 (the Commission's regulations implementing NGPA § 401).

With the introduction of stand-alone firm-transportation service in Order No. 436, the Commission distinguished for the first time between supply curtailment and capacity curtailment. Transportation service can suffer from a capacity interruption (such as a force majeure loss of capacity due to pipeline system failure or a pipeline's overbooking of capacity), whereas sales service can suffer from a shortage in the supply of gas. *See* Order No. 436, P 30,665, at 31,515; Order No. 436–A, P 30,675, at 31,652. The Commission's subsequent approach was to allow pipelines to adopt pro rata capacity curtailment (allocation proportional to the amount reserved, without regard to end use), *see, e.g., Texas Eastern Transmission Corp.*, 37 F.E.R.C. 61,260, at 61,692–93 (1986), *order on reh'g*, 41 F.E.R.C. P 61,015 (1987), *aff'd sub nom. Texaco, Inc. v. FERC*, 886 F.2d 749 (5th Cir.1989), unless the parties agreed to end-use capacity curtailment on a particular pipeline, *see, e.g., Florida Gas Transmission Co.*, 51 F.E.R.C. P 61,309, at 62,010–11, *order on reh'g*, 53 F.E.R.C. 61,396 (1990).

In *City of Mesa v. FERC*, 993 F.2d 888 (D.C.Cir.1993), the court ... found that different treatment of supply and capacity curtailment was reasonable because high-priority users can "generally 'fend for themselves' " to protect against capacity interruption:

Supply shortages usually lead to prolonged periods in which there is simply too little gas to serve the needs of all users. In contrast, capacity constraints occur when there is enough gas in the market but an unexpected event has caused a brief interruption in the movement of the gas to consumers. Additionally, capacity constraints, unlike supply shortages, may only affect the movement of gas on part of a pipeline, thereby allowing customers to receive their quota of gas by using alternate routes that skirt the pipeline bottleneck. These differences mean that pipeline customers can more easily adopt self-help measures to protect their high-priority end-users against the harmful effects of capacity curtailments than supply shortages.

City of Mesa, 993 F.2d at 894–95.

Although *City of Mesa* upheld the limitation of title IV of the NGPA to supply shortages, the court acknowledged that the NGA provided protections for capacity shortages. The court stated that "implicit in the consumer protection mandate is a duty to assure that consumers, especially high-priority consumers, have continuous access to needed supplies of natural gas." 993 F.2d at 895. This duty arises because " 'no single factor in the Commission's duty to protect the public can be more important to the public than the continuity of service provided.' " *Id. (quoting Sunray Mid–Continent Oil Co. v. FPC*, 239 F.2d 97, 101 (10th Cir.1956), rev'd on other grounds, 353 U.S. 944 (1957)). The court emphasized that "since the NGA gives the FERC no specific guidance as to how to apply its broad mandates in a particular case, our review of the FERC's actions here is, again, quite limited." *Id.* In *City of Mesa*, the court concluded that the Commission had failed to engage in reasoned decision making when it approved a curtailment plan that protected "most" high-priority users rather than all such users. 993 F.2d at 896–97. The court noted that in Order No. 636–A the Commission had held that "self-help strategies were generally sufficient to assure protection of end-users and thus to meet NGA mandates" but did not further examine whether self-help measures were adequate to protect against capacity curtailment. *Id.* at 897.

In Order No. 636, which was issued before the court's decision in *City of Mesa*, the Commission continued without change its curtailment policies since Order No. 436. First, the Commission acknowledged that, as a policy matter, it chafed at the title IV end-use curtailment scheme for supply shortages but stated that it was bound by the statute. Order No. 636, P 30,939, at 30,430; *see also Transcontinental Gas Pipe Line Corp.*, 57 F.E.R.C. P 61,345, at 62,117 (1991). The Commission reiterated its reading of § 401(a) that limited its scope to pipelines' sale of gas. Order No. 636–A, P 30,950, at 30,586–89. Second, the Commission maintained that self-help measures would allow the consumer-protection mandate of the NGA to be satisfied by pro rata capacity curtailment:

The Commission believes that with deregulated wellhead sales and a growing menu of options for unbundled pipeline service, customers should rely on prudent planning, private contracts, and the marketplace to the maximum extent practicable to secure both their capacity and supply needs. In today's environment, LDC's [*sic*] and end-users no longer need to rely exclusively on their traditional pipeline supplier. Rather, to an ever-increasing degree they rely on private contracts with gas sellers, storage providers, and others; a more diverse portfolio of pipeline suppliers, where possible; local self-help measures (e.g., local production, peak shaving and storage); and their own gas supply planning through choosing between an increasing array of unbundled service options.

Id. at 30,590.

* * *

We [also] review the Commission's policy on pro rata curtailment to determine whether it is "just and reasonable" under § 4 and whether it serves the "present or future public convenience and necessity" under § 7(e). *See City of Mesa*, 993 F.2d at 895. The Commission decided that the consumer-protection mandate of the NGA did not require it to adopt end-use capacity curtailment across the board and promised to address the issue in each pipeline restructuring proceeding. Order No. 636–A, P 30,950, at 30,591–92. Indeed, the Commission has broad latitude on whether to effectuate its policies in generic rulemakings or in individual-pipeline adjudications. *Mobil Oil*, 498 U.S. at 230. The issue presented to us, then, is whether the Commission's decision that the NGA does not require end-use curtailment in all circumstances is " 'reasoned, principled, and based upon the record.' " *Great Lakes Gas Transmission Ltd. Partnership v. FERC*, 984 F.2d 426, 432 (D.C.Cir.1993) (*quoting Columbia Gas Transmission Corp. v. FERC*, 628 F.2d 578, 593 (D.C.Cir.1979)).

The Commission explained that Order No. 636 had allowed the development of market structures that would enable customers to take independent, market-based steps to avoid the need for Commission-mandated end-use curtailment. Order No. 636–A, P 30,950, at 30,590. Moreover, the Commission found that since the enactment of the NGPA in 1978 "the industry has not experienced shortages beyond isolated, short-lived dislocation," *id.* at 30, 591, and "gas has always flowed according to the dictate of the market, i.e., to the heat sensitive users who need it most and who are thus willing to pay the prevailing market price for it." *Id.* at 30,592. This experience with the industry provides substantial evidence for the Commission's conclusion that end-use curtailment is not required in all circumstances.

We are unpersuaded, particularly in light of the Commission's own actions in the restructuring proceedings, that pro rata capacity curtailment would adequately protect all high-priority customers on all pipelines. *Cf. City of Mesa*, 993 F.2d at 896–97. The Commission's market-based alternatives for customers to avoid curtailment fall into the following categories: (1) arrangements with other pipelines; (2) arrangements with other gas sellers; (3) arrangements for gas storage; (4) arrangements with other customers (including the capacity-release mechanism); and (5) "peak shaving."[50][15] First, arrangements with other pipelines are more widely available after Order No. 636, such as by using different pipelines that connect to one "market center," but a capacity constraint on a pipeline will still cut

---

15. Peak shaving is "the practice of adding propane air mixtures to augment supplies of natural gas during periods of peak demand." *Atlanta Gas Light*, 756 F.2d at 195 n.5.

off delivery to any "captive customers," no matter how many transportation options some other customers may have. Second, arrangements with other gas sellers are by definition relevant only to supply curtailment, not to capacity curtailment. Third, arrangements for gas storage are unhelpful if the capacity interruption occurs at a point between the contract-storage area and the customer's receipt point. Fourth, obtaining gas from other customers, whether through the capacity-release mechanism or otherwise, depends upon the willingness of lower-priority customers to forgo deliveries. Fifth, practices such as "peak shaving" (letting a little gas go a longer way) can temporarily help to alleviate curtailment problems but cannot ensure continuous service if the interruption lasts too long. None of these market-based solutions, therefore, can guarantee continuous service to all high-priority customers in cases of capacity interruptions. Many of the market-based solutions fail to acknowledge that many customers have far less control over access to pipeline capacity than they do over gas supply. In addition, some of the self-help mechanisms will be more readily available to larger pipeline customers. *City of Mesa*, 993 F.2d at 897.

Yet the Commission has not applied Order No. 636 in the restructuring proceedings to preclude the development of curtailment plans that provide more protection to higher-priority users. For example, on remand from *City of Mesa*, the Commission reiterated its general policy that "customers can, and should, avail themselves of self-help methods to obtain their needed supplies" but, in light of the decision in *City of Mesa*, ordered El Paso to "include provisions giving relief to any high priority shipper when that shipper has exercised all other self-help remedies in times of bona fide emergencies." *El Paso Natural Gas Co.*, 69 F.E.R.C. 61,164, at 61,624 (1994), *order on reh'g*, 72 F.E.R.C. P 61,042, *reh'g denied*, 73 F.E.R.C. P 61,074 (1995). In another restructuring proceeding, the Commission approved a settlement and found its curtailment plan consistent with City of Mesa because it "provides an exemption from pro rata curtailment whenever necessary to avoid irreparable injury to life or property." *Florida Gas Transmission Co.*, 70 F.E.R.C. 61,017, at 61,061 (1995). On occasions, the Commission has suggested that "there may be extraordinary circumstances when reasonable self-help efforts are insufficient, even for large customers," such that some emergency protections may always be required for certain force majeure capacity interruptions. *El Paso*, 69 F.E.R.C. 61,164, at 61,624; *see also United Gas Pipe Line Co.*, 65 F.E.R.C. P 61,006, at 61, 092, *reh'g denied sub nom. Koch Gateway Pipeline Co.*, 65 F.E.R.C. P 61,338, at 62,630–31 (1993).

We need not reach the issue whether the adoption of a pure pro rata capacity-curtailment scheme on a generic basis would comply with the Commission's duty under the NGA to ensure that "high-priority consumers have continuous access to needed supplies of natural gas." *City of Mesa*, 993 F.2d at 895. All the Commission did in Order No. 636 was to decide not to require end-use capacity curtailment for all pipelines. Because the Commission expressly declared that it would re-examine the suitability of pure pro rata capacity curtailment for customers on each pipeline, Order No. 636–A, P 30,950, at 30,591–92, we construe any indications that pro rata curtailment will be the default as unreviewable policy statements under § 4(b)(A) of the Administrative Procedure Act, 5 U.S.C. § 553(b)(A). *See Pacific Gas & Elec. Co. v. FPC*, 506 F.2d 33, 39 (D.C.Cir.1974). The manner in which the Commission has applied its curtailment policy in the restructuring proceedings supports our conclusion that any preference for pro rata schemes is not suitable for review. *See Public Citizen, Inc. v. NRC*, 940 F.2d 679, 682–83 (D.C.Cir.1991). Accordingly, the compliance of specific curtailment plans with the NGA's consumer-protection mandate remains open on review of the restructuring proceedings.

We uphold the Commission's decision not to require end-use curtailment on a generic basis for capacity curtailment but to proceed instead on a case-by-case basis.

III. Capacity Release

In this part of the opinion, we address challenges to the voluntary capacity release provisions of Order No. 636, which permit holders of firm transportation rights on a gas pipeline to resell them. 18 C.F.R. § 284.243 (1995). Petitioners challenge the Commission's jurisdiction to institute its capacity release program generally.... We conclude that each of petitioners' claims is either incorrect on the merits or is not suited for review in these proceedings.

* * *

Among the central goals of Order Nos. 436 and 636 has been the conversion of bundled sales arrangements into separate transportation and gas sales transactions. On the transportation side, the Commission recognized that while much of the nation's interstate pipeline capacity was reserved for firm transportation, those transportation rights ultimately were not being utilized. *See supra* Part I.C. FERC therefore sought to develop an active "secondary transportation market," with holders of unutilized firm capacity rights reselling them in competition with any capacity offered directly by the pipeline. According to the Commission:

> Capacity reallocation will promote efficient load management by the pipeline and its customers and, therefore, efficient use of the pipeline capacity on a firm basis throughout the year. Because more buyers will be able to reach more sellers through firm transportation capacity, capacity reallocation comports with the goal of improving nondiscriminatory, open-access transportation to maximize the benefits of the decontrol of natural gas at the wellhead and in the field.

> Order No. 636, P 30,939, at 30,418.

Understanding petitioners' challenges to the capacity release program requires a brief review of related policies that the Commission has employed in the past to accomplish a similar end.

If a firm capacity holder does not ship gas under its transportation right, it pays the pipeline a "reservation fee," but does not pay a "usage fee." Historically, FERC prohibited such holders of unutilized firm capacity rights from transferring those rights to other shippers, and shippers were therefore able to purchase capacity rights only directly from pipelines. *See generally United Gas Pipe Line Co.*, 46 F.E.R.C. 61,060 (1989) (approving first experimental capacity brokering program). Beginning with the *Texas Eastern Transmission Corp.* proceedings, 48 F.E.R.C. 61,248, *order on reh'g*, 48 F.E.R.C. 61,378 (1989), *order on reh'g*, 51 F.E.R.C. P 51,170, *order on reh'g*, 52 F.E.R.C. 61,273 (1990), however, the Commission authorized shippers on some pipelines to engage in nondiscriminatory "capacity brokering." Brokering arrangements allowed a holder of firm capacity rights (the "releasing shipper") to sell those rights to a "replacement shipper." The transaction took place directly between the two parties, and the replacement shipper essentially stepped into the shoes of the releasing shipper.

Three years later, in the Order No. 636 and companion *Algonquin Gas Transmission Corp.* proceedings, 59 F.E.R.C. 61,032 (1992), FERC concluded that it could not ensure that the extant capacity brokering programs were operating in a nondiscriminatory manner. When transactions occurred directly and privately between shippers, there was no way to verify that certain purchasers were not being favored unreasonably over others. "Simply put, there [were] too many potential assignors of capacity and too many different programs for the Commission to oversee capacity brokering...." Order No. 636, P 30,939, at 30,416. In FERC's view, fairness could be secured only if capacity resale transactions were both centralized on each pipeline and subject to open bidding. Moreover, uniformity among the various pipelines was necessary to "prevent any pipeline or firm shipper from achieving an undue advantage, or incurring an undue disadvantage, compared to firm shippers on other pipelines." *Id.*

Accordingly, in Order No. 636, the Commission instituted a uniform national "capacity release" program, and exercised its power under NGA § 5 to conform pipelines' existing capacity brokering certificates to that program. *Id.* While both capacity brokering and capacity release arrangements involve the releasing shipper's decision to sell excess capacity, capacity release requires the central involvement of the pipeline in the transaction. Specifically, under capacity release, each interstate pipeline is required to establish and administer an electronic bulletin board ("EBB"), which is a computer through which putative releasing and replacement shippers may communicate. *Id.* at 30,418. The EBB carries information about available and consummated capacity release transactions. For example, holders of excess firm capacity rights may "post" their available capacity on the EBB. Further, they may establish nondiscriminatory conditions on the sale, including a minimum price and any terms under which the release may continue. Pipelines are also required to post on the EBB any firm capacity that they have available for sale, where the capacity competes for buyers against capacity made available for resale by shippers. "Potential purchasers of capacity will then be able to choose from among the pipeline and the releasers the service that best suits their needs." *Id.* at 30,419. In addition, shippers that wish to acquire firm capacity rights may post offers to purchase capacity on the EBB. 18 C.F.R. § 284.243(d); Order No. 636–A, P 30,950, at 30,565.

With two exceptions, the pipeline must sell the capacity to the highest bidder. First, "short-term transactions," i.e., those for capacity releases of less than one month, may be arranged between shippers without competitive bidding. 18 C.F.R. § 284.243(h)(1); Order No. 636–A, P 30,950, at 30,554. Second, a releasing shipper may identify a replacement shipper on its own and enter into a "pre-arranged" deal. 18 C.F.R. § 284.243(b); Order No. 636, P 30,939, at 30,418. In such a transaction, the selected replacement shipper need only match—rather than outbid—the highest offer made by any other shipper. 18 C.F.R. § 284.243(e). The net effect is that a shipper may ensure that it will receive certain capacity by entering into a pre-arranged deal that both conforms to the releasing shipper's conditions and matches the maximum allowable rate for the capacity. No matter what form the capacity release transaction takes, however, the purchase price for released capacity may not exceed the maximum rate set by FERC for the capacity. 18 C.F.R. § 284.243(e); Order No. 636, P 30,939, at 30,420.

After the replacement shipper has been identified, the pipeline enters into a contract with it for firm capacity rights. The pipeline then may elect to excuse completely the releasing shipper's obligation to pay the reservation fee and related costs. Order No. 636, P 30,939, at 30,419. Otherwise, the releasing shipper is credited for those costs unless the replacement shipper defaults. 18 C.F.R. § 284.243(f); Order No. 636–A, P 30,950, at 30,553. In no instance, however, is the releasing shipper liable for costs associated with the replacement shipper's transportation of gas.

[The court then addresses the jurisdictional challenges to the capacity release program].

Various petitioners challenge both FERC's jurisdiction to institute a uniform capacity release program and its jurisdiction over specific transactions and entities. We begin, then, by outlining the Commission's jurisdiction under § 1(b) of the Natural Gas Act of 1938. Ultimately, we conclude that FERC's capacity release program is a legitimate exercise of its jurisdiction over the interstate transportation of natural gas.

In the early part of this century, state regulatory agencies actively involved themselves in structuring the natural gas industry. The Supreme Court, however, severely cabined those efforts in a series of decisions that interpreted the dormant Commerce Clause to preclude state regulation of both the interstate transportation of natural gas and its ensuing sale in wholesale markets. Congress enacted the Natural Gas Act of 1938 to fill the resulting regulatory gap. The Act, as provided in § 1(b), applies

> [1] to the transportation of natural gas in interstate commerce, [2] to the sale in interstate commerce of natural gas for resale for ultimate public consumption for domestic, commercial, industrial, or any other use, and [3] to natural-gas companies engaged in such transportation or sale, but [does] not apply [4] to any other transportation or sale of natural gas or [5] to the local distribution of natural gas or to the facilities used for such distribution or [6] to the production or gathering of natural gas.

15 U.S.C. § 717(b).

Petitioners' jurisdictional challenges require us to interpret the first and fifth provisions of § 1(b), which address the interstate transportation and "local distribution" of natural gas. In truth, the two provisions are a unity. "It is well established that the ["local distribution"] proviso was added to the Act merely for clarification and was not intended to deprive [FERC] of any jurisdiction otherwise granted by § 1(b)." *Louisiana Power & Light*, 406 U.S. at 637 n.14; *see also East Ohio Gas*, 338 U.S. at 469–70 ("What Congress must have meant by 'facilities' for 'local distribution' was equipment for distributing gas among consumers within a particular local community, not the high-pressure pipe lines transporting the gas to the local mains."). . . .

Petitioners' first jurisdictional challenge is the claim of the LDCs that FERC lacks any authority whatsoever to regulate shippers' resale of firm capacity rights. "LDCs' capacity assignments," they maintain, "involve sales of LDCs' rights to transportation service but do not involve interstate transportation or sale for resale of gas itself." As we understand their position, the LDCs would limit FERC's regulatory authority over transportation to the rendition of interstate gas transportation services, as opposed to authority over the rights to receive those services. As their theory goes, the Commission has jurisdiction over the pipelines' initial sales of transportation capacity—given that it is the pipelines that render transportation services—but is without jurisdiction over resales of those same capacity rights by third parties—given that those third parties do not render transportation services.

Initially, we believe that the distinction drawn by the LDCs between the "rights to" and "rendition of" interstate transportation services is not a meaningful one. While the pipeline provides transportation only when a party utilizes capacity rights to transport gas, the pipeline provides transportation services throughout the capacity release process. Specifically, the pipeline operates the electronic bulletin board on which all prospective transactions are posted and consummated. The pipeline also selects the winning bidder in the transaction. Moreover, unlike capacity brokering arrangements, which occur directly between releasing and replacement shippers, capacity release requires the pipeline to contract with the replacement shipper. "In effect, the pipeline is temporarily abandoning service to the releasing shipper and instituting service to the replacement shipper. Both of these activities are subject to the Commission's jurisdiction under NGA section 1(b). . . ." Order No. 636–A, P 30,939, at 30,551. In sum, the capacity release regulations operate as a term or condition of pipeline service, with which its customers must comply.

As an entirely separate matter, the Commission's jurisdiction attaches to the subject of the capacity resale transaction: interstate transportation rights. "By controlling such capacity, the assignors are effectively determining by whom, and under what circumstances, gas will be transported and are using the pipeline's facilities as if they were the assignors' facilities." *Id.* (quotation marks, alteration, and citation omitted). In contrast, under the regulatory system envisioned by the LDCs, holders of capacity rights could engage in resales without regard to the principles of open access and nondiscrimination that are at the heart of the uniform capacity release system. Such a result is directly contrary to Congress' intent in enacting the Natural Gas Act. Responding to the Supreme Court's conclusion that the Constitution's dormant Commerce Clause prohibited state regulation of the interstate transportation of natural gas, the federal government interceded to ensure stability and protect the interests of the consuming public. It thereby occupied the field, which necessarily includes both the sale and resale of interstate transportation rights. . . .

We also find compelling the acknowledged jurisdictional arrangement prior to the implementation of either capacity brokering or capacity release. At that time, shippers acquired firm capacity rights directly from pipelines on a first-come, first-served basis. Resales of capacity by shippers, including municipalities, simply did not occur. We therefore conclude that the Commission has jurisdiction to require open, nondiscriminatory capacity release by municipalities. . . .

The final jurisdictional challenge to the capacity release mechanism involves "buy/sell" transactions, which FERC professed to bar in Order No. 636 and the companion *El Paso Natural Gas Co.* proceedings, 59 F.E.R.C. 61,031, *reh'g denied*, 60 F.E.R.C. 61,117 (1992). "Buy/sells" occur in three stages. First, an end-user of gas either purchases or identifies certain natural gas at the point of production. The LDC that services the end-user then purchases the gas and transports it first under its own transportation rights on an interstate pipeline and later across its local distribution facilities. The end-user then receives the gas from the LDC. The "buy/sells" reviewed by the Commission in the El Paso proceedings were conducted under the authority and oversight of the California Public Utility Commission.

FERC acknowledges that "buy/sell" transactions implicate legitimate state regulatory interests. *El Paso Natural Gas Co.*, 60 F.E.R.C. P 61,117, at 61,383–84. That said, given the transactions' intermediate stage—in which the end-user expressly arranges for the interstate transportation of specifically identified gas—the Commission contends that it has authority to preempt such state regulation. . . .

We consider petitioners' arguments regarding "buy/sell" transactions under the branch of pre-emption doctrine that concerns "conflicts" between state and federal law, and particularly state law that "stands as an obstacle to the accomplishment and execution of the full purposes and objectives of Congress," *Hines v. Davidowitz*, 312 U.S. 52, 67 (1941). The Commission's goal in preempting "buy/sell" transactions was to preserve the integrity of its uniform capacity release program. *See El Paso Natural Gas*, 60 F.E.R.C. P 61,117, at 61,385. Specifically, the Commission concluded that "buy/sells" offer a ready means of circumventing the open, nondiscriminatory bidding process central to capacity release. Under Order No. 636, an end-user seeking firm interstate transportation for gas that it has identified or acquired at the point of production must attempt to purchase capacity by contracting on the open market. In a "buy/sell" transaction, in contrast, the end-user can contract with an LDC without being forced to compete with other shippers that value the capacity. FERC reasoned that because "buy/sells" occur without open bidding, and result in the tying-up of interstate pipeline capacity, they circumvent and distort the transportation market envisioned by Order No. 636.

The LDCs contend that preemption is inappropriate in this instance because the Commission's prohibition on "buy/sells" constitutes a regulation of the retail sale of natural gas, which Congress reserved to the jurisdiction of state regulatory bodies. While the Commission emphasizes the intermediate, transportation stage of the transaction, the LDCs focus on the terminal stage, describing "buy/sell" agreements as a classic instance of an LDC making a retail sale to a retail customer. *Cf. AGD I*, 824 F.2d at 995 ("LDCs purchase gas for resale to end users, large and small. Their services and prices are subject to state regulation but not to that of FERC."). As the LDCs characterize the transaction:

> A retail customer participating in a buy/sell arrangement with an LDC purchases the same product purchased by other retail gas customers: natural gas, delivered to the point of consumption, at a state-regulated price that includes the cost of (a) the gas; (b) the inter-and intrastate transportation required to move the gas from the market or production area to the point of consumption; and, (c) all other local distribution services, such as balancing and metering costs.

LDCs' Reply Br. at 8. Further, given the express terms of NGA § 1(b), the LDCs maintain that the Commission's jurisdiction cannot arise merely by means of some effect of "buy/sell" agreements on interstate transportation; such an interpretation of the Act would dramatically expand FERC's jurisdiction because almost all gas travels interstate and therefore almost all retail sales of gas affect interstate transportation. *See also Schneidewind v. ANR Pipeline Co.*, 485 U.S. 293, 308 (1988) ("Of course, every state statute that has some indirect effect on rates and facilities of natural gas companies is not preempted."). Thus, conflict pre-emption analysis must be applied with particular care in those instances in which the Commission seeks to preempt state regulation merely because it has some effect on the interstate transportation of natural gas. *Northwest Central Pipeline v. State Corp. Comm'n*, 489 U.S. 493, 515–16 & n. 12 (1989).

We believe that the LDCs have confused two separate issues. While the Commission's rationale in preempting "buy/sells" is the transactions' effect on interstate transportation—namely, that "buy/sells" facilitate circumvention of the capacity release program—the Commission's authority is grounded in the transaction itself. In the intermediate stage of a "buy/sell" transaction, the LDC carries the gas identified by the end-user on its own firm capacity and under its own title on an interstate pipeline. Contrary to the LDCs' characterization, FERC's jurisdiction arises from the transportation itself; interstate transportation of gas selected by the end-user is a central element of the parties' agreement. As FERC states in its brief, "buy/sells" are "at bottom nothing more than agreements by which firm shippers allocate space on an interstate pipeline to customers who negotiate their own wellhead transactions." Transactions that do not include this transportation element are not "buy/sells" and are not preempted.

In a standard retail sale, by contrast, the end-user purchases gas from an LDC at the local delivery point without regard to aspects of gas transportation at points further upstream. *See id.* at 97 ("Traditional LDC retail sales consisted of sales of gas to local customers from generic system supply through local distribution facilities after the gas had completed its interstate journey."). Order No. 636 does not prohibit or condition such sales. Nor does the Order preempt state regulatory agencies from modifying an LDC's rate structure to accommodate differences in local conditions. Further still, LDCs remain free to sell gas to retail customers under the terms and conditions set by state regulators. Under Order No. 636, an end-user that would previously have engaged in a "buy/sell" transaction will still purchase the gas from the producer and still receive the gas at its delivery point. The crucial difference is that the end-user must purchase capacity rights from the LDC in the open market through the capacity release mechanism rather than by transferring title to the gas to the LDC and regaining title at the local delivery point.

Accordingly, we sustain the Commission's determination to pre-empt state regulation of "buy/sell" transactions. FERC's effort to avoid circumvention of its capacity release regulations "represents a reasonable accommodation of conflicting policies that were committed to [its] care" under the Natural Gas Act. *City of New York*, 486 U.S. at 64. Further, given that the regulations do not impinge upon state control over retail gas sales, it appears that the Commission's accommodation is one that Congress would have sanctioned. *See id.*

V. Transition Costs

Order No. 436 ... authorized interstate gas pipelines to convert to blanket-certificated "open-access" transportation service. In exchange, however, customers of those pipelines that did convert were permitted both (1) to convert their firm sales obligations into firm transportation contracts and also (2) to reduce their obligations to purchase gas from the pipelines. Pipeline customers in large numbers exercised their right under the Order to buy less gas from the pipelines, and secured gas supplies from less expensive sources. The pipelines themselves were then left with massive obligations to purchase high-priced gas at the wellhead.

The conditions under which the NGPA began to relax wellhead price controls—namely acute gas shortage and sharply rising prices for alternative fuels—tended to divert pipeline attention from the hazards of incurring long-term obligations to buy high-priced gas. Under pressure from the Commission, the pipelines had typically purchased gas under contracts for very long terms. Besides incorporating high prices (and provisions for escalation upward), the contracts commonly included "take-or-pay" provisions, requiring the pipeline to pay for some specified percentage, say 75%, of the deliverable gas even if it took less. While usually subject to recoup-

ment later, and while a perfectly natural allocation of risk between producer and purchaser, the take-or-pay provisions effectively committed the
pipelines to high gas costs in what by 1982 proved to be a time of falling
prices, both for competing fuels and for substitute supplies of gas not
covered by contract.

Thus arose the "take-or-pay" liabilities addressed by the Commission
in Order No. 436 and its successors, as well as by this court in a variety of
opinions. Specifically, because most customers could purchase gas more
cheaply from other sources, pipelines essentially were unable to pass
through the costs of their own supply obligations. With purchases sharply
reduced, pipelines owed massive "take-or-pay" liabilities to gas producers,
which they had to either "buydown"—i.e., reduce—or "buyout"—i.e.,
eliminate. In Order No. 436, the Commission refused to set a general policy
on whether or how pipelines could attempt to recover these costs. We
vacated and remanded the Order, concluding that, in this regard, it was not
based on reasoned decisionmaking, primarily because it appeared to grossly
underestimate the financial impact of take-or-pay liability on pipelines. *Id.*
at 1021–30. Of great concern to the court was the likelihood that even
higher gas prices would simply cause more customers to switch suppliers,
thereby exacerbating the take-or-pay crisis. This cycle of ever increasing
prices and ever shrinking customer base—a phenomenon that petitioners
label the "death spiral"—made it very unlikely that the pipelines would in
fact recoup their take-or-pay liabilities absent some mechanism for separately passing those costs through to their customers.

In subsequent proceedings, the Commission adopted and this court
approved various measures designed to address that concern and allow
pipelines to pass through some of their take-or-pay liabilities to a broader
range of customers. Most pertinent to our analysis here, under Commission
policy, a pipeline could agree to absorb between 25% and 50% of its take-or-
pay costs in exchange for the right to bill customers an equal share through
a fixed charge, and recover the remaining amount through a volumetric
surcharge based on total throughput. Customers, and in turn the consuming public, ultimately reimbursed pipelines for approximately $6.4 billion in
take-or-pay costs, while the pipelines themselves absorbed $3.6 billion.

After Order No. 436, all of the major interstate pipelines converted to
open-access transportation. Not all customers on those pipelines, however,
exercised their right to unbundle their sales agreements and reduce their
gas purchase obligations. Several years later in Order No. 636, the Commission mandated unbundling and authorized sales customers to reduce their
pipeline gas purchases. When customers exercised that right and secured
gas supplies from other sources, the pipelines once again incurred substantial take-or-pay liabilities; though the Commission labeled these liabilities
"gas supply realignment costs" in Order No. 636, they arose from the same
type of producer-pipeline contract provisions as the "take-or-pay" costs
considered in Order No. 436. [ ]

In allocating recovery of GSR costs, however, the Commission adopted
a policy more advantageous to the pipelines. Instead of refusing to establish

a mechanism for pipelines to recover their take-or-pay costs, as it originally had in Order No. 436, FERC authorized pipelines to bill their customers separately for 100% of their GSR costs. This policy was, in fact, a substantial change from even Order No. 500, which permitted pipelines to surcharge their transportation customers for take-or-pay costs only if they agreed to absorb between 25 and 50% of those costs. The Commission set forth the mechanisms available to pipelines under Order No. 636 as follows:

> . . . The Commission will permit pipelines full cost recovery of prudently incurred gas supply realignment costs deemed to be eligible under this rule. To recover those costs, a pipeline will be permitted to use either a negotiated exit fee, or a reservation fee surcharge recoverable from Part 284 firm transportation customers. . . .

Under this rule, a firm entitlement holder has options as to how to react to gas supply realignment costs: it may remain a sales customer of the pipeline; otherwise, it may take an assignment of the pipeline's existing contracts or pay an exit fee/reservation fee surcharge for costs approved by the Commission. On rehearing, FERC modified this ruling somewhat, and required pipelines to bill 10% of their GSR costs to interruptible transportation customers. . . .

While we owe the Commission substantial deference in matters predictive and economic, we cannot ignore the Commission's unwillingness to address an important challenge to its stated benefit rationale for charging transportation customers. It most emphatically remains the duty of this court to ensure that an agency engage the arguments raised before it—that it conduct a process of reasoned decisionmaking. The deference we owe FERC's expert judgment does not strip us of that responsibility. Indeed, . . . we will uphold an agency's decision "if, but only if, we can discern a reasoned path from the facts and considerations before the [agency] to the decision it reached." *Id.* at 1303 (citations omitted) (second emphasis added).

In this instance, we cannot discern the Commission's path from its view that interruptible transportation customers should bear some of the burden for GSR costs to the conclusion that the share should be 10%. *Cf.* Walt Whitman, Leaves of Grass, Darest Thou Now O Soul ("Darest thou now O soul, Walk out with me toward the unknown region, Where neither ground is for the feet nor any path to follow?"). And, while we are sympathetic to the Commission's view that "the task of determining fair allocations of transition costs is ultimately thankless, even though [it] brings all [its] experience and best judgment to bear on it," Order No. 636–B, P 61,272, at 62,034, the law requires more than simple guesswork. We therefore . . . hold that FERC did not err by failing to exercise its NGA § 5 authority so as to force gas producers to bear part of the transition costs. Furthermore, we sustain the Commission's application of GSR costs to the full range of blanket-certificated transportation customers. We remand the case to the Commission, however, for further consideration of the appropriate share of those costs to be paid by interruptible transportation customers and the gas pipelines.

VI. Conclusion

In its broad contours and in most of its specifics, we uphold Order No. 636. However, we remand certain aspects of Order No. 636, ... to the Commission for further explanation....

Until the Commission takes final action on remand, however, we leave these measures in place as currently formulated.■

NOTES AND COMMENTS

1. Despite its 150–page length, the D.C. Circuit opinion is largely congratulatory of FERC's effort to deregulate natural gas. Several requests for rehearing of the D.C. Circuit's opinion were filed, but all were rejected by the court. On remand, FERC issued Order 636A responding to the few issues on which the court required rehearing.

2. Order 636 was a great event in regulatory history and its appeal made for great theater. Roughly 250 parties intervened. The oral argument was allocated an entire day—375 minutes of scheduled argument by nearly two dozen lawyers on 22 issues grouped into six different categories. By contrast, most oral arguments last between 20 minutes and an hour. An attorney remarked, "It looked like a federal energy bar meeting." *See* Bruce D. Brown, Gashouse Gang, Legal Times, Feb. 26, 1996, at 6.

3. The D.C. Circuit plays an important policy-making role in administrative law. This role is particularly evident in natural gas regulation. This court has often overruled FERC, as the opinion notes. FERC decisions of this type are appealed directly to a circuit court of appeals, not to a district court. As a result of Byzantine multi-district litigation procedures, this case came to oral argument 3½ years after Order 636 was issued and after most of the restructuring had already taken place.

4. Rate design had been a long-simmering issue in the pipeline industry until it was largely resolved by Order 636. Interruptible industrial customers had always complained that they should not be required to pay any of the pipelines' fixed costs because they were not guaranteed any capacity. Consumer groups and many state PUCs wanted to keep local rates down for heating users by making industrials pay some of these costs. FERC had long sided with the consumer interests by making industrials pay some of the fixed costs through use of a "modified fixed variable (MFV)" rate design. But in Order 636, FERC switched to charging all of the fixed costs to firm users by adopting the "straight fixed variable (SFV)" rate design. The court found that FERC's findings that SFV would increase efficiency and competition was supported by substantial evidence as this excerpt shows:

> For several decades, FERC's ratemaking regime has included some portion of a pipeline's fixed costs in the pipeline's commodity and usage charges. Over the years, it varied the specific percentage of fixed costs actually included in those charges, but it generally followed the

principle that some portion of fixed costs should be recouped through quantity-dependent charges.. . .

The PUCs argue that the switch to SFV rate design "will frustrate, rather than promote, the goals of maximizing efficiency and competition." Their complaint centers on the claim that because pipelines under SFV rate design will be able to collect all their fixed costs, including return on investment and taxes, in the demand charge, they will have no incentive to assure that gas actually flows through the pipeline under firm service arrangements. That is, because a pipeline will recover no fixed costs or return on investment through the commodity or usage charge, it will have no incentive to transport any gas.

FERC recognized this potential incentive problem in Order No. 636, but determined that "the pipelines will now have much less influence on the use of their systems because they are transporting gas to, rather than selling gas at, the city-gate." Order No. 636, P 30,939, at 30,436. Accordingly, "transportation volumes will mainly be a function of the needs of gas purchasers and the prices offered by gas sellers in the production areas." *Id.* In any case, "the goals to be accomplished via SFV outweigh generally the goal of allocating fixed costs to annual throughput." Order No. 636–A, P 30,950, at 30,606. We find these explanations sufficiently convincing to meet the substantial evidence standard for rate design in the face of the PUCs' incentive argument. Id. at 1167–69.

To mitigate the effect of the rate design change on customers who would now bear a greater share of the pipeline's fixed costs, FERC had adopted several mitigation measures. For example, if the switch to SFV resulted in a ten percent or greater rate increase for a particular customer class, FERC required that the pipeline phase in SFV rate design over four years for that class, allowing it to avoid "rate shock". The court upheld these mitigation measures. *Id.* at 1170–73.

5. Although producers and pipelines had settled many take-or-pay claims before Order 636, after the order more customers canceled contracts to buy gas from the pipelines, forcing the pipelines to pay more take-or-pay charges, now labeled "gas supply realignment costs" (GSR), to producers. This time, as noted in the excerpts, FERC authorized the pipelines to pass along all of these charges to customers, unlike the earlier orders which sought to force pipelines (and indirectly producers) to share some of the realignment costs. FERC's earlier policy had permitted pipelines to surcharge their transportation customers for take-or-pay costs only if the pipelines agreed to absorb between 25 and 50 percent of those costs.

In the end, it appears that many groups shared the TOP transition costs which totaled about $50 billion, or almost 60 percent of the 1985 value of final gas sales to final consumers. Interstate pipeline companies filed to recover about $10.4 billion in TOP costs, of which about $3.6 billion will be absorbed by the pipeline company shareholders. The bulk of the debt was negotiated away in settlements between the pipeline companies and producers over the years. In many cases, the gas producers, or the parties who held the gas contracts as collateral, had to adjust their wealth by accepting lower values for the contracts they held. Some costs were spread to the creditors of those pipelines that went bankrupt, and some costs may have been partially shifted to general taxpayers if losses were used as credits in calculating income taxes. Margaret Jess, "Restructuring Energy Industries: Lessons from Natural Gas", A Natural Gas Monthly Special Report available from the Energy Information Administration website at ftp://ftp.eia.doe.gov/pub/oil_gas/natura . . ._energy_industries_lessons /html/peg.html>

2. CONTINUING ISSUES UNDER ORDER 636

The implementation of Order 636 has not been without its problems. Three of the most contentious areas have been functional unbundling, rate design, and capacity release.

a. FUNCTIONAL UNBUNDLING

To comply with Order 636's functional unbundling requirements, most pipelines set up separate marketing entities. These marketing entities were not to receive any information from the pipeline that was not also made available to competitors. *See generally Tenneco Gas v. Federal Energy Regulatory Commission*, 969 F.2d 1187 (D.C.Cir.1992).

Compliance with this type of directive is understandably difficult even for a company with the best intentions. The employees of the marketing entity will probably be long-time former employees of the pipeline company and will have both a long institutional memory and close personal relationships with the employees who remain with the pipeline. If the pipeline is small, the practical necessity of sharing some employees complicates the problem. *See, e.g., In re Caprock Pipeline Co.*, 58 FERC P 61,141 (1992).

Shippers have filed a number of complaints with FERC alleging violations by pipelines and their marketing affiliates of the Chinese wall requirements. Many of these have been resolved through negotiations (*see, e.g., In re Transcontinental Gas Pipeline Corp.*, 55 FERC P 61,318 (1991)), but a few have resulted in the assessment of penalties against the pipelines.

For example, in *Amoco Production Co. v. Natural Gas Pipeline Co. of America*, 82 FERC ¶ 61,038 (1998), shippers alleged that the pipeline had violated Standard of Conduct G which states that "to the maximum extent practicable [a pipeline's] operating employees and the operating employees of its marketing affiliate must function independently of each other." 18 C.F.R. § 161.3(g) (1997). The FERC found that the pipeline had created a System Optimization Group, composed of employees who had day-to-day duties and responsibilities for planning, directing, and carrying out gas-related operations including gas transportation, gas sales, or gas marketing activities, for both the pipeline (Natural Gas Pipeline Co.) and for MidCon Gas, its marketing affiliate.

FERC also found that the System Optimization Group decided whether to accept transportation discounts from nonaffiliated shippers, helped determine whether the pipeline would conduct auctions, provided MidCon Gas with pricing inputs for its auction bids, and then evaluated all bids received by the pipeline. FERC assessed civil penalties of $8,840,000 against the pipeline but suspended half the penalty if the pipeline did not violate the rules again during the next two years. 83 FERC P 61,197 at 3 (1998).

Do you understand why the practices condemned above are anti-competitive?

b. RATE DESIGN

SFV rates. In *Union Pacific Fuels v. FERC*, 129 F.3d 157 (D.C.Cir. 1997) the court considered whether contracts that pre-dated Order 636 and required by their terms that rates be designed on the MFV basis, could automatically be changed to SFV basis by Order 636. The court rejected the argument that FERC could only change the rate if it found the contract rate to be "unjust, unreasonable, unduly discriminatory or preferential."[2] Because the contracts provided that they were subject to FERC rate regulation, the court found that the change in rates was not inconsistent with the terms of the contract.

Rolled-in rates. Another issue of rate design that continues to be contentious is the issue of rolled-in versus incremental rates. When a pipeline builds a new segment of its system, should the cost of that segment be paid solely by the customers who will be served by it, or should those costs be "rolled-in" to the overall rate base and distributed among all of the pipeline's customers? *See, e.g., "Complex" Consolidated Edison Co. of New York v. Federal Energy Regulatory Comm'n*, 165 F.3d 992 (2d Cir. 1999)

In *Midcoast Interstate Transmission, Inc. v. FERC*, 198 F.3d 960 (D.C.Cir.2000), the court held that FERC had properly authorized rolling-in the cost of new pipeline construction into a company's system-wide rates because there would be system-wide benefits to consumers and because the impact on system-wide rates would be minimal. This case starkly illustrates how the choice between rolled in and incremental rates can affect competing pipelines. Midcoast and Southern Colonial were both competing to bring new pipeline capacity to the same Alabama market. FERC granted Southern's application to construct a new pipeline. Midcoast appealed this FERC order as an aggrieved party. It argued that if FERC had required incremental pricing, Southern would have had to charge users of the new pipeline an incremental rate of $10.00 in addition to its system-wide rate of $8.80 per decatherm per month. Midcoast proposed to charge only $8.60. If Southern were allowed to roll in the costs of the new pipeline, rates would not rise by more than 5 percent because large pipeline systems, like

---

2. [Editors' note:] This is the standard that FERC must meet if it wants to change a rate set by contract. It is known as the *Mo-bile-Sierra* test and is discussed in Chapter 10.

Southern's can spread the costs over its existing system-wide customers. The cost of the new facilities is subsidized by existing users, to the detriment of smaller competitors like Midcoast.

c. CAPACITY RELEASE

Order Nos. 636 and 636–A outlined a basic transportation capacity release program that each interstate pipeline must implement. Now any shipper that has a firm contract requiring the pipeline to carry its gas has the opportunity to resell that contract to the highest bidder upon the terms and conditions the releasing shipper chooses (*e.g.*, recall terms, volume, term of release, etc.), as long as those terms and conditions are not unduly discriminatory or preferential. Offers to release for a term of more than 30 days must be posted on the electronic bulletin board maintained by the pipeline to provide information to market participants. Short-term releases of firm transportation capacity (releases for a term of less than 30 days) can be done as prearranged deals, and do not have to be posted for competitive bidding.

The capacity release program seems to have been more difficult to implement than envisioned, and has created considerable dissatisfaction among almost all segments of the industry and at FERC itself. FERC has issued a notice of proposed rulemaking and notice of inquiry on short-term and long-term releases, respectively (RM98–10 and RM98–12). The various segments of the industry asked for additional time to respond and held extended negotiations in the hope of reaching a consensus, but negotiations collapsed, and in April, 1999, a wide range of extended comments were filed by virtually every industry participant.

The issues are complex and detailed. Most contracts for natural gas pipeline capacity have been individually negotiated based on the particular needs of the shippers and the pipeline, which tend to vary greatly from place to place. Yet for active markets to develop, a product usually needs to be fungible so that it can be sold in standardized lots. Just as the grain traders promoted the regulation of grain elevators in order to provide a fungible commodity for trading,[3] gas traders would like capacity releases (*i.e.*, shares of pipeline space) to be as fungible as possible Many of the detailed issues in dispute relate to the extent to which a greater degree of uniformity can or should be introduced into contracts for natural gas pipeline capacity.

C. Pricing of Natural Gas

Although some concern has been expressed about the impact of re-structuring on the natural gas industry, negativism is decidedly a minority sentiment at this time. The industry is riding a wave of optimism about its future. The optimism is fostered, not just by the transition to new light-

---

3. *See Munn v. Illinois* and the discussion that follows it in Chapter 3.

handed regulation, but by trends in the supply and demand of natural gas and in the rapid development of spot and futures markets for this commodity.

1.   SUPPLY AND DEMAND

Supply. Until natural gas gained recognition as a premium fuel in the past two decades, its second-class status resulted in a long history of poor government data on the size of gas fields and poor estimates of future gas supplies. The low prices for gas under federal regulation gave producers little incentive to contest official estimates. Today, the most widely used estimate of the amount of natural gas that can be economically recovered within the United States at current prices is almost twice the amount that was estimated just ten years ago. Conservatively, most experts agree that at present rates of use and current technology we have enough natural gas to last at least a half century.

The Environmental Law Institute (ELI) recently studied government and industry gas supply forecasts to assess the nation's ability to switch from dirty coal to clean gas. Official estimates of recoverable gas reserves, based on current prices and little technological growth, total 1,331 trillion cubic feet (tcf) or about 60 years of supply. However, technical progress measured by the historical trend, adds another 100 years to future gas supplies. If technological progress instead advances at the rapid rate of the last decade, then it will unlock enormous gas resources currently considered economically unrecoverable in coal bed methane (300 tcf), tight sands (6,600 tcf), deep gas deposits (3,200 tcf), and geopressurized aquifers (5,700 tcf). The potential gas stored in methane hydrates could add an astounding 200,000 tcf of gas to the resource base. Thus, the ELI concludes that gas could be used as an abundant energy source for centuries, depending on technology and one other factor–price. If the price of gas drops significantly lower than the current average of about $2 per thousand cubic feet (mcf), technology advances will slow and supply will fall below even the official reserve estimate of 1,331 tcf. On the other hand, a price of $4 per mcf would trigger major new supplies around the world and would allow liquefied natural gas (LNG) from large foreign reserves to enter U.S. coastal markets. This price would also make large Alaskan gas reserves, now trapped at Prudhoe Bay, marketable via a gas pipeline to the lower 48. ELI Research Report, "How Abundant? Assessing the Estimates of Natural Gas Supply" at www.eli.org/bookstore/rrgas99.htm.

Given the source, would you take the ELI's forecasts with a grain of salt? Would you be wary of anyone's forecasts, given that the consensus forecast made in the 1970s projected the price of oil in the year 2000 to be $70 per barrel (versus the actual price of about $30)? How accurate are the predictions of the future of natural gas made in the 1978 article by Bryan Hodgson, excerpted in Chapter 7?

Canadian gas has also become a major factor in the gas market in the United States. Not long ago, Canada was reluctant to export its natural gas, preferring to conserve it for future Canadian needs. Exploration continued to find new sources, not only in the west around Alberta, but in eastern Canada, both onshore and offshore. Canada has become eager to export gas to the U.S. market. New pipelines have been built into this market, and Canadian gas is likely to supply 20 percent of the U.S. market in the near future.

Demand. Fortunately for gas producers, the increased supply of gas is matched by a growing increase in demand. A major reason for this growth is the fact that gas combustion is so much cleaner than coal and even oil . In areas where compliance with Clean Air Act standards is a problem, it is much easier to obtain approval for a new gas-fired plant than for a plant using other fossil fuels. Indeed, the EPA's latest crackdown on the pollution from coal-fired power plants in the Midwest, which drifts to the east and contributes to smog in New England, New York and other states, is expected to hasten the demise of these older plants. Their likely replacements will be gas turbine plants. As another example, a Florida utility, charged by the EPA with violating the Clean Air Act, agreed to switch one of its coal-fired power plants to gas. The new plant would produce electricity for about the same price as the old while reducing emissions of sulfur dioxide by 60 tons a year, particulates by 2,000 tons per year, and nitrogen oxide by 30 tons per year. New York Times, Mar. 1, 2000, at A21.

If the Kyoto Protocol on Climate Change becomes an effective treaty to reduce greenhouse gases, it will increase the demand for gas, and "severely tax" the ability of the gas industry to build new infrastructure to meet the demand, according to a study prepared for the Edison Electric Institute. Foster Electric Report No. 182, p. 14 (Jan. 19, 2000). The carbon content per Btu of natural gas is only 55 percent of that for coal and 70 percent of that for oil. Climate Change is discussed in Chapter 17.

The most significant technology in terms of current demand is the combined-cycle turbine that converts natural gas into electricity. Gas turbine generators have been used to generate electricity for many years. The mechanics are simple: gas is burned in the functional equivalent of an airplane's jet engine which turns the wheels of an electric generator. Both small and large scale models are equally feasible, and they can be turned on and off quickly. Power companies have used gas turbine plants for years as sources of "peaking" power, turning them on when temperatures rise and air conditioners hum, and turning them off when the weather cools.

More recently, however, improved plant design and lower gas prices have lowered the price of electricity derived from gas to levels below that of coal, oil and even hydropower. (The competition among fuels for electricity generation is discussed more fully in the chapters on electricity, *infra*). The combined-cycle plant includes both a gas turbine and a steam turbine that utilizes the excess heat thrown off by the gas turbine to create steam which also turns an electric generator. These plants are able to produce energy efficiencies higher than competing technologies and at lower cost. Gas turbines are expected to constitute about 80 percent of the new power generating capacity added in the United States over the next 10–15 years. BNA Daily Report for Executives Feb. 22, 2000, at A–22.

In February 2000, the Department of Energy and GE Power Systems unveiled a new-generation "H System" with turbines two percentage points more efficient than the most efficient combined-cycle power plants in existence (60% versus 58%). Breaking the 60 percent efficiency threshold is tantamount to the first runner breaking the four-minute mile, according to DOE. The increased efficiency could translate into savings of $30 to $40 million over the lifetime of a plant, in addition to reducing pollution from less fuel use. The new system was developed by a public-private R and D effort that started ten years ago; upon its completion DOE will have contributed about $100 million and GE Power about $500,000,000.

Another technology that could greatly increase the demand for natural gas is the gas-powered automotive engine. Experimentation with gas-powered trucks and buses is in the early stages, but today's prototype vehicles are far more efficient and safe than those of a decade ago. If natural gas could replace even a small share of the market for gasoline, this would bring a big increase in the demand for natural gas nationwide. *See* Chapter 15.

Finally, extensive research is underway in the development of fuel cells powered by natural gas. The fuel cells are electrochemical devices in which electric current is created directly by the combination of oxygen and hydrogen ions without the need for a mechanical generator. The development of cost-effective fuel cells on a large scale may be one of the by-products of the space program, which has been using small fuel cells to provide power for spacecraft. *See* Chapter 10).

Many giants of the energy industry have also launched major R & D projects aimed at converting gas to liquid in "GTL" plants. In early 2000, Conoco announced its plans to build a $35 to $50 million plant to test its technology for converting gas to a synthetic petroleum. Conoco has identified 1,200 "stranded gas fields" worldwide, largely fields which have no pipeline access. Amoco and Exxon have gas-to-liquid projects in Alaska; Chevron has a GTL joint venture in Nigeria; and Shell has projects in Malaysia and Bangladesh. Converting gas to a liquid would make it transportable to markets via pipelines, truck, or tankers. If Alaskan gas can be converted to synthetic oil, then the TransAlaskan Pipeline System can be used for another 25 years. Syntroleum Corporation in Tulsa, Oklahoma has a GTL technology that produces synthetic gasoline and diesel fuels. These fuels were recently tested by a manufacturer of fuel cell components and found to be so clean that they could lower the cost of manufacturing and operating fuel cells. Conoco estimates that its GTL technology will be profitable if oil prices are about $25 a barrel. Monica Perin, "Is It Gas? Is It Liquids? It's Both and It's Big," Houston Bus. J., Feb. 18–24, 2000, at 1A and 24A.

In summary, estimates of the supply of and demand for natural gas have been increasing. The principles governing the pricing and availability of natural gas are likely to play an increasingly important role in the energy markets of the coming years.

2. THE SPOT AND FUTURES MARKETS

Today, most natural gas is purchased through contracts of thirty days or less. This means that the price of gas could change dramatically if new "oil shocks" occurred, caused by the geopolitics of the international oil industry or other macroeconomic events. To date, however, the price of gas has remained stable with a downward trend since the restructuring.

Distributors and pipelines have had to radically readjust their thinking about gas prices since restructuring took place. Instead of negotiating twenty-year contracts, they have had to learn the ways of the commodity exchanges. Price volatility has become a significant business risk, leading to the creation of both a spot market and a futures market for natural gas.

Spot market transactions are short-term (*i.e.*, for a term of less than a year, usually 30 days) and are generally interruptible. These factors make the contracts responsive to current market prices, but also expose the parties to the risks of price volatility or service interruption.

The New York Mercantile Exchange (NYMEX) operates a natural gas futures market that allows buyers and sellers to hedge their price risks for up to 18 months in the future. The NYMEX prices are quoted daily and provide reliable price signals for the operation of more complex futures transactions.

These more complex transactions consist of a wide variety of over-the-counter derivatives offered by gas marketers. Derivatives are financial risk-management contracts, such as swaps, options, caps, floors, and collars. The details of the derivative market are beyond the scope of this book, but the bottom line is that LDCs and other large users of natural gas now have a wide array of products and services available to help them insure their business operations against losses from rapid future fluctuations in the price of natural gas.[4] How successful these risk management tools will be remains to be tested because prices have been relatively stable in recent years compared to the shocks of the 1970s and 1980s. [Review Figures 6–1 and 7–4.]

3. POTENTIAL PROBLEMS

a. OVERRELIANCE ON SPOT MARKETS

The switch to a competitive gas market became possible because so many new pipelines had been built that most market areas had reasonably good access to more than one pipeline, and because pipeline capacity had largely caught up with demand. Thus, few pipelines had monopoly positions and there was less need for major new capital facilities that could be financed only on the basis of long-term contracts.

---

4. For a more complete analysis of natural gas derivatives, *see* Mark E. Haedicke & Alan B. Aronowitz, Gas Commodity Markets, in David J. Muchow & William A. Mogel, 4 Energy Law and Transactions, Ch. 88 (1999).

Will these conditions continue? Professor Richard Pierce, a long-time proponent of deregulation, argues that the spot market cannot be the permanent answer for the long-term future of the industry:

A high proportion of transactions in the US gas market today are made on the spot market or pursuant to short-term or interruptible contracts. A healthy US gas market always will include considerable trade in these categories, but the US market seems not yet to have reached a stable equilibrium in this respect. Increased use of long-term, firm contracts is required in the US to encourage adequate investment in exploration and production, pipelines, and gas-burning combustion equipment.

Many participants in the US market seem unusually reluctant to enter into long-term contracts at present. This reluctance is due to the bad experiences with long-term contracts many market participants had in the past. Regulators abrogated or modified contracts; changes in regulatory policies altered the effects of contracts; and many parties refused to comply with contracts because of changes in regulatory policies.

Richard J. Pierce, Jr., Experiences with Natural Gas Regulation and Competition in the US Federal System: Lessons for Europe, in Natural Gas in the Internal Market 125 (Ernst J. Mestmäcker, ed., 1993).

b. UNBUNDLING VERSUS VERTICAL INTEGRATION

Implicit in the natural gas restructuring policy discussion is the premise that unbundling, or separating, services traditionally performed by the same pipeline is desirable as a matter of policy and economic efficiency. Order No. 636 unbundles pipeline sales and transportation, despite the fact that firms had historically found it to be efficient to provide both functions under the umbrella of the same corporation. As FERC noted, the rationale for unbundling was to minimize distortions in the sales market, facilitated by the market power which pipeline companies had over transportation.

Similarly, when antitrust enforcers broke up AT&T in the early 1980s, they not only separated the company "horizontally" into several franchise-based areas (known as the "Baby Bells"), but they also sought to undo the high degree of vertical integration AT&T had historically achieved by providing both long distance and local telephone service. Initially, following its break-up under the consent decree, AT&T was prohibited from participating in local telephone markets. Long distance and local telephone service were effectively unbundled. See W. Kip Viscusi, John M. Vernon & Joseph E. Harrington, Jr., Economics of Regulation and Antitrust 503–04 (2d ed. 1995).

Yet, at the same time, it is well recognized that vertical integration can be efficient. The major oil companies found efficiencies in developing their own crude oil supplies to feed their own refineries to supply their own service stations. Vertical integration internalizes within the firm those transactions costs which otherwise must be incurred through contracting in the open market. In industries that demand high degrees of fixed capital, the internalization of such transactions costs by building company-owned production or distribution infrastructures is often an efficient response to market uncertainties that cannot be easily contracted away. *See* Oliver E. Williamson, Transaction Cost Economics: The Governance of Contractual Relationships, 22 J. L. & Econ. 233 (1979); Ronald H. Coase, The Nature of the Firm, 4 Economica 386 (1937). Vertical integration is likely under circumstances in which assets are specific (or cannot be deployed to alternative uses because of sunk costs), transactions are frequent, and there is a high degree of uncertainty. *See* Oliver E. Williamson, The Mechanisms of Governance (1996).

Thus, while drilling high-cost wells to find oil and gas can be financed through long-term sales contracts with refineries, a firm can save itself the costs associated with negotiating, implementing and enforcing these contracts by operating its own refineries. Likewise, pipeline companies usually need to negotiate long-term contracts with many LDCs or endusers to finance expensive long-distance lines. The costs of enforcing these contracts, especially during periods of volatile energy prices, might be so high as to encourage pipelines to integrate forward and enter the local sales markets themselves.

In addition, operating and engineering (or network) efficiencies can be gained through vertical integration. For example, pipelines must coordinate the shipping of natural gas with expected consumption patterns, so that supply is available to meet customer demand. Changes in customer demand simply cannot be accurately foreseen. Many long-term purchase agreements in the natural gas industry are requirements contacts, which obligate the pipeline to bear the risks of any increase in customer demand. To better cope with these risks, pipelines must keep gas reserves above current demands. Allowing the pipeline to provide both sales and transportation services would let the pipeline spread the costs and risks of keeping such reserves among several sales markets, rather than building them into each sales contract.

Finally, a pipeline with integrated sales and transportation functions has internalized information regarding changes in customer demand, facilitating the communication of such information to the valve operators and other engineers who physically direct the flow of gas through the lines. *See* Alfred E. Kahn, The Economics of Regulation: Principles and Institutions 157–58 (1988).

From the perspective of economic efficiency, then, the question is whether the costs of vertical integration exceed its benefits. If the costs exceed the benefits in the context of integrated pipelines sales and transportation, then FERC's effort to unbundle are justified. Are you convinced? Might a pipeline company have a valid argument that its services are more efficient if bundled together?

c.   WHAT WILL HAPPEN IN A GAS SHORTAGE?

The potential problems which might arise because of overreliance on short-term markets and unbundled sales naturally lead to the question:

What will happen if gas shipments are curtailed because of force majeure events or other operational necessities? The D.C. Circuit was asked to review aspects of FERC's curtailment policy in the following case.

Process Gas Consumers Group v. Federal Energy Regulatory Comm'n

158 F.3d 591 (D.C.Cir.1998)

■ WILLIAMS, J.: In Order No. 636, FERC exercised its authority under § 5 of the Natural Gas Act, 15 U.S.C. § 717d, to require that natural gas pipeline companies unbundle their gas transportation and sales services and file tariffs in compliance with the order. The tariff filing at issue here provides that in the event of certain curtailments customers with specified emergency conditions can secure exemption from curtailment. This of course increases the curtailment of the pipeline's other customers, which would otherwise have been pro rata. The tariff also calls for some compensation to be paid by the exempted customers to the customers who are additionally deprived. But the petitioners argue that the compensation approved by the Commission is so limited that it gives customers inadequate incentives to plan ahead to reduce the likelihood and severity of gas curtailment emergencies. As the Commission's explanation fails to come to grips with the petitioners' contentions, we remand the case for want of reasoned decision-making.

Texas Eastern Transmission Corporation ("Tetco") made its compliance filing in 1992. The proposed tariff would have allowed Tetco to curtail service—even to "firm" transportation customers—in certain situations of force majeure or operational necessity. Such "capacity curtailment" was to be borne pro rata with two exceptions: first, to protect high priority end-uses, as defined by §§ 401 and 402 of the Natural Gas Policy Act, 15 U.S.C. §§ 3391–92, and second, to provide gas to customers for "emergency" situations, defined as ones where gas was necessary "to avoid irreparable injury to life or property (including environmental emergencies) or to provide for minimum plant protection." Prompted by the comments of NUI Corporation (Elizabethtown Gas Division) ("NUI/Elizabethtown"), the Commission rejected Tetco's first proposed exception to pro rata curtailment, finding that the priorities in the NGPA did not apply to capacity curtailment. *See Texas Eastern Transmission Corp.*, 62 F.E.R.C. P 61,015 at 61,119 (1993). The Commission allowed the second exception, but required that Tetco's revised tariff "include compensation by the customer seeking the short term [emergency] exception to any other customer receiving more than its pro rata share of the capacity curtailment." *Id.* Tetco filed a revised tariff, including such a compensation measure, in February 1993.

The compensation provided, however, was quite limited. The tariff calls for increases in the exempted customer's bill by "the aggregate curtailment adjustment quantity requested by the Customer pursuant to [the emergency exemption] multiplied by the Reservation Charge Adjustment for the applicable rate schedule per Dth [Dekatherm] for the applicable zone"; this amount is then distributed to the customers who were curtailed more than pro rata because of the exemption. As we understand this, it means that although the advantaged customers have already paid a reservation charge for their entitlement to transportation, they pay a premium, proportional to that charge, for the transportation they enjoy above pro rata curtailment levels by virtue of their emergency condition. The proceeds go to the more deprived customers, in proportion to their deprivation.

Despite the protests of NUI/Elizabethtown, The Process Gas Consumers Group, and The American Iron and Steel Institute (the latter two collectively "the Industrial Groups") that the compensation provided was inadequate, the Commission accepted Tetco's filing. Upon denial of their request for rehearing on this issue, NUI/Elizabethtown and the Industrial Groups petitioned for review in this court.

Petitioners objected below on two grounds. NUI/Elizabethtown argued that the compensation was inadequate, particularly for local distribution companies ("LDCs"). The increased curtailment for non-exempt customers removes these customers' regular access to part of their gas supply; this supply must be rerouted or replaced, often at a much higher cost. If no replacement can be found, the LDC customers lose the profit they would have made on the resale of the gas. NUI/Elizabethtown therefore proposed setting compensation either by these actual damage amounts (net replacement cost or lost margin) or by a "generic cost" calculated as "a stated percentage in excess of the spot gas price." The Industrial Groups raised an additional argument: that Tetco's compensation scheme gave bad incentives to its customers. Because an emergency exemption aids only customers without some backup capabilities of their own (such as "peak shaving" facilities), the low compensation rate allows these customers to free-ride on the costly contingency preparations of others. Between the grasshopper and the ant, in other words, Tetco's scheme favors the grasshopper and thus encourages his feckless ways. To correct this incentive problem, the Industrial Groups proposed compensation at "a predetermined amount that exceeds the cost of the most expensive gas sources or alternative fuels available to customers."

The Commission gave two reasons for rejecting these suggestions. First, the Commission pointed to the tariff's imbalance resolution procedures as an "adequate remedy" for the loss of gas supply. 63 F.E.R.C. P 61,100 at 61,496; 64 F.E.R.C. P 61,305 at 63,301. This seems to be a red herring. So far as appears, the imbalance procedures impose no cost on customers receiving emergency relief.

Second, the Commission claimed that "no party has put forth a plausible compensation scheme that could be adequately monitored by the Commission." 64 F.E.R.C. P 61,305 at 63,301. But the Commission's two opinions say nothing to explain how any of the petitioners' proposals is either implausible or impractical to monitor. And, so far as concerns NUI/Elizabethtown's spot gas proposal, the Commission itself has in related contexts embraced a compensation device tied to the spot gas price: first in the very same proceeding, as the cash-out price used to resolve imbalances, *see* 62 F.E.R.C. P 61,015 at 61,116–17, and second, in a later case, as compensation paid by those enjoying an emergency exemption from gas supply curtailment, *see Transcontinental Gas Pipe Line Corp.*, 72 F.E.R.C. P 61,037 at 61,237–38 (1995). While we recognize that capacity curtailment and supply curtailment are not identical, *see, e.g., City of Mesa v. FERC*, 301 U.S. App. D.C. 226, 993 F.2d 888, 894–95 (D.C.Cir.1993), the Commission has nowhere explained why the differences render use of a spot-price solution inappropriate here. *Cf. Florida Gas Transmission Co.*, 70 F.E.R.C. P 61,017 at 61,063 (1995) (approving settlement providing capacity curtailment compensation based on alternative fuel cost). Nor, to repeat, has it offered any explanation of the supposed deficiencies of the petitioners' other proposals.

If the Commission had grounds to reject petitioners' proposed alternatives, it has not revealed them. We accordingly remand the case for reconsideration.

So ordered.■

NOTES AND COMMENTS

1. Judge Richard Cudahy of the Seventh Circuit Court of Appeals is a former energy law practitioner and member of the Wisconsin Public Services Commission. He brings a wealth of insight to energy issues. In commenting on the current euphoria about the future of natural gas prices, he reminds us that nuclear power was once greeted as promising a pollution-free source of electricity "too cheap to meter."

> At that time, if memory serves, popular theory conceived a need for 800 nuclear power plants—or possibly as many as 1600. A view that it would be better to build these plants in clusters of about 10 or 25, possibly including reprocessing facilities and the like, also enjoyed some attention. Such a disposition promised to concentrate the safety and environmental problems in sites away from populous areas.... Almost everyone—not merely "government" or "management"—entertained these ideas. Yet, after all that, we now view nuclear power, not as the energy giant on the horizon, but as the most obvious candidate to become a "stranded asset" in the new era of competition.

> Presumably, combined-cycle gas turbine generation will establish the marginal cost—and hence the market price—of electricity under a competitive regime. Natural gas plants are both the cheapest and the fastest plants to build—and the costs of fuel are currently favorable....

> At the time nuclear power parks were drawing the attention of the "interested" community, popular thought placed natural gas on the endangered species list. The then current wisdom suggested that the supply of gas was shrinking and that prices were mounting in the face

of all government efforts to suppress them. Natural gas was a "premium" fuel to be saved for home-heating or agricultural use; using it at a power plant was thought to verge on criminal behavior. In any event, the price of natural gas was rising so rapidly that the thought of competition with nuclear generation was absurd. Gas turbines were as cheap and as fast to build as they are now, but certainly no one saw them as a major factor in fashioning the energy future. All the emphasis was on coal and nuclear generation as best comporting with national security objectives—not to mention cost. Almost everyone thought that dependence on Middle Eastern oil put the nation at risk— if not of an actual embargo, at least of an exorbitant price. Then, all estimates of oil and gas prices for the future assumed a rising trend.

The course of events since 1975 is, of course, well known. A number of huge baseload nuclear plants became redundant because electric demand fell far short of forecasts. Nuclear costs—whether due to poor construction management or to regulatory waffling—climbed out of sight. Meanwhile, natural gas, freed of an earlier regulatory regime, began to fill the interstate pipelines. Gas surpluses and price declines developed. Gradually, there seemed to be enough of the "premium" fuel to find a broad range of satisfactory uses—even in power plants.... Now there appears to be sufficient oil and gas to last literally forever—and at cheaper and cheaper prices.... In 20 years, conventional thought, which was by no means confined to government regulators or the electric power industry, has suffered a total reversal.

I wish I could believe that we are really smarter in 1995 than we were in 1975. But I think the real lesson of history is that prediction is a very imperfect science; it is virtually impossible to provide an accurate 20–year forecast. This is one reason a competitive regime faces what I consider unusual difficulties in the electric power industry. Perhaps these problems are no more serious in a competitive regime than in a regulated one. Yet these problems make one wonder just how different one regime may be from the other.

Richard D. Cudahy, The Choice of Fuel in Competitive Generation, Public Utilities Fortnightly, June 15, 1995, at 6–9.

2. This would be an appropriate time to reflect again on the classic *Charles River Bridge* and *Munn* cases (*see* Chapter 3). To what extent should new natural gas-based technologies be allowed to put older, less efficient technologies out of business when people were induced to invest in the older technologies by explicit or implicit promises of government support? Is the use of natural gas still a business affected with a public interest, as it was when *Munn* was decided, or does it now have so many competitors that the need for regulation has vanished? These issues will surface again in the chapters on electricity *infra*.

3. Canada's parallel experiences with the deregulation of the natural gas industry are described in Leigh Hancher, Energy Regulation and Competition in Canada, 15 J. of Energy & Nat. Res. L. 338 (1997). *See also* Barry

Barton, From Public Service to Market Commodity: Electricity and Gas Law in New Zealand, 16 J. of Energy & Nat. Res. L. 351 (1998).

D.   HAS RESTRUCTURING BEEN A SUCCESS?

FERC's Order 636 has elicited a wide range of comments, from enthusiastic support to harsh condemnation. Two excerpts, the first from an economist who supports deregulation and the second from a lawyer who is concerned about the small consumer, indicate the range of comments in the literature.

Robert J. Michaels The New Age of Natural Gas: How the Regulators Brought Competition,

Regulation Winter 1993, at 68, 70, 74.

Although there were several credible candidates for the title, fifteen years ago natural gas was probably American's most misregulated industry. Interstate pipelines and local distributors were natural monopolies governed by the most stereotypical commission procedure. Price controls on gas production had created shortages that exacerbated the energy crises of the 1970s. Today, the controls are gone, and gas prices are about half those of a decade ago. The pipelines have been restructured into competitive entities by—of all people—federal regulators. State-regulated distributors are next in line for the same shock treatment. . . .

. . . Since the pipelines and distributors were obvious natural monopolies, economists relegated them to the backwaters of incompetent regulation and redistributionist politics. But by the late 1980s the regulators had brought competition to them. The interstate pipelines are no longer resellers of gas who can force distributors to accept and pass on the cost. Almost overnight, nearly 90 percent of their business became the transportation of gas owned by others. Their former captives now make their own deals with producers and use the pipeline only for delivery. Smaller producers and inexperienced customers have at their disposal a growing industry of gas marketers and brokers, who can familiarize them with the market and individualize their transactions. Over two-thirds of all gas sales are now effectively in "spot" markets, with terms of thirty days or less. Pipeline interconnections have grown in capacity and complexity to open up a national market. Futures contracts and options are traded on the New York Mercantile Exchange.

The changes have reached the state-regulated distributors. In the era of shortages many of their industrial customers installed fuel-switching capabilities. Industry's new sensitivity to prices meant that state regulators would find it increasingly difficult to force industrial users to subsidize residential customers. Federal policy adds to the state regulators' problem. FERC now allows industrial users to bypass their local distributors, purchase gas from producers, and have interstate pipelines deliver it. In a growing number of states regulators have responded by allowing distributors to turn themselves into transporters of their customers' own purchases. In some states small end-users can free themselves from dependence on their distributor by hiring brokers to make group purchases that would be uneconomic if made individually.

* * *

... Order 636 levels the playing field by forcing the "unbundling" of pipeline services and symmetric treatment of the pipeline and its customers. Transport customers will have specific rights to the pipeline's main line capacity, storage, and rights on upstream pipelines. With those rights a transport customer can duplicate virtually any service the pipeline can offer a resale customer ..... On their side pipelines will have the right to resell gas at "market-based" rates—they are free to sell at competitive prices, subject to existing regulation of affiliate relationships.■

Joseph Fagan, From Regulation to Deregulation: The Diminishing Role of the Small Consumer Within the Natural Gas Industry

29 Tulsa L.J. 707 at 726–27 (1994).

Organizations representing small customers have responded quickly to Order No. 636. Generally, their concerns reflect the belief that this segment of the industry is the least able to take advantage of the opportunities presented by open-access. This inherent inflexibility will not only deny captive customers the benefits of the new competitive marketplace, it will also shift onto them a disproportionate share of the transition burden.

Several aspects of Order No. 636 raise troubling questions for those who represent small consumers. One such aspect concerns the increasing phenomenon of bypass. As large LDCs and industrial end-users continue to bypass with the FERC's encouragement, the cost of gas will inevitably increase for the captive customers. Secondly, the restructuring rule does not appear to contain any mandatory requirements for the pipelines to contain the costs of their restructuring. To be sure, the Commission urges pipelines to try to accommodate the concerns of the captive customers, but accommodation is not necessary. Finally, consumer groups view Order No. 636 with alarm. Its provisions for transition cost recovery and straight fixed variable (SFV) rate design seem to undermine FERC's statutory duty to protect the natural gas consumer.

One of the provisions of Order No. 636 which met with the most resistance allows pipelines to recover one hundred percent of their prudently incurred transition costs. This provision undoubtedly represents the FERC's efforts to ease the impact which mandatory unbundling and open access will have on the individual pipelines. Nevertheless, the provision holds stark implications for the captive customer. Switchable pipeline customers, knowing that their cost of gas will necessarily increase as these transition costs are recovered, will surely bypass in favor of another supplier. With a smaller customer base left to absorb the full brunt of the restructuring transition, pipelines will have little choice but to pass through these costs to their remaining residential and other captive customers.

The Commission did modify the initial rule somewhat by adding a requirement that pipelines must recover ten percent of their gas supply realignment costs (GSR) from their interruptible customers. These same customers, however, are the same customers who can readily switch away from natural gas in favor of another energy source at any time. This provision will still leave captive customers responsible for 90 percent of pipeline transition costs. If it is a truthful assertion that overall transition costs will approach five billion dollars, surely a mere 10 percent "discount" for captive customers will hardly relieve them of their disproportionate burden. . . .

. . . No one disputes that a free, unregulated market for natural gas will benefit all concerned. However, until that point is finally reached, the transition will be a painful one. The traditional linchpins of the industry, the interstate pipelines, have staggering costs, such as take-or-pay, which must be resolved before full deregulation can take hold. In a system of open access and unbundled service, the pipelines can only truly influence the behavior of the small customers. Yet, it is they who are the most vulnerable and the most incapable of bearing these transition costs. Unless more comprehensive steps are taken to ensure that these customers do not absorb the full impact of deregulation, the brave new world envisioned by Order No. 636 will be a bleak one for them indeed.■

NOTES AND COMMENTS

1.   Is the best measure of the success of gas restructuring the fall in the price of natural gas? In real terms (adjusted for inflation), on-system sales of natural gas showed a price decline of 13 percent from 1990 to 1995. Over the same period, average real electric prices to final consumers fell by almost 9 percent. Residential natural gas and electricity prices fell between 1990 and 1995 everywhere but in New England. Still, big industrial users and power plants have experienced much greater price reductions than retail consumers. Jess, *supra*.

2.   What other non-price factors should be rated to measure the success of gas restructuring?

E.   FREE MARKETS AND FEDERALISM

The U.S. Supreme Court has not had an opportunity to comment directly on the FERC restructuring of the gas industry, but the case below suggests that the Court shares a concern for the captive customer. This case, like the *Transco* case in Chapter Seven, addresses the federalism issues that are a recurrent theme in energy law.

General Motors Corp. v. Tracy

519 U.S. 278 (1997).

■ SOUTER, J.: The State of Ohio imposes its general sales and use taxes on natural gas purchases from all sellers, whether in-state or out-of-state, except regulated public utilities that meet Ohio's statutory definition of a "natural gas company." The question here is whether this difference in tax treatment between sales of gas by domestic utilities subject to regulation and sales of gas by other entities violates the Commerce Clause or Equal Protection Clause. We hold that it does not.

[Ohio levied a 5% tax on the in-state sales of goods, including natural gas, and a parallel 5% use tax on goods purchased out-of-state for use in Ohio. Local jurisdictions were authorized to levy certain additional taxes that increased these sales and use tax rates to as much as 7% in some municipalities. The state exempted natural gas sales by natural gas utilities from all state and local sales taxes, but the supreme court of Ohio interpreted the statute to deny the exemption to other gas sellers, such as producers and independent marketers. *See Chrysler Corp. v. Tracy*, 73 Ohio St. 3d 26, 652 N.E.2d 185 (1995).]

During the tax period in question here, petitioner General Motors Corporation (GMC) bought virtually all the natural gas for its Ohio plants from out-of-state marketers, not LDCs. Respondent Tax Commissioner of Ohio applied the State's general use tax to GMC's purchases, and the State Board of Tax Appeals sustained that action. GMC appealed to the Supreme Court of Ohio on two grounds. GMC first contended that its purchases should be exempt from the sales tax because independent marketers fell within the statutory definition of "natural gas company."... GMC also argued that denying the tax exemption to sales by marketers violated the Commerce and Equal Protection Clauses.

[The Ohio Supreme Court denied relief and certiorari was granted. In part II of the opinion the Court found that plaintiff had standing to raise the constitutional issues on behalf of the sellers.]

III

A

The negative or dormant implication of the Commerce Clause prohibits state taxation or regulation that discriminates against or unduly burdens interstate commerce and thereby "impede[s] free private trade in the national marketplace," *Reeves, Inc. v. Stake*, 447 U.S. 429, 437 (1980). GMC claims that Ohio's differential tax treatment of natural gas sales by marketers and regulated local utilities constitutes "facial" or "patent" discrimination in violation of the Commerce Clause, and it argues that differences in the nature of the businesses of LDCs and interstate marketers cannot justify Ohio's differential treatment of these in-state and out-of-state entities. Although the claim is not that the Ohio tax scheme distinguishes in express terms between in-state and out-of-state entities, GMC argues that by granting the tax exemption solely to LDCs, which are in fact all located in Ohio, the State has "favored some in-state commerce while disfavoring all out-of-state commerce," Brief for Petitioner 16. That is, because the favored entities are all located within the State, "the tax exemption did not need to be drafted explicitly along state lines in order to demonstrate its discriminatory design," *Amerada Hess Corp. v. Director, Div. of Taxation*, N. J. Dept. of Treasury, 490 U.S. 66, 76 (1989). Assessing these arguments requires an understanding of the historical development of the contemporary retail market for natural gas. . . .

B

Since before the Civil War, gas manufactured from coal and other commodities had been used for lighting purposes, and of course it was understood that natural gas could be used the same way. *See* Dorner, Initial Phases of Regulation of the Gas Industry, in 1 Regulation of the Gas Industry §§ 2.03–2.06 (American Gas Assn. 1996) (hereinafter Dorner). By the early years of this century, areas in "proximity to the gas fields," *West v. Kansas Natural Gas Co.*, 221 U.S. 229, 246 (1911), did use natural gas for fuel, but it was not until the 1920's that the development of high-tensile steel and electric welding permitted construction of high-pressure pipelines to transport natural gas from gas fields for distant consumption at relatively low cost. By that time, the States' then-recent experiments with free market competition in the manufactured gas and electricity industries had dramatically underscored the need for comprehensive regulation of the local gas market. Companies supplying manufactured gas proliferated in the latter half of the 19th century and, after initial efforts at regulation by statute at the state level proved unwieldy, the States generally left any regulation of the industry to local governments. *See* Dorner §§ 2.03, 2.04. Many of those municipalities honored the tenets of laissez-faire to the point of permitting multiple gas franchisees to serve a single area and relying on competition to protect the public interest. Ibid. The results were both predictable and disastrous, including an initial period of "wasteful competition," followed by massive consolidation and the threat of monopolistic pricing. The public suffered through essentially the same evolution in the electric industry. Thus, by the time natural gas became a widely marketable commodity, the States had learned from chastening experience that public streets could not be continually torn up to lay competitors' pipes, that investments in parallel delivery systems for different fractions of a local market would limit the value to consumers of any price competition, and that competition would simply give over to monopoly in due course. It seemed virtually an economic necessity for States to provide a single, local franchise with a business opportunity free of competition from any source, within or without the State, so long as the creation of exclusive franchises under state law could be balanced by regulation and the imposition of obligations to the consuming public upon the franchised retailers.

Almost as soon as the States began regulating natural gas retail monopolies, their power to do so was challenged by interstate vendors as inconsistent with the dormant Commerce Clause. While recognizing the interstate character of commerce in natural gas, the Court nonetheless affirmed the States' power to regulate, as a matter of local concern, all direct sales of gas to consumers within their borders, absent congressional prohibition of such state regulation. At the same time, the Court concluded that the dormant Commerce Clause prevents the States from regulating interstate transportation or sales for resale of natural gas. Thus, the Court never questioned the power of the States to regulate retail sales of gas within their respective jurisdictions.

When federal regulation of the natural gas industry finally began in 1938, Congress, too, clearly recognized the value of such state-regulated monopoly arrangements for the sale and distribution of natural gas directly to local consumers. Thus, § 1(b) of the NGA, 15 U.S.C. § 717(b), explicitly exempted "local distribution of natural gas" from federal regulation, even as the NGA authorized the Federal Power Commission (FPC) to begin regulating interstate pipelines. Congress's purpose in enacting the NGA was to fill the regulatory void created by the Court's earlier decisions prohibiting States from regulating interstate transportation and sales for resale of natural gas, while at the same time leaving undisturbed the recognized power of the States to regulate all in-state gas sales directly to consumers. *Panhandle Eastern Pipe Line Co. v. Public Serv. Comm'n of Ind.*, 332 U.S. 507, 516–522 (1947). Thus, the NGA "was drawn with meticulous regard for the continued exercise of state power, not to handicap or dilute it in any way," *id.*, at 517–518; "the scheme was one of cooperative action between federal and state agencies" to "protect consumers against exploitation at the hands of natural gas companies," *id.*, at 520 (internal quotation marks omitted); and "Congress' action ... was an unequivocal recognition of the vital interests of the states and their people, consumers and industry alike, in the regulation of rates and service," *id.*, at 521. Indeed, the Court has construed § 1(b) of the NGA as altogether exempting state regulation of in-state retail sales of natural gas from attack under the dormant Commerce Clause....

For 40 years, the complementary federal regulation of the interstate market and congressionally approved state regulation of the intrastate gas trade thus endured unchanged in any way relevant to this case. The resulting market structure virtually precluded competition between LDCs and other potential suppliers of natural gas for direct sales to consumers, including large industrial consumers. The simplicity of this dual system of federal and state regulation began to erode in 1978, however, when Congress first encouraged interstate pipelines to provide transportation services to end users wishing to ship gas, and thereby moved toward providing a real choice to those consumers who were able to buy gas on the open market and were willing to take it free of state-created obligations to the buyer. The upshot of congressional and regulatory developments over the next 15 years was increasing opportunity for a consumer in that class to choose between gas sold by marketers and gas bundled with rights and benefits mandated by state regulators as sold by LDCs. But amidst such changes, two things remained the same throughout the period involved in this case. Congress did nothing to limit the States' traditional autonomy to authorize and regulate local gas franchises, and the local franchised utilities (though no longer guaranteed monopolies as to all natural gas demand) continued to provide bundled gas to the vast majority of consumers who had neither the capacity to buy on the interstate market nor the resilience to forgo the reliability and protection that state regulation provided.

To this day, all 50 States recognize the need to regulate utilities engaged in local distribution of natural gas. Ohio's treatment of its gas utilities has been a typical blend of limitation and affirmative obligation. Its natural gas utilities, during the period in question, bore with a variety of requirements: they had to submit annual forecasts of future supply and demand for gas, comply with a range of accounting, reporting, and disclosure rules, and get permission from the State Public Utilities Commission to issue securities and even enter certain contracts. The "just and reasonable" rates to which they were restricted, included a single average cost of gas, together with a limited return on investment. The LDCs could not exact "a greater or lesser compensation for any services rendered . . . than [exacted] . . . from any other [customer] for doing a like and contemporaneous service under substantially the same circumstances and conditions."

The State also required LDCs to serve all members of the public, without discrimination, throughout their fields of operations. *See, e.g., Industrial Gas Co. v. Public Utilities Comm'n of Ohio*, 135 Ohio St. 408, 21 N.E.2d 166 (1939). They could not "pick out good portions of a particular territory, serve only select customers under private contract, and refuse service . . . to . . . other users," *id.*, at 413, 21 N.E.2d at 168, or terminate service except for reasons defined by statute and by following statutory procedures, Ohio Rev. Code Ann. §§ 4933.12, 4933.121 (Supp. 1990). . . .

IV

The fact that the local utilities continue to provide a product consisting of gas bundled with the services and protections summarized above, a product thus different from the marketer's unbundled gas, raises a hurdle for GMC's claim that Ohio's differential tax treatment of natural gas utilities and independent marketers violates our "virtually *per se* rule of invalidity" prohibiting facial discrimination against interstate commerce.

A

Conceptually, of course, any notion of discrimination assumes a comparison of substantially similar entities. Although this central assumption has more often than not itself remained dormant in this Court's opinions on state discrimination subject to review under the dormant Commerce Clause, when the allegedly competing entities provide different products, as here, there is a threshold question whether the companies are indeed similarly situated for constitutional purposes. This is so for the simple reason that the difference in products may mean that the different entities serve different markets, and would continue to do so even if the supposedly discriminatory burden were removed. If in fact that should be the case, eliminating the tax or other regulatory differential would not serve the dormant Commerce Clause's fundamental objective of preserving a national market for competition undisturbed by preferential advantages conferred by a State upon its residents or resident competitors. In Justice Jackson's now-famous words: "Our system, fostered by the Commerce Clause, is that every farmer and every craftsman shall be encouraged to produce by the certainty that he will have free access to every market in the Nation, that no home embargoes will withhold his exports, and no foreign state will by customs duties or regulations exclude them. Likewise, every consumer may look to the free competition from every producing area in the Nation to protect him from exploitation by any. Such was the vision of the Founders; such has been the doctrine of this Court which has given it reality." *H. P. Hood & Sons, Inc. v. Du Mond*, 336 U.S. 525, 539, (1949). . . . Thus, in the absence of actual or prospective competition between the supposedly favored and disfavored entities in a single market there can be no local preference, whether by express discrimination against interstate commerce or undue burden upon it, to which the dormant Commerce Clause may apply. The dormant Commerce Clause protects markets and participants in markets, not taxpayers as such. . . .

. . . Here, natural gas marketers did not serve the Ohio LDCs' core market of small, captive users, typified by residential consumers who want and need the bundled product. *See, e.g.*, Darr, A State Regulatory Strategy for the Transitional Phase of Gas Regulation, 12 Yale J. on Reg. 69, 99 (1995) ("The large core residential customer base is bound to the LDC in what currently appears to be a natural-monopoly relationship"); App. 199 (a marketer from which GMC purchased gas does not hold itself out to the general public as a gas supplier, but rather selectively contacts industrial end users that it has identified as potentially profitable customers). While this captive market is not geographically distinguished from the area served by the independent marketers, it is defined economically as comprising consumers who are captive to the need for bundled benefits. These are buyers who live on sufficiently tight budgets to make the stability of rate important, and who cannot readily bear the risk of losing a fuel supply in harsh natural or economic weather. They are also buyers without the high volume requirements needed to make investment in the transaction costs of individual purchases on the open market economically feasible. Pierce, Intrastate Natural Gas Regulation: An Alternative Perspective, 9 Yale J. on Reg. 407, 409–410 (1992) ("Purchasing gas service [from marketers] requires considerable time and expertise. Its benefits are likely to exceed its costs only for consumers who purchase very large quantities of gas"). The demands of this market historically arose free of any influence of differential taxation (since there was none during the pre–1978 period when only LDCs generally served end-users), and because the market's economic characteristics appear to be independent of any effect attributable to the State's sales taxation as imposed today, there is good reason to assume that any pricing changes that could result from eliminating the sales tax differential challenged here would be inadequate to create competition between LDCs and marketers for the business of the utilities' core home market.

On the other hand, ... there is a possibility of competition between LDCs and marketers for the noncaptive market. Although the record before this Court reveals virtually nothing about the details of that competitive market, in the period under examination it presumably included bulk buyers like GMC, which have no need for bundled protection. ... Eliminating the sales tax differential at issue here might well intensify competition between LDCs and marketers for customers in this noncaptive market.

B

In sum, the LDCs' bundled product reflects the demand of a market neither susceptible to competition by the interstate sellers nor likely to be served except by the regulated natural monopolies that have historically supplied its needs. So far as this market is concerned, competition would not be served by eliminating any tax differential as between sellers, and the dormant Commerce Clause has no job to do. There is, however, a further market where the respective sellers of the bundled and unbundled products apparently do compete and may compete further. Thus, the question raised by this case is whether the opportunities for competition between marketers and LDCs in the noncaptive market requires treating marketers and utilities as alike for dormant Commerce Clause purposes. Should we accord controlling significance to the noncaptive market in which they compete, or to the noncompetitive, captive market in which the local utilities alone operate? Although there is no *a priori* answer, a number of reasons support a decision to give the greater weight to the captive market and the local utilities' singular role in serving it, and hence to treat marketers and LDCs as dissimilar for present purposes. First and most important, we must recognize an obligation to proceed cautiously lest we imperil the delivery by regulated LDCs of bundled gas to the noncompetitive captive market. Second, as a Court we lack the expertness and the institutional resources necessary to predict the effects of judicial intervention invalidating Ohio's tax scheme on the utilities' capacity to serve this captive market. Finally, should intervention by the National Government be necessary, Congress has both the resources and the power to strike the balance between the needs of the competitive and captive markets.

1

Where a choice is possible, as it is here, the importance of traditional regulated service to the captive market makes a powerful case against any judicial treatment that might jeopardize LDCs' continuing capacity to serve the captive market. Largely as a response to the monopolistic shakeout that brought an end to the era of unbridled competition among gas utilities, regulation of natural gas for the principal benefit of householders and other consumers of relatively small quantities is the rule in every State in the Union.... [A]nd to this day, notwithstanding the national regulatory revolution, Congress has done nothing to limit its unbroken recognition of the state regulatory authority that has created and preserved the local monopolies. The clear implication is that Congress finds the benefits of the bundled product for captive local buyers well within the realm of what the States may reasonably promote and preserve.

. . .

The continuing importance of the States' interest in protecting the captive market from the effects of competition for the largest consumers is underscored by the common sense of our traditional recognition of the need to accommodate state health and safety regulation in applying dormant Commerce Clause principles. State regulation of natural gas sales to consumers serves important interests in health and safety in fairly obvious ways, in that requirements of dependable supply and extended credit assure that individual buyers of gas for domestic purposes are not frozen out of their houses in the cold months. We have consistently recognized the legitimate state pursuit of such interests as compatible with the Commerce Clause, which was "never intended to cut the States off from legislating on all subjects relating to the health, life, and safety of their citizens, though the legislation might indirectly affect the commerce of the country." Huron Portland Cement Co. v. Detroit, 362 U.S. 440, 443–444.... Just so may health and safety considerations be weighed in the process of deciding the threshold question whether the conditions entailing application of the dormant Commerce Clause are present.

2

... Here we have to assume that any decision to treat the LDC's as similar to the interstate marketers would change the LDCs' position in the noncaptive market in which (we are assuming) they compete, at least at the margins, by affecting the overall size of the LDCs' customer base....

To be sure, what in fact would happen as a result of treating the marketers and LDCs alike we do not know....

... [This] Court is institutionally unsuited to gather the facts upon which economic predictions can be made, and professionally untrained to make them. See, e.g., Fulton Corp. v. Faulkner, 516 U.S., at 341–342, 116 S.Ct., at 859, and authorities cited therein; Hunter, Federalism and State Taxation of Multistate Enterprises, 32 Emory L.J. 89, 108 (1983) ("It is virtually impossible for a court, with its limited resources, to determine with any degree of accuracy the costs to a town, county, or state of a particular industry"); see also Smith, State Discriminations Against Interstate Commerce, 74 Calif. L.Rev. 1203, 1211 (1986) (noting that "[e]ven expert economists" may have difficulty determining "whether the overall economic benefits and burdens of a regulation favor local inhabitants against outsiders"). We are consequently ill qualified to develop Commerce Clause doctrine dependent on any such predictive judgments, and it behooves us to be as reticent about projecting the effect of applying the Commerce Clause here, as we customarily are in declining to engage in elaborate analysis of real-world economic effects, or to consider subtle compensatory tax defenses. The most we can say is that modification of Ohio's tax scheme could subject LDCs to economic pressure that in turn could threaten the preservation of an adequate customer base to support continued provision of bundled services to the captive market. The conclusion counsels against taking the step of treating the bundled gas seller like any other, with the consequent necessity of uniform taxation of all gas sales.

3

Prudence thus counsels against running the risk of weakening or destroying a regulatory scheme of public service and protection recognized by Congress despite its noncompetitive, monopolistic character. Still less is that risk justifiable in light of Congress's own power and institutional competence to decide upon and effectuate any desirable changes in the scheme that has evolved. Congress has the capacity to investigate and analyze facts beyond anything the Judiciary could match, joined with the authority of the commerce power to run economic risks that the Judiciary should confront only when the constitutional or statutory mandate for judicial choice is clear.

. . .

. . . The judgment of the Supreme Court of Ohio is affirmed.

■ Scalia, J. concurring:

I join the Court's opinion, which thoroughly explains why the Ohio tax scheme at issue in this case does not facially discriminate against interstate commerce. I write separately to note my continuing adherence to the view that the so-called "negative" Commerce Clause is an unjustified judicial invention, not to be expanded beyond its existing domain. . . .

■ Stevens, J. dissenting:

In Ohio, as in other States, regulated utilities selling natural gas— referred to by the Court as "LDCs"—operate in two markets, one that is monopolistic and one that is competitive.

In the first, they sell a "noncompetitive bundled gas product," to small consumers who have no practical alternative source of supply. . . .

The second market in which LDCs sell natural gas is a competitive market in which large customers like the General Motors Corporation (GMC) have alternative sources of supply. . . .

It may well be true that without a discriminatory tax advantage in the competitive market, the LDCs would lose business to interstate competitors and therefore be forced to increase the rates charged to small local consumers. This circumstance may require the States to find new, and nondiscriminatory, methods for accommodating the needs of small consumers for regular and reasonably priced natural gas service. As the Court recognizes, speculation about the "real-world economic effects" of a decision like this one is beyond our institutional competence. Such speculation is not, therefore, a sufficient justification for a tax exemption that discriminates against interstate commerce.■

NOTES AND COMMENTS

1.   Is it possible to imagine greater competition in the local distribution of natural gas as well as in the long distance transmission? Some states are now exploring the possibility of allowing the so-called "captive" consumers to break their bonds with the local gas distributing company and buy gas from independent suppliers, with the LDC providing transportation service only. The issues that arise in this type of retail competition will be discussed in the context of the electric industry, where such competition has advanced further than in the gas industry. *See* Chapter 13.

2.   As noted earlier, a long line of Supreme Court cases interpreted the Natural Gas Act as designed primarily to insure the reliable delivery of natural gas for home heating at the lowest possible price. The *Tracy* case indicates that the Court will hew to this tradition until Congress unambiguously changes the policy. *See* C. Adam Buck, Note, "General Motors Corporation v. Tracy", 20 Energy L.J. 345 (1999).

3.   To the extent that FERC requires unbundling of transportation and sales services, has it engaged in a "taking" for which just compensation should be required? We will return to this topic when we study electricity.

CHAPTER 10

INTRODUCTION TO ELECTRICITY

Outline of Chapter:

A. HISTORICAL DEVELOPMENT OF THE REGULATED UTILITY

We will now look at some of the key issues in the law relating to one of the most important forms of energy, electricity. The electric industry is in the midst of rapid and ongoing changes. To understand why these changes are taking place and what their impact will be it is necessary to understand some of the history of the industry.

1. INTRODUCTION OF ELECTRIC TECHNOLOGY

Water power, coal, oil and natural gas are primary forms of energy resources. They are found in nature and can be utilized directly into useable energy. Electricity is what is known as a secondary energy resource. Electricity is also found in nature, as Benjamin Franklin proved in the mid–18th century with his famous experiment in which he flew a kite during a thunderstorm to determine whether lightning was in fact electricity. But our ability to harness natural electricity has been very limited. For all practical purposes, we make our electricity from one of the primary energy resources listed above or from nuclear fission, to be discussed in Chapter Fourteen.

James Trefil, A Scientist in the City (Doubleday, 1994)

Electricity is different from other kinds of energy. When you turn on a light or use an electric tool, you don't need the source of the energy in the same building. In fact, the energy that drives the lights that allow you to read this book was probably generated some tens (if not hundreds) of miles from where you are sitting. Electricity provides a way of separating the generation of energy from its use.

Our modern electrically driven society owes its existence to an English scientist named Michael Faraday. In a series of experiments in 1831, he discovered that when a magnet is moved, an electric current will flow in wires near it. This discovery, part of Faraday's basic research into the nature of electricity, made it possible to build machines that could convert the energy stored in coal into electric energy carried in wires.

A simple generator [is] the device that carries out this conversion. A loop of wires is spun around between the poles of a magnet. From the point of view of someone on the loop, the magnet is always moving, so a current will always flow—first one way, then the other. This so-called alternating current (AC) can be run through wires to the place where it is to be used. To get the electricity from a power plant to your house may require that it travel through many miles of wire, from huge power lines on pylons to the smaller wires that bring it into your home to the little cord that runs from the wall to your lamp.

So long as you have an energy source that can make a shaft spin, you can use that energy to produce electricity. The most common technique is to boil water to make high-pressure steam and then squirt that steam against curved blades attached to the spinning shaft (a device like this is called a steam turbine). It makes no difference how you make the steam—it can be (and is) done routinely by burning coal, oil, or gas, or by extracting heat from a nuclear reactor. You can also turn the shaft by damming a river and then letting water fall from a great height onto the turbine blades.

Today, the advantages of electricity for supplying a city's energy are so obvious that there would seem little point in arguing about them. When electricity was first produced commercially in the late nineteenth century, however, it was far from clear that it would prevail over its competitors. The first use of electricity was for lighting, one of the landmarks of urban electrification occurring in Chicago on April 25, 1878, when a jury-rigged system of batteries and lamps lit up Michigan Avenue for the first time. The demonstration showed up both the strengths and weaknesses of the new technology. The lights used weren't the steady incandescent lights we're accustomed to today but, rather, the kind of carbon arc lights now used only for searchlights and stage lighting. They produce light by passing an electric spark between two cone-shaped carbon rods. In the Chicago demonstration, the result was an intense light: the two electric lamps produced an illumination equivalent to over 600 gas lamps. But they required constant adjustment as the carbon rods burned down. In addition, electrical systems in those days were unreliable in the extreme. The night after that first successful illumination in Chicago, for example, the whole system burned out, and it was months before another demonstration could take place.

The first people to use electrical power in a big way were stores and hotels in downtown business districts. At this stage of development, the main question was whether electricity would be generated locally, by each user, or whether there would be a central utility selling electricity to customers. Many businesses (Wanamaker's store in Philadelphia and the Palmer House hotel in Chicago, for example) installed their own generators. The first central power station was built by Charles Brush in San Francisco in 1879, but at that time the price of copper wire was so high that it was only economical to deliver electricity about half a mile—8 city blocks.

You can't imagine a city with generating plants every 16 blocks. Before our modern system could emerge, with its far-flung power plants and long transmission lines, a huge number of engineering advances had to take place. There's no single thing you can point to and say, "Here's the invention that made it all happen." Instead, there was a steady progression of nickel-and-dime developments that made it possible to generate electricity in large amounts and send it out over long distances—a better valve on a generator here, a better switch on a transmission line there. In the end, such developments wound up not only beating out gas lamps but giving our cities an entirely new shape.

There is no question that electricity is the energy form of choice for urban America. The energy history of our cities over the past century has seen the constant displacement of direct burning of fuels by electricity. The gas lamps were the first to go, except in "olde townes," where they are kept for their historical associations. They were followed by steam-powered factories and steam locomotives, and it probably won't be long before the gasoline-powered automobile joins the list. Let's face it: there's something very attractive about having energy available when you want it, while someone else has to deal with the pollution and other social costs of its generation.■

2.   THE GROWTH OF THE CENTRAL STATION

When we think of the history of electricity in the United States the first name on everybody's lips is that of Thomas Alva Edison. After hundreds of hours of failed experiments with different materials, cotton sewing thread was carefully carbonized, inserted into a glass evacuated by suction pump and connected to electricity supply form a dynamo. The light bulb "burned like an evening star," and we have the exact beginning of a new era for civilization: October 21, 1879. Vaclav Smil, Energies 158–159, The MIT Press (1999).

The great inventor of the light bulb, the phonograph and countless other products was also a pioneer in the generation and distribution of electricity. In 1882, when his company's Pearl Street generating station first delivered electric light to buildings throughout Wall Street, he became a national hero. Neil Baldwin, Edison: Inventing the Century (Hyperion, 1995).

Edison's talents were more on the creative side than on the management side. Credit for the development of the management model for delivering electricity that prevailed throughout the 20th century–the vertically integrated public utility monopoly—is generally given to one of Edison's lieutenants, Samuel Insull, who left Edison's employ in 1892 to assume the presidency of Chicago Edison Co. The great depression of 1893 hit the company hard, but Insull pulled it out and led the company, which became Commonwealth Edison, until the depression of the 1930s, turning it into a widely copied model of corporate organization.

As you read the following excerpts from Harold Platt's book on Insull and his successors (a book that is well worth reading in full) ask yourself whether the key ideas that Insull developed are still appropriate to today's conditions; in particular, (1) the "central station" concept, in which electricity is generated at a central power plant and distributed to customers by wires, and (2) the demand/commodity rate design, which was discussed in Chapter Eight.

Harold L. Platt, The Electric City

(University of Chicago Press, 1991).

In spite of Edison's faith in the central station concept, electrical technology seemed to contain inherent diseconomies of scale. Practical experience continued to accumulate in favor of the self-contained, "isolated" plant for the large consumer of electric lighting. Unit costs (and hence rates) were highest for small consumers, since they made the least efficient use of the station's generating equipment. As more lights were burned for longer periods, the cost of a unit of electricity—expressed as a kilowatt-hour (kWh)—declined. When the equipment was used more fully, the utility's huge capital costs were spread over more units of electricity, making each unit cheaper to generate. The resulting equation between rates and costs appeared to point irreversibly toward the eventual triumph of the self-contained system. As a customer's use increased, it would reach a point where significant savings could be gained from disconnecting the utility lines and purchasing a self-contained system of the appropriate size., In response, utility companies could offer discounts to large consumers, but at the expense of shifting a heavier burden of capital costs onto the small consumers. The result would be rates beyond the reach of most city dwellers who badly wanted to install the new technology.

More than any other individual, Samuel Insull solved the problems inherent in electrical technology and put the central station on a sound economic footing. Great ambition, international background, apprenticeship with Edison, and faith in technological progress combined to give the English immigrant a unique perspective on the problems facing local utility operators.... in the years leading up to his arrival in Chicago in 1892....

The state of the electrical industry in Chicago at the time of Insull's arrival can be described simply as one of chaotic growth. He would have to use all his considerable skills and talents to prove the superiority of the central station approach to meeting the city's electrical energy needs.... Within municipal borders alone, the city inspector's report of 1892 listed 18 central stations and 498 self-contained systems that were powering a total of 273,600 incandescent lights and 16,415 arc lamps.

The resulting crazy quilt of small distribution grids growing out from jerry-built central stations raised serious doubts about the ability of any single utility company to attain the economies of scale necessary to beat the competition of the self-contained system and cheaper sources of light and power. Perhaps the greatest shortcoming of the Edison system was its DC distributors. They used low voltage or "pressure," which made transmission at a distance extremely costly in terms of copper wiring and energy losses. The DC grid works much like a system of water mains. Larger and larger mains are needed to pump water to more distant points at a constant pressure, In a similar way, the diameter of the copper cables had to be enlarged in proportion to increases in both the size of the electrical load and the distance of transmission....

Operators of Edison systems faced a challenge even more threatening to their futures after the appearance in 1886 of an entirely new electrical technology using alternating current (AC). As the name implies, a generator creates a flow of electricity that rapidly alternates back and forth in a circuit. In contrast, in a DC system electricity flows in a single direction around a circuit. The critical, practical difference between the two was the unequivocal superiority of AC for transmitting electricity at a distance. Alternating current could be sent efficiently at high voltage or "pressure," which meant that comparatively inexpensive thin copper cables could be used without suffering unacceptable energy losses. The transmission of energy became increasingly efficient as the voltage was raised. To achieve high-voltage transmission, a passive device called a transformer was used, first to boost the voltages at the generator station for long-distance transmission and then to reduce it for local distribution at the service area.

Championed by George Westinghouse, the AC system threatened a fatal economic blow to the backers of Edison's DC technology. In the late 1880s, local companies using Westinghouse equipment began operating in middle-class communities such as Englewood on the South Side and Evanston on the northern border of the city. The applications of the early AC systems were restricted to incandescent lights and did not include practical motors or streetlamps, but the obvious advantages of the AC distribution grids made the technology ideal for the metropolitan area's vast expanse of low-density residential housing.

Over the next five years of depression and crisis between 1893 and 1898, Insull completed his plan to acquire all the central stations and their franchises in the Loop. Hard times undoubtedly helped persuade the small companies to sell out, especially since Insull followed a policy of offering generous terms. In most cases the equipment of these shoestring operators was simply junked, and the customers were connected to the Edison company lines. Added together with new light and power business in the Loop, the growth of the utility was extremely impressive during a period of general economic distress. For example, the Harrison Street Station had to be expanded by 167 percent from a maximum output of 2,400 to 6,400 KW to keep up with the peak demand. The use of electricity rose from 6.6 million kWh in 1893 to almost 11 million kWh in 1897, an average annual increase in consumption of about 18 percent.

But to Insull's dismay, generating all the CBD's electric business by a modern central station did not save enough to undercut the competition of self-contained systems, let alone gas lighting in the home. To be sure, the Harrison Street Station, with its more economical engines, generators, and fuel-handling equipment, could be expected to reduce the company's operating costs. And the growth of demand in the Loop would probably repay the investment capital sunk in the copper transmission line to link the riverfront plant to the Adams Street building. Yet, as Insull admitted, "no one in the central station business at that time really understood its fundamental economics."

During the depression, rates remained at luxury levels. Complaints from businessmen about high prices replaced the initial enthusiasm for the novel technology. Even in the homes of the affluent middle classes, the common practice was to use electric illumination only in the parlor when guests were present. After they left the light bulbs would be turned off, leaving the gas jets lit in the living quarters. The popularity of dual gas-electric chandeliers was a testament to the high cost of better lighting in the home.

The World's Fair of 1893, however, provided important clues on how to remove these supply-side constraints. For the electricians and the scientists, Chicago's exposition had technical as well as cultural lessons [that] demonstrated the principles of a universal system of distribution. Westinghouse employed a recent invention, the rotary convertor, to convert AC to DC for use by the intramural elevated railway. When coupled with the transformer, the rotary convertor provided a technological means of removing the constraints of restricted distribution areas. Electricity generated at a central station could now be boosted to high voltage by a transformer for long-distance transmission and then changed at local substations by transformers and convertors to meet the particular needs of the distribution area. The model city of 1893 taught Insull and other electrical men in Chicago that there was no real "battle of the systems" between AC and DC. The most important lesson of the World's Fair was that the two systems could be harnessed together to deliver a complete range of electrical services throughout the city.

Insull soon applied the lessons of the model city to the real one, making Chicago Edison first or second to put the rotary convertor into commercial use. In August 1897 electricity from the Harrison Street Station was transmitted at 2,300 volts to the Twenty-seventh Street Station, converted back to DC, and fed to the homes and businesses of the Near South Side. Two years later the first true substation, containing no generating equipment, was jerry-built on the North Side to help handle periods of peak demand from 4:00 p.m. to midnight. Within a few months, the cost efficiencies convinced Insull to shut down the nearby Clark Street Station and convert it into a full-time substation.

More important, these experiments proved the feasibility of a metropolitan power network. Insull was quick to appreciate the economic implications of the new technology for supplying electrical energy at a price lower than previously possible. The combined AC–DC system suggested a hierarchy composed of a few efficient power plants and a citywide network of substations where electricity would be transformed to meet the needs of each local district. This novel concept of central station service led Insull almost immediately to expand his monopoly plans from the CBD to encompass the entire city. In just two years between 1897 and 1898, he was able to achieve this major goal owing to his control of key patent licenses and a measure of incredible good luck.... The resulting concept of a central station hierarchy, together with the monopoly he had obtained, put Insull on the threshold of creating a metropolitan network of power. Yet all this technical and business success would mean little unless Insull also found an answer to the riddle of rates for the large consumer as well as the small residential customer. Electric rates had to be cut sufficiently to compete with the self-contained system and cheaper sources of artificial illumination. Only then would the demand for electrical energy reach a point where true economies of scale could be achieved.

As with the rotary convertor, an invention helped Insull solve the equation of utility costs and consumer rates. But in contrast to the hardware displayed at the World's Fair, the Wright demand meter did not directly answer the question of how to undersell both the self-contained plant and the alternative sources of artificial illumination. Instead, this ingenious device provided Insull with an "aha" experience that suddenly made the pieces of the puzzle fit together. All the economic requirements to beat the competition fell into place once he grasped the peculiar, instantaneous relationship between supply and demand that is inherent in electrical systems. As Insull testified, the demand meter "first taught us how to sell electricity."

Insull first heard about the innovative measuring instrument in 1894 while visiting his homeland. Recently invented by Arthur Wright of Brighton, England, the meter recorded not only a customer's amount of consumption but also the timing and the maximum level of his demand. Intrigued by the device, Insull returned to Chicago but sent his chief electrician, Louis Ferguson, to make a thorough study of its use in Brighton. The engineer returned with an enthusiasm for the metering system that soon infected Insull. In September 1897 the Chicago Edison Company started making a practical test of the measuring device. Within a few years, Wright's invention replaced most of the utility's other meters.

The demand meter showed Insull that electric companies did not work "just as the gas companies do." On the contrary, the two were fundamentally different. The storage tanks of the gas companies allowed them to even out their production schedules and make maximum use of the equipment on a twenty-four hour cycle. In this way gas companies could keep their capital investments in central station machinery to a minimum, because there was no need for expensive but little-used equipment to meet brief periods of peak demand on the system. In contrast, electric companies had to keep an instant balance between demand and supply or suffer service blackouts and equipment damage. To be sure, storage batteries could help meet periods of peak demand, but they had serious drawbacks of their own: they were expensive, cumbersome, dangerous, and very inefficient. Whether to purchase batteries or extra generating equipment to meet periods of maximum demand remained a problem.

Helping Insull break free of his mentor's teachings, the demand meter gave him the insight to recalculate the equation between the electric utility's costs and the customers' bills. Wright's invention suggested a new method of ratemaking with a two-part bill to replace the traditional flat charge. A customer's energy consumption (the number of kilowatt-hours of electricity recorded by the meter) corresponded to the company's operating expenses. The measure of peak demand on the meter represented the customer's share of the capital invested in generating equipment that had to stand ready to serve him. The utility would use each customer's maximum demand to apportion equally the cost of financing the utility's plants and equipment. This primary charge serviced the interest payments on the company's bonded indebtedness, which constituted about 70 percent of its total expenses. The demand meter would determine the number of kilowatt-hours for which to charge each customer at the higher primary rate. A much lower secondary charge would be levied for any consumption beyond that monthly minimum number of units of electricity. The primary rates were fixed for all customers, but the secondary rates were discounted on a sliding scale to encourage greater consumption.

In this way a two-tier rate structure promised to cut the bills of both the small household and the large commercial enterprise. In effect, residential customers would pay a smaller proportion of the utility's financial costs because they had relatively small peak demands. The net result of the two-tier system would be a lower effective rate for each kilowatt-hour of energy. For the most part, the heavy burden of the utility's interest payments would be absorbed by the large consumers of light and power. At the same time, they would benefit from the discounts for heavy use of the equipment, which would progressively reduce their net rate of charge for each kilowatt-hour of electricity. In this way a two-tier system of ratemaking was structured to encourage every type of consumer to use more energy.

During the second half of 1899, Insull not only talked about the future, he began taking practical steps to get there as soon as possible.... The Chicago utility announced a two-tier system of rates for light and power. For the average residential customer, the new method of billing translated into an immediate 32 percent savings, or a net reduction from 19.5¢ per kWh to 13.33¢. At the same time, the utility extended a special incentive to new customers by offering to install six lighting outlets free of charge.... During the crisis of the nineties, rapid improvements in central station service offered comforting reassurance to a nation torn with doubt about the power of technology to promote social justice and democracy.■

NOTES AND COMMENTS

1.   Samuel Insull eventually built up a complex of holding companies that exercised operating control over most of the electric utilities in the United States by the 1920s. By making a large share of the stock in the actual operating companies nonvoting, Insull controlled half a billion dollars worth of electric utility assets in 1930 with a capital investment of about 27 million dollars. Leonard S. Hyman, America's Electric Utilities: Past, Present and Future 106 (Public Utilities Reports, Inc., 6th ed. 1997).

2.   The Insull empire collapsed in the depression of the 1930s. Many of the operating companies went bankrupt and their stockholders lost their entire investment. In response, Congress passed the Public Utility Holding Company Act of 1935, which gave the Securities and Exchange Commission oversight responsibility for companies that owned ten percent or more of the shares of an electric or gas utility. 15 U.S.C. § 79.

3.   ELECTRICITY GOES NATIONAL

Once the technology for sending electricity long distances was developed, it soon became clear that the state boundary lines often made no economic sense to an electron. Many communities and businesses found it more efficient to obtain their power from a nearby plant in another state rather than from a plant in their own state that might be farther away or more expensive.

Public Utilities Comm. of Rhode Island v. Attleboro Steam & Electric Co.

273 U.S. 83 (1927)

■ SANFORD, J.: This case involves the constitutional validity of an order of the Public Utilities Commission of Rhode Island putting into effect a schedule of prices applying to the sale of electric current in interstate commerce

The Narragansett Electric Lighting Company is a Rhode Island corporation engaged in manufacturing electric current at its generating plant in the city of Providence and selling such current generally for light, heat and power. The Attleboro Steam & Electric Company is a Massachusetts corporation engaged in supplying electric current for public and private use in the city of Attleboro and its vicinity in that State.

In 1917, these companies entered into a contract by which the Narragansett Company agreed to sell, and the Attleboro Company to buy, for a period of twenty years, all the electricity required by the Attleboro Company for its own use and for sale in the city of Attleboro and the adjacent territory, at a specified basic rate; the current to be delivered by the Narragansett Company at the State line between Rhode Island and Massachusetts and carried over connecting transmission lines to the station of the Attleboro Company in Massachusetts, where it was to be metered. The Narragansett Company filed with the Public Utilities Commission of Rhode Island a schedule setting out the rate and general terms of the contract and was authorized by the Commission to grant the Attleboro Company the special rate therein shown; and the two companies then entered upon the performance of the contract. Current was thereafter supplied in accordance with its terms; and the generating plant of the Attleboro Company was dismantled.

In 1924 the Narragansett Company—having previously made an unsuccessful attempt to obtain an increase of the special rate to the Attleboro Company—filed with the Rhode Island Commission a new schedule, purporting to cancel the original schedule and establish an increased rate for electric current supplied, in specified minimum quantities, to electric lighting companies for their own use or sale to their customers and delivered either in Rhode Island or at the State line. The Attleboro Company was in fact the only customer of the Narragansett Company to which this new schedule would apply.

The Commission thereupon instituted an investigation as to the contract rate and the proposed rate. After a hearing at which both companies were represented, the Commission found that, owing principally to the increased cost of generating electricity, the Narragansett Company in rendering service to the Attleboro Company was suffering an operating loss, without any return on the investment devoted to such service, while the rates to its other customers yielded a fair return; that the contract rate was unreasonable and a continuance of service to the Attleboro Company under it would be detrimental to the general public welfare and prevent the Narragansett Company from performing its full duty to its other customers; and that the proposed rate was reasonable and would yield a fair return, and no more, for the service to the Attleboro Company. And the Commission thereupon made an order putting into effect the rate contained in the new schedule.

From this order the Attleboro Company prosecuted an appeal to the Supreme Court of Rhode Island which [held] that the order of the Commission imposed a direct burden on interstate commerce and was invalid because of conflict with the commerce clause of the Constitution; and entered a decree reversing the order and directing that the rate investigation be dismissed. 46 R. I. 496.

It is conceded, rightly, that the sale of electric current by the Narragansett Company to the Attleboro Company is a transaction in interstate commerce, notwithstanding the fact that the current is delivered at the State line. The transmission of electric current from one State to another, like that of gas, is interstate commerce, and its essential character is not affected by a passing of custody and title at the state boundary, not arresting the continuous transmission to the intended destination.

The petitioners contend, however, that the Rhode Island Commission cannot effectively exercise its power to regulate the rates for electricity furnished by the Narragansett Company to local consumers, without also regulating the rates for the other service which it furnishes; that if the Narragansett Company continues to furnish electricity to Attleboro Company at a loss this will tend to increase the burden on the local consumers and impair the ability of the Narragansett Company to give them good service at reasonable prices; and that, therefore, the order of the Commission prescribing a reasonable rate for the interstate service to the Attleboro Company should be sustained as being essentially a local regulation, necessary to the protection of matters of local interest, and affecting interstate commerce only indirectly and incidentally.

The order of the Rhode Island Commission is not a regulation of the rates charged to local consumers, having merely an incidental effect upon interstate commerce, but is a regulation of the rates charged by the Narragansett Company for the interstate service to the Attleboro Company, which places a direct burden upon interstate commerce. Being the imposition of a direct burden upon interstate commerce, from which the State is restrained by the force of the Commerce Clause, it must necessarily fall, regardless of its purpose. It is immaterial that the Narragansett Company is a Rhode Island corporation subject to regulation by the Commission in its local business, or that Rhode Island is the State from which the electric current is transmitted in interstate commerce, and not that in which it is received. The forwarding state obviously has no more authority than the receiving State to place a direct burden upon interstate commerce. Nor is it material that the general business of the Narragansett Company appears to be chiefly local. The test of the validity of a state regulation is not the character of the general business of the company, but whether the particular business which is regulated is essentially local or national in character; and if the regulation places a direct burden upon its interstate business it is none the less beyond the power of the State because this may be the smaller part of its general business. Furthermore, if Rhode Island could place a direct burden upon the interstate business of the Narragansett Company because this would result in indirect benefit to the customers of the Narragansett Company in Rhode Island, Massachusetts could, by parity of reasoning, reduce the rates on such interstate business in order to benefit the customers of the Attleboro Company in that State, who would have, in the aggregate, an interest in the interstate rate correlative to that of the customers of the Narragansett Company in Rhode Island. Plainly, however, the paramount interest in the interstate business carried on between the two companies is not local to either State, but is essentially national in character. The rate is therefore not subject to regulation by either of the two States in the guise of protection to their respective local interests; but, if such regulation is required it can only be attained by the exercise of the power vested in Congress.

The decree is accordingly affirmed.

■ BRANDEIS, J., dissenting: The business of the Narragansett Company is an intrastate one. The only electricity sold for use without the State is that agreed to be delivered to the Attleboro Company. That company takes less than 3 per cent. of the electricity produced and manufactured by the Narragansett, which has over 70,000 customers in Rhode Island. The problem is essentially local in character. The Commission found as a fact that continuance of the service to the Attleboro Company at the existing rate would prevent the Narragansett from performing its full duty towards its other customers and would be detrimental to the general public welfare. It issued the order specifically to prevent unjust discrimination and to prevent unjust increase in the price to other customers. The Narragansett, a public service corporation of Rhode Island, is subject to regulation by that State. The order complained of is clearly valid as an exercise of the police power, unless it violates the Commerce Clause.

The power of the State to regulate the selling price of electricity produced and distributed by it within the State and to prevent discrimination is not affected by the fact that the supply is furnished under a long-term contract. If the Commission lacks the power exercised, it is solely because the electricity is delivered for use in another State. That fact makes the transaction interstate commerce, and Congress has power to legislate on the subject. It has not done so, nor has it legislated on any allied subject, so there can be no contention that it has occupied the field. Nor is this a case in which it can be said that the silence of Congress is a command that the Rhode Island utility shall remain free from the public regulation—that it shall be free to discriminate against the citizens of the State by which it was incorporated and in which it does business. That State may not, of course, obstruct or directly burden interstate commerce. But to prevent discrimination in the price of electricity wherever used does not obstruct or place a direct burden upon interstate commerce....

In my opinion the judgment below should be reversed.■

NOTES AND COMMENTS

1. Would the test proposed by Justice Brandeis, that a state could "prevent discrimination in the price of electricity wherever used," have been as effective a means of ensuring fair pricing as the creation of a federal regulatory system? Do the principles of rate design seem clear enough that they could serve as a constitutional standard?

2.   After the Supreme Court limited the ability of the states to regulate interstate sales of electricity in the *Attleboro* case, Congress passed the Federal Power Act, which gave to the Federal Power Commission[1] the power to regulate the "sale of electric energy at wholesale in interstate commerce." 16 U.S.C. § 824.

3.   By the 1950's, the nation was blanketed with a few hundred investor-owned electric utilities on the Insull model. In addition, there were a few large federal electric generation and distribution agencies, such as the Tennessee Valley Authority, a host of publicly owned municipal electric agencies (the "municipals") and hundreds of rural electric cooperatives created under the federal Rural Electrification Act (the "REA co-ops").

Each of the larger entities operated primarily as an independent, vertically integrated unit. It generated its own power, transmitted it over high voltage lines to its own substations, and from there distributed it along lower voltage wires to the end users. Most rural co-ops and some smaller utilities did not have their own generating plants and relied on power purchased from the larger entities.

Since the 1930s, the interconnection of these separate entities had been overseen by the Federal Power Commission. In the 1960s, the issue of interconnection assumed new importance as rapid economic growth left some areas subject to power shortages.

Throughout the 1950s and 1960s, demand for electricity was constantly increasing. Until approximately 1965, utilities were able to meet this increasing demand simply by expanding their base-load capacity and passing through these costs to customers in rate base. During this period, electricity generation was believed by regulators to have been characterized by significant economies of scale. Generation capacity was increased—often without question—to meet this demand. In 1965, the FPC published an extensive survey, the National Power Survey, which suggested that closely coordinated plant constructions and operations by electric utilities could produce power far more cheaply than expansions of capacity and operations by individual utilities.

Many regulators were becoming concerned that sufficient capacity did not exist to meet consumer demand. On November 2, 1965, a relay on the Ontario Hydro system broke. The system was tied into the network of interconnected lines that covered the entire Northeast United States and parts of Canada. Surges of power cascaded through the system, overloading lines and knocking them out of commission. The Northeast Blackout of 1965, as it came to be known, was the worst power failure the electric industry had ever seen. Within a quarter-hour over 30 million people lost their electricity. The FPC responded with recommendations to form "relia-

---

1.   The Federal Power Commission was previously in existence, having been created under the Federal Water Power Act of 1920 to oversee the construction of hydroelectric dams on interstate rivers. *See* Chapter Four.

The new statute was combined with the old into a new Federal Power Act. In a subsequent reorganization, the Commission's name was changed to the Federal Energy Regulatory Commission.

bility councils" on a regional basis with representatives from the various utilities and government agencies.

Stephen Breyer[2] & Paul MacAvoy, Energy Regulation by the Federal Power Commission

Brookings Institution, 1974.

Electricity service is customarily viewed as consisting of (a) production of power by water or steam turbines, (b) transmission over high-voltage lines of the energy produced, and © local distribution for short distances over low-voltage lines to final consumers. By the accounting methods of the industry, more than half the costs are charged to production of electricity, one-eighth to transmission, and the rest to distribution. Several hundred firms owned by private investors provide approximately three-quarters of the nation's electricity supply. The remainder is produced by local, state, or federal installations. Nearly all private firms are vertically integrated, providing generating, transmitting, and distributing services as a single entity or through separate firms controlled by the same holding company. . . .

. . . [C]hanging technology [in the electric utility industry] provoked similar change in the pattern of regulation. As technology made large-scale operation more efficient, competition between companies within a single city began to disappear, and municipalities sought to regulate prices and service quantity through their prerogatives in issuing franchises. Then, between 1905 and 1920, local franchising gave way to comprehensive control by state regulatory boards.

More recently, regulatory control has ceased to mirror the scale of operation that technology makes possible. . . . [T]oday as in the 1930s electricity regulation takes place primarily at the state level; state commissions control the prices of retail sales and review all construction plans. Restraints imposed by the commission or other federal agencies are typically viewed as supplementary forms of regulation.

With the growth of scale in capacity, power companies recognized the importance of coordinating generation and transmission by combining them across regions larger than the single retail distribution area. Recent technological change increasing the size of efficient generating units has in all probability increased the need for coordination. Operation of a group of generating units and a network of interconnecting transmission lines for service to multiple population centers as if the parts were one system can, in principle, produce cost savings in six categories.

Operating costs can be held to a minimum through a program to select for dispatch the power from the those generators capable of producing it most cheaply. The program is formulated by tabulating the power stations

---

2. Some two decades after co-authoring this book with economist Paul MacAvoy, Stephen Breyer was appointed to the Supreme Court of the United States by President Clinton.

in ascending order of marginal operating costs, the "first" station being the one with lowest marginal costs, and then by loading the plants on the system in that order as demand increases. Each plant is "started up" for power production when total demand exceeds full capacity of the operating plants already on line with lower marginal costs.

Costs for meeting peak demands for electricity can be reduced by taking advantage of the fact that demand varies according to the time of day and the season of the year. Two regions in which peak demands occur at different times can save generating capacity by using the peaking capacity in one to supply some part of the peak demand in the other. If in winter demand peaks sharply at about 5:00 P.M., two adjacent systems in different time zones may be able to share the equipment needed to supply their respective peaks. The same principle suggests the possibility of exchanges between areas which have summer peaks because of air conditioning and those where peaks occur in winter because of heating demand. Coordination across companies with different peaks results in what is sometimes referred to as demand-diversity cost savings.

Reserve costs are also reduced by coordination. Reserve generating capacity is kept in case peak demand has been underestimated or in case operating units break down and for use during periods of maintenance. Interconnection can save on the capacity needed to allow maintenance work if firms in a coordination group can stagger their maintenance schedules to allow each to use the same spare generator to substitute for the generator being overhauled. Coordination can also reduce the risk of underforecasting demand. The larger the interconnected system, the more likely that the effect of unusual weather and changes in industrial demand in one place can be absorbed by reserve capacity from another place.

Coordinating the operations of several systems also reduces the need for breakdown reserves. Pooling reserve capacity allows each firm to call upon the reserves of other firms if a generator outage occurs. And the reserves of the others will be available unless several outages occur simultaneously, a contingency that becomes more remote the larger the number of generators in the system. Sharing such capacity can reduce investment in reserve capacity by an amount sufficient to compensate for the increased costs of interconnecting transmission lines.

Generating costs can be reduced by coordination if it allows firms to take advantage of economies of scale in generator size. Since capacity depends on boiler and turbine volume while costs very roughly depend on metal surface areas, costs per unit of capacity decline with total outlay. The larger the generator, the more cheaply it can produce electricity at the margin. In fact, in estimating the elasticity of costs with respect to capacity, the consensus seems to be that costs increase by only 8 or 9 percent when capacity increases 10 percent. Thus the most efficient way to make electricity usually is to install the largest generator that technology permits—a size that increased from roughly 400 megawatts (400,000 kilowatts) in the early 1960s to approximately 1,000 megawatts in the early 1970s. A large generating unit, however, requires a large backup unit in case it breaks down and recently larger units have tended to break down more frequently. Whereas a smaller firm may not face sufficient demand for its electricity to justify replacing a small generator with a large one, several small firms combined into a single system may be able to do so.

Transmission reliability costs can also be reduced through coordinated planning across a wide geographical area. When a generator breaks down, reserve generators must make up the deficit; but, during the first few seconds after a major breakdown (before the reserve generators can start up), more is needed. Power will rush into the deficit area, and the interconnecting transmission lines must be sufficiently strong to withstand the surge. Similarly, when a major line breaks down, power recoils and spreads itself out through the remaining interconnected lines of the system; those remaining lines must not break down, or they will aggravate the problem. Thus, once firms are interconnected at all, the generating or transmission plans of one will affect the need for lines elsewhere. Company X's installation of a large generator in State A may require the strengthening of Company Y's lines in State B, an area well outside Company X's service area. Unless Companies X and Y and others affected coordinate their plans, there is a risk of power failure, on the one hand, or waste, on the other.

Social costs, such as the adverse environmental effects from power generation, can also be reduced through coordination. Nearly every method of making electricity affects the environment in some way. Fossil-fuel plants pollute the air; nuclear plants heat nearby rivers and lakes; hydroelectric plants and their accompanying transmission lines disturb the biotic equilibrium and scenic attraction of wild areas. Coordinated planning over a wide geographic area can reduce total construction and help to locate the area's plants so as to produce the desired level of power at a lower cost to the environment.■

NOTES AND COMMENTS

1. Throughout the late 1960s and the 1970s, blackouts and brownouts began to be a serious concern, especially during periods in which consumer demand "peaked"—such as Summer periods, in which residential and office air conditioning was added to normal demand. Most of us tend to take for granted the ability to throw a switch to provide light, power for appliances, or heat. We tend to underestimate the social impact of energy shortages. Another blackout of New York City on July 13 & 14, 1977, in addition to closing most public transportation facilities and businesses, led to communications shutdown (and the closing of Wall Street), riots and looting, prolonged fires, and many injuries and deaths. The Cost of an Urban Blackout, The Consolidated Edison Blackout, July 13–14, 1977, A Study for the Subcommittee on Energy and Power, Committee on Interstate and Foreign Commerce, United State House of Representatives (June 1978) at 4.

2.   Writing in 1974 in the above-excerpted book, Breyer and MacAvoy went on to encourage the FPC to use its authority to require utilities to interconnect with each other in order to encourage the economies of scale that come with larger generating plants. They noted: "The most efficient way to make electricity usually is to install the largest generator that technology permits—a size that increased from roughly 400 megawatts (400,000 kilowatts) in the early 1960s to approximately 1,000 megawatts in the early 1970s." At that time, regulators were under intense pressure to increase utility capacity to supply electricity in order to meet expected shortages.

Recent economic studies suggest that the optimal size for coal and gas plants never exceeded 500 MW, although the optimal size for a nuclear plant was in the 900–1,100 MW range. *See* Paul L. Joskow & Richard Schmalansee, Markets for Power: An Analysis of Electric Utility Deregulation 51–54 (1983). If regulators during the 1970s were approving new plant construction on the basis of Breyer & MacAvoy's assumptions, would this be likely to lead to unnecessary capital expansion?

Today, the electric industry is the most capital-intensive industry in the US economy: It currently requires $4 in capital investment for every $1 in annual revenues, as compared to a 3/1 ratio for the telephone industry and .6/1 for the automobile industry.

4.   How a Modern Electric System Works

The physical equipment of a modern electric power system is divided into three basic categories: generation, transmission and distribution. Traditionally, in the territory of an investor-owned utility (IOU) or a large municipal utility, the same entity has owned and operated all three parts of the system. Today, however, an increasing share of the generation facilities are operated by independent power producers. And in the future, the transmission and distribution functions may increasingly be handled by separate entities, as discussed in Chapter 11.

a.   GENERATION

Most electric power plants use either coal, oil, natural gas and uranium as fuel. Some plants use renewable resources, such as hydro, geothermal, biomass, wind and solar energy. A bit more than half the electricity in the United States comes from coal-fired plants. About a fifth comes from nuclear power plants. Hydro furnishes around ten percent, depending on the amount of rainfall that has taken place. The use of natural gas as power plant fuel is increasing and is approaching ten percent. The use of fuel oil is dropping and now produces only about three percent. Power from renewable sources other than hydro is increasing, but still amounts to just a few percent.

How To Make Electricity

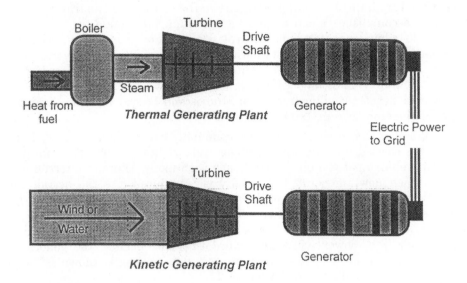

Figure 10–1

Source: www.sledu/nmah/csrl/powering/basics/gen.htm 1999

The type of fuel, its cost, and generating plant efficiency can determine the way a particular generating plant is used. The demand for electricity varies considerably on both daily and yearly cycles. A large electric system will usually contain many different types of generating plant. The system operator will try to keep the mix of plants with the lowest operating costs running at any given time.

For purposes of deciding which plants to operate at any given time, power plants are generally classified into four categories: (1) base load "must run" plants, mostly nuclear or newer coal plants, which have low fuel costs and cannot be turned off and on rapidly; (2) variable "must run" plants, powered by hydro and wind, which have virtually no fuel costs but can operate only if the proper amount of water or wind is available; (3) intermediate load plants, often older coal plants that are more costly to operate than newer models; and (4) peaking plants, typically natural gas or diesel fueled, which have higher operating costs but are relatively inexpensive to build and can be taken on and off line quickly.

The need for this kind of careful balancing of the system results from the fact that electricity cannot be easily stored. This means that whenever customers turn the power on or off the generating load must be increased or decreased almost instantaneously to avoid affecting the voltage significantly.[3] Extensive research is underway in advanced battery design and superconducting magnetic energy storage, but progress is slow.

3. The equivalent of storage can be obtained with "pumped hydro" plants, in which water is pumped up to the reservoir during periods when demand for electricity is low and then released to generate power at peak times. However, there are few potential sites

b.   TRANSMISSION

Power plants are usually large and immovable[4], and their output must be moved from the generating plant site to the consumer. The transmission system accomplishes much of this task with an interconnected system of lines, distribution centers, and control systems. For example, the ERCOT transmission system that covers most of the state of Texas has over 48,000 miles of transmission lines, consisting of 7060 miles of 345KV lines, 16,538 miles of 138KV lines, and 11,456 miles of 69KV lines. Guide to Electric Power in Texas 5 (Center for Global Studies and Energy Institute, University of Houston, 2d. ed., 1999).

Transmission lines are the lines commonly called "high-voltage" lines that are carried on high towers along wide rights of way. They form a spider web-like pattern on the landscape with many points of interconnection. When newly generated electricity is introduced into the network it will flow in whichever direction the lines are most lightly loaded. Similarly, where lines intersect, electricity will flow through the junction in a way that tries to even out the line loads. Thus if demand increases on a particular line, power will flow toward that line even if the generator assumed it was going to go somewhere else. This concept is known as "loop flow," and will be discussed in Chapter 11.

The transmission network must be operated in a way that keeps the voltage and frequency constant within very narrow limits. All systems keep a certain ratio of "spinning reserve;" *i.e.,* generating plants that are in operation and ready to be switched onto the network immediately if needed. In addition, a system needs "operating reserve" in the form of generation equipment or curtailable load that can be brought on or off line within ten minutes or so. Finally, to operate properly the transmission system needs voltage control equipment dispersed throughout the system where voltage support is needed, and an overall system operator with authority to determine which generating units go on and off line at any time. These features of the transmission system are known in the trade as "ancillary services." *See* F.E.R.C. Order No. 888–A, 1997.

Standards for the operation of transmission systems have been set by the North American Electric Reliability Council (NERC), a consortium of various electric industry entities representing public and private utilities that account for virtually all of the electricity supplied in the United States and Canada. NERC's technical activities are carried out by committees on adequacy, security, and market interface. See www.nerc.com/about/

The transmission systems of the United States and Canada are divided into three giant networks. (1) Beginning at about the Rocky Mountains and extending throughout the Western United States and Canada is the Western Interconnection. It's operation is governed by the Western Systems

---

for such plants and the cost of operating them is not cheap.

4. The universality of this proposition is subject to change with the development of smaller scale plants known is the trade as "distributed generation." *See* Section E, *infra.* Nevertheless, for all practical purposes the great bulk of generating capacity will remain immovable for the foreseeable future.

Coordinating Council, a non-profit entity controlled by representatives of the various utilities in the region. (2) Most of Texas has its own Texas Interconnection. These lines are operated by the Electric Reliability Council of Texas, a corporation created pursuant to state statute.[5] (3) The rest of the United States and Canada is part of the Eastern Interconnection, which is one giant network. Operation of the Eastern Interconnection is not centralized, however, but is managed by seven separate regional reliability councils. The future of the system of management of the transmission network is under considerable discussion (*See* Chapter 11).

Construction of transmission lines increased at a rapid rate during the 1970s but began to slow down after about 1985. Hyman, *supra.*, at 144, 161. Construction of new transmission lines today often encounters opposition from neighbors or environmental agencies, and may require a long period of negotiation. The *Florida Power* case in Chapter 2 is an example of the difficulties encountered in transmission line siting.

c. DISTRIBUTION

Substations are located at various points on the transmission system. These substations contain transformers that reduce the voltage and send the power to the 120 and 240 volt lines that serve homes and businesses. (Large industries often bypass the distribution system and take electricity directly from the transmission network if they need higher voltages.)

The distribution system consists of the substations, poles and wires common to many neighborhoods as well as underground lines found in many other areas. Maintenance of these systems must respond to tree growth, sudden wind or ice storms, nesting eagles, and dozens of other local problems that frequently arise.

The distribution function also includes the billing of customers, reading of meters, customer service, and many of the common activities that the average person associates with the work of an electric utility. As a public utility, the distributing company has an obligation to provide service to all customers at published rates. State laws sometimes make it difficult to terminate service to a customer even when he is not paying his bill.

Many rural cooperatives and small municipal utilities operate only a distribution system without either generating or transmitting power. They purchase power in "wholesale" transactions from other utilities or from Federal marketing entities.

B. CURRENT STRUCTURE OF THE INDUSTRY

The next three chapters will discuss the ongoing changes taking place in the electric industry. These include extensive mergers within the electric

---

5. Texas has traditionally tried to limit the interconnections between its lines and those of the rest of the country in order to discourage federal jurisdiction. *See generally* Guide to Electric Power in Texas (Center for Global Studies and Energy Institute, University of Houston, 2d. Ed., 1999)

industry itself, both in the United States and overseas, as well as combinations of traditional electric companies with gas companies, energy marketers and a wide range of other companies. And they also include the entry into the electricity business of other independent companies that may engage in more limited roles than the traditional vertically integrated electric utility.

As background for these changes, however, it is important to understand who the major players are as we enter this period of rapid change.

Table 1. Major Characteristics of Electricity Providers by Type of Ownership, 1998

Ownership	Major Characteristics
Investor-Owned Utilities (IOUs) IOUs account for about three-quarters of all utility generation and capacity. There are 239 in the United States, and they operate in all States except Nebraska. They are also referred to as privately owned utilities.	• Earn a return for investors; either distribute their profits to stockholders as dividends or reinvest the profits • Are granted service monopolies in specified geographic areas • Have obligation to serve and to provide reliable electric power • Are regulated by State and Federal governments, which in turn approve rates that allow a fair rate of return on investment • Most are operating companies that provide basic services for generation, transmission, and distribution
Federally Owned Utilities There are 10 Federally owned utilities in the United States, and they operate in all areas except the Northeast, the upper Midwest, and Hawaii.	• Power not generated for profit • Publicly owned utilities, cooperatives, and other nonprofit entities are given preference in purchasing from them • Primarily producers and wholesalers • Producing agencies for some are the U.S. Army Corps of Engineers, the U.S. Bureau of Reclamation, and the International Water and Boundary Commission • Electricity generated by these agencies is marketed by Federal power marketing administrations in the U.S. Department of Energy • The Tennessee Valley Authority is the largest producer of electricity in this category and markets at both wholesale and retail levels

Other Publicly Owned Utilities
 	
Other publicly owned utilities include:
  Municipals
  Public Power Districts
  State Authorities
  Irrigation Districts
  Other State Organizations
 	
There are 2,009 in the United States.
	• Are nonprofit State and local government agencies
	• Serve at cost; return excess funds to the consumers in the form of community contributions and reduced rates
	• Most municipals just distribute power, although some large ones produce and transmit electricity; they are financed from municipal treasuries and revenue bonds
	• Public power districts and projects are concentrated in Nebraska, Washington, Oregon, Arizona, and California; voters in a public power district elect commissioners or directors to govern the district independent of any municipal government
	• Irrigation districts may have still other forms of organization (e.g., in the Salt River Project Agricultural Improvement and Power District in Arizona, votes for the Board of Directors are apportioned according to the size of landholdings)
	• State authorities, such as the New York Power Authority and the South Carolina Public Service Authority, are agents of their respective State governments

Cooperatively Owned Utilities There are 912 cooperatively owned utilities in the United States, and they operate in all States except Connecticut, Hawaii, Rhode Island, and the District of Columbia.	• Owned by members (rural farmers and communities) • Provide service mostly to members • Incorporated under State law and directed by an elected board of directors which, in turn, selects a manager • The Rural Utilities Service (formerly the Rural Electrification Administration) in the U.S. Department of Agriculture was established under the Rural Electrification Act of 1936 with the purpose of extending credit to co-ops to provide electric service to small rural communities (usually fewer than 1,500 consumers) and farms where it was relatively expensive to provide service
Nonutilities There are 1,934 nonutility power producers in the United States.	• Generate power for their own use and/or for sale in wholesale power markets • Can be subcategorized as qualifying facility (QF) cogenerators, non-QF cogenerators, QF small power producers, exempt wholesale generators, and/or non-QF other. • Also generally referred to as independent power producers
Power Marketers Approximately 400 have filed with FERC.	• Some are utility-affiliated while others are independent • Buy and sell electricity • Do not own or operate generation, transmission, or distribution facilities

Source: Energy Information Administration, Office of Coal, Nuclear, Electric and Alternate Fuels.

Figure 10–2

1. THE PRESENT MIX

The electric industry is made up of six major groups: (1) investor-owned utilities (IOUs); (2) federal agencies that generate, transmit or market power; (3) publicly owned systems, mostly operated by cities and known as "municipals" or "public power;" (4) rural electric cooperatives funded through the Department of Agriculture; (5) independent power producers and (6) power marketers. See Figure 10–2.

a. INVESTOR–OWNED UTILITIES

In 1998 the 239 investor-owned utility (IOU) operating companies dominated the electric power industry, generating some 68 percent of the nation's power. Although referred to as *public* utilities, IOUs are private, shareholder-owned companies ranging in size from small local operations serving a customer base of a few thousand to giant multistate corporations serving millions of customers. The larger IOUs have always been vertically integrated, owning or controlling all the generation, transmission, and distribution facilities required to meet the needs of the customers in their assigned service area, although recent trends suggest that this vertical integration may become less prevalent. See Chapter 13.

IOUs can be found in every State except Nebraska. Their local operations and retail rates are usually highly regulated by State Public Utility Commissions, but their wholesale power sales and power transmission contracts fall under the jurisdiction of the Federal Energy Regulatory Commission (FERC).

Control over IOUs is further concentrated because many of them are actually subsidiaries of utility holding companies. Nearly one-quarter of the IOU operating companies are subsidiaries of registered electric utility holding companies regulated under the Public Utility Holding Company Act of 1935 (PUHCA), 15 U.S.C. § 79, by the Securities and Exchange Commission and FERC. Major utility holding companies include companies such as American Electric Power Co. and Entergy Corp. In addition to the registered holding companies, many other utilities are also part of holding company systems consisting of affiliated utility subsidiaries operating intrastate or in contiguous States and, thus, are exempt from detailed oversight under PUHCA.

b. FEDERAL POWER SYSTEMS

The Federal Government generates electric power at federally owned hydroelectric facilities. It is primarily a wholesaler, marketing its power through five Federal power marketing agencies: 1. Bonneville Power Administration, 2. Western Area Power Administration, 3. Southeastern Power Administration, 4. Southwestern Power Administration, and 5. Alaska Power Administration. Together, Federal systems accounted for just under 8 percent of the nation's power generation in 1998. All Federal power systems are required under existing legislation to give preference in the sale of their output to other public power systems and to rural electric cooperatives.

Federally owned or chartered power systems also include the Tennessee Valley Authority,[6] and facilities operated by the U.S. Army Corps of Engineers, the Bureau of Reclamation, the Bureau of Indian Affairs, and the International Water and Boundary Commission. Jurisdiction over Federal power systems operations and the rates charged to their customers is established in the various authorizing legislation in Title 16 of the U.S. Code.

c.   PUBLIC POWER

The more than 2,000 public power systems include local, municipal, State, and regional public power systems ranging in size from tiny municipal distribution companies to giant systems like the Los Angeles Department of Water and Power. Some states, such as Nebraska and New York, operate electric systems that cover all (in the case of Nebraska) or part of the state. Public power systems generated about 9 percent of the Nation's power in 1998. Many public systems are involved only in retail power distribution; they purchase power supplies from other utilities.

The extent of regulation of public power systems varies among states. In some states the public utility commission exercises jurisdiction in whole or part over operations and rates of publicly owned systems. In other states, public power systems are regulated by local governments or are self-regulated. Municipal systems are usually run by the local city council or an independent board elected by voters or appointed by city officials. Other public power systems are run by public utility districts, irrigation districts, or special state authorities.

d.   RURAL ELECTRIC COOPERATIVES

Electric cooperatives are electric systems owned by their members, each of whom has one vote in the election of a board of directors. The Rural Electrification Act of 1936, 49 Stat. 1363, created the Rural Electrification Administration (REA) to bring electricity to rural areas and subsequently gave it broad lending authority to stimulate rural electricity use. The Act authorizes federal loans at no interest or very low interest to cooperatives for the purpose of "financing the construction and operation of generating plants, electric transmission and distribution lines or systems for the furnishing of electric energy to persons in rural areas who are not receiving central station service." 7 U.S.C. § 904.

In the early 1930s, 9 out of 10 rural homes were without electric service. Today, 99% of rural homes have electricity service. Rural co-ops often act as buying and distribution agents for utility-generated power or for generation and transmission co-ops (G & Ts), which own both generat-

---

6. The Tennessee Valley Authority is an independent government corporation that   sells power within its statutory service area. 16 U.S.C. § 831.

ing and transmission facilities. Early REA borrowers tended to be small cooperatives that purchased wholesale power for distribution to members. Over the past 20 years, however, many expanded into generating and transmission cooperatives in order to lessen their dependence on outside power sources.

Regulatory jurisdiction over cooperatives varies among the States, with some States exercising considerable authority over rates and operations, while other States exempt cooperatives from State regulation. In addition to State regulation, cooperatives with outstanding Federal loans fall under the jurisdiction of the Rural Utilities Service (RUS), successor to REA, which imposes various conditions intended to protect the financial viability of borrowers. *See* 7 U.S.C. § 901 et seq.

e.   INDEPENDENT POWER PRODUCERS

Most independent power producers began operation because of the Public Utility Regulatory Policies Act of 1978 (PURPA), Pub.L. 95–617, 92 Stat. 3117ff., and its requirement that utilities purchase power from certain defined qualifying facilities (QFs). In addition, many state public utility commissions helped the independent power business by persuading utilities to put major generating capacity additions out to bid. Independents often found that they could underbid the traditional utilities, which brought even more independents into the business.

The National Energy Policy Act of 1992, Pub.L. 102–486, 106 Stat. 2776, extended the conditions under which an independent power producer could build and own projects itself without becoming regulated as a public utility. It encouraged the regulated utilities to set up their own unregulated subsidiaries to act as independent builders and operators of generating plants outside the utility's jurisdiction. And it gave FERC greater authority to compel utilities to provide transmission services for wholesale transactions between independent power producers and distant distributing utilities. Such service is known in the trade as "wheeling" and will be discussed in the next Chapter.

f.   POWER MARKETERS

Since the passage of the Energy Policy Act of 1992, many new companies have been created to serve as marketers and brokers of electric power. These companies do not own or operate any electric facilities. They buy and sell electricity on the open market. Some IOUs have created subsidiaries to operate as marketers, but many marketers are independent. Marketers are discussed in Chapter 11.

2.   JURISDICTIONAL ISSUES

The relationship of the investor-owned utilities with the federal agencies, municipals and REA co-ops has had its ups and downs. The cases that follow illustrate some of the issues that pervade the borderline between federal and state regulation of the electric industry.

FPC v. Southern California Edison introduces the relationship of the various segments of the industry. Southern California Edison is a major investor-owned electric utility that generates, transmits, and distributes electricity. The federal government generates power from its hydroelectric facilities, some of which is sold to Edison. The City of Colton is a small municipally-owned facility; like many municipal utilities, it distributes, but does not generate, electricity. This case involves Colton's attempt to obtain federal regulation of the price it had to pay to buy power from Edison. The case involves the interpretation of the key statutory provisions in section 201 of the Federal Power Act, 16 U.S.C. § 824:

> (a) It is declared that the business of transmitting and selling electric energy for ultimate distribution to the public is affected with a public interest, and that Federal regulation of matters relating to generation to the extent provided in [cited sections] and of that part of such business which consists of the transmission of electric energy in interstate commerce and the sale of such energy at wholesale in interstate commerce is necessary in the public interest, such Federal regulation, however, to extend only to those matters which are not subject to regulation by the States.

> (b) (1) The provisions of this Part shall apply to the transmission of electric energy in interstate commerce and to the sale of electric energy at wholesale in interstate commerce, but except as provided in paragraph (2) shall not apply to any other sale of electric energy or deprive a State or State commission of its lawful authority now exercised over the exportation of hydroelectric energy which is transmitted across a State line. The Commission shall have jurisdiction over all facilities for such transmission or sale of electric energy, but shall not have jurisdiction, except as specifically provided in [cited sections], over facilities used for the generation of electric energy or over facilities used in local distribution or only for the transmission of electric energy in intrastate commerce, or over facilities for the transmission of electric energy consumed wholly by the transmitter. . . .

> (d) The term "sale of electric energy at wholesale" when used in this subchapter, means a sale of electric energy to any person for resale.

Federal Power Comm. v. Southern California Edison Co.

376 U.S. 205 (1964).

■ BRENNAN, J.: Petitioner City of Colton, California (Colton), purchases its entire requirements of electric power from respondent Southern California Edison Company (Edison), a California electric utility company which operates in central and southern California and sells energy only to customers located there. Colton applies some of the power purchased to municipal uses, but resells the bulk of it to thousands of residential, commercial, and industrial customers in Colton and its environs. Respondent Public Utilities Commission of California (PUC) had for some years exercised jurisdiction over the Edison–Colton sale, but petitioner Federal Power Commission (FPC), on Colton's petition filed in 1958, asserted jurisdiction under § 201 (b) of the Federal Power Act which extends federal regulatory power to the "sale of electric energy at wholesale in interstate commerce." 16 U.S.C. §§ 791a, 824–824h.

Some of the energy which Edison markets in California originates in Nevada and Arizona. Edison has a contract with the Secretary of the Interior under which, as agent for the United States, it generates energy at the Hoover power plants located in Nevada. This contract allocates to Edison 7% of the total firm generating capacity of Hoover Dam. Edison is also a party to a 1945 contract with the United States and the Metropolitan Water District of Southern California under which it is entitled to a portion of the unused firm energy allocated to the Water District from Hoover Dam. Payment for this energy is made to the United States for the credit of the Water District. Also, Hoover Dam, Davis Dam in Arizona, and Parker Dam in California are interconnected by a transmission line from which Edison has drawn energy by agreement with the Water District.

The FPC found, on the extensive record made before a Hearing Examiner, that out-of-state energy from Hoover Dam was included in the energy delivered by Edison to Colton, and ruled that the "sale to Colton is a sale of electric energy at wholesale in interstate commerce subject to Sections 201, 205 and 206 of the Federal Power Act." 26 F.P.C. 223, 231.

The Court of Appeals did not pass upon the question whether the finding that out-of-state energy reached Colton has support in the record. The court assumed that the finding had such support, but held nevertheless that § 201 (b) did not grant jurisdiction over the rates to the FPC. It ruled that the concluding words of § 201 (a)—"such Federal regulation, however, [is] to extend only to those matters which are not subject to regulation by the States"—confined FPC jurisdiction to those interstate wholesales constitutionally beyond the power of state regulation by force of the Commerce Clause, Art. I, § 8, of the Constitution. Accordingly, it held that the FPC had no jurisdiction because PUC regulation of the Edison–Colton sale was permissible under the Commerce Clause. Because of the importance of the question in the administration of the Federal Power Act we granted the separate petitions for certiorari of the FPC and Colton. 372 U.S. 958. We reverse. We hold that § 201 (b) grants the FPC jurisdiction of all sales of electric energy at wholesale in interstate commerce not expressly exempted by the Act itself, and that the FPC properly asserted jurisdiction of the Edison–Colton sale.

The view of the Court of Appeals was that the limiting language of § 201 (a), read together with the jurisdictional grant in § 201 (b), meant that the FPC could not assert its jurisdiction over a sale which the Commerce Clause allowed a State to regulate. Such a determination of the permissibility of state regulation would require, the Court of Appeals said, an analysis of the impact of state regulation of the sale upon the national interest in commerce. The court held that such an analysis here compelled the conclusion that the FPC lacked jurisdiction, because state regulation of the Edison–Colton sale would not prejudice the interests of any other State. This conclusion was rested upon the view that the interests of Arizona and Nevada, the only States other than California which might claim to be concerned with the Edison–Colton sale, were already given federal protection by the Secretary of the Interior's control of the initial sales of Hoover and Davis energy. Since the first sale was subject to federal regulation, and since the energy subsequently sold by Edison to Colton for resale was to be consumed wholly within California, there was said to be a "complete lack of interest on the part of any other state," and the sale was therefore held to be subject to state regulation and exempt from FPC regulation. 310 F.2d, at 789.

The Court of Appeals expressly rejected the argument that § 201 (b) incorporated a congressional decision against determining the FPC's jurisdiction by such a case-by-case analysis, and in favor of employing a more mechanical test which would bring under federal regulation all sales of electric energy in interstate commerce at wholesale except those specifically exempted, and would exclude all retail sales. In reviewing the court's ruling on this question we do not write on a clean slate. In decisions over the past quarter century we have held that Congress, in enacting the Federal Power Act and the Natural Gas Act, apportioned regulatory power between state and federal governments according to a test which this Court had developed in a series of cases under the Commerce Clause. The Natural Gas Act grew out of the same judicial history as did the part of the Federal Power Act with which we are here concerned; and § 201 (b) of the Power Act has its counterpart in § 1 (b) of the Gas Act, 15 U.S.C. § 717 (b), which became law three years later in 1938.

The test adopted by Congress was developed in a line of decisions, [the last of which] and the one which directly led to congressional intervention, was *Public Utilities Comm'n v. Attleboro Steam & Elec. Co.*, 273 U.S. 83. There the Public Utilities Commission of Rhode Island asserted jurisdiction over the rates at which a Rhode Island company sold energy generated at its Rhode Island plant to a Massachusetts company, which took delivery at the state line for resale to the City of Attleboro. The Court held that the case did not involve "a regulation of the rates charged to local consumers," and that since the sale was of concern to both Rhode Island and Massachusetts it was "national in character." Consequently, "if such regulation is required it can only be attained by the exercise of the power vested in Congress." 273 U.S., at 89–90.

Congress undertook federal regulation through the Federal Power Act in 1935 and the Natural Gas Act in 1938. The premise was that constitutional limitations upon state regulatory power made federal regulation essential if major aspects of interstate transmission and sale were not to go unregulated. *Attleboro*, with the other cases cited, figured prominently in the debates and congressional reports. In *Illinois Natural Gas Co. v. Central Illinois Public Service Co.*, 314 U.S. 498, we were first required to determine the scope of the federal power which Congress had asserted to meet the problem revealed by Attleboro and the other cases. The specific question in that case was whether a company selling interstate gas at wholesale to distributors for resale in a single State could be required by that State's regulatory commission to extend its facilities and connect them with those of a local distributor, or whether such extensions were exclusively a matter for the FPC. The Court noted that prior to the Natural Gas Act there had been another line of cases which adopted a more flexible approach to state power under the Commerce Clause; these cases had been "less concerned to find a point in time and space where the interstate commerce in gas ends and intrastate commerce begins, and [have] looked to the nature of the state regulation involved, the objective of the state, and the effect of the regulation upon the national interest in the commerce." 314 U.S., at 505. But the Court held that Congress, rather than adopting this flexible approach, which was applied by the Court of Appeals in the instant case, "undertook to regulate ... without the necessity, where Congress has not acted, of drawing the precise line between state and federal power by the litigation of particular cases." *Id.*, at 506–507. What Congress did was to adopt the test developed in the Attleboro line which denied state power to regulate a sale "at wholesale to local distributing companies" and allowed state regulation of a sale at "local retail rates to ultimate consumers." 314 U.S., at 504.

In short, our decisions have squarely rejected the view of the Court of Appeals that the scope of FPC jurisdiction over interstate sales of gas or electricity at wholesale is to be determined by a case-by-case analysis of the impact of state regulation upon the national interest. Rather, Congress meant to draw a bright line easily ascertained, between state and federal jurisdiction, making unnecessary such case-by-case analysis. This was done in the Power Act by making FPC jurisdiction plenary and extending it to all wholesale sales in interstate commerce except those which Congress has made explicitly subject to regulation by the States. There is no such exception covering the Edison–Colton sale.... [The Court also rejected the argument that Congress had exempted sales of Hoover Dam Power from FPC jurisdiction.]■

NOTES AND COMMENTS

1. The terms "wholesale" and "retail" are important words of art in energy law. The rule in the Colton case still remains in effect under the Federal Power Act. A wholesale transaction is one between two entities who are not the ultimate users of the electricity. A retail sale is a sale directly to an end user. Wholesale sales are regulated by the Federal Energy Regulatory Commission (the successor to the FPC, *See* Chapter 4) while retail sales are regulated by the state in which the transfer occurs.

2. The other qualifier that limits federal jurisdiction is that the sale must be in interstate commerce. When power is generated by a source that does not also own transmission lines, or by a source that owns transmission lines but these lines do not reach the geographic area in which customers

are located, it is necessary for the distribution utility to interconnect its lines with the source. In addition, as Breyer and MacAvoy note, it is common for adjacent utilities which own transmission lines to interconnect in order to coordinate power generation and distribution.

In *FPC v. Florida Power & Light Co.*, 404 U.S. 453 (1972), the Supreme Court allowed the FPC to exercise jurisdiction over power sold by Florida Power & Light (FP&L), the major investor-owned utility serving South Florida. All of FP&L's generation and transmission facilities were located within the state of Florida and none of its facilities connected directly with out-of-state utilities, customers or power sources. Nevertheless, FPC contended that electrons generated by FP&L reached the interstate market in Georgia since FP&L's transmission lines were connected with those of another Florida utility, Florida Power Corporation (Corp) which in turn connected with Georgia Power Company.

The Court addressed what would determine FPC jurisdiction over the interstate transmission of electricity:

> ... The FPC may exercise jurisdiction only if there is substantial evidentiary support for the Commission's conclusion that FP&L power has reached Georgia via Corp or that Georgia's power has reached FP&L because of exchanges with Corp. What happens when FP&L gives power to Corp and Corp gives power to Georgia (or vice versa)? Is FP&L power commingled with Corp's own supply, and thus passed on with that supply, as the Commission contends? Or is it diverted to handle Corp's independent power needs, displacing a like amount of Corp power that is then passed on, as respondent argues? Or, as the Commission also contends, do changes in FP&L's load or generation, or that of others in the interconnected system, stimulate a reaction up and down the line by a signal or chain reaction that is, in essence electricity moving in interstate commerce?

Federal jurisdiction clearly would have been present if FP&L directly exchanged power with Georgia. Jurisdiction would have also been present, the Court held, if Corp, the intermediate utility, "could be shown to be sometimes no more than a funnel." Even though neither of these circumstances was true in this case, the Court held that FP&L's power was commingled with Corp power and exported across the Georgia line. As the Court observed, "the elusive nature of electrons renders experimental evidence that might draw the fine distinctions in this case practically unobtainable." The Court upheld FPC's assertion of jurisdiction. (*See also* the *Fairfax County Water Authority* case in Chapter 4).

3.   Utilities from the State of Texas have exempted themselves from much federal regulation by avoiding the shipment of power across state lines. Many of their activities, however, are regulated by the Electric Reliability Council of Texas (ERCOT). In 1996 the Texas Public Utilities Commission established ERCOT as an Independent System Operator (ISO) that is separate from, and largely independent of, the utilities that own the transmission network. The reconstituted ERCOT board will establish policies for operating the transmission network on a nondiscriminatory basis

for all power producers and users. The ERCOT board of directors has representatives from the IOUs, public power entities, coops, independent power producers and power marketers. See Guide to Electric Power in Texas, *supra.*

The following case, FPC v. Conway Corp., examines the scope of federal ratemaking authority and introduces the tensions between IOUs and smaller municipal and co-op systems that do not generate power. Although these municipals and co-ops tend to be small in relation to the typical IOU, they have always exerted considerable influence in the making of energy policy by congress and the executive branch through the American Public Power Association. See www.appanet.org.

Federal Power Commission v. Conway Corp.

426 U.S. 271 (1976).

■ WHITE, J.: The question in this case is this: When a power company that sells electricity at both wholesale and retail seeks to raise its wholesale rates, does the Federal Power Commission (Commission) have jurisdiction to consider the allegations of the company's wholesale customers that the proposed wholesale rates, which are within the Commission's jurisdiction, are discriminatory and noncompetitive when considered in relation to the company's retail rates, which are not within the jurisdiction of the Commission? We hold that it does.

Arkansas Power & Light Co. (Company) is a public utility engaged in the sale of electric energy at wholesale in interstate commerce under the meaning of § 201 of the Federal Power Act, 16 U.S.C. § 824. Its wholesale rates are thus within reach of the Commission's powers under § 206(a) of the Act to establish rates which are just, reasonable, and nondiscriminatory. 16 U.S.C. § 824e(a). The Company also sells at retail and seeks industrial sales in competition with some of its wholesale customers. These wholesale customers include the seven municipally owned electric systems and the two electric power cooperatives which are respondents here. Each of these respondents (Customers) operates in the State of Arkansas and each borders on or is surrounded by the territory served by the Company.

In June 1973, the Company filed with the Commission a wholesale rate increase pursuant to § 205(d). The Customers sought to intervene before the Commission, urging that the rate increase be rejected. Among other grounds, it was asserted that the Customers and the Company were in competition for industrial retail accounts and that the rate increase was "an attempt to squeeze [the Customers] or some of them out of competition and to make them more susceptible to the persistent attempts of the company to take over the public[ly] owned systems in the State." It was alleged that the proposed wholesale rates would make it "impossible for the [Customers] to sell power to an industrial load of any size at a competitive price with [the Company], since, in many cases, the revenues therefrom would not even cover the incremental power costs to [the Customers]." It was also asserted that the rate filing was "plainly discriminatory against the single class of customer which [the Company] has historically attempted to drive out of business, without justification on any ordinary cost of service basis...."

The Company opposed the petition. The Commission permitted the Customers to intervene but ruled that it would "limit Customers' participation in this proceeding to matters other than the alleged anti-competitive activities" because the Customers had failed to demonstrate that the relief sought was "within this Commission's authority to direct." The Commission also denied the Customers' amended petition to intervene, again refusing to consider the tendered anticompetitive and discrimination issues. Inasmuch as the Commission's authority is limited to wholesale rates and does not reach sales at retail, the Commission's opinion was that "the relief sought by [the Customers] is beyond the authority granted to us under the Federal Power Act."

Section 201(b) of the Act, 16 U.S.C. § 824(b), confers jurisdiction on the Commission with respect to the sale of electric energy at wholesale in interstate commerce. The prohibition against discriminatory or preferential rates or services imposed by § 205(b) and the Commission's power to set just and reasonable rates under § 206(a) are accordingly limited to sales "subject to the jurisdiction of the Commission," that is, to sales of electric energy at wholesale. The Commission has no power to prescribe the rates for retail sales of power companies. Nor, accordingly, would it have power to remedy an alleged discriminatory or anticompetitive relationship between wholesale and retail rates by ordering the company to increase its retail rates.

As the Commission is at great pains to establish, this is the proper construction of the Act, the legislative history of § 205 indicating that the section was expressly limited to jurisdictional sales to foreclose the possibility that the Commission would seek to correct an alleged discriminatory relationship between wholesale and retail rates by raising or otherwise regulating the nonjurisdictional, retail price. Insofar as we are advised, no party to this case contends otherwise.

Building on this history, the Commission makes a skillful argument that it may neither consider nor remedy any alleged discrimination resting on a difference between jurisdictional and nonjurisdictional rates. But the argument, in the end, is untenable. Section 205(b) forbids the maintenance of any "unreasonable difference in rates" or service "with respect to any ... sale subject to the jurisdiction of the Commission." A jurisdictional sale is necessarily implied in any charge that the difference between wholesale and retail rates is unreasonable or anticompetitive. If the undue preference or discrimination is in any way traceable to the level of the jurisdictional rate, it is plain enough that the section would to that extent apply; and to that extent the Commission would have power to effect a remedy under § 206 by an appropriate order directed to the jurisdictional rate. This was the view of the Court of Appeals, and we agree with it.

The Commission appears to insist that a just and reasonable wholesale rate can never be a contributing factor to an undue discrimination: Once the jurisdictional rate is determined to be just and reasonable, inquiry into discrimination is irrelevant for § 206 (a) purposes, for if the discrimination continues to exist, it is traceable wholly to the nonjurisdictional, retail rate. This argument assumes, however, that ratemaking is an exact science and that there is only one level at which a wholesale rate can be said to be just and reasonable and that any attempt to remedy a discrimination by lowering the jurisdictional rate would always result in an unjustly low rate that would fail to recover fully allocated wholesale costs. As the Court of Appeals pointed out and as this Court has held, however, there is no single cost-recovering rate, but a zone of reasonableness: "Statutory reasonableness is an abstract quality represented by an area rather than a pinpoint. It allows a substantial spread between what is unreasonable because too low and what is unreasonable because too high." *Montana-Dakota Util. Co. v. Northwestern Pub. Serv. Co.*, 341 U.S. 246, 251 (1951). The Commission itself explained the matter in *In re Otter Tail Power Co.*, 2 F.P.C. 134, 149 (1940):

> It occurs to us that one rate in its relation to another rate may be discriminatory, although each rate per se, if considered independently, might fall within the zone of reasonableness. There is considerable latitude within the zone of reasonableness insofar as the level of a particular rate is concerned. The relationship of rates within such a zone, however, may result in an undue advantage in favor of one rate and be discriminatory insofar as another rate is concerned. When such a situation exists, the discrimination found to exist must be removed.

The Commission thus cannot so easily satisfy its obligation to eliminate unreasonable discriminations or put aside its duty to consider whether a proposed rate will have anticompetitive effects. The exercise by the Commission of powers otherwise within its jurisdiction "clearly carries with it the responsibility to consider, in appropriate circumstances, the anticompetitive effects of regulated aspects of interstate utility operations pursuant to ... directives contained in §§ 205, 206...." *Gulf States Util. Co. v. FPC*, 411 U.S. 747, 758–759 (1973). The Commission must arrive at a rate level deemed by it to be just and reasonable, but in doing so it must consider the tendered allegations that the proposed rates are discriminatory and anticompetitive in effect.

We think the Court of Appeals was quite correct in concluding:

> When costs are fully allocated, both the retail rate and the proposed wholesale rate may fall within a zone of reasonableness, yet create a price squeeze between themselves. There would, at the very least, be latitude in the FPC to put wholesale rates in the lower range of the zone of reasonableness, without concern that overall results would be impaired, in view of the utility's own decision to depress certain retail revenues in order to curb the retail competition of its wholesale customers.

510 F. 2d, at 1274. Because the Commission had raised a jurisdictional barrier and refused to consider or hear evidence concerning the Customers' allegations, the Court of Appeals could not determine whether a wholesale

rate, if set low enough partially or wholly to abolish any discriminatory effects found to exist, would fail to recover wholesale costs. The case was therefore remanded to the Commission for further proceedings.

We agree with this disposition. It does not invade a nonjurisdictional area. The remedy, if any, would operate only against the rate for jurisdictional sales. Whether that rate would be affected at all would involve, as the Court of Appeals indicated, an examination of the entire "factual context in which the proposed wholesale rate will function." *Id.*, at 52, 510 F. 2d, at 1273. These facts will naturally include those related to nonjurisdictional transactions, but consideration of such facts would appear to be an everyday affair. As the Commission concedes, in determining whether the proposed wholesale rates are just and reasonable, it would in any event be necessary to determine which of the Company's costs are allocable to its nonjurisdictional, retail sales and which to its jurisdictional, wholesale sales—this in order to insure that the wholesale rate is paying its way, but no more. . . .

Furthermore, § 206(a) provides that whenever the Commission finds that any rate, charge, or classification, demanded, observed, charged, or collected by any public utility for any transmission or sale subject to the jurisdiction of the Commission, or that any rule, regulation, practice, or contract affecting such rate, charge, or classification is unjust, unreasonable, unduly discriminatory or preferential, the Commission shall determine the just and reasonable rate, charge, classification, rule, regulation, practice, or contract to be thereafter observed and in force, and shall fix the same by order.

The rules, practices, or contracts "affecting" the jurisdictional rate are not themselves limited to the jurisdictional context. In [*Panhandle Co. v. FPC*, 324 U.S. 635, 646 (1945),] decided under the almost identical provision of the Natural Gas Act, 15 U.S.C. § 717d(a), the Court emphasized the same aspect of the section, and went on to hold that because it was "clear" that a gas company's "contracts covering direct industrial sales" are contracts "affecting" jurisdictional rates, [t]he Commission, while it lacks authority to fix rates for direct industrial sales, may take those rates into consideration when it fixes the rates for interstate wholesale sales which are subject to its jurisdiction.■

NOTES AND COMMENTS

1. When one utility tries to pick off the best customers of another utility it is commonly referred to in the trade as "cherry-picking." The *Conway* case made it quite difficult for IOUs to pick off the best customers of the municipals by offering lower rates because the IOUs might be forced to offer the same rates to the municipal itself.

2. Municipal utilities sometimes get into conflicts with rural cooperatives as well as with investor-owned utilities. For example, if a city served by a municipal utility expands into an area formerly served by a rural cooperative, state statutes may authorize the municipal utility to use the eminent

domain power to acquire the existing facilities of the co-op that are located in the expansion area. This can give rise to difficult issues of valuation of the acquired facilities and the measurement of the damages incurred by the co-op. *See, e.g., City of Stilwell v. Ozarks Rural Electric Cooperative Corp.,* 166 F.3d 1064 (10th Cir.1999).

3. REGULATION AND CONTRACT

Wholesale electricity rates are determined in two different ways: 1) by contracts between utilities, or between utilities and customer; or 2) by the regulatory provisions of the Federal Power Act. Traditionally, energy companies have relied heavily on long-term contracts. Financial institutions often insisted on such contracts as a condition for financing major capital facilities.

The United States Supreme Court has held that wholesale rates arrived at by contract are presumed to reflect fair bargaining. Therefore, under the Court's so-called "Mobile–Sierra doctrine," FERC cannot change a rate set by contract unless it first finds that the contract rate is "unjust, unreasonable, unduly discriminatory or preferential." *See United Gas Pipe Line v. Mobile Gas Serv. Corp.,* 350 U.S. 332 (1956) and *FPC v. Sierra Pacific Power Co.,* 350 U.S. 348 (1956). The Mobile–Sierra doctrine applies to both the gas and electric side of FERC's operations.[7]

Today, electric utilities are less likely to prefer long term contracts than they were in earlier times. The volatility of energy prices that began in the mid–1970s meant that many electric utilities, like the natural gas utilities, found themselves stuck with long-term contracts that had been entered into under much different market conditions. The *Mobile-Sierra* doctrine made it difficult to modify or terminate these contracts. The following case addresses the application of this doctrine in the context of a contract between two electric utilities.

San Diego Elec. & Gas Co. v. Federal Energy Regulatory Comm.

904 F.2d 727 (D.C.Cir.1990).

■ WILLIAMS, J.: This dispute arises out of the lurching energy prices of the past two decades. An energy purchase contract that looked good for both parties on the date signed (November 4, 1985) soon afterwards looked

---

7. Today, wholesale contracts may specify that they are subject to FERC regulation. For example, in *Union Pacific Fuels v. FERC,* 129 F.3d 157 (D.C.Cir.1997) the court upheld FERC's power to change the rate for transportation on the Kern River gas pipeline from modified fixed/variable to straight fixed/variable in response to the industry-wide shift mandated by Order 636. The Court held that where the contract between the shippers and the pipeline contained a clause specifying that rates were subject to FERC regulation, the Mobile–Sierra doctrine allowed regulatory rate revisions initiated by FERC even though the contract also contained a clause by which the parties agreed not to initiate any such changes themselves.

dismal to the buyer. The Federal Energy Regulatory Commission declined to lower the price, but at the same time declined to relieve the seller from a delay of the effective date stemming from what may seem a technical default. We affirm the Commission against attack by both sides.

The contract obligates San Diego Gas & Electric Company to buy 100 megawatts of generating capacity and associated energy from Public Service Company of New Mexico for a 13–year period starting May 1, 1988. At the time it was entered into, the seller was awash in excess generating capacity and the state Public Service Commission had ordered the unnecessary capacity excluded from its retail rate base. Worse still, more unwanted capacity loomed from New Mexico's interest in a nuclear generating station whose three reactors would start up over the next two years. San Diego needed more capacity and wanted to diversify its mix of power sources by securing entitlements to power from coal and nuclear plants. The price offered by New Mexico was the most favorable available to San Diego and was in line with then prevailing market prices.

November 1985 proved, however, to be something of a crest in the wave of energy prices. Oil prices fell from nearly $30 a barrel in November 1985 to $12 in March 1986. J.A. 208. The plunge triggered a drop in the bulk electric power market as well. As oil is used to produce electricity, a fall in its price (and that of close substitutes such as natural gas, whose price is directly affected by that of oil) drives power production costs down; variable costs fall and electricity producers are able to shift away from relatively capital-intensive nuclear and coal sources.... New contracts in 1988 evidently called for much lower prices—with demand charges (the charge for the purchasing utility's entitlement to take electricity) about half or one-third that specified in the contract.

Under § 205 of the Federal Power Act, 16 U.S.C. § 824d (1988), New Mexico could not collect rates under the contract until it had been accepted for filing with the Commission. When New Mexico filed, San Diego tried to persuade FERC to reject the contract as unjust and unreasonable, but the Commission refused. On the other hand, it also refused New Mexico a waiver that proved necessary if New Mexico was to be able to collect the demand charge starting on the date provided by contract, May 1, 1988. As a result of the refusal New Mexico was unable to collect the $3.3 million contract demand charge accrued from May 1 to June 13. Both parties appeal....

San Diego claims that the Commission did not give enough weight to market changes between the execution of the agreement and the time for its performance. These changes were so great, it argues, as to require that the Commission set the contracts aside under its statutory obligation to ensure that interstate wholesale power rates are just and reasonable. *See* Federal Power Act § 205, 16 U.S.C. § 824d.

In fact the Commission was far from blind to the prevailing market conditions:

Given our statutory obligation to judge the justness and reasonableness of the rate in the Agreement, we are required to explore [San Diego's arguments]. The freedom of the parties to contract in this instance must yield to the Commission's duty to ascertain the justness and reasonableness of the rates.

Order, 43 FERC at 62,153. Against this it placed great weight on the policy considerations behind contract stability:

The certainty and stability which stems from contract performance and enforcement is essential to an orderly bulk power market. If the integrity of contracts is undermined, business would be transacted without legally enforceable assurances and we believe that the market, the industry and ultimately the consumer would suffer.

Id.

This has long been the Commission's position.... Indeed, the Supreme Court has insisted on great Commission deference to freely arrived at contract prices. *See United Gas Pipe Line Co. v. Mobile Gas Service Corp.*, 350 U.S. 332 (1956); *FPC v. Sierra Pacific Power Co.*, 350 U.S. 348 (1956).

As the Commission recognized, the purpose of this contract was to allocate the risk of market price changes between the parties:

The volatility of oil and gas prices, often reflecting large and dramatic swings, is old news. Indeed, this is the very reason that San Diego pursued a long-term purchase from [New Mexico] at rates reflecting [New Mexico's] nuclear and coal units.

Order, 43 FERC at 62,153.

San Diego wanted to diversify its mix of power sources, so to reduce the risk from further surges in the cost of oil and gas. J.A. 256. But each source carries its own set of risks. That is an inevitable part of energy production in a world where sources are varied and their relative prices subject to constant change. Scanning all the sources to which it had access, San Diego selected what it viewed as the optimal mix. On the other side, the contract gave New Mexico partial protection from the risk it had taken in investing heavily in precisely the sources that San Diego (in 1985) felt it needed. San Diego's current conclusion that it got the mix wrong is no reason to allow it to shift the risk (now the loss) back to New Mexico.

We note that New Mexico is no great winner either. The capital-intensive coal and nuclear plants to which it committed itself cannot generate the once-expected revenues. Nothing suggests that New Mexico is a more efficient bearer of the risks that the literal terms of the contract shifted to San Diego. Indeed, San Diego's participation in the 1985 contract as part of a systematic, deliberate program of diversifying risks would seem to mark it as an efficient risk bearer. See Richard A. Posner and Andrew M. Rosenfield, Impossibility and Related Doctrines in Contract Law: An Economic Analysis, 6 J. Legal Stud. 83, 91–92 (1977) (promisor's inferior ability to diversify risks may make it less efficient risk bearer and justify its discharge).

San Diego invokes our decision in *Associated Gas Distributors v. FERC,* 824 F.2d 981 (D.C.Cir.1987), where this court required FERC to proffer adequately "reasoned decisionmaking" for its decision not to use § 5 of the Natural Gas Act, 15 U.S.C. § 717d (1988), to relieve pipelines of enormous take-or-pay liabilities under contracts that had become uneconomic. But the root of that decision was the Commission's failure to face directly the effects of its own decision, Order No. 436, restructuring the gas pipeline industry and for the first time subjecting pipelines as gas-sellers to competition from gas sold by others but transported by the pipelines themselves.... Our ultimate conclusion was that on remand the Commission "must more convincingly address the magnitude of the problem and the adverse consequences likely to result from the nondiscriminatory access and CD adjustment conditions [i.e., the Commission's own regulatory interventions]." *Id.* at 1044. And, although asking for more reasoned decisionmaking, we acknowledged that even in the context of risks that the Commission itself had severely exacerbated, FERC's pro-contract policy arguments were "powerful and well grounded in the statutes it is authorized to enforce." *Id.* at 1027. San Diego here offers nothing remotely comparable to the AGD petitioners' plea for regulatory relief; the Commission's reasoning amply served the case at hand.

The petitions for review are Denied.■

NOTES AND COMMENTS

1.   As the above case illustrates, the oil shocks of the 1970s and 1980s had a significant impact on the electricity industry. Many utilities saw the rising fuel prices of the 1970s and early 1980s as a signal to increase their investment in nuclear power. When fuel prices fell in the mid 1980s, that signal changed, but many utilities thought they were too far down the nuclear road to respond. *See* Chapter 14.

2.   In an earlier case, *Metropolitan Edison Co. v. FERC,* 595 F.2d 851 (D.C.Cir.1979) the court considered a contract entered into in the year 1906 by which an IOU agreed to provide electricity to the Borough of Middletown, Pennsylvania, for one cent per kilowatt-hour until such time as the Borough chose to terminate the contract. The court upheld FERC's determination that the contract was not subject to revision under the Mobile–Sierra doctrine despite the fact that the price was far below current market rates. The court found that the overall impact of the contract on the utility's revenues was minimal. See also *Potomac Electric Power Company v. FERC*, 210 F.3d 403 (D.C.Cir.2000) (rate disparities alone do not justify abrogation of conduct).

3.   As this case indicates, the courts tended to read the Natural Gas Act and the Federal Power Act *in pari materia.*

C.   EXTERNALITIES OF ELECTRICITY

Traditional rate regulation of electricity generation and transmission has, in recent years, been subject to criticism for not reflecting the full social costs of power production and delivery. These activities create externalities in two distinct respects: 1) they may impose costs on adjacent or nearby users by emitting pollutants, influencing property prices, or creating risks; and 2) they may fail to fully reflect the actual costs of the fuel inputs utilized for production, leading to overuse—and potential depletion—of certain energy inputs. In recent years, the generation and transmission of electricity has been subject to environmental regulation designed to internalize the full costs of production and delivery.

1. GENERATION EXTERNALITIES

Electricity generation has a greater impact on air quality than any other single industry in the U.S. (other than the transportation sector, which is discussed in Chapter 15). Electricity generation accounts for approximately 75% of U.S. sulfur dioxide (SO2) emissions. Local SO2 emissions are associated with respiratory health problems and regional SO2 emissions contribute to reduced visibility and acidic rainfall. Utility plants also emit significant quantities of toxic organics and metals such as mercury, cadmium, selenium, lead, arsenic, and beryllium.

The environmental impact of electricity is considered at a number of separate places in this book. The impact of coal-burning power plants on air quality was discussed in Chapter 5. Externalities created by nuclear generation are addressed in Chapter 14. Utilities also account for about a third of man-made greenhouse gas (CO2) emissions in the United States, a subject discussed in Chapter 17. The impact of hydro-electric generation on wildlife habitat and commercial fishing was discussed in Chapter 4. And the environmental impact of windpower was discussed in Chapter 2.

2. TRANSMISSION EXTERNALITIES

When the United States was founded, energy was highly immobile. If you wanted to build a factory, you built it at the specific site along the river where you could build a dam that would give you the water power to turn a mill.

The discovery of the steam engine provided more mobility. Coal and then oil could be brought to the site of the factory, though not without considerable expense. Over time, the technologies for shipping fossil fuels have reduced the cost of transportation. Safety and environmental impact, however, are problems that continue to plague such shipments. (*See* the discussion of transportation of oil by tanker in Chapter 6.)

During the last century, the ability to transmit electric current through wires at high voltage has made it possible to interconnect most of the nation's electric systems. Continuing improvements in the technology have steadily reduced the cost of long distance electric transmission. The ability to transmit energy over long distances at relatively modest cost has enhanced even further the mobility of industries, office complexes and residential communities. This dispersal of new development throughout the nation has had a major impact on American society.

In recent years, however, concern has been rising about the possibility that electric transmission lines have adverse health impacts. Biologists have discovered that proximity to certain types of electric current can cause changes in the formation of cells for reasons that no one can easily explain. This led to some initial studies that appeared to find "clusters" of cancer in a few areas near high-power lines, and these studies were widely reported in the media. The public fear of the electromagnetic field (EMF) created by high-voltage lines is a serious problem for the industry.

A number of scientific organizations have undertaken extensive studies of the EMF issue. A committee of the American Physical Society found no evidence that the electromagnetic fields that radiate from power lines cause cancer. The strength of magnetic fields is measured in "gauss". Magnetic fields radiating from power lines and appliances are measured in milligauss (thousandths of a gauss). A nearby powerline can radiate fields of 5 to 40 milligauss. By contrast, home appliances at a distance of one foot radiate fields from about 1 to 280 milligauss—the highest figure for an electric can opener. Council of the American Physical Society, Power Line Fields and Public Health, Public Statement issued April 22, 1995.

The National Research Council ("NRC") published a report in 1997 entitled "The Possible Health Effects of Exposure to Residential Electric and Magnetic Fields." In this report, the NRC concluded that the "current body of evidence does not show that exposure to these fields presents a human health hazard." The NRC found no conclusive and consistent evidence linking exposure to EMF's with cancer, adverse neurobehavioral effects, and reproductive and developmental effects. *See* Patsy W. Thomley, EMF at Home: The National Research Council Report on the Health Effects of Electric and Magnetic Fields, 13 J. Land Use & Envtl. L. 309 (1998).

Then, in June 1998, another expert panel came to a different conclusion. A panel of experts from the National Institute of Environmental Health Studies (NIEHS) recommended that low frequency EMF radiation be classified as "possibly carcinogenic" based on some potential correlation with incidence of childhood leukemia. Working Group Report, Assessment of Health Effects from Exposure to Powerline Frequency Electric and Magnetic Fields (Christopher Portier and Mary Wolfe, eds., 1998).

Legally, the EMF issue tends to arise in two different contexts. First, it arises when utilities seek to condemn land for a transmission line right of way. If landowners near the right of way claim that their property values have been reduced because of the public fear of EMF, should they be entitled to compensation even if the fear is unreasonable? For example, if an electric utility takes part of your land for a right-of-way, but leaves your home in usable condition, but you claim that the value of the home has been reduced because of the public's unwillingness to live near high-voltage lines, do you have to prove that the public's fear is a reasonable one? State courts have split on this issue. A minority view holds that damages caused by the public's fear are never compensable. An intermediate view holds that damages caused by the public's reasonable fear may be compensable.

The majority view holds that damages caused by the public's fear are always compensable. *See* Comment, The Power Line Dilemma: Compensation for Diminished Property Value Caused by Fear of Electromagnetic Fields, 24 Fla. St. U. L. Rev. 125 (1996); David R. Bolton & Kent A. Sick, Power Lines and Property Values: The Good, the Bad, and the Ugly, 31 Urb. Lawyer 331 (1999).[8]

A second and potentially even more serious problem for utilities is the possibility of damage awards based on theories of personal injury. Numerous personal injury suits have been filed against electric utilities, but few have been successful. EMF personal injury lawsuits generally allege that EMF exposure has caused various forms of cancer, although a few cases have alleged that EMF causes birth defects and other illnesses. The personal injury claims are toxic torts cases based on the theory that an EMF can be toxic. Exposure to ionizing EMF radiation can clearly be toxic, but the controversy in EMF litigation is over whether non-ionizing radiation produced by high-voltage lines is also toxic. Michael C. Anibogu, The Future of Electromagnetic Field Litigation, 15 Pace Envtl. L. Rev. 527 (1998).

In order to support their position, plaintiffs must be able to offer evidence that will pass the standard adopted by the Supreme Court in *Daubert v. Merrell Dow Pharmaceuticals*, 509 U.S. 579 (1993). Under *Daubert*, a trier of fact must consider several factors when determining the validity of scientific evidence: whether the evidence has been or can be tested; if the evidence has been subjected to peer review and publication; the potential or known rate of error; and whether there is general acceptance in the relevant scientific community. Plaintiffs have had difficulty finding expert EMF testimony that meets this standard. *See Indiana Michigan Power Co. v. Runge*, 717 N.E.2d 216 (Ind.App.1999);.

Most of the EMF personal injury claims to date have been negligence-based, with the plaintiff alleging a duty to warn of EMF health risks and/or a duty to take steps to mitigate such risks. Other lawsuits have raised strict product liability claims, emotional distress claims, and a variety of other claims. For example, in *Zuidema v. San Diego Gas & Electric Company*, the plaintiff, Mallory Zuidema, contracted a rare childhood kidney cancer known as Wilm's Tumor. The plaintiff alleged that SDG & E was negligent in failing to warn the Zuidemas of health risks attributable to EMF from power lines adjacent to the Zuidema home, and that but for SDG & E's alleged negligence the Zuidemas would have moved and Mallory would not have developed cancer. After four hours of deliberation, the jury returned a defense verdict on all counts. No appeal was filed. ABA Section of Public

---

8. Resistance to the construction of high-voltage lines may also arise from sources unrelated to EMF, including environmental agencies (*See* the *Florida Power* case discussed in Chapter Two) and neighbors who may think the new power lines will be taking away "their" power to benefit people elsewhere. *See* Robert Wasserstrom et. al., Against the Odds: Building new power lines in a deregulated world, Electric Light & Power, June, 1999.

Utility, Communications and Transportation Law, 1996 Annual Report, p.201.

Electric utilities have often argued that tort claims based on EMF are within the primary jurisdiction of the state's public service commission. The California Supreme Court agreed with this argument in *San Diego Gas & Electric Co. v. Covalt*, 920 P.2d 669 (Cal.1996). For a critique of the *Covalt* opinion *see* Paul Lacourciere, Environmental Takings and the California Public Utilities Commission: the *Covalt* Decision, 5 West by Northwest 115 (1998). An Indiana court came to the opposite conclusion. *Indiana Michigan Power Co. v. Runge*, 717 N.E.2d 216 (Ind.App.1999);.

Although EMF tort claims have floundered for the most part, the NIEHS report may provide plaintiffs' attorneys with support for continued pursuit of these claims, at least in childhood leukemia cases. Electric utilities have spent large sums on research, education programs, design changes, and litigation fees, which they recover from consumers through increased rates. *See* Lisa M. Bogardus, Recovery and Allocation of Electromagnetic Field Mitigation Costs in Electric Utility Rates, 62 Fordham L. Rev. 1705 (1994). A conclusive scientific determination of the health effects of EMF would save ratepayers a great deal of money, if it were favorable, or might dramatically reshape the industry, if it were not.

D.   ENERGY CONSERVATION

Most of our fossil fuel reserves began to form over 500 million years ago, when the earth's oxygen content was too low to sustain mass fires and plant foliage was added layer by layer to the earth's surface. Since then, many areas with significant plant life have sustained mass fires on a regular basis and fossil fuel build-up has slowed to a snail's pace, while demand for fossil fuel has increased drastically—particularly in the last 300 years. On current estimates of supply and demand, the U.S. will exhaust most of its supply of petroleum and natural gas by the year 2050. While there will likely be adequate coal reserves to meet energy demand for several subsequent generations, wide-spread usage of coal is not without its impact on land and the environment (See Chapter 5).

Does the traditional system of ratemaking encourage electric utilities to invest more capital in generating facilities than is economically efficient, environmentally sound and socially desirable? Does traditional ratemaking push utilities to sell more electricity at a time when national policy suggests that the conservation of electricity is a more appropriate goal? Has the traditional pricing of fossil fuels encouraged over-consumption of these precious resources?

These questions have had a major impact on electric industry regulation in recent years. In particular, four regulatory mechanisms[9] have raised

---

9.   In many states, various combinations of, and variations on, these four regulatory mechanisms are used. There is a great deal of variation among the states, and the examples given in this book are illustrative only.

significant issues regarding the conservation of fossil fuels and usage of new fuel sources: 1) demand-side management (DSM): incentives designed to reduce the demand for electricity, especially during peak periods; 2) cogeneration: the use of a single power source to generate heat and power; 3) integrated resource planning (IRP): programs which consider demand and supply options prior to approving utility expansions; and 4) renewable portfolio standards: incentives for utilities and other power generators to utilize renewable sources rather than fossil fuels.

1. DEMAND-SIDE MANAGEMENT

Electric utility companies have promoted the use of electricity since the days of Thomas Edison and Samuel Insull. Traditional ratemaking methodologies have created an incentive for companies to exceed their own estimates for electricity sales each year because any such increase in sales directly improves that year's profits. And like most business people, utility executives like to believe they are producing a product that is of value to society.

During the 1960s, the electric utilities were being criticized for failing to provide adequate, reliable service. They naturally responded by significantly increasing the construction of new generating plants and other facilities. In the 1970s it came as a shock to the electric industry, therefore, when organized groups of ratepayers, such as major industrial users, began to complain that the utilities' emphasis on growth was driving up rates unnecessarily. If the utilities taught their customers to use electricity more efficiently, they argued, it would not be necessary to add so many expensive new power plants.

The ratepayers were supported in this argument by environmental groups that saw new nuclear power plants as too dangerous and new coal-fired plants as too dirty. When events in the Middle East brought home the possibility that our supply of imported petroleum might be at risk, the combination of these factors created strong pressures on the electric industry to consider ways by which the use of electricity could be conserved.

Today, most electric utilities have at least some programs designed to encourage their customers to either (1) reduce total electricity usage, or (2) reduce usage at peak hours. For example, Houston Lighting and Power Company works with home builders to encourage tighter, better insulated construction that will reduce the amount of electricity needed for both heating and air conditioning. It also offers incentives to air conditioning users who agree to cycle their air conditioning units on and off during periods of peak electricity demand.

The extent to which the electric utilities employ serious efforts toward these so-called "demand-side management" (DSM) programs varies with the corporate culture of each company. The incongruity of using electric utilities to "anti-sell" their own product may be compared to using ice cream manufacturers to sell their customers on dieting. But the decision to use the utilities to promote DSM evolved as the result of many years of Congressional debate over various potential ways to promote energy conservation. Beginning with the Energy Policy and Conservation Act of 1975, 42 U.S.C. §§ 6201–6422, Congress almost annually tinkered with legislation designed to encourage users of electricity to use it more efficiently. Current policies for promoting conservation are found in the Public Utility Regulatory Policy Act (PURPA) as amended by the Energy Policy Act of 1992, 42 U.S.C. §§ 6801–6892. This approach addresses the development and implementation of electric power rate structures with incentives for electric utilities to invest in energy conservation.

PURPA "encourages" the states to adopt regulatory policies that improve electric power conservation, encourage the efficient use of electric power generation facilities and fuels, and promote the adoption of equitable rates for electric power. PURPA outlined six fundamental policies for retail electric power rates and services: (i) rates should reflect the actual cost of electric power generation and distribution; (ii) rates should not decline with increases in electric power use unless the cost of providing the power decreases as consumption increases; (iii) rates should reflect the daily variations in the actual cost of electric power generation; (iv) rates should reflect the seasonal variations in the actual cost of electric power generation; (v) rates should offer a special "interruptible" electric power service rate for commercial and industrial customers; and (vi) each electric utility must offer load management techniques to their electric consumers that will be practicable, cost effective and reliable, as determined by the state public utility commission.

PURPA requires the state commissions to "consider each standard . . . and make a determination concerning whether or not it is appropriate to implement such standard . . . within three years from the law's enactment. PURPA also sets up five standards for retail electric power rates and services. First, the provision of services should ordinarily exclude the installation of 'master meters' for multi-unit residential buildings. Second, the rates should not increase under automatic adjustment clauses, unless specific requirements are met. Third, services should provide information to electric utility customers concerning electric power rates. Fourth, the services may not terminate electric power service except in accordance with specified procedures. Finally, '[n]o electric utility may recover from any person other than the shareholders . . . of such utility any direct or indirect expenditure by such utility for promotional or political advertising.' " *See* Louis B. Schwartz *et. al.*, Free Enterprise and Economic Organization: Government Regulation 806–829 (Foundation Press, 6th ed. 1985)

PURPA was upheld in *FERC v. Mississippi.*, 456 U.S. 742 (1982). Mississippi and the Mississippi Public Service Commission argued that the statute usurped the traditional state prerogative to regulate the retail rates and services of public utilities in violation of the Constitution's Commerce Clause and the Tenth Amendment. With respect to the Commerce Clause, the Court first observed that, in Section 2 of PURPA, Congress had invoked "the proper exercise of congressional authority under the Constitution to regulate interstate commerce." The Court concluded that the legislative history of PURPA supported Congress' view that the policies and standards of Title I were needed to promote the conservation and efficient use of electric power, which were essential elements of interstate commerce.

With respect to the Tenth Amendment, the Court noted that numerous cases had upheld the federal government's power to compel the states to engage in regulatory activities. The Court said that "the commerce power permits Congress to preempt the States entirely in the regulation of private utilities." Therefore, Congress could choose not to preempt the traditional state prerogative to regulate the rates and services of public utilities, but choose instead to allow the states to take part in the adoption and implementation of federal policies and standards. Accordingly, the Court concluded that the requirements of Title I "simply establish requirements for continued state activity in an otherwise preemptible field."

The Energy Policy Act of 1992 added three new electric rate policies. First, that "[t]he rates allowed to be charged . . . shall be such that the utility's investment in and expenditures for . . . demand[-side] management measures are at least as profitable, giving appropriate consideration to income lost from reduced sales . . . as its investments in and expenditures for the construction of new generation, transmission, and distribution equipment." Second, that "[t]he rates charged . . . shall be such that the utility is encouraged to make investments in, and expenditures for, all cost-effective improvements in the energy efficiency of power generation, transmission and distribution." Third, that all electric utilities adopt least-cost or integrated resource plans.

An example of the type of programs typically set up in response to PURPA's policy of encouraging Demand Side Management is the following:

Kauai Electric's (KE's) Commercial Retrofit (CR) Program is designed to promote energy efficiency improvements in existing commercial buildings. It targets all existing nonresidential customers. It offers energy audits (analysis), customer education, cash incentives, and low cost financing for energy efficiency measures. The primary program measures are high efficiency air conditioning systems and equipment, high efficiency lighting measures, solar water heaters and heat pumps, and energy management systems.

Commercial customers are grouped into small, medium, and large customers. Those in the small customer category are users of less than 30 kilowatts (kW); those in the medium customer category are users of 30 to 100 kW; and those in the large customer grouping are users of over 100 kW. For small and medium-sized customers, KE will conduct on-site analyses of energy usage, identify energy efficient retrofit opportunities, and assist in implementing appropriate measures through qualified installation subcontractors. KE will buy-down the installed measure cost in an amount equivalent to a two-year customer payback and provide three-year financing of customer contribution at an 8.0 per cent annual rate, with no down payment or prepayment penalty. In the event that a measure does not qualify for an incentive because the payback is two years or less, KE will, nonetheless, provide financing.

For large commercial customers, KE will conduct engineering studies to identify opportunities for increased energy efficiency and develop a phased energy improvement plan. It will negotiate the measures to be installed and the incentives with each large customer. To avoid oversubscription to the program, KE intends to (1) set the initial incentives at a relatively low level and gradually increase them over time, (2) apportion the CR program budget over the three market segments, and (3) establish a cap on the amount of incentives that any one customer can receive in a year (without KE's review).

The CR program is KE's largest DSM program and is expected to account for over one-third of its total DSM savings. KE anticipates that this program will produce energy savings of 33,064,857 kilowatt-hours (kWh) per year and demand savings of 5,583 kW. KE estimates a net resource benefit of $11,460,000 and a benefit-cost ratio of 2.42. The budget for the first year of full scale operation of the CR program is $403,723.

Re Kauai Electric Division of Citizens Utilities Co. Hawaii Public Utilities Comm., Docket #94–0337 (August 5, 1997).

As indicated above, in 1992 Congress directed that the states should provide incentives for electric utilities to engage in DSM programs. Traditional ratemaking methods, however, discouraged utilities from undertaking programs that increased expenses and reduced revenues. State public utilities commissions were therefore required to re-examine their ratemaking methodologies to comply with the Congressional directive.

Georgia Power Company v. Georgia Industrial Group

447 S.E.2d 118 (Ga.App.1994).

■ Pope, C.J.: Georgia Power appeals the superior court's order reversing three orders of the Georgia Public Service Commission (Commission) authorizing Georgia Power to recover through riders or surcharges the costs of certain energy conservation programs and "interruptible service credits" paid to customers to reduce their supply of electricity during peak periods.

The issue in this case is whether such costs may be recovered through riders or whether they must be recovered through base rates utilizing the accounting procedure specified in OCGA § 46–2–26.1 for determining the rates to be charged. This case arose out of the legislature's passage in 1991 of a statute that [the Integrated Resource Planning Act (IRP), OCGA § 46–3A–1 et seq. The IRP requires utilities to file long-range energy plans for review and approval by the Commission. OCGA § 46–3A–2. It also requires certification by the Commission before a utility can construct or sell an electric plant, enter into a long-term power purchase, or spend money on "demand-side capacity options" (programs that reduce the demand for electricity). OCGA §§ 46–3A–1(4); 46–3A–3(a). The IRP] allows a utility to recover, inter alia, its costs for any certified demand-side capacity option and an additional sum as determined by the Commission to encourage the development of such demand-side programs. OCGA § 46–3A–9.

... In September 1992, Georgia Power filed revised demand-side programs for its residential customers and sought a proposed residential demand-side cost recovery rider to recover the costs of such programs. The rider proposed to pass through to residential customers (except low income customers) the expected program costs through 1993, subject to a true-up against actual program costs in a future proceeding at the end of 1993. Any over or under collection would be used, together with projected costs for 1994, to set the rider for 1994.... On January 4, 1993, the Commission ... held that Georgia Power should be allowed to recover the costs of its "interruptible service credits" through a rate rider since the credits were relatively new and there would be a time period necessary to determine participation levels and customer responses.

Appellee Georgia Industrial Group appealed to the Superior Court of Fulton County [from the ruling that allowed] Georgia Power to recover the costs of its demand-side programs and its "interruptible service credits" through a rider mechanism. The superior court reversed the Commission's orders, finding that such expenses are recoverable only through the test year rate case procedure prescribed by OCGA §§ 46–2–25 and 46–2–26.1, which was not followed in this case. Georgia Power brought this appeal from the superior court's order, and we reverse.

Georgia Power argues ... that the superior court's ruling is erroneous because the future test year accounting method set forth in OCGA § 46–2–26.1 only applies to general rate cases, which these proceedings do not involve, and because [the IRP] requires use of an accounting method different from the test year statute since the test year statute bases rates on estimated costs and the new statute requires recovery of actual costs.

OCGA § 46–2–26.1 ("Accounting methods to be used by electric utilities in ratemaking proceedings") provides in pertinent part:

"(b) In any proceeding to determine the rates to be charged by an electric utility, the electric utility shall file jurisdictionally allocated cost of service data on the basis of a test period, and the commission shall utilize a test period, consisting of actual data for the most recent 12 month period for which data are available, fully adjusted separately to reflect estimated operations during the 12 months following the utility's proposed effective date of the rates...."

Thus, pursuant to this future test year method, utility rates are established after an analysis of combined revenue, expenses and investment forecasted for a future 12–month period. We agree with Georgia Power that § 46–2–26.1 sets forth the accounting method to be used in determining the general rates to be charged customers rather than issue-specific rates or riders to be charged a particular group of customers. In support of this conclusion, we note that Georgia Power has cited in the record to a number of occasions in which the Commission has approved rate riders without utilizing the test year method. For the reasons discussed below, we further hold that § 46–3A–9 of the IRP gives the Commission the authority to approve recovery of demand-side costs outside of a general rate case and the test year statute.

Traditionally, electric utilities have been concerned with selling electricity and building new power plants to meet increased demands for electricity. Thus, under traditional ratemaking principles (the test year method), a utility's revenues are tied directly to how much electricity it sells. With the advent of integrated resource planning, however, the focus has been on ensuring the efficient use of electricity and the resources used to produce it. As noted earlier, demand-side programs are those which encourage customers to reduce their demand for electricity; often they involve incentives paid to customers to buy more energy efficient equipment for their homes and businesses. However, because demand-side investments result in less electricity being sold, they necessarily reduce the utility's revenues and earnings. For this reason, the legislature enacted OCGA § 46–3A–9, which allows utilities to recover the cost of demand-side programs plus an additional amount as an incentive to develop such programs:

> "The approved or actual cost, whichever is less, of any certificated demand-side capacity option shall be recovered by the utility in rates, along with an additional sum as determined by the commission to encourage the development of such resources. The commission shall consider lost revenues, if any, changed risks, and an equitable sharing of benefits between the utility and its retail customers."

We read this provision to say that a utility may recover the actual or approved costs of its demand-side programs by passing along such costs directly to its ratepayers along with an additional sum or incentive (as determined by the Commission) to encourage it to develop such programs. It seems clear to us that the legislature intended to treat demand-side costs outside of general ratemaking procedures by virtue of the fact that it provided for the utility to recover through rates not only its costs of such programs but an additional financial incentive to develop such programs over and above its overall rate of return. We further note that in providing for utilities to recover the cost of constructing new power plants, the legislature specified in OCGA § 46–3A–7(a) that a utility should be permitted to include in its "rate base" the full amount of approved construction costs absent a showing of "fraud, concealment, failure to disclose a material fact, imprudence, or criminal misconduct." By contrast, § 46–3A–9 simply says that the utility shall recover its demand-side costs "in rates." Had the legislature intended for recovery of demand-side costs to be accomplished through traditional ratemaking principles, it would have specified that such costs could be put in the rate base as it did with power plant construction costs.

Finally, utilization of the test year method for calculating recovery of demand-side costs is unnecessary and would likely preclude the legislative mandate that utilities be allowed to recover their actual costs of such programs. OCGA § 46–3A–9. First, the purpose of the test year method is to analyze a utility's revenues, expenses and investment forecasted for an entire year and determine whether it is earning an appropriate return. *See* OCGA § 46–2–26.1. Since § 46–3A–9 authorizes a utility to recover the exact costs of its demand-side programs plus an incentive, there is no need to utilize the test year analysis to look at its overall earnings.

Second, use of the test year method will not allow a utility to recover its exact costs of such programs plus an additional amount as an incentive because the test year method is not tied to recovery of specific costs but to an overall rate of return. However, under the rider mechanism approved by the Commission, which contains a true-up provision for factoring in any over or under collection of program costs in setting the rider for the next year, the stated purpose of recovering the actual or approved costs of such programs will be met. *See* OCGA § 46–3A–9.

Because use of the test year statute for calculating recovery of demand-side costs would frustrate the legislature's stated intent in encouraging utilities to develop such programs, we conclude the superior court erred in holding recovery of such costs must be accomplished pursuant to OCGA § 46–2–26.1 and that the Commission could not effectuate recovery of such costs through the use of a rider mechanism.

Judgment reversed.■

NOTES AND COMMENTS

1. An Illinois court construed the Illinois statutes to reach the opposite result in *A. Finkl & Sons Co. v. Illinois Commerce Commission*, 620 N.E.2d 1141 (Ill.App.1993) ("The rule against single-issue ratemaking recognizes that the revenue formula is designed to determine the revenue requirement based on the aggregate costs and demand of the utility. Therefore, it would be improper to consider changes to components of the revenue requirement in isolation.")

2. How much energy are DSM programs actually saving? The question does not have an easy answer. As fuel prices and electricity rates have dropped beginning in 1986, the impetus behind DSM has been lessened. Most businesses have become aware of the value to them of energy efficiency, at least during times of high prices, and many businesses feel that the need for these programs has passed. For example, large industrial users in Minnesota are seeking an exemption from DSM requirements on the ground that they have exhausted all the possibilities for projects that make economic sense. Big Minnesota Industrials Opt Out Of State Energy Conservation Program, Industrial Energy Bulletin, March 5, 1999.

On the other hand, some companies believe that DSM programs are avoiding the need for new generating plant construction. For example, in projections filed with the Florida Public Service Commission, Florida Power and Light Co. says that it expects its DSM programs to reduce total peak summer demand by the end of the next decade by 765 MW. This means, the company claims, that it will not have to construct two new generating units that otherwise would have had to be put into service during that period. Conservation Plans Will Cut Demand Nearly 1,300 MW by 2009, Energy Services & Telcom Report, March 11, 1999.

The Energy Information Administration ("EIA") released in December 1997 its report entitled "U.S. Electric Utility Demand Side Management 1996." The EIA compiled information regarding the success of demand side management ("DSM") programs in six broad categories: (1) energy efficiency, (2) direct load control, (3) interruptible load, (4) other load management, (5) other demand side management, and (6) load building. In 1996, 1003 of 3199 electric utilities in the United States reported having one or more of these DSM programs. The 573 largest operators reported saving 61,842 million kWh. Consumer characteristics, which include knowledge, awareness, and motivation, often influence the success of a program. External influences, such as energy prices, technologies, and regulations, also affect the success of a DSM program.

(1) Programs relating to energy efficiency work to reduce the amount of energy consumed at specific end-use devices without considering the quality of the service provided. This is often achieved by substituting more advanced technology to use less electricity to produce the same levels of energy services. For example, use energy saving appliances and high-efficiency heating. It is common to use financial incentives to encourage participation.

(2) Direct load control involves consumer loads that can be turned off during peak load hours. The power utility operator directly shuts off the power supply to individual appliances or equipment, such as air conditioners.

(3) Interruptible load programs involve contractual agreements with the consumer that service can be interrupted during peak load hours, either by direct control of the utility operator or by the consumer at the request of the operator. For instance, large commercial and industrial consumers may get discounted interruptible rates for agreeing to reduce electrical loads upon request from the utility.

(4) Other load management programs include technologies that shift part or all of a load from one time of day to another and may affect overall energy consumption of space heating and water heating storage systems. If time-of-day metering is used, these programs can implement real time pricing. (5) Other demand side management programs include consumer substitution of other types of energy for electricity and self-generation of electricity. (6) Load building involves increasing the use of existing facilities instead of building new facilities.

3. In the 1990s, the emphasis of national energy policy switched from electricity conservation to promotion of the restructuring of electric utili-

ties to promote more competition. The impact of this restructuring on DSM will be discussed in Chapter 13.

2.   COGENERATION

In a traditional power plant, over half of the energy produced from the burning fuel is lost in the form of waste heat. Engineers have long recognized that if the power plant could be built at a place where additional heat was needed, the energy efficiency of the operation would be greatly improved. They began to develop smaller scale generating plants that could be located in large buildings such as industrial plants, hospitals, etc., where the heat could be used to heat the building or in industrial processes. This process is known as "cogeneration."[10]

Cogeneration has been one of the categories of independent power production encouraged under PURPA, and it has accounted for well over three-quarters of the independent power projects created under that statute. Builders of large buildings now routinely review the potential costs and benefits of cogeneration in comparison to purchased power. As will be discussed in Chapter 13, the interconnection between "cogen" projects and the electric utility's distribution network has sometimes been a contentious issue.

On a volume basis, the most extensive use of cogeneration is found in the wood and paper industries. For example, a lumber or paper mill can use heat to treat its products and use the same heat source to cogenerate their own electricity. If the process creates sawdust, it may be fed back into the process as fuel.

Independent power producers have argued that the monopoly powers of the regulated electric utilities are often used to discourage customers from building cogeneration projects. One such IPP executive, Thomas Casten, argues that the electric utilities became "stultified" prior to PURPA:

> The original entrepreneurs who built electricity from a concept to one of the truly important businesses in every country are long since gone—dead and buried. The aggressive organization built by Samuel Insull took no prisoners and grew in every way possible. His excesses led to PUHCA in 1935, but he sped the development and availability of electricity. Forty years of regulated and protected monopoly prior to PURPA deadened that early entrepreneurial culture throughout the industry and replaced it with a risk-averse, caretaker culture.

Thomas Casten, Turning Off the Heat: Why America Must Double Energy Efficiency to Save Money and Reduce Global Warming 60 (Prometheus Books, 1998).

---

10. A similar way of utilizing the heat produced in the generation of electricity is the combined-cycle gas generating facility, which has become increasingly popular for small plants. See Chapter 9.

The incineration of municipal solid waste is another popular form of cogeneration. After the second oil shock on 1979, many local governments built waste-to-energy plants that would incinerate their solid waste and use the heat to generate electricity. Many of these plants are now in financial difficulty because the rates they charge to solid waste haulers are not competitive with out-of-state landfills, and the Supreme Court has ruled that state and local governments may not favor local waste disposal sites over those from other states without violating the dormant commerce clause. *C & A Carbone, Inc. v. Town of Clarkstown* 511 U.S. 383 (1994). Local governments that have invested large sums in solid waste combustion plants have tried a variety of maneuvers to maintain a supply of local trash despite the lower cost of other disposal methods, but many courts have tended to read the *Carbone* decision broadly. *See,* Comment, The Need for a Rational State and Local Response to *Carbone*, 18 Va. Envt'l L. J. 129 (1999).

In addition, suspicion has focused on the possible emission of toxic air pollutants from solid waste incinerators. For example, mercury from discarded flashlight batteries may end up in the air from incineration. The Toxic Release Inventory (TRI) established under the Emergency Planning and Community Right-to-Know Act of 1986 42 U.S.C. § 11001 *et seq.*, required all generating plants to report releases annually beginning in 1999.

3.   INTEGRATED RESOURCE PLANNING

While demand-side management has had modest success in promoting conservation by consumers, it was not directed toward promoting conservation by the utilities themselves. The program designed to do that goes under the name of "Integrated Resource Planning" (IRP).

Traditionally, state PSC's have regulated the supply of electricity provided by electric utilities. This was done, to a certain extent through rate regulation doctrines, such as the "used and useful" principle, as is discussed in Chapter 8. However, supply regulation has also historically been achieved through condemnation[11], siting, and permitting proceedings.

However, this is just the first step in the power plant or natural gas pipeline development process. Traditionally, most states have required electric utilities to obtain certificates-of-need (CONs) (sometimes called a CCN—"a certificate of convenience and necessity") before building power plants, transmission lines or pipelines. Typically, the CON is only issued following a siting proceeding—a hearing before the state PSC during which a utility makes its proposal and consumer and environmental groups may be allowed to participate as intervenors. Traditionally, the subject matter of

---

11. Ownership of land is often necessary for development of a power project by an electric utility. As is discussed in Chapter 3, in most states electric utilities have the power of eminent domain which is frequently used to build transmission lines for purposes of reaching consumers.

power plant and transmission line siting proceedings was a specific utility-sponsored proposed project.

In recent years, states have begun to experiment with more comprehensive programs of evaluating supply-side alternatives. These are known as least-cost planning or integrated resource planning (IRP). As described by one of the leading advocates of IRP, a utility's planning program should operate as follows:

> The utility system must, in effect, take inventory of its residences, appliances, heating systems, commercial floor-space, and industrial processes, securing estimates of both absolute numbers and average efficiencies. Many utilities have made substantial progress along these lines already, although additional surveys may be needed.

> The next step is to develop low and high case projections of additions to these inventories over the forecast period. The range should bound the universe of plausible growth rates for the major end use categories.... Electricity needs for the high and low scenarios should then be calculated by summing existing and new uses, less anticipated retirements, over the forecast period.

> This calculation will yield a diverging "jaws" forecast comparable to that produced by the econometric methods reviewed earlier, with one crucial difference: the new forecast is rooted firmly in the instrumentalities of demand, allowing planners to track the effects of investments and policies designed to upgrade efficiencies of some or all of those instrumentalities. In parallel with this forecast, planners should develop a comprehensive assessment of opportunities for improving end use efficiencies. What is the "state of the art" existing and anticipated for delivering the services performed by the system's end uses at the lowest possible electricity consumption?

> The question then shifts to how much of this unexploited conservation resource is worth attempting to secure. The answer requires a rigorous methodology for comparing the life-cycle costs of incremental amounts of conservation for each end use with the costs of the most expensive displaceable generating unit in the utility's acquisition plans. In performing that assessment, planners should explicitly credit conservation for its advantages on indices of scale, lead-time, and uncertainty-reduction; the cost column for both the conservation options and the generation alternative should also include quantifiable environmental costs associated with each. The calculation should take specific account of the avoidance of line losses, additional transmission construction, and additional reserve capacity that conservation makes possible when it displaces or defers a new power plant.

> From this process will emerge a decision on which efficiency improvements are worth pursuing; it remains, however, to determine how much of the cost-effective conservation resource the system can count on securing. That inquiry focuses on mechanisms for getting the conservation installed; here planners can draw on numerous prece-

dents. Options include state-imposed efficiency standards for some end uses, supplemented by direct utility investment through incentive programs. Planners must anticipate the success of such programs in convincing end users to take advantage of efficiency opportunities. Again, substantial empirical data are already available.

Using those predictions, planners can narrow the "jaws" of the forecast by inserting assumptions about increases in the efficiency of the end use inventories for the "high" and "low" forecasts. Both forecasts will drop, but the high forecast will drop by more because there are more end uses to upgrade. The high forecast then represents the maximum plausible "post-conservation" system needs: the low forecast represents the minimum requirements that will have to be met.

The gap between the two forecasts which conservation has narrowed but not eliminated represents a range of outcomes with which the utility must be prepared to deal. The enterprise is analogous to purchasing an insurance policy; the goal is to minimize the cost of coping with contingencies of varying probability. New generating units may be one element of the response, but other options will bear close scrutiny. Load management programs that shift consumption away from peak periods, without necessarily affecting total consumption, are an obvious example. Also worth investigating is the willingness of large industrial and commercial customers to sell interruption rights to the utility system, which would provide additional reserves in the event of unexpected shortfalls.

In addition, some options, clearly inferior on cost grounds to baseload generators if markets were assured, may look more attractive as a hedge against possible but unlikely growth in demand. Combustion turbines come readily to mind as a generating alternative with relatively high fuel costs, but shorter lead-times and lower capital costs than baseload plants. Obviously, the more certain the system is that it will need significant "post-conservation" additions of energy supply, the better the high-capital-cost, low-operating-cost baseload systems will look. But the converse is also true and most existing forecasts do not permit an informed evaluation of utilities' investment alternatives.

Ralph C. Cavanagh, Least Cost Planning Imperatives for Electric Utilities and Their Regulators, 10 Harv. Envtl. L. Rev. 299–324 (1986).

Bangor Hydro–Electric Co. v. Public Utilities Comm.

589 A.2d 38 (Me.1991).

■ WATHEN, J.: Bangor Hydro–Electric Company ("Bangor Hydro") appeals a final order of the Maine Public Utilities Commission ("PUC") denying without prejudice Bangor Hydro's petition for certificates of public convenience and necessity for two independent hydroelectric generating projects. Bangor Hydro contends that the PUC arbitrarily ignored its own rules and precedents, made findings of fact that were not supported by the evidence, and erred in denying the certificates due to uncertainties created by their premature filing. Finding no error, we affirm the order of the PUC.

On November 22, 1989, Bangor Hydro filed petitions for certificates of public convenience and necessity requesting the PUC to approve three hydroelectric projects along the Penobscot River. The Basin Mills project, which was expected to provide 32 MW of additional capacity by 1999, involved the construction of a new dam and power facility. Construction on the project was not to begin until 1996. The Veazie project, which was expected to add 6 MW of capacity by 1996, and the Milford project, which was expected to add 2 MW of capacity by 1993, were to provide for an increase in the generating capability of currently existing hydroelectric facilities.

On August 17, 1990, the PUC denied without prejudice the Basin Mills and Veazie petitions [and approved only the Milford project]. *Re Bangor Hydro–Electric Company,* Nos. 89–193 and 89–195 (Me.P.U.C. Aug. 17, 1990). While the PUC found that this decision was warranted solely on grounds of the petitions' prematurity, it also cited Bangor Hydro's failure to pursue least-cost options and demand-side resource planning as an alternative to the projects. In its order, the PUC described the standard used in evaluating petitions for certificates of public convenience and necessity:

> [T]he utility must demonstrate that the power from the new source is needed and that the resource being considered is the most economical or at least it is a part of an overall least cost plan. In addition, the utility must demonstrate that the timing is reasonable. This ... standard ... is consistent with the PUC's longstanding policy of encouraging the development of qualifying facilities ("QFs")[3][12] while requiring utilities to pursue a least-cost plan as required by the Maine Energy Policy Act of 1988, 35–A M.R.S.A. § 3191 (Supp.1990) ("MEPA").[13]

12. QFs are non-utility entities of co-generation and small power production facilities which, as unregulated electric generation sources, market their power to electric utilities. In 1978, Congress enacted the Public Utilities Regulatory Policies Act, section 210 of which was designed to encourage the development of QFs. Pursuant to section 210, the Federal Energy Regulatory Commission promulgated regulations which, among other things, required electric utilities to purchase electricity from QFs at prices not to exceed their avoided costs and required state regulatory agencies to administer the rules. "Avoided costs" are the incremental costs to an electric utility of electric energy, capacity, load management, and/or conservation measures which, but for the purchase from the

QF or QFs, such utility would obtain from another source. Public Utilities Commission Rules and Regulations Chapter 36 § 1(A)(3).

13. The MEPA states: The Legislature finds that it is in the best interests of the State to ensure that Maine and its electric utilities pursue a least-cost energy plan. The Legislature further finds that a least-cost energy plan takes into account many factors including cost, risk, diversity of supply and all available alternatives, including purchases of power from Canadian sources. When the available alternatives are otherwise equivalent, the commission shall give preference first to conservation and demand management and then to power purchased from qualifying facilities. 35–A M.R.S.A. § 3191.

Bangor Hydro argues that the PUC erred in finding that the company did not allow independent power producers to bid against the Basin Mills and Veazie projects and it did not use the bidding process to minimize costs.... The PUC found that, although Bangor Hydro had issued a request for proposals, the bidding and negotiation process was far from complete, and the company had no intention of completing the process until the PUC proceeding was over. The PUC could reasonably have based these findings on the evidence presented, including the testimony of Jeffrey A. Jones, Bangor Hydro's Manager of Power Supply, who stated that, although a bidding process had begun, it would probably not be completed before this case was concluded. He further admitted that the company had not given bidders an opportunity to bid against these particular hydro projects because these projects were already priced below the avoided costs. Thus, the PUC's findings of fact were basically supported by the totality of the evidence of record and not clearly erroneous....

The "All Ratepayers Test" is an analysis of the overall economic efficiency of the use of ratepayer resources to produce end uses,[6][14] to determine whether the same end uses can be provided more efficiently with a demand side energy management program than without it, considering the costs and benefits of the program to the utility and to the ratepayers, taken together. A program satisfies this test if the present value of program benefits exceeds the present value of program costs, at the time of analysis.

Chapter 380 § 2(A). Under the MEPA, a DSM program satisfying the All Ratepayers Test should be implemented in preference to additional supply-side projects, including even QFs. Applying these standards, the PUC found that Bangor Hydro had not pursued its required least-cost plan in the area of conservation and demand-side management. Bangor Hydro argues on appeal that the PUC ignored its own rules and the evidence before it in making this finding....

The PUC based its finding primarily on the testimony of Steve Linnell and Carroll Lee who presented Bangor Hydro's criteria for determining the cost effectiveness of DSM programs. Bangor Hydro had the burden of persuading the PUC that its proposed projects were superior to conservation or demand-side measures. The PUC's finding may not be overturned unless Bangor Hydro can demonstrate that the finding was unreasonable, unjust, or unlawful. Examining the totality of the evidence of record, we find no error.

Bangor Hydro fails to show that the PUC ignored the evidence regarding the manner in which the company screens DSM programs. Taken in its entirety, Lee's testimony supports the conclusion that Bangor Hydro conducts its DSM planning according to its own cost-effectiveness criteria, not in compliance with Chapter 380 or the MEPA. When asked whether Bangor Hydro viewed as its responsibility the obligation to implement all cost-

---

14. "An 'end use' is the light, heat, motor drive, industrial process, or other useful work resulting from electricity supplied by an electric utility or from a non-electric source provided through a demand side energy management program." Chapter 380 § 2(L).

effective programs that it could under the All Ratepayers Test, Lee responded, "No, I don't think that is correct." He also indicated that, "as a general rule, as long as long-run marginal rates exceed a utility's long-run marginal costs, it is not appropriate to pay customers to conserve." Because, as Lee testified, Bangor Hydro's long-run marginal rates currently exceed its long-run marginal costs and are likely to continue to do so, the company would not purchase conservation even if the direct costs of conservation were less than the company's avoided cost. Linnell testified concerning the criteria Bangor Hydro uses in selecting programs for inclusion in the company's DSM plan. These criteria are clearly more stringent than the All Ratepayers Test. Bangor Hydro has failed to prove that the PUC erred in finding that its DSM resource planning was inadequate.■

NOTES AND COMMENTS

1.   Some IRP statutes require the public utility commission to evaluate potential new power sources in terms not only of their direct economic cost but in terms of the indirect costs of the environmental damage the source would create. Each year, power plants cause millions of dollars in damage to the environment but these costs, such as the medical costs produced by air pollution, are not included in the market price of electricity. The burden of "paying" for these environmental externalities falls on society in the form of increased medical expenses, depleted agricultural resources, and a reduced quality of life. Currently, in the United States, coal is the main source of electricity production and contributes significantly to air pollution.

One way to internalize these environmental costs is to add environmental cost values to each potential new source. Such values are sometimes referred to as "environmental adders." Currently about half of the state utility commissions take environmental externalities into consideration in their planning process. Of these, seven states have specified monetary externality values for designated air emissions from power plants. Energy Information Agency, Electricity Generation and Environmental Externalities: Case Studies (1998).

Two methods may be used to calculate the value of environmental externalities. One way is to calculate the environmental damage of a pollutant by examining the real world costs of future climate change, illness, and crop damage. This method is called "damage-cost estimate." Kenneth Rose, et al., The National Regulatory Research Institute, Public Utility Commission Treatment of Environmental Externalities 2 (1994). Public utilities commissions often use another method in which the externality values are based on the costs to the power plants of installing air emissions control technologies. This is called the "control cost method." *Id.* Proponents of these types of regulation argue that they will show that renewable power is really cheaper than fossil fuel when all costs are taken into account. The utility companies should want to choose the resource mix that will achieve the lowest cost, and therefore will be more attracted to renewable energy sources to meet future energy needs. Clinton A. Vince et al., Integrated Resource Planning: The Case for Exporting Comprehensive Energy Planning to the Developing World, 25 Case W. Res. J. Int'l L. 371, 373 (1993).

Minnesota is one state that has enacted renewable resource energy legislation. In 1991, Minnesota legislators passed a statute prohibiting new nonrenewable energy plants unless an applicant could demonstrate renewable energy alternatives were researched and the proposed plant was "less expensive (including environmental costs) than power generated by a renewable energy source." Minn. Stat § 216B.243(3)(a)(1994). The environmental externalities law requires the Minnesota Public Utilities Commission to "quantify and establish a range of environmental costs associated with each method of electricity generation." Minn. Stat. § 216B.2422(3)(a). Monetary values were set based on the values adopted by other jurisdictions and on a 1990 study of externalities. Re Quantification of Environmental Costs, 150 Pub. Util. Rep. 4th (PUR) at 137. The Minnesota courts upheld the values on appeal. *In the Matter of Quantification of Environmental Costs,* 578 N.W.2d 794 (Minn.App.1998). *See* Kirsten H. Engel, The Dormant Commerce Clause Threat to Market-based Environmental Regulation: The Case of Electricity Deregulation, 26 Ecology L. Q. 243, 282–287 (1999).

2.   Many states are now encouraging competition among electricity generators in order to bring about lower prices. Such competition allows individual customers to choose which electricity generator they want to buy power from. To what extent can IRP operate effectively in this type of competitive environment? The issue is discussed in the following article, and again in Chapter 13.

3.   In forecasting energy demand, should we assume that the increasing sophistication of information technology will increase energy efficiency and therefore slow the growth of demand.? Joseph Romm, the Executive Director of the Center for Energy and Climate Solutions, argues that the increasing use of the internet has already increased energy efficiency and is likely to continue to do so. The Center's report on The Internet Economy and Global Warming is available at www.cool-companies.org.

4.   RENEWABLE PORTFOLIO STANDARDS

From earlier material, it is obvious that concern over the supply of fossil fuels and over the safety and reliability of nuclear energy have stimulated an extensive search for alternative energy sources. To the extent that the sources are renewable—i.e., do not deplete with use—they avoid some of the intergenerational issues discussed in Chapter 8.

An increasingly common practice of state public utility commissions is to require that all generators, or all sellers or both, obtain a certain percentage of their power from renewable resources. These rules are referred to as "renewable portfolio standards" (RPS) because they typically specify that a certain percentage of the company's product must be renewable, but allow the company to choose among a variety of sources. The following article describes how a national RPS program might operate, using existing state programs as a model.

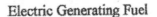

Electric Generating Fuel

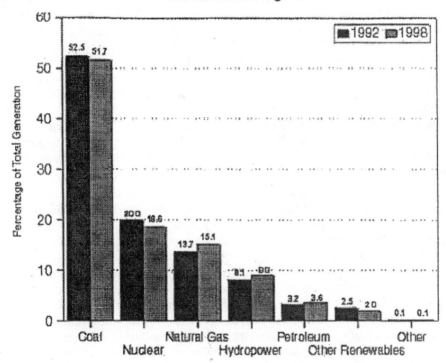

Figure 10–3

At the present time, the share of electric generation fueled by renewable resources other than hydropower is quite low. The challenge of increasing that share is thought to be dependent on the development of regulatory standards that would allow interstate trading of renewable shares.

Brent M. Haddad & Paul Jefferiss, Forging Consensus on National Renewables Policy, 12

Electricity Journal No. 2, March, 1999.

The renewables portfolio standard requires all sellers (or generators) of electricity in the United States to show that they have provided a small but growing percentage of their sales from renewable-energy resources such as wind, solar, biomass, and geothermal. In this way, the RPS creates for electricity a widely used minimum-content-type standard similar to insulation requirements for new buildings and minimum standards for recycled paper content. More than this, the RPS is designed to use market forces to reduce the cost of the program in much the same way that the Environmental Protection Agency's SO[2] allowance trading system reduces the cost of the acid rain program, and that other programs use air pollution permit trading to reduce air emissions at the lowest possible cost.

It would be inconvenient to require every retail seller of electricity in the country to purchase renewably generated power up to a minimum standard. The RPS provides an alternative mechanism that provides minimal inconvenience and improved efficiency. First, a program administrator awards to producers of renewable-resource electricity currency-like renewable energy credits (RECs) that specify when, where, and how much renewable electricity they have generated, and what type of renewable resource was used. RECs represent all of the values of renewable energy not currently paid for by consumers [such as greenhouse gas mitigation and national energy independence]. Instead of having to generate or buy renewable energy, retail sellers could purchase RECs from renewable energy producers and submit them once each year to the program administrator in amounts equal to the required percentage of their total electricity sales.

For renewable energy producers, the RPS therefore creates a second commodity and a second market that supplements the income they receive from selling renewable power itself. They would sell their renewable power locally at the market rate, just like all other power producers. They would sell their RECs nationally to retail suppliers anywhere in the country who need RECs to comply with the law. The price of RECs is expected to be that increment of additional revenue needed to keep competitive renewable power producers in business and to attract new renewables producers into the business. New renewables development, up to the minimum standard, will take place wherever in the country that increment of revenue is lowest. As happened with SO[2] allowances, a vibrant market for RECs is likely to arise, driving their cost down, making renewable-resource generators more competitive, and lowering the cost of our national commitment to renewable energy.

When California's Public Utilities Commission became the first such commission to endorse the RPS, it was endorsing a concept, not a completed blueprint for a program. Now, after 3 years of development involving a collaboration of academic specialists, industry participants and representatives, NGO activists, and state and federal regulators, the concept of the RPS has been refined to the point where it can effectively deal with practical implementation issues. In the following paragraphs, we summarize these refinements and demonstrate how they not only overcome hurdles to implementation but do so in ways that enhance the overall efficacy and political viability of the policy.

One concern that has been raised is that it is difficult to predict or cap the cost of the program. The argument is that if there is a scarcity of renewable energy credits, then retail suppliers who need to purchase RECs may come up short. In this hypothetical scenario, retail suppliers who needed to buy RECs would then be forced to pay either exorbitant prices for scarce RECs or high penalties for non-compliance with the program.

Buyers of RECs can be fully protected from the risk of scarcity. First, we believe that it is quite possible to predict the cost of achieving particular standards in particular years, at least within a range. This means that policymakers can choose to set the initial level of the RPS and its subsequent ramp-up rate at levels that are unlikely to lead to credit scarcity or high prices. At the start, the level of the standard would be quite modest, increasing gradually but steadily over time in a manner consistent with a predetermined balance between our national commitment to renewable energy and our concern about limiting public expenditure. In practice, this means there will be ample advanced warning (years, in fact) to ramp up renewable-energy production to meet the growing requirement to purchase RECs. however, even if projections prove wrong, and credit shortages and high prices occur, a creative price-cap mechanism has been developed for the RPS. The proposed price-cap mechanism solves the issue of trading scarcity without reducing the effectiveness of the market mechanism. In the case of a national RPS, the RPS program administrator would issue a standing offer to sell "proxy" RECs to retail suppliers at a price administratively predetermined to reflect the maximum desired public expenditure on the whole program. If the price of RECs on the market remains below the capped price of the administrator's proxy RECs, retail suppliers will purchase those. But if for any reason (not just scarcity) the market price for RECs exceeds the capped price, retail suppliers can choose to purchase some or all of their requirement from the program administrator. The retail seller would fill out a one-page form stating how many RECs it wishes to purchase and would attach a check. Retail sellers will be able to identify in advance with complete precision their maximum cost of compliance simply by multiplying their REC-purchase requirement in KWHs by the price-cap price.

If retail sellers take advantage of the program administrator's standing offer, a fund would accumulate. The administrator would use this fund to purchase RECs on the market. Fewer RECs would be purchased than the required percentage, but the RPS market would consistently reward the least-cost generators of renewable energy until cost-cap funds run out. In the unlikely scenario that no RECs are available, the administrator could disburse the fund exactly like the trust fund, by auctioning production credits, or supporting R & D.

In practice, of course, retail suppliers will seek, and find, some lower-cost RECs on the market. In this way the certainty of a maximum cost turns the cost uncertainty of a market-based mechanism like the RPS into a defining virtue. The actual cost can only turn out to be equal to or less than the maximum. When one is faced with a choice between a fixed total cost and a maximum cost of equal value that is entirely likely to be much lower than the maximum, one would choose the latter option every time. This is the raison d'etre of market-based mechanisms. Society thus guarantees that it will achieve the goal it has set for itself (in this case, a minimum percentage of renewable-resource electricity as part of the overall electricity mix) at the lowest possible cost.

There is ample opportunity to structure a portfolio standard to ensure more even regional distribution of renewables development, an outcome that would spread out the economic and environmental benefits of renewables. With national credit trading and a relatively low RPS requirement, renewables development is likely to take place in locations where the difference between the local marginal cost of power and the cost of producing renewable energy is lowest. By creating an opportunity for "local content" in the federal program, states (or regions) could ensure that future renewable power development, with its attendant local benefits, occurs locally and, consequently, throughout the nation.■

NOTES AND COMMENTS

1. As of January, 2000, eight states have adopted renewable portfolio standards. Ryan Wiser et. al., Emerging Markets for Renewable Energy: The Role of State Policies during Restructuring, Electricity Journal (January, 2000). To what extent will it be possible to trade credits under RPS programs on an interstate basis without violating the dormant commerce clause? *See* Engel, *supra* at 287–295.

A number of other states have sought to promote renewable power through the use of "System Benefit Charges," through which all customers pay a fee based on volume of electricity used, which is collected at the state level and distributed to support renewable energy projects. *Shea v. Boston Edison Company,* 727 N.E.2d 41 (Mass.2000) (upholding validity of benefit charges under state constitution). Twelve states have adopted such programs. Wiser, *supra.*

2. Financial investment in renewable resources by both the public and private sectors is continuing to increase. The federal government has announced a "Million Solar Roofs" initiative designed to encourage property owners to install solar systems on a million homes and businesses by the year 2010. The federal government has committed to install solar systems on 20,000 of its own buildings within this time period. Government-supported loans are available for program participants. *See* the Department of Energy's web site at http://www.eren.doe.gov/millionroofs.

Some of the major oil companies have made large investments in solar power technology because they are anticipating the expansion of the markets for such power in developing countries. Royal Dutch Shell has announced a plan to invest up to $250 million in its plant in the Netherlands to produce 100,000 square meters of solar cells each year. *See* Utility Environment Report, October 10, 1997, at 9.

3. The State of California has taken the lead in encouraging the use of wind power to generate electricity. Certain mountain passes in California offer some of the most reliable sources of consistently high winds. The California Energy Commission allocated $540 million in state funds in fiscal 1998 to support new renewable energy sources, much of which will be used for windpower projects. The Department of Energy also awards

contracts to help develop improved technologies for the utilization of windpower.

Private utilities outside California are showing increasing interest in the development of windpower farms. Oregon utilities are building a $60 million windpower project in Wyoming that is designed to generate 41.4 MW of electricity. Sixty-nine wind turbines will be erected on a 2100 acre tract of ranchland between Laramie and Rawlins, an area that has an average windspeed of 25 miles per hour.

E. DISTRIBUTED GENERATION

There is a new group of smaller scale generation technologies on the horizon that are attracting a great deal of attention. By providing individual generating plants that are small enough to meet the needs of a home or business, they may reopen the issue that Samuel Insull thought he had settled: Is the central station the most efficient way to generate electricity?

These technologies have been grouped under the term distributed generation (DG). DG includes generation, generation-like and storage devices that are connected to the distribution grid on either the system side or customer side of the meter. These new technologies enable incumbent electric distribution utilities, their non-regulated utility affiliates, independent power producers and consumers to break from the central station paradigm of electricity generation and distribution.

Interest in DG is particularly keen in those businesses for whom a loss in power supply is especially costly. Banking and financial facilities, hospitals, manufacturing and assembly plants, grocery stores and restaurants are seen as the key market for DG, particularly in areas where older utility distribution systems have often caused blackouts. Distributed Generation Could Hit 20% of New Generation in 20 Years, Electric Utility Week, January 3, 2000.

DG includes small generating facilities that can be installed on-site or as part of the distribution network to generate additional power. DG technologies evolved from emergency back-up generators. Indeed, several DG technologies are just back-up generators re-engineered for constant generation at efficiencies comparable to larger central station generation, but others use a wide range of new technologies such as microturbines, reciprocating engines, fuel cells, and even the next generation of wind generators, photovoltaics, etc.

These units are usually generators ranging from about 1 megawatt down to a capacity sized for a single home. They can be used by industrial, commercial and residential customers. They are fueled by natural gas, oil, gas, solar and wind energy, of which natural gas is currently the most popular fuel.[15]

---

15. In addition, companies are developing natural gas-powered fuel cells that will serve many of the same functions as DG. Regina R. Johnson, Fuel Cells: White Knight

The future impact of the addition of DG on generation, distribution and independent power production systems may be significant. DG may be implemented in several different ways in the present distribution structure.

First, DG may take the form of an on-site generator owned by a single customer to meet its on-site needs. In that capacity, DG may also provide co-generated heat and emergency back up power. However, at the present state of the technology an on-site DG may not be an efficient way of meeting all of a customer's generation needs because, although on-site DG units can be used to meet the peak load of summer air conditioning, it is not economical to size a unit that can generate the far greater power needed to start up today's air conditioning units (ten times running load). A DG unit with sufficient capacity to meet such high loads would be under-utilized most of the time.

Second, DG could be interconnected to the distribution grid. A DG unit connected to the grid could generate all base load power, and draw off the grid for the critical cycling loads. Alternatively, a DG unit could be slaved to a certain device, such as a refrigerator or air conditioner and thereby flatten out the generation requirements of the customer throughout the year.

Third, DG could be bi-directionally interconnected to the grid. The bi-directional connection would allow the DG to generate power for the grid. In this role a network of on-site DG units can be used to generate peak-shaving power and voltage support.

Fourth, DG units can be directly installed by the electric utility as part of the distribution grid to perform peak-shaving and voltage support functions or other ancillary services. DG units could replace higher cost or aged peak-load generation facilities and allow utilities to increase generation incrementally to meet instant needs.

Fifth, DG may be used as an alternative to expansion of the distribution network or even the transmission network. Utilities can avoid the cost of constructing a new line to remote customers by siting DG close by them, thus avoiding line-losses resulting from long distance electricity transmission. Indeed, a nearby lower efficiency DG unit may be more efficient than a high efficiency central station generator several miles away.

Finally, one specific instance of this would be serving geographically remote customers by a single DG station in a distribution strategy called "islanding". Islanding could be especially beneficial for industrial parks and small communities, which could take advantage of the high efficiency co-generated heat. Such a generation island could be owned by the utility

for Natural Gas? Public Utilities Fortnightly, March 15, 2000, at 22. Fuel cells have made great improvements in efficiency, mostly due to the collateral benefits of research and development toward efficient automobile fuel cells. (See Chapter 15.) In addition, research into the development of a more efficient storage battery continues. Some commentators suggest that improved storage has even more potential than actual generation devices. Mark P. Mills, Micro Gen? Think Again, Public Utilities Fortnightly, June 1, 1999, at 16.

serving the territory, or, if state legislation permits, by an independent electricity service provider or by the community served.

Although DG is on the horizon, it still needs to resolve a number of important issues before it can expect widespread usage. The technology and standards for uni-directional and bi-directional interconnection need to be fully developed. With current technology and under the present regulations, DG is limited to an unconnected back-up or full capacity generating unit for an unconnected customer, or to units owned by a utility and used as part of the distribution grid. Several things are required before other possibilities will be available.

First, there is a need to agree upon proven technology for either uni-directional or bi-directional interconnection of DG to the grid. Technologies must be developed to allow small scale interconnection. Uni-directional interconnection is the closest technology to realization, because it is the least different from traditional connection to the grid. Bi-directional, however, will be much more difficult to develop, because the utility will need to be able to control it for worker safety and for the anticipated sale of power or grid maintenance to the utility. Additionally, advanced metering technologies will be required to correctly bill customers for reduced use or credit them for grid benefits.

Second, currently there are also no regulations or standards for interconnection of DG. The closest match to this is the large generation connections required to implement PURPA contracts. The procedures under PURPA are too time consuming and expensive to be economically practical for small scale DG.

Third, electricity rates do not reflect the actual cost of generation and delivery of power for different times of day and year. Rather, all costs are aggregated into a single rate, thereby removing all price signals to customers. Without adequate price signals customers cannot determine whether DG is the more efficient manner of generation. Again this goes against the tenets of a competitive market. DG can only thrive in an environment where customers are subject to the actual cost of generation and distribution. Such rates would reveal when DG will be likely to be more efficient than peak power generation or remote customer distribution. Advanced metering technology will be necessary to implement actual time of day rates.

Finally, state commissions must address who may own and operate DG.[16] Specifically, to what extent utilities may do so, and what require-

---

16. In California, independent power producers and industrial users have asked the California Public Utilities Commission to determine whether it would be fair to allow utilities to compete in the DG market. *See* www.cpuc.ca.gov./distgen. The independents and industries argue that under current regulations, utilities can refuse interconnection to any DG unit, but the utilities may install DG units for their own benefit. This seems to go against the competitive goals espoused by the California Commission. In order to remedy this, they argue, state commissions will have to mandate equal access for all DG units regardless of ownership in order to provide a level playing field for the new DG market. The independents claim that allowing utilities to compete and control interconnection

ments they must meet. Related to this issue is the extent to which natural gas distributors will be allowed to enter the DG market. As the provider of the most prevalent DG fuel, natural gas distributors could have a substantial impact on the DG market.

If DG technology really becomes the wave of the future, electric utilities will face new "stranded cost" problems (see Chapter 12). And to what extent will they be compensated for maintaining "spinning reserves"?

DG offers the prospect of many new ways of providing power that depart from the central station model. The low capital investment and small generation capacity of DG makes it the ideal vehicle for independent electricity service providers to enter the electricity generation market. However, the current regulatory structure has long been geared toward large scale central station generation by regulated monopolies. The uncertainties cited above must be addressed before DG will be able to fulfill its potential in the coming competitive distribution market. *See* Chris Holly, Distributed Generation's Big Potential Faces Big Barriers, Energy Daily, June 24, 1999.

will result in a fox guarding the hen-house scenario. If a competitive market is desired, an independent standard of interconnection must be created. Richard Stavros, Last Big Battle for State Regulators, Public Utilities Fortnightly, Oct. 15, 1999.

CHAPTER 11

WHOLESALE ELECTRIC POWER COMPETITION

Outline of Chapter:

A. COMPETITION IN ELECTRICITY AS A GLOBAL TREND

Electricity Reform Abroad and U.S. Investment, Energy Information Administration, U.S. Department of Energy (1997)

<http://www.eia.doe.gov/emeu/pgem/electric/es.html>

Over the past decade a number of nations have restructured their electricity industries. Several nations have also significantly reduced the government's role in the ownership and management of domestic electricity industries both at the state and at the national level. The Energy Information Administration selected Argentina, Australia, and the United Kingdom (UK) for this study partly because of the extent to which these nations have undergone electricity reforms but also because of the major role that U.S. companies have played as investors in these nations' reformed and privatized electricity sectors. Understanding how Argentina, Australia, and the United Kingdom each addressed the issues of primary importance to their country's electricity sector reform may be informative to those who will fashion the structure of similar reforms in the United States. This understanding may be all the more important because of the experiences that U.S. electric companies will have gained from their investments in these countries.

Since the early 1990's, investment in overseas electricity assets has been a rapidly growing target of U.S. companies' foreign investment. The predominant share of this investment has been directed at the United Kingdom and Australian electricity industries. The investment expenditures of U.S. companies in the electricity industries of the United Kingdom and Australia alone far exceed all U.S. overseas electricity investment in the rest of the world combined. Electric utilities from the United States have also been the most prominent foreign investors in the recently-privatized Argentine electricity companies although the dollar value of investment in Argentina's electricity industry has been smaller relative to the investment dollars flowing to Australia and the United Kingdom.

In Argentina, Australia, and the United Kingdom, electricity reform has involved a combination of the following issues:

— an unbundling of electricity assets;

— the creation of electricity pools;

— the creation of independent system operators;

— the privatization of electricity assets through sale or public auction;

— the deregulation of electricity and the implementation of a more restrained form of regulation where regulation was retained;

— the adoption of price cap regulation and movement away from rate-of-return regulation;

— the realization of a competitive market in generation;

— the separation of the "wires" function of distribution from the "marketing" function;

— the gradual introduction of competition in electricity marketing;

— an opening up of domestic electricity assets to foreign investment; and

— determination of the degree of recovery of stranded costs.

In each of the three case study countries, issues surrounding electric industry restructuring, competitive electricity pools, privatization, deregulation, and stranded costs are unique to each country's electricity reform experience. However, there are often more commonalities than differences, particularly in the case of Australia and the United Kingdom. In all three countries, electricity reform involved a greater opening to foreign investment in electricity.

In Argentina, Australia, and the United Kingdom, electricity restructuring and privatization were carried out in an atmosphere of general economy-wide restructuring and privatization. In all three countries, a primary goal motivating electricity reform was to achieve lower electricity costs for consumers through encouraging efficiency improvements in the electricity industry. Reduced costs were also to serve the purpose of improving the efficiency of the overall economy. In all three countries, raising revenues for the treasury to reduce public borrowings was another overriding motive. In Argentina, obtaining badly needed capital for electricity infrastructure improvement and expansion was an additional motivating factor for reform and privatization. . . .

Figure ES3 [included as Figure 11–1] depicts a hypothetical "model" of what a national electric utility restructuring might look like. Figure ES3 shows an electricity industry as a single nationalized entity prior to the restructuring. The restructuring involved the separation of all electricity industry functions along separate lines of business (i.e., generation, transmission, distribution, and marketing) into newly created organizations. It should be stressed that Figure ES3 is a much simplified (and not entirely representative) model of restructurings that have taken place in several nations. Figure ES3 is more illustrative of the United Kingdom experience where the electricity industry prior to restructuring was owned and managed primarily by the central government. In contrast, in Australia statewide electricity restructuring largely preceded nation wide reforms and was predominate. Argentina is also distinct in that Argentina's restructuring involved a wide-scale consolidation of electricity operations.

In the United Kingdom, electricity reform initially involved the complete restructuring (unbundling) of the industry along segmental lines: electricity generation, transmission, distribution, and marketing all became separate operations. Prior to privatization, the United Kingdom created two large power generation companies, one national transmission company, and twelve regional generation companies. A newly-evolving electricity marketing segment was to be gradually developed, where sales, brokerage, and billing operations each became a separate function. In its restructuring, however, the United Kingdom created an industry that from its infancy was dominated by the two large generation companies whose predominant market share and predominant role in the electricity pool has often given rise to concerns over whether generation was adequately competitive.

Although Australian reforms borrowed heavily from the UK experience, there have been several notable distinctions. In contrast to reform in the United Kingdom, electricity reform in Australia was undertaken several years later and at both the state and national levels. In general, several of the Australian state governments restructured their electricity industries in a fashion similar to the United Kingdom: separating generation, transmission, distribution, and supply into different operations. However, although Australia's reform efforts are more recent (and therefore more difficult to appraise), it appears that Australia may have avoided the kind of public concerns that have occurred in the United Kingdom over a lack of competition in electricity generation. Victoria, the second most populous of the Australian states but with a population less than one-fifth that of the UK attempted to create more competition in generation through the creation of five generation companies. Various Australian governments have also encouraged the development of an independent electricity marketing function, thus as in the United Kingdom allowing customers to bypass traditional distribution companies.

In Argentina, as in the United Kingdom, restructuring was primarily a central-government-led operation. The Argentine government unbundled generation operations from transmission and distribution. Electricity marketing, however, was not separated out as a distinct business company or operation. However, due to the dispersed population concentrations in Argentina, several regional transmission companies were created. The regional companies act as spurs connecting otherwise isolated areas to the main electricity grids.

Competitive Electricity Pools

All three countries created national electricity pools. The United Kingdom was first to create a national electricity pool, which has been in operation since 1990. The UK electricity pool is operated by the National Grid Company, which is also responsible for electricity transmission. The UK pool has generally operated efficiently, although concerns have been raised over its tendency to produce price volatility and an unfair playing field between electricity suppliers (again, primarily the two now-privatized dominant generation companies) and electricity consumers. A secondary market, called a contract for differences market, has evolved in the United Kingdom. This secondary market allows participants to hedge a large fraction of their pool purchases.

In Australia, the National Electricity Pool was largely based on the UK model, but with some noteworthy variations. The Australian National Pool is a fairly recent operation, having started in May 1997. (Preceding the creation of the national pool, a couple of Australian state governments created their own electricity pools and these have been in operation for several years.) The Australian National Pool is operated by an independent system operator, the central-government-owned National Electricity Market Management Company, which is separate from any transmission operation. As in the United Kingdom, pool price volatility has been an important concern in Australia, and a contract for differences market has been created to manage this risk. However, due to the relatively large number of generators participating in the supply end of the business, less concern has been raised over a lack of competitiveness.

In Argentina, a national electricity pool was also based upon the UK model. Pool operations began in 1992, and pool prices have been considerably beneath the comparable wholesale price of electricity existing prior to the commencement of pool operations. Again in contrast to the United Kingdom, no generator in Argentina is allowed to control more than ten percent of the system's generation capacity. Further, in Argentina an independent system operator operates the pool.

Asset Privatization

In the United Kingdom, widespread privatization of electricity assets followed shortly after the restructuring. These privatization were achieved through public auctions. Eventually, virtually the entire UK electricity industry was privatized with the exception of some relatively old nuclear generation plants. Much controversy surrounded the sale of UK electricity assets. With the exception of the sale of nuclear assets, UK electricity auctions were oversubscribed, leading to allegations that the government had not obtained a fair value in the sale of public goods. Further, energy companies from the United States were eventually to acquire roughly one half of all UK electricity assets.

In Australia, only the state of Victoria has gone nearly as far as the United Kingdom in its privatization efforts. Other Australian state governments were either slower to privatize or decided to retain ownership while reducing control over their electricity industries. During the initial public auction of Victoria's electricity assets, U.S. companies purchased controlling interests in all five of the privatized regional distribution companies and three of the five generation companies. Sizable premiums over book value were paid in all cases, an indication of the relatively high value U.S. companies placed on these takeover targets.

The Argentine central government also employed an auction to transfer ownership of the national government's holdings in electricity companies to the private sector. Interestingly, in the Argentine auction, bidders were required to submit levels of service standards they were committing to meet along with bid prices. Again, U.S. companies were the dominant foreign investors in Argentine electricity.

Deregulation

All three governments employed a less intrusive form of regulatory authority than that which had existed in the past. The United Kingdom's electricity reform efforts embraced two fairly radical departures from previous electricity regulation. One involved the nature of the regulator. One of the first acts of electricity reform created a national electricity body, the Office of Electricity Regulation (OFFER). In order to reduce regulatory costs and allow industry more discretion in investment and operational matters, the OFFER was lightly staffed and was headed only by a single individual (not a commission). Similar institutions were adopted in Argentina and Australia.

A novel form of price-cap regulation was adopted in the United Kingdom and emulated in Argentina and Australia. Price-cap regulation attempts to restrain costs via the application of price ceilings. Price-cap regulation is a marked contrast to the rate of return regulation employed in the United States. In terms of encouraging efficiency, price-cap regulation appears to have been successful in all three nations but has become a highly controversial matter with regard to whether it promotes equity and fairness for consumers.

Energy Subsidies and Stranded Costs

In the United Kingdom, the issue of energy subsidies (mostly those related to coal) and the disposition of stranded costs (mainly nuclear-related) greatly complicated efforts at electricity privatization. The UK electricity industry had long sustained the UK coal industry through its purchases of domestic coal at highly inflated prices. As both industries became privatized and deregulated, these subsidies were severely reduced. The stranded costs associated with nuclear power investment in the United Kingdom represent the difference in the book value of nuclear power facilities and the market value of these facilities. In contrast to the situation in the United States, where the issue of who should bear the burden of stranded costs associated with nuclear power investments is between rate payers and shareholders, in the UK (where, prior to privatization, all nuclear generating assets were owned by the national government), the issue of allocating the burden of stranded costs was between rate payers and tax payers. In the end, both parties paid: tax payers through the government's auctioning off nuclear electricity assets at heavily discounted prices; and rate payers, through a nuclear surcharge attached to electricity bills.

In Australia, stranded costs were largely unimportant due to Australia's having a very competitive coal industry (by world standards) and never having developed a nuclear power industry. In Argentina, much as in the United Kingdom, part of the failure to successfully privatize the federal government's nuclear plants stemmed from the issue of stranded costs. However, unlike the United Kingdom, Argentina has had to resolve stranded costs associated with past investments in hydroelectric power as well. Even though the marginal costs of operating Argentina's two large binational (i.e., jointly held with Paraguay and Uruguay) hydroelectric facilities are low, it is doubtful that the Argentine government will be able to recover the large capital costs associated with these facilities because of their large construction cost overruns.■

NOTES AND QUESTIONS

1. This summary of an extensive report, prepared for the Department of Energy, discusses restructuring developments in other countries. Are there any institutional aspects of the U.S. energy sector that will make the implementation of competition in the U.S. more of a challenge for regulators? For example, how should the fact that we have so little government ownership of the electricity sector influence the regulatory solution in the U.S.?

2. In Australia, an independent system operator operates a "pool"–an arrangement that facilitates coordination of power transmission decisions and helps to ensure reliability and open access. The pool model is an approach to implementing competition that can involve both markets and government regulation, as regulators sometimes need to evaluate who

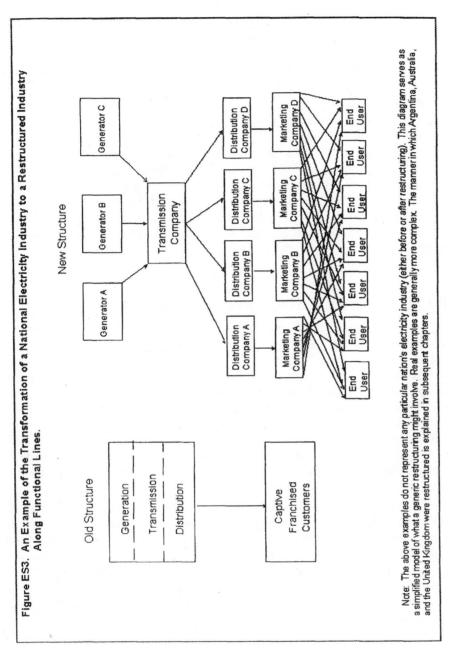

Figure ES3. An Example of the Transformation of a National Electricity Industry to a Restructured Industry Along Functional Lines.

Note: The above examples do not represent any particular nation's electricity industry (either before or after restructuring). This diagram serves as a simplified model of what a generic restructuring might involve. Real examples are generally more complex. The manner in which Argentina, Australia, and the United Kingdom were restructured is explained in subsequent chapters.

Figure 11–1

http://www.eia.doe.gov/emeu/pgem/electric/es3.gif

participates in the pool, who makes decisions regarding the market, and how well the pool works at achieving regulators' goals. Later in this Chapter, the independent system operator, an pooling approach endorsed by U.S. regulators, is discussed as a way of managing transmission. In Chapter Thirteen, the power pool approach is discussed as an approach for implementing retail competition in states such as California.

3. Of course, as with natural gas, stranded costs are a major issue in electricity restructuring. Stranded cost recovery is discussed in detail in Chapter Twelve.

4. Other issues in U.S. electricity regulation, such as price caps and merger activity, are discussed in Chapter Eighteen.

5. Following the U.K.'s privatization and liberalization of its energy industry, foreign investors made large profits in the newly constituted energy services markets. In the late 1990s, the U.K. passed legislation designed to tax the profits of some these firms as "windfalls." This has created a large degree of uncertainty for investors regarding the risks in the restructured U.K. electric power market. For discussion, see Thomas W. Waelde & Abba Kolo, Renegotiating Previous Governments' Privatization Deals: The 1997 U.K. Windfall Tax on Utilities and International Law, 19 J. Intl. L. Bus. 405 (1999). Some investors have left the U.K. market due to this uncertainty.

B. U.S. FEDERAL REGULATION BEFORE 1978

An economic basis for the treatment of firms in the electricity industry as regulated public utilities was because of the assumption that the industry constituted a "natural monopoly." However, in fact that monopoly was never complete. Since its initial development as an energy resource, competition has existed between electricity and alternative energy sources, such as oil and natural gas. For example, as the price of electricity rises, residential consumers in many areas have the option of switching to natural gas for purposes of heating and cooling. In this sense, the availability of alternative energy sources worked as a competitive check on electricity. In addition, competition among various suppliers of electricity has always existed to some degree.

The power of federal regulators to enhance competition in the electric utility industry is limited, largely because federal jurisdiction over competition policy has largely been restricted by statute to wholesale utilities and transactions. Nevertheless, federal regulators have played an integral role in redefining the structure of the utility industry. The application of the antitrust laws, designed to protect competition from monopolistic behavior, to the electricity industry was discussed by the Supreme Court in the landmark case of *Otter Tail Power v. United States*:

Otter Tail Power v. United States
410 U.S. 366 (1973).

[Otter Tail Power was the major IOU in Minnesota, North Dakota, and South Dakota. Like most IOUs, it engaged in the generation, transmission, and distribution of power. It served the large majority of towns in these three states, but in a number of towns power was distributed through a municipal power company which did not generate power itself. These municipal distribution utilities could purchase power at a low rate from federal Bureau of Reclamation projects. However, the purchased power had to be transmitted ("wheeled") over the lines owned by Otter Tail. The municipals alleged that Otter Tail had sought to take over service in the municipal areas by anticompetitive means in violation of the Sherman Act. The civil antitrust suit alleged that Otter Tail had refused to sell wholesale power, had refused to wheel power, had discouraged other suppliers from dealing with the municipals, and had begun litigation to delay the establishment of municipal power systems. The District Court found in favor of the U.S. and the municipals.]

I.

■ Douglas, J.: Otter Tail contends that by reason of the Federal Power Act it is not subject to antitrust regulation with respect to its refusal to deal. We disagree with that position.

"Repeals of the antitrust laws by implication from a regulatory statute are strongly disfavored, and have only been found in cases of plain repugnancy between the antitrust and regulatory provisions." *United States v. Philadelphia National Bank*, 374 U.S. 321, 350–351. *See also Silver v. New York Stock Exchange*, 373 U.S. 341, 357–361. Activities which come under the jurisdiction of a regulatory agency nevertheless may be subject to scrutiny under the antitrust laws.

In *California v. FPC*, 369 U.S. 482, 489, the Court held that approval of an acquisition of the assets of a natural gas company by the Federal Power Commission pursuant to § 7 of the Natural Gas Act "would be no bar to [an] antitrust suit." Under § 7, the standard for approving such acquisitions is "public convenience and necessity." Although the impact on competition is relevant to the Commission's determination, the Court noted that there was "no 'pervasive regulatory scheme' including the antitrust laws that ha[d] been entrusted to the Commission." *Id.*, at 485. Similarly, in *United States v. Radio Corp. of America*, 358 U.S. 334, the Court held that an exchange of radio stations that had been approved by the Federal Communications Commission as in the "public interest" was subject to attack in an antitrust proceeding.

The District Court determined that Otter Tail's consistent refusals to wholesale or wheel power to its municipal customers constituted illegal monopolization. Otter Tail maintains here that its refusals to deal should be immune from antitrust prosecution because the Federal Power Commission has the authority to compel involuntary interconnections of power pursuant to § 202 (b) of the Federal Power Act. The essential thrust of § 202, however, is to encourage voluntary interconnections of power. *See* S. Rep. No. 621, 74th Cong., 1st Sess., 19–20, 48–49; H. R. Rep. No. 1318, 74th Cong., 1st Sess., 8. Only if a power company refuses to interconnect voluntarily may the Federal Power Commission, subject to limitations unrelated to antitrust considerations, order the interconnection. The standard which governs its decision is whether such action is "necessary or appropriate in the public interest." Although antitrust considerations may be relevant, they are not determinative.

There is nothing in the legislative history which reveals a purpose to insulate electric power companies from the operation of the antitrust laws. To the contrary, the history of Part II of the Federal Power Act indicates an overriding policy of maintaining competition to the maximum extent possible consistent with the public interest. As originally conceived, Part II would have included a "common carrier" provision making it "the duty of every public utility to . . . transmit energy for any person upon reasonable request. . . ." In addition, it would have empowered the Federal Power Commission to order wheeling if it found such action to be "necessary or desirable in the public interest." H. R. 5423, 74th Cong., 1st Sess.; S. 1725, 74th Cong., 1st Sess. These provisions were eliminated to preserve "the voluntary action of the utilities." S. Rep. No. 621, 74th Cong., 1st Sess., 19.

It is clear, then, that Congress rejected a pervasive regulatory scheme for controlling the interstate distribution of power in favor of voluntary commercial relationships. When these relationships are governed in the first instance by business judgment and not regulatory coercion, courts must be hesitant to conclude that Congress intended to override the fundamental national policies embodied in the antitrust laws. *See United States v. Radio Corp. of America*, supra, at 351. This is particularly true in this instance because Congress, in passing the Public Utility Holding Company Act, which included Part II of the Federal Power Act, was concerned with "restraint of free and independent competition" among public utility holding companies. *See* 15 U. S. C. § 79a (b)(2).

Thus, there is no basis for concluding that the limited authority of the Federal Power Commission to order interconnections was intended to be a substitute for, or to immunize Otter Tail from, antitrust regulation for refusing to deal with municipal corporations.

II.

The decree of the District Court enjoins Otter Tail from "refusing to sell electric power at wholesale to existing or proposed municipal electric power systems in cities and towns located in [its service area]" and from refusing to wheel electric power over its transmission lines from other electric power lines to such cities and towns. But the decree goes on to provide:

The defendant shall not be compelled by the Judgment in this case to furnish wholesale electric service or wheeling service to a municipality except at rates which are compensatory and under terms and conditions which are filed with and subject to approval by the Federal Power Commission.

So far as wheeling is concerned, there is no authority granted the Commission under Part II of the Federal Power Act to order it, for the bills originally introduced contained common carrier provisions which were deleted. The Act as passed contained only the interconnection provision set forth in § 202 (b). The common carrier provision in the original bill and the power to direct wheeling were left to the "voluntary coordination of electric facilities." Insofar as the District Court ordered wheeling to correct anti-competitive and monopolistic practices of Otter Tail, there is no conflict with the authority of the Federal Power Commission.

III.

The record makes abundantly clear that Otter Tail used its monopoly power in the towns in its service area to foreclose competition or gain a competitive advantage, or to destroy a competitor, all in violation of the antitrust laws. *See United States v. Griffith*, 334 U.S. 100, 107. The District Court determined that Otter Tail has "a strategic dominance in the transmission of power in most of its service area" and that it used this dominance to foreclose potential entrants into the retail area from obtaining electric power from outside sources of supply. 331 F. Supp., at 60. Use of monopoly power "to destroy threatened competition" is a violation of the "attempt to monopolize" clause of § 2 of the Sherman Act. *Lorain Journal v. United States*, 342 U.S. 143, 154; *Eastman Kodak Co. v. Southern Photo Materials Co.*, 273 U.S. 359, 375. So are agreements not to compete, with the aim of preserving or extending a monopoly. *Schine Chain Theatres v. United States*, 334 U.S. 110, 119. In *Associated Press v. United States*, 326 U.S. 1, a cooperative news association had bylaws that permitted member newspapers to bar competitors from joining the association. We held that practice violated the Sherman Act, even though the transgressor "had not yet achieved a complete monopoly." *Id.*, at 13.

When a community serviced by Otter Tail decides not to renew Otter Tail's retail franchise when it expires, it may generate, transmit, and distribute its own electric power. We recently described the difficulties and problems of those isolated electric power systems. *See Gainesville Utilities v. Florida Power Corp.*, 402 U.S. 515, 517–520. Interconnection with other utilities is frequently the only solution. *Id.*, at 519 n. 3. That is what Elbow Lake in the present case did. There were no engineering factors that prevented Otter Tail from selling power at wholesale to those towns that wanted municipal plants or wheeling the power. The District Court found— and its findings are supported—that Otter Tail's refusals to sell at whole-sale or to wheel were solely to prevent municipal power systems from eroding its monopolistic position.

Otter Tail relies on its wheeling contracts with the Bureau of Reclamation and with cooperatives which it says relieve it of any duty to wheel power to municipalities served at retail by Otter Tail at the time the contracts were made. The District Court held that these restrictive provisions were "in reality, territorial allocation schemes," 331 F. Supp., at 63, and were per se violations of the Sherman Act, *citing Northern Pacific R. Co. v. United States*, 356 U.S. 1. Like covenants were there held to "deny defendant's competitors access to the fenced-off market on the same terms as the defendant." *Id.*, at 12. We recently re-emphasized the vice under the Sherman Act of territorial restrictions among potential competitors. United

States v. Topco Associates, 405 U.S. 596, 608. The fact that some of the restrictive provisions were contained in a contract with the Bureau of Reclamation is not material to our problem for, as the Solicitor General says, "government contracting officers do not have the power to grant immunity from the Sherman Act." Such contracts stand on their own footing and are valid or not, depending on the statutory framework within which the federal agency operates. The Solicitor General tells us that these restrictive provisions operate as a "hindrance" to the Bureau and were "agreed to by the Bureau only at Otter Tail's insistence," as the District Court found. The evidence supports that finding. . . .

V.

Otter Tail argues that, without the weapons which it used, more and more municipalities will turn to public power and Otter Tail will go downhill. The argument is a familiar one. It was made in *United States v. Arnold, Schwinn & Co.*, 388 U.S. 365, a civil suit under section 1 of the Sherman Act dealing with a restrictive distribution program and practices of a bicycle manufacturer. We said: "The promotion of self-interest alone does not invoke the rule of reason to immunize otherwise illegal conduct." *Id.*, at 375.

The same may properly be said of section 2 cases under the Sherman Act. That Act assumes that an enterprise will protect itself against loss by operating with superior service, lower costs, and improved efficiency. Otter Tail's theory collided with the Sherman Act as it sought to substitute for competition anticompetitive uses of its dominant economic power.

The fact that three municipalities which Otter Tail opposed finally got their municipal systems does not excuse Otter Tail's conduct. That fact does not condone the antitrust tactics which Otter Tail sought to impose. Moreover, the District Court repeated what we said in *FTC v. National Lead Co.*, 352 U.S. 419, 431, "those caught violating the Act must expect some fencing in." The proclivity for predatory practices has always been a consideration for the District Court in fashioning its antitrust decree. *See United States v. Crescent Amusement Co.*, 323 U.S. 173, 190.

We do not suggest, however, that the District Court, concluding that Otter Tail violated the antitrust laws, should be impervious to Otter Tail's assertion that compulsory interconnection or wheeling will erode its integrated system and threaten its capacity to serve adequately the public. As the dissent properly notes, the Commission may not order interconnection if to do so "would impair [the utility's] ability to render adequate service to its customers." 16 U.S.C. § 824a (b). The District Court in this case found that the "pessimistic view" advanced in Otter Tail's "erosion study" "is not supported by the record." Furthermore, it concluded that "it does not appear that Bureau of Reclamation power is a serious threat to the defendant nor that it will be in the foreseeable future." Since the District Court has made future connections subject to Commission approval and in any event has retained jurisdiction to enable the parties to apply for "necessary or appropriate" relief and presumably will give effect to the policies embodied in the Federal Power Act, we cannot say under these circumstances that it has abused its discretion.■

NOTES AND COMMENTS

1. The Sherman and Clayton Acts contain various sections that prohibit anticompetitive conduct. Section 1 of the Sherman act prohibits agreements in restraint of trade. Section 2 of the Sherman Act prohibits monopolization and attempts to monopolize. The Clayton Act condemns mergers that tend to substantially lessen competition.

In the *Otter Tail Power* case, Otter Tail claimed that it was exempt from the Sherman Act because of the regulated industries exception—where an enterprise's competitive activities are already scrutinized under a pervasive regulatory scheme, courts or agencies may, under the doctrine of primary jurisdiction, defer to that regulatory scheme rather than apply the antitrust laws. As the Court notes, however, such deference is unlikely where a regulatory scheme is not directly concerned with the anticompetitive implications of an enterprise's activities.

A similar exemption applies to regulated enterprises at the state level, where retail transactions in the electricity industry have historically been regulated. The state action doctrine exempts from federal antitrust laws anticompetitive conduct where a state has explicitly adopted an active regulatory policy to displace competition with regulation or a monopoly franchise. Thus, state PSC price regulation of a state-franchised public utility may be exempt from antitrust challenge. However, like the regulated industries exception, the state action doctrine is not automatic. *See, e.g., City of Lafayette v. Louisiana Power & Light Co.*, 435 U.S. 389 (1978); *Cantor v. Detroit Edison Co.*, 428 U.S. 579 (1976). The doctrine is discussed further in Chapter Thirteen.

2. *Otter Tail* considered the authority of the FPC to order interconnection or wheeling of power. The benefits of interconnection are summarized in *Gainesville Utilities v. Florida Power Corp.*, 402 U.S. 515 (1971):

> The demand upon an electric utility for electric power fluctuates significantly from hour to hour, day to day, and season to season. For this reason, generating facilities cannot be maintained on the basis of constant demand. Rather, the utility's generating capacity must be geared to the utility's peak load of demand, and also take into account the fact that generating equipment must occasionally be out of service for overhaul, or because of breakdowns. In consequence, the utility builds certain "reserves" of generating capacity in excess of peak load requirements into its system. The practice of a utility that relies completely on its own generating resources (an "isolated" system in industry jargon) is to maintain equipment capable of producing its peak load requirements plus equipment that produces a "reserve" capacity equal to the capacity of its largest generating unit.

The major importance of an interconnection is that it reduces the need for the "isolated" utility to build and maintain "reserve" generating capacity. An interconnection is simply a transmission line connecting two utilities. Electric power may move freely through the line up to the line's capacity. Ordinarily, however, the energy generated by each system is sufficient to supply the requirements of the system's customers and no substantial amount of power flows through the interconnection. It is only at the times when one of the connected utilities is unable for some reason to produce sufficient power to meet its customers' needs that the deficiency may be supplied by power that automatically flows through the interconnection from the other utility. To the extent that the utility may rely upon the interconnection to supply this deficiency, the utility is freed of the necessity of constructing and maintaining its own equipment for the purpose.

Gainesville Utilities upheld an FPC order that directed interconnection between a municipal utility and a larger, adjacent investor-owned system. The Court reversed the Court of Appeals' decision, which required the municipal system to provide substantially greater compensation for the interconnection than the FPC had required.

3. The Public Utilities Holding Company Act of 1935 (PUHCA), 15 U.S.C. § 79 *et seq.*, mentioned in the Otter Tail case, regulates the ownership structure of public utilities. During the 1920s and 1930s, public utility holding companies had gained effective control over many operating electric utility companies, primarily by controlling voting with far less than 100 percent ownership. PUHCA was aimed at breaking up the trusts that controlled U.S. gas and electric utilities. At the time PUCHA was enacted into law, financial pyramid schemes were common. These schemes allowed utilities in many different areas of the country to fall under the control of a small number of holding companies. Before PUHCA, almost half of all electricity was controlled by three huge holding companies.

Samuel Insull's investments in the industry, a target during the hearing that lead to the enactment of PUHCA, are a good example:

The Insull interests (which operated in 32 states and owned electric companies, textile mills, ice houses, a paper mill, and a hotel) controlled 69 percent of the stock of Corporation Securities and 64 percent of the stock of Insull Utility Investments. Those two companies together owned 28 percent of the voting stock of Middle West Utilities. Middle West Utilities owned eight holding companies, five investment companies, two service companies, two securities companies, and 14 operating companies. It also owned 99 percent of the voting stock of National Electric Power. National, in turn, owned one holding company, one service company, one paper company, and two operating companies. It also owned 93 percent of the voting stock of National Public Service. National Public Service owned three building companies, three miscellaneous firms, and four operating utilities. It also owned 100 percent of the voting stock of Seaboard Public Service. Seaboard Public Service owned the voting stock of five utility operating companies and one ice company. The utilities, in turn, owned eighteen subsidiaries.

L.S. Hyman, America's Electric Utilities: Past, Present and Future 102 (5th ed. 1994).

The Securities and Exchange Commission (SEC) was charged with the administration of PUHCA, including the regulation of holding companies. PUHCA authorized the SEC to break up the massive utility holding companies by requiring them to divest their holdings until each was a single consolidated system serving a defined geographic area. PUHCA also limited the businesses that utility holding companies could engage in to utility-related functions. All holding companies were required to register with the SEC. Through the registration process, the SEC determines whether each holding company will be regulated or exempt from the requirements of PUHCA. The SEC defines a utility holding company as a company which directly or indirectly owns 10 percent or more of the outstanding securities of a single utility company. The SEC has taken a very aggressive approach to interpreting this requirement, but there is a safety valve in PUHCA for holding companies that are entirely intrastate in character. *See* Energy Information Administration, The Public Utility Holding Company Act of 1935: 1935–1992 (1993).

C.   THE GROWTH OF WHOLESALE COMPETITION IN ELECTRIC GENERATION

Competition in electricity generation has brought about certain economic efficiencies, although the net degree of efficiency improvement is a subject of considerable controversy. A recent report by the Energy Information Administration concludes that if full scale competition in electricity generation began, retail prices for electricity would be reduced as much as 6 to 13 percent within 2 years compared to prices under the current approach to regulation. Under conditions of intense competition, the same study predicts that prices could fall as much as 24 percent. The study notes, however, that there are significant differences across regions of the U.S. *See* Energy Information Administration, Electricity Prices in a Competitive Environment: Marginal Cost Pricing of Generation Services and Financial Status of Electric Utilities—A Preliminary Analysis Through 2015 (August 1997).

To understand the current degree and future growth of competition in the "electric power" industry (which as a business area has now displaced its predecessor, the "electric utility" industry), it is useful to explore some of the legal and policy issues that have been addressed at the federal level since the 1970s. In evaluating these legal and policy issues, it is important to recognize how the services historically provided by a single, vertically-integrated utility—generation, distribution and transmission—are no longer regarded as possessing similar economic characteristics. Generation is seen as a structurally competitive industry, one that can accommodate multiple competing suppliers. Distribution and transmission, however, are considered to possess many natural monopoly characteristics.

1. PURPA AND THE GROWTH OF INDEPENDENT POWER PRODUCERS (IPPs)

The various factors that caused electricity prices to increase in the 1970s and 1980s—increased oil prices, environmental standards, and nuclear costs—increased pressure for competition in the electric industry for a number of reasons. First, increased costs did not impact electric utilities uniformly, increasing the disparity of electric rates among different utilities and causing some customers to look enviously at the rates their neighbors were paying. Second, new companies that were not burdened with old plants and had access to a fuel other than oil (such as natural gas) were in a position to build new plants and undercut the prices charged by the older utilities.

In 1978, Congress adopted the Public Utilities Regulatory Policy Act (PURPA), Pub.L. 95–617, 92 Stat. 3117, as a part of President Carter's national energy plan. PURPA's enactment in 1978 showed that Congress was responsive to the desire of customers to explore new options. PURPA endorsed the potential for efficiency and conservation in the energy conversion process and the promotion of efficiency in the pooling, interconnection and "wheeling" (i.e., off-system customer or supplier transmission) of power. Two provisions in PURPA were of significance in jump-starting competition among wholesale power suppliers.

First, PURPA included provisions to encourage efficiency and conservation by non-utility generators of electricity. Section 210 of PURPA authorized FERC to prescribe rules to encourage cogeneration and small power production (known as "qualifying facilities", or QFs) by authorizing FERC to require utilities to purchase or sell electricity from such facilities. The statute provided that the rate of purchase from QFs 1) would be just and reasonable and in the public interest; and 2) shall not discriminate against cogenerators or small power producers. Rules FERC promulgated in 1980 encouraged the growth of QFs by requiring utilities to purchase their power at a price known as "avoided costs," requiring interconnection with the electric utility grid, and exempting the new facilities from certain federal and state regulations, including traditional rate regulation. *See* 18 C.F.R. Pt. 292. FERCs rules were challenged but upheld by the U.S. Supreme Court. *See FERC v. Mississippi*, 456 U.S. 742 (1982) (holding that Congress, in enacting PURPA, did not exceed its power under the Commerce Clause or violate states' rights under the Tenth Amendment); *American Paper Institute, Inc. v. American Electric Power Service Corp.*, 461 U.S. 402 (1983) (holding that FERC's avoided cost rules are not arbitrary, capricious or an abuse of discretion).

PURPA's QF certification scheme jump-started the growth of an independent energy sector. After a period of decades of declining electricity prices, between 1973 and 1982 electricity prices increased by about 60 percent in real (inflation adjusted) terms. US DOE, DOE/S–0057, Energy Security, A Report to the President of the U.S., at 154 (1987). This created strong economic incentives for large consumers of electricity to reduce their energy costs. With PURPA's scheme cogeneration, which had supplied nearly 50 percent of power produced in the U.S. around the turn of the century, again became a viable economic alternative for many industrial and commercial energy users. By 1990, non-utility generation had grown to supply more than half of the marginal generation capacity added to the industry, and more than 10% of cumulative generation capacity. For a discussion of states' roles in implementing this aspect of PURPA, *see* Deirdre Callaghan & Steve Greenwald, PURPA from Coast to Coast: America's Great Electricity Experiment, Natural Resources & Environment, Winter 1996, at 17.

The second major competition-enhancing provision PURPA added to federal law authorized FERC to mandate wheeling for wholesale customers and suppliers. PURPA added Sections 211 and 212 to the Federal Power Act. As *Otter Tail* observed, the FPA did not originally authorize the Commission to require one utility to transmit off-system power. The sections added by PURPA in 1978 allowed FERC to mandate wholesale wheeling only where it would not result in a "reasonably ascertainable uncompensated economic loss" and would not place "an undue burden," "unreasonably impair the reliability of any electric utility," or will not impair adequate service to customers.

In part because of narrow agency and judicial interpretation, however, the version of Sections 211 and 212 enacted in 1978 was never fully utilized to require a utility to transmit power from an off-system source. The Second Circuit held that Section 211 clearly indicated that wheeling could not be ordered solely on the basis of the public interest and the enhancement of competition. *New York Elec. & Gas Co. v. FERC*, 638 F.2d 388, 402 (2d Cir.1980). In addition, the Fifth Circuit rebuked an effort by FERC to foster competition through mandatory wheeling, noting that although FERC's goal was "laudable," the agency "is without authority under the FPA to compel wheeling." *Florida Power & Light Co. v. FERC*, 660 F.2d 668, 677–79 (5th Cir.1981). Following these decisions, FERC itself interpreted Section 211 to "prohibit[] the issuance of wheeling orders that have a significant procompetitive effect." *Southeastern Power Administration*, 26 FERC ¶ 61,127 at 61,323 (1984). Although FERC noted that it may have been willing to require wholesale wheeling to address fuel shortages or to promote the coordination of electricity among utilities, *Southeastern Power Administration*, 25 FERC ¶ 61,204 at 61,539 (1983), FERC did not issue a single order requiring procompetitive wheeling.

Even though the 1978 version of Sections 211 and 212 were never directly used to enhance competition, they may have had some indirect effect on competition in the industry. First, the threat of compulsory wheeling may have nudged utilities to negotiate voluntary transmission agreements with other suppliers and wholesale customers.

Second, FERC used indirect regulatory mechanisms to implement section 211 and 212. FERC's ability to implement "open access" was severely limited by Section 211(c)(1) of the FPA, which barred FERC from requiring wholesale wheeling service "unless the Commission determined that such order would reasonably preserve existing competitive relationships." Despite FERC's narrow jurisdiction under the 1978 version of Section 211 of the FPA to require wheeling, in recent years FERC has issued procompetitive transmission access orders in the adjudicative context as a voluntary condition to a benefit or approval conferred under other sections of the FPA.

For example, FERC has imposed open access transmission terms as a condition to approval of "market-based" rates under its general rate regulation authority, contained in sections 205 and 206 of the FPA. FERC initiated this policy with a flexible pricing experiment in bulk power transactions known as the "Southwest Experiment" in the early 1980s. Later, FERC developed a general market-based pricing policy in a number of adjudicative cases, routinely requiring wholesale transmission access as a condition to its approval of market-based rates.

FERC also used its merger approval authority to develop transmission policy on a case-by-case basis. In the 1980s, electric utility mergers increased dramatically and FERC took the opportunity to act on merger applications. These proceedings have served as an important vehicle for the development of transmission policy. FERC has consistently imposed "open access" transmission terms as a condition to its approval of mergers under section 203 of the FPA. *See* Jim Rossi, Redeeming Judicial Review: The Hard Look Doctrine and Federal Regulatory Efforts to Restructure the Electric Utility Industry, 1994 Wis. L. Rev. 763 (1994).

2.   MARKET–BASED RATES AND OTHER REFORMS TO RATE REGULATION

With the growth of competition, federal regulators have considered moving away from the traditional approach of setting rates based on costs. *See* Chapter Eight. Two approaches, still dependent on regulatory oversight by FERC or state commissions, are market-based rates and incentive rates.

a.   MARKET–BASED RATES

In addition to transmission access, in the late 1980s, FERC adopted additional regulatory strategies to increase competition in the independent energy sector, jump-started by PURPA. Two significant measures adopted by FERC were: 1) the approval of market-based rates for independent power producers that lacked significant market power, effectively relieving these generators of the regulatory burden imposed by cost of service regulation; and 2) the exercise of "light-handed" regulation for independent power producers, which relieved these generators from other costly reporting requirements. Several states have adopted similar market-based rate and light-handed regulation mechanisms. In addition, state programs designed to encourage or require competitive bidding for approval of new generation capacity increased from only a few in 1988 to more than 30 by 1993. The *Dartmouth Power* case provides an overview of some of the concerns raised by market-based and light-handed regulation at the federal level:

Dartmouth Power Associates Limited Partnership

53 F.E.R.C. ¶ 61,117 (1990).

■ Before COMMISSIONERS: MARTIN L. ALLDAY, CHAIRMAN; CHARLES A. TRABANDT, ELIZABETH ANNE MOLER and JERRY J. LANGDON.

On March 21, 1990, as completed on October 5, 1990, Dartmouth Power Associates Limited Partnership (Dartmouth) submitted a Power Purchase Agreement (the Agreement) between Dartmouth and Commonwealth Electric Company (Commonwealth Electric), and an Amendment to the Agreement (Amendment). The rates from Dartmouth to Commonwealth Electric were negotiated between the parties and, as discussed infra, Dartmouth requests that the Commission find that its rates are just and reasonable as market-based rates....

Negotiations leading up to the Agreement began in the spring of 1987. The Agreement was executed September 5, 1989, and was filed March 21, 1990. The Agreement originally provided that Dartmouth would construct, own and operate a 168.8–MW combined cycle, gas-fired unit, and would sell 50 MW of capacity and energy to Commonwealth Electric. Dartmouth states that in February 1990, it decided to reconfigure the unit to reflect a smaller, 67.6–MW combined cycle unit, and notified Commonwealth Electric of this proposed change....

According to Dartmouth, the unit will be located in Commonwealth Electric's service territory and will be fully dispatchable by the New England Power Pool (NEPOOL). Dartmouth states that it will own only those transmission facilities used to interconnect the unit with Commonwealth Electric's system....

Dartmouth is a limited partnership. Dartmouth's sole general partner, EMI Dartmouth, Inc., is a Massachusetts Corporation owned entirely by an individual, James Gordon. According to Dartmouth, Mr. Gordon "will also own at least 50% of the limited partnership interests in Dartmouth." Currently, five other individuals hold limited partnership interests in Dartmouth, and Dartmouth states that other limited partnership interests may be sold in the future. In this regard, the respective interests of Dartmouth's general and limited partners have yet to be determined.

Through Mr. Gordon, Dartmouth will be affiliated with Pawtucket Power Associates Limited Partnership (Pawtucket), an entity which will own a 62–MW cogeneration facility. Dartmouth states that Mr. Gordon owns a 100% interest in EMI Management, Inc. (EMI), the developer of Dartmouth and Pawtucket. According to Dartmouth, EMI has also developed a cogeneration facility which will sell electricity to Commonwealth Electric. . . .

Dartmouth states its price to Commonwealth Electric "was negotiated over an extended period of time," and that "[t]he history of the negotiations between [Commonwealth Electric] and Dartmouth and [Commonwealth Electric's] access to alternative sources of wholesale electric power demonstrate the existence of a competitive market supporting market-based rates." In this regard, in support of its request for approval of market-based rates, Dartmouth argues that the New England electricity market is characterized by an active market for new QF capacity, and that Commonwealth Electric participates in this market both through formal QF bid solicitations and through nonbid negotiations. . . .

Dartmouth argues that negotiations between Dartmouth and Commonwealth Electric took place in the context of a competitive market in which Commonwealth Electric had numerous supply alternatives. In this regard, Dartmouth notes that Commonwealth Electric has had numerous supply alternatives to choose from as evidenced by: (1) the responses to Commonwealth Electric's solicitation for QF capacity in RFP 1 (where bids totaling over 920 MW were received, constituting more than ten times the amount of capacity sought); (2) the responses eight other New England utilities received to 1987 and 1988 solicitations (where bids totaled over 11,000 MW, twelve times the capacity solicited); (3) the response Boston Edison Company (BECO) received in its fall 1989 QF solicitation (where bids totaled 2,837 MW, fourteen times the capacity solicited); and (4) the fact that, according to Dartmouth, 6,200 MW of independent power capacity is currently under construction or development in New England. . . .

Dartmouth argues that, since neither it nor its parent or affiliates own or control transmission facilities (other than those required to interconnect the facility with the purchaser's system), it cannot restrict Commonwealth Electric's access to competing suppliers. Furthermore, Dartmouth states that it does not control any other resources by which it could erect barriers against the entry of other suppliers. Dartmouth also states that it has no affiliations or business relationships which could result in self dealing.

Based on the foregoing arguments, Dartmouth concludes that it lacks market power over Commonwealth Electric, when its proposal is judged against the standards used by the Commission in approving other market-based rates.

Dartmouth requests that the Commission grant waivers of its regulations, considering the market-based nature of Dartmouth's rates. . . .

In Commonwealth Atlantic Limited Partnership (Commonwealth Atlantic), the Commission determined that market-based rates are acceptable if the seller can demonstrate that it lacks market power over the buyer. In addition, the Commission has carefully scrutinized transactions involving nontraditional sellers affiliated with franchised utilities, or affiliated with any other entities that own or control resources that could be used to create barriers to other suppliers who seek to enter the market. Accordingly, we have analyzed Dartmouth's proposal consistent with the analysis used in our prior cases.

In both Enron and Commonwealth Atlantic, the Commission noted that it had previously approved long-term power sales at market-based rates where the seller demonstrated that it had no market power over the buyer (or that the seller had adequately mitigated its market power) and where there was no evidence of potential affiliate abuse. *E.g., Enron*, 52 FERC at p. 61,708 & n.41 (*citing Commonwealth Atlantic*, 51 FERC P61,368 (1990); *Public Service Company of Indiana, Inc.*, 51 FERC P61,367 (1990); *Doswell Limited Partnership*, 50 FERC P61,251 (1990); *Ocean State Power Company*, 44 FERC P61,261 (1989)). In *Enron* and *Commonwealth Atlantic*, the Commission noted that it had previously stated that a seller has market power when it can significantly influence the price in the market by restricting supply or by denying access to alternative sellers. *E.g., id.* (*citing Commonwealth Atlantic*, 51 FERC at p. 62,244 & n.43; *Doswell*, 50 FERC at p. 61,757 & n.12 (1990); *Citizens Power & Light Corporation*, 48 FERC P61,210 (1989)).

Specifically, the criteria set forth in the Commission's prior decisions require that the seller provide evidence that: (1) neither the seller nor any of its affiliates is a dominant firm in the sale of generation services in the relevant market; (2) neither the seller nor any of its affiliates owns or controls transmission facilities which could be used by the buyer in reaching alternative generation suppliers, or they have adequately mitigated their ability to block the buyer in reaching such alternative suppliers; and (3) neither the seller nor any of its affiliates is able to erect or otherwise control any other barrier to entry. The Commission has also analyzed whether there is evidence of potential abuses of self dealing or reciprocal dealing. As discussed below, we find that Dartmouth's filing meets these standards, and thus we will accept Dartmouth's rates for filing....

Neither Dartmouth nor its affiliates own or are affiliated with utilities that own transmission facilities in the region. Neither Dartmouth nor its QF affiliates can erect barriers preventing others from entering the relevant market; in this regard, Dartmouth has stated that it controls no major input factors (e.g., land sites, gas pipelines, or fuel supplies).

Finally, we find that there is no evidence of self dealing or reciprocal dealing abuse. Dartmouth is not affiliated with Commonwealth Electric. Although Dartmouth is affiliated with a developer which is constructing a QF which will serve Commonwealth Electric, there is no evidence that Dartmouth, because of this affiliation, was able to influence the price at which Commonwealth Electric purchased power....

We find that Dartmouth's market-pricing proposal will result in rates to Commonwealth Electric that are within the legally mandated zone of reasonableness. We note that we will have the opportunity to reassess this finding if changes to the rate are proposed. The Dartmouth/Commonwealth Electric Agreement is a formula rate. While the rate charged Commonwealth Electric will vary over time, the adjustments will be pursuant to the approved formulae, which our review has shown were determined through negotiations in which Dartmouth lacked market power. The formulae cannot be changed without a further filing with the Commission. Accordingly, if Dartmouth in the future acquires market power over Commonwealth Electric and tries to exercise that power through modifications to the formula rate, it will need the Commission's approval for such changes. The Commission would review Dartmouth's proposal de novo in light of the then existing circumstances, and would not approve continuation of a market-based rate unless we were assured that Dartmouth continued to lack market power, or had adequately mitigated its market power.

■ CHARLES A. TRABANDT, COMMISSIONER, concurring:

I join in approving the market rate that Dartmouth Power Associates Limited Partnership (Dartmouth Power) proposes to charge Commonwealth Electric Company under the contract before us. I write in order briefly to explain why.

[I take] issue with the majority's approach to approving market rates for independent power producers (IPPs), generators unaffiliated with utilities. [T]he Federal Power Act and the cases contain three requirements: finding a workable competitive market; imposing a just and reasonable price ceiling; and creating a monitoring mechanism to account for changed conditions. Specifically, I disagreed with the Commonwealth holding that we need not subject rates IPPs negotiate to just and reasonable ceilings.

Here, we all agree that the Dartmouth Power contract emerged from a competitive market. As to the second criterion, in this case, the majority keeps to its rejection of a rate ceiling. I adhere to my view. Nevertheless, I agree with approving the contract before us. . . . ■

b. INCENTIVE REGULATION

While FERC and many state PSCs will allow market based rates where a firm lacks market power, most utilities with market power continue to base rates on the cost of service. However, in recent years new regulatory mechanisms designed to encourage more efficient utility rate setting have emerged. One of the most popular of these is incentive rates.

In a policy statement issued in 1992, FERC announced that it will allow electric utilities with market power to propose incentive rate systems in order to advance two efficiency-enhancing results: lower rates to consumers and increase shareholder returns. *Incentive Ratemaking for Interstate Natural Gas Pipelines, Oil Pipelines, and Electric Utilities*, 61 FERC ¶ 61,168.

FERC's 1992 policy statement permitted electric utilities and natural gas pipelines to propose incentive rate mechanisms as alternatives to cost-of-service ratemaking. The Commission's incentive rate policy was premised on two overriding principles. First, incentive rate mechanisms should encourage efficiency by optimizing operating efficiency, allocating services to the highest valued uses, investing new capital when economically warranted, and capturing expanding markets. Second, the initial rates under the incentive rate mechanism must conform to the Commission's just and reasonable standard.

FERC required incentive rates to adhere to the five principles. They must:

1) be prospective;

2) be voluntary;

3) be understandable;

4) result in quantifiable benefits for consumers, subject to the constraint that they not exceed the rates that would apply under cost-of-service regulation; and

5) maintain or enhance incentives to improve the quality of service.

FERC indicated that it would rely on incentive rates on a case by case basis. To date, few utilities have availed themselves of the incentive rate mechanisms FERC has made available.

Most experimentation with incentive rates has occurred at the state level. In addition to cost of service regulation, discussed at length in Chapter Eight, state PSC rate experiments include: benchmarking—giving rewards or penalties to a utility's earning opportunity based on comparison with a pre-set standard, the value of which become known in the future; and price caps—setting a maximum price to be charged which is determined by formula based on factors not within the utilities control, such as inflation, or factors under the utilities control, such as costs. *See* J. Robert Malko & Richard J. Williams, Traditional and New Regulatory Tools, 93, 99 in Reinventing Electric Utility Regulation (Gregory B. Enholm & J. Robert Malko, eds. 1995).

Although under the present laws states have jurisdiction over retail restructuring, discussed in Chapter Thirteen, many states have also experimented with incentive rates. Like FERC's policy statement, many state efforts are designed to encourage more efficient internal decisionmaking by utility managers, resulting in lower customer rates and increased shareholder returns. These performance-based incentive rates come in a variety of different forms. Consider the following proceeding, which approves a form of performance-based incentive rates:

Re San Diego Gas and Electric Company

154 PUR 4th 313 (Cal.P.U.C.1994).

1. Summary

In this decision we consider a proposal by San Diego Gas & Electric Company (SDG&E), joined by Division of Ratepayer Advocates (DRA) and Federal Executive Agencies (FEA), for an experimental base rates regulatory mechanism. . . .

We find that the current program for regulating SDG&E's gas and electric base rates through triennial general rate cases (GRCs) may not provide the most appropriate or effective means of achieving our basic regulatory objective of the lowest reasonable rates consistent with safe, reliable, environmentally sensitive utility service. Moreover, traditional regulation may not be well-suited for the increasingly competitive energy services industry. The Joint Proposal represents an opportunity to take a conservative yet significant step away from traditional cost-of-service regulation. We find that, with minor modification, the proposed experimental, five-year base rates mechanism has a reasonable potential for improving on the attainment of our basic regulatory objective. While that result is not guaranteed, we are satisfied that the program does not represent a significant risk to ratepayers.

Key elements of the adopted experimental program are the following:

1. SDG&E is excused from filing a test year 1996 GRC. In the absence of this authorization, SDG&E would be required to file a GRC application later this year. Subject to further order of the Commission, SDG&E's next GRC will be for test year 1999.

2. During the 1994–1998 experiment, SDG&E's base rates will be capped by a revenue requirement formula which is comparable in some ways to the current operational attrition mechanism, but should yield more accurate revenue requirement forecasts.

3. A revenue-sharing mechanism which allows both shareholders and ratepayers to benefit when SDG&E's financial performance results in earnings in excess of the authorized rate of return plus 1%, yet requires shareholders to absorb the full impact of low earnings when the company earns less than its authorized rate of return.

4. A comprehensive system of performance incentives with as much as $19 million in rewards and $21 million in penalties at stake each year. This system is designed to provide SDG&E's management with additional incentives for reducing electric rates relative to a national rate index while maintaining system quality as represented by employee safety, customer satisfaction, and system reliability.

5. A program of monitoring and evaluation (M & E) designed to ensure the availability of data that will be required to evaluate the experiment, and to systematically provide for such evaluation.

We emphasize our intent that the adopted experiment is applicable to SDG&E only. Southern California Edison Company (Edison) and Pacific Gas and Electric Company (PG&E) have now filed PBR proposals as well. Today's decision is not determinative of the appropriate PBR program components for other utilities. . . .

We begin with a review of our fundamental and longstanding purpose for regulating monopoly utilities. "The function of the Commission is to regulate public utilities and compel the enforcement of their duty to the public." *Atchison, Topeka and Santa Fe Railway Company v. Railroad Commission* (1916) 173 C. 577, 582. "Created by the Constitution in 1911, the commission was designed to protect the people of the state from the consequences of destructive competition and monopoly in the public service industries." *California Motor Transport Co., Ltd. v. Railroad Commission* (1947) 30 C.2d 184, 188. The Commission regulates SDG&E's rates pursuant to the Public Utilities Act, whose "primary purpose is to insure the public adequate service at reasonable rates without discrimination ..." *City and County of San Francisco v. Public Utilities Commission* (1971) 6 C.3d 119, 126....

Here, SDG & E perceives that under current regulation it has an incentive to focus too much on short-term savings, since longer-term savings are captured by ratepayers every third year of the GRC cycle. SDG&E sees this as a flaw of current regulation, and its primary reform objective is to lengthen its planning horizon. Its specific reform proposal is to eliminate its 1996 GRC. However, simply reducing or eliminating the Commission oversight that occurs in a GRC for a five-year period poses a risk to ratepayers (and to shareholders). One possible condition that could protect ratepayers, by compensating them for the assignment of greater risk, is a sharing mechanism that assures that ratepayers receive some of the benefit the utility expects to realize from its new-found impetus for longer-term planning and investment. Within this example, the point is that the sharing mechanism is not the primary objective of the experiment; it is a condition that we might attach to our approval....

We find that current regulation either has caused or has failed to prevent a situation where SDG&E's rates are too high. The evidence is that SDG&E electric rates were recently 136% above the national average. Utility Consumers Action Network (UCAN) witness Navarro reminds us that achieving the goal of least-cost, environmentally sensitive, reliable service "is not just a matter of fairness to ratepayers and the broader public ... [i]t is a matter of economic survival for the state of California."

The evidence does not show that traditional regulation is solely responsible for high rates or a situation where SDG&E lacks the right incentives to control costs and reduce rates, and it does not show that the situation cannot be improved with continuation of traditional approaches to regulation.... The fact remains that high rates developed on traditional regulation's watch. There is little argument that the company can do better in reducing its costs and rates if given the right incentives. If more can be done, then more must done to reduce the company's rates. We therefore believe that reduction of SDG&E's rates, especially electric rates, is an appropriate and necessary objective for regulatory reform. In particular, we want to see a mechanism that provides greater incentive than the current system does for the company to reduce its rates. We agree with DRA's priorities, and hold this to be a primary objective for reform. And while we seek a reduction of SDG&E's rates, eventually to competitive levels, we do not, for purposes of specifying our objectives, require that reductions be accomplished by means of incentives or revenue-sharing....

We find that current regulation places incorrect incentives before utility management to cut cost, find efficiencies, and reduce rates. It is time to place more emphasis on managerial performance in achieving efficiencies and cost reductions, and less emphasis on rate base expansion. Bearing both of these problematic areas of regulation in mind, and recognizing that any new regulatory program is bound to create a new set of incentives for managerial actions, some unintended, that could work at cross-purposes, we adopt as our second broad reform objective a more rational system of incentives to drive utility planning and investment which better serves the overall interests of ratepayers as well as shareholders and the public.

Meeting this second broad objective should help to create an environment which more closely replicates that of a competitive market. Thus, the proposed objective of preparing SDG&E for the increasingly competitive electric services industry is arguably subsumed within the broader objective of proper incentives.

Also, as we have already noted, SDG&E's management needs to respond to new challenges in the industry.... However, we also seek consistency and compatibility of this experiment with our restructuring efforts, whose theme is competition. Accordingly, we adopt the objective of preparing of the company for competition. This means that the company should be at greater risk for the consequences of its actions even as it stands to gain from those actions, and that there should be greater flexibility for management. SDG&E's objective of flexibility and UCAN's objective of loosened regulation are consistent with this objective.

Finally, we recognize that base rate regulation creates significant administrative costs for the utility, the Commission and its staff, and other parties. GRC proceedings, the hallmark of traditional base rate regulation, are burdensome and expensive. SDG & E needs to assemble a team of 150 to 200 people including support personnel to prosecute a GRC. DRA agrees that the regulatory process associated with GRCs has become "burdensome, litigious, and costly." Our own experience is that GRCs are major procedural events that sometimes require weeks of hearings; we have had to create a rate case processing plan to deal with scheduling impact of GRCs on the Commission and on parties. We agree with DGS that reducing this burden should not be the sole or even the primary purpose of this experiment, yet we think it is reasonable to search out ways to reduce the administrative burden and cost of regulation while pursuing the terms of the regulatory compact. That is our objective.

To summarize, our objectives for improving regulation with respect to SDG&E's proposed base rates experiment are as follows:

1. To provide greater incentive than exists under current regulation for the utility to reduce rates.

2. To provide a more rational system of incentives for management to take reasonable risks and control costs in both the long and short run. This includes extending the relatively short-term planning horizon associated with the three-year GRC cycle, and reducing the company's incentive to add to rate base to increase earnings.

3.   To prepare the company to operate effectively in the increasingly competitive energy utility industry. This entails providing greater flexibility for management to take risks combined with a greater assignment of the consequences of those risks to the company.

4.   To reduce the administrative cost of regulation. . . .

The Joint Proposal includes three nonprice performance indicators which reward or penalize the utility's ability to control employee safety, system reliability, and customer satisfaction. There is also a price performance indicator which sets rewards and penalties based on the utility's system average rate as compared to a national index. The maximum yearly reward under the Joint Proposal is $19 million, and the maximum yearly penalty is $21 million. . . .

. . . In addition to the aggregate limits on rewards and penalties noted above, each indicator has an individual limit on rewards and penalties. For employee safety, the maximum reward is $3 million and the maximum penalty is $5 million. The other indicators specify equal maximum rewards and penalties, which are, for customer satisfaction, system reliability, and rate comparison, $2 million, $4 million, and $10 million, respectively. . . .

As already noted, the overall concept of a performance incentives system with predetermined shareholder rewards and penalties that depend on utility management performance, and conditionality between price and nonprice performance, is uncontested. We deem such a system not only reasonable, but essential for achieving the objectives and criteria of regulatory reform. The electric price performance indicator provides an important incentive for achieving the objective of rate reduction. It helps prepare the company for competition in that it begins to decouple rates from costs. Nonprice indicators are necessary to help assure that rate reductions and cost savings do not come at the expense of system quality in the short term or the long term. We will include a performance incentive system as part of the adopted base rates mechanism. . . .

We conclude that the Joint Proposal provides a balanced, appropriately conservative reform package which should prove to be an improvement over current regulation. Since there are risks to ratepayers and shareholders in adhering to the status quo of current regulation, we conclude the only reasonable course of action is to approve the Joint Proposal with the few modifications discussed herein.■

NOTES AND COMMENTS

1.   Many other states have considered incentive rates. For example, Central Maine Power Co.'s incentive rates impose a price cap, utilizing current rates as a starting point. The utility is not able to recover dollar for dollar through its fuel adjustment clause or for purchased power, as it has in the past. The incentive rates contain a service reliability component which establishes an earnings-reduction mechanism, allowing imposition of penalties ranging from $250,000 to $3 million if net service quality or customer

satisfaction declines. In addition, the utility is allowed to pass through to ratepayers a share of the savings and costs associated with the buyout of (QF) power purchase contracts. The utility has also secured a pricing flexibility component, which allows it to select from a variety of pricing options, typically between a marginal cost floor and the price cap, subject to safeguards designed to protect core customers, avoid undue discrimination, and preserve its previously-established rate design policy. Docket No, 92–345, Jan. 10, 1995 (Maine PUC). A similar price flexibility program without a full-fledged price cap was approved in *Re Bangor–Hydro Electric Co.*, 159 P.U.R.4th 460 (Me.PUC 1995).

2. Incentive rate mechanisms may run afoul of traditional cost of service principles. In *Stewart v. Utah*, 885 P.2d 759 (Utah 1994), the Utah Supreme Court held that incentive rates which were designed to encourage investment in the Utah telecommunications infrastructure by providing for an adjustable rate of return and revenue sharing between shareholders and customers of U.S. West, a regulated utility, violated cost-of-service principles:

> We turn now to the legality of the plan promulgated by the Commission under § 54–4–4.1(1). The Commission made no findings in support of the percentage breakdowns that determine the sharing of revenues between the utility and the ratepayers. Revenue sharing begins at a rate of return of 12.2%, the rate the Commission erroneously found to be just and reasonable based on cost-of-service standards. Under the plan, USWC [U.S. West Communications] retains 20% of all overearnings between 12.2% and 13.2%; 40% of all overearnings between 13.2% and 14.2%; and 50% of all overearnings between 14.2% and 17%. Earnings in excess of 17% were to be returned to the ratepayers. Thus, notwithstanding the 12.2% authorized rate of return fixed by the Commission, USWC has an incentive to earn up to a 17% rate of return.

> The Commission's order is defective for a number of reasons. First, it was entered without notice to any party or a hearing on the merits of the plan. Second, the plan essentially forsakes cost-of-service principles as required by Title 54 of the Public Utilities Code. The sharing of revenue begins at 12.2%, but all earnings over and above that percentage that USWC can retain are necessarily excessive because they are not justified by any cost-of-service principle. Nor can they be justified on the ground that they provide an "incentive" for USWC to invest in Utah.... In fact, the incentive to earn higher profits can be achieved as easily, or more easily, by false economics such as cutting maintenance expenses, reducing customer services, and deferring necessary investments. On that score, we emphatically note that the Commission has allowed USWC accelerated depreciation rates to induce USWC to invest in Utah and USWC has not made the investments contemplated. Unjustifiable accelerated depreciation rates translate into unjustifiable charges against ratepayers that inure to the benefit of the shareholders.

Nor can the Commission's plan be justified on the ground that it enables ratepayers to share in some of USWC's excess earnings. Given the Commission's extraordinary default in the regulation of USWC's earnings over the past years, that might well seem a desirable objective, but it is hardly a rationale for institutionalizing and legalizing exorbitant rates. Even if it is possible to justify a sharing of earnings in excess of an authorized rate of return because of a necessary and inevitable lag in rate-fixing procedures, it is certainly not justifiable for a utility to retain excess earnings in increasingly larger percentages above the authorized rate of return on equity. Finally, the Commission's plan in effect assumes that another rate-making proceeding need not take place unless and until USWC earns in excess of 17%, a prescription for regulatory neglect and exploitive rates.

For all the above reasons, the Commission's incentive plan is arbitrary, capricious, and unlawful.

3. Performance-based incentive rates focus on incentives for the utility to improve performance. Other "incentive" rates are more concerned with local economic development than improved utility performance. These economic development incentive rates are designed to entice new and preserve existing industries and business. To the extent that these allow the pricing flexibility necessary for utilities to continue to compete in emerging power markets, such rates are not necessarily inefficient. For example, Massachusetts Electric has filed an incentive rate plan, pursuant to Massachusetts Department of Public Utilities incentive ratemaking guidelines, that would increase customer rates by $30 million. The filing includes a discount program, based on participation in a real-time pricing program, for large industrial customers in the manufacturing, computer and biotech sectors of the economy. Massachusetts Electric Files State's First Incentive Rate Plan, Electric Light & Power, May 1995, at 4.

3.   THE ENERGY POLICY ACT OF 1992 AND THE EMERGENCE OF WHOLESALE SUPPLY COMPETITION

With the enactment of the federal Energy Policy Act of 1992 (EPAct), a statute adopted following the U.S. crisis with Iraq, Congress gave even more emphasis to the promotion of competition among various components of the electric power industry. Two developments were significant in promoting more widespread wholesale power supply competition. First, the EPAct clarified and broadened FERC wholesale wheeling authority. Second, the EPAct removed some of the restrictions on the growth of the independent power industry imposed by PUHCA.

a.   CLARIFICATION AND EXTENSION OF FERC'S WHEELING AUTHORITY

Since passage of the Energy Policy Act, dozens of requests for wholesale transmission service have been filed with FERC. Despite a spirited opposition by the utility industry, FERC's initial treatment of these requests has erased any remaining doubt that it would, in certain circumstances, use its new authority under section 211 to push the industry towards open access and increased competition.

In a watershed decision issued in October 1993, FERC voted unanimously to require Florida Power & Light (FP & L) to provide network transmission service to members of the Florida Municipal Power Agency. *Florida Mun. Power Agency*, 65 F.E.R.C. ¶ 61,125 (1993) (granting request for transmission service as establishing further proceedings to investigate the rates, terms, and conditions of such service). Interpreting its new authority broadly, FERC noted that section 211(c)(2) of the FPA did not bar issuance of a wheeling order due to pre-existing transmission contracts, effectively allowing existing transmission customers the opportunity to "upgrade" the service they received under existing contracts. Given the FPA's purpose of "encourag[ing] the orderly development of plentiful supplies of electricity . . . at reasonable prices," FERC found the public interest in favor of issuance of a wheeling order to be compelling under the circumstances:

> As a general matter, the availability of transmission service (or increased flexibility to use transmission) will enhance competition in the market for power supplies over the long run because it will increase both the power supply options available to transmission customers (thereby benefitting their customers) and the sales options available to sellers. This should result in lower costs to consumers. In addition, if a transmission customer determines that flexible service, such as network service, will allow it to serve its customers more efficiently, we believe that the public interest will be served by requiring that service to be provided so long as the transmitting utility is fully and fairly compensated and there is no unreasonable impairment of reliability.

Id. FERC's order emphasized that the rates, terms, and conditions under which the service is offered must be nondiscriminatory and comparable to what the utility provides other customers. This represents the first step in imposing on the industry the "comparability" standard FERC had adopted in the natural gas context. This precedent-setting decision was widely recognized by industry experts as a clear message that FERC was serious about "leveling the competitive playing field" between transmission users and transmission-owning utilities. FERC has continued to adopt competitive transmission mechanisms by requiring transmission to the distribution level and requiring the open access tariffs filed in merger proceedings to provide network service.

b. FURTHER PROMOTION OF POWER GENERATION BY INDEPENDENT POWER PRODUCERS (IPPs)

The EPAct also recognized the limits of PURPA for encouraging independent power production. PURPA applies only to certified QFs which met the strict small power production or cogeneration described in the statute and FERC's regulations. However, independent power producers which do not comply strictly with these criteria do not qualify for PURPA benefits. Prior to 1992, one significant impediment to the growth of non-PURPA independents was the regulatory morass of a New Deal statute, PUHCA. PUHCA required many power production projects to comply with costly SEC reporting regulations. The EPAct suspended PUHCA for certain independent power producers by creating what is known as a PUHCA exempt wholesale generator (or EWG, pronounced "e-wog").

By 1992, competition in the independent power production sector and open access transmission at the wholesale levels were common, but still not pervasive. In large part, the traditional single, vertically-integrated firm structure had been replaced with a multiplicity of power supply options provided through a single transmitting utility, typically an investor-owned utility (*see* Figure 11.1). In the U.S., most individual end use customers, such as residential users of electricity, do not have a choice from whom they purchase electricity. (The issue of retail competition is discussed in Chapter Thirteen. Regardless of retail competition policies, if electricity prices were to become too high, consumers have the option, as they have in the past, to shift large-load appliances from electricity to natural gas). Large customers, such as industrial users, have many options: they can purchase from their local utility, self-generate pursuant to PURPA, or, if they are able to negotiate transmission terms, purchase their power requirements from an independent generator or other non-utility source.

By the 1990s, however, dissatisfaction with some of the approaches federal regulators embraced in encouraging the growth of the independent power production sector of the industry were widespread. Consider the following case, which discusses PURPA's QF certification criteria:

Brazos Electric Power Cooperative, Inc. v. Federal Energy Regulatory Commission

205 F.3d 235 (5th Cir.2000).

Tenaska is a privately-held partnership engaged in the production of wholesale electric power. Tenaska developed and owns a cogeneration plant in Cleburne, Texas. A cogeneration plant is a facility which produces electric energy and either steam or some other form of useful energy which is used for commercial, industrial, heating, or cooling purposes. See 16 U.S.C. § 796(18)(A). Brazos is an electric utility cooperative engaged in the generation and transmission of electric power. The utility is comprised of individual electric cooperatives in Texas and provides power to those cooperatives. Currently, Brazos is purchasing electricity from Tenaska pursuant to the facilities' Power Purchase Agreement. The Power Purchase Agreement was certified under a Texas statute that granted certification of such contracts only if the cogeneration facility met the requirements of the Public Utilities Regulatory Policies Act of 1978 ("PURPA"), 16 U.S.C. § 823a et seq. Brazos seeks to undo the contract, arguing that Tenaska no longer meets PURPA's requirements.

A further understanding of the facts of this case requires some explanation of the statutes and regulations that control the relationship between a private producer such as Tenaska and public utility corporation such as Brazos. PURPA was enacted in response to the nation's fuel shortage, and its primary aim was to promote conservation of oil and natural gas in electricity generation. *See FERC v. Mississippi*, 456 U.S. 742, 745–46, 102 S.Ct. 2126, 72 L.Ed.2d 532 (1982). To those ends, PURPA required FERC to promulgate rules encouraging the development of alternative generators of electricity, such as cogeneration facilities. *See* 16 U.S.C. § 824a–3(a). The rationale behind encouraging cogeneration is that the production of electricity frequently results in the production of thermal energy as a byproduct; by using small amounts of additional fuel, cogenerators can produce large amounts of thermal energy to be used in other processes. Congress created regulatory benefits to provide economic encouragement to such nontraditional power producers. For example, qualifying cogenerators are exempt from wholesale rate regulation under all federal and state public utility statutes, see 18 C.F.R. §§ 292.601, 292.602, and utilities can be compelled to interconnect with them, paying rates no greater than the utility's full avoided costs, see 18 C.F.R. §§ 292.303, 292.308, 292.101(b). In this way, PURPA ensures the cogenerator a market for its electricity production and allows it to make a profit when it can produce power at an average cost lower than the utility's avoided cost.

Of relevance to the instant appeal are PURPA's guidelines for the certification of facilities as "qualifying cogeneration facilities," and FERC's rules prescribing the standards for that certification. The statute defines "cogeneration facility" as one that produces "(I) electric energy, and (ii) steam or forms of useful energy (such as heat) which are used for industrial, commercial, heating, or cooling purposes." 16 U.S.C. § 796(18)(A). To determine which nontraditional power producers could receive benefits, PURPA created a category of "qualifying cogeneration facilities," or QFs, which includes any facility FERC determines has met the regulatory requirements. See 16 U.S.C. § 796(18)(B)(I).

FERC's regulations prescribe operating, efficiency, and ownership standards for facilities seeking QF status. See 18 C.F.R. § 292.205 (operating and efficiency standards); 18 C.F.R. § 292.206 (ownership criteria). Relevant here is the requirement that electric utilities hold less than 50% of the equity interest in the cogeneration facility. See 18 C.F.R. § 292.206. In addition, the cogeneration facility must "produce electric energy and forms of useful thermal energy (such as heat or steam), used for industrial, commercial, heating, or cooling purposes, through the sequential use of energy." 18 C.F.R. § 292.202(c) (emphasis added).

... [FERC] applies one of three economic tests in determining whether a thermal output is useful for purposes of QF certification. First, if a cogenerator proposes to use its thermal energy in a common industrial or commercial process, that energy is considered presumptively useful. *See id.* at ¶ 61,279. A process, or thermal application, will be deemed "common" after the Commission has received a satisfactory number of QF applications proposing the same use for the thermal output. *See Kamine/Besicorp Allegany*, L.P., 63 FERC ¶ 61,320, ¶ 63,158 (1993). The Commission reasons that, if a thermal application is a common one, the technology involved must be established and there must be a market for the application's end-product. *See Arroyo Energy, L.P.* (Arroyo II), 63 FERC ¶ 61,198, ¶ 62,545 (1993); *Polk Power Partners, L.P., et al.*, 61 FERC ¶ 61,300, ¶ 62,128 (1992). As such, when a facility's proposed use of thermal energy is common in the industry, FERC presumes the energy used in that application is useful and performs no further analysis regarding the economics of the thermal application. *See Bayside Cogeneration*, L.P. (Bayside II), 67 FERC ¶ 61,290, ¶ 62,006 (1994).

When the facility proposes an uncommon application, i.e., one that involves a new technology or creates an end-product without an established market, FERC's analysis is different. *See Electrodyne*, 32 FERC at ¶ 61,278. It employs separate analyses depending on whether the purchaser of the thermal energy—the "thermal host"—is an entity unaffiliated or affiliated with the cogenerator. If an independent entity, unaffiliated with the cogenerator, purchases the thermal energy, FERC considers the energy useful because it assumes no entity would purchase the thermal output, or the end-product produced with the aid of the thermal output, unless it served some legitimate purpose. *See Liquid Carbonic Industries Corp.* v. FERC, 29 F.3d 697, 700 (D.C.Cir.1994). In other words, purchase by the thermal host establishes that there is an arm's-length market for the output. *See Kamine*, 63 FERC at ¶ 63,158; *Electrodyne*, 32 FERC at ¶ 61,279. FERC, therefore, deems the thermal energy useful and performs no further analysis regarding the economics of the thermal application. *See LaJet Energy Co.*, 44 FERC ¶ 61,288, ¶ 61,194 (1988); *Electrodyne*, 32 FERC at ¶ 61,279. . . .

FERC's certification process occurs prior to the construction of the facility, and QF status is granted or denied based on the representations in a facility's application. The regulations provide, however, that FERC may revoke the QF status of a previously-certified facility if the facility, when operational, fails to comply with any of the statements in its application. *See* 18 C.F.R. § 292.207(d)(1).

Brazos challenges Tenaska's certification as a QF. Tenaska and Brazos entered their Power Purchase Agreement ("PPA") in 1993, which obligated Brazos to purchase electric power from Tenaska for twenty-three years, with a seventeen-year rollover, at prices fixed in the PPA. This was not a situation where Brazos was compelled under PURPA to purchase electricity from a QF. Rather, both parties were equally interested in Tenaska's becoming certified as a QF. Tenaska wanted to qualify for PURPA benefits. Brazos wanted the best rates. According to Philip Segrest, Brazos' attorney at the time, the only power sources in Texas were public utilities and QFs. As a QF, Tenaska would only be able to charge rates up to Brazos' avoided costs. The public utilities, however, were currently charging rates above Brazos' avoided costs. Thus, because Tenaska's rates were favorable and because the option of building its own plant was impractical, Brazos "insist[ed] that the PPA be certified by the [Public Utility Commission of Texas] pursuant to PURA [the Public Utility Regulatory Act]...." Under PURA, certification of power purchase agreements was permitted only if the power was being purchased from a QF, as that term was defined in PURPA. *See* Tex.Rev.Civ. Stat. Ann. art. 1446c (West Supp.1994) (repealed 1995).

Therefore, on October 20, 1994, Tenaska applied to FERC for QF certification, obviously with Brazos' blessing. According to its application, Tenaska intended to sell its electrical output to Brazos, while its thermal output, steam, was to be converted into distilled water for sale to "a third party." FERC published notice of Tenaska's application in the Federal Register but received no protests or requests for interventions to Tenaska's certification. Therefore, on January 13, 1995, the Commission granted Tenaska QF status. In doing so, FERC determined, in relevant part, that Tenaska fulfilled its ownership requirement that utilities own less than 50% equitable interest in the facility. More importantly, FERC also concluded that the conversion of steam to distilled water was a common industrial process and application of thermal energy for that use was, therefore, presumptively useful.

Tenaska entered into an arrangement with the City of Cleburne (the "City") in which Tenaska would (1) purchase the City's potable water for use in its steam generator, (2) recover the reject water stream from the steam generator's boiler makeup water treatment system and use it to supply the distilled water system, (3) sell the distilled water to the City, and (4) purchase effluent water from the City's wastewater treatment facility for use in its cooling tower. Under this arrangement, the City gave Tenaska a ten-dollar credit on its water bill for its production of the distilled water, and the City was obligated to construct the facilities necessary for transporting both the effluent water to Tenaska and the distilled water from Tenaska. The City was responsible for the initial financing of the construction, including the issuance of tax-exempt municipal bonds, for which Tenaska would reimburse the City in monthly payments when the debt service was owed. The facility became operational in January 1997.

The City had originally agreed to purchase Tenaska's distilled water in order to attract industries to an industrial park near Tenaska's facility, by offering the ready supply of distilled water for sale as process water. Water which was not resold was to be used to augment the flow of Buffalo Creek, a stream running near the City's business district whose stagnant waters were encouraging nuisance conditions and an increased mosquito population. While negotiations continued with potential occupants of the industrial park, the City ran into difficulty garnering permits from the Environmental Protection Agency to increase Buffalo Creek's flow with distilled water. Initially, therefore, the City had no specific use for the distilled water it was purchasing from Tenaska, and it released its purchase into the City's sewer system. An occupant of the industrial park began purchasing the distilled water in September 1997.

On August 22, 1997, Brazos filed with FERC a motion and petition for revocation of Tenaska's QF status. According to Brazos, the use of Tenaska's thermal output for the production of distilled water had not proven to be "useful." The presumption of usefulness on which Tenaska's QF status was certified, Brazos argued, was rebutted by actual operation of the facility—notably, by the fact that the City paid only ten dollars a month for thousands of gallons of water and then dumped the water in the sewer. Meanwhile, Brazos was being forced under the PPA to pay fixed rates which, five years into the deal, were no longer below the market price. In addition, Brazos contended that Tenaska did not satisfy the ownership requirements for QF status. Although utilities owned less than 50% of Tenaska, Brazos alleged that the utilities' 45% interest gave them effective control in a voting procedure requiring a 70% vote to take action.

FERC denied Brazos' motion. FERC stated that once it determines the proposed use of thermal energy is common, it presumes the thermal energy is useful. FERC would not inquire thereafter into how the thermal host used its purchase, nor would it question whether the cogeneration facility was actually making money from its sale. FERC also found that Tenaska satisfied the ownership requirements for QF status, noting that the utilities' 45% interest was insufficient to effect day-to-day action without the votes of 25% of the non-utility owners. Additionally, the Commission noted that Tenaska's ownership structure had not changed since its certification, and because Brazos failed to object then, its complaint now was untimely.

Subsequently, Brazos filed a request for rehearing and its request was denied. Brazos now petitions this Court for review of FERC's order denying the revocation of Tenaska's QF status.

We must affirm FERC's order unless it is "arbitrary, capricious, an abuse of discretion, or otherwise not in accordance with law." 5 U.S.C. § 706(2)(A). The scope of review under this standard is narrow; it does not authorize a reviewing court to substitute its judgment for that of the agency. *See Motor Vehicle Mfrs. Ass'n v. State Farm Mutual Ins.* Co., 463 U.S. 29, 43, 103 S.Ct. 2856, 77 L.Ed.2d 443 (1983). Rather, we must examine " 'whether the decision was based on a consideration of the relevant factors and whether there has been a clear error of judgment.' " *Id.* (quoting *Bowman Transp., Inc. v. Arkansas–Best Freight Sys., Inc.*, 419 U.S. 281, 285, 95 S.Ct. 438, 42 L.Ed.2d 447 (1974)). Where an agency has considered the relevant factors and provided a satisfactory explanation for its actions, its decision will be upheld.

Noting that FERC regulations allow for post-operational challenges to a QF's certification, Brazos maintains that Tenaska is not entitled to benefits under PURPA because, after its facility was certified and became operational, Tenaska failed to uphold the regulatory requirements for QF status in accordance with projections contained in its application for QF certification. Brazos advances the same arguments it did below: the Commission should revoke Tenaska's QF status because the production of distilled water has not proven to be useful, and because Tenaska does not meet PURPA's ownership requirements. We address each contention in turn.

A.   Useful Thermal Output

The thrust of Brazos' argument is that the Commission's precedent has not established an irrebuttable presumption of usefulness. Brazos does not take issue with the use of the presumption during certification, before the facility is even built; then, Brazos reasons, the Commission is justified in relying on hypothetical facts and an applicant's claim that, because the proposed thermal use is common, the thermal energy will be useful. Rather, Brazos asserts that the Commission was obligated to consider post-operational facts that could rebut the presumption of a thermal output's usefulness. Specifically, Brazos avers first that, although Tenaska represented in its application for QF status that distilled water would be produced for sale to a third party, the sale of water to the City is a "sham" sale designed only to retain PURPA benefits; it is not a sale serving an independent business purpose that could be economically justified. Second, Brazos contends that the water was not useful because before the City found a purchaser, it was pouring the water in the sewer.

In response, FERC asserts that Tenaska continues to satisfy PURPA's regulatory requirements, as represented in its application for QF status. First, Tenaska's sale of water was one piece of a legitimate, integrated financing package. Second, Tenaska's thermal energy has been useful since the day it was certified, for Tenaska has used "an established technology to produce a common product with an existing market." *Arroyo*, 63 FERC at ¶ 62,545 n. 4. According to the Commission, there is no statutory or precedential requirement that, upon the facility's operation, it examine how each individual thermal host is using its purchases or how economically sound every transaction turned out to be. In fact, FERC argues, doing so would undermine its directives under PURPA, for conditioning the maintenance of QF status on investigations into the economics of a thermal host's purchase would impede the development of cogeneration. We agree that Brazos has misconstrued the Commission's prior holdings. Further, to the extent that the present factual scenario differs from that of the Commission's precedents, FERC's use of its presumption here furthers its congressional mandate under PURPA consistently with its regulations promulgated thereto. . . .

Given the consistency with which FERC has denied further inquiry into common thermal applications, nothing in these precedents persuades us that FERC's presumption of usefulness is rebuttable, even post-operation, by the two sets of facts Brazos presents. . . . The Commission has previously opined that treating its presumption as rebuttable would be inconsistent with PURPA's goals, in that "[p]roviding an opportunity for evidentiary hearings before the Commission . . . would seriously impede the very development of cogeneration . . . that Congress sought to facilitate." *Id.* at 62,006 n. 5 (*quoting American Paper Institute, Inc. v. American Electric Power Service Corp.*, 461 U.S. 402, 420, 103 S.Ct. 1921, 76 L.Ed.2d 22 (1983)) (internal quotations omitted). Nonetheless, even if we were to look behind the presumption here, we, like the Commission, are not persuaded that the sale to the City is a sham. Tenaska correctly points out that it received much more than ten dollars in its transactions with the City, for the Distilled Water Supply Agreement was only one piece of their arrangement's puzzle: Tenaska purchased potable water from the City for use in its steam generator, the reject stream from the generator was turned into distilled water, the City purchased the distilled water to attract industrial customers to an adjacent industrial park, the plant's blowdown water was transported to the City's sewage treatment center, and Tenaska purchased the treated sewage effluent from the City for use in the cogenerator's cooling tower. In addition, Tenaska received tax abatements, as well as access to the City's debt for construction of its water facilities so all of this could take place. Seen in the context of a complex project financing, Tenaska's arrangement with the City garnered it more than ten dollars a month. Thus, as proposed in its QF application, Tenaska has sold its product to a third party.

In addition to the economics of Tenaska's transaction with the City, Brazos urges the Commission to examine the City's use of the distilled water during its first year of operation because, according to Brazos, the City's actual use would rebut the Commission's initial presumption of the thermal energy's usefulness. Relying heavily on *Arroyo II*, 63 FERC ¶ 61,-198 (1993), Brazos contends that, before determining that a thermal output is useful, the Commission must be satisfied that the thermal host's use of its purchase is a bona fide industrial or commercial use. When Tenaska first became operational, it was pouring its distilled water into a sewer, which Brazos maintains was not a bona fide use and renders the thermal energy used to create the water non-useful. Brazos contends that the Commission's failure to take into account the City's actual use of the water was an unexplained departure from its precedents.

In *Arroyo II*, the cogenerator's thermal output, steam, was to be used in absorption refrigeration (AR) equipment to provide ice to an adjacent ice rink. The utility complained that the use of thermal output to help create and maintain an ice rink was a novel use requiring application of the independent business purpose test. The Commission declined to apply the test because it found that AR technology was a common use for steam, and the steam was therefore useful. Brazos, however, relies on several passages in the opinion as evidence that the Commission has tempered its presumption of usefulness by also examining the proposed end-use to which the thermal product would be put:

> Our review of the evidence compiled in this proceeding confirms that the proposed use of the Arroyo [cogeneration] facility's thermal output for refrigeration purposes is indeed bona fide. SDG & E [the utility] presents us with no new reason to upset our earlier determination that the technology to be applied by Arroyo, as well as the end product, are established and, accordingly, that the thermal output of the facility is presumptively useful.

Arroyo II, 63 FERC at ¶ 62,545 (citation omitted) (Brazos' emphasis added). This passage does not support Brazos' contention that FERC examines the thermal host's end-use of its purchase in determining the usefulness of a cogenerator's thermal output. It is the cogenerator's use of thermal energy that must be bona fide, not the thermal host's end-use of the end-product, and the cogenerator's use is bona fide when it is common in the industry. Thus, the passage states that the thermal energy was useful because the thermal output (steam) was put to a bona fide use in a common application (AR technology) and created a common product (ice). This passage does not say that the cogenerator's thermal energy was useful because the thermal host's use of ice to build an ice rink was bona fide. The passage does not refer at all to the thermal host's end-use of the thermal product. Nor should it. As the Commission has noted, "if a cogenerator produces a product that has already met the Commission's usefulness requirement, there is no further inquiry to determine if the product is being used by the recipient for a common purpose." *Brooklyn Navy Yard*, 74 FERC at ¶ 61,046.

In this way, Brazos' complaint that the distilled water was not "useful" misses the point. The distillation of water is common, so the steam used to create it is useful. The use an unaffiliated thermal host makes of its arm's-length purchase is irrelevant. *See Arroyo I*, 62 FERC at ¶ 62,723 ("The fact that this is the first instance before the Commission in which this common refrigeration technology is associated with a common refrigeration product for end-use in an ice rink is irrelevant."). This is because the Commission, as the arbiter of "usefulness," has defined the concept in terms of economics. If an application is common, the technology is established and there is a market for the product. If the technology is established and there is a market for the product, that which is used in the application to create the product is "useful." Once the energy used in the established technology or the product with the established market is purchased by a thermal host, FERC has no further involvement. The purchaser bears the market risk of its purchase, not the seller, and whatever use or profit the purchaser makes of its purchase, whether by pouring it in a sewer or reselling it, is of no moment to the seller. *See Bayside II*, 67 FERC at ¶ 62,006 n. 7 (stating that "PURPA does not require that the Commission ensure that a thermal host make as much money as possible, or make any money at all; all PURPA requires is that the Commission ensure that the thermal host takes useful thermal energy that is used for industrial, commercial, heating, or cooling purposes." (internal quotations omitted) (emphasis added)). The point is that the seller has successfully sold its output in an arm's-length market and the purchaser has access to the same market for resale. There is, of course, proof of this point in the instant case—two weeks after Brazos filed its motion and petition for revocation, the City found a purchaser for its distilled water from among those industries it was trying to attract with the supply of that water. . . .

Although this case presents us with what, at first blush, appears to be the proverbial "peppercorn" scenario—a party paying ten dollars for thousands of gallons of distilled water that for nine months it poured into the sewer—we are, for a number of reasons, hesitant to look beyond FERC's presumption of usefulness to release Brazos from its contractual obligations. First, Tenaska and the City entered an arm's-length contract, one amongst many contracts in which the risks and benefits of the typical project finance arrangement were traded. That Brazos now finds itself paying above-market prices for electricity because it entered a "front-loaded" contract fails to undermine the utility of the Commission's presumption of the usefulness of thermal energy in common applications. A front-loaded contract means that the utility's payment rates are determined at the time the obligation to buy from the cogenerator is incurred, rather than at the time of delivery. Such contracts are often used because they allow the QF to finance the construction and operation of the facility in the early years of the contract. As the Ninth Circuit observed in *Independent Energy Producers Ass'n, Inc. v. California Pub. Util. Comm'n*, 36 F.3d 848, 858 (9th Cir.1994), such contracts have been upheld notwithstanding the recognized risk that the prices set by the contract might at times exceed the utility's actual avoided costs, because "certainty as to rate was important." By ensuring a predictable flow of income, such contracts encourage the development of alternative facilities that might never be built. In FERC's words:

> The Commission recognizes this possibility [that current avoided costs might be lower than the rates provided in the contracts] but is cognizant that in other cases, the required rate will turn out to be lower than the avoided cost at the time of purchase.... Many commentators have stressed the need for certainty with regard to return on investment in new technologies. The Commission agrees with these ... arguments, and believes that, in the long run, "over estimations" and "under estimations" of avoided costs will balance out.

Small Power Production and Cogeneration Facilities; Regulations Implementing Section 210 of PURPA, 45 Fed.Reg. 12224 (1980) (quoted in *Independent Energy Producers Ass'n*, 36 F.3d at 858).

Second, allowing post-operation rebuttal of FERC's presumption of a thermal output's usefulness on these grounds would impede the development of cogeneration facilities, a development PURPA was enacted to encourage. *See Arroyo II*, 63 FERC at ¶ 62,546 (explaining that performing economic analyses on common applications would discourage cogeneration). By sanctioning such rebuttal, we would ensure that every time the market for electricity fluctuated and the utility that was the QF's only market recipient was suddenly displeased with its rates, the utility could back out because it thought either the QF or the thermal host was not being as economically wise or efficient as it should be. This scenario poses several problems.

Owners of QFs would have little incentive to sell electric energy if they had to go through an evidentiary hearing before FERC in Washington, D.C., every time a utility claimed someone else was behaving inefficiently with a common application. ... Neither the statute nor the regulations insist or presuppose that FERC should engage in such heavy-handed oversight as to keep tabs on QFs' arm's-length purchasers. If we were to hold otherwise, we would embrace the very form of micro-management that the Commission has determined QFs are supposed to be freed from, and we would "impute to Congress a purpose to paralyze with one hand what it sought to promote with the other." *Clark v. Uebersee Finanz–Korporation, A.G.*, 332 U.S. 480, 489, 68 S.Ct. 174, 92 L.Ed. 88 (1947).

More importantly, FERC's presumption of usefulness is meant to enable cogeneration facilities to obtain financing. The presumption provides certainty for investors that their investment is duly certified under PURPA and entitled to the benefits of PURPA's statutory imperatives, including the presence of a utility to purchase the facility's output. Because the value of a facility's hard assets is usually less than the project debt, debt repayment and anticipated equity returns depend on performance under project contracts. The contracts constitute the framework for project viability because the ability of the project sponsor to produce revenue from project operation is the foundation of a project financing. The PPA is the principal source of project revenue. Therefore, banks lend money for construction and permanent financing on the strength of the utility's obligation to purchase power from a QF. Revocation of a facility's QF status releases the utility from its obligation under the PPA. It leaves the facility without a market recipient and thus without a revenue source for debt repayment. We would be hard pressed to imagine the investor who would contribute to a project so susceptible to such a scenario. In sum, both FERC's precedents and PURPA's mandates persuade us that Tenaska continues to produce useful thermal energy in accordance with the representations in its application for QF status.

B. Ownership Criteria

In order to obtain QF status under PURPA, a cogeneration facility must not be owned by persons primarily engaged in the generation or sale of electric power. *See* 16 U.S.C. § 796(18)(B). The Commission clarified this requirement, determining that electric utilities may own no more than 50% of the equity interest in a QF. *See* 18 C.F.R. § 292.206(b). FERC's regulations thus equate "ownership interest" with "equity interest," but they do not define the term "equity interest." *See Ultrapower 3*, 27 FERC ¶ 61,094, ¶ 61,183 (1984). Cases discussing the Commission's ownership criteria emphasize the stream of benefits accruing to each partner, but the voting interests of each partner have also been examined to avoid a utility partner's manipulation of those benefits. *See id.* at ¶ 61,184. Accordingly, "a utility partner may not have more than 50% control of a qualifying facility." *Brooklyn Navy Yard*, 74 FERC at ¶ 61,048.

According to Brazos, Tenaska has not satisfied the ownership criteria for QF status because utilities have effective control over the facility's operation. Affiliates of three utilities own a 45% interest in Tenaska and have a 38.9% voting interest in the facility, in conformity with the regulatory limits. Before FERC, however, Brazos contended that the utilities' 45% interest in the facility gives them effective control over the facility's operation, because a 70% vote of Tenaska's Executive Review Committee is needed to take significant actions. The Commission disagreed, pointing out that the utility affiliates would still need the approval of the non-utility owners to take significant action. The Commission also pointed out that Tenaska's ownership structure had not changed since it was certified as a QF. Because Brazos was listed as the utility-purchaser in QF application and failed to object when the application was noticed for comment, the Commission determined that Brazos' challenge was untimely.

.... We agree with the Commission that "[a]llowing such belated challenges to QF certifications despite unchanged facts would undermine the contractual reliance QFs need in order to finance and build their projects." *Brazos Electric Power Cooperative v. Tenaska IV Texas Partners, Ltd.*, 85 FERC ¶ 61,097, ¶ 61,348 (1998)....

Briefly, even if we were to give Brazos the benefit of the doubt, its challenge is still without merit. As noted, FERC's ownership criteria are intended to prevent utilities from diverting to themselves the stream of benefits flowing from a QF, such that the utilities would gain some undue advantage vis-a-vis non-utility partners. *See Dominion Resources, Inc.*, 43 FERC ¶ 61,079, ¶ 61,251 (1988). In order to accrue such benefits, "control" requires action, not inaction. That is, a minority interest's ability to block significant actions does not garner the benefits the controlling interest can manipulate by taking significant actions. Furthermore, if the ability to block significant action constituted "control," then Brazos is actually contending that utilities may not have more than 30% control—a proposition that finds no support in the Commission's precedents. See id. at ¶ 61,251 (stating that "a facility will meet the ownership requirements of PURPA ... so long as the interest in the stream of benefits and control by a utility or utilities, by whatever mechanism used, does not exceed 50%"). The utility affiliates' equity and voting interests in Tenaska satisfy the Commission's ownership requirements for QF status.

■ EMILIO M. GARZA, CIRCUIT JUDGE, specially concurring:

The majority opinion reflects a wholesale endorsement of both the result reached by the Federal Energy Regulatory Commission ("FERC") and the methodology used to reach that result. I agree with the former, but not with the latter. Accordingly, I concur in the result reached by the majority, but write separately because the method by which FERC disposed of this case could, if repeated, produce results clearly in conflict with the language and intent of the Public Utility Regulatory Policies Act of 1978 ("PURPA"), 16 U.S.C. § 823a et seq.

In this case, the majority is correct in rejecting Brazos's claim that any "usefulness" from cogeneration in the Tenaska facility is "flushed down the sewer." The evidence shows that the thermal energy produced by the Tenaska facility is used to distill water which is sold to the city or directed into Buffalo Creek to attract customers to an adjacent industrial park. Accordingly, the thermal energy produced by Tenaska is "useful" in any sense of the word, and we defer to FERC's interpretation.

However, Brazos's allegations, when considered relative to FERC's treatment of petitions to revoke QF certification, beg the question: what if Tenaska's cogenerated energy was used to distill water which was promptly flushed down the sewer? Clearly, nothing "useful" would result from the cogeneration, but since the cogenerated energy was "used in a common process," FERC would rely on its presumption of usefulness and the facility would retain QF certification. I fully agree with the majority's statement that "PURPA and its implementing regulations require only that the thermal energy be useful; they do not demand that the sale of every end-product be profitable." However, under FERC's procedural rationale, the Commission cannot ever be sure that the thermal energy is "useful" in the everyday sense of the word. In some cases, FERC's failure to even address claims that a facility's thermal energy is not "useful" could contravene both the language and the intent of PURPA. *See Liquid Carbonic*, 29 F.3d at 706 ("Congress intended PURPA to encourage the development of cogeneration facilities ... [but][t]he encouragement of the goal must, but its nature, limit entry to those who actually further the goal by producing useful energy....").

FERC's irrebuttable presumption of usefulness is justified in the context of petitions for initial certification, upon which financing to build such facilities often depends. As the majority notes, in this context "[p]roviding for evidentiary hearings before the Commission ... would seriously impede the very development of cogeneration ... that Congress sought to facilitate." However, FERC and the majority exaggerate the possibility that an evidentiary hearing years after a facility has been in operation to determine whether the facility truly produces "useful" thermal energy would impede the initial development of the facility. Any hesitancy that this potential future evidentiary hearing might produce is mitigated, if not eliminated, by the fact that FERC already performs evidentiary investigations into other issues of technical compliance (for example, into the 5% mandate). The alternative to allowing post-certification evidentiary hearings on "usefulness," which currently exists, allows facilities to retain QF benefits even if they are not (in fact, even if they never were) the type of facilities to which Congress wanted to afford such benefits. In many cases, this is a clear departure from the statutory mandate, and therefore an impermissible construction of PURPA.

Tenaska has proven that the energy it produces as a co-product to electricity is "useful" in producing distilled water which benefits the community at large, and thus that the benefits afforded it as a QF are justified. Accordingly, I concur in the decision allowing Tenaska's Cleburne facility to retain QF status. However, I cannot agree with the majority's endorsement of the procedure by which FERC summarily dismissed this case. Congress wanted to encourage the production of cogeneration facilities because, in developing alternative sources of "useful" energy while producing electricity, they improved the energy efficiency of electricity generation facilities in particular and the nation in general. By establishing an irrebuttable presumption that prevents it from ever examining whether a facility's co-produced energy is ever "useful," FERC has opened the door to facilities who meet FERC's technical requirements but defy the language and spirit of PURPA.■

NOTES AND COMMENTS

1.   The Fifth Circuit's decision focuses on FERC's very detailed operation and ownership criteria, which appear in PURPA as well as FERC's regulations implementing the statute. Facilities that were built or remain in operation solely by virtue of the fact that they comply with PURPA's QF requirements–and thus qualify for PURPA benefits, such as avoided cost rates–are sometimes referred to as "PURPA machines." Do the benefits of such generation outweigh any imposition of their costs on utilities and/or consumers?

2.   While the facility at issue in the Fifth Circuit decision was a PURPA cogeneration facility, similar issues arise in the context of FERC's approval process for small power production facilities that burn renewable fuels. Here reviewing courts have not always been as deferential towards FERC's approval process. PURPA defines a small power production facility as one that "produces electric energy solely by use, as a primary energy source, of biomass, waste, renewable resources, geothermal resources, or any combination thereof," 16 U.S.C. § 796(17)(A)(I). Some flexibility in fuel use is allowed to these facilities, subject to FERC's approval, in the event of express situations defined in PURPA, including shortages and to prevent electric power outages that affect the public safety, health, and welfare. FERC has adopted regulation that prohibits the use of oil, gas and coal by such a facility in excess of "25 percent of the total energy input of the facility during the 12–month period beginning with the date the facility first produces electric energy and any calendar year subsequent to the year in which the facility first produces electric energy." 18 C.F.R. § 292.204(b)(2).

While initially intended to provide flexibility in fuel use to promote innovative generation technologies, this requirement has recently posed a problem for some small power production facilities, particularly those burning waste and biomass. An example is Laidlaw Gas Recovery Systems, Inc., which owns and operates several landfill gas-to-energy plants which burn methane produced by decomposition to generate electricity. Laidlaw sought to permission to burn natural gas at an amount up to 25% of its output to increase operation of a plant from 17 to 20 MW, in order to alleviate the effects of forced outages and landfill maintenance. At the same time, Laidlaw was seeking a 20 MW output from the facility to meet its contractual supply obligations with a utility, Southern California Edison. Laidlaw also asserted that state environmental regulations in California limited its ability to influence the rate of decomposition and produce methane at its facility. FERC issued a declaratory ruling that would allow Laidlaw to burn natural gas, but Southern California Edison appealed FERC's decision. On appeal, a panel of the D.C. Circuit held that FERC's ruling violated the plain meaning of PURPA, which the court held expressly restricts the circumstances under which FERC can allow flexibility in fuel use for small power production facilities. The D.C. Circuit also rejected FERC's appeal to the general purpose of encouraging the development of small power production facilities. *See Southern California Edison Co. v. Federal Energy Regulatory Commission*, 195 F.3d 17 (D.C.Cir.1999). Does the outcome of this case conflict with the Fifth Circuit's opinion? For an argument that FERC should have more flexibility in interpreting this provision of PURPA in order to encourage renewable and independent power generation, see Jim Rossi, Making Policy Through the Waiver of Regulations at the Federal Energy Regulatory Commission, 47 Admin. L. Rev. 255 (1995).

3. *Independent Energy Producers Ass'n, Inc. v. California Pub. Util. Comm'n*, 36 F.3d 848, 858 (9th Cir.1994), discussed in *Brazos*, addressed the issue of avoided cost rates set under PURPA. In Chapter Thirteen, some of the problems in setting avoided cost rates under PURPA in the light of major changes in market conditions—including the introduction of wholesale and retail competition—are discussed.

A NOTE ON PURPA AND PUCHA REFORM

As the *Brazos* case illustrates, even after the EPAct a great deal of uncertainty revolves around the federal regulatory scheme designed to encourage IPPs. The uncertainty surrounds both PUHCA and PURPA. While many believe that PUHCA worked to protect consumers in the mid-twentieth century, today utility industry investors are increasingly skeptical. With the rise of utility mergers [discussed in Chapter Eighteen], many made efficient with the growth of competition, it is often argued that today PUHCA is more of a hindrance than a benefit to consumers, even given the reforms Congress adopted in the 1992 EPAct. PURPA QFs have spurned much competition in generation, but as the *Brazos* case illustrates, they have also created certain incentives for investment in QFs where other projects may have been more efficient. In addition, some utilities attribute a stranded cost problem [discussed in Chapter Twelve] to PURPA QFS, or see PURPA QFS as inhibiting competition [see Chapter Thirteen]. The following excerpted chapter, prepared by the Energy Information Administration, summarizes some of the arguments for and against PUHCA and PURPA reform:

Federal Legislative Initiatives for Change: The Issues, Energy Information Administration, U.S. Department of Energy (1997)

<http://www.eia.doe.gov/cneaf/electricity/chg_str/chapter6.html>

Some groups contend that two particular statutes are irrelevant in an era of competition, and that these statutes are actually hindering the industry's transition from a regulated monopoly. They are the Public

Utility Holding Company Act of 1935 (PUHCA) and the Public Utility Regulatory Policies Act of 1978 (PURPA)....

The Current Debate Over PUHCA

Although a vigorous debate is now taking place as to whether PUHCA's provisions are relevant today, there seems to be little question among the debaters that six decades ago PUHCA was the right law at the right time. PUHCA achieved what it was designed to do—it broke up the large and powerful trusts that abused their powers over the Nation's electric and gas distribution networks. However, in today's environment of increasing electric industry competition, there are those who believe that PUHCA's regulations are antiquated and are now impeding the transition to competition. Conversely, others feel strongly that, until the industry completes the transition, PUHCA's regulations must stay in effect in order to protect consumers.

Arguments for and against the repeal of PUHCA are summarized in the inset below.

Over the years, the petition for PUHCA repeal has, for the most part, been based on two arguments—that PUHCA has already achieved its goal of restructuring in order to make holding companies manageable and regulated, and that it has been rendered obsolete because of changes that have occurred in the latter part of this century which preclude the holding company abuses of yesterday. They are specifically:

— The development of an extensive disclosure system for all publicly held companies

— The increased competence and independence of accounting firms

— The development of accounting principles and auditing standards and the means to enforce them

— The increased sophistication and integrity of security markets and security professionals

— The increased power and ability of State regulators.(4)

In the mid–1980s, the Securities and Exchange Commission (SEC) determined that PUHCA had achieved its purpose and recommended repeal, but no action was taken in Congress. In 1994, the SEC again initiated a study in order to develop a staff recommendation to either repeal or reform PUHCA or to leave the law intact. In July 1994, the SEC conducted a round table discussion concerning whether or not the fundamental premise of the law and its provisions for addressing problems associated with monopolies and anticompetitive behavior were still relevant in the current increasingly competitive marketplace. In an attempt to obtain a broad cross-section of views on the subject, Federal, State, and local regulators and high-level representatives from utilities, consumer groups, trade associations, investments banks, etc., were invited to participate in the discussion. Later in the year, the SEC published a notice in the Federal Register requesting comments on the subject.

The Pros and Cons of PUHCA Repeal

Against Repeal	*For Repeal*
PUHCA regulations can protect consumers until full retail competition is up and running.	PUHCA's provisions are antiquated.
Ratepayers are still at the mercy of the regulated monopolies.	PUHCA is impeding the transition to competition.
PUHCA guards against monopolies and anticompetitive behavior.	Utilities need to be able to diversify in order to improve profits.
Utility monopolies are now taking actions (e.g., mergers) to increase market dominance, and PUHCA can keep them in control.	PUHCA has already achieved its goal by making holding companies manageable and regulated.
Immediate repeal is a piecemeal approach; repeal should be contained in comprehensive industry restructuring legislation.	The Securities and Exchange Commission itself recommends a conditional repeal.
PUHCA guards against interaffiliate transaction abuse.	PUHCA prevents all companies from playing on a level field.
	Various other regulations have since been instituted that prevent holding company abuse.
	Immediate repeal is necessary; it will take too long if it is contained in comprehensive industry restructuring legislation.

Based on the comments received, the earlier round table discussion, and consultations with the National Association of Regulatory Utility Commissioners (NARUC), the SEC's Division of Investment Management released a report listing three legislative options to give utility holding companies more flexibility. The Division recommended an option that dealt with conditional PUHCA repeal in a minimum 1–year transition period. The conditions included access by State regulators to the books and records of companies within a holding company system, FERC authority to exercise oversight of affiliate transactions, and, generally, that energy consumers would not lose the protection of the Federal Government.

Two bills (which are not considered comprehensive restructuring legislation) were introduced in the 104th Congress that would repeal PUHCA ... The bills' supporters believe that speedy passage is of utmost importance, given the rapidly changing makeup of the electric industry. They contend that the original PUHCA prevents all companies from competing on a level playing field, which some believe is a necessity in a competitive market. Under the current law, the SEC imposes the business and financial restrictions which companies feel are unfair in the current changing environment. The major restrictions include: prices for wholesale and retail transactions are set by FERC and State utility commissions, respectively; registered holding companies need SEC approval to own electric and gas operations; mergers and acquisitions require regulatory approval; and the types of businesses in which registered holding companies may engage are severely limited, but EWGs do not have the same limitations. While other comprehensive energy legislation that has been introduced contains provisions to repeal PUHCA along with provisions aimed at addressing other restructuring issues, certain interests feel that such comprehensive proposals will take far too long to move through the system. They argue that repeal of PUHCA must be promulgated now.

Those who are against outright repeal of PUHCA are not arguing that the Act should remain in effect in an open market atmosphere. Rather, they believe that the time is not yet quite right for its repeal. Until the Nation has completed the transition to a fully competitive market, the safeguards that PUHCA provides are necessary. They question the wisdom of removing vital consumer protection mechanisms and leaving the door open to anticompetitive practices by monopolies who are at present aggressively taking actions, such as merging and diversifying, perhaps to increase their market dominance. According to John Anderson, Executive Director of the Electricity Consumers Resource Council (ELCON), "A repeal of PUHCA while the retail franchises remain in place would further expose hostage ratepayers to the risks of interaffiliate abuse and ill-advised utility forays into unrelated businesses."

Most opponents of the legislative proposals to repeal PUHCA stress that what they are against is immediate, standalone action. Instead, they want to see well-thought-out, comprehensive restructuring and deregulation legislation that will deal with all industry issues, including retail wheeling, stranded investment, PURPA, and FERC jurisdiction, as well as with repeal of PUHCA. Still other groups believe that even after a fully competitive market is established, PUHCA-type regulation will continue to be necessary in order to ensure that the market remains competitive.

The Current Debate Over PURPA

PURPA was born of the energy crises of the 1970s, which resulted in an intense desire by Congress to reduce the Nation's dependence on foreign oil (and fossil fuels in general) and to diversify the technologies used for electricity generation. PURPA's goal was to cultivate conservation and the efficient use of resources. It was successful in that it promoted cogeneration, the use of renewable resources, and other energy-efficient technologies, and it was fortuitous in that it also introduced competition by demonstrating that the generation of electricity is not a natural monopoly. But, like PUHCA, PURPA is now being targeted for repeal due to the industry's move to competition. There are many arguments on both sides of the debate over the prudence of eliminating PURPA immediately, eventually, or not at all. Those arguments are summarized in the inset below. Legislation (which is not considered comprehensive restructuring legislation) was introduced into both Houses during the 104th Congress to address Section 210 of PURPA, which requires electric utilities to buy power from qualifying cogeneration and small power production facilities. . . .

Proponents of PURPA reform or repeal contend that the Act's mandatory purchase obligation is grossly anticompetitive and anticonsumer—anticompetitive because the Government created an artificial market by mandating that utilities buy from QFs, and anticonsumer because numerous studies have estimated that the Act caused utilities (and ultimately, consumers) to pay billions of dollars over present market prices for power. They claim that, although the Act introduced competition, it can hardly be said that it did so in an atmosphere of free market participation, a basic tenet of economic theorists who stress that the rules and prices must be established by the market—not by the Government. In addition they assert that, because of EPACT's creation of exempt wholesale generators and its incorporation of competitive policies, PURPA's QF concept has been overtaken by events; i.e., the industry now realizes that nonutilities can, on the whole, cleanly and efficiently provide additional generating capacity.

The Pros and Cons of PURPA Repeal

Against Repeal	*For Repeal*
There is no guarantee that a free market can sustain the goals of PURPA, especially in the use of cogeneration and renewables.	PURPA is anticompetitive because utilities are required to purchase from QFS.
Our Nation must be able to handle another energy crisis through fuel diversity.	EPACT's provisions for exempt wholesale generators render PURPA obsolete.
Incentives must remain in place to conserve energy and to use more environmentally benign fuels.	EPACT's provisions for exempt wholesale generators render PURPA obsolete.
Qualifying facilities (QFS) bring increased reliability and decrease the need for large costly plants.	PURPA has resulted in high prices to consumers because QF contract terms were lengthy and were based on erroneous forecasts of high capital costs and increases in demand and the price of natural gas.
At this point, utilities still have too much market power and PURPA levels the playing field for nonutilities.	PURPA has resulted in high prices to consumers because QF contract terms were lengthy and were based on erroneous forecasts of high capital costs and increases in demand and the price of natural gas.
Immediate repeal is a piecemeal approach—repeal should be included in comprehensive industry restructuring legislation.	PURPA's goals have already been achieved.
	If natural gas will be the fuel of choice as predicted, the environment will not need PURPA's strict protection since natural gas is the least harmful fossil fuel.
	Cogenerators and renewables have already gotten a foothold and do not need further promotion.
	Immediate repeal is necessary; it will take too long if it is contained in comprehensive industry restructuring legislation.

Those who want PURPA eliminated now say that its mandatory purchase clause is anticompetitive and therefore is impeding the transition to competition. Furthermore, QFS have been receiving long-run avoided-cost rates that today substantially exceed current market prices. These rates were based on erroneous forecasts of sharply rising oil and natural gas prices as well as the expectation of future increases in the demand for electricity and construction of new generating capacity. From the perspective of the QFS, rates above current avoided cost (6 cents per kilowatt-hour or higher) and long-term commitments (often 10 years) were essential to establish the QF power market. By the late 1980s and early 1990s, however, oil prices had stabilized, natural gas prices had declined, and excess generating capacity in most regions of the country allowed utilities to buy capacity and energy at much lower prices than had been forecast a decade earlier. The utilities' actual avoided costs dropped lower than in the mid–1980s and were considerably lower than the levels required by the long-term contracts imposed by some State commissions. Many utilities contend that PURPA has caused dramatic hikes in retail electric rates, and many groups along with these utilities now believe that new regulatory action must be taken to correct past misjudgments.

Forecasters have predicted that future power generation will be dominated by natural gas. Reformers argue that, based on these forecasts, PURPA becomes irrelevant because natural gas is inexpensive and the most environmentally benign of all the fossil fuels used in electric power generation. As mentioned earlier, some groups contend that PURPA is no longer necessary because its goals have already been achieved—i.e., cogeneration using improved turbine techniques and the use of renewable resources has not only gotten a foothold but has claimed a rather significant share of electric power production. Proponents of repeal further contend that PURPA's environmental and fuel diversification goals will be maintained by the workings of a free market.

Others are not so sure. While they may agree that a free market can provide a solution to many of the industry's problems, they seriously question the wisdom of relying on competition to continue the strides made in the use of renewables and cogeneration techniques. Currently, 79 percent of 1995 nonutility capacity and 57 percent of planned additions from 1996 through 1999 are PURPA QF facilities. Energy conservation and diversification of generating fuels were mandated by Congress because of our dependence on foreign oil and the Nation's feeling of helplessness as a result of the energy crises of the 1970s. Those fears have faded with the passage of time, but it is argued that it is not out of the realm of possibility that another crisis could occur. Indeed, some believe that it would be shortsighted and irresponsible to regard energy shortages as merely nightmares of the past and to gamble on the unlikelihood of a similar recurrence. They argue that the Nation cannot be without the ability to cope with such a situation in the future.

Even if dependence on foreign energy sources was not an issue, PURPA supporters fervently stress that common sense dictates that energy be conserved and that electricity generation use more environmentally benign fuels in order to sustain a certain quality of life for future generations. In addition, some believe that QF policy corrects a market failure— i.e., the price of fossil or nuclear energy is too low based on the costly damage it does to the environment and the fact that those who create the pollution do not pay for it. In this context, conservation, diversification of fuels, and the use of renewable resources that are not depletable and other fuels that lessen the problems of acid rain and greenhouse gases must continue to be supported. (For example, in the past, California encouraged the development of renewable generating technologies through PURPA by having two-tiered avoided cost for QFS—one for fossil-fueled plants and another for renewable technologies.) To some groups, just as there is no guarantee that competition can further the goals of PURPA, there is also no question that incentives must remain in place to do so. One incentive already in use is "green" pricing—an alternative to electric utility funding of renewable energy projects [discussed in Chapter Thirteen].

In addition to PURPA's merits regarding the environment and fuel diversification, its supporters point out that QFS bring increased reliability while decreasing the need for large, costly plants. In addition, they contend that today's utilities have too much market power, which makes it necessary for PURPA to continue to give nonutilities a competitive advantage, and until every electricity generator is playing on a level field, PURPA's QF provisions are justified.

There are also those who believe that, while PURPA repeal might and probably would be warranted in a competitive electricity supply scenario, we are not there yet. Just as some PUHCA reformers are against immediate piecemeal and standalone action, some PURPA reformers believe that repeal should be included in a comprehensive restructuring bill. They argue that there is no need to push a repeal bill through Congress when there is currently other proposed electricity competition legislation that will comprehensively address the restructuring and regulatory issues that warrant legislative action.■

D.   ORDER NO. 888: OPEN ACCESS TRANSMISSION, UNBUNDLING, AND THE EMERGENCE OF NEW WHOLESALE POWER MARKETS

Creation of the EWG has spawned growth of many IPPs outside of the PURPA framework. The most significant class of new generators with EWG status are often referred to a "merchant" plants. Unlike traditional utilities, merchants plants do not have a duty to serve any retail load, and provide power primarily in the merging wholesale power markets. The relaxation of PUHCA's requirements in the EPAct and creation of the EWG allow many utilities, through affiliates, to begin supplying power in markets outside of their geographic service areas. An example, discussed further in Chapter 13, is the merchant plant proposed by Duke Energy, which has been planned for siting in Florida. Merchant plants, which sell power at wholesale without the mandatory buyback benefits provided by PURPA, seem to have found an adequate market for their power without mandatory buyback at avoided cost rates, as if required under PURPA.

Regulatory developments after the EPAct have encouraged the development of markets for EWG power, as well as the development of merchants plants more generally. After the EPAct, competitive reforms of the electric power industry have proliferated in two respects. First, the EPAct fueled many reform efforts at the state level, as discussed in Chapter 13. Second, the EPAct shifted much debate over competition from wholesale transmission to retail transmission and other issues, by clarifying federal jurisdiction over wholesale transmission. As is discussed below, however, wholesale transmission reliability and pricing remain important federal regulatory issues. FERC endorsed each of these aspects of the movement to competition when it adopted Order 888 in Spring 1996, a massive set of regulations intended to restructure the electricity industry. On appeal, the D.C. Circuit upheld Order 888 in almost all major respects. *Transmission Access Policy Study Group v. FERC*, 2000 WL 762706 (D.C.Cir.2000). Here are some excerpts from Order 888:

Federal Energy Regulatory Commission (FERC), 18 CFR Parts 35 and 385, [Docket Nos. RM95–8–000 and RM94–7–001; Order No. 888], Promoting Wholesale Competition Through Open Access Non–Discriminatory Transmission Services by Public Utilities; Recovery of Stranded Costs by Public Utilities and Transmitting Utilities

61 Federal Register 21540, Friday, May 10, 1996.

SUMMARY: The Federal Energy Regulatory Commission (Commission) is issuing a Final Rule requiring all public utilities that own, control or operate facilities used for transmitting electric energy in interstate commerce to have on file open access non-discriminatory transmission tariffs that contain minimum terms and conditions of non-discriminatory service. The Final Rule also permits public utilities and transmitting utilities to seek recovery of legitimate, prudent and verifiable stranded costs associated with providing open access and Federal Power Act section 211 transmission services. The Commission's goal is to remove impediments to competition in the wholesale bulk power marketplace and to bring more efficient, lower cost power to the Nation's electricity consumers.

EFFECTIVE DATE: This Final Rule will become effective on July 9, 1996.

In the year since the proposed rules were issued, the pace of competitive changes in the electric utility industry has accelerated. By March of last year, public utilities had filed wholesale open access transmission tariffs with the Commission. Today, prodded by such competitive changes and encouraged by our proposed rules, 106 of the approximately 166 public utilities that own, control, or operate transmission facilities used in interstate commerce have filed some form of wholesale open access tariff. In addition, since the time the proposed rules were issued, numerous state regulatory commissions have adopted or are actively evaluating retail customer choice programs or other utility restructuring alternatives. These events have been spurred by continuing pressures in the marketplace for changes in the way electricity is bought, sold, and transported. Increasingly, customers are demanding the benefits of competition in the growing electricity commodity market.

The Commission estimates the potential quantitative benefits from the Final Rule will be approximately $3.8 to $5.4 billion per year of cost savings, in addition to the non-quantifiable benefits that include better use of existing assets and institutions, new market mechanisms, technical innovation, and less rate distortion. The continuing competitive changes in the industry and the prospect of these benefits to customers make it imperative that this Commission take the necessary steps within its jurisdiction to ensure that all wholesale buyers and sellers of electric energy can obtain non-discriminatory transmission access, that the transition to competition is orderly and fair, and that the integrity and reliability of our electricity infrastructure is maintained.

In this Rule, the Commission seeks to remedy both existing and future undue discrimination in the industry and realize the significant customer benefits that will come with open access. Indeed, it is our statutory obligation under sections 205 and 206 of the Federal Power Act (FPA) to remedy undue discrimination.

To do so, we must eliminate the remaining patchwork of closed and open jurisdictional transmission systems and ensure that all these systems, including those that already provide some form of open access, cannot use monopoly power over transmission to unduly discriminate against others. If we do not take this step now, the result will be benefits to some customers at the expense of others. We have learned from our experience in the natural gas area the importance of addressing competitive transition issues early and with as much certainty to market participants as possible.

Accordingly, in this proceeding and in the accompanying proceeding on OASIS, the Commission, pursuant to its authorities under sections 205 and 206 of the FPA:

— Requires all public utilities that own, control or operate facilities used for transmitting electric energy in interstate commerce

— To file open access non-discriminatory transmission tariffs that contain minimum terms and conditions of non-discriminatory service;

— To take transmission service (including ancillary services) for their own new wholesale sales and purchases of electric energy under the open access tariffs;

— To develop and maintain a same-time information system that will give existing and potential transmission users the same access to transmission information that the public utility enjoys, and further requires public utilities to separate transmission from generation marketing functions and communications;

— Clarifies Federal/state jurisdiction over transmission in interstate commerce and local distribution and provides for deference to certain state recommendations; and

— Permits public utilities and transmitting utilities to seek recovery of legitimate, prudent and verifiable stranded costs associated with providing open access and FPA section 211 transmission services.

Open Access

The Final Rule requires public utilities to file a single open access tariff that offers both network, load-based service and point-to-point, contract-based service. The Rule contains a pro forma tariff that reflects modifications to the NOPR's proposed terms and conditions and also permits variations for regional practices. All public utilities subject to the Rule, including those that already have tariffs on file, will be required to make section 206 compliance filings to meet the new pro forma tariff non-price minimum terms and conditions of non-discriminatory transmission. Utilities may propose their own rates in a section 205 compliance filing.

The Rule provides that public utilities may seek a waiver of some or all of the requirements of the Final Rule. In addition, non-public utilities may seek a waiver of the tariff reciprocity provisions.

The Final Rule does not generically abrogate existing requirements contracts, but will permit customers and public utilities to seek modification, or termination, of certain existing requirements contracts on a case-by-case basis. As to coordination arrangements and contracts, the Rule finds that these arrangements and contracts may need to be modified to remove unduly discriminatory transmission access and/or pricing provisions. Such arrangements and agreements include power pool agreements, public utility holding company agreements, and certain bilateral coordination agreements. The Rule provides guidance and timelines for modifying unduly discriminatory coordination arrangements and contracts, and specifies when the members of such arrangements must begin to conduct trade with each other using the same open access tariff offered to others. The Rule also provides guidance regarding the formation of independent system operators (ISOs).

The Rule does not require any form of corporate restructuring, but will accommodate voluntary restructuring that is consistent with the Rule's open access and comparability policies. As discussed in the NOPR, not all owners or controllers of interstate transmission facilities are subject to the

Commission's jurisdiction under sections 205 and 206 of the FPA and therefore are not subject to this Rule's open access requirements. Therefore, the Final Rule retains the proposed reciprocity provision in the pro forma tariff. Without such a provision, non-open access utilities could take advantage of the competitive opportunities of open access, while at the same time offering inferior access, or no access at all, over their own facilities. Thus, open access utilities would be unfairly burdened. We note that some non-jurisdictional utilities have expressed an interest in a mechanism for obtaining a Commission determination that their transmission tariffs satisfy the reciprocity provisions in the pro forma tariffs, and we provide such a mechanism in the Rule.

The Final Rule does not generically provide for market-based generation rates. Although the Rule codifies the Commission's prior decision that there is no generation dominance in new generating capacity, intervenors in cases may raise generation dominance issues related to new capacity. In addition, to obtain market-based rates for existing generation, we will continue to require public utilities to show, on a case-by-case basis, that there is no generation dominance in existing capacity. Further, in all market-based rate cases, we will continue to look at whether an applicant and its affiliates could erect other barriers to entry and whether there may be problems due to affiliate abuse or reciprocal dealing.

Finally, contemporaneously with this Rule the Commission issues an NOPR on capacity reservation tariffs as an alternative, and perhaps superior, means of remedying undue discrimination.

Conclusion

The Commission believes that the Final Rule will remedy undue discrimination in transmission services in interstate commerce and provide an orderly and fair transition to competitive bulk power markets.■

Following Order No. 888, FERC issued Order No. 889, requiring transmission utility participation in its Open Access Same–Time Information System (OASIS) electronic bulletin board system. The FERC's OASIS requirements apply to public utilities and non-public utilities that provide reciprocal open access transmission service, unless a waiver is granted. Order No. 889 requires that such utilities establish, maintain, and operate (either individually or jointly with other utilities) a real-time information network on which available transmission capacity will be posted and on which capacity reservations may be made. Information about a utility's transmission system must be made available to all transmission customers at the same times. OASIS makes that information available to all customers, ensuring that utilities do not use their ownership, operation, or control of transmission to unfairly deny access. Order No. 889 also requires that a public utility and non-public utility providing reciprocal service to adopt standards of conduct. These standards are designed to ensure that the utility's employees engaged in transmission system operations function independently of the utility's employees engaged in wholesale purchases and sales of electric energy in interstate commerce.

It would be foolhardy to speculate about how the electricity industry will actually look in 25 years. However, following Order 888 federal regulators have focused on several issues, including unbundling and the development regional transmission entities. Although FERC has expressed a clear commitment to competition, Congress has considered federal legislation since 1992 and will likely continue to evaluate federal competition policy in the electric utility industry until consumers and the industry perceive clear and consistent courses of action for both federal and state policies.

1. UNBUNDLING OF WHOLESALE TRANSMISSION AND GENERATION

A significant issue regarding competition before FERC and many state regulatory commissions is the extent to which unbundling (applied by FERC to natural gas sales and transportation in Order No. 636) will work in the electricity industry. As discussed in Chapter Ten, there are many economies to vertical integration of generation, transmission and distribution. However, vertical integration also acts as a significant barrier to enhanced competition. (Similar characteristics of the natural gas industry are discussed in Chapter Seven.) So long as the utilities that own and operate bottleneck transmission and distribution facilities also own and operate generation, incentives for creating unequal access to transmission will exist. Unequal access to transmission facilities in inconsistent with the principle of comparability FERC endorsed in Order No. 888.

To disintegrate generation, transmission, and distribution, FERC could attempt to order formal disaggregation of functions through asset divestiture. FERC's proposed rule on electricity restructuring, a slightly modified version of which was adopted as Order No. 888, discusses "functional unbundling" of generation and transmission:

Promoting Wholesale Competition Through Open Access Non-discriminatory Transmission Services by Public Utilities

60 Federal Register 17662. Friday, April 7, 1995.

. . . Unless all public utilities are required to provide non-discriminatory open access transmission, the ability to achieve full wholesale power competition, and resulting consumer benefits, will be jeopardized. If utilities are allowed to discriminate in favor of their own generation resources at the expense of providing access to others' lower cost generation resources by not providing open access on fair terms, the transmission grid will be a patchwork of open access transmission systems, systems with bilaterally negotiated arrangements, and systems with transmission ordered under section 211. Under such a patchwork of transmission systems, sellers will not have access to transmission on an equal basis, and some sellers will benefit at the expense of others. The ultimate loser in such a regime is the consumer....

As a result of Order No. 436, pipelines became primarily transporters of natural gas. However, in Order No. 636, the Commission noted that pipelines were still providing, albeit at a reduced level, a bundled, city gate, sales service in competition with third-party sales and transportation, and concluded that the competition was not occurring on an equal basis. The Commission also noted that pipelines' natural gas sales prices exceeded those of their competitors, much as electric utilities' embedded costs can exceed the cost of new generating capacity and excess generating capacity of others. In this regard, the Commission determined that the transportation service bundled with pipelines' sales service was superior to that made available to third parties and that pipelines and unregulated competitors were not selling the same product. Accordingly, in Order No. 636, the Commission found this behavior anticompetitive and required pipelines to "unbundle" their sales services from their transportation services and to provide open access transportation service that is equal in quality for all gas supplies whether purchased from the pipeline or some other supplier.

Our experience in the gas area influences our decision that, at a minimum, functional unbundling of wholesale services is necessary in order to obtain non-discriminatory open access and to avoid anticompetitive behavior in wholesale electricity markets....

The Commission's preliminary view is that functional unbundling of wholesale services is necessary to implement non-discriminatory open access. Accordingly, the proposed rule requires that a public utility's uses of its own transmission system for the purpose of engaging in wholesale sales and purchases of electric energy must be separated from other activities, and that transmission services (including ancillary services) must be taken under the filed transmission tariff of general applicability. The proposed rule does not require corporate unbundling (selling off assets to a non-affiliate, or establishing a separate corporate affiliate to manage a utility's transmission assets) in any form, although some utilities may ultimately choose such a course of action. The proposed rule accommodates corporate unbundling, but does not require it.

Functional unbundling means three things. First, it means that a public utility must take transmission services (including ancillary services) for all of its new wholesale sales and purchases of energy under the same tariff of general applicability under which others take service. New wholesale sales and purchases are those under any contracts executed on or after the open access tariffs required by this proposed rule become effective. Non-discriminatory service requires that the utility charge itself the same price for these services that it charges its third-party wholesale transmission customers. We seek comment as to the appropriate means to enforce this requirement, such as a revenue crediting mechanism.

Second, functional unbundling means that a transmission owner must include in its open access tariffs separately stated rates for the transmission and ancillary service components of each transmission service it provides. The rates must satisfy the Commission's Transmission Pricing Policy Statement. Third, functional unbundling means that the public utility, in order to provide non-discriminatory open access to transmission and ancillary services information, must rely upon the same electronic network that its transmission customers rely upon to obtain transmission information about its system when buying or selling power.

For example, the proposed rule requires that a public utility unbundle its new wholesale requirements service contracts, and its new wholesale coordination purchase transactions, and take the firm network transmission component of those services under its own firm network transmission tariff. Similarly, the proposed rule requires that a public utility unbundle any new wholesale coordination sales transactions and take the point-to-point transmission component of that service under its own point-to-point transmission tariff. Finally, the proposed rule requires that a utility unbundle ancillary services and take these services under its network and point-to-point tariffs.

Public utilities also must authorize their power pool agents to offer any transmission service available under power pool arrangements to all transmission customers. In addition, public utilities that participate in a power pool that acts as a control area must authorize the power pool's control center to offer ancillary services under a filed tariff, and must take all of their control area services from that tariff. A public utility must take dispatch service and other ancillary transmission services on the same terms and conditions as those offered to its transmission customers.

The requirement to provide ancillary services and to take those services under a tariff is not intended to mandate any federal rules that would prescribe the actual merit order of dispatch. Rather, it is a requirement that public utilities ensure that dispatch practices and procedures applicable to them are also applied to third-party transmission customers.

The proposed requirement that a public utility take transmission service used for wholesale requirements service and wholesale coordination transactions under its own filed tariff means that all wholesale trade, both that of the public utility and its competitors, would be taken under a single wholesale transmission tariff. Our preliminary view is that such a requirement places the correct incentives on the public utility to file a fair tariff since it must live under those terms for wholesale purposes. The Commission invites comment on its approach to functional unbundling. Will it provide strong enough incentives for non-discriminatory access without some form of corporate restructuring? If utilities restructure, how will our proposed rules apply to different types of corporate structures?

While this approach to unbundling creates good incentives with respect to wholesale service, it omits retail service. In other words, it does not require the transmission owner to take unbundled transmission service under the same tariff as third parties in order to serve its retail customers. This will result in service under two separate arrangements—an explicit wholesale transmission tariff filed at the Commission and an implicit retail transmission tariff governed by a state regulatory body. It also raises the possibility that the quality of transmission service for retail purposes will be superior to the quality of transmission service offered for wholesale purposes.■

NOTES AND COMMENTS

1. In Order No. 888, FERC adopted the notion of "functional unbundling." Will functional unbundling work? Would FERC be required to monitor the communication between a utility's generation and transmission operations? Would it be better to erect a "Chinese wall" between the operations, or to require utilities to divest themselves of either their transmission or their generation assets as the courts required AT & T to sell off its local telephone service operations in 1984? For a discussion of how FERC was able to convince utilities of the benefits of unbundling, *see* Jim Rossi, Can FERC Overcome Special Interest Politics, Public Utilities Fortnightly, Oct. 15, 1995.

2. The industry was moving in the direction FERC anticipated even before Order No. 888 was promulgated. Around the time FERC was considering announcement of its proposed rule, New England Electric System had announced a restructuring proposal that went a step beyond FERC's unbundling proposal. NEES proposed selling off its transmission assets at either replacement cost or original cost to a third party that had no generation assets and would ensure comparability of service. Proceeds from the sale would then be used to write-down NEES's stranded generating assets. NEES Restructuring Proposal Calls for Sale of Transmission Assets, Inside FERC, Nov. 7, 1994, at 4. (Stranded costs are discussed further in Chapter Twelve.)

3. Since Order No. 888's adoption, FERC has been presented with several proposals to sell off generation assets by utilities that intend to focus on transmission and distribution. *See, e.g., Bangor Hydro–Electric Co.,* 86 FERC ¶ 61,020 (1999); *Central Maine Power Co.,* 85 FERC ¶ 61,272 (1998). Some of these have involved nuclear plants. *See Boston Edison Co. & Entergy Nuclear Generation Co.,* 87 FERC ¶ 61,053 (1999) (sale of Pilgrim nuclear unit); *Jersey Central Power & Light Co.,* 87 FERC ¶ 61,014 (1999) (sale of Three Mile Island Unit No. 1). From the perspective of evaluating the asset sale, federal regulators have had a fairly easy task, given their commitment to increasing the number of generation sellers in different markets. Their decisions to approve such sales may have been aided, however, by the premium in excess of book value utilities have earned in generation asset sales. This premium can be used to retire stranded investments or to reduce rates to consumers. *See Duke Energy Moss Landing LLC,* 83 FERC ¶ 61,318 (1998), *on reh'g,* 86 FERC ¶ 61,227 (1999) (discussing acquisition premiums resulting from sale of generation assets at a price in excess of book value). Should FERC concern itself with the impact of asset spin-offs on customers of the purchasing utility? What safeguards might protect these customers from bearing the costs of uneconomic new purchases?

2.   Open Access Wholesale Transmission: Independent System Operators and Regional Transmission Organizations

As discussed in Chapter Ten, the transmission of electricity differs in many respects from the transportation of natural gas. Transmission lines, unlike natural gas pipelines, have no valves. Although it is technologically possible to install "phase shifters" to control the physical flow of power on transmission lines, extreme caution must be exercised to determine the optimum location and use of phase shifters to avoid sacrificing reliable service. Absent some sort of flow control, electrons flow in the path of least resistance. Thus, a transmission transaction that appears to involve the flow of electricity from New York to New Jersey may use transmission lines located in other states, such as Ohio, even though these states do not lie in the direct physical path between the generator and customer. Such physical geographical diversions in the transmission of electricity are called "loop flows".

Under traditional cost-of-service regulation, regulators have been able to avoid most of the economic, operational, and policy problems raised by loop flows. Because most utilities were vertically integrated and did not engage in a large number of transactions with third parties, this was not a significant issue. Where utilities were exchanging power, they tended to rely on informal cooperative mechanisms, such a regional power pools, to monitor loopflow problems.

The transition to competition, however, raises the specter of more system loop flow problems. While FERC has been able to implement competition in natural gas markets on a model of bilateral trading, in which consumers negotiate directly with pipelines for natural gas transportation, such a simple market model is likely to be problematic where transmission capacity constraints lead to large and constantly changing congestion costs.

U.S. regulators have looked to the experience of regulators in other countries as they attempt to implement power competition. Many countries have experimented with power pools, as the excerpt at the beginning of this Chapter describes. The experience of other countries with transmission issues is of great importance to federal regulators in the U.S. as they attempt to implement the open access model in electricity. *See* Alex Henney, The Global Evolution of Competitive Power Markets, Public Utilities Fortnightly, January 15, 1995, at 38. Various alternative methods for the governance and regulation of power pools being used in Britain, Australia, Canada and Scandinavia are analyzed in James Barker, Jr., Bernard Tenenbaum and Fiona Woolf, Regulation of Power Pools and System Operators: An International Comparison, 18 Energy L. J. 261 (1997).

FERC has looked to the Independent Service Operator (ISO) as a way of ensuring transmission reliability in competitive markets. The concept has been described as follows:

ISOs are a new concept in the electric utility industry. Their purpose will be to manage the transmission network in such a way as to allow open and equal access to all electricity buyers and sellers. The FERC does not require utilities to have an ISO in order to ensure open and equal access to the transmission network, but by providing standards for approval, FERC encourages companies and regional power pools to explore the concept.

Questions arise as to what exactly an ISO will do to manage the transmission network, and how decisions will be made. The answers to these questions are being worked out by State commissions and utilities considering this option. It is clear, however, that the ISO will be responsible for reliability and security of the transmission system. The ISO will probably oversee all maintenance, even if the transmission owners provide day-to-day maintenance. The FERC guidelines, noted above, provide some light on other functions of an ISO. They include congestion management, administering transmission and ancillary pricing, making transmission information publicly available, and other activities. It is expected that these functions will not be performed by all ISOs; there will be differences from region to region.

The Changing Structure of the Electric Power Industry: An Update, Energy Information Administration, U.S. Department of Energy (1997) http://www.eia.doe.gov/cneaf/electricity/chg_str/chapter9.html>.

As with the divestiture of assets, in Order No. 888 FERC did not require but encouraged the development of ISOs to assist with the management and operation of transmission networks. Independent, third-party operators of regional, multi-utility transmission systems offer assurance to customers of transmission that access is truly nondiscriminatory. Despite the structure of member utilities, since ISOs are independently operated, they have fewer incentives to favor the wholesale generation market of any incumbent utility.

In Order No. 888, FERC identified eleven principles of ISO governance and operation, in hopes that utilities would voluntarily develop and produce filings that satisfy these principles.

Federal Energy Regulatory Commission (FERC), 18 CFR Parts 35 and 385, [Docket Nos. RM95–8–000 and RM94–7–001; Order No. 888], Promoting Wholesale Competition Through Open Access Non–Discriminatory Transmission Services by Public Utilities; Recovery of Stranded Costs by Public Utilities and Transmitting Utilities

61 Federal Register 21540, Friday, May 10, 1996.

ISO Principles

The Commission recognizes that some utilities are exploring the concept of an Independent System Operator and that the tight power pools are considering restructuring proposals that involve an ISO. While the Commission is not requiring any utility to form an ISO at this time, we wish to encourage the formation of properly-structured ISOs. To this end, we believe it is important to give the industry some guidance on ISOs at this time. Accordingly, we here set out certain principles that will be used in assessing ISO proposals that may be submitted to the Commission in the future. These principles are applicable only to ISOs that would be control area operators, including any ISO established in the restructuring of power pools. We recognize that some utilities are exploring concepts that do not involve full operational control of the grid. Without in any way prejudging the merits of such arrangements, the following principles do not apply to independent administrators or coordinators that lack operational control. We do not have enough information at this time to offer guidance about such entities, but recognize that they could perform a useful role in a restructured industry. Because an ISO will be a public utility subject to our jurisdiction, the ISO's operating standards and procedures must be approved by the Commission. In addition, a properly constituted ISO is a means by which public utilities can comply with the Commission's non-discriminatory transmission tariff requirements. The principles for ISOs are:

1.   The ISO's governance should be structured in a fair and non-discriminatory manner. The primary purpose of an ISO is to ensure fair and non-discriminatory access to transmission services and ancillary services for all users of the system. As such, an ISO should be independent of any individual market participant or any one class of participants (e.g., transmission owners or end-users). A governance structure that includes fair representation of all types of users of the system would help ensure that the ISO formulates policies, operates the system, and resolves disputes in a fair and non-discriminatory manner. The ISO's rules of governance, however, should prevent control, and appearance of control, of decision-making by any class of participants.

2.   An ISO and its employees should have no financial interest in the economic performance of any power market participant. An ISO should adopt and enforce strict conflict of interest standards. To be truly independent, an ISO cannot be owned by any market participant. We recognize that transmission owners need to be able to hold the ISO accountable in its fiduciary role, but should not be able to dictate day-to-day operational matters. Employees of the ISO should also be financially independent of market participants. We recognize, however, that a short transition period (we believe 6 months would be adequate) will be needed for employees of a newly formed ISO to sever all ties with former transmission owners and to make appropriate arrangements for pension plans, health programs and so on. In addition, an ISO should not undertake any contractual arrangement with generation or transmission owners or transmission users that is not at arm's length. In order to ensure independence, a strict conflict of interest standard should be adopted and enforced.

3. An ISO should provide open access to the transmission system and all services under its control at non-pancaked rates pursuant to a single, unbundled, grid-wide tariff that applies to all eligible users in a non-discriminatory manner. An ISO should be responsible for ensuring that all users have non-discriminatory access to the transmission system and all services under ISO control. The portion of the transmission grid operated by a single ISO should be as large as possible, consistent with the agreement of market participants, and the ISO should schedule all transmission on the portion of the grid it controls. An ISO should have clear tariffs for services that neither favor nor disfavor any user or class of users.

4. An ISO should have the primary responsibility in ensuring short-term reliability of grid operations. Its role in this responsibility should be well-defined and comply with applicable standards set by NERC and the regional reliability council. Reliability and security of the transmission system are critical functions for a system operator. As part of this responsibility an ISO should oversee all maintenance of the transmission facilities under its control, including any day-to-day maintenance contracted to be performed by others. An ISO may also have a role with respect to reliability planning. In any case, the ISO should be responsible for ensuring that services (for all users, including new users) can be provided reliably, and for developing and implementing policies related to curtailment to ensure the on-going reliability and security of the system.

5. An ISO should have control over the operation of interconnected transmission facilities within its region. An ISO is an operator of a designated set of transmission facilities.

6. An ISO should identify constraints on the system and be able to take operational actions to relieve those constraints within the trading rules established by the governing body. These rules should promote efficient trading. A key function of an ISO will be to accommodate transactions made in a free and competitive market while remaining at arm's length from those transactions. The ISO may need to exercise some level of operational control over generation facilities in order to regulate and balance the power system, especially when transmission constraints limit trading over interfaces in some circumstances. It is important that the ISO's operational control be exercised in accordance with the trading rules established by the governing body. The trading rules should promote efficiency in the marketplace. In addition, we would expect that an ISO would provide, or cause to be provided, the ancillary services described in this Rule.

7. The ISO should have appropriate incentives for efficient management and administration and should procure the services needed for such management and administration in an open competitive market. Management and administration of the ISO should be carried out in an efficient manner. In addition to personnel and administrative functions, an ISO could perform certain operational functions, such as: determination of appropriate system expansions, transmission maintenance, administering transmission contracts, operation of a settlements system, and operation of

an energy auction. The ISO should use competitive procurement, to the extent possible, for all services provided by the ISO that are needed to operate the system. All procedures and protocols should be publicly available.

8. An ISO's transmission and ancillary services pricing policies should promote the efficient use of and investment in generation, transmission, and consumption. An ISO or an RTG of which the ISO is a member should conduct such studies as may be necessary to identify operational problems or appropriate expansions. Appropriate price signals are essential to achieve efficient investment in generation and transmission and consumption of energy. The pricing policies pursued by the ISO should reflect a number of attributes, including affording non-discriminatory access to services, ensuring cost recovery for transmission owners and those providing ancillary services, ensuring reliability and stability of the system and providing efficient price signals of the costs of using the transmission grid. In particular, the Commission would consider transmission pricing proposals for addressing network congestion that are consistent with our Transmission Pricing Policy Statement. In addition, an ISO should conduct such studies and coordinate with market participants including RTGs, as may be necessary to identify transmission constraints on its system, loop flow impacts between its system and neighboring systems, and other factors that might affect system operation or expansion.

9. An ISO should make transmission system information publicly available on a timely basis via an electronic information network consistent with the Commission's requirements. A free-flow of information between the ISO and market participants is required for an ISO to perform its functions and for market participants to efficiently participate in the market. At a minimum, information on system operation, conditions, available capacity and constraints, and all contracts or other service arrangements of the ISO should be made publicly available. This information should be made available on an OASIS operated by the ISO.

10. An ISO should develop mechanisms to coordinate with neighboring control areas. An ISO will be required to coordinate power scheduling with other entities operating transmission systems. Such coordination is necessary to ensure provision of transmission services that cross system boundaries and to ensure reliability and stability of the systems. The mechanisms by which ISOs and other transmission operators coordinate can be left to those parties to determine.

11. An ISO should establish an ADR process to resolve disputes in the first instance. An ISO should provide for a voluntary dispute resolution process that allows parties to resolve technical, financial, and other issues without resort to filing complaints at the Commission. We would encourage the ISO to establish rules and procedures to implement alternative dispute resolution processes.■

* * *

To date, many utilities have filed ISO proposals with FERC, including groups of utilities located in California, New York, New England, and the Mid–Atlantic (PJM) and the Midwest. In addition, many utilities have announced their intent to form single-utility or multiple utility "Transcos," combining ownership with operational control of for-profit, stand-alone transmission companies.

An example of an ISO is the PJM ISO, created by the Pennsylvania–New Jersey–Maryland Interconnection. The PJM ISO is independent because its members are not affiliated with and are not controlled by market participants. Unlike the corporate board of a Transco, which answers first to shareholders, the PJM Board adheres to a public interest standard, regardless of the commercial interests of members. The ISO makes grid management decisions independent of the commercial interests of its members, and it has the authority to direct its members to construct upgrades or additional facilities. FERC approved the PJM ISO, as it complied with its Order No. 888 ISO principles. *See Pennsylvania–New Jersey–Maryland Interconnection*, 81 FERC ¶ 61,257 (1998).

By contrast, consider an alternative proposal submitted by Alliance Companies. The plan was to form two companies, Alliance Publico and Alliance Transco. Members would transfer their high-voltage transmission facilities to Alliance Transco, but no Alliance company would own more than 5 percent of Alliance Transco's stock. Alliance Publico, a registered public utility holding company, would operate as the managing member of the Alliance Transco. FERC conditionally approved the Alliance Companies request to form a for-profit Transco, but noted that the plan failed many of the eleven ISO principles in Order No. 888, including independence, financial interest, nondiscriminatory tariffs, efficient administration and pricing. *See Alliance Companies*, 89 FERC ¶ 61,298 (1999). FERC approved the arrangement, but encouraged the companies to consider an ISO arrangement over the Transco approach.

Does the distinction between an ISO and Transco matter? Although both may promote transmission coordination, many companies in the industry believe that it important whether FERC encourages ISOs only, or both ISOs and Transcos. Order No. 888 spoke primarily to the ISO. As a non-profit entity that separates ownership and control of transmission, the ISO is believed by some to be the best way of promoting the public interest in transmission.

Some utilities in the industry, however, favor a Transco approach on the grounds that the for-profit motive of the company that both owns and operates transmission will create an inherent incentive for the Transco to expand transmission capacity where this is needed. In many areas of the country, the expansion of transmission capacity will be integral to ensuring reliability in wholesale power markets. In addition, the Transco alternative may be more attractive to some companies, since a transmission-owning company may be more comfortable transferring its transmission facilities to a for-profit company over which it may have some influence. To the extent FERC does not have the authority to mandate transmission pooling, voluntary formation of transmission organizations is important so the Transco is not necessarily at odds with FERC's regulatory agenda. In addition, owners may fear that transfer of ownership of transmission assets to an ISO may jeopardize currently allowed rates of return, since a utility's passive ownership of resources under the control of an ISO may be viewed as a lower risk that justifies a lower rate of return. *See* Stephen Angle & George Cannon, Jr., Independent Transmission Companies: The For–Profit Alternative in Competitive Electric Markets, 19 Energy L.J. 229, 238 (1998).

With the proliferation of generation suppliers, many of whom do not own generation, transmission reliability remains a significant issue for federal regulators. FERC continues to evaluate its role in encouraging ISOs or more regional-based approaches to transmission management and operation. Its most recent effort, dubbed "Order 2000," focuses on the promotion of Regional Transmission Groups, which serve an overlapping function with ISOs in the promotion of wholesale competition. Below are excerpts from the proposed rule, which describes the necessity for FERC's rule, as well as a description of the final rule adopted in Order 2000 from FERC's order on rehearing on the rule.

Proposed Rules, Department of Energy, Federal Energy Regulatory Commission, 18 CFR Part 35, [Docket No. Rm99–2–000] Regional Transmission Organizations; Notice of Proposed Rulemaking

64 Federal Register 31390, Thursday, June 10, 1999.

The Federal Energy Regulatory Commission (Commission) is proposing to amend its regulations under the Federal Power Act (FPA) to facilitate the formation of Regional Transmission Organizations (RTOs). The Commission proposes to require that each public utility that owns, operates, or controls facilities for the transmission of electric energy in interstate commerce make certain filings with respect to forming and participating in an RTO. The Commission also proposes minimum characteristics and functions that a transmission entity must satisfy in order to be considered to be an RTO.

As a result [of Order No. 888 and ensuing developments], the traditional means of grid management is showing signs of strain and may be inadequate to support the efficient and reliable operation that is needed for the continued development of competitive electricity markets. In addition, there are indications that continued discrimination in the provision of transmission services by vertically integrated utilities may also be impeding fully competitive electricity markets. These problems may be depriving the Nation of the benefits of lower prices, more reliance on market solutions, and lighter-handed regulation that competitive markets can bring.

If electricity consumers are to realize the full benefits that competition can bring to wholesale markets, the Commission must address the extent of these problems and appropriate ways of mitigating them. Competition in wholesale electricity markets is the best way to protect the public interest and ensure that electricity consumers pay the lowest price possible for reliable service. We believe that further steps may need to be taken to address grid management if we are to achieve fully competitive power markets. We further believe that regional approaches to the numerous issues affecting the industry may be the best means to eliminate remaining impediments to properly functioning competitive markets.

Our objective is for all transmission owning entities in the Nation, including non-public utility entities, to place their transmission facilities under the control of appropriate regional transmission institutions in a timely manner. We seek to accomplish our objective by encouraging voluntary participation. We are therefore proposing in this rulemaking minimum characteristics and functions for appropriate regional transmission institutions; a collaborative process by which public utilities and non-public utilities that own, operate or control interstate transmission facilities, in consultation with the state officials as appropriate, will consider and develop regional transmission institutions; a willingness to consider incentive pricing on a case-specific basis and an offer of non-monetary regulatory benefits, such as deference in dispute resolution, reduced or eliminated codes of conduct, and streamlined filing and approval procedures; and a time line for public utilities to make appropriate filings with the Commission and initiate operation of regional transmission institutions. As a result, we expect jurisdictional utilities to form Regional (RTOs).

As discussed in detail herein, regional institutions can address the operational and reliability issues now confronting the industry, and any residual discrimination in transmission services that can occur when the operation of the transmission system remains in the control of a vertically integrated utility. Appropriate regional transmission institutions could: (1) improve efficiencies in transmission grid management; (2) improve grid reliability; (3) remove the remaining opportunities for discriminatory transmission practices; (4) improve market performance; and (5) facilitate lighter handed regulation.

Thus, we believe that appropriate regional transmission institutions could successfully address the existing impediments to efficient grid operation and competition and could consequently benefit consumers through lower electricity rates resulting from a wider choice of services and service providers. There are likely to be substantial cost savings brought about by regional transmission institutions.

In light of important questions regarding the complexity of grid regionalization raised by state regulators and applicants in individual cases, we are proposing a flexible approach. We are not proposing to mandate that utilities participate in a regional transmission institution by a date certain. Instead, we act now to ensure that they consider doing so in good faith. Moreover, the Commission is not proposing a "cookie cutter" organizational format for regional transmission institutions or the establishment of fixed or specific regional boundaries under section 202(a) of the FPA.

Rather, the Commission is proposing to establish fundamental characteristics and functions for appropriate regional transmission institutions. We will designate institutions that satisfy all of the minimum characteristics and functions as Regional Transmission Organizations (RTOs). Hereinafter, the term Regional Transmission Organization, or RTO, will refer to an organization that satisfies all of the minimum characteristics and functions....

In light of the comments received [from state regulators and other parties in a previous proceeding], we wish to respond to several concerns that were raised.

First, we are not proposing to mandate RTOs, nor are we proposing detailed specifications on a particular organizational form for RTOs. The goal of this rulemaking is to get RTOs in place through voluntary participation. While this Commission has specific authorities and responsibilities under the FPA to protect against undue discrimination and remove impediments to wholesale competition, we believe it is preferable to meet these responsibilities in the first instance through an open and collaborative process that allows for regional flexibility and induces voluntary behavior.

Second, the development of RTOs is not intended to interfere with state prerogatives in setting retail competition policy. The Commission believes that RTOs can successfully accommodate the transmission systems of all states, whether or not a particular state has adopted retail competition. However, for those states that have chosen to adopt retail wheeling, RTOs can play a critical role in the realization of full competition at the retail level as well as at the wholesale level. In addition, the Commission believes that RTOs will not interfere with a state's prerogative to keep the benefits of low-cost power for the state's own retail consumers.

Third, we propose to allow RTOs to prevent transmission cost shifting by continuing our policy of flexibility with respect to recovery of sunk transmission costs, such as the "license plate" approach.

Fourth, the existence of RTOs has not, and will not in the future, interfere with traditional state and local regulatory responsibilities such as transmission siting, local reliability matters, and regulation of retail sales of generation and local distribution. In fact, RTOs offer the potential to assist the states in their regulation of retail markets and in resolving matters among states on a regional basis. They also provide a vehicle for amicably resolving state and Federal jurisdictional issues.

Finally, we do not propose to establish regional boundaries in this rulemaking. Our foremost concern is that a proposed RTO's regional configuration is sufficient to ensure that the required RTO characteristics and functions are satisfied. To this end, the Commission proposes guidance regarding the scope and regional configuration of RTOs.

II. Background

In April 1996, in Order Nos. 888 and 889, the Commission established the foundation necessary to develop competitive bulk power markets in the

United States: non-discriminatory open access transmission services by public utilities and stranded cost recovery rules that would provide a fair transition to competitive markets. Order Nos. 888 and 889 were very successful in accomplishing much of what they set out to do. However, they were not intended to address all problems that might arise in the development of competitive power markets. Indeed, the nature of the emerging markets and the remaining impediments to full competition have become apparent in the three years since the issuance of our orders.

A.   The Foundation for Competitive Markets: Order Nos. 888 and 889

In Order Nos. 888 and 889, the Commission found that unduly discriminatory and anticompetitive practices existed in the electric industry, and that transmission-owning utilities had discriminated against others seeking transmission access. The Commission stated that its goal was to ensure that customers have the benefits of competitively priced generation, and determined that non-discriminatory open access transmission services (including access to transmission information) and stranded cost recovery were the most critical components of a successful transition to competitive wholesale electricity markets. [Stranded cost recovery is discussed in Chapter Twelve.]

Accordingly, Order No. 888 required all public utilities that own, control or operate facilities used for transmitting electric energy in interstate commerce to (1) file open access non-discriminatory transmission tariffs containing, at a minimum, the non-price terms and conditions set forth in the Order, and (2) functionally unbundle wholesale power services. Under functional unbundling, the public utility must: (a) take transmission services under the same tariff of general applicability as do others; (b) state separate rates for wholesale generation, transmission, and ancillary services; and © rely on the same electronic information network that its transmission customers rely on to obtain information about its transmission system when buying or selling power. Order No. 889 required that all public utilities establish or participate in an Open Access Same–Time Information System (OASIS) that meets certain specifications, and comply with standards of conduct designed to prevent employees of a public utility (or any employees of its affiliates) engaged in wholesale power marketing functions from obtaining preferential access to pertinent transmission system information. . . .

B.   Developments Since Order Nos. 888 and 889

In the three years since Order Nos. 888 and 889 were issued, numerous significant developments have occurred in the electric utility industry. Some of these reflect changes in governmental policies; others are strictly industry driven. These activities have resulted in a considerably different industry landscape from the one faced at the time the Commission was developing Order No. 888, resulting in new regulatory and industry challenges.

Order Nos. 888 and 889 required a significant change in the way many public utilities have done business for most of this century, and most public utilities accepted these changes and made substantial good faith efforts to comply with the new requirements. Virtually all public utilities have filed tariffs stating rates, terms and conditions for third-party use of their transmission systems. In addition, improved information about the transmission system is available to all participants in the market at the same time that it is available to the public utility as a result of utility compliance with the OASIS regulations.

The availability of tariffs and information about the transmission system has fostered a rapid growth in dependence on wholesale markets for acquisition of generation resources. Areas that have experienced generation shortages have seen rapid development of new generation resources. For example, New England, where there was deep concern about adequacy of generation supply only three years ago, now has approximately 30,000 MW of generation proposed. That response comes almost entirely from independent generating plants that are able to sell power into the bulk power market through open access to the transmission system. Power resources are now acquired over increasingly large regional areas, and interregional transfers of electricity have increased.

The very success of Order Nos. 888 and 889 and the initiative utilities pursuing voluntary restructuring beyond the minimum open access requirements have put new stresses on regional transmission systems— stresses that call for regional solutions.

1. Industry Restructuring and New Stresses on the Transmission Grid

Open access transmission and the opening of wholesale competition in the electric industry have brought an array of changes in the past several years: divestiture by many integrated utilities of some or all of their generating assets; significantly increased merger activity both between electric utilities and between electric and natural gas utilities; increases in the number of new participants in the industry in the form of independent power marketers and generators; increases in the volume of trade in the industry, particularly as marketers make multiple sales; state efforts to create retail competition; and new and different uses of the transmission grid.

With respect to divestiture, since August 1997, approximately 50,000 MW of generating capacity have been sold (or are under contract to be sold) by utilities, and an additional 30,000 MW is currently for sale. In total, this represents more than 10 percent of U.S. generating capacity. In all, according to publicly available data, 27 utilities have sold all or some of their generating assets and 7 others have assets for sale. Buyers of this generating capacity have included traditional utilities with specified service territories as well as independent power producers with no required service territory.

Since Order No. 888 was issued, there have been more than 20 applications filed with us to approve proposed mergers involving public utilities. Most of these mergers have been approved by various regulatory authorities, including the Commission, although a few have been rejected or withdrawn, and several mergers are pending regulatory approval. Most of these merger proposals have been between electric utilities with contiguous service areas, while some of the proposed mergers have been between utilities with noncontiguous service areas. The Commission has also been presented with merger applications involving the combination of electric and natural gas assets.

There has been significant growth in the volume of trading in the wholesale electricity market. In the first quarter of 1995, according to power marketer quarterly filings, marketer sales totaled 1.8 million MWh, but by the second quarter of 1998, such sales escalated to 513 million MWh. Many new competitors have entered the industry. For example, in the first quarter of 1995, there were eight power marketers (either independent or affiliated with traditional utilities) actively trading in wholesale power markets, but by the second quarter of 1998, there were 108 actively trading power marketers. The Commission has granted market-based rate authority to well over 500 wholesale power marketers, of which some are independent of traditional investor-owned utilities, some are affiliated with traditional utilities, and some are traditional utilities themselves.

[As discussed in Chapter Thirteen, s]tate commissions and legislatures have been active in the past few years studying competitive options at the retail level, setting up pilot retail access programs, and, in some states, implementing full scale retail access programs. As of May 1, 1999, 18 states have enacted electric restructuring legislation, 3 have issued comprehensive regulatory orders, and 28 others have legislation or orders pending or investigations underway. Fifteen states have implemented full-scale or pilot retail competition programs that offer a choice of suppliers to at least some retail customers. Eight states have set in motion programs to offer access to retail customers by a date certain.

Because of the changes in the structure of the electric industry, the transmission grid is now being used more intensively and in different ways than in the past. The Commission is concerned that the traditional approaches to operating the grid are showing signs of strain. According to the North American Electric Reliability Council (NERC), "the adequacy of the bulk transmission system has been challenged to support the movement of power in unprecedented amounts and in unexpected directions." These changes in the use of the transmission system "will test the electric industry's ability to maintain system security in operating the transmission system under conditions for which it was not planned or designed." It should be noted that, despite the increased transmission system loadings, NERC believes that the "procedures and processes to mitigate potential reliability impacts appear to be working reliably for now," and that even though the system was particularly stressed during the summer of 1998, "the system performed reliably and firm demand was not interrupted due to transmission transfer limitations."

An indication that the increased and different use of the transmission system is stressing the grid is the increased use of transmission line loading relief (TLR) procedures.[16][1] NERC's TLR procedures were invoked 250 times between January 1 and September 1, 1998 to prevent facility or interface overloads on the Eastern Interconnection.

It appears that the planning and construction of transmission and transmission-related facilities may not be keeping up with increased requirements. According to NERC, "Business is increasing on the transmission system, but very little is being done to increase the load serving and transfer capability of the bulk transmission system." The amount of new transmission capacity planned over the next ten years is significantly lower than the additions that had been planned five years ago, and most of the planned projects are for local system support. NERC states that, "The close coordination of generation and transmission planning is diminishing as vertically integrated utilities divest their generation assets and most new generation is being proposed and developed by independent power producers."

The transition to new market structures has resulted in new challenges and circumstances. For example, during the week of June 22–26, 1998, the wholesale electric market in the Midwest experienced numerous events that led to unprecedented high spot market prices. Spot wholesale market prices for energy briefly rose as high as $7,500 per MWh, compared to an average price for the summer of approximately $40 per MWh in the Midwest if the price spikes are excluded. This experience led to calls for price caps, allegations of market power, and a questioning of the effectiveness of transmission open access and wholesale electric competition.

The Commission's staff found that the market institutions were not adequately prepared to deal with such a dramatic series of events. Regarding regional transmission entities, the staff report observed: "The necessity for cooperation in meeting reliability concerns and the Commission's intent to foster competitive market conditions underscores the importance of better regional coordination in areas such as maintenance of transmission and generation systems and transmission planning and operation." Support for this view comes from many sources. For example, the Public Utilities Commission of Ohio, in its own report on the price spikes, recommended that policy makers "take unambiguous action to require coordination of transmission system operations by regionwide Independent System Operators."

On September 29, 1998, the Secretary of Energy Advisory Board Task Force on Electric System Reliability published its final report. The Task

---

1. The TLR procedures are designed to remedy overloads that result when a transmission line or other transmission equipment carries or will carry more power than its rating, which could result in either power outages or damage to property. The TLR procedures are designed to bring overloaded transmission equipment to within NERC's Operating Security Limits essentially by curtailing transactions contributing to the overload. *See North American Electric Reliability Council*, 85 FERC 61,353 (1998) (NERC).

Force was convened in January 1997 to provide advice to the Department of Energy on critical institutional, technical, and policy issues that need to be addressed in order to maintain bulk power electric system reliability in a more competitive industry. The Task Force found that "the traditional reliability institutions and processes that have served the Nation well in the past need to be modified to ensure that reliability is maintained in a competitively neutral fashion;" that "grid reliability depends heavily on system operators who monitor and control the grid in real time;" and that "because bulk power systems are regional in nature, they can and should be operated more reliably and efficiently when coordinated over large geographic areas."[25][2]

The report noted that many regions of the United States are developing ISOs as a way to maintain electric system reliability as competitive markets develop. According to the Task Force, ISOs are significant institutions to assure both electric system reliability and competitive generation markets. The Task Force concluded that a large ISO would: (1) be able to identify and address reliability issues most effectively; (2) internalize much of the loop flow caused by the growing number of transactions; (3) facilitate transmission access across a larger portion of the network, consequently improving market efficiencies and promoting greater competition; and (4) eliminate "pancaking" of transmission rates, thus allowing a greater range of economic energy trades across the network.

2. Successes, Failures, and Haphazard Development of Regional Transmission Entities

Since Order No. 888 was issued, there have been both successful and unsuccessful efforts to establish ISOs, and other efforts to form regional entities to operate the transmission facilities in various parts of the country. While we are encouraged by the success of some of these efforts, it is apparent that the results have been inconsistent, and much of the country's transmission facilities remain outside of an operational regional transmission institution.

Proposals for the establishment of five ISOs have been submitted to and approved, or conditionally approved, by the Commission. These are the California ISO, the PJM ISO, ISO New England ISO, the New York ISO, and the Midwest ISO. In addition, the Texas Commission has ordered an ISO for the Electric Reliability Council of Texas (ERCOT). Moreover, our international neighbors in Canada and Mexico are also pursuing electric restructuring efforts that include various forms of regional transmission entities.

The PJM, New England and New York ISOs were established on the platform of existing tight power pools. It appears that the principal motivation for creating ISOs in these situations was the Order No. 888 require-

---

2. Maintaining Reliability in a Competitive U.S. Electricity Industry; Final Report of the Task Force on Electric System Reliability (Sept. 29, 1998) (Task Force Report). The Task Force was comprised of 24 members representing all major segments of the electric industry, including private and public suppliers, power marketers, regulators, environmentalists, and academics.

ment that there be a single system wide transmission tariff for tight pools. In contrast, the establishment of the California ISO and the ERCOT ISO was the direct result of mandates by state governments. The Midwest ISO, which is not yet operational, is unique. It began through a consensual process and was not driven by a preexisting institution. Two states in the region subsequently required utilities in their states to participate in either a Commission-approved ISO (Illinois and Wisconsin), or sell their transmission assets to an independent transmission company (Wisconsin).

The approved ISOs have similarities as well as differences. All five Commission-approved ISOs operate, or propose to operate, as non-profit organizations. All five ISOs include both public and non-public utility members. However, among the five, there is considerable variation in governance, operational responsibilities, geographic scope and market operations. Four of the ISOs rely on a two-tier form of governance with a non-stakeholder governing board on top that is advised, either formally or informally, by one or more stakeholder groups. In general, the final decision making authority rests with the independent non-stakeholder board. One ISO, the California ISO, uses a board consisting of stakeholders and non-stakeholders.

Four of the five ISOs operate traditional control areas, but the Midwest ISO does not currently plan to operate a traditional control area. Three are multi-state ISOs (New England, PJM and Midwest), while two ISOs (California and New York) currently operate within a single state. The current Midwest ISO members do not encompass one contiguous geographic area and there are holes in its coverage. The ISO New England administers a separate NEPOOL tariff, while the other four administer their own ISO transmission tariffs.

Three ISOs operate or propose to operate centralized power markets (New England, PJM and New York), and one ISO (California) relies on a separate power exchange (PX) to operate such a market. The Midwest ISO did not originally envision an ISO-related centralized market for its region. In addition, at least one separate PX has begun to do business in California apart from the PX established through the restructuring legislation.[35][3]

Not all efforts to create ISOs have been successful. For example, after more than two years of effort, the proponents of the IndeGO ISO in the Pacific Northwest and Rocky Mountain regions ended their efforts to create an ISO. More recently, members of MAPP, an existing power pool that covers six U.S. states and two Canadian provinces, failed to achieve consensus for establishing a long-planned ISO. In the Southwest, proponents of the Desert Star ISO have not been able to reach agreement on a formal proposal after more than two years of discussion.

---

3. The California PX offers day-ahead and hour-ahead markets and the ISO operates a real-time energy market. Participation in the PX market is voluntary except that the three traditional investor-owned utilities in California must bid their generation sales and purchases through the PX for the first five years. New York will offer day-ahead and real-time energy markets that will be operated by the ISO. PJM and New England offer only real-time energy markets, although PJM has proposed to operate a day-ahead market. The ERCOT ISO is the only other ISO that does not currently operate a PX.

Various reasons have been advanced to explain why it is difficult to form a voluntary, multi-state ISO. These include cost shifting in transmission capital costs; disagreements about sharing of ISO transmission revenues among transmission owners; difficulties in obtaining the participation of publicly-owned transmission facilities; concerns about the loss of transmission rights and prices embedded in existing transmission agreements; the likelihood of not being able to maintain or gain a competitive advantage in power markets through the use of transmission facilities; and the preference of certain transmission owners to sell or transfer their transmission assets to a for-profit transmission company in lieu of handing over control to a non-profit ISO.

Apart from these efforts to create ISOs, we have received proposals for other types of transmission entities. For example, in October 1998 a group of Arizona entities filed a request with the Commission to create an "independent scheduling administrator" (ISA) in Arizona. Unlike an ISO, this entity would not administer its own transmission tariff nor would it have any direct operational responsibilities. Instead, it appears that its functions would be limited to monitoring the scheduling decisions and OASIS site operation of the Arizona utilities that operate transmission facilities. In case of disputes, the ISA would provide a type of expedited dispute resolution process. The applicants state that the ISA would be a transitional organization that would ultimately evolve or be merged into a stronger, multi-state ISO. In other developments, one public utility has recently made a filing with us to sell its transmission assets to a newly formed affiliate. Another public utility recently filed a request for declaratory order asking us to find that its proposal to transfer its transmission assets (in the form of ownership or a lease) to a "transco" in return for a passive ownership interest in the transco, would satisfy the Commission's eleven ISO principles.[42][4]

As part of general restructuring initiatives, several states now require independent grid management organizations. For example, an Illinois law requires that its utilities become members of a FERC-approved regional ISO by March 31, 1999, and Wisconsin law gives its utilities the option of joining an ISO or selling their transmission assets to an independent transmission company by June 30, 2000. In both states, the backstop is a single-state organization if regional organizations are not developed. Recently, Virginia and Arkansas have also enacted legislation requiring their electric utilities to join or establish regional transmission entities.■

Regional Transmission Organizations

65 Federal Register 12088, Wednesday, March 8, 2000.

The Federal Energy Regulatory Commission (Commission) reaffirms its basic determinations in Order No. 2000 and clarifies certain terms.

---

4. Entergy Services, Inc., Docket No. EL99-57-000 (filed April 5, 1999).

Order No. 2000 requires that each public utility that owns, operates, or controls facilities for the transmission of electric energy in interstate commerce make certain filings with respect to forming and participating in an Regional Transmission Organization (RTO). Order No. 2000 also codifies minimum characteristics and functions that a transmission entity must satisfy in order to be considered an RTO. The Commission's goal is to promote efficiency in wholesale electricity markets and to ensure that electricity consumers pay the lowest price possible for reliable service.

In Order No. 2000, the Commission concluded that regional institutions could address the operational and reliability issues confronting the industry, and eliminate undue discrimination in transmission services that can occur when the operation of the transmission system remains in the control of a vertically integrated utility. Furthermore, we found that appropriate regional transmission institutions could: (1) improve efficiencies in transmission grid management; (2) improve grid reliability; (3) remove remaining opportunities for discriminatory transmission practices; (4) improve market performance; and (5) facilitate lighter handed regulation. We stated our belief that appropriate RTOs can successfully address the existing impediments to efficient grid operation and competition and can consequently benefit consumers through lower electricity rates and a wider choice of services and service providers. In addition, substantial cost savings are likely to result from the formation of RTOs.

Order No. 2000 established minimum characteristics and functions that an RTO must satisfy in the following areas:

Minimum Characteristics:

1. Independence
2. Scope and Regional Configuration
3. Operational Authority
4. Short-term Reliability

Minimum Functions:

1. Tariff Administration and Design
2. Congestion Management
3. Parallel Path Flow
4. Ancillary Services
5. OASIS and Total Transmission Capability (TTC) and Available Transmission Capability (ATC)
6. Market Monitoring
7. Planning and Expansion
8. Interregional Coordination

In the Final Rule, we noted that the characteristics and functions could be satisfied by different organizational forms, such as ISOs, transcos, combinations of the two, or even new organizational forms not yet discussed in the industry or Docket No. RM99–2–001–3 proposed to the

Commission. Likewise, the Commission did not propose a "cookie cutter" organizational format for regional transmission institutions or the establishment of fixed or specific regional boundaries under section 202(a) of the Federal Power Act (FPA).

We also established an "open architecture" policy regarding RTOs, whereby all RTO proposals must allow the RTO and its members the flexibility to improve their organizations in the future in terms of structure, operations, market support and geographic scope to meet market needs.

In addition, the Commission provided guidance on flexible transmission ratemaking that may be proposed by RTOs, including ratemaking treatments that address congestion pricing and performance-based regulation. The Commission stated that it would consider, on a case-by-case basis, innovative rates that may be appropriate for transmission facilities under RTO control. Furthermore, to facilitate RTO formation in all regions of the Nation, the Final Rule outlined a collaborative process to take place in the Spring of 2000. Under this process, we expect that public utilities and non-public utilities, in coordination with state officials, Commission staff, and all affected interest groups, will actively work toward the voluntary development of RTOs. Lastly, under Order No. 2000, all public utilities that own, operate or control interstate transmission facilities must file with the Commission by October 15, 2000 (or January 15, 2001) a proposal to participate in an RTO with the minimum characteristics and functions to be operational by December 15, 2001, or, alternatively, a description of efforts to participate in an RTO, any existing obstacles to RTO participation, and any plans to work toward RTO participation. That filing must explain the extent to which the transmission entity in which it proposes to participate meets the minimum characteristics and functions for an RTO, and either propose to modify the existing institution to the extent necessary to become an RTO, or explain the efforts, obstacles and plans with respect to conforming to these characteristics and functions.■

NOTES AND QUESTIONS

1. Many commented on FERC's proposed rule to promote RTOs. The economist Paul Joskow argued that FERC's approach risks shortchanging consumers. His position has been summarized as follows:

> "Transmission regulatory reform," says Joskow, "should not be viewed primarily as a 'carrot' ... to entice reluctant utilities to form and participate in RTOs." ... "Regulators," Joskow notes, "will not be doing consumers any favor at all if the small price reduction they receive in the short run as a result of cutting a couple of points off the expected rate of return ... destroys the transmission owner's incentives to invest." But even if the FERC should cave and offer higher ROEs, as the industry wants, Joskow still warns against putting too much faith in ROE incentives as a way of enticing grid expansion: "Indeed, proceeding under the assumption that, at the present time,

'the market' will provide needed transmission network enhancements is the road to ruin. 'There is abundant evidence that market forces are drawing tens of thousands of megawatts of new generating capacity into the system [but] there is not evidence that market forces are drawing ... entrepreneurial investments in new transmission capacity.' "

See Bruce W. Radford, RTOs: Road to Ruin, Public Utilities Fortnightly, Sept 15, 1999, at 4.

2. Other commentators focus on the form of the transmission operator. Professor Charles Koch favors the ISO over the for-profit Transco model, since he believes that the ISO will be less inclined to act as a monopolist. He argues, however, that ISOs need enhanced authority and carefully structured governance design. *See* Charles H. Koch, Jr., Control and Governance of Transmission Organizations in the Restructured Electricity Industry, 27 Fla. St. U. L. Rev. ___ (1999).

By contrast, Professor Robert Michaels believes that the ISO will face very similar incentives to the Transco, since the ISO is made up of for-profit firms who will face market incentives. He believes that the focus on the form of the transmission operator has focused too much on profit versus not-for-profit. Instead, he urges attention to the nature and consequences of the governance of ISOs and Transcos. According to Michaels, "ISOs are supported by those who have been best at playing the politics of traditional regulation, and opposed by those who have generally been less successful." Michaels fears that ISOs are likely to become barriers to entry (see discussion of California's ISO in Chapter Thirteen), and that they may impair innovation vis-a-vis a Transco. *See* Robert J. Michaels, The Governance of Transmission Operators, 20 Energy L.J. 233 (1999).

In the end, does FERC favor either the ISO or Transco model? One author has recently argued that, despite Order No. 2000's professed neutrality on the ISO/Transco issue, FERC favors ISOs over Transcos. *See* Jeremiah D. Lamdert, Order 2000: A Subtle But Clear Preference for ISOs, Public Utilities Fortnightly, Mar. 1, 2000, at 36. But others, including a member of FERC during Order No. 2000's adoption, argue that FERC has paved the way for Transcos. *See* Curt L. Hebert, Jr. & Joshua Z. Rokach, Order 2000: Exposing Myths on What the FERC Really Wants, Public Utilities Fortnightly, Mar. 1, 2000, at 42.

3. The availability of transmission access means little to generators and customers who do not have information regarding a transmitting utility's transmission capacity and load. The EPAct also required FERC to promulgate rules on the reporting of transmission information. FERC's regulations require transmission-owning utilities to report hourly "system lambda" data, which is closely associated the marginal cost of producing power and provides a good indicator of the price for competitive energy. This information, once available only to the transmission owning firm and power pool operators, will undoubtedly provide vital information for both buyers and sellers of power. *See* William C. Booth & Judah L. Rose, Using Hourly

System Lambda to Gauge Bulk Power Prices, Public Utilities Fortnightly, May 1, 1995.

4. As is discussed in opening excerpt to this Chapter, one way in which most of the other countries experimenting with electricity markets have attempted to deal with transmission reliability problems is by creating pool-based electricity markets. Timothy Hogan, an economist, has proposed a model for implementing a pool-based market in the U.S. Pool-based markets will contain both long-term contracts and spot markets. Long-term bilateral contracts, however, would exist for financial reasons only, not as mechanisms for controlling the physical delivery of electricity. A system of spot prices would reflect disparities in congestion conditions throughout the grid. The short-term transmission price from point A to point B would represent the difference between the location-specific spot price at each point. In congested time or areas, it would be very large, representing the difference between the marginal cost of a low cost generating unit that cannot operate because of transmission capacity constraints, and the marginal cost of the more expensive unit that displaces the lower cost option. *See* William H. Hogan, Electric Transmission: A New Model for Old Principles, Electricity Journal 18 (1993). Coupled with futures and options contracts, such markets could provide adequate incentives for investments in power plants. In the case of FERC's RTO rulemaking, Hogan's view has been described as follows:

> For Hogan, everything rests on efficiency of dispatch. He dismisses the transco-ISO debate as a distraction, and tries to avoid using either term: "With deference to Alfred Kahn, who popularized the practice when referring to a term of art that has become politicized, let us call the entity that provides these [grid] services a 'banana,' and explore what must be done." If nothing else, Hogan insists that the banana must coordinate generation prices with market interference caused by transmission constraints, . . ., with locational marginal pricing to allocate congestion rights. Do that, says Hogan, and everything falls into place, including the mystical debate between the transco and ISO models. He sees FERC's role as imposing the efficiency that's lacking when property rights are ambiguous.

See Bruce W. Radford, RTOs: Road to Ruin, Public Utilities Fortnightly, Sept 15, 1999, at 4.

3. OPERATION OF EMERGING WHOLESALE POWER MARKETS

Emerging wholesale electricity markets raise an operational challenge for buyers and suppliers, many of whom need to secure power on a firm basis to meet contractual obligations. Because the transmission system is interrelated in complex and interactive ways, supply and purchase arrangements do not operate in isolation, as they may in other contractual or market settings. A recent EIA report summarizes how competitive bulk power markets have impacted power prices, for both utilities and industrial customers:

The Changing Structure of the Electric Power Industry: Selected Issues, Energy Information Administration, U.S. Department of Energy (1998)

<http://www.eia.doe.gov/cneaf/electricity/chg_ str_issu chg_ str_ iss_ rpt/chapter2.html>

Over two-thirds of the electric utilities in the United States do not generate electricity and depend upon other utilities for their supply of electricity. These utilities, known as requirement utilities, have historically shown a willingness to pay significant premiums for assurance of supply (that is, for requirements service). Even with electricity markets opening to competition and with changes in trading practices, these utilities will be operating under the terms of existing long-term contracts.

Accordingly, it is not certain that the premium for firm power supplies (for requirement contracts) will decline in the immediate future. To the extent that firm power purchases represent a unique market product, premiums for firm requirement contracts (other things being equal) may continue to exist for the foreseeable future.

Non-firm electricity sales and purchases are priced lower than firm energy because of the limited availability of this category of electrical energy and the interruptible nature of the power supply. As part of the managed acquisition of future energy supplies, and as a means to cap the overall price paid for electrical supply, the acquisition of both firm and non-firm supplies of electricity can be expected to continue.

Industrial customers, in the aggregate, have secured price reductions during the 1992–1996 time frame, paying prices that are approximately equal to the wholesale prices for firm power. During the same time period, the per-kilowatt-hour price for retail customers in the residential and commercial sectors has increased. The large investor-owned electric utilities have also responded by cutting internal costs, and the average wholesale selling price has shown a corresponding decline.

Regional electricity markets are characterized by price differences. The competitive push to acquire cheaper electricity will result in more trade among divergent price regions. This development may strain wholesale transmission carrying capability, with associated impacts on reliability standards. If competitive electricity markets are unable to resolve these issues, alternative methods of resolution may become necessary.■

———

As is mentioned in FERC's proposed rule on RTOs, the Midwest price spikes that accompanied a heat wave in Summer 1998 posed a particular stress to the wholesale transmission system. Did emerging new markets in power supply contribute to this problem, or did they help utilities avoid disaster?

As the events of Summer 1998 have been reported, operators for Commonwealth Edison Company, the utility that serves Chicago, faced some difficult choices. Although Commonwealth Edison owns many generation facilities, it still needs to depend on bulk power purchases to serve some of its customer load. With the heat wave during Summer 1998, Commonwealth Edison was required to purchase power on a short term basis from bulk power markets. In a single hour, Commonwealth Edison spent $4 million for power that would normally cost $200,000. At their extreme, prices surged to nearly 100 times their normal level. Utility managers faced the following choice: "either black out areas of Chicago to conserve power during a severe heat wave, just as storms had knocked out some plants and key transmission lines in the Midwest, or buy extra power at sky-high prices." *See* Agis Salpukas, Deregulation Fosters Turmoil in Power Market, The New York Times, July 15, 1998, at D1. During the same period, other companies made some very profitable sales. Enron, a company that specializes in marketing and selling wholesale power, sold large amounts of power to utilities at high prices, and when it reported its earnings, it had a doubling of revenue to $5.86 billion, and an 85 percent rise in income, to $241 million. As has been described, "This was all a marked contrast with the old days, when utilities sold power to one another at reasonable prices during emergencies, and it provides a vivid glimpse of the challenges facing this industry." *Id*. While some of this volatility may be due to the growth of competition, there were other events contributing to the power shortage. "A heat wave was moving across the region, causing a surge in demand for electricity. Violent storms had knocked out key transmission lines and a nuclear plant in Ohio, causing further shortages." *Id*.

After the Midwest power shortage, FERC investigated the reliability of emerging competitive markets in wholesale power. Following an investigation into the events, FERC issued a report. *See* Staff Report to the Federal Energy Regulatory Commission on the Causes of the Wholesale Electric Pricing Abnormalities in the Midwest During June 1998 <available at http://www.ferc.fed.us/electric/mastback.pdf>. FERC's report acknowledged that in competitive markets the price of wholesale power will be high in periods of peak demand, but determined that the conditions during the Summer of 1998 were "unusual." Some criticized FERC for downplaying the lesson of the Summer 1998 shortage, leading to some calls for more regulation of transmission and generation reliability, or alternative calls for more deregulation with warnings to the public about impacts on reliability:

> If we continue to move forward half-regulated and half-unregulated (i.e., with the wholesale market deregulated and the retail market regulated), then one of two transition strategies is required. Planning reserve margins sufficient to protect end users should be put in place and enforced with clear penalties, as in NEPOOL. In the alternative, policy makers should rely on the market alone to set reserves. If the market route is chosen, the public should be warned of the potential for rolling generation shortage-caused blackouts, especially in major urban areas, and especially during the transition.

Judah L. Rose, Missed Opportunity: What's Right and Wrong in the FERC Staff Report on the Midwest Price Spikes, Public Utilities Fortnightly, Nov. 15, 1998, at 48. Others saw the events of Summer 1998 as the new wholesale power market working itself pure:

> Certainly it is true that bulk power markets in the Midwest are relatively underdeveloped. However, our data show that they functioned quite effectively under extreme conditions. A relatively undeveloped market adapted quickly and efficiently to events never before seen. Buyers and sellers reacted rationally to those events in the face of great uncertainty and unfamiliar limits on their abilities to transact.

Robert J. Michaels & Jerry Ellig, Price Spike Redux: A Market Emerged, Public Utilities Fortnightly, February 1, 1999, at p. 40.

The debate over the Summer 1998 price spikes continues to have some impact on the regulatory discussion. The North American Electric Reliability Council (NERC) has proposed new procedures to relieve line overloading, known as transmission load relief protocols. The new TLR rules would relieve the impact of parallel flows on grid systems not located directly on the contract path of the curtailed transaction. FERC encouraged utilities to apply the TLR rules within the Eastern Interconnection pending a final decision, so they were in operation during the period of the Summer 1998 price spikes. The TLR procedures were a significant issue in the rulemaking that culminated in Order 2000, but FERC ultimately deferred to the voluntary approach of the North American Electric Reliability Council in setting protocols, rather adopting its own protocols. FERC's Order 2000 also requires transmission utilities that do not use the NERC TLR protocols to post their own protocol on FERC's OASIS system, so that customers have information regarding TLR.

Does FERC's lack of power over generation load impair its ability to ensure reliable transmission markets? TLR, if mandated, might result in a sort of rationing. Is it better to let a market determine the prices of transmission service? Can this happen? How should transmission be priced? Are there any other jurisdictional weaknesses that might make FERC's job in ensuring a reliable transmission market more difficult?

With the rise of competitive wholesale power markets, FERC has begun to exercise jurisdiction over power marketers, such as Enron. A recent EIA report describes the role power marketers are playing in the industry:

> Power marketers are a relatively new type of firm in the electric power industry. They are different from traditional electric utilities. A power marketer buys electric energy and transmission and other services from traditional utilities, or other suppliers, and then resells these products. The concept of a power marketer first appeared in the mid–1980s. In October 1985, Citizens Energy filed a petition with the FERC seeking approval to purchase and resell electricity. This company was the first to file such a petition. In July 1987, the second petition to buy and resell electrical power was filed with the FERC by Howell

Gas Management. It was not until August 1989, however, that the FERC approved a petition granting the right to buy and resell electric power to Citizens Power and Light. (*Citizens Power & Light Corp.*, 48 Federal Energy Regulatory Commission (FERC) 61,210 (August 8, 1989).) This order was particularly significant because the FERC recognized the existence of a new type of company in the wholesale marketplace and accepted the market-based rate schedules proposed by Citizens. That approval proved to be the foundation for subsequent applications for power marketing status.

Growth in the wholesale power market—estimated to be around 1,343 billion kWh in 1994—has spurred the increase in power marketing companies. EPACT and FERC's movement toward increased competition in the wholesale market by allowing market-based rates were also major factors in the increase in power marketers. Since the first approvals for power marketing status were granted, the number of companies obtaining approval has increased substantially. From a total of 9 in 1992, the number had grown to 180 by the end of December 1995. Most of the companies are gas marketers, who see power generation as a potentially lucrative market. Others types of companies getting into the power marketing business include brokers and financial firms, utility affiliates, independent entrepreneurs, commodity traders and manufactures, and independent power producers.

Presently, only a relatively small number of power marketers are active in the market, but the number of active companies is growing. In 1994, 9 firms sold 7.2 million MWh. In 1995, 40 power marketers sold 26.6 million MWh of electricity. Three companies—Enron Power Marketing, Lewis Dreyfus, and Electric Clearinghouse—accounted for 57 percent of the sales.

In summary, the growth of power marketers signals the potential for a fundamental change in the wholesale electricity business. Since the late 1980s the number of companies approved for power marketing has gone from a few to 180. Presently, only about 10 companies are active in the business of buying and reselling power. It is expected that, as access to transmission lines increases in a competitive environment, more companies will become active in the wholesale electric power business as power marketers.

The Changing Structure of the Electric Power Industry: An Update, Energy Information Administration, U.S. Department of Energy <http://www.eia.doe.gov/cneaf/electricity/chg_str/chapter9.html>. Since Order No. 888, the number of power marketers has continued to grow significantly. As is described in the excerpt below, FERC not only has approved market-based rates for traditional utilities, but has begun to do so for marketers as well. Notice how FERC only exercises it jurisdiction over those engaged in marketing, not those who limit their activities to brokering or aggregating power. FERC does not engage in these regulatory activities for purposes of cost-based ratemaking, but to ensure that rates are just and reasonable and that reliability is maintained.

How to Get Market–Based Rate Approval, Federal Energy Regulatory Commission (March 1999)

<http://www.ferc.fed.us/electric/PwrMkt/PMhow.htm>

Change in the electric utility industry is occurring at a breakneck speed, and a new breed of participant, the power marketer, has evolved to play a key role. Up to now, vertically integrated traditional electric utilities, which had generation, transmission, and distribution systems, were the only entities which bought and sold electricity in bulk. Now, power marketers, which usually do not own any of the traditional assets associated with electric utilities, have emerged as a major player in this emerging competitive market.

Anyone can buy electricity in bulk from traditional electric utilities (which usually own generation, transmission and distribution facilities), power marketers, qualifying facilities (QFs) such as cogeneration facilities or small power production facilities, and some independent power producers (IPPs) such as exempt wholesale generators (EWGs, however, may not sell at retail). Only an entity which has had its rates accepted for filing by the FERC may resell such electricity "at wholesale." If the electricity is to be sold at retail (for example, to a residential, commercial, or industrial establishment), however, the seller needs authorization from the local state public utility commission. Thus, information about making retail sales should be obtained from the public utility commission of the state where the retail sale will be made. The state public utility commission (also sometimes called public service commission, department of public utilities, corporation commission, etc.) is generally located in the state capital.

If the electricity is to be sold for resale (i.e., to another electric utility, including another power marketer, which will then resell it either at wholesale or retail), the seller needs to have its rate schedule "on file" with the Federal Energy Regulatory Commission ("the Commission" or "the FERC"). Regulation of sales for resale were conferred to the Commission in 1935 when Congress enacted the Federal Power Act.

No Federal or state authorization is needed if one only intends to broker power or act as an aggregator of power. Brokers act as an agent, bringing together buyers and sellers; accordingly, they do not take title to and resell the power themselves. Aggregators also generally don't purchase the electricity themselves, but rather act as an agent for a group of retail customers who hope to obtain discounts by purchasing electricity as a group. Any regulation of aggregators, if any, would be by state public utility authorities, not the FERC.

A single entity may engage in any or all of the above described activities; selling at retail, aggregating, brokering, and selling at wholesale. It is not necessary to create a separate entity to engage in each activity.

Sales of electricity by power marketers have grown significantly in recent months. For example, the Edison Electric Institute's Regulatory Briefing Service reports that, during the first quarter of 1995, power marketers sold 2.6 million megaWatt-hours of electricity. By the fourth quarter of 1996, this amount had grown to 95 million megaWatt-hours. If one were to assume an average sale price of $20/MWH, power marketers made $1.9 billion in sales during this quarter alone. The market is still somewhat concentrated, however. During 1996, 73% of all sales were made by only ten power marketers; one marketer, Enron Power Marketing, accounted for about 26% of the market.

Although the wholesale market for electricity is becoming increasingly competitive, that does not mean that it is unregulated. Power marketers whose rates are on file with the Commission are considered to be "public utilities" under the Federal Power Act (just as Pacific Gas and Electric Company and Commonwealth Edison Company are public utilities), and must comply with a number of regulations which apply to all public utilities. However, many of the regulations which customarily apply to traditional public utilities have been waived or relaxed for power marketers. For example, since most power marketers own or control no generation or transmission facilities which could give them market power in their respective markets, they are permitted to charge market-based rates (i.e., whatever is agreed-upon by the buyer and seller. If a seller cannot exert control over the market by exercising market power, then there is no reason for it to charge traditional cost-based rates.) Power marketers need not file their accounting records with the Commission because such records are generally used only for cost-based ratemaking. And, while power marketers are not required to file their individual contracts with the Commission, they ARE nonetheless required to file quarterly summaries of their transactions. If a power marketer has no transactions to report, that marketer must file a report noting that no transactions occurred.

Thus, while there is no charge for a power marketer's initial application for approval of its market-based rates, and FERC fees are assessed only when and if electricity sales occur, the power marketer must nonetheless comply with a variety of ongoing regulatory requirements, EVEN DURING PERIODS THE POWER MARKETER MAKES NO SALES. These requirements continue in force until the power marketer files a notice with the Commission canceling its rate schedule, and it is accepted for filing by the Commission.

A power marketer MUST:

— file quarterly transaction reports. If a power marketer has no transactions to report, that marketer must file a report noting that no transactions occurred;

— file notices of changes in status to report that the power marketer will acquire or will become affiliated with any generation or transmission facilities, or a utility with a franchised service area;

— notify the Commission if its name has changed, if it has merged with another entity, or if its rate schedule has been adopted by another entity (See Section 35.16, Notices of Succession);

— notify the Commission if it desires to cancel its rate schedule and cease marketing activities (See Section 35.15, Notice of Cancellation or Termination);

— notify the Commission if an officer or director is a) an officer or director of more than one public utility, b) an officer or director of a public utility and of any bank, trust company, banking association, or firm that is authorized by law to underwrite or participate in the marketing of securities of a public utility, or c) an officer or director of a public utility and of any company supplying electrical equipment to a public utility.

— annually file with the Commission a list of its 20 largest retail purchasers of electricity; and

— annually file with the Commission information which is used by the Commission to calculate the annual charge for each public utility.

* * *

As wholesale competition evolves, new trading mechanisms are beginning to develop, providing stability against the type of situation that developed in the Summer of 1998. Some of these new markets are described in the following excerpt.■

The Changing Structure of the Electric Power Industry: An Update, Energy Information Administration, U.S. Department of Energy (1997)

<http://www.eia.doe.gov/cneaf/electricity/ chg_str/chapter9.html>

Electricity is becoming a commodity like natural gas, petroleum products (e.g., crude oil, heating oil, gasoline), and other energy products. Electricity at wholesale value is now sold at market centers at market-based rates, and wholesale electricity prices are published daily. Two new electricity futures contracts have been introduced, which can help electricity buyers and sellers manage business risk. These events are relatively new, and they mark the beginning of a new era in the electric power industry.

Wholesale electricity spot markets are now operating at several sites in the western United States. The Pacific Northwest/Pacific Southwest AC Intertie transmission facilities between the California–Oregon Border (referred to as COB), and the Palo Verde Nuclear Power Plant high-voltage switchyard in Arizona are two transfer points with spot markets. Wholesale electricity is also traded at five delivery points spanning approximately a 100–mile area in Washington State (referred to collectively as Mid–Columbia). In Atlanta, Georgia, Continental Power Exchange (CPEX) has started a computerized electricity trading market. According to CPEX, as of March 1996, 30 companies in 28 States across the United States were using the electronic exchange, and CPEX expects the market to grow as the industry becomes more accustomed to electronic trading. The development of market centers for electricity trading is indicative of a change in fundamental business procedures brought about, in part, by restructuring and increased competition in the electric industry.

Public information on prices is necessary for a spot market to function properly. That is, to make informed purchasing decisions, potential electricity buyers need price information on recent transactions. In June 1995, Dow Jones & Company (DJ) met that need for the western markets by compiling peak and off-peak electricity price indices for non-firm power at the COB. Later, DJ began compiling firm and non-firm price indices on transactions at Palo Verde, and now both the COB and Palo Verde indices are published daily in the Wall Street Journal. DJ also compiles price indices, which are available by subscription, for Mid–Columbia and for the North American Reliability Council regions MAIN and ECAR. CPEX has also recently begun publishing a price index in the Energy Daily for transactions occurring during peak hours on the computerized exchange. The DJ and CPEX price indices should help sustain the growth in trading at these market centers, and as the industry becomes more competitive, spot markets and price indices may develop for other areas of the country.

One of the most interesting developments in the industry is the electricity futures contract. On March 29, 1996, The New York Mercantile Exchange (NYMEX) began selling electricity futures contracts for the COB and Palo Verde markets. NYMEX indicated that the futures contract was designed to service a growing wholesale trade at these market centers. The contract which is standard for both COB and Palo Verde, covers 736 MWh delivered over a month. July settlement prices at COB for trading in May 1996 ranged from a low of $11.35 to a high of $12.54 per MWh. The July settlement prices at Palo Verde were slightly higher. On April 26, 1996, NYMEX introduced electricity options contracts at the COB and Palo Verde. An option on a future gives the purchasing party the right, but not the obligation, to buy (in the case of a call option) or sell (in the case of a put option) the underlying futures. It can be thought of as a form of insurance against high or low futures prices. The buyer of the option pays the option writer an up-front premium for this insurance.

It is expected that power marketers will initially be the most likely users of the electricity futures. A power marketer entering into a contract to sell power at a predetermined price runs the risk that the price it must pay for electricity will increase before the power is delivered. The power marketer can hedge its risk by buying electricity futures that match the quantity and timing of the original power contract [See Background Information on Futures Contracts, below]. Under traditional cost-plus regulation, IOUs may not find these risk-management tools very useful. However, in order to participate in the growing wholesale markets, it is expected that many IOUs will submit applications seeking FERC approval to sell wholesale power at market-based rates. FERC Order 888 discusses this issue, and it sets the framework for transmission-owning utilities and their affiliates to participate in these markets. Indeed, FERC's stated goal is to develop more competitive bulk power markets.■

Futures and Options Contracts

Futures contracts are a standardized form of forward contracting that has been practiced for centuries. However, they differ from forward contracts in that they are standardized and traded on an organized exchange, rather than being the result of negotiations between two parties. These contracts have several key features:

— The buyer of a futures contract is said to be in a "long" position, and agrees to receive delivery of the commodity.

— The seller of a futures contract is said to be in a "short" position, and agrees to make delivery of the commodity.

— The contracts are traded on exchanges either by open outcry in specified trading areas or electronically via a computerized network.

— Futures contracts can be terminated by an offsetting transaction executed at any time prior to the contract's expiration. Most futures contracts are terminated by offsetting transactions.

— The same or similar futures contracts can be traded on more than one exchange in the United States or elsewhere.

If you buy a futures contract (go long) and the price goes up, you profit by the amount of the price increase times the contract size; if you buy and the price goes down, you lose an amount equal to the price decrease times the contract size [Figure 11-2]. If you sell a futures contract (go short) and the price goes down, you profit by the amount of the price decrease times the contract size; if you sell and the price goes up, you lose an amount equal to the price increase times the contract size [Figure 11-2].

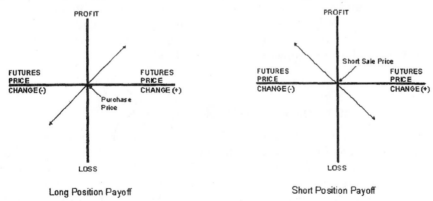

Long Position Payoff   Short Position Payoff

Figure 11-2

Options are another type of financial instrument. Option contracts are usually introduced on a commodity after the futures contract is trading successfully. An option is the right, but not the obligation, to buy or sell a specified number of underlying futures contracts or a specified number of commodity, currency, index, or financial instruments at a price agreed upon on or before a given future date. Options on futures are traded on the same exchanges that trade the underlying futures contracts.

They can be thought of as a form of insurance against high or low prices. The buyer of the option pays the option writer an up-front premium for this insurance. The major difference between futures and options centers on the obligations of the purchaser and the seller. A futures contract obligates the seller to execute the contract, regardless of whether it is profitable or not. In contrast, a purchased option is a limited-risk instrument because, as noted above, the option purchaser has the right, but not the obligation, to buy or sell the underlying futures contract at the option's strike price. At expiration, an option that is worthless will not be exercised, and the option purchaser's loss is limited to the premium paid to buy the option.

Futures markets have evolved and flourished because they serve useful purposes. The two main functions of futures contracts are price discovery and risk transfer. Futures prices are determined through open and competitive bidding among a large number of market participants. Because futures contracts are standardized and traded on a central exchange, prices can be readily observed and compared. The future price of a commodity may be the best indicator of its expected spot price in the future. Indeed, in a stable commodity market, the market price of a commodity must converge to the futures price by the time the futures contract expires, otherwise anyone could engage in arbitrage. Arbitrage occurs when the price of an asset traded on two or more markets is different. Profit is made by buying the asset at the low price in one market and selling it at a higher price in another market. Risk transfer is the other main function of the futures market.

Participants in the futures market are generally classified as hedgers or speculators. Hedgers use futures contracts to offset and minimize the risks of price fluctuations. Speculators, on the other hand, are willing to accept this risk in the hope of earning a profit.■

E.   THE LIMITS OF FEDERAL REGULATION

Under the Federal Power Act, FERC's authority over the electric power industry is limited to jurisdiction over wholesale transactions. Later statutes, such as the Energy Policy Act of 1992, continue to endorse jurisdictional limitations over FERC's power to completely deregulate the industry—especially regarding the provision of retail services (see Chapter Thirteen, discussing state efforts)—but FERC has obviously played a major role in moving the wholesale power industry towards a competitive structure, much as it played a major role in restructuring natural gas.

Even with respect to FERC's jurisdiction over the wholesale operations of the industry, however, FERC's ability to successfully implement a competitive and reliable industry may fall short absent congressional expansion of its authority. In 1999, a panel of the U.S. Court of Appeals for the Eighth Circuit issued a decision that placed additional limits on FERC's authority. We include it here to encourage thought about the intersection between federal and state regulation, and we return to this theme towards the end of Chapter Eighteen. Was this opinion decided correctly?

Northern States Power Co. v. Federal Energy Regulatory Commission

176 F.3d 1090 (8th Cir.1999) certiorari denied 120 S.Ct. 1221, 145 L.Ed. 1121 (2000).

■ Before Fagg, Lay, and Wollman, Circuit Judges.

■ Lay, Circuit J. (Joined on panel by Fagg, J. and Wollman, J.)

On April 24, 1996, the Federal Energy Regulatory Commission ("FERC") promulgated Order No. 888 requiring "all public utilities that own, control or operate facilities used for transmitting electric energy in interstate commerce to have on file open access non-discriminatory transmission tariffs that contain minimum terms and conditions of non-discriminatory service." FERC's stated goal was to encourage competition in the wholesale bulk power market place "and to bring more efficient, lower cost power to the Nation's electricity consumers." Order No. 888 became final and effective on July 9, 1996. Thereafter, Northern States Power Company ("NSP") filed proposed revisions of its Open Access Transmission Tariff ("NSP Tariff")....

FERC rejected the proposed changes to the NSP Tariff's curtailment provisions on the grounds that: 1) NSP had defined curtailment priorities only through general references to unexplained procedures; 2) NSP had failed to demonstrate that the proposed terms were consistent with, or superior to, the pro forma tariff terms required by Order No. 888; and 3) NSP's description of the proposed procedures was misleading. Thereafter NSP filed this petition for review. On August 25, 1998, this court denied NSP's stay request and shortly thereafter denied FERC's motion to transfer the case to the United States Court of Appeals for the District of Columbia, or to hold the case in abeyance pending the omnibus appeal of FERC's Order No. 888 rule-making in the D.C. Circuit....

[The court held that it had jurisdiction to hear the appeal, despite the pending appeal in the D.C. Circuit.]

The fundamental issue to be decided on this appeal is whether FERC may, through its tariff orders, require NSP, a state public utility, to curtail electrical transmission to wholesale (point-to-point) customers on a comparable basis with its native/retail consumers when it experiences power constraints. FERC acknowledges that it cannot permissibly affect state regulation of retail rates and practices. FERC argues that it has simply required that, as to transmission curtailment, NSP may not discriminate against a third party in favor of its own native/retail consumers. Thus, it asserts that Order No. 888 makes clear that a transmission provider must curtail electrical transmission on a comparable and nondiscriminatory basis, including the provider's own use of the system. Under the tariff, public utilities will not be allowed to continue curtailment practices that give priority to bundled, native/retail load consumers over point-to-point users involved in interstate commerce. FERC suggests that there is no justiciable issue here. It reasoned:

> The pro forma tariff requires comparability of curtailments when consistent with Good Utility Practice. The Commission would not expect NSP Companies to violate Good Utility Practice when implementing curtailments. Further, the pro forma tariff allows the Transmission Provider the discretion to curtail firm transmission service when an emergency or other unforeseen condition impairs or degrades the reliability of its transmission system. Absent such system reliability concerns, however, NSP Companies must engage in a pro-rata curtailment.

Order on Requests for Clarification, 83 FERC ¶ 62,338 (1998).

However, the mere fact that the provider may exercise curtailments within its sole discretion is not the problem. The problem arises when NSP exercises its discretion to curtail service, but may then do so only by curtailing both wholesale and native/retail electric sales on an equal basis and not by giving preferential treatment to its native/retail load. Thus, NSP argues, when there exists a power constraint, by providing curtailment to its native/retail consumers on a pro rata basis with wholesale users, NSP will be forced to provide interruptible service to its native/retail consumers. When such power outages occur, a pro rata curtailment will detrimentally affect native/retail consumers who have no other alternatives available to obtain electrical service. NSP urges that when wholesale (point-to-point) customers are curtailed in electrical transmission, the wholesale customer has alternative sources from which to obtain continuous electrical supply, through either the purchase of electricity from another provider, or via their own power generation facilities. Illustrative of this argument, NSP points to the circumstances involving Wisconsin Electric Power Company ("WEP"), an intervenor in this proceeding, and itself when WEP experienced curtailment of electrical transmission by NSP in the summer of 1998. WEP had to resort to alternative power, albeit at a higher price due to the emergency curtailment. Unless we totally miscomprehend the arguments involved, we feel that FERC's observation that no inherent conflict exists between its mandates and practical application is viewed through an adversarial bias.

The more fundamental issue involved here, aside from the practicalities of the situation, is whether FERC has the jurisdiction to affect the curtailment practices of NSP when dealing with NSP's native/retail consumers. FERC argues that it does not, in any way, attempt to affect state regulation of retail rates and practices. At the same time, FERC points out that its jurisdiction over interstate sales is not made in a vacuum. As in *Conway Corp. v. FPC*, 510 F.2d 1264 (D.C.Cir.1975), *aff'd sub nom., FPC v. Conway Corp.*, 426 U.S. 271, 96 S. Ct. 1999, 48 L.Ed.2d 626 (1976), it argues the jurisdiction of the FPC is not "insulated from nonjurisdictional factors." *Id.* at 1272. In *Conway*, an electric utility was engaged in jurisdictional (wholesale) and nonjurisdictional (retail) sales. A portion of the utility's wholesale customers competed against it by reselling gas purchased from the utility to other retail consumers. The wholesale customers alleged that the wholesale price was inflated in order to prevent them from competing for retail business. The Supreme Court held that the Federal Power Act authorized FERC to examine the entire factual context surrounding the wholesale rates, including facts related to the nonjurisdictional retail transactions. *See Conway*, 426 U.S. at 280, 96 S. Ct. 1999.

FERC relies upon the language of the United States Court of Appeals for the District of Columbia in Conway that FERC may take into consideration nonjurisdictional concerns "when germane to the meaningful execution of a jurisdictional function." *Conway*, 510 F.2d at 1272. We have no disagreement with these abstractions. However, one of the problems in the Conway case is the distinction pointed to by then Judge Ginsburg in *Altamont Gas Transmission Company v. FERC*, 92 F.3d 1239 (1996). In *Altamont*, as the result of perceived discrimination against interstate gas shipments, FERC authorized a utility to begin building a new facility, but lowered the utility's allowed rate of return until the utility could demonstrate that its rates and policies no longer discriminated against interstate shippers. In taking note of the Supreme Court's delineation in *Conway*, Judge Ginsburg posited that jurisdictional implications of a nonjurisdictional transaction are germane only "[i]f the undue preference or discrimination is ... traceable to the level of the jurisdictional rate." *Id.* at 1247 (*citing Conway*, 426 U.S. at 277, 96 S. Ct. 1999). We have the same difficulty here, at least by analogy, that the alleged discrimination is traceable to the nonjurisdictional sale of bundled service provided by NSP to the native/retail consumer rather than to the service provided to interstate customers.

As NSP points out, it is given monopolistic control by the five states in which it operates. NSP is a vertically integrated electrical utility and provides electrical service throughout Minnesota, Michigan, North Dakota, South Dakota, and Wisconsin to an estimated two million retail customers. NSP argues that the exclusive grant given by these states to sell to native/retail consumers is on a quid pro quo basis; to wit, that NSP's native/retail consumers may depend on bundled sales without curtailment of service. In Order No. 888, FERC recognizes its own jurisdictional limits and states "[w]e reiterate that we are not requiring the transmission provider to unbundle transmission service to its retail/native load nor are we requiring that bundled retail service be taken under the terms of the Final Rule pro forma tariff." *Id.* at 21,604. This apparent concession is statutorily driven. Under 16 U.S.C. § 824(a), Congress has expressly provided that "Federal regulation ... extend[s] only to those matters which are not subject to regulation by the States." *Id.* Section 824(b)(1) provides:

> The provisions of this subchapter shall apply to the transmission of electric energy in interstate commerce and to the sale of electric energy at wholesale in interstate commerce, but except as provided in paragraph (2) shall not apply to any other sale of electric energy or deprive a State or State commission of its lawful authority now exercised over

the exportation of hydroelectric energy which is transmitted across a State line. The Commission shall have jurisdiction over all facilities for such transmission or sale of electric energy, but shall not have jurisdiction, except as specifically provided in this subchapter and subchapter III of this chapter, over facilities used for the generation of electric energy or over facilities used in local distribution or only for the transmission of electric energy in intrastate commerce, or over facilities for the transmission of electric energy consumed wholly by the transmitter.

Id.

NSP argues that to comply with FERC's interpretation of Order No. 888, as requiring comparable and equal service to point-to-point customers, along with its native/retail consumers, would violate state regulatory laws. For example, in the state of Minnesota NSP may not shed its retail load absent an emergency or when electric supply is limited or unavailable. *See* Northern States Power Company, MINNESOTA ELECTRIC RATE BOOK, GENERAL RULES AND REGULATIONS, Section 6, Curtailment or Interruption of Service, § 6.2 (Add.41); Minn.Stat. § 216B.37–.42. The state tariffs in the other states provide similar limitations. Thus, NSP argues that if it is required to provide comparable transmission to both its retail and wholesale customers on a pro rata basis, that its native/retail consumers will face power outages contrary to the obligation set out in the state tariffs, in turn causing conflict with the long-held position that once a tariff has been approved, it has the force of law and is binding upon the parties. *See Montana–Dakota Utilities Co. v. Northwestern Public Service Co.*, 341 U.S. 246, 251–52, 71 S. Ct. 692, 95 L.Ed. 912 (1951). NSP urges that state authority over its bundled service is jeopardized if FERC requires, under the guise of nondiscrimination, pro rata curtailment of the power supply to NSP's native/retail consumers.

As indicated, when there is a power outage due to power restraints, the wholesale customer may use alternative supplies from other utilities or generate power themselves, and can avoid power outages through such practice. The native/retail consumer, however, is unable to turn to alternative sources of supply. For these reasons, NSP urges that Good Utility Practice requires that wholesale transactions be curtailed before a utility is forced to shed its native/retail load. Thus, we find that NSP, through FERC's interpretation, is placed between the proverbial rock and hard place, and will in effect be in violation of either a state tariff or Order No. 888.

FERC responds simply that it does not operate in a vacuum and that it is not exercising any of its regulatory powers directly, but that through the enforcement of a federal tariff, there could be a lawful, indirect effect upon NSP's services to its native/retail consumers. NSP urges that this allows FERC to do indirectly what it is prohibited from doing directly, intercede in a matter reserved by Congress to the states. *See Altamont*, 92 F.3d at 1248. FERC's ultimate answer to all of this is that where there is a clash between its tariffs and the state law, the federal tariff must prevail under the Supremacy Clause. We cannot agree.

Before reviewing constitutional concerns relating to the Supremacy Clause, it is fundamental that this court must first satisfy itself that FERC has Congressional approval to regulate NSP in the manner now attempted. Congress has drawn a "bright line" between state and federal regulation. Here, there is no conflict between the state and federal regulatory schemes. In fact, FERC concedes that it has no jurisdiction whatsoever over the state's regulation of NSP's bundled retail sales activities. *See* Order No. 888–A, 62 Fed.Reg. 12,274, 12,299 (1997). Additionally, any reliance upon *Nantahala Power & Light Co. v. Thornburg*, 476 U.S. 953, (1986), for the proposition that a state must defer to FERC's decision making for fear of running afoul of the Commerce Clause is also misplaced. In *Nantahala*, the Court applied the "fixed rate doctrine" under which interstate power rates filed with or fixed by FERC had to be given binding effect by state utility commissions in determining intrastate rates. This is not an issue here. In *Nantahala*, the Court was dealing with hydroelectric power and facilities which obtained its power supply from the Tennessee Valley Authority, as well as navigable waters and dams placed thereon. In the present case, we have nothing comparable to the generation of electrical power that was involved in *Nantahala*. *Cf. FPC v. Louisiana Power & Light Co.*, 406 U.S. 621 (1972). We think it obvious that the indirect effect of Order No. 888, as interpreted by the Commission, is an attempt to regulate curtailment of electrical power to NSP's native/retail consumers. Despite FERC's denial as to nonjurisdictional regulation, we find it has transgressed its Congressional authority which limits its jurisdiction to interstate transactions. As such, its attempt to regulate the curtailment of electrical transmission on native/retail consumers is unlawful, as it falls outside of the FPA's specific grant of authority to FERC.

This cause is remanded to FERC to allow amendment to its curtailment orders, as now interpreted under Order No. 888, so as to not encroach upon the authority of the regulatory commissions of the states.■

NOTES AND COMMENTS

1. Consider the following assessment of the *Northern States Power* case:

> ... the Eighth Circuit's decision poses a serious threat of state interference with interstate transmission of electricity. The resulting balkanization of electricity markets would be a major setback both to existing electricity markets and to evolving electric power markets, ultimaely undermining, not enhancing, service reliability for both wholesale and retail customers.

See William H. Penniman & Paul B. Turner, A Jurisdictional Clash Over Electricity Transmission: Northern States Power v. FERC, 20 Energy L.J. 205 (1999).

2. As the opening reading in this Chapter hinted, restructuring of the European Union electric power market is also moving at a rapid pace. An E.U. directive issued in 1996 requires open access to transmission, establishment of a transmission system operator, and financial separation of

generation, transmission and distribution activities. *See* Directive 96/92/EC, www.europa.eu.int/en/comm/dg17/gazeL_en.htm. In addition to the U.K., whose competition plan is discussed in the opening readings of this chapter, Germany has implemented full wholesale and retail competition and Spain has implemented wholesale but not retail competition. The French government is actively studying competition for its markets, in part because the European Commission has taken legal action against France for its failure to end the monopoly of Electricite de France. The E.U. experience illustrates the practical implications of the legal constraints faced by federal regulators in the U.S.:

> The E.C.'s French compliance action illustrates one of the [] most striking differences in U.S. and E.U. power markets. In Europe, the E.C. has ultimate authority over member states to compel the market opening, whereas in the United States there is no national authority nor federal law to require states to open their retail markets. That is rather ironic since a united Europe is a relatively new phenomenon by comparison to the U.S. federal structure.

Shannon Burchett, A Continent United? Some Thoughts on Prospects for a Single Energy Market in Europe, Public Utilities Fortnightly, Jan. 15, 2000, at 32.

CHAPTER 12

STRANDED COSTS

Outline of Chapter:

A. THE NATURE AND SCOPE OF THE STRANDED COST PROBLEM

Although competitive electricity markets will lead to increased efficiencies and, perhaps, lower electricity prices overall, the move towards competitive markets is not what economists would call a "Pareto" move: competition will not make everyone better off and at least some persons or groups will be harmed in the transition. A significant transitional cost regulators face involves the distributional impacts of new competition policy between customers groups, utilities, and investors.

Although, as will be discussed in Chapter Thirteen, regulators restructuring electric utility markets face many distributional issues—including the impacts on consumer and environmental protection—"stranded costs" are one of the most contentious issues in restructuring the utility industry. The issue is not specific to energy, but also arises in the context of telecommunications, railroad and other industries. "Stranded" is an apt metaphor for the phenomenon many utilities experience in deregulated markets. A utility may have incurred large costs under rate regulation, such as its investment in a nuclear plant, with the expectation that these costs would be recovered through regulated rates over a defined term. These costs are not typically recovered in a short period of time, but are recovered over periods ranging from 20 to 50 years; the basic ratemaking principle that customer who are benefitting from the facility also pay for it requires extended depreciation schedules. Yet a lot can happen in a time period than scans approximately half a human life. The "stranded cost" problem arises as regulators announce new policies that do not guarantee rate base or other rate recovery of the costs of assets. These assets or costs may become "shipwrecked," isolated from the traditional revenue streams (of cost or service rates) that have been used to pay for them.

Consider this simple example: If a large investor-owned utility, say Long Island Lighting (LILCO), is required to "wheel" power from a competitor to Widgets Co., a company who was formerly a major customer of LILCO, what is a fair rate for LILCO to charge for the transmission service? Widgets Co. would concede that it should pay for a proportionate share of the cost of operating and maintaining the transmission lines plus a return on the capital invested in those lines. LILCO is likely to argue that the rate should be higher because its loss of Widgets Co.'s business will mean that some of LILCO's generating plant becomes unneeded; and that since the plant was built so that service could be provided to customers such as Widgets Co., a departing customer such as Widgets Co. should continue to pay for its share of the generating plant.

1.   "STRANDED COSTS" DEFINED

It is important to recognize that not all utility investments or expenses qualify as stranded costs. For a cost to be stranded, its economics must differ from the costs faced by other firms in the same market. After all, even new competitors in deregulated markets, such as Independent Power Producers (IPPs), face many costs. These firms make no claim to stranded costs for their expenses associated with even very expensive assets, such as power plants. Clearly, to call all of a utility's costs stranded would far overstate the nature of any regulatory transition problem.

Why do stranded costs arise? Economically, they arise because the cost to the incumbent firm is higher than the costs to new entrants, and differences in cost translate into differences in the prices the incumbent and new firms are able to offer customers. If new entrants, utilizing more efficient technology or taking advantage of a new regulatory structure, are able to offer prices below the incumbent, new entrants can attract customers away from the incumbent.

While this problem could exist in any industry facing technological change (think about how the calculator displaced the slide rule), utility regulation may exacerbate the problem. For example, in the utility context, rate regulation sets the incumbent firm's expectations regarding recovery of the costs of its investments. If rate regulation would have allowed a utility to recover the costs of its investment over a period of, say, 40 years, then prices would be set with this depreciation schedule in mind; yet 20 years later, new technology may allow new entrants to significantly undercut prices based on 20 year-old technology. Other aspects of rate regulation, such as the duty to serve, may also burden the incumbent with disadvantages that new entrants do not necessarily bear.

Even where government has owned utility assets, as it did in the U.K. prior to privatization and market liberalization, a stranded cost problem may still exist. For two reasons, the stranded cost problem may be less pronounced when elecric power markets are liberalized simultaneous with privatization. First, where government rather than private ownership of the industry is pervasive, the tension is between ratepayers and taxpayers. The incurrence of stranded costs by investor-owned utilities in the U.S. poses a tension between the interests of investors, ratepayers, and some-times taxpayers. The tension between ratepayers and taxpayers poses less of a clash—indeed, it may pose none at all—than the conflict between investors and ratepayers. Second, privatization may allow the state an opportunity to place a market value on stranded costs through sale of the assets. This opportunity is often denied to regulators addressing the strand-ed cost problem in the U.S., leading to overestimates of the value of stranded costs and adding to uncertainty in the stranded cost debate. Timothy Brennan and James Boyd identify four types of stranded costs in the electric power sector: "(1) Undepreciated investments in power plants that are more expensive than generators available today. (2) Long-term contracts—most if not all mandated by the 1978 Public Utilities Regulatory Policies Act (PURPA). (3) Generators built but not used, primarily nuclear. (4) expenses related to demand-side management (DSM) and other conser-vation programs that, as substitutes for new plant construction, were charged to the generation side of the business." Timothy J. Brennan & James Boyd, Stranded Costs, Takings, and the Law and Economics of Implicit Contracts, 11 J. Reg. Econ. 41 (1997). Gregory Sidak and Daniel Spulber, strong advocates for stranded cost recovery, define stranded costs as "the inability of utility shareholder to secure the return of, and a competitive rate of return on, their investment." J. Gregory Sidak & Daniel F. Spulber, Deregulatory Takings and the Regulatory Contract 27 (Cam-bridge U. Press 1997). This definition would include both operating expen-ditures incurred by utilities, as well as their capital investments. Other definitions focus on capital outlays, and do not necessarily include ex-penses; for example, Herbert Hovenkamp defines stranded costs as "invest-ments in specialized, durable assets that may seem necessary, or at least justifiable, when constructed and placed into service under a regime of price and entry controls but that have become underutilized or useless under deregulation." Herbert Hovenkamp, The Takings Clause and Im-provident Regulatory Bargains, 108 Yale L.J. 801 (1999).

2. VARIATION IN THE DISTRIBUTION OF STRANDED COSTS

Not all utilities and areas of the country experience the same level stranded costs. Stranded costs vary depending on the geographic area. Here is an estimate of the geographic dispersion of stranded costs:

**Stranded Costs by Region: 1995, From Energy Online
on the Internet, Http://www.energyonline.com/re-
structuring/energydb.strndcst.html**

Region (States)	Estimate
Northeast (Conn., Me., Mass., N.Y., N.H., R.I., Vt.)	$29.5 billion
West (Az., Calif., Colo., Idaho, Montana, Nev., N.M., N.D., S.D., Tex., Utah, Wash., Wyo.)	$28.9 billion
East Central (Ind., Ky., Mo., Ohio, Pa.)	$20.2 billion
Southwest (Ark., Kan., La., Miss., Mo., Okla.)	$14.4 billion
MidAtlantic (Del., Md., N.J., Pa., Va.)	$13.3 billion
Southeast (Ala., Fla., Ga., Miss., N.C., S.C.)	$11.3 billion
Mid–America (Ill., Wis.)	$6.0 billion
Mid Continent (Iowa, Minn., N.D., S.D.)	$632 million

The difference in stranded cost estimate across these regions can be explained by a variety of factors, including: variations in the degree of obsolete or expensive generation capacity, such as nuclear plants; the degree of excess generation capacity more generally; whether regulators have previously allowed full recovery of investments.

It is important to recognize that a cost is not necessarily stranded for utility X merely because utility Y suffers a stranded cost for the same investment. For example, one utility may regard its investment in nuclear plants as stranded costs, while another may regard a similar investment as a successful and very valuable investment, even in emerging restructured environments. Stranded cost is not an absolute concept; its evaluation will depend on the relative viability of a utility's investments in that utility's specific region and market.

Stranded cost estimates vary widely in the industry. The above table estimates stranded costs in the U.S. at under $140 billion. At the time, in 1995, other estimates were higher, some as high as $200 billion. By 1999, however, many of the early estimates of stranded costs had been downward. For example, according to a recent study by Moody's Investors Service, "approximately $102 billion of potentially stranded costs will be eliminated under transition agreements that provide for the sale of generating assets, the collection of transition charges, and securitization of remaining stranded costs." *See* Smoke Mirrors & Stranded Costs: How Stranded Cost Estimates Went From North of $130 Billion Dollars to $10 Billion, Moody's Investors Services, Special Comment, October 1999. The approach of these transition agreements is discussed later in this Chapter.

3.   POLICY ISSUES IN STRANDED COST RECOVERY

Stranded cost issue raises significant policy concerns. Much like the utility ratemaking issues discussed in Chapter 8, stranded cost recovery raises economic and fairness concerns.

a.   ECONOMIC EFFICIENCY

Many utilities and commentators, most notably Gregory Sidak and Daniel Spulber in their book Deregulatory Takings and the Regulatory Contract (Cambridge University Press 1997), argue that compensation for stranded costs is efficient because it sends investors a signal that governmental commits are credible and will be honored. This works to encourage continued investment in energy markets, providing the capital that is necessary for innovation and competition to evolve. Even in competitive markets, energy firms will need to continue to attract capital, and stranded cost recovery ensures that investors have confidence in the regulatory system and are not discouraged to move their dollars away from the industry. *See* Sidak and Spulber, *supra*.

Some advocating stranded cost recovery focus on principles of competitive neutrality. Just as economists recognize that new firms may face barriers to entry in a monopolistic market, utilities facing stranded costs may experience a "negative barrier to entry." *See* William B. Tye & Frank C. Graves, The economics of Negative Barriers to Entry: How to Recover Stranded Costs and Achieve Competition on Equal Terms in the Electric Utility Industry, 37 Nat. Resources J. 175 (1997). Negative barriers to entry may keep incumbent utility companies from innovating in the ways that new entrants can, thus impairing the levels of innovation in competitive markets. Also, since incumbent firms may face burdens that new entrants do not, competition may be tilted towards new entrants, allowing them to engage in predatory or other anti-competitive behavior, so consumers may not have the full benefits of a competitive market.

At the same time, full compensation without some degree of scrutiny could have efficiency consequences. One of the advocates of the relational contract perspective of utility regulation—*i.e.*, utility regulation is an implicit long term contract between utilities and the state—has warned that stranded cost compensation ignores that the history of utility regulation has been characterized by some degree of "strategic opportunism" by utilities in the industry. *See* Oliver Williamson, Response: Deregulatory Takings and the Breach of the Regulatory Contract: Some Precautions, 71 N.Y.U. L. Rev. 1007 (1996). According to Williamson:

> I have long been persuaded that economic organization in general and regulation in particular are usefully addressed in comparative contractual terms. I am furthermore persuaded that both compensation and pricing are usefully addressed in efficiency terms. Thus, were it not for our differences on how to describe regulation, I could end here with the statement that Sidak and Spulber have it right.
>
> As it turns out, our differences on how to describe regulation are consequential. Thus, whereas Sidak and Spulber would award one-hundred-percent recovery to stranded costs, I argue that the degree of compensation "depends." . . .
>
> Sidak and Spulber describe regulation as a contract between a public utility and a regulatory agency in which both behave in stewardship terms. Managers maximize profits subject to regulatory constraints, make full disclosure in all relevant respects, and eschew strategic behavior. Regulators are well-informed and discharge their regulatory assignment in the public interest. . . .
>
> Contrary to Sidak and Spulber, I am not persuaded that the "formality of the regulatory process, with notice and written comments and hearings on the record" should be described as a reliable "mecha-

nism for verifying the mutuality of voluntary exchange and a meeting of the minds." Neither am I persuaded that the investments made by a natural monopolist are assuredly "prudently incurred".... Finally, although this goes unmentioned, Sidak and Spulber appear to assume that regulated firms are operated in least-cost ways (i.e., with an absence of slack). That is unduly sanguine. Suppose instead that regulation is "defective" in all of these respects. What if the managers and workers in regulated natural monopolies acquire deep knowledge about the industry and have more and better information than both the regulatory agencies and, especially, their customers? What if they can and do disclose this information in a selective way, thereby promoting their (sometimes strategic) purposes and covering up possible cost excesses and/or investment mistakes? What if regulators with an eye to future employment opportunities have incentives to be less than vigilant? And what if regulators, like many others, prefer an easy life?....

As the Averch–Johnson effect suggests, utilities (with the acquiescence of regulators) may have overinvested in capital. If utilities are overcompensated, this could send the wrong signal, encouraging them to overinvest in risky projects in the future. In this sense, there is a moral hazard problem with stranded cost recovery. (The moral hazard problem may explain why there is no private insurance market for regulatory risk.) Related to the efficiency arguments in favor of stranded costs, is should be recognized that there are public choice consequences to allowing full compensation for stranded costs.

Although advocates of stranded cost recovery raise some valid concerns about investor confidence, many investors are sophisticated and have an understanding of divergences in regulatory risk. Over the years, state and federal utility commissions have adopted different approaches to the treatment of various regulatory matters, such as nuclear decommissioning. Given the lack of private insurance markets for regulatory risk, investors have developed regulatory risk premiums that take into account the possibilities of different regulatory treatment in different regulatory environments. *See* Lawrence A. Kolbe & William B. Tye, The *Duquesne* Opinion: How Much "Hope" Is There for Investors in Regulated Firms?, 8 Yale J. on Reg. 113 (1991). The risks of different treatment, based on many structural factors in the industry (*e.g.*, a utility's percentage of nuclear generation plants), is often taken into account in investment prices and expected returns. Thus, financial markets may already have adjusted in their prices and expected returns to some of the risks of stranded costs. In addition, investors have at their disposal one of the strongest self-insurance mechanisms against stranded cost recovery, especially since most utilities have historically had a limited business role; the investor is probably more diversified than any actor in the industry, and diversification can help to spread both the risk and the loss of stranded cost disallowances.

Another policy argument against stranded cost recovery is that it risks recreating many of the same problems with ratemaking that may have brought about a need for competitive restructuring of the industry. Utilities will recover stranded costs through fees (paid for by customers) or surcharges (paid for by new entrants or competitors). As with traditional cost of service rate regulation, regulators will need to determine which cost items can be included in such fees or surcharges. And, as occurred with cost of service regulation, utilities may seek inclusion of many items in stranded cost surcharges that consumer advocates and others would find questionable. *See* Robert J. Michaels, Stranded Investment Surcharges: Inequitable and Inefficient. Public Utilities Fortnightly, May 15, 1999, at 21.

Policymakers need to ask what is gained if competition means re-establishing the same regulatory structure that has posed problems in the past. Price regulation creates a system for moving the monopolist's prices towards those of a competitive market, but the regulatory system is imperfect. The Averch–Johnson effect, for instance predicts that utilities may overinvest in capital, leading to higher prices than a competitive market would yield. In addition, utilities may lobby regulators heavily to sustain their monopolies, and the cost of such lobbying may be a loss to consumers.

The degree of benefits to stranded cost recovery depend on how one views the overall benefits of competitive restructuring of the market. Some public choice theorists argue that the shift from rate regulation to competition will be characterized by an effort by the regulated industry to improve their economic position. In other words, industry lobbyists and lawyers have spent resources in a regulated environment to secure regulatory legislation that will protect industry, and these costs are sunk and cannot be recovered through deregulation. Given the expenditure of these resources and the structuring of the firm around them, a move to deregulation is not completely costless. *See* Fred S. McChesney, Of Stranded Costs and Stranded Hopes, 3 The Independent Review 485 (1999). But the question that needs to be assessed is are these costs relevant from a policy perspective in restructuring utility markets? At least some of these costs are nothing more than what economists would call "sunk," and should probably be of no economic efficiency concern as markets are restructured.

An additional economic efficiency issue regarding stranded cost compensation is what is means for future regulatory policies and changes. To the extent the regulatory status quo gives rise to an entitlement of recovery for past investments, regulators may have frozen the status quo in place. This has implications for flexibility and experimentation in regulatory policy, not only in the regulated industries context, but in other areas of the law. If changes to the utility industry give rise to a taking, then why not changes in the tax or bankruptcy laws?

b. FAIRNESS AND EQUITY

As previously discussed, it is a part of the traditional "regulatory compact" between utilities, customers, and regulators that prudently incurred costs are allowed recovery through rates. Utilities who own generation insist on stranded cost recovery because they invested in generation with the expectation of cost recovery under the regulatory compact. Does this compact continue to have any relevance in a competitive electricity market? Should fairness, as a matter of policy, require the government to compensate utilities, whatever the efficiency or public choice consequences?

Fairness issues might also suggest some limitation on stranded cost recovery. For example, is it fair to provide stranded cost recovery to utilities where utilities also receive many benefits from the state? The federal and state governments have provided utilities with many benefits, including tax breaks, subsidies, and an exclusive monopoly franchise. At a minimum, these benefits should be valued and netted from stranded costs.

Even once a determination to compensate utilities for stranded costs is made, regulators need to determine how to pay for stranded cost recovery and here too fairness concerns come into play. One way to pay for stranded costs is through surcharges (also known as a "competitive transition surcharges") on customer bills. However, is it fair to have customers pay for stranded costs when lower cost alternatives may be available in a competitive market? Another way is to impose fees on new entrants; for instance, a utility that owns transmission lines may impose a fee to recover stranded costs on an IPP that needs access to transmission lines. However, is it any fairer to require new entrants to pay for the costs of obsolete or costly technology purchased by the incumbent? Is it fairer simply to pay for stranded costs through the imposition of a general tax on electricity and have it come from the public fisc? Or should stranded costs be paid for through general income taxes? The following report discusses some of these issues, as well as the method for measuring stranded costs:

The Changing Structure of the Electric Power Industry: An Update, Methodologies for Estimating Stranded Costs, Appendix E (1997) (Modified 1999)

<http://www.eia.doe.gov/cneaf/ electricity/chg_str/ append_e.html>

Utilities with power production costs higher than those likely to prevail in the competitive market will be unable to fully recover the fixed costs of generating facilities that they own and operate to meet customer demand. Accordingly, the initial composition of stranded costs will be dominated by assets related to a utility's generating capacity.

A utility can estimate its potential stranded/strandable costs in one of two basic ways. It can compute the present value of its assets and compare the resulting valuation with its sunk or historical costs, or it can look at the loss in revenue (for a given number of years in the future) as a market price for electricity changes and compute the present value of stranded costs. These basic approaches can be varied depending on when the estimates are made, i.e., before or after the commencement of wholesale and retail wheeling and whether the estimates are made administratively or are determined by the market. These varying considerations enable categorization of approaches into bottom-up versus top-down, ex ante versus ex post, and administrative versus market.

Bottom-Up Versus Top–Down

This approach looks at whether stranded costs are estimated for individual assets or for the aggregate of assets. The bottom-up approach computes the amount of each investment (including contracts, regulatory assets, social programs, and other stranded liabilities) that would be stranded. This approach can provide valuable information (for consideration in adopting mitigation strategies) with respect to those cost variables that have critical impacts on costs. Its weakness lies in not being able to encompass certain incumbent burdens.

The top-down approach calculates the difference in revenues under a regulatory regime and those likely to accrue with the commencement of competition. In this approach, the totality of assets (including incumbent burdens) can be taken into account.

Ex Ante Versus Ex Post

These approaches are based on when the estimates for stranded/strandable costs are made, i.e., before or after the commencement of transition to competition.

The ex ante method provides projections (or forecasts) of stranded/strandable costs before the start of competition. It is based on embedded costs and projected market prices from alternative sources. The validity of such forecasts hinges on the legitimacy of a host of assumptions (such as fuel prices, demand growth, load shapes, technological advancements and others) incorporated in the process. Incorrect assumptions could lead to windfall gains or losses.

The ex post approach estimates stranded/strandable costs after competition is introduced and has made a start. Since market prices are known in this approach, a greater degree of confidence can be placed in the estimates. The appeal of this approach lies in its capability to indicate the magnitude of strandable assets that move the utilities to initiate actions toward adoption of feasible mitigation strategies. In addition, the process establishes a benchmark for potential recovery.

Administrative Versus Market Approach

An administrative approach is based on negotiations between the utility and the regulatory agencies in an attempt to estimate the amount of stranded/strandable assets. However, this approach suffers from the same difficulties as the ex ante approach, in which assumptions regarding future prices and asset values need to be made. On the other hand, the market approach starts with observations in the market and minimizes the problems inherent in forecasting. Observed prices can, however, be subject to market volatility, biasing the results in the market approach.

An alternative (in the market approach) is for a utility to put its generating assets up for sale and secure a price offered by the highest bidder. Stranded costs in this approach are immediately determined as the difference between the embedded price and the realized price. Its main disadvantage is that large blocks of assets cannot be sold easily and may tend to depress prices. Its applicability is also limited to marketable assets.

In its recent filing with the Public Service Commission of New York, the Niagara Mohawk Power Corporation (NMPC) opted in favor of a hybrid approach for estimating strandable costs, using several of the above methods. Its preferred method will be ex ante, top-down, and administrative. Revenue projections based on a "business-as-usual" scenario will be compared with what may be sustainable under competitive conditions. NMPC will also use a bottom-up approach to identify the source of deficit. In addition, the utility proposes to make ex post adjustments to market electricity prices in an attempt to fine tune the estimates.

FERC's Methodology for Estimating Stranded Cost Obligations

FERC has adopted the "revenues lost" approach in hopes of avoiding asset-by-asset reviews to calculate recoverable stranded costs. Whether the State regulatory authorities will also adopt this mode remains an open question.

Table E1. Alternative Ways to Compute Stranded Commitments

	Administrative Valuation		Market Valuation	
	Ex ante	*Ex post*	*Ex ante*	*Ex post*
Bottom-up	Asset-by-asset value projections	Assets valued after restructuring	Assets sold at auction	After the fact purchase-price adjustment
Top-down	Projection of regulated rate by customer class	After the fact adjustment of regulated prices	Bundles of assets spun off	Deferred valuation of spun-off assets

Source: Oak Ridge National Laboratory, Estimating Potential Stranded Commitments for U.S. Investor–Owned Electric Utilities, ORNL/CON–406 (Oak Ridge, TN, January 1995), p. 7.

FERC's methodology for estimating the "stranded cost obligation" (SCO) of a departing generation customer takes the following form:

RSR = revenue stream estimate attributable to the departing customer based on the average of three prior year's revenues

SCO = (RSR—CMVE) x L

where

SCO = stranded cost obligation

CMVE = competitive market value estimate either from sale of released capacity or the average annual cost to the customer of replacement capacity and associated energy

L = length of obligation (reasonable expectation period).

The above formula is designed for determining stranded costs associated with departing wholesale-generation customers and retail-turned-wholesale customers. Its application is subject to conditions such as stipulating a cap on SCO, payment options, and others. The formula is designed to ensure full recovery of legitimate, prudent, and verifiable stranded costs subject to the requirement that the utility take steps to mitigate stranded costs. In addition, the results create certainty for the departing customer as well as incentives for parties to renegotiate their existing requirements contracts.

It is just as possible that FERC's formula approach will also raise issues in the process of estimating stranded costs. It will not be easy to estimate the CMVE based on a market analysis. Establishing that the utility had a reasonable expectation of serving the customer may also be controversial.

Mitigation Strategies

Classification Schemes

It is possible to view mitigation strategies from the perspective of whether they are transaction or non-transaction related. This is the approach adopted in a study prepared by the National Regulatory Research Institute (NRRI) as a briefing document (National Regulatory Research Institute, The Regulatory Treatment of Embedded Costs Exceeding Market Prices: Transition to a Competitive Electric Generation Market—A Briefing Document for State Commissions (Columbus, OH, November 7, 1994), pp. 45–56) for state commissions. The classification adopted in the NRRI study is as follows:

Transaction–Related Recovery Devices

— Access charge tied directly to continued transmission or distribution service

— Exit fees charged to departing customers but unrelated to costs incurred on behalf of those customers

— Exit fees charged to departing customers and calculated to recover costs incurred on behalf of those customers

— A share of net generation savings realized by departing customers over time.

Non-Transaction–Related Recovery Devices

— Shifting costs to captive customers

— Charging ratepayers above-cost prices where market exceeds cost

— Accelerated and decelerated depreciation

— Price cap on performance-based rates.

Broader Bases

— Entrance fees charged to new generation

— All sellers pay a per-kilowatthour tax on generation

— Taxes to include credits for financial writedowns or trust funds to subsidize buyout of contracts from nonutility generators.

Each of the above 11 strategies is evaluated to determine its applicability in comparison with other strategies. The criteria used include considerations of static and dynamic efficiency, consistency with evolution to a competitive market, consistency with regulatory quid pro quo, and difficulties in implementation.

The number of suggested mitigation strategies has proliferated since the release of the FERC's declared intent to actively promote electricity competition in the wake of the EPACT. The following recent listing of 34 strategies is based on a review of the filings at FERC, restructuring proceedings, and a survey of the literature. This study classifies them into six major categories.

Market Actions

— Open Markets: Maximizes competitive pressures on electricity suppliers by ensuring a rapid transition to retail wheeling coupled with the elimination of monopoly franchises. The financial consequences of this strategy for utility shareholders are severe.

— Delay Competition: Assumes the retail process to begin in a staged fashion starting with some selected customers getting access to alternative suppliers initially and extending it to others subsequently. A variant of this strategy is to give all customers access at the same time, but to delay the onset of access by several years. This strategy contrasts sharply with the preceding strategy, but reduces financial burdens on utility shareholders.

— Divest Utility Plant: Envisions divestiture of a utility's generating assets to provide a readily identifiable market value for the assets and thus a valuation of its stranded costs. This strategy is deemed necessary to ensure competitive markets and to reduce potential conflicts between unregulated and regulated operations. Reduction of market power is touted as another advantage. Variants of the divestiture strategy include a rate-base spinoff, where the utility retains only that portion of its generation needed to serve its retail customers and sells the remainder. Another version extends divestiture to sale of transmission assets, in the belief that such assets' market value exceeds their book value, and that this may be used to offset losses resulting from the sale of generating assets at below-book market values.

— Mergers: Reduces potential stranded costs by promoting operating efficiencies or improving marketing opportunities.

— Market Excess Capacity or Energy: Assumes that capacity freed by departing customers can be marketed, thereby augmenting revenue accruals and lowering stranded cost estimations.

Depreciation Options

Depreciation accounting enables recovery of original plant cost over the estimated life of the plant of about 30 to 40 years. Nearly 97 percent of the utilities apply a straight-line recovery method for ratemaking purposes. Depreciation expenses are reflected in the prices customers pay for electricity.

— Accelerate Depreciation of Utility Assets: Permits utilities to recover their plants' costs in a shorter period of time in comparison with the straight-line method. Adoption of this procedure tends to raise rates (expenses) over the shortened depreciation schedule, with a corresponding decline later on. Accelerated depreciation techniques are recommended for specific nonmarketable assets, such as those under the category of regulatory assets.

— Transfer Depreciation Reserves: Under this method, depreciation reserves from transmission and distribution categories are transferred to generation assets. Net plant valuation of generating assets is thereby reduced, with a corresponding increase in the net valuation of the above assets.

— Accelerated Depreciation Offset with Decelerated Depreciation: This is the same as "accelerated depreciation" but with a countervailing proviso that decelerates depreciation charges in asset areas that are risk free (such as transmission and distribution assets). This procedure constrains (or offsets) increases in rates.

— Economic Levelization: When a plant or an asset is added to the rate base, a utility recovers depreciation together with income on its full value. The sum of these two is always higher in the initial years and declines continually over time (other things being equal) as the asset valuation is reduced by the amount depreciated each year. This regulatory approach tends to make the process "front-end loaded." Economic levelization keeps the depreciation expense of a resource constant (in real dollars) over time. Thus, economic levelization has the opposite effect of accelerated depreciation and may be viewed as a strategy during the transition to promote sales.

Ratemaking Actions

These strategies are linked with regulatory ratemaking and its linkage with recovery of embedded plant costs.

— Adjust Utility Returns: Reducing a utility's authorized return will lower its revenues, earnings, and rates. For example, reducing the utility's authorized return from 10 percent to 8 percent for a given rate base will reduce earnings to shareholders by 20 percent, thus lowering the utility's revenue requirement and the rates the utility needs to charge to collect that revenue. However, if the utility is instead permitted to hold the rates constant (e.g., at 10 percent), then reducing a utility's authorized return (for reimbursement to shareholders) can be a transition-cost strategy. Shareholders earn the lower return (e.g., 8 percent) and the utility uses the balance (e.g., 2 percent), as embedded in current rates, to offset sunk obligations.

— Eliminate Subsidies: This concept is based on the notion of utilities cross-subsidizing rates from one customer class to the other. Eliminating subsidies and/or discounts will enable "getting the prices right." Elimination of subsidies would permit customers to get a better indication of the utility's cost structure relative to alternative suppliers.

Restructure Rates: The suggested remedy is to design a two-part rate structure for all ratepayers, made up of energy rates approximating the utilities' marginal costs and a fixed charge covering their fixed costs. Such a rate structure reflects prices accurately and allows the utility to compete successfully during the time when it is a low-cost provider, thus avoiding uneconomic bypass of its generation system. It is claimed that this strategy can create a substantial value for the utilities by increasing the level of revenues during the transition to a fully competitive environment. Note that this is one way in which rates could be restructured. There are several other possibilities.

— Unbundle Rates: In addition to the unbundling of rates suggested in the above strategy, rates could be further unbundled to include costs for transmission and distribution and ancillary services. It is claimed that charging unbundled rates for separate categories of services can lead to a reduction in stranded costs during transition.

— Allow Rate Flexibility: The intent is to endow the utilities with flexibility in setting customer rates (prices) with the objective of reducing the level of stranded/strandable costs.

— Performance–Based Ratemaking (PBR): Under this strategy, traditional cost-of-service ratemaking is replaced by either a price or revenue cap, which is adjusted periodically for inflation and a minimum productivity improvement target. This alternative provides the utilities with inducement to reduce costs and improve productivity and tends to shift risks from customers to the utility. To the extent that a portion of the savings can be used to offset potential strandable costs, PBR offers a viable solution.

— Disallow Costs: Regulatory authorities could simply disallow certain costs from the rates. These disallowances could be related to above-market generating costs or other areas of utility operations deemed to be high relative to the industry. This strategy would be effective only in cases for costs not yet included in rates.

— Explicitly Shift Costs to Captive Customers: The intent is to shift costs to captive customers rather than to departing customers. This is a rather unpopular strategy and is unlikely to be implemented because it mitigates stranded costs that might otherwise be allocated to non-captive customers and/or to the utility's shareholders.

— Exit Fees: Requires departing customers to pay exit fees based, for the most part, on the concept of embedded costs. Exit fees could be a lump sum payment or converted into a stream of payments. In dealing with the subject of stranded cost recovery, this strategy enjoys the support of FERC.

— Net Generation Savings: This strategy aims to share the generation savings realized by the departing customers. Net generation savings, in this case, are defined as the difference between a utility's embedded cost of generation and the generation price obtained by the departing customer. Under this approach, a portion of the savings realized by the exiting customer is used to offset stranded costs. Proponents of this approach realize the difficulty in its implementation, since it may require the coordination of more than one regulatory authority.

— Access Charge: An access charge could be levied for transmission and distribution services. This charge, which could be fixed or variable (i.e., depending on the level of usage), could be structured to include an element of stranded cost recovery either on the basis of a lump sum payment or as a regular payment stream. Difficulties may arise in its implementation due to interjurisdictional problems, since transmission rates need to be determined by FERC and distribution rates need to be handled by the States. The appeal of access charges lies in the fact that all customers contribute to the recovery of stranded costs.

Utility Cost Reductions

If savings resulting from utility cost reductions are to be applied to reduce or offset strandable costs, regulatory approval becomes necessary. Cost reductions may be viewed as efficiency gains provided they do not affect the quality or reliability of service to an unacceptable degree. Accordingly, cost reduction measures are welcome, since they do not involve shifting costs among different segments of the economy. Savings resulting from cost reductions could be shared between the ratepayers and the shareholders.

— Reduce Operating Costs: Options available to achieve reductions in operating costs include reducing plant heat rates, trimming other operating and maintenance expenses, or retiring uneconomic plants.

— Reduce Public Policy Program Costs: These include energy efficiency, low-income assistance, and research and development programs. Cutbacks in these programs could result in savings for a utility.

— Reduce Power Purchase Costs: These costs can be reduced either by renegotiating contracts or by using the buyout option where feasible. A number of investor-owned utilities are using this option to lower their overall costs.

— Financial Writedowns: A writedown is a charge against income implying that the extent of the writedown reflects a diminution in earnings for the shareholders. Under a writedown, the possibility of capital cost recovery in the future is eliminated. The strategy, however, permits a utility to take action on its own to become more competitive (by paring historical costs of uneconomic plants).

Tax Measures

Options that include tax measures have an intuitive appeal, because taxes are deemed to be instruments of public policy. Promoters of tax-based options point out that the benefits of promoting competition in electricity trade will be enjoyed by the economy as a whole. Accordingly, the costs of transition should also be borne by the entire economy.

— Consumption Tax: A consumption tax (similar to an excise or a sales tax) could be implemented either at the State or the Federal level. Revenues so received could be segregated in a trust fund for specific uses to include subsidizing the buyout of above-market power purchase contracts and other nonmarketable regulatory assets. Assuming the present value of strandable costs to be $100 billion, a consumption tax of 0.5 cents per kilowatthour will be necessary for a 10–year period. It is unlikely that such a tax will be seriously considered in the near future, because political support may not be secured for its implementation

— National Tax for Nuclear Plants: This strategy is similar to the imposition of a Federal tax, except that it focuses on strandable costs associated with nuclear power plants. Federal taxation is recommended since Federal policies had a major role in the promotion of nuclear power.

— Production Tax: This tax is similar to the consumption tax except for the difference that producers of power pay the tax instead of the customers. This makes the collection process simpler and perhaps less controversial.

— Tax Reduction: A tax-reduction strategy can take many forms. This strategy was initially conceived as a reduction in the utility's marginal income tax rate at the State (where applicable) or Federal level. However, a tax reduction can so target a State's gross revenue tax collected by the utility. Because independent power producers do not collect this tax, a gross revenue tax acts to further differentiate utility prices from prices of alternative suppliers. In addition, some jurisdictions set higher property tax rates for utility-owned generators than for nonutility generators. These higher tax rates contribute to differences between costs (and prices) for utility-owned and nonutility generators. Setting a common property tax rate for all generators within the same jurisdiction (either by lowering the utility's property tax rate or raising the nonutility's rate) will reduce the difference in generation costs (and prices) between suppliers.

— Tax Deduction: Under this strategy, a tax deduction or credit for uneconomic and unamortized investments in utility plants that utilities subsequently retire may be allowed. Such a deduction would have to be beyond (i.e., distinct from) the deduction from the loss against income that a utility takes as a result of writing down generating assets.

Other Options

These are strategies that cannot be conveniently categorized elsewhere. As usual, most of these strategies originated in suggestions for offsetting strandable costs.

— Preserve Retail Franchise: Preservation of retail franchise is recommended as an option because delaying competition may permit utilities to lower the level of stranded costs. Except as another way of delaying or eliminating competition, it is difficult to see how this strategy addresses stranded or transition costs.

— Eliminate Obligation To Serve: In the absence of obligation to serve, utilities may retire uneconomic assets or reduce excess capacity and thereby lower the level of potential strandable costs.

— Statutorily Authorized Recovery: It is possible to enact legislation that would permit statutory recovery of stranded costs. Puget Power in Washington State, for example, has been assured of the recovery of its demand-side management-related expenditures (its largest regulatory asset) in this manner. The legislation enacted in the State of Washington creates a new property right called the "bondable conservation investment," under which customer rates permit the recovery of demand-side management costs incurred by the utility.

— Entrance Fee for Returning Customers: Customers that depart the utility system and subsequently elect to return become liable to be charged an entry fee. The entrance fee could be structured to cover the transition costs incurred during the period the customer purchased power from alternative suppliers.

— Entrance Fee for New Generation: New generation facilities coming on line after restructuring could be charged a fee to enter the market. Practical difficulties are likely to be encountered if this proposal is ever implemented. For example, who will collect this fee without abuse may be a problem. In addition, the procedure may introduce new unacceptable barriers to entry.■

B.   LEGAL ENTITLEMENT TO RECOVERY OF STRANDED COSTS

The U.S. Energy Information Administration estimates that stranded costs could lead to an increase in bankruptcies in the industry if regulators do not find a way to address them. U.S. Department of Energy, Energy Information Administration, Electricity Prices in a Competitive Environment: Marginal Cost Pricing of Generation Services and Financial Status of Electric Utilities—A Preliminary Analysis Through 2015 ix (1997). Not surprisingly, utilities are making vigorous arguments in favor of full or near-full recovery of stranded costs.

States have varied in their solutions to the stranded cost problem. One approach to minimizing the losses associated with stranded costs is to allow full stranded cost recovery. California and Rhode Island, for instance, allow for full stranded cost recovery as a part of their restructuring plans. As a result, California and Rhode Island's plans have been characterized by some consumer advocates as a "bailout." Many believe that less than 100% stranded cost recovery is acceptable. Some states, such as Pennsylvania and New Hampshire, have allowed less than 100% recovery of claimed stranded costs. Is 100% recovery required by law? Which approach is better from an efficiency or social welfare perspective?

Gregory Sidak and Daniel Spulber advance what is perhaps the most forceful argument in favor of full stranded cost recovery in the literature. In 1996, they wrote:

> The competitive transformation of local exchange telecommunications and the electric power industry raises significant takings questions about whether regulators should give a public utility the opportunity to recover its stranded costs. As regulators mandate the unbundling of basic network elements in local telephony or mandate wholesale and retail wheeling in the electricity industry, they introduce competition that denies a utility the opportunity to recover the cost of service; at the same time, those regulators often leave untouched the utility's preexisting incumbent burdens. Such regulatory action threatens to confiscate private property—namely, shareholder value—for the promotion of competition, without just compensation.

J. Gregory Sidak & Daniel F. Spulber, Deregulatory Takings and Breach of the Regulatory Contract, 71 N.Y.U. L. Rev. 851, 857–58 (1996). Following responses from some critics,[1] they clarified their argument in 1997. Although the excerpt below focuses on the implications of "deregulatory takings" for telecommunications regulation, might it also extend to electric utility restructuring?

J. Gregory Sidak & Daniel F. Spulber, Givings, Takings, and the Fallacy of Forward–Looking Costs

72 N.Y.U. L. Rev. 1068, 1074–78 (1997).

Deregulation requires the state to compensate for past contractual obligations made to private investors and to think carefully before creating new ones.

Our analysis can be summarized in four familiar epigrams. First, "a deal is a deal." The government entered into a regulatory contract with utilities in the network industries consisting of entry controls, rate regulation, and obligations to serve. The contract can be renegotiated bilaterally to prepare the ground for competition, but the voluntary exchange inherent in such renegotiation will require compensating utility investors for the loss of their investment-backed expectations.

Second, "there is no such thing as a free lunch." Someone must pay the costs of publicly mandated services. The facilities of the regulated network industries did not fall like manna from heaven, but rather were established by incumbent utilities through the expenditures of their investors. Utilities made past expenditures to perform obligations to serve in expectation of the reasonable opportunity to recover the costs of invest-

---

1. *See* William J. Baumol & Thomas W. Merrill, Deregulatory Takings, Breach of the Regulatory Contract, and the Telecommunications Act of 1996, 72 N.Y.U. L. Rev. 1037 (1997); Stephen F. Williams, Deregulatory Takings and Breach of the Regulatory Contract: A Comment, 71 N.Y.U. L. Rev. 1000 (1996); Oliver E. Williamson, Deregulatory Takings and Breach of the Regulatory Contract: Some Precautions, 71 N.Y.U. L. Rev. 1007 (1996).

ment plus a competitive rate of return. Investors must be compensated for those past costs; it follows a fortiori that investors must be offered additional compensation if existing responsibilities are perpetuated or new burdens are imposed. Reed Hundt, chairman of the Federal Communications Commission, revealed his lack of understanding of that principle when he declared at the end of 1996 that opening the local exchange should not be called a free lunch: "The rate payers paid for this network.... My argument is that it's been a nice lunch for the entire country."[19][2]

Contrary to that reasoning, the benefits of deregulation are the result of free markets, not the expropriation of investor wealth. A telephone customer has acquired no ownership in the local exchange network by virtue of having paid regulated rates for service from an investor-owned LEC, just as he could not expect to have acquired any ownership interest in Texaco by virtue of having purchased gasoline from that company over a period of years. Chairman Hundt's comment fundamentally misapprehends the legal and economic significance, traceable to *Munn v. Illinois* and to earlier English common law, of dedicating private property to a public purpose. In addition, his remarks show that he does not recognize that investment in a network industry does not happen only once.

Third, "an ounce of prevention is worth a pound of cure." If regulators adopt the correct pricing policies for mandatory access to network facilities and accompany such pricing rules with competitively neutral and nonbypassable end-user charges, then they will avoid the takings issue. This advice is consistent with the prudential rule, commonly attributed to Justice Brandeis's famous 1936 concurrence in *Ashwander v. Tennessee Valley Authority*[21],[3] that courts (and a fortiori regulatory agencies, we would add) should read statutes to avoid having to decide constitutional questions. The deregulation of network industries in the United States should not have come to this. Regulators should have taken care to read statutes, such as the local competition provisions of the Telecommunications Act of 1996, in a way that would have obviated litigation over takings questions that have arisen as a result of the FCC's actions. In short, this third epigram is necessary advice to dispense because the FCC and many state PUCs have ignored the constitutional precedent concerning regulated industries that makes clear that investors in public utilities are entitled to the reasonable opportunity to recover their investment and a competitive return.

Fourth, regulators should heed the advice, "look before you leap." Before creating new forms of regulation of network industries, such as the unbundling requirements of the Telecommunications Act of 1996, regulators should compare the costs and benefits. It does little good to protest the high cost of deregulation or the inefficiencies of regulation after the fact. Optimization is achieved as the result of decisions made before

---

2. Mark Landler, The Bells Want F.C.C. to Make Providers Share Internet Costs, N.Y. Times, Nov. 25, 1996, at D1 (quoting Reed E. Hundt, Chairman, Federal Communications Commission).

3. 297 U.S. 288, 347 (1936) (Brandeis, J., concurring).

networks are created and costs are sunk. After costs are sunk, protections against regulatory opportunism and deregulatory takings come into play so as to preserve future incentives for private parties to invest in network infrastructure and to enter into efficient agreements with regulatory agencies.

What does it mean to protect private ownership of the telecommunications network? Ownership of an economic asset has two aspects: rights to residual returns and rights of residual control. Residual returns refer to the returns from an asset after all prior claimants have been paid; thus, equity holders in a corporation obtain the returns after debt holders and other creditors have been paid. Residual control refers to the control of the asset for the purposes of the owners, subject to legal and other prior (contractual) restrictions. Protection of private property from government takings means protection of investors' residual returns, as well as protection of their residual control in the absence of just compensation.■

* * *

How does this argument apply to electric utility industry restructuring? Sidak and Spulber updated and clarified their argument further in a book, entitled Deregulatory Takings and the Regulatory Contract: The Competitive Transformation of Network Industries in the United States (Cambridge U. Press 1997). Their book, more than 500 pages of legal and regulatory analysis, has been invoked in regulatory proceedings a judicial cases across the country. It has been compared in its importance to Robert Bork's The Antitrust Paradox (Basic Books 1978), a controversial book on antitrust policy written before Bork's appointment to the U.S. Court of Appeals for the D.C. Circuit and his failed nomination to the Supreme Court; as Bork advocated a reorientation for antitrust law, it has been suggested that Sidak and Spulber are arguing for a reorientation of regulated industries principles (we consider the merits of this claim below). See Jim Chen, The Second Coming of Smyth v. Ames, 77 Tex. L. Rev. 1535, 1555 (1999). For reviews of the arguments Sidak and Spulber make in their book, see Jim Rossi, The Irony of Deregulatory Takings, 77 Tex. L. Rev. 297, 311–313 (1998); Herbert Hovenkamp, The Takings Clause and Improvident Regulatory Bargains, 108 Yale L.J. 801 (1999). For a forceful argument that stranded cost advocates overstate the extent of a property interest and contract underlying the regulatory arrangement between utilities and the state, see Lois R. Lupica, Transition Losses in the Electric Power Market: A Challenge to the Premises Underlying the Arguments for Compensation, 52 Rutgers L. Rev. __ (forthcoming 2000).

1.   PROCEDURAL CONSIDERATIONS: HOW HAS FERC ALLOWED FOR STRANDED COST RECOVERY IN ITS RESTRUCTURING ORDERS?

Cajun Electric Power Co–op. v. FERC
28 F.3d 173 (D.C.Cir.1994).

Per curiam: Cajun Electric Power Cooperative, Inc., and other wholesale and retail customers of Entergy Corporation (Entergy) petition for review of three electric power tariffs filed by Entergy and approved by the Federal Energy Regulatory Commission. We grant the petition and remand for reconsideration consistent with this opinion.

Entergy is a public utility holding company, whose various wholly-owned subsidiaries collectively deal in both the transmission and generation of electric power. On August 2, 1991, one of its subsidiaries, Entergy Services, Inc., submitted three tariffs to the Commission for approval pursuant to section 205 of the Federal Power Act. *See* 16 U.S.C. §§ 824d, 824e (1988). Two were rate schedules which provided for the wholesale sale of power at negotiated, market-based rates. These represented a departure from the regulated, cost-based rates that Entergy was then applying. The third tariff was a rate schedule which purported to provide open access to Entergy's transmission system. This transmission service tariff (TST) provided that any eligible electric utility could purchase transmission service over Entergy's lines at cost-based rates. It also included a provision under which Entergy could recover its "stranded investment costs," which are the costs Entergy incurs due to any surplus in generation (or other) facilities resulting from the introduction of open access to its transmission services; i.e., Entergy's current customers might take advantage of open access to purchase power from competing entities and thereby leave Entergy with excess capacity and the costs which that entails. Entergy's filing—although lengthy—was not supported by either testimony or affidavits.

The critical issue in this case involves Entergy's move from regulated to market pricing for its wholesale sales of electric power. As both parties agreed at oral argument, the primary source of Entergy's market power in generation sales is its bottleneck monopoly in transmission services. Given this market power, a classic tying problem exists: Entergy could use its monopoly over transmission services to eliminate competition in the market for generation services. *Cf. Eastman Kodak Co. v. Image Technical Services*, 119 L. Ed. 2d 265, 112 S. Ct. 2072, 2079 (1992) ("A tying arrangement is "an agreement by a party to sell one product but only on the condition that the buyer also purchases a different (or tied) product, or at least agrees that he will not purchase that product from any other supplier," "and is illegal under the Sherman Act" if the seller has "appreciable economic power' in the tying product market and if the arrangement affects a substantial volume of commerce in the tied market.") (citations omitted).

When faced with these kinds of concerns, FERC only approves market-based rates when a utility demonstrates that its market power is sufficiently mitigated in the relevant markets. Hence, the core question here is whether the open-access transmission tariff truly mitigates Entergy's market power; accordingly, FERC approved Entergy's tariffs only after concluding that Entergy "will not dominate generation in any relevant market" and "will have adequately mitigated its market power in transmission" after having implemented the TST.

In declining to hold a hearing or request additional evidentiary submissions before rendering its decision, FERC concluded that the petitioners had not demonstrated in their intervention motion that there were any genuine issues of material fact that required a trial-type hearing. FERC believed that by granting competitors access to Entergy's transmission services, the TST would "provide sufficient assurance that Entergy will not exercise market power under the new tariffs." The idea was that "open access" to Entergy's transmission grid would effectively mitigate production-related market power. To facilitate this result, FERC modified Entergy's proposed TST. For example, FERC required Entergy to file all transmission service requests with FERC, to maintain an electronic bulletin board of available transmission capacity and requests for transmission service, and to submit an updated market analysis every three years. FERC also permitted customers to file complaints under section 206 of the Federal Power Act if they believed that Entergy was exercising market power. Finally, FERC also required that any stranded investment costs levied against users of Entergy's transmission grid be "legitimate and verifiable." Satisfied with these adjustments, FERC declined to conduct hearings on the TST, and maintained that a "hearing would only speculate about what Entergy might do in the future."

In general, FERC must hold an evidentiary hearing "only when a genuine issue of material fact exists," *Vermont Dept. of Public Service v. F.E.R.C.*, 260 U.S. App. D.C. 20, 817 F.2d 127, 140 (D.C.Cir.1987), and even then, "FERC need not conduct such a hearing if [the disputed issues] may be adequately resolved on the written record." *Moreau v. F.E.R.C.*, 299 U.S. App. D.C. 168, 982 F.2d 556, 568 (D.C.Cir.1993). Moreover, "mere allegations of disputed fact are insufficient to mandate a hearing; a petitioner must make an adequate proffer of evidence to support them." *Woolen Mill Associates v. F.E.R.C.*, 286 U.S.App.D.C. 367, 917 F.2d 589, 592 (D.C.Cir.1990). We review FERC's decision to deny an evidentiary hearing for an abuse of discretion. *Woolen Mill*, 917 F.2d at 592. Notwithstanding this deferential standard of review, we conclude that FERC erred in summarily approving Entergy's tariffs.

The petitioners proffered several facts that raise serious doubts concerning the mitigation of Entergy's market power—doubts that FERC has not adequately addressed and upon which an evidentiary hearing may shed light. Although FERC's analysis of Entergy's market power was not cursory, *see* 58 F.E.R.C. ¶ 61,234 at 61,754–60, we think its determination that the TST would sufficiently mitigate Entergy's market power is seriously flawed. The petitioners raised several factual issues which indicate that Entergy might retain significant market power notwithstanding the TST.

The most problematic of these involves the "stranded investment" provision, concerning which the Commission stated as follows:

> The Commission believes that Entergy should be able to recover legitimate and verifiable stranded investment costs and that such cost recovery does not constitute the collection of monopoly rents. By filing the open access transmission tariff in this proceeding, Entergy provided an opportunity for wholesale power market participants in its relevant market area to trade with each other more easily. However,

this opportunity may result in certain transition problems, such as Entergy's stranded investment. Entergy negotiated its existing power contracts with Captive Cities and Individual Cities when these entities were its full and partial requirements customers respectively. They had limited, if any, options other than purchasing Entergy's generation services. By offering the open access transmission tariff, Entergy has now expanded the supply options available to these customers so that they can, in many cases, purchase their requirements elsewhere as soon as the tariff becomes effective. If Entergy has made investment decisions based on a contractual commitment or a reasonable expectation at that time that it would continue to serve these customers, it should be able to recover from them the legitimate and verifiable costs invested on their behalf. 60 F.E.R.C. ¶ 61,168 at 61,631.

Section 9a of the TST provides that Entergy may recover its stranded investment costs from certain competitors who use its transmission services. These costs—which must be generation-related since the customer will be employing Entergy's transmission services in any case—are to be included in the rates charged for the transmission service. In other words, if Entergy loses a customer of generation capacity to a competitor but the customer continues to employ Entergy's transmission grid, the charge for the transmission will include not only costs directly associated with it, but also the cost of Entergy's generation capacity idled by the switch. "The customer's cost liability for stranded investment" is, however, limited to "what the customer would have contributed to fixed costs under its existing rate had the customer remained on Entergy's system."

This is, in essence, a tying arrangement, *see Jefferson Parish Hospital Dist. No. 2 v. Hyde*, 466 U.S. 2, 12, 80 L. Ed. 2d 2, 104 S. Ct. 1551 (1984) ("the essential characteristic of an invalid tying arrangement lies in the seller's exploitation of its control over the tying product to force the buyer into the purchase of the tied product"), and it might be fine if the purpose of the arrangement were not to cabin Entergy's market power. The Commission argues that this is not a tying arrangement because it "is not a situation in which Entergy is requiring a customer to purchase generation in the future in exchange for transmission in the future." 60 F.E.R.C. ¶ 61,168 at 61,632 (1992). But if a company can charge a former customer for the fixed cost of its product whether or not the customer wants that product, and can tie this cost to the delivery of a bottleneck monopoly product that the customer must purchase, the products are as effectively tied as they would be in a traditional tying arrangement. By analogy, suppose a certain Company A both owned the roads and sold cars. Section 9a of the TST is equivalent to a rule whereby former car customers of Company A, who decide instead to purchase a car from Company B, must pay a toll for road use that covers not only the cost of the road, but also the cost of the displaced productive capacity that would have built the cars they no longer buy from Company A. At any rate, it is hard to imagine that such limited and costly access to the "roads"—that is, to Entergy's transmission grid—will serve to effectively mitigate its market power, especially in the context of electricity generation where fractions of a cent per kilowatt hour can make the difference among competitors.

Permitting a transmission monopolist to impose generation-related charges on competitors who seek only transmission services may actually serve to increase the entity's market power, for it creates an odd asymmetry. That is, while Entergy can compete for generation sales outside its transmission grid without concern for a stranded investment charge, Entergy's competitors cannot compete for the customers on its transmission system on the same basis.

As a theoretical matter, then, the petitioners would appear to be correct that the stranded investment provision is anticompetitive. The Commission admitted as much at oral argument stating "if you're charged these costs, there's some dampening of competition ... I cannot deny that." The question of how much competition in fact is dampened goes to the heart of the complicated issues the Commission faces in these tariffs. The petitioners adequately flagged this issue for the Commission as a specific disputed material issue of fact. We think that there should have been an evidentiary hearing to address it.

The Commission attempted to avoid the issue altogether by declaring that decisions on stranded investment will be made on a case-by-case basis. It argued that the issue is raised "prematurely," since "affected parties may challenge Entergy's recovery of such costs in the particular cases in which they are claimed." Moreover, the Commission prescribed "procedures in conjunction with a particular stranded investment charge, so that a potential transmission customer will know the potential stranded investment for which the customer might be liable and will be able to assess whether to contract for new generation service from another supplier." The Commission described the procedures as follows:

> Entergy shall provide, within thirty days of a request for transmission service, the specific stranded investment charge, if any, which Entergy would propose to charge the requester. If a requester finds the proposed stranded investment charge unreasonable, the requester shall have thirty days in which to respond to Entergy, explaining why it disagrees with the charge. Entergy and the requester shall then have ninety days to attempt to resolve the dispute. If Entergy and the requester have not resolved the matter after ninety days, the requester may: (1) file the dispute directly with the Commission for resolution ... or (2) wait until the proposed stranded investment charge is filed as part of Entergy's proposed transmission rate under section 205 of the FPA, and contest at that time. *Id.* at 61,631–32.

In short, the Commission argues that the issue of whether stranded investment cost will reduce access to transmission is not susceptible of final resolution by a hearing at this point, because legitimate and verifiable stranded investment can only properly be determined on a case-by-case basis and appropriate procedures have been made available for doing just that.

But central to the Commission's approval of the tariffs was its finding that Entergy's market power would be mitigated by the TST upon its implementation. It follows that the question of whether Entergy's recovery of stranded investment cost precludes mitigation of its market power must be faced squarely by the Commission at this juncture. The provision of procedures to determine stranded investment cost on a case-by-case basis at a later date is no answer if the provision has a present anticompetitive effect. Assurances that stranded investment cost is legitimate, verifiable and accurately calculated do not in themselves resolve whether the imposition of such production-related costs on transmission services precludes the mitigation of Entergy's market power.

Moreover, the procedures themselves hang over any prospective deal like the sword of Damocles. To be forced to litigate to determine the price of a product introduces deal-killing transactional costs and uncertainties. If Entergy claims a stranded investment cost that a customer finds unreasonable, it will be at least 150 days (30 + 30 + 90) before the Commission even receives the complaint, much less resolves it.

What is inescapably before the Commission at this juncture is its validation of the concept of stranded investment, because—not surprisingly really—its view on this matter may itself dictate market structure. The Commission must address whether the TST's provision of a process for recovery of stranded investment costs is itself a deal killer that, perhaps ironically, precludes genuine open access to Entergy's transmission system. In short, the question that must be asked now is whether the TST allows for "meaningful access to alternative suppliers." *Western Systems Power Pool*, 55 F.E.R.C. ¶ 61,099 at 61,317 (1991) (emphasis added).

Petitioners argue that the concept of stranded investment has no meaning in a competitive market, since a surplus of productive capacity can always be readily eliminated simply by lowering price. That is, a price can always be found that is low enough that it increases demand sufficiently to eliminate any excess in productive capacity. In the instant case, Entergy always has the option to reemploy any temporarily unemployed productive resources by making off-system sales at market-based prices. Hence, there really is no such thing as stranded investment, only a failure to compete. Of course, the point of introducing competition is to reap the benefits associated with just such market forces. In this sense, a stranded investment provision is the antithesis of competition.

The Commission suggested at oral argument that if there is no such thing as a legitimate stranded investment cost, then the petitioners have nothing to worry about, since the Commission only permits the recovery of such costs if they are, in fact, legitimate. But if the Commission is wrong at the outset concerning the possibility of legitimate stranded investment cost, it is not fair or reasonable to create such a mechanism for recovery. It generates uncertainty over costs that may completely bar competitive transactions, not to mention the expense of the process itself which could also prove to be prohibitive.

Other provisions of the TST may also lessen the mitigation of Entergy's market power. Entergy retains sole discretion to determine the amount of transmission capability available for its competitors' use, 58 FERC at 61,739 (section 7 of the TST provides that Entergy "is the sole judge of transmission availability for a specified transaction"), which may prove problematic in light of the fact that Entergy need only provide "transfer capability . . . in excess of that needed to accommodate" its own transmission needs. *Id.* Other provisions of the TST that may restrain competition include the point to point service limitation, the failure to impose reasonable time limits on Entergy's response to requests for transmission service, and Entergy's reservation of the right to cancel service in certain instances, even where a customer has paid for transmission system modifications.

Taken as a whole, the TST seems to provide Entergy with the means to stifle the very competition it purports to create. We think it plain that there may never be any competition if Entergy decides to open only a slight amount of transmission capability to its competitors. At the very least, Entergy's ability to determine whether and when it has surplus transmission capability creates an uncertainty that impedes competition. Any competitor willing to bear this uncertainty, moreover, is then confronted with another: the potentially high stranded investment costs that it might have to bear in using Entergy's transmission services. No competitor could be but somewhat leery of depending on the TST in light of these concerns.

The Commission suggests that the stranded investment provision is necessary to lure Entergy into competition: "any utility would be reluctant to open its transmission system voluntarily if it meant being subjected to self-inflicted stranded investment." There are two answers to this. First, while the Commission argues that the stranded investment charge "provides an equitable recovery of costs from the parties for which the costs were incurred," this is irrelevant if the tariffs do not mitigate Entergy's market power sufficiently that the resulting market-based prices will be "just and reasonable" under section 205 of the Federal Power Act. 16 U.S.C. § 824d (1988).

Second, this case may take on a different cast in light of recent amendments to the Federal Power Act. Specifically, the Commission can now order transmission services pursuant to the Energy Policy Act of 1992. *See* 16 U.S.C.A. §§ 824j and 824k (1992). As the legislative history explains:

> The title clarifies FERC's authority to order utilities to provide transmission service. It directs FERC to require wheeling that is in the public interest, maintains system reliability, and serves one or more additional goals—including the promotion of wholesale competition, conservation, efficiency, and the prevention of discriminatory practices. The transmitting utility is entitled to payment for the cost of providing such service, plus a reasonable rate of return.

Comprehensive National Energy Policy Act: Report of the Committee on Energy and Commerce House of Representatives, 102d Cong., 2d Sess., Rept. 102–474, Part 1, at 140 (March 30, 1992).

In light of the substantial controversies evoked by Entergy's tariff filing, the Commission's failure to conduct an evidentiary hearing was arbitrary and capricious. Moreover, the substantive decision is flawed in that the Commission failed to adequately explain its approval of the stranded investment provision, among others. Accordingly, we grant the petition for review and remand this matter to the Commission to conduct further proceedings.

So ordered.■

———

In Order No. 888, which followed the D.C. Circuit's *Cajun* decision, FERC allowed utilities to recover a large portion of their stranded costs:

> With regard to stranded costs, the Final Rule adopts the Commission's supplemental proposal. It will permit utilities to seek extra-contractual recovery of stranded costs associated with a limited set of existing (executed on or before July 11, 1994) wholesale requirements contracts and provides that the Commission will be the primary forum for utilities to seek recovery of stranded costs associated with retail-turned-wholesale transmission customers. It also will allow utilities to seek recovery of stranded costs caused by retail wheeling only in circumstances in which the state regulatory authority does not have authority to address retail stranded costs at the time the retail wheeling is required. The Rule retains the revenues lost approach for calculating stranded costs and provides a formula for calculating such costs.

While FERC's decision to allow stranded cost recovery seems uncontroversial, it needs to be understood in the context of how FERC has treated this problem elsewhere. FERC's approach to allowing recovery of stranded costs for electric utilities may conflict with its policies in the natural gas context. Although Order No. 636 is FERC's major natural gas pipeline restructuring rule, Order No. 500 addressed the stranded cost issue in natural gas, by articulating FERC's principle for deciding how to allocate take or pay costs. The basic issue FERC attempted to resolve in Order No. 500 is how the blame for uneconomic contracts would be shared:

> The causes of the pipelines' take-or-pay problems are many and complex. It is undoubtedly true that some pipelines independently entered into contracts incorporating both high prices and high take-or-pay levels. At the same time, pipelines entered into contracts, which were based on the anticipated demands of their customers, and whose terms reflected those which producers were able to obtain under the then prevailing market conditions. . . . The Commission recognizes that it is difficult to assign blame for the pipeline industry's take-or-pay problems. In brief, no one segment of the natural gas industry or particular circumstance appears wholly responsible for the pipelines' excess inventories of gas. As a result, all segments should shoulder some of the burden of resolving the problem.

Order No. 500, 52 Fed. Reg. at 30,337. Consistent with this general statement, FERC opted for cost sharing of the stranded costs in the natural gas pipeline industry pursuant to an equitable formula. FERC made pipelines (and their shareholders) absorb between twenty-five percent and fifty percent of high-priced natural gas costs and allowed them to pass an equal amount (from twenty-five percent to fifty percent) on to their customers through a fixed charge. Any residual costs (for instance, fifty percent if a pipeline chose to absorb just twenty-five percent and pass through twenty-five percent) could be added to the ordinary rate and recouped to the extent that customers would buy the pipeline's expensive gas.

FERC's differing approaches to stranded cost recovery in electricity and natural gas industries raises the question of whether FERC can justify the stranded cost recovery it allowed electric utilities in Order No. 888.

John Burritt McArthur, The Irreconcilable Differences Between FERC's Natural Gas and Electricity Stranded Cost Treatments

46 Buff. L. Rev. 71 (1998).

One way to picture the problem with the new rule for electricity is to imagine that Order Nos. 888 and 500 had been issued on the same day. FERC would have had to admit that while it was requiring equitable sharing in natural gas, this was an exception to the cost-causation principle that it thinks should apply generally, including to the electricity industry. FERC would say, "We are going to rely on cost responsibility for incurring stranded costs in natural gas, but ignore that principle in electricity and focus instead on the bargain utilities say is represented by their service commitment, their financial exposure, and what we enjoy calling cost causation." The Commission would have had to argue that it was giving pipelines this special burden because contract renegotiation was so far along and admit, in turn, that this was because the Commission had thwarted all pressures to address the take-or-pay problem sooner. And it would have had to hold, inconsistently, that the "extraordinary" magnitude of high gas costs required equitable sharing in Order No. 500, that the smaller size of later gas transition costs warranted full recovery in Order No. 636, and that the company-threatening size of the costs (i.e., the extraordinarily large costs) required full pass-through in electricity....

The fact that FERC and state commissions only can reach a fair allocation of stranded electric costs by deciding the responsibility that utilities bear for their mistakes, over-investments, and discrimination, does not mean that the electric industry would end up with the same proportionate burden as pipelines. To the extent that FERC and state regulators played a larger role by requiring utilities to sign QF contracts and in other electricity market distortions, electric companies could get more protection under a cost-responsibility standard. The Commission thus far has avoided measuring the distortions due to company mistakes, but there is no reason to expect that this balance would be the same in electricity as in gas.

One big distinction between the two industries is the painful cure already doled out to electric utilities for unwanted nuclear plants. Nuclear plants provide a lot of the nation's electric power-twenty-two percent by the early Nineties. Utilities wrote off something like $20 billion for these plants in the 1980's. To the extent that commissions already had adjudicated the blame that utilities should bear for these costs, the residual costs presumably would be passed through to customers in their entirety. At least many of these costs already should be discounted for cost responsibility.

A second distortion more direct than in natural gas comes from QF contracts. These contracts forced utilities to buy very uneconomic power. Under the peculiar structure of PURPA, states set avoided-cost standards under which utilities had to purchase power that matched their own "avoided costs." . . . State commissions also overestimated the amount of power needed. SoCal, one of the country's largest utilities, has claimed that QF contracts will be its largest source of stranded costs, with its above-market QF payments having a net present value of about $5 billion. The Edison Electric Institute (EEI) estimates the net present value of QF contracts at $38 billion nationally. . . . In many states, the level of government involvement in these contracts is higher than in the ordinary take-or-pay contract.

Another large group of costs come from "regulatory assets," which can include everything from approved storm property losses to deferred fuel charges. The EEI's figure for these costs is at least $75 billion. Though companies have every incentive to inflate their regulatory-asset account with ordinary business expenses, these costs include a number of legitimate but deferred costs whose recovery already has been guaranteed by commissions. Many demand-side management expenses may fall into this category.

It is not possible to know how far utilities really should be held responsible for their stranded costs because FERC has not developed the record needed to make this determination. But it is unwise to take the regulatory victim argument at face value. It turns out, for instance, that half of SoCal's QF purchases were made from Mission Energy, a wholly owned affiliate. In another category of stranded costs, Bernard Black and Richard Pierce claim that utilities exploited demand management programs once they realized that these programs offered a way to inflate their ratebase. Thus even costs that look as if they were foisted on utilities by regulators deserve a closer look before anyone decides how far they should be recovered.

Even though a test of cost responsibility might let electric companies recover a higher percentage of their stranded costs than pipelines, this does not mean that Order No. 888's full recovery represents a prudential decision to avoid the difficult and costly question of how much. There is no sign that the Commission was making a prudent, if implicit, judgment that the benefits of making electric companies bear some of their losses would be outweighed by the costs of litigating the right allocation. One problem with such a theory is that FERC did not develop any record at all on the stranded costs that it blames on electric companies. Nor did it project the cost of litigation. So there was no basis for guessing how these factors balance each other.

Moreover, a decision that utilities are to blame for only an insignificant share of stranded costs is inconsistent with the justification for deregulating. If that is so, then these companies, with all the benefits of their large scale, established networks, and deep experience, might as well remain our electric suppliers. We have deregulated because FERC does not believe that electric companies have been efficient. They have made too many mistakes. That is why their markets have been opened up.

If costs are stranded from utility mistakes, subsidizing those mistakes by passing the costs along to departing customers, to all customers, or to competing generators through an added transmission surcharge has efficiency costs. Such indulgence rewards the inefficient and delays, perhaps in some cases prevents, the shift of demand to better run companies. This subsidy has unwarranted wealth-transfer effects as well as efficiency problems.

Finally, careless, unjustified pass-through, a pass-through inconsistent with the stated rationales for deregulating, undermines (and should undermine) the legitimacy of the regulatory process. Every government decision can add to or subtract from the assent upon which agency action relies for implementation. Major decisions that come into the public eye generally have a disproportionate effect on beliefs about agencies. Agencies have to fight for legitimacy by making the fairness of their orders transparent to the larger society upon which those orders will be imposed. A stranded cost rule so at odds with the theory of deregulation can only damage the Commission's support.

The fact that FERC has not been consistent as it moved from natural gas to electricity does not mean automatically that Order No. 888 is wrong. Consistency is not a god to be pursued slavishly. The natural gas rules might be ill-founded, or there might be some other distinction between the two industries. Or something fundamental might have changed in the economy between the late 1980's and today, in a way that justifies different treatment of electric companies.

Nonetheless, such a marked difference in approach, with outcomes so contradictory, justifies at least the presumption that something is wrong with Order No. 888. And in fact, there is no obviously relevant difference between deregulation in natural gas and in electricity, in spite of FERC's claims.... And there is no large economic change under way across the country that seems to justify the differences.

The worst problem is that full recovery is so at odds with the goals of deregulation, which should reflect the Commission's first and most deep-seated duty, its duty to serve consumers. The Commission's obeisance to alleged utility reliance and financial integrity and its allegiance to "cost causation" reject the insight of deregulation. As FERC understood in natural gas but has forgotten in electricity, the rationale for opening industries to the market is the inefficiency of regulated decisionmaking. Industries are exposed to competition because the core duty of agencies in American economic regulation is to protect consumer welfare, not to shield careless utility investment. Unbundling and open access do not deny regulated companies their right to recovery. They merely make those companies prove that their investments were efficient. If not, the loss is supposed to fall on the investing company.

Making regulated companies bear the risk of bad investments performs several functions. It ensures that they have every incentive to operate at maximal efficiency. It clears the way for new entrants to appear and force competition into the industry. And it guarantees that consumers will get the benefits of lower prices that competition can bring. Cost-based recovery would not have to saddle utilities with mistakes that regulators foisted on them, but it would make a fair effort at distinguishing that impairment from mistakes that should be lodged with utility decisionmaking.

In contrast, the decision to protect stranded plants and supply contracts of electric utilities, even when the inefficiency of these investments and discrimination in shielding them from market forces has risen to a level that requires deregulation, is inconsistent with the decision to deregulate.■

2. DOES THE TAKINGS CLAUSE GUARANTEE STRANDED COST RECOVERY?

The stranded cost debate echoes the takings issues discussed in the ratemaking cases in Chapter 8. Under the Takings Clause of the U.S. Constitution, it is unconstitutional for the government to take private property for public use without just compensation. As Justice Holmes stated, "We are in danger of forgetting that a strong public desire to improve the public condition is not enough to warrant achieving the desire by a shorter cut than the constitutional way of paying for the change." *Pennsylvania Coal Co. v. Mahon*, 260 U.S. 393 (1922).

Sidak and Spulber advance the argument that attempts to deregulate the industry operate as a "taking" if stranded costs are not completely recovered by utilities:

> Courts will soon face a third genre of takings cases that will make the analysis of regulatory takings seem simplistic by comparison. Regulatory change is precipitating the competitive transformation of network industries served by public utilities long presumed to be natural monopolies and subjected to extensive rate regulation. The takings issue arises because those utilities assumed obligations to serve in return for the regulator's assurance that the utilities would have the opportunity to earn a competitive return on invested capital, along with the compensation for the full cost of providing service. Regulators

protect the utility's opportunity to earn a competitive return by controlling entry into its market. . . .

. . . [W]hen the state removes entry regulation, it will jeopardize the financial solvency of the public utility unless it simultaneously allows the utility to "rebalance" its rate structure to eliminate the implicit subsidies and unless the costs of incumbent burdens are either shared by all firms in the market or explicitly reimbursed by some third party.

See J. Gregory Sidak & Daniel F. Spulber, Deregulatory Takings and Breach of the Regulatory Contract, 71 N.Y.U. L. Rev. 851, 857–58 (1996); see also J. Gregory Sidak and Daniel F. Spulber, Givings Takings and the Fallacy of Forward–Looking Costs, 72 N.Y.U. L. Rev. 1068 (1997); Leigh H. Martin, Note: Deregulatory Takings: Stranded Investments and the Regulatory Compact in a Deregulated Electric Utility Industry, 31 Ga. L. Rev. 1183 (1997).

The takings argument does play an important role in the context of mandated open access of network facilities. Notions of physical invasion hold a grip on the definition of what constitutes a taking in the American legal mind. In, *Loretto v. Teleprompter Manhattan CATV Corp.*, 458 U.S. 419 (1982), the Supreme Court found that the use of a few square inches of property on the outside of a building for a cable television cable connection constituted a taking. The smallest physical invasion, according to *Loretto*, can constitute a taking. Thus, mandated open access of network facilities, such as power transmission lines, without compensation may be held to be a taking. In the context of a physical occupation, courts have not had the same reluctance they seem to have in finding a taking for failure to compensate stranded costs. *See Gulf Power Co. v. United States*, 998 F.Supp. 1386, 1394–95 (N.D.Fla.1998) (relying upon Sidak & Spulber to support the proposition that a permanent physical occupation of property constitutes a per se taking); *GTE Southwest, Inc. v. Public Utility Commission of Texas*, 10 S.W.3d 7 (Tex.Ct. of App., Austin 1999) (finding a taking based on *Loretto* where the Commission ordered GTE to revise its tariff to ensure reasonable, nondiscriminatory bases for decisions affecting access to customers by alternate service providers, including "the relocation of multiple demarcation points to a single point of demarcation on multi-unit premises").

However, that a physical invasion taking may exist under *Loretto* does not imply that stranded cost compensation is constitutionally mandated in all cases where stranded costs remain uncompensated. According to Stephen Williams, a judge on the U.S. Court of Appeals for the D.C. Circuit:

[Sidak and Spulber's] sketch of takings law strikes me as somewhat more protective than the present reality. For example, the authors observe that physical invasions generate an automatic entitlement to compensation, and in a way that is true. The article notes that sending a train down someone else's tracks is a physical invasion, and that invading a wire with particles is similar. But some regulations that look to me very much like government licenses for physical invasions by third parties, such as rent-control laws, are not treated as such, but rather as regulations of land use. I am not saying anything about the merits of the authors' position, only that it may not map perfectly onto the Supreme Court's previous analyses.

See Stephen F. Williams, Deregulatory Takings and Breach of the Regulatory Contract: A Comment, 71 N.Y.U. L. Rev. 1000, 1006 (1996).

Assuming that a regulators did remove entry barriers without providing full compensation for such stranded costs, what result would you predict given cases such as *Charles River Bridge*, *Market Street Railway*, and *Duquesne*? Are there any limitations on the constitutional case for recovery of stranded costs? If so, what are they? Is there any instance in which the constitutional claim recovery is a meritorious one? Consider the following case:

In the Matter of Energy Association of New York State v. Public Service Commission

169 Misc.2d 924, 653 N.Y.S.2d 502 (Sup. Ct., Albany Cty. 1996).

In March 1993 the Public Service Commission of the State of New York ("PSC") commenced the Herculean task of smoothing New York's transition to an increasingly competitive electric industry by instituting Phase I of an administrative proceeding designed to discuss, investigate and address relevant issues.

Phase II commenced in August 1994 "to identify regulatory and ratemaking practices that will assist in a transition to a more competitive electric industry designed to increase efficiency in the provision of electricity while maintaining safety, environmental, affordability, and service quality goals." This involved a broad and intensive collaboration on the part of the electric utilities and the PSC to develop potential models for restructuring the electric industry, culminating on May 20, 1996 with the issuance by the PSC of Opinion 96–12.

Opinion 96–12 contains three steps: (1) orders electric utilities to file plans on how they would restructure in a competitive marketplace; (2) rejects the utilities' claim that consumers, as a matter of law, must pay rates designed to recover every dollar of stranded costs, regardless of origin and ratepayer impact, reserving the issue for a factual case-by-case analysis and determination; and (3) sets forth a PSC policy statement on electric competition ("Vision Policy")....

In their petition, petitioners ask the Court to declare that the PSC may not direct retail wheeling, generation deregulation or asset divestiture....

The Commission policy statement adopted the principle of retail wheeling (utilities carrying electricity to end users in return for a reasonable "retail wheeling" rate) (without directing same), and established, as a goal, a January 1, 1998 implementation date. No direction was necessary because electricity rates have yet to be "unbundled" (i.e., disassembled and broken into their component parts), open transmission access has not yet taken effect, and given the "essential facilities" doctrine of the antitrust laws and anti-discrimination provisions of the Public Service Law, a retail wheeling directive ought not to be necessary.

[T]he PSC [is not] preempted from effectuating retail wheeling by any federal law. Section 201(b) of the Federal Power Act limits the jurisdiction of the Federal Energy Regulatory Commission ("FERC") to "the transmission of electric energy in interstate commerce and to the sale of electric energy at wholesale in interstate commerce." (16 U.S.C., sec. 824(b)). Further, section 201(a) of the Federal Power Act declares that ". . . federal regulation . . . extend[s] only to those matters which are not subject to regulation by the states." (16 U.S.C., sec. 824(a)). Finally, that retail wheeling is the province of state jurisdiction, becomes crystal clear from section 212(g) of the Federal Power Act, wherein it is stated that "no order [requiring transmission service] may be issued . . . which is inconsistent with any state law which governs the retail marketing areas of electric utilities." (16 U.S.C., sec. 824k(g)). [*See* also, Energy Policy Act of 1992 in which Congress reaffirmed that the regulation of retail electric sales is a matter of state jurisdiction].

Petitioners' constitutional claims against retail wheeling center around their contention that requiring them to carry competitors' electricity would amount to a "taking", even though said competitors would be required to pay "just and reasonable" rates. The argument then switches to the contention of petitioners that they must be afforded full "stranded costs."

In *Loretto v. Teleprompter Manhattan CATV Corp.*, 458 U.S. 419, 102 S.Ct. 3164, 73 L.Ed.2d 868 (1982) the U.S. Supreme Court did indeed hold a New York statute mandating a permanent attachment of cable television wires to a private building, amounted to a taking, but carefully emphasized the vital distinction between a permanent, physical occupation by a private enterprise and "a regulation that merely restricts the use of property." [Ibid., p. 430, 102 S.Ct. p. 3164]. Retail wheeling is not affected by this holding inasmuch as the carrying of a competitor's electricity is not a permanent, physical occupation, and further, that utilities are quasi-public. In *Rochester Gas and Elec. Corp. v. PSC*, 71 N.Y.2d 313, 525 N.Y.S.2d 809, 520 N.E.2d 528 (1988) the New York Court of Appeals rejected the argument that to require a utility to carry a competitor's natural gas resulted in a physical invasion of RG & E's distribution system, holding that to require a regulated utility to carry that which it has always carried does not amount to a taking inasmuch as the utility is not being forced to provide services beyond its original commitment, but is only being required to furnish services it has always provided (*See also, In re Pennsylvania Gas Co.*, 225 N.Y. 397, 122 N.E. 260 [1919], aff'd 252 U.S. 23, 40 S.Ct. 279, 64 L.Ed. 434 [1920]); *Pipeline Cases*, 234 U.S. 548, 34 S.Ct. 956, 58 L.Ed. 1459 [1913]; *Kansas City Power and Light Co. v. State Corp. Comm'n*, 238 Kan. 842, 715 P.2d 19 [1986], appeal dismissed, 479 U.S. 801, 107 S.Ct. 41, 93 L.Ed.2d 4 [1986], wherein the Court held that legislation mandating that electric utilities interconnect their facilities with those of private cogenerators did not constitute a taking. . . .

Opinion 96–12 encourages utilities to divest themselves of generation assets in order to facilitate the development of a competitive market place "not subject to the abuses of dominant market power" (168 PUR 4th 587, at n. 98). It does not, however, in fact direct divestiture. Nevertheless petitioners petition the Court for a declaration that the Commission lacks authority to do so. Though academic questions are not a proper subject for judicial review (*Cuomo v. Long Island Lighting*, 71 N.Y.2d 349, 525 N.Y.S.2d 828, 520 N.E.2d 546 [1988]), it is meaningful to note that divestiture may be effected through exercise of powers inherent in the PSC's discretion to set rates. . . .

In Opinion 96–12 the Public Service Commission rejected a claim by the utility industry that rates, as a matter of law, must be designed to reimburse them for every dollar that the utilities may lose due to competition.

The electric utility industry repeatedly professed recognition that a competitive electric marketplace was inevitable and in the public interest; it, however, conditioned its cooperation on an assurance that ratepayers would underwrite all stranded costs—in the context of this case, competitive losses. Having, as a matter of law, been denied that assurance, the utilities brought this petition denying a jurisdictional base for the other aspects of Opinion 96–12.

One of the arguments made by petitioners in support of their claims for total recovery of their stranded costs (as against the PSC decision, based on the law, to examine the recoverability of stranded costs on a case-by-case basis) is that they contracted with New York State to provide safe and reliable service in return for prudent cost recovery; that this constituted a "regulatory compact"; and that failure to guarantee full recovery of stranded costs constitutes a breach of contract. These arguments are contradicted by the Public Service Law and have repeatedly been rejected by the courts. (*See*, Public Service Law, sec. 72; *Abrams v. Public Serv. Comm'n*, 67 N.Y.2d 205, 212, 501 N.Y.S.2d 777, 492 N.E.2d 1193 [1986], which has interpreted section 72 as empowering the PSC to deny utilities recovery of prudent costs; *Matter of Consolidated Edison Co. of N.Y. v. PSC*, 53 A.D.2d 131, 134, 385 N.Y.S.2d 209 [3rd Dep't 1976], motion for leave to appeal denied, 40 N.Y.2d 803, 387 N.Y.S.2d 1030, 356 N.E.2d 482 wherein the court stated "other than the accomplishment of a just and reasonable result there is no requirement in law that any specific factor should be considered in fixing utility rates . . .").

Since the turn of the century, electric utilities have been on notice that they are required to serve the public need for electricity, not in return for a particular ratemaking method, but in return for a variety of powers traditionally reserved to the sovereign, including eminent domain and the use of public rights-of-way. (*Tismer v. The New York Edison Co.*, 228 N.Y. 585, 127 N.E. 923 [1920] (". . . the duty to serve would exist without the statute, for it results from the acceptance of the franchise of a public corporation".) *See also, In re Pennsylvania Gas Co.*, 225 N.Y. 397, 406, 122 N.E. 260 [1920]). If utilities fail to provide service, regardless of their rate levels, the PSC may take preventive, corrective or remedial action (PSL, sections 25, 65(1), 72); (*Matter of the PSC v. Jamaica Water Supply Co.*, 54 A.D.2d 10, 386 N.Y.S.2d 230 [1976], *aff'd* 42 N.Y.2d 880, 397 N.Y.S.2d 784, 366 N.E.2d 872 [1977]).

The basis of agency ratemaking authority has traveled a path from "fair value" of "used and useful" assets (*see Smyth v. Ames*, 169 U.S. 466, 18 S.Ct. 418, 42 L.Ed. 819 [1898]), this language giving way to "prudent investment" language, to specific valuation methods based on an "end-result test", which enables agencies to use any ratemaking method of their choosing provided that the "end result" of the process is "just and reasonable" rates. (*See Federal Power Comm'n v. Hope Natural Gas Co.*, 320 U.S. 591, 601–2, 64 S.Ct. 281, 287–88, 88 L.Ed. 333 [1944]).

"Just and reasonable" rates do not necessarily guarantee utilities net revenues nor do they immunize utilities from the effects of competition. "The due process clause ... has not and cannot be applied to insure values or to restore values that have been lost by the operation of economic forces." (*Mkt. St. Ry. Co. v. Railroad Comm'n of Cal.*, 324 U.S. 548, 567, 65 S.Ct. 770, 780, 89 L.Ed. 1171 [1945], *reh'g denied* 324 U.S. 890, 65 S.Ct. 1020, 89 L.Ed. 1438 [1945]). "Regulation does not insure that the business shall produce net revenues, nor does the Constitution require that the losses of the business in one year shall be restored from future earnings." (*Federal Power Commission v. Natural Gas Pipeline Co. of America*, 315 U.S. 575, 590, 62 S.Ct. 736, 745, 86 L.Ed. 1037 [1942]; *San Diego Land and Town Co. v. Jasper*, 189 U.S. 439, 447, 23 S.Ct. 571, 574, 47 L.Ed. 892 [1903]; *see also, Covington and Lexington Turnpike Rd. Co. v. Sandford*, 164 U.S. 578, 596, 17 S.Ct. 198, 205, 41 L.Ed. 560 [1896], wherein the court held that the public need not be subject to unreasonable rates so that stockholders may earn dividends; rather, in order to be "just and reasonable", rates simply must reflect a fair balancing of ratepayer and shareholder interests).

In *Los Angeles Gas and Electric Corp. v. Railroad Comm'n of Cal.*, 289 U.S. 287, 306, 53 S.Ct. 637, 644, 77 L.Ed. 1180 [1933], the Court wrote that "while cost must be considered, the Court has held that it is not an exclusive or final test. The public have not underwritten the investment." And in *PSC of Mont. v. Great Northern Utilities Co.*, 289 U.S. 130, 135, 53 S.Ct. 546, 548, 77 L.Ed. 1080 [1933], the Court expounded "[t]he loss of, or the failure to obtain, patronage, due to competition, does not justify the imposition of charges that are exorbitant and unjust to the public. The Constitution ... does not protect public utilities against such business hazards."

The New York Public Service Commission generally has based rates on projections of prudent costs, but when necessary it has deviated from that procedure in order to avoid excessive or unreasonable rates. (*See: Matter of Rochester Gas and Electric Corp. v. PSC*, 108 A.D.2d 35, 488 N.Y.S.2d 303 [3rd Dep't 1985]; *Matter of St. Lawrence Gas Co. v. PSC*, 42 N.Y.2d 461,

398 N.Y.S.2d 868, 368 N.E.2d 1234 [1977], wherein the Court confirmed a Commission decision denying a utility rate recovery of losses due to competition; *PSC Case 27032, Central Hudson Gas and Electric Corporation (Central Hudson), Opinion No. 77–6*, 17 N.Y. PSC 401, 408–9 [1977], wherein the Commission denied a utility rate recovery of a portion of carrying charges on excess capacity that was prudently constructed; *PSC Case 26943, Niagara Mohawk Corporation, Opinion 76–23*, 16 N.Y. PSC 908, 923–930 [1976]).

The rule of *Smyth v. Ames, supra*, does not prevail today. "In 1942 in its decision in *Power Comm'n v. Pipeline Co.*, 315 U.S. 575, 62 S.Ct. 736, 86 L.Ed. 1037, the Supreme Court overruled so much of *Smyth v. Ames* as prescribed a requirement for valuation based on 'fair value.' The Court held that 'the Constitution does not bind the ratemaking bodies to the service of any single formula or combination of formulas' (*Id.* at p. 586, 62 S.Ct. at p. 743). Two years later, in the landmark decision of *Power Comm'n. v. Hope Gas Co.*, 320 U.S. 591, 64 S.Ct. 281, supra), the Court reaffirmed the rules stated in Power Comm'n v. Pipeline Co., supra and added that 'it is the result reached not the method employed which is controlling' (*Id.*, at p. 602, 64 S.Ct. at p. 288). Unless shown to be 'unjust and unreasonable,' the rates are valid." (*Abrams, supra*, at p. 213, 501 N.Y.S.2d 777, 492 N.E.2d 1193).

> "In New York, the courts and the PSC have availed themselves of the latitude afforded by Hope Gas Co., supra and have not insisted upon a rigid approach (cites omitted) . . . there is no Federal proscription against the use of the "prudent investment" test . . . Of course, the New York Public Service Commission is not bound under Hope Gas Co., supra to use the "prudent investment" approach and, indeed, it has not always done so (cites omitted). . . . But if the end result is a just and reasonable balancing of consumer and investor interests, the PSC may employ the "prudent investment" test or any other formula or combination of formulae without offending the Federal Constitution or decisional law." (*Abrams, supra*, pp. 214–215, 501 N.Y.S.2d 777, 492 N.E.2d 1193).

When the wheat is separated from the chaff, the one immutable rule of ratemaking comes down to this: Is the "end result" "just and reasonable"—and fair as between the utilities' customers and their stockholders. That is a determination of the regulatory body, subject only to the prohibition against arbitrary and capricious decisionmaking. The Courts must otherwise defer to the expertise of the regulatory body!■

———

As the New York case suggests, the constitutional case for recovery of stranded costs may have been greatly overstated by some advocates, such as Sidak and Spulber. According to Jim Chen,

> Judicial endorsement of [Sidak and Spulber's argument for] *Deregulatory Takings* would reinvigorate not only the confiscatory ratemaking doctrine [of *Smyth v. Ames*] but also another economically charged

constitutional doctrine of the early twentieth century—the substantive due process analysis of Lochner v. New York. "Within the modern legal academy, '*Lochner*' has become an epithet used to characterize an outmoded, over-narrow way of thinking about ... economic regulation." *Smyth* and the confiscatory ratemaking doctrine played a central role during the *Lochner* era. Indeed, ratemaking controversies were arguably "[t]he most significant cases in the [*Lochner*-era] Court's campaign to expand the definition of property and takings." But confiscatory ratemaking survived the uprising against *Lochner* because of, not in spite of, its basis in the Takings Clause. This independent constitutional foundation shielded *Smyth* and its kin during "the demise of economic substantive due process in the federal courts."

Jim Chen, The Second Coming of *Smyth v. Ames*, 77 Tex. L. Rev. 1535, 1555 (1999) (cited sources omitted). It has also been noted that Sidak and Spulber argument gives short shrift to key cases in the history of utility regulation, such as *Charles River Bridge* (*see* Chapter Three, *infra*). *See* Herbert Hovenkamp, The Takings Clause and Improvident Regulatory Bargains, 108 Yale L.J. 801 (1999) (book review). What do you think?

If accepted as a principle of constitutional law, the entitlement to stranded cost recovery has serious implications for regulatory policy generally, not only for deregulation. Recall, for example, the history of hydroelectric power. Early in the twentieth century, the federal government approved many public power projects. An example is the Tennessee Valley Authority (TVA), established as a part of FDR's New Deal programs in the 1930's. Many private utilities (as well as coal and ice companies) challenged TVA on the grounds that government-produced electricity would cause irreparable economic harm to them. A series of constitutional challenges against TVA was mounted, but the appellate courts rejected these challenges. Although not expressly framed as taking cases, a trial court hearing a series of challenges by nineteen utilities took the position that the utilities were threatened with future economic harm; however, the court also noted that the injury would be *damnun absque injuria* unless TVA itself was unlawful. The court reasoned:

> Since the United States has acquired these dam sites and constructed these dams legally, the water power, the right to convert it to electric energy, and the energy produced constitute power belonging to the United States.... This electric energy may be rightfully disposed of.... While the Government, in selling property of the United States, performs many functions that would be performed inn the operation of a private business trading in similar property, inasmuch as the energy sold is created at dams lawfully erected within the Federal power, the Government in performing these functions is not entering into private business. It is merely using an appropriate method of disposing of its property. The Government may sell land belonging to the United States in competition with a real estate agency, carry parcels in competition with express companies, and manage and control its thousands of square miles of national parks even as a private company. The

Government has an equal right to sell hydroelectric power, lawfully created, in competition with a private utility....

Tennessee Electric Power Co. v. TVA, 21 F.Supp. 947, 959–61 (E.D.Tenn. 1938). This case was appealed to the U.S. Supreme Court but the Court dismissed the case for lack of standing. Although not quite as quote-worthy, the Supreme Court's opinion basically holds that a legal right is necessary for standing, but that there is no legal right to be free from competition resulting from the activities of the federal government. *Tennessee Electric Power Co. v. TVA*, 306 U.S. 118 (1939). The Court reasoned (citing *Charles River Bridge* and other cases), "The local franchises, while having elements of property, confer no contractual or property right to be free of competition either from individuals, other public utility corporations, or the state or municipality granting the franchise. The grantor may preclude itself by contract from initiating or permitting such competition, but no such contractual obligation is here asserted." *Id.* at 138. For discussion of the TVA cases, *see* Joseph Swildler & Robert Marquis, TVA in Court: A Study of TVA's Constitutional Litigation, 32 Iowa L. Rev. 296, 197 n.6 (1947); George D. Haimbaugh, Jr., The TVA Cases: A Quarter Century Later, 41 Ind. L.J. 197 (1965).

In *Evac v. Pataki*, 89 F.Supp.2d 250 (N.D. N.Y. 2000), a private medical air transport company sued the state of New York, alleging that its establishment of free transport service was unconstitutional. The court dismissed the claim, rejecting the procedural and substantive due process claim because there is no protectable property interest in customers. In addition, the takings claim was rejected. After examining the *Penn Central* factors, the court stated, "An examination of these factors indicates that because the State did not physically invade, permanently appropriate, or nullify all economically viable uses of Evac's property, the State's provision of free medical transport services does not amount to a compensable taking."

Even if stranded cost claims succeed in their substance, they may face significant practical litigation barriers. One such barrier is the ripeness requirement in takings cases. How can utilities prove damages that have not yet ben fully realized? In *Texas Office of Public Utility Counsel v. FCC*, 183 F.3d 393 (1999), it was held that a stranded cost challenge to the FCC's universal service financing mechanism was not ripe for a constitutional challenge because the company challenging the FCC policy had not proved any lost revenue. GTE challenged the FCC's decision to leave incumbent local telephone utilities exposed to local competition without first implementing the new universal service plan results in a severe reduction of its revenues from local service. GTE argued that a regulated entity cannot be forced to operate one segment of its business at a loss on the expectation that it can make up the shortfalls from another competitive line of business. The Fifth Circuit rejected GTE's argument, reasoning:

GTE has failed to meet the requirements of Duquesne, because it cannot show that it will lose any revenue at all, much less enough to constitute a taking under more recent precedent. Its attempt to distinguish Duquesne is misguided because, contrary to GTE's claim, the Duquesne Court did not base its finding of takings on the fact that the market was no longer closed to competition.

Rather, Duquesne stands for the proposition that "no single rate-making methodology is mandated by the Constitution, which looks to the consequences a governmental authority produces rather than the techniques it employs." *Duquesne, 488 U.S. at 299* (Scalia, J., concurring). Duquesne does not require courts to engage in a takings analysis whenever an agency opens a previously regulated market to competition.

Texas Office of Public Utility Counsel v. FCC, 183 F.3d 393, 437 (5th Cir. 1999). This may not be the last word on how the ripeness doctrine applies in deregulatory takings cases, as the Supreme Court has granted certiorari to hear an appeal of this case. *See GTE Service Corp. v. FCC*, 120 S.Ct. 2214 (2000).

Consider, for example, recent litigation raising a takings challenge to deregulation policies for the electric utility industry in Pennsylvania. PECO Energy, a utility, drafted a partial settlement that would have established a competitive transition charge to recover what it claimed were over $5 billion in stranded costs. The Pennsylvania Public Utility Commission (PUC) rejected PECO's compromise, which contained a mandated rate reduction, in large part because it believed the utility was overreaching in its claim for stranded costs. In the end, the Commission allowed recovery of some stranded costs, but substantially less than the utility had sought. Although the case has since settled, the facts raise several difficult legal issues.

First, could PECO establish the existence of a regulatory compact? Whether deregulation is a "taking" will depend upon a showing of a regulatory compact, a commitment on behalf of government to bear the bulk of the risk of regulatory change. The evidence of such a commitment proffered by PECO would include statutes, regulations, orders approving plant construction projects, rate orders, and tariffs. In other words, PECO would have to rely almost entirely on sources of public law to establish the existence of a contract, but probably would not have an express government statement—and certainly would not have unmistakably unambiguous language in these sources of law—that government will protect industry from regulatory change. Instead, as with most statements of law, some ambiguity as to the future would likely be implicit. It is hardly going to be easy for utilities to prove the existence of a government commitment, which will be necessary to compel compensation under the deregulatory takings jurisprudence Sidak and Spulber advocate.

Second, could PECO prove that the PUC's breach of the regulatory compact is causally related to the damage it claims it suffered? Causation complications arise, because endogenous changes in regulation are often the result of—or at least occur simultaneously with—changing technological and economic conditions, which Sidak and Spulber characterize as exogenous. According to Sidak and Spulber, "Exogenous shocks are external effects such as fluctuations in market demand, variations in the cost of labor, equipment, and technology, and environmental factors such as the effects of weather on electric power usage, or the effects of adverse weather conditions on the operation of the utility's facilities. Endogenous shocks are determined by the effects of the regulator's actions on the riskiness of the utility's stream of earnings over time." Sidak and Spulber suggest that changes in economic and technological conditions, as in *Market Street Railway*, do not necessarily warrant compensation, but that independent government changes in regulation do. Yet separating endogenous from exogenous factors is not a task that a court will be able to perform easily. The task will be greatly complicated to the extent that endogenous government regulation is a reaction to—or an effort to mitigate—the very exogenous shocks that the authors claim do not necessarily warrant compensation as a matter of law and policy.

Third, and related to the causation issue, what is the damage that PECO incurred? PECO followed the Commission's decision by taking a $3.1 billion write-off, in anticipation of losses it claimed to be a result of the Commission's decision. Yet PECO's common stock prices were $22.93 a share before it filed its settlement, and $23.96 a share immediately after the Commission's decision. The day after the PUC's decision and again later, Standard & Poor's affirmed its ratings of PECO. Several months later, PECO's stock had climbed to $30 a share. Assuming a taking can be established, damages will be extremely difficult, if not impossible, to prove ex ante. While ripeness and finality requirements are satisfied as soon as regulators have adopted specific plans for deregulation, it could take years for a taking to materialize for purposes of measuring compensation.

Sidak and Spulber argue that efficient investment markets will immediately recognize losses due to deregulation. Two problems, however, plague investment market data measures of damages. To begin, what today is considered obsolete technology may still have some substantial economic value in a deregulated environment. For example, while "many predict that nuclear power will not be able to compete in the increasingly deregulated electricity market," utilities that possess such assets have engaged in serious negotiations aimed at selling them. Not all generation assets that utilities today claim as stranded by deregulation will necessarily lack economic value in the competitive environment. Due to loss aversion, the potential losses from changing the status quo are more likely to influence investors than are uncertain gains. Uncertainty about the future may lead investors to discount the benefits to the firm of a competitive market.

A second problem that complicates the analysis relates to the proof of damages. Aggregate, firm-wide financial data will be of little assistance to regulators because deregulation will bring benefits to many utilities that also claim losses. For example, many utilities that own inefficient or obsolete generation facilities also will incur stranded benefits in a competitive industry due to their valuable distribution and transmission systems, including their rights of way. Without complete data, courts would be foolish to compensate utility write-offs taken for strategic economic reasons in the face of future uncertainty about the nature and degree of competition in the industry. Strategic behavior by utilities may bias the information regarding losses available to investors today, leading to exaggerations in the costs of deregulation as measured by investor behavior data.

See Jim Rossi, The Irony of Deregulatory Takings, 77 Tex. L. Rev. 297, 311–313 (1998) (book review); *see also* Steve Isser & Steven A. Mitnick, Enron's Battle With PECO, Public Utilities Fortnightly, Mar. 1, 1998, at 38 (discussing Pennsylvania litigation).

Although courts have been reluctant to endorse the argument, the prospect of takings claims for failing to allow or consider stranded cost recovery remains a legitimate legal concern for regulators as they restructure the industry. Ratemaking takings cases, such as *Duquesne* (Chapter 8), suggest that courts routinely defer to regulators' judgments about which cost recovery mechanisms are best for the industry. As Richard Pierce has stated:

> Detailed judicial review of ratemaking has little, if any, effect in constraining the political process. Moreover, the judicial review process imposes high error costs and high judicial resource costs. Thus, the "end results" test announced in Hope can be seen as a decision to allocate to the political institutions of government near total power to protect the constitutional values underlying the takings clause in the ratemaking context. This is required by the severe institutional limitations of the judiciary as a potential source of protection for these values.

Richard J. Pierce, Jr., Public Utility Regulatory Takings: Should the Judiciary Attempt to Police the Political Institutions, 77 Geo. L.J. 2031, 2032 (1989). As with utility ratemaking, courts might decide to defer to the political process, which an agency or legislature, for the best solution to the stranded cost recovery problem. Arguably, however, a different set of takings principles could apply in a restructured industry, especially if regulation is no longer the norm. In a totally deregulated environment, the Supreme Court's regulatory takings jurisprudence could apply. And if recent land use cases suggest any trend, the Court might be less willing to defer to regulatory action if it is not considered to be ratemaking.

3. BREACH OF CONTRACT

In *United States v. Winstar Corp.*, the Supreme Court allowed the U.S. government to be sued for breach of contract following Congress's enactment of a statute eliminating the government's contractual obligations with savings and loan institutions. 518 U.S. 839, 843 (1996). Sidak and Spulber *see Winstar* case as providing another legal basis for compensation of stranded costs:

J. Gregory Sidak & Daniel F. Spulber, Givings, Takings, and the Fallacy of Forward–Looking Costs

72 N.Y.U. L. Rev. 1068, 1147–50 (1997).

The Supreme Court's 1996 decision in *United States v. Winstar Corp.*, while not addressing a regulated network industry, does indicate how the

Court would likely view a case involving recovery of stranded costs arising from breach of the regulatory contract in such an industry.... To appreciate Winstar's relevance to the regulatory contract, it is necessary first to review the essential facts of the case.

Three thrifts sued the United States for breach of contract after they had been declared in violation of the capital requirements of the new Financial Institutions Reform, Recovery, and Enforcement Act of 1989 (FIRREA). The thrifts argued that savings and loan regulators had promised to indemnify them from the type of regulatory change that FIRREA produced. During the savings and loan crisis of the 1980s, the Federal Home Loan Bank Board sought to induce healthy thrifts to merge with failing ones. The Board signed agreements with the healthy thrifts that allowed them to count the excess of the purchase price over the fair market value of the acquired assets as an intangible asset—"supervisory goodwill"—that counted toward fulfilling capital reserve requirements.

The Board agreed to allow the healthy thrifts to amortize supervisory goodwill over twenty-five to forty years—an extended period that would give the healthy thrifts a reasonable opportunity to recover their costs of rehabilitating the sick thrifts. Without those regulatory agreements, the thrifts created by the mergers would have violated the capital reserve requirements. Thus, the healthy thrifts' investment in the sick thrifts never would have happened. Overall, however, the Board's practice of encouraging such merged thrifts turned out to be a failure and promised to lead to the insolvency of federal deposit insurance funds for the thrifts. Eventually, Congress enacted FIRREA, which forbade thrifts from counting supervisory goodwill toward capital requirements. Regulators promptly seized and liquidated two of the three plaintiff thrifts in Winstar for failing to comply with the new capital reserve requirements; the third avoided seizure only by aggressively recapitalizing.

A plurality of the Supreme Court upheld the determination by the U.S. Court of Appeals for the Federal Circuit that the government had breached contractual obligations to the thrifts and was liable for breach of contract. One of the government's defenses was the "unmistakability" doctrine, under which surrenders of sovereign authority, to be enforceable, must appear in unmistakable terms in a contract. Justices Souter, Stevens, O'Connor, and Breyer found that the defense did not apply to the contracts at issue, because the plaintiffs were suing not to stop the government from changing capital reserve requirements applicable to thrifts, but only to compel the government to indemnify them for the effects of such changes. Justices Scalia, Kennedy, and Thomas did not accept that distinction between injunctive relief and damages but nonetheless found that the particular contracts at issue established that the government had unmistakably agreed to indemnify the thrifts. Chief Justice Rehnquist dissented in an opinion partially joined by Justice Ginsburg.■

NOTES AND COMMENTS

1. The Court remanded *Winstar* for determination of damages. *See* 518 U.S. at 843. In two cases nearly identical cases on remand, two courts

arrived at vastly different damages awards; one court awarded $909 million the other awarded $24 million. *See* Steve France, Goodwill Hunting, ABA Journal, June 1999, at 38. The resolution of these damages on appeal will significantly impact the savings and loan institutions; they have filed more than 120 related suits against the government. *See id.* Their resolution may also significantly impact other industries, including the electric utility industry. *See, e.g.* J. Gregory Sidak & Daniel F. Spulber, Deregulatory Takings and Breach of the Regulatory Contract (1997).

2.   In *Winstar*, the Supreme Court allowed the breach of contract claims against the federal government to go forward, although the Court noted that clear and unmistakable language in a contract was a predicate to the suits. As Sidak and Spulber note, to the extent states or the federal government have waived sovereign immunity with respect to the utilities they regulate, the *Winstar* cases raises a possibility for of lawsuits based on breach of contract for failure to allow stranded cost recovery in the utility industry. In the electric utility industry it is likely that breach of contract claims will proceed against the states, rather than the federal government. (Why is this?) Many states have waived sovereign immunity for breach of contract, and the government contract principles articulated in *Winstar* may be applicable by analogy to a breach of contract case against an individual state. In addition to sovereign immunity, however, a variety of legal issues will need to be addressed in order for these claims to succeed.

In a lawsuit involving an alleged breach of contract, the first issue is whether a contract exists. Commentators debate whether the "regulatory compact" (or "regulatory contract") that may exist between the government and the utilities must be based on express terms. *See* William J. Baumol & Thomas W. Merrill, Deregulatory Takings, Breach of the Regulatory Contract, and the Telecommunications Act of 1996, 72 N.Y.U. L. Rev. 1037, 1045 (1997) (criticizing J. Gregory Sidak & Daniel F. Spulber, Deregulatory Takings and Breach of the Regulatory Contract, 71 N.Y.U. L. Rev. 851 (1996)); *see also* Leigh H. Martin, Deregulatory Takings: Stranded Investments and the Regulatory Compact in a Deregulated Electric Utility Industry, 31 Ga. L. Rev. 1183, 1215 (1997). Sidak and Spulber, relying on *Winstar*, argue that the regulatory compact regulators promises utilities to operate as monopolies, recovery for the historical cost of specific investments or investors the opportunity to earn a competitive return on their investment.

William Baumol and Thomas Merrill, in a response, disagree with Sidak and Spulber's reading of *Winstar*.

> At issue in the case was whether the federal government could be sued for breach of contract by the acquiring S & Ls. Four Justices joined in Justice Souter's plurality opinion, which would have recognized an exception to the unmistakability doctrine for government "indemnification" agreements holding entities harmless in the event of future changes in regulation. However, a majority of five Justices rejected such an exception. Justice Scalia, joined by two other Justices, saw no need to create the exception, because in his view the contracts

in question unmistakably promised the acquiring S & Ls they would receive favorable accounting treatment. Chief Justice Rehnquist, joined by one other Justice, also rejected the exception, but found that the doctrine was not satisfied. Thus, by a vote of five to four, Winstar reaffirmed the unmistakability doctrine and rejected Justice Souter's proposed exception. The Court disagreed about the application of the doctrine in the specific context presented, but did not call into question the doctrine's continued validity.

William J. Baumol & Thomas W. Merrill, Deregulatory Takings, Breach of the Regulatory Contract, and the Telecommunications Act of 1996, 72 N.Y.U. L. Rev. 1037, 1046 (1997) Baumol and Merrill's reading of Winstar is consistent with the case law. While promises must be in express terms—according to *Winstar*, "unmistakable"—"in grants by the public, nothing passes by implication." *See* Herbert Hovenkamp, The Takings Clause and Improvident Regulatory Bargains, 108 Yale L.J. 801, 811 (1997) (quoting *Charles River Bridge v. Warren Bridge* 36 U.S. (Pet. 11) 420, 546 (1837); *Winstar*, 518 U.S. at 877 (*citing Merrion v. Jicarilla Apache Tribe*, 455 U.S. 130, 148 (1982) (holding that waiver of the sovereign power to tax could not be inferred from silence); *Energy Ass'n of New York v. Public Serv. Comm'n of New York,* 653 N.Y.S.2d 502, 514 (1996) (including eminent domain and use of public rights-of-way as sovereign powers). Under U.S. case law, there is a presumption that general language in statutes and regulations "is not intended to create private contractual or vested rights but merely declares a policy to be pursued until the legislature shall ordain otherwise." *National R.R. Passenger v, Atchison, Topeka & Sante Fe Ry.*, 470 U.S. 451, 466 (1985) (quoting *Dodge v. Board of Education*, 302 U.S. 74, 79 (1937)). Nevertheless, in some instances utilities may be able to find language in a corporate charter, franchise agreement, public utility statute, or a long-standing judicial doctrine that at least arguably establishes express contractual terms.

3.   Assuming a "regulatory compact" establishes a contractual relationship between government and a public utility, the next issue is whether a breach occurred. Deregulation of an electric utility does not necessarily result in a breach of contract. For example, in *Energy Ass'n of New York v. Public Serv. Comm'n of New York*, the court rejected a utility's argument that the "failure to guarantee full recovery of stranded costs constitutes breach of contract." 653 N.Y.S.2d 502, 513–514 (1996). Instead, the court held "just and reasonable rates do not necessarily ... immunize utilities from the effects of competition." *Id.* Thus, only those utilities expressly contracting for monopolies will be probably be able to have such monopolies recognized and enforced. *See* Herbert Hovenkamp, The Takings Clause and Improvident Regulatory Bargains, 108 Yale L.J. 801, 811 (1997) (citing *In re Binghamton Bridge*, 70 U.S. (3 Wall.) 51, 82 (1865) ("enforcing an explicit monopoly provision in a corporate charter").

4.   Assuming a utility proves breach of contract, the court must address remedies. Courts will look "to the effect of a contract's enforcement" rather than the "particular remedy sought." *Winstar*, 518 U.S. at 880

(discussing the applicability of the doctrine of unmistakability). The three traditional contract damage measures of relief are expectancy, reliance, and restitution. A plaintiff's expectation interest is his "interest in having the benefit of his bargain by being put in as good a position as he would have been had the contract been formed." Restatement (Second) of Contracts § 344(a) (1981). But, in the stranded cost context, these damages are largely speculative; some utilities, for example, have alleged stranded costs in generation assets, only later to sell these generation assets at greater than the book value they claimed was stranded. While post-*Winstar* courts awarded starkly disparate damages to thrifts, they have ruled plaintiffs cannot recover for speculative damages. *See Glendale Federal Bank v. United States*, No. 90–772C, 1999 U.S. Claims LEXIS 70 (Apr. 9, 1999); *see also California Federal Bank v. United States*, No. 92–138C, 1999 U.S. Claims LEXIS 77 (Apr. 16, 1999).

It will be difficult, if not impossible, for monopolistic utilities to prove lost profits. For example, accurately predicting the power consumption of Las Vegas today would have required nothing less than a crystal ball fifty years ago. In *Kenford Co., Inc. v. County of Eerie*, the court addressed whether a plaintiff could recover lost profits for the contemplated 20–year operation of a stadium. 493 N.E.2d 234 (N.Y.1986). "The multitude of assumptions required to establish projection of profitability over the life of this contract require speculation and conjecture, making it beyond the capability of even the most sophisticated procedures to satisfy the legal requirements of proof with reasonable certainty." *Id.* at 236. In addition, the uncertainties inherent in lost profit models pose challenges in distinguishing between objective and subjective probabilities about future. *See* Franco Modigliani and Kalman Cohen, The Role of Anticipations and Plans in Economic Behavior and Their Use in Economic Analysis and Forecasting, Studies in Business Expectations and Planning No. 4, University of Illinois Bulletin, Jan. 1961, Vol. 58 No. 38 at 66–67 (discussing the expected utility theory and subjective probability distributions). Thus, it is highly unlikely utilities will recover lost profits until they are realized.

Utilities will also seek reliance damages, and this may be their strongest claim to a loss for breach of contract. A party's reliance interest is his "interest in being reimbursed for loss caused by reliance on the contract by being put in as good a position as he would have been in had the contract not been made." Restatement (Second) of Contracts § 344(b) (1981). To recover reliance damages, utilities must "prove losses for actual outlay and expenditure." *See Glendale* at *12 (quoting *United States v. Behan*, 110 U.S. 338, 345 (1884). Yet, lower prices under deregulation may increase demand for power. "Power plants that had been written off as stranded by deregulation are in fact finding strong market demand." Hovenkamp, *supra*, at 804. As a result, awarding a utility the full costs of its investments may bestow a windfall upon it by placing it in better a position than they would have been had there been no contract. Therefore, damage awards must be made on an ad hoc basis.

Even utilities with express monopolies may face one last hurdle. Under *Hadley v. Baxendale*, the consequences of a breach of contract must be foreseeable by the parties at the time of contracting. 9 Ex. 341 (1854). "When the California Public Utilities Commission announced that it would begin proceedings that would lead to the introduction of retail wheeling ... three major utilities experienced twenty percent declines in share prices almost overnight." Hovenkamp, *supra*, at 833 (citation omitted). "If the shareholders reasonable expectation was that they would be perfectly compensated for these losses, however, then shareholder price should not have declined at all." *Id.* Consequently, sales of stock by utilities (and their top management) following deregulation announcements may demonstrate whether utilities believed they were actually granted monopolies.

Although the breach of contract claim seems questionable, it is not without some merit. But courts to date have required clear contracts as a basis for protection of the utility's interest in stranded cost recovery. For example, the Public Service Company of New Hampshire had been promised by the State of New Hampshire recovery of a specific investment of $2.3 billion in a bankruptcy proceeding. PSNH successfully obtained an injunction against a New Hampshire restructuring plan that did not guarantee recovery of the costs of this investment. In reviewing the district court injunction, the U.S. Court of Appeals for the First Circuit determined that there was a likelihood of success on the merits, given the specific agreements between the utility and state and federal regulators. The court also noted that the possibility of irreparable harm from bankruptcy made issuance of a preliminary injunction appropriate. *See Public Service Co. of New Hampshire v. Patch*, 167 F.3d 15 (1st Cir.1998). However, the First Circuit held that the district court was incorrect in its decision to issue an injunction against implementation of New Hampshire's plan for all New Hampshire utilities:

> The district court's extension of the injunction to protect all other New Hampshire electric utilities is more troublesome. Although the other utilities have joined in attacks on the Final Plan similar to those made by PSNH, it is not clear that they can assert the Contracts Clause or bankruptcy reorganization arguments that made PSNH's case so appealing to the district court. Nor is it evident that utilities are constitutionally insulated against losses that result merely from a change in rate regulation that introduces competition.

Id. at 28. *See also Public Service Co. of New Hampshire v. Patch*, 167 F.3d 29 (1st Cir.1998) (rejecting federal preemption claim based on the "filed rate doctrine," arguing that tariffs filed with FERC preclude New Hampshire from denying stranded cost recovery, and rejecting injunction claim by utilities that lack clear contract guaranteeing recovery from previous bankruptcy reorganization).

C. MITIGATING DAMAGES: ASSET SECURITIZATION

The damages utilities face due to the stranded cost problem are very uncertain. Numerous power plants have been sold by utilities at above book value, suggesting that many assets will have value above utilities' expectations even in a competitive environment. *See* Power Plant Sales Raise Questions About Stranded Costs, Consumers' Bills, Antitrust and Trade Reg. Daily (FNA) (Feb. 6, 1998). Thus, overcompensation of the loss caused by the stranded cost problem is a real risk, especially given uncertainties in the total amount of the harm utilities and investors may suffer.

Given this uncertainty, even if the legal and policy arguments supporting recovery of stranded costs are successful, utilities will likely be subjected to an obligation to mitigate any damages they expect to suffer due to restructuring. To mitigate costs and secure stranded cost recovery, many utilities are experimenting with a novel regulatory solution called "asset securitization." Sidak and Spulber have defended securitization:

> The proceeds from the bond issuance would enable the incumbent utility to recoup its stranded costs immediately. The utility would use the bonds to shift the risk of stranded cost recovery from current shareholders to a new class of consenting bondholders, whose recourse relative to other creditors would presumably be limited to the stream of revenues [from consumer surcharges]. The incumbent utility could no longer oppose immediate competitive entry on grounds of cost recovery.

J. Gregory Sidak & Daniel F. Spulber, Givings, Takings, and the Fallacy of Forward–Looking Costs, 72 N.Y.U. L. Rev. 1068, 1154 (1997). To understand why many utilities are finding this option attractive, some explanation of asset securitization is first necessary.

1. CONVENTIONAL ASSET SECURITIZATION

Securitization is a financing tool that is utilized by a company to lower its cost of funds. Securitization involves the financing of an underlying asset of some value (*e.g.*, a mortgage or an automobile loan). "In securitization, a company partly 'deconstructs' itself by separating certain types of highly liquid assets from the risks generally associated with the company." *See* Steven L. Schwarcz, The Alchemy of Asset Securitization, 1 Stan. J.L. Bus. & Fin. 133, 134 (1994). "The company can then use these assets to raise funds in the capital markets at a lower cost than if the company, with its associated risks, could have raised the funds directly by issuing more debt or equity." *Id.* Securitization is also defined as

> the sale of equity or debt instruments, representing ownership interests in, or secured by, a segregated, income-producing asset or pool of assets, in a transaction structured to reduce or reallocate certain risks inherent in owning or lending against the underlying assets and to ensure that such interests are more readily marketable and, thus, more liquid than ownership shares against the underlying assets.

Joseph C. Shenker & Anthony J. Colletta, Asset Securitization: Evolution, Current Issues and New Frontiers, 69 Tex. L. Rev. 1369, 1374–75 (1991).

Securitization is a process that begins with the identification of a sponsor's assets that can be used to raise funds. *See id.* at 1376 (referring to a "sponsor' as the economic owner of the asset and to an "originator" as the entity that created the asset). "Assets most suitable for securitization are those with standardized terms, delinquency and loss experience that can support an actuarial analysis of expected losses, and uniform underwriting standards and servicing procedures satisfactory to rating agencies and investors." *See id.* at 1377. Once the assets are chosen, the sponsor transfers the assets (typically called "receivables") to a legally separate entity referred to as a special purpose vehicle (SPV). Steven L. Schwarcz, The Alchemy of Asset Securitization, 1 Stan. J.L. Bus. & Fin. 133, 135 (1994). "To raise funds to purchase these receivables, the SPV issues securities in the capital markets." *Id.* The SPV then uses the receivables it acquired to repay investors in the future. *See id.* at 136.

The goal of securitization is to obtain lower cost funds by the separating the sponsor's receivables from the sponsor's risks. *See id.* The SPV's lower cost of funds is passed on to the sponsor through a relatively higher selling price for the sponsor's receivables. *See id.* To determine whether a company should employ securitization, the sponsor should weigh the anticipated cost savings from securitization against the transaction costs of securitization (e.g., underwriters' fees). *Id.* at 137–138. Transaction costs aside, securitization is most valuable when the cost of funds obtained through securitization is less than the cost of the sponsor's other sources of funding. *See id.* at 136.

The structure of the transfer of assets from the sponsor to the SPV is important to investors and rating agencies from a bankruptcy standpoint. The sponsor frequently structures the transfer as a "true sale" to remove the receivables from the sponsor's bankruptcy estate. *See id.* at 135 (citations omitted). The sponsor also structures the SPV so that it is "bankruptcy remote" to prevent creditors from filing an involuntary bankruptcy petition against the SPV. *See id.* "To achieve bankruptcy remoteness, the SPV's organizational structure strictly limits its permitted business activities." *Id.*

Asset-backed securities resulted from the federal government's desire to increase the availability of funds for housing finance. *See* Joseph C. Shenker & Anthony J. Colletta, Asset Securitization: Evolution, Current Issues and New Frontiers, 69 Tex. L. Rev. 1369, 1383 (1991). "In 1971, The Federal Home Loan Mortgage Corporation issued the first mortgage . . . security backed by conventional loans." *Id.* Later developments in the evolution of securitization include collateralized mortgage obligations (CMO's):

> The earliest asset backed securities were based upon mortgage obligations and employ large pools of mortgage loans to 'collateralize' the securities being issued. Development of these securities permitted mortgage lenders to access the security markets and thereby obtain greater capital available for mortgage loans at lesser cost. Examination of the payment history of like mortgage loans was performed which employed statistical methods to identify the expected magnitude of defaults and late or early payments. Sufficient loans were then includ-

ed in the collateral pool to provide assurance of recovery of the security's face value and interest, and to obtain thereby a desired AAA or AA credit rating and associated lower cost. The interest and principal repayment terms of the CMO were then established to match the anticipated cash flow from repayment of the mortgage loans.

Walter R. Hall, Securitization and Stranded Cost Recovery, 18 Energy L.J. 363, 378 (1997) (citations omitted).

2.   SECURITIZATION OF STRANDED ASSETS

It should come as no surprise that the utility industry finds securitization an attractive option. Much, but not all, discussion of stranded costs is focused on recovery of the costs of assets, which can be securitized using similar techniques to conventional asset securitization. (Securitization is more questionable when applied to those aspects of the stranded cost problem that are not assets.) Moody's Investors Service, a credit rating agency, estimates that utility securitizations in 1999 could be between $50 and $75 billion. *See* Lori A. Burkhart & Philip S. Cross, News Digest: Stranded Costs; Securitization, Pub. Util. Fort., Feb. 15, 1999 at 12.

Securitization of stranded costs enables a utility to receive cash "today, as opposed to a revenue stream generated ... over time." Calvin R. Wong, Emerging and Nonstandard Products: A Rating Agency's Prospective, 759 PLI/Comm 347, 371 (1997). As with stranded costs more generally, "[t]he recovery mechanism typically is either a customer charge or a usage-based charge that is imposed even if the retail customer ceases to purchase its electric supply from the historic utility." *Id.* Public utility commissions generally must approve these charges. Once approved, the utility transfers the rights to the charges to a special purpose vehicle (SPV). The SPV then purchases the rights to the charges with funds raised by issuing securities in the capital markets. The securities issued are often called "rate reduction bonds." Utilities may be required to obtain ratings from credit ratings agencies. In addition, utilities may need to obtain Internal Revenue Service rulings and issuance approvals from the Securities and Exchange Commission. Proceeds from the sale of rate reduction bonds may reduce interest expenses if they used to retire more expensive existing debt.

Yet, while asset securitization of stranded costs has some benefits from a cost mitigation perspective, securitization of stranded costs is different from securitization of conventional assets in a number of ways. First, and most importantly, traditional securitized assets are "already an enforceable contract right at the time of their securitization and require only collection by the servicing organization." Walter R. Hall, Securitization and Stranded Cost Recovery, 18 Energy L.J. 363, 385 (1997). However, in the utility restructuring context, the stranded cost issue suggest that property or contractual interests in recovery of the costs of the asset are often uncertain. Created by a *new* property interest, "stranded costs ... are to be collected only in connection with the provision of future electric service by the servicer or another organization." *Id.* Even where no new property interest is created, regulators have to concede the level of stranded cost recovery utilities are entitled to.[4]

But, "[e]stimating all future recovery *today* ignores future market price changes, provides poor incentives to mitigate uneconomic costs and locks in a payment stream for the utility that may prove completely inappropriate in the future." *See* Kenneth Rose, Securitization of Uneconomic Costs: Whom Does It Secure?, Pub. Util. Fort., June 1, 1997 at 32. Utility securitization is also subject to a periodic "true up" mechanism, which assures appropriate principal and interest collections when sales vary from projections. *See* Walter R. Hall, Securitization and Stranded Cost Recovery, 18 Energy L.J. 363, 385 (1997). But even adjustment mechanisms may be inadequate to protect remaining customers. For example, recovering exit fees from customers who leave the service territory may be difficult. *See* Calvin R. Wong, Emerging and Nonstandard Products: A Rating Agency's Prospective, 759 PLI/Comm 347, 372 (1997). This could lead to an (increased) securitization charge spread over a smaller customer base, causing customer rates to rise. *Id.*

A second difference is that one general objective of securitization is to remove securitized assets (and associated debt) from a company's balance sheet. However, the Securities and Exchange Commission's Office of Chief Accountant informed California's utilities that stranded costs cannot be removed from balance sheets. *See* Dean E. Criddle, Fundamental Principles of Electric Utility Securitization, 1082 PLI/Corp 617, 643 (1997) (citing Letter Rulings 9750017, 9750018, 9750019, 9814007).

Third, politically motivated securitization may place incumbent utilities in a relatively more competitive position than newer competitors. *See* Kenneth Rose, Securitization of Uneconomic Costs: Whom Does It Secure?, Pub. Util. Fort., June 1, 1997 at 32; *but see* Daniel William Fessler, Facts, Fairness and Securitization, Pub. Util. Fort., Sept. 15, 1997 at 16 ("securitization . . . *should* reduce the costs to the consumer of dealing with the

---

4. According to Sidak and Spulber,

Under the Pennsylvania plan, the Commonwealth does not guarantee the transition bonds. Nonetheless, the capital markets would provide, through the price that it set for those marketable securities, a continuous estimate of the likelihood that the state would renege on its promise embodied in the rate order authorizing the securitization and the ITC. Moreover, services such as Moody's and Standard & Poor's would continuously rate the risk that the state would interfere with the sole revenue stream servicing the transition bonds. Through bond prices and bond ratings, the capital markets would quantify the expectation of regulatory opportunism on a state-by-state basis, much in the way that the premiums for political risk insurance vary from one country to the next. The issuance of transition bonds would create a security for which the principal risk would be relatively free from "noise" and causal ambiguity. Risk would not arise from competitors or from exogenous changes in technology or market demand, but rather from regulatory opportunism. Transition bonds, in short, would enable the capital markets to regulate the regulators.

J. Gregory Sidak & Daniel F. Spulber, Givings, Takings, and the Fallacy of Forward-Looking Costs, 72 N.Y.U. L. Rev. 1068, 1154–55 (1997).

past while accelerating the emergence of significant competition in generation") (emphasis added).

Given these differences between asset securitization in the utility industry and in other contexts, at a minimum, as with other stranded cost recovery mechanisms, stranded cost securitization may require ongoing regulatory review of the uses of funds raised from securitization. Even with continued regulator oversight, securitization may be an imperfect mitigation technique, as it requires regulators to establish a contractual or property-based entitlement to recovery for an asset, conceded that full stranded cost recovery may be required.

Nevertheless, many states are allowing utilities to proceed with securitization of stranded assets. In 1995, new legislation enabled Puget Sound Power & Light to become the first utility to securitize an intangible asset. *See* J. Michael Parish, Securitization: An Easier Way?, Pub. Util. Fort., Oct. 1, 1998 at 28 (the intangible asset was demand-side management—a conservation tool unrelated to stranded costs). In 1996, California became the first state to provide for securitization of stranded costs, as a part of its electric utility restructuring plan. *See id.* Since then, other states such as Pennsylvania and Illinois have enacted distinctive legislation allowing for the securitization of stranded costs. State utility commissions are placing restrictions on the use utilities can make of case they raise in securitization of stranded assets. For example, Pennsylvania requires utilities to use proceeds from securitization "principally to reduce the electric utility's transition or stranded costs and to reduce the related capitalization." James W. Durham & Ward L. Smith, Utility Restructuring: Negotiating, Structuring and Documenting the Deal–Securing Lower Costs for the Present and Future, 1082 PLI/Corp 607, 613 (1997). To protect consumers, "Pennsylvania mandates a 54 month rate freeze . . . for non-generation costs and a 9 year rate freeze . . . for the energy supply component." Walter R. Hall, Securitization and Stranded Cost Recovery, 18 Energy L.J. 363, 373 n.23 (1997) (citing 66 Pa. Cons. Stat. Ann. 2804 (West Supp. 1997)). "Such freezes are subject to lengthening or shortening depending upon how quickly the utility recovers approved stranded costs and provides full retail access." *Id.* "Transition costs must be collected during these rate freeze periods." *Id.*

Illinois utilities have also experimented with securitization to reduce a utility's cost of capital, although there too restrictions have been imposed on utility use of the proceeds. *See* Ill. Power Withdraws Bid to Securitize $1.728–Billion After ICC Staff Objects, Electric Utility Week, May 11, 1998 at 3. "At least 80% of the proceeds [from the sale of securitized bonds] must be used to refinance existing debt or equity, or both." *See* ComEd Seeks Approval for $3.4–Billion Securitized Bond Issue; IP, $1.7–Billion, Electric Utility Week, Mar. 30, 1998 at 5. "No more than 20% can be used to repay or retire fuel contracts or spent nuclear fuel obligations, or to pay labor-related and other specified costs." *Id.* Stranded costs are "recovered on a lost-revenue basis using a formula that assures a utility it will recoup revenues equivalent to those paid by full-requirements customers, minus a mitigation factor ..." To Buy Back Stock, Redeem Debt, ComEd Seeks $3.4–Billion in Securitized Bonds, Electric Utility Week, May 4, 1998 at 17. "For the first year that residential customers are authorized to shop for power, this [mitigation] factor is 6% of the bundled service rate; it ramps up to 10% over the transition period to a competitive environment." ComEd Seeks Approval for $3.4–Billion Securitized Bond Issue; IP, $1.7–Billion, Electric Utility Week, Mar. 30, 1998 at 5.

RETAIL COMPETITION IN ELECTRIC POWER

A. OVERVIEW OF RETAIL COMPETITION ISSUES

1. THE LIMITS OF FEDERAL JURISDICTION

FERC's jurisdiction extends to wholesale sales only. It can order the owner of an electric transmission system to transport ("wheel") power from a competitor to another utility such as a municipal or a coop who will resell it, but it has no jurisdiction to order wheeling directly to an end user. Thus, for example, if a large user such as Widgets Co. thought it could get cheaper power by buying it from the New York Power Authority and having it wheeled by Long Island Lighting, FERC would have no authority to direct Long Island Lighting to provide the service. Only the New York Public Service Commission would have jurisdiction over such a sale because it is a sale at retail.

State utility commissions have not traditionally required electric utilities to engage in this type of transaction, which is referred to in the trade as "retail wheeling." The question of whether to allow customers to obtain retail wheeling, and if so under what conditions, is one of the hot issues in current energy law. In Order No. 888, FERC reaffirmed state jurisdiction over retail wheeling when it stated:

> While we reaffirm our conclusion that this Commission has exclusive jurisdiction over the rates, terms, and conditions of unbundled retail transmission in interstate commerce by public utilities, we

nevertheless recognize the very legitimate concerns of state regulatory authorities as they contemplate direct retail access or other state restructuring programs. Accordingly, we specify circumstances under which we will give deference to state recommendations. Although jurisdictional boundaries may shift as a result of restructuring programs in wholesale and retail markets, we do not believe this will change fundamental state regulatory authorities, including authority to regulate the vast majority of generation asset costs, the siting of generation and transmission facilities, and decisions regarding retail service territories. We intend to be respectful of state objectives so long as they do not balkanize interstate transmission of power or conflict with our interstate open access policies.

This Chapter addresses several of the issues related to the general division of power between the federal government and the states regarding competition policy. What are the limits of state ability to implement retail electric power competition? Will federal antitrust laws continue to protect consumers in light of state restructuring, or will states need to develop their own active consumer protection programs to replace the traditional protections that accompanied price regulation? What if state environmental regulations associated with power plant and transmission line siting pose a tension with federal or state competition policy? To the extent the division of authority between the federal government and the states acts as a barrier to pursuing competition policy, this issue is likely to be reassessed by Congress as it considers national restructuring legislation in coming years.

2. Municipalization and "Sham" Wholesale Wheeling

Although, as is discussed later in this Chapter, many states have adopted comprehensive retail competition plans, even where states have not endorsed retail competition end users frequently attempt to wrangle state and federal public utility laws to provide for retail options. Municipalization, a trend discussed below, has successful worked to bypass the incumbent utility in several instances. At some level, however, even municipalization may effectuate "sham" wholesale wheeling, another trend discussed below (but one that FERC has disfavored in its recent decisions).

a. MUNICIPALIZATION

Municipalization refers to the replacement of utility service provided by an incumbent utility with service provided by a municipality. Municipalization is attractive to the extent the municipal utility can provide an end user a better deal on its energy costs than the incumbent utility.

Municipal governments can use their condemnation powers to offer residents new retail power options, but incumbent utilities may resist this development. In *El Paso Electric Co. v. Federal Energy Regulatory Commission*, 201 F.3d 667 (5th Cir. 2000), FERC's ability to require an investor-owned utility to cede its service territory to a municipal utility was addressed. El Paso Electric Company, the investor-owned utility, sought review of FERC's decision requiring the utility to sell power at wholesale to the City of Las Cruces, New Mexico. The City had filed a complaint under Section 202(b) of the Federal Power Act (the "Act"), requesting that FERC issue a temporary order requiring EPE to sell wholesale power to the City. Section 202(b) of the Federal Power Act provides:

> Whenever the Commission, upon application . . . of any person engaged in the transmission or sale of electric energy, . . ., finds such action necessary or appropriate in the public interest it may by order direct a public utility (if the Commission finds that no undue burden will be placed upon such public utility thereby) to establish physical connection of its transmission facilities with the facilities of one or more other persons engaged in the transmission or sale of electric energy, to sell energy to or exchange energy with such persons: Provided, That the Commission shall have no authority to compel the enlargement of generating facilities for such purposes, nor to compel such public utility to sell or exchange energy when to do so would impair its ability to render adequate service to its customers.

16 U.S.C. § 824a(b) (emphasis in original). El Paso argued that FERC exceeded its authority under the statute because the City is not "engaged in the transmission or sale of electric energy" and because the Act does not grant to FERC the same "public interest" authority to order sales of electricity as it does to order interconnection of electric facilities. The Fifth Circuit rejected this argument, but held that an evidentiary hearing was necessary prior to FERC's decision to require the sale of power.

The following excerpt discusses some additional law and policy issues raised by municipalization:

Suedeen G. Kelly, Municipalization of Electricity: The Allure of Lower Rates for Bright Lights in Big Cities

37 Nat. Resources J. 43 (1997).

Municipalization is the replacement of utility service provided by an investor-owned utility (IOU) with service provided by the municipality itself. Today, many municipalities are pondering whether to take over their local electric IOU. Their goal is to lower electric rates by taking advantage of changes made in 1992 to federal law that make it easier to procure cheaper, wholesale electric power. In the last four years, at least 33 cities across the United States have seriously considered electric municipalization. Of these, six have decided not to municipalize. The two cities of Clyde, Ohio, and Broken Bow, Oklahoma, have completed the municipalization process. Municipalization efforts have usually been encouraged by the electric ratepayers, particularly large industrial electric consumers, who are anxious to lower their utility costs.

Cities typically begin the municipalization process with a legal, economic and engineering feasibility study. Often, implementation of a municipalization plan requires pre-approval by the voters through a referendum. The city must also anticipate that the IOU to be ousted will fight back with a public education campaign and litigation. Because of the potentially high costs of municipalizing in the face of stiff opposition from the incumbent IOU, municipalization may not prove economically feasible for many cities. However, the mere pursuit of the municipalization option may bring about enough political pressure to achieve the desired result of lower, long-term electric rates through state regulatory reform of the electric industry.

This article describes some of the reasons for the recent increase in municipalization efforts. In addition, it discusses legal and economic hurdles that a city must overcome in order to municipalize. Part I of the article defines municipalization as it broadly applies to various techniques for accessing lower rates. Part II analyzes two ways in which municipalization, or attempts at municipalization, can lower rates in areas with traditionally higher rates. The economic and legal challenges to municipalization are discussed in Part III. Part IV briefly describes the type of reaction that one can expect from an IOU facing possible municipalization in one of its service territories. The article concludes that even though municipalization may be expensive, cities in some areas face rates that are high enough to make consideration of the option worthwhile. Indeed, as various regions of the country move toward competition in the electric industry, those areas not embarking on regulatory reform will face additional pressures to municipalize so that they too may take advantage of the lower rates.

I. THE TERM MUNICIPALIZATION COVERS VARIOUS METHODS FOR ACQUIRING OWNERSHIP AND CONTROLLING DISTRIBUTION FACILITIES

The term "municipalization" describes efforts by cities across the United States to substitute electric utility service provided by an IOU with electric service provided by the municipality itself. The city municipalizes by acquiring ownership and operational control of the facilities necessary to distribute electricity to its residents. A city can do this in a number of ways. Traditionally, a city buys or condemns the existing distribution facilities within the city limits owned by the IOU presently providing electric service. For example, the city of Las Cruces, New Mexico, is pursuing the condemnation of El Paso Electric Company's distribution facilities that are located within the city limits. A city could also build its own new and redundant electric distribution facilities. This occurred in the town of Clyde, Ohio, and is under consideration in Monroe Township, New Jersey. Recently, cities have been experimenting with becoming a municipal electric utility by owning less than all the distribution facilities. Those in the know call this "municipalization lite", or even better, "muni lite." For example, the cities of Palm Springs, California, and Falls Church, Virginia, have considered merely installing their own meters at the end of the IOU's distribution line to each house and business receiving electric service. The legality of this strategy for purposes of being able to obtain transmission service to import power, a factor critical to the ultimate goal of lowering electric rates, is discussed infra.

Whether a city has the authority to acquire, condemn or build electric distribution facilities depends on local municipal law. However, since the mass distribution of electricity began in the 1880s, cities have routinely formed publicly-owned, municipal utilities to provide electric service. Even so, the state legislature may also have given the state public utility commission, state finance department, or a related agency a role in approving the acquisition, condemnation, or substitution of the IOU by the municipal utility. If so, the municipality may face an uphill battle in getting approval of a takeover of an IOU's service from the state public utilities commission which is likely to be concerned about the impact of municipalization on the financial health of the IOU and its ability to continue to render quality service to its remaining service areas.

II. THE MUNICIPALIZATION MOVEMENT AIMS TO LOWER ELECTRIC RATES

The impetus behind cities' interest in municipalizing their electric utility service is the prospect of lowering electric rates. Rates can be lowered by municipalization efforts in at least two ways. First, by becoming an electric distribution utility, cities hope to put themselves in a position to buy wholesale power from newer, lower-cost generation sources, and transmit it to the municipal distribution facility at a price lower than their IOU charges. Second, attempts at municipalization may induce efforts by the IOU or state government to reduce rates....

[Changes in technology and federal law] have jump started the municipalization movement and are dictating the form that municipalization of electric service is taking. Municipalities realize they must qualify as legitimate resellers under the Federal Power Act to avail themselves of access to cheaper generation over utility-owned transmission lines. Specifically, in the words of the Federal Power Act, they must "own or control" distribution facilities and use them to import cheaper wholesale power to their residents. In this effort they are usually encouraged by large industrial electricity consumers located within the municipality. For example, in Clyde, Ohio, the Whirlpool Corporation strongly supported the municipalization effort, but only after the initial push toward municipalization had been made by the town. Anchor Glass Container Corporation initiated the municipalization process when it encouraged Aberdeen, New Jersey to finance a municipalization feasibility study. Similarly, in the Village of Romeo, Michigan, the Ford Motor Company funded the preliminary municipalization study. In other instances, the industrial customers have, at least initially, been the only beneficiaries of municipalization. Broken Bow, Oklahoma formed the Broken Bow Public Works Authority to serve only one large customer, Pan–Pacific Industries. Similarly, the city of Darlington, South Carolina is considering municipalizing and initially serving only five industrial customers. West Valley City, Utah considered creating a municipal utility in an industrial park, initially serving only one customer.

Large industrials are not the only groups supporting municipalization efforts. Other classes of consumers are often demanding that the city go after cheaper power on their behalf. Power marketers, power brokers and competitive wholesale generators are also likely to be supportive. For example, the Modesto Irrigation District of California, which apparently has authority to distribute electric power within and outside of its boundaries, hopes to serve large industrial customers in non-adjoining areas with power supplied to it by Destec Energy, a power marketer. Enova Power Marketing has been working with the city of Victorville, California in connection with its interest in creating a municipal electric utility.

Sometimes municipalization attempts do not have to come to fruition in order to realize the overarching goal of lower electric rates. Often, merely a concerted effort by a city or town to consider the feasibility of municipalization will compel the local IOU to lower rates, either for the large industrial customer or for the entire town. Either way the town usually benefits. For example, in Brook Park, Ohio, the community's attempt to municipalize had stalled over a dispute with the utility until Ford Motor Company got involved. As a result of Ford's intervention, Cleveland Electric agreed to price controls which would save Ford $8 million per year over five to seven years. Although the town did not municipalize, Ford agreed to share its savings with the town. Moreover, when the settlement period ends, Brook Park will have access to the power distribution system to operate as a municipality. In other instances, the state public utility commission may order rate-discounting by the local IOU.

On a larger scale, the drive to gain access to cheaper power has been so strong that many states are now considering retail wheeling which would allow retail competition for generation.... Certainly, the likelihood that retail wheeling, or significant rate discounting, will become a local reality will affect a given city's deliberations on the subject of municipalization. For example, a group of more than 22 southern California towns has banded together to form the Southern California Cities Joint Powers Committee to lobby the public utilities commission and state legislature for competitive electric benefits rather than pursue establishing their own municipal utilities. However, the possibility of achieving lower electric rates through alternatives may not dissuade a city from seriously pursuing municipalization because the very act of considering a takeover of the local IOU will likely increase the political pressure in favor of implementing retail wheeling or rate-discounting reform. Victorville, California put its municipalization plan on hold when Southern California Edison began negotiating electric rates with a large glass manufacturer, AFG Industries, located within Victorville.

Cities may also view municipalization of electric service as providing other benefits, such as a better quality of service or freedom from state public utility commission oversight. The possibility of rate-discounting or retail wheeling may not dissuade some cities from pursuing municipalization if they have reasons for municipalizing other than lower rates. Las Cruces, New Mexico, for example, conducted its municipalization feasibility study even before EPAct made lower-cost generation most easily available to municipal utilities. At any rate, the mere possibility, or even the likelihood, that retail wheeling will be introduced or that the local IOU will offer rate-discounting will often not stop the municipalization process, although it is a factor to consider.

III.   MUNICIPALIZATION MUST BE ECONOMICALLY AND LEGALLY FEASIBLE

Cities typically begin consideration of municipalizing the electric service with a study of the legal, economic and engineering feasibility of one or more possible means of accomplishing it. If a municipalization plan emerges from the study, it may need to be approved by the voters through a referendum. The outcome of the vote will often be dependent on what types of savings the residents can hope to receive from municipalizing. Because the largest cost is most often the cost of acquiring distribution facilities, either by duplicating the existing facilities or obtaining them through purchase or condemnation, the plan must first address what facilities it will obtain.

A.   Possible Forms of Municipalization: Traditional and Muni–Lite

Municipalization can be accomplished by purchasing or condemning the local IOU's distribution facilities or building new, duplicative facilities. The feasibility study will focus on precisely what distribution facilities must be acquired or built. As discussed above, in order to be able to obtain open access transmission service over transmission lines of a hostile utility connecting the generator with the city, a municipality must "own or control" distribution facilities and use them "to deliver all" the wholesale power it resells to the ultimate consumers of the electricity. The purpose of the provision is to limit wheeling rights to entities undertaking legitimate wholesale transactions, not retail transactions masquerading as wholesale transactions. However, the law remains unclear as to what distribution facilities cities must own or control to avoid the sham wholesale transaction prohibition. Given the high cost of acquiring electric distribution facilities, many municipalities will be looking to own or control the least necessary to qualify for wholesale transmission access.

A number of IOU's have filed complaints with FERC against municipalities whose municipalization efforts involve acquisition of less than all the distribution facilities. The IOUs argue that these are sham wholesale transactions. In the first and only one of these cases yet to be decided by FERC, FERC has agreed with the IOU. In City of Palm Springs, California, 76 FERC para. 61,127 (1996), FERC ruled that Palm Springs owned or controlled insufficient distribution facilities to save it from falling into the sham wholesale transaction category. Palm Springs had purchased electric meters and installed them between the end of the distribution lines owned by the IOU currently serving city residents, Southern California Edison Company, and the main circuit breaker of each electric consumer in the city. These meters measured the flow of power, duplicating meters already installed by Southern California Edison. In deciding the case, FERC acknowledged that meters may be classified as part of distribution facilities for cost classification and jurisdictional purposes but found that, because meters do not accomplish the physical delivery of power, they do not meet the "delivery of power" requirement of section 212 of the Federal Power Act. FERC added that to find otherwise would be inconsistent with the purpose of the statute, which is to prohibit a wholesale sale that is merely "a subterfuge intended to circumvent the ban on the Commission's ability to order retail wheeling." However, FERC specifically declined to discuss what would be the minimum distribution facilities needed to be owned or controlled by an entity in order to survive a sham wholesale transaction challenge. Therefore, a city considering municipalization must consider how much of the distribution facilities it must purchase, condemn or construct, balancing the cost against the possibility that FERC might not authorize the municipality, as a wholesale purchaser under Section 212 of the Federal Power Act, to access lower rates.

B. Legal Authority to Undertake Municipalization

A legal review of the feasibility of municipalization begins with an assessment of the municipality's authority under state law to purchase or condemn, own, and operate an electric utility. Often the state provisions can provide express authorization for purchase or condemnation of utility facilities. Other times, however, the law is not so clear. In such cases, the city must either seek clarification of the law or lobby the legislature to clarify the city's rights under the statutes by providing for express authorization. Other legal issues include the legal status and effect of the current IOU's franchise with the city as well as any other relevant contracts it might have with the city. Typically, an IOU serving a municipality has a franchise agreement with the city that entitles the IOU to use city streets and rights of way to operate and maintain the IOU's distribution and transmission facilities located within city limits. The franchise agreement is most often not a franchise to serve the residents of the city with electricity; rather, the right to serve particular areas or customers is usually granted an IOU by the state public utility commission. Sometimes an IOU enters into a contract with a municipality to provide electricity and specialized electric services at specific rates to city offices and public improvements (street lights, for example).

The legal review would also address the municipality's authority to: (1) finance the purchase, construction or condemnation of an electric utility; (2) enter into wholesale power supply agreements; (3) enter into wholesale transmission agreements; and (4) obtain, if necessary, a wholesale wheeling order from FERC, as described above.

C. Economic Feasibility of Municipalization

The economic feasibility study weighs the anticipated costs of municipalization against the anticipated benefits. Costs can be assessed across the time line of municipalization, i.e., for the study of municipalization, the implementation of the plan and the operation of the resulting municipal utility. Costs connected with the feasibility study include primarily the costs of services to complete the review, including, for example, legal, planning, economic, engineering, accounting, and public relations/education costs. Public relations might seem like an unlikely cost to have on the study list, but it can be an expenditure of great magnitude particularly if the proposal will ultimately be voted upon by city residents or is likely to be opposed by the incumbent IOU.

Costs of implementing a municipalization plan include the usual costs associated with the start-up of any business: costs of services to form the entity, negotiate contracts, obtain financing, purchase (or engineer and construct) its plant and equipment and hire employees. Implementation costs would also include those associated with any public referendum on the plan and with litigating any challenges to the plan. Litigation costs should not be underestimated, particularly if the resident IOU opposes the municipalization.

Costs of operating a municipal electric utility include the usual costs associated with the operation of any electric utility that buys power on the wholesale market, wheels it over transmission lines and distributes it to the ultimate electric consumers. Additionally, two other operational costs might be incurred by a city forming a municipal electric utility today: (1) costs associated with any loss accruing to the IOU that served the city prior to municipalization (i.e., "stranded costs" of the IOU resulting from the municipalization), and (2) costs associated with any loss accruing to the municipal utility itself from the implementation of retail electric competition in the future (i.e., "stranded costs" resulting from future retail wheeling).

A municipal utility could be held accountable for the recovery of stranded costs incurred by the previously-serving IOU as a result of the municipalization. If the new municipal utility uses the transmission line of the previously-serving IOU to reach a new generation source, FERC permits the IOU to recover its stranded costs from the municipal utility. FERC reasons that where an IOU has prudently incurred costs that would not be stranded but for mandatory wholesale wheeling over its transmission line under the new statutory and regulatory requirements, the retail-turned-wholesale customer (i.e., new municipal utility) should be responsible for recovery of these costs....

Any city considering municipalization today must also take into account the likelihood that state or federal regulatory reform will mandate retail wheeling sometime in the not-too-distant future. The city should factor into its cost assessment any risk that retail wheeling will cause it to incur stranded costs. These costs, whether they are ultimately recoverable from customers departing the municipal utility or not, will lessen anticipated overall benefits of municipalization.

The primary benefit of municipalization lies in the prospect that the municipal utility's long-term costs of serving its residents will be less than those of the currently-serving IOU. As the previous discussion reveals, the savings is most likely to arise from the muni's ability to procure significantly cheaper generation sources without also incurring a significant stranded cost obligation to the ousted IOU. Obviously, the probability that this outcome can be achieved will vary from case to case. But FERC's assessment that significant benefits ($3.8 billion to $5.4 billion per year of cost savings) will accrue from wholesale electric competition on a nationwide basis is encouraging to many cities thinking about municipalization

IV. THE RESIDENT IOU WILL FIGHT BACK

Cities considering municipalization must be prepared for the likelihood that the resident IOU will oppose their efforts. They must expect IOU-supported public relations and education campaigns against municipalization. These campaigns would likely emphasize the costs and risks associated with municipalization, particularly those involved in: (1) construction, purchase or condemnation of distribution facilities; (2) efforts to obtain cheaper long-term wholesale power; (3) efforts to obtain wholesale transmission access; and (4) paying wholesale wheeling rates that might include a stranded cost obligation. For example, Aberdeen, New Jersey, both the city of Aberdeen and the resident IOU, Jersey Central Power & Light Co. performed feasibility studies of municipalization, and the IOU led a public relations campaign against it. The subsequent referendum on municipalization was soundly defeated.

It is also quite possible that the resident IOU will challenge the municipality's authority to implement its municipalization plan in appropriate state, federal agency and judicial forums. In the event the city pursues condemnation, a heated disagreement will likely erupt over the compensation due the IOU for property taken as well as property rendered surplus by the municipalization.

CONCLUSION

Even though municipalization may be an expensive option to study and implement, many cities are experiencing high enough electric rates that they have an incentive to pursue it. Indeed, as retail wheeling reform spreads across the country, it is likely that citizens in "unreformed" states will exert even more pressure on their cities to municipalize, with the hope that they too will soon have lower electric rates.■

b. "SHAM" WHOLESALE WHEELING

Professor Kelly refers to "sham" wholesale transactions, which FERC generally disfavors. A sham transaction occurs when an applicant uses FERC's authority to require wholesale transmission orders to effectuate what is really a retail transmission arrangement. FERC has concluded that the use of a "middleman" that is not a bona fide wholesale customer is a "sham" wholesale arrangement—outside of the jurisdiction of federal regulators—and has refused to entertain jurisdiction over such wheeling requests. The following case provides an example.

Prairieland Energy, Inc.

88 FERC ¶ 61,153, (August 2, 1999).

On May 21, 1999, Prairieland Energy, Inc. (Prairieland) applied for an order from the Commission pursuant to section 211 of the Federal Power Act (FPA). As discussed below, we will deny Prairieland's application.

Background

This is Prairieland's second request for a section 211 order requiring the Commonwealth Edison Company (Commonwealth Edison) to provide firm, point-to-point transmission service to Prairieland under the terms and conditions of Commonwealth Edison's open access transmission tariff (Commonwealth Edison OATT).

Prairieland is an Illinois corporation. It was established and is wholly owned by the University of Illinois (UI). Prairieland was created by UI, among other purposes, to acquire and sell electricity to UI, which is currently a retail customer of Commonwealth Edison. To facilitate its proposed sales to UI, Prairieland states that it applied for firm point-to-point transmission service under the Commonwealth Edison OATT, but that its request was rejected on the grounds that Prairieland does not qualify as an eligible customer under Section 1.11 of the Commonwealth Edison OATT.

In the December 28 Order, the Commission found that Prairieland failed to demonstrate that it is an "electric utility" eligible to seek a section 211 order because it failed to demonstrate that it "sells electric energy."

In this filing, Prairieland again seeks a section 211 order from the Commission, based on additional documentation not previously filed. Prairieland submits, among other things, an executed agreement, dated May 18, 1999, which contemplates the sale of electric power by Prairieland to UI (UI Precedent Agreement). Prairieland also submits an executed lease agreement, dated April 1, 1999 (UI Lease). Prairieland contends that under the UI Lease, it will operate and control UI's distribution facilities....

Under section 211 of the FPA, an "electric utility" may request an order from the Commission requiring a transmitting utility to provide transmission services to the applicant. An "electric utility" is defined as "any person or State agency (including any municipality) which sells electric energy...."

In prior cases, we have determined whether an entity sold electric energy by considering whether the transactions at issue possess sufficient indicia of a sale. We have considered a number of factors. For example, we have considered whether the entity at issue: (I) has established its own rate schedules and terms and conditions of service; (ii) takes title to the electric energy it intends to transmit to its customers; (iii) owns or controls transmission or distribution facilities used to serve its customers; or (iv) is a legal entity separate and distinct from the entities to whom it seeks to transmit electric energy.[10][1]

The weight to be given to each of these factors in a given case may vary, depending on the specific facts presented. For example, a power marketer may be found to sell electric energy at wholesale or retail, even though it does not own or control transmission or distribution facilities. On

1. *See People's Electric Cooperative,* 84 FERC 61,229 at 62,124–30 (1998), reh'g pending.

the other hand, the absence of ownership or control of transmission or distribution facilities may be important where, as here, the proposed sale depends upon the applicant's ownership or control of facilities in order to consummate the proposed sale and other factors also indicate that there is no true sale of electric power.

We conclude that Prairieland has not shown that it is an electric utility. Neither the UI Precedent Agreement nor the UI Lease disclose the terms necessary for a finding that Prairieland's proposed transfer of electric energy to UI would be a bona fide commercial transaction. The UI Precedent Agreement, for example, states only that Prairieland will transfer electric energy to UI and that it will be obligated to do so at, or below, cost. Specifically, the UI Precedent Agreement states that the "rates and charges [payable by UI to Prairieland for electric energy] shall not exceed the rates and charges for comparable service then available to [UI] from [Commonwealth Edison]." Moreover, while Prairieland contends that it may sell electric power to parties other than UI in the future, as an electric utility might, the UI Lease would require that any such transaction be approved by UI first and be limited to non-profit institutions or governmental entities.

In addition, the UI Lease suggests that any "sales" made by Prairieland to UI would be regulated and controlled entirely by UI, pursuant to rates, terms and conditions that presumably could be established by UI, at will. For example, the UI Lease makes clear that Prairieland "is intended to be and to remain an instrumentality of [UI] for federal income tax purposes," and that "[t]he activities of [Prairieland] shall be limited to activities which further the governmental purposes of [UI]." The UI Lease further limits Prairieland's control of UI's facilities in ways that could fundamentally rig the terms and conditions of any "sales" made to UI. Specifically, the UI Lease states that Prairieland may not operate its leased facilities without "obtaining the prior written consent of [UI] ... [and] complying with any other requirements reasonably imposed by [UI]." In addition, the UI Lease would permit UI, at its sole discretion, to alter or improve Prairieland's facilities, as UI may deem to be necessary or desirable, and further bestows upon UI the right to staff and operate Prairieland consistent with UI's management policies.

Under these circumstances, Prairieland's conveyance of electric energy to UI bears little resemblance to a sale. Rather, the transaction proposed by Prairieland would be more analogous to the type of interdepartmental transfer that has been held not to constitute a sale.

We conclude, therefore, that Prairieland is not eligible to request transmission service under section 211 because it is not an electric utility under the FPA.■

3. AN ILLUSTRATION OF STATE RETAIL COMPETITION: CALIFORNIA'S RETAIL COMPETITION PLAN

Municipalization may provide rate relief for customers, but since the municipality replaces the incumbent utility it does not fully effectuate retail competition. For many years, states have considered plans to implement retail wheeling, or direct access to electricity supply markets. Most of these plans were focused on providing direct access for large retail customers, such as industrial plants. By the mid–1990s, however, state "retail wheeling" plans were being displaced by much more comprehensive efforts to implement "retail competition." Unlike retail wheeling, which focuses solely on the issue of retail transmission access, retail competition plans address a range of additional issues, including consumer protection, stranded cost recovery, and green pricing.

California has been a leader among the states in movement towards retail wheeling. California's efforts to adopt retail wheeling began in 1994, when the California Public Utilities Commission, prodded by electrical rates 50 percent higher than the national average, adopted a rule designed to allow all customers in the state a choice of their electricity supplier by the year 2002. In 1996, the California Legislature adopted, and California Governor Pete Wilson signed, AB 1890, a bill designed to facilitate the transition to retail wheeling in the state. The California act spells out in detail 1) stranded cost recovery, 2) organization of the new industry structure, 3) protection of system reliability, 4) funding of public purpose and environmental programs, and 5) consumer protection.

To facilitate the transition to retail competition, the California act envisions that state-chartered, non-profit institutions will play an integral role in the new industry structure. Independent System Operators (ISOs) will "ensure efficient use and reliable operation of the transmission grid." A power exchange, open to all sellers on a nondiscriminatory basis, will operate an "efficient, competitive auction" for the buying and selling of power. There will also be an Oversight Board, which will oversee the ISO and the Power Exchange. The new California Act requires both investor-owned and publicly-owned utilities to commit control of their transmission facilities to the ISO and jointly file pricing schemes for their use with FERC. Direct bilateral transactions between electricity suppliers and end-use consumers began in Spring 1998. The following brochure, designed by California regulators for lay consumers, explains the California restructuring plan:

How Electric Industry Change Affects You (Electric Restructuring in Plain English), California Public Utilities Commission

<http://WWW.CPUC.CA.GOV/divisions/CSD/ELECTRIC/ lainEnglish981030.htm> (Visited March 15, 2000).

Goals of a competitive electric industry

— Consumer choice in electric services, and

— Competition among utilities and other electricity providers to reduce electric rates in California. (Current electric rates are 30 to 50 percent higher than the national average.)

To improve customer choice and lower rates, the Legislature enacted, and Governor Wilson signed, Assembly Bill 1890 in September 1996 to make California's electric competitive. The CPUC is implementing a four-year transition period to this new competitive market. As of March 31, 1998 consumers from all customer classes (residential, commercial, agricultural, industrial) are able to buy electricity from either their current utility or another electricity supplier. The industry will be fully competitive by 2002.

PG & E, SCE, and SDG & E customers as well as customers of Southern California Water Company Bear Valley District, Kirkwood Gas and Electric, and the California customers of Sierra Pacific Power and PacifiCorp are now able to buy electricity from their current utility or from a non-utility electric service provider. If you are a customer of one of these utilities, (now known as utility distribution companies) whether you decide to continue buying electricity from your utility or choose to buy from another supplier, your utility will continue to deliver electricity to your home or business. But for the first time, you will be able to purchase that electricity from whatever company will give you the service options and/or prices you want.

The California Public Utilities Commission, working closely with the Federal Energy Regulatory Commission, utilities and other entities, will assure continued delivery of safe, reliable, and environmentally-sensitive electric service. The CPUC also ensures fair competition and that residential and small commercial customers are educated about the competitive electric industry and protected from unfair business practices.

More Customer Choice

— Whether you are a residential, commercial, agricultural or industrial customer, you have more choices for purchasing electricity.

— If you don't want to buy electricity from another supplier, you can continue to buy electricity from your current utility. It's your choice.

— You can buy electricity from a company other than your current utility and have it delivered through the lines of your utility.

— You may be able to contract with your city, country, an association, a broker or an aggregator to purchase electricity for you. Each entity offering electric service to residential and small business customers must register with the CPUC. And you can check to see if a company is registered before you do business with the company.

— You may wish to install a special meter so you can purchase and use electricity on an hourly basis at a time when it is least expensive.

— You can choose the supplier that offers the pricing plan you want. Some suppliers may offer different rates for day and for night, or for different seasons.

Lower Electric Rates

The electric rates of PG & E, SCE, SDG & E, PacifiCorp and Sierra Pacific Power are frozen at the rates in effect on June 10, 1996. By law, these utilities were also required to reduce residential and small commercial electric rates by 10 percent on January 1, 1998.

PG & E, Edison and SDG & E must purchase electricity from a competitive spot market called the Power Exchange. The Power Exchange will determine the price of electricity hourly according to demand for and supply of electricity. It will publish the price of electricity so consumers can shift their energy use to times when it is less expensive.

Utility plants and other obligations will be paid off earlier, and at a reduced rate of return. This will reduce rates by April 2002. Under monopoly regulation, electric rates, in part, reimbursed utilities for their costs of building power plants and buying electricity from independent power producers to serve their customers. The CPUC reviewed and approved these costs as reasonable, and authorized utilities to recover them in rates over many years. To ensure recover these costs during the transition to a competitive electric industry, all utility customers will pay a competition transition charge-most of which will be collected through March 31, 2002.

Having everyone pay a competition transition charge is important.

It means that residential and small commercial customers won't end up paying higher rates to make up revenue lost from customers who leave the utility system and choose service from a competing company.

Other Advantages of a Competitive Electric Industry

— Electricity producers will not build generation facilities unless demand for electricity shows more facilities are needed.

— Electricity producers, including utilities, will have an incentive to operate as efficiently as possible so they can be competitive, remain financially viable, and earn a profit for their shareholders. Increased efficiency should produce lower electric rates in the long run.

— The cost of electricity is a key cost for businesses, as well as residential customers. Reducing this cost will encourage businesses to remain, expand, and locate in california. This means more jobs and more business investment. Two non-utility companies already plan to build new generation plants in california using the latest gas turbine technology.

— Having more time-of-use options will give consumers more incentive to use electricity efficiently to lower their costs.

— Electrical appliance manufacturers will have incentive to produce products which satisfy consumer needs but use as little electricity as possible.

Public Purpose Programs

The Legislature and CPUC have established public purpose programs to encourage energy conservation and efficiency, and research and development of energy efficient technologies and products. These programs will continue to be funded through a public goods charge, which all customers will pay. Low-income assistance programs will continue to be funded through a separate charge.

Itemized Bills

Your monthly electric bill is itemized so you can easily see how much you are paying for electricity, delivery of electricity, the competition transition charge, the rate reduction bonds, and the public goods charge. However, your rates during the four-year transition period will not be higher than they were in June 1996. Rates for residential and small commercial customers were reduced by 10 percent on January 1, 1998.

Why the Electric Industry has Become Competitive

1. The 1978 Federal Public Utilities Regulatory Policies Act required utilities to buy power from unregulated generators. The purpose was to encourage development of smaller generating facilities, and use of new technologies and alternative fuel sources such as wind, solar, water, and waste to produce electricity.

2. Use of alternative fuel reduces the demand for and reliance on, fossil fuels. It also reduces reliance on importing fossil fuels from other countries, and is better for the environment.

3. The 1992 National Energy Policy Act allowed more types of unregulated companies to generate and sell electricity. Like California, other states also are exploring opening their electric

markets to competition. Congress is now considering legislation to make the nation's electric market competitive.

4. New technology such as fuel cells, micro generation plants, and photovoltaic systems enable consumers to buy electricity directly from local producers, or build a small, efficient plant to fuel their business or factory.

5. In May 1995, after analysis of the changing electricity industry and many hearings around the state to get input from industry experts, utilities, consumer organizations, and the public, the CPUC proposed a policy for introducing competition in California's electric industry. December 1995, after additional public comment, the CPUC adopted a final policy and began to plan transition to the new market.

6. In April 1996, the Federal Energy Regulatory Commission ordered electric utilities nationwide to allow other electricity providers to transmit electricity through utility transmission systems. Utilities and other companies in areas where electricity is less costly to produce will be able to sell cheaper electricity to areas where it is more expensive to produce electricity.

7. In September 1996, AB 1890 was enacted. This landmark legislation fundamentally changed California's electric industry by introducing competition and customer choice.

How California's Electric Market Has Changed

PG & E, Edison, and SDG & E will continue to own their transmission facilities, but have turned operation of these facilities over to an Independent System Operator (ISO). The Federal Energy Regulatory Commission regulates the ISO. The ISO, functioning like an air traffic controller for energy, operates the state's transmission system to ensure electricity flowing into it reaches all customers when they need it so they continue to have reliable service. The ISO will also ensure that all generators have equal opportunity to send their electricity through the transmission system to their customers. Generators who ship electricity through the system will pay a fee to cover system costs and to ensure reliability.

Utility distribution companies continue to have the "obligation to serve the public," and they will continue to deliver electricity to your home or business regardless of who you choose to sell you electricity.

Distribution lines link your business or home to the transmission system. PG & E, Edison and SDG & E will continue to operate distribution lines and be responsible for reliable, safe delivery of electricity to your home or business. The CPUC will continue to make sure they fulfill this responsibility, and regulate their transmission and distribution rates using performance-based, rather than cost-of-service ratemaking.

A Power Exchange, regulated by the Federal Energy Regulatory Commission, became operational on March 31, 1998. PG & E, Edison and SDG & E must sell their power to the Power Exchange. If they wish to, municipalities, independent power producers, irrigation districts, and out-of-state producers may also sell power to the Power Exchange.

PG & E, Edison and SDG & E must also buy their power from the Power Exchange for four years to resell to customers who buy electricity from the utility distribution companies. They will pay a price determined by the Power Exchange based on the market demand for power. This will assure fair competition between utilities and other electricity suppliers. To ensure PG & E, Edison, and SDG & E do not continue their traditional monopoly advantage by controlling generation, transmission and distribution, the ISO and Power Exchange are independent of the utilities.■

* * *

For historical and geographical reasons, prior to restructuring California was a state in which the cost of electricity is relatively high. Separated by the Sierra mountains from the coal fields of the high plains, and with limited local supplies of hydro and oil, Californians pay much more for electricity than their neighbors in Oregon and Washington who have benefitted from the big Columbia River hydro projects. The three primary companies that distribute electricity in California are Pacific Electric and Gas Co. (PG & E), which covers northern California, Southern California

Edison and San Diego Gas & Electric, which serve the southern parts of the state. In addition, there are some substantial municipal systems, including the City of Los Angeles.

The state's major utilities have been under great pressure from major industrial users to allow them to import power from other sources. After prolonged negotiations, the three major utilities and some of the larger users agreed on a proposal for an ISO and submitted it to FERC for approval in April of 1996. The California legislature effectively endorsed that proposal by passing AB 1890, but the bill also included the creation of a state oversight board with two members from the legislature.

In two opinions in late 1996, FERC approved the basic structure of the ISO and the Power Exchange. *See In Re Pacific Gas and Electric Company* et. al., 77 FERC ¶ 61,204 (1996); *In Re Pacific Gas and Electric Company* et. al., 77 FERC ¶ 61,265 (1996). The following order describes the operation of California's Power Exchange:

In Re Pacific Gas and Electric Company et al.

77 FERC ¶ 61,204 (1996).

PANEL: Before Commissioners: Elizabeth Anne Moler, Chair; Vicky A. Bailey, James J. Hoecker, William L. Massey, and Donald F. Santa, Jr.

I. Introduction

On April 29, 1996, Pacific Gas and Electric Company (PG & E), San Diego Gas & Electric Company (SDG & E), and Southern California Edison Company (SoCal Edison) (collectively, the Companies) filed in Docket No. EC96–19–000 a Joint Application for Authorization to Convey Operational Control of Designated Jurisdictional Facilities to an Independent System Operator (ISO). Also on that date, the Companies filed in Docket No. ER96–1663–000 a Joint Application for Authority to Sell Electric Energy at Market–Based Rates Using a Power Exchange (PX).

Overview of the Proposed PX in Docket No. ER96–1663–000

The Companies state that the PX will establish a competitive spot market for electric power through a day-ahead and hour-ahead auction of generation and demand bids using transparent rules and protocols. This auction will bring together buyers and sellers who have not arranged all of their needs through bilateral contracts. The auction will also allow the PX to reveal day-ahead and hour-ahead market-clearing prices in coordination with the ISO. According to the Companies, the day-ahead market is needed to accommodate the lead times required for start-up of fossil plants to meet load reliably, and the hour-ahead market provides flexibility to account for changed circumstances. Commitments will be treated as forward sales and purchases. They state that, "at times, the PX will need to iterate with the ISO to ensure that transmission constraints are not violated and over-generation conditions do not exist."

Day-ahead demand bids, and any associated price limits, will be submitted to the PX from buyers on behalf of their end-use customers or by end-use customers themselves. All generators wishing to supply energy may bid, including baseload, intermediate load, cycling units, and intermittent energy producers such as solar and wind units. Generation and demand bids will be binding on the bidders when they are submitted to the PX, although the generation and demand schedules are subject to adjustment by the ISO for reliability and congestion management purposes. The PX will conduct a day-ahead auction of bids from generators to serve the demand bids at or below the bid-in demand price.

The PX will rank and evaluate generation bids in merit order, based on both price and operational capabilities, and will then submit its preferred, balanced day-ahead schedules of generation, load, and associated transmission losses to the ISO. The PX's schedules will include generation, the Companies' loads bid into the PX and which are not served by other means, together with demand bids submitted from other buyers, including but not limited to, municipal utilities, other scheduling coordinators, and utilities outside the ISO's control area. The PX's preferred schedules will also include reserve and regulation ancillary services sufficient to meet the PX's pro rata share of the requirements for the ISO's control area. The PX will bid both to supply ancillary services to, and to buy its full ancillary services requirements from, the ISO.

Prior to the PX's submission of its preferred schedule, the PX will participate in the ISO's management of over-generation conditions. The ISO will also receive balanced schedules from non-PX scheduling coordinators and will perform analyses to determine if transmission congestion will occur as a result of the combined schedules of the PX and other scheduling coordinators, and to arrange for required ancillary services. The scheduling coordinators will have an opportunity to adjust their schedules to account for transmission congestion. Upon final acceptance of all schedules by the ISO, the PX will notify the PX generators and buyers of the accepted generation and load schedules. These accepted schedules will become the day-ahead generation and load schedules and will be the basis on which the PX reveals the day-ahead market-clearing price in each zone and the corresponding price at each generator location in each zone.

The Companies state that a similar process, not including an iteration, will be used for hour-ahead scheduling. These final day-ahead and hour ahead schedules are used in the PX's settlement process, and are financially binding.

Participation in the PX will be voluntary, except that for a five-year transition period, the Companies must bid all of their generation into the PX and must purchase through the PX all of the electric energy required to serve their utility service retail customers. After the transition period, the Companies' participation in the PX will be voluntary.

Once the PX is in operation, the filing parties will authorize the PX to file on their behalf under section 205 any new rate schedules and amended contracts, rules, and protocols that change the rights, duties or operations of the PX. The PX will have exclusive filing authority, since the governing contracts will prohibit any party from making unilateral filings unless that party has exhausted its remedies under the PX's dispute resolution process.

The PX as an entity itself will be a public utility under section 201(e) of the FPA, 16 U.S.C. 824(e) (1994). The PX will bill and collect revenue from energy purchasers at uniform marginal energy prices (averaged over a transmission zone) and disburse this revenue to the energy sellers and the ISO. All generators in a zone will be paid the bid price of the last winning marginal generator. The ISO will be paid for transmission losses, ancillary services, and congestion costs. Moreover, subject to the ISO's grid-management protocols, the PX auction will determine which buyers and sellers will sell or purchase through the PX, as well as the price and other terms under which these transactions will be made. In this sense, the PX will effectively exercise control, including unit-commitment and scheduling control, over transactions made through the PX....

A variety of agreements and tariffs (ISO/PX Implementing Agreements) will include the rules, protocols or procedures which the PX will adopt to develop the preferred generation dispatch schedule in the forward market; and agreements between the PX and market participants dealing with entity-specific aspects of market participation. The Companies state that agreements between the PX and market participants will be standardized to the extent possible.

Bidding Rules and Bid Evaluation Procedures

The PX will evaluate generation and demand bids and establish a day-ahead preferred schedule by taking into account both the prices offered for service from each bid-in generating unit and the operating capabilities of each unit together with the demand bids for quantity of load and price. The PX will consider operating constraints, and it will not include in its final schedule any demand which had an associated bid price below the market-clearing price.

Based on the final PX dispatch schedule accepted by the ISO, the PX will reveal its market-clearing prices for PX energy. A uniform market-clearing price for PX buyers in a congestion-management zone will be established based on the cost of the marginal generator in that zone for each hour. Hourly prices will be established based on the PX's 24–hour optimization. However, the Companies state that notwithstanding the existence of different market-clearing prices in specific congestion management zones, the California Commission Decision envisions that the Companies will average the costs paid for energy within or among the utility service customers the Companies serve.

The PX price-determination methodology will establish a price in each hour that will match supply and demand according to five principles: (1) the loss-adjusted market-clearing price paid to the marginal generator in each hour will be no less than the combined energy and no-load bid price of the marginal generator; (2) the loss-adjusted market-clearing price may include all or a portion of the start-up cost of the marginal unit such that each generator scheduled to operate during the day will be paid no less than its full bid price for its scheduled operation; (3) no demand bidder whose demand is included in the schedule will pay more than its bid in each hour; (4) if supply is sufficient to meet demand at or below the demand price bid, (as defined by the Companies, a demand price bid states the maximum price for each hour at a which a customer is prepared to take a specified amount of energy in the day ahead schedule) the market-clearing price will be set by the marginal generating unit; and (5) if demand at a price exceeds supply, the market-clearing price will be set by the lowest winning demand price bid. In the absence of adequate demand price bids, demand will be curtailed to match supply, and the market-clearing price will be set equal to an administratively pre-determined cap. . . . ■

As states have moved towards retail competition, two basic approaches to establishing competitive power markets have evolved. One approach allows competitive markets to evolve by virtue of contracts between buyers and sellers of power, perhaps arranged with the assistance of marketers, brokers and aggregators of power. This approach, often referred to a "bilateral contracting," seems attractive, especially to the extent that we are uncertain how power markets are likely to evolve structurally.

In contrast to this bilateral contracting approach, has established a power exchange—a mandatory pool for purchasing power. California's power exchange began trading on April 1, 1998. (The website for California's power exchange is http://www.calpx.com/.) Under California's system, distribution utilities that also own generation are required to sell their generation to the power exchange and repurchase it at the spot market price prior to selling it to their incumbent customers. This is nothing more than a paper transaction, but it works to ensure that the customers of the distribution company are not harmed from the company's ownership of generation facilities. In this sense, power pooling through a mandatory power exchange markets can work to effectively unbundle generation and distribution. For more on the topic, *see* Peter Fox–Penner, Electric Utility Restructuring: A Guide to the Competitive Era 211–13 (1997). California's power exchange does not preclude bilateral transactions, but it creates a retail spot market in electric power to supplement them. In addition, private markets have emerged to compete with California's government-established power exchange. One example is Automated Power Exchange, Inc. (APX), which operates a computerized marketplace in which buyers and sellers of electric energy enter into short-term power supply contracts at prices displayed by the APX computer, subject to the buy and sell limits established by market participants. APX requested that FERC disclaim jurisdiction over APX's operations, but FERC concluded that APX is a public utility, subject to filing requirements with FERC. *See Automated Power Exchange, Inc. v. Federal Energy Regulatory Commission*, 204 F.3d 1144 (D.C.Cir.2000) (upholding FERC's assertion of jurisdiction).

In Summer 2000, California's regulators voted to allow utilities to purchase power from qualified exchange sources other than the California

Power Exchange, subject to the approval of the California Public Utilities Commission. California's PX: Monopoly No More, Public Utilities Fortnightly, July 1, 2000 at 16.

Whether California's consumers are benefitting from the new availability of competitive retail electricity supply continues to be an issue of some debate. Have small customers benefitted from California's restructuring plan, or has it worked primarily to the benefit of larger commercial and industrial customers? According to the California Public Utilities Commission, as of January 15, 2200 California has 209,752 direct access customers (2.1%) out of 10,157,716 possible utility distribution customers. The direct access customers represent 13.8% of the total load. Almost one-third of the demand by large industrial customers is being served by competitive companies, whereas only about 2.1% of residential load is on direct access. One of the impediments to the development of retail competition for residential customers in California may have been the withdrawal from the California market of Enron, an energy service provider marketing retail power to residential customers, early after California's retail competition plan commenced. It has been observed:

> One useful way of thinking about the degree to which rapid change can be expected in the new electricity market is to look at the experience in telephony. In the first year after the 1984 breakup of the Bell system, for example, AT & T's share of the interstate telephone market declined by less than 4 percent, despite aggressive marketing on the part of its challengers. (Presumably, AT & T's share of the residential market declined at an even slower rate.) Though AT & T still commands 50 percent of the long-distance market, over time consumers have become more familiar with the process of switching long-distance carriers, causing AT & T's market share to decline. Seen in this light, the results to date of residential switching in California's electric market hardly appear surprising. We believe those results should not be looked upon as an indication of a stagnant or failing market.

Ryan Wiser, William Golove, and Steve Pickle, California's Electric Market: What's in it for the Consumer?, Fortnightly, Aug. 1998, at 38.

While large commercial and industrial customers have benefitted some from California's plan, out of state suppliers have also gained access to a larger market at lower prices than were previously available. Some suggest that California's plan may have had more of an impact on wholesale competition than retail competition:

> [T]he most far-reaching impacts have occurred at the wholesale end of the market. This finding is surprising, moreover, because the mechanism described in the program's enabling legislation, Assembly Bill 1890, was not designed to intervene in wholesale markets....
>
> ... California's out-of-state suppliers may be ahead. They are receiving better prices since they can participate in the PX and ISO on equal terms with California players. A conservative estimate is that

California has transferred approximately $100 million in additional revenues to out-of-state suppliers. Our best detailed guess is that the losses are at least twice that. Savings of this magnitude are more than sufficient to reimburse outside suppliers for purchasing firm supplies in a more risky market.

California does not fare so well. Changing the terms of trade costs California $100 million to $200 million per year—and Californians have to bear the costs of additional volatility to some degree.

Robert McCullough, Electric Competition One Year Later: Winners and Losers in California, Fortnightly, Mar. 1, 1999, at 24.

Adding to the difficulty with implementing retail competition in California is limited participation in its ISO, due to terms defined primarily by transmission-owning utility corporations. According to Professor Robert Michaels, California's ISO may be acting as a barrier to entry for municipal utilities, excluding "nearly half" of the state's import-export-capability. "The Los Angeles Department of Water and Power has chosen not to join the ISO after learning that it would pay a cost-based average of 88 cents/kWh to access the grid while corporate systems are paying under 35 cents/kWh." *See* Robert J. Michaels, The Governance of Transmission Operators, 20 Energy L.J. 233, 247 (1999).

4. OTHER STATE RESTRUCTURING PLANS

Although California is seen as a national and international innovator in its comprehensive plan for electricity restructuring, most other states have considered moving forward with retail competition, and many have already adopted competition plans. States already adopting retail competition plans include many larger states, such as New York, Illinois and Texas. Other states at the front end of the restructuring movement are Pennsylvania and New Hampshire. The following summaries, prepared by the U.S. Energy Information Administration, available at http://www.eia.doe.gov/cneaf/electricity/chg_str/tab5rev.html>, describe the features of some of these plans:

Texas (1999):

6/99: Restructuring legislation, SB 7, was enacted to restructure the Texas electric industry allowing retail competition. The bill requires retail competition to begin by 1/02. Rates will be frozen for 3 years, and then a 6% reduction will be required for residential and small commercial consumers. This will remain the "price to beat" for five years or until utilities lose 40% of their consumers to competition. The bill will also require a reduction of NOx and SO2 emissions from "grandfathered" power plants over a 2–year period. All net, verifiable, nonmitigated stranded costs may be recovered. Securitization will be allowed as a recovery mechanism. Utilities must unbundle into 3 separate categories, using separate companies or affiliate companies, the generation, the distribution and transmission, and the retail electric provider. Utilities will be limited to owning and controlling not more than 20% of installed generation capacity in their region (ERCOT). Municipals and cooperatives are not affected by the law, unless they choose (after 1/02) to open their territories to competition. The law also requires an increase in renewable generation and 50% of new capacity to be natural gas-fired.

Illinois (1997):

7/99: Legislation, SB 24, was enacted to amend the restructuring law. The amendment moves up the transition to customer choice. The first third of commercial and industrial consumers will have retail access by 10/1/99, the second third by 6/1/00, and the final third by 10/1/00. Residential customers will receive a 5% rate reduction by 10/1/01, seven months earlier. The rate cap for utilities is increased by 2%, cogeneration is promoted, and ComEd is required to allocate $250 million to a special environmental initiatives and energy-efficiency fund.

12/97: HB 362, "The Electric Service Customer Choice and Rate Relief Act of 1997," enacted. The bill provides for rate cuts for ComEd and Illinois Power effective 8/98. The law accords some commercial and industrial customers choice by October 1999, and all customers, including residential, choice for their generation supplier by 5/02. Transition charges may be collected through 2006. Most residential customers will receive a 15% rate reduction by 8/98, and another 5% reduction in 5/02.

Pennsylvania (1996):

5/99: The PUC finalized rules for full consumer choice in the retail electricity market. By 9/99, utilities will mail information packages to all consumers that have not chosen a competitive supplier. The packages will contain information about consumer choice, the "price to compare," and a list of competitive suppliers serving their rate class and location.

12/96: HB 1509, the Electricity Generation Customer Choice and Competition Act, was enacted. The law allows consumers to choose among competitive generation suppliers beginning with one third of the State's consumers by 1/99, two thirds by 1/2000, and all consumers by 1/2001. Utilities are required to submit restructuring plans by 9/97.

New York (1996):

6/98: PSC set rules for a Systems Benefit Charge to fund R & D related to energy service, storage, generation, the environment, and renewables; pilot programs for energy management for low-income consumers; and environmental protection.

1997 to 1998: The PSC approved restructuring orders for six utilities in the State.

5/96: The PSC issued its decision to restructure NY's electric power industry. The Competitive Opportunities Case adopted the goal of having a competitive wholesale market by 1997, and a competitive retail market by early 1998. Electric utilities are required to submit restructuring plans by

10/96. It also states that utilities should have a reasonable opportunity to recover stranded costs consistent with the goals of restructuring.

New Hampshire (1996):

4/99: Restructuring in NH is at a standstill due to Federal court rulings concerning the PUC's efforts to set stranded costs and rates for PSNH. The continuing Federal court cases further delay restructuring efforts in the State.

1/98: The PUC delayed the start of competition, due to begin 1/98, until 7/98 due to the continuing litigation between the PUC and the Public Service of New Hampshire.

3/97: PSNH filed a complaint in Federal District Court requesting a stay against the PUC's stranded cost recovery plan, claiming the PSNH would be forced into bankruptcy. The stay was issued, halting implementation of the restructuring plan as it applied to PSNH. The stay was extended until a trial is completed, which is expected to begin in February 1999.

2/97: The PUC issued a final plan and legal analysis for restructuring the electric power industry in NH. Among the issues addressed by the plan are market structure, unbundling electric services, stranded costs, and public policy issues such as universal service, renewable energy, and customer protections.

5/96: HB 1392 was enacted, requiring the PUC to implement retail choice for all customers of electric utilities under its jurisdiction by 1/1/98 or at the earliest date which the Commission determines to be in the public interest, but not later than 7/1/98.

Has your state restructured its electric power industry? How?

Is the state-by-state approach to restructuring working, or is there a need for federal intervention? Suedeen Kelly, a former regulatory commissioner in New Mexico, suggests that the slow, incremental approach of state regulators towards electricity restructuring has been well paced.

Suedeen G. Kelly, the New Electric Powerhouses: Will They Transform Your Life?

29 Envtl. L. 285 (1999).

Over the last thirty years the price of electricity has soared. This spurred experimentation with competition in the generation of electricity. In 1992, Congress promoted wholesale competition in the generation of electricity with the passage of the Energy Policy Act. The year 1999 finds seventeen states embarking on retail competition in generation. They are looking for choice, lower costs, and innovation—typical attributes of a competitive market—but they do not want to lose the reliability, universal service, and environmental protection that the regulated generation monopoly brought us. Trying to achieve all of these goals poses an enormous challenge for state policy makers. The issues they must resolve are difficult ones, and some of them are novel to regulatory policy. They include recovery of stranded costs, criteria for approval of mergers and acquisitions, and cost-shifting from large to small electricity consumers. So far the states have worked to solve these uncommon problems with uncommon sense. They are proceeding slowly, on a state-by-state basis, using consensus-building processes, and showing willingness to devise creative solutions that will also be politically acceptable. While this is the very process that foretells a successful transition to a restructured industry, it is threatened by objections that it is too slow, lacks uniformity, and results in solutions at odds with our economic models. These objections have merit. However, they should not be heeded because their merits are outweighed by their costs. . . .

A dream of many people is that the Summer of the Future in the electric industry can be even better than the Summer of' 98, and they have acted to realize that dream. To wit, twelve states [as of Summer 1999] have passed legislation to restructure their electric companies. These states include the usual suspect, California; but also the unusual, Arizona, Montana, and Oklahoma; and the unusually thoughtful, Connecticut, Illinois, Maine, Massachusetts, New Hampshire, Pennsylvania, Rhode Island, and Virginia; as well as the uncategorizable, Nevada.[44][2] Another five states are embarking on restructuring by regulatory order,[45][3] and at least seven other states have initiated pilot projects.[46][4]

The states that have developed restructuring plans have, by and large, tried to keep the benefits of regulation we have talked about (reliability, universal service, environmental protection) while also seeking the benefits of competition. Of course, it is one thing to want change and another thing to succeed with it. With the exception of California, none of these states has gone beyond the threshold of restructuring, so it is difficult to predict whether they will succeed. But, by and large, they seem to have gone about solving the problems associated with restructuring in a promising way.

2.   Cal. Pub. Util. Code § 391 (West 1998); Ariz. Rev. Stat. Ann. § 30–803 (West 1998); Mont. Code Ann. §§ 69–8–101 to 69–8–104 (1998); Okla. Stat. tit. 17, §§ 190.1–190.9 (1998); Conn. Gen. Stat. Ann. § 16–244 (West 1998); 220 Ill. Comp. Stat. 5/16–101 to 5/16–130 (West 1998); Me. Rev. Stat. Ann. tit. 35–A, §§ 3201–3217 (West 1998); Mass. Gen. Laws ch. 164, § 1A (1998); N.H. Rev. Stat. Ann. § 374–F:1 to 374–F:7 (1998); 66 Pa. Cons. Stat. Ann. §§ 2801–2812 (West 1998); R.I. Gen. Laws § 39–1–43 (1998); 1998 Va. Acts ch. 633; Nev. Rev. Stat. Ann. § 704.976 (Michie1998).

3.   These states are: Maryland, Michigan, New Jersey, New York, and Vermont.

181 P.U.R.4th 185 (Md.P.S.C. Dec.3, 1997) (Nos. 8738, 73834); 177 P.U.R.4th 201, (Mich.P.S.C. June 5, 1997) (No. U–11290); Docket No. EX94120585Y (N.J.B.P.U. April 3, 1997); 168 P.U.R.4th 515 (N.Y.P.S.C. May 20, 1996) (Nos. 94–E–0952, 96–12); 174 P.U.R.4th 409 (Vt.P.S.B. Dec. 30, 1996) (No. 5854).

4.   These states include: Idaho, Iowa, Missouri, New Mexico, Ohio, Texas, and Washington. See U.S. Energy Info. Admin., Status of Electric Industry Restructuring by State (last modified Feb. 1, 1999) <http:// www.eia.doe.gov/cneaf/electricity/ chg_str/tab5rev.html> [hereinafter U.S. Energy Info. Admin., Restructuring by State].

A. Common Sense Can Be a Mistake

Always using common sense to solve problems is sometimes a mistake. I believe this is particularly true with the restructuring of the electric industry, where the goals are so uncommon. To succeed in this effort, we need decision makers with uncommon sense. There are three uncommon things going on in restructuring efforts across the states that lead me to believe we may succeed with reform.

1. Uncommon Characteristic Number One: Proceeding Slowly

First, we are proceeding very slowly—with, of course, the exception of California. However, we thank California for its bold experiments that so richly benefit the rest of us. Restructuring has been under consideration to some degree in most states since Congress passed the Energy Policy Act in 1992. While seventeen states have announced industry restructuring, sixteen of them are only just getting started. In short, there's been no rush to abandon the old and bring in the new, a sometimes uncommon response in the face of strong political pressure to change.

2. Uncommon Characteristic Number Two: Restructuring State-by-State

Second, we are restructuring on a state-by-state basis rather than at the federal level. Although there have been more than a dozen bills introduced in the House and Senate of Congress to restructure at the federal level, the word out of Washington is that, at least for the time being, the leadership is not going to move this legislation.

3. Uncommon Characteristic Number Three: Using Consensus–building Processes

Third, it seems in most states, reform is occurring through a variety of attempt-to-build-consensus processes. For example, even in California, which moved quicker than any other state, the administrative proposal was on the table for public comment and rearrangement for twenty months before a final administrative plan was adopted. Then, the legislature scrutinized it for nine months and replaced it with legislation that was the product of a three-week-long, eighteen-hour-a-day, give-and-take marathon negotiation among the California legislative leadership and all the stakeholders in the industry. The restructuring legislation ended up being passed unanimously by both houses of the legislature.

B. Three Common Sense Threats to This Approach

This restructuring process, which involves moving slowly on a state-by-state basis and taking into account the interests of the many stakeholders in this business, holds promise for successful reform because it fosters novel and creative solutions to the many issues that are implicated by restructuring. However, this uncommon approach is being assaulted on three fronts by objections that are, arguably, common-sense ones.

First, the frustration of some with the slowness and diversity of a state-by-state process is creating pressure in Congress to mandate a universal solution. Second, the common knowledge that there is no pre-existing solution to some of these first-ever problems is creating pressure to duck these issues and restructure without first resolving all the problems. Third, the belief that some problems are plausibly susceptible to solution using existing models is creating pressure to abandon real problem solving and substitute "the model."

I'd like to discuss three restructuring issues that illustrate what I'm talking about, that is, successfully using uncommon solutions for a problem that, arguably and unsuccessfully, could be solved with common solutions.

1. Uncommon Example Number One: Stranded Costs—Who Pays?

Common sense is the knowledge a person attains based on society's conventional wisdom. But, as Chris Marianetti, only sixteen years old but a national oratory finalist, put it, "Too often common sense serves as a sort of thoughtless mastery, and that is not an oxymoron." In electric industry restructuring, stranded costs are an uncommon problem that cannot be eliminated with a common solution. Stranded costs are what many of today's utility generators are going to have when competition comes to electricity. For example, today generators may need to be paid, say, six cents per kilowatt-hour (KWH) to cover all the costs of having built, and now having to operate, an electric generator. Today, that's not a problem because they have a monopoly on the sale of electricity, and the regulator will set the price to allow them to recover the six cents per KWH they need. Tomorrow, however, when the competitive market takes hold and the lower cost generators start producing, the market price might well be just four cents per KWH. By market definition, today's utility will only be able to sell its power at four cents, although to make ends meet it needs to sell it at six cents. The two cents per KWH difference is the utility's stranded cost. Who is going to carry this loss? There are only three potential payers: the utility's shareholders, if it's an investor-owned utility, the consumers of electricity, or the taxpayer—or some combination of these.

Different states have approached this issue differently, and with unusual ideas. In California and Massachusetts, for example, utilities are potentially going to be able to recover all stranded costs associated with their own generation facilities from consumers. Although, in California the recovery period is four years, while in Massachusetts it is ten years.

In Connecticut, in order to recover from consumers the stranded costs associated with their generation facilities, utilities must first sell their generation assets. They must sell their nonnuclear generation by January 2000 and their interest in nuclear generation by January 2004. Each state has a variation on how stranded costs will be determined and how they will be recovered.

The threat to continuing to solve the stranded-cost problem in this case-by-case mode is the notion that a universal solution to this issue would expedite the restructuring process and add certainty of outcome for all stakeholders. Indeed, this is a common sense solution, but it is a thoughtless one because the issue of stranded costs is much more than an economics issue. It is a big values issue, especially to consumers. Many of today's consumer advocates were involved in administrative disputes in the 1970s and 1980s over the building of these generators. They took the position that they were too costly to build. They lost the cases then. Now they are in an "I told you so" mood. They are angry at having had to pay high costs, and they don't want to take it anymore. Many utilities with high-cost generation have suffered, too. Often, rates were set at a level insufficient to recover totally the costs they incurred and their stock values and bond ratings tumbled. They don't want to be handicapped with stranded costs at the same time they look to compete with new entrants in the generation market.

In short, the country's stranded cost problems are local, historical, and ideological, as well as economic. They need to be solved in individual and uncommon ways.

2.   Uncommon Example Number Two: Utility Mergers—Good or Bad?

In order to achieve all the economic objectives of restructuring (i.e., choice, lower costs, and innovation) the market for generation has to work when all is said and done. Unfortunately, there is a lot we do not yet know about the relationship between the structure of a market and its performance. However, we do know that highly concentrated markets do not usually perform as well as less concentrated markets. If we are to have a competitive market in generation, we need to be concerned about the expected competitive effects of proposed utility mergers, especially with respect to likely future concentration. This is not an easy issue with which to grapple.

Although our antitrust history provides us with quite a bit of data regarding the likely competitive effects of proposed mergers in existing unregulated, competitive markets, there is little available on proposed mergers in new markets being formed by regulators out of regulated markets. This is different because when a market is just forming, particularly when it is forming under a regulatory regime, regulators can and will take regulatory actions that will affect it. For example, in the electric industry, if regulators are willing to take action to force utilities' transmission systems to eliminate transmission constraints regionally or nationally, the electricity market will be broadened and a particular merger might then pose less of a concentration threat.

The bottom line is that developing criteria for approving mergers in the emerging new market is going to be a difficult and complex undertaking. Today, most utility mergers must be approved by the Federal Energy Regulatory Commission (FERC) as well as by the state public utility commissions of the states affected by the merger. FERC only looks at the likely effects of the merger on wholesale competition. The states have exclusive jurisdiction over the effects of the merger on retail competition.

Because this will be a difficult issue to decide, the danger is that state decision makers will forego a serious attempt at analysis and adopt a reflex reaction that could either be that bigger is better, or bigger is worse.

Certainly, in some instances bigger will be better, like when it is necessary to create a new entrant in the market. But in some instances bigger will not be better because it will have an anticompetitive effect.

About a year ago, in one state, which should go nameless but which I can tell you is situated next to Washington, D.C., and is not Virginia, a merger of the two largest utilities in the state was approved with absolutely no evaluation of the likely effects on retail competition. It might be said that it was a common sense approach to the merger (not to analyze anticompetitive effects on retail competition) because the state did not have any retail competition in place. However, shortly after the commission approved the merger, which resulted in the newly combined utility serving over eighty percent of the state's market in generation, it announced that it was going to actively consider restructuring the industry in the state.

Needless to say, if the state had initially acted in considering the merger with some thoughtfulness, it likely would not have ended up with the handicap it now has in trying to introduce competition successfully into generation in the state. To quote John Wooden, UCLA's legendary coach with extraordinary success in competitive endeavors, "It's what you learn after you know it all that counts."

In restructuring the electric industry, we are likely going to face numerous problems whose solutions will demand knowledge beyond that which we already have acquired. Success will lie in forcing ourselves to learn more than we now know.

3. Uncommon Example Number Three: Cost–Shifting—From Regulated Rates to Market Rates, or Something In–Between?

In their book, For the Common Good, Herman Daly and John Cobb, Jr., have observed that "[o]utside the physical sciences no field of study has more fully achieved the ideal form of academic discipline than economics." And precisely because of its success, it has been particularly liable to the commission of the "Fallacy of Misplaced Concreteness." The fallacy of misplaced concreteness, as Daly and Cobb explain it, is the application of tried and true economic conclusions to the real world—without recognizing that the seemingly concrete conclusions are actually the product of a high level of abstraction and sometimes are not appropriately applicable. The fallacy of misplaced concreteness is a threat to devising creative solutions to the cost-shifting problem in electric industry restructuring.

The cost-shifting problem arises from the fact that electric utilities have forever been subject to rate regulation. Rate regulators do not like to raise rates, particularly residential rates, because of the political fallout that always occurs. I learned this lesson painfully with one of my decisions as a novice rate regulator. A particular utility had sought a rate increase. My fellow commissioners and I ultimately determined the facts necessitated a rate decrease. It would be the first time anyone could recall a New Mexico utility regulator ordering a rate decrease. We announced the decision with great relief that we did not have to order residential rates increased and deal with the usual attendant political fallout. Naively, we thought the residential customers would be happy. But we were quite anxious about the political fallout that might occur at the behest of angry shareholders. We were right to be anxious, but we were wrong about what to be anxious about. The State Attorney General, the advocate for residential consumers, was the angry and vocal one—for our failure to lower residential rates enough. Ah, the pitfalls associated with acting on misplaced conventional wisdom.

One more observation on the subject of residential utility rates: regulators almost universally have tried to keep residential rate increases to a minimum by raising industrial rates a bit more than a politically blind cost analysis would peg them. In economic terms, in today's regulated world, the larger consumers more often than not subsidize the smaller ones. When generation becomes competitive (i.e., when the market sets electricity rates) this will change. Smaller consumers will feel the burden of the shifting costs from the larger consumers to them.

Whether smaller consumers will actually feel a rate increase in a particular jurisdiction in a new market setting is difficult to predict. One New Mexico legislator has said that if it were to happen, it would be political suicide for the legislators or regulators deemed responsible for restructuring. Indeed, even the possibility that residential consumers might not see as big a rate decrease as industrial consumers is a big political concern. In sum, the fact that there will be cost-shifting is an issue that must be addressed in planning for restructuring.

The traditional economics-based solution would be to accept the shifting of costs to smaller consumers as a fact of economic life—indeed a necessary development of the efficient marketplace. "Homo economicus" would say the problem is not the shifting of costs but the negative perception of the shifting of costs. As "Hamlet the Economist" might argue "there is nothing either good or bad but thinking makes it so." The economist's response would be to focus on the negative perception as the problem and solve it by educating the public, or by spin-doctoring, or a combination of both. Thus, the economic argument goes, if the worst happens (such as the rates rise so that the most needy among us cannot afford the new cost of electricity), devise a safety net through the welfare or tax system. "Homo politicus" would respond that allowing the market to handle this issue as it saw fit would be committing the fallacy of misplaced concreteness, not to mention political suicide.

So far, most states have rejected the common sense economic solution of letting the market handle the cost-shifting issue in its conventional and efficient wisdom. For example, in California the legislature ordered all utilities to freeze customer rates at levels in existence on June 1996, except that rates for residential and small commercial customers must be lowered by ten percent. To allow utilities to accomplish this without losing money, the legislature authorized a secure stranded cost recovery mechanism that resulted in the utilities actually being able to lower their costs. In other words, as the restructured industry moves forward, small customers have been guaranteed a rate decrease.

Cost shifting has been held at bay by a guaranteed rate decrease in a number of states. It is not an elegant mechanism; it is not an efficient mechanism. It is an unconventional mechanism. Will it work? It is too soon to say, but I cannot help but think about the first air-conditioner that Arthur Miller described. A cooling machine rolling about on casters was certainly unconventional. Having to fuel it with pitchers of water was not very efficient. The fact that it spurted water everywhere upon its filling was hardly elegant. But it did come to change our lives, for the better.

Reordering an industry that began one hundred sixteen years ago, that came of age sixty years ago, and that hit productive middle age thirty years ago is an unconventional development. The process going on in the states to restructure the industry is likewise unconventional but seems to be working uncommonly well. . . .■

NOTES AND COMMENTS

1. The stranded cost issue, integral to most state restructuring plans (and a major impediment to the implementation of New Hampshire's plan), is discussed in detail in Chapter 12.

2. Federal retail wheeling legislation, intended to allow retail choice by the year 2000, was introduced in 1996 (One bill is HR 3790, July 11, 1996, sponsored by Rep. Dan Schaefer). It did not pass either chamber and later legislation, introduced in 1998 and 1999, allows states the choice to implement retail competition but requires them to consider it within the next several years. No clear federal statement on the topic, from Congress or FERC, has been made.

3. If too many customers "switch"—leaving the incumbent utility to purchase in a competitive market—or switch power supply providers due to short term changes in price, this could cause serious problems with the reliability of distribution. What constraints, if any, are there on the customer's ability to return to the original incumbent utility? One way some states are addressing this issue is to assess exit fees (also used to compensate for stranded costs), or reentry penalties for customers who switch power suppliers too often and thus impose costs on other customers of the power distribution system. Other states require a minimum period in power purchase options offered by the utility or others. In Illinois, where power purchase options offered by utilities are required by law to run for at least twelve months, competitive markets have been slow to develop because the prices for such contracts (determined by an independent consulting firm) have been set at what many consider artificially low levels, deterring many customers from leaving the incumbent utilities and encouraging some customers that once used other retail suppliers to return to the utility. *See* Steve Daniels, A Jolt to Electricity Deregulation: Pricing Glitch is Restoring ComEd's Market Power, Crain's Chicago Business, Mar. 13, 2000.

4. Market power problems similar to those that developed in Illinois have been identified in California and several other markets that have imple-

mented retail competition. This issue is described in the discussion of federal merger policy in Chapter 18.

5. Concerns with high electricity prices have driven the restructuring debate and the push for retail access in states such as California and Texas. However, recent data shows that overall U.S. utility rates have declined dramatically in real dollar terms between 1982 and 1992. The largest drop has been in the rates for industrials—the biggest proponents of retail wheeling. NRDC Releases New Study of Trends in U.S. Electric Rates, May 17, 1995 (press release). As figure 13–1 illustrates, states like California have relatively high retail electricity prices, probably contributing significantly to the demand for regulatory reforms.

6. In many states, "pilot programs" have been pursued as a gradual way of implementing retail competition. For example, in early May, 1996, New Hampshire marketing groups began competing for 15,000 customers as a part of a two-year retail wheeling pilot program. *See* J. F. Schuler, Jr., Residential Pilot Programs: Who's Doing, Who's Dealing?, Fortnightly Jan. 1, 1997. The Department of Energy monitors state restructuring efforts and compiles information about state programs on a web site. *See* U.S. Energy Information Administrative, Status of Electric Industry Restructuring by States, <http://www.eia.doe.gov/cneaf/electricity/chg_str/regmap.html>. Many states have commenced an investigation of the benefits of retail wheeling, but have not yet adopted comprehensive restructuring plans.

7. Some states, including Florida and several other states in the Southeast, refer to themselves "low cost power" states, suggesting that retail competition is far off on the regulatory horizon. *See* Figure 13–1. Low cost power states see no need to restructure, since they do not believe that consumers will be better off with retail competition. Other than low cost power, what characteristics would power markets in states reluctant to move towards retail competition likely have? Will these states be able to avoid implementing retail access markets, or will the failure to do so impair the development of wholesale competition?

8. Perhaps the most successful experiment to date with retail competition comes from Germany. In Germany, as in many U.S. states, industrial customers clearly benefitted from the introduction of competition; some industrial customers received discounts of 30 to 40 percent without even switching suppliers. Lower prices have fueled economic growth. A German utility wooed a Swedish paper mill customer from France by slashing rates 25 percent below those available within the French system. Residential customers also faced tangible reductions in price. Residential customers have seen cut throat competition between different "brands" of electricity—department stores are selling electric power brands across the counter—and for some customer segments, 39 percent reductions in price were made available by alternative brands. The German experiment is said to have been aided by three structural phenomena. First, Germany's prices were very high—almost twice the average in the U.S. Second, the German

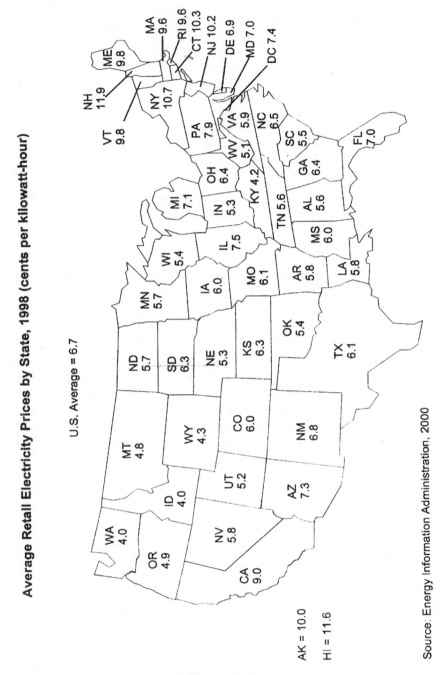

Figure 13–1

market faced excess capacity of up to 30 percent. Third, even before restructuring the German market was highly decentralized, with no one utility possessing significant market power. *See* Branko Terzic, Berthold Wurm & Yorck Dietrich, Germany: Taking the Lead in Electricity and Gas, Public Utilities Fortnightly, Jan. 15, 2000, at 22.

In addition, Germany may have benefitted from a no-nonsense approach to adding stranded cost and other social program surcharges on to power rates. According to one account:

> Though American customers have far lower rates than their German counterparts, prices in states proceeding with deregulation continue to be inflated by surcharges demanded by state regulators. The surcharges, which have applied in other countries, too, are intended to let utilities recover "stranded costs"—the costs of power plants built when prices were regulated that could not operate profitably in an open market. By contrast, German officials did not bother, deciding instead to let all utilities sink or swim on their own.

Edmund L. Andrews, Cheaper Power to the People: In Germany, a Radical Deregulation Benefits Households, New York Times, Oct. 28, 1999, at C1.

5.   CONSUMER PROTECTION

Many state restructuring plans promise consumers rate reductions or attempt to hold residential consumers harmless. (See Chapter 18.) Illinois and California, for example, promised customers rate reductions with the adoption of retail competition. Another approach, implemented in Pennsylvania and Texas, is the "price to beat." As implemented in Pennsylvania, this approach works as follows:

> Kevin Cadden, spokesman for the Pennsylvania Public Utility Commission, explains it this way. "The shopping credit is what customers shop off of. For example, on an average basis in Philadelphia for a residential customer, it's 5.65 cents per kilowatt-hour. Anything under that, which customers buy transmission for, is money in their pocket. Anything over that, they're paying extra. The shopping credit, then, is the combination (in most areas of Pennsylvania), of what they would pay their existing electric distribution company for generation and transmission." Cadden clarifies that in most areas the shopping credit applies to generation and transmission, "but in certain territories, like Allegheny, the shopping credit is generation only." (For detail, see Application of PECO Energy Company for Approval of its Restructuring Plan under Section 2806 of the Public Utility Code and joint petition for partial settlement, Pennsylvania PUC, R–00973953.)

Courtney Barry, Texas Passes a Restructuring Bill: Even Bubba Likes It, Public Utilities Fortnightly, Sept. 1, 1999, at 32. A Texas regulator has described their version of the price to beat as follows:

> You have an existing and a fully vertically integrated utility that has generation, transmission and distribution. We take that company and we divide [it] into three companies: 1) the distribution and transmission, which remains fully regulated; 2) the power generation, who is only a wholesaler; and 3) the retail electric provider [REP], who sells to the public and they can buy on the market or they can buy from their affiliated generation company.

We functionally unbundled—[we] made all the generation go to the affiliate and then said 'OK, [retail] affiliate, you can't compete in your service territory at a price higher or different than the price to beat.' They [REPs] can't compete in their service territory. They can only charge the price to beat and the price to beat is more or less an arbitrary price. It's a reduction of 6 percent off the price from the day before.

And in Texas, we stayed away from the California deal—we didn't cut prices in the transition period. We froze them because we wanted that difference in the gain to go toward stranded costs. So these prices are fairly inflated; the 6 percent cut will bring it down but it doesn't bring it down so low that competitors cannot come in.

Id.

Despite these promises of lower prices, with the rise of retail competition many of the consumer protections taken for granted under the traditional approach to state utility regulation may be at risk. As is discussed in Chapter 8, price regulation allowed private gain to converge with the public interest in consumer service obligations in the utility industry. Retail competition creates a tension between private gain and the public interest in universal access, requiring regulators to reassess their role. Also, as traditional state regulatory structures are transformed, new questions regarding the role of federal antitrust laws in protecting consumers will arise.

a. THE DUTY TO SERVE AND RETAIL COMPETITION

In a competitive retail market, the DisCo, or incumbent distribution utility, is the natural bearer of service obligations, since it remains a natural monopoly. Regulators need to carefully assess their relationship with the DisCo and other institutional actors in competitive retail power markets. One of the primary goals that needs to be taken into account in developing this relationship is consumer protection.

Jim Rossi, The Common Law 'Duty to Serve' and Protection of Consumers in an Age of Competitive Retail Public Utility Restructuring

51 Vand. L. Rev. 1233 (1998).

The dawn of competition in electricity raises a tension for the common · law duty to serve, historically protected by public utility franchise and price regulation.... If viewed purely from the economic efficiency perspective, the content of the traditional public utility duty to serve should be reassessed to fit the structure of a competitive power supply market. To the extent extraordinary service obligations are continued for natural gas and electricity in the same manner that they have been for the past hundred years, regulators will need to articulate alternative justifications outside of economic efficiency, such as fairness or distributive justice.

Yet, regardless of the reasons supporting the perpetuation of extraordinary service obligations, extraordinary service obligations can facilitate access to power supply without undermining efficiency gains, despite the warnings of free marketeers who look askance at the continuation of a duty to serve in a competitive era in emerging competitive retail power markets. At the same time, proposals endorsed by many consumer advocates that suppliers or marketers assume extraordinary service obligations are specious. Equal application of a duty to every institutional actor providing electric utility services in competitive retail markets will pose significant economic costs and may thwart the development of retail power markets. Regulators must acknowledge a need for new approaches to financing extraordinary service obligations. The introduction of competition will create a demand for distinct interim and longer-term mechanisms for financing the duty to serve.

... Current state retail wheeling plans require, at a minimum, that the power distribution sector of the industry assume some extraordinary service obligation. There is little agreement among the states, though, about whether the various market institutions interacting with the DisCo in retail markets should also bear extraordinary service obligations. After evaluating some various state approaches, I conclude that, in emerging retail power markets, a duty to serve can continue to apply in competitive retail power markets with little disruption to retail competition, but initially this obligation should be limited to DisCos. Efficient financing of this obligation will require an appropriately set system benefits charge ("SBC") on power distribution, unbundling or mandated use of a PoolCo power exchange to facilitate supply access, and properly set exit fees. The lesson of electricity markets is generalizable to other network industries, such as telecommunications and natural gas: In these industries, too, unbundling or the development of a robust supply competitive market clearinghouse, such as the PoolCo, can work to minimize the structural inefficiencies of imposing a duty to serve and concomitant financing mechanisms on incumbent distribution utilities.

At the same time, I conclude that in the long run, as retail power markets flourish, the power distribution industry will face—and, indeed, is already facing—increased pressure to become competitive or contestable. As this pressure grows, regulators will be forced to consider alternatives to an incumbent distribution utility SBC to finance the duty to serve. Thus, I conclude that eventually power markets will need to apply taxation mechanisms to power consumption or supply in order to continue financing the duty to serve. If appropriately structured, financing mechanisms can work to minimize the distortions of the duty to serve in retail power markets, allowing retail competition and the duty to serve to coexist.

A.   Continuation of the Duty to Serve in Retail Markets: the Limits of Economic Efficiency and the Importance of Distribution

Wholesale transmission access and competition among wholesale suppliers has not posed any immediate threat to the public utility duty to serve, but the introduction of retail competition requires some reassessment of the intellectual foundations for and practical application of the traditional duty to serve. The California Public Utility Commission's first order leading to the adoption of retail choice legislation acknowledged the need for consideration of this issue as customers begin to shop for power:

> To allow eligible customers to choose without restriction between the regulated price for bundled utility service and the price offered by the generation services market may severely reduce the utility's ability to plan for, and reliably serve, its remaining customers. Absent modifications to the compact's traditional duty to service, consumers may make choices about electric services which they find economically attractive, but which are undesirable with respect to the broader goal of allocating society's resources efficiently.

The possibility of such uneconomic bypass—bypass that might work to lower costs for a single shopping customer while raising average costs for other customers—may necessitate some consideration of the costs of the traditional duty to serve. Moreover, a system that allows power suppliers and customers to choose to deal with each other, especially if left unregulated, may allow suppliers or distributors to elect never to serve certain classes of customers, such as low-income residents, or to cease service however they wish consistent with retail power sales agreements. In at least one state, concerns over the implications of competition for the duty to serve and for service quality more generally were cited as reasons not to pursue retail competition for the present. It should come as no surprise that, in the telecommunications context, many observe a "conflict" between the telecom analog to the duty to serve—universal service—and retail competition.

1. The Challenge of Simultaneous Competition and Access

Of course, perceived conflicts between vigorous retail competition and customer access can be avoided to the extent that one of these seemingly incompatible goals is simply abandoned. Because it is not likely that the movement towards retail competition in traditional public utility industries will cease, one option in the face of the tension between retail competition and common law service obligations is to abandon the duty to serve for electric power markets, treating electricity service as any other service in a competitive market. After all, as retail markets open up, it will be increasingly possible for suppliers and distributors to provide a variety of service qualities to end users. Without a duty to serve, the electricity market might operate much like other deregulated markets, such as trucking and banking, which rely on contractual obligations and general consumer protection laws to ensure service delivery. If a supplier refuses service to a customer, the customer must find alternative suppliers, and competition in power generation will likely provide customers a range of power supply qualities. And, should a power distributor refuse to extend or continue service to a customer because it is not profitable, the customer may attempt to find alternatives. For example, alternatives such as self-generation or wheeling around the DisCo may be cost feasible for large, heavy load customers of electricity. Markets, after all, flourish with bilateral relationships; the duty to serve imposes a unilateral obligation on the incumbent utility. Customers in such markets already have a variety of legal protections, including credit financing and consumer protection statutes, such as the Uniform Commercial Code.

Yet, though a challenge, it is not an impossible task for regulators to establish extraordinary service obligations in competitive retail industries. Many insurance industries provide for universal service through various sorts of assigned risk pools. For example, the property insurance industry has developed Fair Access to Insurance Requirements ("FAIR") plans. In the hospital industry, the obligation of hospitals to serve the indigent is explicitly made a condition in the awarding of federal construction grants. Nonprofit health care providers take on an obligation to provide indigent health care, in part as a condition to the grant of certain governmental benefits, such as federal, state, or local tax benefits. Although it may be questionable how successful these approaches to promoting universal service have been, the experience in these industries suggests that the conflict between retail competition and universal service is not new. Those who look askance at the duty to serve in the age of competition refuse the enormous challenge it poses, but the challenge is not an insurmountable barrier.

To date, those states that have addressed retail competition in power markets express an awareness of the potential tension between the common law duty to serve and competitive retail markets without abandoning either goal. The preamble to California's 1996 retail wheeling legislation states, "(I)t is the further intent of the Legislature to continue to fund low-income ratepayer assistance programs ... in an unbundled manner" and maintains 1996–level low-income and universal service expenditures. New Hampshire, which considered similar legislation, is more explicit:

A restructured electric utility industry should provide adequate safeguards to assure universal service. Minimum residential customer service safeguards and protections should be maintained. Programs and mechanisms that enable residential customers with low incomes to manage and afford essential electricity requirements should be included as a part of industry restructuring.

The task of formulating extraordinary service obligations should not preclude consideration of retail competition by states, nor should it necessarily lead to the abandonment of extraordinary service obligations. In fact, the introduction of retail competition may even lead to enhancement of consumer protection obligations, perhaps from fear of the abuses markets may yield. In Ohio, for example, the consideration of retail competition has mobilized consumer protection interests, leading to the proposal of minimum electricity service standards for the first time in the state's history.

2.   Rationales for the Duty to Serve and Its Application to the DisCo

At least in the short run, for small load customers, such as residential customers, small business, and single location offices, power distribution is considered to remain a natural monopoly service. Put another way, a single utility will continue to provide distribution to power supply for the large bulk of power customers. So, for most smaller customers who do not have access to capital financing markets or own rights of way to build transmission lines, it is cost prohibitive to duplicate distribution lines if the incumbent DisCo itself owns the facilities. Thus, even in competitive retail markets, DisCos will initially remain natural monopolies for residential and small commercial customers, at least with respect to the horizontal distribution market. Following California's approach, to date every state retail wheeling plan treats power distribution in this manner by defining a de jure monopoly for distribution, subject to fairly traditional regulation, effectively defining a new regulatory compact that is limited to power distribution.

Further, to date every state that has seriously considered moving to retail competition in the sale of electricity has determined that the DisCo must provide a "basic service" option to those who do not choose an alternative supplier for electricity, are refused service by a retail supplier, or have been disconnected. In some states, this will be regulated at a rate established to be less than the rates immediately prior to competition, thus minimizing the impact of stranded costs on small residential customers.

For example, according to Vermont's retail competition restructuring order, "exclusive franchises for distribution" remain necessary. The DisCo "will retain its obligation to plan, build, and operate its local distribution system in a manner that ensures safe and reliable service to customers." Vermont defines the "Basic Service Offer" as "(s)ervice offered to customers by the distribution company but provided by a retail service provider through contract." This service "(m)ay be priced either to float with the spot market or fixed on a longer-term basis." After the transition to retail competition this offer, which is limited to franchised customers of DisCos, "will be made available over a contracted period" and "through a retail service provider."

Since retail competition envisions the fragmentation of utility service into different markets, from generation to transmission to distribution, the implications of continuing the duty to serve will need to be assessed in the context of each of these markets. Given power distribution's de jure monopoly status under state retail wheeling plans, most state regulators, with little or no analysis, look initially to the DisCo as the primary bearer of the traditional duty to serve. However, given the inapplicability of the traditional rate regulation framework for understanding service obligations in the competitive market structure and the mobilization of interests likely to support imposition of new service obligations, the economic efficiency rationales for continuing to impose an extraordinary service obligation on the incumbent utility require reassessment.

Consider, first, the economic rationales for imposing service extension obligations. Because the DisCo maintains a horizontal monopoly with respect to rights of way and essential network facilities, most customers will continue to require its distribution service. At the same time, the

DisCo will be in a better position than suppliers or others to spread the costs of service extension, minimizing the economic impact of the distribution network on customers, particularly the poor. Customers, on average, are likely to have higher marginal utilities of money than the DisCo, so imposing upon the DisCo an obligation to provide service and spread the costs may maximize social welfare. Even in a competitive retail market, economic efficiency rationales for requiring the DisCo to extend its distribution network to customers seem relevant. It should be noted, though, that in a deregulated environment where power supply is competitive, the access and cost spreading rationales for the extension obligation apply to distribution service only, not to competitively provided power supply. Put another way, despite an economic rationale for requiring the DisCo to assume some distribution service extension obligation, economic analysis does not necessarily require the DisCo to also provide power supply. Thus, without further exploration of the structure of retail power markets, there does not appear to be a strong economic rationale for requiring the DisCo to build generation facilities or procure power supply to serve customers. Nevertheless, to the extent regulators decide to impose basic service obligations on some institutional actor in competitive power markets, the DisCo may also be in the best position to spread the costs associated with basic service.

With respect to service continuation, the second obligation of the traditional duty to serve, the economic efficiency rationales behind the obligation also require some reassessment. [O]ne of the primary economic efficiency rationales for imposing extraordinary service continuation obligations relates to the utility's status as the superior risk-bearer vis-a-vis the customer. In deregulated power markets, however, the long-term contract analogy, which undergirds application of superior risk-bearer analysis to the regulatory compact, loses much of its relevance, since customers themselves may select power suppliers on a month-to-month basis.

Further, in a competitive retail market, the same rationales cannot justify imposition of an obligation on a private firm to provide full service below cost, as often applied under rate regulation. Now, as has been observed, there may be some continuing advantage to avoiding power shut-off to the extent that a customer is able to pay the variable portion of the costs associated with the supply and distribution of power. This cost sharing advantage, however, is significantly reduced in a competitive market in which power suppliers face alternative customers for their capacity; it may apply to distribution service, but, absent excess capacity committed to DisCo customers, it does not apply to power supply.

Despite these structural and regulatory differences between a competitive market and the traditional regulated industry, some efficiency arguments support imposition of a service continuation obligation on the DisCo or other suppliers in a competitive environment. First, with respect to service discontinuation, the physics of power flow may require the DisCo to bear some responsibility if its grid has not been modernized. Once power is supplied to a distribution grid without computerized customer metering, the DisCo is automatically the supplier of last resort to the retail customer; the customer will continue to receive power until it is physically disconnected by the DisCo. In certain areas, technology may necessitate some DisCo service continuation obligation.

A second rationale for imposition of a service continuation obligation is that power markets may yield poor information. Assuming that customers have good information about power supply options and the terms of power supply sales contracts, when compared to the DisCo, the customer will be the superior bearer of the risks of service shut-off. The customer can purchase supply plans that provide for early warning or, if necessary, insurance to cover the risks of property or other damage due to a loss of power. Many customers, though, may not have adequate information about power supply markets so as to react to the risks of shut-off, particularly where shut-off is due to technological failure or emergencies. In addition, in competitive power markets, consumers are unlikely to immediately possess the knowledge or experience to react to this information when some action, such as the purchasing of power insurance or backup supply options, is in order. Poor information or consumer discounting of risks may require the DisCo or a supplier to assume some service continuation obligation, even in a competitive power supply market. This will especially be true as these markets initially evolve and as regulators embark on the task of educating consumers.

Further, given that a welfare system already exists in our market economy, the imposition of service continuation obligations in a competitive power supply market might work to mitigate the incentives the welfare system produces for taking excessive credit risks. As competitive power markets evolve, consumers are likely to be offered credit financing plans for electricity akin to many of the financing plans available for other purchases, such as purchase of an automobile. Offerers of such sales are likely to provide creative financing options, often offering consumers who are poor credit risks high-cost financing plans. Such risks, to the extent they are repeatedly presented to low-income consumers in a competitive power supply market, will also increase the incidence of default, especially because utilities will not face the same incentives as under rate regulation to continue service with acceptance of partial payment. As customers increasingly default and lose the basic necessities of life, such as electricity service, over time this could both drive up the cost of the welfare system and undermine its poverty reduction goal. Thus, imposition of a service continuation obligation, even in a competitive market, might be seen as a way of reducing the costs of other public welfare programs.

Though some reassessment is necessary, economic efficiency arguments for continuing with some extraordinary service obligations in competitive markets are not completely irrelevant. To the extent economic arguments exist, though, they relate primarily to horizontal integration and the quality of information consumers will likely possess, because with retail competition, the market facilitates many of the transactions which the traditional public utility previously coordinated within a single, vertically integrated firm. Weaknesses with the economic efficiency rationales for the traditional duty to serve aside, to the extent regulators continue to adhere to the constituent obligations of the common law duty to serve, they will also likely need to articulate non-efficiency justifications, such as fairness or distributive justice. In this sense, retail competition is likely to force more explicit discussion of the costs and benefits of extraordinary service obligations than occurred under the traditional regulatory compact. For example, in Ohio the discussion of consumer service protections has become explicit with the dawn of competition, while previously consumer protections were sometimes built into utility tariffs on a voluntary basis.

To the extent a duty to serve continues to apply to the industry, for whatever reasons, competitively priced retail power markets will work to minimize many of the price distortions of cross-subsidization historically associated with extraordinary service obligations. Under a rate regulation regime, utility service obligations were paid for through cross-subsidization, but rate regulation helped to minimize the market distortions caused by this practice. Utilities generally were not opposed to taking on service obligations, especially where they worked to enlarge the customer base, so long as they could recover the costs of these obligations from some customers. With retail competition and a movement to market-based pricing, cross-subsidization will continue to exist, but power supply markets will require DisCos to minimize the impact of subsidies on customers or risk losing customers, especially larger ones, to bypass or other suppliers wheeling on the DisCo system. Most DisCos are attempting to cover some or all of the cost of extraordinary access (along with the costs of environmental programs) through an SBC for which the retail customers who have power delivered via the distribution system pay. FERC has observed, "the authority of state commissions to address retail stranded costs is based on their jurisdiction over local distribution facilities and the service of delivering electric energy to end users." So long as states are regulating distribution service, there is some basis for a state-imposed charge and it is unlikely that this will be preempted under the Federal Power Act.

While imposition of extraordinary service obligations on the DisCo is a common and noncontroversial element of each state retail wheeling plan to date, its implementation poses new problems for regulators. First, is limiting imposition of extraordinary service obligations to the DisCo the best way to ensure an efficient power supply, or should regulators attempt to find ways to shift some of the extraordinary service obligations to power suppliers or marketers? Second, absent the traditional levels of vertical integration, how is the DisCo to obtain basic service power and ensure reliability for incumbent customers? Will it have an obligation to provide power supply from generators it owns or operates, or should the DisCo have some other mechanism for shifting the risk of supply shortage to power suppliers or others? If the former should be the case, residential and small commercial customers are unlikely to see many of the benefits of retail competition. However, because DisCos may have little notice of power needs—and no time to notify suppliers—it may be a challenge for them to plan for reliable power. Third, and most important, how will service obligations be paid for? Structuring this SBC is likely to be the subject of rate design debate, but in the long run the SBC will become unworkable if power distribution becomes structurally competitive. Regulators, then, will be required to look to alternative financing mechanisms for consumer access.■

NOTES AND COMMENTS

1. Why are power generation companies, suppliers, marketers and brokers different from distribution companies? Should these actors also bear a duty to serve? If so, how would this be implemented?

2. How will power be provided for the "basic service" plan that is used to meet consumer service obligations in a competitive market? Various proposals focus on establishing a mandatory power supply pool, mimicking the Telecom model, competitive bidding, allocating basic service based on market share, or pure competition through a power exchange. The mandatory supply pool would require each generating company wishing to compete in a retail market to set aside a portion of its capacity for "basic service." This approach is consistent with those who argue that "[a]ffirmative [service] obligations should attach to each part of the industry." *See* Roger D. Colton, The 'Obligation to Serve' and a Competitive Electric Industry 45 (DOE Office of Economic, Electricity and Natural Gas Analysis, May 1997). The Telecom model, implemented by federal regulators following the breakup of AT & T, allows each customers to select its preferred long distance carrier. Applied to electricity supply, each customer could be mailed a ballot to select its power supplier; absent consumer selection of a power supplier, the customer's basic service plan is assigned the incumbent DisCo. Regulators could also conduct a competitive bidding procedure for basic service, choosing one or more basic service suppliers for a defined term. A fourth approach, endorsed by the National Consumer Law Center, would assign basic service obligations to generators based on market share. *See* Barbara Alexander, Consumer Protection Proposals for Retail Electric Competition 32 (1996). For discussion and criticism of the various approaches to ensuring basic service, see Jim Rossi The Common Law "Duty to Serve" and Protection of Consumers in an Age of Competitive Retail Public Utility Restructuring, 51 Vand. L. Rev. 1233, 1301–14 (1998). How does California ensure basic service will be provided?

3. With the adoption on comprehensive retail competition plans, state regulators are required to embark on massive consumer education programs. In addition, as retail markets emerge, state regulators need to actively police against abuses such as "slamming" and "cramming," as have developed in competitive telecommunications markets. How should regulators perform this role? What will this mean for the traditional state PSC? While the PSC may have the authority to punish the handful of utilities it regulated through incentive regulation for service disruptions and other problems, how will it perform its role in a competitive retail market where there are hundreds or thousands of energy companies

providing services to customers? California requires energy service providers to register with the state commission. California Public Utilities Commission, D.98–03–072, Opinion Regarding Consumer Protection (Mar. 26, 1998).

4. With the rise of retail competition, consumer bills have become increasingly complex. In states such as California, consumers are sent a monthly bill that contains itemized accounts of generation, distribution, and transmission charges. They may also pay renewable fees and other "transition" charges to cover stranded costs. A systems benefits charge (or SBC) refers to a catchall charge designed to fund consumer protection and environmental programs.

5. The rise of microturbines, or distributed generation, challenges the necessity of the DisCo's monopoly. What if distribution is no longer a natural monopoly? Have the economic arguments for service obligations lost their relevance? In the telecommunications industry, wireless services challenge the traditional monopoly that attached to the "wires" of the local telephone company, but universal service has survived. Why? Is a physical energy market, such as electricity or natural gas, any different? For criticism of the widely-held position that distribution remains a natural monopoly in a competitive power supply market, even without microturbines, see Vernon L. Smith, Can Electric Power "Natural Monopoly" Be Deregulated?, in Making National Energy Policy (Hans H. Landsberg, ed. 1993).

b. STATE ACTION IMMUNITY FROM ANTITRUST LAWS

The antitrust laws are designed to protect against anti-competitive and monopolistic conduct. The overarching purpose of antitrust law is to promote competition. Most modern antitrust laws in the United States derive from important antitrust statutes passed during the late nineteenth and early twentieth centuries, such as the Sherman Antitrust Act of 1890 ("the Sherman Act"). The wording of the Sherman Act's two substantive sections—Sections 1 and 2—reflects Congress's broad public policy against anti-competitive behavior. Another statute, the Clayton Act, was adopted several years later. A variety of offenses are included under the Sherman Act and Clayton Act, including combinations in restraint of trade, price fixing, price squeeze, and other anticompetitive acts. The antitrust laws also allow courts (and the Department of Justice) to scrutinize mergers; in the electric utility context, FERC has merger authority, which is discussed further in Chapter 18.

Unlike many industries, electric utilities have not been afforded an explicit exemption from antitrust liability. Instead, the industry had traditionally been granted immunity because of the view that the industry is comprised of natural monopolies—to the extent natural monopoly regulation dominates, the protection of competition is considered inappropriate. Because the purpose of antitrust laws is to support competition but competition was deemed to be inappropriate for the electric utility industry, the courts developed antitrust immunity the activities of most electric utilities under the state action doctrine. The following case illustrates the application of this doctrine:

TEC Cogeneration, Inc. v. Florida Power & Light Co.,

76 F.3d 1560 (11th Cir. 1996).

This is an appeal from the denial of a motion for summary judgment by the district court. Two questions are presented: first, whether a public utility is immune from antitrust liability under the state-action doctrine of *Parker v. Brown*, 317 U.S. 341, (1943), for its allegedly anti-competitive conduct concerning a cogenerator in the areas of wheeling, rates, and interconnection; and second, whether lobbying of a county legislative body by the utility is protected from antitrust liability under the Noerr/ Pennington doctrine. *Eastern R.R. Presidents Conference v. Noerr Motor Freight, Inc.*, 365 U.S. 127, (1961); *United Mine Workers of America v. Pennington*, 381 U.S. 657, (1965). The district court found that the utility was not entitled to immunity from antitrust sanctions for its actions. We disagree. The denial by the district court of the utility's motion for summary judgment is reversed.

Appellant Florida Power & Light Company (FPL) is an investor-owned public electric utility engaged in three functions: generation, transmission, and distribution and sale of electric energy. It services southern and eastern Florida, including most of Dade [County]. FPL is regulated by the Florida Public Service Commission (PSC). It owns and controls ninety percent of the total electrical generating capacity in its service area and the electrical grid with which [the Miami Downtown Government] Center can interconnect. FPL has monopoly power within its service area both as to the purchase of wholesale power and the sale of retail power.

In 1981, Dade issued requests to bid on the Center cogeneration facility. Cogenerators' proposal was selected and in late 1983, Dade and the Cogenerators entered into contracts providing for the construction and operation of a twenty-seven megawatt cogeneration facility at Center and for the supply of cogeneration equipment for the project. The Cogenerators agreed to operate Center for Dade for sixteen years. The Cogenerators also contracted to supply electrical and thermal power to Dade. Dade and the Cogenerators were to share in the profits, if any, from operating the Center; the Cogenerators were to absorb the losses. The final contract allowed for excess power, if any, from Center, to be dispensed to Dade facilities outside Center, such as to the Jackson Memorial Hospital/Civic Center complex (Hospital). Practically speaking, excess power could be dispensed only one of two ways, either via a wheeling arrangement with FPL or by constructing a separate transmission line. A separate line would require the approval of the local legislative body, i.e., the Dade County Board of Commissioners (Commission). With these parameters in place, construction of the cogeneration facility commenced in mid–1984 and the facility became fully operational at the end of 1986.

To reduce their losses, the Cogenerators sought a logical use for the excess power. Under rules promulgated by the PSC, two options were immediately available: (1) the Cogenerators could either sell the surplus electricity to FPL at a rate equal to FPL's avoided cost; or (2) the Cogenerators could force FPL to transmit or wheel the excess power to another Florida utility, who in turn would purchase it at its own avoided cost rate.

At avoided cost rates, it appeared that the Cogenerators could not break even with either option. FPL alleges that the Cogenerators deliberately ignored their two legitimate options and pursued a third, allegedly illegitimate, alternative in order to obtain higher prices for their power: the Cogenerators approached FPL to wheel their surplus power to other Dade facilities outside Center, most notably, to Hospital, two miles northwest. Believing that the Cogenerators' request violated the PSC's self-service wheeling rules,[17][5] FPL declined to wheel.

Rebuffed by FPL, the Cogenerators then turned to the best efforts clause in its contract with Dade. They directed Dade, in effect, to petition the PSC for an order compelling FPL to wheel power from Center to other Dade facilities, including Hospital.

After an eleven-month administrative proceeding, the PSC denied Dade's petition. The PSC found that Dade could not comply with the PSC's self-service wheeling rules because Dade did not actually own the generating equipment that produced the power to be wheeled; did not generate the power to be wheeled; and was contractually bound to purchase the electricity from the Cogenerators. Hence, the PSC found, by definition, that Dade could not "serve oneself." Petition of Metropolitan Dade County for Expedited Consideration of Request for Provision of Self–Service Transmission, Order No. 17510, Docket No. 860786–EI, 87 FPSC 5:32, 35–37 (May 5, 1987).

After the PSC wheeling disallowance, the Cogenerators played their fourth and final card: what can't be sent indirectly, send directly. They approached Dade with a proposal to construct a separate transmission line from Center to Hospital. A separate line would reduce surplus electricity without being dependent upon wheeling by FPL at avoided cost rates. A joint submission was made by the Cogenerators and Dade to Commission for its approval. The Cogenerators lobbied Commission for approval; FPL lobbied against. The Commission voted five-to-one against the construction of the separate transmission line.

Within weeks, the Cogenerators filed this suit....

---

5. Under PSC regulations, the Cogenerators can ask FPL to wheel electricity from Center to Hospital only if they qualify under the self-service wheeling rules: (1) there must be an exact identity of ownership between the generator and the consumer of the electricity; and (2) wheeling will not increase rates to utility, i.e., FPL ratepayers. Fla.Admin.Code R. 25–17.0882. Under Florida law, a cogenerator may not sell electricity at retail. *PW Ventures*, 533 So.2d at 281.

FPL's motion for summary judgment relies principally on two immunity doctrines: the state action immunity doctrine and the Noerr/ Pennington immunity doctrine. The district court denied summary judgment under both.

We review each of these findings de novo.

B. The State Action Immunity Doctrine

The Supreme Court first articulated the state-action immunity doctrine in *Parker v. Brown*, 317 U.S. 341 (1943). In Parker, the Court grappled with the applicability of the Sherman Act to a California agricultural statutory program intended to restrict competition among private producers of raisins in order to stabilize prices and prevent economic waste. Relying on principles of federalism and state sovereignty, the Court refused to find that the Sherman Act was "intended to restrain state action or official action directed by a state" and determined that "[t]here is no suggestion of a purpose to restrain state action in the Act's legislative history." Id. at 351. The Court held, therefore, that federal antitrust laws were not intended to reach state-regulated anticompetitive activities. Id. at 350–52, *City of Columbia v. Omni Outdoor Advertising, Inc.*, 499 U.S. 365, 370 (1991).

Thirty-seven years later, in *California Retail Liquor Dealers Ass'n. v. Midcal Aluminum, Inc.*, 445 U.S. 97 (1980), a unanimous Court established a two-pronged test to determine when private party anticompetitive conduct is entitled to state action immunity from antitrust liability: (1) the conduct had to be performed pursuant to a clearly articulated policy of the state to displace competition with regulation; and (2) the conduct had to be closely supervised by the state. Id. at 105; see also *F.T.C. v. Ticor Title Ins. Co.*, 504 U.S. 621 (1992). These two prongs are addressed below.

1. Clearly Articulated Policy of the State.

The Court set out the first element of state action immunity in *Southern Motor Carriers Rate Conference, Inc. v. U.S.*, 471 U.S. 48 (1985). There, the Court determined that a private party acting pursuant to an anticompetitive regulatory program need not "point to a specific, detailed legislative authorization" for its challenged conduct. Id. at 57, 105 S.Ct. at 1726. As long as the State as sovereign clearly intends to displace competition in a particular field with a regulatory structure, the first prong of the *Midcal* test is satisfied. Id. at 64.

In this case, the district court found that Florida has two statutory policies regarding power generation and transmission: a policy favoring monopoly power in Florida electric utilities, and a policy of encouraging development of Florida cogeneration facilities, complemented by the implementation of PSC regulatory guidelines. Fla.Stat. § 366.051 (1991). The district court found that these statutes set out clearly articulated policies regarding utilities and cogenerators. Accordingly, the district court found that FPL had satisfied the first prong of the *Midcal* test, except as to its Strategic Energy Business Study or SEBS.

We agree with the district court that Florida has an obvious and clearly articulated policy to displace competition with regulation in the area of power generation and transmission and that FPL's conduct has been performed pursuant to that policy. The Florida legislature gave the PSC broad authority to regulate FPL. See Ch. 366, Fla.Stat. Further, the relationship between Florida utilities and cogenerators has been subject to pervasive state regulation through statute and regulatory rules. Fla.Stat. § 366.05(1), . 04(1), (5), .06(1), .051 (1994); Fla.Admin.Code R. 25–17.080–.091 (1988). A myriad of agency proceedings have transpired. The field has not been left to the parties' unfettered business discretion. In addition, the Florida Supreme Court has been active in its role of judicial review. See *C.F. Industries, Inc. v. Nichols*, 536 So.2d 234 (Fla.1988) (standby rates for qualifying facilities); *PW Ventures, Inc. v. Nichols*, 533 So.2d 281 (Fla.1988) (third-party sales by qualifying facilities); *Storey v. Mayo*, 217 So.2d 304, 307 (Fla.1968), cert. denied, 395 U.S. 909 (1969) ("The powers of the Commission over ... privately-owned utilities [are] omnipotent within the confines of the statute and the limits of organic law.").

We disagree, however, with the district court's exclusion of SEBS from its finding. It is clear that Florida intended to displace competition in the utility industry with a regulatory structure, Southern Motor Carriers, 471 U.S. at 64, 105 S.Ct. at 1730, and FPL's internal SEBS study has no relevance to the issue of Florida's clearly articulated policy of regulation. Contrary to the district court's ruling, we conclude that the first prong of the state action defense is satisfied here, without qualification, that is, including SEBS.

2.   Conduct Actively Supervised by the State.

This second prong of the state action defense applies when the challenged conduct is by a private party rather than a government official. *Ticor*, 504 U.S. at 630. Active state involvement is the second precondition for antitrust immunity; the conduct by the private party has to be closely supervised by the state. *Midcal*, 445 U.S. at 105–06. The active supervision requirement is designed to ensure that the state has "ultimate control" over the private party's conduct, with the power to review and disapprove, if necessary, particular anticompetitive acts that may offend state policy. *Patrick v. Burget*, 486 U.S. 94, 101 (1988).

The district court considered FPL's conduct in three areas alleged to be anticompetitive by the Cogenerators: (1) FPL's refusal to wheel; (2) its use of rates; and (3) its alleged interference with interconnection. It determined that for FPL to meet the second prong of the state action defense, Florida, through the PSC, must have "actively supervised, substantially reviewed, or independently exercised judgment and control" over FPL's "overall anti-competitive campaign."

In each of the three areas, the district court found that, while the PSC had the power to review FPL's conduct, it was not given the opportunity to exercise its power to review FPL's conduct. Therefore, the district court determined that the PSC's regulatory authority (in application or as applied) did not satisfy the second prong of the state action immunity standard.

As we conclude that the PSC did in fact exercise active supervision over FPL, we do not discuss these areas separately, as the same rationale applies to each.

3.   The Active Supervision in this Case.

In 1987, the PSC denied Dade's petition to allow the Cogenerators to wheel power to Hospital because they could not satisfy the PSC self-service wheeling rules. *In re: Petition of Metropolitan Dade County*, Order No. 17510 (1987).

The district court notes that FPL stands behind this PSC ruling as conclusive evidence of active state supervision. The district court finds this reliance misplaced. It focuses instead on the circumstances leading up to the PSC hearing: FPL's acts that have their genesis in the embryonic stages of Center when FPL participated in the early negotiations of the Cogenerator–Dade agreement. That is, under an estoppel-like analysis, the district court found that, when FPL ostensibly gave its blessing to the contract (with full knowledge that it contemplated: (1) the wheeling of excess power by FPL to other Dade locations; (2) the conveyance of power to other Dade facilities through a direct transmission line; or (3) the sale of excess power to FPL at avoided cost rates), it can't be heard to complain now. The district court's determination is based, not on whether the PSC had the power to actively supervise and review FPL's conduct, but on whether it was ever given the opportunity to exercise its power to supervise and review (and possibly disapprove), these early acts of FPL.

That is not the issue. The issue is this: Has the State of Florida, through its state regulatory agency, the PSC, actively supervised FPL in the areas of wheeling, rates and interconnection? The answer is clearly yes, as to each. The fact that FPL didn't complain about wheeling or rates or interconnection when it first reviewed the Center contract is not material as to whether or not the PSC had the power to actively supervise FPL. That power is insulated. FPL's failure to object does not take away from the PSC its opportunity to exercise the power of active supervision. Failure by the parties to commence an action or proceeding (at the time when the district court apparently thought they should have objected), does not constitute the nullification of the PSC's power to act.

The PSC exercises its powers only when called upon to do so. No call was made. For example, the decisions of this circuit govern or control a plethora of legal issues—but if a particular issue is never brought before us—it doesn't mean we don't have control. We don't have opportunity—but we still have control. We still have active supervision.

The record is clear—the doors to the PSC were open to all with standing to complain. Being met with a complaint, the PSC had the full power to actively supervise. Whether or not the State, through the PSC, exercises its control sua sponte is not material, unless, of course, there is an apparent devious design to abdicate or obstruct control, and that is not the case here. The record shows that, when the PSC was called upon, they acted. We, the judiciary, do not have to take a walk with the PSC members to see if they visit FPL's offices every morning.

In sum, Florida has clearly articulated policies regarding the relationship between FPL and the Cogenerators. In addition, the record is clear that the PSC actively supervised all aspects of FPL's alleged anti-competitive conduct. We conclude, therefore, that both prongs of the state action immunity doctrine are satisfied here and FPL's conduct is immune from antitrust liability in each of the three areas of wheeling, rates and interconnection.■

NOTES AND COMMENTS

1. An official with the U.S. Department of Justice Antitrust Division has stated:

> "If a state opens its retail market to competition, then the state action doctrine would not apply to conduct that relates directly to retail competition," says the attorney, Milton A. Marquis. "So I think it's becoming less relevant in electricity, certainly with respect to wholesale [power], which is not a state matter anyway, but with respect to retail competition in those states that have decided to open their retail markets to competition. Because you can't have both. You can't have the state action doctrine and retail competition."

Joseph F. Schuler, State Action Doctrine Losing Relevance, Department of Justice Attorney Says, Fortnightly, May 15, 1999, at 70. Would the TEC Cogeneration case be decided differently today in a state like California, which has adopted a comprehensive retail competition plan?

2. Despite the national movement towards competition, some appellate courts continue to decide cases consistent with the approach of the Eleventh Circuit in *TEC Cogeneration. See North Star Steel Co. v. MidAmerican Energy Holdings Co.*, 184 F.3d 732 (8th Cir. 1999) (examining Iowa's regulatory scheme and concluding that state action immunity applies).

Under the case law, however, the case for erosion of the state action doctrine for at least some aspects of the industry, if deregulated, seems strong. In *Cantor v. Detroit Edison Co.*, it was held that a utility could be subject to antitrust liability for illegally tying the "sale" of free light bulbs to the sale of electricity. 428 U.S. 579 (1976). There, the Court found the state action doctrine inapplicable for two reasons: (1) the decision to engage in the program and to recover the costs through the company's electric rates was more the decision of the company than the state public service commission; and (2) the bundling of light bulbs to electric sales, although approved and supervised by the state agency, was not integral to the state's interest and policy in the regulation of electric utilities.

Similarly, in *Columbia Steel Casting Co., Inc. v. Portland General Electric Co.*, 111 F.3d 1427 (9th Cir.1996), a court found that the state action doctrine did not protect an agreement between two utilities to divide the city of Portland into separate service territories. The court observed that technology and deregulation have recently been exerting competitive pressures into markets where utility monopolies once dominated. The court determined that the state commission's orders were not specific enough to meet the clearly articulated policy requirement of the *Midcal* test. In addition, the court looked to a city ordinance that disapproved of exclusive territories and instead favored competition.

For discussion of application of the state action doctrine to a deregulated electric power industry, see Jeffery D. Schwartz, The Use of the Antitrust State Action Doctrine in the Deregulated Electric Utility Industry, 48 Am. U. L. Rev. 1449 (1999).

B.   The Tension Between Competition and Environmental Regulation

While most of the debate over transition costs centers around the issue of stranded investment and its impacts on consumers and investors (*see* Chapter 12), widespread retail competition will also have a significant impact on environmental regulation of the industry. Environmental and conservation mechanisms are addressed above in Chapter 10; the following readings address the conflict between many of these mechanisms and competition in the electricity industry.

1.   Federal Competition Policy and the Environment

Some see competition in the electric power industry as leading to a reduction in certain air pollutants that have contributed to global warming. For example, one author argues that competition will encourage the development of more efficient combined-cycle generation technologies, which will displace out of date and inefficient technologies, such as single-cycle coal generation. This, the author argues, will lead to a reduction in emissions of greenhouse gases that contribute to global warming. *See* Thomas R. Casten, Turning Off the Heat: Why America Must Double Energy Efficiency to Save Money and Reduce Global Warming (Prometheus Books 1998). Many others, however, are not as optimistic about the prospects of competition for environmental regulations. For example, a report by the Congressional Research Service gives the following account of the impacts of competition in power on air pollution:

Congressional Research Service (Larry Parker and John Blodgett), 98–615: Electricity Restructuring: The Implications for Air Quality

(Updated July 16, 1999) <http://www.cnie.org/nle/eng-43.html> (last visited Mar. 15, 2000).

[T]he general scenario goes as follows. A competitive generating sector would result in a revaluation of generating assets—i.e., moving from a traditional embedded-cost valuation scheme to a market valuation scheme, which would increase the value of some generating capacity and decrease the value of other generating capacity. Competition would tend to move the value of generating capacity to the marginal cost of constructing new capacity, generally represented at the current time by a new natural gas-fired, combined-cycle facility. In general, older facilities that have been fully depreciated would tend to have market values greater than their current book value under regulation; in contrast, newer, capital intensive facilities (such as some nuclear plants) would have market values less than their current book value. (Case-by-case valuation would be affected by location, availability of alternatives, and electricity demand.) In addition, the Clean Air Act typically imposes its most stringent pollution controls on new powerplant construction, permitting existing capacity to meet less stringent and less costly standards. This differential impact may give some older facilities a competitive operating cost advantage to complement their low, depreciated cost basis.

The new valuation, combined with low operating costs, would encourage operators to maximize generation from their existing facilities. For example, over one-half the increase in electricity generation projected for 2005 (about 64,000 MW) could be obtained if operation of coal-fired capacity increased from its 62% capacity factor in 1995 to 75%. However, the economic and environmental advantages of new technology, such as natural gas-fired, combined-cycle technology (a very clean technology) may be sufficient in some case to overcome the advantages of expanding use of existing plants.

Environmental Implications. It is this renewed attractiveness of existing capacity under restructuring, specifically of coal-fired capacity, along with the potential that demand for electricity may rise (and energy conservation slacken) if prices decline, that raises environmental concerns. Absent effective controls, burning more coal will produce more emissions than alternative sources of electricity generation—and much of that coal capacity is in the Midwest, which is currently a center of attention for reducing NOx emissions.

Except for CO2, the regulatory regimen of the Clean Air Act provides authorities for controlling the potential increase in emissions—assuming they are effectively implemented. Existing controls "cap" SO2 emissions in the 48 contiguous states and the District of Columbia, and there is no reason to question the effectiveness of the cap in the future, regardless of the changes underway in the utility industry. For NOx emissions, control and implementation is more complicated, primarily because implementation of much of the process lies with the states. Any increase in NOx emissions in the Midwest could complicate an already difficult process underway to reduce the region's NOx emissions, which contribute to ozone nonattainment in the Northeast. How this regional, state-implemented process would be affected by restructuring is not certain.

CO2 is not currently regulated. Any increase in fossil fuel-fired generation will increase CO2 emissions, with coal producing about 75% more carbon emissions than natural gas on a Btu basis. If the U.S. were to ratify the Kyoto Agreement, which would require the U.S. to reduce greenhouse gas emissions to below 1990 levels, any increases would have to be rolled back or offset. The effort required would be increased if restructuring differentially advantaged coal. Ultimately, whether developments in electricity generation and demand lead to increased emissions of air pollutants depends on the implementation of the CAA (and on any new requirements that might be enacted); while for CO2, increases are likely unless Congress ratifies the Kyoto Agreement and enacts implementing legislation (an uncertain prospect). Those who are focused on preventing environmental deterioration tend to take a precautionary stance, to propose immediate preventative measures, and to argue that such measures be attached to available legislative vehicles. In contrast, those who doubt that there will be significant environmental effects and/or who are focused on the substantial regulatory structure in place tend to take a wait-and-see position.

The current attention on increased emissions from coal-fired generation may address the clearest and most quantifiable risk to the environment from restructuring, but with so many changes underway, the ultimate outcome remains uncertain. Some trends are already manifest, such as renovation of existing coal-fired capacity. Others are just emerging, such as a "green market" in California, in which consumers can take into account environmental costs in their purchasing decisions. Some effects remain to be determined in the future, such as the implications of new price signals for demand and conservation; the implication of new cost valuations for the choice of new generating technologies; developments in transmission capacity; and the effectiveness of ongoing environmental programs.■

NOTES AND COMMENTS

1. As the Congressional Research Service excerpt suggests, it could be a mistake to conclude that environmental concerns are irrelevant to the federal wholesale power competition policies discussed in Chapter 11. Nor are they irrelevant to state retail competition policies, discussed earlier in this Chapter, or to stranded cost compensation, discussed in Chapter 12. Stranded cost computation, for example, may affect the economic viability of generation from older polluting sources. The environmental transition costs of competition were a significant issue in the process of adoption of Order No. 888. FERC stated in its final rule:

> The Commission has prepared a Final Environmental Impact Statement (FEIS) evaluating the possible environmental consequences of changes in the bulk power marketplace expected to occur as a result of the open access requirements of this Final Rule. The FEIS focuses, as do most commenters, on possible increases in emissions of nitrogen oxides (NO[X]) from certain fossil-fuel fired generators, which could affect air quality in the producing region and in areas to which these emissions may be carried.

In response to comments on the Draft EIS, the Commission performed numerous additional studies. The FEIS finds that the relative future competitiveness of coal and natural gas generation is the key variable affecting the impact of the Final Rule. If competitive conditions favor natural gas, the Rule is likely to lead to environmental benefits. Both EPA and the Commission staff believe this projected scenario is the more likely one. If competitive conditions favor coal, the Rule may lead to small negative environmental impacts. However, even using the most extreme, unlikely assumptions about the future of the industry, the negative consequences are not likely to occur until after the turn of the century. Because the impacts will remain modest at least until 2010, there is no need for an interim mitigation program. In addition, even if the data showed more significant negative consequences requiring mitigation, the Commission does not have the statutory authority under the Federal Power Act or the expertise to address this possible far-term problem. The Commission believes, however, that there is time for federal and state air quality authorities to address any potential adverse impact as part of a comprehensive NO[X] regulatory program under the Clean Air Act.

Despite our conclusions regarding the lack of environmental impacts expected to result from the Rule, the Commission has examined a wide variety of proposals for mitigating possible adverse effects. We share the view of most commenters that the preferred approach for mitigating increased NO[X] emissions generally is a NO[X] cap and trading regulatory program comparable to that developed by Congress to address sulfur dioxide emissions in the Clean Air Act Amendments of 1990. The Commission has examined various means of establishing such a program, including use of existing federal authorities under the Clean Air Act, cooperative efforts by state and federal air quality regulators, and development of a new emissions regulatory program administered by the Commission under the Federal Power Act. The Commission has concluded that a NO[X] regulatory program could best be developed and administered under the Clean Air Act, in cooperation with interested states, and offers to lend Commission support to that effort should it become necessary.

Initially, the EPA disagreed with FERC. EPA decided in May 1996 not to approve the final environmental impact statement conducted by FERC on Order No. 888. EPA's major concern was that competition will result in increased generation at higher polluting power plants, resulting in greater emissions of pollutants such as nitrogen oxides. *See, e.g.*, Stephen C. Fotis & Ann P. Southwick, The Price of Switching, Legal Times, May 13, 1996, at 23. Consequently, EPA desired that FERC include environmental mitigation measures in Order No. 888. This resulted in a referral of FERC's actions to the White House Council on Environmental Quality (CEQ), as is allowed under the National Environmental Policy Act. FERC maintained, however, that it did not have the jurisdiction under the Federal Power Act to impose such measures on the industry, and that the EPA was the appropriate agency to adopt mitigation measure. In this context, should a

CEQ recommendation that mitigation measure be imposed trump FERC's decision? Can CEQ require FERC to mitigate the environmental consequences of competition, even if, as FERC suggests, the FPA does not authorize FERC to regulate air pollution?

2. Another environmental transition cost issue associated with federal restructuring policy involves PURPA, the reform of which is discussed in Chapter 11. PURPA's avoided cost rates, many have complained, increase consumer electricity rates because utilities are contractually required to continue purchasing power at these rates even though the costs of generating electricity have subsequently dropped significantly. In many states, consumers are bearing the cost of long-term contracts with non-utility generators which qualify for buybacks of surplus power at avoided costs. As competition becomes more pervasive, mandatory buyback programs risk becoming, as some have suggested, a type of stranded investment. For example, some states have attempted to deal with this problem by allowing utilities to buy-out or sell off their contracts with PURPA facilities and pass these costs on to consumers in rate base.

California is one state where QF avoided cost rates have been challenged by utilities. In *Independent Energy Producers Association, Inc. v. California Public Utilities Commission*, 36 F.3d 848 (9th Cir. 1994), the problem was acknowledged:

> In 1985 and 1986, CPUC recognized that the avoided cost rates provided in standard offer contracts Nos. 2 and 4, which were calculated in part based on the cost of fuel needed to generate electricity, were higher than the actual avoided cost rates in 1985. In projecting future avoided costs at the time the contracts were executed, the CPUC had considered the anticipated cost to the utility of its own fuel sources, primarily fuel and natural gas, and had assumed that fossil fuel prices would continue to rise into the 1980's. Instead, these prices declined. As a consequence, the avoided cost rates provided in the contracts were higher than the then current actual avoided cost rate. The CPUC has suspended the availability of these fixed price contracts for future contracts, but previously-signed contracts remain in effect.

Id. at 852. To address previously signed contracts, California implemented a QF monitoring program:

> Under this program, the CPUC authorized the Utilities to monitor the compliance of the QFs from which they purchase electric energy to ensure that they are in compliance with federal operating and efficiency standards. The program provides that if a Utility determines that a QF is not in compliance with operating and efficiency standards, the Utility is authorized to suspend payment of the avoided cost rate specified in the standard offer contract, and to substitute an "alternative" avoided cost rate equal to 80% of the Utility's avoided cost for short term economy power.

> The Utilities are also permitted to collect from the QFs payments above the 80% "alternative" avoided cost rate for any time period that

the QF has not been operating in compliance with federal efficiency standards, retroactively for a period up to three years from the last date on which efficiency data was submitted. Finally, the Utilities are permitted to suspend parallel operation with any "non-complying QF" if the utility determines that continued parallel operation represents a burden to the utility or its customers.

Id. at 852–53. The Ninth Circuit held that this avoided cost monitoring plan was preempted by PURPA:

We conclude that the CPUC program is preempted by PURPA insofar as it authorizes the Utilities to determine that a QF is not in compliance with the Commission's operating and efficiency standards and to impose a reduced avoided cost rate on that QF. Moreover, to the extent that the CPUC program authorizes the Utilities to disconnect from parallel operation a "non-complying" QF, and thus to prevent such a QF from selling energy to and purchasing energy from the Utility, it is also preempted under federal law. *See* 18 C.F.R. § 292.303(c) (requiring electric utilities to interconnect with QFs as necessary to accomplish sales and purchases with the QFs).

However, insofar as the CPUC's program requires QFs to submit operating data to the Utilities for monitoring, and insofar as the monitoring requirements do not impose an undue burden on the QFs, the program is not preempted. Because reasonable monitoring by the state and by utilities does not by itself effect a determination of status, it falls within the state's broad ratemaking authority. In fact, in promulgating the federal regulations, the Commission acknowledged that information routinely flowing between QFs and utilities would allow the utilities to determine if the QF met federal operating and efficiency standards. Small Power Production and Cogeneration Facilities—Qualifying Status, 45 Fed.Reg. 17959, 17962 (1980). If based on this data, a utility believes that the QF is not in compliance with federal standards, it may petition the Commission to revoke the cogenerator's QF status.

Id. at 859.

The following case illustrates the continuing conflict between competition and PURPA's scheme to encourage renewable power and cogeneration:

Southern California Edison Company v. San Diego Gas & Electric Company

70 F.E.R.C. ¶ 61,215 (1995).

Introduction

On January 6, 1995, Southern California Edison Company (Edison) filed a petition for enforcement pursuant to section 210(h) of the Public Utility Regulatory Policies Act of 1978 (PURPA), 16 U.S.C. 824a–3(h) (1988). On January 18, 1995, San Diego Gas & Electric Company (San

Diego) filed a petition for enforcement pursuant to section 210(h) of PURPA or, in the alternative, for a declaratory order.

Both utilities state that the California Public Utilities Commission (California Commission) has ordered them to sign long-term, fixed-priced contracts with qualifying facilities (QFs) to purchase significant amounts of unneeded QF capacity at prices far in excess of their avoided costs. They argue that this new directive is in violation of PURPA and this Commission's implementing regulations. The California Commission responds that the two utilities challenge only a small part of a complex and comprehensive resource plan that is entirely within its implementation role under PURPA. Numerous intervenors support or challenge all or portions of the challenged program.

While we have grave concerns about the need for this capacity and the staleness of the data relied upon by the California Commission, we do not reach a definitive conclusion on these issues because we decide the cases on other grounds. We do, however, find that the California program at issue violates PURPA and our implementing regulations because the California Commission did not consider all sources in reaching its avoided cost determinations.

Edison's Enforcement Petition

Edison states that the California Commission has ordered Edison to sign long-term, fixed-price contracts with QFs to purchase 686 MW of new capacity that will come on line in 1997–1999. Edison states that these contracts will require payments demonstrably more expensive than alternative sources of power, will require Edison to purchase capacity before it is needed, and will dramatically increase stranded costs in a soon-to-be-restructured electric utility industry.

Edison explains that these obligations are the result of the California Commission's Biennial Resource Plan Update (BRPU), which, pursuant to section 210(f) of PURPA, implements this Commission's rules governing the purchase by electric utilities of electricity from QFs. According to Edison, the BRPU has three stages. First, following the latest projections of energy and capacity needs of California utilities (Edison, San Diego, and Pacific Gas and Electric Company (PG & E)) made by the California Energy Commission (CEC), the utilities file a resource plan identifying potential resource additions. The California Commission examines these plans and determines what new resources the utilities would add. Second, after the utilities have supplied certain data, the California Commission determines the utilities' assumed costs, known as "benchmark prices", for these resource additions, and determines which of the additions could be avoided. Third, QFs are then allowed to bid against the utilities' benchmark prices for the new resources. If bids received by the QFs are below the utilities' benchmark prices for the new resources, the utilities are then directed by the California Commission to enter into standard contracts (called "Final Standard Offer 4" or "FSO4" contracts) with the winning bidders with respect to each avoided resource. The winning bidders are paid the price bid by the second lowest bidder with respect to each avoided resource. (This procedure is referred to as a second-price auction.) Certain winning bidders receive additional payments to reflect the assumed value to society of reduced air emissions.

Based on the CEC's 1990 electricity report, the California Commission concluded in 1992 that Edison would construct 624 MW of new generation from 1997 to 1999 as follows: two new geothermal plants, one wind farm, and the repowering of an existing steam plant. The California Commission also estimated Edison's costs for construction of each of these projects, which were given the name "Identified Deferrable Resources" (IDRs). Edison states that even though the estimated costs were many times larger than the capital costs of constructing new gas-fired turbines, the California Commission concluded that the IDRs were economic by imputing massive environmental compliance costs to the alternative, gas-fired resources.

In 1993, pursuant to California Commission directive, Edison solicited bids for 624 MW of new capacity, broken down into four separate IDRs. Only QFs were allowed to bid. The California Commission, in implementing a California statute, required that half of the capacity for three of the four IDRs be reserved solely for renewable bidders. The solicitation produced bids lower than the IDR benchmarks.

Edison argues that the California program is in conflict with PURPA and the Commission's rules implementing PURPA. Edison states that a fundamental flaw in the solicitation structure is its assumption that any QF contract that is priced below the utility's assumed cost of providing the same power to itself through the construction of new resources (the benchmark price) is necessarily below avoided cost. Edison states that the California Commission ignores this Commission's regulations, which define avoided costs as the costs of replacement energy the utility could generate itself or "purchase from another source." 18 C.F.R. § 292.101(b)(6) (1994). Edison also states that lower-cost alternatives were readily available for 4.0 cents/kWh or less, even though it was required to execute contracts with QFs at initial rates as high as 6.6 cents/kWh.

Edison argues that this result also is the product of the California Commission's intention to favor "renewable" QFs. Edison explains that the California Commission segmented the solicitation into four separate IDRs (274 MW repower, 50 MW wind, 100 MW geothermal, and 200 MW geothermal), and that a QF was required to bid separately against each IDR. Compounding this segmentation, half of the renewable IDR capacity was set aside for bidding only by renewable QFs. A related flaw, in Edison's opinion, was the mandate that winning bidders be paid an air emissions adder/subtracter based on the difference in projected emissions between the bid-winning QF project and the IDR. Edison also criticizes the California Commission for failing to determine the utility's avoided cost calculated at the time the power is delivered or "at the time the obligation is incurred." 18 C.F.R. § 292.304(d)(2)(ii) (1994). Edison claims that the California Commission's avoided cost determination was made with stale data.

Finally, Edison argues that the California QF program is inconsistent with the California Commission's ongoing proposal to restructure the electric utility industry, whereby certain retail customers will be able to opt for "direct access", i.e., retail wheeling. Edison states that the failure to address the effect of restructuring on avoided costs, and the failure to allow a means to address stranded costs in the standard offer contracts, violates PURPA and the Commission's implementing regulations.

Edison states that it is required under the BRPU to execute contracts with the QFs by March 29, 1995. Edison requests that the Commission act as expeditiously as possible. Specifically, Edison asks that the Commission either relieve it of its obligation to enter into contracts with the QFs by March 29, 1995 or, if the Commission declines to take action, to issue a notice of intent not to act in time to allow Edison to seek appropriate injunctive relief from a federal district court before it is required to sign the contracts. . . .

Discussion

Pursuant to Rule 214 of the Commission's Rules of Practice and Procedure, 18 C.F.R. 385.214 (1994), the notices of intervention filed by the California Commission and DOE serve to make them parties to the proceedings in Docket Nos. EL95–16–000 and EL95–19–000. Additionally, the timely, unopposed motions to intervene summarized above serve to make the entities which filed the motions parties to the proceedings in Docket Nos. EL95–16–000 and EL95–19–000. Further, we find good cause to grant all of the motions to intervene out-of-time in the proceedings in Docket Nos. EL95–16–000 and EL95–19–000, and will consider all supplemental pleadings, in light of the interests they raise and in order to complete all of the arguments of the parties.

Preliminary Observations

Before addressing the merits of Edison's and San Diego's petitions, we believe that some preliminary observations are in order to provide a better understanding of the action we take today.

When Congress enacted PURPA in 1978, there was very little non-utility generation. In 1978 virtually all new generating capacity was provided by traditional electric utilities. In fact, one of the principal reasons Congress adopted section 210 of PURPA was because electric utilities had refused to purchase power from non-utility producers. In contrast to 1978, non-traditional producers, including QFs, now provide well in excess of half of all new generating resources, and the Commission has determined that there is no longer any dominance in the provision of new generating capacity.

One of the reasons for the dramatic growth of the QF industry was the Commission's policy decision in 1980 to set the maximum rate permissible under PURPA section 210(b), i.e., a full avoided cost rate. While such rates do not result in direct benefits to ratepayers, they nevertheless are fully consistent with PURPA section 210(b)'s requirement that the rates be just and reasonable to ratepayers and in the public interest. Nevertheless, PURPA does not permit either the Commission, or the States in their implementation of PURPA, to require a purchase rate that exceeds avoided cost.

Since 1980, the Commission has given the States wide latitude in implementing PURPA. We have done so partly in recognition of the important role which Congress intended to give the States under PURPA, as well as to avoid unnecessary interference with state efforts to maximize the development of QFs. However, as noted above, the QF industry is now a developed industry and the need for integration of policy objectives under PURPA and other federal electric regulatory policies is pronounced. This is particularly the case given the fact that the electric utility industry is in the midst of a transition to a competitive wholesale power market, and some States, including California, are considering direct access for retail customers.

As the electric utility industry becomes increasingly competitive, the need to ensure that the States are using procedures which ensure that QF rates do not exceed avoided cost becomes more critical. This is because QF rates that exceed avoided cost will, by definition, give QFs an unfair advantage over other market participants (non-QFs). This, in turn, will hinder the development of competitive markets and hurt ratepayers, a result clearly at odds with ensuring the just and reasonable rates required by PURPA section 210(b).

We believe it is incumbent upon regulators, Federal and State, to avoid the creation of transition costs where possible. California's decision to consider a major restructuring of its retail electricity market significantly heightens our concern with stranded costs arising from above-avoided-cost rates. We believe it is inconsistent with our obligation under PURPA to ensure just and reasonable rates, and our goals to encourage development of competitive bulk power markets, to permit the use of PURPA to create new contracts that do not reflect market conditions for new bulk power supplies.

Finally, in acting today, we acknowledge California's ability under its authorities over the electric utilities subject to its jurisdiction to favor particular generation technologies over others. We respect the fact that resource planning and resource decisions are the prerogative of state commissions and that states may wish to diversify their generation mix to meet environmental goals in a variety of ways. Our decision today does not, for example, preclude the possibility that, in setting an avoided cost rate, a state may account for environmental costs of all fuel sources included in an all source determination of avoided cost. Also, under state authority, a state may choose to require a utility to construct generation capacity of a preferred technology or to purchase power from the supplier of a particular type of resource. The recovery of costs of utility-constructed generation would be regulated by the state. The rates for wholesale sales would be regulated by this Commission on a cost-of-service or market-based rate basis, as appropriate. Our decision here simply makes clear that the State can pursue its policy choices concerning particular generation technologies consistent with the requirements of PURPA and our regulations, so long as such action does not result in rates above avoided cost.

Commission Response

Edison and San Diego have asked this Commission to declare that the California Commission orders at issue are in conflict with PURPA and this Commission's implementing regulations because the orders require the utilities to purchase from QFs at rates in excess of their avoided costs. Their reasons include the fact that the California solicitations brought in bids from cogeneration facilities at prices below what was awarded for some renewable capacity; that portions of the solicitations were set aside for renewable bidders; that the bids were segmented into separate capacity blocks; that bid prices are distorted by adders or subtracters to reflect environmental externalities; that the final orders ignore updated need projections; that the solicitations were not open to non-QF bidders; and that the orders may result in stranded costs in a restructured electric utility industry. There is no need to address most of Edison's and San Diego's arguments because we find as a threshold matter that the California Commission's method of determining avoided costs is inconsistent with PURPA and our regulations.

While we are reluctant to interfere in California's implementation of PURPA and our regulations, as we explained in *Connecticut Light and Power Company*, 70 FERC ¶ 61,102 (1995) (CL&P), PURPA expressly directed this Commission, and not the states, to prescribe rules governing QF rates. PURPA gave the states responsibility for "implementing" the statute and the Commission's rules. As a result, a state may prescribe a particular per unit charge only if the process it uses to establish the per unit charge is in accordance with the Commission's rules.

Section 210(b) of PURPA explicitly provides that no Commission rule on QF rates "shall provide for a rate which exceeds the incremental cost to the electric utility of alternative energy." The "incremental cost of alternative electric energy" is defined in section 210(d) of PURPA as "the cost to the electric utility of the electric energy which, but for the purchase from such cogenerator or small power producer, such utility would generate or purchase from another source." The Supreme Court stated that PURPA "sets full avoided cost as the maximum rate that the Commission may prescribe." The Commission's regulations, tracking the statutory language, in turn expressly provide that QF rates must "be just and reasonable to the electric consumer of the electric utility" and "not discriminate against qualifying cogeneration and small power production facilities," and that "nothing in [the Commission's regulations] requires any electric utility to pay more than the avoided cost for purchases." The Commission's regulations define avoided costs as "the incremental costs to an electric utility of electric energy or capacity or both which, but for the purchase from the qualifying facility or qualifying facilities, such utility would generate itself or purchase from another source."

As pointed out by the California Commission, IEP, and numerous other intervenors, the Commission gives great latitude to state commissions as to procedures selected to determine avoided costs. The Commission has not, and does not intend in the future, to second-guess state regulatory authorities' actual determinations of avoided costs (i.e., whether the per unit charges are no higher than incremental costs). Rather, the Commission believes its role is limited to ensuring the process used to calculate the per unit charge (i.e., implementation) accords with the statute and our regulations.

As noted above, under PURPA an avoided cost (incremental cost) determination must permit QFs to participate in a non-discriminatory fashion and, at the same time, assure that the purchasing utility pays no more than the cost it otherwise would incur to generate the capacity (or energy) itself "or purchase from another source" (the language of section 210 of PURPA, emphasis added). Congress in this language did not in any way limit the sources to be considered. The consequence is that regardless of whether the State regulatory authority determines avoided cost administratively, through competitive solicitation (bidding), or some combination thereof, it must in its process reflect prices available from all sources able to sell to the utility whose avoided cost is being determined. If the state is determining avoided cost by relying on a combination of benchmark and bidding procedures, as here, this means that the bidding cannot be limited to certain sellers (QFs); rather, it must be all-source bidding.

For this reason, we find that the California Commission's process of determining avoided costs did not comply with PURPA. Under the California Commission's procedures, as explained above, a benchmark price was determined for the acquisition of certain capacity. Only QFs were then permitted to bid against the benchmark. Such a procedure could not properly determine avoided costs, because it excluded potential sources of capacity from which the utilities could purchase, in contravention of the requirements of section 210 of PURPA and our regulations.

Because the California Commission's procedure was unlawful under PURPA, Edison and San Diego cannot lawfully be compelled to enter into contracts resulting from that procedure. At this juncture, there are no executed contracts. However, in order to avoid parties spending further time and resources in pursuing contracts that would be unlawful under PURPA, we believe it would be appropriate for the California Commission to stay its requirements directing Edison and San Diego to purchase pending the outcome of further administrative procedures in accordance with PURPA. We also encourage the utilities and QFs to reach a settlement that would be consistent with PURPA.

Finally, based on the record before us at this time, we have grave concerns about the need for this capacity and the staleness of the data relied upon by the California Commission. Because we are deciding these cases on other grounds, we do not need to reach a definitive conclusion on these issues.

Applicability of Decision

Many other states now also use some sort of bidding procedure to establish avoided cost. We do not know whether these states engage in all-source bidding procedures, or whether they, as California, limit bidding to QFs. However, we do not believe it would be in the public interest to invalidate the QF contracts that have resulted from prior solicitations in California or elsewhere that have not been challenged and are pending. Consistent with our recent order in CL & P, we will not entertain requests to invalidate preexisting contracts in which avoided costs were established pursuant to a state bidding procedure that did not allow all-source bidding unless such issue has been raised and is pending or is raised in a timely appeal of a state decision. We believe that the appropriate time in which to challenge a state-imposed rate for a QF purchase is up to the time the purchase contract is signed, not years into a contract.

■WILLIAM L. MASSEY, Commissioner, concurring: I concur in today's order. My concurrence is driven by essentially two factors. First, as competition emerges, the QF contracts at issue here would increase the amount of stranded costs ultimately borne by the utilities' ratepayers and/or shareholders. That is a step in the wrong direction. Stranded cost is the central issue in the debate over the future structure of the electric industry and it is time for regulators, federal and state, to face it squarely and boldly. We need to find ways to reduce, not increase, the industry's potential stranded cost problems.

Second, in today's wholesale market, QFs should compete head-on with other power suppliers. The power supply industry has become much more competitive since the enactment of PURPA. PURPA has been a success in this respect. The QF industry has matured sufficiently that QFs can and should compete on the merits with other supply options. QFs can, for example, often assist utilities to meet long-term environmental compliance requirements, and I believe the market and state regulators can recognize and integrate the value of such assistance in the all-source determination process.

Our order stands for two principles. First, while avoided costs may be determined administratively, through bidding or some combination thereof, the determination must consider prices available from all sources able to sell to the affected utility. Thus, our order does not preclude administrative determinations of avoided costs, so long as all sources are considered. I believe bidding may be the best way for states to comply with PURPA, but it is not the only way. Second, if avoided costs are determined through a combination of bidding and benchmark procedures, the bidding phase must be open to all sources, not just QFs. The parties addressed many other issues but, beyond establishing these two principles, we do not resolve those issues in this order.

I want to underscore that our decision today does not preclude states from considering environmental costs in determining avoided costs under PURPA. The order expressly leaves open the possibility that states may account for the environmental costs of all fuel sources included in an all-source determination. The order also says that states can pursue their policy choices concerning particular generation technologies consistent with PURPA and our regulations, so long as such action does not result in rates above avoided cost. Indeed, a primary purpose of PURPA is to encourage the development of alternative generation, including non-fossil generation, and today's order must be read with that in mind.

The consideration of environmental costs and other non-price factors under PURPA is consistent with a recent amendment to PURPA. In the Energy Policy Act of 1992, Congress amended PURPA to require states to consider mandating the use of "integrated resource planning." The amendment of PURPA to include this requirement supports construing PURPA's avoided cost standard as allowing consideration of the non-price factors essential to integrated resource planning.

The consideration of environmental costs and other non-price factors under PURPA is also consistent with this Commission's past statements. In proposing procedures in 1988 to allow bidding under PURPA, the Commission stated:

Terms and conditions for electricity production and delivery cannot be described by a single facet of the sale, such as price. Rather, a variety of factors which affect the continued security and operational integrity of the purchasing utility's system, including fuel diversity and reliability, must be taken into consideration in selecting purchases. Congress was aware that many attributes need to be taken into account in determining the value of purchases from QFs.

The Commission also stated then that one permissible way to rank bids under PURPA would be based on price alone, but "there are severe drawbacks to focusing solely on price because of the multiple attributes of electricity." The Commission stated: "It is precisely for this reason that this rulemaking proposes to condition the use of bidding on nonprice factors being taken into account in the selection of winning bids." While the Commission has since terminated the 1988 [competitive bidding] rulemaking, the Commission has never disavowed its interpretation of PURPA as allowing consideration of nonprice factors, and does not do so in today's order.

One shortcoming I see in today's order is the lack of guidance to the states on how to determine avoided costs. We tell California they did it wrong. But we offer little guidance on how to do it right. I support opening a generic proceeding, to elicit input from all interested parties and to explore fully how PURPA should work in a competitive power supply industry. One of PURPA's primary goals is to encourage the development of alternative fuel generation such as geothermal, wind power and others. As long as PURPA is the law of the land, we owe it to the state regulators, the QFs and the utilities to provide additional guidance with respect to how PURPA's goals can be accomplished in a competitive era.

In hindsight, the Commission should have initiated a generic proceeding sooner. If we had, perhaps we could have avoided the surprise that some will argue we are imposing today. We should flesh out a number of issues by rulemaking to give the states guidance on how to implement PURPA in a lawful manner. Providing such guidance will help to ensure that this Commission is not regularly called upon to second-guess state decisions under PURPA.

Finally, our order in no way affects the authority of states to adopt and implement power supply policies outside of PURPA. Our order today construes only the requirements of PURPA, and does not (indeed, could not) purport to limit the authority of states beyond the context of PURPA. Our order says only that states cannot act under PURPA to require utilities to pay more than their avoided costs.■

Michael J. Zucchet, Renewable Resource Electricity in The Changing Regulatory Environment, Feature Article in 1995 Renewable Energy Annual, U.S. Department of Energy, Energy Information Administration (Dec. 1995)

<http://www.eia.doe.gov/cneaf/pubs_html/rea/feature2.html>

While the States set and mandate the avoided-cost rates paid to QFs, the process used by each State to set these rates is subject to review by FERC.

In response to several cases involving utilities appealing to overturn mandated QF rates, FERC has made rulings that may change the way QF power is purchased and will affect the ability of State commissions to dictate the resource energy mix of their future capacity. In separate cases involving Connecticut Light & Power Company and two California utilities (Southern California Edison Company and San Diego Gas & Electric Company), FERC refused to allow the State to set rates above the current avoided cost of capacity and energy. The most significant of these cases for renewables was the California case, where FERC disapproved the Biennial Resource Plan Update (BRPU) of the California Public Utilities Commission (CPUC). BRPU structured a bidding process where only QFs bid against one another for new capacity, and it required renewable "set-asides," forcing utilities to purchase a certain percentage of energy from renewable sources. FERC disallowed the plan, ruling that BRPU forced utilities to pay above avoided costs by excluding some potential generation sources from the bidding for the QF segment of the bid. Citing Section 210(b) of PURPA, FERC ruled that the States must include all alternative sources of capacity and energy in their calculations of avoided cost.

While the utilities involved in the cases were satisfied, independent power producers and the CPUC were stunned. CPUC, which has been a leader in the evolution of electric markets, claimed that the FERC order was irreconcilable with California's progressive State energy policy. CPUC further asserted that the FERC rulings limited the ability of States to initiate set-asides or other resource planning activities, which is not a proper role for FERC, according to CPUC. The FERC rulings regarding QF treatment under PURPA are especially critical given the terms of many QF contracts. The majority of QFs in California and, to a much lesser extent, in other States, are now facing an avoided cost "cliff," as 10–year contracts written at rates in the 6–9 cents per kilowatt-hour range in the mid–1980s expire over the next few years. With current avoided costs in the 3–4 cent range, rolling over the contracts at today's rates would create financial problems for QFs.

Although FERC has since reaffirmed its California decision rejecting QF rates above avoided cost, it has also asserted that States can favor specific energy sources as long as such action does not result in rates above avoided cost. For example, FERC said that States may influence costs incurred by utilities through taxes or tax credits on generation produced by a particular fuel. What FERC explicitly disallowed was the addition of "externality adders" in avoided-cost calculations. Since renewable energy production is environmentally benign relative to most fossil fuel energy technologies, some States have included these adders in their avoided-cost calculations to level the playing field between renewables and fossil fuels. FERC ruled, however, that policies that constitute environmental externality adders that result in rates above avoided cost would not be acceptable.

In short, if a State wishes to encourage renewable generation, FERC has indicated that it may do so through the tax code (or some other broad policy measure), but it may not use a rate-setting mechanism that results in a rate that is above avoided cost. CPUC has responded to this directive by considering a proposal mandating that utilities that sell at retail in the State obtain 12 percent of their energy from renewable resources. This approach is designed to support renewables and circumvent the FERC orders rejecting QF rates above avoided cost.

In other cases brought before FERC, the Commission has repeatedly rejected utilities' requests to abrogate existing QF contracts. In unrelated cases involving Niagara Mohawk Power Corporation and New York State Electric and Gas Corporation, FERC reaffirmed its unwillingness to cancel existing QF contracts simply because avoided-cost rates have changed and the deals have gone sour in changing electricity markets. FERC ruled that it will not disturb existing above-avoided-cost QF contracts if they were not challenged at the time they were signed.

In rejecting these petitions, FERC made several key findings. First, it affirmed that PURPA regulations permit QF rates to remain in effect even if avoided cost rates decline over time. Second, it affirmed the policy of relying on States to do the factual determination of avoided cost. And finally, the Commission plainly stated its disposition not to disturb executed contracts.

While the positions of most utilities and QFs are quite evident (and opposite), State public utility commissions and residential and industrial energy consumers are not necessarily decided on the issue of favorable QF treatment. Most State commissions are in favor of the States' ability to control their own energy planning, although not all have endorsed the idea of above-avoided-cost QF contracts as a means to their planning ends. The Nevada Public Service Commission, for example, recently disallowed the rates set for a geothermal development because they were deemed too far above avoided cost to be reasonable, even though the QF and the utility both supported the rates. Many consumers, especially large industrial consumers, do not necessarily favor or oppose renewables but want to ensure both that power purchases are competitive and that utilities cannot exert monopoly power over QFs and independent power producers. On the other hand, some smaller consumers, especially residential consumers, have shown a willingness to pay for environmentally benign electricity.■

* * *

A bill proposed to Congress in 1995 (S. 708, introduced by Senator Nickles from Oklahoma) proposed the repeal of Section 210 of PURPA—the buyback and avoided cost provision for renewable and cogeneration facilities. Then Undersecretary at DOE, Elizabeth Moler, testified in opposition to the bill:

> First, there is an increasing tension between PURPA's encouragement of cogeneration and renewable technologies and PURPA's requirement that utilities purchase QF power at avoided cost. It is becoming increasingly difficult to reconcile PURPA's avoided cost requirements with encouraging higher priced renewable technologies, particularly in light of the goal of the Energy Policy Act to encourage competitive wholesale power markets.

> Second, repealing PURPA Section 210 is premature given the market power over transmission that utilities have today. While competition clearly is coming to the electric industry, full competition is not yet here. At a minimum, those who control the Nation's transmission grid must provide comparable open access before we can have competitive wholesale power markets. Repeal of PURPA section 210 is premature until we open the transmission grid, on a fair basis, to all wholesale buyers and sellers of electric energy.

> Third, as we move to competitive wholesale power markets, we must honor obligations entered into under the prior regulatory regime. We must deal responsibly with all uneconomic prior investments and contracts; these include both utility investments, and QF contracts. As of 1993, PURPA producers were supplying 47,774 megawatts of capacity to electric utilities and sales comprised 267.6 billion kilowatt hours of electricity annually. Thus, PURPA power is an important component of our Nation's electric supply, contributing approximately six percent of our generating capacity.

> The tensions between PURPA and the emerging competitive wholesale market have become evident in the Commission's recent PURPA workload. Many traditional utilities that have been required to purchase QF power now find themselves with billions of dollars of uneconomic QF contracts. Some have asked the Commission to invalidate those contracts retroactively. Other utilities find themselves facing state PURPA programs requiring them to enter into additional uneconomic QF contracts, that is, contracts that even under today's calculations are above the avoided cost of alternative power. Several utilities have asked us to find that such state programs conflict with

PURPA and our rules. We are also facing a growing number of cases in which QFs cannot meet the technical requirements for QF status and seek temporary waivers of PURPA and our regulations. Utilities, on the other hand, are seeking stricter monitoring programs to ensure that QFs do indeed meet the technical requirements. When they do not, utilities argue for lower rates for the periods when QFs are out of compliance.

The Commission has responded to these requests by reviewing certain state programs—notably those in Connecticut and California. We found the Connecticut program violated PURPA because it mandated rates above a utility's avoided cost. We also concluded the most significant—and certainly the most controversial—of these cases, the California Biennial Resource Plan Update (BRPU) case, last week. In that case, we considered whether California's recent QF bidding process is lawful under PURPA. We found that, under PURPA, a state determination of avoided cost must take into account all potential sources of capacity, which means all technologies and all types of sellers (i.e., QFs and non-QFs, including the purchasing utility). The rationale for this decision is that PURPA very clearly sets an avoided cost cap on QF rates, and that Congress, in enacting PURPA, did not intend for electric consumers to be worse off with PURPA than without PURPA. The California proceeding did not meet that test, and we therefore found that it violated PURPA.

The Commission recognizes that many utilities face above-market QF contracts, and that implementing PURPA may now conflict both with its goal of not causing harm to consumers and with the competitive goals of the Energy Policy Act. However, I believe that repeal of section 210 of PURPA is premature at this time because we have not yet achieved competitive wholesale power markets.

One of the findings on which S. 708 is premised is the increasingly competitive wholesale electric marketplace being brought about by the Energy Policy Act. There is no doubt that we are seeing an increasingly competitive marketplace. However, we have a lot of work ahead of us before we can achieve competitive wholesale generation markets. The key to that goal is to open the transmission grid, on a fair basis, to all wholesale buyers and sellers of electric energy. Until we remove the linchpin of utility monopoly power, we simply will not have a fair opportunity for all sellers, including cogeneration and renewables, to compete.

The Commission is attempting to address the transmission market power issue in our recently issued open access notice of proposed rulemaking. We are committed to eliminating undue discrimination and market power in transmission services. I believe that the PURPA requirement to purchase at rates no higher than avoided cost should be retained until transmission market power has been mitigated. In the meantime, however, we must ensure that the PURPA avoided cost requirement is properly implemented, and that consumers are not harmed.

There is a second concern which S. 708 raises. There is a price tag that comes with achieving competitive electricity markets. Some utility investments, as well as some QF contracts, are not economic in today's competitive world. These above market resource commitments have become known as stranded costs.

The Commission has stated unequivocally that utilities are entitled to an opportunity to recover prudently incurred costs. A fair transition from one regulatory regime to another honors the contractual and extra-contractual expectations of the parties under the prior regime. The Commission's recently issued notice of proposed rulemaking on open access and stranded costs addresses this issue and applies to all types of stranded costs, including those associated with mandatory QF contracts.

Past contracts and expectations should be honored. Even so, utilities and QFs should nonetheless attempt to mitigate the problem of uneconomic contracts. The Commission has encouraged utilities to try to buy-out or buy-down uneconomic QF contracts to help lower rates. With respect to uneconomic utility investments, the Commission similarly has proposed in its proposed stranded cost rule that utilities must attempt to mitigate stranded costs, for example by trying to market the "stranded" assets.

I emphasize that what we are dealing with here is a transition issue in the move to competitive markets. Both traditional utilities and QFs are now caught between the old rules of regulation and the new rules of competition. Once we move beyond this generation of uneconomic assets and contracts, and once we achieve open transmission access, we will have overcome the most difficult transition issues.

By the year 2000, most federal legislative proposals to restructure the electric utility industry included some repeal of PURPA avoided cost benefits for QFs. Is the QF issue a type of stranded cost problem? If so, should regulators recognize the environmental tension in compensating this type of stranded cost, as opposed to other types of stranded cost, such as older generating plants?

2.   ENVIRONMENTAL CONCERNS IN THE STATES: DSM AND IRP

Increased competition has also called into question the continued necessity of DSM and IRP programs. The following readings explore this issue:

Bernard S. Black & Richard J. Pierce, Jr., The Choice Between Markets and Central Planning in Regulating the U.S. Electricity Industry

93 Colum. L. Rev. 1339 (1993).

The structure, methods of operation, and forms of government intervention that have dominated the electricity industry since its birth are no longer viable. The industry has begun a period of radical change. When that process is complete, the electricity industry and its regulation will bear little resemblance to the patterns that have become familiar over the past century. The defenders of the old regime, recognizing that the status quo ante is dead, have changed their allegiances to one of two competing revolutionary armies. Those armies, led by policy wonks with radically different visions of the post-revolutionary state of the industry, are assaulting the ramparts at state utility commissions, state legislatures, a variety of federal agencies, and the U.S. Congress.

The results to date are surprising. Both armies have won almost every battle! Over the past five years, government institutions have begun to implement a combination of four revolutionary changes in the structure, operation, and regulation of the electricity industry. These changes are competitive contracting for electric power, negawatt acquisition programs (NAPs) (utility subsidies for energy-efficiency investments by their customers), market-based environmental regulation (emission fees and marketable pollution permits), and environmental adders (shadow prices reflecting pollution harm that utilities add to power costs when choosing new power sources).

These revolutions cannot continue indefinitely on their present paths. Neither large-scale negawatt programs nor environmental adders can coexist with competitive retail power markets. Environmental adders double-count pollution harm for most pollutants given market-based methods of controlling pollution that are already in place. Taken together, NAPs and environmental adders undermine our ability to achieve the economic gains from competitive contracting and market-based pollution control, while offering small environmental gains.

We must choose between two revolutionary visions of the future of the electricity sector of the U.S. economy. The first vision, embodied in competitive contracting and market-based environmental regulation, relies where possible on markets, private incentives, and decentralized decisions to produce optimal pricing and consumption of electric power and least-cost pollution control. This vision resembles the deregulatory trend that has produced huge benefits in the telephone, transportation, and natural gas sectors of our economy. The second vision, embodied in NAPs and environmental adders, distrusts consumer choice and relies on central planners, housed in regulated utilities, state utility commissions, and federal regulatory agencies, to correct perceived large-scale imperfections in the electricity market. This vision's faith in central planning ("integrated resource planning" is the new phrase) bears an uncomfortable resemblance to the systems previously used to govern the economies of eastern Europe and the former Soviet Union.

As this analogy suggests, we have strong views concerning the best path for revolutionary change. * * * ■

Re Electric Services, Market Competition, and Regulatory Policies, Case No. 8678 Order No. 72136

86 Md.P.S.C. 271, 163 P.U.R.4th 131 (Md.P.S.C.1995)

The Commission intends to take a measured approach to restructuring Maryland's electric utility industry. Maryland consumers currently enjoy electricity rates below both national and regional averages. Moreover, Maryland's electricity rates are globally competitive compared to those in most other industrialized countries. Unlike some other states, there has been no clamor among Maryland consumers over exorbitant electricity rates. Also, unlike many other states, Maryland's electricity rates are not inflated by an abundance of expensive nuclear power plants or many high-cost PURPA contracts. As such, Maryland's electric utility industry is not in need of dramatic fixes at this time. On the other hand, the Commission does see the need to begin a process of sensible and progressive change, designed to protect the interests of our residential consumers, businesses, the utility industry, and other stakeholders.

E.   IRP, DSM, Renewables, and Social Programs

1.   Position of the Parties

It is believed by many that increasing competition and the resulting restructuring of the electricity industry will, or should, affect the current regulatory treatment of IRP, DSM, renewables, and social programs. In this proceeding, the commenters were asked to address these issues.

All of the State's investor-owned utilities believe that the burdens of environmental and social programs should be applied to all competitors, eliminated altogether, or supplied by the State. The IOU's contend that utility responsibility for these programs puts them at a competitive disadvantage vis-a-vis alternate power suppliers, such as independent power producers....

2.   Commission Findings

The Commission's goal is to preserve the benefits of IRP, DSM, renewables, and social programs within the context of a more competitive environment, while at the same time not disadvantaging the State's electric utilities in competitive markets.

Specifically, the Commission reaffirms its commitment to IRP. We believe IRP is in the public interest, and has continued importance even given the changes outlined elsewhere in this Order. IRP has resulted in significant benefits in Maryland, including lower costs, greater efficiencies, and reductions in demand for capacity and energy (with attendant reductions in pollutant emissions). We recognize, however, that the IRP process will have to evolve along with the rest of the industry.

The Commission agrees that current notions of IRP may be incompatible with full retail competition. As such, we anticipate the need for additional changes to the IRP process should retail wheeling become a reality. However, this is not a current issue in Maryland because retail wheeling will not be instituted at this time.

Rather, we endorse competitive bidding as a means of taking advantage of generation and other resources available on the competitive wholesale market. In a wholesale competition environment, IRP can play an important role in a utility's procurement function.

Furthermore, we have previously indicated that environmental factors, inter alia, must be considered in any competitive bid.

The Commission continues to also believe that DSM offers important benefits to ratepayers and the industry. The reduction in the demand for electricity achieved by these programs has resulted in the need for less capacity. This, in turn, has significant collateral benefits in terms of reducing pollution and other negative environmental impacts.

The Commission is aware of complaints that DSM programs are not cost-effective. We also are aware of arguments that utilities have a conflict of interest in administering DSM, which often detracts from the success of these programs.

As previously mentioned, the Commission will allow DSM resources to bid against supply-side proposals pursuant to its competitive bidding policy for all new capacity. This will ensure that cost-effective DSM is given full and fair consideration. If DSM is more cost-effective, and meets the other necessary requirements, it will win the solicitation.

However, DSM's consideration in future competitive bidding does not address reducing the immediate consumption of electricity. As such, the Commission continues to support existing DSM programs. We emphasize that such programs are administered at the retail level, and, therefore, will not hinder Maryland utilities in competing in the wholesale power market. The Commission reiterates that DSM must also be cost-effective.

While the Commission is aware that the energy services industry has grown considerably in the past several years, we continue to believe that appropriate incentives to encourage ratepayer participation in DSM programs are necessary. While several energy service companies market conservation and energy efficiency services to Maryland ratepayers, the availability and affordability of these services to the average consumer is unclear. We direct our Staff to investigate this matter, and report its findings to us. On the other hand, most larger customers already have the sophistication and the means to take advantage of these opportunities, and many in fact do so. The Commission will carefully monitor the development of the energy services industry, and this may cause it to revise its view of the need for DSM incentives.

In the meantime, we encourage utilities to develop innovative ways of increasing efficient and cost-effective consumer participation in DSM. One proposal we find interesting involves providing financing for energy-efficiency and conservation measures, as opposed to direct rebates.

The Commission has already provided its views on renewables in its discussion on competitive bidding. In short, we support the continued development of renewable technologies, but will not force this State's utilities to purchase or implement uneconomic resources, renewable or otherwise. As such, we will not approve any preferences or set-asides favoring renewable technologies. We also decline to engage in any process of internalizing environmental costs over and above those internalized as a result of environmental laws. However, the Commission strongly supports the utilization of cost-effective renewable resources. All of the State's IOU's, and several other utilities, indicate that they are actively researching and experimenting with renewable technologies. The Commission encourages them to continue this development.

Many of the commenters, particularly the IOU's, express concerns over utility responsibility for other social and environmental programs. The concern is that utility responsibility for these matters inhibits their ability to provide inexpensive electricity services, and thereby to compete with alternate suppliers (or self-generation) in a more competitive electricity industry. To remedy this, the IOU's recommend that any such burdens either be applied to all competitors, eliminated altogether, or provided by the State through its powers of general taxation.

The Commission does not believe that the reforms outlined in this Order will affect the current treatment of social and environmental programs. This Order primarily contemplates fostering wholesale competition through competitive bidding for future power supplies. The costs for social and environmental programs, however, are allocated to retail ratepayers. Since the Commission is not instituting retail wheeling, we envision the continuation of the aforementioned programs in their current form. We reemphasize that this will not inhibit a Maryland utility's ability to compete in any bid for power, including its own.

Finally, we will make every effort to ensure that the State's utilities are not unduly or unfairly burdened with regulatory obligations which could hinder the move to a future industry paradigm (such as retail competition). As such, any new programs to be funded through utility rates will receive added scrutiny.█

NOTES AND COMMENTS

1.   While Professors Pierce and Black see a conflict between competition and environmental programs, not all are as pessimistic about the implications of competition for environmental programs such as DSM and IRP. Consider the following:

Regulation must evolve with the transformation of markets for electric generation. One way that regulation can evolve is to recognize its role as a facilitator of information. A critical barrier to this new role is jurisdictional ambiguity. Jurisdictional ambiguity must be resolved, and federal and state regulatory authorities must adopt a cooperative relationship in place of the current antagonistic relationship. As a facilitator, the regulatory commission must recognize the value of alternative costing theories. Bidding is a vehicle that can be used to facilitate information flow. However, for bidding to work, new models must be developed that are not encumbered by techniques that result in model-limited choice. Providing access to models and encouraging active participation (by reducing the transactions costs of participation) expands future options.

Carl Pechman, Regulating Power: The Economics of Electricity in the Information Age (1993).

2.   Does the Maryland PSC agree with Pierce and Black, or with Pechman? A recent Energy Information Administrative article on the topic concludes:

As the industry considers major restructuring, the scope and character of electric utility DSM are likely to change. Market interventions designed to accelerate the commercialization of new energy-efficient technologies or practices may continue to be justified as a means of reducing market failures. . . . At the same time, restructuring could greatly expand other demand-side activities including the use of real time pricing, time-of-use pricing, automated energy management, energy information services, and other services designed to expand the ability of customers to respond to changing price signals. Providing service packages that include generation, management of the price risks associated with competitive generation markets, and demand-side services could help attract and retain customers in a competitive market. The future of DSM will be determined by the choices that consumers, utilities, other service providers, regulators, and legislators make during the transition to competitive electric power markets.

U.S. Electric Utility Demand–Side Management: Trends and Analysis, U.S. Department of Energy, Energy Information Administration <http://www.eia.doe.gov/cneaf/pubs_html/feat_dsm/contents.html>   (last visited March 15, 2000).

3.   If retail wheeling were adopted, would the Maryland PSC be forced to reconsider how environmental regulation will coexist with competition? What would its options be?

3.   DORMANT COMMERCE CLAUSE AND FEDERAL PREEMPTION PROBLEMS

With the rise of competition, some states are positioning themselves to limit the importation of power produced from low-cost coal fired plants. Northeastern electricity producers, for instance, are at a disadvantage compared to those in the Midwest, who have access to low-cost, high sulfur coal. At the same time, it is feared that increased emissions of particulates, ozone and other pollutants in the Midwest will travel to the Northeast, imposing even greater costs on Northeast electricity suppliers. The dormant commerce clause protects commerce from protectionist regulation by states, and may pose a barrier to efforts to limit the importation of power. *See* Student Note, Commerce Clause Implications of Massachusetts' Attempt to Limit the Importation of "Dirty" Power in the Looming Competitive Market for Electricity Generation, 38 B.C. L. Rev. 811 (1997).

The Pennsylvania Public Utility Commission issued an order under the state's Electricity Generation Customer Choice and Competition Act, 66 Pa. C.S. 2801–12, authorizing PECO Energy, a Philadelphia-based electric utility, the authority to recover stranded costs from transmission customers through a transition charge. Indianapolis Power & Light Co., an Indiana utility that wanted to sell power in Pennsylvania, appealed the Commission's decision to the Commonwealth Court of Pennsylvania, arguing that the order violated the dormant commerce clause because it discriminated against companies from outside Pennsylvania. The Court upheld the validity of the order, saying that the power to authorize the recovery of these costs came within the scope of the regulatory powers traditionally assigned to the states. *Indianapolis Power & Light Company v. Pennsylvania P.U.C.,* 711 A.2d 1071 (Pa.Cmwlth.1998).

One author, concerned with the impact of state system benefits charges designed to promote environmental goals, observes:

> Many states are plunging ahead to implement the quickest or most controllable option, without analyzing the legality of their initiatives in advance. California, for example, has earmarked $540 million by legislative action for renewable energy projects. . . . The Wisconsin Public Service Commission has allocated $210 million annually for energy conservation, development of renewable resources, and support of low-income customer assistance. All of these initiatives would impose a systems benefit charge, a levy on each kilowatt-hour of retail electricity sales, to fund in-state renewable energy development, as an avowed purpose of the programs. This raises two potential problems. First, the Supreme Court prohibits the imposition of a levy on sales in interstate commerce to subsidize in-state industries. The Supreme Court allows distinctions in the imposition of a tax on fundamentally different regulated and unregulated commodities. However, in a deregulated market, an in-state subsidy funded by levies on interstate electricity sales (especially where the state does not own the generating equipment) is legally suspect.

Steven Ferrey, Renewable Subsidies in the Age of Deregulation; State-imposed Preferences May Have Come to the Wrong Place at the Wrong Time, Fortnightly, Dec. 1997.

Kirsten H. Engel, The Dormant Commerce Clause Threat to Market–Based Environmental Regulation: The Case of Electricity Deregulation

26 Ecology L.Q. 243 (1999).

If a governor, under pressure during hard economic times to save her state's struggling dairy industry, signed into law a bill banning the import of out-of-state milk products, such a law would surely be struck down in court under the dormant Commerce Clause. Indeed, the principle against protectionism in interstate trade applies to all articles traded in interstate commerce, including those related to the environment.

Imagine instead that two states, for example, California and Maine, wish to reduce local levels of pollutants attributable to the generation of electricity from fossil fuels. They therefore adopt programs to foster their states' renewable power industries. According to each program, ten percent of the energy supplied to end-use customers within the state must consist of renewable power such as wind, solar, geothermal, or biomass. In developing strategies to implement this renewable power mandate, each state toys briefly with a traditional regulatory approach according to which each individual energy retailer must alter its energy sources to ensure that a minimum percentage of its portfolio consists of renewable power. Each state rejects this option, however, due to opposition from a subset of suppliers obligated under long-term fossil fuel supply contracts. Instead, each state implements a tradable obligation mechanism, a variation on the increasingly popular emissions trading programs recently adopted by federal, state, and local governments. Under such a program, energy retailers can meet renewable energy requirements through the purchase of renewable energy credits from other generators or retailers without altering their own energy portfolio. Conversely, retailers who overcomply by purchasing more renewable power than the mandated minimum percentage may sell their extra credits to suppliers whose percentage of renewable power falls below the minimum. Marketable renewable energy credits thus efficiently spread the cost of satisfying the ten percent renewable requirement among the state's energy retailers.

Suppose that sometime later a California energy retailer purchases renewable energy credits from a biomass company in Maine and proffers such credits under California's minimum renewable energy mandate. Upon learning of the sale, the California legislature prohibits the use of out-of-state renewable energy credits under the California standard. California's legislators reason that accepting out-of-state credits will undermine the state's objective of improving air quality. Upset that the legislature has spoiled their trade, both the California energy credit importer and the Maine energy credit exporter sue California, claiming that the state's ban violates the dormant Commerce Clause.

What result? Can California's hypothetical ban on importing out-of-state renewable energy credits be distinguished from the New Jersey ban on importing out-of-state waste that was struck down in Philadelphia v. New Jersey? Both constitute facial discrimination against articles of commerce, which the Supreme Court has generally held "virtually per se" invalid. Nevertheless, California is guilty of nothing more than trying to ensure clean air in an efficient manner. California provides such clean air benefits when it adopts a renewable energy mandate, and it provides those benefits more efficiently by using a tradable obligation mechanism to implement that mandate. If California does not also prohibit credits from out-of-state renewables generators, it may subsidize clean air in distant areas such as Maine. To be sure, California could capture the clean air benefits simply by refusing to use a tradable obligation mechanism, but it would then lose the efficiencies gained by such a market-based approach. If California's ban on out-of-state credits is considered facial discrimination, the Commerce Clause would require California to choose either inefficient regulation that provides clean air only within the state or efficient regulation that may improve the air quality of distant states rather than its own. . . .

States have many options for retaining the environmental or economic benefits of an incentive-based mechanism while deregulating their electricity industries. [M]any of these options are constitutionally permissible. Others, however, unavoidably burden interstate trade and hence could be struck down under the dormant Commerce Clause under either the test for regulation that is facially discriminatory or the test for regulation that is facially neutral and yet places an excessive burden on interstate trade.

Application of these tests reveals that state market-based environmental legislation may be invalidated under the dormant Commerce Clause in at least three situations. First, a state acts unconstitutionally if it creates a marketable permit or obligation scheme and employs facial discrimination to retain the environmental public goods for its own residents. A state might, for example, restrict its energy credit program to renewables generators located within its boundaries. Second, a state violates the dormant Commerce Clause if it requires that the environmental costs of economic activity be internalized, and such internalization results in a significant discriminatory effect against out-of-state producers. Mechanisms such as nondiscriminatory environmental externality values, emissions portfolio standards, and hybrid emissions and consumption taxes raise such problems. Third, a state might unconstitutionally divert funds generated through a nondiscriminatory tax to a subset of local industry, as with a system benefits charge used to subsidize in-state renewables generators.

A state probably does not act unconstitutionally if it takes a less burdensome approach. For example, a state might restrict the legal value of a tradable environmental permit according to the location of the ultimate use of the permit (for example, limiting renewable energy credits that satisfy a renewable portfolio standard to credits that are sold to in-state consumers). Similarly, a state might subsidize environmentally sensitive industries through general tax revenues, rather than through a system benefits charge. A state might thus implement some of the incentive-based options in a manner that minimizes the constitutional risk. Nevertheless, these approaches are not foolproof, and a state may still fear constitutional challenges to such regulations.

For this reason, many policymakers wish to adopt a nonregulatory approach to reduce the environmental threats of electricity deregulation. Green marketing is such an approach. Through green marketing, corporations encourage consumers to patronize environmentally sensitive products by using standard marketing techniques to emphasize a good's environmental advantages. Green marketing is premised on the idea that fully informed consumers will switch to less polluting and habitat-destroying products. As a consequence, it is believed, producers will shift their purchases away from environmentally destructive production processes and toward environmentally benign processes because environmental consciousness will be more profitable. Green marketing thus moves environmental protection away from the realm of government regulation to individual choice in the marketplace.

Many large electricity companies are pursuing green marketing as a business strategy. At least twelve United States electric utilities support renewable power generation through "green pricing," and another thirty have considered, or are planning to offer, such an option. Nevertheless, fewer than twenty megawatts of renewable electricity are currently supported through green pricing programs. Perhaps more promising are the green marketing proposals of electricity retailers in states that have already deregulated their electricity industry. Deregulated retailers might be expected to market green power more aggressively than would a monopolistic public utility.

Unfortunately, economics and equity prevent the successful substitution of green marketing for state incentive-based environmental regulation. As a stand-alone mechanism to reduce the harmful environmental impacts of electricity production, green marketing suffers from numerous drawbacks. The first problem is that the benefits of renewable power, clean air, for instance, are public goods. Hence consumers have little incentive to purchase renewable power, given that they can enjoy (that is, free-ride off of) this clean air benefit when renewable power is purchased by others. The result of the free-riding activity associated with purchases of public goods such as renewable power is that the good will be under-supplied in relation to its net social benefits. The simple economic lesson here is that renewable power will be under-supplied if its support is left solely to the workings of the market.

Various pilot programs intended to test the demand for green power have demonstrated this basic law of economics. Although as many as seventy percent of residential customers claim that they are willing to pay more for renewable power, utility green pricing programs typically draw less than three percent of residential customers and an even smaller percentage of commercial customers. In a Massachusetts electric retail competition pilot program, residents were offered a choice between various energy options, some of them consisting of green power sources, and were provided with complete and comparable information about each option. Only four percent of eligible residential customers chose to participate in the Massachusetts pilot program. Of the four percent who enrolled, thirty-one percent chose a green option. Overall then, slightly more than one percent of eligible consumers subscribed to a green power option. In short, while people support clean energy, they have little incentive to purchase it out of their own pocketbook, since they can always enjoy its benefits if it is purchased by someone else.

Green marketing also raises equitable considerations. First, because the benefits of green energy are public goods, all of society gains from the purchasing decisions of a subset of environmentally conscious consumers. Thus, those who are willing to pay for environmental benefits subsidize a clean environment for those who are not. Second, industrial energy purchases have the largest environmental impacts (simply as a result of their larger energy demand), but green marketing appeals are not likely to make much of a difference in corporate decision making. To date, interest in environmentally friendly electricity is found primarily among residential consumers. Because it relies solely on individual choice to shape the energy market, green marketing ensures that residential consumers will pay to offset the environmental harms caused by the largest electricity consumers. Not only is funding for renewable power likely to decrease in such a scenario, but it is plainly inequitable for those least responsible for the environmental problems of electrical production to pay for the environmental restorative measures of those who are most responsible. For that reason, green marketing can be seen as a reversal of the principle endorsed by most environmental groups—the polluter pays principle. Despite this reversal, several prominent environmental organizations are promoting green marketing as a key component of their strategy to combat the possible adverse environmental impacts of electricity deregulation, prompting a vigorous debate within the environmental community.

The above criticisms all assume a green marketing mechanism that is functioning perfectly. But for a market to be efficient, consumers must have access to complete and accurate information concerning the goods being traded. Generators must inform consumers about the source of the energy offered as well as the impacts of its generation upon the environment. Obtaining such information is extremely difficult. In promotional literature, electricity companies stress their reliance upon renewable power and their record of environmental leadership. Many of the claims of green marketers, however, may be misleading, and purchasers of green energy may provide no net improvement in environmental quality.

Given these controversies, consumer groups are advocating truth-in-advertising laws specifically related to the green marketing claims made by retailers of electricity. Such laws would supplement the Federal Trade Commission's general restrictions upon green marketing claims. States are beginning to respond. Recently, California passed a law requiring that entities offering electric services disclose accurate, reliable and easy-to-understand information on the generation attributes of the electricity they propose to sell. Under this law, electricity suppliers must disclose this information to all potential end-use consumers "in all product-specific written promotional materials" distributed to consumers through print or electronic media. Moreover, several attorneys general recently urged states to adhere to consumer protection green marketing guidelines in electric industry restructuring legislation.

Other proposals include certification programs in which sellers of green energy compete for a seal or other stamp of approval from regulators.

Certification programs call for a state agency or private organization to verify that the type and percentage of renewable power being advertised by retail sellers corresponds to the characteristics of their actual renewable power supplies. Green power certification programs are now being implemented in several states. California has enacted one of the most aggressive of such programs. Under California's electricity restructuring law, the state is required to "implement a process for certifying eligible renewable resource providers." Customers who purchase certified renewable resources gain earlier access to the deregulated market. Certification programs advance not only consumer right-to-know objectives but also the marketing goals of retail sellers by assuring customers of the true greenness of the products they purchase.

Green marketing alone is thus an insufficient and, arguably, even inequitable method of addressing the environmental problems caused by the deregulated electricity market. If green marketing cannot provide the answer, is there any way to avoid the problems for incentive-based environmental regulation posed by the dormant Commerce Clause? . . .

The desirability of state market-based environmental regulation warrants several reforms in the Court's current tests for identifying unconstitutional burdens upon interstate commerce. First, state market-based mechanisms that employ facial discrimination should not be presumed invalid where the discrimination is part of a state's attempt to correct for market failures that create or exacerbate environmental degradation and where the discrimination is necessary to prevent a state from losing to other jurisdictions the benefits associated with correcting a market failure. Second, the market participant exception should be expanded to encompass state legislation dictating particular consumer preferences and again designed to prevent the loss to other jurisdictions of public environmental goods. Finally, the rule prohibiting extraterritorial regulation should be expanded to allow state decision makers to consider the environmental costs of their decisions, regardless of whether these costs will be incurred within or without the state's territory.■

NOTES AND COMMENTS

1. How would the dormant commerce clause cases, studied in the context of coal regulation, apply to state environmental programs, such as those being considered by Northeastern states and those discussed by Ferrey and Engel? Professor Engel proposes some modifications to how courts apply the dormant commerce clause analysis. Do you believe that these modifications are necessary? How would you assess the constitutionality of the hypothetical program Professor Engel presents at the beginning of her article?

2. One way regulators are attempting to ensure the coexistence of retail competition and environmental protection is by adopting renewable portfolio standards, requiring that a specified percentage of the energy in a retailer's portfolio be derived from renewable power sources. Many of these

portfolio plans are accompanied by a market in renewable credits, allowing suppliers with an excess to sell credits and those with a deficit to buy them. Proposed federal electricity restructuring legislation has also contained renewable portfolio standards. For discussion, see Kirsten H. Engel, The Dormant Commerce Clause Threat to Market–Based Environmental Regulation: The Case of Electricity Deregulation, 26 Ecology L.Q. 243, 262–65 (1999).

3. With restructuring, "green pricing" has emerged as one way to promote environmentally safer ways of generating electricity. Many utilities are encouraging the development of renewable energy through "green pricing" programs for residential, commercial, and industrial consumers. These programs offer a potential market solution to the funding of future renewable technologies, in which electricity consumers would voluntarily pay for renewable energy development. For instance, some utilities already offer consumers willing to pay a price premium for renewable energy an option by allowing them to participate in a program that allows them to add some incremental amount of money to their regular electricity bills or another program which rounds up consumers' bills to the nearest dollar, with the added quantity going to support renewable energy. One market survey concluded that customers are willing to pay $10 more per month to purchase green power. See Kari Smith, Customer Driven Markets for Renewably Generated Electricity, California Regulatory Research Project (CRRP/1–96 August 1996). According to the Natural Resources Defense Council, nearly 2 megawatts of power is generated today through green pricing programs in the United States. See NRDC Analysis Finds Green Pricing Programs Total Less Than 2 MW, Utility Environment Report, April 12, 1996, at 14.

How well will these programs work in a competitive environment? Is there a need for additional funding to encourage renewable power? Consider the following comparison of green power options in the California and Pennsylvania markets, from a report prepared by the California Regulatory Research Project:

> After an initial burst of marketing activity and growth during the first half of 1998, the green retail market showed virtually no growth during the remainder of the year. In 1999, the green market expanded rapidly, showing approximately 10 percent growth per month. As of September 30, 1999, approximately 85% of the 162,000 direct access small customers (residential and small commercial) in California are being served with green power.

> The rapid growth of California's green market in 1999 is dependent on a state incentive program called the Renewable Customer Credit. These incentives allow green power to be sold at a discount to incumbent utility pricing, making green power the only discounted power option available to small customers in California.

> A steep drop in the level of Renewable Customer Credit incentives will occur in the year 2000 if current levels of green market growth are

sustained. This is likely to result in a return to premium pricing for green power and a marked slowing of green market growth....

The deregulation of retail electricity in California spurred a tremendous initial response on the part of businesses seeking to carve out their niche in this $22 billion market. When the switch was finally thrown to open the market on April 1, 1998, over 250 companies had registered to conduct business as retail energy service providers (ESPs). Over time, 15 registered to sell renewable or "green power." By April 1, 1999, however, fewer than ten companies remained active as ESPs and only six were actively selling green power. Total penetration into the small customer segments was poor, at only 120,000 customers or roughly 135 average megawatts of demand, corresponding to 1.7% percent of total utility load for these segments.

From the perspective of ESPs that collectively invested an estimated 250 million dollars in marketing to small customers in California, these results are disastrous. They also indicate severe structural problems with the California market, particularly when California's numbers are compared to results in Pennsylvania, where over 358,000 or 7.8 percent of residential customers switched in less than a six months. It is also estimated that some twenty percent of those switching in Pennsylvania, or approximately 72,000 customers, chose green products.

Whereas the residential and small commercial direct access market in California has done poorly overall, on a relative basis, green power has done very well. What most business leaders expected to be a relatively insignificant niche now dominated dominates the small customer market. Of the 120,000 small customers that switched through April 1999, it is estimated that approximately 85% were being served with green power. From April through August 1999, the green power market grew rapidly, at approximately 10% per month.

Warren W. Byrne, Green Power in California: First Year Review from a Business Perspective (2000) <available on the Internet at http://www.cleanpower.org/crrp/b.htm> (last visited March 24, 2000). This report mentions the Renewable Customer Credit, a publicly funded program paid for through surcharges on distribution. The same report is skeptical about how well this credit program will encourage growth in green power in the future:

The 1.5 cent per kilowatt-hours Customer Credit (CC) subsidy is the single most important driving factor to the current Phase III expansion in the green market. This level of subsidy allows ESPs to sell green power at a discount to standard utility tariffs. However, the design of the CC program is such that the levels of support are likely to decline rapidly sometime during the year 2000, forcing the market to back into a position where only green power sales at a premium will be profitable for ESPs. As the most active green ESPs testified in hearings on the issue on September 23, 1999, this is likely to cause a substantial a substantial decrease in market growth, further handicapping its chances for long-term success.

The CC program allocates $75.6 million to be spent from 1998 through 2001 to support the sales of renewable power to retail customers. It is allocated in monthly allotments of $900,000 for the first year, $1.35 million for the second, $1.80 million for the third, and $2.25 million for the fourth. The incentive is applied in the form of a 1.5 cent payment for every kilowatt-hour of qualifying renewable power sold by a registered "green ESP" to a qualifying customer. The incentive is designed to remain at 1.5 cents per kilowatt-hour until such time as demand for the credit exceeds supply, at which point the CEC [California Energy Commission] will need to develop an alternate method for setting the credit level. Given that the date when demand will outpace supply is forecast to occur sometime in early 2000 at current market growth rates, the CEC has begun hearings seeking ESP input on what method should be used to set the credit level. Regardless of method chosen, the level is likely to drop to near one half its current size during the year 2000.

While creating tremendous opportunity for the green market, the design and implementation of the CC program has also been the source of substantial margin uncertainty for ESPs, significantly hampering the development of a green market that is stable over the long term. CC program related uncertainty falls into three categories: "supply procurement roulette," "subsidy sunset," and "accelerated shrink shock."

"Supply procurement roulette" stemmed from the fact that the CEC limited eligibility to a type of generation for which no reliable wholesale market existed at the time. Retail choice had been scheduled to open in January of 1998 and several ESPs were aggressively marketing green power as early as the fourth quarter of 1997. These ESPs needed to finalize their supply procurement in 1997 in order to price their products effectively and to make sure that their sales as of January 1998 would be backed with sufficient energy. Accordingly, several of the leading green ESPs were forced to purchase renewable power from out-of-state or utility owned resources. Because ESPs were unable to include reliably the value of the subsidy in their forecasts and pricing, without "rolling the dice" in a volatile short term eligible supply market, this uncertainty also maintained significant upward pressure on retail green power prices, therefore also reducing market size. Had the rules been less restrictive, the green market might have benefitted from an estimated $1 to $3 million in additional CC incentives.

The "subsidy sunset" problem stems from the CC program's scheduled termination of fund collection at end of March 2002. This means that just as an ESP might expect to see profitability from current investments in customer acquisition, funding for the CC incentive is expected to end, pulling out the cornerstone of that profitability. There is a reasonable probability that funding for the CC program may be extended. However, continuity is uncertain, as is the level at which the funding might be continued. This kind of uncertainty is a strong deterrent to investment and market growth.

In addition to the "subsidy sunset" issue, the market will face a "credit cliff" sometime in the year 2000. Without careful analysis, one might expect that the CC level will decline slowly as demand catches up and gradually overtakes funding supply. However, that is not the case. Through May 1999, the CC program was undersubscribed, meaning that demand started significantly lower than supply. The resulting unspent allocations of monthly funding have been rolled forward to the next month as a surplus. The surplus peaked in May 1999 at approximately $9.8 million. At that time, demand crossed the point of equaling ongoing monthly funding allocations and began to cut into the surplus dollars. By the time the surplus is fully consumed at the 1.5 cent level, demand is likely to be more than double the quantity that can be supported at the 1.5 cent per kilowatt-hour level by monthly allocations alone. If CC funding levels remain the same, and demand continues to grow, the credit level will inevitably shrink by close to 50 percent during 2000.

What "credit cliff" will mean to the market is that customers who had signed up for green power at a 0.1 cent per kilowatt-hour discount may have their prices raised to a significant premium. An ESP would need to charge an approximate 0.6 cent per kilowatt-hour or higher premium in order to remain margin neutral on customers that are now receiving a discount if the CC level drops as much as can be reasonably expected in 2000. For an ESP not to raise prices if CC incentives drop below 1.0 cent per kilowatt-hour would mean that they are certain to lose money on each customer they serve. Price hikes would be likely to cause some level of customer reversion back to default service. Such reversion in turn would have a further negative impact on the profitability of ESPs.

Insight into how many customers might revert in the case of price hikes can be gained by looking at how many current green customers signed up to discount service versus premium service. We can assume that some percentage of discount customers value the discount more highly than they do the product's "green-ness." This is likely to be particularly true of commercial customers. The extent to which individual customers value savings more than green-ness should be a good predictor of their probability of switching if prices are raised.

As of April 1999, approximately 30 percent of green demand is from commercial customers purchasing discount products. Residential customers purchasing discount products constitute an additional 25 percent of total green demand. In all, approximately 55 percent of current green demand is receiving discounted service. When incentives decline and green ESPs are forced to raise prices such that these customers are paying a premium, it is possible that a high percentage of the discount commercial customers and some portion of the discount residential customers will choose to revert to default service. This could mean the green market might lose up to 50 percent of its demand base.

However, there are several reasons why raising prices for existing customers should not cause a significant number of them to switch back to default service. The amount of the discount that customers are receiving today is negligible, approximately 1% of the total bill, or 60 cents per month for the average residential customer, $1.00 for the average small commercial customer, and $6.65 for the average commercial/industrial customer over 20kw in demand. Due to the masking influences of seasonal usage and PX price variability, it would be unlikely for customers to detect a price increase of even five percent on their total bill. Therefore, unless they are otherwise informed that their price has increased by one or two percent, they are unlikely to catch it and switch of their own accord.

If they are informed of a price increase by some other means, they are reasonably likely to value the green component over this negligible amount of money, particularly if the ESPs customer education has been effective. Commercial customers may be more bottom line oriented, but the amount of savings in question remains negligible. Inertia will also work in favor of customer retention. Switching takes time and effort on the part of a customer and saving a negligible amount of money is not likely to be worth the effort for a large percentage of customers.

Id.

4.   Many states also actively police the environmental aspects of utility regulation through power plant siting and integrated resource planning statutes. Such regulatory proceeding may also include some assessment of the "need" for power plants or transmission lines. However, if markets, rather than regulation, are the norm for decisions about power supply, does discussion of "need" continue to make sense?

The following case was decided against the backdrop of such concerns in Florida. Two issues are raised by the case, but not discussed at length: 1) whether using a state siting statute to preclude approval of a merchant power plant owned by an out-of-state utility violates the dormant commerce clause; and 2) whether the federal policy of competition in the Energy Policy Act of 1992 preempts state consideration of nonenvironmental factors (e.g., reliability and "need") in power plant siting and integrated resource planning. Will the federal courts assess these issues in the same way as the Florida Supreme Court? What might this mean for the future of state utility regulation?

Tampa Electric Co. v. Florida

200 P.U.R. 4th 370, 2000 WL 422871 (Fla. Supreme Court 2000)

The issue presented concerns the statutory authority of the PSC to grant a determination of need under the Florida Electrical Power Plant

Siting Act (Siting Act) and the Florida Energy Efficiency & Conservation Act (FEECA) for an electric power company's proposal to build and operate a merchant plant in Volusia County. [Editor's note: The PSC granted a determination of need for Duke Energy's proposed merchant power plant, at issue in this appeal.] We reverse the order of the PSC for the reasons stated herein.

The construction of any new electrical power generating plant with a capacity greater than seventy-five megawatts is required to be certified in accord with the various requirements of the Siting Act in chapter 403, Florida Statutes. As part of the process, an applicant seeks a determination of need from the PSC for a proposed power plant. *See* § 403.519, Fla. Stat. (1997). The PSC's granting of a determination of need for a proposed power plant creates a presumption of public need. *See* § 403.519, Fla. Stat. (1997). This determination serves as the PSC's report required by section 403.507(2)(a) 2, Florida Statutes (1997), as part of the permitting procedure.

On August 19, 1998, the Utilities Commission of the City of New Smyrna Beach (New Smyrna), and Duke Energy New Smyrna Beach Power Co., Ltd. (Duke) filed in the PSC a joint petition for determination of need for the New Smyrna Beach Power Project, a proposed natural gas fired combined cycle generating plant with 514 megawatts of net capacity to be built and operated by Duke in New Smyrna Beach. Duke is not presently subject to PSC regulation as a public utility authorized to generate and sell electric power at retail rates to Florida customers. Duke is a subsidiary of an investor-owned utility based in North Carolina. As a company offering electrical power for sale at wholesale rates, Duke is subject to the regulatory jurisdiction of the Federal Energy Regulatory Commission (FERC) and is classified as an exempt wholesale generator (EWG). New Smyrna is a Florida municipal electric utility that directly serves retail customers. In the present petition for determination of need, Duke proposed to build a 514–megawatt plant, with thirty megawatts of that capacity and associated energy committed to be sold to New Smyrna and the remaining megawatts uncommitted and intended to be made available for sale at competitive wholesale rates to utilities that directly serve retail customers.

Prior to filing the present joint petition, Duke and New Smyrna entered into an agreement requiring Duke to finance, design, build, own, and operate the plant and to sell to New Smyrna thirty megawatts of Duke's proposed plant's capacity at a discount wholesale rate. New Smyrna agreed to provide the site for the plant, a wastewater treatment facility, water, and tax reductions. New Smyrna intends to sell to its retail customers the energy it has committed to purchase from Duke. The agreement also provides that Duke will make available for sale the remaining 484 megawatts of power in the competitive wholesale electrical power market primarily, but not exclusively, for ultimate use in Florida.

The seven intervenors as to the petition included present appellants Tampa Electric Co. (Tampa Electric), Florida Power Corp. (FPC), and Florida Power & Light Co. (FP & L). After a hearing in December 1998, three members of the Commission voted to deny motions to dismiss by FPC and FP & L and voted to grant the joint petition. In re Joint Petition for Determination of Need, No. PSC–99–0535–FOF–EM (March 22, 1999) (Order). Commissioner Clark dissented, concluding that Duke was not a proper applicant. Commissioner Jacobs concurred and dissented, stating that he believed Duke was a proper applicant but that Duke had not proven its proposed plant to be the most cost-effective option.

In this appeal, appellants are public utilities that are regulated and authorized by the PSC to generate and sell electrical power to users of the power in Florida. Appellants designate themselves as Florida retail utilities. Appellants contend that section 403.519, Florida Statutes, from its initial adoption in 1980 through subsequent legislative changes and up to the present date, does not authorize the PSC to grant a determination of need to an entity other than a Florida retail utility regulated by the PSC whose petition is based upon a specified demonstrated need of Florida retail utilities for serving Florida power customers.

Appellants point out that the recent national movement toward the construction of power plants intended to generate power to be sold in competitive wholesale markets stems from recent federal legislative initiatives. This movement began with the Public Utilities Regulatory Policies Act of 1978 (PURPA). Subsequent relevant federal legislation includes the Energy Policy Act of 1992, which exempts certain wholesale generators from some regulatory requirements. Another milestone is a FERC order issued in 1996 which affects power distribution. Appellants note that these federal initiatives occurred subsequent to the Legislature's enactment of the Siting Act of 1973. Appellants also emphasize that the Legislature has not amended section 403.519 to authorize the PSC to grant a determination of need for a power plant in Florida that would generate power intended to be sold in the competitive wholesale market which is developing as a result of these federal legislative and regulatory changes.

Appellants contend that Duke is not an authorized applicant under section 403.519 because Duke is not a Florida retail utility. Appellants contend that joining with New Smyrna, which is a proper applicant, does not cure the fact that Duke is not a proper applicant in view of the commitment to New Smyrna of just thirty megawatts of the 514–megawatt capacity of the plant. Appellants contend that the proposed plant is not authorized by section 403.519 because all but the thirty megawatts that New Smyrna has agreed to buy is uncommitted. Therefore, there is no demonstrated specific need committed to Florida customers who are intended to be served by this proposed plant.

In support of their position, appellants cite PSC orders in proceedings that led to this Court's decisions in *Nassau Power Corp. v. Beard*, 601 So.2d 1175 (Fla.1992) (Nassau I), and *Nassau Power Corp. v. Deason*, 641 So.2d 396 (Fla.1994) (Nassau II) (collectively, the Nassau cases).

In the proceedings below, the five members of the PSC were divided in their conclusions as to the decision to grant the determination of need. The three-member majority's rationale is presented by the PSC as an appellee in this Court. In the PSC order at issue here, the PSC majority finds that Duke and New Smyrna are proper applicants pursuant to the Siting Act, FEECA, and the Florida Administrative Code. Order at 18–29. The majority construes section 403.519 as requiring, pursuant to section 403.503(4), Florida Statutes (1997), that an applicant may be any "electric utility." *Id.* at 19. Utilities are defined in section 403.503(13), Florida Statutes (1997), as "regulated electric companies." *Id.* The majority finds that Duke is a regulated electric company pursuant to federal regulatory statutes because the statutes do not expressly provide that "regulated electric companies" are to be state-regulated. Id. at 20. The majority finds that even though Duke is not a Florida retail utility, it is a regulated electric company subject to federal regulation and certain other Florida regulation. *Id.* at 19, 22–24. The majority also finds that a determination of need properly could be based upon the projected needs of utilities throughout peninsular Florida rather than committed megawatt needs of specific retail utilities. *Id.* at 53–54. The majority finds the Nassau cases not to be on point here because those cases concerned a wholly different issue. *Id.* at 29–32. In the Nassau cases, the PSC was asked to determine the need and standing of qualified facilities under PURPA, the federal law regulating cogenerators. The PSC points out that it specifically limited its decision to the facts of those qualified-facilities cases. *Id.* at 32.

In her dissenting opinion, Commissioner Clark construes the Siting Act and FEECA to mean that a proper applicant under section 403.519 is defined for purposes of FEECA, of which section 403.519 is a part, as "any person or entity of whatever form which provides electricity or natural gas at retail to the public." Order at 58 (quoting Ch. 80–65, § 5 at 214, Laws of Fla.) (alteration in original). She concludes that a utility's sale of electrical power must be a retail sale in order for that utility to be subject to PSC regulatory authority. *Id.* at 66. She notes that "wholesale sales are a matter within the sphere of federal regulation." Id. Commissioner Clark cites this Court's Nassau cases in support of her interpretation of the term "applicant" in section 403.519. *Id.* at 68. She finds those cases to be relevant in that this Court's rationale focused on the types of entities enumerated in section 403.503, Florida Statutes, and "concluded that the common denominator present in each was an obligation to serve customers." *Id.* at 68. Thus, "the need to be examined under section 403.519, Florida Statutes, was a need resulting from the duty to serve those customers." *Id.* Commissioner Clark concludes her dissenting opinion by stating:

> Our task in this case was to decide what the law is, not what it ought to be. In my view, the law is clear that Duke New Smyrna is not a proper applicant under section 403.519, Florida Statutes, and the petition must be dismissed. We should, however, move forward with our workshop so that we can make recommendations to the Legislature as to what the law ought to be.

Order at 71. In his dissenting opinion, Commissioner Jacobs agrees with the majority that Duke is a proper applicant but finds that Duke and New

Smyrna "failed to provide the weight of evidence required to depart from the Commission's long-standing policy of relying on its own cost effectiveness analysis of a proposed plant." Order at 74.

In this Court, Duke and New Smyrna, who are joint appellees with the PSC, argue that a need determination as part of the permitting process for the proposed Duke plant does fall within the parameters of section 403.519. They argue that the primary determinant as to Duke's applicant status is whether Duke is a regulated utility. The appellees maintain that Duke qualifies as a regulated utility because it is regulated under federal regulatory procedures, and if Duke receives permits to operate its proposed plant in Florida, the plant's operation will be regulated in part by the PSC. Duke and New Smyrna maintain that the Nassau cases were decided in the context of need for power demonstrated by cogenerators and that those cases do not apply here. The appellees also rely upon the fact that Duke has filed a joint application with New Smyrna.

New Smyrna additionally presents two constitutional arguments and argues that prohibiting Duke from applying directly for a need determination would violate the dormant Commerce Clause of the United States Constitution because such action would unconstitutionally discriminate against out-of-state commerce and burden interstate commerce. New Smyrna also argues that any state requirement that Duke first obtain a contract with a retail utility to build the project is preempted by the federal Energy Policy Act of 1992, which mandates a robust competitive wholesale market. . . .

The precise question we consider here is: Does section 403.519, Florida Statutes, authorize the granting of a determination of need upon an application for a proposed power plant for which the owner and operator is not a Florida retail utility regulated by the PSC and for which only thirty megawatts of the plant's 514–megawatt capacity have been committed by contract to be sold to a Florida retail utility regulated by the PSC?

While we recognize that the PSC is correct in pointing out that the Nassau cases were decided upon different facts and were intended to resolve different issues, we conclude that our analysis of the Siting Act, articulated in those decisions, is applicable to the present case. In Nassau II, we stated:

In *Nassau Power Corp. v. Beard*, 601 So.2d 1175, 1176–77 (Fla.1992), we recently explained:

The Siting Act was passed by the legislature in 1973 for the purpose of minimizing the adverse impact of power plants on the environment. See § 403.502, Fla. Stat. (1989). That Act establishes a site certification process that requires the PSC to determine the need for any proposed power plants, including cogenerators, based on the criteria set forth in section 403.519, Florida Statutes (1989). Section 403.519 requires the PSC to make specific findings for each electric generating facility proposed in Florida, as to (1) electric system reliability and integrity, (2) the need to provide adequate electricity at a reasonable cost; (3) whether the proposed facility is the most cost-effective alternative available for supplying electricity; and (4) conservation measures reasonably available to mitigate the need for the plant. (Footnote omitted).... Only an "applicant" can request a determination of need under section 403.519. Section 403.503(4), Florida Statutes (1991), defines the term "applicant" as "any electric utility which applies for certification pursuant to the provisions of this act." An "electric utility," as used in the Act, means cities and towns, counties, public utility districts, regulated electric companies, electric cooperatives, and joint operating agencies, or combinations thereof, engaged in, or authorized to engage in, the business of generating, transmitting, or distributing electric energy. Sec. 403.503(13), Fla. Stat. (1991). The Commission determined that because non-utility generators are not included in this definition, Nassau is not a proper applicant under section 403.519. The Commission reasoned that a need determination proceeding is designed to examine the need resulting from an electric utility's duty to serve customers. Non-utility generators, such as Nassau, have no similar need because they are not required to serve customers. The Commission's interpretation of section 403.519 also comports with this Court's decision in *Nassau Power Corp. v. Beard*. In that decision, we rejected Nassau's argument that "the Siting Act does not require the PSC to determine need on a utility-specific basis." 601 So.2d at 1178 n. 9. Rather, we agreed with the Commission that the need to be determined under section 403.519 is "the need of the entity ultimately consuming the power," in this case FPL. *Id*.

641 So.2d at 397, 398–99 (footnote omitted). Based upon our Nassau analysis of the Siting Act, we conclude that the granting of the determination of need on the basis of the present application does exceed the PSC's present authority. A determination of need is presently available only to an applicant that has demonstrated that a utility or utilities serving retail customers has specific committed need for all of the electrical power to be generated at a proposed plant.

Our decision is founded upon our continuing recognition that the regulation of the generation and sale of power in Florida resides in the legislative branch of government. The PSC, successor to the Florida Railroad and Public Utilities Commission, is an arm of the legislative branch in that the Commission obtains all of its authority from legislation. Originally, the Legislature did not include among the PSC's responsibilities the authority to approve the siting of new power plants but left such authority to local government entities. In 1973, the Legislature enacted the Florida Electrical Power Plant Siting Act, to preempt local government action and to consolidate approval of most state agencies into a single license. Within that law was a requirement that each utility submit a ten-year site plan estimating the utility's power generating needs and the general location of its power plants. In enacting the Siting Act, the Legislature recognized a need for statewide perspective in selecting sites for power plants because of the "significant impact upon the welfare of the population, the location and growth of industry and the use of the natural resources of the state." *See*

Ch. 73–33, § 1 at 73, Laws of Fla. At that time, the role of the PSC was to prepare a "report and recommendation as to the present and future needs for electrical generating capacity in the area to be served by the proposed site." *Id.* at 77 . . . .

Our reading of th[e] statutory history leads us to continue to conclude that the present statutory scheme was intended to place the PSC's determination of need within the regulatory framework allowing Florida regulated utilities to propose new power plants to provide electrical service to their Florida customers at retail rates. This need determination, pursuant to section 403.519, contemplates the PSC's express consideration of the statutory factors based upon demonstrated specified needs of these Florida customers. The need determination is part of the process that the Legislature intended by its plain language to balance "the pressing need for increased power generation facilities" with the necessity that the state

> ensure through available and reasonable methods that the location and operation of electrical power plants will produce minimal adverse effects on human health, the environment, the ecology of the land and its wildlife, and the ecology of state waters and their aquatic life.

§ 403.502, Fla. Stat. (1997).

Accordingly, we find that the statutory scheme embodied in the Siting Act and FEECA was not intended to authorize the determination of need for a proposed power plant output that is not fully committed to use by Florida customers who purchase electrical power at retail rates. Rather, we find that the Legislature must enact express statutory criteria if it intends such authority for the PSC. Pursuant only to such legislative action will the PSC be authorized to consider the advent of the competitive market in wholesale power promoted by recent federal initiatives. Such statutory criteria are necessary if the Florida regulatory procedures are intended to cover this evolution in the electric power industry. The projected need of unspecified utilities throughout peninsular Florida is not among the authorized statutory criteria for determining whether to grant a determination of need pursuant to section 403.519, Florida Statutes. Moreover, we agree with appellants that the fact of Duke's joining with New Smyrna in this arrangement for a thirty-megawatt commitment does not transform the application into one that complies with the Siting Act and FEECA.

We find no merit in the constitutional arguments advanced by New Smyrna. As to any alleged preemption or interference with interstate commerce, we find that power-plant siting and need determination are areas that Congress has expressly left to the states.

Accordingly, we reverse the order of the PSC on the basis that the granting of the determination of need exceeds the PSC's authority pursuant to section 403.519, Florida Statutes (1997).

It is so ordered.

■Anstead, J., dissenting.

I cannot concur in the majority's conclusion that the Florida Legislature has clearly prohibited the proposed action of the Commission. Indeed, it appears to me that the prohibition is based upon a strained and artificial construction of various provisions of the legislative scheme that have little bearing on the issue before us today. In fact, even under the strained construction of the majority the issue would be not whether the petitioning utilities were proper applicants, but whether the capacity required should be permitted.

I am especially concerned with the majority's conclusion that it will not find Commission authority to act absent "express statutory criteria" for the specific circumstances presented here. Clearly, the Commission was created to regulate utilities seeking to operate in Florida. In my view that is precisely what the Commission is doing here.■

CHAPTER 14

NUCLEAR ENERGY

A. THE DEVELOPMENT OF NUCLEAR POWER

The nuclear weapon tests in South Asia have brought renewed media attention to nuclear energy. But although peaceful uses of nuclear power attract less attention, nuclear energy continues to be used throughout the world for a wide variety of purposes ranging from nuclear medicine to the generation of electricity in nuclear power plants.

Nuclear energy was first utilized in the latter days of World War Two when the atomic bomb was invented and then quickly used against the Japanese cities of Hiroshima and Nagasaki. In the aftermath of the war, the United States emphasized the importance of peaceful uses of atomic energy. One of the most obvious possibilities was the use of nuclear fission as a source of heat for commercial power plants.

In the years immediately following the war, the United States was the only nation that had demonstrated its ability to create nuclear fission. The government hoped that it could maintain that monopoly, but it soon became apparent that the Soviet Union was also capable of producing nuclear weapons.

As nuclear capabilities spread, the United States gave up hope of isolating nuclear technology and decided to encourage the spread of peaceful uses of nuclear energy. The "Atoms for Peace" program, initiated by President Eisenhower shortly after his election, transferred nuclear technology from the military forces to the private companies that specialized in power plant construction, such as Westinghouse and General Electric.

From the beginning of nuclear energy, the United States federal government kept close tabs on all of the domestic uses of this energy. The Atomic Energy Act of 1954, 42 U.S.C. § 2011 et. seq., opened up the use of nuclear power to more private companies and encouraged the development of nuclear power, but under close regulation by the Atomic Energy Commission (now the Nuclear Regulatory Commission), which exercises supervision over even the most detailed aspects of nuclear energy.

Because the insurance industry refused to bear the risk of nuclear accidents, the large scale nuclear power plants began to be built only after Congress passed the Price–Anderson Act in 1957, which capped the liability of private companies and made the federal government the reinsurer of the nuclear industry. The Price–Anderson Act, as currently amended, not only limits liabilities arising out of any "nuclear incident or precautionary evacuation," 42 U.S.C. § 2014(w), it provides a mechanism for consolidating all claims in the nature of "any public liability action arising out of or resulting from a nuclear accident" in a single federal court proceeding. 42 U.S.C. § 2210(n)(2).

The first nuclear power plant came on line in 1957 in Shippingport, Pennsylvania, near Pittsburgh. Stephen E. Atkins, Historical Encyclopedia of Atomic Energy 329–330 (Greenwood Press, 2000). In the late 1950s and early 1960s some three dozen small nuclear plants were built in various parts of the world. Initial experience with these plants suggested that the resulting cost of nuclear power would decline steadily with improvements in the technology. In the mid–1960s, optimistic supporters of nuclear power extrapolated that decline into the future and bragged that soon nuclear power would be "too cheap to meter."

Power companies throughout the world then rushed to jump on the bandwagon. From 1965 until 1975, they ordered almost 300 nuclear power plants. Companies in Japan, Sweden, Britain, France, Germany and Canada joined four big American companies in the race to build nuclear plants as fast as the orders could be filled.

In the United States, the decline of domestic oil reserves and the rapid growth of energy demand during this period gave a patriotic flavor to the move toward nuclear power. It was seen as an important element in the ability of America to maintain energy self-reliance. With existing and potential regional wars disrupting world trade, American industry was increasingly nervous about its growing reliance on oil that had to be imported from the Middle East.

Uranium, the metal used to make nuclear power plant fuel, has been found in ample quantities in the United States. One of the most prevalent sources was in Southeast Utah, where huge piles of tailings along the bed of the Colorado River remain as the residue of mines and mills that produced uranium oxide, the first step in creating nuclear fuel. The uranium oxide, which is then enriched to increase the percentage of the isotope uranium 235, is eventually transformed into "fuel rods" which produce heat that boils water and creates steam that drives the turbines that generate electricity. The boilers and turbines, two of the main elements of a nuclear power plant, are essentially the same as those in all other steam generating plants. It is in the source of the heat that creates the steam that the nuclear power plant is unique.

The uniqueness of nuclear power's heat source did not go unnoticed. Throughout this period the United States was continuing to develop and test nuclear weapons, including a "hydrogen bomb" that far exceeded the power of the weapons used on Japan in 1945. Moreover, other nations including the Soviet Union, China and France were actively testing such weapons.

Public reaction to nuclear power was initially dominated by patriotic pride in American technology that submerged the nagging fears about accidental or hostile misuse of the power. As the public became aware of the long range impact of radiation sickness on residents of Hiroshima and Nagasaki, the fear of nuclear power began to spread more widely. As the growing numbers of nuclear plants began to rise on the horizon, an increasing number of people began to doubt their safety.

In the 1970s, the temper of nuclear regulation changed. People were no longer complacent about nuclear power safety, or convinced by environmental claims made by industry and government. Throughout the 1960's and into the early 1970's, nuclear power not only remained economically desirable, it was also given a prominent position in national energy plans. Still, a rift in the government-industry partnership started to develop which would first manifest itself in a bureaucratic realignment.

The AEC had conflicting functions: promoting the use of nuclear technology and, at the same time, insuring that the technology was applied safely. In 1974, realizing the cross purpose of both promotion and safety oversight, Congress split the AEC. It created the Nuclear Regulatory Commission (NRC), an independent agency responsible for safety and licensing, and formed the Energy Research and Development Administration (ERDA), later absorbed by the Department of Energy, responsible for promotion and development of nuclear power. Energy Reorganization Act of 1974, P.L. 93–438, 88 Stat. 1233 (1974) (codified as amended at 42 U.S.C.A. §§ 5801–79). This alignment did not completely remove a fundamental regulatory conflict for the NRC. The NRC had the responsibility both for licensing plants and for safety oversight. If the NRC too vigorously exercises its safety role, then the attendant compliance costs act as a disincentive to invest in nuclear plants, which cuts across the NRC's licensing grain.[1]

The NRC responded to the growing discomfort about the safety of nuclear power by steadily tightening safety requirements. New rules were often applied to plants already under construction. The procedures for licensing of new plants involved a multitude of layers, and the NRC responded to anti-nuclear groups by permitting them to intervene at many stages of the process.

B.   THE FUTURE OF NUCLEAR POWER

The first generation of nuclear power plants are up and operating in the United States and providing about a fifth of the nation's electricity.

Location of Nuclear Power Plants

Figure 14–1

Source: NCR, 1999

Although they have not lived up to all of the high expectations of their promoters, these plants are delivering a significant share of our power requirements. The industry now needs to decide what to do in the future.

---

1.   Jan G. Laitos and Joseph P. Tomain, Energy and Natural Resources in a Nutshell 465–466 (West Group, 1992).

1. NEW POWER PLANT CONSTRUCTION

Should another generation of nuclear plants, perhaps incorporating new safety and economy features, be started? The major designers of such plants believe that they can now build plants that avoid the mistakes of the past and produce safe and economical power.

a. UNITED STATES

Congress has agreed that streamlined design standards should be adopted, but to date no domestic power company has elected to buy a plant designed pursuant to the new standards. No nuclear power plants are now under construction in the United States.

Nicholas S. Reynolds & Robert L. Draper, The Future of Nuclear Power

Natural Resources & Environment, Winter 1994, at 9

Elements within the nuclear power industry, and the federal government, are currently devoting considerable resources to the development of advanced nuclear reactor designs capable of being built on a schedule commensurate with those demand projections.... In some respects, the prospects for a second generation of nuclear power plants will depend on the success of the current generation. Compilation of a solid safety record is necessary to continue to build public confidence. A serious nuclear accident, or any operational incident arousing broad public concern, could be devastating to the prospect for new growth. In addition, continued strong economic performance is necessary to boost investor confidence and minimize a loss of "market share" to alternative generating sources in the short term.

... [T]here is considerable agreement on the principal hurdles that must be cleared if a second generation of reactors is to be realized. These issues have revealed themselves over the course of the history of reactor operations, from the earliest plant licensing proceedings up through the most recent efforts to provide temporary spent-fuel storage. The nuclear power industry sponsored the development of the "Strategic Plan for Building New Nuclear Power Plants" in 1990 to identify clearly and assign responsibility and a schedule for addressing these prerequisites to future growth. Nuclear Power Oversight Committee, Strategic Plan for Building New Nuclear Power Plants (Strategic Plan) (1990).

The nuclear power industry's Strategic Plan identified fourteen "building blocks" for the development of a second generation of nuclear power plants, including:

- development of a predictable, streamlined regulatory process for plant construction and licensing;
- availability of high-level (including spent fuel) and low-level radioactive waste disposal capacity;

- equitable and predictable rate treatment for nuclear power projects, and a structure for financing, ownership, and operation of plants which reasonably compensates owners and investor; and

- broad public acceptance of nuclear power.

Several of these objectives have already been met, and progress continues to be made on those not fully addressed.

A statutory and regulatory framework for streamlined, or "one-step," plant licensing is in place. NRC regulations (in Title 10, Part 52 of the Code of Federal Regulations) were revised in 1989 to provide for issuance of a combined construction permit and operating license for a nuclear power plant. Under this approach, which has yet to be tested, all design issues would be resolved before construction begins. There would be an opportunity for a post-construction hearing, but only on the question of whether the nuclear power plant as constructed complies with the acceptance criteria in its combined license. This framework should do much to minimize the threat of delay inherently associated with post-construction hearings in the past, which paralyzed the operation and escalated the cost of several plants built in the 1970s and 1980s.

NRC's streamlined licensing process has been affirmed and bolstered by Congress. Through EPAct of 1992, Congress enacted long-awaited legislation which provides clear authority for NRC to issue combined licenses. *See* 42 U.S.C.A. § 2235 (West 1993). . . .

A uniform regulatory framework is also in place (again, in 10 C.F.R. Part 52) to support generic NRC approval (certification) of standardized advanced reactor designs. Under NRC's design certification regulations, a plant vendor may seek one-time NRC approval of an "essentially complete" nuclear power plant design through rulemaking. 10 C.F.R. Part 52, subpart B. A potential licensee could then select a certified design "off the shelf" and reference the reactor vendor's design certification in its own combined license application, and thereby avoid duplicative review of all but the remaining site-specific design issues. (10 C.F.R. Part 52 similarly provides for incorporation by reference in a combined license of a previously issued plant site permit.)

In addition to simplifying the plant licensing process, standardized designs would facilitate generic (and hence more efficient) regulation of operations and sharing of experience across the industry, and eliminate many of the regulatory complexities and hardware peculiarities of today's unique-design plants. Standardized advanced plant designs would improve the economic viability of new nuclear-generating capacity in at least four more ways:

- capital cost reductions (some speculate at least 50 percent) through design modularization and standardization;

- shortened construction schedules (existing plants required an average of eight years to complete);

- reductions in radioactive waste generation, risk of core-damage accidents, and personnel exposures; and

- improvement of plant availability rates, which translates into increased safety and reliability.

Thus many of the problems inherent in the construction and operation of the current generation of plants would be eliminated or minimized through advanced designs alone. . . .

A second generation of plants would most likely consist of advanced light water reactors (improved versions of the same general water-cooled designs utilized in existing plants) of two types—"evolutionary" designs (large units combining the best features of existing plants) and "passive" designs (smaller, simpler plants employing natural forces such as gravity and convective flow, rather than engineered systems such as pumps and valves, to correct abnormal operating conditions). These new plants are intended to be safer (as defined by accident probabilities and personnel exposure) and more reliable (fewer unplanned automatic shutdowns and a longer plant life) than the current generation of light water reactors. . . .

A new generation of nuclear plants could be financed privately, as turn-key projects through, for example, partnerships among entrepreneurial investors of joint ventures among reactor vendors, architect/engineers, constructors, and plant operators. The new era of competition and deregulation in the electric power industry has expanded the opportunities for alternative ownership and power sales arrangements. Plant operation could be undertaken by an independent power producer, which could be an unregulated affiliate of a utility.

At the same time, state rate regulatory bodies are being encouraged to employ cost recovery approaches which reduce the risk to ratepayers, shareholders, and potential investors in backing new nuclear power projects. One example is the concept of "rolling prudence," under which construction costs and schedules are reviewed periodically, so that any disallowances will be identified promptly, and the prudence of continuing a project can be considered incrementally. *See, e.g., Connecticut Light & Power Co.,* No 92–11–11, 1993 WL 347545 (Conn.D.P.U.C.). While public opposition could still hinder plant siting and licensing efforts in some areas, those aspects of the process have been significantly improved, as discussed above, to avoid unwarranted delay in plant operation.

Finally, environmental legislation should be mentioned as one factor that could weigh in favor of nuclear power as a second-generation technology. It is projected that, after the turn of the century, electric utilities will need to add a significant amount of new capacity to replace retired plants and to satisfy increasing demand for electricity. As utilities look to replace coal-fired capacity, many additions will likely incorporate "clean coal"-generating technologies that satisfy sulfur dioxide emissions limits imposed under recent clean air legislation. In addition, one could expect that the environmental effects of greenhouse gases (e.g., global warming) will continue to receive both public and scientific attention. These concerns could cause utilities to consider seriously nuclear power as a viable alternative for future baseload generating capacity.■

NOTES AND COMMENTS

1. The Nuclear Regulatory Commission has now approved standard designs and streamlined permit procedures. 10 C.F.R. Part 52. There have not been any applicants to build plants under the new procedures.

2. Some of the earliest nuclear power plants will be needing license renewals in the early part of the twenty first century. Renewal procedures are found in 10 C.F.R. Part 54.

b. OVERSEAS

The expansion of nuclear power may be at a standstill in the US, but many developing countries find it an attractive and affordable solution to their growing need for electrical power. Russia has become the major player involved in exporting nuclear technology and materials, earning over $2 billion from nuclear exports in 1996. Russia's wealth of nuclear material comes from extracting uranium from nuclear warheads.

Hans Blix Nuclear Energy in the 21st Century

Nuclear News (Sept. 1997) at 34.

[Hans Blix was the Director General of the International Atomic Energy Agency.]

Global energy use will increase considerably in the decades to come. Even if a more efficient use of energy will somewhat slow the additional demand, billions of people in Asia and elsewhere in the developing world wanting a higher living standard will sustain a high demand. This calls for more energy—particularly electricity for trains, industry, light, refrigerators, washing machines, TV sets, and much more. The World Energy Council forecasts that the world use of electricity will increase by 50 to 75 percent by 2020. It is one of the safer predictions in the energy field.

At present, China uses close to 1000 kWh per person per year. In my country, Sweden, it is about 15 000; in the Republic of Korea, 5000; and in Japan, 7500 kWh per capita per annum. In the not-so-distant future, per capita consumption in China and in other developing Asian countries will surely reach a level similar to present consumption in the Republic of Korea. In China, electricity generation has had an average increase of 10 percent a year over the last 10 years, and future demand in China as a whole looks set to expand at a rate of 16 GW per year.

How is this huge increase to be met? For good reasons, the nuclear power option is attracting growing attention in China, and in other countries with rapidly expanding economies in East and Southeast Asia.

In the Republic of Korea, only one 600–MWe reactor was operating in 1980; today, installed nuclear capacity is 15 times higher. In China, the first power reactor was commissioned a few years ago. Today, three reactors are operating in China, two of them in Guangdong province. In the near future, other provinces may also want to develop nuclear power. Decisions have already been taken to construct eight reactors nationwide, and four of these are currently under construction. At Qinshan (Qinshan Phase 2), the construction of two new 600–MWe pressurized water reactor (PWR) units of Chinese design started in June 1996, with commercial operation expected by mid–2002. At Lingao, close to Daya Bay, civil engineering work started in 1996 for two 1000–MWe PWRs to be supplied under agreement with Framatome, with commercial operation scheduled in the second half of 2002.

Agreements have been signed for four other reactors. Two 700–MWe Candu 6 reactors, supplied by Atomic Energy of Canada Limited, will be built at Qinshan (Qinshan Phase 3). Construction should start in mid–1998 and commercial operation is expected in early 2003. Also, two 1000–MWe units (VVER–1000) are to be built with a Russian supplier at Lianyungan in the province of Jiangsu.

At the IAEA, we see this ambitious nuclear program as part of China's desire to reduce its dependence on electricity generation by fossil fuels and reduce the need for the transport by rail of vast quantities of coal, which now accounts for about 70 percent of China's electricity output. Nuclear power and hydro power will allow China to meet some of its growing electricity demand without pollution and without CO_2 emissions, which may contribute to global warming. . . .

As I hope is clear from the foregoing, nuclear power should have a significant future in the global energy mix. There are certain factors that will help or hinder the wider adoption of nuclear power.

Economic factors and growing public opposition—especially after the Chernobyl disaster—have slowed the expansion of nuclear power in many countries, and have led to a stagnation in the construction of nuclear plants in Western Europe and in the Americas. Slow economic growth and overcapacity in the generating industry in these regions are additional reasons that there has been very little major baseload construction of any kind in recent years. Construction of nuclear plants is currently continuing vigorously only in East Asia.

Despite this recent history, nuclear power remains a viable and, in my view, indispensable part of our global energy future for several reasons:

1. The cost of energy production remains important to countries, utilities, and consumers. As I have indicated, nuclear power is at present roughly on a par with coal, and in some cases can be competitive with natural gas in terms of generating costs. The large up-front investment required for nuclear plants is admittedly a drawback in capital-starved developing countries, but where governments are able to provide resources and leadership, the potential long-term returns can be great. The plant is

expensive to build, but the uranium fuel is relatively cheap. Reactors now tend increasingly to stay in operation past the end of their depreciated economic life—40 years or more—increasing their profitability while requiring no more investment. Moreover, the prices of fossil fuels are likely to increase over time. Nuclear generation can thus be expected to keep its competitive edge in various countries over the long run. Uranium-based fuel resources are not a problem for the near future. Also, nuclear technology is relatively young, and so there is still scope for rationalization, standardization, modular construction, higher burnup, and simplification—all of which will result in greater efficiency and lower cost. China's strategy for long-term standardization on an advanced PWR design should ensure that these economies are realized.

2.   Energy independence is another important factor. Not all countries have abundant energy resources, whether fossil fuels or hydropower. On the other hand, if several years' worth of nuclear fuel is imported, it can be stored for use over that time period. Some 25 tonnes is all that is needed for one full year of operation, and the space required for its storage is insignificant. Since fuel costs represent only about one-sixth of the overall cost of nuclear electricity, the cost of storing several years' worth of fuel remains very affordable. For countries without oil and gas, such as France, Japan, and the Republic of Korea, nuclear power offers a measure of self-reliance and immunity against international crises.

3.   The increasing safety and reliability of nuclear technology can be seen in the improved production figures for nuclear power plants around the world, lower doses to plant personnel, and fewer unplanned outages. The availability factor for the world's nuclear power reactors is now close to 80 percent. Unplanned outages, on average below 5 percent, can be compared favorably with what is occurring at fossil-fueled plants. This makes nuclear energy an excellent candidate for baseload power generation.

By the end of 1996, more than 8100 reactor-years of operating plant experience had been accumulated by the current nuclear energy systems of the world. New generations of nuclear power plants have been or are being developed, building on this background of success and applying lessons learned from the experience of operating plants.

Advanced designs currently under development comprise three basic types:

* Water-cooled reactors, using water as coolant and moderator.

* Fast reactors, using liquid metal, e.g. sodium, as coolant.

* Gas-cooled reactors, using gas, e.g. helium, as coolant and graphite as moderator.

About 90 percent of the nuclear power reactors now in operation are water-cooled, mostly light-water reactors (LWRs) with ordinary water as moderator—either boiling water reactors (BWRs) or PWRs. The rest are heavy-water reactors (HWRs). While the designs of advanced LWRs (ALWRs) resemble those of their predecessors, they incorporate new passive safety systems, as well as plant simplifications. The first BWR of advanced design was connected to the Japanese grid last year.

Liquid metal-cooled fast reactors (LMFRs), or breeders, have been under development for many years. With breeding capability, fast reactors can extract up to 60 times as much energy from uranium as can thermal reactors. The successful design, construction, and operation of such plants in several countries, notably France and the Russian Federation, has provided more than 200 reactor-years of experience on which to base further improvements. In the future, fast reactors may also be used to burn plutonium and other long-lived transuranic radioisotopes, allowing isolation time for high-level radioactive waste to be reduced.■

NOTES AND COMMENTS

1. The multilateral Convention on Nuclear Safety (CNS), which entered into force on October 24, 1996, set forth internationally recognized nuclear safety standards. CNS, adopted on June 17, 1994, IAEA Doc. INFCIRC/449/ Annex, 33 I.L.M. 1518. The objective of the agreement is an attempt to regulate international nuclear energy through the use of the peer review process under the auspices of the autonomous intergovernmental organization International Atomic Energy Agency (IAEA). Both general and specific safety standards are set out that guide radiation protection, emergency preparedness, siting, design, construction, and operation of nuclear power plants. CNS, art. 17, INFCIRC/449/Annex at 6, 33 I.L.M. at 1521. The benefit of peer review lies in its voluntary nature. The review process consists largely of national reports and review meetings and; when practiced, feels more like persuasion than compulsion. *See* Note, The Practice of Peer Review in the International Nuclear Safety Regime, 72 N.Y.U. L. Rev. 430 (1997).

2. As of 1997, ten countries met at least 40% of their total electricity demand from nuclear power, including France, Belgium and Lithuania. Over the long term, however, the International Atomic Energy Agency projects net additions to nuclear power generating capacity only in Japan and the developing countries. "In other regions, countries that are operating older reactors and have other, more economical options for new generating capacity are expected to let their nuclear capacity fade as current nuclear units are retired." EIA, International Energy Outlook, 1999.

3. China expects to increase significantly its reliance on nuclear power. Ling Zheng, Nuclear Energy: China's Approach Towards Addressing Global Warming, 12 Geo.Int'l Envtl.Rev. 493 (2000).

2. ADVANTAGES OF NUCLEAR POWER

One of the nation's leading energy scholars, Donald Zillman, suggests that it is time to re-examine the beneficial attributes of nuclear power. "Global warming can produce as catastrophic harms to the earth as significant radiation release from a nuclear accident," he points out. Increased use of nuclear energy may be the most practical current method of reducing consumption of fossil fuels." He says that nuclear energy was overpraised in the 1950s and over-condemned in the 1980s but that "it might take its place as a technology in which the real risks are outweighed by the benefits in the new century." Donald N. Zillman, Nuclear Power, in James E. Hickey, Jr. et. al., Energy Law and Policy for the 21st Century 10-2 (Rocky Mountain Mineral Law Foundation, 2000). *See also* William C. Sailor et al., A Nuclear Solution to Climate Change?, 288 Science 1177 (May 19, 2000).

In view of the current hostility of environmental organizations toward nuclear energy, it surprises many people to learn that nuclear power plants were once welcomed by many environmental groups as a pollution-free alternative to smoky, coal-burning power plants. The waste that nuclear power plants generate is all contained and none of it is released into the environment, while a typical 1000–megawatt coal-burning plant emits 100,000 tons of sulphur dioxide, 75,000 tons of nitrogen oxides, and 5000 tons of fly ash into the environment every year. In addition, such plants also emit great quantities of carbon dioxide, which is increasingly seen as a contributor to climate change. Neal Cabreza of the Department of Nuclear Engineering at the University of California concludes that the United States' use of electricity generated by nuclear power plants averted the cumulative emission of 1.6 billion metric tons of carbon dioxide, 65 million tons of sulphur dioxide, and 27 million tons of nitrogen oxides.

Although many people seem to believe that nuclear power plants emit radiation, Cabreza says that the use of nuclear power plants only add a very tiny fraction of radiation exposure to the more common types of radiation (i.e. cosmic rays from outer space, radon gas, television sets, watch dials, smoke detectors, etc....). In numbers, the average radiation dose rate people get from the common types of radiation is about 360 millirem. Nuclear power plants would increase this dosage rate by only 1 millirem.

In addition, because the fuel used in nuclear power plants exists in abundant supply, the price is very cheap, unlike for fossil fuels where the supply is finite and slowly diminishing. A typical fuel pellet cost about $7. This one fuel pellet has an equivalent energy of three barrels of oil, which cost $84, or one ton of coal, which cost $29. In 1993, the fossil fuels displaced by nuclear energy totaled: 470 million tons of coal and 96 million barrels of oil which translated to about $17 billion. By using nuclear energy at $7 per pellet, a savings of about $13 billion was generated in just one year. Www.nuc.berkeley.edu/thyd/ne161/ncabreza/sources.hmtl

The Editor of Power magazine argues that the fact that the global warming issue "continues to stream through the political hallways" is a big potential boost for nuclear power. When compared to the leading competition, the natural-gas fired power plants that are currently the most economical for new generation, nuclear plants not only produce less carbon dioxide but create no risk of methane leaks. Methane is a more powerful gas than carbon dioxide. Jason Makansi, Bet on nuclear for the new century, Power, January–February, 2000.

3. DETERRENTS TO NUCLEAR POWER PLANT CONSTRUCTION

Despite the apparent advantages of nuclear power, electric companies in the United States currently have no plans to begin construction of nuclear units. The arguments against such construction can be divided into two categories: arguments based on (1) cost, and on (2) risk.

a. HISTORY OF COST OVERRUNS

Chapter Eight reviewed the financial problems experienced by many electric utilities in connection with the construction of the first generation of nuclear power plants. In general, these projects were plagued by complex health and safety regulations that were often applied retroactively to plants under construction. Lawsuits by project opponents and multi-level review procedures at the NRC resulted in expensive delays at a time of rising construction costs.

In addition, the wild fluctuations in the costs of competing energy sources that took place during this period caused electricity users to institute conservation measures, thus reducing the demand for electricity. This made some of the power plants under construction appear to be unnecessary, and a number of plants were canceled before they were completed.

The utilities were forced to raise electric rates sharply during this period, both to cover the costs of the nuclear plants and the rise in the prices of other fuels. Consumer resistance to these increases put great pressure on state utility commissions, which often forced utility shareholders to swallow expenditures for plants that went dramatically over budget or were never completed. The result was that many electric utilities were forced to cut dividends and face the wrath of both unhappy shareholders and unhappy customers. And their attempts to challenge regulatory cutbacks in court proved fruitless after the Supreme Court's *Duquesne* decision.

The rush to embrace the new technology produced economic factors that drove up costs. The shortage of trained labor led to enough faulty construction to scare even advocates of nuclear power. And the dominance of a few firms limited competition and contributed to dramatic cost increases. *See generally* Robert J. Duffy, Nuclear Politics in America (University Press of Kansas, 1997). By the 1990's, it became apparent that nuclear power had become an economic disaster:

> The nuclear power plant debacle destroyed the status quo ante in the electricity industry. In the 1970s, with enthusiastic encouragement from state and federal regulators, utilities began construction of over one hundred nuclear power plants. Utilities and regulators predicted continuation of the historic pattern of a doubling in electricity demand every decade. Moreover, nuclear plants were expected to drive the cost of electricity to new lows. The massive nuclear construction program, predicated on forecasts of low costs and high demand, became instead an economic nightmare for all concerned. Actual costs of nuclear power

plants vastly exceeded estimates, sometimes by as much as 1000%. At the same time, electric rate increases dramatically slowed the growth in demand for electricity. As the power plants approached completion, it became apparent that they were both unneeded and extravagantly expensive. Consumers were outraged at the huge rate increases that would result from letting utilities recover their massive investments in nuclear power plants. Regulators and their political superiors responded to the outpouring of populist sentiment by disallowing tens of billions of dollars in utility investments—approximately 20% of total utility investments in nuclear power plants. Most utilities suffered significant financial harm from these disallowances.

The massive disallowances of utility investments in nuclear power plants dramatically changed utility incentives. The high perceived risk of future disallowances reversed utilities' incentives to overinvest, and made utilities extremely reluctant to build new power plants. Shareholders are not compensated for this risk through the allowed rate of return. Disallowances also place utility managers' jobs in jeopardy. As a result, utilities now systematically underestimate future demand to justify not building new generating capacity. The unwillingness of utilities to invest in new power plants created a void that must be filled with a new industry structure and new forms of government oversight.

Bernard S. Black & Richard J. Pierce, Jr., The Choice Between Markets and Central Planning in Regulating the U.S. Electricity Industry, 93 Colum. L. Rev. 1339 (1993).

Given this experience, it is probably not surprising that surveys of electric utility executives find little support for the construction of a new round of nuclear power plants today, despite the fact that there is considerable concern about the need for additional generating capacity.

b. THE RISK FACTOR

A 1979 accident at the Three Mile Island plant near Harrisburg, Pennsylvania, brought extended media attention to the risks associated with the potential malfunction of nuclear power plants. The accident also brought litigation which remained unresolved even at the end of the century.

In Re TMI Litigation

193 F.3d 613 (3d Cir.1999).

■ MCKEE, J.: [Plaintiffs sued the owners, operators and contractors of the Three Mile Island nuclear power plant, alleging that they suffered neoplasms as a result of radiation released into the environment as a result of an accident at the plant. For background purposes, the court described the accident as follows:] What has been described as the "nation's worst nuclear accident"[2][74] at about 4:00 a.m. on Wednesday, March 28, 1979. Ironically, the "nation's worst nuclear accident" grew out of a minor malfunction, or transient that occurred in the nonnuclear part of the system. For some reason, several feedwater pumps, that normally drew heat from the pressurized water reactor's (PWR's) cooling water, shut-off automatically. The system was designed so that when the feedwater pumps tripped, the main turbine and electrical generator also tripped. Thus, by design, the turbine and generator tripped approximately one second later. Three seconds after the turbine tripped, the pressure in the reactor coolant system increased to a level that caused the power-operated relief valve (PORV) to open in order to release the pressure. When the PORV opened, the fission process in the reactor core automatically shut down. Consequently, the heat generation in the reactor core dropped to decay heat levels.

However, the PORV did not close as it should have when the system pressure was reduced to acceptable levels. Instead, it remained open for approximately 2 hours. Unfortunately, the personnel operating Unit 2 did not realize that the PORV had not closed. They believed that it had automatically closed when the system was depressurized. Because the PORV remained open, reactor coolant water flowed from the reactor coolant system into the reactor coolant drain tank, which is designed to collect reactor coolant that is released from the reactor coolant system through the PORV during power operation. The continued flow of reactor coolant water into the reactor coolant drain tank caused a safety valve to lift on the drain tank and a drain tank rupture disk to burst. This rupture disk burst allowed the reactor coolant water to be discharged directly into the reactor building, which overfilled along with its sump pumps. The reactor building sump pumps were on automatic and aligned with the auxiliary building sump tank. When the reactor building sump pumps overfilled, some coolant water was transferred to the aligned auxiliary building sump tank. For some reason, there was no rupture disk on the sump tank and reactor coolant water was discharged directly into the auxiliary building. The contaminated coolant water continued to flow from the reactor building into the auxiliary building for several days. Estimates of the amount of radioactive water discharged into the reactor and auxiliary buildings range from 700,000 gallons to 5,000,000 gallons.

Approximately 2 minutes into the accident, the emergency core cooling system ("ECCS") began pumping water into the reactor core. However, operations personnel, still believing that the PORV had closed, and therefore unaware that reactor coolant water was escaping from the reactor coolant system, turned off most of the water flowing to the core through

2. Prior to the TMI–2 accident, there were "major" reactor accidents at the National Reactor Testing Laboratory in Idaho in 1955 and 1961, at the Fermi Reactor in Detroit, Michigan in 1966 and at Browns Ferry 1 in Alabama in 1975. Major accidents outside of the United States occurred at Chalk River, Canada in 1952, Windscale, England in 1957, Lucens, Switzerland in 1969 and, perhaps the most famous of all reactor accidents, at Chernobyl, in Ukraine about 30 miles south of the border with Belarus, (both of which were then part of the former USSR) in 1986.

the ECCS. They did so believing that they were preventing the reactor system from becoming filled with water—a condition they were required to prevent.

However, there was not enough coolant water being circulated through the reactor coolant system to cool the reactor core because reactor coolant water was being discharged into the reactor building. Consequently, the core reaction was producing more heat than the coolant system was removing, and the core began to heat up. The loss of reactor coolant water allowed the reactor core to become uncovered. Within three hours of the beginning of the accident, as much as two-thirds of the twelve-foot high core was uncovered. Temperatures reached as high as 3500 to 4000 degrees Fahrenheit or more in parts of the core during its maximum exposure.

About 2–1/2 hours into the accident, some of the fuel rods in the reactor cracked, releasing xenon and other fission product gases, which had accumulated in the fuel rod gap between the fuel and the cladding, into the coolant water. Over the next few hours, more fuel rods cracked, releasing radioactive iodine and cesium into the primary coolant water as well as additional noble gases.

A series of events then unfolded involving various reactions, valves and controls. The end result was that, nearly 10 hours into the accident, there was a sudden spike of pressure and temperature in the reactor building. Initially, the spike was dismissed as some type of instrument malfunction. However, operations personnel learned on March 29th that the spike was caused by the explosion of hydrogen gas in the reactor building. Fears of another hydrogen explosion developed when a hydrogen gas bubble was later found in the reactor system. Presumably, there was a concern that another hydrogen explosion would damage the reactor vessel, leading to further releases of radioactive material. However, the fears about another hydrogen explosion were later learned to be unfounded.

During the last days of March and the first week of April, operations personnel began to regain control and contain the radioactive releases caused by the accident. However, it was not until the afternoon of April 27, 1979 that stable conditions were finally established in TMI–2.

The parties generally agree that the radioactive fission products released to the environment as a result of the accident escaped from the damaged fuel and were transported in the coolant through the letdown line into the auxiliary building. Once in the auxiliary building, the radioactive fission products were released into the environment through the building's ventilation system. Because of the volatility of noble gases and radioiodines, those elements were the primary radionuclides available for release from the auxiliary building. Two krypton isotopes, 87 and 85, were not released in significant quantities because of the short half-life of 87Kr and because of the small amount of 85Kr in the reactor core. Nonetheless, despite the various filters, radioiodines were released. After the first day, the quantities of 88Kr and 135Xe were reduced by radioactive decay. All of the 133I contained in the coolant which was released to the auxiliary building eventually decayed to 133Xe and 133mXe. These radionuclides were the predominate ones released from the plant to the environment. TMI–2 also contained a treatment system, called the "liquid radwaste treatment system", which was designed to collect, process, monitor and recycle or dispose of radioactive liquid wastes prior to discharge to the environment. After the system processed the liquid radwaste, it was discharged into the Susquehanna River. However, because the primary coolant water flowed into the auxiliary building during the accident, the liquid radwaste treatment system was overwhelmed and radioactive materials were released to the Susquehanna River. The Nuclear Regulatory Commission's Special Inquiry Group concluded that the quantity of radioactive materials contained in the liquid released into the Susquehanna River was not significant. None of the plaintiffs here claim harm as a result of the releases of liquid radwaste into the river.

[In an exhaustive opinion, covering 116 pages in the Federal Reporter, the court of appeals affirmed the district court's grant of summary judgment in favor of defendants in regard to ten plaintiffs that had been selected as trial plaintiffs. It held that the district court acted properly in excluding much of plaintiffs' expert testimony under the standard set forth in *Daubert v. Merrell Dow Pharmaceuticals, Inc.*, 509 U.S. 579 (1993).]■

NOTES AND COMMENTS

1. The Three Mile Island accident also focused attention on the issue of emergency evacuation of the area around a nuclear power plant in case of an accident. In 1980, Congress added new requirements for emergency evacuation plans as a condition for the issuance of power plant licenses. *See* 94 Stat. 780. This led to a series of conflicts between utilities and nearby local governments that opposed a plant and sought to torpedo the evacuation plan by refusing to participate in the planning process. Eventually, after additional legislation, the NRC adopted the so-called "realism doctrine" and concluded that the Commission could assume that each local government would really cooperate in the utility's evacuation plan if an emergency arose, even if the local government claimed that it wouldn't. The NRC rules incorporating these assumptions were upheld in *Commonwealth of Massachusetts v. United States*, 856 F.2d 378 (1st Cir.1988).

2. In 1986, an explosion at the Chernobyl nuclear power plant in the Ukraine caused the release of large amounts of radiation into the atmosphere. Some thirty people died as a result of the explosion and acute radiation poisoning in the immediate neighborhood. Radiation in amounts that caused concern spread over much of Northern and Eastern Europe. The Chernobyl reactor, like many Russian-constructed reactors, was in the open rather than in a pressurizable containment structure used in American nuclear plants. Nevertheless, the Chernobyl accident heightened public fears of nuclear power plants throughout the world. Atkins, *supra* at 81–84.

3. The fear of accidents at nuclear power plants has spawned a subspecialty of risk evaluators who have tried to develop credible means of predicting the likelihood of such accidents. *See* National Research Council, Risk

Assessment in the Federal Government: Managing the Process (National Academy Press, 1993). In addition, a new field of "risk communication" has arisen, involving specialists in informing decisionmakers and the public about the relative likelihood and gravity of various kinds of risks. National Research Council, Understanding Risk: Informing Decisions in a Democratic Society (National Academy Press, 1996). For an analysis of the application of risk-communication techniques to the NRC procedures, *see* Center for Strategic and International Studies (CSIS), The Regulatory Process for Nuclear Power Reactors: A Review 31–38 (August, 1999).

4.   The Nuclear Regulatory Commission, which oversees all safety issues relating to nuclear power plants in the United States, is based at One White Flint North, Rockville, Maryland 11555. The regulatory process is primarily handled by the commission's Office of Nuclear Reactor Regulation. Inspections and investigations are handled by the commission's regional offices in Philadelphia, Atlanta, Chicago and Dallas.

4.   DECOMMISSIONING NUCLEAR POWER PLANTS

Like any factory, a nuclear power plant has a limited life expectancy. How long will the existing plants continue to operate safely and economically? Some nuclear power plants have been retired by their operators before the end of their expected lives. In 1998, two units at Zion, Illinois, and a unit at Millstone, Connecticut, were retired prematurely because of high costs. The San Onofre plant on the California coast was being dismantled in 2000, in part because of worries about earthquake risks.[3]

What do you do with an abandoned nuclear power plant? The cost of removing irradiated materials and making the site available for other uses is estimated to be in the range of $400 to $600 million per plant. To assure that funds will be available to cover these costs, ratepayers served by nuclear plants have been paying special fees into trust funds which are intended to accumulate enough money to be able to pay these costs of decommissioning when they occur.

Citizens Awareness Network v. Nuclear Regulatory Commission

59 F.3d 284 (1st Cir.1995).

■ TORRUELLA, C.J.: Citizens Awareness Network ("CAN") petitions for review of a final order and opinion of the United States Nuclear Regulatory Commission ("NRC" or "the Commission") denying CAN's request for an adjudicatory hearing regarding decommissioning activities taking place at

---

3. On the other hand, in a few other cases utilities have filed applications for 20-year extensions of the operating lives of particular licensed plants. Baltimore Gas and Electric Company is seeking a renewal for its Calvert Cliffs plant and Duke Power Co. has sought a renewal of the license for the Oconee plant. For an analysis of the issues arising in the license renewal process, *see* CSIS, *supra* at 32–38.

the Yankee Nuclear Power Station ("Yankee NPS"). CAN's petition for review rests on three grounds. First, CAN contends that the Commission's order violates CAN members' right to due process under the Fifth Amendment and § 189a of the Atomic Energy Act ("AEA"), 42 U.S.C. § 2239 (1988). Second, CAN argues that the NRC's action violates the National Environmental Policy Act, ("NEPA"), 42 U.S.C. § 4321 *et seq.* (1988) by failing to conduct an environmental analysis ("EA") or an environmental impact statement ("EIS") prior to decommissioning. Finally, CAN argues that the Commission's actions violate its own precedents and regulations, in violation of the Administrative Procedure Act ("APA"), 5 U.S.C. § 501 *et seq.* Although we reject CAN's Fifth Amendment arguments, we grant CAN's petition for review on the other grounds stated.

Operators of nuclear power plants must have a license issued by the NRC. That license describes the facility and the authorized activities that the operator may conduct. If the operator, called the "licensee," wishes to modify the facility or take actions not specifically authorized by the license, the licensee may seek an amendment to its license from the Commission. *See* 42 U.S.C. §§ 2131–2133, 2237 (1988). Section 189a of the AEA provides that:

> In any proceeding under this chapter, for the granting, suspending, revoking, or amending of any license or construction permit, or application to transfer control, and in any proceeding for the issuance or modification of rules and regulations dealing with the activities of licensees, ... the Commission shall grant a hearing upon the request of any person whose interest may be affected by the proceeding, and shall admit any such person as a party to such proceeding.... 42 U.S.C. § 2239(a)(1)(A).

The Commission has issued regulations specifically allowing a licensee to modify its facilities without NRC supervision, unless the modification is inconsistent with the license or involves an "unreviewed safety question." 10 C.F.R. § 50.59(a)(1). If the proposed change is inconsistent with the license, or does involve an unreviewed safety question (as that term is defined in 10 C.F.R. § 50.59(a)(2)(ii)), the licensee must apply to the Commission for a license amendment, 10 C.F.R. § 50.59(c), and only then are the statutory hearing rights of § 189a triggered. The procedures for decommissioning[4][1] a nuclear power plant are set forth principally in 10 C.F.R. §§ 50.82, 50.75, 51.53, and 51.95 (1990). The formal process begins with the filing of an application by the licensee, normally after the plant has ceased permanent operations, for authority to surrender its license and to decommission the facility. Five years before the licensee expects to end plant operations, the licensee must submit a preliminary decommissioning plan containing a cost estimate for decommissioning and an assessment of the major technical factors that could affect planning for decommissioning. 10 C.F.R. § 50.75. Within two years after "permanent cessation of opera-

---

4. "Decommissioning" means those activities necessary "to remove [a facility] safely from service and reduce residual radioac-tivity to a level that permits release of the property for unrestricted use and termination of the license." 10 C.F.R. § 50.2.

tions" at the plant, but no later than one year prior to expiration of its license, a licensee must submit to the Commission an application for "authority to surrender a license voluntarily and to decommission the facility," together with an environmental report covering the proposed decommissioning activities. 10 C.F.R. §§ 50.82, 50.83. This application must be accompanied by the licensee's proposed decommissioning plan, which describes the decommissioning method chosen and the activities involved, and sets forth a financial plan for assuring the availability of adequate funds for the decommissioning costs. 10 C.F.R. § 50.82(b). The Commission then reviews the decommissioning plan, prepares either an environmental impact statement ("EIS") or an environmental assessment ("EA") in compliance with NEPA, and gives notice to interested parties. 10 C.F.R. § 51.95. If the NRC finds the plan satisfactory (i.e., in accordance with regulations and not inimical to the common defense or the health and safety of the public), the Commission issues a decommissioning order approving the plan and authorizing decommissioning. 10 C.F.R. § 50.82(e).

The Commission has stated that its regulations allow a licensee to conduct certain, limited decommissioning activities prior to obtaining NRC approval:

> It should be noted that [10 C.F.R.] § 50.59 permits a holder of an operating license to carry out certain activities without prior Commission approval unless these activities involve a change in the technical specifications or an unreviewed safety question. However, when there is a change in the technical specifications or an unreviewed safety question, § 50.59 requires the holder of an operating license to submit an application for amendment to the license pursuant to § 50.90....
>
> This rulemaking does not alter a licensee's capability to conduct activities under § 50.59. Although the Commission must approve the decommissioning alternative and major structural changes to radioactive components of the facility or other major changes, the licensee may proceed with some activities such as decontamination, minor component disassembly, and shipment and storage of spent fuel if these activities are permitted by the operating license and/or § 50.59.

53 Fed. Reg. at 24025–24026.

The Commission adhered to this position from the issuance of this statement in 1988 until 1993. *See, e.g., Long Island Lighting Co.*, 33 N.R.C. at 73 n.5 ("Major dismantling and other activities that constitute decommissioning under the NRC's regulations must await NRC approval of a decommissioning plan"); Sacramento Mun. Util. Dist. (Rancho Seco Nuclear Generating Station), 35 N.R.C. 47, 62 n. 7 (1992) (same).

On February 27, 1992, licensee Yankee Atomic Electric Company ("YAEC") announced its intention to cease operations permanently at Yankee NPS, a nuclear power plant located near Rowe, Massachusetts. One month later, YAEC applied for a license amendment to limit its license to a POL, a possession-only license, thus revoking YAEC's authority to operate the plant. The NRC published a Notice of Proposed Action informing the public of its opportunity to be heard on the license amendment request, pursuant to § 189a of the AEA. 57 Fed. Reg. 13126, 13140 (April 15, 1992). There were no hearing requests; accordingly, the NRC issued the requested amendment to YAEC's license on August 5, 1992. 57 Fed. Reg. 37558, 37579 (Aug. 19, 1992). In the cover letter accompanying YAEC's amended license, the Commission reminded YAEC that "the NRC must approve ... major structural changes to radioactive components of the facility...." ...

At a meeting between YAEC and NRC representatives on October 27, 1992, YAEC proposed that the NRC grant permission for YAEC to initiate an "early component removal project" (the "CRP"), prior to submission and approval of its decommissioning plan, and hence prior to conducting an environmental assessment of decommissioning at the site. YAEC explained that it wished expeditious commencement of this early CRP because of the unexpected availability of space in the Barnwell, South Carolina Low-level Waste Disposal facility. If made to wait for submission and approval of a decommissioning plan, YAEC would lose its chance to use the Barnwell facility.

Pursuant to this proposed CRP, YAEC would first remove the four steam generators and the pressurizer from the nuclear reactor containment, remove core internals from the reactor pressure vessel, and transport all of these radioactive components to the Barnwell facility. After this dismantling, YAEC proposed to then cut up the nuclear reactor core baffle plate (which is too radioactive to meet low-level waste criteria and thus cannot be dumped in the Barnwell site), and store the pieces in canisters in the spent fuel pool for future delivery to a U.S. Department of Energy waste site. Finally, YAEC planned to remove and transport the four main coolant pumps to the Barnwell site. These CRP activities would result in the permanent disposal of 90% of the nonfuel, residual radioactivity at Yankee NPS, all prior to approval of the actual decommissioning plan.

On November 25, 1992, YAEC sent a letter to the NRC which set forth YAEC's arguments as to how NRC regulations, Statements of Consideration issued with those regulations, and Commission precedents could be "interpreted" to allow approval of the early CRP, despite the fact that the Commission's interpretative policy at that time explicitly required NRC approval for major structural changes. During this period, CAN also wrote two letters to the NRC, on November 2, 1992 and again on December 21, 1992, requesting inter alia that the Commission halt or postpone any and all dismantling activities at Yankee NPS until a decommissioning plan was submitted, moved through the public notice-and-comment process, and approved. In a December 29, 1992 letter to CAN, Kenneth Rogers, the Acting Chairman of the Commission, responded that the Commission was "considering a public meeting in the vicinity of the plant early in 1993 to provide information to the public on NRC's review of decommissioning in general and on expected site activities which will occur prior to the licensee's submittal of a decommissioning plan in late 1993." On January 14, 1993, following internal review of its decommissioning policies, the Commission issued a Staff Requirements Memo ("SRM"), setting forth a significant, substantial change from previously held agency positions on decommissioning activities, and essentially adopting YAEC's proposed "interpretation" of prior agency precedents and positions. Without any explanation for the substantial modification, or any further analysis, the SRM stated:

> Notwithstanding the Commission's statements in footnote 3 of CLI–90–08 [*Long Island Lighting Co.*, 33 N.R.C. 61 (1991)] and the Statements of Consideration for the decommissioning rules at 53 Federal Register 24025–26, licensees should be allowed to undertake any decommissioning activity (as the term "decommission" is defined in 10 C.F.R. 50.2) that does not—(a) foreclose the release of the site for possible unrestricted use, (b) significantly increase decommissioning costs, (c) cause any significant environmental impact not previously reviewed, or (d) violate the terms of the licensee's existing license (e.g., OL, POL, OL with confirmatory shutdown order etc.) or 10 C.F.R. 50.59 as applied to the existing license.... The staff may permit licensees to use their decommissioning funds for the decommissioning activities permitted above ..., notwithstanding the fact that their decommissioning plans have not yet been approved by the NRC.

Shortly after the Commission issued this SRM, YAEC advised the NRC that it planned to begin its CRP activities in accordance with this new policy.[5][2]

On June 30, 1993, the Commission issued another SRM reiterating its new decommissioning policy, and stating that it had voted to formally amend 10 C.F.R. § 50.59 to reflect this new position. This proposed rulemaking is still underway. The Commission also stated that approval of a decommissioning plan is not an action that triggers hearing rights under § 189a of the AEA, but that the Commission staff could, in its discretion, formulate an informal hearing process for decommissioning plan approval.

On September 8, 1993, CAN again wrote to the NRC, again requesting a hearing on the CRP at Yankee NPS. CAN also generally alleged that the NRC was in violation of its own regulations, and in violation of "the rule making process," by allowing a licensee to engage in a CRP without prior Commission approval. The Commission responded to these allegations in a letter dated November 18, 1993, stating that CAN had "failed to identify the proposed action that might be taken by the NRC Staff that requires the offer of a hearing."

The next day, CAN filed a petition for agency review requesting that the NRC halt the CRP activities pending an investigation by the Inspector General's office. In the petition, CAN reiterated its position that the CRP constitutes decommissioning, and that the NRC was thus in violation of its own regulations in allowing CRP activities at Yankee NPS prior to approval of a decommissioning plan. The NRC responded by letter dated December

---

5. Later, YAEC submitted a decommissioning plan, which is currently under NRC review. YAEC completed most of the CRP activities, however, before it ever submitted its decommissioning plan to the Commission, and well before any environmental assessment was performed.

29, 1993, explaining its policy change as set forth in the SRMs, and concluding that CAN's petition "does not provide any new information regarding why public health and safety warrants suspension of the CRP and therefore does not meet the threshold for treatment under 10 CFR 2.206."

After a flurry of letters, in which CAN repeatedly requested formal hearings on the CRP and the Commission consistently denied these requests on the grounds that the CRP was in accord with the new policy, CAN filed this petition for review.

We review agency actions and decisions with substantial deference, setting them aside only if found to be "arbitrary, capricious, an abuse of discretion, or otherwise not in accordance with the law." 5 U.S.C. § 706(2)(A).... This deference is especially marked in technical or scientific matters within the agency's area of expertise. While this is a highly deferential standard of review, it is not a rubber stamp; in order to avoid being deemed arbitrary and capricious, an agency decision must be rational. *Puerto Rico v. Sun Oil Co.*, 8 F.3d at 77. Moreover, when an administrative agency departs significantly from its own precedent, "it must confront the issue squarely and explain why the departure is reasonable." *Davila-Bardales v. INS*, 27 F.3d 1, 5 (1st Cir.1994). This is not to say that agencies must forever adhere to their precedents; agencies may "refine, reformulate and even reverse their precedents in the light of new insights and changed circumstances." *Id*. An agency changing its course must, however, supply a reasoned analysis for the change. With these principles in mind, we turn to the merits of CAN's petition....

CAN contends that the NRC's unexplained change in its decommissioning policy was irrational and contrary to its own duly-promulgated regulations, in violation of the procedural requirements of the APA. CAN argues that the Commission's significant policy shift, manifested in its two Staff Requirements Memos, improperly revoked duly-promulgated Commission regulations, interpretations and precedents, without the benefit of rulemaking procedures or even a rational explanation for the change. By allowing YAEC to commence the CRP activities notwithstanding its own precedents and regulations, CAN contends, the Commission acted arbitrarily and capriciously, in violation of the APA.

In defense of the unexplained change in its decommissioning policy, the NRC maintains that the former policy had never been incorporated into the regulations themselves, and, in any case, that agencies are free to alter their interpretations of their own regulations.

While this is certainly true, any such alteration or reversal must be accompanied by some reasoning—some indication that the shift is rational, and therefore not arbitrary and capricious.... While this is not a difficult standard to meet, the Commission has not met it here.

The prior Commission policy regarding decommissioning, embodied in 10 C.F.R. § 50.59 and explicated in the Commission's published Statement of Consideration, required NRC approval of a decommissioning plan before a licensee undertook any major structural changes to a facility. This policy was developed through a lengthy notice and comment period, with substantial public participation. *See* 53 Fed. Reg. 24018, 24020 (a total of 143 individuals and organizations submitted comments on proposed rule). The Commission adhered to this policy for almost five years, reiterating its position in at least two adjudicatory decisions.

Then, rather suddenly, the Commission circulated two internal staff memos that completely reversed this settled policy, without any notice to the affected public. More troubling, however, was the Commission's failure to provide in those memos, or anywhere else, any justification or reasoning whatsoever for the change. The memos did not set forth any new facts, fresh information, or changed circumstances which would counsel the shift. Nor did they provide any legal analysis of how the new policy comported with, or at least did not conflict with, existing agency regulations. With nothing more than a breezy "notwithstanding," the Commission abruptly disposed of five years' worth of well-reasoned, duly-promulgated agency precedent.

Moreover, the NRC's actions are inconsistent with the plain terms of the AEA, the NRC's enabling statute, which provide that "in any proceeding for the issuance or modification of rules and regulations dealing with the activities of licensees, . . . the Commission shall grant a hearing upon the request of any person whose interest may be affected by the proceeding. . . ." 42 U.S.C. § 2239(a)(1)(A). While the NRC's policy shift involved an interpretation of its regulation, and not the regulation itself, it was an interpretative policy that provided a great deal of substantive guidance on the rather ambiguous language of the regulation, by specifically delineating the permissible activities of licensees.

We think that the statute's phrase "modification of rules and regulations" encompasses substantive interpretative policy changes like the one involved here, and therefore that the Commission cannot effect such modifications without complying with the statute's notice and hearing provisions. *See Natural Resources, Etc. v. NRC*, 695 F.2d 623, 625 (D.C.Cir. 1982) ("Fair notice to affected parties requires that the Commission not alter suddenly and *sub silentio* settled interpretations of its own regulations.").

Finally, we agree with the petitioners that the Commission's new policy appears utterly irrational on its face. By allowing licensees to conduct most, if not all, of the permanent removal and shipment of the major structures and radioactive components before the submittal of a decommissioning plan, it appears that the Commission is rendering the entire decommissioning plan approval process nugatory. Why should a licensee be required to submit such a plan if its decommissioning is already irreversibly underway? Why offer the public the opportunity to be heard on a proposed decommissioning plan if the actual decommissioning activities are already completed? In short, the Commission's new decommissioning policy seems to render any regulatory oversight of the decommissioning process moot. Perhaps a rational basis for this policy exists, but we cannot see one, and the Commission has not provided one.

The Commission's failure to provide any explanation for its seemingly irrational change in policy renders its new policy arbitrary and capricious, and not in accordance with the requirements of 42 U.S.C. § 2239(a)(1)(A). We therefore remand the issue of the NRC's change in decommissioning policy for further proceedings, in accordance with the AEA's hearing requirements and this opinion.

[The court also held that the Commission violated the National Environmental Policy Act by failing to perform the required environmental analyses on the change in policy, but the court rejected the due process claim.]■

NOTES AND COMMENTS

1. As the above case indicates, the problems of decommissioning a nuclear power plant are severely complicated by the difficulties associated with the disposal of both the highly radioactive fuel rods and the large volumes of less radioactive "low-level" waste found in any nuclear facility. These issues are discussed at greater length in the second half of this chapter.

Given the difficulty of finding disposal sites for nuclear waste, was the NRC reasonable in trying to shortcut the procedural process to enable the company to take advantage of an opportunity to dispose of waste that might be lost as a result of delays? What did the citizens group hope to gain by insisting on compliance with the procedures? The hostility of environmental organizations to nuclear power remains intense. For information on the position of opponents of nuclear power, the web site of the Nuclear Information and Resource Service is a useful resource: www.nirs.org

2. The case also illustrates the painfully slow procedures that have been the rule for NRC proceedings. For a practical analysis of some of the problems of government attorneys who must cope with these procedures, see Peter L. Strauss, The Internal Relations of Government: Cautionary Tales from Inside the Black Box, 61 L. & Contemp. Prob. 155 (1998).

3. Some utilities have become insolvent as a result of investments in nuclear facilities. One such utility is a rural cooperative in Louisiana, Cajun Electric Power Cooperative. Like all cooperatives, it received financing from the Department of Agriculture on very favorable terms. When Cajun's nuclear investments proved unmanageable, the Department demanded that Cajun raise its rates to enable it to pay off its federal loan, but the Louisiana PSC refused to allow the rate increases. The U.S. sued, claiming that the Rural Electrification Act gave the Secretary of Agriculture the authority to demand that a co-op raise its rates, but the Fifth Circuit held that the federal statute did not allow the secretary to preempt state rate regulation–at least not on a case-by-case basis. *In re Cajun Electric Power Cooperative*, 109 F.3d 248 (5th Cir.1997). The company was in bankruptcy proceedings, and the magnitude of its financial problems were set out in

another Fifth Circuit opinion (*In re Cajun Electric Power Cooperative*, 119 F.3d 349 (5th Cir.1997)) approving a settlement of the bankruptcy:

Cajun's largest creditor is the federal government's Rural Utilities Service ("RUS") (formerly the Rural Electrification Administration), which provided Cajun with loans and loan guarantees for its investment in the River Bend nuclear plant. RUS asserts that it has secured claims against Cajun of $4.2 billion. Cajun's second-largest creditor is the nuclear plant's builder and principal owner, Gulf States Utilities Co. ("Gulf States"), which through its corporate successor, Energy Gulf States, Inc., asserts unsecured claims of $400 million.

Cajun and Gulf States were bitter rivals who in 1980 united in a common endeavor: construction of the River Bend nuclear reactor. Cajun invested $588 million in River Bend in exchange for a 30 percent ownership stake. RUS lent Cajun a substantial amount of capital for its investment in River Bend and guaranteed the remainder of Cajun's River Bend loans.

If the settlement is affirmed, Cajun first and foremost would be freed of any future involvement in River Bend. Cajun would be obligated, however, to pay $107 million toward its share of the reactor's decommissioning trust fund. Cajun would be absolved of any further liability for the plant's decommissioning, but would be barred from recovering any excess if the decommissioning fund proves to be overfunded.

Cajun, unshackled from its River Bend investment, would drop its suit against Gulf States seeking (1) rescission of the River Bend agreement on grounds of fraud and error; or, in the alternative, (2) damages for breach of contract, breach of fiduciary duty, and mismanagement. A four-month trial was held in district court on the fraud suit; it ended with the district court ruling in Gulf States' favor, although a final written opinion has not issued. The breach of contract suit has not yet gone to trial; the trustee has estimated that Cajun might recover $200 million in damages. [Other litigation would also be dropped.] Cajun transfers two transmission lines worth $20 million to Gulf States, which agrees to transmit Cajun power through its lines.

Also under the settlement, RUS succeeds to Cajun's interest in River Bend. RUS can keep this "asset," sell it, or force Gulf States to take it. In the unlikely event that the plant is sold to a third party, Cajun will deduct the sale price from its debt to RUS. The eventual owner of Cajun's interest in River Bend would receive any proceeds from litigation over design defects, estimated by the trustee to be about $10 million.

The Committee representing the trade creditors [who had claims totaling about $7 million] requested that the court defer approval until confirmation of a bankruptcy plan, or, in the alternative, approve the settlement conditionally, pending confirmation of a plan. The district court denied these requests and approved the settlement on August 27, 1996. The Committee appeals....

The appellate court held that the bankruptcy court correctly decided that the settlement was fair and equitable. The court noted that past precedent required that the court "consider the reasonable views of a majority of the creditors," and that "the vast numerical majority of creditors is represented by the Committee [of trade creditors], which opposes the settlement.... The appellees point out, however, that the trade creditors' aggregate claim against Cajun is only a drop in the bucket—by some estimates less than one percent of Cajun's total debt." But, said the court, "given also the relatively small amount of the trade creditors' claims, the district court did not clearly err by finding the settlement in the creditors' interests. In any event, given that all of the other factors in the equation overwhelmingly favor the settlement, the wishes of the trade creditors do not compel us to reject the settlement."

3. The existing rules requiring funding for decommissioning nuclear power plants are found in 10 C.F.R. § 50.75. The Commission amended its rules relating to the decommissioning process after the CAN decision in SECY–96–086.

C. THE EFFECT OF ELECTRICITY RESTRUCTURING

As the restructuring of the electric power industry gives companies more options, the question of whether to buy or sell nuclear power plants has become a reality for many companies for the first time. A few electric utilities have apparently decided to shop around to purchase nuclear power plants owned by other utilities, hoping that economies of scale can be achieved through management of a sizable number of plants. AmerGen Energy Company, a U.S.-British joint venture, purchased the first Three Mile Island unit from General Public Utilities, and the holding company, Entergy Corporation, bought the pilgrim nuclear plant from Boston Edison. Commonwealth Edison and PECO have proposed a merger based largely on a common desire to operate a fleet of nuclear plants.

With increasing competition in the electricity market, the Nuclear Regulatory Commission has had to evaluate the extent to which new players in the market are qualified to operate nuclear power plants. In addition, the extent to which unregulated companies will be responsible for the financial obligations of decommissioning has raised new issues regarding proof of financial responsibility. Originally, it was always assumed that the operators of nuclear plants would be regulated utilities that would be able to pass along to their customers any costs imposed by NRC rules. What happens if ownership passes to a non-regulated company?

In the Matter of North Atlantic Energy Service Corp., (Seabrook Station, Unit 1)

49 N.R.C. 201 (1999).

The Montaup Electric Company ("Montaup") seeks to transfer its 2.9–percent ownership interest in [a nuclear power plant named] Seabrook

Station, Unit 1, to the Little Bay Power Corporation ("Little Bay"). Montaup is one of eleven co-owners of the Seabrook Station, Unit 1. Little Bay is a wholly-owned subsidiary of BayCorp Holdings, Ltd. ("BayCorp"), which is also the holding company for the Great Bay Power Corporation (the holder of a 12.1–percent ownership interest in Seabrook). On Montaup's behalf, Seabrook's licensed operator, the North Allantic Energy Service Corporation ("NAESCO"), submitted the transfer application to the Commission for approval. The Atomic Energy Act ("AEA") requires Commission approval of transfers of ownership rights. See AEA, § 184, 42 U.S.C. § 2234. Recently-promulgated NRC regulations ("Subpart M") govern hearing requests on transfer applications. See Final Rule, "Public Notification, Availability of Documents and Records, Hearing Requests and Procedures for Hearings on License Transfer Applications," 63 Fed. Reg. 66, 721 (Dec. 3, 1998), to be codified at 10 C.F.R. §§ 2.1300 et seq.

Pursuant to Subpart M, the New England Power Company ("NEP")— a 10–percent co-owner of the Seabrook plant—has filed a timely intervention petition opposing the Montaup-to-Little Bay transfer application as well as a petition for summary relief or, in the alternative, a request for hearing.

Pursuant to Section 184 of the AEA and section 50.80 of our regulations, Montaup and Little Bay seek approval of the proposed transfer as part of Montaup's efforts to divest all of its electric generating assets pursuant to the restructuring of the electric utility industry in Massachusetts and Rhode Island. Under the transfer arrangement, Little Bay would (among other things) assume full responsibility for Montaup's remaining share of Seabrook's future costs, including obligations for capital investment, operating expenses and any escalation of decommissioning obligations in excess of Montaup's pre-funded contribution (described immediately below).

In their application, Montaup and Little Bay offer the following two forms of assurance that the decommissioning and operating expenses associated with the 2.9–percent ownership interest will be fully paid. First, Montaup offers to provide an $11.8 million pre-funded decommissioning payment—an amount which, assuming 4–percent inflation plus 1.73–percent rate of real return, would purportedly grow by the year 2026 to equal the amount required to satisfy the decommissioning funding obligation associated with Montaup's 2.9–percent interest in Seabrook. Montaup compares its proposed 1.73–percent rate of real return to the 2–percent rate provided for in the NRC's Final Rule, "Financial Assurance Requirements for Decommissioning Nuclear Power Reactors," 63 Fed. Reg. 50,465 (Sept. 22, 1998), corrected, 63 Fed. Reg. 57,236 (Oct. 27, 1998), to be codified at 10 C.F.R. § 50.75(e)(1)(I).

Second, Little Bay submits estimates for the total operating expenses at Seabrook attributable to Montaup's 2.9–percent ownership share of Seabrook for the first five years of Little Bay's ownership and the sources of funds to cover those costs. Little Bay also proffers favorable revenue predictions for the future, based on the assumptions that Seabrook will operate until its current license expires in 2026 and that market revenues through the year 2026 should be sufficient to cover Little Bay's share of the plant's decommissioning expenses and operating expenses, even if the estimates for those costs are later revised upward. As a further indication of the adequacy of Little Bay's financial assurances, the application points out that Little Bay's take-or-pay sales contract with Great Bay requires the latter to pay for all of Little Bay's Seabrook-related costs, whether or not Great Bay succeeds in reselling the electricity it buys from Little Bay.

Under the license transfer, NAESCO would remain the managing agent for the facility's eleven joint owners and would continue to have exclusive responsibility for the management, operation and maintenance of the Seabrook Station. The license would be amended only for administrative purposes to reflect the transfer of Montaup's ownership interest to Little Bay.

The Commission, in its December 14, 1998, Federal Register notice of Little Bay's and Montaup's application (63 Fed. Reg. 68,801), indicated that the proposed transfer would involve no changes in the rights, obligations, or interests of the other ten co-owners of the Seabrook Station, nor would it result in any physical changes to the plant or the manner in which it will operate.

(1) Financial Assurance regarding Satisfaction of Decommissioning Funding Obligation

On the facts and allegations of this case, we see no conceivable violation of our regulation, 10 C.F.R. § 50.75, requiring licensees to show sufficient assurance of adequate decommissioning funding. When Little Bay and Montaup filed their license transfer application in September 1998, they calculated an $11.8 million prepayment amount based on the assumption that the plant's total decommissioning costs would total $489 million (in current dollars), and that, by 2026, the $11.8 million would grow into the $14.2 million (again, in current dollars) necessary to meet Montaup's 2.9–percent share of Seabrook's decommissioning costs. That assumption derived from the cost formula set forth in section 50.75(c), using NUREG–1307 (Rev. 7, Nov. 1997). Although the applicants' calculations were based on then-current information when submitted in September 1998, the Commission staff in December created an alternate method for calculating expected costs of low-level waste disposal, with the result that the estimated decommissioning cost for plants of Seabrook's type now can be decreased considerably, from $489 million to $289 million.

As a result of the recent revision, the $11.8 million committed by Montaup already exceeds, by a healthy margin, the minimum amount required to fully fund its 2.9–percent share of Seabrook's decommissioning costs, as calculated under section 50.75(c) and the new decommissioning cost alternative—an amount of less than $8.4 million. This renders NEP's concerns, including Seabrook's allegedly high risk of early closure, inconsequential for our financial assurance determination.

Montaup's promise to prepay considerably more than the minimum amount currently prescribed by the NRC financial assurance formula leaves NEP without any plausible decommissioning funding grievance, and (particularly in view of Montaup's minuscule share of the plant) gives us no reason to think that the public health and safety might in any respect be left unprotected. Prepayment is in fact the strongest and most reliable of the various decommissioning funding devices set out in section 50.75(e)(1). We conclude here, as a matter of law, that Montaup's prepayment provides sufficient assurance for its share of decommissioning costs and that there exists no genuine issue of material fact or law necessitating a hearing on decommissioning funding assurance. See 10 C.F.R. § 2.1306(b)(2)(iv).

(2) Financial Qualifications for Meeting Operating Expenses

NEP meets the requirements set out in Subpart M regarding the admissibility of the "operating expenses" issue. See 10 C.F.R. §§ 2.1306, 2.1308. Its petition and reply clearly set out the claim that Little Bay will lack sufficient financial resources to fulfill its obligations for operating expenses. NEP's pleadings, and the applicants' own vigorous responses, demonstrate that a genuine dispute exists regarding this issue. NEP's arguments are certainly relevant and material. Indeed, they go to the very heart of the question whether applicants' financial qualifications are adequate to pass statutory and regulatory muster. When promulgating Subpart M a few months ago, we expressly recognized that NRC review of license transfer applications "consists largely of assuring that the ultimately licensed entity has the capability to meet financial qualification and decommissioning funding aspects of NRC regulations." See 63 Fed. Reg. at 66,724. NEP's claims, in short, lie at the core of the NRC's license transfer inquiry. . . . In sum, NEP does not claim that five-year cost-and-revenue projections are per se inadequate to meet financial qualification requirements—such a claim would be precluded as a collateral attack on NRC rules. Rather, NEP simply contends that, as NRC rules themselves contemplate, the circumstances of this particular transfer call for more detailed or extensive financial protection. We thus conclude that NEP's petition for a hearing does not constitute an impermissible collateral attack on section 50.33(f)(2) but instead raises an admissible issue for a hearing under Subpart M.

(3) Scope of Proceeding

For the reasons set forth above, we grant NEP's intervention petition and hearing request. The scope of the hearing will be limited to the following issue: whether the Montaup-to-Little Bay license transfer application meets NRC rules for financial qualification regarding Seabrook's operating expenses (10 C.F.R. § 50.33(f)). Given the early stage of the proceeding and the existence of outstanding factual questions, however, we will hold in abeyance NEP's alternative request for the imposition of conditions.

Our grant of NEP's hearing request by no means suggests that NEP necessarily will succeed in its challenge to the transfer application. It faces a formidable task in persuading us that factors peculiar to Seabrook call for modification or rejection of what NEP acknowledges are financial qualifica-tion plans of the type ordinarily found acceptable by the Commission. See, e.g., NEP's Intervention Petition at 2. Some aspects of NEP's position seem to us particularly troublesome. We will set out our concerns to guide the parties as they proceed to a hearing in this case.

First, as a general matter, NEP cannot insist that applicants provide the impossible: absolutely certain predictions of future economic conditions. To be sure. safe operation of a nuclear plant requires adequate funding, but the potential safety impacts of a shortfall in funding are not so direct or immediate as the safety impacts of significant technical deficiencies. Gener-ally speaking, then, the level of assurance the Commission finds it reason-able to require regarding a licensee's ability to meet financial obligations is less than the extremely high assurance the Commission requires regarding the safety of reactor design, construction, and operation. The Commission will accept financial assurances based on plausible assumptions and fore-casts, even though the possibility is not insignificant that things will turn out less favorably than expected. Thus, the mere casting of doubt on some aspects of proposed funding plans is not by itself sufficient to defeat a finding of reasonable assurance.

At the same time, though, funding plans that rely on assumptions seriously at odds with governing realities will not be deemed acceptable simply because their form matches plans described in the regulations. Relying on affidavits and various forms of financial data, NEP asserts that Little Bay's cost-and-revenue estimates fail to provide the required assur-ance because they do not reflect a realistic outlook for Little Bay itself or for the nuclear power industry in New England. As in other cases (e.g., *River Bend,* 40 NRC at 51–53), we cannot brush aside such economically-based safety concerns without giving the intervenor a chance to substanti-ate its concerns at a hearing, but we note that NEP's arguments ultimately will prevail only if it can demonstrate relevant uncertainties significantly greater than those that usually cloud business outlooks.

Finally, we cannot accede to NEP's seeming view that Little Bay inherently cannot meet our financial qualification rules because its rates are not regulated by a state utilities commission. This view runs counter to the premise underlying the entire restructuring and economic deregulation of the electric utility industry, i.e., that the marketplace will replace cost-of-service ratemaking. In our view, unregulated electricity rates are not incompatible with maintaining sufficient financial resources to operate a nuclear power reactor.■

NOTES AND COMMENTS

1. Under 10 C.F.R. § 50.75(e) of the Commission's regulations, a company acquiring an interest in a nuclear power plant has five different options for demonstrating that it will be financially responsible for meeting its decom-missioning obligations. For a non-regulated company, prepayment may be

the only feasible option, since it cannot count on ratepayers' legal obligations in the way that is possible for regulated public utilities.

2. The continuing financial stability of existing public utility operators of nuclear power plants is also a matter of concern as competition brings new, lower cost generating sources into the market. The NRC intends to monitor the financial condition of existing operators and to request additional financial assurances if needed to assure that decommissioning obligations are met. SECY-98-164, Final Rule on Financial Assurance Requirements for Decommissioning Power Reactors, July 2, 1998. The General Accounting Office has suggested that NRC should clarify the standards and criteria by which it will be reviewing the financial reports of the operators. GAO, Nuclear Regulation: Better Oversight Needed to Ensure Accumulation of Funds to Decommission Nuclear Power plants (May, 1999).

The Market Value of Nuclear Power, Nainish K. Gupta & Herbert G. Thompson, Jr.,

Electricity Journal, October, 1999.

Illinois Power Co. announced in April 1999 that it had reached an interim agreement to sell its Clinton Nuclear Power Plant to AmerGen Energy Co., perhaps by the end of the year. AmerGen Energy would pay Illinois Power $20 million for the 950 MW plant, or $21 per kW. The plant has a book value of $1.6 billion and a capital cost of $4.833 billion. The sale would be the third involving AmerGen, the joint venture between PECO Energy Co. and British Energy. AmerGen is working through the regulatory approval process to acquire the undamaged Three Mile Island Unit 1 from GPU Inc. for $23 million, or $28.4 per kW. Recently, owners said they were in exclusive talks with AmerGen to sell the single-unit, 530 MW Vermont Yankee station. That plant could have a market value of anywhere from $20 million to $50 million, based on prior sales. In the only other nuclear sales completed to date, Great Bay Power Corp. paid $3.2 million, or $95 per kW, for a 3 percent interest in the Seabrook generating station, and Entergy Nuclear paid $27 million, or $40.5 per kW, for BEC Energy's Pilgrim station.

Earlier, in February, GPU Inc. put its 637 MW Oyster Creek station back on the market. In July 1998, GPU announced both the agreement to sell its Three Mile Island Unit 1 and its inability to find a buyer for Oyster Creek. At that time, GPU officials said the company was left with two options for Oyster Creek: early retirement or continued operation until its license expires in 2009. A generally more active market for nuclear plants later led the company to rethink its strategy and put the plant back on the market.

This dismal scenario for nuclear plant market valuation may be coming to an end, however. As of this writing, the most recent announced sale, on June 24, was for a prospective purchase by AmerGen of Nine Mile Point 1 and 2 (NM1, NM2). These units, owned largely by Niagara Mohawk and New York State Electric and Gas (NYSEG), are selling for around $135 per kW, or $91.45 million for the 59 percent of NM2 owned by these two utilities and $71.7 million for the 100 percent of NM1 owned by Niagara Mohawk. This price, although still short of the remaining book value, is far above the prices offered in earlier nuclear plant sales. This is significant in part because these units are of vastly different vintages (NM1 start of operations in 1969, NM2 in 1988), and uncertainty exists for any attempts at life extension. As with other nuclear plant sales, this agreement calls for the sellers to purchase power from these units at negotiated prices for up to five years.

[Nuclear plants are selling at lower values than other generating plants.] As we see it, (1) Nuclear plants do not provide the same opportunities for conversion to other fuels as fossil fuel plants provide. Hence nuclear assets do not fit the trading strategies of many of the new integrated energy companies which place value on fuel arbitrage opportunities.(2) Nuclear power's history of mishaps, inappropriate regulatory responses, and increased regulatory scrutiny has not only increased the direct cost of doing business, but has also heightened the perception of risk and uncertainty throughout the industry. (3) Successfully operating a nuclear plant requires a unique set of skills that all utilities do not possess. This is evident by the significant number of nuclear plants sitting idle around the country. Only a few utilities, such as Entergy, PECO, and BG&E, have the experience and skill required to be a top-notch nuclear operator and perform O & M enhancements. (4) Based on past experience, nuclear plant expansion and upgrade requests are not likely to be looked upon favorably by regulators. Also, environmental factors and production technology differences at the site, such as the fuel rods disposal problem and the uncertain plant life, can lower the site value of the plant. (5) There remains uncertainty associated with the tax consequences (and time requirements) of transferring ownership, revaluing the asset, and transferring the decommissioning funds.

These factors, among others, drastically reduce the number of able and willing buyers and, in turn, discourage utility owners from putting nuclear plants up for sale. The result is the observed lackluster market for these assets to date.... It is our view that many plants will play little or no positive role in this future world. Some past mistakes will require more than a miracle to overcome. But a number of nuclear plants will be active players and command higher market prices.... A number of nuclear plants have low and improving operating costs, sometimes well below those of their fossil fuel counterparts. These low-cost units will allow their owners to significantly reduce the burdens of past construction costs. Some plants have made recent technological improvements which have reduced costs and/or extended the life of the plant. Baltimore Gas & Electric's Calvert Cliffs provides a recent example: there are plans to replace the steam generators with new units, and BGE has already requested an extension of the operating license from the Nuclear Regulatory Commission for an additional 20 years. If in addition Calvert Cliffs can maintain the recent trend of high capacity factor and low operating cost, it will find its future market value improved. The economics of relicensing a nuclear facility look extremely attractive when compared to building a new combined-cycle natural gas power plant. Relicensing costs are estimated between $10 million and $50 million per plant for an estimated production cost of $10 to $50 per kW, compared with $350 to $450 per kW to build the most efficient combined-cycle natural gas plant.

A higher market price for electricity in certain regions will, of course, improve the economics of nuclear plants. What factors might cause this to come about even beyond current expectations? One obvious answer is that fossil fuel prices could significantly increase. It has happened before. In addition to the usual historical reasons, one likely cause of fuel price escalation can be a burdensome carbon dioxide tax or penalty. In these events, nuclear power could start to look like a bargain. Other changes in environmental policy could similarly favor nuclear power.

The long-awaited institutional reforms affecting nuclear power's prospects are still overdue. The industry is still waiting for a viable solution to the storage problem for nuclear fuel and other high-level waste. Also, new licensing, license extension, and license exchange reforms are badly needed. Finally, tax reforms are needed, both at the federal and local government level. The tax impact of the exchange of the decommissioning fund, along with property tax reforms, are among the taxes that most impacted the recent sales of nuclear plants. Finding the public will to positively address these issues would undoubtedly increase the attractiveness of the nuclear power market.■

NOTES AND QUESTIONS

1. In the Matter of Kansas Gas and Electric Co., (Wolf Creek Generating Station, Unit 1), 49 N.R.C. 441 (1999), the Commission decided that there was no need to undertake an antitrust review upon the transfer of a nuclear license: "After consideration of the arguments presented in the briefs, and based on a thorough de novo review of the scope of the Commission's antitrust authority, we have concluded that the structure, language and history of the Atomic Energy Act cut against our prior practice of conducting antitrust reviews of post-operating license transfers. It now seems clear to us that Congress never contemplated such reviews." The NRC's authority to deal with antitrust issues "as it deems appropriate" has previously been interpreted to give the Commission considerable flexibility in deciding whether to grant or deny original licenses based on earlier antitrust violations. *Alabama Power Co. v. N.R.C.*, 692 F.2d 1362 (11th Cir. 1982), *cert. denied* 464 U.S. 816 (1983).

2. The issue of the financial responsibility of a company to operate and maintain the nuclear power plant is separate from the issue of its responsibility to cover decommissioning costs. The NRC plans to maintain continuing oversight to ensure that operators' budgets for maintenance and safety, for example, are not unduly reduced. Nuclear Regulatory Commission, Final Policy Statement on Restructuring, 62 Fed. Reg. 44,071 (Aug. 19, 1997).

In practice, it appears that a relatively small number of companies with extensive nuclear power plant operation experience are planning to acquire many of the existing plants. Entergy Nuclear, a subsidiary of the Energy system, recently purchased two nuclear plants from the New York Power Authority for $967 million, and has indicated that it wants to purchase other plants in the region. David W. Chen, Agency Votes to Accept Bids for 2 A–Plants, New York Times, March 29, 2000. In addition, the proposed merger of Commonwealth Edison and PECO is said to be based on the economies of scale that would result from unified management of many nuclear power plants. Rebecca Smith, Fissionaries: Two Utility Executives See Potential Riches In Nuclear Stepchildren, Wall St. J., Oct. 28, 1999.

To what extent is the consolidation of nuclear power plant operations likely to raise antitrust issues? Is it in the public interest to have many companies, or few companies, engaged in such operations? Is this an issue that should be dominated by economic considerations or safety considerations?

3. During the late 1990s, many United States electric companies expanded through acquisition of companies abroad, and a number of European energy companies began to acquire electric companies in the United States. The Nuclear Regulatory Commission is currently reexamining the statute and regulations to determine whether new rules are needed regarding the extent to which foreign entities may participate in the operation of nuclear plants in the United States. Martin S. Malsch, The Purchase of U.S. Nuclear Power Plants by Foreign Entities, 20 Energy L. J. 263 (1999).

D. FEDERAL PREEMPTION

Nuclear energy was initially developed during World War II as part of the federal government's national defense effort. The concern about the potential conversion of nuclear energy to military purposes by foreign governments or guerilla groups remains an important issue. Consequently, the federal government continues to play a key role in the control of nuclear energy.

The dominant nature of this federal role has led to a series of cases testing the extent to which the federal government has pre-empted the field and barred state and local regulation affecting the industry.

1. SAFETY OR ECONOMICS?

The Atomic Energy Act specifically said that the federal agency (now the NRC) would have the exclusive authority to regulate safety of nuclear facilities. State and local governments retained, however, the right to enforce all other forms of regulation. In regard to nuclear power plants in particular, it was recognized that the electric industry was heavily regulated by state public utility commissions, and Congress intended to leave this regulatory system in place. The line between safety and other regulatory objectives is not crystal clear, and the following case indicated that the Supreme Court was willing to interpret the distinction generously in favor of state regulation.

Pacific Gas & Elec. Co. v. Energy Resources & Development Comm'n

461 U.S. 190 (1983).

■ WHITE, J.: The turning of swords into plowshares has symbolized the transformation of atomic power into a source of energy in American society. To facilitate this development the federal government relaxed its monopoly over fissionable materials and nuclear technology, and in its place, erected a complex scheme to promote the civilian development of nuclear energy, while seeking to safeguard the public and the environment from the unpredictable risks of a new technology. Early on, it was decided that the states would continue their traditional role in the regulation of electricity production. The interrelationship of federal and state authority in the nuclear energy field has not been simple; the federal regulatory structure has been frequently amended to optimize the partnership.

This case emerges from the intersection of the federal government's efforts to ensure that nuclear power is safe with the exercise of the historic state authority over the generation and sale of electricity. At issue is whether provisions in the 1976 amendments to California's Warren–Alquist Act, Cal. Pub. Res. Code §§ 25524.1(b) and 25524.2 (West 1977), which condition the construction of nuclear plants on findings by the State Energy Resources Conservation and Development Commission that adequate storage facilities and means of disposal are available for nuclear waste, are preempted by the Atomic Energy Act of 1954, 42 U.S.C. § 2011, *et seq.*

I

A nuclear reactor must be periodically refueled and the "spent fuel" removed. This spent fuel is intensely radioactive and must be carefully stored. The general practice is to store the fuel in a water-filled pool at the reactor site. For many years, it was assumed that this fuel would be reprocessed; accordingly, the storage pools were designed as short-term holding facilities with limited storage capacities. As expectations for reprocessing remained unfulfilled, the spent fuel accumulated in the storage pools, creating the risk that nuclear reactors would have to be shut down. This could occur if there were insufficient room in the pool to store spent fuel and also if there were not enough space to hold the entire fuel core when certain inspections or emergencies required unloading of the reactor. In recent years, the problem has taken on special urgency. Some 8,000 metric tons of spent nuclear fuel have already accumulated, and it is projected that by the year 2000 there will be some 72,000 metric tons of spent fuel. Government studies indicate that a number of reactors could be forced to shut down in the near future due to the inability to store spent fuel.

There is a second dimension to the problem. Even with water-pools adequate to store safely all the spent fuel produced during the working lifetime of the reactor, permanent disposal is needed because the wastes will remain radioactive for thousands of years. There are both safety and economic aspects to the nuclear waste issue: first, if not properly stored, nuclear wastes might leak and endanger both the environment and human health; second, the lack of a long-term disposal option increases the risk that the insufficiency of interim storage space for spent fuel will lead to reactor-shutdowns, rendering nuclear energy an unpredictable and uneconomical adventure.

The California laws at issue here are responses to these concerns. In 1974, California adopted the Warren–Alquist State Energy Resources Conservation and Development Act, Cal. Pub. Res. Code §§ 25000–25986 (West 1977 and Supp.1981). The Act requires that a utility seeking to build in California any electric power generating plant, including a nuclear power plant, must apply for certification to the State Energy Resources and Conservation Commission (Energy Commission). The Warren–Alquist Act was amended in 1976 to provide additional state regulation of new nuclear power plant construction.

Two sections of these amendments are before us. Section 25524.1(b) provides that before additional nuclear plants may be built, the Energy Commission must determine on a case-by-case basis that there will be "adequate capacity" for storage of a plant's spent fuel rods "at the time such nuclear facility requires such . . . storage." The law also requires that each utility provide continuous, on-site, "full core reserve storage capacity" in order to permit storage of the entire reactor core if it must be removed to permit repairs of the reactor. In short, § 25524.1(b) addresses the interim storage of spent fuel.

Section 25524.2 deals with the long-term solution to nuclear wastes. This section imposes a moratorium on the certification of new nuclear plants until the Energy Commission "finds that there has been developed and that the United States through its authorized agency has approved and there exists a demonstrated technology or means for the disposal of high-level nuclear waste." "Disposal" is defined as a "method for the permanent and terminal disposition of high-level nuclear waste. . . ." Cal. Pub. Res. Code § 25524.2(a), (c). Such a finding must be reported to the state legislature, which may nullify it.

Petitioners Pacific Gas and Electric Company and Southern California Edison Company filed this action . . . alleging that the two provisions are void because they are preempted by and in conflict with the Atomic Energy Act. . . . The Court of Appeals for the Ninth Circuit [held that the California statutes . . . were not preempted because §§ 271 and 274(k) of the Atomic Energy Act, 42 U.S.C. §§ 2018 and 2021(k), constitute a Congressional authorization for states to regulate nuclear power plants "for purposes other than protection against radiation hazards."[6][11] . . . .

III

It is well-established that within Constitutional limits Congress may preempt state authority by so stating in express terms. . . .

Petitioners, the United States, and supporting amici, present three major lines of argument as to why § 25524.2 is preempted. First, they submit that the statute—because it regulates construction of nuclear plants and because it is allegedly predicated on safety concerns—ignores the division between federal and state authority created by the Atomic Energy Act, and falls within the field that the federal government has preserved for its own exclusive control. Second, the statute, and the judgments that underlie it, conflict with decisions concerning the nuclear waste disposal issue made by Congress and the Nuclear Regulatory Commission. Third, the California statute frustrates the federal goal of developing nuclear technology as a source of energy. We consider each of these contentions in turn.

A

Even a brief perusal of the Atomic Energy Act reveals that, despite its comprehensiveness, it does not at any point expressly require the States to construct or authorize nuclear power plants or prohibit the States from deciding, as an absolute or conditional matter, not to permit the construction of any further reactors. Instead, petitioners argue that the Act is intended to preserve the federal government as the sole regulator of all matters nuclear, and that § 25524.2 falls within the scope of this impliedly preempted field. But as we view the issue, Congress, in passing the 1954 Act and in subsequently amending it, intended that the federal government should regulate the radiological safety aspects involved in the construction and operation of a nuclear plant, but that the States retain their traditional responsibility in the field of regulating electrical utilities for determining questions of need, reliability, cost and other related state concerns.

Need for new power facilities, their economic feasibility, and rates and services, are areas that have been characteristically governed by the States. . . . The Nuclear Regulatory Commission (NRC), which now exercises the AEC's regulatory authority, does not purport to exercise its authority based on economic considerations, 10 CFR § 8.4, and has recently

---

6. Section 271, 42 U.S.C. § 2018, provides that: "Nothing in this chapter shall be construed to affect the authority or regulations of any Federal, State or local agency with respect to the generation, sale, or transmission of electric power produced through the use of nuclear facilities licensed by the Commission: Provided, That this section shall not be deemed to confer upon any Federal, State or local agency any authority to regulate, control, or restrict any activities of the Commission." Section 274(k), 42 U.S.C. § 2021(k), provides that: "Nothing in this section shall be construed to affect the authority of any State or local agency to regulate activities for purposes other than protection against radiation hazards." The role of these provisions in the federal regulatory structure is discussed *infra*, at 1724–1726.

repealed its regulations concerning the financial qualifications and capabilities of a utility proposing to construct and operate a nuclear power plant. 47 Fed.Reg. 13751. In its notice of rule repeal, the NRC stated that utility financial qualifications are only of concern to the NRC if related to the public health and safety. It is almost inconceivable that Congress would have left a regulatory vacuum; the only reasonable inference is that Congress intended the states to continue to make these judgments. Any doubt that ratemaking and plant-need questions were to remain in state hands was removed by § 271, 42 U.S.C. § 2018 which provided:

> "Nothing in this chapter shall be construed to affect the authority or regulations of any Federal, State or local agency with respect to the generation, sale, or transmission of electric power produced through the use of nuclear facilities licensed by the Commission...." ...

From the passage of the Atomic Energy Act in 1954, through several revisions, and to the present day, Congress has preserved the dual regulation of nuclear-powered electricity generation: the federal government maintains complete control of the safety and "nuclear" aspects of energy generation; the states exercise their traditional authority over the need for additional generating capacity, the type of generating facilities to be licensed, land use, ratemaking, and the like....

The above is not particularly controversial. But deciding how § 25524.2 is to be construed and classified is a more difficult proposition. At the outset, we emphasize that the statute does not seek to regulate the construction or operation of a nuclear powerplant. It would clearly be impermissible for California to attempt to do so, for such regulation, even if enacted out of non-safety concerns, would nevertheless directly conflict with the NRC's exclusive authority over plant construction and operation. Respondents appear to concede as much. Respondents do broadly argue, however, that although safety regulation of nuclear plants by states is forbidden, a state may completely prohibit new construction until its safety concerns are satisfied by the federal government. We reject this line of reasoning. State safety regulation is not preempted only when it conflicts with federal law. Rather, the federal government has occupied the entire field of nuclear safety concerns, except the limited powers expressly ceded to the states. When the federal government completely occupies a given field or an identifiable portion of it, as it has done here, the test of preemption is whether "the matter on which the state asserts the right to act is in any way regulated by the federal government." Rice v. Santa Fe Elevator Corp., *supra*, 331 U.S., at 236. A state moratorium on nuclear construction grounded in safety concerns falls squarely within the prohibited field. Moreover, a state judgment that nuclear power is not safe enough to be further developed would conflict directly with the countervailing judgment of the NRC that nuclear construction may proceed notwithstanding extant uncertainties as to waste disposal. A state prohibition on nuclear construction for safety reasons would also be in the teeth of the Atomic Energy Act's objective to insure that nuclear technology be safe enough for widespread development and use—and would be preempted for that reason.

That being the case, it is necessary to determine whether there is a non-safety rationale for § 25524.2. California has maintained, and the Court of Appeals agreed, that § 25524.2 was aimed at economic problems, not radiation hazards. The California Assembly Committee On Resources, Land Use, and Energy, which proposed a package of bills including § 25524.2, reported that the waste disposal problem was "largely economic or the result of poor planning, not safety related." ... The Committee explained that the lack of a federally approved method of waste disposal created a "clog" in the nuclear fuel cycle. Storage space was limited while more nuclear wastes were continuously produced. Without a permanent means of disposal, the nuclear waste problem could become critical leading to unpredictably high costs to contain the problem or, worse, shutdowns in reactors. "Waste disposal safety," the Reassessment Report notes, "is not directly addressed by the bills, which ask only that a method [of waste disposal] be chosen and accepted by the federal government." ...

Petitioners and amici nevertheless ... maintain that § 25524.2 evinces no concern with the economics of nuclear power. The statute states that the "development" and "existence" of a permanent disposal technology approved by federal authorities will lift the moratorium; the statute does not provide for considering the economic costs of the technology selected. This view of the statute is overly myopic. Once a technology is selected and demonstrated, the utilities and the California Public Utilities Commission would be able to estimate costs; such cost estimates cannot be made until the federal government has settled upon the method of long-term waste disposal. Moreover, once a satisfactory disposal technology is found and demonstrated, fears of having to close down operating reactors should largely evaporate.

Second, it is suggested that California, if concerned with economics, would have banned California utilities from building plants outside the state. This objection carries little force. There is no indication that California utilities are contemplating such construction; the state legislature is not obligated to address purely hypothetical facets of a problem.

Third, petitioners note that there already is a body, the California Public Utilities Commission, which is authorized to determine on economic grounds whether a nuclear power plant should be constructed. While California is certainly free to make these decisions on a case-by-case basis, a state is not foreclosed from reaching the same decision through a legislative judgment, applicable to all cases. The economic uncertainties engendered by the nuclear waste disposal problems are not factors that vary from facility to facility; the issue readily lends itself to more generalized decisionmaking and California cannot be faulted for pursuing that course.

Fourth, petitioners note that Proposition 15, the initiative out of which § 25524.2 arose, and companion provisions in California's so-called nuclear laws, are more clearly written with safety purposes in mind.[7][27] It is

7. The 1976 amendments to the Warren–Alquist Act were passed as an alternative to Proposition 15, an initiative submitted to California's voters in June of 1976. (By their

suggested that § 25524.2 shares a common heritage with these laws and should be presumed to have been enacted for the same purposes. The short answer here is that these other state laws are not before the Court, and indeed, Proposition 15 was not passed; these provisions and their pedigree do not taint other parts of the Warren–Alquist Act.

Although these specific indicia of California's intent in enacting § 25524.2 are subject to varying interpretation, there are two further reasons why we should not become embroiled in attempting to ascertain California's true motive. First, inquiry into legislative motive is often an unsatisfactory venture. *United States v. O'Brien*, 391 U.S. 367, 383 (1968). What motivates one legislator to vote for a statute is not necessarily what motivates scores of others to enact it. Second, it would be particularly pointless for us to engage in such inquiry here when it is clear that the states have been allowed to retain authority over the need for electrical generating facilities easily sufficient to permit a state so inclined to halt the construction of new nuclear plants by refusing on economic grounds to issue certificates of public convenience in individual proceedings. In these circumstances, it should be up to Congress to determine whether a state has misused the authority left in its hands.

Therefore, we accept California's avowed economic purpose as the rationale for enacting § 25524.2. Accordingly, the statute lies outside the occupied field of nuclear safety regulation.

B

Petitioners' second major argument concerns federal regulation aimed at the nuclear waste disposal problem itself. It is contended that § 25524.2 conflicts with federal regulation of nuclear waste disposal, with the NRC's decision that it is permissible to continue to license reactors, notwithstanding uncertainty surrounding the waste disposal problem, and with Congress' recent passage of legislation directed at that problem.

Pursuant to its authority under the Act, 42 U.S.C. §§ 2071–2075, 2111–2114, the AEC, and later the NRC, promulgated extensive and detailed regulations concerning the operation of nuclear facilities and the handling of nuclear materials....

Congress gave the Department of Energy the responsibility for "the establishment of temporary and permanent facilities for the storage, management, and ultimate disposal of nuclear wastes." 42 U.S.C.

terms, these provisions would not have become operative if Proposition 15 had been adopted. Cal. Pub. Res. Code § 25524.2, Historical Note (West 1977). The proposition was rejected.) Like § 25524.2, Proposition 15, among other things, barred the construction of new nuclear power plants unless a permanent method of waste disposal was developed, though Proposition 15 gave as the reason for its concern the threat of harm to "the land or the people of ... California." Similarly, Cal. Pub. Res. Code § 25524.3(b) (West 1982 Supp.), requires the state Energy Commission to undertake a study of underground placement and berm containment of nuclear reactors, to determine whether such construction techniques are necessary for "enhancing the public health and safety...."

§ 7133(a)(8)(C). No such permanent disposal facilities have yet to be licensed, and the NRC and the Department of Energy continue to authorize the storage of spent fuel at reactor sites in pools of water. In 1977, the NRC was asked by the Natural Resources Defense Council to halt reactor licensing until it had determined that there was a method of permanent disposal for high-level waste. The NRC concluded that, given the progress toward the development of disposal facilities and the availability of interim storage, it could continue to license new reactors. *Natural Resources Defense Council, Inc. v. NRC*, 582 F.2d 166, 168–169 (2d Cir. 1978).

The NRC's imprimatur, however, indicates only that it is safe to proceed with such plants, not that it is economically wise to do so. Because the NRC order does not and could not compel a utility to develop a nuclear plant, compliance with both it and § 25524.2 are possible. Moreover, because the NRC's regulations are aimed at insuring that plants are safe, not necessarily that they are economical, § 25524.2 does not interfere with the objective of the federal regulation.

Nor has California sought through § 25524.2 to impose its own standards on nuclear waste disposal. The statute accepts that it is the federal responsibility to develop and license such technology. As there is no attempt on California's part to enter this field, one which is occupied by the federal government, we do not find § 25524.2 preempted any more by the NRC's obligations in the waste disposal field than by its licensing power over the plants themselves.

After this case was decided by the Court of Appeals, a new piece was added to the regulatory puzzle. In its closing week, the 97th Congress passed the Nuclear Waste Policy Act of 1982, Pub. L. No. 97–425, 96 Stat. 2201 (1982), a complex bill providing for a multi-faceted attack on the problem. Inter alia, the bill authorizes repositories for disposal of high-level radioactive waste and spent nuclear fuel, provides for licensing and expansion of interim storage, authorizes research and development, and provides a scheme for financing. While the passage of this new legislation may convince state authorities that there is now a sufficient federal commitment to fuel storage and waste disposal that licensing of nuclear reactors may resume, and, indeed, this seems to be one of the purposes of the Act, it does not appear that Congress intended to make that decision for the states through this legislation.

C

Finally, it is strongly contended that § 25524.2 frustrates the Atomic Energy Act's purpose to develop the commercial use of nuclear power. It is well established that state law is preempted if it "stands as an obstacle to the accomplishment of the full purposes and objectives of Congress." *Hines v. Davidowitz*, 312 U.S. 52, 67 (1941).

There is little doubt that a primary purpose of the Atomic Energy Act was, and continues to be, the promotion of nuclear power.... [But] the promotion of nuclear power is not to be accomplished "at all costs." The elaborate licensing and safety provisions and the continued preservation of state regulation in traditional areas belie that. Moreover, Congress has allowed the States to determine—as a matter of economics—whether a nuclear plant vis-a-vis a fossil fuel plant should be built. The decision of California to exercise that authority does not, in itself, constitute a basis for preemption. Therefore, while the argument of petitioners and the United States has considerable force, the legal reality remains that Congress has left sufficient authority in the states to allow the development of nuclear power to be slowed or even stopped for economic reasons. Given this statutory scheme, it is for Congress to rethink the division of regulatory authority in light of its possible exercise by the states to undercut a federal objective. The courts should not assume the role which our system assigns to Congress.

IV

The judgment of the Court of Appeals is: Affirmed.

■ BLACKMUN, J., with whom JUSTICE STEVENS joins, concurring in part and concurring in the judgment: I join the Court's opinion, except to the extent it suggests that a State may not prohibit the construction of nuclear power plants if the State is motivated by concerns about the safety of such plants. Since the Court finds that California was not so motivated, this suggestion is unnecessary to the Court's holding. [The dissent went on to explain why it believed California could prohibit nuclear power plants even if it were motivated by safety concerns.]■

NOTES AND COMMENTS

1. The background of the events that led to this case is discussed in Thomas R. Wellock, Critical Masses: Opposition to Nuclear Power in California, 1958–1978 (University of Wisconsin Press, 1998).

2. Given the Court's limited interpretation of Congress' intent to preempt state regulation, is it likely that any state that wants to prevent the construction of additional nuclear power plants will be able to do so? Do you agree with Donald Zillman's observation that "It does not take a very adept state legal counsel to advise the Legislature how to draft a 'no more nukes' statute that would be based on economic or planning reasons rather than on safety concerns."? Zillman, supra at 10–23. Are there sound policy reasons why Congress might want to override state objections to nuclear power plants? For an analysis of preemption issues from a law and economics perspective, see David B. Spence & Paula Murray, The Law, Economics, and Politics of Federal Preemption Jurisprudence: A Quantitative Analysis, 87 Calif. L. Rev. 1125 (1999).

2.   RADIATION OR POLLUTION?

Kerr–McGee Chemical Corp. v. City of West Chicago

914 F.2d 820 (7th Cir.1990).

■ CUMMINGS, J.: This is the latest appeal in a string of litigation concerning the planned disposal of radioactive waste at the Kerr–McGee Chemical

Corporation's Rare Earths Facility, located partly within the corporate limits of the City of West Chicago (the "City") in DuPage County, Illinois. Kerr–McGee appeals from the district court's denial of its motion for a preliminary injunction. The injunction would have barred the City from requiring Kerr–McGee to obtain approval under a municipal ordinance for certain aspects of the construction of a disposal cell for radioactive material. Because the relevant federal statute does not preempt a municipal ordinance that on its face targets only health and safety hazards unrelated to hazards created by radiation, the judgment of the district court is affirmed.

I

From 1932 to 1973, Kerr–McGee and its predecessor companies used the property in question to recover thorium from radioactive ores. One by-product of this process was waste material referred to as tailings, which were stored on the site. In 1978, five years after Kerr–McGee shut down the processing operation, the federal Nuclear Regulatory Commission (NRC) issued an order requiring Kerr–McGee to submit a plan for decommissioning the facility, covering proper disposal of the tailings. The following year Kerr–McGee responded with a plan that called for encapsulating the tailings in an earthen disposal "cell" on the same property. Estimated to cost approximately $23 million to construct and maintain, this project would involve covering the tailings with layers of clay, rock, and soil eight feet high. The structure is alleged to be suitable for use for the next 1,000 years. . . . As part of its effort to convince the NRC of its position in favor of on-site disposal, Kerr–McGee prepared and submitted a 12–volume engineering report that described the design and construction of the cell. The report included discussion of methods that could be used to control such problems as erosion, runoff, and dust.

The NRC [issued the license in 1990.] On March 5, 1990, a Kerr–McGee official informed the City's mayor that it would begin work on its "stabilization program" the next day. The City responded to this announcement by informing Kerr–McGee that it planned to hold Kerr–McGee to compliance with the Erosion and Sedimentation Regulations contained in Article IV of the West Chicago Code. The relevant provisions of the Code involve such issues as dust control and erosion problems. The next day City officials posted a stop work notice at the site, stating that all persons ignoring the notice "are liable to arrest."

Kerr–McGee officials and workers did not test that threat, nor did they apply for a permit. Instead on March 7, 1990, Kerr–McGee filed its complaint for declaratory and injunctive relief in federal court against the City. The next day Kerr–McGee moved for a temporary restraining order and for a preliminary injunction.

The district court denied the request for a preliminary injunction after finding that Kerr–McGee had not made a minimal showing of some likelihood of success on the merits. The court relied heavily upon a finding that Kerr–McGee, in its license request, represented to the NRC that its disposal plans would conform strictly to the City's Code. *Kerr–McGee Chemical Corp. v. City of West Chicago*, 732 F.Supp. 922, 927 (N.D.Ill. 1990). Judge Holderman found that the City's enforcement of its Code could not conflict with federal law on the ground that the NRC's amendment of the Kerr–McGee license explicitly required compliance with the Code. *Id.* at 927–928. The district court further found that Kerr–McGee has adequate remedies at law, that it has failed to demonstrate that it will suffer irreparable harm if the preliminary injunction is not granted, and that the public interest would not be served if the injunction were granted. *Id.* at 928–929.

II

This appeal does not present questions concerning the cost or safety ramifications of on-site stabilization of tailings in West Chicago or the validity of the NRC licensing scheme.... Here the NRC is completing a lengthy review and appeals process focused directly on the risk of radiation contamination presented by Kerr–McGee's project, a project which was undertaken in response to the NRC's demand for a stabilization program for the tailings now stored on the West Chicago site.

Despite this restraint on the City, Kerr–McGee asks that we unmask the City's true motivation in requiring Kerr–McGee to obtain City approval. Given the City's well-documented opposition to on-site encapsulation and what Kerr–McGee calls a Not–In–My–Back–Yard attitude to the project, Kerr–McGee asserts that the City cannot pretend that it will treat Kerr–McGee's project as just another local development. It is not clear how heavily legislative purpose is to be weighed in determining preemption. *Pacific Gas*, 461 U.S. at 197–198. But it would require us to pile one speculation upon another to find that the City plans to use the Code to frustrate the NRC licensing program. The Code itself is "radiation neutral." The City has not applied its Code, so it has not even had the chance to do so in a manner intended to subvert the federal licensing scheme. The mere exercise of jurisdiction by the City does not create an irreconcilable conflict with the objectives of federal law.

The NRC and Kerr–McGee agree that references to the City's regulations in the NRC license are intended "to be enforced by federal means" and that Kerr–McGee is required by the NRC only to "meet the substantive parameters concerning the control of radioactive dust and runoff, and the like" (NRC Br. at 17–18; Pl.'s Reply Br. at 2). Indeed the NRC may lack authority under the various relevant federal statutes to incorporate a generally worded local standard into an NRC license in the way the City claims it has. Thus Kerr–McGee did not bind itself to submit its plans to the City through its representations to the NRC. Nevertheless it remains to be seen whether the City's attempt to apply its Code to the Kerr–McGee project will in any way frustrate the federal statutory scheme and interfere with Kerr–McGee's rights under its federal license. Kerr–McGee's claim is ripe because the City is prepared to apply its Code immediately in a way that may affect the project. It would be improper, however, to prejudge the

City's actions on the grounds that the Supremacy Clause might be violated at some future date. The City does indeed have the power to say "no" to aspects of the project that violate the Code, if they do not directly involve radiation hazards (including those "inextricably intermixed" with non-radiation hazards) and are not selected for scrutiny by the City merely to delay or frustrate the project as a whole.

For the foregoing reasons, the judgment of the district court denying Kerr–McGee's motion for injunctive relief is affirmed.■

NOTES AND COMMENTS

1. The above case illustrates how a determined local government can use the authority provided to the states by the *Pacific Gas* opinion to control the operation of nuclear facilities. Eventually, Kerr–McGee gave up and shipped all of the spoil material by rail to a disposal site in Utah. The continuing history of the Kerr–McGee fight with West Chicago is set forth in *Carey v. Kerr–McGee Chemical Corp.*, 999 F.Supp. 1109 (N.D.Ill.1998) (holding that a resident's claim for personal injury damages from the tritium dust blowing from the site was barred by the statute of limitations because of the extensive publicity regarding the potential damage beginning in 1976).

2. Unlike regulatory issues, jurisdiction over public liability issues is strictly preempted to actions in the federal courts under the Price–Anderson Act, which the Supreme Court has characterized as invoking "complete preemption doctrine" that converts an ordinary common law complaint into a federal cause of action. *El Paso Natural Gas Company v. Neztsosie*, 526 U.S. 473 (1999). On the other hand, the Court upheld an award of punitive damages under state law to an employee of a nuclear fuel fabrication facility licensed by the NRC. *Silkwood v. Kerr–McGee Corp.*, 464 U.S. 238 (1984).

E. DISPOSAL OF NUCLEAR WASTES

The most troublesome issue dogging nuclear power continues to be the disposal of nuclear waste. Almost twenty-five years have passed since the adoption of the California statute at issue in the *Pacific Gas & Electric* case, *supra*, but the industry is still unable to predict with assurance what will be done with used fuel rods. In addition, the disposal of less radioactive forms of radioactive waste continues to pose difficult political and legal problems.

1. THE NATURE OF NUCLEAR WASTES

The process by which nuclear fuel is created leaves radioactive waste behind at various stages of the process. The mining and milling of uranium creates piles of debris known as mill tailings, which contain small amounts of radioactive material. The handling of the material during the various stages of the process turns clothing, tools etc. into low-level sources of radioactivity. And when the fuel loses enough of its potency that it must be replaced, it still remains highly radioactive.

As the cases in the previous section indicate, concern with the disposal of waste materials from operations using nuclear energy have had a major impact on the willingness of people to develop new facilities using such energy. As radioactive material emits radiation it gradually loses its radio-active property. Some materials lose almost all of their radioactivity within a matter of days, while other materials will remain dangerously radioactive for thousands of years.

Humans and other animals are exposed to radioactivity in small amounts in everyday life from cosmic rays, elements such as radon in the soil, and other sources. But when radiation exceeds certain levels it can be very hazardous to health. In some cases, the gradual accumulation of radioactivity in the body can cause radiation sickness in people who never even knew they had been exposed.

When radioactive materials are used for medical or industrial purposes, they typically exhaust their productive radioactive capability over a period of time. At the end of that time they remain radioactive, though no longer producing the kind of radiation needed to perform the tasks for which they were intended. At that point, the user often seeks to dispose of the material, and it becomes categorized as radioactive waste. For almost half a century, Americans have been debating what to do with radioactive waste.

Under United States law, various categories of radioactive waste are treated under separate statutes and regulations. In general, the categories consist of (1) the waste from uranium mining, (2) military waste, (3) low-level waste, and (4) high-level waste.

a. URANIUM MILL TAILINGS

When ore is processed to remove uranium, the ore that remains is referred to as uranium mill tailings. Such tailings contain low but significant levels of radioactivity. Most uranium mining in the United States has ceased production, but huge piles of uranium mill tailings remain near the mining sites.

The Uranium Mill Tailings Radiation Control Act of 1978, 42 U.S.C. § 2000 *et. seq.*, provides that the Nuclear Regulatory Commission is to control the disposal of radioactive waste from uranium mill tailings. The Environmental Protection Agency adopted standards to be met by such disposal facilities (*see* American Mining Congress v. Thomas, 772 F.2d 640 (10th Cir.1985) cert. denied 476 U.S. 1158 (1986)), but it is the NRC that issues the permits. The ninth circuit rejected arguments of a citizen group that disposal of uranium mill tailings required an NPDES permit under the Clean Water Act. The court found that the legislative intent of Congress in adopting the Uranium Mill Tailings Radiation Control Act of 1978 precluded joint jurisdiction under the Clean Water Act. *Waste Action Project v. Dawn Mining Corp.*, 137 F.3d 1426 (9th Cir.1998).

Probably the most controversial uranium mill tailings site is located in Moab, Utah, and is now owned by Atlas Minerals Corporation, which is bankrupt. The site is adjacent to the bed of the Colorado River, and there are questions about the extent to which the site is contributing radioactivity to the waters of the river. Moab is a center for a growing tourist economy in southeast Utah, so the community is eager to see the problem resolved.

The company originally proposed a plan to decontaminate the tailings pile on-site by capping it. Opponents demanded that the tailings be moved to a site away from the river. On January 14, 2000, the Department of Energy announced that it would ask Congress for $300 million to remove the 10.6 million tons of tailings to a site away from the River. Joe Bauman, DOE Unveils Tailings Plan, Deseret News, January 15, 2000.

One of the few sites that is currently licensed to take uranium mill tailings is in Tooele County in northwestern Utah. It is owned by Envirocare, Inc., a company that has had a controversial history. The company is a defendant in a number of lawsuits alleging that it has conspired to prevent competitors from obtaining permits for radioactive waste disposal sites. *See Waste Control Specialists v. Envirocare of Texas, Inc.*, 199 F.3d 781 (5th Cir. 2000). As a result of inquiries into the licensing of the company's own site in Utah, the Department of Energy refused to ship materials to the site until the company changed management. Envirocare is currently seeking to obtain permits to increase the level of radioactive wastes that it is authorized to handle at its Tooele County site.

b. MILITARY RADIOACTIVE WASTE[8]

Large amounts of radioactive waste are being stored at the various sites used for defense-related research and development activities. Most of these sites are under the control of the Department of Energy. The DOE has begun shipments of this radioactive waste to the Waste Isolation Pilot Plant (WIPP) near Carlsbad, N.M. This is an underground storage facility located in a salt formation. *See* www.wipp.carlsbad.nm.us. The facility has been designed to store both transuranic waste (primarily materials contaminated by plutonium from weapons plants) and "mixed waste," defined as a mixture of hazardous chemicals and low-level radioactive waste.

Initially, WIPP will be receiving shipments from Los Alamos, N.M., the Idaho National Engineering and Environmental Laboratory, and the Rocky Flats site near Denver. Eventually, shipments will come from DOE sites in 15 states. The material is being shipped by truck. The regulations provide for tracking of the trucks by satellite, and call for cooperation with state and local authorities to ensure the safety of the shipments. Some New Mexico state officials have sought to prevent shipments to the plant but

---

8. For a more complete analysis of the entire complex interrelationship of the military services with the environment, see Stephen Dycus, National Defense and the Environment (University Press of New England, 1996.)

without success. *State of New Mexico ex rel. Madrid v. Richardson,* 39 F.Supp.2d 48 (D.D.C.1999).

The costs of clean-up at commercial power plants pales in comparison to the cost of cleaning up some of the sites where early military nuclear work was done, such as Hanford, Washington and Rocky Flats, Colorado. *See* Michele Stenehjem Gerber, On the Home Front: The Cold War Legacy of the Hanford Nuclear Site (University of Nebraska Press, 2d. Ed., 1997). Programs for military purposes have created some of the most contaminated sites in the country with cleanup costs in the billions of dollars. The estimate for cleaning up the Rocky Flats plant, near Denver, is $7.3 billion. More than a ton of plutonium is unaccounted for and believed to be lodged in the equipment and the ducts of the buildings. For a discussion of the cleanup problems at Hanford, *see* Gerald F. Hess, Hanford: Cleaning Up the Most Contaminated Place in the United States, 38 Ariz. L. Rev. 165 (1996); John S. Applegate & Stephen Dycus, Institutional Controls or Emperor's Clothes? Long–Term Stewardship of the Nuclear Weapons Complex, 28 Envt'l L. Rptr. 10631 (1998).

c.   LOW–LEVEL RADIOACTIVE WASTE

Congress, through the Low–Level Radioactive Waste Policy Amendments Act of 1985, 42 U.S.C. § 2021b *et seq.*, tried to implement a national policy for low-level nuclear waste disposal without preempting all of the states' traditional authority over the use of land within their jurisdictions. Relying largely on a report submitted by the National Governors' Association, Congress declared a federal policy of holding each State "responsible for providing for the availability of capacity either within or outside the State for the disposal of low-level radioactive waste generated within its borders," and found that such waste could be disposed of "most safely and efficiently ... on a regional basis." § 4(a)(1). The 1980 Act authorized States to enter into regional compacts that, once ratified by Congress, would have the authority beginning in 1986 to restrict the use of their disposal facilities to waste generated within member States. § 4(a)(2)(B). The 1980 Act included no penalties for States that failed to participate in this plan.

By 1985, only three approved regional compacts had operational disposal facilities, and these were pre-existing facilities in South Carolina, Nevada, and Washington. No new facilities had been sited. The 1980 Act would have given these three compacts the ability to exclude waste from nonmembers, and the remaining 31 States would have had no assured outlet for their low level radioactive waste. To avoid that prospect, Congress passed the Low–Level Radioactive Waste Policy Amendments Act of 1985.

The 1985 Act was again based largely on a proposal submitted by the National Governors' Association. It required the existing facilities to continue to accept waste from any other state for seven years, but after 1992 "Each State shall be responsible for providing, either by itself or in cooperation with other States, for the disposal of ... low-level radioactive waste generated within the State," 42 U.S.C. § 2021c(a)(1)(A), with the exception of certain waste generated by the Federal Government, §§ 2021c(a)(1)(B), 2021c(b). The Act authorizes States to "enter into such [interstate] compacts as may be necessary to provide for the establishment and operation of regional disposal facilities for low-level radioactive waste." § 2021d(a)(2). After the seven-year transition period expires, approved regional compacts may exclude radioactive waste generated outside the region. § 2021d(c).

The Act provides three types of incentives to encourage the States to comply with their statutory obligation to provide for the disposal of waste generated within their borders. (1) Monetary incentives. One quarter of the surcharges, which states in which disposal facilities are located are entitled to collect, is to be transferred to other states that meet certain statutory deadlines. § 2021e(d)(2)(A). (2) Access incentives. The second type of incentive involves the denial of access to disposal sites. States that fail to meet the statutory deadlines may be denied access to disposal facilities thereafter. § 2021e(e)(2). (3) The take title provision. The Act provides: "If a State (or, where applicable, a compact region) in which low-level radioactive waste is generated is unable to provide for the disposal of all such waste generated within such State or compact region by January 1, 1996, each State in which such waste is generated, upon the request of the generator or owner of the waste, shall take title to the waste, be obligated to take possession of the waste, and shall be liable for all damages directly or indirectly incurred by such generator or owner as a consequence of the failure of the State to take possession of the waste as soon after January 1, 1996, as the generator or owner notifies the State that the waste is available for shipment." § 2021e(d)(2)(C).

Despite the fact that the statute was written by the state governments themselves, the Supreme Court held that the Tenth Amendment was violated by the section of the act that would have required each state government to "take title" to all low-level waste in the state if it could not find a workable disposal site. *New York v. United States*, 505 U.S. 144, 112 S.Ct. 2408 (1992):

> The take title provision appears to be unique. No other federal statute has been cited which offers a state government no option other than that of implementing legislation enacted by Congress. Whether one views the take title provision as lying outside Congress' enumerated powers, or as infringing upon the core of state sovereignty reserved by the Tenth Amendment, the provision is inconsistent with the federal structure of our Government established by the Constitution. . . .

> Respondents note that the Act embodies a bargain among the sited and unsited States, a compromise to which New York was a willing participant and from which New York has reaped much benefit. Respondents then pose what appears at first to be a troubling question: How can a federal statute be found an unconstitutional infringement of

State sovereignty when state officials consented to the statute's enactment?

The answer follows from an understanding of the fundamental
purpose served by our Government's federal structure. The Constitution does not protect the sovereignty of States for the benefit of the
States or state governments as abstract political entities, or even for
the benefit of the public officials governing the States. To the contrary,
the Constitution divides authority between federal and state governments for the protection of individuals. State sovereignty is not just an
end in itself: "Rather, federalism secures to citizens the liberties that
derive from the diffusion of sovereign power." *Coleman v. Thompson*,
111 S.Ct. 2546, 2570 (1991) (Blackmun, J., dissenting). "Just as the
separation and independence of the coordinate Branches of the Federal
Government serves to prevent the accumulation of excessive power in
any one Branch, a healthy balance of power between the States and the
Federal Government will reduce the risk of tyranny and abuse from
either front." *Gregory v. Ashcroft*, 111 S. Ct., at 2400 (1991). *See* The
Federalist No. 51, p. 323.

Where Congress exceeds its authority relative to the States, therefore, the departure from the constitutional plan cannot be ratified by
the "consent" of state officials. . . .

State officials thus cannot consent to the enlargement of the
powers of Congress beyond those enumerated in the Constitution.
Indeed, the facts of this case raise the possibility that powerful incentives might lead both federal and state officials to view departures from
the federal structure to be in their personal interests. Most citizens
recognize the need for radioactive waste disposal sites, but few want
sites near their homes. As a result, while it would be well within the
authority of either federal or state officials to choose where the
disposal sites will be, it is likely to be in the political interest of each
individual official to avoid being held accountable to the voters for the
choice of location.

The Court said that state officials could not negate the Constitution's
allocation of authority by purporting to submit to the direction of Congress
to avoid the appearance of personal responsibility.

Whether the Act would have succeeded in obtaining approval of numerous disposal sites if the take-title provision had been upheld is a question
that will remain unanswered. What is clear is that in the absence of that
provision the Act has not provided enough carrots or sticks to persuade
state and local government officials to take the unpopular step of approving
the permits necessary to bring these sites into operation. The experience of
the Midwestern states is typical:

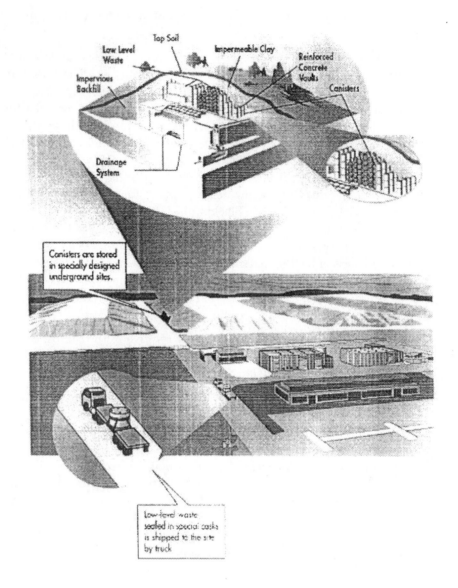

Labels in figure: Top Soil; Low Level Waste; Impermeable Clay; Reinforced Concrete Vaults; Impervious Backfill; Canisters; Drainage System; Canisters are stored in specially designed underground sites.; Low-level waste sealed in special casks is shipped to the site by truck

Figure 14–2

Figure 31. Diagram of a Low–Level Waste Disposal Site
Source: NCR, 1999

Tom Uhlenbrock, Midwestern States Abandon Proposal to Set up Dump[9] for Radioactive Waste

St. Louis Post Dispatch, Nov. 4, 1997, at D1.

Missouri and five other Midwestern states have given up on efforts to build a landfill for low-level radioactive wastes. Instead, they will ship them

9. [Ed. note] For some reason the news media consistently refers to any disposal site as a "dump" even though these facilities typically involve highly sophisticated storage techniques.

to a landfill in South Carolina. As a result, Union Electric Co. of St. Louis will get nearly $1 million back from the fund set up to build the landfill. The refund, eventually, could benefit UE customers because it will be considered in future rate considerations.

The rebate marks the failure of the Low–Level Waste Policy Act of 1980, which directed states to form "compacts" and build landfills to hold the wastes they produced. Not one compact has built a landfill since the law was passed. The Midwestern states spent $12.2 million in their unsuccessful effort. Illinois spent $90 million courting Martinsville for a landfill, only to have the site declared unfit geologically. Its efforts are on hold.

Missouri initially joined with Michigan, Ohio, Indiana, Iowa, Minnesota and Wisconsin to form the Midwest Compact. The utility companies that had nuclear power plants in each state were assessed fees to finance the project. The fees were to be paid back from receipts once the landfill was set up.

Because it had the most nuclear power plants, Michigan was chosen the "host" state for the landfill. But Michigan balked at locating a facility there and was kicked out of the compact. Ohio then took over and was searching for a site when the states decided in June to abandon the effort because the volume of low-level waste was decreasing and the cost of building a landfill was increasing.

The commissioners met Monday in St. Louis and voted to return the money paid by the utility companies by Dec. 31. Union Electric will get back $963,942. Kay Drey, an anti-nuclear activist from University City, attended the meeting and said the failure of the Midwest Compact showed the problems of dealing with nuclear waste. "Nothing is resolved," Drey said. "It's not just a political problem. It's also a technical and geological problem."

Missouri has about two dozen generators of radioactive waste, ranging from swabs and gloves used at medical schools and research labs to filters and sludges from Union Electric's Callaway County nuclear plant. Those generators produced 27,307 cubic feet of radioactive waste in 1986, when the Midwest Compact was formed, compared with just 2,944 feet last year. Most of what is produced now goes to Chem–Nuclear's landfill in Barnwell, S.C.

UE, the state's top producer, dropped its output from 5,900 cubic feet in 1986 to 2,061 cubic feet last year. That figure will grow considerably when the Callaway County plant is decommissioned. The 40–year license for the Callaway County plant ends in 2024, meaning it could be closed and dismantled, with much of the debris taken to a low-level radioactive waste landfill. The current cost estimate for decommissioning the plant is $451 million. "And that figure is expected to escalate 4 percent a year every year to 2033, when the work would be finished," said UE's Mike Cleary.

The utility is required to maintain a decommissioning fund. As of Sept. 30, the fund held $119 million. The fund is calculated to grow, Cleary said, with the estimates of the total de-commissioning cost. ■

NOTES AND COMMENTS

1. Maine, Vermont and Texas reached an agreement by which low level nuclear waste from Maine and Vermont will be sent to a site in Texas for disposal. Vermont and Maine will pay $25,000,000 each for the right to dispose of waste in Texas. Texas authorities originally approved an underground disposal site near Sierra Blanca, a tiny town about ninety miles east of El Paso. Mexican authorities filed a complaint with President Clinton about the proposed Sierra Blanca site, arguing that if the site leaks it would contaminate an area extending up to the Mexican border. Eventually, the Texas Natural Resources Commission denied a permit for the Sierra Blanca site. Envirocare, Inc. is currently seeking the approval of Texas authorities for an "assured isolation storage facility" at another Texas site. Texas Advisory Board to Review Envirocare's LLW Application, Nuclear Waste News, February 10, 2000. Some groups have questioned whether this kind of storage constitutes "disposal" within the meaning of the interstate compact.

2. Throughout the 1990s, all low level radioactive waste was disposed of at three sites: Barnwell, S.C., Clive, Utah, and Richland, Washington. Only the Richland site was designated pursuant to an interstate compact authorized by 42 U.S.C. § 2021b. Barnwell and Clive are privately operated sites that were approved under state law. However, the federal statute sets limits on the total amount of waste that may be stored at each of these sites. The governor of South Carolina has appointed a task force to consider whether the state should enter into a compact with a few other states. Under the Act, this would then permit South Carolina to deny waste from states that were not members of the compact, thus extending the life of the Barnwell facility. Sue Anne Pressley, In S.C., Rethinking an Atomic Waste Welcome Mat, Washington Post, Nov. 23, 1999.

3. The state of California sought to acquire federal land in a remote section of the Mojave desert on which the state could construct a low-level radioactive waste disposal facility. *See, e.g., Fort Mojave Indian Tribe v. California Dept. of Health Services*, 38 Cal.App.4th 1574, (1995); *California Department of Health Services v. Babbitt*, 46 F.Supp.2d 13 (D.D.C.1999). Increased efficiency in the use of radioactive materials substantially reduced the amount of waste being generated, and the state may conclude that the site is unlikely to be needed. What Will 2000 Offer For LLW Industry?, Nuclear Waste News, January 6, 2000.

4. The Central Interstate Compact succeeded in obtaining a preliminary injunction against the state of Nebraska that prevents the state from interfering with an application for a license for a disposal facility that Nebraska is obligated to provide under the terms of the compact. *Entergy, Arkansas, Inc. v. Nebraska*, 210 F.3d 887 (8th Cir.2000).

5. A study by the General Accounting Office in 1999 found that "the efforts by states to develop new disposal facilities have essentially stopped." It found that although the rate of waste disposal had dropped to less than half of the rate during the 1980s, the capacity of the Barnwell facility is likely to be used up in ten years. GAO, Low-level Radioactive Wastes: States Are Not Developing Disposal Facilities (Sept., 1999). A working group of the National Conference of State Legislatures is said to be

exploring the idea of repealing the federal statute in favor of "free market solutions." State Legislators Talk of Possible "Free Market" in LLW Disposal, Nuclear Waste News, February 3, 2000.

2. Disposal of High-Level Nuclear Waste

The problems associated with the disposal of low-level nuclear waste have been frustrating. The gravity of the low-level waste issue, however, pales in comparison to the problem of disposal of high-level waste.

The policy of the United States government since the late 1970s has been based on the desire to bury all of the fuel rods from nuclear power plants at an underground disposal site. The Nuclear Waste Policy Act of 1982 (NWPA) 42 U.S.C. § 10101 *et seq.*, gave the Department of Energy the responsibility of finding a site for the permanent disposal of high-level nuclear waste and it listed potential sites in Mississippi, Nevada, Texas, Utah and Washington.

Congress reacted to a storm of opposition to these sites by narrowing the selection to the single site at Yucca Mountain. *See* 42 U.S.C. § 10172 (1987). If the exploratory work at the site satisfies the DOE, NRC and EPA that it is safe, the President is to submit a recommendation to Congress that the site be approved. If the site is not found to be safe, it is back to square one. Extensive exploration of the site has been undertaken, but it will be many years before the agencies will be ready to decide whether to certify it as safe.

Regarding the disposal of high-level waste, significant concerns have been raised about (1) the time, place and method of disposal, and (2) the transportation of the material to the site.

a. THE DISPOSAL METHOD

Underground burial of nuclear waste reflects a kind of natural logic. "The uranium at the heart of those wastes was once an ore brought up from deep beneath the ground, and even though humankind has fired that ore into something truly awesome, it seems to make intuitive sense to put it back. Ashes to ashes, dust to dust. Besides, we are creatures of the surface in much the same way that aquatic animals are creatures of the deep and we find it easy to suppose that we have disposed of something, rid ourselves of something, if it is lifted above or sunk below the plane on which we live." Kai Erickson, 12,000 A.D.: Are You Listening?, The New York Times Magazine, March 6, 1994.

Today, however, there is not unanimous support for the idea of permanent burial of nuclear waste. The cost of the preliminary studies and testing of the Yucca Mountain site have been enormous.[10] Some commenta-

---

10. For fiscal year 2001, the Doe requested an appropriation of $358.3 million, an increase of $77.1 million over the prior year. Nuclear News, March, 2000, p. 17.

tors believe that a wiser policy would be to leave the waste on the surface so that it can be more easily monitored over the many millennia that will be needed to render it harmless. These observers, therefore, see continued inaction on the Yucca Mountain project as advantageous.

Many nuclear engineers, however favor a different approach. Fuel rods can be recycled through the use of "breeder reactors." Atkins, *supra* at 59–60. India has such a reactor in operation and is bringing a larger one on line in order to use its plentiful supply of thorium as a fuel. Peter E. Hodgson, Nuclear Power, Energy and the Environment 59 (Imperial College Press, 1999). Many other countries have used this method to avoid the need either to mine new uranium or to dispose of used fuel rods. The British operate a facility at Sellafield that recycles fuel from many countries, but the facility has recently experienced difficulties, apparently because of labor problem. Matthew L. Wald, A Lapse at Home Comes to Haunt a British Export, New York Times, March 22, 2000.

Denise Renee Foster, Utilities: De Facto Repositories for High–Level Radioactive Waste?

5 Dick. J. [Envtl.]. L. Pol. 375, 376–79 (1996).

Nuclear power plants and nuclear technology have been used in the United States for over thirty years. Until the late 1970s, the standard procedure for handling waste was to use a system of on-site storage subject to government regulation. By 1980, however, it had become apparent that although such an approach was adequate as a short-term solution, a permanent method of disposal was needed.

Congress enacted the Nuclear Waste Policy Act (NWPA) in 1982 to establish a national program for disposal of high-level nuclear waste.... Since the enactment of the NWPA, utilities that will use the disposal facilities have been making payments into this fund at a rate of one mill per kilowatt-hour produced with nuclear fuel. These payments have gone into a Nuclear Waste Fund established in the Treasury Department....

Although the concept of a permanent repository for nuclear waste has been widely accepted, much controversy has resulted regarding the decision about where to locate the repository. The NWPA called for the Department of Energy (DOE) to investigate a large number of potential sites and then to narrow the list to the three most scientifically viable locations.

The NWPA was amended in 1987. The 1987 NWPA amendments authorize the Secretary of the DOE to enter into contracts with the owners and generators of spent nuclear fuel of domestic origin (a category which includes utilities) for the acceptance and disposal of spent nuclear fuel. The 1987 amendments also provide that the contracts require the Secretary of the DOE to take title to the spent nuclear fuel as expeditiously as practicable after a repository commences operation. In return for the payment of fees that go into the Nuclear Waste Fund, the 1987 NWPA amendments also stipulate that the Secretary, beginning no later than January 31, 1998, will dispose of such spent nuclear fuel. In addition, the 1987 NWPA amendments direct the DOE to investigate only Yucca Mountain, Nevada as a potential site for a permanent repository.

Congress decided to abandon the process of careful scientific investigation of a few sites as originally required by the NWPA when it was enacted because pressure to deal with the issue of nuclear waste was growing. Under the 1987 amendments, if the DOE determines that the Yucca Mountain site should not be recommended after the site characterization is completed, the Yucca Mountain site will not be selected as the site of the nuclear repository. Congress would then have to amend the NWPA again to allow for another site to be selected to host the repository.

Nevada is concerned, however, that the same political pressures that led to the 1987 NWPA amendments will lead to the acceptance of Yucca Mountain as the repository site, regardless of the results of the site characterization process. A poll taken in Nevada when the 1987 NWPA amendments were being debated revealed that seventy-five percent of the people in Nevada opposed the creation of a high-level repository in the state. In fact, all of Nevada's representatives and senators also vehemently opposed the selection of Yucca Mountain. Nevada, unfortunately, had less political clout than did Texas and Washington, the other states then being considered to host the repository under the 1982 NWPA site selection scheme.

The state of Nevada claims that the decision to place the nuclear repository at Yucca Mountain is scientifically unsound and politically suspect. The DOE argues, to the contrary, that the Yucca Mountain site is a well-chosen location for the repository because, among other reasons, of its proximity to the site where nuclear weapons were tested.[11] At the very least, the DOE believes the government should be permitted to conduct extensive investigation of Yucca Mountain to make further scientific assessments. The DOE contends that the only basis for Nevada's complaints is that the state does not want the repository in its "back yard." ■

Alan Chapple[12], Used Nuclear Fuel: Deadline Looms–but Where's the Plan?

Nuclear News, May, 1997.

It is less than a year until the Department of Energy's January 31, 1998, deadline to start moving used fuel from U.S. nuclear power plant

---

11. [Editor's note]: New concerns have arisen about the weapons testing site, however. Groundwater studies suggest that radioactivity from the underground explosions of nuclear weapons will travel beyond the site boundaries, perhaps affecting wells in nearby towns, though there is disagreement about how imminent any problem is. Martin For-

stenzer, Concerns Arise Over Aquifer Near Nuclear Test Site, New York Times, March 21, 2000.

12. Alan Chapple is senior writer at the Nuclear Energy Institute, the nuclear industry's Washington, D.C.-based energy policy organization.

Yucca Mountain is about 100 miles northwest of Las Vegas, Nevada.

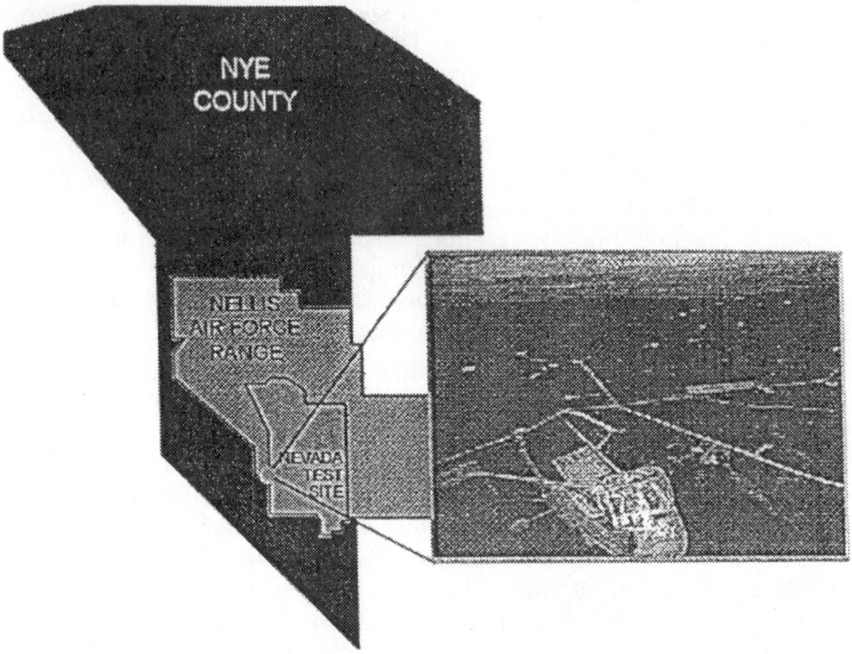

Figure 14–3

http://www.ymp.gov/reference/maps/vipmap.htm

sites. And, despite a court ruling last July that affirmed the DOE's obligation, the department says it has no place to store or dispose of used fuel from the nation's 109 operating plants and the handful of those that have shut down.

That's a problem—one that can be measured in billions of dollars, and one whose affected parties include the nuclear energy industry, many of the nation's governors and state utility commissions, members of Congress, labor unions, and the public.

This diverse group has seen 15 years of consumer payments into the Nuclear Waste Fund produce precious little. Despite having a waste fund that recently topped $13 billion, the federal government will miss by more than a dozen years its scheduled 1998 opening of a permanent repository. The most troubling aspect of this situation is the absence of a plan that would enable the DOE to fulfill its 1998 obligation until a repository opens.

This situation was not what Congress envisioned in 1982, when it passed the Nuclear Waste Policy Act. That legislation established a simple deal between the federal government and Americans who receive electricity from nuclear power plants. In return for customer payments of one-tenth of a cent per kilowatt-hour of nuclear-generated electricity into the waste fund, the DOE would build a permanent repository. The act mandated that the DOE begin accepting used fuel by the end of next January.

But the DOE acknowledges that it won't meet the deadline—despite utility customers' having upheld their end of the bargain by committing billions of dollars to the waste fund. In fact, the agency's most optimistic estimates have a repository opening in 2010; others believe 2015 to be a more realistic projection. Even if the Energy Department manages to open a repository in 2010, 78 U.S. nuclear plants will have run out of storage capacity in their used fuel pools.

To cope with the DOE's delay, some nuclear utilities are building aboveground storage facilities, where the used fuel is contained in massive concrete-and-steel canisters. Thirteen utilities have built onsite storage facilities or plan to do so by the end of 1997. Although a simple and safe solution, in engineering terms, expanded onsite storage is expensive. Moreover, the need for onsite storage has brought protests from consumers and state utility regulators, outraged that the public might be charged twice for used fuel management (once for the waste fund, and again to pay for onsite storage). A recent study found that storing used fuel at a central interim facility—instead of building more onsite storage—would save consumers $7 billion if the interim facility were operating by 2000 and a permanent repository were opened in 2015.

That's why Congress needs to fix the nation's used fuel management program....■

Indiana Michigan Power Co. v. Department of Energy

88 F.3d 1272 (D.C.Cir. 1996).

■ Sentelle, J.: The Nuclear Waste Policy Act ("NWPA") of 1982 authorized the Secretary of Energy ("Secretary") to enter contracts with owners and generators of high-level radioactive waste and spent nuclear fuel ("SNF") under which the private parties were to pay the Secretary statutorily imposed fees in return for which the Secretary, "beginning not later than January 31, 1998, will dispose of the high-level radioactive waste or [SNF] involved...." 42 U.S.C. § 10222(a)(5)(B) (1994). Petitioners are utilities and state commissions who paid fees to the Secretary under the statute. They seek review of the Department of Energy's ("DOE") final interpretation declaring that the Department has no obligation to perform its part of the contractual bargain. We conclude that the Department's interpretation is not valid and we therefore allow the petition for review.

In the NWPA, Congress created a comprehensive scheme for the interim storage and permanent disposal of high-level radioactive waste generated by civilian nuclear power plants. NWPA establishes that, in return for a payment of fees by the utilities, DOE will construct repositories for SNF, with the utilities generating the waste bearing the primary responsibility for interim storage of SNF until DOE accepts the SNF "in accordance with the provisions of this chapter." 42 U.S.C. § 10131(a)(5).

The NWPA requires the utilities to enter into standard contracts with DOE for the disposal of the waste. According to the statute, the contracts shall provide that "the Secretary shall take title to the high-level radioactive waste or spent nuclear fuel" and "in return for the payment of fees established by this section, the Secretary, beginning not later than January 31, 1998, will dispose of the high-level radioactive waste or spent nuclear fuel as provided in this subchapter."42 U.S.C. § 10222(a)(5). The final standard contract adopted by DOE, following notice and comment, states that "the services to be provided by DOE under this contract shall begin, after commencement of facility operations, not later than January 31, 1998 and shall continue until such time as all SNF . . . from the civilian nuclear power reactors specified . . . has been disposed of." 10 C.F.R. § 961.11, Art. II (1996).

In February 1994, DOE's Secretary, Hazel O'Leary, indicated that, while at the time NWPA was enacted DOE "envisioned that it would have a waste management facility in operation and prepared to begin acceptance of [SNF] in 1998," DOE subsequently concluded it did not have "a clear legal obligation under the [NWPA] to accept [SNF] absent an operational repository or other facility constructed under the [NWPA]." . . . On April 28, 1995, DOE issued its Final Interpretation (Final Interpretation of Nuclear Waste Acceptance Issues, 60 Fed. Reg. 21,793 (1995)) that it would not be able to begin taking SNF by January 31, 1998, that it did not have an unconditional statutory or contractual obligation to accept high-level waste and spent fuel beginning January 31, 1998 in the absence of a repository or interim storage facility constructed under the NWPA, [and] that it had no authority under the NWPA to provide interim storage in the absence of a facility that has been authorized, constructed and licensed in accordance with the NWPA.

Petitioners and intervenors then filed their petitions for review of the Final Interpretation. In reviewing an agency's construction of a statute entrusted to its administration, we follow the two-step statutory analysis established in *Chevron U.S.A., Inc. v. Natural Resources Defense Council, Inc.*, 467 U.S. 837, 842–43 (1984). First, we ask whether Congress has spoken unambiguously to the question at hand. If it has, then our duty is clear: "We must follow that language and give it effect." *Wisconsin Elec. Power Co. v. DOE*, 778 F.2d 1, 4 (D.C.Cir.1985). If not, we consider the agency's action under the second step of *Chevron*, deferring to the agency's interpretation if it is reasonable and consistent with the statute's purpose. We now apply that review to the Department's interpretation of section 302(a)(5)(B).

Section 302(a)(5)(B) states that "in return for the payment of fees . . . [DOE], beginning not later than January 31, 1998, will dispose of the [SNF]. . . ." The states and utilities contend that this provision means what it says: in return for the payment of fees to the utilities, DOE will begin accepting SNF not later than January 31, 1998. DOE argues that this language does not in fact require it to begin to dispose of SNF by January 31, 1998; rather, the agency contends that this obligation is further conditioned on the availability of a repository or other facility authorized, constructed, and licensed in accordance with the NWPA. DOE contends that this is the only interpretation possible when one examines the statute as a whole.

To support this interpretation, the Department first argues that Congress's use of the term "dispose" in section 302(a)(5)(B), which provides that DOE "will dispose of the high-level radioactive waste or spent nuclear fuel involved as provided in this subchapter," presupposes the availability of a repository. Although conceding that the statute does not define "dispose," DOE notes that the statute does define "disposal" as "the emplacement in a repository of . . . spent nuclear fuel . . . with no foreseeable intent of recovery." 42 U.S.C. § 10101(9). DOE contends that "dispose" is simply a different grammatical form of "disposal," and that Congress must have intended the two terms be interpreted consistently. Thus, it argues, section 302 must require a repository be operational before DOE may begin accepting SNF.

We disagree. The phrase "dispose of "is a common term. It has a common meaning. For example, Webster's Third New International Dictionary Unabridged 654 (1961) defines it as meaning, among other things, "to get rid of; throw away; discard." Admittedly, that and other dictionaries list other definitions. Each of those definitions, however, is consistent with the one set forth and not consistent with a limitation for placing the object of the phrase "in the disposal." There is no indication in the statute that Congress intended the words to be used in any but their common sense. Indeed, the very fact that Congress defined "disposal" restrictively and did not define "dispose" bears mute testimony to the strong possibility that Congress intended the former as a term of art, the latter as common English. . . .

Perhaps more importantly, we must interpret the section in light of the whole statutory scheme. See *Bailey v. United States,* 116 S. Ct. 501, 506 (1995) (observing that a court must "consider not only the bare meaning of the word but also its placement and purpose in the statutory scheme.") In the scheme before us, indeed in another subsection of the very section under review, Congress used even the elsewhere narrowly defined "disposal" to encompass more than "emplacement in a repository of . . . spent nuclear fuel . . . with no foreseeable intent of recovery." That is, in section 302(d), 42 U.S.C. § 10222(d), Congress authorizes the Secretary to make expenditures "for purposes of radioactive waste disposal activities," and expressly includes within the ambit of authorized "disposal" activities those conducted not only in connection with repositories, but also with "any . . . monitored retrievable storage facility or test and evaluation facility constructed under this chapter." 42 U.S.C. § 10222(d)(1). Therefore, even if we look to Congress's use of "disposal" to enlighten our interpretation of "dispose of," we still find that Congress has not evidenced limited usage for which the Department argues.

DOE next argues that subsections (A) and (B) of 302(a)(5) are not independent provisions, but rather must be read together because taking title to the waste cannot be separated from the disposal activities. To support this proposition, DOE cites section 302(a)(1), which describes the Standard Contract as "for the acceptance of title, subsequent transportation, and disposal of such waste or spent fuel" and section 123, which provides that "delivery and acceptance by the Secretary, of any high-level radioactive waste or spent nuclear fuel for a repository constructed under this part shall constitute a transfer to the Secretary of title to such waste and spent fuel." 42 U.S.C. § 10143. Respondent contends that these provisions evince Congress's intent that DOE take title to the waste before proceeding with disposal. According to DOE, any other interpretation of these sections would result in an anomaly in which one party would have ownership of the SNF while another party would have physical control of it.

We do not find this argument persuasive. Sections 302(a)(5)(A) and (B) clearly set forth two independent requirements. These separate obligations are independent of whether DOE holds title to SNF when it begins to dispose of the material. The duties imposed on DOE under subsections (A) and (B) are linked to different events and are triggered at different times. DOE's duty under subsection (A) to take title to the SNF is linked to the commencement of repository operations and is triggered when a generator or owner of SNF makes a request to DOE. DOE's duty under subsection (B) to dispose of the SNF is conditioned on the payment of fees by the owner and is triggered, at the latest, by the arrival of January 31, 1998. Nowhere, however, does the statute indicate that the obligation established in subsection (B) is somehow tied to the commencement of repository operations referred to in subsection (A). . . .

The Department's treatment of this statute is not an interpretation but a rewrite. It not only blue-pencils out the phrase "not later than January 31, 1998," but destroys the quid pro quo created by Congress. It does not survive the first step of the *Chevron* analysis. 467 U.S. at 842–43. Under the plain language of the statute, the utilities anticipated paying fees "in return for [which] the Secretary" had a commensurate duty. She was to begin disposing of the high-level radioactive waste or SNF by a day certain. The Secretary now contends that the payment of fees was for nothing. At oral argument, one of the panel compared the government's position to a Yiddish saying: "Here is air; give me money," and asked counsel for the Department to distinguish the Secretary's position. He found no way to do so, nor have we.

Finally, respondent asserts that reading subsection (B) as creating an unconditional obligation cannot be reconciled with other requirements of the statute, noting that the NWPA provides a complex scheme for the authorization, construction and licensing of a repository or monitored retrieval storage facility. DOE contends that "many contingencies facing the commencement of repository operations strongly undercut the assumption that Congress intended to require disposal by 1998 no matter what the outcome."

Although Congress anticipated the existence of a repository by 1998, the fact that such a repository does not exist does not make subsection (B) illogical; it simply affects the remedy we can provide. We agree with DOE that Congress contemplated a facility would be available by 1998; however, that Congress contemplated such a facility would be available does not mean that Congress conditioned DOE's obligation to begin acceptance of SNF on the availability of a facility. It does not make sense to assert that Congress would express an intent to exempt DOE from the January 31, 1998 deadline by including specific statutory procedures regarding the siting and development of a repository in the NWPA. Rather, these prerequisites evince a strong congressional intent that DOE's various obligations be performed in a timely manner. DOE's interpretation of the provisions does not harmonize them. Instead, its interpretation reads into section 302(a)(5)(B) language that appears only in section 302(a)(5)(A) and reads out of section 302(a)(5)(B) language that actually appears in that provision.

It is premature to determine the appropriate remedy, particularly as to the interaction between Article XI and Article XVI of the Standard Contracts, as DOE has not yet defaulted upon either its statutory or contractual obligation. We therefore will remand this matter for further proceedings consistent with this opinion.

In conclusion, we hold that the petitioners' reading of the statute comports with the plain language of the measure. In contrast, the agency's interpretation renders the phrase "not later than January 31, 1998" superfluous. Thus, we hold that section 302(a)(5)(B) creates an obligation in DOE, reciprocal to the utilities' obligation to pay, to start disposing of the SNF no later than January 31, 1998. The decision of the Secretary is vacated, and the case is remanded for further proceedings consistent with this opinion.■

NOTES AND COMMENTS

1. In a subsequent order issued on November 14, 1997, the D.C. Circuit decided that the appropriate remedy was an action for damages against the DOE for breach of contract: "Although petitioners have a clear right to relief, and the Department has a clear duty to act, we decline to issue the broad writ of mandamus sought by petitioners because they are presented with another potentially adequate remedy. Although the statute does not prescribe a particular remedy in the event that the Department fails to perform on time, the Standard Contract does provide a scheme for dealing with delayed performance. 10 C.F.R. § 961.11, Art. IX. Specifically, Article IX of the Standard Contract outlines how the parties are to proceed if one party is unable to fulfill its obligations in a timely manner. Under Article IX, unavoidable delays are to be treated differently than avoidable delays. A failure to perform is considered 'unavoidable' only if such failure 'arises out of causes beyond the control and without the fault or negligence of the

party failing to perform.' *Id.* at Art. IX.A. If a party's delay is determined to be unavoidable, that party is not liable for damages caused by the failure to perform in a timely manner. *Id.* An avoidable delay, in contrast, is caused by 'circumstances within the reasonable control' of the delinquent party. *Id.* at Art. IX.B. If a party's delay is avoidable, the charges and schedules in the contract must be equitably adjusted to reflect additional costs incurred by the other party. *Id.* The contract also provides a mechanism for resolving disputes of fact that the parties may encounter along the way. *See id.* at Art. XVI. Petitioners have not convinced us that this contractual scheme is inadequate to deal with DOE's anticipated delay in accepting the SNF.... Accordingly, we conclude that petitioners must pursue the remedies provided in the Standard Contract in the event that DOE does not perform its duty to dispose of the SNF by January 31, 1998." *Northern States Power Co. v. D.O.E.*, 128 F.3d 754 (D.C.Cir.1997). *See also Wisconsin Elec. Power Co. v. U.S.*, 211 F.3d 646 (D.C.Cir.2000). A recent Supreme Court decision has enhanced the rights of government contractors to seek damages if the government breaches the contract. *United States v. Winstar*, 518 U.S. 839 (1996) (allowing Savings & Loans to sue the government for damages).

2.   The Department of Energy published a draft environmental impact statement on the Yucca Mountain site in August, 1999. The study concludes that the risks associated with construction and use of the facility are substantially less than the risks associated with leaving the wastes at the various power plant sites around the country. DOE's Draft EIS an Important Milestone, Nuclear News, October, 1999. Storage of such highly radioactive material underground has never been attempted before. Could the radiation leak into the water table? What if the climate changes?

Both houses of Congress have approved bills approving the interim storage of waste at the Yucca Mountain site. *See* Note, Tipping the Scales: Why Congress and the President Should Create a Federal Interim Storage Facility for High–Level Radioactive Waste, 19 J. Land, Resources, & Envtl L. 293 (1999). However, the Clinton Administration opposes the legislation, and the bills have not passed with a veto-proof margin. Art Pine, Senate OKs Nevada Site for Storing U.S. Nuclear Waste but Veto Looms, Los Angeles Times, February 11, 2000.

3.   The interim storage of high-level waste has outgrown the water-filled pools that were included as part of the plants' original designs. The NRC has now authorized the use of dry cask storage, which can be undertaken by a plant operator if an NRC-approved cask design is used. *See Kelley v. Nuclear Regulatory Commission*, 42 F.3d 1501 (6th Cir.1995). These casks are kept above ground on the power plant site. Federal district court in Maine relied on *Kerr–McGee*, supra, in allowing the state to exercise regulatory jurisdiction over non-radiological issues involved in the transfer of spent fuel to dry cask storage. *Maine Yankee Atomic Power Company v.*

Bonsey, ___ F.Supp.2d ___, ___ WL ___ [2000 U.S.Dist. Lexis 6865] (D.Me. 2000).

4. Fed up with the long delays in the Yucca Mountain project, some utilities have been supporting a private venture to store fuel rods on Indian lands in Northwestern Utah. *See www.privatefuelstorage.com* A band of the Goschute Indian Tribe has approved a plan by a Wisconsin company, Private Fuel Storage, to store spent nuclear power plant fuel on the Goshute Indian Reservation in Skull Valley, Utah. The company is a joint venture of Northern States Power Co. and seven other electric utilities. The lease to the company has been approved by the Bureau of Indian Affairs, and the staff of the NRC has issued a safety evaluation report that was generally favorable. NRC Gives Backing to Storage Plan, Nuclear Engineering International, February 24, 2000. Utah state authorities have vowed to fight the project, but their direct control over reservation land is limited. *State of Utah v. United States Department of the Interior,* 45 F.Supp.2d 1279 (D. Utah 1999).

b. TRANSPORTATION METHODS

When spent fuel is moved from a power plant site, it must be encased in an NRC-approved cask. The casks that have been approved for transportation weigh about 40 tons (for road transport) and 100 tons (for rail transport). Through the end of 1995, approximately 1300 shipments of spent fuel have been made, about 90% by road and 10% by rail. Accidents occurred on four of these shipments, but in none of them were the contents of the casks released.[13]

One of the most intensive programs for the movement of spent fuel occurred when the Shoreham nuclear power plant on Long Island was closed down after it had been loaded with fuel and tested. (The plant was closed because of uncertainties about the ability to evacuate people from the heavily populated neighborhood in which it was located.) The fuel, which had been used only in the start-up tests, was transported by barge around Long Island and up the Delaware River to a power plant in Philadelphia. From there it was transferred to special railroad trains that carried it through central Philadelphia to the Limerick power plant. The movement of 560 fuel assemblies was completed over a one-year period in 1993–94 without serious incident. For the history of the ill-fated Shoreham project, *see* Joan Aron, Licensed to Kill? The Nuclear Regulatory Commission and the Shoreham Power Plant (University of Pittsburgh Press, 1998).

At those nuclear power plants where the quantity of spent fuel has outrun the capacity of the pools in which the fuel was originally stored, the NRC has approved the use of dry cask storage, but the casks used for such storage differ from those that would be used for transportation of the spent fuel. Applications are currently pending before the NRC for the approval of

---

13. Presentation by James D. McClure, Sandia Laboratories, to the Nuclear Waste Technical Review Board, Nov. 19, 1997. For a summary of the complex federal laws governing the transportation of radioactive waste, *see* Dan W. Reicher, Nuclear Energy and Weapons, in Celia Campbell–Mohn et. al., Environmental Law: From Resources to Recovery 559, 609–613 (West Publishing, 1993).

a cask that would serve both the needs of storage and those of transportation.

When the time comes to move the spent fuel now stored at nuclear power plants to a central disposal site, the shipments will extend over a long period of time. Some shipments will go by rail and some by truck. The State of Nevada has estimated that close to 80,000 truck trips and almost 13,000 rail trips would be needed if the shipments took place in 1999. While this estimate may be high, the volume of traffic will certainly be substantial enough to attract a great deal of public attention.

Many state and local governments have adopted regulations designed to exercise supervision over, or prohibition of, the transportation of nuclear materials. In a number of instances the courts have held that such regulations are preempted by federal law. *See* e.g. *Washington State Building and Construction Trades Council v. Spellman,* 684 F.2d 627 (9th Cir.1982). However, as the prospect of actual transportation looms, the elected officials of the states through which the material must pass may grow increasingly nervous.

CHAPTER 15

ENERGY IN TRANSPORTATION

Outline of Chapter:

A. INTRODUCTION

American-born columnist Bill Bryson, who worked in England for twenty years before moving back to the United States in 1995, noted that "Not long after we moved here we had the people next door round for dinner and–I swear this is true–they drove. I have since come to realize that there was nothing especially odd in their driving less than a couple of hundred feet to visit us. Nobody walks anywhere in America nowadays." Bill Bryson, Notes from a Big Country 131 (1998).

Americans consume vast quantities of energy in the course of moving themselves and their goods about. Europeans, who have approximately the same standard of living as Americans, each consume about a third of the amount of energy for transportation as a resident of the United States. The Japanese get by on about a fifth of our transportation energy per person. Office of Technology Assessment, Saving Energy in U.S. Transportation 32 (1994). And, like Bryson, they are typically amazed at the tendency of Americans to drive even short distances to get wherever they want to go.

Is it inevitable that the occupants of such a large and prosperous country must expend such a high proportion of their energy on transportation? Are we, as many foreign observers claim, simply inefficient in the way we move about our country? Or are our travel practices the leading edge of worldwide trends.[1]

From the early days of European colonization of North America, concern about linkage among the widespread sections of the country has been a matter of national debate. Could the interests of the separate colonies be unified without an efficient transportation network? Could we realize our "manifest destiny" of controlling the western part of the continent without effective ways to move people and goods there? How much energy should we expend in integrating the different parts of the country?

The terms of that debate have been modified over time as technology has brought new modes of transport. And today the dramatic changes in information technology raise questions about the extent to which electronic transfer of information will displace a share of the movement of people and goods. But the basic question remains high on the national agenda. How much energy should we be devoting to transportation and its impacts?

This chapter looks at the way debates about transportation have shaped and are continuing to shape energy law and policy. It begins with a brief reminder that the technology of engines and fuels has always set the parameters of potential policy, a topic of particular relevance today as we appear to be nearing new breakthroughs in automotive engine technology. In that connection, the network of gasoline stations that serves as the source of fuel for modern automobiles and trucks plays a key role. And the chapter briefly addresses the potential impact of new technology in producing a more efficient and less polluting motor vehicle.

The chapter then looks at the present pattern of highway-oriented transportation with its high energy consumption ratio and serious air pollution consequences. After briefly summarizing the social and economic

---

1. Much of the world is experiencing growth in motor vehicle transportation that resembles past trends in the United States. National Research Council, Transportation Research Board, Toward a Sustainable Future 61 (National Academy Press, 1997) (hereinafter "Sustainable Future").

factors that have produced the current pattern, it looks at the attempts to use the law to ameliorate the pollution and energy consumption problems resulting from our current patterns of development and transportation.

The chapter then briefly recounts the history of the way in which different technologies have created different patterns of transportation and land development, and explores the litigation generated by highway construction. Finally, the chapter explores current pressures, growing out of public dissatisfaction with traffic congestion, to use the law to change "urban sprawl."

B. ENGINES AND FUELS IN TRANSPORTATION

One of the key factors that affects the use of energy in transportation is the kind of engine being used and the type of fuel consumed by that engine. The twentieth century saw a gradual shift from coal-fired steam engines to internal combustion, jet and diesel engines fueled by petroleum derivatives, so that by the end of the century these oil-based engines drove virtually all forms of transportation. This means that as domestic oil supplies have leveled off, and we have become increasingly dependent on foreign oil, the dependency of our transportation sector on these overseas oil supplies has played a major role in our international relations. See Chapter 16, *infra*.

1. THE EMERGENCE OF AUTOMOTIVE DOMINANCE

From a broad historical perspective, the use of energy in transportation has gone through three phases. In each phase there has been one dominant form of power used to propel transportation. In the first phase animals dominated. In the second phase the steam engine; today it is the internal combustion engine. Whether we are at the dawn of a new phase remains to be seen.

The pre-industrial era. In the early days of the republic, animal power and wind power were the predominant sources of energy for transportation. Oxen pulled the covered wagons that brought settlers to the West; mules towed barges along the Erie Canal; horse-driven coaches carried the mail. Western cowboys managed cattle drives on horseback.

In urban areas, horses were everywhere, especially after about 1840 when the horse-drawn streetcar began to be the most popular form of urban transportation. The livery stable, with its noise and odors, became a common target of nuisance litigation. *See, e.g., Sheldon v. Weeks*, 51 Ill.App. 314 (1893). Even well into the late 19th Century, horse-drawn railways were one of the main forms of urban transportation. And we still use "horsepower" as a measure of the ability of an engine to perform work.[2]

---

2. *See* Chapter 2, § A.

On the oceans, transportation and trade were carried on by "tall ships" that captured the wind with dozens of sails. The ability to use our sailing vessels to trade with Europe and the Caribbean was one of the goals of the American revolution. Clipper ships from American ports carried goods all over the world in the mid 19th Century.

Internally, an intricate network of canals was built in the first half of the nineteenth century to transport goods to and from the interior of the country. Along the towpaths, mules pulled the barges at a stately pace. By mid-century, however, there were clear signs that animals would no longer remain the dominant form of transportation either on water or on land.

The industrial revolution. Steam engines fueled by coal were developed late in the 18th century, but it wasn't until the first half of the 19th Century when they were installed on wheeled vehicles that came to be known as railroad trains. Peter Cooper attracted national attention to steam railroad engines when he made a widely publicized bet that his locomotive, Tom Thumb, could win a race with a horse-drawn wagon. In 1830, the race was a "media event" that attracted national attention. The locomotive was in the lead but a broken drive belt gave the horse the victory. Nevertheless, the event made the public aware of the steam engine's capabilities. Russell Bourne, Americans on the Move 69 (Fulcrum Publishing, 1995).

It was not the speed of the railroad engine but its power that proved to be the key factor in establishing the railroads' dominance in the period after the Civil War. The railroads revolutionized transportation by making it possible to carry heavy loads over long distances much faster and cheaper than older forms of transportation.

In the cities, electricity became the driving force in rail transportation as the old horse-drawn streetcars were replaced by electrified trolleys. Between 1890 and 1920, the use of electric streetcars rose from 2 billion to 15.5 billion trips annually. Mark S. Foster, From Streetcar to Superhighway 14 (Temple University Press, 1981).

Passenger travel on long distance railroads also became common. The trains provided increased comfort and convenience in comparison to the stagecoaches they replaced, and the volume of passengers and speed of travel was increased while the cost was substantially reduced. In 1882, just three years after the intercontinental railroad was completed, a million passengers rode between Omaha and San Francisco. Bourne, *supra* at 97.

The steam engine also had a significant impact on water travel. Robert Fulton first attracted wide attention to the possibility of steamboats when he made his well publicized journey up the Hudson River from New York to Albany in 1807. Within a few decades the paddlewheel steamboats became a familiar sight on rivers such as the Ohio and Mississippi, carrying passengers and towing barges. Towards the end of the century, steamships became the dominant force in international travel as well.

The automotive era. The end of the nineteenth century saw the development of the internal combustion engine using gasoline as a fuel. Internal combustion ushered in the third phase of American transportation, as automobiles and trucks began to supplant steam-driven railroads except for the heaviest loads or the most frequently used routes.

In 1886, when Carl Benz obtained a German patent on a motorcar with an internal combustion engine of his design and named the car after a

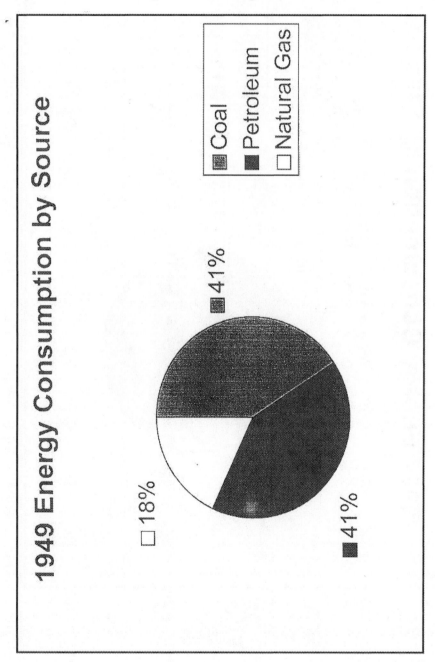

Figure 15–1

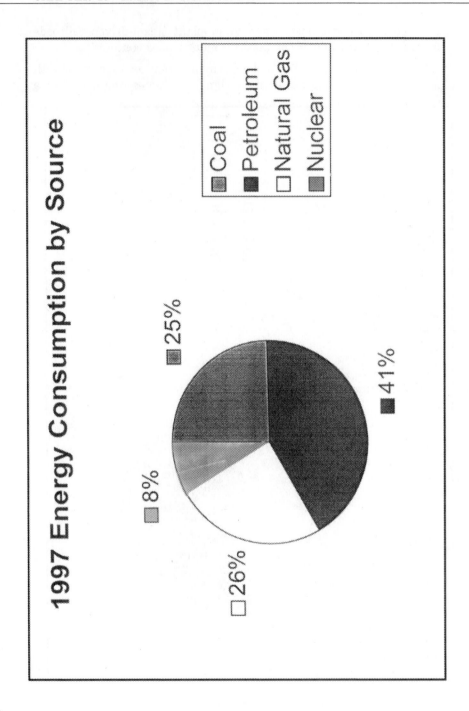

Figure 15–2

Source: E1A

friend's daughter, Mercedes, few people recognized the revolution that was to come. Autos began to be made in the United States during the next decade; the Duryea Brothers opened the first American automobile manufacturing plant in 1895, followed quickly by a number of others, and by 1905 the most popular song in the country had everyone singing "Come away with me Lucille ... in my merry Oldsmobile." Three years later, Henry Ford started producing the Model T, and the auto industry never looked back. Clay McShane, The Automobile 19–39 (Westport, Ct.: Greenwood Press, 1997).

It didn't take long to begin putting the internal combustion engine in trucks as well as cars, and the newly formed trucking industry quickly began to compete with railroads and barge lines for the transport of goods. In the 1950s, the efficiency of trucking was further enhanced by the widespread use of diesel engines and diesel fuel, a more economical method of transporting heavy cargoes. Between 1965 and 1980, the number of tractor-trailers in the national fleet nearly doubled, and their total miles traveled per year grew at a rate nearly double that of passenger car travel, which was itself growing significantly. Sustainable Future, *supra* at 41.

In the air, early airplanes used internal combustion engines that relied on gasoline. In the mid–20th century, jet engines using jet fuel began to replace the older propeller-driven planes. Today, mid-size jet planes are increasingly taking over shorter routes formerly being flown by propeller aircraft.

There are a great many engineering differences among automobile, truck and airplane engines, but they have one important thing in common. They all run on fuel derived from petroleum. Diesel engines have also replaced steam engines on ships and railroad trains, reducing the steam engine to the status of a nostalgic toy for rail buffs. This means that as the 21st Century begins, virtually all of the mechanized transportation in the world is dependent on petroleum.

2. THE DISTRIBUTION AND MARKETING OF PETROLEUM

Modern automobile and truck transportation has been possible because gasoline and diesel fuel are readily available all over the nation, and throughout most of the world. If changes are to be made in the engines and fuels used on the highways, they will need to take into account the existing system through which motor vehicle fuels are distributed.

a. THE CHANGING GAS STATION

Early in the Twentieth Century, when it became apparent that the gasoline-fueled automobile was going to be a major source of business for the oil companies, each of the major oil companies began creating a network of "gas stations" to sell its product. These vertically integrated companies wanted the oil that they explored for and produced to remain within the company's control until it actually reached the consumer.

The result was the competing networks of gas stations that are familiar sights all over the world. Over time, some companies dropped out of certain markets to concentrate their sales in other markets, and a variety of independent distributors of various sizes have joined in the competition, but the major oil companies continue to control a significant share of the market.

Most early gas stations not only sold gas but performed repair work as well. Early autos needed lots of work, and the gas station operator was often a skilled mechanic. Gas stations contained bays for car repair and carried an extensive selection of tools and parts. Many gas stations operated tow truck fleets to bring stranded motorists to the facility.

After World War II, the major oil companies competed ferociously with each other for the best locations for gas stations. Frequently the location of gas stations became an issue under local zoning laws. Many communities tried to limit the number of gas stations, both to preserve the land for other uses and to respond to pressure from the local operators of the stations who complained that the bitter rivalry among the oil companies for more stations meant that local operators were making less profit. Local governments passed laws providing that no new gas station could be built within, e.g., 500 feet of any other gas station. *Compare Stone v. City of Maitland*, 446 F.2d 83 (5th Cir.1971) (upholding such an ordinance) with *City of Miami v. Woolin*, 387 F.2d 893 (5th Cir.1968) (striking down an ordinance requiring an even greater separation).

As oil and gasoline prices fell in the 1980s, most of the major oil companies lost some of their competitive zest in marketing. Most companies cut back on the number of regions in which they operated to reduce distribution costs. Local operators began to complain about the closing of gas stations rather than the proliferation of them.

In addition, local dealers have complained that the major oil companies are increasingly opening company-owned stations that compete with their own dealers. Some states have passed laws that try to protect local dealers. Divorcement, or outright prohibition of refiners from direct operation of gasoline stations, has been in effect for a number of years in Connecticut, Delaware, Maryland, Nevada, and in the District of Columbia. Some commentators suggest that these laws tend indirectly to increase prices and reduce service.

> The most carefully studied experience of divorcement relates to Maryland, where divorcement legislation prohibiting refiners from directly operating retail gasoline stations was enacted in 1974 and has been in force since 1979. About 200 stations (less than 100% of the Maryland market) were affected. The best available empirical evidence on the effects of divorcement comes from a study by Barron and Umbeck [who] obtained a data set consisting of periodic surveys of prices charged and hours open for 178 of the 210 stations subject to divorcement under Maryland's divorcement law. The surveys covered the period from January 1977 to January 1982, extending, therefore, from before to after divorcement. The data set also included surveys of prices and hours of operation of nearby competitor stations. In all, about 600 stations were in the original sample.

The authors found that divorcement caused full service gasoline prices to rise 5–7 cents per gallon at the stations subject to forced divestiture, and about 1 cent per gallon at the competitor stations. The also found that hours of operation fell about 8–9 hours per week at the stations subject to divorcement. Thus, this study indicates that, while the competitors of integrated stations benefitted, it was the consumers who were harmed by Maryland's divorcement law.

Larry Goldstein et. al., Divorced from the facts, The Oil and Gas Journal, Nov. 9, 1998

Modern cars need repairs less often, with the result that the nature of the modern gas station has become quite different from its original counterpart. Self-service gas pumps have replaced attendants, and an increasing number of stations provide facilities for inserting credit cards right at the pump. This has made the purchase of gas less time-consuming for the customer.

In addition, gas stations today often obtain a large share of their revenue from selling other commercial products. The line between the traditional convenience store and the gas station has become blurred as many traditional convenience stores have started to sell gas and many gas stations sell the products typically found at convenience stores. This has led to local zoning battles over whether a facility zoned for a gas station could operate a convenience store as an "accessory use" (*See, e.g., Exxon Corp. v. Board of Standards and Appeals*, 542 N.Y.S.2d 639 (App. Div. 1989)) and whether convenience stores could install gas pumps as an accessory use in areas that were not zoned for gas stations (*See, e.g., Eubanks v. Board of Adjustment*, 768 S.W.2d 624 (Mo.App.1989)).

Although these changes appear to have been popular with some consumers, not everyone would agree. A Houston resident recently wrote a letter to the popular trade publication, Oil & Gas Journal, complaining that on "May 22, my wife and I were running some errands, which included filling the gas tank of her SUV and adding some air to a rear tire. It sounds very simple, does it not? Well, it ain't!." They went to "three major-brand (Shell, Chevron, Exxon) "filling" stations—you noticed I did not say 'service' stations—but the air hoses at none of them were functional. When one goes into the commercial areas of these stations that are packed with Twinkies, cola, etc., to report the problem, the attendant, who is undoubtedly working for minimum wage, either shrugs and says, 'that's not my responsibility', or, 'I'll report it, and maybe someone will fix it soon.' I would add that this is a rather upscale area of Houston, the 'oil capital' of the world."

We hear a lot of bleating by various industries leaders about our poor public image and how no one understands us, but the one area where the public sees us the most (filling stations) is in horrific condition. A few years ago, there was a big push to put in fancy stations, but many of them are very dingy, dirty, and neglected. Of course, you can still buy Twinkies, cola, etc., there, but air? Ha! ...

Why is it so difficult for the leaders of industry to understand simple public relations? . . . I would be most interested in hearing some comments from industry leaders on our continued failing public relations efforts, and why this easy contact area is so neglected.

Letter from Stan S. Thurber, Oil & Gas Journal, June 14, 1999, p.6.

The major oil companies, on the other hand, increasingly question whether they want to continue to distribute gasoline through franchise relationships with dealers. They are increasing rents to dealers, opening more company-operated outlets, or simply delivering gasoline to wholesalers and abandoning direct retail marketing. Allen Barrionuevo, Service Stations Muddle Merger of Exxon, Mobil, Wall St. Journal, p.B1, Nov. 22, 1999. It is now commonly believed that the modern consumer no longer retains any brand loyalty. "Today, consumers want gasoline, quick and cheap, regardless of brand," together with "their soft drink, chips, and an assortment of convenient services." Jim Dudley, Integration seen as best business model for US refining-marketing, Oil & Gas Journal, Jan. 31, 2000.

The difficulty of predicting the future of the gas station is underscored by the network of federal laws and regulations governing gas station operations, and by questions about the nature of the fuels that will be needed for new engines that will be developed in the twenty-first century.

b.   FRANCHISE REGULATION

Oil companies often operate some gas stations themselves, but a large proportion of the gas stations are still operated by local franchisees, who operate them pursuant to a contract that requires them to sell the company's products. Such franchising arrangements are quite common in other retail businesses such as restaurants.[3]

Relationships between the franchisee and the franchisor are not always harmonious. The franchisees often feel overwhelmed by the size and expertise of the large companies with which they deal. And the oil companies are sometimes frustrated when they need to modify national marketing strategies to adapt to the franchisees' local problems. In the field of gasoline retailing, the franchisees have persuaded Congress to adopt a federal statute, the Petroleum Marketing Practices Act, 15 U.S.C. § 2801 et. seq., that limits the right of the oil companies to terminate a franchise agreement in certain circumstances,[4] and provides that if the agreement is terminated the company must offer to sell the property to the franchisee.

---

3. It is estimated that over one third of all of the retail sales of all kinds in the United States are made at franchised outlets. Robert W. Emerson, Franchise Terminations: Legal Rights and Practical Effects When Franchisees Claim the Franchisor Discriminates, 35 Amer. Bus. L. J. 559, 561 (1998).

4. For a discussion of the PMPA standards with which a company must comply if it seeks to get out of the gasoline marketing business, see Unocal Corporation v. Kaabipour, 177 F.3d 755 (9th Cir. 1999) cert. denied 120 S.Ct. 614 (1999) (oil company properly complied with PMPA rules governing sale of its marketing assets).

Rhodes v. Amoco Oil Company

143 F.3d 1369 (10th Cir. 1998).

■ HOLLOWAY, J.: Plaintiff-appellant Brad Rhodes (Rhodes or plaintiff) brings this appeal from the district court's final order granting summary judgment to defendant Amoco Oil Company (Amoco or defendant). *Rhodes v. Amoco Oil Co.*, 955 F. Supp. 1288 (D.Kan.1997). Jurisdiction in the district court was asserted under the Petroleum Marketing Practices Act (the PMPA), 15 U.S.C. §§ 2801–2841. Our jurisdiction arises under 28 U.S.C. § 1291.

The facts are set out in the district court's opinion. A brief overview will suffice to provide the background for our discussion of the issues raised on appeal. Rhodes operated a service station in Derby, Kansas, just outside Wichita, as lessee and franchisee of Amoco. In 1993, Amoco decided to sell all of its retail stations in the Wichita area. Amoco retained a certified appraiser, David Hopkins, to appraise all of its properties in the Wichita area, including that leased by plaintiff. Hopkins initially appraised the property leased by Rhodes at $180,477. Based on that appraisal, Amoco offered to sell the property to plaintiff for $180,000.

Plaintiff declined that offer and hired his own appraiser, Roger Turner, who like Hopkins was independent, experienced, and a certified appraiser. Turner appraised the property at $77,500. Plaintiff then made a counteroffer of $77,000 to purchase the station. Thereafter, the parties continued to negotiate, with Amoco several times extending Rhodes's lease so that the negotiations could continue. These dealings are described in the district court's opinion, 955 F. Supp. at 1289–90, and need not concern us now. For our purposes, we should focus only on Amoco's final offer. Amoco eventually asked Hopkins to update his appraisal of the property, and Hopkins' second appraisal concluded that the fair market value of the property was $132,000. Amoco then offered the property to Rhodes at that price on February 24, 1995. Rhodes made a final counteroffer of $90,000, which Amoco rejected.

Rhodes then commenced this action on April 28, 1995. His complaint alleges that Amoco had not made, during the required 90–day period after notification of nonrenewal, a bona fide offer to sell, transfer or assign to plaintiff Amoco's interest in the Leased Marketing Premises. Plaintiff prayed, *inter alia*, for preliminary and permanent injunctive relief, declaratory relief, and damages under the PMPA provisions. *Id.* at 10–11.

Holding that Amoco's February 1995 offer of $132,000 satisfied Amoco's statutory duty to make a "bona fide" offer to sell the property to its franchisee, Rhodes, the district court granted a motion by Amoco for summary judgment. On review, we conclude that on this record the summary judgment must be reversed.

Congress has seen fit to regulate the relationships between franchisors such as Amoco and their franchisees through the PMPA. The PMPA affords protection to franchisees because "Congress found that [franchisors] had been using their power over franchisees to further their own self-interest." *Slatky v. Amoco Oil Co.*, 830 F.2d 476, 482 (3d Cir.1987) (en banc). In remedying the disparity in bargaining power of the parties, "Congress protected the franchisee's interests by curbing those of the [franchisor]. Senate Report at 18, U.S. Code Cong. Ad. News 1978, at 876." *Id.*

The statute creates two basic mechanisms to protect the franchisees. First, the statute proscribes termination or nonrenewal of franchises except on specified grounds. 15 U.S.C. § 2802(b)(3). This limitation generally prohibits "the arbitrary and discriminatory termination or nonrenewal of a franchise." *Sandlin v. Texaco Refining and Marketing, Inc.*, 900 F.2d 1479, 1480 (10th Cir.1990). This part of the PMPA does not concern us here; Rhodes has never contended that the initial decision not to renew his franchise agreement was made in bad faith or for other than permissible reasons.

We are concerned on this appeal only with the second protective mechanism afforded by the PMPA—that the franchisor make "a bona fide offer to sell, transfer or assign" its interest in the premises to the franchisee. 15 U.S.C. § 2802(b)(3)(D)(iii)(I).[2][5] In connection with this second protective mechanism requiring a bona fide offer, this court has pointed out that the bona fide offer provision therefore serves as a second, and distinct, layer of protection, assuring the franchisee an opportunity to continue to earn a livelihood from the property while permitting the distributor to end the franchise relationship. *Sandlin*, 900 F.2d at 1481 (*quoting* 830 F.2d 476 at 484.

As we held in *Sandlin*, "we use an objective test to decide whether an offer is bona fide." *Sandlin*, 900 F.2d at 1481, [and] we must determine if there is a genuine issue of material fact whether Amoco's February 1995 offer at $132,000 was bona fide, considering the circumstances objectively. Thus considering this record, we are convinced that the evidence and reasonable inferences therefrom do reveal such a factual issue concerning that offer.

In the first place, the magnitude of the difference between the Hopkins appraisal, on which the $132,000 offer was based, and the Turner appraisal cannot be ignored in reviewing this summary judgment. Mr. Turner's appraisal, prepared at the request of plaintiff Rhodes, was for $77,500. The lowest appraisal obtained by Amoco from Mr. Hopkins was $132,000. Amoco's lowest appraised value is thus some 70% higher than the Turner appraisal obtained by plaintiff.

Viewing this factual record and reasonable inferences therefrom in the light most favorable to the party opposing summary judgment, the appraisal of Rhodes' expert, Turner, must be considered as evidence showing an accurate estimate of fair market value. It is important to note that Amoco offered no criticism of the Turner appraisal in its motion for summary

---

5. This bona fide offer requirement applies where an oil company terminates or fails to renew a franchise for a permissible business purpose unrelated to the franchisee's misconduct. *Slatky*, 830 F.2d at 478.

judgment and supporting papers. Instead, Amoco emphasized the process by which it made various earlier offers to Rhodes, suggesting that they prove the bona fides of its offer at issue. That evidence about earlier offers is not persuasive. Under the objective standard enunciated in *Sandlin*, the only issue here is whether a genuine issue of material fact was raised concerning whether Amoco's final $132,000 offer was bona fide. While "there may be a range of prices with reasonable claims to being fair market value," *Slatky*, 830 F.2d at 485, the evidence here clearly raises factual issues on the bona fide offer question. Amoco has provided nothing other than the Hopkins appraisal which would cast doubt on the analysis and conclusion reached by Turner. Amoco has provided no evidence as to the degree of discrepancy between the two appraisals in question which could be considered "normal" or reasonable.

Moreover, there is no response addressing plaintiff's other evidence. These specific points were developed by Mr. Turner in his affidavit, offered by Rhodes, each of which identifies asserted deficiencies in the 1995 Hopkins appraisal submitted by Amoco:

1. Although the primary structure of the service station was erected in 1953 and the car wash bay was added in 1975, Mr. Hopkins concluded, without explanation or documentation, that the "effective age" of the property was 15 to 18 years.

2. Hopkins did not account for the trend of declining sales at plaintiff's location over recent years, nor did he take into account the declining profit margins of retail service stations generally.

3. Hopkins did not consider the impact of two new, major competitors in the immediate vicinity of the subject property and their influence on traffic patterns.

4. In evaluating sales of comparable properties, Hopkins made adjustments to the sales prices on three properties without proper explanation or documentation.

5. In applying the cost approach, Hopkins used a replacement cost of $80 per square foot, while Turner recommended, based on his information and experience, a figure of about $58 per square foot.

6. Depreciation estimates given by Hopkins were mere opinion without supporting data.

7. Hopkins' cost approach reflects a lack of understanding of the changing business climate.

8. In using the sales comparison approach, Hopkins used the other sales in the area by Amoco, without adjustment for the fact that all of the buyers were "under duress" because of their relationships with Amoco; none of these sales should have been considered normal, arms' length transactions. App. at 282–85.

Plaintiff Rhodes also submitted an affidavit from Mr. Steve Martens, also a certified appraiser. A checklist was attached and incorporated in Martens' affidavit, which also identified a number of alleged deficiencies in the Hopkins appraisal. Among other things, Mr. Martens questioned why Mr. Hopkins had relied only upon the cost approach of estimating the market value. The standard procedure, he explains, is to prepare estimates using the cost approach, the income approach, and the comparable sales approach, before selecting the estimate which best represents fair market value. Mr. Martens concluded that the Hopkins appraisal was not acceptable. App. at 286–87, 293–94.

In sum, considering the record evidence before us in the light favorable to Rhodes, as we must in reviewing this summary judgment, we hold that there is a genuine issue of material fact whether Amoco's $132,000 offer in question was bona fide under the PMPA requirement. Accordingly, we reverse the summary disposition of that controlling factual issue without trial.

■ BALCOCK, J., dissenting: In enacting the Petroleum Marketing Practices Act, Pub. L. No. 95–297, 92 Stat. 322 (1978) (codified as amended at 15 U.S.C. §§ 2801–2841) (hereinafter PMPA), "Congress did not intend to intrude courts into the marketplace." *Sandlin v. Texaco Refining and Marketing, Inc.*, 900 F.2d 1479, 1481 (10th Cir.1990). Rather, Congress enacted the PMPA "to equalize the . . . disparity in bargaining power" between gasoline station franchisors and franchisees. *Doebereiner v. Sohio Oil Co.*, 880 F.2d 329, 331 (11th Cir.1989) (citing S. Rep. No. 95–731 (1978), reprinted in 1978 U.S.C.C.A.N. 873), amended on rehearing, 893 F.2d 1275 (11th Cir.1990). Regrettably, this court's opinion thwarts the intent of Congress by effectively tipping the bargaining scales in favor of the franchisee, and thrusting courts (at least in this circuit) into the franchise relationship.

To be sure, the question of whether a franchisor's offer to sell is "bona fide" as required by the PMPA, *see 15 U.S.C. § 2802*(b)(3)(D), addresses the fairness of the franchisor's treatment of the franchisee under an objective standard. *See Sandlin*, 900 F.2d at 1481. By requiring a "bona fide offer to sell," Congress undoubtedly intended to protect the franchisee from an unreasonably high offer price which would preclude the franchisee's purchase of the business and frustrate the franchisee's expectation of continuing the franchise relationship. Yet there can be little doubt that Congress' did not use the term "bona fide," with its notions of subjective good faith, *see Roberts v. Amoco Oil Co.*, 740 F.2d 602, 607 (8th Cir.1984), to place the franchisor at an obvious disadvantage. Rather, Congress' use of the term "bona fide" suggests that courts afford "some degree of deference" to a franchisor's valuation of its property. *Slatky v. Amoco Oil Co.*, 830 F.2d 476, 485 (3d Cir.1987) (en banc) (emphasis added). Otherwise, the PMPA would afford no protection to the franchisor's legitimate property rights and economic interests. While in this case the court's opinion gives lip service to Amoco's legitimate rights and interests, it effectively ignores them. Surely this was not Congress' intent.

This court's decision turns solely upon the disparity between Amoco's final independent appraisal of $132,000 and Rhodes' independent appraisal of $77,500. Twenty-three years of law practice taught me, however, that independent appraisers will typically appraise the value of property consistent with their clients' wishes, using the method of appraisal which most benefits their clients' interests. This is so because "the word 'value' almost always involves conjecture, a guess, a prediction, a prophecy." *Amerada Hess Corp. v. Commissioner*, 517 F.2d 75, 83 (3d Cir.1975) (internal quotations omitted). "There is no universally infallible index of fair market value. All valuation is necessarily an approximation." *Id*. After today, I can envision few cases in this circuit where a disgruntled franchisee will be unable to generate an appraisal sufficiently disparate from the franchisor's to require a jury trial, despite the ongoing objective good faith efforts of the franchisor to reach an agreement. Thus, a franchisor will "rarely rest comfortably" that its offer to sell is "bona fide." *Slatky*, 830 F.2d at 485. Because I believe based on the law and facts of this case that the appraisers' difference of opinion alone is insufficient to require a jury determination as to whether Amoco's offer to sell was "bona fide," I would affirm the district court's grant of summary judgment to Amoco. Accordingly, I dissent. [Judge Baldock's detailed analysis of the facts is omitted.]■

NOTES AND COMMENTS

1.   In a trial involving a local gas station operator and a major oil company over the value of the property, which party is more likely to request a jury? Are local juries the most appropriate bodies to determine value of real estate in their area? Will a jury easily be able to separate the value of the station that is created by the franchisee's own goodwill from other elements of value, as the court requires? Do you see why it is necessary to make such a separation?

2.   What is the policy rationale for giving the federal courts the responsibility of determining the price at which an oil company offers to sell a gas station to the local operator? Which interest groups would prefer such a forum? What arguments could be made in favor of (a) resolving these disputes in the state courts rather than the federal courts? (b) creating a remedy before some administrative agency such as the U.S. Department of Transportation? (c) leaving these disputes to be resolved by the private market?

The next time that you are tempted to complain about how long it has taken the federal court to reach your case, remember that the judge has the awesome responsibility of weighing different appraisals of gas stations. Chief Justice Rehnquist has consistently complained about the extent to which the Congress has assigned relatively minor issues to the federal courts, thereby aggravating the court congestion problem.

3.   On the other hand, although the issues under the PMPA may seem trivial today, the importance of legal control of the fuel distribution network may increase significantly if new engines are developed that use fuels other than gasoline. Assume, for example, that major car manufacturers were prepared to develop virtually pollution-free automobiles that were fueled by liquid hydrogen. In order to make it practical to use such engines

for anything except very localized transportation, it would be necessary either to arrange to supply the needed fuel throughout the existing network of gas stations, or else to set up an independent network of stations. This issue may need examination relatively quickly if technological advances in engine design proceed on their current course. See § 3, *infra*.

4.   As part of its general relaxation of earlier strict antitrust principles, the Supreme Court has held that it is not an antitrust violation for an oil company to fix the price at which its franchisee may sell gasoline or other fuels. *State Oil Co. v. Khan*, 522 U.S. 3 (1997). Will the ability to exercise this power have an effect on the future availability of alternative fuels at gas stations? *See also Portland 76 Auto/Truck Plaza, Inc. v. Union Oil Co. of California*, 153 F.3d 938 (9th Cir. 1998) (franchisee's lease of truck stop was not a "facility" within the protection of the Robinson–Patman Act.)

5.   State legislators have sometimes tried to respond to complaints by gas station operators about their treatment by the oil companies, but the oil companies have challenged rules that appear to favor local interests. In Chevron U.S.A., Inc. v. Cayetano, 57 F.Supp.2d 1003 (D.Haw.1998), the court held invalid a Hawaii statute that limited the rents that oil companies could charge dealers. The court found that the statute violated the Fifth and Fourteenth Amendments because it failed to advance a legitimate state interest for two reasons: (1) new dealers receive no protection because existing dealers could capture the value of the reduced rent in the form of a premium upon sale of their interest, and (2) incumbent dealers are not protected because the oil companies can offset rent reductions by increasing the wholesale price of gasoline.

c.   LEAKING UNDERGROUND STORAGE TANKS

The United States Environmental Protection Agency has been trying to deal with the millions of underground gasoline storage tanks at gas stations around the country that were beginning to corrode. A number of celebrated incidents occurred in which gasoline from rusted tanks leaked into drinking water wells or caused serious explosions underneath buildings.

Beginning in 1984, the Resource Conservation and Recovery Act (RCRA) authorized a special Underground Storage Tank (UST) program targeted specifically on this problem. 42 U.S.C. § 9001 *et. seq.* State governments may assume responsibility for administering the program if their program is approved by the EPA. 42 U.S.C. § 9007.

The EPA regulations adopted in 1988 gave gas station owners ten years to either upgrade their existing tanks, install new tanks meeting EPA standards for corrosion protection, or close down. 40 C.F.R. Part 280 and Part 281. Thus towards the end of the year 1998 gas stations all over the country were being ripped apart and put together again. Over a million tanks were closed between 1990 and 1998 and over 300,000 cleanups were undertaken. Bureau of Transportation Statistics, Annual Report 132 (1999).

Although there were some significant instances in which leaking underground tanks caused major health and safety problems, these were a very small percentage of the tanks that had to be replaced. The industry felt that the cost of the cleanup efforts required by the EPA far exceeded the relatively small amount of property damage that typically occurred.

The U.S. Environmental Protection Agency implemented a regulation requiring all underground storage tanks (USTs) in the U.S. to meet new specifications by December 1998. By the time the rule took effect, gas station owners had come a long way toward compliance. According to EPA's Sept. 30, 1998, tally, 1,236,007 underground storage tanks had been closed by the time the rule took effect—a larger number than the 891,686 still active tanks that had been equipped to comply with EPA's new requirements.

Many tanks were found to have been leaking (leaking underground storage tanks are called LUSTs). EPA reports 371,387 confirmed releases from LUSTs. As of early this year, a total of 314.965 cleanups had been initiated, and 203,247 of those had been completed. These compliance efforts have been costly. The average tank upgrade has cost about $125,000 recently. Indeed, the cleanup cost seems conceivably equal to the life savings of a gas station owner if one visualizes a sole proprietorship with an owner-operator. Where leaks had occurred, EPA mandated "free product removal." This meant that dirt was excavated and, if affected, groundwater was pumped from specially drilled cleanup wells in order to remove free product "to the maximum extent practicable." If only a small amount of dirt was contaminated, the cost was as low as $10,000. More extensive soil contamination cost up to $125,000. If groundwater was involved, costs ranged from $100,000 to over $1 million for drilling wells, pumping and treating water, monitoring, and so-forth. It was especially hard to eliminate spilled petroleum products from substrata and groundwater by pump-and treat methods. It was like trying to get gasoline or oil out of a rag by gently rinsing the rag with tap water.

[A California study by Lawrence Livermore Laboratory found] that, to recover a perceived property-value loss of a few tens of thousands of dollars, cleanup efforts can cost millions of dollars at a site with groundwater that poses a minimal risk or has limited beneficial use. The average cost of pump-and-treat groundwater cleanups has been $637,000/acre-ft of California water. New water supply sources can normally be developed at a cost of $700–900/acre-ft in California. The water that is affected by leaking underground fuel tanks is almost always shallow groundwater that was originally not recommended for use due to susceptibility to contamination from sewers, septic fields, etc. The total volume of California groundwater affected by leaking underground fuel tanks is less than 0.0005% of California's groundwater resources.

Craig S. Marsen, Costs of remediating underground storage tank leaks exceed benefits; Oil and Gas Journal, Aug. 9, 1999.

3. DEVELOPMENTS IN ENGINE TECHNOLOGY

The automobile industry has gradually been improving the efficiency of auto and truck technology. They have improved the rolling resistance of tires and added lockup torque conversion to transmissions to eliminate slippage at highway speeds. Engines have been improved by switching from carburetors to fuel injection, improving combustion control, and adding valves to improve engine breathing. These efficiency gains have been offset, however, by consumer switches to larger vehicles. Bureau of Transportation Statistics, Annual Report 105 (1999).

Continuing concern over air pollution from gasoline-burning internal combustion engines, aggravated by the awareness that over a quarter of United States greenhouse gas emissions come from the transportation sector's consumption of petroleum, has led to extensive research and development efforts to find clean, efficient substitutes for the traditional automobile and truck engines. These efforts have included attempts to produce electric cars and cleaner burning diesel engines, but at the present time the two most promising technologies appear to be (a) hybrid vehicles, that combine an electric motor and an internal combustion engine, and (b) fuel cell vehicles.

a. HYBRID VEHICLES

Toyota has been selling a hybrid automobile in Japan and plans to introduce it into the United States in the year 2000. The Japanese version of the Toyota Prius combines a 1.5 liter gasoline engine with an electric motor and a battery pack. When accelerating, the car uses the battery-powered electric motor. At higher speeds, the gasoline engine takes over, and uses excess power to recharge the batteries. In Japanese tests, the Prius got 67 miles per gallon in mixed city-country driving. It emitted about 90% less nitrogen oxides and carbon monoxide than comparable cars, and it reduced carbon dioxide emissions by 50%.

Honda is also introducing a hybrid vehicle in the United States. The two-seat Honda Insight also combines a gasoline engine and an electric motor. Tests by the EPA certified that the Insight got 61 miles per gallon in city driving and 70 miles per gallon on the highway. Most other auto manufacturers are also working on hybrid vehicles and are expected to introduce models soon. By comparison, many of the larger sport utility vehicles, which have been increasingly popular in the 1990s, get about 12 miles per gallon in city driving and 16 miles per gallon on the highway.

A joint venture of the automobile companies and several federal research laboratories has been working on the design of an energy-efficient vehicle since 1993 with the hope of introducing a prototype in 2004. The venture has focused on the design of a hybrid vehicle using diesel fuel. But the increasingly tight emission requirements being proposed by EPA may make it difficult to expand the use of diesel engines, as discussed in § 4, *infra*.

b. FUEL CELL CARS

Although fuel cells have been in widespread use for specialized applications, attempts to design automobile engines based on fuel cell technology were widely assumed to be far from any current relevance. In 1999, these assumptions began to change.

In March 1999, Daimler–Chrysler demonstrated a model of a hydrogen-fueled car that was much farther along than others in the industry had expected. The reaction in the industry was immediate: The Wall Street Journal said "not long ago, the fuel cell was dismissed as an environmentalist's pipe dream [but now] it is the subject of a heavily-financed research-and-development race among some of the world's biggest auto makers" Wall Street Journal, March 15, 1999, at 1.[6]

Georgetown University has built and operated a fuel cell bus pursuant to a Federal Transit Administration demonstration grant. The bus uses a 100 kW fuel cell manufactured by a Connecticut company, International Fuel Cells. The fuel cell is supplemented by a battery, which provides additional power for acceleration.

The Chicago Transit Authority operates three buses powered by hydrogen-powered fuel cell engines. The buses store compressed hydrogen in tanks mounted on the roof. The buses are refueled at a central station from tanks of liquid hydrogen.

For current educational information on fuel cell cars, a good source is the Los Alamos National Laboratory: www.education.lanl.gov/resources/fuelcells. Information on European research and development of hydrogen fuel cell vehicles can be found at www.hydrogen.org/index-e.html.

c. THE FUELS OF THE FUTURE

The demonstration of the prototype fuel cell car by Daimler–Chrysler led the refiners' trade journal *Octane Week* to editorialize that this "amazingly compact, fuel-efficient, prototype 2004 model year hydrogen fuel cell car signals a potentially devastating future for oil refiners. Unless they can come up with a fuel cell friendly fuel, such as zero-sulfur, zero-aromatics naphtha or a similar 'gasoline,' refiners may be unwise to assume the gasoline/diesel infrastructure guarantees their products have a place in the fuel cell fleet of the future." Fuels Industry May Be Turned Upside-down by Fuel Cell Revolution, Octane Week, March 22, 1999. On the other hand, the Oil Daily quoted the chairman of Chevron: "People have been predicting the death of the internal combustion engine for a very long time, and it hasn't happened.... But as I've said for years, if automobiles are going to run on milk, then we'll be in the milk business." Analysts Have Trouble Predicting Future Route for Fuel Cell Vehicles, 49 Oil Daily #60, March 30, 1999.

---

6. The development of vehicles powered by fuel cells is only one element, though a very important element, of a longstanding campaign of environmentalist Amory Lovins to transform the automobile industry. *See* Amory B. Lovins, L. Hunter Lovins & Paul Hawken, A Road Map for Natural Capitalism, 76 Harvard Business Review 145 (1999).

Milk is not currently in the cards, but extensive research is underway on virtually every other possible fuel alternative. It is too early to predict the eventual outcome, but many expert observers believe that there could be a substantial change in the mix of fuels by 2020. *See, e.g.,* Louella E. Bensabat, U.S. Fuels Mix to Change in the Next Two Decades, Oil and Gas Journal, July 12, 1999, p.46.

Among the alternatives is the continued use of gasoline, although it may need to be a cleaner gasoline, perhaps refined through the use of gas-to-liquids conversion methodology. Research is underway to try to develop a fuel cell that will generate electricity from gasoline. The German auto manufacturer BMW is working on a Solid Oxide Fuel Cell that will evaporate the gasoline, obtaining hydrogen through a splitting process in a reformer, which then reacts with oxygen in the air fed in during the process, generating electricity and, as a waste product, water. *See* BMW joins race to develop gasoline fuel cell vehicles, 14 Octane Week #18 (May 3, 1999).

Methanol is another alternative being given consideration. Currently, methanol is being refined for use as a gasoline additive (known as MTBE) that is required in areas with high ozone pollution. That additive is likely to be phased out because of concern about its potential for causing water pollution (*see* § 4, *infra*), which will force closing of methanol production facilities unless new uses are found. This has stimulated research into the use of methanol as an on-board fuel for fuel cell cars.

In California, a joint venture of auto and oil companies, in cooperation with the state government, has been formed to test fuel cell vehicles and determine how to make fuel available. ARCO, Texaco and Shell joined with Ford and Daimler–Chrysler to "address the fuel and infrastructure needs to support some 50 fuel cell vehicles planned for delivery between 2000 and 2003. Refiners offer oxidation, gasification, GTL fuels to fuel cell alliance, 14 Octane Week #17, April 26, 1999. Some of the demonstration vehicles will run on methanol, and the use of cleaner blends of gasoline will also be explored. See their web site, www.drivingthefuture.org, for the most current developments.

The use of liquid or compressed hydrogen is also being given consideration. This is assumed to be the most efficient power source for fuel cell operation, but it would require major changes in refining and distribution systems. In addition, major advances in technology are still needed in order to make the large-scale production of hydrogen economically efficient. Nevertheless, research in hydrogen technology is given high priority because the potential of this fuel would be so advantageous from an environmental perspective.

Other fuels for transportation that could possibly be the beneficiaries of scientific breakthroughs include liquefied or compressed natural gas, ethanol, propane, and new varieties of diesel fuel. *See* Bensabat, *supra.*

4.   AIR POLLUTION CONTROLS

Research and development of engine technology has been driven by two objectives, which are sometimes compatible but at other times seem to work at cross purposes. One is economic efficiency, heightened by the desire to reduce dependence on overseas sources of petroleum; the second is concern with air pollution caused by motor vehicles. The pollution-reduction objective is the charge of the United States Environmental Protection Agency, which lacks a strong mandate to improve energy efficiency. That goal is in the purview of the United States Department of Energy. The private sector sometimes finds itself pulled in two different directions by these two agencies.

a.   MOBILE SOURCE REGULATIONS

The EPA is authorized by the Clean Air Act to regulate emissions of harmful pollutants from mobile sources (motor vehicles). The Act gives the EPA the general power to promulgate "standards applicable to the emission of any air pollutant from any class or classes of new motor vehicles or motor vehicle engines, which in the EPA Administrator's judgment cause, or contribute to, air pollution which may reasonably be anticipated to endanger public health or welfare." 42 U.S.C. § 7521(a)(1). These standards apply for the useful life of the car. Currently that life is ten years or 100,000 miles starting in 1990, but vehicles are not tested after 7 years or 75,000 miles.

The EPA originally was slow to establish sulfur and particulate emissions standards as required by the 1977 amendments to the Clean Air Act. Indeed, the EPA failed to set such standards for over six years for autos, and for even longer periods for heavier vehicles, necessitating litigation by environmental organizations that forced EPA to meet court-imposed time-tables. *See, e.g., Natural Resources Defense Council v. Thomas,* 805 F.2d 410 (D.C.Cir.1986).

The EPA has promulgated separate standards for light duty passenger vehicles, light duty trucks, heavy duty vehicles and motorcycles. The Act requires that standards for carbon monoxide, hydrocarbons, nitrous oxides and particulates require the greatest degree of emission reduction technologically achievable. Indeed, EPA may set standards that are currently technologically feasible, or promulgate a higher technology-forcing standard. *Natural Resources Defense Council v. EPA,* 655 F.2d 318 (D.C.Cir. 1981). However, the EPA must consider whether these emission standards will be cost-effective, or endanger public safety.

Every new vehicle model and new emission control device must be tested by the EPA. § 206(a)(1),(2). The EPA may also randomly test new vehicles that have already been certified in conformity with the standards. If the vehicle does not pass, the EPA may suspend or revoke the certificate of conformity unless the manufacturer pays a non-conformance penalty ("NCP"). An attempt by EPA to avoid recall of nonconforming vehicles by requiring offsetting reductions of future year models was held invalid by the D.C. Circuit, but the court indicated that EPA had some discretion to consider offsets as part of an enforcement policy. *Center for Auto Safety v. Ruckelshaus,* 747 F.2d 1 (D.C.Cir.1984).

The Act preempts state regulation of mobile source emissions with the exception of California. (§ 209(a)) As a single experimental program, California may promulgate different emission standards subject to a waiver from EPA standards. The EPA may not require other states to adopt the California standards, *Commonwealth of Virginia v. EPA,* 108 F.3d 1397 (D.C.Cir.1997), but any state may voluntarily choose to adopt the California standards. *See* subsection c, *infra.*

While the CAA allowed other states to opt in to the California program (§ 209(e)(2)(B)), that power was voluntarily waived in 1998 by all of the Northeastern states as part of a National Low Emission Vehicle program, for which the EPA has now adopted regulations. www.epa.gov/orcdizux/lev-nlev.htm This program, after being approved by the Northeastern states and all auto manufacturers, disallowed those states from opting into the California emission standards, allowing the auto manufacturers to avoid having to meet California standards outside of California. In exchange the auto manufacturers agreed to produce and distribute certain quantities of LEVs to the Northeastern states by model year 1999 and the rest of the country by model year 2001.

A substantial obstacle to lower mobile source pollution is the proliferation of minivans and sport utility vehicles ("SUVS"), which are currently regulated under the lower light truck standard for emissions. The EPA has proposed that the light truck emission standard be brought into line with the passenger vehicle requirements. Auto manufacturers are understandably resisting this action. However, California has already brought light truck emission standards up to that of passenger cars for 2004, and Ford currently produces SUVs that meet those standards. Therefore it will be difficult for the other manufacturers to argue the technological unfeasibility of the higher standards. Indeed the California Air Resources Board (CARB) states that the new standards are attainable for $60 for passenger cars and $220 for SUVs.

The EPA is currently considering more stringent emission standards for mobile sources and requirements that petroleum refiners drastically reduce the sulfur content of gasoline as part of the "Phase II" emission regulations for mobile sources. The proposal seeks to lower sulfur levels in gasoline from the current average of 340 ppm to 30 ppm between 2004 and 2006. (This proposal will apply to all states except California, which already has the 30 ppm sulfur standard.) Reducing sulfur levels to 30 ppm would be the equivalent to removing 54 million cars nationwide. As with other emissions programs, refineries can earn credits for meeting the 30 ppm requirements early or by exceeding those requirements. These credits may be sold or used in to offset future shortfalls.

In response to this, oil companies have suggested their own plan, which would allow sale of 300 ppm sulfur gas in western states through 2004, and 150 ppm sulfur in eastern states with all states reaching 30 ppm by 2010.

The regulation split relies on the logic that western states should have more relaxed regulations because those states currently have low populations with fewer Clean Air Act violations. Additionally, the oil companies claim that this retooling will increase gas prices by up to six cents a gallon, while their plan would only raise prices 3 cents a gallon. The EPA, on the other hand, estimates an increase of a mere 1.7 to 1.9 cents per gallon to reach 30 ppm by 2004.

In apparent contradiction to their early stance on emission reductions, the auto manufacturers currently support the EPA's proposal to require oil refineries to retool to produce lower sulfur gasoline. This proposal would enable light trucks to lower emissions without applying new technologies because sulfur has been shown to inhibit the performance of catalytic convertors. However, auto manufacturers insist that advanced emission-control technologies being developed can only achieve lower emissions with even lower sulfur gasoline. Indeed, both domestic and foreign auto manufacturers have asked the EPA to further reduce allowable sulfur levels to 5 ppm.

Under the "phase II" plan, passenger cars will have to lower emissions to 0.07 gram per mile by 2007 and light trucks under 8,500 pounds will have to meet that same 0.07 gpm standard by 2009. Several passenger car classes already meet these new standards. This plan has been applauded by some environmental groups for "closing a 30–year loophole" and criticized by others for allowing less stringent emission standards for minivans and SUVs, and for allowing manufacturers ten years to apply technology that exists today. BNA Environment Reporter, May 7, 1999, at 7.

Problems regarding this new standard and the sulfur reduction proposal have come from unexpected directions and introduce a new balancing problem. First, advanced diesel engines, which will be capable of achieving 80 mpg by 2004, will not be able to meet the new emission standards. The Partnership for a New Generation of Vehicles, under which these cars are being developed, has been charged with establishing a policy regarding the trade off between fuel standards, emission regulations, and fuel economy, but has not yet done so. Second, refineries that retool to meet the 30 ppm standard will likely produce higher levels of sulfur in the refining process. *See* Gerald Parkinson, Refiners Ride a Rough Road, 106 Chemical Engineering #8, p. 48 (Aug. 1999). This increase may necessitate revised pollution permits from state and local authorities. In response, the EPA has encouraged states to streamline their re-permitting process and suggested that states allow refineries to offset the sulfur increases against the expected mobile emission reductions. For current information on the mobile source emissions program, see *http://www.epa.gov/ocfo-page/cj/g01all.htm*. For a thorough analysis of the history and current operation of the mobile source control program, *see* Arnold W. Reitze, Jr., Mobile Source Air Pollution Control, 6 The Envtl Lawyer 309 (2000).

b. FUEL COMPOSITION STANDARDS

Section 211 of the Clean Air Act ("CAA") (42 U.S.C. § 7545) gives the EPA authority over the composition of fuels. Historically, this section of the

CAA was first used to ban the sale of leaded gasoline. *Ethyl Corp. v. EPA,* 541 F.2d 1 (D.C.Cir.1976). Presently, every fuel manufacturer must register all fuels and additives that it wishes to sell. The manufacturer must provide the EPA with the name of each additive contained in the fuel, the concentration of that additive, and purpose for which the additive was added. Where the EPA finds that a fuel or additive may detrimentally effect the public health or the emission control system of any vehicle, it may control or prohibit its manufacture or sale.

The EPA's ability to prevent the use of certain additives under the CAA was challenged in *Ethyl Corp. v. EPA.* 51 F.3d 1053 (D.C.Cir.1995) (preventing use of MMT). While the court found that the EPA had improperly relied on a provision requiring that an additive not damage or impair a vehicle's emission control system (sec. 211(f)(4)), an earlier case between the same parties held that the EPA had the duty to consider public health in the evaluation of additives under section 211(a) and (c)). *Ethyl Corp. v. EPA,* 541 F.2d 1 (D.C.Cir.1976) (regarding EPA's ability to ban lead as gasoline additive). That interpretation of the CAA was reiterated by the 1977 amendments to the CAA which explicitly authorized the EPA to regulate fuels or fuel additives "which may reasonably be anticipated to endanger the public health or welfare." H.R. Rep. No. 95–294, 95th Cong. 1st Sess. 43–50 (1977). Current EPA regulations adopted pursuant to § 211(f)(1)(B), added in 1990, impose numerous restrictions on fuel additives for the purpose of protecting emission control devices.

In addition to regulating additives, the EPA enforces the requirements that reformulated gasoline ("RFG") be used in specified non-attainment areas. RFG must not have greater emissions than conventional gasoline, must contain at least 2.0% oxygen by weight, and some form of detergent to prevent efficiency-damaging deposits. Additionally, RFG may not contain any lead or other heavy metals, cannot contain more than 1.0% benzene by volume, and cannot exceed an aromatic hydrocarbon content of 25% by volume. Finally, during the high ozone season RFG volatile organic compound emissions must be 15% lower than that of conventional gasoline, and year round toxic emissions must be 15% lower than conventional gasoline. Manufacturers that exceed these minimum requirements are granted credits, which may be used for future production or sold to other manufacturers for the same non-attainment area.

The future of the RFG gasoline program is in some doubt because of growing concerns that MTBE (methyl tertiary butyl ether), which has been the additive favored by the oil industry for meeting oxygen requirements, has been the source of water pollution problems. In response to a recent University of California study concluding that adding MTBE to gasoline produces significant health risks while only minimally reducing emissions, California has banned the use of MTBE from gasoline sold in the state beginning in 2002.

The refiners claim that MTBE cannot readily be replaced. First, the other ether compounds, (ethyl tertiary butyl ether ("ETBE") and tertiary amyl methyl ether ("TAME")) that could replace MTBE, will likely also be found to cause similar health risks. If these ether compounds are allowed there is a question of how much can be produced in time to meet the 2003 deadline. Second, ethanol is the only other available additive that would allow the refiners to meet the 2 percent by weight oxygen requirement discussed in section . Ethanol suppliers are currently producing at full capacity to meet the needs of Midwest gasohol. These suppliers may not be able to increase production to meet the sizable additive requirements of all of California.

c. THE CALIFORNIA MODEL: STRICTER CONTROLS ON VEHICLES AND FUELS

The Clean Air Act contained a special provision allowing California to set its own mobile source standards without being preempted by the federal legislation Other states may opt into California's exception if they: 1) adopt standards identical to California's; 2) California receives a waiver from EPA for those standards; and 3) both California and opting state give manufacturers at least two model years to comply with new standards. The opt-in strategy was established so that auto manufacturers need only produce two different standards of vehicles, while allowing each state to mandate its own requirements would conceivably result in 51 different standards. Note that the opt-in states may still vary the target number of sales as long as the vehicle standards are equal to California's. *See American Automobile Manufacturers Assoc. v. Cahill,* 973 F.Supp. 288 (N.D.N.Y.1997).

California has set a fleet average requirement for non-methane organic ("NMOG") emissions, which becomes stricter each year. Auto manufacturers may meet these requirements by selling Low Emission Vehicles ("LEV"). The manufacturers also earn credits for selling more LEVs than required to meet the NMOG standard. The manufacturer may use these credits to offset future fleet emissions. In addition, unlike the federal fuel efficiency credits, the manufacturer may sell the emission credits to other manufacturers.

California had also originally required auto manufacturers to sell a specific number of Zero Emission Vehicles ("ZEVs") that produce no emissions directly from the vehicle. However, California has since repealed its ZEV sales quotas for 1998 (2%) through 2002 (5%), because of the limited range and performance of battery operated cars (the only currently available ZEV). California has not repealed its 10% quota for 2003, in expectation that new fuel cell technologies will allow manufacturers to produce a more commercially viable ZEV.

American Automobile Mfrs. Ass'n v. Cahill

152 F.3d 196 (2d Cir.1998).

■ WINTER, J.: In 1990, California adopted new regulations designed to reduce vehicle emissions. The regulations established, inter alia, a system under which new vehicles are classified into different low-emission categories according to the amount of pollution they emit ("LEV program"). Under the California regulations, the average emissions from the mix of the different vehicles sold in California by a given manufacturer in a given year must comply with an overall "fleet average" emissions standard. However, manufacturers have the flexibility to decide how many vehicles within each low-emission category they will produce and sell. Manufacturers can also meet the fleet average requirement through the use of credits, which can be obtained by producing more low-emission vehicles than required for a particular model year or which can be purchased directly from other manufacturers. The only limitation on the flexibility accorded manufacturers is a sales quota imposed for one category of vehicles, ZEVs. Under the regulations, two percent of all new vehicles certified for sale in California for model years 1998–2000, five percent for model years 2001–2002, and ten percent for model year 2003 were required to be ZEVs. The EPA approved California's plan and granted it the requisite waiver on January 7, 1993.

In 1992, New York adopted California's LEV program for light-duty vehicles pursuant to the Clean Air Act's opt-in provision. See *Motor Vehicles Mfrs. Ass'n v. New York State Dept. of Envtl. Conservation,* 17 F.3d 521, 529–30 (2d Cir.1994). New York's classification system, fleet average requirements, and ZEV sales requirements were identical, with one exception, to those of California for model years 1998–2003. That exception concerned medium-duty vehicles, which were included in California's ZEV requirements but not in New York's. We upheld the New York regulations in the face of a claim that they were preempted, holding that New York's LEV program fell within the "opt-in" provision of Section 177 (17 F.3d at 532–33).

California's classification system and fleet average requirements are still, with one exception, in force for model years 1998–2002. The exception is that California has abandoned the ZEV sales requirement for model years 1998–2002. It has replaced the ZEV sales requirement for those years in part with individual Memorandums of Agreement ("MOAs") with the seven largest automobile manufacturers, requiring specific numbers of ZEVs to be sold during calendar years 1998–2000. . . .

In the original Clean Air Act, Congress exempted California from federal preemption. The exception for California was in recognition of the fact that it, alone among the states, already had a regulatory scheme in place and that it faced special air pollution problems. The exception, however, was limited to California, in recognition of the burden on commerce that would result from allowing other states to set their own individual emissions standards. *See* H.R. Rep. No. 95–294, at 309 (1977), reprinted in 1977 U.S.C.C.A.N. 1077, 1388.

In 1977, Congress decided to amend the exception for California to allow other states "to adopt and enforce new motor vehicle emission standards which are identical to California's standards." *Id.* at 310, 1977 U.S.C.C.A.N. at 1389. The legislative history is clear that, under the broadened exception, "States are not authorized to adopt or enforce standards other than the California standards." *Id.* Finally, in recognition of the size of California's economy and demand for autos, Congress concluded that "this new State authority should not place an undue burden on vehicle manufacturers who will be required, in any event, to produce vehicles meeting the California standards for sale in California." *Id.*

If other states may adopt a "California standard" that is not in force in California, the consequences will be wholly at odds with congressional intent. First, under such a scheme, the Manufacturers will not "be required, in any event, to produce vehicles meeting the California standards for sale in California." Id. Instead, they might have to produce vehicles meeting the requirements of a single, much smaller state. Second, the Manufacturers might be required to comply with more than two—perhaps several—sets of emissions regulations. *See Commonwealth of Virginia v. EPA,* 108 F.3d 1397, 1401 (D.C.Cir.1997) ("There are two [federal and California], and only two, permissible sets of regulations limiting emissions from new cars sold in the United States."). Indeed, New York's ZEV sales requirement does not apply to medium-duty vehicles, as did the original California requirements. Were we to uphold New York's ZEV sales requirement under Section 177, then a third state might adopt ZEV sales requirements as to medium-duty vehicles, as California did originally, leading to at least four different regulatory schemes: federal, California, New York, and the third state.

We hold, therefore, that New York's ZEV sales requirement is preempted by Section 209 of the Clean Air Act and reverse. In view of our disposition of this matter, we need not reach the other arguments raised by the Manufacturers.■

NOTES AND COMMENTS

1. The state of Massachusetts has also tried to tighten auto standards by adopting a variation of the California standards for ZEVs. The First Circuit, by a circuitous route, eventually reached the same conclusion as the Second Circuit did in the above case; that the variation from the California standard rendered the Massachusetts standard invalid. *Association of International Automobile Manufacturers v. Comm'r, Massachusetts Dept. of Environmental Protection,* 208 F.3d 1 (1st Cir.2000). EPA has now reached agreement with the Northeastern states and the auto manufacturers on a National Low Emission Vehicle program, under which the Northeastern states have waived their right to adopt the California emission standards in exchange for agreements by auto manufacturers to produce and distribute certain quantities of LEVs.

2. As with emissions, California has its own plan for implementing reformulated gasoline ("RFG"). However, presently California does not have express authority to disregard the federal RFG rules. The federal oxygenate requirements are only required in federal emission non-attainment areas such as the Los Angeles basin and San Diego. California has set its own phase 2 RFG oxygenate requirements within the range of 1.8 to 2.2 percent by weight for the entire state of California. These requirements exceed

federal emission attainment areas standards, but do not satisfy the non-attainment standards.

The state has requested a waiver of federal oxygenate requirements, which would allow refiners to produce MTBE–free RFG without violating federal law and allow refiners to meet California's more flexible standards with a wider variety of additives.

Because of the questionable ability of ethanol or the other ethers to fully replace MTBE, California's phase 2 standards will depend on a decision of the EPA and/or Congress regarding the oxygenate waiver. If the waiver is not granted, California may not be able to simultaneously ban MTBE and meet the federal oxygenate requirement.

3. California also has its own standard for on-board emission diagnostic devices (OBDs). These devices monitor the operation of the emission control system and warn motorists if the system is not working properly by flashing a "check engine" light on the dashboard. Equipment manufacturers challenged certain anti-tampering provisions of the rules, but the rules were approved by EPA and upheld by the D.C. Circuit. *Motor & Equipment Manufacturers Ass'n v. Nichols*, 142 F.3d 449 (D.C.Cir.1998).

C. CONSTRUCTION OF TRANSPORTATION FACILITIES

Although the growing use of mountain bikes and all-terrain vehicles has made it possible for a certain amount of travel to take place without construction of on-the-ground transportation facilities, the vast majority of travel requires and will continue to require the construction of roads, railroads, seaports, airports or other such facilities. The nature and amount of the energy used in transportation is heavily dependent on the type of facilities that are constructed and their location and design.

1. TRANSPORTATION PATTERNS

As the United States evolved through the three phases of engine dominance, the vehicles propelled by those engines used a growing variety of routes over which to travel. The geography of the country reflected continually evolving transportation patterns. Post roads[7] and canals gave way to railway and streetcar lines, which in turn gave way to the highway network and hub airports that dominate American transportation today.

Early roads and shipping routes. In colonial times, post roads, river boats and coastal shipping connected the various colonies. With the formation of the federal government in 1789, Americans realized the need for transportation improvements that would tie the new nation together. In 1795, our first "superhighway," the Philadelphia to Lancaster turnpike, was constructed on a stone and gravel base with bridges across the

---

7. A post road was a road over which mail was carried by coach or horseback. Many post roads had stables situated at regu- lar intervals so that mail carriers could change horses.

numerous waterways, enabling year round travel without reliance on ferries. It stimulated construction of many other toll roads, and by the early years of the new century one could travel by stagecoach on improved roadways from Portland to Baltimore and inland as far as Carlisle, Utica and Rutland. D. W. Meinig, Atlantic America, 1492–1800 363–366 (Yale University Press, 1986).

From the outset, the federal government was given a significant role in the development and regulation of transportation. Of the three federal departments that were created initially, two had significant transportation responsibilities: The Post Office was authorized to establish post roads to assist in the delivery of mail; and the Department of the Army (which at that time employed virtually the only engineers in the nation) was charged with implementing the responsibility the framers gave to the federal government for facilitating interstate commerce.

President Jefferson promoted the construction of a "national road" that would open up the Northwest Territories. Begun in 1808, it eventually extended all the way to Vandalia. Bourne, *supra* at 6–10. Thus the framework was established at the outset for a strong federal presence in the development and regulation of highway transportation, though the importance of the federal role would wax and wane over the next two centuries.

The early years of the new United States also saw improvements in travel over water. Chaotic relations with Europe in the last quarter of the eighteenth century led American traders to expand connections with Asia. Trade with China and India required construction of larger sailing vessels, which increased the growing prosperity of eastern ports.

Meanwhile, an extensive program of canal-building was undertaken to facilitate the internal shipment of goods. When New York's Governor Clinton opened the Erie Canal in 1825 the cost of shipping goods from the Great Lakes region to New York City dropped dramatically. The canal was the clincher for the growing preeminence of New York City as the nation's commercial capital. And its success stimulated countless imitators in what became known as the American Canal Era of the 1830s and 1840s. In 1848, Chicagoans completed the canal that joined Lake Michigan with the Mississippi River, creating the last link in an inland waterway that stretched form New York City to New Orleans.

Railroads. With the development of the steam engine, tracks of iron rails were needed to bear the great weight of the railroad cars. The rail network that was created in the mid-nineteenth century greatly facilitated the shipment of goods around the country. In the years leading up to the Civil War, numerous privately financed railroads, aided by government land grants, connected much of the eastern half of the country with major western termini at St. Louis and Chicago.

But the aspiration that attained symbolic significance was the construction of a transcontinental railroad that would link California, with its burgeoning goldfields, with the rest of the nation. The railroads that joined together in Utah in 1869 to create the first transcontinental rail line "wrought a revolution in Western travel. It fixed in place the first full axis and quickened the pulse of the nation in all its Western extremities." D. W. Meinig, Transcontinental America, 1850–1915 27–28 (1998).

With the coming of the railroads, the shipment of goods was largely taken over by the railroads. Many of the turnpike companies went into bankruptcy, and their facilities were taken over by the government.[8] Canal companies also suffered in the competition with the railroads.

The railroad companies prospered, however, and the "tycoons" who ran them became both admired and despised as representatives of the no-holds-barred capitalist culture that dominated the United States during the latter half of the nineteenth century. With steam railroads providing competitive year-round transportation, and steam manufacturing producing competitive supplies of goods, the free market that the early political economists had hypothesized began to become a practical reality.

In the cities, construction of street railway networks (originally designed for horse-drawn cars and later electrified) created the opportunity for wide-ranging urban expansion. The construction of the first subway (in Boston in 1897) was followed by similar systems in New York, Chicago and Philadelphia. The first two decades of the century saw the expansion of streetcar and interurban lines throughout the country. Many of them were operated by private companies, though corrupt interrelationships with city politicians left the business with a bad odor.

Highways. With the country's attention and capital focused on railroads, roadbuilding languished. As the twentieth century began, however, pressure for better roads began to appear from a new source–bicyclists. The introduction of pneumatic tires for bicycles created heavy demand, and by 1896 a million bicycles were being sold every year. The League of American Wheelmen was formed to lobby for better roads. Bourne, *supra* at 110–111.

As quickly as 1910, however, it was apparent that it was the automobile that was going to be the vehicle that most needed roadways. The United States Department of Agriculture had created an Office of Road Inquiry in 1893 in response to the interests of bicyclists, and it had engaged in promotional activities to encourage local governments to build better roads. But at the outset of World War I, automobile production in America was running at about 200,000 per year and these drivers were getting tired of being stuck in the mud.

Automotive transportation began to promise the public a greater degree of flexibility than was available by rail. In response, a stronger federal highway agency was created to tie together the road networks being developed by the various states. After the end of World War I, President Wilson implemented the act that created the Federal Bureau of Public Roads as successor to the Office of Road Inquiry.

8. *See* the discussion of the extent to which investors in existing technology should be protected against technological changes in *Charles River Bridge Co. v. Warren Bridge Co., supra* Chapter 3.

The need for better roads was made apparent by the heavy influx of militarily-related truck traffic that had occurred during the war. The success of trucking for military goods inspired the birth of the interstate trucking industry, which joined in the demand for more and better highways. Tom Lewis, Divided Highways 10–11 (Viking Penguin, 1997). The Lincoln Highway, linking New York and San Francisco, was followed by other named routes that were motivated by tourism promotion.

The 1920s saw the creation of the framework of federal-state agency cooperation that continues to characterize the roadbuilding program. By this time, each state had created a road building agency to oversee construction of all major roads in the state. The federal government provides money, conducts research and sets standards, while the actual road construction and maintenance is undertaken by state highway officials. James A. Dunn, Jr., Driving Forces: The Automobile, Its Enemies, and the Politics of Mobility 28–29 (Brookings Inst. Press 1998).

By the end of the decade, agreement had been reached on the places where each state's roads would link up with those of its neighbors. Common systems of signage and numbering were established. As public fascination with the automobile grew, the federal money for highway construction increased each year.[9] The chief of the Bureau of Public Roads proclaimed the goal to "be able to drive out of any county seat in the United States at thirty-five miles an hour and drive into any other county seat–and never crack a spring." Lewis *supra* at 19. By 1930, American auto production had reached five million vehicles per year.

The depression that began in 1929 only increased the demand for road construction as a method of providing jobs for the unemployed. Presidents Hoover and then Roosevelt continually increased the flow of federal money into highway construction during the 1930s. Congress ensured that the federal money was spread throughout every congressional district, creating a network that emphasized extensiveness rather than capacity.

Airports. Air travel is bringing the regions of the country closer together. The widespread introduction of the jet plane into commercial aviation in the 1960s made it possible to conduct business in any two large cities in the country on the same day. With the deregulation of the airline industry in the late 1970s, the larger airlines established "hub" cities into which a high volume of travel was funneled, thus serving as stimulants to growth in those regions.

As airports expanded they frequently encountered conflicts with neighboring landowners and the local governments in which they lived. In *United States v. Causby*, 328 U.S. 256 (1946) the Supreme Court established the rule that government airports were liable under the taking clause only if they caused airplanes to fly so low over neighboring land that

---

9. As the demand for highways grew, the need for rural and branch railroad tracks declined. In the 1920s, the railroads began a pattern of track abandonment that has continued until the present day. Sarah H. Gordon, Passage to Union: How the Railroads Transformed American Life 344–345, (Ivan R. Dee, 1996.)

it prevented any reasonable use of the land. Nevertheless, under many state laws the neighbors of airports were successful in bringing nuisance actions that effectively forced airports such as Los Angeles International to acquire and destroy hundreds of homes in the flight path.

In addition, controversy has arisen about the extent to which local governments may impose controls on the hours of operation and flight path characteristics of airports without falling afoul of federal preemption.

Today, complaints about airport traffic are just as likely to relate to automobiles as airplanes. During busy periods, automobile traffic jams are a standard feature at major airports around the world. In many cases, air pollution buildups have become matters of increasing concern.

Many communities have turned to railroad connections as a means of solving airport traffic problems. At more than 140 airports around the world, new rail links are under discussion, in the planning stage or being built. Today, more than 70 of the world's airports have rail connections. See Andrew Sharp, Airport, Mainport, or Greenport, Airports International, May, 1999.

2.   LOCATION AND DESIGN REGULATIONS

Until the last 30 years or so, the law played only a minor role in the construction of transportation facilities. The government used the power of eminent domain to acquire the needed land, but except for land acquisition the lawyer played only a minor role in transportation. But the massive construction generated by the Interstate Highway program that began in the 1950s led to statutory changes that imposed new restrictions on the construction process.

a.   HIGHWAYS

During World War II, it became apparent that American highways were quite primitive in comparison with those of Europe. After the war ended, a broad coalition of trucking companies, auto manufacturers and oil companies lobbied for better roads. President Eisenhower persuaded Congress that an extensive upgrade of the highway system was essential to national defense. Kenneth T. Jackson, Crabgrass Frontier: The Suburbanization of the United States 248–251 (Oxford University Press, 1985).[10] Extensive debate was needed, however, before a way to pay for the program was settled.

The program came to fruition with agreement on the creation of the Highway Trust Fund. Dunn, *supra* at 34–35. Federal taxes were increased on gasoline, tires and other automotive supplies but the money was to be sequestered in a special fund to be used only for highway construction.

---

10. President Eisenhower often recounted how his recognition of the need for better highways was shaped by two personal experiences. In 1919, he was a participant in the first U.S. Army convoy to travel coast to coast–taking 62 days at an average speed of 5 miles per hour. And during World War II he saw how the autobahns made it possible for the German army to move troops and equipment efficiently. *See* Lewis, supra *at 89–91*.

Once this compromise was settled, the Interstate Highway program was shepherded through Congress in 1956 by Tennessee's Senator Gore and Baltimore's Congressman Fallon with little dissent. Lewis, *supra* at 115–117.

One key element of the compromise was that the new interstate system would be designed for trucks as well as automobiles. The trucking industry would be paying a significant share of the taxes going into the trust fund, so they argued that the system should be designed to meet their needs, including adequate vertical clearance and interchanges designed to enable a semi to barrel through without slowing down–a standard that greatly increased the total amount of land needed for interchanges.

Since the authorization of the interstate highway system, the dominance of trucking over railroads has gradually but steadily increased. The railroads have had to obtain federal legislation giving them indirect subsidies, and have merged in order to reduce competitive pressures (*see* Chapter 5). Trucks now account for well over four-fifths of the energy used in transportation of goods. Sustainable Future, *supra* at 43.

The beginning of construction of the Interstate system in the late 1950s was a time of considerable satisfaction. There were various controversies over the location of the routes and the bypassing of small towns, but in most rural areas the recognition of the value of greater accessibility outweighed the complaints.

Controversy erupted, however, when construction began on Interstate highways through urban areas. The wide highways and extensive interchanges required destruction of large amounts of housing and public facilities and the relocation of a great many unhappy people. In addition, the highways themselves were designed to move vehicles quickly, creating high noise volumes for neighboring properties. The urban interstates also cut off access to neighborhoods and destroyed the charm of many urban landscapes. The Department of Transportation enlisted the help of design professionals to assist the traditional engineers. Their proposals for such enhancements as sound barriers and visual amenities gradually worked their way into the engineers' bag of tools. See Department of Transportation, The Freeway in the City: Principles of Planning and Design, (G.P.O., 1968).

To reduce the cost of land acquisition and relocation, early highway builders often tried to map the route through low-income neighborhoods where property values and political savvy were low. Coming at a time of intense concern about civil rights issues, this practice was widely condemned as racially discriminatory, and allegations of differential impact of highways on racial groups continue to pose contentious issues of environmental justice. *See, e.g., The Jersey Heights Neighborhood Ass'n v. Glendening*, 174 F.3d 180 (4th Cir. 1999).

Even more attractive to highway builders was parkland. If the road could be built through a park no one would have to be relocated at all. However, this raised the ire of the advocates of urban recreation, who persuaded Congress to try to limit the use of parks for highways. This led to a famous decision of the Supreme Court:

Citizens to Preserve Overton Park v. Volpe

401 U.S. 402 (1971).

■ MARSHALL, J.: The growing public concern about the quality of our natural environment has prompted Congress in recent years to enact legislation designed to curb the accelerating destruction of our country's natural beauty. We are concerned in this case with § 4 (f) of the Department of Transportation Act of 1966, as amended, and § 18 (a) of the Federal–Aid Highway Act of 1968, 82 Stat. 823, 23 U.S.C. § 138 (1964 ed., Supp. V) (hereafter § 138). These statutes prohibit the Secretary of Transportation from authorizing the use of federal funds to finance the construction of highways through public parks if a "feasible and prudent" alternative route exists. If no such route is available, the statutes allow him to approve construction through parks only if there has been "all possible planning to minimize harm" to the park.

Petitioners, private citizens as well as local and national conservation organizations, contend that the Secretary has violated these statutes by authorizing the expenditure of federal funds for the construction of a six-lane interstate highway through a public park in Memphis, Tennessee. Their claim was rejected by the District Court, which granted the Secretary's motion for summary judgment, and the Court of Appeals for the Sixth Circuit affirmed. After oral argument, this Court granted a stay that halted construction and, treating the application for the stay as a petition for certiorari, granted review. 400 U.S. 939. We now reverse the judgment below and remand for further proceedings in the District Court.

Overton Park is a 342–acre city park located near the center of Memphis. The park contains a zoo, a nine-hole municipal golf course, an outdoor theater, nature trails, a bridle path, an art academy, picnic areas, and 170 acres of forest. The proposed highway, which is to be a six-lane, high-speed, expressway, will sever the zoo from the rest of the park. Although the roadway will be depressed below ground level except where it crosses a small creek, 26 acres of the park will be destroyed. The highway is to be a segment of Interstate Highway I–40, part of the National System of Interstate and Defense Highways. I–40 will provide Memphis with a major east-west expressway which will allow easier access to downtown Memphis from the residential areas on the eastern edge of the city.

Although the route through the park was approved by the Bureau of Public Roads in 1956 and by the Federal Highway Administrator in 1966, the enactment of § 4 (f) of the Department of Transportation Act prevented distribution of federal funds for the section of the highway designated to go through Overton Park until the Secretary of Transportation determined whether the requirements of § 4 (f) had been met. Federal funding for the rest of the project was, however, available; and the state acquired a right-of-way on both sides of the park. In April 1968, the Secretary announced that he concurred in the judgment of local officials that I–40 should be built through the park. And in September 1969 the State acquired the right-of-way inside Overton Park from the city. Final approval for the project—the route as well as the design—was not announced until November 1969, after Congress had reiterated in § 138 of the Federal–Aid Highway Act that highway construction through public parks was to be restricted. Neither announcement approving the route and design of I–40 was accompanied by a statement of the Secretary's factual findings. He did not indicate why he believed there were no feasible and prudent alternative routes or why design changes could not be made to reduce the harm to the park.

Petitioners contend that the Secretary's action is invalid without such formal findings and that the Secretary did not make an independent determination but merely relied on the judgment of the Memphis City Council. They also contend that it would be "feasible and prudent" to route I–40 around Overton Park either to the north or to the south. And they argue that if these alternative routes are not "feasible and prudent," the present plan does not include "all possible" methods for reducing harm to the park. Petitioners claim that I–40 could be built under the park by using either of two possible tunneling methods, and they claim that, at a minimum, by using advanced drainage techniques the expressway could be depressed below ground level along the entire route through the park including the section that crosses the small creek. . . .

Section 4 (f) of the Department of Transportation Act and § 138 of the Federal–Aid Highway Act are clear and specific directives. Both the Department of Transportation Act and the Federal–Aid Highway Act provide that the Secretary "shall not approve any program or project" that requires the use of any public parkland "unless (1) there is no feasible and prudent alternative to the use of such land, and (2) such program includes all possible planning to minimize harm to such park. . . ." 23 U.S.C. § 138 (1964 ed., Supp. V); 49 U.S.C. § 1653 (f) (1964 ed., Supp. V). This language is a plain and explicit bar to the use of federal funds for construction of highways through parks—only the most unusual situations are exempted. Despite the clarity of the statutory language, respondents argue that the Secretary has wide discretion. They recognize that the requirement that there be no "feasible" alternative route admits of little administrative discretion. For this exemption to apply the Secretary must find that as a matter of sound engineering it would not be feasible to build the highway along any other route. Respondents argue, however, that the requirement that there be no other "prudent" route requires the Secretary to engage in a wide-ranging balancing of competing interests. They contend that the Secretary should weigh the detriment resulting from the destruction of parkland against the cost of other routes, safety considerations, and other factors, and determine on the basis of the importance that he attaches to these other factors whether, on balance, alternative feasible routes would be "prudent."

But no such wide-ranging endeavor was intended. It is obvious that in most cases considerations of cost, directness of route, and community disruption will indicate that parkland should be used for highway construction whenever possible. Although it may be necessary to transfer funds from one jurisdiction to another, there will always be a smaller outlay required from the public purse when parkland is used since the public already owns the land and there will be no need to pay for right-of-way. And since people do not live or work in parks, if a highway is built on parkland no one will have to leave his home or give up his business. Such factors are common to substantially all highway construction. Thus, if Congress intended these factors to be on an equal footing with preservation of parkland there would have been no need for the statutes.

[The Court remanded the case to the district court with instructions to review the case under the Administrative Procedure Act.] Section 706 (2)(A) [of the Administrative Procedure Act] requires a finding that the actual choice made was not "arbitrary, capricious, an abuse of discretion, or otherwise not in accordance with law." 5 U.S.C. § 706 (2)(A) (1964 ed., Supp. V). To make this finding the court must consider whether the decision was based on a consideration of the relevant factors and whether there has been a clear error of judgment. Although this inquiry into the facts is to be searching and careful, the ultimate standard of review is a narrow one. The court is not empowered to substitute its judgment for that of the agency.■

NOTES AND COMMENTS

1. The *Overton Park* case came at the outset of the wave of environmental legislation that the 1970s produced. By indicating that the courts would review "informal" agency actions that had traditionally been thought subject to the agency's unreviewable discretion, the decision paved the way for the extensive role that the federal courts would play in reviewing environmental issues in ensuing years. The edited version of the opinion omits the discussion of the administrative law issues. For a fuller discussion, *see* Anderson, Glicksman, Mandelker & Tarlock, Environmental Protection: Law and Policy 149–161 (Aspen Publishing, 3d. ed. 1999).

2. In 1969, Congress adopted the National Environmental Policy Act (*see* Chapter 4, *supra*), which was soon interpreted to require environmental impact statements for the construction of segments of the interstate highway system. This led to extensive litigation on the issue of whether a particular segment of the system could be evaluated only in regard to its own direct impacts, or whether it would be necessary to consider the impact of other related segments as well, even at a stage when the location of related segments was still undetermined. Thus when Nebraska used federal funds to build a highway up almost to the boundary of a recreation area and planned to build the highway through the recreation area with state money, the District Court held that the impact of the state road on the park must be considered pursuant to NEPA because the segmented part of the highway did not have an independent utility separate from the project as a whole. *Patterson v. Exon*, 415 F.Supp. 1276 (D.Neb.1976). *See*

generally Daniel M. Mandelker, NEPA Law and Litigation § 9.04 (2d ed. 1992).

Congress has given many smaller highway projects categorical exemptions from NEPA. The DOT reports that 91.5% of highway projects fit within one of the categorical exemptions; 6.1% of the projects were the subject of environmental assessments but resulted in a finding of no significant impact; and only 2.4% required full scale environmental impact statements. Tom Ichniowski, The pace is slow on TEA–21's streamlining provision, 242 Engineering News Record, June 21, 1999 at 9.

3. In the 1960s, when it became apparent that the construction of the urban segments of the interstate highway system was going to be controversial, the federal government adopted a policy of shifting funds into the quick completion of the less controversial rural segments of the system. *See* Lewis *supra* at 162–163. The result was that the long stretches of rural interstate highways were largely completed during the 1970s while some of the most difficult urban segments were still not resolved in the 1990s.

A particular problem exists in regions that have failed to attain one or more of the standards for ambient air quality under the Clean Air Act. Here transportation projects cannot be approved unless they conform to the State Implementation Plan adopted pursuant to that statute. EPA regulations grandfathered many projects that had been in the planning stage during the 1980s, but these regulations were held invalid in a 1999 decision of the D.C. Circuit, forcing a halt to a significant number of complex projects. *Environmental Defense Fund v. Environmental Protection Agency*, 167 F.3d 641 (D.C.Cir.1999).

4. Highway construction is also often affected by the National Historic Preservation Act, 16 U.S.C. § 470 *et seq.* In a number of cases, litigants have used the act to force the redesign of major highway facilities to avoid destruction of historic buildings or interference with historic neighborhoods. *See* Comment, Old Stuff Is Good Stuff: Federal Agency Responsibilities Under Section 106 of the National Historic Preservation Act, 7 Admin. L. J. Amer. U. 697 (1993/94). The case law under the act tracks closely that of NEPA and § 4(f) of the highway act. *See* William H. Rodgers, Jr., Environmental Law 984–993 (West Group, 2d.ed. 1994).

In addition, state statutes modeled on NEPA frequently play a major role in the location and design of highways. *See, e.g., Montana Environmental Information Center, Inc. v. Montana Department of Transportation*, [2000 Mt. 5] 994 P.2d 676 (Mont.2000) (supplemental state EIS should have been prepared for highway interchange when patterns of development had changed since original EIS was prepared).

The interrelationship of all of the various laws has meant that the average time needed to obtain approval of a new transportation project is in the range of four years. *See*, e.g., *City of South Pasadena v. Slater*, 56 F. Supp.2d. 1106 (C.D.Cal.1999), relating the thirty-five year history of attempts to complete the 710 freeway. As part of the 1998 transportation legislation, Congress directed the Department of Transportation to adopt regulations designed to simplify and shorten the planning period. *See* § E 2 b, *infra*.

5. Highway agencies usually use "mitigation" as a way of reaching agreement on a project; i.e., they try to create new values similar to the values they will destroy so that they can show that the net effect is positive. In many cases, state highway departments end up buying substantial amounts of private land to be converted to conservation purposes in mitigation of their impact on park and open space land. *See, e.g., Illinois Dept. of Transportation v. Callender Construction Co.*, 711 N.E.2d 1199 (Ill.App.1999) (state highway dept. has authority to condemn private land to secure conservation areas to trade for areas to be taken for highway.)

b. AIRPORTS AND SEAPORTS

Construction of other kinds of transportation facilities also has faced new legal hurdles. The jet engine brought dramatically increased noise levels to airports, giving rise to increased complaints from neighbors, who have frequently challenged the environmental impact of airport expansions. *See, e.g., City of Los Angeles v. Federal Aviation Administration*, 138 F.3d 806 (9th Cir. 1998); *City of Richfield v. Federal Aviation Administration*, 152 F.3d 905 (8th Cir. 1998). In some areas, neighbors have prevailed in nuisance complaints against airport operators. *See, e.g., Seale v. Pearson*, 736 So.2d 1108 (Ala.Civ.App.1999).

In addition, airports have had to comply with federal regulations governing flight paths, which have determined what parts of the surrounding area would be exposed to the airplane noise. *See Morongo Band of Mission Indians v. Federal Aviation Administration*, 161 F.3d 569 (9th Cir. 1998). Local governments have often adopted ordinances seeking to impose limits on airport operations, such as curfews that prevented nighttime takeoffs or landings. *See, e.g., National Helicopter Corp. of America v. City of New York*, 137 F.3d 81 (2d Cir.1998). This has led to legislation and litigation about the extent of federal preemption, the standard for which was established in *City of Burbank v. Lockheed Air Terminal, Inc.*, 411 U.S. 624 (1973).

Seaports also face both NEPA compliance and compliance with the Coastal Zone Management Act, 16 U.S.C. § 1451 et seq. The act requires federal and federally funded facilities to be consistent with a state's coastal zone management plan. It gives state governments a greater say in the location and operation of federal facilities than is typically found outside the coastal zone. *See* Rutherford H. Platt, Land Use and Society 410–418 (Island Press, 1996).

D. The Energy Cost of "Sprawl"

Technological changes in transportation have greatly influenced patterns of land development in the United States. The greater mobility that people obtain from modern transportation technology has led to a dramatic change in the American landscape. Americans are increasingly living in thinly scattered and decentralized locations, with the result that Americans each year expend more energy getting from place to place. Awareness of the influence of transportation on the quality of life has grown gradually:

> Transportation planning tends to be oriented to future conditions, because new projects take so long to build. But it is difficult to get the public interested in long-term plans if no problem exists currently. The public generally responds best when there is a crisis. Traffic congestion became that crisis in the 1980s, especially in those new suburban centers that blossomed.... The traffic attracted to edge cities and the new fringe beehives of business and commerce quickly expanded to fill up the remaining highway capacity, and caused lengthy traffic delays. Traffic congestion became a media topic, locally and nationally.

Robert T. Dunphy, Moving Beyond Gridlock: Traffic and Development 1–2 (Urban Land Institute, 1997). Ironically, the construction of those office and commercial complexes on the urban fringe was originally stimulated by the hope of attracting employees who wanted to avoid the traffic congestion that they then associated with the older cities.

At the present time, the transportation sector uses about one-fourth of all of the energy consumed in the United States. The transportation sector uses over 65% of the petroleum consumed in the United States, and highway vehicles account for 84% of that amount. This means that transportation uses the equivalent of all of the domestically produced oil and 40% of our oil imports. Bureau of Transportation Statistics, Annual Report 104–106(1999).

Studies of alternative transportation patterns employing higher building densities and more mass transit suggest that dramatic savings in energy use would be achieved by changes in land use patterns. Analyses of European cities that use such patterns, and model simulations of American cities, all suggest that substantial savings could be achieved. *See* Judy S. Davis & Samuel Seskin, Impact of Urban Form on Travel Behavior, 29 Urban Lawyer 215 (1997). Whether such changes can be accomplished, however, is a serious question.

1. Automobile-Oriented Decentralization

In modern times, land development has been extending far out into the countryside as residential and commercial developers open up new areas to the driving public. People are driving longer and longer distances and the traffic is continually getting worse. This pattern of decentralized urbanization is commonly referred to as "sprawl."

Modern development patterns contrast sharply with those that prevailed when the country was founded. The cities of the eighteenth century tended to be small and compact. Horsedrawn vehicles' limitations made it impractical to travel long distances to work on a daily basis.

In the nineteenth century, railroads made it possible to move goods to central locations for consolidation and transshipment. This spurred the expansion of port cities such as New York and San Francisco. And "Chicago's location at the breaking point between eastern and western rail networks ... maintained Chicago's railroad hegemony for the rest of the century." William Cronon, Nature's Metropolis 83 (Norton, 1991).

The most significant technological innovation that triggered the expansion of cities was the streetcar. Development of land on the outer fringes of urban areas was stimulated by the availability of streetcar lines that made it easy to reach the downtown area.

Automobiles brought a new mobility, unhindered by the need for extensive track systems. As the road network grew, buses replaced streetcar lines as the most common form of mass transportation. As more people acquired their own automobiles, the pattern of urban development began to change.

Many promoters of road construction saw themselves as providing a healthier alternative to the "teeming cities," which they saw as increasingly overcrowded. Henry Wallace, the Secretary of Agriculture in President Roosevelt's cabinet, said that "decentralization properly worked out in connection with concrete roads and electricity will have a lot to do with providing a more satisfactory life for the next generation." Lewis, *supra* at 52. Roads were widened into highways and connected by interchanges that greatly increased the speed of travel, but only for a while. Retailers began to move out of downtown areas into new shopping centers scattered throughout the urban areas. Jackson, *supra* at 257–261.

Meanwhile, the federal government stimulated new housing developments in outlying areas through federally guaranteed home loans. Federal tax laws, which permitted homeowners to take a tax deduction for home mortgage interest, stimulated families and individuals to invest in a home. And if they sold the home, they were required to invest the proceeds in another equally expensive home or pay capital gains tax, thus providing further stimulation to the housing market. Christine A. Klein, A Requiem for the Rollover Rule: Capital Gains, Farmland Loss, and the Law of Unintended Consequences, 55 Wash. & Lee L. Rev. 403 (1998).

High inflation in the 1970–85 period further stimulated homeownership as the values of homes went up dramatically. An entire generation came to believe that the best way to keep up with inflation was to buy a home because home prices always went up at a rate exceeding the inflation rate.

Most of the new homebuilding was in outlying areas rather than in the cities. Older housing in the cities was suffering from neglected maintenance during the depression and the war, and urban renewal programs were seen as ways to clear out the slums so that people could move to a better life in new housing. Robert Moses, the master builder of transportation facilities, saw highway building as one element in a desirable program to replace slums with highways, move slum dwellers into better high rise public housing, and open up the suburbs for the middle classes.

Office buildings also started seeking locations on the fringes of urban areas where land was less expensive. As traffic generators scattered throughout metropolitan areas, the radial network of rail and road ways that had been typical of early 20th century cities became unsuited to the non-radial travel patterns that were becoming typical. Frequently a "beltway" circling the metropolitan area became one of the most heavily traveled routes. Highways that were built to bring workers downtown ended up carrying their heaviest traffic in the opposite direction as city workers commuted to suburban jobs. Dunphy, *supra* at 33–35.

In summary, current patterns of land development emphasize single family homes at relatively low densities in developments designed on the assumption that virtually all residents would travel by private automobile. The great amount of space needed to accommodate this pattern has meant that the mileage traveled per household has increased rapidly. And with trucks replacing railways as the primary means of goods transport, the road network has absorbed a growing share of American energy consumption.

2. Factors That Have Fostered Current Trends in Transportation

In the twentieth century, Americans' energy choices have affected every area of production and consumption, but it is in transportation where these choices have most dramatically increased our energy consumption. As David Nye puts it, "Most farmers abandoned horses and oxen for tractors, [and] motorists preferred large cars with poor fuel economy; [while the federal government] spent billions of dollars on interstate highways instead of on mass transit. And during the 1970s the federal government signally failed to develop a coherent energy policy. As the result of all these decisions, made by the people or their institutions, the United States became the largest consumer of energy in the world's history." David Nye, Consuming Power 255–56 (MIT Press, 1998).

The reasons why the people of the United States have chosen to expend such a large share of their budgets for transportation are many and complex. Any listing of them would include the following dozen:

[1] Automobile merchandising. The American's reputed love affair with the automobile is often cited as the cause of our increasingly decentralized pattern of development. In comparison with other industrialized countries, such as Japan or the European countries, Americans take far fewer trips by public transportation. Is our lifestyle simply a matter of what the economists would call a "taste" for private transportation? Or are there factors about American society at the turn of the millennium that make our development pattern more efficient than its critics recognize?

[2] Growth in trucking. It was the trucking industry's powerful political support for federal gasoline taxes to fund federal spending on highways has facilitated the rapid development of the federal interstate highway network. Although automobile drivers must share the network with more and heavier trucks, the network's increased efficiency has made it possible to extend significantly the mileage that drivers are willing to commute, thus greatly increasing total energy consumption.

More recently, the growth of the trucking industry was been facilitated by the deregulation of most shipments and the development of more entrepreneurial management. The deregulation of the trucking industry has brought about significant competition in trucking while railroad ownership is becoming increasingly concentrated.

The volume of truck movements has also grown as a result of the increased emphasis in American industry on the use of sophisticated logistics to move resources and products so that they are the right place at the right time. *See* W. Bruce Allen, The Logistics Revolution and Transportation, 553 Annals of the American Academy of Political and Social Science 106 (1998).

[3] Workforce expansion. Another factor that has driven up the usage of energy in transportation is certainly the growth of the workforce. The so-called baby boom generation began to reach driving age in the 1960s and began entering the workforce around 1965. The number of licensed drivers doubled between 1960 and 1980; and between 1965 and 1985 the labor force grew at a rate of 2.1% per year, nearly twice the rate of growth from 1950 to 1965. Sustainable Future, *supra* at 44–45.

Equally striking was the increase in two-income families. In early 1999, 46.4% of the working population was female, and the ratio has been increasing steadily. Bureau of Labor Statistics, Employment and Earnings (February, 1999) p. 8. With two people in the household traveling to employment, a homesite located near one particular jobsite becomes less important than a location conveniently situated for access to the overall highway network.

And the automobile makes it possible to combine trips for work and shopping or pleasure in ways that are difficult on public transportation; this efficiency is particularly valuable to the time-sensitive two-income family. Among two-parent families with children, the amount of time spent on paid work increased by 18% between 1969 and 1996. Council of Economic Advisers, Families and the Labor Market, 1969–1999: Analyzing the "Time Crunch" (May, 1999).

[4] Privacy and security. Traditionally, Americans have sought a higher degree of personal space and privacy than people in other cultures, and the private automobile satisfies this desire. Charles L. Wright, Fast Wheels, Slow Traffic 115–118 (1992). Psychologists have observed, for example, that a group of Americans who converse with each other will stand farther apart than similar groups from most other cultures. This demand for more private space is rewarded on American roadways where the vast majority of cars carry a single occupant.[11] .

11. "At first, electricity and the automobile enlivened the city, reinforcing its density and bringing mobility and kinetic excitement to its daily round. Eventually, however, they were used to undermine the central city as Americans moved to suburbs and em-

[5]   The climate-controlled lifestyle. The pervasiveness of air conditioning in homes and businesses has also increased the demand for the kind of air conditioned door-to-door travel that the automobile can provide. The EIA's 1997 Residential Energy Consumption Survey showed that 72% of American households have air conditioning. The downtown business districts of cities with climates as varied as Minneapolis and Houston have invested significant sums in the creation of enclosed walkways among office buildings that preserve the climate-controlled environment, and the enclosed regional shopping mall has become a fixture throughout the country.

These trends are responding to the fact that white collar workers, who make up a growing segment of the population, seek to avoid exposure to weather-related inconveniences. The executive who commutes from the climate-controlled garage attached to her single-family house to the climate-controlled garage attached to her office building may be able to dress with complete disregard for outside weather conditions.

[6]   Perception of safety. Although nearly 50,000 people each year are killed in auto accidents in the United States, people tend to downplay the danger. Howard Margolis, Dealing With Risk 38 (University of Chicago Press, 1996). Despite the high risk of automobile accidents, many Americans say that they actually feel safer in their car than in public transportation. Accidents involving public transportation tend to receive more media coverage than the routine fatalities in auto accidents. And the fear of contact with criminal behavior on public transportation is one of those risks that ranks higher in public perception than statistics would support.

[7]   Cellular telephones. The development of extensive networks of towers that facilitate the use of cellular telephones in most of the populated areas of the United States has meant that automobile drivers can conduct business or otherwise engage in "multi-tasking" while driving their vehicle. This makes the traffic jam less of a threat to productivity than it was a decade earlier. Although the safety implications of this practice are somewhat alarming, it continues to be popular.

[8]   Job-shifting. Increasing job mobility has accentuated the need for flexibility in housing location. The number of people who predict that they will remain at the same job for a long period of time has been declining steadily, and the 1990s' downsizing of large corporations and growth of entrepreneurial start-ups has continued to encourage the trend to seek flexibility over stability in home location.

[9]   Greater affluence. Reliance on the private automobile is also simply a product of increased wealth. All industrialized countries have seen increases in automobile ownership, but the increase in the United States has been particularly notable. In 1950 there were just under 7 automobiles in the United States for every 10 licensed drivers; by 1980 the ratio had passed 1 to 1. Sustainable Future, *supra* at 41.

braced a more private form of popular culture." Nye, *supra* at 158.

Although many of the newly affluent are more conscious of environmental issues than members of preceding generations, that has not necessarily lead to reduced energy consumption. Every improvement in gas mileage was counteracted by more cars and more mileage driven per car. In the decade preceding 1997 annual motor vehicle travel increased nearly 30%. *Id.* Environmentalists might jog for their health but rarely walked to work, and a love for the outdoors often meant wanting to live as far from the city as possible.

[10] Information technology. The rapid growth of advanced information technology in the 1990s has also contributed to new transportation and development patterns. The need for centralized locations for "office work" has begun to diminish, and increasing numbers of people work at home for part of the week Dunphy, *supra* at 36–37.

As this trend continues it will reduce the importance of home-to-work transportation in the selection of a residence, which may benefit both rural and urban locations at the expense of traditional suburbs. A growing number of individuals who work in e-commerce out of their homes have wide-ranging choices of where to live. Some Western states that once relied on resource extraction as their economic base are coming to realize that it is "resource attraction" that is bringing in new entrepreneurs who can work from any place that a satellite can see. *See* Thomas Michael Power, Lost Landscapes and Failed Economies 41–43 (Island Press, 1996).

[11] Cheap land. Much new development takes place at the edge of metropolitan areas in "a peripheral zone, perhaps as large as a county, that has emerged as a viable socioeconomic unit. Spread out along its highway growth corridors are shopping malls, industrial parks, campuslike office complexes, hospitals, schools and a full range of housing types. Its residents look to their immediate surroundings rather than to the city for their jobs and other needs; and its industries find not only the employees they need but also the specialized services." Robert Fishman, Bourgeois Utopias: The Rise and Fall of Suburbia 184 (Basic Books, 1987). The name "edge city" has become commonly used for these areas. *See* Joel Garreau, Edge City: Life on the Urban Frontier (Doubleday, 1991).

[12] The highway lobby. Such a wide range of interest groups are so well organized in support of government money for road construction that it has long been difficult to obtain support for any other mode of transportation. Automobile manufacturers, oil companies, truckers, farmers, land developers; all are comfortable with a system that provides extensive financial support for the maintenance of the network on which the existing pattern of development is dependent. *See* Dunn, *supra* at 23–30.

* * *

All of these factors have stimulated increasing movement into formerly rural areas, thereby stretching out the time of travel if not its frequency. If we are going to reduce our consumption of energy for transportation, we must either begin to reverse these development patterns, or find new technological ways of traveling within the current pattern without using so much energy, or both.

Americans' preferences for sprawling growth, automotive movement, and individualistic heating and housing impose conditions on their future energy choices. As the United States prepares to enter a new century, the federal government and the major automobile manufacturers are investing billions of dollars in electric cars, hybrid cars, solar cars, and smart cars that will drive themselves. Such planning makes sense so long as consumers choose to remain spread out. Nye, *supra* at 257–58.

But are current trends inevitable? Dissatisfaction with existing modes of transportation and development patterns is increasing for a variety of reasons.

3.   FACTORS CREATING PRESSURE FOR CHANGES IN TRANSPORTATION

Despite the reasons for continuing support of a pattern of development of spread-out living with ever-increasing reliance on automobiles and trucks to connect everything together, a backlash has been gradually developing. It has developed on two fronts: (a) attempts to accommodate to the current development pattern but expend less energy, and (b) attempts to promote a more concentrated development pattern that would facilitate more use of mass transit.

[1]   **Air pollution.** Motor vehicles are recognized as a serious source of air pollution. Motor vehicle exhaust includes carbon monoxide, nitrogen oxides, volatile organic compounds and particulate matter. Nitrogen oxides and volatile organic compounds are the major contributor to smog, which can be hazardous to people with many common breathing disorders, as can particulate matter. In the concentrations found in some traffic "hot spots," carbon monoxide can slow peoples' reflexes and contributes to safety problems.

[2]   **Climate change.** Recently attention has been focused on the extent to which transportation is responsible for the emission of greenhouse gases that may be contributing to climate change. (See Chapter 17.) If future trends continue, transportation within the United States will be contributing a third of the nation's emissions of atmospheric carbon dioxide, the most prevalent of the greenhouse gases. James J. MacKenzie, Driving the Road to Sustainable Ground Transportation 121, 126–27 in Frontiers of Survival (World Resources Institute, 1997).

[3]   **Concern about oil imports.** Americans have been nervous about the extent to which the national economy, and particularly the transportation system, has become increasingly dependent on imported oil. The overall transportation system is the largest user of oil in the U.S. economy and is almost completely dependent (97%) on oil. About two thirds of the oil we use goes directly into transportation. And, as indicated in

Chapter 16, the percentage of our oil that comes from overseas is projected to rise each year.

Our reliance on imported oil has led us to become involved diplomatically and at times militarily in the affairs of those parts of the world from which we get our oil. This has not only contributed to high defense budgets but has frequently embroiled us in hostile relations with countries that have turned potential trading partners into enemies.

[4] Safety. Highway safety became a growing concern of the federal government under pressure from Ralph Nader, whose book Unsafe at Any Speed (Grossman, 1965) attained wide popularity. Congress created the National Highway Traffic Safety Administration and authorized it to set safety standards and order recalls. The automobile manufacturers were required to install airbags and undergo safety testing of vehicle models. In 1974, Congress adopted national speed limits designed to increase safety and reduce energy consumption in response to the first oil shock, but these were relaxed after gasoline prices came down.

[5] Noise. People who live near transportation facilities have become increasingly vocal objectors as transportation volumes have increased. Most large scale forms of transportation create noise that can be unpleasant at close range. Residents of areas near airports have often persuaded authorities to impose curfews and specific takeoff and landing patterns designed to reduce noise. Highway departments are increasingly installing sound barriers alongside freeways to reduce the noise level in residential neighborhoods.

[6] Traffic congestion. The users of the highways are also expressing frustration with steadily growing traffic congestion and increased home-to-work travel time. Recent studies show that there continues to be an increase in (1) the number of licensed drivers, (2) the number of trips per driver, and (3) the length of the average trip. MacKenzie, *supra* at 151–152. As economist Paul Krugman puts it, "when few people have cars, the one-car family is king, but when everyone has two, a lot of time is spent in traffic jams." Paul Krugman, Money can't buy happiness. Er, can it?, New York Times, June 1, 1999, p.23, col. 2.

[7] Alienation. Concern about loss of a sense of community is also part of the growing dissatisfaction with current land use patterns. It is commonly believed that people are spending less time in social or civic pursuits and more time alone. A "tendency for social life to become 'privatized,' and to a reduced feeling of concern and responsibility among families for their neighbors ..." has been noted by many observers. Jackson, *supra* at 272.

[8] Lack of open areas. In many parts of the country, voters are beginning to protest the lack of open space and natural habitat in metropolitan areas. Throughout the West, for example, people speak of their fear of their community becoming "Los Angelized." In the late 1990s, voters began to show solid support for bond issues to protect open space through land acquisition.

[9]   **Sprawl.** The word "sprawl" has become a common opprobrium for the pattern of land development that relies on the private automobile for transportation. Voters have been expressing a growing dissatisfaction with the phenomenon of widely dispersed low-density land development. "Sprawl is self-perpetuating: the dominance of the automobile among our transportation choices makes low-density development possible; low-density development, in turn, makes us more dependent on automobiles for access to increasingly dispersed locations for employment, services, and recreation. This is bad news for all, but especially for those who are unable to use cars as a primary mode of transportation, including the poor, the disabled, the elderly, and children." F. Kaid Benfield, Running on Empty: The Case for a Sustainable National Transportation System, 25 Envtl. L. 651, 657 (1995).

Although the interrelationship of highway projects and sprawling development is widely assumed[12], few governmental units in the United States have successfully managed systems for identifying and regulating the growth-inducing impacts of transportation projects. Marie L. York, Dealing with Secondary Environmental Impacts of Transportation, 51 Land Use L. & Zoning Digest 3 (March, 1999). New growth management initiatives continue to seek to integrate transportation and land development. *See* § F, *infra.*

[10]   **Tax resistance.** Perhaps the most important cause of dissatisfaction with the existing patterns of transportation and land development has simply been the voters' resistance to spending money on the public works projects that would be needed to reduce congestion and improve efficiency. During the first two oil shocks between 1979 and 1981, the high rates of inflation doubled the cost of highway construction and maintenance, causing great political reluctance to raise the taxes needed to keep highway construction going. Mark H. Rose, Interstate: Express Highway Politics, 1939–1989 113 (University of Tennessee Press, rev. ed., 1990).

This aversion to expenditures affected public works projects of all sorts. Lester Thurow points out that "public infrastructure investment has been cut in half over the past twenty-five years and has fallen to the point where the stock of public capital is now declining relative to the GDP–falling from 55 to 40 percent of GDP in the last decade. Less is being invested in public infrastructure in the United States than in any of the [developed] countries–one third as much as Japan." Lester Thurow, The Future of Capitalism 291 (1996).

During the Reagan administration, a policy decision was made to use virtually all federal highway funds for repairs rather than new roads, with the result that between 1981 and 1989 total highway mileage increased only 0.6% while total vehicle miles driven went up over 33%. Anthony Downs, Stuck in Traffic: Coping with Peak–Hour Traffic Congestion 11 (Brookings Institution, 1992). Most capital spending today is on renovation,

12.   Not everyone shares the conviction that the automobile is primarily to blame for   decentralization, which in fact began a century ago. *See* Dunn, *supra* at 146–147.

rehabilitation and widening of existing highways rather than on new route construction. Sustainable Future, *supra* at 51. Whether the increased public spending projected in the 1998 federal highway legislation will begin to reverse this trend remains to be seen.

E.   FEDERAL LEGISLATIVE RESPONSES

In response to these concerns, Congress has adopted a number of new programs designed to reduce the energy consumption and pollutant output of motor vehicles. Congress has been very reluctant to address the issue of land use patterns[13], which has traditionally been considered an area of state and local policy, and some state and local governments have begun to address these issues (*see* section F, *infra*).

1.   FUEL ECONOMY STANDARDS

In response to the first oil shock, the Congress adopted in 1975 the Corporate Average Fuel Economy (CAFÉ) program designed to require vehicle manufacturers to sell more fuel-efficient automobiles. The program set minimum miles-per-gallon requirements for automobile and light truck manufacturers based on total vehicle sales. It requires auto manufacturers to produce a total output of cars that averaged over the minimum standards for miles-per-gallon, but left the companies the discretion to create whatever mix of vehicles they chose as long as the average complied with the standard.

In 1975, the federal government set the average fuel economy for passenger automobiles, at 27.5 miles per gallon (mpg). 49 U.S.C. § 32902. This regulation went into force for the 1985 model year. The fuel economy program enumerated exceptions for emergency vehicles, dedicated alcohol or natural gas vehicles and manufacturers of less than 10,000 autos per year. More importantly, the program provided mechanisms to modify the average mpg across the board or to provide exemptions from the national standard for individual manufactures to reflect the maximum feasible average for that model year. The Secretary of Transportation could lower the average down to 26.0 mpg before she must submit an amendment to Congress. Any increase above 27.5 must also be submitted before Congress for approval. *Id.* The Secretary lowered the average down to 26.0 in 1986, but the average has remained at 27.5 since 1990.

Where a manufacturer is unable to meet the national standard it must either pay a $5 fine for each .1 mpg that the manufacturer's fleet is below the standard multiplied by the number of cars in the fleet (49 U.S.C. § 32912) or it can elect to submit a plan to the Secretary of Transportation.

---

13. The indirect impact of federal programs on patterns of land development is significant but also complex. *See* William W. Buzbee, Urban Sprawl, Federalism, and the Problem of Institutional Complexity, 68 Fordham L. Rev. 57 (1999).

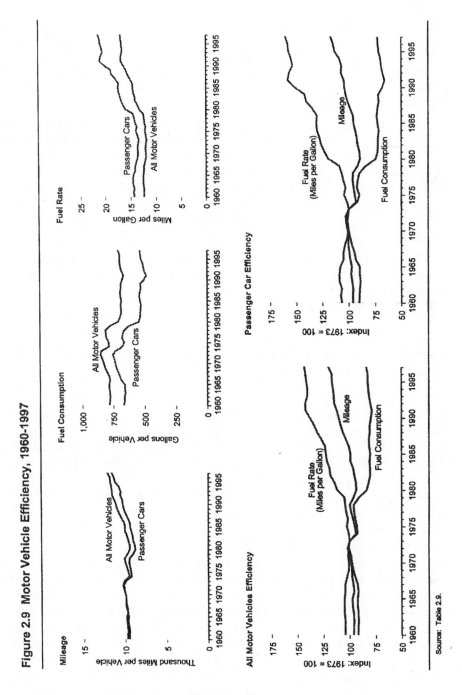

Figure 2.9 Motor Vehicle Efficiency, 1960-1997

Source: Table 2.9.

Figure 15-3

This plan provides for efficiency credits, whereby a manufacturer earns credits for exceeding the national standard, which may be used to remedy past standard violations. The plan must demonstrate that the manufacturer will, within the next three model years, earn enough efficiency credits to cover its deficiency for the current year. The program also allows a manufacturer to apply credits to any of the three consecutive model years following the year the credits are earned, but may only do so if it has already met the national standard, by meeting the standard or applying credits, for any preceding three consecutive model years: 49 U.S.C. § 32903. These credits are only available for the same class of automobile.

This program also factors in the benefits to the manufacturers' fleets derived from electric cars (49 U.S.C. § 32904) and hybrid vehicles. 49 U.S.C. § 32906. However, the program limits a manufacturer's fleet average increase due to hybrid vehicles to 1.2 mpg until 2004 and .9 mpg until 2008. Presently those limits are not in danger of being met. In terms of current development, purely electric cars are taking a backseat to the new hybrid vehicles, but even these hybrids have only been introduced for a short time.

The federal program preempts state law in this area unless the state adopts identical standards. The only exception to this rule allows states to mandate a different efficiency standard for automobiles obtained for the state's own use. 49 U.S.C. § 32919.

Competitive Enterprise Institute v. National Highway Traffic Safety Admin.

45 F.3d 481 (D.C.Cir.1995).

■ GINSBERG, J.: The Competitive Enterprise Institute and Consumer Alert (hereinafter referred to jointly as the CEI) petition for review of the National Highway Traffic Safety Administration rulemaking setting the corporate average fuel economy (CAFÉ) standard for 1990 passenger cars. The petitioners claim that the agency arbitrarily and capriciously failed to acknowledge significant adverse safety effects of setting the standard at 27.5 rather than 26.5 miles per gallon or somewhere in between. Finding that the agency adequately rooted its decision in the record of the rulemaking, we deny the petition for review.

In response to the then-restricted world supply of oil, the Congress enacted the Energy Policy and Conservation Act of 1975, which was intended, among other things, to induce automobile manufacturers to improve the fuel economy of their cars. The Act set a CAFÉ standard for passenger cars that increased several times and then leveled off at 27.5 miles per gallon for model years 1985 and beyond. 15 U.S.C. § 2002(a)(1). The NHTSA is authorized to raise or lower the standard for a particular model year, however, in order to achieve the "maximum feasible average fuel economy," taking into account technological feasibility, economic feasibility, the effect upon fuel economy of other federal motor vehicle standards, and the need of the nation to conserve energy. *See* 15 U.S.C. § 2002(e) (listing factors); *15 U.S.C. § 2002*(a)(4) (granting Secretary of Transportation discretion to amend CAFÉ standard); 49 C.F.R. § 1.50(f) (delegating authority to NHTSA). Although the Act does not list safety as a factor that the agency is to consider in setting the CAFÉ standard, the NHTSA has previously considered safety as an aspect of technological or economic feasibility. *See Competitive Enterprise Institute v. National Highway Traffic Safety Admin.*, 956 F.2d 321, 322 (D.C.Cir.1992) ("CEI II").

Under the Act, a manufacturer that fails to meet the CAFÉ standard is liable for a monetary penalty. *15 U.S.C. § 2008*(b)(1). A manufacturer may, however, offset its shortfall in meeting the CAFÉ standard one year with credits it earns by exceeding the standard in other years. *15 U.S.C. § 2002(l)*. A manufacturer may carry credits backward or forward up to three model years.

Each manufacturer must meet the CAFÉ standard separately for its domestically manufactured fleet and for its "not domestically manufactured" fleet, which is defined to exclude cars built in the United States from imported parts. In 1988 the NHTSA was concerned that the 27.5 mpg standard might lead American automobile manufacturers to shift some of their large-car manufacturing activity overseas in order to average the fuel economy of those cars with more of their small cars, thereby raising the average fuel economy of their domestic fleets and lowering the comfortably high average fuel economy of their non-domestic fleets. Notice of Proposed Rulemaking: Passenger Automobile Average Fuel Economy Standards for Model Years 1989 and 1990, 53 Fed. Reg. 33,080, 33,080–81 (1988). Foreseeing the job loss and "potential economic harm" that might occur, the NHTSA proposed to lower the MY 1989 and 1990 CAFÉ standards from 27.5 mpg to not less than 26.5 mpg. *Id. at 33,083.*

Later in 1988 the NHTSA lowered the CAFÉ standard for MY 1989 from 27.5 mpg to 26.5 mpg. Final Rule: Passenger Automobile Average Fuel Economy Standards for Model Year 1989, 53 Fed. Reg. 39,275 (1988). We affirmed. *See Competitive Enterprise Institute v. National Highway Traffic Safety Admin.*, 901 F.2d 107, 110 (D.C.Cir.1990) ("CEI I"). In 1989, however, the agency terminated the MY 1990 aspect of the rulemaking without changing the CAFÉ standard for that year. "This decision [was] based largely on the increasing need of the nation to conserve energy and a conclusion by the agency that retention of the 27.5 mpg standard for MY 1990 [would] not have a significant adverse effect on U.S. employment or on the competitiveness of the U.S. auto industry." Termination of Rulemaking: Passenger Automobile Average Fuel Economy Standard for Model Year 1990, 54 Fed. Reg. 21,985, 21,989 (1989). The NHTSA also concluded, contrary to the submission of the CEI, that leaving the MY 1990 CAFÉ standard at 27.5 mpg would not have an adverse effect upon automotive safety. *Id.* at 21,992–94. [On review, the D.C. Circuit remanded the MY 1990 standard to the agency to address the issue of whether the standard would cause manufacturers to discourage purchase of larger cars by raising their price. *CEI II, supra.* The agency reopened the rulemaking but concluded that there would be no such impact. CEI now petitions for review of that decision]

The CEI contends that the NHTSA, on remand, failed to give adequate consideration to the petitioners' contention that retaining the statutory

CAFÉ standard for MY 1990 would have significant adverse safety effects. Specifically, the CEI claims that the agency failed to consider that (1) the CAFÉ standard causes automobile manufacturers to downsize passenger cars, resulting in significantly more traffic fatalities because larger, heavier cars are safer than smaller, lighter cars; and (2) the CAFÉ standard constrains automobile manufacturers from upsizing cars, thereby pricing consumers out of the market for larger, heavier, and (presumably) safer cars. The substance of the CEI's position is intuitively appealing. We must deal here, however, not with our intuition and not with the petitioners' position in the abstract, but with the concrete record before us and with the conclusions that the agency drew from it. That record adequately supports the NHTSA's conclusion that maintaining the 27.5 mpg CAFÉ standard for MY 1990 would not significantly affect the safety of the motoring public.

First, the NHTSA reasonably concluded from the evidence before it that the MY 1990 CAFÉ standard did not cause automobile manufacturers either to downsize or to refrain from upsizing their cars. In its notice reopening the rulemaking proceeding, the agency asked commenters to address:

> What specific actions [manufacturers would] actually take, if any, depending upon whether the MY 1990 CAFÉ standard remained at 27.5 mpg or were reduced to some level between 26.5 mpg and 27.5 mpg? If the standard remained at 27.5 mpg, would manufacturers downsize vehicles, refrain from upsizing vehicles[,] or change the mix or pricing policies of the vehicles they offer for sale?

Reopening of Rulemaking Proceeding: Passenger Automobile Average Fuel Economy Standard for Model Year 1990, 57 Fed. Reg. 48,777, 48,778 (1992). Further, recognizing that a regulatory change made in 1992 would not affect the production of vehicles in MYs 1990–92, the NHTSA asked the automobile manufacturers to state what specific actions they would take with respect to any model year (presumably by carrying credits backward or forward) were the agency to lower the 1990 standard. *Id.*

No manufacturer identified any change that it would make in the size or weight of its vehicles, in its product mix, or in its pricing strategy—for any model year—if the NHTSA were to lower the MY 1990 CAFÉ standard. In fact, the Ford Motor Company asserted that it "did not reduce its average car size over what would have been offered absent such 1990 standard." The General Motors Corporation stated that "relaxing the standard could in some cases generate credits giving manufacturers more flexibility to offer larger, safer cars in later model years," but did not go so far as to suggest that it would be one of the beneficiaries. Accordingly, the NHTSA reasonably decided that maintaining the MY 1990 CAFÉ standard would have no appreciable effect upon the size or weight of automobiles offered for sale in any model year.

Second, the factual record simply does not support the CEI's contention that consumers are priced out of the market for larger, heavier cars by reason of the 27.5 mpg standard. As part of the rulemaking for the MY

1986 CAFÉ standard, the NHTSA analyzed the cost-effectiveness of various technological changes that manufacturers have used to meet fuel economy standards. That analysis showed that most of the technological changes paid for themselves with fuel savings over the first four years of ownership and that all but one were cost-effective over the life of the vehicle. *See* Final Regulatory Impact Analysis for MY 1986 Passenger Car CAFÉ Standard III–32, III–33 (1985). Moreover, the NHTSA noted that the technological changes—including improved aerodynamics, substitution of lighter materials, fuel injection, electronic engine control, wide ratio gearing, reduced lubricant viscosity, and reduced rolling resistance—are widely available on large and small cars alike. Therefore, any increase in the purchase price of cars owing to those features would not impose a relative penalty upon the purchase of a large car. Finally, while the NHTSA recognized that a manufacturer could attempt to induce a shift in its product mix either by reducing the price of its small cars or by increasing the price of its large cars (or both), *see* 58 Fed. Reg. at 6944, the agency noted that no manufacturer commented in the rulemaking on remand that it had taken either step in order to meet the MY 1990 CAFÉ standard of 27.5 mpg.

Finally, the NHTSA considered the study upon which the CEI rested its contention that the MY 1990 CAFÉ standard had a significant effect on safety. *See* Robert W. Crandall & John D. Graham, The Effect of Fuel Economy Standards on Automobile Safety, 32 J. of L. & Econ. 97, 109–10 (1989). That study suggests that in the 1980s manufacturers significantly reduced the average weight of their cars due to the CAFÉ standards. Using a model describing the relationship of automobile weight to safety, and explaining weight as a function solely of CAFÉ regulation and of the expected prices of gasoline and steel (as forecast four years in advance), Crandall and Graham estimated that the CAFÉ program caused a "500–pound or 14 percent reduction in the average weight of 1989 cars," which was "associated with a 14–27 percent increase in occupant fatality risk." *Id.* at 111.

The NHTSA did not directly dispute the general finding of the Crandall and Graham study, i.e., that there is a relationship between safety and the size or weight of automobiles. *See* 58 Fed. Reg. at 6946 ("The agency ... fully agrees ... that all other things being equal, a large car is safer than a small car"). Instead the agency faulted Crandall and Graham for failing to take account of factors in addition to gasoline and steel prices—namely, "technological advances," "increased competition," and "changes in consumer preferences"—that in the agency's view would explain almost all of the average car's weight loss that the authors instead attributed to the CAFÉ standard. (Indeed the agency even suggested that "any CAFÉ standard effect [on weight] is negligible." Id.)

Although phrased in a variety of ways, the NHTSA's response to Crandall and Graham comes down to suggesting that a change in consumers' preferences, rather than any constraining effect of the CAFÉ standards, accounts for vehicle downsizing over the period that they studied. (After all, "increased competition" only facilitates the satisfaction of consumers' preferences; nor, if manufacturers were not constrained by the CAFÉ standards to adopt them, are "technological advances" relevant unless consumers demanded them). While the agency speculated that consumers might have preferred "downsized vehicles [because they] offered better handling, easier parking, and potential cost savings associated with reduced materials usage," it offered no reason whatsoever to think that consumer preferences actually did change at all during the relevant time, much less that they changed in the direction of preferring smaller and apparently more dangerous cars. Merely to assert the existence of another possible explanation, which is all that the NHTSA has done, does nothing to undermine the significance of the findings carefully documented by Crandall and Graham. It is like asserting that regulation of the airlines had no effect because it occurred at a time when all consumers preferred amenities such as gourmet meals rather than cheaper fares; that is, of course, possible, but the only evidence is to the contrary.

The NHTSA's failure adequately to respond to the Crandall and Graham study is troubling, but it is not a basis, upon this record, for overturning the agency's decision to adhere to the 27.5 mpg CAFÉ standard for MY 1990. The overwhelming fact is that no automobile manufacturer is on record stating that it would have added weight to its automobiles (or taken any other action) in any model year had the NHTSA relaxed the 1990 CAFÉ standard. Therefore, record evidence documenting a correlation between the safety and the size or weight of a vehicle, and the contribution of the CAFÉ standard to determining size or weight, while potentially relevant to any future decision to retain or amend the CAFÉ standard, simply does not require the NHTSA to amend the MY 1990 CAFÉ standard.

The NHTSA has identified sufficient support in the record for its decision not to amend the MY 1990 CAFÉ standard. The manufacturers did not assert in their comments to the agency on remand that they would implement any design or product mix changes if the NHTSA amended the MY 1990 CAFÉ standard and there is no hard evidence in the record that the MY 1990 CAFÉ standard caused any manufacturer to price any consumers out of the market for larger, safer cars. The petition for review is therefore Denied.■

NOTES AND COMMENTS

1. Department of Transportation reports suggest that the CAFÉ standard program has succeeded, but that such standards may not be the proper method to continue to set fuel conservation goals. Industry groups, on the other hand, claim that CAFÉ has not lived up to expectations. They argue that oil savings have been less than one-tenth of what was predicted. And oil imports have increased from 35% of the oil we used in the mid–1970s to over 50% today. The automobile manufacturers and oil industry, through the Coalition for Vehicle Choice, have lobbied Congress heavily in an attempt to have the CAFÉ standards program repealed. See www.vehicle-

choice.org In the years 1996 through 1999, Congress attached riders to the Department of Transportation appropriations bills barring the use of funds to revise CAFÉ standards. *See* Robert Bamberger, Automobile and Light Truck Fuel Economy: Is CAFÉ Up to Standards? (Congressional Research Service, 1999).

2. In an evaluation of the CAFÉ standards program, the Transportation Research Board concluded that the standards have led to reduced petroleum use but "the magnitude of the effect is subject to debate" because "motorists may respond to higher fuel economy by driving more" and thus might counteract the program's benefits. Sustainable Future, *supra* at 117. A subsequent economic analysis of surveys of motor vehicle use concluded that motorists do drive more when gasoline prices drop or fuel economy improves, and that this phenomenon reduces energy savings of fuel economy improvement by about 20%. David L. Green et. al., Fuel Economy Rebound Effect for U.S. Household Vehicles, 20 Energy Journal 1 (1999).

3. In 1993, the Clinton administration entered into agreements between the automobile manufacturers and a number of federal research laboratories to develop a more energy-efficient and non-polluting highway vehicle engine. The Partnership for a New Generation of Vehicles, as this joint venture is called, intends to produce a production prototype of a "supercar" by 2004. But because the program has focused most of its attention on diesel-electric hybrid cars, there are serious questions about the ability of such an engine to meet the Phase II emission standards for tailpipe emissions proposed by the EPA. *See* Keith Bradsher, Detroit Plays Catch-Up In Race for Hybrid Car, New York Times, January 1, 2000.

2. TRANSPORTATION PLANNING REQUIREMENTS

The historic compromise that produced the Interstate Highway Act of 1956 was interpreted by the "road lobby" as a guarantee that all of the taxes on gasoline and related equipment were to be sequestered in the Highway Trust Fund where they would be used only for road construction. Advocates of other modes of transportation soon began to cast a covetous eye on this fund, arguing that if the fund were used to finance subways, for example, the result would be to reduce the need for highway construction by taking people off the roads.

The auto manufacturers, trucking companies and oil companies adamantly resisted these attempts. There continues to be a strenuous debate between those who think that the existing system contains built-in subsidies for automobiles (*see, e.g.,* World Resources Institute, The Going Rate: What it Really Costs to Drive (1992)) and those who believe that the publicly owned transit systems are an inefficient waste of public funds (*see, e.g.,* Clifford Winston & Chad Shirley, Alternate Route: Toward Efficient Urban Transportation (Brookings Institution Press, 1998)).

This debate has also been regularly heard in the halls of Congress. Since 1962, federal law has required the states to engage in a highway planning process for "urbanized areas" of more than 50,000 people. In response to the desire of local governments to play a greater role in the planning of highways, highway trust funds were given to the states to finance the creation of Metropolitan Planning Organizations, which included representatives of local governments as well as state agencies. These MPOs were staffed with engineers and planners who worked closely with state and federal highway officials in approving the layout of the highway system.

a.   THE 1991 ISTEA LEGISLATION

During the 1990s, Congress began to increase the funding for alternative modes of transportation. Responding to the argument that the construction of new highways just seemed to create more traffic and more traffic jams, Congress passed new legislation in 1991 and again in 1998 that tried to stimulate "multi-modal" transportation planning that considered not only roads but mass transit and other modes of transportation.

The ready availability of cash from the highway trust fund has frequently meant that the highway planners have had better financing than the planners of other types of public facilities. This led to many complaints that highways were being built without consideration of alternative modes of transportation, particularly rapid transit. In addition, the growing concern about air pollution from motor vehicles meant that state environmental agencies were required by the Clean Air Act to engage in a separate planning process to try to attain the standards for ozone and nitrogen oxides established by the U.S. Environmental Protection Agency.

Congress responded to these concerns in 1981 by passing the Intermodal Surface Transportation Efficiency Act of 1991, commonly called "ice tea" (ISTEA). The act adopted the policy that transportation planning should consider not only roads but travel by train, bus, bicycle and on foot. It substantially increased the funds available for non-highway modes of transportation. It also required the states to make many detailed changes in the planning process, which were designed to ensure that all modes of transportation were given fair consideration and to integrate the transportation planning with air quality planning. 23 U.S.C. § 135. Comparable changes to the air quality planning requirements were made in the Clean Air Act amendments of 1990. 42 U.S.C. § 7506 (c).

Different urbanized areas developed their own administrative structures to carry out these planning processes. Some saw the need for change as a high priority, while others tried to change as little as possible. On balance, the ISTEA legislation produced a number of significant plans that brought attention to a greater variety of modes of transportation. *See* Daniel Carlson et. al., At Road's End: Transportation and Land Use Choices for Communities (Island Press, 1995).

In general, ISTEA represented a move away from the complete dominance of the highway in transportation planning. The new buzzword became "intermodalism," meaning that planners should consider all different modes of transportation and how they interrelate. Terminals at which people could interchange among transit, highway, bicycle and pedestrian facilities were encouraged.

The act also sought to increase the role of state and local governments in the decisionmaking process with the objective of reaching an earlier consensus among affected groups; "partnerships" became the preferred way of making decisions. State and local agencies were encouraged to "leverage" their funds in combination to maximize the efficiency of federal funding.

But although ISTEA was "a significant symbolic achievement for the anti highway forces" it did not cause dramatic shifts of money from highways to transit. Dunn, *supra* at 43. Its long term impact is likely to result from opening up the planning process to new ideas and new people who approach transportation issues from a broader perspective than traditional highway engineers.

b. THE 1998 TEA–21 LEGISLATION

In 1998, Congress was presented with a potential surplus in the federal budget for the first time in many years. It responded by passing legislation appropriating significantly increased funds for highways and other transportation projects and making further changes in the transportation planning process. Public Law 105–178 was given the high-sounding name of the Transportation Equity Act for the Twenty-first Century, and is referred to as TEA–21.

The TEA–21 legislation supports a variety of initiatives directed to the full range of transportation alternatives, including highways, mass transit, and bicycle paths. 23 U.S.C. § 133. New programs are established for the design and demonstration of advanced technologies, such as fixed guideway vehicles, fuel-cell powered transit vehicles, and magnetic levitation technologies for urban public transportation. The DOT's ITS (Intelligent Transportation Systems) program for advanced transportation technologies for the movement of goods between states and across borders received an authorization of over a billion dollars. Some $9 billion was allocated to individual "demonstration projects" in the districts of influential members of Congress.

As in the 1991 legislation, particular emphasis has been given to the coordination of transportation planning and the reduction of air pollution. Section 1110 of the Act authorizes over $8 billion for the CMAQ (Congestion Mitigation and Air Quality Improvement) program to fund projects and programs that help meet the requirements of the Clean Air Act in areas that are or were failing to attain the National Ambient Air Quality Standards.

The Department of Transportation was also charged with writing regulations with the goal of reducing delay in the environmental review process, using the environmental review process under NEPA as a vehicle for integrating other required environmental reviews and analyses related to the proposed project, including reviews under other relevant state and local laws. TEA–21 also includes a specific provision to require the early identification of all federal agencies, and, in certain instances, state agencies, with jurisdiction by law over issues related to a proposed project. Cooperating agencies can participate in the NEPA process as soon as the identification of a proposal has occurred and they can also assume responsibility for preparation of a portion of the analyses within their area of expertise. Section 1309 also mandates the establishment of timelines, in consultation with all involved federal agencies, and incorporates the criteria set forth in the CEQ regulations for determining appropriate time limits for projects. It also authorizes the Secretary, at the request of a State, to allow federal-aid highway funds to be used to meet the provisions for enhanced environmental streamlining.

On October 18, 1999, the agencies responsible for reviewing environmental documents prepared under the National Environmental Policy Act of 1969 for highway and transit projects[14] executed a Memorandum of Understanding (MOU) on permit streamlining. The MOU is to be implemented by an Environmental Streamlining Action Plan, the initial draft of which proposes several steps to improve environmental review processes, including recognizing and promoting successful efforts by state and local governments; encouraging field organizations to pursue partnering opportunities and programmatic agreements for site specific or project specific (pilot) efforts; developing national dispute resolution procedures; and identifying ways to develop performance measures and to benchmark techniques assessing the effectiveness of the project development processes and practices. The department also plans to publish revisions to environmental impact regulations and related procedures for public comment. *See* www.fhwa.dot.gov/environment/strmlng.htm.

F.   STATE AND LOCAL GROWTH MANAGEMENT

In the United States, local communities have been adopting laws and programs to manage land development in various ways for over a century. In modern terminology this process is called "growth management," and although controversial in some of its forms, it seems to be experiencing a resurgence as the Twenty-first Century begins. For a current analysis of the law of growth management in the United States, *see* Julian C. Juergensmeyer & Thomas E. Roberts, Land Use Planning and Control Law 365–410 (St. Paul, Minn.: West Group, 1998).

Many of these growth management programs hope to improve transportation efficiency and reduce energy consumption. They are a reaction against the dramatic increase in non-urban land development that came in response to the booming economy of the 1990s. The United States Depart-

---

14. The United States Departments of Transportation, Interior, Agriculture, Commerce and Army (Corps of Engineers); the   Environmental Protection Agency: and the Advisory Council on Historic Preservation.

ment of Agriculture reported that almost 16 million acres of land was developed in the 5–years between 1992 and 1997. This was considerably more than the 13 million acres that was developed during the 10–year period from 1982 to 1992. USDA, Natural Resources Inventory: www. nhq.nrcs.bov/land/pubs Virtually all of this development was automobile-dependent, and it contributed to greatly increasing traffic congestion throughout most of the rapidly growing metropolitan areas.

A leading text by Godschalk and Brower defines growth management as a "conscious governmental program intended to influence the rate, amount, type, location, and/or quality of future development within a local jurisdiction." David Godschalk, et al., Constitutional Issues in Growth Management 8 (Washington, D.C.: Planners Press 1979). These five objectives fall into three basic categories of technique:[15] A growth management strategy can work toward all three of these objectives, but many of them put the emphasis on one of the three. (1) Some strategies focus on the *quality* of development, usually with the objective of encouraging only development that meets certain standards. (2) Other strategies manage the *quantity* of development by regulating the rate of growth or ultimate capacity for development. (3) And many strategies emphasize the *location* of development by expanding or contracting existing areas that attract growth or by diverting the growth to new areas.

1.   Regulation of Development Quality.

Today, Americans are so accustomed to a wide array of programs designed to maintain the quality of development that these programs are largely taken for granted. Protection against toxic dumping, poisoned water and unhealthy smog has produced a substantially cleaner environment than that of 25 years ago. Building and zoning codes have so successfully protected neighborhood property values that we are often barely conscious that the codes exist.

This current plethora of quality controls is a product of gradual evolution. They reflect changing ideas of quality, and a growing need to manage conditions in an increasingly crowded environment. Increasingly, the quality of transportation services is seen as a key area of local concern.

Early in the twentieth century, zoning began to be used to control quality by segregating land uses in ways designed to encourage high quality development. New York City's initial zoning tried to protect Fifth Avenue's expensive housing from too close contact with the burgeoning garment industry. And countless suburbs used zoning to insist that large areas be limited to single family housing on a lot of a certain size.

Gradually communities began to expand on the kinds of quality standards they enforced. As motor vehicles became more prevalent, parking

---

15.   For purposes of this discussion, the idea of: "type" is referred to as the *quality* of development; "rate" and "amount" are referred to as the *quantity* of development. *See* Fred P. Bosselman, Craig A. Peterson & Claire McCarthy, Managing Tourism Growth 40–53 (Island Press, 1999).

became an increasing problem in urban neighborhoods. Cities began to require new development to provide off-street parking. Although developers originally protested, they quickly found that residents and customers were greatly attracted by the convenience of on-site parking. Norman Williams, Jr. & John Taylor, 4A, American Land Planning Law 1–26 (Callaghan, 1986). Older downtowns found it very hard to compete with new development in outlying locations where free parking was available.

Today, the most common source of discontent about the quality of new development is its impact on vehicle traffic. The public has gradually come to believe that, in our auto-oriented society, rapid growth can lead to critical congestion on the roadways that defies any cure. Adding more lanes of highway simply attracts more vehicles, creating time-wasting delays and unhealthy air quality.

Increasingly, efforts are being made to manage traffic cooperatively through coalitions of local businesses that stagger hours and combine car pooling efforts. Special lanes for high-occupancy vehicles or buses have been introduced to try to encourage people to travel cooperatively. But traffic remains by far the most common cause of opposition to new development proposals.

A common way by which local governments have sought to improve the quality of transportation available to new development is to require the developer to bear a larger share of the costs of road improvements. By ensuring that new development pays for the share of the new transportation facilities needed to accommodate the new occupants, these programs enhance the quality of life for those moving into the community.

Home Builders and Contractors Ass'n of Palm Beach County v. Board of County Commissioners of Palm Beach County

446 So.2d 140 (Fla.App.1983).

■ DOWNEY, J.: This case involves the validity of a Palm Beach County ordinance imposing an impact fee on new development for the purpose of constructing roads made necessary by the increased traffic generated by such new development.

Appellants, Home Builders and Contractors Association of Palm Beach County, Inc. (hereafter Home Builders), and Ted Satter Enterprises, Inc., filed suit against the Board of County Commissioners of Palm Beach County for declaratory and injunctive relief to invalidate Palm Beach County Ordinance 79–7, as amended, denominated the "Fair Share Contribution for Road Improvements Ordinance." From a final judgment upholding the validity of the ordinance, Home Builders has perfected this appeal.

The Palm Beach 1980 County Comprehensive Plan recognized that in view of the unusual growth rate being experienced in the county and in order to maintain a consistent level of road service and quality of life, extensive road improvements would be necessary, requiring regulation of new development activity which generates additional automobile traffic. The County Commission therefore enacted Ordinance 79–7 in order to finance the necessary road capital improvements and to regulate increases in traffic levels. The ordinance would require any new land development activity generating road traffic to pay its "fair share" of the reasonably anticipated cost of expansion of new roads attributable to the new development.

The ordinance has a formula which takes into consideration the costs of road construction and the number of motor vehicle trips generated by different types of land use. It provides for a fee of $300 per unit for single family homes, $200 per unit for multi-family, $175 per unit for mobile homes with other amounts for commercial or other development, all subject to annual review. The fee is to be paid upon commencement of any new land development activity generating traffic. The ordinance divides the county into forty zones, indicated on a map incorporated by reference into the ordinance, and establishes a trust fund for each zone. Funds collected from building activity in a particular zone may only be spent in that zone, and must be spent within a reasonable time after collection (not later than six years) or returned to the present owner of the property.

The initial question which must be answered is the challenge to the county's authority to enact an ordinance of this kind. [The court quoted the decision of the Florida Supreme Court in Speer v. Olson, 367 So. 2d 207, 210–11 (1978) as follows:] "The first sentence of Section 125.01(1), Florida Statutes, (1975), grants to the governing body of a county the full power to carry on county government. Unless the Legislature has pre-empted a particular subject relating to county government by either general or special law, the county governing body, by reason of this sentence, has full authority to act through the exercise of home rule power."

We know of no general or special act which purports to limit the grant of authority contained in the foregoing constitutional and statutory enactments nor is the ordinance inconsistent with any general or special law. Art. VIII, sec. 1(f), Fla. Const. Accordingly, we hold that Palm Beach County had the power and authority to enact the fee impact ordinance in question, assuming the ordinance involves a regulatory fee rather than a tax.

Home Builders contends the ordinance is invalid because of the disparity between the people who benefit and the people who pay. As stated in its brief: "Our position is that since anyone can drive a vehicle over any of these roads, regardless of whether he lives in the zone or has paid the impact fee, there is too great a disparity between those who pay and those who receive the benefit, making the charge in reality a tax, which the county does not have the power to impose."

If by that argument it is Home Builders' position that the benefits accruing from roads constructed with the impact fees collected must be used exclusively or overwhelmingly for the subdivision residents in question, we would have to differ. It is difficult to envision any capital improvement for parks, sewers, drainage, roads, or whatever, which would not in some measure benefit members of the community who do not reside in or utilize the new development. For example, landowners abutting a subdivision may well derive substantial benefit from intrasubdivision drainage facilities. Parks within subdivisions are not restricted to subdivision residents only. Furthermore, intrasubdivision streets and roads may be extensively used by persons not residents thereof.

A resume of the decisions in this and other jurisdictions demonstrates that those attacking impact fees often rely upon this same argument; it is one frequently found and generally rejected . . .

Next Home Builders contends that the fair share ordinance is arbitrary and discriminatory and thus violates the equal protection provisions of the Federal and State Constitutions. The thrust of the argument is that since municipalities may "opt out" of the ordinance under Article VIII, Section 1(f) of the Florida Constitution, and thirty-three of the thirty-seven municipalities in the county have opted out, equal protection is denied to those subject to the ordinance.

We disagree. Using the rational basis test articulated in *In re Estate of Greenberg*, 390 So.2d 40 (Fla.1980), we believe the evidence demonstrates that the ordinance bears a reasonable relationship to a legitimate state purpose. The Florida Constitution itself provides that county ordinances of non-charter counties shall not be effective in a municipality if it conflicts with a municipal ordinance. Surely that in itself should not render all non-charter county regulatory fees ineffective or impact fees could only be allowed in charter counties. Furthermore, the fact that an impact fee is payable on land located in the county whereas it would not be payable on nearby land in a municipality which has opted out does not offend equal protection. Unequal or different charges or fees assessed in incorporated and unincorporated areas, like different hours for retail liquor sales and other areas of regulation which may lack uniformity, are not improper where such legislation is otherwise a valid exercise of governmental power.

In addition, we would observe that for aught we know any of these municipalities which have opted out may themselves one day enact impact fees, which will tend to lessen the ostensible unequal treatment of land development in different areas.

Finally, appellants maintain that the ordinance is a tax rather than a regulatory fee and thus in violation of Article VII, Section 1(a) of the Florida Constitution. In all candor we concede this is the most difficult point raised in this appeal. As one reads the various cases involving the dichotomy between a fee and a tax the distinction almost seems to become more amorphous rather than less. In any event, some years ago this court decided *Broward County v. Janis Development Corp.*, 311 So.2d 371 (Fla. 4th DCA 1975), and held that a county ordinance imposing an impact fee for roads was in reality a tax rather than a fee. Appellants naturally rely heavily upon Janis to support their argument that this ordinance is a tax in sheep's clothing and that impact fees and roads are simply not compatible. However, the problem with the Janis ordinance was not that it involved an impact fee for roads (as opposed to parks or drainage, etc.) but rather that the legislation had several inherent defects. For example, the money generated by the ordinance far exceeded the cost of meeting the needs brought about by the new development. In addition, the ordinance was lacking in specific restrictions regarding the use of revenue received. These are the features which required this court to hold it was not dealing with a regulatory fee. The amount and use of the funds simply did not jibe with the concept of regulation; it smacked more of revenue raising which is descriptive of a tax.

In *Contractors & Builders Ass'n of Pinellas County v. City of Dunedin*, 329 So.2d 314 (Fla.1976), *cert. denied*, 444 U.S. 867 (1979) the supreme court and this court pointed out the features of the Janis ordinance which kept it from passing muster as an acceptable impact fee ordinance. Consequently, the Palm Beach County ordinance in question here was crafted with *Dunedin's* lessons in mind. The present ordinance recognizes that the rapid rate of new development will require a substantial increase in the capacity of the county road system. The evidence shows that the cost of construction of additional roads will far exceed the fair share fees imposed by the ordinance. In fact the county suggests that under the ordinance the cost will exceed the revenue produced by eighty-five percent. The formula for calculating the amount of the fee is not rigid and inflexible, but rather allows the person improving the land to determine his fair share by furnishing his own independent study of traffic and economic data in order to demonstrate that his share is less than the amount under the formula set forth in the ordinance. Lastly, expenditure of the funds collected is localized by virtue of the zone system.

Thus, it appears that the Palm Beach County ordinance meets the tests laid down in *Dunedin*, which supports the trial judge's findings that the ordinance imposes a regulatory fee and not a prohibited tax.■

NOTES AND COMMENTS

1.   By statute, Florida now requires local governments to ensure that public facilities will be built "concurrent" with private development. *See* Thomas G. Pelham, Adequate Public Facilities Requirements: Reflections of Florida's Concurrency System for Managing Growth, 19 Fla. St. U. L. Rev. 974 (1992). The objective of concurrency programs is to ensure that when residents move into a new development they will have adequate roads and other infrastructure already in place to meet their needs.

2.   Can mass transit be financed through impact fees in the way that highways can? Some communities have required developers to contribute to a fund for the financing of mass transit. In the case of *Russ Building Partnership v. City and County of San Francisco*, 246 Cal.Rptr. 21 (Cal.App. 1987), the court addressed a "Transit Impact Development Fee" that required office building developers in downtown San Francisco to pay a $5 per square foot transit fee. Builders attacked the amount of the transit fee, contending that the methodology used and the assumptions relied upon by the city's consultants were unsupported by the evidence. The board had

fixed the transit fee at $5 per square foot based on a June 1981 estimate of increased transit costs calculated by Bruce Bernhard of the San Francisco Public Utilities Commission Bureau of Finance. This fee was less than Bernhard's calculation of $6.57 per square foot. Prior to trial, which lasted ten weeks, the city retained Touche–Ross as a consultant, and they calculated the increase in the transit costs to be $8.36 per square foot based on a projected use over the next 45 years. The trial court found that the 45–year forecast was reasonable as it "rationally and directly related" to the estimated life of the buildings. The trial court also concluded that the assumptions and figures employed by the consultants in arriving at this amount were rationally based.

On appeal, plaintiffs challenged numerous elements of the city's methodology, but the court eventually rejected each challenge in a detailed opinion:

> Russ Building plaintiff challenges the use of the 45–year projection, claiming that it was not possible to estimate the increased transit costs that far into the future. Plaintiff relies on the testimony of its experts who stated, essentially, that for such a long period of time there were too many variables to consider to make any reliable estimate. Naturally, this conclusion was disputed by the city's experts. While the degree of precision of the costs decreases proportionally with the length of the projection, we cannot state that such long term forecasts are inherently unreliable or are so arbitrary as to be mere speculation. The trial court's decision approving the 45–year term was supported by substantial evidence.

> Next, Russ Building plaintiff argues that Touche–Ross used an improper discount rate in calculating the present transit fee. Touche–Ross applied a discount rate of 1.74 percent in arriving at the net present value of the lump sum fee levied against plaintiff. Plaintiff contends that the discount rate was too low and that it should be based on the rate for the "snapshot year" 1980–1981, the period from which the ridership data was taken. Touche–Ross used an economic forecast which estimated the discount rate over the 45–year projected term, rather than the rate for the "snapshot year." This was the only long-term projection in the record, and there was testimony on both sides concerning its accuracy. The trial court found that there was a rational basis for using this method and we agree.

> Russ Building plaintiff contends this figure is too low and that the discount rate for the snapshot year should have been used. We find no inconsistencies in the use of a snapshot year to predict the amount of increased services needed and the 45–year forecast to estimate the cost of those services over useful lives of the buildings. The increased usage of the transit system can be calculated to a reasonable certainty by selecting a model year, in this case 1980–1981, and extrapolating the need based on known quantities for ultimate office capacity, vehicle capacity, route structure and patronage volume.

In contrast to the future usage figure, the cost of those services is not reasonably ascertainable in any one year, but fluctuates with the economy. The cost for maintaining, repairing and purchasing new vehicles, and the costs of salaries and insurance, to name a few, are variable, subject to influences outside the control of city officials, e.g., gas prices, the inflation rate, etc. Under such circumstances, it would be unreasonable to base the discount rate on a "snapshot year" since it could be a year of unusually high or low inflation and, as we note, the inflation rate has not remained the same. In arriving at the cost of the increased transit services over the projected 45-year life of the building, it is more rational to use a forecast based on historical economic trends. We find substantial evidence to support the trial court's finding.

The court also held that the absence of any mechanism to adjust the rate in the future was not fatal, although such a mechanism had been found to be essential in rent control ordinances in *Birkenfeld v. City of Berkeley*, 550 P.2d 1001 (Cal.1976).

Plaintiff proposes the city collect an annual installment, subject to yearly recalculations of the estimated cost. Plaintiff's reliance on *Birkenfeld* is misplaced. In that case, a City of Berkeley rent control ordinance required a rollback of all controlled rents to those in effect on August 15, 1971; this would become the maximum rent subject to adjustments on a unit-by-unit procedure, which the court held was too cumbersome to be effective. (*Id.*, at p. 136.) In this context, the court held that "[for] such rent ceilings of indefinite duration an adjustment mechanism is constitutionally necessary to provide for changes in circumstances and also provide for the previously mentioned situations in which the base rent cannot reasonably be deemed to reflect general market conditions." (*Id.*, at p. 169.)

There is no similarity between the method for arriving at the maximum rent allowed in *Birkenfeld* and the projected costs for increased transit services in the instant matter. Unlike the Berkeley ordinance, the transit fee was not artificially limited to one particular year, but calculated based on the expected costs over the 45-year period, taking into consideration the fluctuating market conditions and inflation rate. A fair reading of Birkenfeld convinces us that an annual readjustment of the transit fee is not constitutionally mandated in this instance, and plaintiff's contention necessarily fails.

The appellate court did find that the city's consultants erred in two respects in computing the impact of new development on transit. First, the consultants had erroneously underestimated the revenues that the city would derive from the sale of "fast pass" tickets. Second, the consultants had concluded that since the increased numbers of transit riders would use both main line routes and crosstown and feeder routes, the developers should be charged for expansion of all of the routes even though it was only the main line routes that were likely to become overcrowded:

However, we find these errors to be harmless. The difference between the transit fee as originally estimated and the amount using the methodology discussed above would result in an estimated fee well above the $5 figure imposed on the Russ Building plaintiff. Using the Touche–Ross analysis relied on by the trial court, a recalculation of the fast pass revenue figure would result in a $0.60–per-square-foot reduction, from $8.36 to $7.76. If the transfer rate were recalculated to exclude below capacity "policy lines," the fee would be further reduced by 81 cents per square foot; from $7.76 to $6.95; still well above the $5–per-square-foot fee imposed by the city. Accordingly, it would serve no purpose to remand this matter for further findings.

3.   Cases like *Russ* illustrate the fact that many of the general principles of public utility ratemaking discussed in Chapter Eight, *supra*, are also applicable to publicly-owned facilities and services as well as to private companies. In many states, governments that operate transportation facilities are limited by law to charging fees and rates that recover their costs. In some states, however, local governments seek to make a profit off public services, either by charging high rates or imposing local taxes on utility services. Although this form of revenue has a regressive effect, it is often popular in communities where much of the land is owned by charities or other governments and is therefore off the property tax rolls.

4.   Developers have fought long and hard against the expansion of development exactions, arguing that they drive up the cost of housing and discriminate in favor of existing residents of a community. The Supreme Court has held that exactions of land or other specific property are valid only if they have a connection to the impact of the development and if the amount of the exaction is roughly proportional to the extent of the impact. *Dolan v. City of Tigard*, 512 U.S. 374 (1994). More recently, the Court has indicated that these requirements are not applicable to fees payable in cash rather than in the form of land or other property. *City of Monterey v. Del Monte Dunes at Monterey, Ltd.*, 526 U.S. 687, 702–703 (1999). But many states have their own tests that may be as strict or stricter than the Supreme Court's. *See* Fred P. Bosselman, Dolan's Mysteries Explained?, 51 Land Use Law and Zoning Digest #1, January, 1999, at 3.

5.   Another form of quality control by local government involves standards designed to ensure that facilities such as day care and neighborhood shopping are available within walking distance of residential neighborhoods. Incentives for "mixed use" development often involve special procedures for larger subdivisions such as "planned unit developments." *See* Daniel M. Mandelker, Land Use Law § 9.23 et seq. (4th ed. 1998).

2.   REGULATION OF THE QUANTITY OF DEVELOPMENT.

Strategies to manage the quantity of development are not new, but until recently communities have usually wanted more and more development rather than less. Many places throughout America and the world are still desperate for almost any kind of development that will bring enough jobs to the local community to keep normal services and amenities alive.

Many such communities have long had economic development·programs, designed to attract more development to the area. These programs are not undiscriminating about quality—try locating a waste disposal site if you are in doubt of it. But within certain quality limitations, the primary objective of economic development programs is to *increase* the quantity of development in the area. State governments often spend very large sums of public money in support of these programs to attract economic development.

More sophisticated communities in recent years have come to recognize the importance of the overall quantity of development as a key factor in determining whether the transportation system will meet community expectations. This recognition has grown out of the difficulty of dealing with cumulative impact: if the change caused by any individual development proposal seems minor, but it can be seen that a major impact will take place when the impacts of many projected developments are aggregated, how can the overburdening of transportation or other public facilities be avoided?

As a technical matter, it is much easier to devise needed safeguards if one can accurately project the total amount of development that will take place and the time frame during which it will occur. In real life, however, those factors are likely to be speculative projections that are subject to considerable debate. The early developer will have a strong incentive to use estimates that reduce the impact assigned to her proposal. Even where agreement can be reached on the degree of safeguards needed and the appropriate share for each participant, legal and financial considerations may make it very hard to implement methods of providing such safeguards if there is no way to project the quantity of development accurately.

Beginning in the late 1960's, some communities in the United States began to adopt policies to limit and/or control the quantity of increases of their resident population that would otherwise occur. Juergensmeyer *supra* at pp. 369–373. Since that time, states and localities have adopted many growth management programs that emphasize thoughtful coordination of the quantity of land development. Many quantity-oriented growth management programs seek to reduce the cost of public services and facilities.

The late arrival of these quantity limitations reflected lingering doubts about their legal validity in the United States. Juergensmeyer *supra* at 373–374. Early enabling legislation for land use controls did not contain specific authority for regulation of the rate or amount of development. Initially, the legal support for quantity limitations grew out of the local practice of adopting a "moratorium" on development when confronted with a development proposal that caused public outcry. Where the outcry reflected serious public concern about the impact of the proposal on, for example, the adequacy of sewage treatment or the protection of scenic views, the courts allowed communities to halt all development for a reasonable time while they formulated a regulatory strategy. Juergensmeyer *supra* at 377–79.

Burnham v. Monroe County

738 So.2d 471 (Fla.App., 1999).

The Burnhams have owned their property in Monroe County since 1967; they submitted their application for a building permit in July, 1992, after Monroe County's "Rate of Growth Ordinance", commonly referred to as "ROGO" became effective. *See* Monroe County, Fla., Ordinance 16–1992 (June 23, 1992). Under ROGO, Monroe County awards points for certain design features [such as high-efficiency air conditioning systems, hurricane-strength structural windloads, and low-flow plumbing fixtures] included in building plans; building permits are allocated to applicants who have accumulated the most points.

The owners' construction plans did not include enough of the features that ROGO sought to encourage to entitle them to a building permit. The County repeatedly informed them that they could obtain a ROGO allocation, and the ensuing building permit, at any time simply by incorporating simple changes to their plans. At no time did the owners make those changes; they instead chose to challenge the ordinance and sued the County for inverse condemnation ...

It is clear from the record that no taking occurred; all the owners had to do in order to obtain the necessary points for their building permit was to make a few minor changes to their plans. To establish a taking by inverse condemnation, a plaintiff must show that the challenged regulation denies all economically beneficial or productive use of land. *See Lucas v. South Carolina Coastal Council*, 505 U.S. 1003 (1992). The owners made no such showing in this case.

Moreover, the trial court correctly determined that the ROGO ordinance was constitutional, as it substantially advances the legitimate state interests of promoting water conservation, windstorm protection, energy efficiency, growth control, and habitat protection. *See Nollan v. California Coastal Comm'n*, 483 U.S. 825 (1987).■

NOTES AND COMMENTS

1. Once the legal validity of these time-based regulations became established, some communities began to develop more sophisticated use of time factors in their growth management strategies. For example, Pitkin County, Colorado, adopted an ordinance that used a ranking system for each development application based on the impact of the project on the community. The ordinance established an annual quota for new building permits and granted the permits in accordance with the relative rank of each application until the quota was exhausted. The ordinance was upheld in *Wilkinson v. Pitkin County*, 872 P.2d 1269 (Colo.App.1993). *See also Schenck v. City of Hudson*, 114 F.3d 590 (6th Cir.1997) (annual quota for zoning permits upheld.). Where the local government has not backed up the ordinance with careful planning, courts have sometimes thrown out quanti-

tative controls that appeared to be arbitrary. *See, e.g., Rancourt v. Town of Barnstead*, 523 A.2d 55 (N.H.1986).

2.   Quantitative limitations on growth have been most widely accepted when the limits are correlated with programs to expand public services or facilities. In the states of Florida and Washington, for example, the term used for this correlation is "concurrency." New development is supposed to take place at the same time as the public facilities necessary to serve it are built. Juergensmeyer *supra* at 371. Concurrency, like sustainability, sounds great but is hard to define. Difficult timing issues arise over when facilities are deemed to be complete. Is it when financing is assured? Or when construction has started? Or when facilities are open for business? But the concept itself has considerable support despite, or perhaps because of, its indeterminacy.

Strategists who use quantity limitations need to make difficult policy decisions. How do you decide if the level of service demanded by a community reflects realistic objectives? If the local voters continually refuse to vote money to upgrade the schools or the roads, can they legitimately deny development because these facilities are too crowded? On the other hand, if Los Angeles runs low on water, does it need to build desalinization plants in order to accommodate growth?

3.   Limiting the supply of development without reducing the demand has a natural tendency to increase the price that buyers must pay for the product being developed. Where is the line to be drawn between public services that everyone traditionally has a right to receive, such as education and police protection, and scarce resources that can legitimately be conserved by pricing policies?

3.   LIMITING DEVELOPMENT LOCATION.

Some states have concluded that the development of an efficient and environmentally sound transportation system requires the intervention of state or regional policymakers to influence the location of development. For example, in 1999 the Georgia legislature, at the request of Governor Barnes, created the Georgia Regional Transportation Authority, and gave it extensive powers over the location of major developments in the Atlanta metropolitan area. Official Code of Georgia Annotated 50–32–1 et seq. The Authority's initial work plan includes the preparation of a regional transportation plan that will meet federal requirements relating to ozone nonattainment.[16] The Authority also has authority to issue up to $2 billion in bonds for projects that will alleviate air pollution, such as mass transit. See www.grta.org.

Some states have adopted another growth management technique known as "urban growth boundaries." Lines are drawn on a map to delineate where growth will be permitted or encouraged and, conversely,

---

16. For an excellent summary of the   *see* Dunphy, *supra* at 57–72.
history of Atlanta's transportation problems,

where it will not. Hawaii has had such a system for many years, and Oregon, and more recently Washington, have adopted policies at the state level encouraging such boundaries. Urban growth boundaries are designed to encourage growth in places where highways and other costly infrastructure services can reasonably be provided and to preserve from development those areas outside of the line that are rural in character.[17]

Under the Oregon state law mandating growth boundaries for each urban area, local governments are required to set these boundaries in a way that is consistent with various "goals" established by the state. The boundaries must be approved ("acknowledged") by a state agency, the Land Conservation and Development Commission. One of the goals requires each community to plan for the anticipated increase in population that is expected to occur.

Hummel v. Land Conservation and Development Comm'n

954 P.2d 824 (Ore.App.1998).

■ WARREN, J.: Petitioners seek review of an order of respondent Land Conservation and Development Commission (LCDC) on the expanded urban growth boundary (UGB) that the City of Brookings (the city) adopted as part of the periodic review of its comprehensive plan and land use ordinances. In its order LCDC generally approved the expanded UGB but also remanded the periodic review work task concerning the UGB to the city and to intervenor Curry County for certain modifications. Petitioners attack that order to the extent that LCDC approved the expansion of the UGB; the modifications that it required are not in issue. We affirm.

The city is located in the extreme southwest corner of the state. It lies on the northwest side of the Chetco River, which enters the Pacific Ocean at the city's western border. The unincorporated community of Harbor lies directly across the river from the city. The city's current comprehensive plan, which LCDC acknowledged on January 27, 1983, established a UGB that includes the Brookings city limits, the community of Harbor, and a number of additional areas on the edges of those boundaries. That UGB presently contains over 9,000 residents. The Brookings area is expected to grow to over 16,000 people within the next 20 years.

In part because of the anticipated growth, the Department of Land Conservation and Development (DLCD) notified the city in mid–1992 to begin the periodic review process. In late July 1993, DLCD approved the city's periodic review program (work program), which identified a number of specific tasks (work tasks) and gave priorities and target dates for each.

---

17. Urban growth boundaries may be implemented voluntarily by local governments in some states. Douglas Porter's book discusses such programs in such diverse places as Clackamas County, Oregon; Fort Collins, Colorado; King County, Washington; Lexington/Fayette County, Kentucky; Portland, Oregon; and Sarasota County, Florida. Douglas Porter, Profiles in Growth Management, (Urban Land Institute 1996).

The numbered work tasks are: (1) to amend the UGB, among other things in order to provide a 20 year supply of vacant buildable land (priority A); (2) to establish an urban reserve boundary (priority B); (3) to amend the comprehensive plan and land use ordinances to deal with a number of issues, including the extension of the UGB resulting from work task 1 (priority C); (4) to adopt a public facilities plan for the new UGB, including providing for extending public services to the newly included areas (priority D); and (5) to develop a transportation system plan (priority D). Each work task had a separate target date for completion. The later tasks depended in part on the earlier ones; for instance, the city was not to begin work on numbers 4 and 5 until it had completed number 1.

In its preliminary work on work task 1, the city concluded that, in order to accommodate the anticipated population growth and other needs, it had to add 899 acres of buildable land to the existing UGB. The city found some difficulty in locating the needed land because of the geographical character of the Brookings area, which is a narrow flatland between rugged hills on the east and the ocean on the west. Much of the urbanizable flat land was already inside the existing UGB. The city was able to find part of the needed additional land by expanding the UGB to include existing exception areas and a limited amount of resource land on the relatively flat areas north of the city. That additional land, however, was not sufficient to meet the city's need.

It was difficult, if not impossible, for the city to extend the UGB on flat land south of its previous limits, although it did add a few pre-existing exception areas. Other than in those locations, the flat land south of Harbor, known as the Harbor Bench, is a small but highly productive agricultural area that, because of a unique combination of soil and climate, is, for all practical purposes, the only source of Easter lily bulbs and hydrangea stock in the country. The city could not include that agricultural land in the UGB. East of Harbor and the Harbor Bench are the Harbor Hills, which have rugged, unbuildable western slopes and which are the source of the aquifer that supplies the agricultural areas on the Harbor Bench. The Harbor Hills rise directly from the Harbor Bench and are currently zoned forest grazing.

The city decided that the best location for additional vacant buildable acres was in the Harbor Hills. It therefore included a large portion of those hills, beginning directly east of the Harbor Bench agricultural lands and continuing over the top of the hills and down the other side, in the expanded UGB. It recognized that, because of their topography, the western slopes of that portion are not buildable. However, the city found that other sections of the area contain a significant amount of land that is buildable at a variety of price levels. It justified including the unbuildable land in the UGB on the grounds that that land was necessary in order to provide urban services to the buildable land and that excluding it would create a confusing boundary, with non-UGB land surrounding UGB land in an illogical pattern.

Petitioner's arguments are, in one way or another, attacks on the inclusion of the Harbor Hills area in the UGB. . . . In conducting a periodic review, the planning agency does not make one specific change in isolation; rather, it reevaluates the entire situation in order to bring the plan and land use regulations back into compliance with the goals. That process is much closer to the original development and acknowledgment of the plan and regulations than to a plan amendment. At the end of the periodic review process, the entire plan and regulations, including the UGB, must fully comply with all requirements. At this stage of the Brookings process, however, we can determine only whether the UGB complies to the extent that it is possible for it to do so in light of the unknown results of the remaining work tasks.

Petitioners argue that LCDC's qualified acknowledgment of the city's expanded UGB violated Goal 14, the urbanization goal, which describes seven factors to consider in establishing and modifying a UGB:

(1) Demonstrate need to accommodate long-range urban population growth requirements consistent with LCDC goals; (2) Need for housing, employment opportunities, and liability;(3) Orderly and economic provision for public facilities and services; (4) Maximum efficiency of and uses within and on the fringe of the existing urban area; (5) Environmental, energy, economics and social consequences; (6) Retention of agricultural land as defined, with Class I being the highest priority for retention and Class VI the lowest priority; and, (7) Compatibility of the proposed urban uses with nearby agricultural activities.

Petitioners first argue that the expanded UGB violates factors 1 and 2 of Goal 14, the "need" factors, because it includes far more land than the city identified as necessary to provide for its probable growth in the next 20 years. Instead of the 771 acres that, according to petitioners, the city needs, it adopted a UGB that includes an additional 3,491 acres. Petitioners argue that it would be possible to find the needed acres entirely north of the Chetco River without including any part of the Harbor Hills: For that point they focus on two exception areas north of the city. They also attack LCDC's conclusion that it was necessary to add a large amount of unbuildable land in the Harbor Hills in order to reach and serve the buildable land in that area. They concede that that argument would be legitimate if the City was compelled to include the Harbor Hills in order to meet its land needs of 771 acres—in order to reach the flatter, buildable portion of the Harbor Hills at the top of the Hills, urban services such as sewer and water lines would arguably have to be built across the large, unbuildable portion of the Harbor Hills.

By conceding that the city's argument would be legitimate if the city had to include the Harbor Hills to meet its need for buildable land, petitioners necessarily concede that the Goal 14 need factors would be satisfied in that event. That concession resolves this argument because, as respondents point out, petitioners misunderstand the record. The city in fact needs an additional 899 buildable acres, not 771, and the areas that petitioners identify north of the Chetco River are inadequate to satisfy that need. LCDC could also find that the excluded exception areas do not contain the amount of buildable land that petitioners suggest. For those reasons, it was necessary for the city to look to the area south of the river, which as a practical matter means the Harbor Hills. In light of those facts and in light of this concession, petitioners have not shown that LCDC erred on this ground in approving the city's expansion of the UGB in that area.

Petitioners next assert that the revised UGB fails to satisfy factor 3 of Goal 14, because there is no assurance that there will be an orderly provision of public facilities and services to the new area. However, work task 4 requires the city to develop a public facilities plan for the expanded UGB, something that is also necessary to comply with Goal 11. Before adopting the expanded UGB, the city determined that it is feasible to provide the necessary public services to the expanded UGB and that they are in fact likely to be provided. That is sufficient at this point to support LCDC's conclusion that the city satisfied factor 3 of goal 14. Any problems that developing the plan uncovers with the expanded UGB can be considered in connection with work task 4. If it does not prove possible to develop an appropriate plan for the expanded area, the city can then reconsider and modify its action on the UGB. In short, work on matters related to factor 3 will become more precise as the city works on its remaining periodic review work tasks. . . .

We hold, thus, that LCDC did not err in approving the city's expanded UGB at this stage of the periodic review process. We express no opinion on whether actions that the city, DLCD, and LCDC may take at later stages of that process will require any reevaluation of that issue.

Affirmed.■

NOTES AND COMMENTS

1.   The case raises the question of the degree of flexibility that local governments should be given in adapting statewide rules to local conditions. Should the city be forced to pretend that development is feasible on steep hills lacking municipal services when the only other way of meeting state goals for new urban growth would be to destroy a unique agricultural area that "because of a unique combination of soil and climate" is "the only source of Easter lily bulbs and hydrangea stock in the country?"

2.   Location-oriented growth management is by no means dominated by negative attitudes toward growth. The Oregon legislation requires the preparation of transportation plans to promote the efficient location and design of transportation facilities. *See* Dunphy, *supra at 49–50.* Many communities have identified parts of their area that they think are particularly appropriate for development and they focus their strategy on means for increasing these areas' desirability to developers. This strategy is sometimes known as "nodal development."

Communities can offer various financing mechanisms to lure new development to, e.g., industrial parks. Special assessment or taxing districts can help developers defer costs, and many communities offer tax abatement for the most attractive kinds of development. State governments compete actively to provide subsidies to builders of auto or chemical plants.

All of these location-oriented management techniques generally fall under the umbrella of land use planning. Communities identify areas that are appropriate for particular uses and plan to provide the public facilities and services needed by the projected type and quantity of development. One traditional planning technique is capital improvement programming, under which a community develops a list of infrastructure improvements and a time schedule for their construction. Such programs can guide the placement and timing of development because the location of new streets and highways determines where new development will take place. In addition, sewer and water line extensions are often necessary to make housing subdivisions feasible; timing those extensions and deciding where they will go has a large impact on development patterns.

3.   Subdivision regulations can also play a key role in directing development into patterns that will be compatible with surrounding property. Communities will often finance a wide range of local improvements for attractive types of development if they locate in the right area. State and regional agencies may also help to extend public services into rural areas in order to hasten their urbanization.

Zoning can also help attract development to a particular area by keeping out incompatible uses. For example, by barring housing from agricultural or industrial areas a community can help ensure that the desired uses will not be harassed by unhappy neighbors. And despite the traditional kid glove treatment for agriculture, more and more communities are realizing that uses such as hog factories are capable of blighting a wide area in a way that precludes other development.

Some communities seek to attract development by intensifying the use of already developed areas. Sometimes a critical mass is necessary to attract particular types of development, and this can be accomplished by encouraging higher densities in areas in which such development is taking place. A few places like Waikiki and Las Vegas seem to thrive on crowded conditions that most communities would find wholly unacceptable.

G.   FUTURE TRENDS

Throughout the United States a great deal of creative energy is being devoted to devising ways of producing a more energy-efficient, pollution-resistant pattern of transportation and land development. In the next edition of this book the authors hope that it will be appropriate to devote more space to one or more of the following topics, each of which shows promise.

Infill. Energy efficiency is one of the objectives of government programs for the promotion of "infill" development; i.e., the encouragement of new development on vacant or underused land within existing cities. When "brownfields" sites, which have been abandoned by earlier industries, are redeveloped they can take advantage of existing transportation networks and proximity to existing housing. Robert A. Simons, Turning Brownfields into Greenbacks (Urban Land Institute, 1998). If the indirect costs of fringe area development were taken into account, redevelopment of inner city sites may be the more economically efficient alternative. Joel B. Eisen, Brownfields of Dreams: Challenges and Limits of Voluntary Cleanup Programs and Incentives,1996 U. Ill. L. Rev. 883, 1025–26 (1996).

More mass transit. Funding for mass transit has been a significant goal for those who seek to improve energy efficiency. The 1998 TEA–21 law provides a very substantial increase in funding for mass transit. Whether state and local governments will use it to develop new facilities or to maintain aging systems remains to be seen.

Increased urban densities. Land developers have expressed a growing interest in promoting more dense urban development. Downs, *supra* at 79–97. Some architects and planners advocate a "new urbanism" in development design. The concept of new urbanism, sometimes referred to as "neotraditional" development, is based on a desire to reduce the need for automobile travel and to create communities with more social interaction. Neighborhoods are dotted with businesses accessible by foot; networks of bike paths encourage people to leave their cars at home. *See generally* Peter Katz, The New Urbanism: Toward an Architecture of Community (1994).

To date, only a relatively few communities designed according these principles have been completed, and it is too early to evaluate their success. The Disney Company's town in Florida called Celebration has attracted the most attention. But unless these design principles become the new norm among developers, a few demonstration communities are unlikely to have any real influence on patterns of sprawl. Dunn *supra* at 152–155. For information promoting the use of community designs that minimize automotive travel, *see* www.carfree.com.

Increased rail shipments. Increased use of rail for shipments rather than trucks has been one of the goals of environmental groups. *See* Benfield, *supra* at 673. The railroads succeeded in 1992 in persuading Congress to impose a moratorium on increases in the permitted size and weight limits for trucks, but there are some indications that political infighting between the railroad and trucking industry is increasing, and this may trigger further losses of freight volume by the railroads. *See* Frank N. Wilner, Truck–Rail War Looms, Traffic World, February 22, 1999, at 12. And the Transportation Research Board has concluded that diversion of truck traffic to rail is unlikely to have a significant effect on fuel use and pollution emissions. Sustainable Future, *supra* at 122–123.

Peak-hour pricing. Economists have long advocated the establishment of higher prices for traveling at peak times as a way of reducing traffic congestion and improving the overall efficiency of the transportation system.[18] A few communities have undertaken limited experiments with

---

18. For an analysis of a wide array of approaches to value pricing, *see* Roger P. Roess, William R. McShane & Elena S. Prassas, Traffic Engineering 18–27 (2d ed. 1998).

such programs. Felicia B. Young & John T. Berg, Value pricing helps reduce congestion, 62 Public Roads #5 (1999) at 47. Some transit systems do provide discounts for off-peak travel, as do some toll roads and bridges, but the technical problems of implementing such a system on a large scale for automobile travel are daunting. Tirza S. Wahrman, Breaking the Logjam: The Peak Pricing of Congested Urban Roadways under the Clean Air Act to Improve Air Quality and Reduce Vehicle Miles Traveled, 8 Duke Env. L. & Pol'y F. 181 (1998).

Intelligent vehicles. The U.S. Department of Transportation continues to fund research on intelligent vehicle highway systems. Such systems would combine electronic sensors in highways and vehicles with centralized management of traffic flows. Downs, *supra* at 73–74; Lewis T. Branscomb & James H. Keller, Converging Infrastructures: Intelligent Transportation and the National Information Infrastructure (MIT Press, 1996).

Conclusion. Is our present system of virtually total reliance on the automobile a policy that can be sustained indefinitely? In his recent history of American energy consumption, David Nye summarizes:

> The energy choices of the past have brought the United States prosperity, but no more than was achieved by some other countries that use far less. The choices made at the end of the twentieth century will determine whether the US continues to consume more power per capita than any other country. Americans must choose whether to tax gasoline in order to stimulate conversion to alternative energies. They must choose whether deregulation will be used simply to save money in the short term or whether it can be part of a larger strategy of becoming more efficient. They must choose whether to make environmental economics that basis of policy. Individually, they must choose whether they want to drive or to take mass transit, whether they will buy ever-larger houses, how well they will insulate their homes, whether they will invest in low energy light bulbs and appliances, and whether they will adopt solar water heating, heat pumps, and other energy-saving technologies. In designing their cities, Americans can decide whether to encourage cycling, pedestrian traffic, and local shopping. In the workplace, they must decide to what extent computers will be used to reduce commuting. At the polls, they must decide whether to endorse recycling, research on alternative energies, and more fuel-efficient vehicles. In short, they must decide whether they think energy choices matter now, or whether they expect ingenious technologies to solve emerging problems later. They can even choose to believe in technological determinism, which will apparently absolve them from any responsibility to make choices. Whatever Americans decide, in the twenty-first century their economic well-being, the quality of their environment, how to travel, where and how they work, and how they live togther will be powerfully shaped by their consuming power. Nye, *supra* at 273–74.

James Dunn, on the other hand, argues that the "automobile system has been nothing if not sustainable for about a century now," having survived depressions, wars, and energy and pollution crises. Throughout the world, automobiles are "the most popular form of transportation, with people scrambling to own a car in spite of high taxes and bad roads." The "intense popularity and durability" of the automobile means that "calling an as yet nonexistent future system with fewer automobiles more sustainable than the present one would be laughable." Dunn, *supra* at 173–174.

CHAPTER 16

INTERNATIONAL PETROLEUM

Outline of Chapter:

A. INTRODUCTION AND SCOPE

No single chapter can do justice to the legal, political, and socio-economic complexity of international energy transactions. Yet no study of energy law and policy is complete without at least a dip into the wider world of international petroleum. Most of the major American oil companies have shifted their attention and their budgets to international exploration and development. This is where the "elephants"—fields containing over one billion barrels of oil—are to be found. Even large-sized independents have been bitten by the international bug. Many domestic oil and gas lawyers have retooled themselves in international law to work this new frontier.

This chapter is designed to introduce the student to some of the major principles and problems involved when oil companies go abroad to explore for and produce oil and gas, such as:

State ownership of minerals. The United States and Canada are virtually the only countries on earth where minerals can be owned privately. Chapter 6 on Oil analyzed many of the problems which arise under private ownership: the wastefulness of the rule of capture; the need for state conservation legislation; the conflicts between state and federal regulation; the tension between government regulation and unconstitutional takings. Which of these problems disappear and which new ones arise when the state owns all the minerals?

The major forms of international concession agreements between host governments and multinational oil companies. The early concession forms are compared to the oil and gas lease used in the United States on both private and public lands and to modern agreements used today.

The principles of public law used to arbitrate disputes between governments and companies under these concession agreements. Which nation's law will govern the dispute? Can a private company overcome legal barriers to suing a government or a state oil company, such as sovereign immunity and the act of state doctrine?

The environmental and socio-cultural constraints on companies that choose to develop in ecologically sensitive areas like the rainforests or in areas where indigenous peoples still live in pre-industrialized societies. Through the lens of the doctrine of forum non conveniens, which arises when foreign plaintiffs bring suit in U.S. courts alleging environmental or human rights abuses by multinational companies in their native countries, this part discusses whether oil companies can bring sustainable development to rainforest nations.

The overarching theme of this chapter is the interplay of national sovereignty with private rights and, then, their interaction with the international public law of human rights and sustainable development.

Before setting out on this tour of international petroleum transactions, this chapter begins with a summary history of the geopolitics and statistical background of world oil markets. Students should use Figure 6–1 in Chapter 6, showing the price of crude oil from 1880 to the 1990s, as a road map to this next section.

B.   THE HISTORY AND CURRENT STRUCTURE OF INTERNATIONAL OIL

1.   THE GEOPOLITICS OF OIL

a.   THE UNITED STATES: FROM EXPORTER TO IMPORTER

For almost half a century after oil was discovered in Pennsylvania, the United States was the primary source of petroleum and exported its products throughout the world. With little oil production abroad, American oil companies competed only with themselves.

Boom and bust conditions characterized the oil business in the 1860s and early 1870s, but by the 1880s prices began to stabilize when the Standard Oil Company, headed by John D. Rockefeller, obtained control of some 85 to 90 percent of the oil refineries in the United States and was able to establish monopoly prices. The Standard Oil Trust agreement allowed the company to control the production of refined petroleum. In 1889, Congress enacted the Sherman Anti–Trust Act, aimed directly at protecting consumers from the predatory practices of monopolists, especially the Standard Oil Trust.[1] The Standard Oil Trust was "busted" in 1911, and Standard Oil was dissolved into separate entities which ultimately became Exxon, Mobil, Chevron, Sohio/BP, Amoco, Conoco, and ARCO/Sun.

In the 1890s, oil from Russia and Sumatra began to provide competitive sources of kerosene. Standard Oil was forced to compete internationally with various European enterprises, such as the Nobel brothers, the Rothschilds and the newly-formed Royal Dutch Company.

In 1901, oil was first discovered in the region known as the Middle East by British companies in Persia (now Iran). This stimulated the search that located the extensive fields of Iraq, Kuwait, Saudi Arabia and neighboring states. The American dominance in oil production ended after World War II when it became clear that other parts of the world had oil reserves that would far outlast American supplies.

b.   FROM THE 1930s TO 1970s

The following excerpts from Daniel Yergin's history of the oil industry highlight some of the key events leading to creation of an international market in oil.

---

1. *See* Daniel Yergin, The Prize: The Epic Quest for Oil, Money and Power 45, 56–77, 96–110 (1991). The "trust" was formalized in 1882 in the Standard Oil Trust Agreement which created a board of trustees in whose hands was placed the stock of all the entities controlled by Standard Oil. The trustees were charged with "general supervision" of the 14 wholly owned and 26 partly owned companies, and they selected the directors and officers which could include themselves. The trust agreement created a central office to coordinate and rationalize the activities of the different operating entities. This trust was perfectly legal and turned what was once a method for protecting widows and orphans into a device for wielding monopoly power.

Daniel Yergin, The Prize: The Epic Quest for Oil, Money and Power

Simon & Schuster, 1991, at 395–396, 531–32, 544, 567, and 569.

"We're Running Out of Oil!"

The late 1920s and early 1930s had seen an explosive growth in the United States in discoveries and in additions to known reserves. But from the middle 1930s onward, while significant "revisions and additions" were made to existing oil fields, the discovery rate of new fields had fallen off very sharply, leading to the view that additions in the future would be more difficult, more expensive, and more limited. The precipitous decline in new discoveries transfixed and frightened those responsible for fueling a global war. "The law of diminishing returns is becoming operative," said the director of reserves for the Petroleum Administration for War in 1943. "As new oil fields are not being formed and as the number is ultimately finite, the time will come sooner or later when the supply is exhausted." For the United States, he added, "the bonanza days of oil discovery, for the most part, belong to history."

Such gloomy analyses could lead to only one conclusion. Although oil was then flowing out from American ports to all the war fronts, the United States was destined to become a net importer of oil, a transformation of historic dimensions, and one with potentially grave security implications. The wartime gloom about America's recoverable oil resources gave rise to what became known as the "conservation theory" that the United States, and particularly the United States government, had to control and develop "extraterritorial" (foreign) oil reserves in order to reduce the drain on domestic supplies, conserve them for the future, and thus guarantee America's security. . . . And where were these foreign reserves to be found? There was only one answer. "In all surveys of the situation," Herbert Feis, the State Department's Economic Adviser, was to say, "the pencil came to an awed pause at one point and place: the Middle East."

The New Competitors

The proliferation of players in the oil game was remarkable, especially in the Middle East. In 1946, 9 oil companies operated in the region; by 1956, 19; and by 1970, the number reached 81. Yet even this was only part of a larger expansion. Between 1953 and 1972, by one estimate, more than 350 companies either entered the foreign (that is, non-U.S.) oil industry or significantly expanded their participation. Among these "new internationals" were 15 large American oil companies; 20 medium-sized American oil companies; 10 large American natural gas, chemical, and steel companies; and 25 non-American firms. How different this was from the situation at the beginning of the postwar period, when only six American firms, in addition to the five acknowledged American majors, had any active exploration interests anywhere overseas at all. In 1953, no private oil company anywhere in the world, other than the seven largest, had as much as 200 million barrels of proven foreign reserves; by 1972, at least thirteen of the "new internationals" each owned more than 2 billion barrels of foreign reserves. Altogether, the new entrants owned 112 billion barrels of proven reserves a quarter of the free world total. By 1972, the "new internationals" had a total daily output among them of 5.2 million barrels per day.

One of the most obvious results of such a crowded arena was a decline in profitability. The industry had earned high rates of return on its foreign investment until the mid–1950s—the rewards, some would say, for the risks taken in distant, inaccessible regions in the turbulent postwar days, or, others would say, the result of an oligopoly, an industry dominated by a handful of major players. The series of crises in Mossadegh and Iran, the Korean War, and Suez all continued to buoy the profit rate above 20 percent. But with the reopening of the Suez Canal in 1957, the intense competition to sell supplies started to force both prices and profits down. Thereafter, and continuing through the sixties, investment in foreign oil yielded 11 to 13 percent returns, which were pretty much the same as for manufacturing industries. While the exporting countries were counting more money than they had ever seen before, the oil industry itself was no longer being as well rewarded as in the past.

The Conversion of Europe

Part of the reason for oil's victory over coal was environmental, especially in Britain. London had long suffered from "Killer Fogs" as the result of pollution from coal burning, particularly the open fires in houses. So thick were those fogs that confused motorists literally could not find their way home to their own streets and instead would drive their cars onto lawns blocks away from their own houses. Whenever the fogs descended, London's hospitals would fill with people suffering from acute respiratory ailments. In response, "smokeless zones" were established where the burning of coal for home heating was banned, and in 1957 Parliament passed the Clean Air Act, which favored oil. Still, the biggest force promoting the switch was cost; oil prices were going down, and coal prices were not. From 1958 onward, oil was a cheaper industrial fuel than coal.

The End of the Twenty–Year Surplus: To a Seller's Market.

The 1970s also saw a dramatic shift in world oil. Demand was catching up with available supply, and the twenty-year surplus was over. As a result, the world was rapidly becoming more dependent on the Middle East and North Africa for its petroleum....

In the period 1957 to 1963, surplus capacity in the United States had totaled about 4 million barrels per day. By 1970, only a million barrels per day remained, and even that number may have been overstated. That was the year, too, that American oil production reached 11.3 million barrels per day. That was the peak, the highest level it would ever reach. From then on, it began its decline. In March 1971, for the first time in a quarter century, the Texas Railroad Commission allowed all-out production at 100 percent of capacity.... With consumption continuing to rise, the United States had to turn to the world oil market to satisfy the demand.... Imports as a share of total oil consumption [from 1967 to 1973] rose from 19 percent to 36 percent.

Environmental Impact

Another significant shift was taking place in the industrial countries. Man's view of the environment and his relationship to it were also changing.... Beginning in the mid–1960s, environmental issues began to compete successfully for their place in the political process, in the United States and elsewhere. Air pollution prompted utilities around the world to shift from coal to less-polluting oil....

The retreat from coal was accelerated, and reliance on cleaner-burning oil grew. Nuclear power was bruited as an environmental improvement over the combustion of hydrocarbons. Efforts were accelerated to search for new sources of oil, and toward the end of the 1960s, hopes grew for major production offshore of California. There, after all, before the end of the nineteenth century, the very first drilling in water had taken place from piers near Santa Barbara. Now, more than seventy years later, rigs were being positioned along the scenic Southern California coastline. But then, in January 1969, the drilling of an offshore well in the Santa Barbara channel encountered an unexpected geological anomaly, and as a result, an estimated six thousand barrels of oil seeped out of an uncharted fissure and bubbled to the surface. A gooey slick of heavy crude oil flowed unchecked into the coastal waters and washed up on thirty miles of beaches. The public outcry was nationwide and reached right across the political spectrum. The Nixon Administration imposed a moratorium on California offshore development, in effect shutting it down. However great the need for oil, the leak increased opposition to energy development in other environmentally sensitive areas, including the most promising area in all of North American, ... Alaska.■

c.   NATIONALISM, WAR, AND EMBARGOES: THE FIRST OIL SHOCK

The relative stability of oil prices ended with a bang at about two o'clock in the afternoon on October 6, 1973. In the middle of the Jewish holiday of Yom Kippur, Syria and Egypt launched a surprise attack on Israel. The United States, fearful that Israel might be overrun by the combined attack, rushed supplies to the Israeli armed forces. Israel counterattacked, and regained the territory it had lost. In return, Arab nations that had supported Syria and Egypt declared an embargo on the shipment of oil to the United States, the Netherlands, and other countries friendly to Israel. As certain Arab producers cut back production, U.S. refineries scrambled for oil, and shortages sent crude prices soaring. (Review Figure 6–1 in the Oil Chapter).

The events of the 1970s unsheathed the power of the "oil weapon" and led to a radical transformation in the international oil industry. In 1970, large, vertically integrated companies dominated the industry. They owned 94 percent of oil production in the non-Communist world and sold 91 percent of all refined products. By 1984, the companies' share of crude oil ownership had been reduced to less than 40 percent as most African and Middle East countries nationalized their oil reserves and production. The following provides a brief summary of this transformation:

The Center for Strategic and International Studies, The Critical Link: Energy and National Security in the 1980s

Ballinger, 126–27 (pub. rev. ed. 1982).

Nationalization of Production

Up to 1970 the Seven Sisters [Royal Dutch Shell, Exxon, Gulf, Texaco, BP, Mobil and Standard Oil of California (Chevron)] dominated world petroleum trade. They produced the oil, shipped it to major markets in Europe and Japan, refined it and sold the products to the final user. Vertical integration gave the companies extraordinary logistical flexibility. As the main suppliers of crude oil to most refiners worldwide and as distributors of refined products, they could readily adjust supply and demand in most markets. Furthermore, even when a few countries nationalized production—notably Mexico and Iran in the 1930s and 1950s—power over the downstream end of the industry allowed the companies to maintain considerable control over the market for those nations' crude oil. As one historian of the oil industry has noted,

> However successful host governments were in finding technicians to help the oil flowing, they were lost without customers on world markets. These were difficult to find as long as the bulk of the world's refineries have either been owned by the majors or tied to them by long-term supply contracts, and this difficulty was exacerbated by the general world glut of oil in the 1960s.

Thus, with the ability to restrict markets for the producing nations for their crude oil, the major companies could preserve their preeminence in both the upstream and downstream aspects of the industry.

Originally the major oil companies received concessions from the oil-bearing countries of Latin America and the Persian Gulf, under which the companies developed oil fields in certain areas for a given length of time (fifty years, for example). In return the companies paid royalties or excise taxes to their "host" governments. This system gave the companies complete control over the rate of oil production, pricing, and exports. In short, the companies took all the risks of failure and all the financial rewards of success. The countries by contrast received an income from production with little investment of capital or labor.

"The concession system", as one expert has noted, "by its very nature could not satisfy the desire of producing country governments for more influence on the rate at which their oil was produced or on other decisions concerning the exploitation of their resources." Any reduction in prices for crude oil because of market conditions automatically cut revenues to the producing government. Moreover, the gradual depletion of reserves eroded the base for future revenues, especially for the Persian Gulf states, since oil is virtually their sole source of income.

Concerned about the exploitation of their resources, some of the Middle Eastern oil producers—Saudi Arabia, Iran, Iraq, and Kuwait—joined Venezuela in forming the Organization of Petroleum Exporting Countries (OPEC) in 1960. OPEC set out to coordinate long-term policies on production rates, pricing, and taxation of the companies. During the 1960s OPEC wielded little power, largely because of a world oil glut and constant price-cutting as older companies battled with newer companies to preserve or increase markets. The price wars eventually led to a confrontation between the oil companies and the producing countries that would mark the end of oil company control over world oil production.■

* * *

d. THE ERA OF PRICE CONTROLS

The sharp rise in oil prices following the 1973 embargo caused anguished cries of pain from millions of American consumers. The reaction of the various members of Congress was heavily influenced by the particular part of the country they represented. Regional politics had always permeated national oil policy. When foreign oil was cheap, consumers on the east coast sought to import as much as possible. Producers from Texas and other states, however, argued that cheap foreign oil was driving them out of business. Representatives of the producing states demanded limits on oil imports, arguing that national security required a strong domestic industry. Early in the Eisenhower Administration, voluntary quotas on imported oil were tried and failed. Then in 1957, Eisenhower instituted the Mandatory Oil Import Program (MOIP), which limited the amount of foreign oil that could be brought into the country. Despite this program, imports continued to climb because of exemptions in the program that fed America's hunger for inexpensive crude oil and refined products. With the 1973 embargo, foreign oil prices rose to such an extent that MOIP became obsolete. Federal attention instead turned to protecting the consumer from this first oil shock.

Between 1970 and 1981, the federal government maintained a complex system of oil price controls, first as an anti-inflationary measure and then to prevent "windfall profits" to domestic producers whose $3 per barrel oil could sell for $30 a barrel in 1980. Oil prices were regulated at each stage of production, refining, wholesaling, and retailing. These controls were first administered through the President's Cost of Living Council, the now defunct Federal Energy Administration, and finally through the Department of Energy (DOE). The Emergency Petroleum Allocation Act, 15 U.S.C.A. § 751 *et seq.*, authorized the President to allocate petroleum products because of the national oil shortage.

The regulations resulted in an intricate price and allocation structure, involving such complex concepts as "two-tier pricing, entitlements, exception relief, small refiner bias, and the stripper well exemption, to name a few of the arcane terms that have become associated with the regulation of petroleum at the federal level during the 1970s."[2] The general policy of the program was to encourage producers to explore for "new oil" by allowing

---

2. Jan G. Laitos and Joseph P. Tomain, Energy and Natural Resources Law 443 (West 1992).

them to sell such oil at a higher price, while preventing them from raising the price of "old oil" and reaping windfall profits. Thus the legal question of whether any particular crude oil was new or old had great economic significance to the producer. Old oil prices were determined by reference to both historical and current levels of production from a given property (the "base production control level.") Oil produced at or below that level was "old" oil, while oil produced in excess of that level was "new" oil. If producers invested capital in new production, the cost was passed through to the refiners of the new oil and then to consumers, and the price of new oil rose to market levels.

The disparity between the price of controlled oil and uncontrolled new oil had an unequal impact on different groups of refiners. With a dual pricing system, the major integrated oil companies, which as a class had greater access to old oil, had significantly lower refining costs than did small independent refiners. The government's response was the Entitlements Program Regulations under the Energy Policy and Conservation Act, 42 U.S.C.A. § 6201 *et seq.*, which tried to equalize the impact of the two-tier pricing system. Each refiner was required to have an "entitlement" for each barrel of old oil it refined. Refiners were issued monthly entitlements equal to their proportionate share of the national ratio of old oil to new oil. A refiner that used more old oil than the national average had to buy additional entitlements from refiners that were below the national average. Small refiners received special entitlements to cheaper old oil so that they could stay competitive.

The price and allocation controls pitted the majors against the independents, importers against domestic producers, and states with new oil against states with old oil. Virtually no one was happy with the program, and its expiration in 1981 was greeted joyfully by almost everyone.

e. THE AYATOLLAH AND THE SECOND OIL SHOCK

The sharp price increases that followed the Yom Kippur war of 1973 became known as the first oil shock. A second shock hit in 1979, when the Shah of Iran was ousted and replaced by a theocratic government headed by the Ayatollah Khomeini. On November 12, 1979, in response to the taking of hostages by Iran, President Carter banned the importation into the United States of oil produced in Iran. The Iranian government then placed an embargo on the export of its oil to the United States. Oil prices skyrocketed again.

The price increases were fueled by a wave of panic buying at all levels. Industrial users and utilities furiously built inventories as insurance against rising prices and possible shortages. Consumers did the same:

> Before 1979, the typical motorist in the Western world drove around with his tank only one-quarter full. Suddenly worried about gasoline shortages, he too started building inventories, which is another way of saying that he now kept his gas tank three-quarters full. And suddenly, almost overnight, upwards of a billion gallons of motor fuel

were sucked out of gasoline station tanks by America's frightened motorists.[3]

With supply down by about 2,000,000 barrels a day, and demand increased by 3,000,000 barrels of panic buying, the United States suddenly had a five million barrel shortfall. This drove the price of oil from about $13.00 to $34.00 a barrel.

In an effort to alleviate the hardships caused by the shortage, the Department of Energy imposed quotas on the sale of oil products and implemented a new system of mandatory allocations that allowed domestic refiners injured by this embargo to receive cheaper oil from other domestic refiners. A program to ration gasoline was readied, but it was never needed because of the third (and even less expected) oil shock which hit in early 1981. This third shock requires some knowledge about OPEC.

f.   THE ROLE OF OPEC

In 1960, Venezuela had persuaded Saudi Arabia, Kuwait, Iraq and Iran to join together as the Organization of Petroleum Exporting Countries (OPEC) with the goal of increasing their oil revenues.[4] During the 1960s, OPEC was relatively ineffective, but Egypt's seizure of the Suez Canal in 1969 provided a rallying point for the producing nations. When oil production in the U.S. peaked and the Mideast conflicts erupted, OPEC's solidarity made it appear invincible. More nations joined the cartel, and petrodollars filled the coffers of their national treasuries. The following excerpt describes OPEC more fully.

Alfred A. Marcus, The Organization of Petroleum Exporting Countries, in Controversial Issues in Energy Policy 57–61

(Sage, 1992)

The Organization of Petroleum Exporting Countries (OPEC) is a cartel that was formed in 1960 by Iran, Iraq, Kuwait, Saudi Arabia, and Venezuela. OPEC now includes 13 countries—Algeria, Ecuador, Gabon, Indonesia, Libya, Nigeria, Qatar, and the United Arab Emirates in addition to the 5 founding members. Of these 13 nations, 6 are Arab—Iraq, Kuwait, Saudi Arabia, the United Arab Emirates, Libya, and Algeria. Although Iran is not an Arab nation, it is Islamic and borders Arab nations. In 1967–1968, the Arab members of OPEC formed an exclusively Arab organization, the Organization of Arab Petroleum Exporting Countries (OAPEC). Syria and Egypt subsequently joined OAPEC. On October 17, 1973, 11 days after the armies of Syria and Egypt launched a surprise attack on Israel, OAPEC

---

3. Yergin, *supra* at 687.

4. Ironically, the birth of OPEC was brought about by a Venezuelan oil minister, Perez Alfonzo, who had studied the oil industry while living in the United States. He proposed to model a global alliance on the Texas Railroad Commission's system of market demand prorationing. Such an alliance would restrict production and prevent Venezuela's high cost oil industry from being swamped by cheap oil from the Mideast. *See* Yergin, *supra* at 512.

announced a cutoff of oil to Western countries and Japan. The 1973 oil embargo was one of the most dramatic actions taken by a cartel in history, catching nearly all observers by surprise and altering the course of post-World War II history. . . .

On January 1, 1979, oil production in another OPEC nation, Iran, was almost entirely shut down because of the strikes and political disturbances that led to the overthrow of the Shah and the establishment of a fundamentalist Islamic republic. Iraq then invaded Iran, and on September 25, 1980, both countries started to bomb each other's oil facilities. The Iraqis damaged the Iranian refinery at Abadan—the world's largest—and the Iranians retaliated against Iraqi refineries at Basra. Oil tankers and freighters, trapped in the Shatt al-Arab waterway, had nowhere to go. Oil tanker traffic through the Strait of Hormuz was delayed because shipowners feared they would be caught in the conflict. With supplies reduced, the world again faced a major petroleum price hike.

. . . No matter what the effects of the 1973 Arab boycott were, the impetus for the boycott was political. The Iranian Revolution and Iran–Iraq War were not pursued for economic reasons. Indeed, by contributing to a worldwide recession, they weakened the hold of oil on the world economy. The collapse in world oil prices then devastated the economies of the OPEC countries. . . . The economic theory of cartel behavior misses the deep-seated political passions that affect the behavior of Persian Gulf nations. Thus, along with economics, it is necessary to consider political explanations for what OPEC does.

Conditions vary considerably among the OPEC countries. Some are democracies; some are dictatorships. Some are ruled by military juntas and some are governed by traditional monarchies. . . . Population, per capita income, and oil wealth divide the OPEC nations. There are over 150 million Indonesians and almost 100 million Nigerians, but only about 1 million people living in the United Arab Emirates, and only 200,000 in Qatar. Indonesia is a very poor country with GDP per capita under $500, whereas the United Arab Emirates and Qatar are very rich countries with GDP per capita above $20,000. Saudi Arabia, Kuwait, Iraq, and Iran have the largest crude oil reserves in the world. Indonesia possesses less than 6% of the proven Saudi reserves, and Nigeria less than 10%. Some OPEC countries have sufficient production capacity to generate oil revenues to meet their economic development needs, but others cannot meet their economic development requirements with oil revenues alone. Saudi Arabia, Qatar, the United Arab Emirates, and Kuwait belong in the former category; their oil revenues provide all they need for economic development. Indonesia, Nigeria, Algeria, and Venezuela belong in the latter category, with oil revenues insufficient to provide for their economic development needs.

OPEC nations that are able to finance their economic growth with their oil revenues have different economic interests than OPEC nations that cannot. . . . Nations like Saudi Arabia, which are rich in crude oil reserves, do not want prices rising to the point where alternatives to OPEC oil become feasible. They are likely to remain oil exporters for a very long time and therefore have an interest in preserving a healthy oil market over the long term. OPEC nations unable to finance their economic growth with their oil revenues have a different outlook: Their need is to generate revenues as quickly as possible. Their oil reserves are limited and their potential for future oil discoveries slim, so they do not care if prices rise to the point where it becomes feasible to develop alternatives. . . .

Because the nations with small reserves are not likely to be major producers in the future, they have no reason to consider Saudi Arabia's long-term interests. But the price increases they favor can be achieved only if such countries as Saudi Arabia keep oil from the market. The countries with small reserves are not in a position to achieve price increases on their own to help them maximize short-term earnings; thus, it has to be the nations rich in crude oil reserves that withhold the oil. For these nations to withhold oil depends on whether they can earn more money from doing so than from investing abroad. From 1973 to 1979, when oil prices went up more rapidly than the rate of return from investments abroad, it was in their interest not to produce oil. The rate of return on their investments did not match the rate of return from keeping oil in the ground. This situation reversed itself in the 1980s, however. When oil prices declined and interest rates on investments abroad increased, it was no longer profitable for these countries to withhold oil from the market. From a purely economic point of view, OPEC's cohesion diminished in the later period.

For economic reasons, Saudi Arabia, the United Arab Emirates, Kuwait, and Qatar can be expected to pursue a policy of moderation. These countries have extensive investments in the West and do not want to see Western economies hurt or the power of Western governments undermined. The political reasons for a policy of moderation are to maintain the support of the United States and other Western governments. These nations also rely on the United States and the West for military protection. Without weapons and other assistance, the survival of these regimes is in jeopardy. The threat comes from Arab extremists. Politically, however, association with the West is a liability because extremists in the Arab and Islamic world attack them because of it.

For some OPEC countries, economic calculations are not paramount. Iraq, Iran, and Libya are ruled by cliques hostile to Western pragmatism and materialism. (They would say western exploitation and power.) For them, economic prosperity is incidental to political ambitions. Oil can finance terrorism and be exchanged for weapons to fight the West. The ruling cliques of the oil-rich nations also are sympathetic to many of the causes of the extremists (e.g., Palestinian nationalism), supporting them monetarily and in other ways. Without hesitation in 1973, they used oil as a political weapon in a campaign against Western interests, and they remain vulnerable to political blackmail from the extremists. The premise of economic theory is that cartel members are rational, calculating economic actors that seek to maximize their material gain, but the reality of OPEC is that oil is used not only for the purposes of economic development but also for redressing political grievances.■

OPEC functioned rather well as long as Saudi Arabia was willing to produce far less than its capacity in order to maintain high prices. As a country with a small population and huge oil reserves, Saudi Arabia had more flexibility to control production without causing internal hardship than did many other OPEC countries.

In 1979, however, with the price of oil exceeding $30.00 per barrel, the Saudis began to worry that oil might be priced out of the market, or that the consuming countries might "destabilize" the situation by fomenting revolutions or engaging in military activity. They became increasingly reluctant to hold down their production as a means of maintaining such high prices.

g.   THE THIRD OIL SHOCK: PRICES DROP

The Saudis' suspicions proved to be accurate. The third oil shock came when consumers began to switch from expensive oil to other fuels in a big way. Economists had generally assumed that the demand for oil would not vary even if the price went up because oil was a necessity. This theory was tested in the early 1980s and found to be wrong. Although it took a few years, consumers and endusers responded to the high price of oil by implementing conservation practices. Oil consumption began to drop off. The third oil shock was the shock of seeing prices plunge in the early 1980s.

Energy conservation was largely the result of fuel switching and technological innovation. Responding to 1975 legislation that mandated a doubling of the average fuel efficiency of new automobiles, automobile companies created cars that reduced oil consumption by 2 million barrels per day. By 1985, the United States was 25 percent more energy efficient and 32 percent more oil efficient than it had been in 1973. Similarly, Japan became 31 percent more energy efficient and 51 percent more oil efficient. By 1983, oil consumption in the entire noncommunist world was 45.7 million barrels per day, about 6 million barrels less than daily consumption had been at its peak in 1979.[5] The effects of conservation and fuel substitution on the demand for oil in the United States are depicted in Figure 16–1. Daniel Yergin explains further:

"Although OPEC attempted to cut production to help stabilize prices, the various OPEC countries could not agree on how to share the pain, with the result that workable quota reductions were not systematically achieved. In 1985, in an atmosphere of growing animosity between the two largest producers, Iran and Saudi Arabia, the Saudi government increased production. Oil prices, which had been falling gradually since 1981, dropped sharply. Oil prices in Texas plummeted to $10. This was "the Third Oil Shock, but all the consequences ran in the opposite direction. Now, the exporters were scrambling for markets, rather than buyers for supplies.

---

5.   Yergin, *supra* at 718.

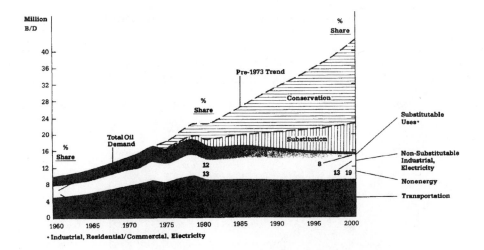

Figure 16–1

U.S. Oil Demand, Actual (1960–79) & Projected (1980–2000), from Exxon Co. USA, Energy Outlook 1980–2000 (1981) as printed in Government Institutes, Inc., Energy Reference Handbook (3rd ed. 1981) p. 296.

And buyers rather than sellers were playing leapfrog, each jumping over the other in pursuit of the lowest price.''[6]

Today, American oil importers are increasingly relying on supplies from Latin America, Canada and the North Sea rather than on oil from the Mideast. Venezuela supplied over 17 percent of U.S. oil imports in 1996 while Saudi Arabia dropped to below 15 percent, slightly behind Canada's 15.05 percent. Mexico supplied over 13 percent and 6.5 percent came from the North Sea. The share from South American countries is still small but growing rapidly. 75 Platt's Oilgram Price Report #56, at 10 (March 21, 1997).

In 1998, the U.S. imported more than 50 percent of its oil consumption. The national security implications of this dependence on imports are discussed in Chapter 18.

h.   OIL ON THE COMMODITY EXCHANGE

Today, the power of oil companies to control prices has vanished, and the OPEC countries have had only limited success in maintaining fixed prices. Oil prices are determined on the commodity markets. The New York Mercantile Exchange (NYMEX) and the International Petroleum Exchange (IPE) trade oil futures daily and ''spot'' markets dominate industry pricing. In recent years, the price of oil has been relatively stable in the range of $15.00 to $19.00 a barrel. This is around the ''consensus'' price discussed by both OPEC and non-OPEC producing nations (such as Norway and Mexico) after the Third Oil Shock.[7] However, this price can fluctuate quite

---

6.   Yergin, *supra* at 750.

7.   Vice President, and then President, George Bush was a former independent oil

widely over shorter periods, as witnessed by the following monthly price chart:

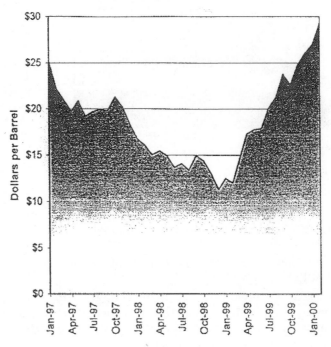

Source: Reuters. The crude oil price is calculated as the monthly average of the daily settlement price for the front month NYMEX crude oil futures price for West Texas Intermediate crude oil delivered at Cushing, OK.

Every major oil company struggled to adapt to the new competitive world of trading oil on the spot market.[8] The major oil companies' control over

man from West Texas. He feared that the unimaginably low prices of the Third Oil Shock would cripple the domestic oil industry. On a trip to Saudi Arabia in April 1986, as Vice President, Bush is reported to have warned the Saudis that the United States would impose a tariff on imported oil if prices remained so low. A tariff would transfer petrodollars from oil exporters to the U.S. Treasury. (The price collapse alone transferred $50 billion from oil producers to oil consumers in 1986). Whether this warning was real or not, the December 1986 meeting of OPEC ministers adopted a "reference price" of $18

a barrel, and agreed to a quota that managed to bring prices up. Yergin, *supra* at 750–64.

8. As Yergin writes: "Not only established modes of operation, but fundamental, deeply held beliefs were being challenged. 'The concept I was taught was that you moved your own crude through your own refining and downstream system,' said George Keller, the chairman of Chevron. 'It was so obvious that it was a truism.' The move to the commodity style of trading would be resisted in many companies by traditionalists who saw this direction as an uncouth, immoral, and inappropriate way to conduct the oil business—almost against the laws of

prices is minimal now that the predominant source of oil for the United States is not domestic but overseas. Oil produced in the United States competes in an international market. Daniel Yergin summarizes:

> Once it had been Standard Oil that had set the price. Then it had been the Texas Railroad Commission system in the United States and the majors in the rest of the world. Then it was OPEC. Now price was being established, every day, instantaneously, on the open market, in the interaction of the floor traders on the Nymex with buyers and sellers glued to computer screens all over the world.... [The Nymex price joined] the gold price, interest rates, and the Dow Jones Industrial Average among the most vital and carefully monitored measures of the daily beat of the world economy. Yergin, *supra* at 725–26.

NOTES AND COMMENTS

1. Iraq invaded Kuwait in August 1990, launching Project Desert Storm which sent U.S. troops to defend Kuwait and other friendly Arab countries against Saddam Hussein's aggression. Iraq set virtually all of Kuwait's 1000 wells on fire. One correspondent described the scene as follows: "Dante would have felt right at home in Kuwait, a desert paradise that has suddenly been transformed into an environmental inferno. Across the land hundreds of orange fireballs roar like dragons, blasting sulfurous clouds high into the air. Soot falls like gritty snowflakes.... From overcast skies drips a greasy black rain, while sheets of gooey oil slap against a polluted shore." Time, March 18, 1991 at p.36.[9]

No fourth oil shock occurred during Desert Storm. Why not?

2. What explains the sharp fall and then rise in crude prices in 1998–2000 in Figure 16–2? With weakened demand in 1998 due to the Asian crisis, oil prices fell throughout the year. But when they plummeted to $10 a barrel in December 1998, a twelve–year low, OPEC ministers resolved to act. OPEC oil export revenues had fallen by 35 percent in just one year, to the lowest point since 1972 on an inflation-adjusted basis. The sharp decline sent OPEC members' budgets into steep deficits. At their March 1999 meeting, both OPEC and non-OPEC countries agreed to cut output by 2.1 million barrels a day. The non-OPEC members, Mexico, Norway, Russia,

nature. They took a lot of persuading, but in due course they were persuaded. What it came down to in most of the companies was the establishment of trading as a separate profit center, a way to make money on its own terms, and not merely as a method for assuring that supply and demand were balanced within the parent company's own operations. If there had been no loyalty on the part of exporters toward companies when supplies were tight, then, in time of surplus, there would be no loyalty on the part of companies toward the exporters. Buyers would shop for the cheapest barrel anywhere in the world, whether to use it themselves or to turn around and trade it again, all in order to be as competitive as possible." Yergin, *supra* at 723.

9. The "Fires of Kuwait" is a stunning documentary of the heroic feats of oil well firefighters from around the world, but especially from Texas, to bring the wells under control. It is often shown in IMAX theaters connected to science museums and is a "must see."

andOman agreed to trim 400,000 barrels and ten of the 11 members of OPEC pledged to cut output by 1.7 million barrels. By July, compliance with their pledges boosted prices to almost $20 a barrel. Nigeria, one of the group's weaker members in compliance, saw output fall by 30,000 barrels a day because of civil unrest. However, Iraq boosted output in July to take advantage of newly approved exports of oil-for-food by the United Nations. A U.N. release reported that Iraq was producing its fields above MER rates, resulting in reservoir damage and lower ultimate yields.

The question is: will the cartel hold? Qatar has said the cartel will be forced to abandon its cuts if skyrocketing prices start to reduce demand. In July 1999, the president of Venezuela's national oil company said that OPEC should increase output if prices climb to $22. The price of crude oil immediately fell 5 percent, the biggest drop in seven months. However, by March 2000, the price of a barrel of crude oil had reached more than $30, and soaring gasoline prices had become part of the presidential primary debates and election-year politics. Secretary of Energy Richardson was dispatched on a whirlwind tour to convince the major OPEC players that they should increase output to moderate the impact on importing countries' economies. In March 2000, the House of Representatives passed legislation requiring the President to consider restrictions on military aid to oil-producing countries engaged in price-fixing.

3.   Daniel Yergin's sequel to *The Prize*, titled *The Commanding Heights* (Simon & Schuster, 1998), documents the battle between governments and the marketplace to control the dominant industries in the world economy.

2.   Statistical Background to International Oil

Between 1953 and 1972, over 300 private companies and more than 50 different state-owned companies either entered or expanded into the international oil business. See Neil H. Jacoby, Multinational Oil: A Study in Industrial Dynamics 120 (1974). In a chapter of the American Association of Petroleum Geologists' book, *International Oil and Gas Ventures: A Business Perspective* (forthcoming 2000), Dr. Michelle Michot Foss, Director of the Energy Institute of the University of Houston, explains the major influences on international exploration. Here are some of the graphs with accompanying "sound bites."

Figure 16–3 shows how the percentage shares of total industry profits reflect the changing structure of the industry. National Oil Companies (NOCs) and governments now take almost 80% of industry profits:

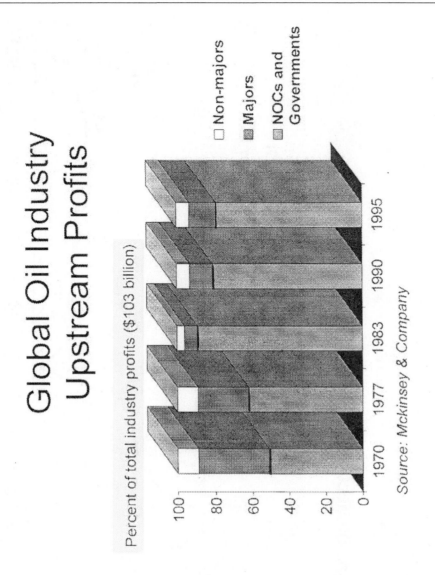

Figure 16–3

Source: Data from Oil & Gas J. (Sept. 8, 1997) adapted and copyrighted by the Energy Institute of the University of Houston; also appearing in Michelle Michot Foss, "Major Influences in the International Exploration Business," in International Oil and Gas Ventures: A Business Perspective (American Ass'n of Petroleum Geologists, forthcoming 2000).

Figure 16–4 shows that return on investment (ROI) for both U.S. and foreign projects has declined significantly since 1980–81. In recent years, the ROI for foreign projects has converged with the ROI domestically:

This fall in rates of return has driven the industry to restructure through mergers and acquisitions and to adopt new technologies like 3–D

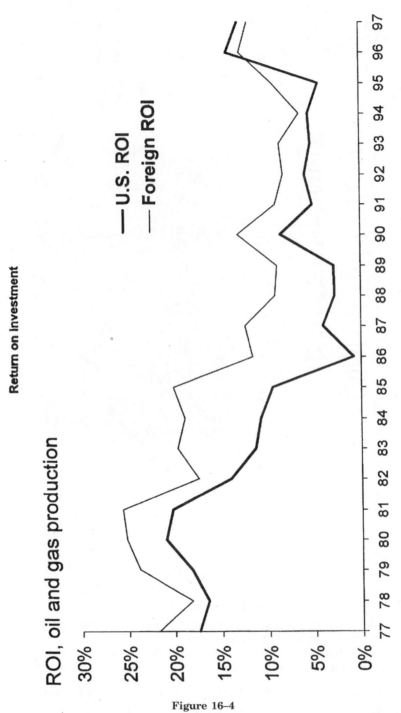

Figure 16–4

Source: Data from EIA, adapted, copyrighted, and also appearing as in Fig. 16–3 *supra*.

seismic to lower costs. Finding costs for oil, both in the U.S. and abroad, have decreased, accompanied by large-scale employment reductions, as shown in Figure 16–5 below:

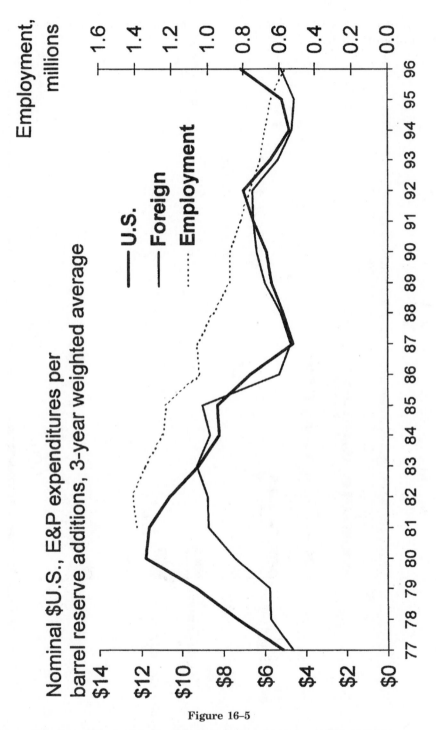

Figure 16–5

Source: Data from EIA adapted, copyrighted, and also appearing as in Fig. 16–3 *supra*.

OPEC and the countries of the former Soviet Union (FSU) continue to dominate world oil reserves, even though South America and Africa show growth in reserves while North America and Europe have lost ground, as seen in Figure 16–6:

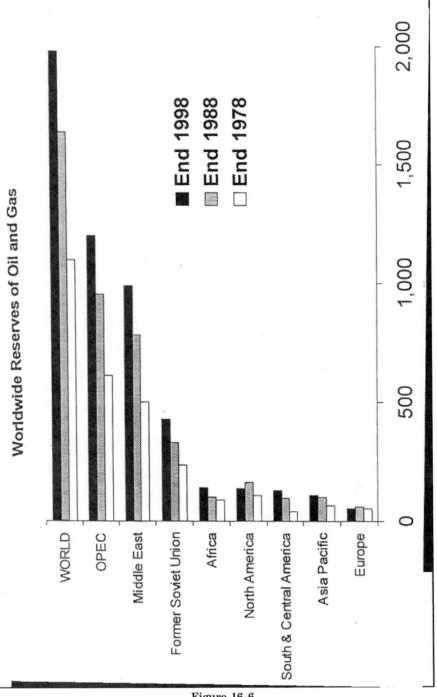

Figure 16–6

Source: Data from BP Amoco, Statistical Review of World Energy (1999).

OPEC's share of world oil production, both past and forecast, is depicted in Figure 16–7 below:

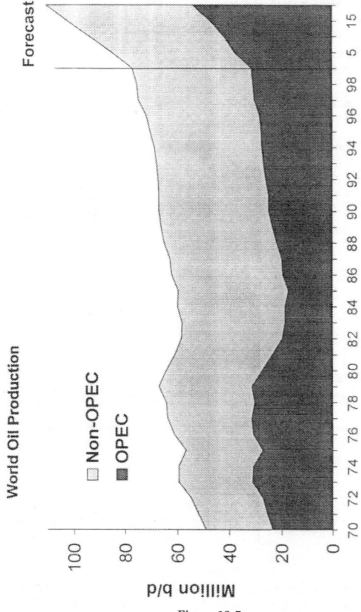

Figure 16–7

Source: Data from EIA, adapted, copyrighted, and also appearing as in Fig. 16–3.

A telling depiction of the distribution of the world's oil potential is in Figure 16–8, adapted from a book by Daniel Johnston. The United States is a "super mature" area with more than 600,000 wells producing an average of 12 barrels of oil a day (BOPD). By comparison, the Middle East has barely been tapped.

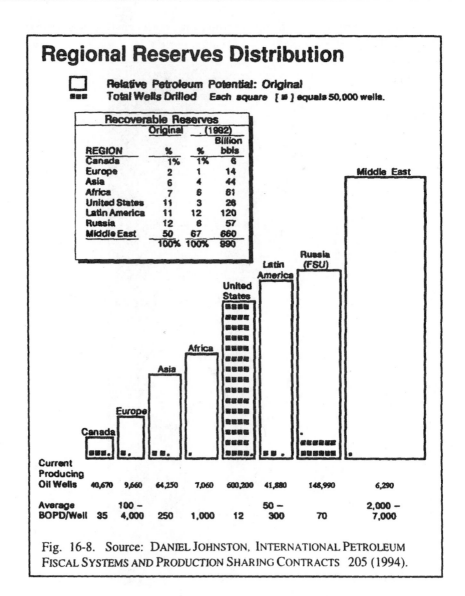

Fig. 16-8. Source: DANIEL JOHNSTON, INTERNATIONAL PETROLEUM FISCAL SYSTEMS AND PRODUCTION SHARING CONTRACTS 205 (1994).

Figure 16–8

What, then explains the fact that foreign direct investment in the U.S. oil and gas industry has tripled since 1980, from about $12 billion to about $40 billion, as companies like BHP (Australia), BP (Britain), Statoil (Norway), and Agip (Italy) have staked out major positions in the U.S. industry? Dr. Foss writes:

A specific lure is the U.S. offshore, a prolific region that is potentially more so as the industry pushes into deeper waters. Companies operating in the U.S. deep water gulf of Mexico can gain invaluable experience to deploy in emerging offshore basins around the world. The second factor, ... is the attractiveness of the huge U.S. market. The risks of offshore development are offset by the relative ease of delivering oil and gas to final customers, because of our tremendous base of pipeline and other infrastructure and our advanced and highly liquid financial markets for energy commodities. For these reasons, the U.S. has continued to be a magnet for investment, as much for the opportunity to hone "field-to-market" skills for companies as for the potential returns. All of this is particularly true for natural gas. The chance to acquire operating knowledge with respect to all segments of the natural gas industry in the world's most intensely developed gas market is especially enticing to foreign investors. Third, while the U.S. is not free of political risk, it can be more manageable because of the transparency of our markets and policy processes. However, no explorationist should underestimate the potential for legal or regulatory changes in the U.S. that can completely alter the economics of a project. Foss, *supra* at ___.

Despite this investment in U.S. oil and gas reserves, our dependence on petroleum imports continues to rise, as shown in Figure 16–9 below:

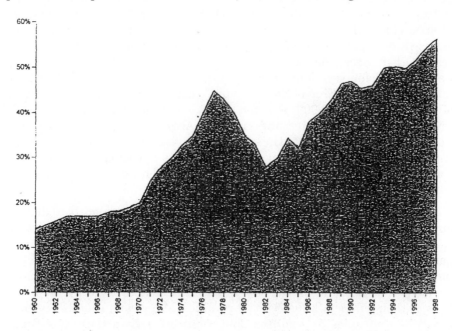

Petroleum Imports as a Percentage of U.S. Petroleum Consumption.

Figure 16–9

Source: EIA

C.   CONCESSIONS THROUGH THE AGES

1.   THE EARLIEST CONCESSIONS

The following article by Professors Smith and Dzienkowsky examines the early history of oil and gas leases executed by private landowners to oil companies in the U.S. and compares these with the early Middle Eastern and Mexican concessions. (The private oil and gas lease is discussed in Chapter 6. The article offers an interesting perspective on the role of the courts in interpreting private contracts in common law countries like the United States.

Ernest E. Smith and John S. Dzienkowsky, A Fifty–Year Perspective on World Petroleum Arrangements

24 Texas Int'l L. J. 13 at 17–23 (1989).

The archetypal Middle Eastern concession was obtained by William D'Arcy from the Shah of Persia in 1901. For a $100,000 "bonus," another $100,000 in stock in his oil company, and a 16% royalty, D'Arcy received exclusive oil rights to 500,000 square miles of Persia for the next sixty years. Other concessions in the region generally followed this format; they were granted for very long terms and covered immense areas. The 1933 concession that the King of Saudi Arabia granted to Standard Oil Company of California for £ 50,000 was for a sixty-six-year term and ultimately covered almost as much territory as the D'Arcy grant. Six years later, the Ruler of Abu Dhabi granted a seventy-five year concession covering the entire country to a consortium composed of five major oil companies. The Kuwait concession was also for a seventy-five-year term and covered the entire country.

These concessions did not specifically obligate the companies to drill on any of the lands granted or to release territory if exploration and drilling were not undertaken. Moreover, the host countries had no right to participate in managerial decisions, including decisions on drilling and development. After the initial consideration and, occasionally, other agreed-upon payments had been made, the sole financial benefit received by the countries or their rulers was the right to royalties. Many early concessions even freed the companies from all tax obligations other than those specifically provided for in the agreement.

The royalty provisions in the Middle Eastern concessions granted in the 1930s were generally less favorable to rulers than those in the original grant to D'Arcy. These later concessions typically provided for a royalty calculated as a flat rate per ton of oil rather than as a percentage of the value of the sale price of production. Thus, both the Ruler of Abu Dhabi and the Sultan of Muscat and Oman received three rupees per English ton of oil produced from their respective concessions; the Arabian concession set the royalty at four gold shillings per ton.

The Middle Eastern concessions were strikingly similar to the oil and gas leases granted in the United States in the first three decades of this century. By 1900, the conditions that had characterized mid-nineteenth century development in Pennsylvania—shallow, inexpensive wells drilled by operators willing to take oil leases on tracts of an acre or less—had largely disappeared in the United States. Lessees, faced with more costly drilling and the need to have greater established reserves for expanding markets, insisted on leasing larger tracts. Although United States oil and gas leases rarely, if ever, covered tracts as immense as those in the Middle East, this difference was attributable to the size of the farms and ranches owned by lessors, rather than to a greater skill in bargaining. Like the Ruler of Abu Dhabi, a landowner in Texas or Oklahoma typically entered into a single oil and gas lease covering all the property he owned, whether it was a forty-acre farm or an 85,000–acre ranch. Moreover, many fixed-term leases, some for as long as ninety-nine years, were still in effect, and new ones were occasionally executed. Other leases, as written, might in theory last forever, even though production was never obtained. These no-term leases permitted the lessee to maintain the lease in effect indefinitely by paying an annual rental. If oil production was obtained, however, royalty clauses in United States leases generally entitled the landowner to a fraction of the oil produced rather than a fixed payment per ton, although the percentages varied considerably from lease to lease. In the case of natural gas, some leases did not base the payment on the volume of production, but merely provided for an annual payment of a fixed amount per gas well.

By the 1930s, however, a standard United States oil and gas lease had emerged that differed significantly from its Middle Eastern counterparts of the same period. Leases covering all property owned by the lessor were still the rule, but fixed-term and no-term leases had disappeared. The lease term had assumed its modern form, providing that the lessee's interest would last for a specified time period, usually five or ten years, and so long thereafter as oil or gas might be produced. Unless drilling and production occurred by the end of the primary term, the lease terminated. Additionally, the royalty clause for both oil and gas had become standardized at one-eighth of production for oil and one-eighth of the sale price or market value for gas.

Rather curiously, the midwestern farmer who leased his land to an oil company was in a better contractual position than the Middle Eastern sheik. Under the typical Middle Eastern concession, the oil company did not risk losing its concession if it failed to drill. The opposite was true under the United States oil and gas lease; the lease format, although it did not guarantee drilling, at least assured the landowner that his land would not be tied up indefinitely by the payment of a small annual rental. If oil was discovered, neither the Middle Eastern concession nor the United States lease imposed upon the oil company any express contractual duty to produce from the well. Under the concession, the company could safely shut in the well if it wanted to do so. The lessee in the United States, however, risked losing the lease for lack of production at the end of the primary term, at least if the shut-in well was the initial discovery well. Finally, if production was obtained, the lessor was not limited to a flat sum per ton, but received one eighth of the production or its sale price.

The lessor in the United States had not only the benefit of the lease format, but also the more significant benefit of the United States courts. The most widely used printed oil and gas leases were drafted for use by oil companies and contained relatively few provisions favorable to the lessor. The courts, however, had long shown their willingness to redress egregious imbalances in contractual rights between the oil companies and their lessors. Judicial hostility to the patent unfairness of the no-term lease was the principal factor leading to its discontinuance. Judicial suggestions that the no-term lease lacked consideration brought into question its enforceability, and the emergence of the implied covenants doctrine assured its demise. Indeed, the judicial doctrine that the lessee impliedly covenants to perform as a reasonably prudent operator and to undertake the various obligations imposed by such a standard provided the lessor with his greatest protection.

By the turn of the century, United States courts had concluded that an oil and gas lessee impliedly covenants to explore, develop, and produce from the leased premises for the mutual benefit of both itself and the landowner. In 1905, the Eighth Circuit commented in *Brewster v. Lanyon Zinc Co.* that "a covenant arising by necessary implication is as much a part of the contract—is as effectually one of its terms—as if [it] had been plainly expressed. Although different rationales were suggested for implying covenants in oil and gas leases, and disagreement existed over the obligations imposed by the implied covenants, the existence of the implied covenants doctrine itself was not open to serious challenge. By the early years of this century, courts had held that a lessee had an implied duty to drill offset wells to protect the leased premises from drainage by wells on adjacent tracts The courts had also construed the no-term lease to contain an implied covenant to drill an initial exploratory well.

The basic format of the modern lease reflected a direct reaction to these rulings. By providing for a fixed, relatively short primary term, a payment for the privilege of deferring drilling during each year of that term, and automatic termination if no drilling or production occurred before the end of the primary term, the lease obviated the need for an implied duty to drill an initial exploratory well. The other implied covenants, however, were unaffected and remained intact under the modern oil and gas lease. In 1934, the United States Supreme Court had no difficulty in stating that the lessee's implied covenant to develop was a generally accepted rule.

The implied covenants gave a lessor in the United States significant legal advantages not available to his Middle Eastern counterparts. Whether the lessor was a Texas rancher or an Arabian sheik, the principal consideration for granting the lease was the right to royalties on production. But neither the concession nor the printed form lease contained express production or developmental obligations. In the Middle East, where some wells might produce over 40,000 barrels of oil a day, low-producing wells, including those producing "only" 10,000 or fewer barrels a day, were commonly shut in as a matter of course. The country (or its ruler) was thus deprived of the income from those wells until the company holding the concession chose to begin production. The Texas rancher, if faced with such a situation, could invoke the implied covenant to operate a well capable of producing oil in paying quantities.

Virtually all commentators agree that the United States lessee had an implied duty to produce from a profitable well, and this position found explicit judicial support....

* * *

The more common problem that lessors faced was a lessee's failure to develop a field after initial drilling discovered a reservoir capable of production. As the leases and concessions were written, a company desiring to hold its proven reserves indefinitely, in hopes of a larger demand at a higher price, was free to do so. Indeed, this strategy was the rule. The Middle Eastern concessions were almost invariably held by consortia with partially overlapping memberships. This interrelationship of the major oil companies resulted in joint offtake agreements limiting the total amount of production from virtually all of the major concessions. Because these agreements limited each company to production of a fixed amount of oil for market, the incentive to drill new wells into an established and proven reservoir was slight. Nothing in the early concessions prohibited these abusive practices by the companies.

In the United States, however, the oil companies were faced with a much different legal environment. The antitrust laws made domestic offtake agreements illegal, and the implied covenant of reasonable development gave the lessor a remedy against a company that had failed to drill additional wells into a proven reservoir. As a general rule, the lessor was required to show that his lessee had delayed unreasonably in drilling additional wells, that the lessee had a reasonable expectation that such wells would be profitable, and that the lessor had given the lessee notice of breach and had demanded compliance. A landowner who successfully met this burden of proof might be entitled to a variety of remedies, ranging from damages to outright cancellation of the undeveloped portions of the lease. Alternatively, the lessor might obtain a conditional decree requiring the lessee to drill a specified number of wells within a specified period of time in order to maintain all or part of the lease. No similar rights or remedies were found in contemporaneously executed Middle Eastern concessions.

[The authors then proceed to contrast the early Mideast concessions with the concession rights asserted by companies in Mexico. In Mexico, the companies claimed fee simple ownership of mineral rights, under Mexican mining laws which provided that petroleum was the "exclusive property of the owner of the soil" and that such ownership was both "irrevocable" and "perpetual". Using these laws, foreign companies bought huge areas of Mexican land. By the time of the Mexican Revolution in 1911, much of the subsoil was claimed by foreign companies as perpetual and exclusive grants of the right to the petroleum].

III.   Changes in the Concession System

In the United States, the doctrine of implied covenants helped to balance the rights of the oil companies and the lessors. lacking such judicial redress, foreign sovereigns inevitably turned to other methods to establish more equitable arrangements. Two principal options appeared available to accomplish this result: expropriation or renegotiation. In some instances no bright line existed between these two methods. Renegotiation under political duress may appear to a company as differing only marginally from outright nationalization; expropriation can take place so gradually that the process may not seem significantly different from ongoing renegotiation. Typically, however, both the changes in petroleum arrangements and the methods used to change them differed markedly. In many ways, the methods of change in Mexico and in the Middle East were at opposite ends of the spectrum of options that sovereigns could use to obtain control over the exploitation of their natural resources.■

NOTES AND COMMENTS

1.   One cause of the Mexican Revolution of 1911 was the extraordinary concentration of Mexico's wealth in foreign hands. Article 27 of the new 1917 Constitution vested ownership of all natural resources such as hydrocarbons in the state of Mexico. The oil companies protested that the post-revolutionary laws were illegal because they were retroactive and deprived the companies of their fee simple ownership by requiring them to transfer their holdings to a concession system. For 20 years, the two sides argued about the transfer to a new concession system until, in 1938, the government simply expropriated the assets of the multinational oil companies and banished them. The companies, in turn, boycotted the purchase of Mexican oil and attempted to deny Mexico access to virtually all foreign oil markets. The Mexican government created Pemex (Petroleus Mexicanos) to take over the assets of the foreign companies and to operate the oil fields without any foreign assistance.

Professors Smith and Dzienkowski assert that Mexico (and Pemex) still suffer from this long history of isolation from joint participation in development with profit-driven multinational oil companies. By contrast, those countries which undertook more gradual expropriation of foreign interests and which allowed foreign companies to continue to participate in the oil and gas industry acquired expertise and knowledge from their working relationship with their multinational partners. This expertise then allowed their state oil companies to move into the profitable downstream end of the oil and gas industry. For example, Saudi Arabia formed a joint venture with

Texaco to operate refineries and gas stations in the United States. By investing in transportation, refining and marketing activities, these countries have secured outlets for their reserves, and have obtained a greater share of profits from the value chain between production and the end use sale. Pemex remains largely a crude oil exporter. *Id.* at 42–46.

2.   The implied covenants imposed on lessees by the courts in oil and gas cases are similar to the implied promise found to exist in the famous case of *Wood v. Lucy, Lady Duff–Gordon*, 222 N.Y. 88, 118 N.E. 214 (1917), read by virtually all students in first-year contracts. In this case, the court inferred a promise on the part of plaintiff Wood to use reasonable efforts to market Lucy's fashionable dresses, thereby rescuing the plaintiff's exclusive agency arrangement with Lucy from the claim that the agency contract lacked consideration or mutuality of obligation. The reasoning of *Wood v. Lucy* has been adopted by the Uniform Commercial Code which requires that both buyers and sellers in exclusive deals use "best efforts" to supply and promote the goods subject to the contract. John D. Calamari and Joseph M. Perillo, The Law of Contracts, sec. 4.12 (4th ed.1998).

Professor Walter Pratt views *Wood v. Lucy* as epitomizing the transformation of contract doctrine from the needs of a rural society in 1870 to the needs of a modern manufacturing society marked by accelerated change, national markets, and large enterprises. He writes:

> Recognizing that the doctrines of the past were not adequate for the needs of a changing commercial world, the judges modified the doctrines to embrace the greater uncertainty that characterized the new agreements. . . . In the language of the courts, the central concept for both enforcement and performance came to be that of "good faith." Through the use of that concept courts strove to preserve some of the moral decency of the rural past [with its localism and face-to-face communication] while allowing the development of commercial practices for the urban future, with as yet undefined morals. Walter F. Pratt, Jr., American Contract Law at the Turn of the Century, 39 S.C. L. Rev. 415 at 418–19 (1988).

> Why did the moral decency of "good faith" and "best efforts" not develop in international petroleum contracting?

2.   Nationalization in the 1970s

The "creeping nationalization" model often used by Middle Eastern countries is described in the following arbitration between Libya and LIAMCO, an American oil company owned by Arco/Sinclair. The Libyan concession at issue was "modern" and advanced compared to D'Arcy's concession. Note that many oil companies "caved in" to the inevitable and accepted the new demands of the host government. LIAMCO did not, and this arbitration ensued. Libya was one of the first countries to assert control over the oil companies. Its position was enhanced in 1970 when the Trans–Arabian pipeline, which carried 500,000 barrels of crude oil per day from Saudi Arabia to the Mediterranean, was shut down for many months because a tractor ruptured the line.[10] This made Libyan oil much more valuable to Europe.

Most disputes between oil companies and host countries are resolved thorough arbitration rather than litigation. This excerpted version of the 173–page award contains many principles of property and contract law used internationally in the settlement of disputes.

ARBITRAL TRIBUNAL: AWARD IN DISPUTE BETWEEN LIBYAN AMERICAN OIL COMPANY (LIAMCO) AND THE GOVERNMENT OF THE LIBYAN ARAB REPUBLIC RELATING TO PETROLEUM CONCESSIONS

International Legal Materials Vol. 20, No.1, Jan. 1981

20 I.L.M. 1 (1981).
[Reproduced from the text filed originally with the U.S. District Court for the District of Columbia in Misc. No. 79–57. Date: April 12, 1977].

(Sole Arbitrator: Dr. Sobhi Mahmassani)

ARBITRATION PROCEEDINGS

1. By its letter dated 2 July 1974 addressed to the President of the International Court of Justice, the Hague, the Claimant Libyan American Oil Company (hereinafter called LIAMCO) stated: that under date of 12 December 1955, the United Kingdom of Libya, now the Libyan Arab Republic (the Respondent herein), pursuant to provisions of its Petroleum Law 1955, adopted 21 April 1955, entered with the Claimant into three Petroleum Concessions Nos. 16, 17 and 20—all of which were in the same form (as prescribed by the Law) as to substantive clauses, relating, inter alia, to the extraction of Petroleum from certain land areas in Libya over a period of fifty years, renewable for an additional ten years.

. . . That by a so-called Nationalization Decree, made public 1 September 1973, the Revolutionary Command Council of the Respondent issued Law Number 66 expressed to provide for the nationalization and transfer to the Respondent of fifty one percent of all properties, privileges, assets, rights, shares, activities and interests of the Claimant under its said Petroleum Concessions.

That this premature and unilateral repudiation in part of the Concession Agreements some thirty-two years before the expiry of the period of the concessions and some forty-two years before the time to which such period could be extended, is a fundamental breach of the Concession Agreements, thereby occasioning a claim by Claimant for restitution in integrum and damages and giving rise to an arbitral dispute within the meaning of Clause 28 of the Concession Agreements.

[A second nationalization decree seized the remaining 49 percent of the interests of the Claimant under the concessions. Liamco exercised the

---

10. The "Libyan squeeze" is colorfully described in Yergin, *supra* at 574–87.

arbitration provision in Clause 28 of the Concession Agreements. The state of Libya refused to respond, and the arbitration proceeded without its participation, as authorized in Clause 28. The President of the International Court of Justice appointed a Sole Arbitrator, Dr. Sobhi Mahmassani, Counselor-at-Law of Beirut].

* * *

FACTS AND EVIDENCE

As the Respondent did not appear, the Arbitral Tribunal had to admit the best evidence available and to rely chiefly on the basic facts as supported by copies of the various official documents and by conclusive technical reports or expert testimony presented by the Claimant.

I. LIBYAN LAW ON CONCESSIONS

1. Petroleum Law of 1955

Libya, a federation of three provinces of Tripolitania, Cyrenaica and Fezzan, was recognized as an independent sovereign State by the United Nations in 1949, effective 2 January 1952. Its form of government was monarchical under King Idriss I.

In order to improve its economic conditions, to encourage foreign capital investment, and to insure the exploitation and protection of its natural resources, Libya enacted Petroleum Law No. 25 of 21 April 1955 (28 Sha'ban 1374 h.), effective 18 August 1955, i.e. 30 days after publication in the Official Gazette.

This Law is a modern enactment which established a framework for the exploration and production of petroleum within the Libyan Kingdom. In its Article 1, it laid down the basic rule that:

"(1) All petroleum in Libya in its natural state, in strata, is the property of the Libyan State;

(2) No person shall explore or prospect for, mine or produce petroleum, unless authorized by a permit or concession issued under this Law".

This Law provided a concessionary system for the exploitation of petroleum products, and established an autonomous Petroleum Commission responsible for the implementation of the provisions of the Law under the supervision of the appropriate Minister (Article 2.3). The Commission was empowered to "grant concession in the form set out in the Second Schedule to this Law and not otherwise, provided that they may contain such minor non-discriminatory variations as may be required to meet the circumstances of any particular case". "Concessions shall be granted for the period of time requested by the applicant provided that such period shall not exceed fifty (50) years. A concession may be renewed for any period such that the total of the two periods does not exceed sixty (60) years" (Article 9.1, 9.4). Under the "working obligations" of the concessionaire, Article 11 provided for an obligation to make certain minimum capital expenditures and that:

"The holder of any concession granted under this Law shall, within eight months of the grant of such concession, commence operations to explore for petroleum within the concession area. He shall diligently prosecute all his operations under the concession in a workmanlike manner and by appropriate scientific methods . . . "

The Law provided for the surrender by the concessionnaire of parts of the concession granted, within a period of five years under conditions detailed in Article 10. The Law provided also for pipeline facilities, exemption from certain import and export duties, payments to the State as taxes, fees, rents, royalties and division of profits (Articles 12–16). It laid down the conditions for the assignment and revocation of permits and concessions, defined the rights and obligations of the parties in the event of force majeure and laid down provisions for penalties, definitions and other regulations (Articles 17–25).

Article 20 also provided that "any disputes between the Commission and the concession holder arising from any concession granted under this Law shall be settled by arbitration in the manner set out in the Second Schedule hereto", i.e. Clause 28 of said Schedule which will be analyzed in its amended form in a later section.

* * *

3.   Royal Decree of 20 November 1965

This legislation was intended to amend the Petroleum Law of 1955 in such a manner as to significantly increase the State's income from the concessionaires, and to secure their consent to such increase. The amendments included the following economic advantages:

a) The royalty of 12½ percent was to be paid no longer on the value of exported oil determined according to the "free competitive market price" at a Libyan port as provided in the original concession, but according to the "posted price", to be determined according to procedures set forth in the Amended Law. (Claimant contends that while the Law called for mutual consultancy prior to setting the "posted price", it is a fact that thereafter the posted price was set at levels higher than the free market price).

b) The amounts of marketing and quality allowances and discounts to be made in determining the "value" for the determination of royalties and taxes was to be fixed by the law and regulations, and not by the concessionaires.

c) The Ministry of Petroleum was to have the right to purchase, at the same price upon which royalties were to be calculated, a substantial amount of, the concession oil.

d) Clause 8 of the Concession Agreements was to be amended to provide that the 12½ percent royalty was no longer to be considered as a credit against the 50% income tax, but simply as an expense in determining taxable profits. The effect was to increase taxes payable to the State in the amount of one-half of the royalties.

On 22 November 1965, an official Explanatory memorandum was issued by the Ministry of Petroleum. It explained that the amended Law was enacted in consistency with the OPEC (Organization of the Petroleum Exporting Countries) settlement reached in 1964 with the major oil companies. It underscored the abovementioned advantages which Libya should enjoy from its oil in a way similar to that enjoyed by other oil producing countries. The Memorandum stated that the new regime should be applied to all companies without exception, and that this application was to be made retroactive to January 1, 1965. It showed by a schedule of figures that due to the resulting increase the government oil revenues for that year would rise from 87.5 to 135.5 in million Libyan pounds.

* * *

The original 1955 law contained a Clause 16 entitled "security of company's rights", whereby the government of Libya assured that it would "take steps necessary to ensure Company's enjoyment of all the rights conferred under this Concession." The 1965 Law amended Article 16 to read:

"(2) This Concession shall throughout the period of its validity be construed in accordance with the Petroleum Law and the Regulations in force on the date of the execution of the agreement of amendment by which this paragraph (2) was incorporated into this concession agreement. Any amendment to and repeal of such Regulations shall not affect the contractual rights of the Company without its consent."

II. LIAMCO'S CONCESSION AGREEMENTS

* * *

2. LIAMCO's concession grants and partial assignments

After adopting its Petroleum Law of 1955, the Libyan Government, in the late summer of 1955, invited applications for exploration permits and concessions from companies which could meet the requirements of the Law, esp. Article 5 thereof. Among the invitees were Texas Gulf and its subsidiary LIAMCO, Sinclair and ARCO, all of which complied with the statutory requirements and belonged to the group called "independents". This group were actively solicited to participate by the Libyan Government, because (according to Claimant) they were noted for their aggressive exploration for oil and offered a counter-weight to the large integrated oil producers, called the "Seven Sisters". Within the framework of the Libyan Petroleum Law, approximately 133 concessions were granted to American, British, German, Italian and French companies prior to the end of 1971. Among the first applicants, LIAMCO was granted, as of December 10, 1955, Concessions 16, 17, 18, 19, 20, 21 and 22.... [LIAMCO, with the consent of the proper Ministers, assigned parts of its concessions to W.R. Grace and to a subsidiary of Exxon].

LIAMCO continued to own that 25.5% undivided interest in said Concessions. It is this interest which was expropriated by the Libyan

Government, and has constituted the subject matter of the present arbitration.

3. The Concession Deeds

Concessions were granted to LIAMCO in the form of "Deeds of Concession", each representing a bilateral agreement concluded between the Petroleum Commission and LIAMCO, and approved by the Minister of Petroleum. All these concessions were dated 12 December 1955, and were executed in contractual form by a member of the Petroleum Commission, by two members of the Council of Ministers and by a representative of LIAMCO.... That prescribed form, and consequently each Concession Agreement, contained thirty clauses entitled successively as follows: grant of concession, surrender of concession area, renewal of concession, working obligations, company to follow good oil field practices, surface rents, royalty, taxation on profits, method of making payments, exemption from certain import and export duties, exchange control, ancillary rights, transport rights, right to occupy land, company's labour, company's rights ensured, savings for rights of Government and others, employment and training of Libyans, water disposal and plugging of boreholes and wells, reports to be furnished, inspection, measurement of petroleum, address of local manager, force majeure, assignment, right to remove property, revocation, arbitration, definitions, fee.

4. Scope of the grant of concession

[The grant of concession in each of LIAMCO's Agreements provided for the enjoyment of exclusive concession rights during the prescribed period of 50 years. The two concessions covered about 8,000 square kilometers].

5. Principal provisions of the Concession Agreements

The LIAMCO Concession agreements of 1955 provided for the payment of rents, royalties and taxes. These were to be calculated as follows:

a) An annual rent, under Clause 6, was to be paid for each 100 square kilometers of concession territory, in the amount of:

— Ten Libyan pounds yearly for the first eight years;

— Twenty Libyan pounds for each of the next seven years, or until the petroleum is discovered in commercial quantities, whichever date shall come first;

— 2500 Libyan pounds for each year thereafter.

b) Royalties, under Clauses 7 and 9, were to be paid quarterly in the amount of 12 1/2% of the value of field production of petroleum during the previous quarter....

c) Annual taxes, under Clause 8, were payable under the Laws of Libya, provided that if the total amount of taxes added to fees, rents and royalties falls short of 50 percent of the Company's profits, the Company shall pay to the Government such sum by way of surtax as will make the total of the Company's payments equal to 50 percent of such profits.

In addition to the above economic obligations, LIAMCO undertook a number of contractual obligations pursuant to the terms of its Concession Agreements. Among the principal of such obligations are the following: a) Clause 4 of the Agreements imposed upon the concessionnaire the obligation to "work" the concession in conformity with Article 11 of the Petroleum Law, whose provisions are set forth above. This obligation entails the necessity to engage the minimum amounts of investment and expenses necessary to actively explore the concession area and to prosecute diligently all operations required thereby.

b) Pursuant to Clause 5 of the Agreements, the Company was required to perform all operations consistent with the exercise of proper field practice prevailing in the industry.

c) In Clause 18, the concessionnaire undertook an obligation to train Libyan national employees and, within ten years of operations, to employ nationals to constitute at least 75% of its total number of employees, as well as to found special training programs for Libyans as soon as exports should be undertaken from the concession area.

d) The concessionnaire likewise undertook to render both technical and economic reports to the Petroleum Commission (Clause 20), and to permit inspection by the Commission of the project and of the Company's books and records (Clause 21).

As a counterpart to the numerous obligations undertaken, the concessionnaire received, pursuant to the terms of the Concessions as initially granted, the following protections: a) "Security of Company's Rights" (Clause 16). This provided, as above set forth, that the contractual rights expressly created by the concession shall not be altered except by mutual consent. . . .

c) "Cancellation of the Concession" (Clause 27). The Petroleum Commission was given the right to terminate the contract for several grounds of non-performance by the concessionnaire and, in particular, failure to pay rents and royalties overdue for at least six months or failure to pay amounts as required by the decision of an arbitral tribunal rendered against it. The Clause particularly provided that: "Whenever the Company disputes the grounds under which cancellation is based and requests arbitration under Clause 28 of this contract, the cancellation shall only become effective subject to and in accordance with the result of tile arbitration."

d) "Arbitration" (Clause 28). The Concession Agreements provided that all disputes arising out of or in connection with the concession shall be finally settled by arbitration as will be explained hereafter. They provided also that the concession shall be governed by and interpreted in accordance with the Laws of Libya and such principles and rules of international law as may be relevant.

6. Modifications of the Concession Agreements

[LIAMCO agreed to amend its Concession Agreements to conform to the Royal Decree of 1965].

III. NATIONALIZATION DECREES

1. Measures prior to LIAMCO's nationalizations

On September 1, 1969, a Revolutionary Command Council, headed by Colonel Muammar el Qadhafi, overthrew the Government of King Idriss, and announced the formation of the Libyan Arab Republic. The new regime, from the outset, assured foreign interests that there would be no specific changes in policy and that the obligations of the State would be respected. Later on, it took gradual measures which were proclaimed as a protection against imperialism and in harmony with the nationalistic aims of the Revolution.

The first measure was the demand that British and American forces evacuate the military bases established by them. Then followed the confiscation of all land, establishments and interests of Italian colonists established in Libya.

At the end of January 1970, the Libyan Government summoned local oil representatives and demanded substantial modifications in the "posted price" of petroleum. During the ensuing negotiations, the Government, acting under the authority of the "conservation" provisions of the above-mentioned Regulation 8 of 1968, took measures to cut back production and increase pressure on the oil companies. In September 1970, LIAMCO agreed to a $0.30 increase in posting and a 55% tax rate. Shortly after the agreement to terms, the production rates which had been cut back as "conservation measures" were restored to their pre-existing levels. Similar arrangements were made with other oil producers.

The September 1970 settlement forced up posted prices to approximately $2.53 per barrel. In January 1971, local representatives of oil companies in Libya were again summoned to the Ministry of Petroleum to agree to even higher posted prices, plus additional increases arising from the then pending Teheran negotiations between Gulf States' governments and petroleum concessionaires. This demand was backed up by threats of complete stoppage of production. Finally, on April 2, 1971, fifteen oil companies, including LIAMCO, signed the Tripoli Agreement, increasing posted prices to $3.44 with assorted other new financial obligations on the companies.

On December 7, 1971, the Arab Government of Libya passed a law nationalizing the entire [50%] interest of British Petroleum (BP) in Concession No. 65. As stated by the Libyan representative in his speech before the United Nations Security Council on 9 December 1971, the motive of this nationalization was in retaliation to the British non-intervention with regard to the Iranian occupation of three islands in the Arabian Persian Gulf.... [Bunker Hunt, an American "independent" company, owned the other 50% of Concession 65; Libya nationalized it in 1973].

* * *

In July of 1973, the Libyan Government announced a general plan for participation in the oil industry. Under pressure pursuant to that plan,

Occidental and three of the four members of the Oasis Group (Amerada, Continental and Marathon, but not Shell) agreed to accept the nationalization of 51% of their concession interests on the terms set forth in Nationalization Laws Nos. 44 and 51 of August 1973. In exchange, they received separate agreements with the Minister of Petroleum giving them certain assurances as to continuing sources of supply in the future, and entailing for them additional financial obligations, constituting very important modifications of their rights in the remaining 49% of the Concession.

2.   Nationalization of 51% of LIAMCO'S concession rights

In summer of 1973, the Libyan Government asked the oil producers to accept a 51% participation by the State in the oil concessions. It set the end of August as a deadline for their acceptance, under threat of taking "appropriate measures."

As no acceptance was made, the appropriate measures were the issuance by the Libyan Revolutionary Command Council on September 1, 1973 of Law No. 66, nationalizing 51% of the concession rights of the following companies (Article 1): Esso Standard Libya Inc., Libyan American Oil Company (LIAMCO), Grace Petroleum Corporation, Esso Sirte Inc., Shell Libya, Mobil and Gelsenberg Libya, Texaco Overseas Petroleum Company and California Oil Company.

The relevant articles for said nationalization were the following:

Article I

"The ownership of 51% of all property, rights, assets, portions, shares, activities and interests in any form ... as regards petroleum concession deeds ... shall be nationalized and transferred to the State....

Article 6

"All property, rights and assets of the Companies, the ownership of which has reverted to the State in accordance with the provisions of Article 1, shall be transferred to the National Oil Corporation".

Article 7

"The nationalized concession areas shall be invested through the National Oil Corporation in association with the Companies referred to in Article 1. The Corporation's share in the participation shall be 51% and the share of these Companies in the participation shall be 49%.

"The operation shall be made through the operating company which was actually operating before the execution of the provisions of this Law. A committee for the management of the operating company shall be appointed by a decision from the Minister of Petroleum. The committee shall consist of three members, two of whom shall represent the government and the other member shall represent the nationalized companies."

The nationalization measures were immediately implemented. The operator of LIAMCO's concessions, Esso Sirte, LIAMCO's co-concessionnaire, was put under control of a management committee as provided in said Article 7. The National Oil Corporation appropriated 51% of all benefits accruing from those concessions, and LIAMCO was deprived of its rights thereunder.

As to compensation, Article 2 of said Nationalization Law provided as follows:

"The State shall compensate people concerned for the property, rights and assets that have reverted to it under Article 1." [Compensation was to be assessed by a committee selected by the Minister of Petroleum, consisting of a Libyan judge, a representative of the National Oil Corporation, and a representative of the Ministry of Treasury.]

* * *

4.   Reactions to said nationalizations

Explaining the principles of the Nationalization Decree of 1973, the Libyan Prime Minister, in a statement of 2 September 1973, defined the basic principles for conducting negotiations with oil companies. The first principle is that Libya cannot buy its own oil which is underground, and consequently, compensation for nationalization should be based on the net book value of the concession. This means the balance of the funds a company brought into Libya and spent on the concession (for studies, exploration, pipe, reports), after deducting the funds it recovered from it.

LIAMCO immediately reacted to the September 1, 1973 Decree. Together with five other oil companies it filed a protest to the 51% nationalization measures, refusing to give its agreement to them.

By note dated September 14, 1973, the State Department of the U.S.A. duly protested through diplomatic channels. It recalled the statement of the Revolutionary Command Council, made on September 1, 1969 to the diplomatic corps, that the new regime would fulfill all its international obligations and would respect the rights of the petroleum companies operating in Libya, and recalled the provisions of the concession agreements that the contractual rights of the concessionaires should not be altered except by mutual consent of the parties. The note stated that the "net book value" formula for compensation did not meet the minimum standards for prompt, adequate and effective compensation required by international law. It further stated that it expected Libya to respond positively to any requests for arbitration under the agreements.

* * *

By a circular letter to all oil companies dated 8 December 1973, the Minister of Petroleum advised that Libya, handling a matter of the heart of the sovereignty, did not accept therein any dispute which would be arbitrable under Clause 28 of the Concession Deeds; and that compensation being guaranteed according to procedures of the Nationalization Law, all arbitration applications should be rejected.

Under these circumstances, some concessionaires finally did agree to compensation terms for the 51% taking and, after agreeing to drop any requests for arbitration, entered into supplemental agreements in respect to the remaining 49% interest.

Moreover, the Libyan Government proceeded to the total liquidation of LIAMCO's interests in Libya by the second nationalization in February 1974.

No compensation was paid or offered to LIAMCO for either the first or the second nationalization measures. . . .

* * *

Meanwhile, by another diplomatic note addressed to the Libyan Government on June, 1974, the State Department of the U.S.A. stated that it was clear that the reason for the nationalization of 1974 was political retaliation. It noted that "under the principles of international law, measures taken by a State against the interests of foreign nationals, which are motivated not by reason of public utility, but of political retaliation against the State of which those nationals are citizens, are invalid and are not entitled to recognition by other States. . . ."

That position of the U.S. State Department was reaffirmed on 30 December 1975 in a press release No. 630 on foreign investment and nationalization. In that Statement it was repeated that:

"Under international law, the United States has a right to expect:

— That any taking of American private property will be nondiscriminatory;

— That it will be for a public purpose; and

— That its citizens will receive prompt, adequate and effective compensation from the expropriating country."

". . . The State Department wishes to place on record its view that foreign investors are entitled to the fair market value of their interests. Acceptance by U.S. nationals of less than fair market value does not constitute acceptance of any other standard by the United States Government."

5.   Summary of LIAMCO's activities

* * *

When LIAMCO entered into its concession agreements in December 1955, it acted as a pioneer in a desert land where no extensive exploration had been undertaken by any company. It faced exceptional difficulties with regard to any facilities that might be utilized in connection with supplies of any kind. There were no machine or repair shops, no roads, no adequate ports, no personnel nor labor, no water, no communications, no fuel and no experienced governmental departments to handle the required formalities and enterprise. LIAMCO was even confronted with the unusual and costly task of clearing abandoned World War II mines.

Under such circumstances, LIAMCO had to operate, and had, moreover, to agree to an expedited discovery program which required it to accept an obligation to commence the drilling of an exploration well by April 30, 1956, i.e. four and one-half months only after the grant of the concessions, subject to forfeiture of all its seven concessions in case of failure to meet that deadline. This was an obligation that the major petroleum companies would not accept.

LIAMCO struggled hard and overcame all those difficulties. Experienced personnel was brought from abroad, including a great number of Egyptians. Water supply was drilled and provided in sufficient quantities, even for Libyan tribes. LIAMCO pioneered these efforts which other companies followed, and even shared with them all its knowledge and experience.

Thus, by very intense day and night toil, the works of the initial operation well were completed on 19 April 1956, and next day the drilling operation began on schedule as agreed with the Petroleum Commission.

* * *

Claimant has summarized the status of Concessions 16, 17 and 20, on the eve of said nationalization measures, as follows: LIAMCO had performed all its obligations to "work" the concessions accorded to it as required by the concessionnaire acting alone and in concert with its co-concessionaires; it had performed extensive scientific survey work, drilled numerous exploratory wells, drilled and completed 79 development or producing wells, constructed a 54–mile crude oil pipeline, and an accompanying gas transmission line and road, drilled two water supply wells and one water injection well; it constructed a 105 million cubic foot per day gas processing plant, and constructed all required supporting facilities necessary to the proper development of the petroleum reserves discovered in the concession area.

As a result of these exploratory and operational activities, LIAMCO and its co-concessionaires discovered and defined a petroleum field containing substantial petroleum reserves, which on the dates of 1973 and 1974 was capable of producing up to 133,000 barrels of crude oil and liquids per day, plus 150 million cubic feet of gas per day.

6. Claimant's characterization of the facts of the case

On the basis of the above facts, the Claimant contends that the Libyan nationalization measures of 1973 and 1974 concerning LIAMCO's 25.5% undivided interest in Concessions Nos. 16, 17 and 20 of 1955 as amended in 1966, were politically motivated, discriminatory and confiscatory in nature, and constituted a denial of justice, a wrongful taking and an unlawful breach of contract, and are illegal as contrary to the principles of the law of Libya common to the principles of international law.

In consequence, Claimant requests the issue of an award ordering: as a principal relief the restoration of its concession rights together with all the benefits accruing from such restoration, and as an alternative relief the payment of adequate damages plus interest as will be detailed later.

PART THREE. CONSIDERATIONS OF LAW AND REMEDIES
I. GENERAL NATURE AND PROTECTION OF CONCESSIONS

The petroleum concession agreements entered into between LIAMCO and the Libyan Government constitute the subject matter of the dispute. These agreements, as other similar agreements, are classified by some international jurists under the type of the so-called "international development contracts."

A contract of this type is a semi-public agreement made between a State and a private individual, whose object covers a project of public utility or the exploitation of certain natural resources, and in which are defined the rights and obligations of the parties in their mutual relationship.

Such a contract has special characteristics of which the most common are the following: The contracting parties are not ordinary private persons, one of them being the State or a Government organ, the other very commonly being a foreign corporation. The object of the contract is usually a long-term exploitation of natural resources, involving expensive plants and installations. . . .

Although a concession contract partakes of mixed public and private legal character, it retains a predominant contractual nature. According to the general rules of the law of concessions, widely accepted by modern jurists, the concessionnaire's activities in mining, petroleum and similar concessions, do not have the character of public service, but are considered as private projects and enterprises, and as such are generally governed by the principles of the private law of contracts (V. Duez et Debeyre, Traite de droit administratif, No. 803 p. 606; et Andre de Laubadere, Traite elementaire de droit administratif, No. 49 p. 45).

This contractual nature has been confirmed in all Libyan petroleum concessions, which took the form of written signed agreements, in which the usual style and language used in contracts were employed, the rights and obligations of each party were set forth "in consideration" of and in reciprocity to those of the other party, and all amendments were made by mutual consent according to an imperative contractual provision.

To strengthen this contractual character in LIAMCO's and similar other concession agreements as a precaution against the fact that one of the parties is the State, it was deemed necessary to ensure a certain protection for the contractual rights of the concessionnaire. Usually, foreign investors before taking the risk of investing substantial amounts of money and labor for "working" their concessions, are anxious to seek sufficient assurance for the respect of the principle of the sanctity of contracts. In other words, they seek to be guaranteed against the possibility of arbitrary exercise by the State of its sovereignty power either to alter or to abrogate unilaterally their contractual rights. Any such alteration or abrogation of concession agreements should be made by mutual consent of the parties.

To ensure such protection in LIAMCO's Concessions, a specific provision has been inserted to that effect in Clause 16 of its Agreements. That

Clause has been legally authorized by and modeled upon the same standard clause of Schedule II annexed to the Petroleum Laws of 1955 and 1965. In its amended final version, it reads as follows:

"(1) The Government of Libya, the Commission and the appropriate provincial authorities will take all steps necessary to ensure that the Company enjoys all the rights conferred by this Concession. The contractual rights expressly created by this Concession shall not be altered except by mutual consent of the parties."

"(2) This Concession shall throughout the period of its validity be construed in accordance with the Petroleum Law and the Regulations in force on the date of execution of the Agreement of Amendment by which this paragraph (2) was incorporated into this Concession Agreement. Any amendment to or repeal of such Regulations shall not affect the contractual rights of the Company without its consent."

The above Clause comes under what has been termed "stabilization" and "intangibility" clauses, which have been considered as legally binding under international law (V. Article of Prosper Weil, "Les clauses de stabilisation on d'intangibilite inserees dans les accords de developpement economique", in Melanges Rousseau, p. 301–328).

Moreover, Clause 16 is justified not only by the said Libyan Petroleum legislation, but also by the general principle of the sanctity of contracts recognized also in municipal* and international law, as will be analyzed at a later stage hereof. It is likewise consistent with the principle of non-retroactivity of laws, which denies retrospective effect to a new legislation and asserts the respect of vested rights (droits acquis) acquired under a previous legislation. The principle of non-retroactivity of laws is also admitted by Islamic law, and is based on the following Koranic verse:

"We never punish until We have sent a messenger" (XVII, 15).(Islamic script)

In addition to the clause protecting contractual rights, most concession agreements contain explicit mandatory provisions: determining the law to be applicable, and providing for arbitration in case of dispute. . . .

II. PRINCIPLES OF LAW APPLICABLE IN THE DISPUTE

1. Validity of the choice of law clause

In a concession agreement, an important question arises regarding the choice of the proper law to be applied for its interpretation and enforcement and for governing any details that are not explicitly provided for in it.

The legal systems of the two contracting parties are usually dissimilar. It is not fair to rely on one of them to the exclusion of the other without infringing the principle of the equality of the parties, unless expressly agreed to by mutual consent either in the original contract or in a later

* [Editors' note:] Municipal law means the internal law of a nation, such as its constitution, statutes, executive regulations and court decisions.

document. Moreover, the two or one of these systems might be vague or insufficient on the various concession issues.

Hence, in a case involving a foreign litigant, the tribunal to which it is submitted has to refer for guidance to the general principles governing the conflict of laws in private international law.

According to said principles, the proper law of a contract is that "by which the parties to a contract intended, or may fairly be presumed to have intended, the contract to be governed; or ... to submit themselves" (Dicey's Digest of the Conflict of Laws, Rule 155; and Lord McNair's article "The General Principles of Law Recognized by Civilized Nations", in British Yearbook of International Law, 1957, p.69–98).

Pursuant to that established rule on the solution of the conflict laws in contracts in general, concession agreements usually contain an explicit provision stating the intention of the parties as to the choice of the proper law to which they submit their contract.

In accordance with that practice, Clause 28, para. 7, of the original LIAMCO Concession Agreements Nos. 16, 17 and 20 of 12 December 1955 provided that:

"This Concession shall be governed by and interpreted in accordance with the Laws of Libya and such principles and rules of international law as may be relevant, and the umpire or sole arbitrator shall base his award upon these laws, principles and rules."

The same Paragraph 7 was modified by the Amendment Agreement of 20 January 1966 as follows:

"This Concession shall be governed by and interpreted in accordance with the principles of law of Libya common to the principles of international law, and in the absence of such common principles then by and in accordance with the general principles of law as may have been applied by international tribunals."

* * *

Moreover, Libyan municipal public law has explicitly authorized the said choice of law clause by Clause 28, para. 7, of the Schedule II annexed to Petroleum Laws of 1955 and 1965.

The two laws were duly promulgated by the appropriate Libyan legislature. They have continued in force after the Libyan Revolution, according to the legal international public rule that the change of government does not, per se, affect the validity of the existing legal system and the rights and liabilities derived from it.

* * *

Therefore, it is an accepted universal principle of both domestic and international laws that the parties to a mixed public and private contract are free to select in their contract the law to govern their contractual relationship.

2. Analysis of the choice of law clause

* * *

Hence, the principal proper law of the contract in said Concessions is Libyan domestic law. But it is specified in the Agreements that this covers only "the principles of law of Libya common to the principles of international law." Thus, it excludes any part of Libyan law which is in conflict with the principles of international law.

To determine the meaning of "the principles of international law," it is useful to refer to those of its sources that are accepted by the International Court of Justice. Article 38 of its Statute provides as follows:

"1. The Court, whose function is to decide in accordance with international law such disputes as are submitted to it, shall apply:

"a. international conventions, whether general or particular, establishing rules expressly recognized by the contesting states;

"b. international custom, as evidence of a general practice accepted as law;

"c. the general principles of law recognized by civilized nations;

"d. subject to the provisions of Article 59 (concerning the relative effects of judgments), judicial decisions and the teachings of the most highly qualified publicists of the various nations, as subsidiary means for the determination of rules of law."

* * *

As to the meaning of "the principles of the law of Libya" in this connection, it is relevant to point out that this comprises any legislative enactment consistent with international legal principles. It includes, inter alia, all Petroleum concessions laws, all consistent relevant sections of any private or public Libyan legislation, including the Civil Code.

In particular, Article 1, para. 2, of the Libyan Civil Code, promulgated on 28 November 1953, provides that:

"(2) If there is no legal text to be applied the judge will adjudicate in accordance with the principles of Islamic law, failing which in accordance with custom, and failing that in accordance with natural law and the rules of equity."

* * *

Moreover, the Revolutionary Government underscored the importance of this source of law in its new legislation. Pursuant to this policy, the Revolutionary Command Council, by Decree dated 28 October 1971 (9 Ramadan 1391 H.), provided that Islamic law shall be the principal source of Libyan legislation, and appointed special commissions to review existing laws and to amend them according to dictates of Islamic Shari'a. Typical examples of such amended laws are the Statute on Wakfs No. 124 of 1972, the Larceny Statute No. 148 of 1972, and the Adultery Statute No. 70 of 1973.

It is relevant to note that the other subsidiary legal sources mentioned in said Article 1 of the Libyan Civil Code, namely custom and natural law and equity, are also in harmony with the Islamic legal system itself. As a matter of fact, in the absence of a contrary legal text based on the Holy Koran or the Traditions of the Prophet, Islamic law considers custom as a source of law and as complementary to and explanatory of the contents of contracts, especially in commercial transactions. This is illustrated by many Islamic legal maxims, of which the following may be quoted:

— "Custom is authoritative". [Eds. Note: This maxim is then written in Arabic script which is noted as "illegible word" by the word processing program].…

— "What is customary amongst merchants is deemed an if agreed upon between them". (Illegible Word)

— "A matter established by custom is like a matter established by law." (Illegible Word) (Articles 36, 37, 43–45 of the Ottoman Majallah Code. V. our book "The Philosophy of Jurisprudence in Islam", 4th Arabic edition, Beirut, 1975, p. 266–7, and its English translation, Leyden, 1961, p. 132–133).

Similarly, equity (Istihsan) is considered as an auxiliary source of law, especially by the Maliki and Hanafi Schools. Further, all Islamic rules of law are based on and influenced by religious and moral precepts of Islam (V. Ibid, Arabic text p. 190….)

* * *

Thus, it has been pointed out that Libyan law in general and Islamic law in particular have common rules and principles with international law, and provide for the application of custom and equity as subsidiary sources. Consequently, these provisions are, in general, consistent and in harmony with the contents of the proper law of the contract chosen and agreed upon in Clause 28, para. 7, of LIAMCO's Concession Agreements, …

Moreover, in the absence of that primary law of the contract, the same Paragraph provides as a secondary choice to apply subsidiarily "the general principles of law as may have been applied by international tribunals."

These general principles are usually embodied in most recognized legal systems, and particularly in Libyan legislation, including its modern codes and Islamic law. They are applied by municipal courts and are mainly referred to in international and arbitral case-law. They, thus, form a compendium of legal precepts and maxims, universally accepted in theory and practice. Instances of such precepts are, inter alia, the principle of the sanctity of property and contracts, the respect of acquired vested rights, the prohibition of unjust enrichment, the obligation of compensation in cases of expropriation and wrongful damage, etc.

III. LEGALITY OF THE ARBITRATION

I. The Arbitration clause and its validity.…

The arbitration Clause 28, in its final modified version, reads as follows:

"(1) If at any time during or after the currency of this contract any difference or dispute shall arise between the Government and the Company concerning the interpretation or performance of the provisions of this contract, or its annexes, or in connection with the rights and liabilities of either of the contracting parties hereunder, and if the parties should fail to settle such difference or dispute by agreement, the same shall, failing any agreement to settle it in any other way, be referred to [arbitration]...."

It is widely accepted in international law and practice that an arbitration clause survives the unilateral termination by the State of the contract in which it is inserted and continues in force even after that termination. This is a logical consequence of the interpretation of the intention of the contracting parties, and appears to be one of the basic conditions for creating a favorable climate for foreign investment.

* * *

It has been contended by the Libyan Government, in its Circular letter of 8 December 1973, addressed to all oil companies and referred to above, that it rejects arbitration as contrary to the heart of its sovereignty. Such argument cannot be retained against said international practice, which was also confirmed in many international conventions and resolutions. For instance, the Convention of 1966 on the Settlement of Investment Disputes between States and Nationals of other States provides, in its Article 25, that whenever the parties have agreed to arbitrate no party may withdraw its consent unilaterally. More generally, Resolution No. 1803 (XV11) of the United Nations General Assembly, dated 21 December 1952, while proclaiming the permanent sovereignty of peoples and nations over their natural resources, confirms the obligation of the State to respect arbitration agreements (Section I, para. I and 4).

Therefore, a State may always validly waive its so-called sovereign rights by signing an arbitration agreement and then by staying bound by it.

Moreover, that ruling is in harmony with Islamic law and practice, which is officially adopted by Libya. This is evidenced by many historical precedents. For instance, Prophet Muhammad was appointed as an arbitrator before Islam by the Meccans, and after Islam by the Treaty of Medina. He was confirmed by the Holy Koran (S IV, 65) as the natural arbitrator in all disputes relating to Muslims. He himself resorted to arbitration in his conflict with the Tribe of Banu Qurayza. Muslim rulers followed this practice in many instances, the most famous of which was the arbitration agreement concluded in the year 657 A.D. (37 H.) between Caliph 'Ali and Mu'awiya after the battle of Siffin (V. our lectures on International law, op. cit., p. 272–273, and Arabic text p. 160–163)....

IV. CLAIMANT'S DEMANDS AND LEGAL ARGUMENTS

[LIAMCO requested the Arbitral Tribunal to issue an award ordering the restoration to LIAMCO of its concession rights; the transfer to LIAMCO of the benefits of the exercise of its concession rights by the National Oil Company of Libya from the time of the purported transfer of such concession rights until the time of effective restoration to LIAMCO of its concession rights; or, as an alternative to the above relief, the payment of $250 million by the Government of Libya to LIAMCO as damages for the irremediable breach and termination of its concession agreements].

The legal arguments presented in support of these claimed remedies may be classified under two groups: unlawful taking of property by unlawful nationalization, and breach of contract.

* * *

V. LAWFULNESS OF THE LIBYAN NATIONALIZATION MEASURES AND THE RESULTANT TAKING OF PROPERTY

This expose will treat successively the following topics, namely: the classical concept of property, evolution of that concept and the right of nationalization, United Nations Resolutions on the subject, concession rights as property, the sanctity of contracts, and the examination of LIAMCO's nationalizations in the light of said legal considerations.

1. The classical concept of property

One of the fundamental rights universally recognized is the right of private ownership or property (Dominium).

The Classical concept of this right defines it as the right to the use, exploitation and disposal (usus, fructus, abusus) of the object owned.

Although this classical definition has been tempered and limited sometimes by reason of public interest, nonetheless the inviolability of the right of property has remained throughout history as a sacred proposition confirmed and reaffirmed by a succession of constitutional and international declarations and charters. The most famous instances of such basic documents are: the English Magna Charta of 1215, the French "Declaration des droits de l'homme et du citoyen" of 1789 which was recently incorporated in the Preamble to the French constitution of 1958, the Fifth amendment to the American constitution of 1789, the two Hague Conventions of 1890 and 1907, the Declarations of the International Law Association of Vienna in 1926 and of Oxford in 1932, and last but not least the United Nations Bill of Human Rights of 1948, the Pan–American Bill of the same name and date, and the Protocol of 1952 annexed to the Convention of Rome on Human Rights of 1950.

The same concept of this absolute right of property was adopted in private law, in particular Roman law, the European civil codes influenced by it, and many other modern codes. For instance, Article 811 of the Libyan Civil Code provides as follows:

"The owner of a thing has alone, within the limits of the law, the right to use it, to exploit it and to dispose of it."

Applied to land (immovable property) the contents of this absolute right extended in theory to the air space above it and to things lying underground, as was often expressed in the Latin maxim: "Cujus est solum ejus est usque ad coelum, et ad inferos" (Whose is the soil, his is also that which is above and below it). Article 812 para. 2, of the Libyan Civil Code incorporates the same rule with the limitations imposed by the special legislation on quarries and mines.

* * *

In comparison with these views on property, it is relevant to record that Islamic law recognized the inviolable character of the right of property, on the basis of the Holy Koranic Verse.

"And do not appropriate unlawfully each other's property" (S II, 188).

Muslim jurists moulded the meaning of this Verse in a general maxim which provides that:

"One is not allowed to take another's property without legal cause" (Article 97 of the Ottoman Majallah Code).

But they limited the generality of that rule by the requirements of public necessity in order to prevent public nuisance. This restriction was couched in another complementary legal maxim which reads thus:

"Private damage has to be suffered in order to fend off public damage."

(Article 26 of the Ottoman Majallah Code. V. our book "The General Theory of Obligations and Contracts under Islamic law", in Arabic, Vol. I p. 93, and our "Philosophy of Jurisprudence in Islam", op. cit., in., Arabic p. 309, English translation p. 157).

2. Evolution of the concept of property and the emergence of the right of nationalization

From the outset of this century and especially after World War I, new political and economic trends have tempered the absolute character of the aforementioned classical meaning of property.

Gradually, property came to be viewed as having a dominant "social function or role," and has as such to be subservient to the public interest of the Community represented by the State. The old sacred character of property has become subject to the influence of social objectives. Its protection has thus been attenuated in domestic as well as in international law.

Moreover, natural resources, in general, do not belong anymore to the owner of the land, but to the Community represented by the State as a privilege of its sovereignty. This view has been adopted in Libya and expressly laid down in its legislation on mines and petroleum. . . .

* * *

Likewise, nationalization by the State of private property began to be practiced on a larger scale than in the past. As differentiated from individual expropriation acts based on administrative law and public necessity, nationalization has taken, in general, the feature of a collective legislative measure motivated by the public social policy of the State. It became thus characterized as a sovereign act, immune from judicial control and subject to international law whenever foreign elements were at issue.

According to the definition formulated in 1952 by the "Institut de droit international":

"Nationalization is the transfer to the State, by a legislative act and in the public interest, of property or private rights of a designated character, with a view to their exploitation or control by the State, or their direction to a new objective by the State." (Annuaire 1952, II p. 279).

The objectives of nationalization vary according to the general political and economic policies of various States.

In communist States, all land and means of production and capital, whether or not foreign-owned, were nationalized on a general scale, often with no compensation. This was done, for instance, by the Soviet State, following the Russian Revolution at the end of World War I.

Nationalization was also frequent in the period between the two world wars, and was even enhanced in some European and American States by express constitutional provisions. As an instance thereof, may be cited the Mexican nationalizations which were effected since 1936 on seventeen oil companies and on foreign-owned land in a program of Agrarian reform.

After World War II, more nationalizations were executed on a very wide level by Eastern European nations, covering land and means of production, and in which only partial indemnities were paid. Even in England and France nationalization of many companies and enterprises was effected, in which the principle of prior, full compensation was not strictly respected (V. Konst. Katzarov, Theorie de la nationalisation, Neuchatel, 1960, p. 412 et s.)

Moreover, during that period and afterwards, many new nations, in particular those forming the so-called "Third World", have emerged and attained their independence. Motivated by a nationalistic spirit to stress their prestige and to control their national economy, many of these new States as well as some other old ones had recourse, especially since 1950, to general measures of nationalization covering chiefly oil concessions and other natural resources and public utilities.

Among such measures were those taken by: Iran in 1951, Egypt in 1956, Indonesia in 1957, Irak, [sic] Ceylon and Cuba in 1961, Algeria from 1963, Syria in 1964, Peru in 1968, Bolivia and Zambia in 1969, Chile in 1970, Libya from 1970, Saudi Arabia in 1972, and Kuwait since 1973. Some of these nationalizations will be discussed hereafter.

This overreaching tendency was implemented and aided by national organizations, such as the Algerian Sonatrach and the National Oil Company of Libya. Further, it was encouraged and systematized after the founding in 1960 of OPEC (Organization of the Petroleum Exporting Countries), in which most oil producing States were regrouped and are still represented. OPEC's tremendous influence is largely felt in the global oil business and consequently in the economic and financial situation all over the world.

On the basis of such frequent precedents, mostly uncontested as to their principle, most publicists to-day uphold the sovereign right of a State to nationalize foreign property, in the sense that a State possesses as an attribute of its sovereignty and supreme power the right to nationalize all things belonging to any person within its jurisdiction. They stress that States possess that right to nationalize in "the manner and form they consider best," and that they "enjoy complete freedom in this field ... Neither international judicial decisions, nor international treaty practice, nor legal principles provide any evidence of a restrictive rule." (V. S. Friedman, Expropriation in International Law, London, 1953, p. 134, 140–142; and Gillian White, Nationalisation of Foreign Property, New York, 1961, p. 35 et s.).

* * *

3.   United Nations Resolutions on Nationalization

The frequency of the above mentioned general measures of nationalization has evoked international attention. Since 1952, The United Nations General Assembly has delivered a series of successive resolutions, in which the sovereign right of States to nationalize and to control their natural resources, as being the pro-property of the Community, has been confirmed and reaffirmed. Hereunder are recalled the provisions of the principal resolutions relevant to the points at issue.

(I) Resolution No. 626 (VII) of 21 December 1952: which reads as follows:

"The General Assembly, Bearing in mind the need for encouraging the under-developed countries in the proper use and exploitation of their natural wealth and resources,

"Considering that the economic development of the under-developed countries is one of the fundamental requisites for the strengthening of universal peace,

"Remembering that the right of peoples freely to use and exploit their natural wealth and resources is inherent in their sovereignty and in accordance with the Purposes and Principles of the Charter of the United Nations,

"1. Recommends all Member States, in the exercise of their right freely to use and exploit their natural wealth and resources wherever deemed desirable by them for their own progress and economic development, to have due regard, consistently with their sovereignty, to the need for maintaining the flow of capital in conditions of security, mutual confidence and economic co-operation among nations;

"2. Further recommends all Member States to refrain from acts, direct or indirect, designed to impede the exercise of the sovereignty of any State over its natural resources."

II) Resolution No. 1803 (XVII) of 14 December 1962; ...

"1. The right of peoples and nations to permanent sovereignty over their wealth and resources must be exercised in the interest of their national development and of the well-being of the people of the State concerned.

"2. The exploration, development and disposition of such resources, as well as the import of the foreign capital required for these purposes, should be in conformity with the rules and conditions which the peoples and nations freely consider to be necessary or desirable with regard to the authorization, restriction or prohibition of such activities."

(III) Resolution of 25 November 1966: which recommends increased participation of developing nations in the operation of projects exploited by foreign companies.

(IV) Resolution No. 3281 (XXIX) of 12 December 1974: in which it was provided, in its Chapter II, Article 2, as follows:

"1. Every State has and shall freely exercise full permanent sovereignty, including possession, use and disposal, over all its wealth, natural resources and economic activities.

"2. Each State has the right:

"(a) To regulate and exercise authority over foreign investment within its national jurisdiction in accordance with its laws and regulations and in conformity with its national objectives and priorities. No State shall be compelled to grant preferential treatment to foreign investment;

"(b) To regulate and supervise the activities of transnational corporations within its national jurisdiction and take measures to ensure that such activities comply with its laws, rules and regulations and conform with its economic and social policies. Transnational corporations shall not intervene in the internal affairs of a host State. Every State should, with full regard to its sovereign rights, co-operate with other States in the exercise of the right set forth in this subparagraph;

"(c) To nationalize, expropriate or transfer ownership of foreign property in which case appropriate compensation should be paid by the State adopting such measures, taking into account its relevant laws and regulations and all circumstances that the State considers pertinent. In any case where the question of compensation gives rise to a controversy, it shall be settled under the domestic law of the nationalizing State and by its tribunals, unless it is freely and mutually agreed by all States concerned that other peaceful means be sought on the basis of the sovereign equality of States and in accordance with the principle of free choice of means."

In response to the invitation proffered by the Arbitral Tribunal, the Claimant commented on the resolutions of the U.N. General Assembly bearing on the subject matter in a Memorial which it submitted to the Tribunal at its meeting of 11 January 1977. Referring to Resolution No. 1803 of 1962, the Memorial concluded that it specifically provided for the respect of foreign investment agreements, and was in contemplation of the

Parties when they entered into their Agreements of 1965. As to the Economic Charter contained in Resolution No. 3281 of 1974, it does not represent a consensus of nations and cannot be invoked as a source of international law.

In this connection, the Arbitral Tribunal has reached the conclusion that the said Resolutions, if not a unanimous source of law, are evidence of the recent dominant trend of international opinion concerning the sovereign right of States over their natural resources, and that the said right is always subject to the respect for contractual agreements and to the obligation of compensation, as will be explained in a later section.

4. Concession Rights as Property

[The arbitrator classified concession rights as incorporeal property, similar to the usufruct recognized by Islamic law].

5. Sanctity of contracts

The right to conclude contracts is one of the primordial civil rights acknowledged since olden times. It was the essence of "commercium" or "jus commercii" of the Roman "jus civile" whose scope was enlarged and extended by "jus gentium". Then it was always and constantly considered as security for economic transactions, and was even extended to the field of international relations.

This fundamental right is protected and characterized by two important propositions couched respectively in the expression that "the contract is the law of the parties", and in the Latin maxim that "Pacta sunt servanda" (pacts are to be observed).

The first proposition means that the contracting parties are free to arrange their contractual relationship as they mutually intend. The second means that a freely and validly concluded contract is binding upon the parties in their mutual relationship.

In fact, the principle of the sanctity of contracts, in its two characteristic propositions, has always constituted an integral part of most legal systems. These include those systems that are based on Roman law, the Napoleonic Code (e.g. Article 1134) and other European civil codes, as well as Anglo–Saxon Common Law and Islamic Jurisprudence (Shari'a).

Libya adopted and incorporated this legal principle in its Article 147 of the Civil Code (Same in Article 147 of the Egyptian code, Article 146 of the Iraki [sic] and Kuweiti [sic] codes, Article 148 of the Syrian code, and Article 221 of the Lebanese Code of Obligations and Contracts), whose paragraph 1 reads as follows:

"The contract is the law of the parties. It cannot be canceled or amended except by their mutual consent or for reasons admitted by the law".

The binding force of the contract is expressed in Article 148, para. 1, of the same Code:

"A contract shall be performed according to its contents and in the manner which accords with good faith".

Moreover, Islamic law, ... underscores the binding nature of contractual relations and of all terms and conditions of a contract that are not contrary to a text of law. This is expressed in the legal maxim:

"A stipulation is to be complied with as far as possible" (Article 83 of the Ottoman Majallah Code).

This maxim is corroborated by the various sources of Islamic law. For instance, a Koranic Verse ordains:

"Oh, you who believe, perform the contracts" (S V, 1). (Illegible Sentence)

"(Al–Jami' As–Sagheer, II, No. 9213).

* * *

Consequently, one of the parties cannot unilaterally cancel or modify the contents of the agreement, unless it is so authorized by the law, by a special provision of the agreement, or by its nature which implies such presumed intention of the parties.

* * *

6. Legal qualification and implications of LIAMCO's nationalizations

Having laid down the views generally held in municipal law which are common to international legal principles on the right of nationalization versus the right of property and the respect for contracts, it is necessary to examine the legal qualification of LIAMCO's nationalization measures in the light of those views.

LIAMCO contends that such measures are wrongful, because they are politically motivated, discriminatory and confiscatory.

As to the contention that the said measures were politically motivated and not in pursuance of a legitimate public purpose, it is the general opinion in international theory that the public utility principle is not a necessary requisite for the legality of a nationalization. This principle was mentioned by Grotius and other later publicists, but now there is no international authority, from a judicial or any other source, to support its application to nationalization. Motives are indifferent to international law, each State being free "to judge for itself what it considers useful or necessary for the public good.... The object pursued by it is of no concern to third parties."

This assertion is easily comprehensible, because nationalization in itself usually presupposes a general policy or political plan in support of which it is executed.

However, ... [i]t is clear and undisputed that non-discrimination is a requisite for the validity of a lawful nationalization. This is a rule well established in international legal theory and practice. Therefore, a purely discriminatory nationalization is illegal and wrongful.

In support of its contention of discrimination in its case, LIAMCO maintains that the nationalizations complained of were "specifically aimed at LIAMCO, an American company, because of its American corporate nationality and due to its insistence, amongst other things, on certain rights guaranteed to it under the concession agreements including the right to have all disputes determined by arbitration. . . ." And they were "part of an overall program of political retaliation against these nations whose politics were contrary to those of the new Libyan regime." In particular, "they were timed to coincide with the opening of the Washington Conference an energy."

[The arbitrator found that, while Libya first nationalized only British Petroleum (BP) and the Bunker Hunt Company in 1973, subsequent nationalization acts covered 51% of LIAMCO's concessions as well as those of Shell, Esso, Grace, Mobil, Texaco and California Oil Company. All these other companies later made arrangements with Libya, and continued to operate in Libya at the time of the arbitration. Some companies, like the American Murphy Oil Co., were not nationalized. . . . In 1974 the second LIAMCO nationalization act took the remaining 49% of LIAMCO's concession interests, apparently motivated by the failure of LIAMCO to agree with the Government as other companies had done].

From the above facts, it appears, that LIAMCO was not the first company to be nationalized, nor was it the only oil company nor the only American company to be nationalized by the first nationalization Act, nor was it nationalized alone on the date of the second nationalization Act. Other companies were nationalized before it, other American and Non–American companies were nationalized with it and after it, and other American companies are still operating in Libya.

Thus, it may be concluded from the above that the political motive was not the predominant motive for nationalization, and that such motive per se does not constitute a sufficient proof of a purely discriminatory measure.

* * *

After putting aside such grounds and the ground of tort (delictual) liability (responsabilite delictuelle), because no fraudulent or purely discriminatory intention has been proved, there remains the contractual liability of Libya towards LIAMCO in connection with its concessions and their nationalization.

VI.   REMEDIES FOR PREMATURE TERMINATION OF CONTRACT

[Having found that Libya was obligated to LIAMCO, the arbitrator addressed LIAMCO's requested remedies. LIAMCO preferred restoration of the concession, called "restitutio in integrum," to the alternative award of damages. The arbitrator found that under general principles of both international law and of Libyan law, obligations are to be performed in kind, if such performance is possible].

[However], impossibility [of performance] is in fact most usual in the international field. For this reason, it has been asserted that "it is impossible to compel a State to make restitution, this would constitute in fact an intolerable interference in the internal sovereignty of States."

Restitutio has thus been considered in international law as against the respect due for the sovereignty of the nationalizing State....

Further, restitution presupposes the cancellation of the nationalization measures at issue, and such cancellation violates also the sovereignty of the nationalizing State. Moreover, nationalization is sometimes qualified as an "Act of State," which is immune from control, judicial or otherwise.

* * *

[For similar reasons, the arbitrator rejected LIAMCO's call for a declaratory judgment that Libya did not have lawful title to oil extracted from LIAMCO's concession until effective payment was made. International precedents from courts in Tokyo, Italy and Britain confirmed the unenforceability of any decree to seize nationalized oil in tankers at various ports.]■

NOTES AND COMMENTS

1. The remainder of the arbitration decree discusses whether LIAMCO could claim damages for lost profits. Libya was clearly obligated to compensate LIAMCO for the value of the physical assets seized. Had the nationalization been an unlawful taking, international law would also allow the grant of lost profits. However, in cases of lawful nationalization, international precedent was decidedly mixed. Frequently in contemporary cases, the state and the private party had agreed to a lump sum payment. Few settlements seemed to have adopted the position of the U.S. State Department that adequate compensation had to include full compensation for lost profits. Instead, a legal doctrine was developing which allowed courts to revise contracts or treaties which had become onerous due to "unforeseen events" by providing "equitable" compensation.

Juxtaposed to the U.S. position was that of Libya's Prime Minister who explained his country's view that compensation should be based on "net book value", as follows:

> The first principle is that I cannot buy my own oil which is underground because this would be like a person who buys his house twice.... The net estimated book value is, for example, when the Occidental Company came and obtained a concession in Libya paying for example 100 million Libyan dinars.... [Assume] that this particular company ... had recovered something like 60 million dinars. The book value at the time of nationalization or participation is 40–million dinars....
>
> The second principle is that anyone who would like to be among us and cooperate with us must realize that the Libyan Arab Republic is not a milk cow... [and] that part of the profits should be utilized in the interest of the Libyan Arab people. 20 I.L.M. at 75.

In light of the opposite positions of the U.S. and Libya, and confusion in international standards, the arbitrator resorted to the principle of Equity, recognized as a supplementary source of law in Libyan law, Islamic law, and international law. The arbitrator decreed that "equitable compensation" for LIAMCO consisted of: $13.8 million for physical plant and equipment, $66 million for lost profits, and interest at the 5% standard set in the Libyan Civil Code. LIAMCO had requested $194 million in lost profits and interest at 12%. 20 I.L.M. at 77–87.

2.   The dispute between Kuwait and Aminoil (the American Independent Oil Company) over nationalization of that company's rich concession is reported in 66 I.L.R. 519, 21 I.L.M. 976 (1982). Aminoil unsuccessfully tried to use contract principles of duress to invalidate its consent to bow to some of Kuwait's increased demands. The arbitral award reads at paragraph 44: "In truth, the Company made a choice; disagreeable as certain demands might be, it considered that it was better to accede to them because it was still possible to live with them." In determining damages, the arbitrators used as a guide the "legitimate expectations" of both parties to the contract. Because of the many years of negotiations with Kuwait in which Aminoil had reluctantly consented to many Kuwaiti demands, the arbitrators found that "Aminoil had come to accept the principle of a moderate estimate of profits, and that it was this that constituted its legitimate expectation." (Para. 160).

In a separate opinion, one of the three appointed arbitrators, Sir Fitzmaurice wrote (Para. 26):

> It is an illusion to suppose that monetary compensation alone, even on a generous scale, necessarily removes the confiscatory element from a take-over.... It is like paying compensation to a man who has lost his leg. Unfortunately it does not restore the leg.... What the company wants is to be able to go on operating its Concession for the agreed term, not to be compensated for having to cease doing so against its will. In being deprived of the right to go on, all sorts of factors enter in that are not simply financial. In this respect, businesses are very like human beings, who do not relish being compulsorily retired and relegated to the side-lines ... even though it may be accompanied by a 'golden handshake' ... Nationalizations may be lawful or unlawful, but the test can never be 'whether they are confiscatory or not' because by virtue of their inherent character, they always are.

Arbitration awards are often kept confidential. Some of the few reported arbitral decisions involving petroleum agreements include Petroleum Dev. Ltd. v. Sheikh of Abu Dhabi, 18 I.L.R. 144 (1951); Ruler of Qatar v. Int'l Marine Oil Co., 20 I.L.R. 534 (1953); Saudi Arabia v. Arabian American Oil Co., 27 I.L.R. 117 (1958); Sapphire Int'l Pet. Ltd, v. National Iranian Oil Co., 35 I.L.R. 136 (1963); British Pet. Explor. Co. v. Libyan Arab Republic, 53 I.L.R. 297 (1973).

3.   Did the succession of United Nations resolutions quoted in the Libyan award invite host countries to institute creeping expropriation of foreign

interests? Note that LIAMCO tried to eliminate UN Resolution No. 3281 from the accepted principles of international law used in its arbitration. Why? Did the arbitrator ultimately adopt this Resolution's method of determining compensation?

While the United States continues to propound a standard of "prompt, adequate and effective" compensation for expropriation, the international community has not wholeheartedly adopted this standard. Rather, the standards of "appropriate" and "just" compensation have often been used. (The Aminoil–Kuwait arbitration used the "appropriate" standard of U.N. Resolution 1803). In the Chilean expropriation of Kennecott Copper, Chile offered to pay compensation after deducting excess profits earned by the company in Chile for several years. The profits exceeded the value of the property, so Chile argued that it owed nothing. Is this "appropriate" or "just"? See generally, Ralph H. Folsom, Michael Wallace Gordon, John A. Spanogle, Jr, International Business Transactions in a Nutshell 411–35 (1992). U.S. companies may be able to buy insurance against expropriation from OPIC, the Overseas Private Investment Corporation or the Export–Import Bank. *Id.* at 436–52.

Some commentators see a recent trend toward "full" compensation as the appropriate international standard as a result of "the now widely accepted need to encourage investment in the Third World [which has] eroded the rationale for a partial compensation standard that appeared so compelling to many observers just a short time ago." Patrick M. Norton, A Law of the Future or a Law of the Past? Modern Tribunals and the International Law of Expropriation, 85 American J. Int'l L. 474 (1991). *See also* Paul D. Friedland and Eleanor Wong, Measuring Damages for the Deprivation of Income–Producing Assets: ICSID Case Studies, ICSID Review–Foreign Investment L. J. 400 (1991).

4.   Compare the principles of property law used in these arbitrations to the analysis used by U.S. courts under the Takings Clause of the U.S. Constitution that private property shall not "be taken for public use without just compensation."

How do the principles announced differ from those used by public utility regulators in the U.S. to determine fair rates of return for utility companies?

Outright expropriations by government take-overs reached a modern high in the mid–1970s, but have diminished greatly in recent years. Investors today more commonly face the risk that a government will seek to void or renegotiate a contract because it results in unconscionably high profits or was the result of a corrupt payoff made by a now-ousted political party. *See* Susan Rose–Ackerman & Jim Rossi, Disentangling Deregulatory Takings, 86 Va.L.Rev. ___ (forthcoming 2000), previously published as Takings Law and Infrastructure Investment: Certainty, Flexibility and Compensation, Working Paper No. 20, Yale Law School Program for Studies in Law, Economics and Public Policy (Aug. 1999).

The Russian Production Sharing Agreement Law of 1996 states that "amendments to the production sharing agreement may be made on the demand of one party in the event that circumstances change significantly provided such changes are in accordance with the civil code of the Russian Federation." Could the 1999–2000 swing in the price of crude oil, as shown in Figure 16–3 allow Russia to unilaterally amend such an agreement? What risk premium would be necessary for foreign investors to invest in the Russian oil industry under such laws? *See* the Conference Proceedings on Investing in Russia Under the Law on Production Sharing Agreements, 20 Houston J. Int'l L. 517 (1998).

5.   How are arbitration awards enforced? The United States is one of more than 80 parties to the 1958 U.N. Convention on the Recognition and Enforcement of Foreign Arbitral Awards, 21 U.S.T. 2517, T.I.A.S. No. 6997 (June 10, 1958), as implemented in the U.S. through 9 U.S.C. secs. 201–208. *See also* 28 U.S.C. secs. 1605(a)(1) and (6) on arbitral agreements with foreign states. The U.N. Convention commits the courts of each signatory nation to recognize and enforce arbitration clauses and agreements in international commercial disputes. The U.S. is also a party to several other bilateral and investment treaties that include provisions recognizing and enforcing arbitral agreements and awards. Some of these bilateral treaties may also contain compensation standards for nationalization that accord better with the U.S. standard of "prompt, adequate and effective."

6.   Arbitration rather than litigation is the major dispute resolution device used in international agreements. The parties commonly choose to use the rules of one of four arbitral institutions: the International Chamber of Commerce, the World Bank's International Center for the Settlement of Investment Disputes (ICSID), the United Nations Commission on International Trade Law (UNCITRAL), or the Arbitration Institute of the Stockholm Chamber of Commerce. Because the arbitration clause is very important to the parties, it should be carefully drafted. *See generally* Michael P. Darden, Legal Research Checklist for International Petroleum Operations 58 (1994).

One of the most important provisions in the clause is the choice of law to be used by the parties in resolving the dispute. Would the result in LIAMCO have been different if the dispute was to be governed by Libyan law only, without reference to international law?

3.   MODERN FORMS OF PETROLEUM AGREEMENTS

a.   OVERVIEW

How do governments today grant rights to develop their oil and gas resources? Professor Gary Conine describes and contrasts the major types of systems used today to grant rights to companies:

Gary B. Conine, International Oil and Gas Transactions: Basic Contracts and Dispute Resolution

State Bar of Texas, Advanced Oil, Gas and Mineral Law Course, Ch. J (1994) at pp. J–1 to J–3.

In general, three legal mechanisms are used by states in granting operating rights to private investors. One involves detailed and rigid legal codes which may go so far as to prescribe not only the conditions under which these rights will be granted but also the form of any agreement between the host government and the oil company. The government is free to negotiate very few terms with the firm. Such legislation is employed in the United States, Canada, Australia, Latin America and most West European countries.

A second regime authorizes a state commission or a national oil company to negotiate and execute *ad hoc* agreements with individual foreign oil companies. For example, the petroleum laws of some countries entrust all petroleum development to a national oil company which, in turn, negotiates contracts with foreign companies to explore for and develop the resource.

An increasing number of countries have adopted a third system that represents a combined, or hybrid, approach that permits a degree of flexibility in formulating each transaction within broad legislative constraints designed to assure adherence to public policies.

There are various advantages and disadvantages to each form of legal system used for issuing petroleum investment agreements. Detailed legislative systems have been credited with affording an opportunity to include general policy objectives in the law and with imposing a standardized system that makes government oversight and enforcement easier and more effective. It reduces the scope of bargaining, which strengthens the government's negotiating position and ensures public policies will be satisfied, while it produces some assurance that all potential operators will be treated alike.

The disadvantage of a detailed code lies in its lack of flexibility. In order to entice companies to invest in a country, the government often must be able to adjust the terms of its agreements to make its offers as attractive as those of other countries.

On the other hand, the *ad hoc* approach gives the state agency considerable latitude in negotiations, enhancing the country's ability to structure attractive proposals. But it often creates uncertainty among investors and bureaucrats over the terms that will be acceptable to the government, complicates the evaluation of competing offers due to the lack of uniformity in terms, and results in highly complex agreements that may be difficult to formulate and monitor or which invite opportunities for corruption and discrimination.

The [third] hybrid system uses a code that delegates authority over mineral resources to a specific agency of the government, establishes the procedures for offering development contracts, and prescribes minimum standards and conditions that are non-negotiable, such as provisions on environmental, safety, labor and tax matters. Factors important to the financial evaluation of a project, such as the allocation of risk and revenues, are assigned to the discretion of the licensing agency to allow it the flexibility to attract companies to specific projects. . . .

B.   Selecting the Licensee or Contractor

World petroleum laws have used, again, one of three procedures for the award of investment agreements. One procedure vests the government with complete discretion over the selection of a licensee or contractor, and the negotiation of contract terms. . . . As with the *ad hoc* approach, the primary advantage of the discretionary award of licenses lies in the ability to adjust license terms to attract investment at various times to different projects. It also allows the government to select the investor that it believes will be best qualified technically and financially to undertake the operations that will be required in specific situations.

A second procedure relies on public auctions to select the licensee. If there is to be any screening of potential bidders, it must be accomplished prior to the auction. Moreover, all terms of the license, with the exception of the one that is the subject of the bid, must be determined in advance. The auction is compatible with detailed legislation that prescribes most terms in the license or requires the use of a prescribed license form. . . . The applicant submitting the highest bid on the open term is awarded the license.

A variant of the auction is the open competition. Here the government may announce the general terms it is seeking for a license in a designated area and permit each applicant to construct its own offer. There is usually more than one open term, so that each proposal must be separately evaluated on the basis of the criteria announced for the competition. While a competition suggests that all proposals are to be submitted on a certain date and evaluated against one another, common practice more often results in a series of proposals from each applicant as the government discloses deficiencies in the offers in an effort to get the applicants to bid against one another.

The auction offers two advantages. First, it minimizes the need for the application of non-quantifiable criteria that permit discretionary decisions, reducing the need for bureaucratic judgment. The most meritorious proposal can be determined by any party based on the stated criterion without explanation or justification. Second, the auction provides greater assurance that the winning bid maximizes the financial benefits that can be extracted by the government for a license under the circumstances. Assuming a sufficient number of participants, competition will force the bidders to offer the best terms that the economics of the project will allow. Where expertise in evaluating competing proposals is unavailable to the government, the auction simplifies the process while providing some assurance that the winning proposal is the best deal for the country.

Yet auctions have also been criticized as a licensing procedure. Like the detailed legislation with which it is often associated, the auction is inherently inflexible. To achieve the benefits of the auction, most terms must be prescribed in advance, leaving only a few terms open for bidding. This precludes the use of more complex selection criteria that could be used to attain public objectives other than enhanced revenues. At the same time, it requires the state licensing agency to have considerable experience in formulating licenses as investment packages and to use that experience wisely to assure widespread interest among potential investors.

It is also charged that the auction does not assure that the highest bidder will be the most competent. Indeed, some assert that it tends to favor major companies that have the resources necessary to make large bonus payments upon the issuance of a license and forgo recovery of that investment for years until the license area can be explored and developed. This factor discourages bidding by independent companies and dilutes the competitive forces relied on to maximize bids. While this makes sense, it does not explain the clear preference among major companies for the award of licenses based on direct negotiations. One can only assume that this preference is related again to the greater resources of the major companies and their resulting ability to compete more effectively in negotiations. Their ability to commit experts from various fields for prolonged periods and to devise numerous financial scenarios to accommodate specific concerns and needs of the host country seem to give them a negotiating advantage. This form of competitive advantage is against other companies and does not necessarily assure the government that it is getting the best possible deal. Contemporary surveys have indicated that auctions are employed by a minority of countries.■

NOTES AND COMMENTS

1. Which method of bidding and selection best guards against bribery and corruption?

2. Four types of petroleum investment contracts are in common use today:

First is the modern *concession or license*. This contract grants exclusive rights to explore, produce and sell petroleum to the licensee, but with extensive provisions governing work commitments and a development program. Revenues to the state generally accrue through royalties, bonus, rentals, and taxes, but the fiscal terms are far more sophisticated than in an oil and gas lease or the early concessions.

The second common contract is a *production sharing agreement* whereby the host country grants a company the right to explore and develop a particular area in exchange for the opportunity to recover its costs and a specific profit share from any production obtained under the contract. The company takes the risk that production revenues will cover costs. The country usually maintains control over the producing properties by creating a state-owned oil company which enters into the contract with the foreign company. The foreign company serves as a "contractor" for the state. The state receives revenues as a share of the "profit oil" remaining after part of the oil, the "cost oil," is used to reimburse the contractor for expenses.

The third type of contract is the *joint venture* or *participation agreement*, whereby the state oil company (or government) and the foreign company form a new entity to develop the oil and gas reserves. A management committee composed of representatives from both parents operates the joint venture. Many concession and production sharing agreements give the government the option of electing to participate.

The final type of agreement is a *service contract*, under which a company agrees to provide certain services or technical assistance to the host country or its state oil company in return for a fixed fee or a share of production.

Why don't U.S. landowners, including the federal government, adopt some of these forms of international petroleum agreements in lieu of the oil and gas lease?

3.   Do you agree with the following observations of one scholar of petroleum agreements?:

> The modern mineral agreement negotiated with host governments ... is an anomaly. It is nominally a contract to conduct certain activities under host government supervision, but since the risk and financing are borne by the contractor, it is a foreign equity investment. The foreign investment is basically the contract itself, since in most agreements title to the resources in the ground and even to the equipment and installations is held by the host government or reverts to the government at the termination of the contract. Moreover, the contracts have not been regarded by most host governments as covenants to be honored throughout their term, but rather as a framework for more or less continuous negotiation as the relative bargaining power and opportunities created by new conditions change in favor of the government.
>
> In the major OPEC countries, such as Saudi Arabia and Kuwait, the position of the original Contractor has diminished to that of a technician and buyer of the oil produced, with little or no control over the amount of oil produced or received, or over the price that must be paid to the host government for the oil. The position of petroleum companies operating in non-OPEC countries, as well as in some of the smaller OPEC producers such as Ecuador and Indonesia, is much stronger since most of these countries need substantial exploration and development to expand their reserves and output, and the governments lack the financial and technical resources to undertake investments on an adequate scale. . . .

Raymond F. Mikesell, *Petroleum Company Operations & Agreements in the Developing Countries* 135 (Resources for the Future 1984).

4.   "Contractor take" is the measure of a contractor's share of profits (gross revenues minus total costs) after royalties and taxes are paid to the government. Contractor take varies from about 10% in Abu Dhabi and Indonesia; to 30% to 40% in China, Colombia, Papua New Guinea; and to 40% or more in Australia, the U.S., and the Philippines. Daniel Johnston, International Petroleum Fiscal Systems and Production Sharing Contracts 14 (1994). The expected contractor's take necessary to attract investors will vary with perceptions of many kinds of risk: the geological risk of finding

reserves; development risks of getting production to a market; political risks; and risks relating to the future price of oil or gas. The book by Johnston provides a good overview of the business side of petroleum contracting.

Countries which impose onerous fiscal terms will find few multinational companies bidding to assist them in exploiting their reserves. Many developing countries initially tried to imitate OPEC countries' fiscal terms. In the absence of OPEC-size fields, these countries attracted little foreign investment until they revised their petroleum contracts and laws. Professor Mikesell *supra* concludes that many countries lost years of potential production, at an enormous cost to the countries.

5. Many countries of the former Soviet Union sought to adopt modern, market-oriented petroleum laws after the fall of Communism. For a description of one such drafting project to develop model laws for Russia in the areas of Licensing, Conservation and the Environment, Pipelines, and Taxation, see the Symposium on the Russian Petroleum Legislation Project at the University of Houston Law Center, published in *15* Houston J. of Int'l L., Nos. 2 and 3 (1993).

A nine-page legal checklist of at least 200 items to research before venturing abroad, with accompanying commentary, appears in Michael P. Darden, Legal Research Checklist for International Petroleum Operations, Monograph No. 20 (Section of Natural Resources, Energy and Environmental Law, American Bar Association,1994).

A casebook on "International Petroleum Transactions" by Professors Smith, Dzienkowski, Anderson, Conine and Lowe (Rocky Mountain Mineral Law Foundation 1993) awaits the intrepid student. Would you expect to find discussions of the rule of capture and unitization in this casebook, as compared to a casebook on U.S. oil and gas law? Why or why not?

6. Many countries that created state oil companies in the 1970s when oil prices were high have had second thoughts. The 1990s have seen a strong trend toward greater privatization and participation by private companies in many countries. Falling oil prices exposed the inefficiency and bloated costs of many state-run operations. Government revenues fell drastically as oil prices dropped, and many states could no longer provide the capital needed to invest in their own oil and gas resources. Private lenders were equally wary of investing in wasteful operations run by state governments. All these forces converged to foster the pendulum swing toward privatization.

Privatization can be accomplished in several ways: by selling company stock to private investors; by selling the company's assets; by downsizing and reorganizing the company into subsidiaries, some of which are sold and some retained; by joint venturing with foreign companies; or by "privatizing" the management of the company by entering into service contracts with private firms who will provide the skills and technology necessary for efficient development. *See, e.g.,* Carlos E. Martinez, Early Lessons of Latin American Privatizations, 15 Suffolk Transnat'l L.J. 468 (1992). Argentina has transformed its once state-controlled energy sector. In 1993, it privatized its national oil company, YPF; shortly thereafter, YPF acquired Dallas-based Maxum Petroleum and now operates in many Latin American countries. *See* Jay G. Martin, Privatization of Latin American Energy, 14 Nat. Resources & Env't 103 (1999). Privatization of industrial enterprises in Russia and the countries of the former Soviet Union has not been nearly as successful. *See, e.g.,* Anne E. Peck, Foreign Investment in Kazakhstan's Mineral Industries, 40 Post–Soviet Geography and Economics 471 (1999).

In *Why Governments Waste Natural Resources* (Johns Hopkins Univ. Press 1999), William Ascher looks at 16 case studies of wasteful resource policies in countries like Mexico, Indonesia, Brazil, Mexico, and Ghana, in an effort to explain the waste. Why, *e.g.,* did the state oil company of Peru go bankrupt in the late 1970s after pursuing questionable Amazonian exploration, leaving the state to refinance a foreign debt of $1 billion? Why were 85% of the contracts of Pemex awarded illegally without competitive bidding in the 1980s, and why did Pemex's debt reach $25 billion by 1982, contributing to Mexico's financial collapse? His careful analysis concludes that the resource failures are not due to ignorance or weak governmental capacity, but to deliberate policy decisions of top government officials who are bent on promoting development initiatives, redistributing wealth and capturing revenues for the central treasury. Ascher concludes that in many cases the restoration of private or communal resource ownership would prevent some of the wasteful practices that have left resource-rich countries poorer rather than better off.

Privatization often results in high unemployment and social unrest as workers in inefficient industries or in bloated bureaucracies are laid off so that the newly privatized firm can compete in the world market against its agile rivals. China's state-owned industries have been losing money since the mid–1990s. In 1998, the government laid off 6 million workers from state-owned enterprises, 4 million more workers were let go in 1999, and predictions are that 6 million more will be laid off in 2000. Only some of these workers are absorbed into the growing private sector, which has risen from 34 percent of China's economy in 1990 to 43 percent in 1998. In some industrialized cities of China, unemployment may be as high as 50 percent. BNA Daily Report for Executives, Jan. 18, 2000, at A–1. [Review Figure 16–5 for employment trends in the U.S. oil industry].

b. CORRUPTION

Increasingly, corruption has come to be recognized as one of the most serious current barriers to investment and growth especially in natural resource industries in developing countries. It is also a serious impediment to democratic institutions. *See generally* Susan Rose–Ackerman, Corruption and Government: Causes, Consequences and Reform (1999); George Moody–Stuart, Grand Corruption: How Business Bribes Damage Developing Countries (1997); and 14 Conn. J. Int'l L., Issue No. 2 (1999) (entire issue devoted to corruption). Russia's economic failure after the fall of Communism has been partly attributed to the vast corruption, bordering on kleptocracy, that appears to have accompanied many efforts to privatize its state industries. The management of Russia's giant oil companies are often former Soviet ministers and ranking Communist Party officials. Five chief executives of Russia's privatized oil companies recently joined the Forbes list of the world's 200 wealthiest people. *See* Tina Obut, Avik Sarkar & Sankar Sudner, "Roots of Systemic Woes in Russian Oil Sector Traceable to Industry Evolution," Oil & Gas J. 27 (Jan. 25, 1999). Russia's production of oil, gas and coal declined significantly between 1992 and 1997. The Energy Information Administration of the U.S. Department of Energy writes excellent country reports on the petroleum industry in every producing nation. See www.eia.doe.gov/emeu/cabs/russia for the sad report on Russia.

Corruption has not been a stranger to resource acquisition in the United States. The Teapot Dome scandal involved the award of leases to two oil companies in 1922 on the Navy's oil reserves at Teapot Dome in Wyoming and Elk Hill in California. The leases were awarded after executives of the oil companies made payments (in the guise of loans or investments) to Albert Fall, the Secretary of the Interior. The Supreme Court canceled the leases and the Secretary was jailed. This scandal notwithstanding, the United States has been a global leader in the fight against corruption since 1977 with the passage of the Foreign Corrupt Practices Act (FCPA), 15 U.S.C.A. secs. 78dd–1, 78dd–2, 78dd–3 and 78m (West 1997 & West Supp. 1999)

This Act owes its birth to the Watergate scandal that ultimately led to the impeachment of President Nixon. The Watergate burglary of the Democratic National Committee's headquarters in 1972 led to a Senate investigation of contributions to Richard Nixon's reelection campaign. The Senate investigating committee found that 15 major corporations had violated the campaign contribution laws by making illegal payments. A report from one of these corporations, Gulf Oil, described an elaborate system of overseas bribes, totaling more than $5 million. A subsequent investigation by the Securities and Exchange Commission (SEC) found that more than 400 U.S. Companies had made "questionable payments" of more than $300 million abroad. No specific law expressly prohibited Americans from paying a bribe to a foreign official. The FCPA was passed to fill the void. The U.S. became the first country in the world to make payments of bribes to foreign officials illegal. The Act also requires that corporations keep accounting records to prevent bribes from being hidden. Individual officers, directors and employees of companies are subject to fines and imprisonment for violating the act.

The Act left America standing alone in the world, with its corporations at a serious disadvantage against foreign competitors who could continue to use bribes to secure valuable contracts. The Department of Commerce reported that U.S. businesses lost 100 foreign contracts valued at $45 billion to overseas competitors during 1994 and 1995. Kari Diersen, Foreign Corrupt Practices Act, 36 Am. Crim. L. Rev. 753 at 764 n. 88 ((1999). The United States undertook a foreign policy campaign to level the playing field by exhorting other countries and international organizations to join the anti-bribery bandwagon. Years of lobbying the Organization for Economic Cooperation and Development (the OECD is a group of leading industrialized countries) finally bore fruit in 1997 when all 29 member countries signed the Convention on Combating Bribery of Foreign Public Officials in International Business Transactions (37 I.L.M. 1(1998)). The Convention entered into force in 1999 and makes it a criminal offense to give a bribe to a foreign public official. The OECD's Centre for Anti–Corruption Compliance has an extensive website on foreign corruption at www.oecd.org/daf/nocorruption/index. In addition, the U.N. General Assembly approved a resolution against corruption in 1997.

Transparency International (TI) is a nongovernmental organization founded to stop international bribery. It publishes a Corruption Perception Index that lists the most and least corrupt countries in the world in terms of taking bribes. It recently added a Bribe Payers Index ranking 19 leading industrialized countries in terms of their paying bribes. TI's homepage is at www.transparency.de. The index is quite useful to firms venturing abroad. Where do you think United States officials and companies rank on the respective lists–as bribe takers and bribe payers–using a scale of 1 to 10 with 10 being negligible corruption?

The World Bank, the International Monetary Fund, the World Trade Organization, the International Chamber of Commerce and the Organization of American States have also undertaken significant anti-corruption initiatives. The World Bank has refused to fund projects in countries with corruption. For example, it suspended a $76 million loan to Kenya for energy development because it could not ensure that the contracts would be awarded fairly and openly. *See* A. Timothy Martin, The Development of International Bribery Law, 14 Nat. Resources & Env't 95 (Fall 1999)

China ranks quite poorly on the indexes. In his opening speech to the Chinese parliament in March 2000, the Chinese Prime Minister repeatedly cited corruption as one of China's most pressing problems. A few days later, China executed a former provincial vice governor for taking bribes worth $600,000. New York Times, Mar. 9, 2000, at A10.

Some key prosecutions in the United States under the FCPA have involved oil companies. In 1986, Ashland Oil was prosecuted for its actions in securing offshore petroleum rights from the Sultanate of Oman. The SEC settled a civil action against Triton Energy in 1997 involving petroleum operations in Indonesia. The FCPA poses special challenges to U.S. companies developing natural resource projects abroad with state-owned oil companies as their joint venturers. *See* Lucinda A. Low and John E. Davis, Coping with the Foreign Corrupt Practices Act: A Primer for Energy and Natural Resource Sectors, 16 J. Energy & Nat. Resources L. 286–320 (1998); and Christopher F. Corr & Judd Lawler, Damned If You Do, Damned If You Don't? The OECD Convention and the Globalization of Anti–Bribery Measures, 32 Vanderbilt J. Transnat'l L. 1249 (1999).

Under the FCPA it is not illegal to pay gratuities to foreign officials who perform "routine governmental action", *i.e.*, "grease" payments for processing permits, visas, providing phone service, etc. Is it easy to draw a line between legal and illegal payments? Steven R. Salbu argues that the "world is not ready to agree about what comprises corruption" and that the FCPA and its progeny unwisely promote the extraterritorial criminalization of bribery when "[t]he world is not sufficiently homogenized to embrace one conceptualization of morality in gray areas." Is the FCPA a "culturally arrogant encroachment" on the international law principle of national sovereignty? *See* Salbu, The Foreign Corrupt Practices Act as a Threat to Global Harmony, 20 Mich. J. of Int'l L. 419 (1999). Is Transparency International's approach a better way to reduce bribery than the FCPA's use of legal fiat?

NOTES AND COMMENTS

1. U.S. oil companies venturing abroad are also subject to federal laws and Executive Orders which may impose trade sanctions against repressive regimes which violate human rights. For example, Congress enacted a law authorizing the President to prohibit U.S. persons from making new investments in Burma if the President certifies that the Government of Burma has maltreated or exiled Daw Aung San Suu Kyi (winner of the Nobel peace prize in 1991) or committed repression or violence against its democratic opposition. In May 1997, the president found that Burma had committed large-scale repression of the democratic opposition, and issued an order imposing trade sanctions on Burma.

Several states of the United States, such as Massachusetts, have passed laws prohibiting the state or its agencies from purchasing goods or services from companies that do business with Burma. In signing the bill into law, the Lieutenant Governor of Massachusetts stated that a steady flow of foreign investment into Burma was allowing the brutal military regime to supply itself with weapons and portray itself as the legitimate government. In *Crosby v. National Foreign Trade Council,* 120 S.Ct. 4545 (2000), the Supreme Court held that Massachusetts' Burma Law unconstitutionally encroached on the federal government's exclusive power over foreign relations and also was preempted by federal law.

Do trade sanctions like this create another "unlevel" playing field for U.S. companies operating abroad, as did the Foreign Corrupt Practices Act? In an opinion ad on the OpEd pages of the New York Times, ExxonMobil states that "Unless broadly adopted by many countries, sanctions do little more than damage U.S. businesses that are unable to compete with foreign companies not similarly constrained. Moreover, government entities in the U.S. have been on a sanctions binge since the 1980s, so that now some form of U.S. sanctions applies to countries with over two-thirds of the world's population. And this leads to more than simply an economic loss for Americans–it can also deprive developing nations of a positive force for change that is often associated with the participation of private U.S. enterprise in their national economies." New York Times, Mar. 9, 2000, at

A29. In 1996, Conoco was awarded a contract worth $1 billion by the National Iranian Oil Co to develop a large offshore field. After the contract was signed, President Clinton issued an executive order imposing trade sanctions on Iran, and Conoco was forced to withdraw from the project, which later was awarded to Total, the French oil company. BNA Daily Report for Executives A–46, Sept. 29, 1999, at A46.

4.   BARRIERS TO LITIGATING DISPUTES: SOVEREIGN IMMUNITY, POLITICAL QUESTION, AND THE ACT OF STATE DOCTRINES

One reason for the prevalence of arbitration as a dispute resolution mechanism in international petroleum agreements is that substantial barriers exist to litigating claims against host governments or their national oil companies. By resorting to arbitration, many of these barriers disappear and private investors are better assured of a forum in which disputes can be resolved. The nationalization of oil company interests by OPEC countries in the 1970s provided a cornucopia of law on the issues of sovereign immunity, political question, and the act of state doctrine. Under these three doctrines, a court will dismiss a cause of action, even though the court has personal jurisdiction and subject matter jurisdiction over the defendant under the principles advanced in *International Shoe* and other cases studied in Civil Procedure or International Law.

a.   SOVEREIGN IMMUNITY

The doctrine of sovereign immunity derives from the "common law" principle of international law that sovereigns are equal and should not be subject to suit in the courts of another nation. Application of the doctrine in the United States was codified in the Foreign Sovereign Immunities Act of 1976, 28 U.S.C. secs. 1330, 1602–1611 after court decisions began restricting the doctrine so that immunity did not apply to commercial activities of states. As state oil companies proliferated and expanded their commercial reach, the Act's usefulness as a tool to bring these companies to court was often tested. The Act grants to federal district courts jurisdiction over any civil action against a foreign state which falls into one of several exceptions to sovereign immunity. These exceptions include:

1.   Waiver of immunity by the foreign state. Sec. 1605(a)(1).

2.   Action based on commercial activity conducted in the U.S. by the foreign state, or conducted outside the U.S. "in connection with a commercial activity of the foreign state elsewhere . . . [which] causes a direct effect in the United States." Sec. 1605(a)(2).

3.   Claims that rights in property were taken in violation of international law, and that property is present in the U.S. in connection with a commercial activity carried on by the foreign state in the U.S.; or that the property is "owned or operated by an agency or instrumentality of the foreign state" which is engaged in commercial activity in the U.S. Sec. 1605(a)(3).

4.   A claim for money damages against a foreign state for personal injury or death, or for damage to property occurring in the U.S. and caused by the tortious act of the foreign state or its officials and employees, as long as the tortious act is not the exercise of a discretionary function by the foreign state. Sec. 1605(a)(5).

See generally Jordan J. Paust, Joan M. Fitzpatrick, & Jon M. Van Dyke, International Law and Litigation in the U.S. 567–638 (West 2000).

Which of these exceptions are likely to be at issue under the following claims? What do you think is the likely result?

— Libya nationalized its oil concessions and then embargoed exports of crude oil to the U.S. To obtain crude oil supplies, a Bahamian refiner entered into new contracts with the Libyan National Oil Corporation at prices triple the previous price. The refiner was a subsidiary of a New England merchant who sold fuel oil in that area. The New England merchant sued the Libyan National Oil company for $1.6 billion in damages for breach of contract and other overcharges. Carey v. National Oil Corp., 592 F.2d 673 (2d Cir.1979).

— LIAMCO (the Libyan American Oil Company) sought to confirm and enforce an arbitration award against Libya for nationalizing its concession rights. LIAMCO had entered into the concession agreement in 1955 and negotiated arbitration and choice of law provisions with Libya in amendments to the original contract in 1966 and 1967. Libyan American Oil Company v. Socialist People's Libyan Arab Jamahirya (Libya), 482 F.Supp. 1175 (D.D.C.1980).

— PEMEX was engaged in drilling a well, the Ixtoc I, in the Bay of Campeche. The well blew out, leading to a massive oil spill which reached the lower Texas beaches, entailing huge cleanup efforts and losses of recreational business. Private plaintiffs and the state of Texas brought suit against PEMEX. In re SEDCO, 543 F.Supp. 561 (S.D.Tex.1982).

— The owner of a shrimp trawler sought damages against a tug owned by PEMEX, which collided with the trawler. See S.T. Tringali Co. v. The Tug PEMEX XV, 274 F.Supp. 227 (S.D.Tex.1967).

b.   POLITICAL QUESTION

If an action in a U.S. court survives analysis under the Foreign Sovereign Immunities Act, it might still be dismissed because it is best left to another branch of government. The Persian Gulf again provides a good example of the "political question" doctrine. In Occidental of Umm al Qaywayn, Inc. v. A Certain Cargo of Petroleum, 577 F.2d 1196 (5th Cir. 1978), Occidental brought an action for conversion of tankers full of crude oil brought to the United States by rival oil companies. Occidental traced its right to the oil from a concession it had signed with the sheikhdom of Umm. Rival Buttes Oil Company entered into a concession agreement with the neighboring sheikhdom of Sharjah. The rulers of the two sheihkdoms then each claimed title to the same tiny island of Abu Musa in the Gulf as part of their territorial waters. Iran also claimed ownership of the island.

Iran teamed up with Sharjah and these two states confirmed Buttes' concession. Then Iran invaded the island, leaving Occidental and Umm without any protection. The rulers of Umm and Sharjah ultimately resolved to share royalties, but Occidental was left out in the cold. Umm terminated its concession. After reciting this history, the court wrote:

> A political question clearly emerges under the proper analysis.... Shorn of its factual complexity, appellants claim a tortious conversion of oil.... [W]e find that to successfully maintain its tortious conversion action, appellant would have to establish its right to possess the oil at the time of conversion. Appellant apparently contends that the conversion occurred when appellant was supplanted by Buttes through the intervention of Iran, sometime after November 30, 1971. Because, as a matter of international law, one who receives an interest in land which is in dispute between sovereigns takes subject to the dispute, ... appellant must necessarily develop Umm's right to undisputed possession of the portion of the continental shelf where the oil was extracted.... Therefore, in order to resolve appellant's right to possess the oil, we would have to resolve the dispute over Abu Musa. The resolution of a territorial dispute between sovereigns, however, is a political question which we are powerless to decide.

> Throughout the history of the federal judiciary, political questions have been held to be nonjusticiable and therefore not a "case or controversy" as defined by Article III.... In Marbury v. Madison, 5 U.S. (1 Cranch) 137, 164–66, 2 L.Ed. 60 (1803), Chief Justice Marshall acknowledged the existence of a class of cases which involve a "mere political act of the executive" and which were placed by the Constitution in the hands of the executive. The Supreme Court therefore appreciated that the genesis of the political question is the constitutional separation and disbursement of powers among the branches of government. *Id.* at 1201–03.

c. THE ACT OF STATE DOCTRINE

More common than the political question is the judicially created act of state doctrine. In 1897, the Supreme Court formulated the doctrine when it held that "the courts of one country will not sit in judgment on the acts of the government of another, done within its own territory." Underhill v. Hernandez, 168 U.S. 250, 252. (1897). The doctrine requires, first, that public acts occurred, and second, that the acts took place in the foreign country.

In the following case, again arising from the Persian Gulf, the court distinguishes the defense of sovereign immunity from the act of state doctrine. The International Association of Machinists and Aerospace Workers (IAM) sued OPEC for violating the U.S. antitrust laws by price-fixing. (Recall that the OPEC embargo and price rises caused large unemployment effects as well as inflation).

International Association of Machinists and Aerospace Workers (IAM) v. OPEC

649 F.2d 1354 (9th Cir. 1981), cert. denied, 454 U.S. 1163 (1982).

■ CHOY, CIRCUIT JUDGE:

The OPEC nations produce and export oil either through government-owned companies or through government participation in private companies. Prior to the formation of OPEC, these diverse and sometimes antagonistic countries were plagued with fluctuating oil prices. Without coordination among them, oil was often in oversupply on the world market resulting in low prices. The OPEC nations realized that self-interest dictated that they "formulate a system to ensure the stabilisation (sic) of prices by, among other means, the regulation of production, with due regard to the interests of the producing and of the consuming nations, and to the necessity of securing a steady income to the producing countries, an efficient economic and regular supply of this source of energy to consuming nations." OPEC Resolution of the First Conference, Resolution 1.1(3), September 1960.

OPEC achieves its goals by a system of production limits and royalties which its members unanimously adopt. There is no enforcement arm of OPEC. The force behind OPEC decrees is the collective self-interest of the 13 nations.

After formation of OPEC, it is alleged, the price of crude oil increased tenfold and more. Whether or not a causal relation exists, there is no doubt that the price of oil has risen dramatically in recent years, and that this has become of international concern. . . .

In December 1978, IAM brought suit against OPEC and its member nations. IAM's complaint alleged price fixing in violation of the Sherman Act, 15 U.S.C. § 1, and requested treble damages and injunctive relief under the Clayton Act, 15 U.S.C. §§ 15, 16. IAM claimed a deliberate targeting and victimization of the United States market, directly resulting in higher prices for Americans.

The defendants refused to recognize the jurisdiction of the district court, and they did not appear in the proceedings below. Their cause was argued by various amici, with additional information provided by court-appointed experts. The district court ordered a full hearing, noting that the Foreign Sovereign Immunities Act (FSIA) prohibits the entry of a default judgment against a foreign sovereignty "unless the claimant establishes his claim or right to relief by evidence satisfactory to the court." 28 U.S.C. § 1608(e).

At the close of the trial, the district judge granted judgment in favor of the defendants. The court held, first, that it lacked jurisdiction over the defendant nations under the Foreign Sovereign Immunities Act. . . .

A. Sovereign Immunity

In the international sphere each state is viewed as an independent sovereign, equal in sovereignty to all other states. It is said that an equal holds no power of sovereignty over an equal. Thus the doctrine of sovereign immunity: the courts of one state generally have no jurisdiction to entertain suits against another state. This rule of international law developed by custom among nations. Also by custom, an exception developed for the commercial activities of a state. The former concept of absolute sovereign immunity gave way to a restrictive view. Under the restrictive theory of sovereign immunity, immunity did not exist for commercial activities since they were seen as non-sovereign.

In 1976, Congress enacted the FSIA and declared that the federal courts will apply an objective nature-of-the-act test in determining whether activity is commercial and thus not immune: "The commercial character of an activity shall be determined by reference to the nature of the course of conduct or particular transaction or act, rather than by reference to its purpose." 28 U.S.C. § 1603(d).

A critical step in characterizing the nature of a given activity is defining exactly what that activity is. The immunity question may be determined by how broadly or narrowly that activity is defined. In this case, IAM insists on a very narrow focus on the specific activity of "price fixing." IAM argues that the FSIA does not give immunity to this activity. Under the FSIA a commercial activity is one which an individual might "customarily carr(y) on for profit." H.R.Rep. No.94–1487, 94th Cong., 2d Sess. 16, reprinted in (1976) U.S.Code Cong. & Ad. News 6604, 6615. OPEC's activity, characterized by IAM as making agreements to fix prices, is one which is presumably done for profit; it is thus commercial and immunity does not apply.

The court below defined OPEC's activity in a different way: "(I)t is clear that the nature of the activity engaged in by each of these OPEC member countries is the establishment by a sovereign state of the terms and conditions for the removal of a prime natural resource to wit, crude oil from its territory." 477 F.Supp. at 567. The trial judge reasoned that, according to international law, the development and control of natural resources is a prime governmental function. Id. at 567–78. The opinion cites several resolutions of the United Nations' General Assembly, which the United States supported, and the United States Constitution, Art. 4, § 3, cl. 2, which treat the control of natural resources as governmental acts.

IAM argues that the district court's analysis strays from the path set forth in the FSIA. The control of natural resources is the purpose behind OPEC's actions, but the act complained of here is a conspiracy to fix prices. The FSIA instructs us to look upon the act itself rather than underlying sovereign motivations.

The district court was understandably troubled by the broader implications of an anti-trust action against the OPEC nations. The importance of the alleged price-fixing activity to the OPEC nations cannot be ignored. Oil revenues represent their only significant source of income. Consideration of their sovereignty cannot be separated from their near total dependence upon oil. We find that these concerns are appropriately addressed by application of the act of state doctrine. While we do not apply the doctrine of sovereign immunity, its elements remain relevant to our discussion of the act of state doctrine.

B. The Act of State Doctrine

The act of state doctrine declares that a United States court will not adjudicate a politically sensitive dispute which would require the court to judge the legality of the sovereign act of a foreign state. . . .

The doctrine recognizes the institutional limitations of the courts and the peculiar requirements of successful foreign relations. To participate adeptly in the global community, the United States must speak with one voice and pursue a careful and deliberate foreign policy. The political branches of our government are able to consider the competing economic and political considerations and respond to the public will in order to carry on foreign relations in accordance with the best interests of the country as a whole. The courts, in contrast, focus on single disputes and make decisions on the basis of legal principles. The timing of our decisions is largely a result of our caseload and of the random tactical considerations which motivate parties to bring lawsuits and to seek delay or expedition. When the courts engage in piecemeal adjudication of the legality of the sovereign acts of states, they risk disruption of our country's international diplomacy. The executive may utilize protocol, economic sanction, compromise, delay, and persuasion to achieve international objectives. Ill-timed judicial decisions challenging the acts of foreign states could nullify these tools and embarrass the United States in the eyes of the world. . . .

While the act of state doctrine has no explicit source in our Constitution or statutes, it does have "constitutional underpinnings." *Banco Nacional de Cuba v. Sabbatino*, 376 U.S. 398, 423 (1964). The Supreme Court has stated that the act of state doctrine

> arises out of the basic relationships between branches of government in a system of separation of powers The doctrine as formulated in past decisions expresses the strong sense of the Judicial Branch that its engagement in the task of passing on the validity of foreign acts of state may hinder rather than further this country's pursuit of goals both for itself and for the community of nations as a whole in the international sphere. *Id.*

The doctrine of sovereign immunity is similar to the act of state doctrine in that it also represents the need to respect the sovereignty of foreign states. The two doctrines differ, however, in significant respects. The law of sovereign immunity goes to the jurisdiction of the court. The act of state doctrine is not jurisdictional. *Ricaud v. American Metal Co.*, 246 U.S. 304, 309 (1918). Rather, it is a prudential doctrine designed to avoid judicial action in sensitive areas. Sovereign immunity is a principle of international law, recognized in the United States by statute. It is the states themselves, as defendants, who may claim sovereign immunity. The act of state doctrine is a domestic legal principle, arising from the peculiar role of American courts. It recognizes not only the sovereignty of foreign states, but also the spheres of power of the co-equal branches of our government. Thus a private litigant may raise the act of state doctrine, even when no sovereign state is a party to the action. See, e. g., *Timberlane Lumber Co. v. Bank of America*, 549 F.2d 597, 606 (9th Cir.1976). The act of state doctrine is apposite whenever the federal courts must question the legality of the sovereign acts of foreign states.

It has been suggested that the FSIA supersedes the act of state doctrine, or that the amorphous doctrine is limited by modern jurisprudence. We disagree.

Congress in enacting the FSIA recognized the distinction between sovereign immunity and the act of state doctrine [citing legislative history of the FSIA]. . . .

The act of state doctrine is not diluted by the commercial activity exception which limits the doctrine of sovereign immunity. While purely commercial activity may not rise to the level of an act of state, certain seemingly commercial activity will trigger act of state considerations. As the district court noted, OPEC's "price-fixing" activity has a significant sovereign component. While the FSIA ignores the underlying purpose of a state's action, the act of state doctrine does not. This court has stated that the motivations of the sovereign must be examined for a public interest basis. *Timberlane*, 549 F.2d at 607. When the state qua state acts in the public interest, its sovereignty is asserted. The courts must proceed cautiously to avoid an affront to that sovereignty. Because the act of state doctrine and the doctrine of sovereign immunity address different concerns and apply in different circumstances, we find that the act of state doctrine remains available when such caution is appropriate, regardless of any commercial component of the activity involved.

The record in this case contains extensive documentation of the involvement of our executive and legislative branches with the oil question. IAM does not dispute that the United States has a grave interest in the petro-politics of the Middle East, or that the foreign policy arms of the executive and legislative branches are intimately involved in this sensitive area. It is clear that OPEC and its activities are carefully considered in the formulation of American foreign policy.

The remedy IAM seeks is an injunction against the OPEC nations. The possibility of insult to the OPEC states and of interference with the efforts of the political branches to seek favorable relations with them is apparent from the very nature of this action and the remedy sought. While the case is formulated as an anti-trust action, the granting of any relief would in effect amount to an order from a domestic court instructing a foreign sovereign to alter its chosen means of allocating and profiting from its own valuable natural resources. On the other hand, should the court hold that OPEC's actions are legal, this "would greatly strengthen the bargaining hand" of the OPEC nations in the event that Congress or the executive chooses to condemn OPEC's actions. Sabbatino, 376 U.S. at 432, 84 S.Ct. at 942.

A further consideration is the availability of internationally-accepted legal principles which would render the issues appropriate for judicial disposition. As the Supreme Court stated in Sabbatino,

> It should be apparent that the greater the degree of codification or consensus concerning a particular area of international law, the more appropriate it is for the judiciary to render decisions regarding it, since the courts can then focus on the application of an agreed principle to circumstances of fact rather than on the sensitive task of establishing a principle not inconsistent with the national interest or with international justice. 376 U.S. at 428, 84 S.Ct. at 940.

While conspiracies in restraint of trade are clearly illegal under domestic law, the record reveals no international consensus condemning cartels, royalties, and production agreements.[11] The United States and other nations have supported the principle of supreme state sovereignty over natural resources. The OPEC nations themselves obviously will not agree that their actions are illegal. We are reluctant to allow judicial interference in an area so void of international consensus....

IV. Conclusion

The act of state doctrine is applicable in this case.... The issue of whether the FSIA allows jurisdiction in this case need not be decided, ...

The decision of the district court dismissing this action is affirmed.■

NOTES AND QUESTIONS

1. Both Bunker Hunt and LIAMCO were thwarted by the act of state doctrine in their quest to be compensated for the loss of their Libyan concessions. Both sought to avoid the doctrine by resort to the Hickenlooper Amendment to the Foreign Assistance Act of 1964. The Hickenlooper Amendment was passed by an angry Congress after the U.S. Supreme Court held that the act of state doctrine precluded the judiciary from examining the legality of the Cuban expropriation of foreign assets in *Banco Nacional de Cuba v. Sabbatino*, 376 U.S. 398 (1964). The Amendment and its application were construed in *Libyan American Oil Company v. Socialist People's Libyan Arab Jamahirya*, 482 F.Supp. 1175 (D.D.C. 1980), as follows:

> Since the ruling in *Underhill*, courts have consistently found a foreign state's act of nationalization to be the classic example of an act of state. "Expropriations of the property of an alien within the boundaries of the sovereign state are traditionally considered to be public acts of the sovereign removed from judicial scrutiny by application of the act of state rubric." *Hunt v. Mobil Oil Corp.*, 550 F.2d 68, 73 (2d Cir.1977), cert. denied, 434 U.S. 984....

---

11. The amici suggest that production quotas and royalties are accepted sovereign practices, citing, inter alia, the Connally Hot Oil Act, 15 U.S.C. § 715; United States' payment to farmers not to produce wheat; and Japan's voluntary reduction of TV and automobile production to maintain prices.

Petitioner argues that even if the act of state doctrine should be applied in this case, the exception embodied in the Hickenlooper Amendment to the Foreign Assistance Act of 1964 would still require this Court to decide this case. The amendment provides that unless the President, for foreign policy reasons, suggests otherwise, courts must not decline on the ground of the act of state doctrine to decide the merits of a claim of title or other right to property ... based upon (or traced though) a confiscation or other taking after January 1, 1959, by an act of that state in violation of the principles of international law. 22 U.S.C. § 2370(e)(2).

The President has made no suggestion in this matter, but petitioner has failed to show that the amendment's requirements have been met.

The contract rights that lie at the heart of petitioner's claim do not constitute property for purposes of the amendment, *Menendez v. Saks & Co.*, 485 F.2d 1355, 1372 (2d Cir.1973), rev'd on other grounds, sub nom. *Alfred Dunhill of London, Inc. v. Republic of Cuba*, 425 U.S. 682 (1976), nor have courts found that the repudiation of contractual obligations amounts to a "confiscation or other taking," as those terms are employed in the statute. *Occidental of Umm al Qaywayn, Inc. v. Cities Service Oil Co.*, 396 F.Supp. 461, 472 (W.D.La.1975). Finally, petitioner has failed to show that the taking was in violation of international law. The nationalization provisions of Libyan law established means for LIAMCO to recover its investment. Because LIAMCO may not have been satisfied with the rate at which Libya was prepared to recompense the company does not render the original nationalization in violation of international law.

For the reasons set forth above, the Court declines to recognize or enforce the arbitral award. An order consistent with this memorandum follows. 482 F.Supp. at 1179.

2. Nelson Bunker Hunt tried to circumvent the act of state doctrine in a suit for conversion against Coastal States, a company which had purchased "hot" oil from Libya after the expropriation of Hunt's concession. In *Hunt v. Coastal States Gas Producing Co.*, 583 S.W.2d 322 (Tex.1979), six judges of the Texas Supreme Court adopted the same narrow reading of the Hickenlooper Amendment. Since Libya was the place of the contract's execution and performance, as well as the location of the subject matter, Libyan substantive law governed the interpretation of Hunt's rights by the Texas court. Under Libyan law, all petroleum belonged to the state, and Hunt had only a contractual right to explore for and produce it. Hunt had no property right to protect under the Hickenlooper Amendment.

A strong dissent argued that "[i]t has long been recognized that contract rights are a form of property protected by the Fifth Amendment" (citing *United States Trust Co. v. New Jersey*, 431 U.S. 1 (1977)), and that the legislative history of the Hickenlooper Amendment showed that Congress contemplated precisely this sort of claim. Furthermore, the Department of State had indicated its belief that the Amendment was passed precisely to allow American courts to entertain such suits; that Libya's expropriation violated international law (because it was discriminatory and offered inadequate compensation); and that Hunt should be supported in his pursuit of remedies. *Id.* at 326–336. *See also Hunt v. Mobil Oil Corp.,* 550 F.2d 68 (2d Cir.1977), *cert. denied,* 434 U.S. 984, 98 S.Ct. 608 (1977) (act of state doctrine precluded Hunt's claim that Mobil, BP, Exxon and the other "Seven Sisters" violated the antitrust laws by conspiring to preserve the competitive advantage of Persian Gulf crude over Libyan crude; their conspiracy allegedly prevented Hunt from reaching any settlement with Libya, thus resulting in nationalization).

It seems clear that the courts are reluctant to intervene in cases involving expropriation of natural resource industries in developing countries.

3.   These cases should give the reader a greater appreciation of the importance of an arbitration clause in an international petroleum agreement. Such a clause allows the parties to choose a forum for arbitration, to select the law which will govern the dispute, and to agree that the arbitration award will be final, without appeal to a court. The parties' agreement on these matters will be upheld in almost all circumstances. *See generally,* Henry P. De Vries, International Commercial Arbitration: A Contractual Substitute for National Courts, 57 Tul. L. Rev. 42 (1982); and David J. Branson & Richard E. Wallace, Jr., Choosing the Substantive Law to Apply in International Commercial Arbitration, 27 Va. J. Int'l L 39 (1986).

4.   Does the Foreign Corrupt Practices Act abrogate the act of state doctrine? In *Clayco Petroleum Corp. v. Occidental Petroleum Corp.,* 712 F.2d 404 (9th Cir. 1983), *cert. denied,* 464 U.S. 1040 (1984), Clayco filed a private antitrust suit against Occidental Petroleum, its subsidiary and its chief executive, Armand Hammer, charging them with making bribes to the rulers of Umm Al Qaywayn. The rulers had allegedly agreed to grant Clayco an oil concession in September 1969, but two months later the concession was granted to Occidental. Clayco first learned of the reasons for losing the concession when the Oakland Tribune published an article reporting that Occidental had made questionable payments of $30 million. The SEC commenced an action against Occidental for violating the reporting requirements of the Security Exchange Act, and a subsequent report prepared for the SEC confirmed that bribes were paid.

The *Clayco* court held that the act of state doctrine prohibited a private suit which would embarrass the political branches of the U.S. in its conduct of foreign policy and which would "impugn or question the nobility of a foreign nation's motivation." 712 F.2d at 407. Clayco then argued that the Foreign Corrupt Practices Act created an exception to the act of state doctrine. The court wrote:

> The FCPA was intended to stop bribery of foreign officials and political parties by domestic corporations. Bribery abroad was considered a "severe" United States foreign policy problem; it embarrasses friendly governments, causes a decline of foreign esteem for the United

States and casts suspicion on the activities of our enterprises, giving credence to our foreign opponents [citing legislative history, with a footnote that it may be "the revelation of bribery, more than bribery itself," which causes these problems]. The FCPA thus represents a legislative judgment that our foreign relations will be bettered by a strict anti-bribery statute. There is also no question, however, that any prosecution under the Act entails risks to our relations with the foreign governments involved....

The Justice Department and the SEC share enforcement responsibilities under the FCPA. They coordinate enforcement of the Act with the State Department, recognizing the potential foreign policy problems of these actions. Therefore, any governmental enforcement represents a judgment on the wisdom of bringing a proceeding, in the light of the exigencies of foreign affairs. Act of state concerns are thus inapplicable....

Here, however, we are faced with a private lawsuit, rather than a public enforcement action. It is the screening of governmental proceedings, with State Department consultation, which distinguishes FCPA enforcement from private suits.... Hence, in private suits, the act of state doctrine remains necessary to protect the proper conduct of national foreign policy. *Id.* at 408–09.

Does this decision make the work of Transparency International more important to private investors? To U.S. officials who do not want the blame for embarrassing corrupt foreign officials?

D. ENVIRONMENTAL, SOCIAL AND CULTURAL IMPACTS ABROAD

1. INTRODUCTION

In 1986, Conoco signed an agreement with Ecuador to explore for hydrocarbons on Block 16, a 500,000–acre tract of nearly virgin forest in the Amazon basin. Within three years, Conoco had found 200 million barrels of oil and proposed to build pipelines to develop the field. Part of Block 16 included a world-famous biological reserve and the traditional territory of the Huaorani Indians. A strategic coalition of environmental groups, led by the Rainforest Action Network, forged an alliance with human rights activists to oppose the access road accompanying the proposed pipeline to the field. Such a road would lure landless peasants from other areas into settlements, destroying the pristine nature of the rainforest and the cultural life of the Indians (by bringing alcoholism, prostitution and disease to the villages). In late 1991, faced with tremendous pressure from such groups, Conoco sold its share of the project and left Ecuador. *See* Robert Wasserstrom and Susan Reider, "Oil Firms in Environmentally Sensitive Areas Learning to Balance Stakeholder Interests." Oil & Gas J. (Aug. 18, 1997), at 23–27.

Should some parts of the world, with ecologically or culturally unique qualities simply be deemed "lands unsuitable" for oil and gas development? The United States uses this approach under the Surface Mining Control and Reclamation Act (see Chapter 5). This global issue is similar to that faced in the United States regarding the opening up of the Arctic National Wildlife Refuge (ANWR) or the imposition of drilling moratoria off the coasts of California and Florida (see Chapter 6).

Many oil companies, usually in partnership with state oil companies, are still actively seeking to drill in the rainforests of South America. After Conoco withdrew from Block 16, Maxus Petroleum took the concession. (Maxus was subsequently acquired by YPF, the Argentinian national oil company, which was then sold to a Spanish company, Repcol). Even companies who have left the area may face trailing obligations. Native citizens of the foreign country, alleging injuries from environmental pollution or human rights abuses, have increasingly sought to vindicate their rights in U.S. courts where they have access to public interest attorneys, the procedural and substantive safeguards of the American judicial system, and the chance of securing larger awards. These foreign plaintiffs must hurdle the doctrine of forum non conveniens in order to bring suit in the United States.

2.   THE DOCTRINE OF FORUM NON CONVENIENS

Jota v. Texaco Inc.

157 F.3d 153 (2d Cir.1998).

▉ JON O. NEWMAN, CIRCUIT JUDGE:

This appeal poses important issues concerning the appropriateness of a United States forum for litigation in which a foreign government is significantly interested. Issues of forum non conveniens, comity, and indispensable party all arise in an unusual context in that the foreign country, the Republic of Ecuador, initially expressed vigorous opposition to the maintenance of this litigation in a United States Court and now, after a change in the government, just as vigorously urges that the litigation proceed here. Two sets of putative class action plaintiffs who sued Texaco Inc. ("Texaco") appeal from the judgments of the District Court for the Southern District of New York (Jed S. Rakoff, District Judge), entered on November 13, 1996, and August 13, 1997, respectively. The Court dismissed both actions on the grounds of (i) forum non conveniens, (ii) international comity, and (iii) failure to join an indispensable party. The Republic of Ecuador and its state-owned corporation, PetroEcuador (together, the "Republic"), appeal from the Court's August 12, 1997, denial of their post-judgment motion to intervene, in order to cure their failure to be joined; one set of plaintiffs also appeals from the contemporaneous denial of its post-judgment motion for reconsideration.

We hold that dismissal on the ground of forum non conveniens was erroneous in the absence of a condition requiring Texaco to submit to jurisdiction in Ecuador and that the dismissal on this ground inappropriately rested entirely on adoption of another district court's weighing of the relevant factors in litigation that is arguably distinguishable. We similarly hold that dismissal on the ground of comity was erroneous in the absence of a condition requiring Texaco to submit to jurisdiction in Ecuador. We also hold that the District Court's reasoning regarding the plaintiffs' failure to join an indispensable party sufficed only to support dismissing so much of the complaint as sought to enjoin activities currently under the Republic's control. Finally, we note that upon the remand that is required as a consequence of our rulings, it will be appropriate for the District Court to reconsider the issues before it in light of Ecuador's changed litigating position. Accordingly, we vacate the judgments and remand for further consideration.

Background

Understanding the issues requires a detailed outline of the procedural history of the litigation.

1. The Complaints

This case involves consolidated appeals from two actions filed on behalf of two putative classes. In one action, *Aguinda v. Texaco Inc.,* Dkt. No. 93 Civ. 7527, 1994 WL 142006 (S.D.N.Y. April 11, 1994), certain residents of the Oriente region of Ecuador—primarily members of indigenous tribes—sued Texaco for environmental and personal injuries that allegedly resulted from Texaco's exploitation of the region's oil fields. In the other action, *Ashanga v. Texaco Inc.,* S.D.N.Y. Dkt. No. 94 Civ. 9266, certain residents of Peru, who live downstream from Ecuador's Oriente region, assert similar injuries resulting from these activities.

Both complaints allege that Texaco polluted the rain forests and rivers in Ecuador and Peru during oil exploitation activities in Ecuador between 1964 and 1992. In particular, they allege that Texaco improperly dumped large quantities of toxic by-products of the drilling process into the local rivers, contrary to prevailing industry practice of pumping these substances back into the emptied wells. Additionally, they allege that Texaco used other improper means of eliminating toxic substances, such as burning them, dumping them directly into landfills, and spreading them on the local dirt roads. They also allege that the Trans–Ecuadoran Pipeline, constructed by Texaco, has leaked large quantities of petroleum into the environment. The named plaintiffs allege that they and their families have experienced various physical injuries, including poisoning and the development of pre-cancerous growths.

The complaints sought money damages under theories of negligence, public nuisance, private nuisance, strict liability, "medical monitoring," trespass, civil conspiracy, and violations actionable under the Alien Tort Act, 28 U.S.C. § 1350 ("ATA"). The plaintiffs also sought "equitable relief to remedy the contamination and spoliation of their properties, water supplies and environment." [Ed. Note: The equitable relief included undertaking environmental cleanup, renovating or closing the Trans–Ecuadoran

Pipeline, creation of an environmental monitoring fund, formulating standards to govern future Texaco oil development, creation of a medical monitoring fund, an injunction restraining Texaco from entering into activities that run a high risk of environmental or human injuries, and restitution].

2. Texaco's Motion to Dismiss

In December 1993, Texaco moved to dismiss on the grounds of (i) failure to join an indispensable party—the Republic of Ecuador, (ii) international comity, and (iii) forum non conveniens. Inherent in all three defenses was the close participation of the Ecuadoran government in the activities for which Texaco was sought to be held liable. Elaborating its grounds for dismissal, Texaco submitted an affidavit by the president of a Texaco subsidiary, averring the following facts. Texaco had participated in oil drilling in Ecuador exclusively through its fourth-level subsidiary, Texaco Petroleum Company ("TexPet"). Beginning in 1965, TexPet operated a petroleum concession for a consortium ("the Consortium") owned in equal shares by TexPet and Gulf Oil. Oil was first discovered in the Oriente in 1969, and was extracted thereafter by the Consortium. In 1974, the Ecuadoran government, through its state-owned oil agency, currently known as PetroEcuador, obtained a 25 percent share of the Consortium. By 1992, PetroEcuador had become the sole owner of the Consortium.[4][12]

In addition to evidence presented by Texaco suggesting that the Republic had been heavily involved in the drilling operations and had eventually become the sole operator, Texaco submitted a copy of a letter written by Ecuador's ambassador to the United States and addressed to the United States Department of State. In that letter, Ambassador Edgar Teran asserted that the Republic considered this action (as well as a similar case brought by other plaintiffs in the Southern District of Texas, *Sequihua v. Texaco, Inc.,* 847 F.Supp. 61 (S.D.Tex.1994), an affront to Ecuador's national sovereignty. Ambassador Teran stated that Ecuador had a paramount interest in formulating its own environmental and industrial policies, and that Ecuador's courts were open to adjudicate such disputes.

3. District Court's Initial Decision

In an order filed in April 1994, the District Court (Vincent L. Broderick, District Judge), reserved decision on Texaco's motion. See *Aguinda v. Texaco, Inc.,* No. 93 Civ. 7527, 1994 WL 142006 (S.D.N.Y.1994). The Court acknowledged that forum non conveniens dismissal might be appropriate as to the claims seeking money damages. Judge Broderick reasoned that "[d]isputes over class membership, determination of individualized or common damages, and the need for large amounts of testimony with interpret-

---

12. In 1974, TexPet and Gulf each owned 37.5 percent shares. In 1976, PetroEcuador acquired Gulf's interest, thereby obtaining a majority stake. TexPet continued to operate the Trans–Ecuadoran Pipeline—a Consortium enterprise—until October 1989, when PetroEcuador assumed that responsi-

bility. TexPet continued to operate the Consortium's drilling operations until July 1990, when PetroEcuador also took over that function. Finally, in June 1992, TexPet surrendered all its interests in the Consortium, leaving it wholly owned by PetroEcuador.

ers, perhaps often in local dialects, would make effective adjudication in New York problematic at best." Id. at *2. However, he stated, any dismissal on this ground would be contingent on Texaco's first agreeing to submit to personal jurisdiction in the courts of Ecuador. The Court further suggested that even if Texaco filed such a stipulation, the Court might retain jurisdiction over the injunctive portions of the action.

The Court also reserved decision as to dismissal on the basis of international comity, but noted that there appeared to be no conflict between the laws of Ecuador and the United States. Finally, the Court declined to consider dismissal for failure to join Ecuador and PetroEcuador, reasoning that the parties had yet to develop a sufficient record.

4.   District Court's Grant of Texaco's Motion to Dismiss

Following Judge Broderick's death, the case was reassigned, ultimately to Judge Rakoff. After a significant period of discovery, Texaco renewed its motion to dismiss. Counsel for the Republic submitted an amicus brief, supporting Texaco's motion to dismiss, once again informing the Court that the Republic objected to United States jurisdiction over the case. That brief was accompanied by an affidavit to the same effect signed by Ambassador Teran, again expressing the Republic's position.

In response, the plaintiffs submitted three documents signed by representatives of the Ecuadoran National Congress, indicating their support for the plaintiffs' action. In one, the President of the Congress and four committee "presidents" wrote to Ecuador's President and Foreign Minister expressing their "concern" over the position that Ambassador Teran had taken. They stated that "[i]n our judgment the Ecuadorian government should not intervene in the development of this trial, much less show bias openly in a way that benefits the interests of the Texaco company." In the second document, Dr. Isauro Puente Davila, a legislator who served as the President of the Special Permanent Commission on Environmental Defense, issued an "official announcement" that

only the adjudication of jurisdiction in the claim filed by Ecuadorians ... in a federal court of N.Y. against the Texaco Company, will bring to those affected the possibility of finding just treatment and a solution to the serious situation that they are going through.

In November 1996, the District Court granted Texaco's motion to dismiss, as it related to the Aguinda plaintiffs. See *Aguinda v. Texaco, Inc.*, 945 F.Supp. 625 (S.D.N.Y.1996). Judge Rakoff stated that he found persuasive the forum non conveniens and international comity holdings made by the Southern District of Texas in the Sequihua litigation. See *Sequihua v. Texaco, Inc.*, 847 F.Supp. 61 (S.D.Tex.1994)....

The Court also dismissed for the "independently-sufficient reason" of failure to join indispensable parties, namely, PetroEcuador and the Republic of Ecuador....

5.   District Court's Denial of Motions (i) to Reconsider Judgment and (ii) to Intervene

The plaintiffs in the Aguinda action moved for reconsideration, representing that the Republic was now willing to participate in that action as an intervenor. Thereafter, the Republic filed a motion to intervene. In an affidavit accompanying that motion, Ecuador's Attorney General stated that he was "summariz[ing] the official judicial position of the Republic of Ecuador," and concluded that

> [t]he intervention ... does not under any concept damage the sovereignty of the Republic of Ecuador, instead it looks to protect the interests of the indigenous citizens of the Ecuadorian Amazon who were seriously affected by the environmental contamination attributed to the defendant company....

In March 1997, the District Court ruled that the Republic's motion to intervene was not sufficiently precise. Plaintiffs' counsel had represented that due to an Ecuadoran election, and a subsequent change of administration, the Republic was now willing to waive sovereign immunity and consent to the jurisdiction of the District Court. However, the Court ruled, the intervention motion filed by the Republic had not "expressly and unequivocally state[d] that [it] was prepared to waive sovereign immunity." The Court requested that the Republic provide fresh written assurances ... that the Republic of Ecuador, if it still desires to intervene in this law suit, is expressly prepared to waive sovereign immunity and submit fully to the jurisdiction of this Court (including jurisdiction over any counterclaims and cross-claims that may be filed against Ecuador in connection with this action).

In response, the Attorney General of Ecuador again wrote the District Court, but stopped short of agreeing to the conditions required by the Court. The Attorney General explained that "Ecuador ratifies it[s] participation in this lawsuit in support of said persons in order to procure the necessary indemnization in order to alleviate the environmental damages caused by Texaco." While the Attorney General agreed, somewhat obliquely, to "allot the entire value of the indemnization to the projects and works of remediation which might be necessary," he made clear that the Republic did not agree to waive its sovereign immunity defense as to any claims made by parties other than the Aguinda plaintiffs. Thus, the Republic appeared unwilling to defend claims presented either by Texaco or by the Ashanga plaintiffs.

In August 1997, the District Court denied both the Aguinda plaintiffs' motion for reconsideration and the Republic's motion to intervene. See *Aquinda v. Texaco, Inc.,* 175 F.R.D. 50 (S.D.N.Y.1997). The Court characterized the Republic's motion as "patently, and prejudicially, untimely." Id. at 51. In Judge Rakoff's view, Ecuador had not shown any reason why the Court should consider its post-judgment change of position in now supporting the Court's jurisdiction over the case. Additionally, the Court ruled that Ecuador was not entitled to place limitations on its participation in the case, and would have to be willing to subject itself to possible counterclaims and cross-claims in order to intervene.

Discussion

The Aguinda and Ashanga plaintiffs appeal from the dismissal of their complaints, and the Aguinda plaintiffs also appeal from the denial of their motion for reconsideration. The Republic of Ecuador appeals from the denial of its motion to intervene. The plaintiffs-appellants challenge each of the three grounds on which the District Court dismissed their action: (1) forum non conveniens, (2) international comity, and (3) failure to join an indispensable party.

1. Forum Non Conveniens

The forum non conveniens doctrine allows dismissal only where the court determines that "an alternative forum is available, because application of the doctrine 'presupposes at least two forums in which the defendant is amenable to process.'" *Murray v. British Broadcasting Corp.,* 81 F.3d 287, 292 (2d Cir.1996) (quoting *Gulf Oil Corp. v. Gilbert,* 330 U.S. 501, 506–07, 67 S.Ct. 839, 91 L.Ed. 1055 (1947)). "Through a discretionary inquiry, the court determines where litigation will be most convenient and will serve the ends of justice." *PT United Can Co. v. Crown Cork & Seal Co.,* 138 F.3d 65, 73 (2d Cir.1998). "[I]n order to grant a motion to dismiss for forum non conveniens, a court must satisfy itself [among other things] that the litigation may be conducted elsewhere against all defendants." Id.

The District Court incorporated the forum non conveniens holding of Sequihua, and appellants contend that Sequihua was inapposite. In particular, the appellants argue that the only defendant in the present case, Texaco, is not subject to suit in Ecuador. Texaco's only response is that TexPet is subject to suit in Ecuadoran courts, and is both a defendant and a plaintiff in various actions currently pending in that jurisdiction. But Texaco does not dispute that Texaco itself is not amenable to suit in Ecuador.

Accordingly, dismissal for forum non conveniens is not appropriate, at least absent a commitment by Texaco to submit to the jurisdiction of the Ecuadoran courts for purposes of this action. Cf. *In re Union Carbide Corp. Gas Plant Disaster,* 809 F.2d 195, 203–04 (2d Cir.1987) (affirming dismissal for forum non conveniens that was conditioned upon defendant's consent to personal jurisdiction in India; such conditions "are not unusual and have been imposed in numerous cases where the foreign court would not provide an adequate alternative in the absence of such a condition").

On remand, in addition to requiring Texaco's consent to Ecuadoran jurisdiction, the District Court should independently reweigh the factors relevant to a forum non conveniens dismissal, rather than simply rely on Sequihua. . . .

2. Comity

International comity is " 'the recognition which one nation allows within its territory to the legislative, executive or judicial acts of another nation.'" *Pravin Banker Associates, Ltd. v. Banco Popular Del Peru,* 109 F.3d 850, 854 (2d Cir.1997) (quoting *Hilton v. Guyot,* 159 U.S. 113, 164, 16 S.Ct. 139, 40 L.Ed. 95 (1895)). Under the principles of comity, United States courts "ordinarily refuse to review acts of foreign governments and defer to proceedings taking place in foreign countries, allowing those acts and proceedings to have extraterritorial effect in the United States." *Id.*

This doctrine "is best understood as a guide where the issues to be resolved are entangled in international relations." *In re Maxwell Communication Corp.*, 93 F.3d 1036, 1047 (2d Cir.1996). The District Court's dismissal on the ground of international comity is reviewed for abuse of discretion. *See Pravin*, 109 F.3d at 856.

In dismissing the complaints in this litigation on the ground of comity, the District Court explicitly adopted the comity considerations articulated by the District Court in *Sequihua* in dismissing a similar case. See Sequihua, 847 F.Supp. at 63. Applying the factors set forth in Restatement (3d) of Foreign Relations § 403 (1986), the Court in *Sequihua* had concluded that "the challenged activity and the alleged harm occurred entirely in Ecuador"; that the conduct at issue was regulated by the Republic and "exercise of jurisdiction by this Court would interfere with Ecuador's sovereign right to control its own environment and resources"; and that "the Republic of Ecuador has expressed its strenuous objections to the exercise of jurisdiction by this Court." *Id.*

When a court dismisses on the ground of comity, it should normally consider whether an adequate forum exists in the objecting nation and whether the defendant sought to be sued in the United States forum is subject to or has consented to the assertion of jurisdiction against it in the foreign forum. That is the approach usually taken with a dismissal on the ground of forum non conveniens, as we noted in Part 1, and it is equally pertinent to dismissal on the ground of comity. Though extreme cases might be imagined where a foreign sovereign's interests were so legitimately affronted by the conduct of litigation in a United States forum that dismissal is warranted without regard to the defendant's amenability to suit in an adequate foreign forum, this case presents no such circumstances.

With the comity issue remanded for lack of conditioning dismissal on Texaco's consent to jurisdiction in Ecuador, it will then be appropriate for the District Court to reconsider the merits of the comity issue in light of Ecuador's changed litigating position. . . .

3. Failure to Join Indispensable Party

The District Court dismissed the complaint under Rule 19(b) on the ground that the Republic's participation was necessary to afford the plaintiffs the full scope of the equitable relief they sought. . . .

In this case, the District Court reasoned that in the absence of the Republic, the plaintiffs would not be able to obtain "complete relief," since their desired equitable relief would require enjoining the Republic (the current owner and operator of the oil drilling equipment). The Court then explained that dismissal was appropriate under Rule 19(b) because, in the absence of the Republic, "any order of this Court granting any material part of the Ecuador-directed equitable relief sought by the plaintiffs would be unenforceable on its face, prejudicial to both present and absent parties, and an open invitation to an international political debacle." *Aquinda*, 945 F.Supp. at 628 (emphasis added). In effect, the Court dismissed the case because the "Ecuador-directed" equitable remedies sought by the plaintiffs would be possible only if Ecuador was joined as a party and, without Ecuador in the case, the Court would be unable to provide the plaintiffs with "complete relief."

Rule 19(a) requires the Court to join any person who is necessary to effect "complete relief," where such joinder is feasible. But Rule 19(b) does not authorize dismissal simply because such a party cannot be joined. Instead, the Court is to determine "whether in equity and good conscience the action should proceed among the parties before it, or should be dismissed, the absent person thus being regarded as indispensable." Fed. R.Civ.P. 19(b). And in making this determination, the Court is to consider, among other things, "the extent to which, by protective provisions in the judgment, by the shaping of relief, or other measures, the prejudice can be lessened or avoided." *Id.* Among the Court's options is to "order a pleading amended ... when by restructuring the relief requested plaintiff is able to change the status of an 'indispensable' party to that of merely a Rule 19(a) party or otherwise prevent the ill effects of nonjoinder." 7 Charles A. Wright, Arthur R. Miller & Mary Kay Kane, *Federal Practice and Procedure* § 1609, at 132–33 (2d ed.1986).

Since some aspects of the equitable relief sought by the plaintiffs would have required substantial participation by the Ecuadoran government, which at an earlier stage had resisted joinder, the District Court had discretion to dismiss some portions of the plaintiffs' complaint. But since much of the relief sought could be fully provided by Texaco without any participation by Ecuador, dismissal of the entire complaint on Rule 19 grounds exceeds that discretion. For example, an injunction might require Texaco to make good faith efforts to institute all, or at least portions, of the relief that the plaintiffs seek, an obligation the performance of which might not encounter any obstruction from Ecuador. A remand to reconsider the dismissal on Rule 19 grounds is required.

[The court then discussed Ecuador's post-judgment motion to intervene and held that the district court on remand should reassess this motion to determine whether granting it would prejudice Texaco and to give Ecuador the opportunity to promptly advise the court of its role and any sovereign immunity claims it intended to retain].

For the above stated reasons, we vacate the judgment of the District Court and remand for proceedings not inconsistent with this decision.∎

NOTES AND QUESTIONS

1. Forum non conveniens is a judicially created doctrine designed to prevent plaintiffs from harassing defendants by filing suit in an inconvenient forum, even though personal jurisdiction and subject matter jurisdiction exist in that forum. The factors to be used in a forum non conveniens analysis are barely discussed in the *Jota* case. One important factor is whether the plaintiff has a fair and adequate forum in the foreign country. On remand, the district court should also look at the following types of

factors, enunciated in the seminal case of *Gulf Oil Corp. v. Gilbert*, 330 U.S. 501, 67 S.Ct. 839 (1947):

> Important considerations [of the private interest of the litigant] are the relative ease of access to sources of proof; availability of compulsory process for attendance of unwilling, and the cost of obtaining attendance of willing, witnesses; possibility of view of premises, if view would be appropriate to the action; and all other practical problems that make trial of a case easy, expeditious and inexpensive. There may also be questions as to the enforcibility of a judgment if one is obtained. The court will weigh relative advantages and obstacles to fair trial....
>
> Factors of public interest also have place in applying the doctrine. Administrative difficulties follow for courts when litigation is piled up in congested centers instead of being handled at its origin. Jury duty is a burden that ought not to be imposed upon the people of a community which has no relation to the litigation. In cases which touch the affairs of many persons, there is reason for holding the trial in their view and reach rather than in remote parts of the country where they can learn of it by report only. There is a local interest in having localized controversies decided at home. There is an appropriateness, too, in having the trial of a diversity case in a forum that is at home with the state law that must govern the case, rather than having a court in some other forum untangle problems in conflict of laws, and in law foreign to itself. *Id.* at 508–09.

How would you apply these factors to the *Jota* facts?

See Aguinda v. Texaco, Inc., 2000 WL 122143 (S.D.N.Y.2000) (memorandum order on remand.)

As an aside, the plaintiff in the *Gilbert* case, was a Virginia citizen whose warehouse had burned after Gulf Oil had allegedly mishandled a delivery of gasoline to the warehouse, resulting in damages of $400,000. The plaintiff brought his action against Gulf in New York, seemingly at the behest of the subrogated insurance companies who feared that a jury of provincial Virginians would be "staggered" by the requested award of $400,000. The court wrote: "This unproven premise that jurors of New York live on terms of intimacy with $400,000 transactions is not an assumption we easily make." *Id.* at 510.

2. Does forum non conveniens make any sense in today's world of widespread jet travel, photocopiers, videographers, and internet access?

The doctrine's international application has been the subject of much commentary. Supporters of the doctrine's usefulness in dismissing claims and sending plaintiffs back to their home courts typically cite Lord Denning in *Smith Kline & French Lab. Ltd. v. Bloch*, [1983] 1 W.L.R. 730. 733 (CA 1982): "As a moth is drawn to the light, so is a litigant drawn to the United States. If he can only get his case into their courts, he stands to win a fortune." The United States judicial system offers the following advantages to a foreign plaintiff: attorneys who will work for contingency fees; no liability for defendants' attorney costs; the world's most extensive pretrial discovery; strict liability laws; the award of damages for many more types of harms, including punitive damages; and the right to a jury. See Russell

J. Weintraub, International Litigation and Forum Non Conveniens, 29 Texas Int'l L. J. 321, 323–24 (1994).

On the other hand, critics of dismissals on the grounds of forum non conveniens often quote Justice Doggett's concurring opinion in *Dow Chemical Co. v. Castro Alfaro*, 786 S.W.2d 674 at 680–90 (Tex.1990) that the doctrine is used to shield alleged wrongdoers: "The refusal of a Texas corporation to confront a Texas judge and jury is to be labeled "inconvenient" when what is really involved is not convenience but connivance to avoid corporate accountability." *Id.* at 680.

In this case, Costa Rican farmworkers sued Dow and Shell Oil Company in a Texas court for personal injuries allegedly sustained as a result of exposure to a pesticide (DBCP) made by them in Texas plants. The EPA had banned the pesticides' use in the United States, but Dow and Shell had allegedly shipped the pesticide to Costa Rica for use in the banana plantations there. In a 5–4 decision, a majority of the court held that the Texas legislature had statutorily abolished the doctrine of forum non conveniens in personal injury cases arising out of events in a foreign country.[3]

Justice Doggett further commented on the doctrine of judicial comity that was designed to show deference to the foreign forum: "There is a sense of outrage on the part of many poor countries where citizens are the most vulnerable to exports of hazardous drugs, pesticides and food products. At the 1977 meeting of the UNEP Governing Council, Dr. J.C. Kiano, the Kenyan minister for water development, warned that developing nations will no longer tolerate being used as dumping grounds for products that had not been adequately tested." *Id.* at 688. In an accompanying footnote, Justice Doggett cited a senior vice president of Monsanto who acknowledged that "[t]he realization at corporate headquarters that liability for any [industrial] disaster would be decided in the U.S. courts, more than pressure from Third World governments, has forced companies to tighten safety procedures, upgrade plants, supervise maintenance more closely and educate workers and communities." *Id.* at 687, note 10.

And finally, Justice Doggett addressed the public policy concerns of the dissent that Texas citizens would bear an undue burden of jury duty as foreign plaintiffs flooded into Texas courts:

> The doctrine of forum non conveniens is obsolete in a world in which markets are global and in which ecologists have documented the delicate balance of all life on this planet.... [The doctrine's parochial] perspective ignores the reality that actions of our corporations affecting those abroad will also affect Texans. Although DBCP is banned from use within the United States, it and other similarly banned chemicals have been consumed by Texans eating foods imported from Costa Rica and elsewhere. *Id.* at 689.

---

3. [Editors' note:] At issue was Section 71.031 of the Texas Civil Practice & Remedies Code. The Texas legislature subsequently amended the law by passage of Sec. 71.051.

Both sides of the dispute over the wisdom of forum non conveniens seem to agree that dismissal of a suit by a U.S. court is outcome determinative. One study showed that fewer than four percent of cases dismissed ever reached trial in a foreign court. David W. Robertson, Forum Non Conveniens in America and England: "A Rather Fantastic Fiction," 103 L.Q. Rev. 398, 409 (1987).

3.   Judith Kimerling, an attorney for the Natural Resources Defense Council, wrote a book titled "Amazon Crude" (NRDC, 1991), in which she chronicles many of the devastating effects of oil development on the lands and peoples of the Oriente region of Ecuador and Peru. Parts of the book are excerpted in Judith Kimerling, Disregarding Environmental Law: Petroleum Development in Protected Natural Areas and Indigenous Homelands in the Ecuadorian Amazon, 14 Hastings Int'l & Comp. L. Rev. 849 (1991). It is bleak reading, as shown by these brief excerpts:

> During seismic studies, noisy helicopters carry equipment and work crews into the forests. They fell trees, clear trails and heliports, destroy crops, drill holes, and detonate explosives, typically without regard for the presence of homes, gardens, streams, lakes, or sacred areas. Indigenous people say these activities make wildlife act "crazy" and flee in terror, abandoning their young. Fish and wildlife also suffer from uncontrolled hunting and fishing (with explosives) by seismic workers. Clearing the forests destroys habitat, foods, medicines, and commercial woods. Erosion in cleared areas can degrade receiving waters.
>
> Before drilling a well, the oil company clears two to five hectares to build a drilling platform. [Ed. note: one hectare is about 2.5 acres]. Up to fifteen hectares of the surrounding forests are disturbed by logging for boards to lie beneath the platform. Wells are typically drilled without regard for the presence of settled areas.... For large helicopters additional lands are sometimes cleared for flight paths....
>
> In the Oriente, virtually all of the produced water wastes, along with spilled oil and chemicals, and wastes from well drilling and maintenance, enter the environment untreated. Most of these wastes initially are dumped into open pits, hundreds of which dot the region.... Rainwater freely enters the pits, swelling the contents and becoming contaminated as it mixes with the water.... Large artificial lakes of spilled petroleum are common near the pits. *Id.* at 862, 869.

4.   Texaco's response to the *Jota* case and many of the issues raised in it can be accessed on their website at www.texaco.com. Texaco asserts that it separated the oil from the produced water before it was discharged into streams, and that other nations, including the U.S., Mexico, Brazil and Nigeria, allow the discharge of produced water rather than reinjection. See Texaco, Inc. Response to Claims (last modified Feb. 1, 2000) <http://www.texaco.com/shared/position/docs/ responsec. html>. Texaco states that it undertook a $40 million remediation program to assure that there would be no lasting environmental damage in Ecuador.

The U.S. EPA imposed zero discharge limits for produced water, produced sand, and drilling wastes in coastal Texas and Louisiana. The industry appealed the EPA's rules as being too stringent. In *Texas Oil & Gas Association v. EPA*, 161 F.3d 923 (5th Cir. 1998), the court agreed with the EPA that zero discharge was the best available technology economically achievable (the BAT standard) for all three effluents. Almost all operators already practiced zero discharge for produced water. The entire coastal category of dischargers had already attained zero discharge of drilling wastes. The Clean Water Act's applicability to oil and gas drilling and production is discussed in more detail in Chapter 6.

Should the zero discharge standard be used as a principle of international law? The Interstate Oil Compact Commission released a study in 1999 by the Bureau for Social Research at Oklahoma State University showing that U.S. oil and gas producers spent more than $2.6 billion a year, or about $2 per barrel of oil equivalent, to comply with environmental regulations. Would a domestic producer argue for stricter international standards? Would a multinational oil company?

5. In January 2000, 250,000 gallons of oil spilled into the bay waters off Rio de Janeiro from a ruptured pipeline operated by the state-owned Petroleo Brasileiro. Miles of shoreline were blackened with oil. The government planned to fine the company $26,500 based on the applicable domestic laws, plus the company is expected to pay for the clean up. The company has been accused of operating without required state licenses and without performing environmental audits. New York Times, Jan. 20, 2000, at 23A.

6. Texaco's website on "Response to Claims" lists the many environmental laws enacted by the Ecuadorian government, many specifically applicable to hydrocarbon development. How does passage of these laws factor into the forum non conveniens analysis?

7. *Jota* cites the well-known Bhopal case of *In re Union Carbide Gas Plant Disaster*, 809 F.2d 195 (2d Cir.1987) which affirmed the dismissal of personal injury and wrongful death suits brought by Indian plaintiffs in U.S. district court on the grounds of forum non conveniens, conditioned on Union Carbide Corporation's consent to personal jurisdiction in India. The district court opinion by Judge Keenan appears at 634 F.Supp. 842 (D.C.N.Y.1986). Over 2000 persons were killed and 200,000 injured by a lethal gas released from a chemical plant in Bhopal, India, operated by Union Carbide India Limited, a company incorporated under India's laws whose stock was traded on the Bombay Stock Exchange. The plant was managed and operated entirely by Indians in India. The U.S. district court found that the Indian judicial system was competent to handle complex technological issues and that the tort law of India was similarly suitable.

In 1989, Union Carbide Corp. entered into a $470 million settlement with the Indian government for claims arising from the Bhopal tragedy. Most claimants received about $600 for injuries and $3000 for death. However, the Indian government has also charged Union Carbide and the chairman of the company at the time of the disaster with the crime of "culpable homicide," equivalent to manslaughter. The ex-chairman and company officials in the United States have refused to subject themselves to the jurisdiction of the Bhopal district court, despite orders to do so from the Indian Supreme Court, and are being tried in absentia along with nine senior Indian executives of the plant. The ex-chairman of Union Carbide seems to have gone into hiding to escape a summons to appear in a New York court in a lawsuit charging him with civil contempt for failing to comply with the lawful orders of the Indian court and of Judge Keenan in his 1986 district court opinion that Union Carbide consent to the jurisdiction of the Indian courts. The Indian government issued an arrest warrant for the ex-chairman and notified Interpol that he is a fugitive. Chris Hedges, "A Key Figure Proves Elusive in a U.S. Suit over Bhopal," New York Times, International Section, Mar. 5, 2000, at 5.

8.   Complex questions of comity and the appropriate judicial forum also arise in the United States on Indian lands. *E.g.*, in *El Paso Natural Gas Co. v. Neztsosie*, 526 U.S. 473 (1999), members of the Navajo Nation filed suit for damages under Navajo tort law in a Navajo tribal court against a company that had operated open pit uranium mines on its land from 1950 to 1965. The Navajos claimed that the mines had polluted their drinking water and exposed them to radioactive materials. The defendant companies filed suit in U.S. district court seeking to enjoin the Navajos from pursuing their claims in the tribal court. Both the district court and the Ninth Circuit Court of Appeals allowed the Indian claims to proceed in tribal court, even to the extent that the tribal court would be allowed to determine whether it had jurisdiction over claims brought under the Price–Anderson Act (discussed in Chapter 14). The Supreme Court held that the Price–Anderson Act gave the district court original jurisdiction over claims arising out of a nuclear incident. The comity rationale used by the lower courts to require the companies to exhaust their claims in tribal courts before they sought jurisdiction in the federal courts was held to be inappropriate for such claims.

A course in American Indian Law is good background for attorneys seeking to practice international energy law. Aboriginal land titles can be a major impediment to investment in natural resources in many countries of the world, including Canada and Australia. *See, e.g.*, G.P.J. McGinley, Natural Resource Companies and Aboriginal Title to Land: The Australian Experience–Mabo and its Aftermath, 28 Int'l Lawyer 695 (1994); D.E. Fisher, Indigenous Interests and Infrastructure Development, 18 J. Energy & Nat. Res. L. 67 (2000); Annotation: Proof and Extinguishment of Aboriginal Title to Indian Lands, 41 A.L.R. 425 (1979). In December 1999, the National Energy Board of Canada approved the operation of a $560 million gas pipeline from offshore Nova Scotia to the northeastern United States, but only after settling legal battles with the Mi'kmaq Indians over environmental monitoring and promotion of aboriginal participation in the project's workforce.

3.   Indigenous Peoples

Kimerling's work paints a similarly bleak picture of the effect of development on the health and culture of native communities and of the colonists who follow the roads and camps of the oil companies. Joe Kane, a journalist-adventurer, lived with the Huaorani for several months and wrote a riveting account of his experiences in "Savages" (Vintage Books 1996). He does not idealize the hunger, cold, disease and dangers of the Huaorani's natural environment, but the "savages" in the title to his book are clearly not the Huaorani. His book also gives a good account of the problems involved in working with native groups who live in small communities of a hundred or so members, scattered throughout dense rainforest. The book contains photos of the Huaorani and of the oil pollution.

In the U.S., clashes over Native American rights to land were ultimately resolved through the reservation system of setting aside specific land areas for the Indians, sometimes by forced removal of the Indians from their homelands. Most first-year law students are familiar with the case of *Johnson and Graham's Lessee v. McIntosh*, 21 U.S. (8 Wheat) 543 (1823) in which the Supreme Court announced that the law of discovery and conquest gave the federal government superior title to lands once owned by the native Indians. The Court wrote:

> The title by conquest is acquired and maintained by force.... Humanity, however, acting on public opinion, has established, as a general rule, that the conquered shall not be wantonly oppressed, and that their condition shall remain as eligible as is compatible with the objects of the conquest. Most usually, they are incorporated with the victorious nation, ... The new and old members of the society mingle with each other; the distinction between them is gradually lost, and they make one people. Where this incorporation is practicable, humanity demands, and a wise policy requires, that the rights of the conquered to property should remain unimpaired; ... and that confidence in their security should gradually banish the painful sense of being separated from their ancient connections, and united by force to strangers. When the conquest is complete, and the conquered inhabitants can be blended with the conquerors, or safely governed as a distinct people, public opinion, which not even the conqueror can disregard, imposes these restraints upon him; and he cannot neglect them, without injury to his fame, and hazard to his power. 21 U.S. at 589–90.

How does the Declaration of Principles appearing below resolve the rights of indigenous groups today? What if native groups want to maintain their identity rather than blend into a "melting pot?"

After reading the Declarations, reconsider the problems of federalism that exist in developing and transporting energy resources in the United States, even with its strong centralized government. (Review, *e.g.*, the cases on offshore oil and gas development in Chapter 6). How are power and financial benefits to be shared between the central government, provinces, and indigenous territories when oil and gas development occurs on native lands ? In the *Jota* case, was there even an effective central government?

Declaration of Principles on the Rights of Indigenous Peoples

(As reprinted in S. James Anaya, Indigenous Peoples in International Law 190–91 (Oxford Univ. Press 1996).

Adopted by representatives of indigenous peoples and organizations meeting in Geneva July 1985, in preparation for the fourth session of the United Nations Working Group on Indigenous Populations; as reaffirmed and amended by representatives of indigenous peoples and organizations meeting in Geneva, July 1987, in preparation for the working group's fifth session. Reprinted in U.N. Doc. ECN.4/Sub.2/1987/22, Annex 5 (1987).

1. Indigenous nations and peoples have in common with all humanity, the right to life, and to freedom from oppression, discrimination, and aggression.

2. All indigenous nations and peoples have the right to self-determination, by virtue of which they have the right to whatever degree of autonomy or self-government they choose. This includes the right to freely determine their political status, freely pursue their own economic, social, religious and cultural development, and determine their own membership and/or citizenship, without external interference.

3. No State shall assert any jurisdiction over an indigenous nation and people, or its territory, except in accordance with the freely expressed wishes of the nation and people concerned.

4. Indigenous nations and peoples are entitled to the permanent control and enjoyment of their aboriginal ancestral-historical territories. This includes air space, surface and subsurface rights, inland and coastal waters, sea ice, renewable and non-renewable resources and the economies based on these resources.

5. Rights to share and use land, subject to the underlying and inalienable title of the indigenous nation or people, may be granted by their free and informed consent, as evidenced in a valid treaty or agreement.

6. Discovery, conquest, settlement on a theory *of terra nullius* and unilateral legislation are never legitimate bases for States to claim or retain the territories of indigenous nations or peoples.

7. In cases where lands taken in violation of these principles have already been settled, the indigenous nation or people concerned is entitled to immediate restitution, including compensation for the loss of use, without extinction of original title. Indigenous peoples' right to regain possession and control of sacred sites must always be respected.

8. No State shall participate financially or militarily in the involuntary displacement of indigenous populations, or in the subsequent economic exploitation or military use of their territory.

9. The laws and customs of indigenous nations and peoples must be recognized by States' legislative, administrative and judicial institutions and, in case of conflicts with State laws, shall take precedence.

10.   No State shall deny an indigenous nation, community, or people residing within its borders the right to participate in the life of the State in whatever manner and to whatever degree they may choose. This includes the right to participate in other forms of collective action and expression.

11.   Indigenous nations and peoples continue to own and control their material culture, including archaeological, historical and sacred sites, artefacts, designs, knowledge, and works of art. They have the right to regain items of major cultural significance and, in all cases, to the return of the human remains of their ancestors for burial according with their traditions.

12.   Indigenous nations and peoples have the right to education, and the control of education, and to conduct business with States in their own languages, and to establish their own educational institutions.

13.   No technical, scientific or social investigations, including archaeological excavations, shall take place in relation to indigenous nations or peoples, or their lands, without their prior authorization, and their continuing ownership and control.

14.   The religious practices of indigenous nations and peoples shall be fully respected and protected by the laws of States and by international law. Indigenous nations and peoples shall always enjoy unrestricted access to, and enjoyment of sacred sites in accordance with their own laws and customs, including the right of privacy.

15.   Indigenous nations and peoples are subjects of international law.

16.   Treaties and other agreements freely made with indigenous nations or peoples shall be recognized and applied in the same manner and according to the same international laws and principles as treaties and agreements entered into with other States.

17.   Disputes regarding the jurisdiction, territories and institutions of an indigenous nation or people are a proper concern of international law, and must be resolved by mutual agreement or valid treaty.

18.   Indigenous nations and peoples may engage in self-defence against State actions in conflict with their right to self-determination.

19.   Indigenous nations and peoples have the right freely to travel, and to maintain economic, social, cultural and religious relations with each other across State borders.

20.   In addition to these rights, indigenous nations and peoples are entitled to the enjoyment of all the human rights and fundamental freedoms enumerated in the International Bill of Human Rights and other United Nations instruments. In no circumstances shall they be subjected to adverse discrimination.

21.   All indigenous nations and peoples have the right to their own traditional medicine, including the right to the protection of vital medicinal plants, animals and minerals. Indigenous nations and peoples also have the right to benefit from modern medical techniques and services on a basis equal to that of the general population of the States within which they are located. Furthermore, all indigenous nations and peoples have the right to

determine, plan, implement, and control the resources respecting health, housing, and other social services affecting them.

22. According to the right of self-determination, all indigenous nations and peoples shall not be obligated to participate in State military services, including armies, paramilitary or "civil" organizations with military structures, within the country or in international conflicts.

Another declaration, the Declaration of San Jose, was adopted by the UNESCO Meeting of Experts on Ethno–Development and Ethnocide in Latin America in San Jose on Dec. 11, 1981 (UNESCO Doc. PS 82/WF.32 (1982), reprinted in Anaya, *supra* at 192). It reads:

For the past few years, increasing concern has been expressed at various international forums over the problems of the loss of cultural identity among the Indian populations of Latin America. This complex process, which has historical, social, political and economic roots, has been termed *ethnocide*.

Ethnocide means that an ethnic group is denied the right to enjoy, develop and transmit its own culture and its own language, whether collectively or individually. This involves an extreme form of massive violation of human rights and, in particular, the right of ethnic groups to respect for their cultural identity, as established by numerous declarations, covenants and agreements of the United Nations and its Specialized Agencies, as well as various regional intergovernmental bodies and numerous non-government organizations.

In response to this demand, UNESCO organized an international meeting on ethnocide and ethno-development in Latin America. . . .

The participants in the meeting, Indian and other experts, made the following Declaration:

1. We declare that ethnocide, that is, cultural genocide is a violation of international law equivalent to genocide, which was condemned by the United Nations Convention on the Prevention and Punishment of the Crime of Genocide of 1948.

2. We affirm that ethno-development is an inalienable right of Indian groups.

3. By ethno-development we mean the extension and consideration of the elements of its own culture, through strengthening the independent decision-making capacity of a culturally distinct society to direct its own development and exercise self-determination, at whatever level, which implies an equitable and independent share of power. This means that the ethnic group is a political and administrative unit, with authority over its own territory and decision-making powers within the confines of its development project, in a process of increasing autonomy and self-management. . . .

11. Disregard for these principles constitutes a gross violation of the right of all individuals and peoples to be different, to consider themselves as different and to be regarded as such, a right recognized in the Declara-

tion on Race and Racial Prejudice adopted by the UNESCO General Conference in 1978, and should therefore be condemned, especially when it creates a risk of ethnocide.

12.   In addition, disregard for these principles creates disequilibrium and lack of harmony within society and may incite the Indian peoples to the ultimate resort of rebellion against tyranny and oppression, thereby endangering world peace. It therefore contravenes the United Nations Charter and the Constitution of UNESCO.

Of what force and effect are such declarations? Recall that the arbitrator in *LIAMCO v. Libya* (discussed earlier in this chapter) used Resolutions of the United Nations General Assembly to discern principles of international law. Some commentators divide international law sources into "hard law" and "soft law." Hard law consists of binding international commitments such as treaties in force, decisions of international courts, and clear customary international law principles. Custom is defined as the general practice of sovereign states. For example, the law of the sea was derived almost entirely from custom before becoming codified in the 1958 and 1972 Conventions on the Law of the Sea. Custom is basically international "common law."

Soft law sources are nonbinding legal instruments that declare principles and aspirational goals or set voluntary standards. U.N. General Assembly Resolutions and declarations of international institutions and conferences generally fall into this category. However, some U.N. resolutions become authoritative evidence of international law as states conform their general practice to the resolution's principles. A resolution which is adopted unanimously, or by a large majority which includes the major powers, and which is relied upon by states can thus become "hard law."

Soft law may also be created by non-state actors. As Professor Hickey writes: "In the energy field, [the generation of soft law] would include the 1990 Valdez Principles on corporate environmental conduct produced by the Coalition for Environmentally Responsible Economics [CERES][4], comprised of individual and corporate investors and environmental organizations. It would also include guidelines issued by the International Maritime Organization (IMO) like its 1989 Guidelines and Standards for the Removal of Offshore Installations and Structures on the Continental Shelf and on the Exclusive Economic Zone." James E. Hickey, Jr. "International Law," in *Energy Law and Policy for the 21st Century* at 4–18 (Rocky Mountain Mineral Law Foundation 2000). Soft law provisions are important because "they begin the process of hard law formation and provoke responses by states, by international organizations, and by other non-state international actors all of which help to shape future acceptable obligations." *Id.* at 4–19.

---

4. [Editors' note:] CERES created the Valdez Principles after the Exxon Valdez oil spill; they pledge *inter alia* the sustainable use of natural resources and compensation for environmental harm. The idea of such a code of conduct came from the Sullivan Principles which were written by a director of General Motors to bring about the end of apartheid in South Africa. *See* Daniel H. Pink, The Valdez Principles: Is What's Good for America Good for General Motors?, 8 Yale L. & Pol'y Rev. 180 (1990).

See also Jose Paulo Kastrup, The Internationalization of Indigenous Rights from the Environmental and Human Rights Perspective, 32 Texas Int'l L. J. 97 (1997).

In November, 1999, an editorial in the Oil & Gas Journal declared that "[i]f the 1990s have been the Decade of the Environment as far as the petroleum industry is concerned, then the next decade is likely to be the Decade of Human Rights." Bob Williams, Human Rights Decade, Oil & Gas Journal, Nov. 1, 1999, at 23. As you read the next section on new approaches to drilling in the rainforest, consider whether the multinational oil companies have adopted some of the soft law in these Declarations.

4.   Sustainable Development and Drilling in the Rainforest

a.   THE VILLANO AND CAMISEA PROJECTS

Large oil and gas fields underlie the rainforests and the offshore areas of several countries of South and Central America, including Peru, Ecuador, Colombia, and Brazil. Shell, Arco, Conoco, Occidental and other multinational companies have licenses to drill in these areas, often in partnership with national oil companies. Indigenous tribes often live in these areas. Undoubtedly stung by the severe public condemnation of past practices, some of these companies are making serious efforts at sustainable development. Much of the information on these sustainable development practices comes from the websites of the oil companies. Shell, in particular, has pledged a policy of openness and public participation in its practices. As an example, Shell maintained a website for the Camisea project in Peru's Amazon which contained a stunning amount of information, broadcast to its "stakeholders" in briefing papers, photos, anthropologist's reports, environmental assessment reports and speeches and contracts with the indigenous groups in the drilling area.[5]

Industry journals also report on the advanced technology being used in rainforests. For example, ARCO's Villano project in Ecuador's rainforest represents the "new paradigm of oil industry sustainable development in the rainforest." Bob Williams, "Arco's Villano Project: Improvised Solutions in Ecuador's Rainforest," Oil & Gas J., Aug. 2, 1999 at 19. In 1988, ARCO and its partner Agip signed a service contract with Ecuador for the exploration and development of Block 10. In 1992, ARCO announced the Villano discovery with estimated reserves of about 200 million barrels of oil. ARCO installed the "small footprint" drillsite used in Alaska's North Slope. (See Figure 6–7 in Chapter 6). No roads access the area. All equipment was brought in by helicopter. The drill site is about 6.2 acres,

---

5. The Camisea website is no longer operational because Shell Prospecting and Development Peru (hereinafter referred to as Shell) withdrew from the project in July 1998. The website (formerly at www.camisea.com) was maintained until April, 2000. Copies of the Camisea/Shell documents cited in this section of the chapter were downloaded and printed in February and March 2000, and are available from Prof. Jacqueline Weaver.

and multiple wells extend from it. Produced water is reinjected. Production is remotely controlled from a central processing facility located 24 miles from the site next to an existing road in an area already disturbed by human intervention. Electricity is generated here and cabled to the drill site.

The greatest challenge was transporting the oil out of a roadless area with minimal impact. The usual pipeline right of way (ROW) is 45 to 90 feet wide, and pipe is laid in trenches using heavy equipment. ARCO determined that its 12–inch flow line to the central processing facility would not be buried because this caused erosion and damage to mature tree roots. Instead, it looked to densely populated countries in Europe and Japan for solutions. While looking for an overhead monorail system for the pipeline, ARCO found a small, walking tractor-excavator used in the Alps on slopes of up to 45 degrees. ARCO modified the machines with special attachments and cleared a ROW in the rainforest with a maximum width of 12 feet. It adapted a cogwheel-based monorack system used to transport harvest loads in vineyards and orchards on hilly slopes. The "invisible pipeline" now snakes through a "green tunnel" in the jungle. Because so few large trees were disturbed, the jungle canopy above the pipeline remains unbroken. A footpath of small logs follows the pipeline through the rainforest.

Six small construction campsites remain with helipads to serve the six shutoff control valves, topped by solar power panels to power the valve controllers. The crude oil from the processing facility is piped to the Trans–Ecuadorian pipeline and from there to a port city. Production from Block 10 is constrained by the lack of pipeline capacity on this trunk pipeline. All the producers feeding into this pipeline are prorated. ARCO Oriente is awaiting the technical and financial studies for a new "world class" $500–600 million trunk pipeline. Much of the information in the Oil and Gas Journal also appears on the internet at <http://www.arco.com?init/villano> with photos of the green tunnel and the machines.

ARCO has encountered two significant non-technical problems. The first is that some indigenous groups demanded that the company build a road to Block 10, delaying the project by 5 months. The second is that the infant mortality and health of the indigenous population around Block 10 improved so dramatically from health services provided to them that the growing population has created environmental problems. The native people cut timber in a circular pattern around their living area. "They want ... a road to get more timber to market, because they have more babies to feed; as a result they run out of trees nearby to cut and then expand the circle broader," but the environmental NGOs (nongovernmental organizations) come "unglued" at the talk of building roads. Oil & Gas J., Aug. 2, 1999 at 26.

Shell Oil's Camisea project in the rainforests of Peru (a joint venture between Shell Prospecting and Development Peru (SPDP) and Mobil) was treated as if it were offshore. *See* 97 Oil & Gas J., Feb. 22, 1999 at 51–54. Work on a well site was commenced when two men were winched down from a helicopter into the forest to carve out a helipad. Shell's greatest challenge was developing mechanisms to work with the indigenous groups. It hired environmental consultants to identify the stakeholders and NGO groups and involved them in meetings and workshops. As a result of these early consultations, Shell voluntarily modified the boundary of its concession to exclude a small area that intruded into a national park. Shell then undertook a "world class" environmental impact assessment. The Smithsonian Institute was invited to do an independent survey of the area to establish its biodiversity and to monitor any effects of the project. Shell undertook a study of the local population's health through the Royal Tropical Institute of Amsterdam. Key Peruvian health agencies also studied the socio-economic base of the region. Shell agreed with Red Ambiental Peruana (RAP), an NGO network of 35 organizations, to perform independent monitoring work. In addition the Peruvian government performed quarterly audits of performance, which Shell requested be made public. Feedback from all of these studies and communication with all the stakeholders led to constant, iterative changes in the design of the project, a process called "adaptive management." Shell frankly acknowledged that its performance in the Camisea area in the 1980s was "unacceptable." See Shell Prospecting and Development Peru, "The Camisea Project, Peru–Sensitive Management in a Sensitive Natural and Social Environment."

To minimize effects on the indigenous people, Shell developed a health passport of required inoculations for all workers going to Camisea. Anyone with signs of the flu or contagious illness could not travel to the project. Shell workers were restricted to project site areas. Only a few people called Community Liaison Officers met regularly with the native communities. Local native people were hired as guides or for field work, so that no settlers or outside workers would come up the river to look for work. This focus on health was due to the fact that a large number of Nahua Indians had died in 1984 from the spread of a western disease, seemingly contacted from loggers. Shell's Community Relations Guidelines, a code of conduct for all project workers at Camisea, were written by an independent anthropologist.

The once-nomadic indigenous people had been encouraged to settle in the Camisea area in 1950. As the settled population increased, it pushed against limited land. The Peruvian Hydrocarbon Law gives licensees the right of eminent domain to acquire surface access to acreage necessary for development. Shell promised in its Camisea agreement that its operation would involve the participation of the local indigenous people and that "net benefits" would accrue to them through contractual agreements for surface use (rather than using condemnation). What local infrastructure and social capital should be developed so that the local population could use and conserve the forest in a sustainable manner?

The "Land Use Transfer Agreement" between Shell and the Shivankoreni Native Community appeared in full at the Camisea website. In summary, the contract reads that Shell, the Transferee, "has assumed a public commitment to carry out the Camisea Project–Block 75—in a sustainable manner, based on good operating practices, the fulfillment of the highest industry standards, and with a net benefit for the region with the dynamic participation and the cooperation of the surrounding communities to the area of the project." Shell agreed to "rigorously" fulfill the technical, safety and environmental protection standards in the Environmental Impact Assessment (EIA) to prevent, minimize or eliminate negative impacts. Payment is a schedule of physical goods (listed below) to be used as infrastructure for health, education, communication, water supply and the social well-being of the community (rather than as benefits to any one individual). In addition, Shell promised to finance the training of members of the Shivankoreni so that they will be able to operate and maintain the physical infrastructure and acquire a sense of autonomy with respect to their own development. The land use agreement could be nullified by the natives if Shell or its workers exceeded the limits of the acreage granted, failed to deliver the promised goods or programs, injured any member of the native group either "physically or morally", or failed to adhere to the stipulations of the environmental management plan for ecological protection. Clause 8 contains an arbitration procedure to resolve disputes. The compensation is listed as follows:

—medications

—school supplies for the primary school

—a scholarship for 3–years of college schooling for one student

—support for a pilot development project

—a water tank, pipe and faucets

—construction of a multi-purpose hall for a community office and Mother's Club

—3 Singer sewing machines and an industrial embroidering machine; 60 machetes, 60 shovels, mosquito netting, 6 pairs of scissors, 4 spools of thread and cooking pans.

—two modules for 100 laying hens each.

—electrical wire, bulbs, and switches.

If a second well were drilled, compensation would include a second college scholarship, solar-powered lighting for the medical post and community hall; a chain saw; an outboard motor; and a solar-powered refrigerator for the medical post (to store vaccines and medicines as part of a "cold chain" of refrigerators owned by native communities scattered in small villages throughout the Camisea rainforest area).

Together, both lists totaled almost $100,000 of goods and services. Seventy registered members of the Shivankoreni community attended a general assembly to analyze the agreement before signing it.

NOTES AND QUESTIONS

1.   Two groups continue to oppose drilling in the Amazon–the Rainforest Action Network (RAN) and Project Underground. Their websites are at

www.ran.org and www.moles.org/projectunderground. Shell states that RAN fails to acknowledge the support which Shell has from the local indigenous communities and the desire of these communities to make social and educational progress and to have an influential voice of their own. The direct views of Mercedes Manriquez, legal advisor of CONAP (the confederation of Amazonian nationalities of Peru) on indigenous rights in Peru are stated as follows: "Achieving a 'Joint Agreement' between the indigenous people of the Urubamba is a process of progress and drawbacks, due to the different expectations of the Communities themselves and their Organizations as well as of some NGO's, which working from the outside with the desire to orient the communities as to the best way to face Shell, end up confusing the native view point and limiting all the initiative of a 'Joint Agreement' that we the natives establish." Manriquez also documents the difficulties that the native communities have in understanding the Environmental Impact Assessment (EIA) and responding to it: "The native communities need the interaction of national and international NGO's that identify with the indigenous cause, but will not impose upon our decisions, and will act in response to our needs. They must also be in agreement with the same principles of respect, consultation and participation that in support of us they demand from the State and the Oil Companies. Our options, priorities and the course of our destiny are decisions for us to make .. We also have the right to make mistakes and learn from our errors." Mercedes Manriquez, "Indigenous Participation in the Current Development Process of the Camisea Project," Camisea website document, last modified Jan. 18, 1999).

2.   The Camisea Briefing Papers on the Camisea website were detailed progress reports, unflinching in their documentation of errors, such as the account of a cement spill in Briefing Paper 14 and its post-event monitoring. Briefing Paper 12 is an account of RAP's fourth independent monitoring visit, documenting the need for greater erosion control at two well sites and the need for more clarity on how scholarships are given. It also described Round 5 of a series of consultations with 44 villages on mitigation measures for the flowline and its gravel needs; and the second round of national and international workshops held in Lima (Peru), Washington D.C. and London to present an overall update on Camisea and receive comments on the next steps of the project.

Briefing Paper 12, dated July 1998, announced Shell's and Mobil's decision to not proceed further with development of Block 88, despite having drilled three very successful gas wells. Briefing Papers 14 and 15 describe the process of demobilizing and restoring the sites. What do you think triggered this decision to withdraw?

3.   Perupetro is the national oil company of Peru. Its website is www.perupetro.com.pe. A click on its homepage index for "Legal Framework" brings up "The Rules of Fair Play" which recite the Peruvian statutory and Constitutional guarantees of stability of contracts and the stability of the tax and currency exchange system in force on the date a contract is signed. Is there any better advertisement to attract investors?

4. In May 1999, heavy rains triggered a landslide which wiped out 13 feet of Perupetro's largest, 530–mile pipeline, sending thousands of barrels of oil gushing into the rainforest. Houston Chronicle, March 24, 1999 at D6.

b. SUSTAINABLE DEVELOPMENT AS A PRINCIPLE OF INTERNATIONAL LAW

Shell pledged a standard of "sustainable development" in its Camisea agreements, defined as "improv[ing] the quality of life while ensuring that renewable resources remain vibrant to benefit future generations and nonrenewable resources are used wisely and efficiently with the benefit of future generations in mind."

How does this definition compare to the principle of sustainable development which has been much discussed and debated in international environmental law? In the following article, Professor Tarlock focuses on timber exploitation rather than oil and gas exploitation and on the preservation of ecosystems rather than indigenous communities. Nonetheless, he offers many insights into the clash between the nearly inviolate "hard" principle of national sovereignty and the "softer" principles of sustainable development in international environmental law. The article proposes that patent laws be reformed to recognize a new type of concession in rainforest countries—a concession that grants royalties in genetic biodiversity.

A. Dan Tarlock, Exclusive Sovereignty Versus Sustainable Development of a Shared Resource: The Dilemma of Latin American Rainforest Management

32 Texas Int'l L.J. 37 (1997) at 38–39, 40–41, 43–44,52–53, 62–66.

The paradox of rainforest destruction is that the emerging global perception of forests as increasingly valuable bioreserves is not as widely shared by the host countries as it is in the developed world. This paradox is not surprising—global concern about the use of rainforests is a product of the scientific nature of environmentalism and the changes in human valuation of tropical resources produced by widely disseminated scientific information among global elites. The net result is that the scientific environmentalism is causing a fundamental global paradigm shift away from a focus on unrestrained, rapid economic growth toward one of environmentally sustainable development. This shift is illustrated in the environmental conception of tropical rainforests. In the past generation what was an inhospitable jungle or a hardwood forest inhabited by savage tribes of "Indians" is now an extremely fragile biodiversity hot spot, extractive reserve, and carbon sink. The responsibility for managing rainforests should be shared between the nation-state in which the forest is located, indigenous peoples living in the forest, and the international community.

* * *

This Article examines the failure of the international legal system to develop an effective legal response to the scientific imperative that nations with rich tropical (and temperate) forest resources replace rapid and destructive exploitation with management strategies that benefit both present and future generations of humankind. The basic argument is that classic international law precludes the development of effective direct international legal restraints because it effectively shields internal policies, such as natural resource management decisions from external standards regardless of the international spillovers. International law cannot solve the host countries' lack of capacity to control destructive uses. If tropical rainforest destruction is to be replaced with sustainable forest use practices, the primary implementation burden falls on the host countries. However, international law can perhaps make a modest contribution to the development of indirect restraints which can influence and reinforce both international and domestic rainforest conservation policies by providing a standard that can measure specific actions, serve as a deterrent to the adoption of destructive policies, and provide a basis for internal and external sanctions.

Rainforest destruction is the product of national policies driven by internal and well as external forces. The main determinants of forest exploitation are population pressures and national development and settlement policies. The creation of counterincentives to the historic pattern of underregulated exploitation involves the highly politically sensitive issues of population control and distribution, economic growth rates, and property entitlement regimes.. : .

II.   The Wall of National Sovereignty

A.   The Right to Develop: A Modern Manifestation of Sovereignty

Focusing on the modification of internal national behavior is always dicey. This is especially true for rainforest destruction. Absolute exclusive territorial sovereignty is commonly identified as the major barrier to effective rainforest management. Sovereignty claims allow nations to shield internal development and management decisions from international law restraints by equating exclusive territorial sovereignty with an absolute right to develop their natural resources. Rapid and intensive exploitation is an exercise of the right to develop—a right which has become an integral part of postcolonial international law. The recognition of national sovereignty and the derivative right to develop is embedded in every modern environmental and natural resources management declaration and convention relevant to rainforest management. The right has been grounded in either "colonial" concepts of sovereignty or the postcolonial principle of the duty of equity owed by the North to the South. Although some rainforest nations have moved away from the heavily subsidized economic development schemes that excited the World Bank's attention in the 1980s, the tension between sovereign (internal) and international (external) management strategies remains the nub of the inability to subject rainforest management to an international legal regime.

Classic international law supports the right to develop because it concerns itself only with minimal standards of external conduct among nations. As long as nation-states respect the territorial sovereignty of other nations, they have the exclusive power to manage natural resources within their borders. Absolute territorial sovereignty reached its apogee in the late nineteenth and early twentieth centuries, when it was accepted as the international organizing principle. The major twentieth century application of this "grundnorm" is the developing world's claim of a right to develop as incidental to the right of self-determination. Since World War II, self-determination has been expanded to encompass a right to exploit natural resources and provides the foundation for the customary right to develop. Western nations initially opposed this claimed right in order to protect foreign mineral concessions, but the Rio Declaration adopted it by consensus for the first time in an international document. Principle 3 states that "[t]he right to develop must be fulfilled so as to equitably meet developmental and environmental needs of future generations."

From many modern perspectives, sovereignty and corollary exclusive rights are archaic remnants of a decaying and accidental international order. There is an increasing consensus among students of international relations that absolute territorial sovereignty is no longer a functional organizing concept given the interdependencies of the modern world. Private global trading, communications, cultural and scientific networks, and the liberal ideals that they support have eroded the vitality of the concept.

The environmental case against exclusive national sovereignty rests on the scientific and economic argument that unacceptable levels of transboundary and global spillovers exist.

On both historical and instrumental grounds, the case is a strong one. Historically, rainforest destruction is a consequence of the nation-state, which arose in Europe by default after the Thirty Years' War. Both the continent's great powers and the Catholic Church were forced to recognize the permanent existence of separate small, as well as large, Catholic and Protestant nations. The great project of international law has been to promote the peaceful coexistence among these accidental territorial divisions and, subsequently, the orderly carving up of the globe in the wake of the failures of the Spanish, Portuguese, English, French, Dutch, German, and Russian colonial empires. This effort has only highlighted the importance of the weakness of the idea of sovereignty when applied to nations with varying capacities to manage their territory and peoples. To accomplish the peaceful transition from a colonial world to a world of independent states, international law reversed the legal order of the Roman Empire: territorial prerogatives are the norm and universal rules the exception. Since World War II, international law has tried to return to universal rules centered around the protection of human dignity, and, more recently, centered around the ecological integrity of the planet.

The basic objective is simple: shared control over rainforest management between the nation-state and private and governmental non-national representatives of the "international community" so that international norms can be applied to internal natural resources decisions.

The argument for shared control proceeds in three stages: (1) the recognition of limitations on the use of a state's territory, (2) the expansion of the category of common or shared resources to include resources conventionally classified as exclusive, and (3) the creation of new norms of conduct that can be adapted to apply to specific state activities that cause internal as well as external adverse environmental consequences. The concept of sustainable development is the current consensus candidate for the new norm. It allows for modification of exclusive sovereignty within the context of classic theories of sovereignty, but it draws support from counter-traditions in international law; specifically, the Grotian vision of international law as a progressive source of idealism, individual as well as state rights, and the recognition that non-state actors (such as international organizations and non-governmental organizations) have legitimate interests in the formulation and application of international law....

[Professor Tarlock then describes the accepted principle of international law that no State has the right to use its territory in a manner that causes injury, such as pollution, to another state. However this principle does little to prevent a state from conducting nonsustainable development within its own territory. In the absence of any binding commitments to preserve forests as CO_2 sinks to prevent global warming, it is difficult to characterize the forests as a shared world resource or as belonging to the "common heritage of mankind." Some types of property have been characterized by the United Nations as areas of "common concern" to mankind, such as the high seas and seabeds. And the European Court of Justice has characterized wild birds as a case where management of the "common heritage" is entrusted to member states. However, tropical countries have been unwilling to "internationalize" their forests unless compensated by North-to-South transfers of wealth and technology. Moreover, forests are not a true "commons". Query for students: Why not?]

In the past decade, the concept of sustainable development has gained widespread acceptance as the organizing principle for the development of new international environmental rights and duties in both developed and developing countries....

The current working definition of sustainable development is contained in the 1987 Bruntland report which defines it as development "that meets the needs of the present without compromising the ability of future generations to meet their own needs." The Bruntland Commission's task was to break the impasse between developed and developing nations that surfaced at the 1972 Stockholm Conference. The Bruntland Commission succeeded in collapsing the dichotomy between environmental protection and development to induce the developing world to accept the legitimacy of environmental protection. Rio indicated the formal success of the Bruntland Commission, thus making sustainable development the organizing principle for all future international efforts. However, like all compromises, the issue is whether it will actually advance the objectives of the exercise or whether it will become a meaningless post-hoc label used to justify the continuation of the status quo.

Sustainable development has been criticized as too vague to be meaningfully implemented, a hopelessly romantic fantasy unsuited to a technological world that may lock many countries into subsistence economies if North–South subsidies fail to materialize, and a way to subordinate environmental protection to development. A cynic might argue that its current success rests on the unspoken assumption that it will never progress to a constraint on the current widespread practices of environmentally unsustainable development.

* * *

The United Nations Conference on Environment and Development identified the five most important principles of sustainable development as: (1) the emphasis on the quality of life rather than commodities, (2) the integration of the whole natural environment when assessing potential damage, (3) the reconceptualization of natural environments as national assets, (4) the recognition that there must be different responsibilities for developed and developing countries, and (5) the idea that all national policies should be tested against the norm of sustainability.

* * *

IV.   The Impact of Sustainable Development on Legal Rules

Sustainable development can serve as a basis to reevaluate and change a number of domestic and international laws that encourage rainforest destruction and other unsustainable resource use practices. The concept is not a magic wand that transforms anticonservation rules into proconservation rules. Sustainable development can, however, provide a rationale for eliminating some deeply entrenched *per se* legal rules that discourage rainforest conservation. This proposition is controversial because the elimination of *per se* conservation barriers represents a substantial power shift to host countries or, conversely, an encroachment of host country prerogatives. . . .

A.   A New Intellectual Property Regime

Sustainable development can help provide justifications for new intellectual property rights regimes that curb the traditional policy of cheap access to rainforest bioriches. The creation of property rights regimes that allow host countries to capture more of the value of rainforests is central to the long-term success of the project of rainforest conservation. Historically, only those who seek to exploit nature in developing new and useful products receive property protection. At the present time, the prevailing rule is that no one owns "biodiversity" until a crop is harvested or a plant, animal, or derivative product is manipulated by a human effort to create something new and useful. The Biodiversity Convention supports sustainable development by an important and extremely controversial change in intellectual property law. However, intellectual property law does not protect "products of nature." This rule prohibits either the host country or the exploiter from claiming a patent in a useful element of biodiversity simply by discovering a useful plant or natural process and marketing it. The Convention reverses this order and seeks to reward "those who exercise forbearance and thus preserve biodiversity." Articles 16 and 17 create sovereign rights in biodiversity that the host nation may exploit by permitting prospecting and capturing a percentage of the royalties from any valuable discoveries. The Convention supports both new patent and concession model regimes.

Concession models are the easiest to implement. Biodiversity can be developed on the mineral concession model or the recognition of "compensation-style rights." A "country which sourced a particular type of genetic material would have a 'right' to a royalty-style payment from the organization that had developed into and marketed the end-product." Countries have long claimed ownership of their mineral resources and licensed prospecting and exploitation concessions to foreign oil companies. This practice can be adapted to biodiversity prospecting. Costa Rica pioneered this idea with the joint venture between Merck Pharmaceutical Company and the nonprofit Costa Rican National Institute for Biodiversity. Merck funded an assessment of Costa Rica's biodiversity resources in return for the chance to evaluate the inventory and use the information. Merck will pay royalties on any commercial products derived from the inventory. The concession idea is promising, but there are two limitations. First, a country's perceived genic resource reserves may not create sufficient incentives for companies to obtain prospecting permits. Second, it will be extremely difficult to create exclusive property rights in biodiversity information, and thus the incentives to seek concessions will again be weak.

Sustainable development equally supports the creation of new patent rights in unmodified nature which may be claimed and licensed by host countries. The United States and Europe have rejected structural patents on chemical compounds in the absence of a demonstrated use for the compound; but, "[d]espite its inequity as a system for compensating human efforts, something resembling a structure patent is exactly the sort of protection needed for biodiversity chemical structures." At the present time, the need for human manipulation bars the recognition of patent rights for discoveries of nature, but the distinction between natural and artificial gene sequences is eroding in patent law as the biotechnology industry progresses. Thus, there will be future pressure to eliminate this barrier and to create an intellectual property regime that recognizes that host countries may claim a "sui generis 'intellectual property-style' right in unmodified genetic sequences...."

      * * *

C. Debt-for-Nature

Sustainable development supports new biodiversity conservation concepts such as debt-for-nature swaps. These swaps are attempts to create financial incentives for rainforest nations to preserve biodiversity. The basic rationale is simple. Rainforest nations are burdened with debt that was incurred to buy oil or finance inefficient public infrastructure in the 1970s. In 1987, a Washington, D.C.-based NGO purchased $650,000 worth of Bolivian debt for $100,000 in return for a government commitment to preserve 3.7 million acres of tropical rainforest. The experiment was not an initial success because the government failed to fund the management account for two years and did not enact the promised reserve protection legislation. The enforcement problem was partially cured by the next swap. Ecuador issued $10,000,000 worth of bonds. NGOs were invited to purchase debt on the secondary market and then repay the bonds. The interest was assigned to Fundacion Natura for the purchase and management of reserves, and $10,000,000 of discounted debt was purchased. Debt-for-nature swaps involve foreign government debt purchases, debt forgiveness, or government grants to NGOs.

Debt-for-nature swaps are usually hailed as creative market solutions to biodiversity protection that result in a voluntary surrender of a country's sovereign right to develop. Some host countries are happy to turn unexploited natural areas into a source of needed cash, but to some countries, debt-for-nature swaps represent an unacceptable forced sale of the country's patrimony. Brazil has a long history of resistance to debt-for-nature swaps because they interfere with sovereignty. This objection can be mitigated by the principle of sustainable development. The acceptance of the concept by most nations of the world represents a partial surrender of sovereignty, despite all the affirmations of national sovereignty in the Rio declarations, because they subject themselves to a standard of conduct in return for the promise of assistance and toleration of differential development practices. Since debt-for-nature swaps can further sustainable development, they fall within the limitations of the North–South bargain.

* * *

V. Conclusion: Toward an Ethic of Stewardship Sovereignty

The ethic of sustainable development can be implemented in international environmental law by modifying the concept of exclusive territorial sovereignty to make clear that nations have primary but not exclusive control over resource decisions with extraterritorial impacts and that nations owe duties to the international community.

In short, sustainable development is enlightened, forward-looking resource stewardship.■

NOTES AND QUESTIONS

1. A World Bank study of a hectare of Peruvian rainforest calculated that the present value of harvesting the hardwood was $1000 but that the present value of a mix of fruit, latex, and selective timber harvesting was $6820. A contingent valuation study of the ecotourism value of the Monteverde Cloud Forest in Costa Rica produced a figure between $2.4 and $2.9 million. Tarlock, *supra* at 53. What is a hectare of Peruvian rainforest worth if it overlies a large oil or gas field? One industry expert posits a 50 million barrel oil field which will cause 100 hectares of necessary forest destruction to develop. The project will also result in an additional 2000

hectares of destruction from squatters and loggers who gain access to new roads and from villagers who contrive crop destruction so that they can collect compensation from the oil company. The oil is worth about $1 billion. Of this, the host country will receive about $780 million in government take and local purchases. This amounts to $370,000 per hectare for all 2,100 destroyed hectares, or $7,800,000 per hectare for the project's necessary destruction. Richard Barry, The Management of International Oil Operations 70–72 (1994).

2. Is Shell's operation in Peru an example of forward-looking resource stewardship? Can private actors be better stewards than host governments? In 1991, the Oil Industry International Exploration and Production Forum issued formal guidelines for operating in tropical forests. Can private codes of environmental conduct developed by multinational companies and their trade associations provide the transfer of technological expertise necessary for sustainable development? Professor Baram writes that "[t]rade associations in particular are capable of weaving a global system of private codes that could be superior in many respects to public sector efforts, which have proven to be cumbersome and inefficient." Michael Baram, Multinational Corporations, Private Codes, and Technology Transfer for Sustainable Development, 24 Environmental Law 33 (1994). His article discusses various strategies to extend the reach of private codes in the developing world, such as integrating and harmonizing codes into a quasi-regulatory international system which uses registration, progress reports, evaluations, and public access to monitor the performance of companies. An international agency, such as the United Nations Environment Programme (UNEP) would enforce the codes with sanctions such as de-registration and adverse publicity directed against companies that fail to make progress.

Another model is the International Organization for Standardization (ISO) which has developed widely used standards for environmental management, audits, labeling and life-cycle assessment. *See* Paulette L. Stenzel, Can the ISO 14000 Series Environmental Management Standards Provide a Viable Alternative to Government Regulation?, 37 Am. Bus. L. J. 237 (2000); Kerry E. Rodgers, The ISO Environmental Standards Initiative, 5 N.Y.U. Envtl. L. J. 181 (1996).

Shell invited a nongovernmental organization called SustainAbility to monitor its health, safety and environmental performance. SustainAbility had significant concerns that Shell's approach was merely a public relations exercise in the wake of media crises spotlighting its complicity with Nigerian police squads and with Greenpeace over the abandonment of the Brent Spar rig in the North Sea. SustainAbility's report on Shell's performance is available at <www.sustainability.co.uk/about-SA/shell-relationship >. The Global Reporting Initiative of CERES seeks to elevate corporate reporting on environmental sustainability to the level of financial reporting, using a standardized set of measures. *See* <www.ceres.org>. Professor Baram's recommendations appear to have been adopted by UNEP and SustainAbility. In 1999, these two organizations issued "The Oil Sector Report" which examines how 50 leading oil companies do environmental and social accounting, as a catalyst for developing a "best practices" reporting framework that will be compatible with the Global Reporting Initiative. The Oil Sector Report found that smaller companies and state-owned companies have poorer accounting than the large multinationals; that most reports do not measure actual impacts such as disturbances to land or biodiversity; and that many of the companies do not use third-party verification which would raise the level of public trust in the companies' voluntary reports. *See* < www.sustainability.co.uk >. Many large accounting firms like Ernst & Young and KPMG now have environmental services groups or "Sustainability Advisory Services" which conduct field audits of their clients' environmental performance.

2. Is eco-tourism less socially and environmentally destructive than oil and gas development? In Managing Tourism Growth: Issues and Applications (Island Press 1999) by Fred P. Bosselman, Craig A. Peterson, and Claire McCarthy, the authors' computer database search of thousands of publications throughout the world since 1995 found thousands of articles reflecting adverse impacts from tourism. Appropriate mitigation strategies were either nonexistent or not being implemented. Moreover, the people in the local economy often did not participate or benefit in the growth from tourism in a meaningful way. For example, a World Wildlife Federation study of ecotourism in the Royal Chitwan National Park in Nepal showed that the 60,000 visiting tourists to the park in 1994 had only a minimal impact on household income. Only six percent of the households earned income directly or indirectly from ecotourism. The average annual salary of these households from ecotourism was $600. A University of Arizona study reported that whalewatching tours in Baja, Mexico returned less than one percent of the tourist's expenditures to the Mexican economy. *Id.* at 7.

3. Paralleling the international movement in the 1970s against Colonialism, American Indian tribes pushed for policies of tribal self-determination in an effort to break out of the vicious poverty which often existed on their reservations. For a thorough account of why some tribes moved forward while others remained behind, *see* Steven Cornell & Joseph P. Kalt (eds.), What Can Tribes Do? Strategies and Institutions in American Indian Economic Development (1992).

4. In Sustainable Development in Mineral Economies (1998), Richard Auty and Raymond Mikesell use environmental and natural resource accounting to measure the performance of many developing countries with resource economies. This accounting deducts the depletion of natural resources stocks and environmental degradation from a country's national product to give a more accurate measure of sustainability. This work contains useful case studies for students of international energy projects.

Some developed countries have also undertaken "green accounting." A 1995 study by the Japanese Economic Planning Agency concluded that air pollution, water pollution and ecosystem damage cost the Japanese economy $100 billion or two percent of Gross Domestic Product in 1990. Daniel H. Cole, Accounting for Sustainable Development, 8 Fordham Envtl L. J. 123 at 131 (1996). A study by two economists found that economic growth initially leads to environmental deterioration followed by a subsequent phase of improvement, with the turning point at about $8,000 per capita GNP. *Id.* at 127.

5.   In April 2000, the National Park Service signed an agreement allowing the Diversa Corporation to "bioprospect" in Yellowstone National Park. Diversa will pay the park service $100,000 over five years plus royalties of 0.5 percent to 10 percent on sales of any commercial products it derives from its search for commercially valuable microbes in the geysers and hot springs of the park. The agreement is suspended pending completion of a court-ordered Environmental Impact Assessment on the National Park Service's new policy of allowing bioprospecting. New York Times, April 25, 2000 at D5. *See also* Elizabeth Pennisi, "Lawsuit Targets Yellowstone Bug Deal," 279 Science 1624 (March 13, 1998). Whether bioprospecting can be a source of private financing for biodiversity conservation is discussed in Gordon C. Rausser and Arthur A. Small, Valuing Research Leads: Biospecting and the Conservation of Genetic Resources, 108 J. of Political Economy 173 (2000).

6.   International efforts to secure recognition of intellectual property rights in natural genetic material culminated in the Convention on Biological Diversity, adopted on May 22, 1992 and opened for signatures at the U.N. Conference on Environment and Development (also called the Earth or Rio Summit) in 1992. By early 1997, the Convention had been ratified by 165 nations, but conspicuously not by the United States. The Convention rejected the previous view that natural materials were the "common heritage" of all mankind and therefore freely accessible. Rather, Articles 3 and 15 of the Biodiversity Treaty recognize the sovereign right of each nation over its own natural resources and access to them. The Convention then obligates all parties to assure that both the countries supplying the genetic material and the countries using it receive economic benefits. "In short, the Convention makes reciprocity–transfer of genetic resources in exchange for compensatory payments and transfer of technology—the basic principle of biodiversity prospecting." Roger W. Findley, Legal and Economic Incentives for the Sustainable Use of Rainforests, 32 Texas Int'l L. J. 17 at 32 (1997). For further reading, *see* William Lesser, Sustainable Use of Genetic Resources under the Convention on Biological Diversity: Exploring Access and Benefit Sharing Issues (1998).

E.   CHAPTER REVIEW PROBLEM

Your client is an American oil company doing business in Burma as a joint venturer with the Burmese national oil company in the construction of a gas pipeline. Your client has been served with a complaint filed in a U.S. district court in the district where your client is headquartered, naming your client, its chief executive, the State Oil Company, and the Burmese military junta as defendants. The complaint alleges that the State Oil Company is controlled by the junta that seized control of Burma (Myanmar) in 1988. The junta arrested all the democratic leaders of Burma who had captured 82 percent of parliamentary seats in an election in 1991. Plaintiffs seek to represent a class of thousands of Burmese who want injunctive, declaratory and compensatory relief for international human rights violations perpetrated by the joint venturers.

Plaintiffs allege that the defendant junta's military and police forces use violence, intimidation, and torture to relocate villages, seize private property and enslave farmers as forced laborers on the pipeline project, in violation of state, federal and customary international law. There is no functioning judiciary in Burma and any suits filed in Burma would result in terrible reprisals against the plaintiffs.

The complaint further contends that your client negotiated a production sharing contract with the junta's Council on State Law and Order Restoration in 1991, resulting in a joint venture with the State Oil Company. The parties agreed that the Council, acting as an agent for the joint venture, would clear land and provide labor for the pipeline. Your client company has allegedly subsidized these activities, and its executives continue to make major decisions involving the project at its U.S. headquarter offices, knowing that serious human rights abuses are occurring. Plaintiffs seek an order directing your client to cease paying money to the Council and to cease its joint venture with State Oil Company.

On what grounds would you move to dismiss this complaint for lack of subject-matter jurisdiction?

1. Under the Foreign Sovereignty Immunity Act are the junta's Council and the State Oil Company immune from suit? Are your American clients?

2. If the Council and State Oil Company are immune, should the court dismiss the suit for failure to join an indispensable party?

3. Your research uncovers the Alien Tort Claims Act which states that "the district courts shall have original jurisdiction of any civil action by an alien for a tort only, committed in violation of the law of nations or a treaty of the United States." Is the law of nations a part of federal common law? Where do you find the norms of the law of nations? Assume that one such customary norm is a prohibition against official torture. Can your client be deemed to have participated in state acts of torture as a joint venturer? Can your client be privately liable for violations of international law even absent any participation in state action? Assume that your research shows that forced labor, piracy, and slave trading are included in the handful of crimes for which the law of nations attributes individual responsibility.

4. Does the act of state doctrine apply to dismiss the suit in part or in whole? Is there an international consensus condemning torture (but not cartels)? Of what import are the federal law and executive orders which prohibit only "new investment" in Burma? Does the act of state doctrine prohibit plaintiffs' claims based on expropriation of property?

The answers to all of these questions can be derived from the materials studied in the chapter. If you want to check your advice to your American clients, read *Doe I v. Unocal Corp.*, 963 F.Supp. 880 (C.D.Cal.1997). In addition, ask yourself if your client company would have less exposure to liability if it had entered a service contract rather than a joint venture with Burma. How would liability exposure change if the alleged acts were inflicted on members of an indigenous tribe?

If this fact pattern seems far-fetched, consider that many multinational oil companies operate in areas where dictatorships and ethnic and military conflicts are a way of life. Shell has extensive investments in Nigeria, the world's sixth largest oil exporter. When members of the Ogoni tribe attacked its oil field facilities to protest environmental damage to their land in 1996, Shell requested protection from Nigeria's military government. The government sent the notoriously brutal mobile police to the area. Shell paid for the transportation and salary bonuses of some troops who acted as "oil field guards." The police laid waste to whole villages and the government of General Abacha executed the most prominent Ogoni, a political activist and writer named Ken Saro–Wiwa, after a rigged secret trial. Paul Lewis, "Nigeria's Deadly Oil War: Shell Defends its Record," New York Times, Feb. 13, 1996, at A1. After being accused of complicity in the murder of Ken Saro–Wiwa, Shell turned to Amnesty International for help in drafting a code of conduct regarding human rights. *See* Armin Rosenkranz & Richard Campbell, Foreign Environmental and Human Rights Suits Against U.S. Corporations in U.S. Courts, 18 Stanford Envtl L. J. 145, 207 (1999). In March 2000, Nigeria's newly elected government announced a crackdown on sabotage of oil facilities. It is creating a new police unit that is authorized to shoot vandals on sight. The unit will be subsidized by the Nigerian National Petroleum Corp. Houston Chronicle, Mar. 23, 2000, at 24A.

In Colombia, the leftist guerilla group, the Revolutionary Armed Forces of Colombia (FARC) dynamited a major oil pipeline 64 times between January and November 1999. This sabotage caused considerable environmental damage from oil spills and killed nearby villagers in explosive fires. Another rebel group, ELN, stated that it would stop kidnaping oilfield workers if the foreign oil companies paid ELN the money they now pay for security. FARC justified its attacks on the oil sector as retribution for foreign oil company collaboration with right-wing paramilitary forces which protect oil company facilities. *See* John Wade, "Violence, Crime Continues to Cast Shadow over Future Oil Investment in Colombia, Oil & Gas Journal, Jan. 17, 2000, at 32.

Meanwhile, Occidental Petroleum was granted a license in late 1999 to explore for oil just two miles from the territory of the U'wa tribe, on a block which might contain 2.5 billion barrels of oil. The U'wa threatened mass suicide in 1997 to prevent drilling on their land. The U'Wa now fear that the Occidental project will attract this same kind of violence and environmental sabotage and bring in thousands of government soldiers to guard the oil facilities. *See* "Colombia Permits Exploration for Oil," Houston Chronicle, Sept. 22, 1999, at C3.

CHAPTER 17

THE CLIMATE CHANGE ISSUE

Outline of Chapter:

A. THE CLIMATE CHANGE ISSUE'S IMPACT ON THE ENERGY SECTOR

No environmental issue poses as many potential difficulties for the energy industries as the possibility that the combustion of fossil fuels is contributing to a change in the world's climate: a change that will cause a gradual increase in the temperature levels each year for a century or more.

The key points of mainstream scientific opinion on climate change can be summarized succinctly: The combustion of fuels containing carbon: coal, oil and natural gas, known collectively as the "fossil fuels," emits carbon dioxide (CO_2) to the atmosphere. These emissions have increased the levels of carbon dioxide (CO_2) in the atmosphere. Carbon dioxide lets radiant energy into the atmosphere more freely than it lets it out. The effectiveness of this atmospheric heat retention increases with increases in CO_2. This increase has the potential to warm the earth's climate. Computer models predict that the climate will warm significantly over the next century.

Measurements of CO_2 in the atmosphere have shown a steady increase of about 0.5% per year, rising from 315 ppm in 1958 to about 365 ppm in 1997. Gayle Christianson, Greenhouse 167 (Walker & Co. 1999). There is growing evidence of a warming climate over the past 100 years that is consistent with the progressively increasing concentration of greenhouse gases, especially CO_2, in the atmosphere. Although scientists do not yet know how much of the current climatic change is natural and how much is due to human activity, there is no question that the burning of fossil fuels is the dominant mode of human CO_2 production. Because the amount of CO_2 in the atmosphere far exceeds that of the other greenhouse gases, many of the studies of the problem have focused solely on CO_2, assuming that if it can be controlled the problem will largely be solved.

When the concern about global warming began to be voiced in the 1980s, the energy industries sought out people who had serious questions about the mainstream theories. Funding for the work of many of these skeptics has been provided by the Global Climate Coalition, a joint venture financed primarily by the oil, coal, and automobile industries. Mainstream scientists have been quite disdainful of these industry-funded experts. For a critical view of the role of the energy industries in the climate change debate, *see* Ross Gelbspan, The Heat Is On: The High Stakes Battle Over Earth's Threatened Climate, (Addison–Wesley 1997).

The position of the energy industries on climate change is less consistent than it was in the early 1990s, when the industry almost uniformly dismissed concern about the issue as premature. Two of the three of the world's largest oil companies, Royal Dutch Shell and British Petroleum, have quit the council, as has Texaco; furthermore, both Ford and Daimler–Chrysler have also withdrawn from the group. *See* Climate change group loses second major automaker, 15 Octane Week #4, January 24, 2000.

A growing number of energy companies are taking action on their own initiative to reduce their own greenhouse gas emissions. Peter Cameron, From Principles to Practice: The Kyoto Protocol, 18 J. of Energy & Natural Resources Law 1, 2 (2000). Shell has joined the Business Environmental Leadership Council, a group of twenty-two companies "committed to greater understanding and action on the climate change issue," Three Energy Firms Join Pro–Action Group, National Journal's Daily Energy Briefing, Feb. 11, 1999. British Petroleum has committed to a reduction in its own greenhouse gas emissions to 10% below 1990 levels by 2010, and has retained outside consultants to conduct an emissions audit of the company and monitor its progress. BP Signs Up for Emissions Audit, 49 Oil Daily #122, June 28, 1999. Almost 200 companies reported to the Energy Information Agency in 1998 that they had projects to reduce greenhouse gas emissions underway or planned. US greenhouse gas emission growth slows, Oil & Gas Journal, Feb. 14, 2000, p. 30.

Although the views of the energy companies are now more diverse, this does not mean that they are less concerned about both the accuracy and the impact of global climate projections. (*See* for example the American Petroleum Institute position at www.api.org/globalclimate.) As the Twenty-first Century begins, the federal and state governments in the United States have adopted only a few legal rules and principles based on the objective of avoiding climate change. But some other nations are moving forward more aggressively, and the industry no longer assumes that the possibility of United States laws on the topic is more remote than a cold day in the nether world.

B. HAS THE EARTH BECOME WARMER?

Records of temperatures at the earth's surface have been kept in great detail throughout the world in recent years. The farther back in time one searches for such records, the more questionable they become. Nevertheless, most scientists are confident that we have reliable temperature records at least for the Twentieth Century. And modern scientific methods of examining ice cores and other buried materials give us increasing confidence that we can estimate climate conditions even in prehistoric times.

1. GEOLOGICAL TIME

Geologists, paleontologists and astronomers all have produced theories about why the earth's climate appears to have fluctuated dramatically over hundreds of thousands of years. Astronomers, for example, believe that glaciers have advanced and retreated based on slight changes in the earth's axis and orbit, producing cycles that last 41,000, 23,000 and 19,000 years. William K. Stevens, A Change in the Weather 24–26 (Delacorte Press, 1999). Fluctuations on this kind of time scale seem irrelevant for practical purposes.

The completion of two sets of ice core records from locations in Greenland has given scientists one of the best sets of climate records that go back about 110,000 years. These records indicate that there have been abrupt climate shifts in the last few thousand years, and that these shifts have often occurred within a decade or less and have often lasted for centuries. National Research Council, Global Environmental Change: Research Pathways for the Next Decade 131, 237 (National Academy Press, 1999) (Hereinafter "Research Pathways"). Similar records of warming since the end of the "little ice age" of the fourteenth through the sixteenth centuries are found in the studies of Antarctica's paleoclimatic ice-core record. C. Lorieus et al., The ice-core record: climate sensitivity and future greenhouse warming, 347 Nature 139 (1990). Reconstructions of the climate record over the last millennium, using "various sets of Paleoclimate data, from tree rings and ice cores to corals, sediments, and historical records," suggest that the "rapid warming over the last century . . . has no counterpart in the millennial record." Ray Bradley, 1000 years of climate change, 288 Science 1353 (May 26, 2000).

The National Research Council has concluded that the recent paleoclimatic data is more consistent with the mid-to upper range of consensus estimates of climate sensitivity to increases in carbon dioxide. Research Pathways, *supra* at 266. Few people argue, however, that we can derive principles to guide today's actions solely from the observations of millennia past. Instead, much of the current thinking focuses on changes that have taken place from the beginning of the twentieth century to its end.

2. THE TWENTIETH CENTURY

In 1996, the computer models suggested that over the past century, Earth's surface has warmed by about 0.5°C (±0.2°C). In January, 2000, a panel of the National Academy of Sciences reviewed the data and agreed that the earth's surface temperature had increased by between 0.4 and 0.8 degrees Celsius in the past century. National Research Council, Reconciling Observations of Global Temperature Change (National Academy Press, 2000).

Global average surface temperature, 1860–1998

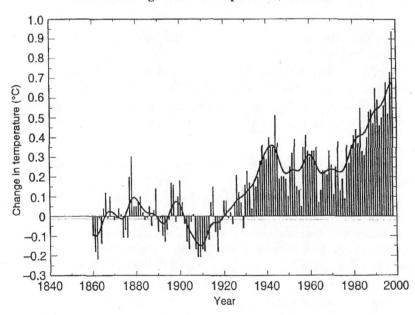

Figure 17–1

Source: Hadley Centre, *Climate Change and its Impacts*, Bracknell: UK Meteorological Office, 1998.

Note: The bars show the annual global average surface temperature; the smoothed curve represents the 5–year average.

The fact that the climate at the surface of the earth has warmed over the period of a century is not really seriously debated, though the extent of that increase is still subject to differing views. But until recently, there was great doubt that the activities of puny humans could have any discernible impact on the climate of the massive planet earth. Some doubt still remains, but the events of the last two decades of the century has swung scientific and public opinion heavily toward the view that humans are at least partially responsible.

3. THE 1980S AND 1990S

During the period from 1980 to 1999, the world, and particularly the Northern Hemisphere, experienced the hottest years in the century. The 1990s were the warmest decade over recorded; the top 6 warmest years of the century were in the 1990s, and each year in the decade of the 1990s ranked among the top 15 in the century, according to reports from the National Climatic Data Center. Www.ncdc.noaa.gov/ol/climate/research /1999/ann/ann99.html.

Based on measurements taken on land rather than in the ocean, 1998 and 1999 were the warmest and second warmest years in the century. When ocean temperatures are factored in, 1998 and 1997 were the two warmest years, but 1999 remains the 5th warmest year even taking account of the cooling effect of dramatic changes in the Pacific ocean oscillation described in Chapter 2. *Id* Scientists have noted that these unusually warm temperatures include especially warm winter temperatures in the Northern Hemisphere. This is referred to as the cool ocean warm land (COWL) pattern. Periods of these COWL conditions have occurred in the past, and it is not clear to what extent this current episode has been aggravated by greenhouse gas emissions. Research Pathways, *supra* at 137–147.

In the United States, at least, the warm conditions carried over into the winter of 1999–2000. The weather conditions from December 1999 through February, 2000, were the warmest since the government began keeping weather statistics 105 years ago. Every state in the continental United States was warmer than average. The national standardized temperature index for March–May 2000 also tied the record for the warmest Spring period since record keeping began in 1895. Except for a few scattered reporting sites, the entire country experienced above normal temperatures. Satellite readings from the lower half of the atmosphere also found record warm temperatures for the January–May 2000 period, 2 degrees F. above the long-term mean. National Climatic Data Center, March–May 2000, U.S. National Analysis, June 16, 2000.

Scientists are quick to point out that a few years or even a couple of decades is too short a time to be confident that a long term trend has been observed. Nevertheless, during the 1990s public opinion swung sharply toward support of the mainstream scientific theory that supports human responsibility for global warming. And the news media has begun to abandon the position that it must not discuss climate change without giving equal time to interest groups that seek to discredit mainstream theories. *See* Frank Houston, Covering the Climate: Beware of False Conflict, Columbia Journalism Review, March–April, 2000, at p. 52.

C. What Causes Climate Change?

Although the fact that the climate has warmed is generally accepted, the cause of the warmer temperatures is still hotly debated. The great majority of climate scientists believe that human-caused emission of greenhouse gases is a major factor, but the extent of that relationship is difficult to prove, and some scientists argue that the relationship is either unproven or at best minor. Before trying to understand the dissenters, who expound a variety of different theories and often disagree among themselves, it is necessary to appreciate the position of the great majority of the scientific community.

1. Climate models: The International Panel on Climate Change (IPCC)

The growing recognition in the 1970s and 1980s of the possibility that increases in greenhouse gases were triggering climate change came at the time that high-powered computer modeling was beginning to be widely used. In various parts of the world, global climate models began to be developed by academic and governmental institutions. These institutions realized that there was a need for international cooperation if the scientific research was to proceed efficiently.

Much of the science of global warming has been developed by the International Panel on Climate Change (IPCC), a group established in 1988 by the World Meteorological Organization (WMO) and the United Nations Environment Program (UNEP). The IPCC contains representatives of all of the model builders, as well as other academic and governmental agencies with expertise in climate science. The panel consists of about 2,500 scientists from around the world.

The IPCC was directed to prepare a report every five years that would indicate the consensus of the views of the expert community about the extent of climate change that was likely to take place, and its causes. The IPCC's first report was issued in 1990, and their second report in 1995 reflected the development of new data and analyses that improve our understanding of climate change. In their 1995 report, the IPCC determined that there is a discernible human influence on climate and a link between the concentration of CO_2 and increase in temperature. Summary for Policymakers: The Science Of Climate Change IPCC Working Group I, Chapter 8 (John T. Houghton et al., eds., Cambridge University Press 1996).

The predictions made by the IPCC are based on sophisticated computer climate models created to distinguish between natural and anthropogenic influences on climate. This is achieved by a comparison of the modeled and observed spatial and temporal patterns of climate change. In the United States, some of the prominent models are located at the National Center for Atmospheric Research, the Lawrence Livermore Laboratory, the Goddard Institute for Space Studies, and the Geophysical Fluid Dynamics Laboratory. Other models are operated by institutions in other countries.[1]

The current projection, using 1990 and current emission trends as a baseline, predicts that the average global temperature will rise by about 2 degrees Celsius by 2100. This prediction accounts for climate feedbacks and the effects of sulfate aerosols. However, due to the complexity and fragility of earth's climatic system, the current warming estimate ranges from 1–3.5 degrees Celsius. Confidence in the predictions of the climate models would be improved with a reduction in the present uncertainties, but "[a] statistically significant climate change signal was nevertheless detected in the models relied on by the IPCC," K. Hasselman, Are We Seeing Global Warming?, 276 Science 934 (May 9, 1997).

Most analyses of North American conditions suggest that the temperature increases across most of North America will be greater than the global average. Preliminary indications from the National Assessment Synthesis Team, which was asked to prepare an evaluation of the potential consequences of climate variability and change for the United States through the end of the Twenty-first Century, suggest that average warming over the United States during the century will be 5 to 10 degrees F. For current information on the national assessment, consult www.atcscc.faa.gov. For the Western United States, the preliminary assessment suggests an even

---

1. Like all complex models, they are continually in need of updating. The National Academy of Sciences has criticized the inadequacy of the funding levels provided by the United States government for this research. "When the U.S. Global Change Research Program (USGCRP) recently began to look at what greenhouse warming might mean for different regions of the United States, it quickly ran up against a problem: No U.S. modelers had simulated changing regional climate in enough detail. So USGCRP policy analysts had to rely on climate models from Canada and Britain until one U.S. model finally made the grade. Even then, that model had to be partly run on computers in Japan and Australia because the United States doesn't have enough computer power at its climate centers. The obvious, but surprising, conclusion is that even as the United States tries to shape the world's greenhouse warming policy, it lags in the race to simulate climate." Richard A. Kerr, Research Council Says U.S. Climate Models Can't Keep Up, 283 Science Feb. 5, 1999 at 766. A study by the National Research Council suggests that more money needs to be invested in climate models that will be sufficiently fine-tuned that they can project regional differences. U.S. Global Environmental Change Research Program, Global Environmental Change: Research Pathways for the Next Decade (National Academy Press, 1999). Indeed, the official national assessment by the United States government is relying on a Canadian and a British model as primary sources on which to base predictions.

greater rate of increase; by the 2030s temperatures would increase by about 3 or 4 degrees F., while by the 2090s they would increase by 8 to 11 degrees. On the other hand, the heat in the Southeastern states would increase more slowly than the national average.

Figure 17–2 illustrates how the climate of particular North American cities might change if these predictions prove to be accurate. For each city in the first column, the next three columns represent cities that currently have temperatures 3–4, 6–7, and 9–10 degrees F. higher than the city in the first column. Note that the table considers only annual average temperature. It is not intended to suggest that increases in such temperature would cause the other climate conditions in the cited cities to be replicated.

Cities with annual temperatures illustrative of potential increased warming.

Cities with annual mean temperatures illustrative of potential increased warming

Current city	3-4 degree F. increase	6-7 degree F. increase	9-10 degree F. increase
Winnipeg	Quebec	Montreal	Toronto
Bismarck	Sioux Falls	Toledo	Columbus OH
Burlington VT	Youngstown	Boston	Wilmington DE
Buffalo	Pittsburgh	Philadelphia	Paducah
Denver	Topeka	Amarillo	Charlotte
Chicago	Indianapolis	Asheville	Washington DC
Portland OR	San Francisco	Tulsa	Fresno
New York City	Washington DC	Birmingham	Jackson MS
St. Louis	Oklahoma City	Columbia SC	Shreveport
San Francisco	Sacramento	Fresno	Waco
Nashville	Wichita Falls	Dallas	Austin
Atlanta	Columbus GA	Jacksonville	Daytona Beach
El Paso	Tallahassee	Galveston	Tampa
Los Angeles	Galveston	Orlando	Miami
New Orleans	Corpus Christi	West Palm Beach	Honolulu
Austin	Phoenix	Kahului	Key West

Figure 17–2

Source: Annual average temperatures taken from Gilbert Schwartz, The Climate Advisor, 1987; table compiled by authors.

Spirited, and occasionally acrimonious, colloquy, has ranged over many aspects of the credibility (or lack thereof) of the mathematically and physically based climate models that are used to project the climate changes resulting from a sustaining buildup of atmospheric CO_2. Some skeptics ask why should we believe such models' attempts to describe changes in such a dauntingly complex system as Earth's climate, especially given the difficulty they have had in simulating present temperature conditions without making arbitrary "flux corrections? But since 1995, some of the models have improved their accuracy and eliminated the need for such corrections. And Britain's Hadley Centre, one of the most respected modelers, now says that without any such corrections its models predict about 3 degrees Celsius warming over the next century, slightly more than the IPCC mean estimate from 1995. Michael Grubb et. al., The Kyoto Protocol: A Guide and Assessment 23 (Royal Institute of International Affairs, 1999).

Further confirmation of the models came when oceanographers assembled an array of early deep-ocean temperature data that had never been previously analyzed systematically. They reported that a large part of the warming that the models had predicted, but had not previously been found, had taken place in the deep oceans. Sydney Levitus, Warming of the World Ocean, 287 Science 2225 (March 24, 2000).

Although arguments about the models will persist, given the staggering array of variables with which they must deal, mainstream scientists such as Princeton climatologist Jerry Mahlman say that there are no credible alternatives, and that "the climate models do a reasonably good job of capturing the essence of the large-scale aspects of the current climate and its considerable natural variability on time scales ranging from 1 day to decades," while recognizing that the models contain weaknesses that add important uncertainty to the very best model projections of human-induced climate changes. J.D. Mahlman, Uncertainties in Projections of Human-Caused Climate Warming, 278 Science 1416 (Nov. 21, 1997). For an explanation of the mechanics of the climate models, *see* Martin Parry and Timothy Carter, Climate Impact and Adaptation Assessment: A Guide to the IPCC Approach (Earthscan Publications, 1998).

The IPCC's 1995 report achieved a broad consensus on what science can say about the causes of climate change. For a readable summary of the report, *see* John Houghton, Global Warming: The Complete Briefing (Cambridge University Press, 2d. Ed. 1997). Although the report based its detailed projections on modern computer models, the models were based on an underlying scientific theory, known as the "greenhouse effect," that has been known and accepted for a long time.

2. THE GREENHOUSE EFFECT

The "greenhouse effect" is the name given to the process that occurs when greenhouse gases accumulate in the atmosphere and trap heat at the surface of the earth, thus contributing to increases in temperature levels. The existence of the greenhouse effect is not denied outside of some place like the Flat Earth Society. Jean–Baptiste–Joseph Fourier hypothesized its existence in the 1820s, *see* Christianson, *supra* at 11–12, and the Swedish chemist Svante Arrhenius was awarded the Nobel prize for his calculations of the greenhouse effect as early as 1903. *Id.* at 105–115.

In addition to CO_2, other greenhouse gases include N_2O, SO_2, chlorofluorocarbons (CFCs) and tropospheric ozone. And methane, the chemical name for natural gas, is itself a powerful greenhouse gas that on a molecule for molecule basis has ten times the heat retention power of carbon dioxide. Christianson, *supra* at 219–221.[2]

Energy from the sun enables life to exist on the planet. The net effect of the greenhouse gas accumulation is that the earth's atmosphere acts as a blanket to retain the sun's heat and maintain the earth's average surface temperature of about 15°C. This heat retention is principally due to the action of the particles and gases that give rise to the greenhouse effect. The greenhouse effect is actually one of the most well-established theories in the atmospheric sciences. Venus, with its very dense carbon dioxide atmosphere, has oven-like temperatures at its surface, while Mars, with its very thin carbon dioxide atmosphere, has temperatures comparable to Antarctica in the winter. Carbon dioxide, and certain other gases, preferentially allow sunlight to filter through to the surface of the planet relative to the amount of radiant energy that the atmosphere allows to escape back up through the atmosphere to space. A certain amount of greenhouse gas is needed to keep a planet at a habitable temperature; the earth would be much colder in the absence of any greenhouse warming. But when the amount of greenhouse gases increase, there is an increase in the planet's temperature because more heat is trapped.

To summarize, the unchallenged facts about the greenhouse effect include three key propositions: (1) Atmospheric levels of greenhouse gases are increasing because of human activities; (2) Greenhouse gases absorb and re-radiate infrared radiation in a way that heats the planet; and (3) Atmospheric changes are long-lasting, because the major greenhouse gases remain in the atmosphere for periods ranging from a decade to centuries, and the climate itself has considerable inertia, mainly because of the high heat capacity of the world ocean. Mahlman, *supra,* at 1419.

3. Other Possible Causative Factors

There is little dispute that the increased atmospheric concentration of greenhouse gases is largely attributable to human activities like the burning of fossil-fuels. The debate hinges on the impact of these increased concentrations. What is being extensively debated is (1) the *degree* to which the greenhouse effect is causing the observed climate changes; (2) whether

---

2. Of course methane is ordinarily burned rather than emitted into the atmosphere. While modern methods of using natural gas can reduce unintentional methane emissions, the cumulative effect of the emissions can be substantial. And the slight leakage of natural gas that typically accompanies every stage of its use from extraction to combustion also adds substantial amounts of methane to the atmosphere, as do the operation of hog farms and cattle feedlots.

the greenhouse effect will be counteracted by other changes in world climate; and (3) what we should do about it, if anything.

Some critics challenge the conclusions of the IPCC report because they believe that it is virtually impossible to accurately predict the behavior of the global climate, and that the recent warming trend may simply be earth's natural variation at work.[3] Other commentators accept the possibility that the models may be correct, but argue that (1) future warming will probably be slow, small, and partly beneficial, or (2) the accuracy of computer models is not yet sufficiently great to justify large expenditures in reliance on them. Stevens, *supra* at 242–243. Murray Weidenbaum, a former chairman of the Council of Economic Advisers, says: "Clearly, the massive and unprecedented scale of emissions of CO_2 (the major and most durable greenhouse gas) into the atmosphere is a source of genuine worry." But he suggests that the "effects of those human-originated emissions ... can be and often have been swamped by serious natural fluctuations, such as activity related to the sun." He finds this to be just one of "many continuing uncertainties involved in developing global warming policies." Murray Weidenbaum, An Agnostic Examination of the Case for Action on Global Warming (National Policy Association, 1997).

One of the most difficult arguments to either prove or disprove is that the trends in climate change are not largely influenced by natural climatic variation that has produced cycles of warm and cold periods in the past. The natural variability of climate adds confusion to the effort to diagnose human-induced climate changes. Apparent long-term trends can be artificially amplified or damped by the contaminating effects of undiagnosed natural variations.

Some astronomers who study the sun's sunspot cycles have speculated that there may be a connection between these cycles and climate change. Princeton climatologist Jerry Mahlman says that it "is difficult, but not impossible, to construct conceivable alternate hypotheses to explain this observed warming. Using variations in solar output or in natural climate to explain the observed warming can be appealing, but both have serious logical inconsistencies." Mahlman *supra* at 1420. But some studies of tree-ring records suggest that the climate models do need to be adjusted both for changing solar variability and for periods of high-level dust following major volcanic eruptions. Rosanne D'Arrigo et. al., Northern Hemisphere Temperature Variability for the Past three Centuries: Tree-ring and Model Estimates, 42 Climatic Change 663, 671–73 (1999).

Some oceanographers have hypothesized that changes in the alignment of the moon with the sun and earth affect the earth's temperature on a 1500 to 1800 year cycle. The strength of the tides varies with the moon's alignment, and when the tides are stronger, more cold water from lower

3. For journalistic advocacy based on some of the skeptical views, *see* Antony Milne, Beyond The Warming: The Hazards Of Climate Prediction In The Age Of Chaos, (Prism Press 1996); M. L. Parsons, Global Warming: The Truth Behind The Myth (Ple-num 1995). However, politically charged characterizations of the views of scientists on these issues need to be read with caution. Each of the more well-respected dissenting scientists has an individual viewpoint that is distinct from the others.

ocean levels becomes mixed with upper level water, causing a cooling effect on the atmosphere. Fred Pearce, Is the Moon Turning up the Earth's Thermostat, New Scientist, April 1, 2000, at 12.

One of the more difficult issues posed for the model builders is to explain the discrepancies between temperature levels at the surface of the earth, which have been rising, and temperatures in the troposphere, which have been almost steady.

> Since 1979, polar orbiting satellites have monitored atmospheric temperatures on a global scale.... There is an apparent difference between the thermometer-estimated surface warming of roughly 0.20 degree Celsius per decade since 1979 and the much smaller temperature trend in the lower troposphere estimated from satellites and radiosondes.

B.D. Santer et. al., Interpreting Differential Temperature Trends at the Surface and in the Lower Troposphere, 287 Science 1227 (February 18, 2000).

It is the surface temperatures that have the impact on human activities, of course, but if the increased heat is caused by the greenhouse effect, then the temperatures in the upper air should be rising also. Mainstream scientists have been puzzled by these differences, and some sceptics have argued that changes in the network of surface recording stations have affected the global temperature value and that satellite data suggest that no real increase in global temperature has been observed.[4] However, other analysis of the satellite data indicates that when gradual changes in the satellites' orbits are taken into consideration, the data does show a steady increase. Frank J. Wentz & Matthias Schnabel, Effects of Orbital Decay on Satellite–Derived Lower–Tropospheric Temperature Trends, 394 Nature 661 (August 13, 1998).

Nevertheless, scientists still cannot fully explain why the differences exist. A review by a panel of the National Academy of Sciences concluded that the differences between surface and upper air measurements are real and not simply data glitches. The committee concluded that "major advances are needed in our modeling and interpretation of temperature profiles, along with considerable improvements in data acquisition, documentation and distribution of the data, and their analysis by the scientific community worldwide." David E. Parker, Temperatures High and Low, 287 Science 1216, 1217 (February 18, 2000).

4. POTENTIAL COUNTERVAILING FACTORS

Some sceptics of the mainstream theories of climate change argue that the greenhouse effect will be largely negated by other changes in climate

---

4. There is also a possibility that the temperature records have been affected by increasing urbanization. One recent study compared the difference between a long record of deep soil temperatures, which had been maintained at the University of Illinois, with the surface temperatures reported during that period. It supports the position that current models may be understating the "urban heat island" effect. Stanley A. Chagnon, A Rare Long Record of Deep Soil Temperatures Defines Temporal Temperature Changes and an Urban Heat Island, 42 Climatic Change 531, 535 (1999).

that will be taking place. One of the biggest hurdles for the modelers is prediction of future cloud cover. The computer modelers are the first to admit that the science of modeling is still relatively young and will undoubtedly improve with time. Some sceptics have suggested that increased cloudiness will counteract greenhouse heating. The most prominent of these is MIT meteorology professor Richard Lindzen.

> According to Lindzen and scientists of a like turn of mind, additional cloud cover will boost negative feedback by reflecting more light and cooling the planet, thus short-circuiting the glum scenario advanced by environmentalists. Yet many of Lindzen's peers are skeptical. Their research indicates that a substantial increase in clouds will contribute to a warming of the air and sea, bringing about a number of positive feedbacks such as the melting of the polar ice.

Christianson, *supra* at 202–203.

The substitution of cloudier weather for warmer weather does not necessarily cheer the average person. Jerry Mahlman suggests that projections of increased water vapor in the atmosphere have a greater than 99 out of 100 chance of being true within the predicted range. "Global mean amounts of water vapor will increase in the lower troposphere (0 to 3 km) in approximately exponential proportion (roughly 6% per 1°C of warming) to the global mean temperature change. The typical relative humidities would probably change substantially less, in percentage terms, than would water vapor concentrations." Mahlman, *supra* at 1417. Because the climate models do not agree with Lindzen's predictions, and because Lindzen does not have his own computer model of the impact of greater cloud cover, there has apparently been no consensus on what the impact of increased cloud cover would be if it occurred. Christianson, *supra* at 201–203.

Nevertheless, we know that changes in other radiatively active substances offset somewhat the warming effect of increased greenhouse gases. There have been decreases in lower stratospheric ozone and increases in sulfate particles, and both of these factors should have produced cooling effects in the stratosphere, and such a trend has been observed, consistent with model predictions. Mahlman, *supra* at 1420.

> The stratosphere will continue to cool significantly as CO_2 increases. If ozone continues to decrease, the cooling will be magnified. There is no known mechanism to prevent the global mean cooling of the stratosphere under these scenarios. Global mean amounts of water vapor will increase in the lower troposphere (0 to 3 km) in approximately exponential proportion (roughly 6% per 1°C of warming) to the global mean temperature change. The typical relative humidities would probably change substantially less, in percentage terms, than would water vapor concentrations. *Id.*

On the other hand, the increase in sulfate particles in the air that accompanied the Twentieth Century is likely to be reversed, at least in the United States, as increasingly strict environmental regulations kick in during the early years of the Twenty-first Century. This means that the cooling influence of these particles will lessen over time. Tom M. L. Wigley, The Science of Climate Change: Global and U.S. Perspectives 16, 21 (Pew Center on Global Climate Change 1999).

On balance, do the various other possible causes or countervailing factors raise sufficient questions about mainstream climate change theory that the theory does not produce reliable evidence for reliance by policy makers? One court has been presented directly with that issue:

In the Matter of the Quantification of Environmental Costs Pursuant to Laws of Minnesota 1993, Chapter 356, Section 3

578 N.W.2d 794 (Minn.App.1998).

■ RANDALL, J.: The Minnesota Legislature directed the Minnesota Public Utilities Commission (the commission) to determine environmental cost values for each method of electricity generation and required utilities to use those values in proceedings before the commission. The commission set interim environmental cost values for five air pollutants on March 1, 1994, including carbon dioxide (CO_2). The commission also initiated a contested case proceeding to set final environmental cost values and appointed an administrative law judge (ALJ) to preside over the proceedings. On January 3, 1997, the commission set final values for six air pollutants. The commission established four separate geographic ranges to more accurately represent environmental costs corresponding to pollutants emitted in urban, metropolitan fringe, rural areas, and areas "within 200 miles of the Minnesota border." Several parties objected to the commission's decision concerning the value set for CO_2 and requested reconsideration. Upon reconsideration, the commission removed the cost value for CO_2 in the 200 mile range, but did not change the values for other pollutants in that range. The relators filed a certiorari appeal alleging that the commission's decision to set values for CO_2 was improper. Other parties filed notices of review on separate issues. We affirm.

The relators, Lignite Energy Council (LEC), and the Environmental Coalition (the EC) assert challenges to the commission's order setting environmental cost values for CO_2. The relators argue that (1) the commission should not be entitled to great deference because the commission was acting outside of its realm of expertise; (2) the commission decision to set values for CO_2 was not supported by substantial evidence and/or its decision was arbitrary and capricious because the testimony of Dr. Ciborowski, an expert witness, (and the bases for his testimony) was grounded in incomplete data, speculation, conjecture, and uncertainty; and (3) there is no substantial evidence that CO_2 causes or contributes to serious environmental damage. We address each contention in turn.

Was the commission acting within its realm of expertise? The relators argue that no special deference is due to the commission because it was not acting within its realm of expertise in evaluating global economic conditions, the scientific properties and analysis of CO_2, and the effects of CO_2 on the environment. We disagree. Here, the legislature assigned the task of determining environmental cost values to the administrative agency it presumably thought would be most appropriate to take on this responsibility. There is no challenge that the legislature made an improper delegation of authority to the agency, and it is fundamental that the courts cannot take on the functions of administrative agencies without violating the separation of powers. Thus, this court will not substitute its judgment for the commission's in such a situation.

Was the commission's decision concerning the CO_2 values proper? There is considerable debate as to which standard of review applies. Here, the ALJ heard evidence in the form of oral and written testimony, weighed the evidence on a preponderance of the evidence standard, and made findings of fact concerning environmental cost values. Further, the commission chose to employ a contested case procedure. Given these circumstances, the commission acted in a quasi-judicial capacity in determining facts and in resolving the rights of the parties, and as such, its decision is subject to the substantial evidence test.

The relators argue that the speculative nature of the evidence (specifically Dr. Ciborowski's testimony) on which the commission relied in setting the CO_2 values shows that commission's decision is not supported by the record. We disagree. Here, the record shows that Dr. Ciborowski's testimony and recommendations, as relators contend, are based on some assumptions, speculations, and uncertainties in data. But the ALJ conducted a careful review of (1) Intergovernmental Panel on Climate Change (IPCC) research and the peer review process; (2) research on CO_2 values by other scientific review panels; (3) the uncertainties in the scientific reports and how the uncertainties are acknowledged in the scientific community; (4) Dr. Ciborowski's testimony and the basis for his testimony; (5) damage estimates; (6) discount rates; (7); the Minnesota Pollution Control Agency's and the Attorney General's recommended values; and (8) several parties' recommendations that a zero value be used. The ALJ determined that some testimony and suggestions were supported by the evidence and others were not, and explained the bases for his determinations.

Further, the ALJ noted that the parties had a sufficient opportunity for thorough cross-examination in his determination that Dr. Ciborowski was qualified to give an expert opinion. This determination appears to be within the ALJ's broad discretion.

Furthermore, in its order, the commission explained its decision to set the values on the following factors: (1) the IPCC report was the most accurate and useful source available; (2) some expert testimony and suggested ranges were more strongly supported by the evidence than others; (3) Dr. Ciborowski's approach was supported by the evidence; (4) the experiences of New York in setting environmental costs; and (5) the uncertainties inherent in the research would be taken into account by using a lower estimate of global damage and a higher damage discount rate. The commission also argues that it believed it should attempt to do what was practicable, given the uncertainties, instead of doing nothing as LEC's argument implies. Under these circumstances, the commission based its decision on sufficient evidence in the record (primarily the IPCC report and Dr. Ciborowski's testimony and recommendations) and has given an adequate and reasonable explanation of its decision.

Was the commission's decision that CO_2 negatively affects the environment supported by the evidence? Given the above analysis, the commission properly relied on Dr. Ciborowski's expert testimony and the IPCC report. Here, the ALJ and commission made findings of fact and adequately explained the basis underlying the determinations. Additionally, the commission acted pursuant to a valid delegation of authority from the legislature in an area in which the courts are not accustomed to dealing. Accordingly, we conclude that the commission's determination that CO_2 negatively affects the environment was proper.

While we acknowledge the concerns about the uncertain and speculative nature of the available data, we are disinclined to prohibit the state from directing its instrumentalities to engage in environmentally-conscious planning strategies. Hopefully, the administrative process ensures the use of the best information available and takes precautions to guard against the dangers surrounding the use of such data. Here, the process adequately explained its decisions....

Affirmed and motion granted.■

NOTES AND COMMENTS

1.   Quite a number of states now use a procedure similar to Minnesota's in which the decision to build a particular type of electric generating facility must take into consideration the environmental externalities of the various alternative technologies. This "environmental adder" process is discussed in Chapter 10.

2.   The coal industry presented expert testimony by a number of the prominent sceptics about climate change in the administrative proceeding that led up to this Minnesota litigation, and all of the witnesses were subject to extensive cross-examination. Some of this testimony is discussed critically in Gelbspan, *supra* at 39–61.

D.   POSSIBLE IMPACTS OF CLIMATE CHANGE

Concern about future warming of the planet has led to a good deal of speculation about what the effects of such warming would be. One obvious category of direct effects of climate warming is changes in crop yields and the range or numbers of pests that affect plants, or diseases that threaten animals or human health. Water supplies may be affected by changes in the probability of catastrophic episodes of drought and flooding if climate warming alters the number and character of destructive storms. The effect on natural ecosystems, such as the tropical forests, has also been a matter of concern.

1. TEMPERATURE AND RAINFALL CHANGES

The aspect of climate change that has captured most of the public attention is the idea that there will be "global warming." This sound bite fails to capture the complex nature of the scientists' predictions, either at the global level or at the regional level. Nevertheless, it is accurate to say that on average the mainstream theory predicts that there will be a gradual increase in average global temperature as the accumulation of greenhouse gases in the atmosphere increases.

a. GLOBAL AVERAGES

In his summary of the IPCC projections, Jerry Mahlman asserts that the following projections have a 90% likelihood of being accurate:

> A doubling of atmospheric CO_2 over preindustrial levels is projected to lead to an equilibrium global warming in the range of 1.5° to 4.5°C. These generous uncertainty brackets reflect remaining limitations in modeling the radiative feedbacks of clouds, details of the changed amounts of water vapor in the upper troposphere (5 to 10 km), and responses of sea ice. In effect, this means that there is roughly a 10% chance that the actual equilibrium warming caused by doubled atmospheric CO_2 levels could be lower than 1.5°C or higher than 4.5°C. For the answer to lie outside these bounds, we would have to discover a substantial surprise beyond our current understanding.

Mahlman, *supra* at 1418.

Of course average weather is not what we experience. We experience a wide range of hot and cold periods that average out over a period of time. It would be important to know whether climate change would bring greater or less deviation from the norm in the form of extreme hot or cold spells. The models are less conclusive on this issue, but on balance they suggest that the standard deviations of the natural temperature fluctuations of the climate system would not change significantly. This means that there would be an increased probability of extreme heat events and a decreased probability of extreme cold events, simply because of the higher mean temperature, but not a greater frequency of such events. *Id.* Changes is the nature and extent of extreme weather events will "probably not become evident in a statistically convincing way for many decades, with the exception of temperature extremes, which should become evident sooner." Wigley *supra* at 5.

Scientists also predict that, on the global scale, increases in temperature would be accompanied by comparable increases in precipitation. Thus the IPCC projects that with the warming of the climate there would be an increase in the rate of evaporation, which would lead to an increase in global mean precipitation of about 2 ± 0.5% per 1°C of global warming.

Some increase in average precipitation, and in the incidence of heavy precipitation events, has already been observed. Stevens, *supra* at 200–201.

Mahlman goes on to criticize some of the journalistic accounts of climate change for projecting changes for which there is little if any scientific support:

> There are assertions that the number of tropical storms, hurricanes, and typhoons per year will increase. That is possible, but there appears to be no credible evidence to substantiate such assertions. Assertions that winds in midlatitude (versus tropical) cyclones will become more intense do not appear to have credible scientific support. It is theoretically plausible that smaller-scale storms such as thunderstorms or squall lines could become stronger under locally favorable conditions, but the direct evidence remains weak.

Mahlman, *supra* at 1421. However, some research suggests that tropical storms, once formed, might tend to become more intense in the warmer oceans, at least in circumstances where the storms can remain over open water for extended periods. *Id.*

b.   REGIONAL EFFECTS

A person who was looking out solely for his own self interest might well take a different view of climate change if he lived on the plains of Saskatchewan than if he lived on the Maldive Islands. The prospect of a longer growing season in Canada might bring both economic and lifestyle advantages, although that is by no means certain, but the prospect of rising sea levels on low-lying islands would surely mean disaster. How can these regional differences be analyzed and taken into account?

For example, if a lengthened growing season caused the prime area for growing corn to move northward by a few hundred miles, a billion dollars a year lost by Iowa farmers could eventually become Minnesota's billion-dollar gain. To the extent such changes crossed international boundaries, they could have the potential to disrupt international relations, as happened in the dispute between the United States and Canada over acid rain. The perception that the economic activities of one nation could create climatic changes that would be detrimental to another nation has the potential for causing serious arguments about environmental justice.

The following material is one small portion of an interdisciplinary study by Texas scientists and economists that attempts to forecast the effect of climate change on the state of Texas. It illustrates the complexity of any attempt to forecast the effects of climate change at the regional level.

Judith Clarkson et. al. Urban Areas, In The Impact of Global Warming on Texas 170–180

(Gerald North et. al., eds., University of Texas Press 1995).

Evidence suggests that a changing climate will not introduce new phenomena to the regions of Texas, but merely intensify already existing conditions. The Houston–Galveston urban region, with its high groundwater table, subsidence, and long history of severe flooding along its coastline and bayous, will be particularly vulnerable and could experience permanent loss of urban land in sensitive areas, necessitating extensive relocation programs.

In addition, a rise in sea level would enable salt water to penetrate farther inland and upstream into rivers, bays, wetlands, and aquifers. Were sea level to rise, water intake facilities would have to be relocated far upstream at great expense. Coastal cities, such as those in Ford Bend County that withdraw their water directly from rivers, could be affected and may have to relocate their intake structures to a point farther upstream. The city of Corpus Christi, which withdraws water from the river following its release from Lake Corpus Christi, had to build a saltwater barrier to protect its intake structure from salt water at high tides. An additional impact of sea-level rise could be saltwater intrusion of coastal aquifers, particularly in areas where extensive withdrawal of groundwater has taken place in the past. Thus, in many different ways, the water supplies of coastal cities may be vulnerable to sea-level rise.

Along the Texas coast, the Houston–Galveston area is particularly vulnerable because of subsidence caused by groundwater withdrawal. Subsidence has exceeded 1.5 feet (0.5 m) in a bowl-shaped region more than 70 miles (110 km) across, and a few isolated spots have subsided nearly 10 feet (3 m).

Another factor increasing the vulnerability of the area to flooding is coastal erosion, which is also exacerbated by subsidence. The Gulf Coast states have the highest average annual coastal erosion rate in the nation, exceeding 5 feet per year. Of the 370 miles (600 km) of Texas Gulf shoreline, approximately 60 percent is eroding at rates between 1 and 50 feet (1–15 m) per year....

Texas experienced a devastating drought in the 1950's. Given the major population growth since that time, a repeat of such climatic conditions could be very serious for many of the state's major metropolitan areas. Even under current conditions, some metropolitan areas will have difficulty meeting future water needs (assuming continued population growth), despite the fact that municipal demand would have priority of use....

Potential water-supply problems were documented in a recent study of global warming in Texas. The study used water budgets based on the drought of record for the state of Texas in the years 1951—1960. A global warming scenario based on an average temperature increase of 3.5°F and a precipitation reduction of 5 percent was added to the 2030 demand scenario. The study determined that the municipal reservoir volume of Zone I of the Trinity River would decline to below 20 percent of capacity in the seventh year of a severe drought. The Rio Grande would be fully depleted by the seventh year—even under demand predictions for the year 2000, *without* additional global warming or precipitation change. In fact, under current conditions, the Rio Grande is seriously vulnerable in a severe drought. The study also projected that municipal reservoir volume in Zone

2 of the Colorado River would fall as low as 30 percent of capacity in the seventh year of the model drought. Thus, three important sources of surface water, which serve a major portion of the state's urban population, including Dallas and Austin, are at risk if climate change increases the frequency, duration, and/or severity of droughts. . . .

San Antonio is completely dependent on the Edwards aquifer for its supplies, and in 1990 it was within 1 day of instituting mandatory water rationing. Because withdrawal of water from the aquifer is currently unregulated, the city competes with local irrigators for limited supplies. Conflicts between user groups are likely to intensify with global climate change, as demand for water increases and recharge of the aquifer from surface water sources declines. Better management of the region's water supplies is in everybody's interest. If local entities cannot agree on a plan, there is little doubt that one will be imposed on the region by some higher level of government. As a last resort, the federal government may be forced to intervene, perhaps under the Endangered Species Act, to protect species dependent upon the spring flows at San Marcos.

Another closely related issue is water quality. Because of large surface water withdrawals, river flow below both El Paso and Dallas is reduced to a trickle in summer months and consists primarily of treated effluent from municipal wastewater treatment plants. Increasingly saline municipal and agricultural return flows and highly saline inflows from tributaries have resulted in high salinity levels in much of the Rio Grande. The water in Falcon Reservoir, the major source of supply for the Lower Rio Grande Valley, has an average value for total dissolved solids of 600 mg/1. This is more than double that found in the majority of drinking water supplies in the United States as a whole. Surface water supplies in the area are limited, and groundwater also has high levels of total dissolved salts.

While global warming may result in warmer winters and reduce demand for heating in northern regions, it most likely will increase the demand for cooling in the summer in southern states. In Dallas, for instance, a 4–5° increase in temperature will increase the number of days with highs above 100° from 19 to 78 per year. Many studies suggest that a number of climate-related factors, including increased energy use for air conditioning, will lead to relatively higher energy prices. One study, which should be considered speculative, suggests that climate change induced energy generation will increase by 7–33 percent in Texas. However, as discussed in Chapter 9, a 10–15 percent increase may be a more realistic figure for an average rise in temperature of 2°C. This increase in demand will naturally place an upward pressure on energy prices.

Another factor that could result in higher energy prices is a reduction in the use of coal as a source of electrical power. Coal has been a cheap source of power, but environmental considerations, including the fact that it produces the highest levels of CO_2 per unit of energy, may make it a less desirable option in the future. As a result of amendments to the Clean Air Act that require reductions in sulfur dioxide emissions, the capital cost of building and retrofitting coal plants has increased dramatically. Similar requirements to control CO_2 emissions and/or a carbon tax on energy sources could make coal uncompetitive with other fuels.∎

NOTES AND COMMENTS

1.   There is a large demand for specific climate change predictions at the regional and local scales where life and life support systems are actually affected. Unfortunately, our confidence in predictions on these smaller scales will likely remain relatively low. Much greater fidelity of calculated local climate impacts will require large improvements in computational power and in the physical and biological sophistication of the models. For example, the large uncertainty in modeling the all-important responses of clouds could become even harder at regional and local levels. Major sustained efforts will be required to reduce these uncertainties substantially. Mahlman, *supra* at 1421.

2.   Such regional studies that have been done offer some tentative ideas about the varying effects of climate change on different parts of the world. Model studies suggest that it is likely, though by no means certain, that the temperate regions of the Northern Hemisphere will experience decreases in soil moisture in response to increases in summer temperatures. This result remains somewhat sensitive to the details of predicted spring and summer precipitation, as well as to model assumptions about land surface processes and the offsetting effects of airborne sulfate particles in those regions. Mahlman, *supra* at 1420.

3.   The National Assessment of the Potential Consequences of Climate Variability and Change for the United States is in the process of an extensive research program that attempts to break down the impacts on the United States by region. To follow the work of the National Assessment, *see* www.atcscc.faa.gov.

4.   An exceptionally strong trend of warming temperatures in Arctic regions has raised concerns about the impact of melting permafrost that could become an impenetrable morass. Christianson, *supra* at 216–217. By 2050 or so, the high latitudes of the Northern Hemisphere are also expected to experience temperature increases well in excess of the global average increase. In addition, substantial reductions of northern sea ice are expected. Precipitation is expected to increase significantly in higher northern latitudes. This effect mainly occurs because of the higher moisture content of the warmer air as it moves poleward, cools, and releases its moisture. Mahlman, *supra* at 1420. The IPCC's analysis of the regional studies is in Robert T. Watson, ed., The Regional Impact of Climate Change: an Assessment of Vulnerability (Cambridge University Press, 1998).

2.   SEA LEVEL RISE

Small island nations, such as the Bahamas or the Maldives, have been particularly concerned about the potential of rising sea levels. Sea level rise is projected to be gradual but eventually substantial. The IPCC's projections of 50 ± 25 cm by the year 2100, at a gradual rate of 5 millimeters a year, reflect primarily the thermal expansion of sea water. Long-term melting of landlocked ice carries the potential for considerably higher increases, but with less certainty. Mahlman, *supra* at 1419.

In the United States, the areas most at risk from sea level rise are the areas along the Gulf Coast and the mid-Atlantic and South Atlantic coastal areas. In these regions the land along the coast is low and flat, and is already subsiding gradually from other causes. James E. Neumann et. al., Sea-level Rise & Global Climate Change: A Review of Impacts to U.S. Coasts 3 (Pew Center on Global Climate Change, 2000).

Concern about potential sea-level rise is the dominant theme of a group of small island states that have formed a coalition to participate in the international negotiations over climate change issues. For example, 80% of the Bahamas are five feet or less above sea level, and about 35 other countries find themselves in roughly similar positions. Stevens, *supra* at 258–259

3.   PLANT GROWTH

The higher concentrations of carbon dioxide in the air should stimulate greater plant growth. This will have both beneficial and adverse impacts on agriculture. Experiments in greenhouses have demonstrated that plants grow faster when the amount of carbon dioxide in the air is increased significantly. However, agronomists point out that plant growth is limited by available nutrients like nitrogen and phosphorus, and by water (although carbon dioxide stimulation also makes plants use water more efficiently). Faster growth may simply make plants less nutritious by diluting the nutrient content. The need for fertilizer and pesticides would increase. "Finally, some scientists believe that eventually a saturation point is reached, at which forest trees and perennial plants gain no more benefit from more carbon dioxide." Stevens, *supra* at 247.

The range of insects and other disease vectors are likely to spread as the climate warms. The complex interrelationship of all of these and other factors make it difficult to predict the extent to which a particular regional impact will be beneficial or harmful. Christianson, *supra* at 251–253. In a 1998 report, a panel of the IPCC concluded that the ability of agricultural interests to adapt to changing climate conditions would vary greatly from one part of the world to another. It suggested that the areas that would be most vulnerable would be those that (1) are already having difficulty coping with extreme weather events, (2) lack good markets or other institutions to facilitate redistribution of deficits and surpluses, or (3) lack resources to finance adaptation. Watson, *supra* at 6. Also, *see generally* George Frisvold & Betsey Kuhn, Global Environmental Change and Agriculture: Assessing the Impacts (Edward Elgar, 1999).

4. ENERGY DEMAND

In regions where temperatures become warmer, the growing season will increase and the cost of heating will be reduced. On the other hand, energy costs for air conditioning, which accounts for peak usage in most parts of the United States, will increase. The consortium of Texas academics concluded that that state would experience substantial increases in energy demand. Clarkson et. al., *supra* at 179–181.

Macroeconomists have found it difficult to model the impact of climate change on energy usage, concluding that the relationship between energy consumption and carbon dioxide emissions must be analyzed in terms of individual fuels. In addition, the capital intensive nature of the energy industries makes short term shifts in fuel usage complex and difficult. Terry Barker et. al., Global Warming and Energy Demand 311–312 (Routledge 1995).

5. BIODIVERSITY

Would the result of a changing climate be increased rates of extinction of species? The prospect concerns biologists, but studies have been inconclusive until recently. "Now biologists are ... compiling an impressive array of data suggesting that climate changes big and small can have profound effects on species. Climate's fingerprints are turning up in observations compiled over years and decades." Bernice Wuethrich, How Climate Change Alters the Rhythms of the Wild, 287 Science 793 (February 4, 2000). A Panel of the IPCC Working Group identified many regions in which ecosystem shifts were a serious concern. Watson et. al., *supra* at 4–5.

A review of the various studies by Adam Markham and Jay Malcolm concluded that eight categories of ecosystem were most at risk: (1) mangrove forests, (2) boreal forests, (3) tropical forests, (4) alpine/montane ecosystems, (5) Arctic ecosystems, (6) coastal wetlands, (7) coral reefs, and (8) island ecosystems. Adam Markham and Jay Malcolm, Biodiversity and Wildlife: Adaptation to Climate Change, in Adapting to Climate Change: An International Perspective 384 (Joel B. Smith et. al., eds., Springer, 1996).

In some parts of the world the changes in climate that have already taken place have produced noticeable changes in the composition of natural areas. In the sub-Arctic regions of North America, for instance, the warming of the 1980s and 1990s have produced substantial changes in forest composition. "The permafrost is thawing, and clouds of insects that have been proliferated in a warmer climate are killing vast stretches of Alaska's evergreen forest." Stevens, *supra* at 173.[5] Subtropical areas also stand to

---

5. Melting permafrost causes other problems as well. Extensive oil and gas facilities are located in these Arctic areas, and in many cases they have used the permafrost as a solid base for constructing buildings and pipelines. Moreover, when permafrost melts it releases extensive quantities of methane, a gas whose greenhouse impact is many times that of carbon dioxide. O.A. Anisimov & F. E. Nelson, Permafrost and Global Warming: Strategies of Adaptation, in Adapting to Climate Change: An International Perspective

lose significant ecological values. See, e.g., Eugene O. Box et. al., Predicted Effects of Climatic Change on Distribution of Ecologically Important Native Tree and Shrub Species in Florida, 41 Climatic Change 213, 238 (1999).

6. Is There a Risk of Sudden Catastrophe?

The changes most scientists predict are very gradual in nature. Although steady and inexorable, they hardly invoke in the average person the terror expected from veteran watchers of disaster movies. Some commentators have suggested, however, that more catastrophic results of climate change are possible. Although most scientists discount these possible disasters heavily, there is some scientific support for the suggestion that at least two of these theories are possible: (1) collapse of Antarctic ice shelves, and (2) sudden shifts in ocean currents.

a. ANTARCTIC ICE FIELD COLLAPSE

One of the most threatening warnings from those who condemn the failure to reduce greenhouse gas emissions is the threat that large ice shelves in the Antarctic will collapse into the sea, causing an immediate and catastrophic rise in sea levels all over the globe. Most of the Arctic polar ice is already floating in the ocean, so if it melts it would not cause the sea to rise. But much of the ice in Antarctica rests on land, as does the ice cap that covers most of Greenland. The Greenland ice cap has shrunk markedly during the 1990s, but the IPCC's forecasts suggest that in the future this may be partially offset by precipitation increases in Greenland. Stevens, *supra* at 260.

In Antarctica, scientists have found that the West Antarctic ice sheet did collapse during a warm period some 400,000 years ago, at a time when the sea level was some sixty to seventy feet higher than it is now. *Id.* At 262–63. The Worldwatch Institute claims that if the West Antarctic Ice Sheet were to melt, sea levels around the world would rise 20 feet. Geoffrey Lean, The Seas Keep Rising but the World Looks Away, the Independent (London), March 12, 2000, at 19. However, most of the models imply that the oceans around Antarctica are quite resistant to warming, unlike the Northern polar oceans. Therefore, little change in sea-ice cover is predicted to occur in Antarctica, at least over the next century or two. Mahlman, *supra* at 1419.

b. OCEAN CURRENT SHIFTS

Another widely discussed possible result of climate change is a sudden change in ocean currents. The example often cited is the possibility that the Gulf Stream might change, robbing the Northeastern United States and all of Europe of its moderating influence.

Wally Broecker of Lamont–Doherty has been the chief proponent of the idea that the on-again, off-again behavior of the ocean conveyor was

440 (Joel B. Smith et. al., eds., Springer, 1996).

> responsible for sharp, rapid climatic changes in the past.... If the world warms as much as the IPCC projects, he says, it could set in motion a train of events that would weaken or halt the conveyor. Some computer models have supported this hypothesis.

Stevens, *supra* at 285. The projected precipitation increases at higher latitudes act to reduce the ocean's salinity and thus its density. This effect inhibits the tendency of the water to sink, thus suppressing the overturning circulation. Mahlman, *supra* at 1420. The Hadley Centre's most recent model "projects some slow-down, but no collapse, of the Gulf Stream that determines weather patterns in Europe and the eastern United States and Canada–though this continues to remain a point of divergence between the models." Grubb, *supra* at 23.

Another big question mark is the interrelationship between climate change and *el niño* events. The repeated onset of extremely powerful *el niño* events (*see* Chapter 2) during the 1980s and 1990s led some observers to hypothesize that the warming of the earth's climate was responsible for the trend. Scientists have not documented any clear evidence that the overall climate change contributed to the warming of the Pacific Ocean that triggers *el niños*, but their studies have confirmed the correlation. Richard A. Kerr, Big *El Niños* Ride the Back of Slower Climate Change, 283 Science 1108 (February 19, 1999). The ability of scientists to predict *el niños* continues to improve, so that they now feel confident of their ability to predict these events a year in advance. Research Pathways, *supra* at 87.

E. Should We Attempt to Control Climate Change?

Are the likely impacts of greenhouse gas build-up so serious that we should take immediate steps to change our patterns of energy use? In any event, are the impacts at least sufficiently inevitable and serious that we need to try to adapt to the changing conditions we will be encountering? If so, what should those efforts entail?

The choices range from massive alteration of lifestyles to complete inaction. The issue has taxed the creative minds of some of the best scientists, economists and engineers. Proposed responses tend to fall into two categories: (a) prevention strategies, which would reduce the amount of greenhouse gas buildup in the atmosphere, and (b) adaptation, which would reduce the adverse effects of the greenhouse gas buildup.

1. Prevention Strategies

The lag time between greenhouse gas buildup and climate change, and the lag time in any strategy for reducing greenhouse gas emissions, means that it is almost impossible to imagine any strategy that we might undertake that would affect the climate within the first ten years after its adoption. Beyond that, there are a wide range of proposals to bring about an eventual reduction in the emission of greenhouse gases.

a. PHASING OUT FOSSIL FUELS

Some students of the problem, like journalist Ross Gelbspan, believe that almost superhuman efforts should be undertaken to reduce the build-up of greenhouse gases.

> To reduce greenhouse emissions by 60 percent will take, in whatever form, a massive, sweeping change whose proportions are as monumental as the threat itself. And it must be driven by an urgency that recognizes that planetary systems change not gradually but with abrupt and devastating shifts.
>
> What will it take? In an ideal world we would have a ten-year plan to phase out all fossil fuel burning. We would have a brain trust–of industrial leaders, engineers, government officials, energy specialists, and parents–who would evaluate the various alternative energy forms. They would decide which kinds of renewable, climate-friendly energy are appropriate for different uses and different settings. Business planners and engineers would determine how best to produce and install them. And the public relations industry would put its extraordinary expertise to positive use to promote the acceptance of renewable energy around the world.

Gelbspan, *supra* at 187.

No government has endorsed such a radical social restructuring in response to the climate change issue. Some countries, however, have begun rather extensive efforts to cut back on fossil fuel usage. In March, 2000, the British government proposed very large cuts in greenhouse gas emissions, hoping to reduce emissions to 21.5% below 1990 levels by the year 2010.

> U.K. carbon dioxide emissions dropped dramatically from 1990 to 1999, nearly 15 percent, due to a major shift from coal to natural gas in electric power production. But, facing complaints from coal miners, the British government essentially put a hold on new gas-fired generation. As a result, CO_2 emissions are projected to begin rising next year. The proposed new measures include an energy tax; negotiated agreements with energy-intensive sectors, including electric power; a voluntary agreement already secured with European car manufacturers to reduce carbon dioxide by 25 percent in new cars; and a requirement that sources of electricity include 10 percent from renewables. Continuing increases in a controversial petrol tax escalator are also on the table, the government says. The proposal is available at http://www.environment.detr.gov.uk/climatechange/

Brits Outline Massive Cuts in CO_2 Emissions, Electricity Daily, March 15, 2000.

Although these proposals were initiated by the Labor government, it was Margaret Thatcher, the long-time Conservative prime minister, who initiated serious research into the climate change issue in Britain back in the 1980s. Mrs. Thatcher, whose background was in chemistry, was responsible for the creation of the Hadley Center for Climate Prediction and

Research, one of the leading centers for climate research. Stevens, *supra* at 162.

Other European countries have also supported substantial reductions in greenhouse gas emissions, at least if they can be averaged throughout the European Union as a whole. In March, 2000, the European Commission released details of a European Climate Change Programme requiring detailed responses from individual member countries by September. Many old industrial facilities in Eastern Europe are being phased out, which will facilitate these reductions. Oil companies in Europe have been among the leaders in seeking ways to reduce emissions, especially BP and Shell, which are based in Europe and have extensive European investments. There has been little public skepticism in Europe about the potential problem of climate change.

Elsewhere in the world, however, the prospect of drastic reductions seems quite unpalatable. Developing countries such as China plan substantial increases in energy consumption as they industrialize, and they are unwilling to give up cheap resources of fossil fuel in exchange for nuclear or renewable technologies. The United States has also shown little appetite for dramatic reductions. Greenhouse emissions in the United States have continued to increase, though the rate of increase has slowed. Between 1990 and 1998, total emissions increased about 15%, but the increase between 1997 and 1998 was only 0.5%. EPA Report Will Become Basis For Tracking Kyoto, Electricity Daily, March 16, 2000.

Because of the unlikelihood that Americans would opt for sharp reductions in fossil fuel usage, attention has been focused on efforts to reduce emissions in less spectacular fashion through energy conservation and the sequestration of greenhouse gases.

b.   REDUCING EMISSIONS THROUGH ENERGY EFFICIENCY

An early study by the National Academy of Engineering recommended that the best strategy for addressing climate change, given the uncertainties that surround it, is simply to generate, distribute, and use energy as efficiently and cleanly as possible. Energy efficiency is a "tie-in strategy" because climatic change is only one of several good reasons to consider a policy of energy efficiency. What would be wasted by an energy efficiency strategy if serious global warming never materialized?

One of the simplest ways to increase energy efficiency is to encourage the use of natural gas and discourage the use of coal, which emits twice as much carbon dioxide per unit of energy produced as does natural gas. However, it will be important to ensure that uncontrolled release of methane, itself a powerful greenhouse gas, is adequately controlled.

In addition, nuclear power plants emit no CO_2 during actual plant operation. Is there a greater risk from enormous volumes of low-activity waste (CO_2) or small volumes of high-activity waste (fission products)?

The development of hydrogen-rich fuels (see Chapter 15) could also bring about substantial gains in energy efficiency as well as reduction of greenhouse gas emissions. Murray Weidenbaum argues that the economically preferable response to climate change is to wait. "Time may really be on our side. Engineers working on improving the efficiency of energy utilization say that imminent advances in technology promise important advances in the years ahead." Weidenbaum, *supra* at 8.

Thomas Casten, a leading entrepreneur in the development of cogeneration systems, argues that more efficient technologies are already available and should be utilized more frequently. He says that increasing use of cogeneration would quickly enhance energy efficiency. He contends that the deregulation of the electricity industry would have a powerful and beneficial influence on energy efficiency. Existing monopoly power reduces the need for electric utilities to employ efficient technologies, and allows them to erect anticompetitive barriers against more efficient competitors. Ending electric monopolies would force the closure of obsolete coal-burning plants in favor of more efficient combined-cycle natural gas plants that produce usable heat as well as electricity, thus reducing greenhouse gas emissions in two ways. Thomas R. Casten, Turning Off the Heat: Why America Must Double Energy Efficiency to Save Money and Reduce Global Warming 146–197 (Prometheus Books, 1998).

The EPA is promoting energy efficiency in commercial and industrial buildings through a voluntary partnership, the EPA Energy STAR Buildings partnership. The program involves conversion of buildings to energy efficient lighting and improvements in heating and air conditioning efficiency. US firms press greenhouse gas initiatives, Oil & Gas Journal, January 31, 2000, p.37.

c. SEQUESTRATION OF GREENHOUSE GASES

One appealing but questionable potential response to greenhouse gas buildup that is undergoing intense scientific study is the planting of more forests. Forests, and to a lesser extent other forms of plant life, are known to absorb CO_2 in the process of photosynthesis. Some studies suggest that the total impact of forests is significant while other studies view it as relatively minor. Research into the issue has been difficult because of a lack of baseline data on the amount of existing forest cover and the rate of its carbon absorption. Scientists are now just beginning the baseline studies needed to quantify reliably the effects of forests on CO_2. Jocelyn Kaiser & Karen Schmidt, Coming to grips with the world's greenhouse gases, 281 Science 504 (July 24, 1998). Preliminary data suggests that in the 1990s the forests sequestered between 1 and 2 billion tons of carbon annually, but in the 1980s very little sequestration took place, suggesting that sequestration is highly variable. Carbon sinks large but unreliable, says science, Electricity Daily, March 31, 2000.

A number of large multinational corporations have instituted so-called "carbon sequestration" forestry projects in the hopes that they will be able to offset the benefits from such projects against their own carbon dioxide emissions or use them in some future emissions trading program. Vanessa Houlder, Emissions Trading: Salvation or Hot Air, Financial Times, April

15, 1999. However, many biologists have expressed concern about whether the potential replacement of the natural landscape with plantation forests may lead to a loss of biodiversity or other unforseen ecological effects. Joy E. Hecht and Brett Orlando, Can the Kyoto Protocol Support Biodiversity Conservation?, 28 Envtl L. Rptr. 10508 (1998). The IPCC's Special Report on Land Use, Land Use Change and Forestry (2000) emphasizes the difficulties of measuring the impact of forestry on the release of carbon dioxide and other greenhouse gases. The capacity of forest systems for additional carbon uptake may be limited by nutrients and other biophysical factors, and increased temperatures may cause the rate of heterotrophic respiration to rise at a rate faster than the rate of photosynthesis. *Id.* at 4.

Another way of preventing CO_2 from reaching the atmosphere is to sequester it underground or in the oceans. Carbon dioxide is sometimes used in the secondary recovery of oil fields. The gas is pumped into oil-bearing formations in order to increase the amount of oil that can be recovered (*see* Chapter 6). More CO_2 could be sequestered if it were injected into other sealed aquifers independent of oil production needs. Since 1996, the Norwegian oil company Statoil has been piping a million tons of CO_2 per year into a salt dome under the North Sea. Karen Schmidt, A Way to Make CO_2 Go Away: Deep–Six It, 281 Science 505 (July 24, 1998).

Other experiments designed to pipe the gas into deep ocean waters are also being explored. Peter G. Brewer, et al., Direct Experiments on the Ocean Disposal of Fossil Fuel CO_2, 284 Science 943 (May 7, 1999). The United States Department of Energy is offering substantial research grants for work on carbon dioxide sequestration. CO_2 sequestration, offset projects grow, 143 Power #6, November–December 1999, at 8.

d. GEOENGINEERING

Could modern engineering technology counteract the effect of greenhouse gases by reconstituting the oceans and atmosphere? Some scientists have suggested adding iron to the oceans to help plankton absorb more CO_2, but there is likely to be strong opposition to the idea because of concern about unforeseen chemical and biological consequences. Vanessa Houlder, Carbon Sequestration: Not Yet Out of the Woods, Financial Times, April 15, 1999.

Relatively little serious attention has been paid to a variety of ideas to counteract the greenhouse effect by the physical emission into the atmosphere of substances that would have the effect of blocking sunlight, thus counteracting the warming influence of the greenhouse effect. When global temperatures dipped in the early 1990s, the sceptics saw support for their argument that global warming is far from imminent. However, the atmospheric scientists argued that the eruption of Mount Pinatubo in the Philippines, and the consequent rise in sulfate aerosols, explained this apparent cooling trend.[6] Stephen Henry Schneider, Laboratory Earth 64 (Weidenfeld & Nicholson 1996).

---

6. For an extended analysis of the Pinatubo eruption, see Alwyn Scarth, Vulcan's Fury: Man Against the Volcano 253–273 (Yale University Press, 1999). As Pinatubo's

Sulfate aerosols stored in the ocean and released by volcanic eruptions help combat the effects of increased greenhouse gases by acting as a type of neutralizing agent, but they are short-lived and create serious low-level air pollution. *Id.* Could we find a way to produce similar results artificially? The aerosols produced by industrial pollution presumably have some cooling and drying effect on the climate. Owen B. Toon, How Pollution Suppresses Rain, 287 Science 1763 (March 10, 2000). The risks associated with the promotion of such activities on a large scale will undoubtedly discourage serious implementation. However, for an extensive discussion and endorsement of the concept, *see* Jay Michaelson, Geoengineering: A Climate Change Manhattan Project, 17 Stan. Envtl. L. J. 73 (1998).

2.   THE NEGOTIATION OF THE KYOTO PROTOCOL

When the scientific community began to reach a consensus about the causes of climate change, the major nations of the world began a process of deciding how to react to the issue. Could international law provide a vehicle by which the countries of the world could agree upon a coordinated approach to the climate change issue? The first steps in getting the nations together to formulate a consensus on the issue were taken by various United Nations organizations.

a.   THE INTERNATIONAL POLITICS OF CLIMATE CHANGE

At the 1992 United Nations Conference on Environment and Development, the Rio Agreement was signed, pledging a commitment from the world's industrial leaders and developing nations to reduce greenhouse gases emissions. However, voluntary implementation of the goal to reduce emissions to 1990 levels by the year 2000 proved ineffective due to lack of UN funding and unimpressive performance by the Commission for Sustainable Development (CSD). In fact, not only will most states fail to reduce greenhouse gas emissions, the international energy agency has predicted "significant increases in worldwide emissions over the next 15 years," Sean T. Fox, Responding to Climate Change: The Case for Unilateral Trade Measures to Protect the Global Atmosphere, 84 Geo. L. J. 2499, 2500 (1996). *See* also Alex G. Hanafi, Legal and Institutional Issues for an Effective Program to Combat Climate Change, 22 Harv. Envtl L. Rev. 441, 457–59 (1998).

The following book review summarizes some of the political issues that have made diplomatic negotiation so difficult.

volcanic dust dissipated, the upward march of temperatures began again. The year 1997 was the hottest on record until 1998, which broke the record again. The ten hottest years of the Twentieth Century all occurred between 1986 and 1998. Christianson, *supra* at 234, 275. Although scientists caution against making long term judgments based on short term trends, the increasing heat has had a powerful impact on public attitudes toward the climate change issue.

Alan E. Boyle, Book Review: Negotiating Climate Change: the Inside Story of the Rio Convention.

(Irving M. Mintzer and J. Amber Leonard, Eds., Cambridge University Press 1994).
89 Amer. J. Int'l L. 864 (1995).

The development of a body of international law dealing with the environment is one of the more remarkable features of international law in the past twenty-five years. Starting almost from nothing, it is today an increasingly large and complex subject; its global dimensions are apparent in the instruments of the 1992 UN Conference on Environment and Development (UNCED) in Rio de Janeiro, and it has implications at various levels for North–South relations, international trade, economic development and human rights.

One of the reasons for the importance of the Rio Conference instruments, including the Climate Change Convention, is that together they set out a framework of global environmental responsibilities, distinct from earlier concerns with merely regional or transboundary responsibilities. The nature of these global environmental responsibilities is subtle and not easily expressed in terms of rights and obligations. They involve notions of sustainability and intergenerational equity; a recognition of the limitations of science and prediction, in the form of a precautionary approach to the control of potential global risks; and the institutionalization of a North–South relationship, expressed in the principle of "common but differentiated responsibility." This principle is a recognition of the reality that the contributions of developed and developing states to global environmental problems are historically different, and that their economic and technical capacity to tackle these problems also varies widely.

The Climate Change Convention, whose negotiation is the subject of this book, exemplifies these elements of global environmental responsibility. Although at one level it is correct to see the Convention as part of a lawmaking process, comparable to others that constitute most of contemporary international environmental law, the Convention is arguably much more significant for what it says about international political and economic relations than for its international law. This is most obvious in (1) its formulation of the common but differentiated responsibilities of developed and developing states; (2) the limited commitments made by developing states; and (3) the provision for access to funding and technology on which these commitments are expressly conditional. An understanding of the Convention thus requires, rather more than a lawyer's skills of interpretation, an appreciation of its political, scientific and economic context and of the dynamics of the negotiation process. . . .

Jean Ripert of France, Chair of the Intergovernmental Negotiating Committee, poses at the outset the still-unanswered question whether the universality of support for a Convention concluded after very difficult negotiations reflects a real balance of interests or merely "a legal void created by agreement to a text of no significance." The committee's Vice–Chair, Ahmed Djoghlaf, while emphasizing the important role played by developing states, remarks also on their inability to reach coordinated positions. Divisions of policy between oil producers like Saudi Arabia and the members of the Association of Small Island States were clearly apparent in the negotiations.

The developed states found it no easier to coordinate their positions. Speaking for India, Chandrashekhar Dasgupta gives a good account of how these various differences were overcome, partly because of the high political priority attached to agreeing to a text for UNCED, and partly because of the negotiating process, with its use of consensus procedures, small working groups and activist Chairs (reminiscent of the UNCLOS negotiations). This view is echoed by Bo Kjellen from Sweden, who, like others, points to the many and complex unresolved issues, which will require continuing negotiation. Goldenberg, from Brazil, points out the most important omission of all—"without 'targets and timetables' the implementation of the Convention will depend on the goodwill of OECD countries."[7] That so much depends on good will is a measure of the success of the United States in resisting any concrete commitments; but, as Nitze observes, this will be a continuing source of tension in U.S. foreign policy. Precisely because the lack of concrete commitments is the largest part of the problem, the United States must also be the largest part of the solution if the Convention is to stand any chance of success.

Thus, the prospects for the Convention, which several authors address in the latter part of the book, remain clouded and contingent on maintaining a coalition of interests that is at the same time capable of moving things forward. The process is one of "equitable dialogue" among diverse interests, but the problem is one of avoiding an outcome similar to that of UNCLOS III, without abandoning the goal of universality and common commitments. What this book does make clear about the Climate Change Convention is that, as with the French Revolution, any assessment of its long-term significance is still very premature.■

NOTES AND COMMENTS

1. The unwillingness of developing countries to make commitments to stem future greenhouse gas emissions has been the major stumbling block to meaningful participation by the United States government in programs to reduce emissions.

> All countries could suffer from climate change, although it is likely that poor countries will suffer most, due to their vulnerable geographies and economies. In addition, it is the economically developed countries of the so-called global North that have generated the most greenhouse gases since the advent of the Industrial Revolution, and they have thereby benefitted from using the global atmosphere as a sink for the harmful by-products of their economic development. Dur-

---

7. [Editors' note:] The members of the Organization for Economic and Cultural Development (OECD) are all of the major developed nations.

ing the negotiations for the Climate Convention, developing countries were unified in emphasizing the historical responsibility of developed countries for climate change. They agreed to participate in the climate negotiations only on the condition that they not be required to accept any substantial commitments of their own.

Paul G. Harris, Common but Differentiated Responsibility: the Kyoto Protocol and United States Policy, 7 N.Y.U. Envtl. L.J. 27, 30–31 (1999).

Is the developing countries' argument—that the industrial nations caused the problem and must remedy it—a persuasive one? For the view that equity requires that developing countries have a right to increase greenhouse gas emissions as a corollary of their right to economic development, *see* Christine Batruch, "Hot Air" as Precedent for Developing Countries: Equity Considerations, 17 UCLA J. Envtl. Law and Policy 45 (1998–1999).

At the present time, the United States and European countries are the largest generators of CO_2. Some estimates, however, suggest that by the year 2015 China and India will be the two leading emitters of CO_2. Christianson, *supra* at 264. *See* Note: The Kyoto Protocol and China: Global Warming's Sleeping Giant, 11 Geo. Int'l Envtl. L. Rev. 401 (1999).

2. Five years later at the "Rio Plus 5," a special session of the UN General Assembly, still no substantive commitments resulted. This led to the third conference of the parties (COP) to the U.N. Framework Convention On Climate Change held in Kyoto, Japan in December 1997.

ABA Section of Natural Resources, Energy and Environmental Law, Special Committee on Climate Change and Sustainable Development, 1997 Annual Report

On December 11, 1997, in Kyoto Japan, the Conference of Parties to the UN Framework Convention on Climate Change (FCCC) unanimously adopted the "Kyoto Protocol to the United Nations Framework Convention on Climate Change" (Kyoto Protocol). The FCCC concluded nearly two years of international negotiations involving various FCCC subsidiary bodies and resulted in an international agreement calling for binding obligations on Annex I Parties (developed countries) to reduce their greenhouse gas emissions at least five percent below 1990 levels by 2008–2012.

The U.S. will have, during the first commitment period of 2008–2012, binding obligations to reduce its 1) carbon dioxide, methane and nitrous oxide emissions seven percent below 1990 levels and 2) hydrofluorocarbon, perfluorocarbon and sulfur hexafluoride emissions seven percent below 1990 or 1995 levels. The same base years or base periods apply to all Annex I Parties except for countries with economies in transition (EITs), which are allowed some flexibility in the selection of a base year or base period. The "assigned amounts" (targets) are set forth in Annex B to protocol and include the following:

Iceland	110%
Australia	108%
Norway	101%
Russia, Ukraine, New Zealand	100%
Croatia	95%
Japan, Canada, Poland, Hungary	94%
U.S.	93%
European Union (EU) collectively, Switzerland, other EITs	92%

Targets and timetables and binding obligations. Known as Quantified Emission Limitations and Reduction Objectives (QELROs), the binding commitments and targets and timetables for Annex I parties are set forth in Article 3 and Annexes A and B. The key compromise was the EU as a bloc agreeing to a collective eight percent reduction under its so-called "bubble" (*see* Article 4 and discussion in I.A.2, *infra*), with the U.S. agreeing to a seven percent reduction level and Japan agreeing to a six percent reduction level. Thus, the commitments are politically differentiated but were not determined by any formulaic means.

Critical components of the agreement on targets and timetables were agreements on coverage of gases–the so-called "basket" approach–and "sinks," or forestry-based offsets. Coverage of all six gases was crucial to the U.S. The option of being able to elect a different baseline for the second set of gases was important to Japan and other countries. No clear consensus could be reached on sinks, so the Parties agreed to limit removals by sinks to afforestation, reforestation and deforestation since 1990, subject to later decisions by the conference, taking into account work by the Intergovernmental Panel on Climate Change. *See* Articles 3.3, 3.4 and 3.7.

"Banking" of excess reductions from the first commitment period to meet obligations in a subsequent commitment period was allowed, but "borrowing" of reductions from a subsequent commitment period to meet obligations in the first commitment period was not. *See* Article 3.13.

Policies and measures, and the EU bubble. Under Article 4, the EU received its bubble, under which it collectively will be responsible for an eight percent reduction but will also have the flexibility to assign different targets to individual Parties. Thus, some EU countries will be able to increase their emissions, while others (such as the United Kingdom and Germany) will bear a larger share of reductions. Failure by the EU to meet the collective eight percent target will mean that each Party shall be responsible for meeting its own level of emissions set out in the EU agreement. *See* Article 4.5. However, the EU was only able to obtain a weakened version of policies and measures (PAMs) in Article 2. While there is still mandatory language in Article 2, implementation or "elaboration" of such PAMs appears to be discretionary in accordance with individual Parties' national circumstances.

Emissions trading and commitments for developing countries. These two issues threatened to crater the negotiations in the early hours of December 11. Ultimately, the U.S. and other Annex I Parties insisted on emissions trading, and the non-Annex I Parties (developing countries) acceded in order to avoid total collapse of the negotiations. Later, however, although many Annex I Parties and some non-Annex I Parties sought to include a U.S.-sponsored provision so that advanced developing countries could "opt in" to Annex I commitments, the U.S. acceded to developing countries' insistence that the protocol exclude binding obligations for developing countries, the opt-in provision, and even establishment of a process for developing such commitments for developing nations.

Emissions trading, joint implementation and the Clean Development Mechanism. Because no clear consensus could be forged on many critical issues, numerous framework, shell or placeholder provisions are scattered throughout the Kyoto Protocol. Notable among these are the following provisions: emissions trading (Articles 3.10, 3.11 and 16 bis); joint implementation among Annex I Parties (Articles 3.10, 3.11 and 6); the so-called Clean Development Mechanism (Articles 3.12 and 12), which became a substitute for joint implementation between Annex I and non-Annex I Parties and for the Brazil-sponsored Clean Development Fund; credit for early action from the year 2000 (Article 12.10); and enforcement and noncompliance (Article 17).■

NOTES AND COMMENTS

1. An extensive analysis of the Kyoto Protocol is found in Michael Grubb et. al., The Kyoto Protocol: A Guide and Assessment (Royal Institute of International Affairs, 1999). President Clinton signed the Kyoto treaty, but said that he would not submit it for Senate ratification until there was a meaningful level of participation from developing countries. The Buenos Aires meeting in November, 1998, set a time frame for discussions on this issue to conclude in a two-year period, in order to try to resolve the issue. Some progress was made at Buenos Aires when Argentina and Kazakhstan became the first developing countries to announce that they were prepared to take on emissions reduction targets similar to those of the industrialized countries.

Perhaps the key question in the international politics of climate change is whether the developing countries will remain unified in their present posture. At one point during the Kyoto negotiations, some 35 developing countries supported a proposal to provide an explicit path by which developing countries might voluntarily adopt quantified commitments, but Brazil, India, China and the OPEC countries lined up solidly against it and it was withdrawn. Grubb, *supra* at 110. For a relatively optimistic look at the possibilities for reductions by developing countries, *see* Jonathan Baert Wiener, On the Political Economy of Global Environmental Regulation, 87 Geo. L. J. 749 (1999). For a critique of Kyoto from a deep ecology perspective, see Prue Taylor, An Ecological Approach to International Law: Responding to Challenges of Climate Change (Routledge, 1998).

2. The United States Congress has strongly indicated that it will not ratify the Kyoto accord unless the developing countries are brought under

the agreement. In July 1997, by a vote of 95–0, the U.S. Senate adopted Senate Resolution 98 (SR–98), the so-called Byrd–Hagel Resolution., S. Res. 98, 105th Cong., 143 Cong. Rec. S8138–39 (daily ed. July 25, 1997).

SR–98 stated, inter alia, that the United States should not be a signatory to any protocol to, or other agreement regarding, the Climate Convention that would

(A) mandate new commitments to limit or reduce greenhouse gas emissions for the Annex I [developed country] Parties, unless the protocol or other agreement also mandates new specific scheduled commitments to limit or reduce greenhouse gas emissions for Developing Country Parties within the same compliance period, or

(B) would result in serious harm to the economy of the United States....

The Byrd–Hagel Resolution reflected concerns about the effects of any climate treaty on the U.S. economy and distrust among both Republican and Democratic senators of an agreement that would exclude the developing countries. On a first reading, the Resolution sounds ominous, [but instead of] focusing on the rhetoric of the most outspoken anti-Climate Convention senators, it is instructive to look at the meaning of the Resolution made explicit by senators in floor debate.... First, rightly or wrongly, there was a concern that developing countries would have an unfair economic advantage because they would not be facing the same restrictions on economic output as the United States. Gross National Product is, for better or worse, still largely proportional to energy use and thus to GHG emissions (especially carbon dioxide). There was also the concern that U.S. manufacturing, and hence U.S. jobs, would move abroad to take advantage of relaxed environmental regulations there. Second, the Senate believed that an effective climate treaty absolutely required developing country participation. During floor debate on the Resolution, senator after senator cited the future emissions of China as justification for their position.

Harris, *supra* at 36–39.

b.   THE TRADING PROPOSALS

Economists have long advocated flexible, market-based processes for dealing with environmental issues. Several potential market-based international economic policies have emerged as a response to the climate change problem: e.g., carbon taxes, joint implementation, and international tradeable permits. Carbon taxes have generally fallen out of favor because of their tendency to aggravate distortions associated with remaining taxes on investment or labor. *See* Ian W. H. Parry, Carbon Abatement: Lessons from Second–Best Economics, in Frisvold & Kuhn, *supra* at 327–342.

The Kyoto conference gave symbolic support to "joint implementation," a system where industrialized countries receive benefits from helping developing countries with their emissions reduction commitments. Some commentators suggest that this may present a "free-rider" problem. See Hanafi, *supra* at 460, 467–69. For additional commentary on joint implementation, *see* Note: Joint Implementation: Legal and Institutional Issues for an Effective International Program to Combat Climate Change, 22 Harv. Envtl. L. Rev. 441 (1998).

The "Clean Development Mechanism" (CDM) for allowing intergovernmental transfers also received preliminary support.

> A new mechanism was set out in Article 12 to assist Parties not included in Annex I to achieve sustainable development and attain the ultimate objective of the Convention. It was also designed to assist those Parties to Annex I in achieving compliance with their quantified emission limitation and reduction commitments under Article 3 of the Protocol. The credits acquired in this way effectively raise the number of tons the acquiring country may emit above its Article 3 "assigned amount".

Peter Cameron, From Principles to Practice: The Kyoto Protocol, 18 J. of Energy & Natural Resources Law 1, 8 (2000). The CDM has been called "the Kyoto surprise" and described as the "most enigmatic and complex" part of the document. In general, the objective is to allow industrialized countries to achieve some of their emission reductions through projects undertaken in developing countries. "Quite simply, industrialized countries scent a way of alleviating their commitments, and developing countries scent money." But "so much is left open that it could take many forms." Grubb *supra* at 226. Until substantive and procedural principles are agreed upon, extended comment on the CDM and related "Joint Implementation" mechanisms would be premature.

A strong majority of the countries represented at the Kyoto conference were opposed to the idea of emission permits that could be traded internationally. Many developing countries saw the idea as "a way for rich countries to export their pollution and evade their obligations," Vanessa Houlder, Emissions Trading: Salvation or Hot Air, Financial Times, April 15, 1999. International tradable permits are being strongly pushed by the United States government, and they are attractive to private industry because the system creates a tradable asset, as opposed to taxes which create only liabilities. Christiaan Vrolijk, The Kyoto Protocol: Implications for the Electricity Sector, Power Economics, January 31, 2000. *See* also Jae Edmonds et. al., International Emissions Trading & Global Climate Change (Pew Center on Global Climate Change, 1999).

> The EU approach to emissions trading has some interesting aspects. There has been an insistence upon a Europe-wide solution. If Member States were to go ahead with different trading arrangements, this would be damaging to the idea of an internal market. Specifically, pnvate companies could face differently economic conditions in one Member State from what comparable businesses face in another Member State. There would be important state aid implications. If a state were to purchase permits on the open market and transfer them to specific enterprises free or without conditions, this might constitute

state aid and would have to be authorized in advance by the European Commission. It would otherwise distort competition with enterprises in other Member States that had to purchase permits themselves on the open market. This raises another issue: the possibility of conflicts arising between measures taken to liberalize energy markets and programs aimed at reducing greenhouse gas emissions. We might ask whether there is likely to be a "coming collision" between such measures and economic liberalization? Deregulation of electric utilities in the USA may, for example, have the potential for increasing carbon dioxide emissions over the next decade, making it more difficult for the USA to ratify.

Cameron *supra* at 13.

Potential schemes for international emissions trading have been the basis of extensive scholarly discussion. *See generally* Jonathan Baert Wiener, Global Environmental Regulation: Instrument Choice in Legal Context, 108 Yale L. J. 677 (1999); David M. Driesen, Free Lunch or Cheap Fix? The Emissions Trading Idea and the Climate Change Convention, 26 B. C. Envtl. Aff. L. Rev. 1 (1998); Comment: An Analysis of a Global CO_2 Emissions Trading Program, 14 J. Land Use & Envtl. L. 125 (1998); David M. Driesen, Choosing Environmental Instruments in a Transnational Context, 27 Ecology L. Q. 1 (2000).

The World Bank is setting up a global emissions trading fund, which it says could eventually provide industrialized nations with emissions credits. Four governments and nine companies will participate in an initial Prototype Carbon Fund, which has raised over half of a $150 million target. The Bank plans to invest the money in about 20 projects over three years and will broker negotiating prices for the emissions reductions between buyers and sellers. Emissions Trading, Electrical Utility Week, January 24, 2000.

Many economists in both the developing and the developed countries have questioned the advisability of using a system of permits that could be traded internationally. P.K. Rao believes that the high transaction costs and the high degree of uncertainty "suggest that the principle of market-based emission trading may have a long way to proceed before being effective in any sense." P.K. Rao, The Economics of Global Climate Change 128–131 (M.E. Sharpe, 2000). Murray Weidenbaum suggests that an economic analysis of the distributional effects of international emissions trading "shows the unexpected result that emissions trading among nations is, in effect, a massive shift of income and wealth from the economically advanced societies of the West to China, India, and other poor but rapidly growing nations. I do not see any support among Americans for that type of stealthy cross-border philanthropy." Weidenbaum *supra* at 7.

So, assuming that the political objections to international emissions trading can be overcome, will the technical difficulties be surmounted? University of Dundee law professor Peter Cameron summarizes:

(1) Will such a trading system evolve? Most observers believe that there are a number of significant and difficult problems that must be

settled before progress can be made. (2) If you have an emissions trading scheme, to what extent will that fit with existing regulatory mechanisms'? (3) Should a trading permit be a transferable property right? (4) How should permits for emissions trading be allocated and how can they be traded in an international marketplace? (5) How will a domestic emissions trading scheme mesh with regional and international emissions trading? (6) How will it be possible to ensure that emissions trading is transparent, low-cost and efficient? (7) How can verification of greenhouse gas emissions or sinks be ensured? (8) How can compliance with an international emissions trading regime be enforced?

In any case, regardless of whether the Kyoto Protocol ever creates binding obligations for developed states, national commitments to the principle of sustainable development and recognition of the links between a clean environment, tourism and community well-being, indicate that GHG reduction programs and emission trading schemes will develop at national and regional levels. Indeed, it is likely that national efforts to regulate emissions trading will provide models for international emissions trading in the future.

Cameron, *supra* at 17–18. The European Commission's proposal will authorize trading among members of the EU if the technical details can be worked out.

3. THE COST AND EFFECTIVENESS OF CONTROLS

Many economists have analyzed the economic impact of a cap on carbon dioxide. "It is no surprise that each analyst comes up with a different set of numbers," since they make different assumptions and use different data and models, says Murray Weidenbaum. "Yet, one overriding point emerges from examining these impact studies: the costs of meeting the proposed caps on carbon dioxide usage will be very substantial, ranging from tens of billions to hundreds of billions of dollars a year." Weidenbaum, *supra* at 5.

Most estimates of the implementation cost of greenhouse gas reduction have focused on reductions by large emitters, such as power plants. *See* Hanafi, *supra* at 450–57. But to achieve the kinds of reduction called for by advocates of major change, it would be necessary to regulate the small scale emissions of individual buildings and vehicles, which are responsible for the great majority of carbon dioxide emissions. The cost of measuring and monitoring reductions of small sources is an imposing hurdle for any system to overcome. Hanafi, *supra* at 488–95. David Fleming, the director of the Lean Economy Initiative, a British environmental group, has proposed a system of "Domestic Tradable Quotas" that would allow the "industrial economy to reinvent itself with a completely new way of meeting its energy needs," Every person would be given a Domestic Tradable Quota (DTQ), which would be an "equal per capita entitlement of 'carbon units' to cover domestic needs for fuel for all purposes, including private transport," People could trade their units in the market. Over time, the total quantity of carbon units made available would be gradually reduced. Carbon units "would be surrendered–as virtual ration coupons–to cover the purchase of all types of fuel and domestic energy," The greater the carbon emissions of the fuel or energy source, the more carbon units would have to be surrendered. "The whole transaction and all the calculations needed would be carried out using technology which is already commonplace for credit cards and direct debit systems," David Fleming, Your Climate Needs You, Town & Country Planning 302 (October, 1998).

Fleming's proposal illustrates the fact that the ubiquitous nature of carbon dioxide emissions means that virtually every aspect of our lives has some impact on the problem. Unlike the acid rain program, which is often discussed as a model for an international emissions trading program, it would be difficult to provide meaningful and equitable remedies by focusing only on the largest polluters. It is not easy to imagine public acceptance of a regulatory system as pervasive and Orwellian as the one Fleming proposes, but can meaningful reductions of CO_2 be achieved without affecting such basic activities as home heating and automobile driving? Will advances in technology make it possible to achieve reductions at this scale without the kind of restrictions that Fleming advocates?

F.   ADAPTATION TO A CHANGING CLIMATE

The other major category of potential responses to greenhouse gas buildup is adaptation. Many energy industry analysts argue that democratic societies will never accept the cost of major reductions in fossil fuel consumption. They say that the prudent course of action is carefully planned adjustment to environmental changes. Even people who advocate prevention strategies often agree that those strategies may take effect so far in the future that some degree of adaption is also necessary.

Some economists believe that the gradual nature of the changes in climate will allow us to cope with many of the changes without undue disruption. *See* Robert Mendelsohn & James E. Neumann, The Impact of Climate Change on the United States Economy 321 (Cambridge Univ. Press 1999). The key element of their argument is that, in comparison with the naturally rapid rate at which society rebuilds and changes, the relatively slow rate of predicted climate change should not be very serious. By phasing in adaptive measures over many decades the cost of the adjustment could be significantly reduced.

1.   AGRICULTURAL READJUSTMENT

One of the most obvious areas in which there are possibilities for adaptation is agriculture. Some forms of adaptation may be relatively easy to implement; *e.g.,* planting alternative crop strains that would be more suited to a wide range of plausible climatic futures, or building coastal barriers to block the advance of a rising ocean. But the application of these strategies may encounter strong opposition if they are perceived as having other adverse impacts. Construction of seawalls, for example, often destroys coastal wetlands.

A study by two economists of the potential impact of climate change on the United States (funded by the Electric Power Research Institute, an industry group) suggests that if sensible adaptation measures are implemented gradually, "moderate warming over the next century would result in a much diminished economic impact compared to" previous estimates. They suggest the agricultural sector would benefit, while the impact on energy prices and the availability of water resources would be adverse. Mendelsohn & Neumann, *supra* at 328.

> Some of the science surrounding impacts has changed. Sectors dependent upon the ecosystem appear not to be as threatened by climate change as first thought. Agronomic studies suggest that carbon fertilization is likely to offset some if not all of the damages from warming. Models of forest ecology suggest that increases in productivity and in the land base of productive forests in the Southeast could more than offset any reductions elsewhere in timber production regions. Further, estimates of the magnitude of climate change have moderated over the last decade. Whereas earlier impact studies examined the implication of climate changes of 4.5°C or more with sea levels rising a full meter, doubling projections now center on 2°C with sea level rising 0.4 m or less for the next century.[8]

Ibid at 321. They also forecast that Southern states would suffer while Northern states would benefit. *Ibid.* at 325. Other studies suggest that it is the center of the United States that would suffer the most because of drought. Kathryn S. Brown, Taking Global Warming to the People, 283 Science 1440 (March 5, 1999).

The preliminary views of the scientists conducting the national assessment of climate change in the United States are that the consequences of climate change for agriculture hinge on changes in the frequency and intensity of droughts, flooding and storms. It is these extreme weather events, rather than average conditions, that will have the greatest impact. Hopefully, the ability to predict these events over a longer range will partially alleviate any increase in their severity and frequency.

2.   PROTECTING NATURAL AREAS

As discussed in Chapter 2, most of our governmentally protected natural areas have been selected to preserve the type of habitat that was present in the area at the time protection was initiated. What will happen if climate change effectively moves habitats to new locations?

---

8. [Editors' note:] Careful reading is always advisable in interpreting statistics in the literature on climate change. Note that the authors refer to earlier studies that examined a range of numbers that included 4.5 degrees, while current studies "center on" 2 degrees. Is this a comparison of apples and oranges?

Studies of the impact of climate change on animal species are beginning to show significant geographical movements already taking place that appear to be the result of changes in climate. For example, amphibians in Costa Rican cloud forests have significantly declined in the face of warmer and drier conditions. A study of 34 European butterfly species found that their ranges had shifted to the north by from 35 to 240 kilometers. And the worldwide decline of several coral species has been linked by some scientists to climate change. Wuethrich, *supra* at 795.

Could we redesign our methods for protecting natural areas to cope with the needed changes? Flexible location of reserve boundaries is an appealing idea in principle, but it "has little precedent in the real world." Markham & Malcolm, *supra* at 392. Corridor systems that connect natural areas may become particularly important, and "fragmentation" of habitats may be "the single biggest barrier to ecosystem adaptation to a changing climate." *Id*. At 392–393.

G. CONCLUSION

It is clear that much is known about the climate system and about how that knowledge is expressed through the use of models of the atmosphere, ocean, ice, and land surface systems. This knowledge makes it obvious that human-caused greenhouse warming is not a problem that can rationally be dismissed or ignored. However, the remaining uncertainties in modeling make it evident that we cannot yet produce a sharp picture of how the warmed climate will proceed, either globally or locally.

None of these recognized uncertainties can make the problem go away. It is very likely that human-caused greenhouse warming is going to continue to unfold, slowly but inexorably, for a long time into the future. "The decades-long lag between emission of the gases and their effect on the atmosphere has not yet been fully played out. Moreover, it seems unlikely at best that atmospheric concentrations of greenhouse gases are going to stop building up anytime soon." Stevens, *supra* at 309. The severity of the impacts can be modest or large, depending on how some of the remaining key uncertainties are resolved through the eventual changes in the real climate system, and on our success in reducing emissions of long-lived greenhouse gases.

CHAPTER 18

CONTINUING ISSUES IN ECONOMIC REGULATION

Outline of Chapter:
A. Regulatory Efforts to Maintain Low Energy Prices
    1. Low Energy Prices: A Means to What Ends?
    2. Controlling Supply to Maintain Low Prices
    3. Price Caps
    4. Subsidies
B. National Merger Policy
C. Federal and State Authority Over Economic Regulation

Many of the economic issues in regulatory policy, particularly in the natural gas and electric power contexts, deal with ratemaking (Chapter 8), open access (Chapters 9 and 11), unbundling (Chapters 9 and 11), and stranded costs (Chapter 12). Other continuing issues in energy economic policy, such as efforts to maintain low energy prices and national merger policy, extend beyond the natural gas and electric power industries to oil and other resources, although regulators may use these regulatory mechanisms in the natural gas and electric power contexts too. Regardless of the energy resource being regulated, federal regulators also continue to struggle with the division in authority between national and state regulators; the concluding readings in this Chapter illustrate some of the similarities and differences between federal and state jurisdiction in the regulatory structures in the natural gas and electric power industries.

A. REGULATORY EFFORTS TO MAINTAIN LOW ENERGY PRICES

1. LOW ENERGY PRICES: A MEANS TO WHAT ENDS?

For years, federal regulators have focused on the economic policy goal of keeping energy prices as low as possible. Whether the policy involves federal hydropower (*e.g.*, the Niagara Dam), gas pump prices, or natural gas prices, federal regulators have made persistent efforts to allow consumers access to the resources. While some economists may advocate lower energy prices as a way of putting increased emphasis on efficiency, low energy prices are also a means for the promotion of other regulatory ends. Low energy costs are seen as furthering many other important national policy goals, some independent of the consumers and business goals narrowly defined within the energy sector.

First, low energy prices are intricately tied to growth in the industrial sector of the economy. For example, industrial customers consumer more electric power and natural gas than any other customer class. In many industries, such as the electro-chemical sector, energy costs are one of the largest operating expenses that businesses face. Low energy costs may make a difference in the profitability of a business operation. They may also mean that a plant will stay in operation, or that it will continue to operate in a given region or state. It is not uncommon for manufacturing plants to consider energy costs as a major factor in deciding where to locate—and relocate—their operations.

Second, low energy costs are tied to social welfare policy. For example, historically cheap access to electricity in rural areas is tied to major improvements in living conditions. Many federal programs provide assistance for low-income customers, allowing low cost access to heat and electricity.

Third, low energy prices may indirectly promote national security. For example, to the extent the U.S. depends on foreign sources of supply of oil, domestic regulators will have little ability to ensure low prices. Promoting domestic supply of oil provides some degree of insulation with the U.S. from price shocks due to foreign supply limitations. The increase in supply due to domestic sources helps to keep prices low, and at the same time low prices due to multiple sources of supply reduce the influence of foreign source countries on U.S. energy policy and security decisions more broadly.

Fourth, Americans also see low energy prices as tied to individual freedom and autonomy. The long summer drive in the family station wagon to Yellowstone or another national park is a summer memory for many of us. Without low gas prices such memories would fade from our collective consciousness. Access to energy, whether gas or electricity, allows us a far broader range of choices as consumers. We can purchase a gas or electric lawn mower, we have choices in our kitchen range, and we have options how to travel on our vacation. Low cost access to a variety of energy resources make these options possible.

So it is important to keep in mind that low energy prices, while a primary goal of national energy policy, is but a means to other ends. As is discussed in Chapter Eight, many energy resources, particularly in the electricity and natural gas sectors have historically been regulated on a cost-of-service basis by both federal and state regulators. This has worked to keep energy prices low, and has also helped further other ends. For example, cost-of-service regulation allows regulators to charge high-load industrial customers lower rates per kilowatt hour based primarily on the energy bill component (the "interruptible rates" discussed in Chapter Eight), allowing them lower average per-unit rates than other customers. Cost-of-service regulation also allows regulators to subsidize service for customers who may not be able to fully pay for the cost of service to them. Recall, for example, the writings about the duty to serve and universal service in electricity in Chapter Eight. As long as low-income customers are willing to pay the variable component of their bill, it is good business for utilities in a price regulation regime to offer them service despite their inability to pay for the full cost of service.

National efforts to deregulate the natural gas and electric power industries may also be understood as efforts to promote the national policy of low energy prices. As competition emerges in these industries, however, regulators will need to assess how effectively competitive power markets serve the other ends related to low energy prices. Does competition in electricity spurn industrial growth, or is this only true if industrial customers are offered sweetheart deals at the cost of incumbent residential customers? Will access and reliability continue in a competitive environment, or will regulators need to step in with new rules? While competition if often embraced for furthering the goal of lower energy prices, regulators must not lose sight of the policy ends low energy prices are intended to further. If they do so, they risk throwing the baby out with the bathwater of cost-of-service regulation.

2.   CONTROLLING SUPPLY TO MAINTAIN LOW PRICES

Perhaps more than any other sector of the energy industry, government regulation of oil has been dominated by the policy of keeping prices low. Oil illustrates how the policy of low prices is tied to other goals, many reverberating far beyond the energy sector of the economy. Here, regulators have shied away from cost of service regulation—historically favored in the natural gas and electric power industries—to apply a basic lesson in microeconomics: The less supply for any good, the higher prices will be, assuming that every thing else remains equal. In the oil industry, regulators have pursued the policy of low prices indirectly, by government efforts to control and monitor supply. As a public policy matter, these efforts to maintain low prices have been linked closely with the policy goal of national security.

The 1973 OPEC oil embargo (see Chapter Six on the Geopolitics of Oil) caused profound social and economic disruptions to the United States and other Western nations. In the U.S., unemployment rose from 4.7 percent in the fall of 1973 to over 8.5 percent by the end of 1974. Inflation jumped from an annual rate of 6.1 percent to 11.4 percent over the same period. One econometric study estimated that 53 percent of the loss in national output and 29 percent of the inflation was due to the embargo. A new term was coined to name the combination of high unemployment and high inflation: stagnation. The Second Oil Shock of 1979 led most forecasters to believe that world oil prices would be at the mercy of the Mideast oil exporters for decades to come.

How could the nation be weaned from this dependence on insecure oil imported from unfriendly nations? Presidents Nixon and Ford launched Project Independence; President Carter called the energy crisis the "Moral Equivalent of War" (unfortunately acronymed as MEOW) and pushed for major energy initiatives in Congress; and the nation actually did go to war in the Persian Gulf in 1991 to counter Saddam Hussein's invasion of Kuwait with Operation Desert Storm. Imports did start to fall as a percentage of U.S. consumption in 1977, but by 1983, the percentage had turned sharply upwards again. In 1999, the U.S. was more than 50 percent dependent on foreign oil compared to 32 percent on the eve of the embargo.

Perhaps the current ample supplies of energy and the fact that oil prices did not rise during the Gulf War in 1991 signal that we do not need a national energy policy focused on energy security. Nonetheless, no American wants to live through the serious macroeconomic impacts of another energy shortage, and the geopolitical vagaries of world oil supplies are not easy to dismiss. Should our nation do anything to protect its national security against supply disruptions in imported oil? Two economists discuss whether there is a rationale for government intervention in energy markets and then discuss the various options available and which ones are optimal:

James M. Griffin and Henry B. Steele, Energy Economics and Policy 216–17 (1986)

The Rationale for Government Intervention

The fact that the industrialized nations are highly susceptible to future supply disruptions does not automatically prove that a market failure exists and that government intervention is called for. After all, the vagaries inflicted by the weather on many agricultural crops are neither less severe nor more predictable than supply disruptions for oil. There is no public outcry for strategic orange juice or wheat reserves. What is so special about oil? Is it that oil is essential for life while wheat for bread is merely a want? No, obviously not, as we shall soon see.

A close look at a wide variety of commodity markets such as wheat shows active futures markets and numerous speculators who maintain substantial speculative inventories. Speculators acquire buffer inventories, which they hope to sell later at much higher prices. Is there any evidence that the levels of such speculative inventory holdings for these commodities are too small? After all, private investors can assess the probability of a shortage, weighing the probable gain against the inventory holding costs, just as accurately as the government can.

In contrast, a look at U.S. private inventories of crude oil and petroleum products reveals an inventory level just sufficient to enable the smooth day-to-day operations of the oil industry. The absence of large speculative inventories seems at first bizarre given the instability of the world oil market. But is there an explanation? The experience of domestic producers in the 1970s with oil price controls, and before that with natural gas price controls, suggests that price controls would likely be imposed in response to a supply disruption, preventing one from reaping large speculative profits.

Paradoxically, the primary argument favoring government intervention to increase emergency supplies is that private investors under-invest because they assume that price controls would likely be imposed to prevent their earning "obscene" profits. There is another prominent explanation given for the tendency to underinvest in inventories. The social value of emergency supplies during a disruption may well exceed the private value, which is the basis for the private firm's inventory level decision. For example, private demand schedules for oil may not include the external effects brought about by macroeconomic linkages. Put another way, providers of emergency supplies may not be able to appropriate the full social benefits of their inventories. They may receive only a $20 per barrel profit due to the crude price increase, but the full social benefit of that incremental oil in an emergency situation may be $30 or $40 when the macroeconomic effects are factored in. . . .

[Having discovered a source of market failure, the economists discuss the selection of an optimal set of national security programs at pp 229–38:]

Conservation. An integral part of all national security programs for dealing with embargos is oil conservation. Fortunately, conservation does not necessarily require an elaborate bureaucracy because conservation naturally occurs as a consequence of higher prices. . . . Lower-valued uses of oil will necessarily be curtailed when the market price exceeds the value of such uses.

A conservation program need not be limited to those actions which occur voluntarily in response to higher prices. Particularly when prices are controlled during a disruption, nonprice rationing devices must be used. Other conservation devices include quantity rationing, speed limit reductions, and mandatory thermostat reductions. Policies such as these were employed during the 1973 Arab oil embargo and probably will be utilized again in an impending disruption situation. . . .

The important point in a conservation policy is recognizing that it has limits. At current consumption rates, a small reduction in consumption can be achieved with minimal changes in life styles. In fact, the loss in social benefits is approximated by the market price, since at the margin the consumer is indifferent between purchasing an oil product and other goods worth the same money. As one moves up the demand curve, achieving greater and greater conservation, the foregone marginal social benefit of each additional percentage of oil saved becomes greater. At some point the foregone marginal social benefits exceed the costs of providing for emergency oil supplies. This defines the limits to a conservation policy. . . .

Self-Sufficiency in Domestic Oil Production: Drain the United States First. For Japan and the European countries, excepting the United Kingdom and Norway, domestic self-sufficiency in oil production is virtually an impossibility. Nature did not endow these countries with sizeable deposits of even higher cost oil. Consequently, to be self-sufficient in energy production, these countries would have to convert almost completely to other energy forms. At current price differentials among fuels and current technology, such a conversion would inflict impractical costs upon these economies.

For the United States, the choice is a different one. Physical limitations on the petroleum resource base are not as serious. Significant conventional oil reserves and shale oil reserves can be developed providing one is willing to pay the higher cost. Thus the United States probably has the physical reserves to raise domestic production enough to achieve self-sufficiency. Self-sufficiency would likely entail the rapid exploitation of existing conventional oil reserves, extensive exploration in offshore areas, and development of a large scale shale oil industry. The real question is not the physical capability, but the cost of this additional oil production. United States oil production is already high-cost compared to worldwide costs, and the additional oil production to reach self-sufficiency is likely to result in oil costs well above world prices.... There exist other, lower-cost alternative methods of providing security.

Another difficulty with pushing domestic oil production up to self-sufficiency is that, because it would exhaust the reserves of lower-cost oil, future generations would have to produce still higher cost reserves to achieve security. The policy of draining America first would significantly increase the cost of national security for future generations.

Drain OPEC First. If it is unwise to embark on self-sufficiency programs that would drain America first, what are the merits of a security program that would drain OPEC first, leaving domestic reserves in the ground? ... Even though undeveloped U.S. oil reserves would be formidable, the necessary oil wells, drilling equipment, and pipeline construction could not be developed instantaneously in the event of an embargo. To awaken such a dormant industry might take many years. Thus in the event of an embargo, the United States would have to rely on other methods of achieving national security.

[Furthermore] the increased costs of complete vulnerability in the interim would seem to far outweigh any future benefits.... [T]his increased vulnerability would increase the probability of an embargo, raising the expected marginal damage function. Thus, just as "drain America first" makes no sense as a long-run strategy, "drain OPEC first" makes no sense as a short-run strategy.

Long–Term Contracts. From any one country's view, a seemingly complete solution to a supply disruption problem is to arrange long-term contracts with secure oil exporters.... Since the long-term contract price would be set previously at pre-embargo levels, it would seem that a country with such contracts could be completely insulated from the apocalypse surrounding it.

But such a narrow view of the world overlooks two basic realities. First, the world's existing oil production can be seen as coming from the same bathtub. Even though one country can establish the right to purchase some portion of the secure oil present in the bathtub, the total amount of secure oil is not increased. Consequently, from a world perspective, security is not enhanced.

Second, it is unrealistic for a country to assume that it can remain unaffected by a worldwide supply disruption.... Even if a country chose to hoard its oil, the severe macroeconomic dislocations affecting its trading partners would ultimately spread to it.

There are situations where long-term contracts with secure producers can actually enhance world security. Continuing the analogy of the bathtub, if the long-term contract puts more water (oil) in the tub, security is enhanced. Suppose the long-term contract leads to the development of additional productive capacity in secure areas. The existence of such contracts could provide funds necessary for the development of additional productive capacity earmarked for purposes of fulfilling a long-term contract.

International Sharing Agreements. The International Energy Agency was formed as the consuming nations' response to the 1973 Arab oil embargo. All of the major consuming nations except France have agreed that in the event of an embargo against any one member country, all other members will share oil, so as to spread the effect of the embargo evenly over the various members. Additionally, each IEA member agrees to maintain oil storage equal to 90 days of imports, thereby significantly increasing the world's emergency oil supplies. In principle, such an agreement substantially reduces the cost of emergency supplies to any one country and reduces the probability of an embargo against any single country. Some might even argue that it completely resolves the national security problem because participants would realize that an embargo against any one nation would not be able to cripple it, so the embargo tool would never be employed.

Doubts about the effectiveness of the IEA center on the political realities of an embargo and the problems with the pricing of shared oil. While the IEA is no doubt some deterrent to an embargo, agreements among sovereign nations are frequently violated with complete impunity. Suppose country A, a nonembargoed member of IEA, were threatened by embargoing nations that it too would be embargoed if it shared oil with country B, the object of the embargo. It is entirely possible that country A would withdraw from the IEA.

The other objection raised about the IEA is the pricing of shared petroleum. Under the IEA formula, an embargoed country receives rights to purchase a predetermined quantity of the other members' crude oil. Apparently the price of the crude could be set by the IEA secretariat at levels well below world spot prices, giving incentives to purchase more crude than would be the case if world spot prices guided the decision. In effect, mechanical sharing formulas with prices set below world spot levels would only add distortions. An alternative to mechanical sharing formulas, which would fulfill the intended purpose of sharing, would be an agreement among IEA members that no country would impose limitations on its oil companies that would prohibit the reexportation of crude. In effect, the IEA could simply agree to a free market in crude trade among its member countries—a novel idea!

Reserve Standby Capacity. A frequently advocated policy offered by casual observers of the oil industry is to develop large quantities of reserve standby capacity. Owners of existing oil wells could be paid not to produce, saving this production for an emergency. Just as the agricultural soil bank took domestic farm land out of production, oil fields could be shut down until needed. Obviously, government payments would have to be large enough to compensate producers to defer production and to maintain the pumping equipment and the pipeline facilities to transport the oil to the refinery.

. . . [O]nly fields having the following characteristics are likely to have acceptably low maintenance costs per barrel: high daily production rates, reasonably low drilling costs per well (to enable infill drilling to increase production), and a location near a major refining center. Clearly, even though Alaskan North Slope wells have high daily production rates, they are very costly to drill, and the expenses of maintaining the pipeline to Valdez on standby would be exorbitant.

There are, however, some fields that meet these conditions, yielding reasonably low costs. Professors Mead and Sorensen show that the Elk Hills field, a part of the Naval Petroleum Reserve located in southern California, could be economically attractive as a reserve standby facility. . . .

At present, production from the Naval Petroleum Reserve would add perhaps only 200,000 to 300,000 barrels per day to domestic production; in general, few fields would be suited for a standby-reserve basis. . . .

Oil Storage. The single most important aspect of U.S. emergency supply policy was the creation of a strategic petroleum reserve, using salt domes located along the Gulf Coast as huge storage facilities. After the mining of salt, great sealed caverns are left deep in the earth's crust that make excellent natural storage facilities with costs only a fraction of those of above-ground steel storage tanks. The major cost of these facilities is simply the interest cost of the stored oil. Standby pipeline facilities are generally near refineries, so that transportation costs are not large.

Oil storage has long been a favorite strategy of European countries, where it is not uncommon to see storage equal to more than 90 days' consumption. In Europe, oil refiners are required by law to maintain 90 or more days' supply. Until explicit government action was taken, U.S. refiners held perhaps 20 to 25 days' consumption or less, which is the amount needed for standard operations. The National Emergency Petroleum Storage Act of 1976 provided for the creation of the Strategic Petroleum Reserve equal to one billion barrels, to have been achieved by 1980. But by 1983, the total stockpile was only about 325 million barrels, and the total goal had been revised downward to 750 million barrels to be achieved by 1989. By 1985, with reserves standing at 500 million barrels, additional purchases were suspended in order to reduce the government deficit. At the 1985 oil import level of about 5 million barrels per day, the actual stockpile would replace fully embargoed imports for a period of 100 days.

Since the supply of available salt domes is very large and imported oil can be purchased at a given price for storage, the long-run supply schedule of emergency supplies from this source tends to be flat over a considerable range. Recent estimates place the annual cost per barrel of this method of storage (including interest costs) at between $3.25 to $4.00 per barrel. In effect, oil storage places a ceiling price on emergency supplies. Other methods, such as reserve standby capacity, should be utilized up to the point that their costs equal the ceiling implied by storage.

Two major questions arise regarding the strategic petroleum reserve (SPR) as the primary element in the U.S. oil security plan. First, what is the optimal size of the SPR? Second, what is or should be the trigger mechanism to initiate withdrawals from the SPR? The answer to the question of the optimal SPR size requires a complicated analytical framework employing dynamic programming techniques together with a host of assumptions regarding the frequency, intensity, and duration of likely future embargos. Almost all studies recommend a reserve greater than 750 million barrels and most recommend a reserve greater than 1 billion barrels.

The trigger mechanism to initiate withdrawals from the SPR currently rests with the President. On the face of it, it would appear to be a simple matter to know when to begin selling oil from the SPR and at what rate, but imagine yourself as President of the U.S. facing the following situation: The Iran–Iraq war spreads as routed Iraqi troops pour into Kuwait and Iranian forces pursue, cutting off all oil shipments from Iran, Iraq, and Kuwait. The loss of 3 million barrels per day of oil supply from world markets sends spot prices up by $10 per barrel. Your economic advisors argue that since in the very short run supply and demand are most inelastic, SPR shipments should begin immediately in volumes of at least 1.5 million barrels per day, offsetting at least half of the shortfall. They argue that such a move would stabilize spot prices and bring about orderly supply and demand adjustments. But your National Security Advisor and Secretary of Defense argue that the SPR should be saved for potentially worse days to come. They fear the conflict will spread into Saudi Arabia, resulting in the loss of another 5 million barrels per day of production. In such event, they argue, war damage and sabotage of these fields will prevent any flow of oil from the Persian Gulf for at least two years. They argue that SPR reserves should be saved until the war picture is more certain. As President you opted for the "wait and see" strategy. The war is then confined to Kuwait and, by the time this becomes apparent, spot prices have risen by $30 above predisruption levels. By the time you begin production from the SPR four months later at a rate of .5 million barrels per day, the economic damage has been done.

Due to the inherent tendency to underutilize the SPR, observers have attempted to formulate a simple set of rules regarding when and how much to withdraw from the SPR. It is extremely difficult to specify the full set of rules that would apply for a large number of situations. The most appealing plan uses the options market as a signaling device for the intensity and duration of supply disruption. [The authors then describe how to use the options market as the trigger. The options system allows the aggregate expectations of the private sector about future market conditions to control rather than the expectations of government officials .. The oil is sold to the highest bidder so that it goes to the highest valued uses]. ∎

NOTES AND COMMENTS:

1. Griffin and Steele also analyze the relative merits of an oil import tariff versus oil import quotas as devices to reduce dependence on foreign oil. Both tariffs and quotas would raise the price of domestic oil; the first does so directly, like a tax, and the second does so indirectly by creating a deliberate shortage. Either way, the higher price of oil sold in the United States would then reflect a security premium and more accurately represent its market value. *See id.* at 238–42.

2. In 1999, crude oil prices (in real terms) fell to their lowest level, since 1973. The federal government took the following actions regarding the SPR:

> Deep in the ground below Bayou Choctaw, La., and Big Hill, Texas, the federal government's stockpile of oil floats in a salty brine filling a hollowed-out salt cavern.
>
> For the first time in five years, the federal government is adding to the Strategic Petroleum Reserve using a novel appeal to oil companies to restore the supply. The government has been accepting crude in lieu of a cash payment of royalties from companies producing crude on federal land [from OCS leases in the Gulf of Mexico].
>
> The government plans to pour 28 million barrels into the reserve.... This will replace the crude sold in 1996 to help balance the federal budget.
>
> While Congress has been unwilling to allocate cash to buy oil for the reserve, under this new program, the managers of thereserve are able to take in crude but no cash, as it would in a royalty-in-kind program. In the case of the [SPR], the Energy and Interior Departments could take in the oil without congressional appropriations, since the project does not require any new funds ... The effort to take oil off market began at a time of low prices, with crude trading at $12 a barrel. Since then, the price of crude is now trading at more than $18 a barrel, which is still far less than the average price the government has paid in the past.
>
> The Department plans to have [28 million barrels of new] crude in the reserve by March 2000. Oil can be withdrawn from the reserve at 4.1 million barrels per day. So the 28 million barrels added represents seven days' worth of supply [on top of the existing 565 million barrels in storage]....
>
> Congress had asked the Energy Department to sell some oil to put cash into the 1998 budget, just as it had done in 1996. But before the oil could be sold, it became clear that prices were dropping very low, very quickly, and Congress canceled the order.

Robin Brown, Royalty-in-Kind Helping Fill Reserve, Houston Chronicle, June 26, 1999, at C1.

2. It is clear that the SPR has been used for domestic political purposes other than national security, i.e., deficit reduction. The SPR has also been

caught up in the geopolitics of the United States' efforts to sustain a good relationship with Saudi Arabia, the largest of the Mideast producers, and a country ruled by a royal family that is relatively pro-Western. In the late 1970s, the U.S. was importing Saudi oil which, inevitably could be used to replace domestic supplies that were going to fill the reserve. Morris Adelman, a noted authority on world oil markets, describes the following events in his book The Genie Out of the Bottle: World Oil since 1970 at pp. 181–82 (MIT Press 1995)[citations omitted]:

> The United States stopped purchases for the SPR in November 1978. SPR imports ceased by September 1979. By then, the world market was in growing surplus. But the United States would not resume purchase without prior Saudi approval. The Saudis urged delay, which they said was "necessary to help bolster the power of pro-American Saudi officials and offset the efforts of militant pro-Arab groups seeking to gain control of the kingdom." It was said in the United States that many Saudi "senior officials are anxious to cut exports as soon as possible to placate conservative Moslems, who regard high oil production as an unsound concession to the U.S."

> ... DOE refused a Venezuelan offer to sell oil for the SPR "out of fear it might compromise Energy Secretary Charles Duncan's agreement with Saudi Arabia not to resume filling of the strategic reserve."

> ... Congressional impatience was building. SPR imports were finally resumed in September 1980, but at a very low level.... Later the GAO [General Accounting Office of the U.S. government] recommended faster filling of the SPR: "Despite abundant supplies, the United States has refrained from bidding for oil in the open market. This is widely thought to reflect a sensitivity to the wishes of Saudi Arabia."

3. Figure 18–1 shows data about the Strategic Petroleum Reserve.

4. The low oil prices of 1999 were short-lived. Between January 1999 and March 2000, oil prices soared from $11 a barrel to over $30 a barrel. With the 2000 presidential election around the corner, it should not come as a surprise that politicians exerted enormous pressure on the President to tap into the Strategic Petroleum Reserve. As of March 2000, the President had not tapped into the reserves, but had proposed the creation of a reserve for heating oil in the Northeast and requested reauthorization from Congress of presidential authority to tap into reserves. See Clinton Proposes Modest Steps to Ease Fuel Crunch; President Will Not Open Petroleum Reserve, Washington Post, Mar. 19, 2000, at A2.

Strategic Petroleum Reserve, 1977-1998
(Million Barrels, Except as Noted)

Year	Crude Oil Imports	Domestic Crude Oil Deliveries	Domestic Crude Oil Sales	End-of-Year Stocks			Days of Net Petroleum Imports [3]
				Quantity [1]	Share of Crude Oil [2] Stocks (percent)	Share of Total Petroleum Stocks (percent)	
1977	7.54	[4]0.37	0.00	7.46	2.1	0.6	1
1978	58.60	0.00	0.00	66.66	17.8	5.2	8
1979	24.43	(s)	0.00	91.19	21.2	8.8	11
1980	16.07	1.30	0.00	107.80	23.1	7.7	17
1981	93.30	28.79	0.00	230.34	38.8	15.6	43
1982	60.19	3.79	0.00	293.83	43.7	20.5	68
1983	85.29	0.42	0.00	379.09	52.4	26.1	88
1984	72.04	0.05	0.00	450.51	58.6	28.9	96
1985	43.12	0.17	0.00	493.32	60.6	32.5	115
1986	17.56	1.21	0.00	511.57	60.7	32.1	64
1987	26.52	2.69	0.00	540.65	60.8	33.6	91
1988	18.78	0.01	0.00	559.82	62.9	35.0	85
1989	20.35	0.00	0.00	579.86	62.9	36.7	81
1990	9.77	0.00	3.91	585.69	64.5	36.1	82
1991	0.00	0.03	1.72	568.51	63.7	33.2	86
1992	3.89	2.60	0.00	574.72	64.4	36.1	83
1993	5.37	6.96	0.00	587.08	63.6	36.6	77
1994	4.49	0.11	0.00	591.67	63.7	35.8	73
1995	0.00	0.00	0.00	591.64	66.1	37.8	76
1996	0.00	0.00	25.82	565.82	66.6	37.5	67
1997	0.00	0.00	2.33	563.43	64.9	36.1	[4]62
1998	0.00	0.00	0.00	571.41	63.9	34.7	66

R=Revised.   (s)=Less than 0.005 million barrels.
Web Page: http://www.eia.doe.gov/oil_gas/petroleum/pet_frame.html.

[1] Stocks do not include imported quantities in transit to Strategic Petroleum Reserve terminals, pipeline fill, and above-ground storage.
[2] Including lease condensate stocks.
[3] Derived by dividing end-of-year Strategic Petroleum Reserve stocks by annual average daily net imports of all petroleum. Calculated prior to rounding.
[4] The quantity of domestic fuel oil which was in storage prior to injection of foreign crude oil.

Sources: Domestic Crude Oil Deliveries and Domestic Crude Oil Sales: U.S. Department of Energy, Assistant Secretary for Fossil Energy; unpublished data.   All Other Data: 1977-1980—Energy Information Administration (EIA), Energy Data Report, Petroleum Statement, Annual. • 1981-1997—EIA, Petroleum Supply Annual. • 1998—EIA, Petroleum Supply Monthly (February 1999).

Figure 18-1

3.   Price Caps

One policy tool for ensuring low energy prices is price caps, mentioned by Professors Griffin and Steele and in previous chapters. A price cap limits the retail or wholesale price that a supplier can charge. Many price caps are benchmarked to inflation, allowing some flexibility in their implementation. Regulators have experimented with price caps in the context of nearly every energy resource, from gasoline to natural gas and electricity. In nearly every context in the energy sector, they have failed to achieve their overall policy goal, yet they are often embraced by federal and state regulators as a way of keeping energy prices low. Consider the following critique:

Richard J. Pierce, Price Level Regulation Based on Inflation Is Not An Attractive Alternative to Profit Level Regulation

84 NW. U. L. Rev. 665 (1990).

When the British government privatized its telecommunications industry in 1984, it was forced to confront for the first time the issue of how, if at all, to regulate that industry. It rejected traditional cost-of-service regulation in favor of a system of price level regulation. Price level regulation relies entirely on a price cap that changes automatically over time in accordance with a formula that incorporates expected future changes in costs and in productivity. The changes in regulated price are unrelated to actual changes in firm costs or profits. British Telecommunication's ceiling price at any time is determined through application of a simple formula: present price equals initial price, plus inflation, minus a three percent productivity adjustment factor (CPI-3)....

In their 1989 book, Price Level Regulation for Diversified Public Utilities, Professors Jordan Jay Hillman and Ronald Braeutigam of Northwestern University urge serious consideration of price level regulation as a substitute for profit level regulation of all natural monopolies.... I conclude that price level regulation based on the CPI-3 formula holds little realistic promise of yielding acceptable results.

Proponents of price level regulation refer to the British Telecom experience to demonstrate the viability of the concept. I doubt the predictive value of this experience for three reasons: (1) it is limited to a single context; (2) we have only four years of experience; and (3) it may constitute de facto profit level regulation disguised as price level regulation.

Recent experience with real price level regulation has much greater predictive power. The United States adopted price level regulation for important purposes in the Natural Gas Policy Act (NGPA), Crude Oil Windfall Profits Tax Act (COWPT), and the Public Utility Regulatory Policies Act (PURPA). The experience under each of those statutes is not encouraging.

In the NGPA Congress imposed price ceilings at varying levels on each of several categories of natural gas. Each price ceiling consisted of an initial price and an automatic price adjustment mechanism designed to further several goals simultaneously. The price ceiling applicable to "new natural gas'" illustrates the NGPA approach. In 1978, Congress chose an initial price ceiling slightly higher than the pre-existing price ceiling derived from profit level regulation and somewhat lower than what Congress perceived to be the price that would exist in a competitive market. Congress then selected a price adjustment mechanism based on its desire to achieve parity between the "new gas" ceiling price and the market-clearing price of gas by 1985. To accomplish this purpose the price adjustment clause was designed to reflect simultaneously four factors: (1) expected increases in nominal costs; (2) expected increases in real costs attributable to the depleting resource effect; (3) expected productivity increases; and (4) the need to close the perceived gap between the initial ceiling price and the efficient price. Based on extensive testimony, Congress ultimately selected a price adjustment mechanism that consisted of the Gross National Product implicit price deflator minus 0.2%, plus 3.5%. The first term in the adjustment mechanism was intended to reflect changes in nominal costs, while the second term was intended to reflect the net effect of the other three factors.

Even with perfect hindsight, it is difficult to determine the relationship between the initial price level Congress chose and the "efficient price" in 1978. It is easy, however, to assess the performance of the automatic price adjustment mechanism Congress chose. That mechanism performed miserably, largely because it was incapable of reflecting major changes in demand factors. The quantity of gas demanded at the new gas ceiling price soared in 1979 in response to changes in the closely related oil market in the wake of the Iranian Revolution. For two years, it appeared that Congress had seriously underestimated the rate of change in the "new gas" ceiling price necessary to yield an efficient price.

That concern was replaced quickly in 1981 with the opposite concern. The world price of oil began to decline, yielding a rapid decrease in the quantity of gas demanded at the "new gas" ceiling price. In the meantime, that ceiling price continued its inexorable climb as a function of the operation of the automatic adjustment mechanism. The costs of the factors of production later declined in response to the change in demand factors. The automatic adjustment mechanism was incapable of reflecting either the downward changes in demand or the ensuing reductions in factor costs. The ceiling price kept increasing as the efficient price decreased rapidly. Eventually, the ceiling price was more than double the efficient price.

This experiment with price level regulation in the gas industry had devastating effects on all market participants. Gas consumers were particularly hard hit, faring far worse than they would have if the government had withdrawn completely from any attempt to regulate even those components of the gas industry that possess some degree of natural monopoly power. Regulation through the use of price ceilings yielded prices higher than would have resulted from the unconstrained exercise of natural monopoly power by pipelines and distributors. Ineffective price regulation was combined with the typical anticompetitive features of economic regulation to minimize both regulatory and market constraints on prices and output. The regulated market intermediaries, pipelines and distributors, enjoyed considerable insulation from competitive pressures through the usual array of tariff provisions, regulatory barriers to entry, and regulatory barriers to exit that create barriers to entry.

This experience suggests the possibility that adoption of price level regulation in other contexts also has the potential to create allocative inefficiencies worse than those resulting from unconstrained monopoly if the typical anticompetitive features of economic regulation are retained. This raises an important issue—if we move from profit level regulation to price level regulation, do we simultaneously discard all of the constraints on competition that usually accompany regulation based on perceived natural monopoly? If we do not, the NGPA experience suggests the existence of one set of significant risks. Yet, if we abandon those aspects of economic regulation, we risk the very problems that originally caused us to impose regulatory barriers to entry, exit, and competition in natural monopoly markets.

It is tempting to dismiss the NGPA experience with price level regulation as attributable merely to a one-time error in selecting an appropriate price adjustment formula. Yet, it is not so easy to suggest ways in which Congress could have avoided its error. Congress assumed that the real costs of exploration and production attributable to the depleting resource effect would increase at a level sufficient to offset any productivity gains and to yield a net real cost increase of 3.5% per year. That assumption seemed plausible at the time. Congress can be criticized for failing to incorporate changes in demand factors in the automatic adjustment mechanism. It is difficult even today, however, to conceive of any method of accomplishing that important goal through a price adjustment mechanism designed to further the primary goal of tracking expected changes in costs.

Congress was not alone in making enormous errors in the process of implementing price level regulation under NGPA. Congress delegated authority to the Federal Energy Regulatory Commission (FERC) to identify new categories of gas produced under conditions that justified a price ceiling at or near the market price. FERC exercised this authority in 1980. It determined that gas produced from "tight sands" merited a special price ceiling. FERC decided that the incentive price applicable to this new category should be based on FERC's approximation of the present and expected future market price of gas—the "efficient price" in the parlance of price level regulation. It chose for this purpose an initial price level of $4.50 per million Btus, subject to an automatic price adjustment of twice the level of inflation. Ex post, it is easy to conclude that both the initial price and the automatic adjustment mechanism chosen by FERC were wrong. The ceiling price rose to $7.00, while the efficient price declined to less than $2.00. In this case it is also easy to criticize FERC's decision ex ante. Its estimates were naive even in 1980. It is much more difficult, however, to suggest a price adjustment mechanism that would have performed acceptably. Any of the mechanisms used or proposed for use in the new systems of price level regulation would have produced a ceiling price far higher than the efficient price.

The federal government tried a different version of price level regulation in COWPT. The "windfall profit" subject to tax was based on the difference between the market price at which a barrel of oil was sold and the "adjusted base price" applicable to that barrel. Each of three "tiers" of oil was subject to a different adjusted base price. The initial base prices selected in 1979 were $16.55, $15.20, and $12.81 per barrel. In the case of the lower two base prices, the automatic price adjustment mechanism was the level of inflation. For the higher base price category, the adjustment mechanism was inflation plus two percent, again reflecting the expected net effect of real cost increases and expected productivity increases.

The adjusted base price in this system was not intended to be the "efficient price"; Congress relied on the market for that purpose. The adjusted base price applicable to the high base price category—$16.55 plus inflation plus two percent—was intended, however, to parallel the market price, thereby yielding a steady flow of tax revenue each year. Thus, the automatic price adjustment mechanism applicable to Tier Three Oil in COWPT was designed to perform a function analogous to the automatic price adjustment mechanism in a system of price level regulation. The government expected to raise revenues of $227.3 billion through COWPT between 1979 and 1991. Its total revenues to date are a tiny fraction of that amount. The large disparity between expected and actual tax revenues is attributable entirely to one feature of COWPT. The automatic price adjustment mechanism Congress chose as a surrogate for expected future changes in the costs of finding and producing crude oil was incapable of reflecting changes in demand factors. Demand for domestically produced crude oil plummeted, while the adjusted base price increased. Eventually, finding costs also fell significantly, but the price adjustment mechanism was incapable of reflecting that change either. The adjusted base price applicable to Tier Three Oil, which was intended always to lie below the market price, has been well above the market price since 1981.

The final recent experience with a version of price level regulation arose under PURPA. Section 210 of PURPA requires state utility commissions to compel electric utilities to purchase power from qualified cogenerators and small power producers at a price that represents each utility's "full avoided cost" of generating electricity. Since cogeneration and small power production projects depend for their financial viability on continuity of markets at predictable prices, the statute required each state agency to reflect in long-term contracts the agency's projection of the utility's "full avoided cost" of generation for the next several decades. The pricing provisions of the mandated contracts typically included an initial price and an automatic price adjustment mechanism based on the agency's best estimate of expected future changes in the utility's costs. In a high proportion of cases, the price adjustment mechanism chosen by the agency produced a mandatory price to the utility far above the utility's actual avoided cost. Again, the adjustment mechanism was incapable of reflecting either major changes in demand factors or the resulting major changes in firm costs.

All of these descriptions of recent disastrous experiences with inflation-based price level regulation are drawn from the energy context. Based on these experiences, I feel confident in urging complete rejection of any inflation-based form of price level regulation for potential application to electric and gas utilities. This experience also explains in part my extreme skepticism that the CPI–3 version of price level regulation represents an alternative to profit level regulation worthy of serious consideration in any context. . . .

Having acknowledged the high social costs of profit leve regulation and criticized the theoretically promising alternative of CPI–3 price level regulation, I feel obligated to identify other alternatives that offer greater promise. The approach that offers the highest probability of improving allocative and productive efficiency depends critically on the present and expected future characteristics of a market that is now subject to profit level regulation. The alternatives to price level regulation that are likely to enhance social welfare in some contexts include: (1) plain vanilla deregulation; (2) deregulation of sales markets combined with mandatory equal access to significant sunk cost facilities; (3) deregulation combined with reliance on relational contracts; and (4) flexible pricing within boundaries. . . . ■

NOTES AND COMMENTS

1. Price caps have been integrated into many state retail restructuring plans, to the extent they limit the prices that can be charged for power. Many of the state retail electric plans discussed in Chapter Thirteen guarantee residential consumers a rate decrease or set limits on future rates. Do you think that price caps in this context will pose some of the problems Pierce discusses? Why or why not?

2. Jordan Jay Hillman and Ronald Braeutigam responded to Professor Pierce:

> Our position can be described more fully as follows: Given the serious deficiencies of profit level regulation and the potential efficiency benefits of price level regulation, especially in the case of diversified public utilities serving both natural monopolies and other markets with varying price elasticities, we should continue efforts to minimize certain impediments to the success of price level regulation in the natural monopoly markets.
>
> Pierce initially seems to agree with us about the serious deficiencies of profit level regulation and the substantial potential benefits of price level regulation. In the end, however, his views and ours on the potential comparative efficacy of the two systems diverge in two major respects: (1) we attach greater weight to the identified deficiencies of profit level regulation, and (2) we are more hopeful that credible economic standards and decisional processes important to the success of a price level regime can be established. . . .
>
> We do not differ from Pierce in finding substantial impediments to the success of price level regulation. In the case of our shared concerns, however, we sense a greater possibility of workable solutions. Other of his concerns to us seem inapposite. In particular, we find little predictive value in the notable failures he cites in the regulation or

taxation of energy commodities by rigid price formula. As Pierce notes, these prices were subject to unusual volatility. These energy commodities involve competitive markets in which the price of any single commodity is greatly affected by changes in alternative fuel prices. In the case of natural gas, the question is whether any regulation was warranted in 1978, when Congress imposed a rigid, wholly formulaic price adjustment mechanism on a commodity whose market price was driven by the price of oil. We find no analogy in this experience to the more flexible price adjustment mechanisms proposed for the retail markets of regulated public utilities with relatively stable demand. . . .

Jordan Jay Hillman & Ronald Braeutigam, The Potential Benefits and Problems of Price Level Regulation: A More Hopeful Perspective, 84 N.W. U. L. Rev. 695 (1990). But, if competition is presented as an alternative to cost-of-service regulation, do Hillman and Braeutigam's proposals still have relevance for regulators?

4. SUBSIDIES

While many federal programs have focused on keeping prices as low as possible, other economic goals also come into play. For example, federal regulators have often taken an interest in encouraging conservation or certain types of energy resource use, and have done this through a variety of subsidies and tax breaks. Subsidies and tax breaks have the advantage of spreading the costs of low energy prices across the general tax source; everyone pays for the resource, not just those who use it. They also coexist well with the broader goal of lower energy prices, as regulators are not required to increase overall prices to discourage consumption. At the same time, subsidies may raise independent problems as a regulatory tool:

> . . . [S]avings resulting from intervention in one sector could induce consumption in another. Grants, tax breaks, and below-market-rate loans encourage people to winterize their houses, thereby reducing the costs of home heating. But, unlike the workings of a general fuel-price increase, such subsidies have also enabled people to apply the savings in heating toward greater energy expenditures on everything else–not including such uses as warmed outdoor swimming pools and motorboats. . . .

Pietro S. Nivola, The Politics of Energy Conservation 5 (Brookings 1986). Consider the following critique of many of the subsidies in Carter's energy legislation:

> [T]he reliance on government sanctions and subsidies to rein in demand [has] invited a burgeoning pork barrel. . . . Truckers lobbied for extra incentives to pay for windscreens on cabs and trailers. The inter-city busline industry came mighty close to getting its axles greased with $1 billion in special tax benefits. Inland barge operators had long enjoyed the advantages of leaving to taxpayers the multibillion-dollar annual expense of constructing and maintaining the water-

> ways; now, by trotting out the argument that barges saved oil, the operators fended off renewed efforts to levy users fees.
>
> Other peculiar players reaped rewards from the logrolling free-for-all in which conservation measures were swept up. Several times, opponents of school integration managed to graft anti-busing amendments onto major energy bills on the theory that, *mirabile visu*, they would spare fuel.

Id. at 7. A question often ignored in the formulation of subsidies is whether they are cost-effective. In other words, can the outcome of changed supply or demand justify the costs that have been spent on the program. Many federal subsidies have failed to meet basic cost-effectiveness criteria, rendering in question any reliance on general tax base and spending programs to further national energy policy goals:

> A defect in almost any program of investment tax credits is that the program may support projects that would be undertaken even without government aid. Residential conservation credits for home improvements have illustrated this proclivity ... By 1980, items such as storm doors were being financed by the Treasury at a tax loss per barrel of oil saved equal to $91.93 in 1975 dollars.
>
> The potential for similar false economies hung over the system of low interest loans sponsored by the federal Solar Energy and Conservation Bank, established in 1980. The kinds of investments that qualified, and the degree to which subsidized loans departed from market rates and time frames, were such that critics feared the bank would be defraying as much as 60 percent of the costs of, say, solar hot tubs and barbeques, at an implicit price of at least $70 per barrel expressed in oil equivalents.

Id. at 7–8.

While economists have been particularly skeptical of subsidies design to change consumer behavior patterns, they have been more welcoming of technological development subsidies, such as tax breaks for innovative new fuels or generation technologies. The economic arguments for these supply-side subsidies focus on growing infant industries (such as the solar power industry) and on alleviating many of the barriers to entry that new, technologically innovative entrants face—especially in a monopolistic market. How well as PURPA worked as a subsidy program? See Chapters Eleven and Thirteen.

Discussion of subsidies in the face of the competitive restructuring of the energy sector invokes many of the same issues discussed in the context of the stranded cost problem, in Chapter Twelve.

B.   National Merger Policy

Not surprisingly, the rapidly changing structure of the energy industry has encouraged many energy companies to reevaluate their corporate holdings. Many companies have found it economically advantageous to merge with their competitors, joining forces to build a stronghold to diversify into new markets. This has an impact on the concentration of market power in the industry. The electric power industry provides an example:

> One effect of [] mergers is that the industry is becoming more concentrated. In 1992 the 10 largest IOUs owned 36–percent of total IOU-held generation capacity, and the 20 largest IOUs owned 56 percent of IOU-held generation capacity. By 2000, the 10 largest IOUs will own an estimated 51 percent of IOU-held generation capacity, and the 20 largest will own an estimated 73 percent.

Energy Information Administration, U.S. Department of Energy, The Changing Structure of the Electric Power Industry, 1999: Mergers and Other Corporate Combination ix (Dec. 1999). A movement towards concentration seems to contradict some of the goals of competitive reforms to electric power markets. But even areas that have undergone major competitive reforms still have market concentration problems. A Department of Energy Report observes:

> There is strong evidence that market power has been exercised in the electricity context. In both the United Kingdom (U.K.) And California, where data from competitive electricity markets are now available, researchers have found that wholesale power prices have been as much as 75 percent above competitive levels at times. Other studies examining electricity markets in Australia, New Jersey, and Colorado identify potential market power issues in those areas as well.

U.S. Department of Energy, Horizontal Market Power in Restructured Electricity Markets v (Mar. 2000). That report distinguishes between markets with "high" market power potential—in which a single company owns more than 75% of the capacity in the power control area and transmission import capability into the area is less than 40% of the company's capacity—and markets with low to modest market power potential—in which a single company owns 20 to 50% of capacity in the power control area and transmission import capability into the area is more than 100% of the company's capacity. *Id.* at 9.

In energy industries with little or no cost of service regulation, such as oil and coal, the Department of Justice and Federal Trade Commission evaluate mergers between energy companies under Section 7 of the Clayton Act and the Hart–Scott–Rodino Antitrust Improvements Act. In these merger proceedings, broader policy issues are often implicated. These agencies may also take an active role in the electric power and natural gas industries. Consider the testimony of a recent Chair of the Federal Trade Commission:

> The [Federal Trade] Commission has committed considerable resources to addressing the wave of consolidation in the petroleum and gasoline industry. In fiscal years 1999 and 2000 to date, the FTC's Bureau of Competition used a staggering one-third of its enforcement

budget to address issues in energy industries. In February of this year, we filed an action in federal district court in San Francisco seeking a preliminary injunction against the proposed merger of BP Amoco p.l.c. and Atlantic Richfield Company ("ARCO").

The complaint alleges that the merger would combine the two largest firms exploring for and producing crude oil on the North Slope in Alaska; that BP already exercises market power in the sale of crude oil on the West Coast; and that by acquiring ARCO, BP would eliminate as an independent competitor the firm most likely to threaten BP's market power. ARCO, the pioneer on the North Slope, has been the most aggressive explorer for oil in Alaska's history. The Commission's suit has been joined by suits filed by the States of California, Oregon, and Washington. This is the latest of a number of enforcement actions in which the Commission worked with various states in pursuit of our common interest in protecting American consumers. Last week, the Commission, the states and the parties obtained an order from the Court adjourning the preliminary injunction hearing while the Commission evaluates the parties' proposal to sell all of ARCO's Alaska operations to Phillips Petroleum Co.

The BP/ARCO case comes on the heels of the Commission's investigation of the merger between Exxon and Mobil. After an extensive review, from oil fields to the gas pump, the Commission required the largest retail divestiture in FTC history-the sale or assignment of 2,431 Exxon and Mobil gas stations in the Northeast and Mid–Atlantic, and California, Texas and Guam. The Commission also ordered the divestiture of Exxon's Benicia refinery in California; light petroleum terminals in Boston, Massachusetts, Manassas, Virginia, and Guam; a pipeline interest in the Southeast; Mobil's interest in the Trans–Alaska Pipeline; Exxon's jet turbine oil business; and a volume of paraffinic lubricant base oil equivalent to Mobil's production. The Commission coordinated its investigation with the Attorneys General of several states and with the European Commission (about 60% of the merged firm's assets are located outside the United States).

There are several particularly noteworthy aspects of the Exxon/Mobil settlement. First, the divestiture requirements eliminated all of the overlaps in areas in which the Commission had evidence of competitive concerns. Second, while several different purchasers may end up buying divested assets, each will purchase a major group of assets constituting a business unit. This is likely to replicate, as nearly as possible, the scale of operations and competitive incentives that were present for each of these asset groups prior to the merger. Third, these divestitures, while extensive, represent a small part of the overall transaction. The majority of the transaction did not involve significant competitive overlaps. In sum, we were able to resolve the competitive concerns presented by this massive merger without litigation.

The Commission also required divestitures in the merger between BP and Amoco, and in a joint venture combining the refining and marketing businesses of Shell, Texaco and Star Enterprises to create at the time the largest refining and marketing company in the United States.

The Commission challenged potentially anticompetitive mergers in other energy industries as well. Three recent matters served to protect emerging competition in electric power generation. Two of these cases were so-called "convergence mergers," where an electric power company proposed to acquire a key supplier of fuel used to generate electricity. One involved PacifiCorp's proposed acquisition of The Energy Group PLC and its subsidiary, Peabody Coal. PacifiCorp's control of certain Peabody coal mines allegedly would have enabled it to raise the fuel costs of its rival generating companies and raise the wholesale price of electricity during certain peak demand periods. The Commission secured a consent agreement to divest the coal mines, but the transaction was later abandoned by the parties. In another case, Dominion Resources, an electric utility that accounted for more than 70% of the electric power generation capacity in the Commonwealth of Virginia, proposed to acquire Consolidated Natural Gas ("CNG"), the primary distributor of natural gas in southeastern Virginia and the only likely supplier to any new gas-fueled electricity generating plants in that region. Dominion allegedly could have raised the cost of entry and power generation for new electricity competitors. Working closely with Commonwealth officials, the Commission required the divestiture of Virginia Natural Gas, a subsidiary of CNG. In a third matter, the Commission challenged CMS Energy Corporation's proposed acquisition of two natural gas pipelines. CMS itself was a transporter of natural gas, whose customers could purchase the gas from other suppliers, either for their own use or to generate electricity. The Commission alleged that the acquisition would have enabled CMS to raise the cost of transportation for its gas and electric generation customers. This case did not require divestitures, but the Commission's consent order assures that CMS cannot restrict access to its pipeline network, thus allowing new entry that should maintain a competitive market.

Prepared Testimony of Robert Pitofsky, Chairman of the Federal Trade Commission, Before the Senate Committee on the Judiciary Subcommittee on Antitrust, Business Rights, and Competition, March 22, 2000.

In more regulated energy industries, such as natural gas and electric power, FERC also plays an active role in evaluating industry mergers. FERC issues approvals of mergers designed to protect against the concentration of market power and ensure compliance with the Sherman and Clayton Acts, discussed above in the *Otter Tail* case in Chapter Eleven. Although FERC has enjoyed a modest success in implementing structural unbundling, especially from the seller's perspective, it faces a larger challenge where utilities are combining their assets in the hopes of remaining competitive. As is discussed above, the Department of Justice and Federal Trade Commission, with chief responsibility for enforcing the antitrust laws, sometimes also plays a major role in the approval of utility mergers. In addition, the Internal Revenue Service may need to evaluate mergers to determine tax liability, the Nuclear Regulatory Commission may need to approve mergers involving the transfer of nuclear facilities, the SEC may need to assure PUHCA compliance, and state public utility commissions or attorney general's offices generally have authority to allocate merger savings between ratepayers and shareholder. It is important that a consistent and quick process be in place, to encourage firms to innovate with new technologies and new mixes of assets, and to enter into new markets.

When the pace of electric utility merger filings increased in the 1990's, FERC reassessed and streamlined its approach to approving utility mergers in the electric power industry. FERC has issued a policy statement and has proposed a rulemaking with the principal goal of speeding up its approval process. *See* Inquiry Concerning the Commission's Merger Policy Under the Federal Power Act, 61 Fed. Reg. 68,595 (1996); Notice of Proposed Rulemaking, Revised Filing Requirements Under Part 33 of the Commission's Regulations, 63 Fed. Reg. 20,340 (1998). Yet, FERC has not yet adopted its proposed rule on merger filing requirements as a regulation, and the guidelines in its policy statement appear to have had more lasting influence on its approach to utility mergers. The industry continues to see FERC's merger policy as a significant impediment to corporate alignments and combinations. However, as electric utilities consider aligning with telecommunications companies, merger policy will play an extremely important role in defining the industry.

Part of the reason FERC's merger approval process is sluggish is that it often imposes conditions on the approval of mergers designed to protect against market concentration. While before Order No. 888 FERC may have conditioned mergers on market based rates or open access conditions, after Order No. 888 FERC has conditioned mergers on divestiture of generation facilities or participation in regional, multi-utility transmission entities. Of course, if a utility agrees to these conditions, it may also be conceding market power. Consider the following case:

Western Resources, Inc. and Kansas City Power & Light Company

86 Ferc ¶ 61,312, Order Setting Merger and Tariff for Hearing Issued March 31, 1999.

Western Resources, Inc. (Western Resources) and Kansas City Power & Light Co. (KCPL) have applied for Commission approval of their proposed merger under Section 203 of the Federal Power Act (FPA). The Applicants propose the creation of a new public utility, Westar Energy, Inc. (Westar), that would own and operate the electric power facilities now owned by Western Resources, KCPL, and Kansas Gas and Electric Company (KGE), a public utility that is now a subsidiary of Western Resources. Western Resources would own Westar. The Applicants also filed an open access transmission tariff for service over their combined systems. We will set the merger for an evidentiary hearing on the issues of market power and customer protection. We will set the tariff for hearing on rate issues, to become effective when the merger is consummated.

Section 203(a) of the FPA provides as follows:

> No public utility shall sell, lease, or otherwise dispose of the whole of its facilities subject to the jurisdiction of the Commission, or any part thereof of a value in excess of $50,000, or by any means whatsoever, directly or indirectly, merge or consolidate such facilities or any part thereof with those of any other person, or purchase, acquire, or take any security of any other public utility, without first having secured an order of the Commission authorizing it to do so.

The Commission must approve a proposed merger if it finds that the merger "will be consistent with the public interest."

The Commission has updated and clarified its procedures for reviewing public utility mergers in light of the changes in the electric power industry in the Merger Policy Statement, in which the Commission determined to focus its review of three issues: (1) the effect of the merger on competition; (2) the effect of the merger on rates; and (3) the effect of the merger on regulation. In analyzing this merger, the Commission will apply these three factors.

In their original analysis, the Applicants identify non-firm energy and short-term capacity as the relevant product. The Applicants identify and define relevant geographic markets using two different methods: a "regional" geographic market approach, and the destination market approach prescribed by Appendix A of the Merger Policy Statement. They argue, however, that their regional approach is preferable. This is because it would be difficult for the Applicants to target specific customers for price increases (i.e., engage in price discrimination), an assumption that is implicit in the destination market approach. They argue that systematic and sustained price discrimination is unlikely in the post-Order No. 888 world because increased transmission access and trading reduces such opportunities. The Applicants also offer analyses of power flows and price correlations to support their argument that the geographic market is regional in scope.

The Applicants' "regional" approach defines non-firm energy and short-term capacity as the relevant product. In defining the geographic market, the Applicants include as suppliers all utilities in the SPP, Union (which is now Ameren Corporation and is in Mid–America Interconnected Network (MAIN)) and all Mid-Continent Area Power Pool (MAPP) utilities that sell into the SPP. They then perform an "economic capacity test," by which they calculate the delivered cost of power from each supplier to the border of the SPP/Union area. The Applicants account for one transmission constraint from MAPP into SPP and one constraint from Southwestern Public Service Company (SPS) to the rest of the SPP.

The Applicants then evaluate pre-and post-merger concentration in the regional geographic market using several measures of a supplier's ability to provide products. These measures include: economic, marginal economic, total, and baseload coal/nuclear capacity. The Applicants further evaluate the effect of the merger on market concentration at varying price levels for economic and marginal economic capacity. Their results show that pre-to post-merger changes in market concentration exceed the Guidelines' thresholds at four of 16 price levels using economic and marginal economic capacity and in the only case for baseload capacity. In these cases, the post-merger markets are moderately concentrated and generally, changes in market concentration only slightly exceed the thresholds.

The Applicants' destination market analysis (which they assert is unnecessary) identifies 16 destination markets. Their results show that pre-to post-merger changes in market concentration exceed the Guidelines' thresholds for moderately concentrated markets in 34 of 128 (27 percent of) cases using economic and marginal economic capacity.

The Applicants conclude from their analyses that the proposed merger raises no competitive concerns and that no further analysis is warranted because pre-to post-merger changes in concentration exceed the thresholds primarily in off-peak periods. In such periods, the Applicants argue, the potential exercise of market power is of less concern because supply curves are more elastic.

The Applicants also contend that the combination of Western Resources' interests in gas transportation (through its interest in ONEOK) with KCPL's generation capacity poses no vertical competitive concerns. This is because the generators interconnected with the ONEOK gas delivery system in Oklahoma are also connected with at least one other pipeline and because Western Resources has less than a 10 percent voting interest in ONEOK....

In the Merger Policy Statement, the Commission stated that:

> ... if an adequately supported screen analysis shows that the merger would not significantly increase concentration, and there are no interventions raising genuine issues of material fact that cannot be resolved on the basis of the written record, the Commission will not set this issue for hearing. If the thresholds are exceeded, then the application should present further analysis consistent with the Guidelines. The Commission will also consider any applicant-proposed remedies at this stage. If none is presented, or if the analysis does not adequately deal with the issues, we will need to examine the merger further.

The Commission will set for hearing the competitive effects of merger proposals if they fail the above screen analysis, if there are problems concerning the assumptions or data used in the screen analysis, or if there are factors external to the screen which put the screen analysis in doubt. We may also set for hearing applications that have used an alternative analytic method the results of which are not adequately supported.

We find that several aspects of the Applicants' competitive analysis warrant further investigation at an evidentiary hearing. Foremost, the Applicants' analysis fails the screen. Pre-to post-merger changes in concentration exceed the thresholds in a significant number of instances. The fact that these instances occur across a range of relevant markets, load/price levels and capacity measures indicates potentially significant adverse effects of the proposed merger and thus, further investigation at hearing is warranted.

With regard to the Applicants' data and assumptions, we note in particular that the Applicants do not explain how transmission interfaces that will become internal to the merged firm are treated in their analysis. If the Applicants assume, without basis, that internal interface capacity is available to third parties (i.e, TDUs), then their analysis likely understates the magnitude of threshold violations in the highly concentrated Western Resources and KCPL markets. This would compound our concern that the merger might create or enhance the Applicants' incentive and ability to operate their system so as to exercise the potentially significant market power in generation indicated by their own analysis. On the other hand, if the Applicants make the conservative assumption that internal interface capacity is not available for third party use, then their analysis likely overstates the magnitude of threshold violations in their own destination markets. In that case, we may be less concerned about the potential adverse competitive effects of the merger. However, without additional information, we are unable to determine whether the Applicants' commitment to treat TDU customers like native load is appropriate and/or adequate to mitigate potential adverse competitive effects in the Applicants' own destination markets. In addition, the Commission disagrees with the Applicants' reliance on market concentration results based on a single (i.e., marginal economic) capacity measure. Rather, we believe that various capacity measures generally provide useful information regarding the effect of the merger on market concentration and should be considered in rendering a decision regarding the competitive effects of a proposed merger.

We agree with intervenors that the Applicants have not adequately supported their alternative regional analysis. The Commission is open to considering credible, well-supported alternative approaches to defining relevant geographic markets. However, the Applicants' method has not been sufficiently supported. In particular, we are concerned that the Applicants account for transmission constraints inconsistently in their regional and destination market analyses. For example, the Applicants identify only two transmission constraints in their regional market analysis, but in their revised destination market analysis, they identify over thirty instances where transactions would be limited by transmission availability. We note that disparities in system lambdas in the region affected by the merger may indicate the presence of transmission constraints that could narrow the scope of trade and, therefore, relevant geographic markets—regardless of whether a regional or destination market approach is used. Accordingly, we believe that the Applicants' regional market analysis must be further explored at hearing. At hearing, the Applicants may further develop and support their claim that the markets affected by the proposed merger have evolved to the point where price discrimination would be difficult. . . .

The Merger Policy Statement explains our concern that there be adequate ratepayer protection from adverse rate effects as a result of a merger. It describes various commitments that may be acceptable means of protecting ratepayers, such as hold harmless provisions, open seasons for wholesale customers, rate freezes, and rate reductions.

The Applicants state that they contacted their wholesale customers before filing the merger, as the Policy Statement requires, to find out their concerns. They propose a customer protection plan to ensure that customers will not have to pay increased rates as a result of the merger. The Applicants commit not to file rate increases for current full and partial requirements service customers for four years after consummation of the merger. They claim that the customer protection plan protects transmission customers in several ways. First, within 90 days after consummation of the merger, the Applicants propose to allow any customer taking transmission service from either applicant under a bilateral agreement to switch to the new single-system open access tariff. Second, for customers who do not make this switch, the Applicants will not increase rates for four years. Third, customers taking service under Western Resources' or KCPL's existing open access tariff will automatically be switched to the new single-system tariff. The Applicants will cap the rates of those that were using KCPL's tariff and that continue to use only KCPL's facilities at the rate in the existing KCPL tariff. Finally, as noted above, in the Amended Application the Applicants provided protection for KCPL's customers to ensure that they would not face higher fuel costs as a result of the merger. . . .

We will set the Applicants' wholesale ratepayer protection plan for hearing. The Applicants have not adequately demonstrated that the plan will protect their customers from merger-related harm, and intervenors raise a number of issues of material fact that, absent settlement, need to be explored at hearing.

The Applicants estimate that the merger will cost $61.9 million (transition costs), which the Applicants intend to amortize over a five-year period. This estimate does not include transaction costs. Under the Applicants' four-year wholesale ratepayer protection plan, it is unclear whether the Applicants intend to recover merger-related costs in the fifth year of the amortization period. In addition, transmission customers that either (1) voluntarily switch from stand-alone transmission agreements, or (2) are forced to switch from Western Resources' or KCPL's individual transmission tariff to the Applicants' open access merger tariff could face an increase in transmission costs through higher transmission rates and additional ancillary service charges. Therefore, the Applicants' wholesale ratepayer protection plan may not protect wholesale customers from merger-related harm.

As explained in the Merger Policy Statement, the Commission's primary concern with the effect on regulation of a proposed merger involves possible changes in the Commission's jurisdiction when a registered holding company is formed, thus invoking the jurisdiction of the Securities and Exchange Commission (SEC). We are also concerned with the effect on state regulation where a state does not have authority to act on a merger.

The Applicants say that the merger will not adversely affect regulation. With regard to this Commission's jurisdiction, the Applicants say that since Western Resources is and will remain a public utility holding company that is exempt from regulation under PUHCA, there will be no change in the Commission's authority to regulate the Applicants. With regard to state regulation, they say that the public utility commissions of Kansas and Missouri have authority to act on the merger.

We are satisfied that the merger will not have an adverse effect on regulation. Accordingly, we will not set this issue for hearing.

Intervenors raise a number of objections to the proposed tariff. For example, MJMEUC argues that the rates are unjust and unreasonable. It asks that the filing be suspended and put into effect, subject to refund, upon consummation of the merger, and that the filing be set for hearing. It says that the proposed rate of return on equity of 12.9% is excessive, since the transmission/distribution side of the business is less risky than the generation side. Moreover, the Applicants have improperly failed to directly assign certain facilities to themselves, to be recovered from customers who buy power from the Applicants. The proposed tariff is unclear as to which voltage levels are covered by the proposed rates (as opposed to being treated as distribution). MJMEUC argues that the various proposed loss factors for different voltage levels are unsupported. Finally, the charges for ancillary services are allegedly excessive.

The Applicants argue in response to KEPCO that they filed abbreviated cost support data, as the Commission's regulations allow where only moderate rate increases are sought. They say that the information KEPCO wants can only be supplied after the combined system has been operated for some time. For instance, data on losses on the combined system will only be available when the combined system has operated for a time. Until some actual experience has occurred, the Applicants say that it is reasonable to base losses on historical data on Western Resources' system. The Applicants argue that they have submitted all the information required by the Commission's regulations, since their filing qualifies for the abbreviated filing requirements.

Moreover, the Applicants argue, KEPCO's criticism of the non-rate terms and conditions of the tariff is really an attempt to relitigate the Commission's open access tariff requirements. The Applicants say that KEPCO misstates the Form 1 data filed by the Applicants. They defend their proposed rate of return on equity, arguing that it is consistent with recent Commission precedent. They also point out that their proposed network operating agreement is subject to negotiation with particular customers and argue that KEPCO's problems with it should be worked out in such negotiations rather than in this proceeding.

In response to MJMEUC's concerns about increased transmission rates, particularly for ancillary services, the Applicants argue that MJMEUC its adequately protected. They point out that the rates of KCPL customers who continue to use only KCPL's system are capped for four years after the merger. The Applicants also defend their proposed tariff rates on the issues of tax allocation, Account 565 expenses, and other arguments raised by KEPCO and MJMEUC.

Our preliminary analysis of the proposed tariff indicates that it has not been shown to be just and reasonable and that it may be unjust, unreasonable, unduly discriminatory or preferential, or otherwise unlawful. Accordingly, we will accept the proposed tariff for filing, suspend it, and make it effective on the date of consummation of the merger, subject to refund. In addition, in light of the intervenors' arguments, we will set the tariffs for hearing, as ordered below. Finally, we will waive the 120–day advance notice requirement to allow the tariff to become effective as requested by the Applicants.

Commissioner Bailey concurred in a separate statement.

■ VICKY A. BAILEY COMMISSIONER, concurring:

I am disappointed that the Commission is unable to assess the adequacy of the Applicants' commitment to alleviate any potential adverse merger-related effects on competition. In particular, I do not understand the perceived inadequacy of the Applicants' commitment: (1) to join an ISO or similar organization within one year of the date of closing of the merger; and (2) to allow TDUs to participate in future transmission planning decisions and to receive access to the internal interface of the merged company's system on a basis equivalent to the Applicants' native load customers. I am not convinced that the Commission is truly unable to assess the value of the proposed mitigative measures absent a hearing on the competitive effects of the proposed merger.

Nevertheless, I understand that the Commission's review is hampered by the perceived inadequacy of the Applicants' supporting data and assumptions. I am not in a position to doubt the judgment of the Commission, its staff, and intervenors as to the utter inadequacy of the Applicants' presentation.

I note only that a similar rationale—problems with the data and assumptions employed by the Applicants in their competitive analysis—justifies the Commission's decision to set for hearing the competitive implications of another recent merger application. *See American Electric Power Co. and Central and South West Corp.*, 85 FERC P 61,201 at 61,818–19 (1998). I understand that the process of both preparing and reviewing a merger application can, at times, resemble more of an art than an exact science. Nevertheless, I am increasingly concerned that, after more than two years of experience processing merger applications under the Commission's Merger Policy Statement, the Commission's criteria might not be specific enough. It appears that merger applicants still may lack sufficient guidance as to what the Commission is looking for when it receives a merger application and what type of presentation a merger applicant need make to ensure processing of its application in a timely manner.■

Richard D. Cudahy, The FERC's Policy on Electric Mergers: a Bit of Perspective,

8 Energy L.J. 113 (1997).

I. Introduction

Now that we have the Merger Policy Statement of the Federal Energy Regulatory Commission (FERC), the last obstacle to deregulation of the electric utility industry seems to have dissolved in bureaucratic smoke. It was not ever thus. The movement for deregulation and competition in electric power began as far back as the *Otter Tail* decision in 1973, and surely by 1978 with the independent power provisions of PURPA. The movement was nourished by the astonishing differences in rates and costs from one utility service area to another in the 1980's. But along the way, the struggle to introduce competition into the electric power industry has encountered a series of stubborn obstacles. At various times, considerations of transmission access, of the obligation to serve, of fairness among the customer classes, of stranded costs and even of the waywardness of electric flows have seemed to block the deregulatory path. The passage of the Energy Policy Act of 1992 leveled the chief obstacle still standing by opening the way to mandatory access to transmission grids. The promised land of free competition loomed on the horizon, and the advance party of large industrial customers pressed forward to reach it.

Just as it looked as if a whole new world of ruthless rivalry was about to emerge, a cloud no bigger than a man's hand appeared on the horizon. At the edge of the cloud one could barely make out the letters of a word—"Merger." For when the electric power people awoke from their long night of natural monopoly, they began to rush into each other's arms to attempt an unprecedented number of corporate couplings.

II. The FERC's New Merger Policy

During the past sixty years when electric power has been a pervasively regulated industry, no comparable epidemic of mergers or related consolidations has broken out. There have been a few sporadic efforts at merger, but nothing like the present phenomenon. While pervasively regulated, electric utilities apparently saw little advantage in merger. They also probably correctly thought that their regulators, especially the state regulators, would not view merger activities with great favor. But above all, the utilities did not perceive the risk—the risk of bankruptcy—that deregulation has brought....

Strength through union is a natural response. At least two dozen electric utilities have announced plans to merge in the past few years.

Forty-five percent of utility executives and power marketers report being involved in merger activities. And two-thirds of utility executives do not expect their companies to remain "intact" over the next decade. Faced with the task of evaluating this torrent of proposed mergers, the FERC elected to seek public comment with a view to issuing a new merger policy.

The Commission has set out two goals for its Policy Statement: to focus its merger policy on competitive concerns in wholesale power markets, and to provide greater regulatory certainty. The Commission has been successful in pursuing the goal of safeguarding competition. In doing so, the FERC has not veered perceptibly from its views in recent merger cases. Its approach has been cautious, conservative and certainly orthodox. How adequate this approach will prove for a deregulating electricity industry is a matter this article will touch upon later.

The Commission has grounded its restated merger policy on three pillars. Taking its cue from the six Commonwealth factors that have governed the Commission's evaluation of mergers since 1966, it has collapsed these factors into a surviving trio, the nucleus of its merger analysis. These key factors are the effect on (1) competition, (2) rates and (3) regulation.

The Policy Statement places by far its greatest emphasis on competition and specifically on competition in generation. The foundation stone of competitive generation is the Commission's Open Access Rule, Order No. 888. The Rule defines the market available to any given customer within boundaries set by the cost of transmission, line losses and the carrying capacity of the lines. Some analysts have taken the position that Open Access alone is enough to mitigate market power in generation (as well as in transmission).[19][1] The Commission has not adopted this view. Instead, it has adopted, without modification, the 1992 Horizontal Merger Guidelines of the Department of Justice (DOJ) and the Federal Trade Commission (FTC).[20][2]

As adopted by the FERC, the Guidelines set out five steps in merger analysis: (1) assess whether the merger would significantly increase concentration; (2) assess whether the merger could result in adverse competitive effects; (3) assess whether entry could mitigate the adverse effects of the merger; (4) assess whether the merger results in efficiency gains not achievable by other means; and (5) assess whether, absent the merger, either party would likely fail, causing its assets to exit the market. What

---

1. *See, e.g.*, Robert J. Michaels, Market Power in Electric Utility Mergers: Access, Energy, and the Guidelines, 17 Energy L.J. 401 (1996). Professor Michaels takes the position that open access is enough to preclude market power, provided that transmission constraints are minimized and other obstacles to the free flow of electricity are removed. His seems to be a sort of potential competition or contestability approach: access in and out of a market, not concentration of generation ownership, better assays the risk of anti-competitive conduct. *Cf.*, William B. Tye, The Theory of Contestable Markets: Applications to Regulatory and Antitrust Problems in the Rail Industry (1990).

2. Department of Justice and Federal Trade Commission 1992 Horizontal Merger Guidelines, 57 Fed. Reg. 41,552 (1992).

the Commission calls its "Competitive Analysis Screen" involves primarily the Guidelines' first step—checking for increasing concentration. The screen can be broken down into two sub-steps: first, the definition of product and geographic markets, and second, the calculation of the Guidelines' concentration thresholds, indicating suspect mergers. In re-drawing the definition of product and geographic markets, the FERC first mentions the need to define product markets based on their cross-substitutability. Then the Commission defines geographic markets as including sources of supply that offer a competitive delivered price and are accessible within the physical constraints of the system.

The Policy Statement next calculates horizontal seller concentration in that market, using the Guidelines' well-worn Herfindahl–Hirschman Index (HHI). This method assigns a single number to describe the market's level of concentration by summing the squares of firms' market shares. If the post-merger sum or its increase (relative to before the merger) indicates competitive problems, the Commission will look to further relevant analysis supplied by the applicant. Additional analysis could address the potential for adverse competitive effects, the potential for entry and the role entry could play in mitigating market power. If applicants satisfy the analytic screen in their filings, they will typically be able to avoid a hearing on competition. On the other hand, the Commission will set for hearing any merger proposals that fail the screen analysis, raise problems of assumptions or data, or present questionable external factors.

If an application of the Guidelines discloses potential market power, the FERC suggests a grab bag of mitigating measures. For example, divestiture of generation is an obvious means of alleviating potential market power in generation. In other cases, elimination of transmission constraints may lessen market power in generation by widening the set of potential power suppliers and thereby reducing market concentration. The FERC will also consider the commitment of transmission to an Independent System Operator (ISO) as possibly being an effective way to dampen market power in generation.

While the Policy Statement goes into some detail about the screen (step one), it does not spell out explicitly what will happen to mergers that flunk the screen. Presumably the FERC will turn to the four Guidelines steps after the first one, concentration. Step two of the Guidelines requires the FERC to assess whether adverse competitive effects will flow from the merger. This suggests that the Commission will delve deeper into real competitive conditions rather than relying solely on raw concentration. As it stands, however, the Policy Statement leaves the specifics of its post-screen scrutiny to speculation.[28][3]

---

3. One scholar whose own proposal closely prefigured the Policy Statement has described some market characteristics that the FERC might examine in this context. They include ease of entry (the Policy Statement's step three), degree of excess capacity, proportion of fixed costs versus variable costs, degree of product homogeneity, buyer-side structure, extent of sellers' knowledge of each other's prices and costs degree of transparency of any exercise of market power and extent of potentially available economies of

The FERC in its stated views tries to maintain a determined neutrality between encouraging and discouraging mergers. But, although it mentions as step four the possibility of "efficiency gains that reasonably cannot be achieved by the parties through other means," the Statement's implicit thrust is negative. It takes the approach of the trustbuster. The Statement emphasizes why mergers might be bad—and offers suggestions for making them less bad—but fails to list any specific benefit, save one, that they might confer. This single specified advantage to be gained from a merger is the rescue of a "utility in severe financial distress" to "ensure reliable electricity service." This is, perhaps, an unintended reminder that electric power is an infrastructure industry, and no one really wants to pursue the competitive paradigm to the point of turning out the lights.

III.   The Inevitability of Consolidation After Deregulation

Viewing the FERC's new policy and the commentary of academics and industry, one might get the impression that the FERC and the industry in its charge are braving virgin territory. They are not. Power generation is not the first infrastructure industry to undergo deregulation; it is one of the last. There may well be something to learn about the electric industry's future from other deregulated industries' past.

Competition is a powerful solvent of inefficiencies and its advocates rejoice in that fact. But its onset is turbulent and disorderly. Deregulation is bound to roil a regulated market structure and to push an industry toward some new competitive equilibrium. As one deregulated industry after another has sought a new equilibrium, an undeviating sequence has emerged. When a capital-intensive industry is deregulated, market concentration inevitably rises. This has been the story in all the major deregulated, capital—intensive, infrastructure industries: passenger air travel, less-than-truckload motor carriage, air cargo, railroads, natural gas and even telecommunications.[37][4] And the primary mechanism in boosting concentration, though not the only one, is merger.

One perceptive scholar, Almarin Phillips, showed remarkable prescience in describing how the very process of deregulation would alter the

scale. Richard J. Pierce, Jr., Antitrust Policy in the New Electricity Industry, 17 Energy L.J. 29, 48 (1996).

4. This pattern of consolidation is not confined to physical infrastructure industries. It exists, too, in commercial banking, the principal industry outside the physical infrastructure to be deregulated. Although commercial banking remains deeply fragmented along state lines and within market segments, Congress and federal regulators have steadily chipped away at the legal partitions within commercial banking. In direct response, the number of U.S. banks fell from 14,407 in 1985 to 9,941 in 1995. Peter Martin, Comment & Analysis: Banks That Drag

Their Feet, Fin. Times, at 18 (July 25, 1996). Mergers have been the key mechanism for boosting banks' market concentration; their pace has been "little short of frenzied." Fewer Banks, Bigger Banks, Fin. Times, at 23 (June 20, 1995). This staggering consolidation of this highly capital-intensive business is set to continue, particularly if further regulatory barriers fall. If the wall with investment banking comes down, for example, Federal Reserve Chairman Alan Greenspan opines, "We'll see inevitably various types of mergers." Tim Carrington, Greenspan Backs Ending Glass–Steagall, Wall St. J. A2 (Mar. 1, 1995).

structure of a regulated industry. Although he directed his work specifically at the airlines, it has much broader significance. Not long after the passage of the Airline Deregulation Act of 1978, Phillips argued that, although airline deregulation was a major step forward, there was little understanding of the forces that it would unleash. The architects of deregulation were, he wrote in 1981, "hopelessly naive in their often implicit, always sanguine evaluations of the structural consequences of deregulation."[38][5]

What the airline industry in the early 1980s was being driven toward, and what electric power will soon be driven toward, has been called "equilibrium." Equilibrium exists for competitors in a market when workable competition can be sustained and competition disciplines prices but the number of competitors remains roughly stable. Under regulation, there is no equilibrium or need for equilibrium. When deregulation occurs, a search for equilibrium is set off. This may result in competitors of a wholly different size and number than existed under regulation. In the case of electric utilities, why would one expect a system in which the production units are now basically defined by state lines (presumably because of state regulation) to maintain its structure in a regime of interstate competition? There is every reason to expect the advent of a new equilibrium characterized by a new structure.

Merger policy, Phillips believed, ought to incorporate the fact of this search for a new equilibrium. Remember that the forces driving consolidation in the airlines perhaps were not fully appreciated. "The vision [held by deregulation's proponents] of the deregulated airline industry as effectively competitive suggested that merger policies developed under the antitrust laws would suffice for whatever mergers and acquisitions might transpire," Phillips observed. "In this the proponents of deregulation were wrong."

The roots of the failure to appreciate the full dimensions of the merger problem lie deep in American merger law. The paradigm that most deeply informs modern merger policy is entitled "structure-conduct-performance."[44][6] This is to say, industry structure determines firms' conduct, or at least the choices open to firms; and conduct in turn shapes an industry's performance. This principle is central to the FERC's Policy Statement, for the significance of concentration statistics is, of course, derived from this paradigm. That approach assumes, in line with the great bulk of expert opinion, that in the case of horizontal mergers, the likely

---

5. Almarin Phillips, Airline Mergers in the New Regulatory Environment, 129 U. Penn. L. Rev. 856, 856 (1981) (emphasis added); *accord*, George Williams, The Airline Industry and the Impact of Deregulation 11 (1993) ("The clear expectation of those advocating total economic deregulation was that the sector would be transformed into a highly efficient, competitive, and consumer orientated marketplace.... That this idealistic vision was flawed was a result of the response of the existing carriers to the real competition imposed upon them.").

6. Herbert Hovenkamp, Federal Antitrust Policy: The Law of Competition and Its Practice § 1.7 (1994). Although the 1992 Horizontal Merger Guidelines have retreated from the purer structuralism of the 1968 Guidelines, principally in the opportunities to rebut inferences drawn from the concentration statistics, the "analysis remains mainly, although not exclusively, structural." *Id.*

conduct of firms depends in large measure on how many and how big the firms are in the relevant market.[45][7]

Yet as far as its structural consequences are concerned, deregulation is different. As an industry moves from a pervasively regulated setting to loosely fettered competition, orthodox principles may no longer adequately describe the forces at work. "Even if it is true that a highly concentrated market structure tends to produce poor economic performance under relatively static market conditions," Phillips argued, "this truth obscures the more important relationships between structure and performance in a dynamic setting." And, as Phillips saw with remarkable clarity, "[d]eregulation creates such a setting."

Phillips contended that deregulation reverses a causal link that orthodox antitrust policy assumes. "The traditional view has been that industry structure gives rise to specific types of conduct," he wrote. "In the deregulated airline industry, the exact opposite is true." The analysis must therefore address the question of how the actual and perceived changes in the performance of the carriers are likely to "feedback" to private decisions affecting the hitherto regulated and unregulated aspects of structure and conduct.

The Phillips Thesis in Electricity Generation

To establish the relevance of Phillips' insight for electricity deregulation, take one problem that electric power may soon encounter. Phillips describes the same problem in airlines after that industry's own deregulation: the proclivity of carriers to take on new routes and to undertake new services on the basis of short-run incremental cost. This may make sense from the point of view of the individual airline. Incremental revenue may exceed incremental cost for, at worst, a contribution to overhead. But other carriers are led by competition to take on like business on a similarly short-run basis. Soon many carriers are operating at a loss. If the carriers cannot make up the shortfall elsewhere—presumably in the inelastic demand sectors—there will be none of the long-run profits needed for survival. In Phillips' words: "To the extent that mergers yield more efficient operations—or shield carriers from such ruinous rivalry—mergers will be encouraged by the threats to survival."

It is not difficult to shift this scenario into the world of electric generating companies. In electricity generation, short-run incremental cost is generally only a fraction of average total cost. It seems likely that many generation operators, focused on the recovery of incremental cost, will fall short of total cost recovery—and for them there will be a major risk of failure. In theory, the problem of widespread below-cost operation would not arise unless there were excess capacity. But, of course, that is the present condition.

---

7. "[A] consensus among economists attaches great significance to the degree of market concentration" as a prime way of assessing the anti-competitive effects of a horizontal merger." Phillip Areeda & Donald Turner, Antitrust Law § 910b (1996).

For a number of reasons, excess capacity may persist. Marginally efficient or even inefficient capacity may not be purged promptly from the market. First, there are economic reasons. Power plants have a single use. The capital tied up in them has little value except to produce electricity. This is a practical guarantee that marginal plants will be run to recover running costs alone. Even if the running costs of electric generators are not quite competitive, firms might still run them to escape the considerable cost of decommissioning and scrapping them. Second, even after deregulation, concerns about the adequacy of bulk power supply may cause regulators to continue to require approval of withdrawals of a plant from service. Analogous plant in other industries—for example, branch railroad lines—proved very difficult to abandon for many years.

Finally, the limited experience with electric utilities in bankruptcy has shown that, while owners and creditors may change, electricity flows on. In the airline industry there was a similar experience: the practice of bankrupt carriers' continuing to operate in bankruptcy was a source of anguish to their solvent competitors. With respect to electric power, there used to be a clearer reason to prop up a bankrupt utility (serving retail customers) than might be the case for an unbundled power generator. Public policy grounds, however—maintaining the bulk power supply—might still argue for keeping the generators in business, even if insolvent.

The overhang of excess capacity, then, threatens the financial livelihood of many electricity firms. True, recovery of stranded costs will presumably cushion the write-off of uneconomic assets, but it remains to be seen whether these adjustments will fully compensate for excess capacity's downward pressure on electricity prices. Particularly given the possible continuation of at least some regulatory restraints on electric plants leaving the market, excess capacity may turn out to be a long-lived albatross around the industry's neck. For many utilities faced with this problem, the choice may be between an early consolidation or a later shotgun marriage under threat of bankruptcy....

The Phillips thesis suggests that there will be many electric power mergers—probably sooner rather than later. If appropriate mergers are blocked, the antitrust laws can be by-passed. "Efficient" firms can grow internally, while other, less efficient, firms fall by the wayside. These less efficient firms, denied an avenue to efficiency by merger, may lurch toward failure and later seek merger under the failing-firm doctrine. This process could leave only a few very large, not necessarily efficient quasi-monopolies in the industry. The FERC therefore would be well-advised to consider the Phillips thesis as a "public interest" factor to be weighed along with inferences drawn from measures of concentration.

IV.   The Phillips Thesis in Airlines and Railroads

If the Phillips thesis fits as suggested into the "public interest" part of the merger analysis, how much weight should the FERC give it? For comparative purposes, it may be useful to look at the approach of other regulatory agencies overseeing industries comparable with electric power.

For comparable industries, this article selects the transportation businesses—principally airlines and railroads—which are sufficiently capital-intensive to be economically analogous. In addition, the processes of deregulation and of consolidation are well enough along in these industries to be instructive.

A. Airlines

From the 1930's until the late 1970's, the airlines were subject to a regulatory scheme designed to protect them as an infant industry from "excessive" competition, yet also to maintain a managed rivalry thought to promote efficiency. Under regulation, the Civil Aeronautics Board (CAB) oversaw the airlines' fares and determined their route structures and several other essential features. The demise of a trunk (major) airline or the rise of a new one was disfavored. A leading element of this regime was the handicapping of competition: the CAB expected the airlines to use some profits from lucrative routes to subsidize marginal ones, and it provided the weaker carriers with enough route awards to keep them in the race without necessarily making them winners. As a protectionist arrangement, the system worked splendidly. Almost all the original trunk (major) airlines survived from 1938 until the coming of deregulation, and no new airlines joined the list.

After dissatisfaction with the system led to abandonment of the old regulatory regime in 1978, the popularity of mergers and acquisitions skyrocketed. After deregulation, the number of airlines in many city pair markets increased significantly, but this initial burst of competitive zeal fizzled after 1983 as the measures of firm concentration rose inexorably. The market share of the three leaders has at times approached 60 percent.

To a significant degree, higher concentration has been achieved by merger. Between 1979 and 1988, there were 51 airline mergers and acquisitions. Some of these after 1982 were monsters—shrinking the number and inflating the size of the survivors. And in a reverse of the view that prevailed on the eve of deregulation, most observers now expect massive additional consolidation in the airlines. A possible union of Delta and Continental has been seriously considered and may be revived. TWA, Northwest, and USAir are themselves prime merger targets.

This record confirms the Phillips thesis that deregulation itself, by making a new equilibrium necessary and by enhancing risk, creates a powerful force for consolidation. And these risks are real. In the years after deregulation, the industry rang up losses that exceeded all its prior earnings since the inception of commercial aviation. A number of lines simply went bankrupt and out of business, like Pan American (old-timers) and Midway and Air Florida (new post-deregulation carriers). Others dwelled for a long time in a twilight world in-and-out of Chapter 11, such as America West and Continental. Plenty in good times is no guarantee of survival in bad. This bit of airline wisdom helps explain why Continental, which has been in bankruptcy twice, would apparently like to find a safe harbor at a time when it is doing well.

How has the Department of Transportation (DOT) dealt with mergers among airlines? Under the Airline Deregulation Act of 1978, this agency was required to approve mergers under a standard reflecting a modification of the Clayton Act. The Deregulation Act, however, mandated more than a pure antitrust approach. The DOT had to weigh the probable anti-competitive effect of a merger against the obligation of "meeting significant transportation conveniences and needs of the public . . . unless . . . such significant transportation conveniences and needs may . . . be satisfied by a reasonably available alternative having materially less anti-competitive effect." Under this standard, the DOT approved "nearly every merger the airlines proposed to it." With concern mounting about the DOT's permissive review, Congress allowed the DOT's authority over domestic airline mergers to expire, which automatically shifted it to the Department of Justice and the Federal Trade Commission. Congress left mergers involving foreign commerce to the DOT.

This was a classic case of closing the barn door long after the horse had escaped for good. Let us take an example or two of how the DOT applied this statutory mandate (ways which Alfred Kahn was to call "unconscionable").[78][8] In the Northwest Airlines–Republic Acquisition Case in 1986, the DOT noted that the merging carriers' combined share of emplanements at their would-be joint hub of Minneapolis–St. Paul was 80%. The DOJ intervened to oppose the merger on the grounds that it was anti-competitive.

The DOT rebuffed the DOJ. It held that the controlling statute, rather than using concentration figures as the "pivotal inquiry, . . . requires a functional analysis focusing directly on the structure, history, and probable future‘ of the industry involved." In a bow to contestability theory, the DOT said that low entry barriers meant that "measures of concentration in that market will provide little insight into market power." Very significantly, in rejecting the received antitrust wisdom, the DOT observed that, "[A]irline markets are nearly always concentrated by traditional antitrust standards, yet most are competitive in performance." This view conflicts directly with the principle that structure determines conduct, which, in turn, determines performance.

In the later TWA–Ozark case, the DOT reiterated that "airline markets are nearly always concentrated under traditional antitrust standards, yet they perform competitively." As these examples show, the DOT was inclined to weigh economies, efficiencies, and other "public interest" factors heavily in the balance with purportedly anti-competitive aspects of proposed mergers—and certainly more heavily than would the FERC under its Policy Statement.

B. Railroads

Railroads also provide a case history of deregulation as a signal for relentless merger activity. Only one industry is more capital-intensive than

---

8. Alfred E. Kahn (Speaker), in Donald L. Flexner (Moderator), To Regulate or De- regulate: An Article of Faith or Analysis?, 55 Antitrust L.J. 205, 206 (1986).

railroads, and that is electric generation. The two industries are economically comparable. The rails were partially deregulated under the 4–R Act in 1976 and, more significantly, under the Staggers Act in 1980. There had been considerable merger activity among the railroads before deregulation, but since the Staggers Act, the number of significant U.S. railways has shrunk from 26 to 9. Only five giants remain. The merger of the Union Pacific and the Southern Pacific (involving almost 25,000 miles of track) leaves only two major rail systems in the West. In the East, two systems—CSX and Norfolk/Southern—which had been bidding for the third—Conrail—now are set on dismembering the latter. CSC and Norfolk/Southern will then acquire the Conrail pieces, leaving only two major systems in the East. Already there is newspaper and industry speculation of an East–West merger to create the nation's first transcontinental railroad.

Railroad mergers must be approved by the Surface Transportation Board (STB) in the Department of Transportation. This agency is the successor to the Interstate Commerce Commission (ICC). In reviewing rail mergers, the STB applies the same statutory standard that the FERC must use for electric utility mergers: the proposed combination must be "consistent with the public interest." The STB has issued no merger "policy statement" comparable to the FERC's, but its approach is clear from its recent order approving the merger of the Union Pacific and Southern Pacific, two parallel railroads. The DOJ intervened there to allege an annual competitive injury to shippers of $800 million—more than the railroads' claimed annual savings from the merger. In the words of the Antitrust Division's chief, the combination would be "the most anticompetitive rail merger in our history."

The STB labeled the DOJ's claim of harm "totally without foundation." Rejecting the DOJ's proposed ameliorative merger condition—divestiture of more than a thousand miles of track—the STB criticized the DOJ's entire approach:

> Our statutory mandate, which requires us to balance efficiency gains against competitive harm, sharply contrasts with the approach to mergers taken by DOJ and the Federal Trade Commission (FTC). The policies embodied in the antitrust laws provide guidance, but are not determinative.

And in a separate opinion, Commissioner Owen pointed to the long history of railroad regulation in asserting the antitrust laws' diminished relevance:

> Since the passage of the Transportation Act, 1920, it has been the public policy of the United States to encourage railroad mergers and consolidations that are in the public interest.... Railroads were the first major industry where merger and consolidation were promoted by the federal government.... Moreover, Congress repeatedly has directed that railroad merger and consolidation applications be measured by a different standard than is used by the Justice Department....

V. Possible Competitively Neutral or Pro-competitive Benefits to Merger

There are many reasons for firms and their managers to seek mergers—including, of course, the prohibited motive of acquisition of market power. Some of these reasons go by the name of "savings" or "economies" (e.g., of scale or of scope). These sometimes can be quantified. There are other reasons that are meaningful but cannot be quantified. Sometimes these reasons go under the rubric of synergies. Occasionally the purpose is simply to get bigger or to preclude a takeover. We have already noted a transcendent reason for merging in the course of deregulation—to cope with risk and to achieve equilibrium. Bearing in mind that the mere acquisition of market power is forbidden, we will look into some of the many permissible reasons, ranging from the obvious to the fanciful.

With respect to mergers, economies of scale or scope (or sometimes density) are sought after by the proponents. In electric power generation at the plant level, economies of scale are not usually decisive since, in current thinking, these are exhausted at 500 megawatts or so, and most modest-sized utilities can support this. Some authorities set 1600 megawatts as the maximum capacity from which savings can be realized through placing multiple plants at a single site. This seems easy to achieve without raising market concentration concerns. Current thinking also sees a much bigger role for combined-cycle gas turbine generation, where economies of scale are exhausted early. At the firm level, some economies of scale in the form of labor and other savings usually can be claimed as a result of combining operations and eliminating jobs. There might also be some advantages in combined buying of fuel or materials.

Despite the relatively unexciting prospects for economies of scale, everyone, or almost everyone, is impressed with the expectations for economies of scope and coordination at the firm level. These would include efficiencies achieved through the classic diversities associated with electric power. Merging companies serving complementary classes of customers (particularly adding industrial load to a company without it) may be helpful. Or, for example, a major economy can be realized through demand diversity, combining a company with a summer peak with a winter-peaker. And there are, of course, major benefits to be obtained by the central dispatch of a large number of diversified plants. Presumably, a horizontal merger, by increasing the number and diversity of the plants within the system, can increase the benefits. Access to a larger array of plants through merger may also reduce reserve requirements and thereby lower the costs of reliability.

Professor Pierce has pointed out that the same coordination benefits may be obtained by adopting a strongly integrated power pool with an Independent System Operator (ISO). In theory, at least, this is correct, but it remains to be seen how the interactions of these institutions actually play out. . . .

The effect of consolidation in furthering diversification can also lower business risk and concomitantly reduce the cost of capital. The competitive generation of electric power, unless fortified with a full portfolio of long-term contracts (a presumably anticompetitive arrangement), will be fraught with business risk. Diversifying that risk by consolidation would seem to make business sense and would reduce the cost of capital. Larger blocks of generating facilities are likely to offer a broader range of types of generating plants, thereby reducing the risk of failure of any one type. A large inventory of plants of different types also provides an opportunity for one-stop shopping by customers. Regulatory risk, of course, varies from state to state. Even after deregulation, the potential for state intervention is significant in areas such as choice of fuel, plant siting, environmental requirements, demand-side management, integrated resource planning and the like. A geographically dispersed plant mix could provide a distinct advantage in the event of severe regulatory problems in particular jurisdictions.

Some commentators have written of the benefits of mergers of generating companies operating in different regional markets. Apparently, mergers like this could increase size and diversity without increasing concentration. Ironically, this approach flies in the face of the principle incorporated in the Public Utility Holding Company Act of 1935, which forbids holding companies from owning several utilities unless they can be electrically integrated—usually meaning that the companies must be contiguous.

Another factor relevant to the size of a power-generating enterprise, and one not much investigated in connection with deregulation, is the matter of planning. One of the premises underlying the deregulation of generation is that the market in its wisdom will determine when capacity has to be built and what kind of capacity it ought to be. Contrary to today's conventional wisdom, it is hard to imagine that generating companies will assume this responsibility without substantial regulatory oversight. Extensive externalities burden electricity generation. There are crucial environmental considerations—thermal impact, clean air, clean water, distance from population centers and all the rest. Then there are questions of domestic and international fuel supply, which have major public dimensions. Energy security considerations may be important—like the long-standing and so far unsuccessful effort to diminish reliance on foreign oil. These and more prosaic matters will require planning both by the generation suppliers and by the government. There will have to be cooperative planning with each party displaying a comparable degree of sophistication. And there will have to be appropriate input from the public. All this would seem to require, on the part of generating companies, substantial staffing and expertise to operate smoothly. The point has been made that competition will pare overhead to the bone. That may be true, but a large generating company can absorb essential planning staff more economically than a smaller company....■

NOTES AND COMMENTS

1. Judge Cudahy endorses a progressive reading of FERC's role in enforcing antitrust policy. Is this view consistent with repeal of PUHCA and

movement towards competitive wholesale power markets, as Congress endorsed in the Energy Policy Act of 1992? Should FERC play a role at all, given that DOJ continues to police mergers where there is significant market power?

2.   Two recent industry trends are not discussed by Judge Cudahy. First, electric utilities are increasingly diversifying into other markets, such as energy services, while other firms, such as telecommunications operators, are also entering into energy markets. Would this trend change his recommendations? Second, many utilities are reinventing themselves as multinational firms. Many large U.S. utilities own or are developing power generation facilities in Europe, Eastern Europe, Asia, and developing countries. And increasingly, foreign firms own shares in U.S. utilities and IPPs. With increasing internationalization of electric utilities, how should merger policy evolve?

C. FEDERAL AND STATE AUTHORITY OVER ECONOMIC REGULATION

As was raised in Chapter 11, there are some limits on FERC's authority over implementing competition in the electric utility industry. As the following excerpt suggests, the natural gas industry did not pose the same jurisdictional limits.

Richard J. Pierce, Jr., The State of the Transition To Competitive Markets in Natural Gas and Electricity

15 Energy L. J. 323 (1994).

... The FERC cannot control the path and rate of progress of the electricity transition to the extent it exercised control over the gas transition because it lacks many of the regulatory tools it applied to the gas industry. The differences lie in three principal areas: (1) retail wheeling; (2) transmission rates and conditions; and, (3) construction and expansion of transmission lines.

When Congress authorized the FERC to mandate third party access to transmission lines for wholesale transactions in the Energy Policy Act of 1992 (EPAct), it specifically denied the FERC the power necessary to mandate access for retail transactions. No such jurisdictional dichotomy exists in the gas industry. The FERC has the power to authorize an interstate pipeline to bypass a local distribution company, a power broadly analogous to the power to authorize retail wheeling of electricity. Early in the gas transition, the FERC indicated its willingness to authorize LDC bypasses expeditiously in virtually all cases. FERC's power and willingness to authorize LDC bypasses had a major impact on the policies and practices of the LDCs and PUCs ... The FERC cannot initiate an analogous sequence of actions and reactions in the electricity industry because it is prohibited from ordering retail wheeling. [State efforts to implement retail competition are discussed in Chapter Thirteen.]

Statutory distinctions between wholesale and retail transmission services also will give rise to many related jurisdictional disputes. When is a putatively wholesale transmission service actually a prohibited sham retail service? This issue arises in many contexts. When a group of formerly retail customers of Utility A become wholesale customers of Utility B, what institution has the power, and arguably the responsibility, to authorize Utility A to collect a portion of its stranded investment from that group of customers? The institutional candidates include the FERC, the PUC, the state legislature, a state court, all of the above, and none of the above ... We will not have clear answers to these questions for many years.

The distinction between wholesale and retail wheeling also will exacerbate the pre-existing uncertainty with respect to the allocation of rate jurisdiction over transmission services. By the time the FERC began the gas transition, courts had already held that it had plenary power over all "interstate" transportation of gas, whether for retail or wholesale, and that all high pressure pipelines that contained some gas destined for an "interstate" market were subject to FERC's regulatory control. The case law with respect to FERC's power over transmission lines is not as clear. With most electricity traditionally transmitted as part of a bundled sales transaction, the FERC and reviewing courts have had little occasion to resolve disputes concerning jurisdiction to set transmission rates. For purposes of FERC's jurisdiction over electricity wholesales, courts have interpreted "interstate" broadly to include any transaction within a single state if the transaction makes use of interconnected transmission lines in which the potential exists for commingling with electricity from an out-of-state source. As a practical matter, those holdings give the FERC plenary power over virtually all electricity wholesales in the continental United States. The FERC has asserted jurisdiction over pure transmission transactions in analogous conditions, but no court has addressed this somewhat different issue.

Ultimately, courts are likely to establish a new "bright line" test that confers on the FERC plenary power over the rates and conditions of service for all transactions that use a high voltage transmission line in the continental United States, including retail wheeling transactions and transactions that purport to involve only transmission from one point to another in a single state. Such a test would avoid one serious version of the "two drivers of one car" problem. The transmission grid would not function effectively if it were subject to potentially conflicting rates and conditions of service imposed by the FERC and the PUCs. The existence of ubiquitous loop flows renders the PUCs poor candidates to exercise any power over high voltage transmission services. For instance, a transmission transaction that putatively involves use of a single line between Harrisburg and Philadelphia, PA, can effect the available capacity of lines in New York, New Jersey, Maryland, etc. Loop flows have much broader implications....

By avoiding one version of the "two drivers of one car" problem, however, courts will create another version of that problem. The FERC will have plenary power to determine the rates and conditions applicable to retail wheeling transactions to the extent those transactions require use of high voltage transmission lines, but states will have the exclusive power to require retail wheeling. However, this version of the problem is somewhat more manageable. A state PUC can order its utilities to apply to the FERC for authorization to provide retail wheeling service, subject to whatever rates and conditions of service the FERC approves. Conflicts will arise only if a PUC attempts to impose on a high voltage line rates or conditions of service that differ from those imposed by the FERC. The Supremacy Clause will resolve all such conflicts in favor of the FERC.

There is no uncertainty with respect to one critical jurisdictional issue. The FERC has no power to authorize construction or expansion of transmission lines. States have exclusive jurisdiction over this aspect of the industry's activities, and many states have delegated all or part of this regulatory power to local governments. By contrast, the FERC has plenary and preemptive power to authorize construction or expansion of gas pipelines. [See *Louisiana Ass'n of Indep. Producers & Royalty Owners v. FERC*, 958 F.2d 1101 (D.C.Cir.1992).] This difference in allocation of jurisdictional power over the two industries will prove to be the source of major problems when attempting to implement the electricity transition. . . .

FERC's plenary and preemptive power to authorize construction or expansion of gas pipelines was critical to the success of the gas transition. The Iroquois Pipeline project illustrates the point well. The FERC authorized construction of a large new pipeline from Canada to the northeastern United States over the strenuous objections of market incumbents and a handful of rich and powerful citizens of Connecticut and New York. From FERC's perspective, that decision was easy. The project would produce hundreds of millions of dollars in benefits to millions of consumers by eliminating the effects of transportation capacity constraints and enhancing consumers' access to competitive sources of supply. The cost to affected local residents was trivial in comparison with the regional benefits. If the project had required approval by each state, it might never have been built. At least it would have been delayed for many years. The project would have had no chance of receiving approval if it required approval by each affected unit of local government.

. . . The best solution to the problem would be an amendment to the Federal Power Act (FPA) conferring on the FERC the same powers with respect to transmission projects that the Natural Gas Act (NGA) gives it for gas pipeline projects. Congress eventually will take that action, but probably not for many years. Only a federal agency is in a position to balance the costs of a project to a few local residents against the benefits of the project to millions of consumers in several states. Transmission capacity constraints are already producing unnecessarily high electricity prices in some areas, but the causal relationship is difficult to demonstrate in the present environment in which lack of effective competition produces widely varying electricity prices independent of capacity constraints. As competition begins to yield a convergence of electricity prices, the causal relationship between aberrantly high prices in some areas and capacity constraints will become more apparent. Eventually, that phenomenon will become so obvious, so large, and so widespread that Congress will feel compelled to act. In the intervening years, however, millions of consumers will have borne billions of dollars in unnecessarily high electricity prices, and capacity constraints will have induced a geographically inappropriate pattern of investments in generating plants. Transmission capacity constraints can double the cost of electricity in a market by forcing the grid operator to substitute a high cost generating plant for a low cost generating plant. Such congestion costs have the potential to dwarf all other components of the cost of transmission.■

* * *

Richard Pierce's excerpt raises some serious concerns with the current status of FERC's authority to successfully guide the transition to competition in the electric power industry. A further issue, not discussed by Pierce, but raised by recent concerns over wholesale power reliability, is FERC's lack of jurisdiction over wholesale power generators. *See* Chapter 11. Given the interrelationship between generation and transmission in electricity, if FERC is unable to order the expansion of generation, will it ever be in the position it needs to ensure reliability of the system? Will new legislation be needed? What issues will Congress likely need to focus its attention on?

How do limits on federal authority manifest themselves in other energy industry contexts, such as coal and oil?

INDEX

References are to pages

1–56662–900–4

90000